THE INTERNATIONAL LAW OF THE SEA:

CASES, DOCUMENTS AND READINGS

THE INTERNATIONAL LAW OF THE SEA:

CASES, DOCUMENTS, AND READINGS

by

GARY KNIGHT

*Former Campanile Professor of
Marine Resources Law
Louisiana State University Law Center*

and

HUNGDAH CHIU

*Professor of Law
University of Maryland, School of Law,
Baltimore, Maryland, USA*

With a Foreword by
Professor Louis B. Sohn

Published by
ELSEVIER APPLIED SCIENCE
LONDON and NEW YORK
and
UNIFO PUBLISHERS, Inc.

ELSEVIER SCIENCE PUBLISHERS LTD
Crown House, Linton Road, Barking, Essex IG11 8JU, England

Sole Distributor in the USA and Canada
ELSEVIER SCIENCE PUBLISHING CO., INC.
655 Avenue of the Americas, New York, NY 10010, USA

WITH 4 TABLES AND 64 ILLUSTRATIONS

© 1991 ELSEVIER SCIENCE PUBLISHERS LTD and UNIFO PUBLISHERS, INC.

British Library Cataloguing in Publication Data

Knight, Gary
The international law of the sea: cases,
documents and readings.
I. Title II. Chiu, Hungdah, 1936–
341.45

ISBN 1-85166-703-2

Library of Congress CIP data applied for

Printed in Great Britain by Galliard (Printers) Ltd, Great Yarmouth

PREFACE

The first edition of this casebook, edited by Professor Gary Knight of the Louisiana State University, was published in 1969, two years after the seabed question had been raised in the United Nations. Because of the rapid changes in the law of the sea, Professor Knight had used the loose-leaf format to keep the casebook updated in later editions. The last edition was published in 1980, two years before the final adoption of the 1982 United Nations Convention on the Law of the Sea. After Professor Knight left the Louisiana State University in the mid-1980's, there has been no law of the sea casebook published, and his book remains the only one available. In 1988, Professor Knight agreed to have me undertake a thorough and updated revision of his casebook.

Notes, questions and references have been supplied to facilitate discussion of the issues raised by the materials and to assist further research where interests or assignments so dictate. The "references" are not exhaustive and are confined to English language materials only. Because the *Uniform System of Citations* used in legal writings is not used outside the legal field or the United States, in this revised edition, I have decided to use the conventional form of citation. For the book, the place of publication and the publisher is provided; for articles, the complete titles of the journals and the beginning and ending pages of the article are provided. The references are chronologically arranged and within a calendar year, books or articles are arranged according to alphabetical order of the last names of the authors.

All treaties, conventions or agreements referred to in the book have been provided with proper sources. However, the source of the following frequently cited treaties are provided below and will not be repeated in the text:

> Convention on the Territorial Sea and the Contiguous Zone, Done at Geneva on April 29, 1958, 1500 U.S.T. 1606, T.I.A.S. 5639, 516 U.N.T.S. 205.

> Convention on the High Seas, Done at Geneva on April 29, 1958, 13 U.S.T. 2312, T.I.A.S. 5200, 450 U.N.T.S. 82.

> Convention on the Continental Shelf, Done at Geneva on April 29, 1958, 15 U.S.T. 471, T.I.A.S. 5578, 499 U.N.T.S. 311.

> Convention on Fishing and Conservation of the Living Resources of the High Seas, Done at Geneva on April 29, 1958, 559 U.N.T.S. 285.

> United Nations Convention on the Law of the Sea, Done at Montego Bay on December 10, 1982, U.N. Doc. A/CONF.62/122 and Corr. 1 to 11.

The organization of this book is primarily the same as the 1980 edition of Knight's loose-leaf version, though more than 50% of the materials are new. In Chapter 1, it provides general background information on the nature of oceans and seas and their jurisdictional zones. This is followed by the history of the law of the sea (Chapter 2) and the sources of the international law of the sea (Chapter 3). Then, it deals with maritime boundary problems (Chapters 4 and 5) and the legal status and related problems of the regimes of internal waters, territorial seas, straits and contiguous zones (Chapter 6), the high seas (Chapter 7), the continental shelf (Chapter 8), and the exclusive economic zone (Chapter 9). The next four chapters of the book cover the legal regimes and problems associated with the exploitation of the non-living ocean resources (Chapter 10), exploitation of living resources (Chapter 11), marine pollution (Chapter 12) and scientific research (Chapter 13). Chapter 14 covers the settlement of disputes relating to the law of the sea. The chapter on military use of the ocean, as it appears in Knight's 1980 edition, is omitted and is replaced by a new Chapter 15 on the law of war and neutrality in warfare at sea. In view of the recent maritime warfare at the Falkland Islands and the Persian Gulf, it appears that the traditional law of maritime warfare and neutrality cannot be ignored in a law of the sea book.

Virtually all important articles of the 1982 United Nations Convention on the Law of the Sea are distributed throughout the book under the relevant subject matter heading. A special index to this Convention is prepared in the index section of this book. A highly selected bibliography is also prepared to the convenience of users. Since I am responsible for preparing this edition of the book, please direct all your comments, inquiries and suggestions to me.

HUNGDAH CHIU
January 1, 1991

ACKNOWLEDGEMENTS

I am grateful to Professor Louis B. Sohn, formerly of Harvard Law School and now with the University of Georgia Law School, for contributing the foreword to this book and for his encouragement in the course of the preparation of the manuscript. Professor Sohn is my former teacher and the experience and training received from taking his course on the United Nations Law and seminar on international law at Harvard Law School have provided me with a solid background in research in international law.

In the course of preparing this revised edition of Gary Knight's *International Law of the Sea: Cases, Documents and Readings*, I was ably assisted at the various stages of its development by Andrew Stone, Christopher G. Raffaele, Rachel C. Tadmor, Mary M. Hogans-Ott, all former students at the University of Maryland School of Law, Ms. Ching-Chane Hwang of the Department of Government and Politics of the University of Maryland at College Park, Ms. Shaiw-chei Chuang of the Institute of International Relations of the National Chengchi University in the Republic of China, and Faye Ku of Georgetown University School of Foreign Service. The tedious work of typing and proofreading was ably performed by Lu Ann Marshall and Kathy Montroy, the administrative work by Ms. Chih-Yu Wu and the compilation of index and miscellaneous research assistance by Ms. Su Yun Chang. I would like to express my sincere thanks to each of them.

Professor Martin Ira Glassner of the Department of Geography of the Southern Connecticut State University read the manuscript and offered many valuable suggestions. Major Steven T. Lynch of the USAF read part of manuscript and made many useful editorial suggestions. Maxine Z. Grosshans, Research Librarian of the Marshall Law Library of the University of Maryland Law School, provided valuable assistance in locating various research materials used in this book. Dean Michael J. Kelly of the University of Maryland School of Law provided three summer research grants in the course of preparing this manuscript and the Asia Pacific Educational Fund provided support for preparing the manuscript for publication. I thank them as well.

I, on behalf of Gary Knight and myself, am greatly indebted to many authors and publishers for permission to reprint materials used in this casebook. I acknowledge with appreciation the permission granted to reprint copyrighted materials by the following authors and publishers:

American Bar Association: W.L. Griffin, "The Emerging Law of Ocean Space," *International Lawyer*, Vol. 1 (1969), pp. 556-560.

American Law Institute Publishers: *Restatement of the Law, Second, Foreign Relations Law of the United States*, 2nd ed., 1965, pp. 161-162; *Restatement on the Foreign Relations Law of the United States*, 3rd revision, Vol. 1, 1987, pp. 24-29, 35-36, 38-39, 50, 55, 65-66; Vol. 2, 10-11, 16-17, 49, 56-57, 62-63, 67-69, 81, 83-87, 89-90.

American Society of International Law: "Contemporary Practice of the United States Relating to International Law," *American Journal of International Law*, Vol. 57 (1963), pp. 403-404; Arthur H. Dean, "The Second Geneva Conference on the Law of the Sea: The Fight for Freedom of the Seas," *American Journal of International Law*, Vol. 54 (1960), pp. 772-773, 775-776 (reprinted with permission also of the author); Claims Commission--United States and Mexico, "The Oriental Navigation Company v. The United Mexican States (Docket No. 411)," (Opinion rendered October 3, 1928), *American Journal of International Law*, Vol. 23 (1929), pp. 434-437; "Conference for the Codification of International Law, The Hague, March-April, 1930, Report of the Second Committee (Territorial Sea), Annex I ("The Legal Status of the Territorial Sea"),"

vii

American Journal of International Law, Vol. 24 (1930), Supplement, pp. 234, 250-251; "Conference for the Codification of International Law, The Hague, March-April, 1930, Report of the Second Committee (Territorial Sea), Annex I ("The Legal Status of the Territorial Sea")," *American Journal of International Law*, Vol. 24 (1930), Supplement, pp. 248-250; Hugo Caminos and Michael R. Molitor, "Progressive Development of International Law and the Package Deal," *American Journal of International Law*, Vol. 79 (1985), pp. 879, 887-889 (reprinted with permission also of Hugo Caminos); "Johnson v. Mexico (The Daylight) (U. S.-Mexican Claims Commission; April 15, 1927)," *American Journal of International Law*, Vol. 21 (1927), pp. 794-795; John Norton Moore, "The Regime of Straits and the Third United Nations Conference on the Law of the Sea," *American Journal of International Law*, Vol. 74 (1980), pp. 95-971(reprinted with permission also of the author); Myres S. McDougal, "The Hydrogen Bomb Tests and the International Law of the Sea," *American Journal of International Law*, Vol. 49 (1955), pp. 356-359(reprinted with permission also of the author); "Map of Guinea-Bissau/Guinea Maritime Boundary," *International Legal Materials*, Vol. 25 (1986), p. 306-307; "Sketch Map Showing Approximate Outlines of Exclusive Economic Zone of the United States, Commonwealth of Puerto Rico, Commonwealth of the Northern Mariana Islands and United States Overseas Possessions," *International Legal Materials*, Vol. 22 (1983), p. 463.

Anderson Publishing Co.: Andrew W. Anderson, "Jurisdiction over Stateless Vessels on the High Seas: An Appraisal Under Domestic and International Law," *Journal of Maritime Law and Commerce*, Vol. 13 (1982), pp. 327-328, 329-330, 334-337(reprinted with permission also of the author); Douglas A. Jacobsen and James D. Yellen, "Oil Pollution: The 1984 London Protocols and the AMOCO CADIZ," *Journal of Maritime Law and Commerce*, Vol. 15 (1984), pp. 467, 483-485(reprinted with permission also of the authors).

Appleton-Century-Crofts, Inc., Prentice Hall: Herbert W. Briggs, ed., *The Law of Nations, Cases, Documents, and Notes*, 2nd ed., 1952, p. 991.

Association of American Geographers: G.E. Pearcy, "Geographical Aspects of the Law of the Sea," *Annals of the Association of American Geographers*, Vol. 49 (1959), p. 5.

Blackwood Pillan & Wilson Co.: Thomas Wemyss Fulton, *The Sovereignty of the Sea*, 1911, pp. 3-6.

Boston University International Law Journal: Kimberly S. Davis, "International Management of Cetaceans Under the New Law of the Sea Convention," *Boston University International Law Journal*, Vol. 3 (1985), pp. 484-488. Reprinted with permission also of the author.

Butterworths & (Publishers) Co., Ltd.: J. G. Starke, *Introduction to International Law*, 9th ed., 1984, pp. 497-498, 498-499, 561-566, 566-568, 568-569.

Carnegie Endowment for International Peace: Max Sorensen, "Law of the Sea," *International Conciliation*, No. 520, November, 1958, pp. 201-206.

Chinese Society of International Law: *Chinese Yearbook of International Law*, Vol. 3 (1983), p. 213; Hungdah Chiu, "Some Problems Concerning the Delimitation of Maritime Boundary Between the Republic of China and the Philippines," *Chinese Yearbook of International Law and Affairs*, Vol. 3 (1983), pp. 10-12.

Columbia Journal of Environmental Law: Gregory M. Travalio and Rebecca J. Clement,

"International Protection of Marine Mammals," *Columbia Journal of Environmental Law*, Vol. 5 (1979), pp. 207-213(reprinted in modified form).

Duke University School of Law: Margaret G. Wachenfeld, "Reflagging Kuwaiti Tankers: A U. S. Response in the Persian Gulf," *Duke Law Journal*, Vol. 1988, pp. 181, 183, 184, 185-187(reprinted with permission also of the author).

Elsevier Science Publishers B. V., Social and Humanities Section: Robert H. Stansfield, "The Torrey Canyon," *R. Bernardt, Encyclopedia of International Law*, Vol. 11, *Law of the Sea, Air and Space*, 1989, pp. 333-334. Reprinted with permission also of R. Bernardt.

Encyclopedia Britannica, Inc.: "Oceans and Seas," *Encyclopedia Britannica*, Macropaedia, Vol. 13, 15th ed., 1974, 1982 reprint, pp. 482-484, c 1982 by Encyclopedia Britannica, Inc.

Facts on File, Inc.: "U. S. Attacks, Seizes Iranian Mine Ship," *Facts on File*, Vol. 47, No. 24444 (September 25, 1987), p. 685.

Fred B. Rothman & Co.: Wyndham L. Walker, "Territorial Waters: The Cannon Shot Rule," *British Yearbook of International Law*, Vol. 22 (1945), pp. 210, 230-231.

Grotius Publications Ltd.: Croft v. Dunphy (Case No. 82) *Annual Digest of Public International Law Cases 1931-1932*, pp. 157-160; *Re* Martinez and Others, *International Law Reports*, Vol. 28, pp. 170-175; The Corfu Channel Case (United Kingdom v. Albania), Judgment on the Merits, April 19, 1949, *I.C.J. Reports 1949*, pp. 18-20.

Harvard International Law Journal: Patrick M. Norton, "Between the Ideology and the Reality: The Shadow of the Law of Neutrality," *Harvard International Law Journal*, Vol. 17 (1976), pp. 249-252, 276-277, 307, 309-311.

Hemisphere Publishing Corp.: Boleslaw Adam Boczek, "Law of Warfare at Sea and Neutrality: Lessons from the Gulf War," *Ocean Development and International Law*, Vol. 20 (1989), pp. 247-248; John Copper, "Delimitation of the Maritime Boundary in the Gulf of Maine Area," *Ocean Development and International Law*, Vol. 16 (1986), p. 77.

Philip Caryl Jessup, Jr.: P.C. Jessup, *The Law of Territorial Waters and Maritime Jurisdiction*, New York: G.A. Jennings, 1927, pp. 3-5, 7. Reprinted by permission of Philip Caryl Jessup, Jr., heir and executor of P.C. Jessup.

Kluwer Academic Publishers Group: Alfred H. A. Soons, *Marine Scientific Research and the Law of the Sea*, Deventer, The Netherlands: Kluwer Law and Taxation Publishers, 1982, pp. 16-20, 20-23, 23-26, 28-29, 30-33; F. V. Garcia-Amador, *The Exploration and Conservation of the Resources of the Sea*, The Netherlands: A. W. Sijthof, 1959, pp. 59-65; L. J. Bouchez, *The Regimes of Bays in International Law*, The Hague: Martinus Nijhoff, 1964, pp. 116-117, 198; Shigeru Oda, "International Law of the Resources of the Sea," *Hague Recueil des Cours*, Vol. 127 (1970), pp. 384-387.

Law of the Sea Institute, University of Hawaii Law School: Jorge Vargas, "Marine Scientific Research and Transfer of Technology," in Jon M. Van Dyke, ed., *Consensus and Confrontation: The United States and the Law of the Sea Convention*, 1985, pp. 453-455, 458-460; Boleslaw A. Boczek, *The Transfer of Marine Technology to Developing Nations in International Law*, 1982, pp. 23-24, 26, 28-30, 33-34; R. D. Hodgson and Lewis Alexander, *Toward an Objective Analysis of Special Circumstances: Bays, Rivers, Coastal and Oceanic Archipelagos and Atolls*, Kingston: University of Rhode Island, Law of the Sea Institute, Occasional Paper No. 13 (1972), p. 3.

Little, Brown & Company: William W. Bishop, Jr. *International Law, Cases and Materials*, 3rd ed., 1971, pp. 926-928.

Longmans, Green & Co.: Pitman Benjamin Potter, *The Freedom of the Sea in History, Law and Politics*, 1924, pp. 27, 30-35; *International Law*, Vol. 1, 8th ed. by H. Lauterpacht, 1955, pp. 508-509; C. John Colombos, *The International Law of the Sea*, 6th ed., 1967, p. 470.

Louisiana Law Review: John A. Knauss, "The Effects of the Law of the Sea on Future Marine Scientific Research and of Marine Scientific Research on the Future Law of the Sea," *Louisiana Law Review*, Vol. 45 (1985), pp. 1208-1211.

Louisiana State University: Gary Knight, "International Law of Fisheries," *Marine Science Teaching Aid*, Issue No. 2, January 1973, published by the Center for Wetland Resources, Louisiana State University, Baton Rouge, Louisiana, and is sponsored by the Office of Sea Grant, NOAA, U.S. Department of Commerce.

Macmillan Publishers Ltd.: Coleman Phillipson, *The International Law and Custom of Ancient Greece and Rome*, 1911, pp. 376-378.

Manchester University Press: D. W. Bowett, *The Law of the Sea*, 1967, pp. 52-55, 56-58; R. R. Churchill and A. V. Lowe, *The Law of the Sea*, 2nd ed., 1988, pp. 42-43, 43-44, 132, 136-137, 227-231, 242-244, 245-247, 349-351.

Maryland Journal of International Law and Trade: Hungdah Chiu, "Some Problems Concerning the Application of the Maritime Boundary Delimitation Provisions of the 1982 United Nations Convention on the Law of the Sea Between Adjacent or Opposite States," *Maryland Journal of International Law and Trade*, Vol. 9 (1985), PP. 4-6(reprinted with permission also of the author).

Naval Law Review, Naval Justice School, Newport, R.I. 02841: J. R. Brock, "Hot Pursuit and the Right of Pursuit," *JAG Journal*, March-April, 1960, pp. 19-20. Views expressed in this article are of the author's and do not purport to represent the views or policies of the Department of the Navy.

New Haven Press which holds the copyright of the following book: Myres S. McDougal and William T. Burke, *The Public Order of the Oceans*, New Haven, Connecticut and London: Yale University Press, 1962, pp. 306-308. Reprinted with the permission of the authors.

Oceana Publications, Inc.: Kenneth R. Simmonds, ed., *New Directions in the Law of the Sea*, New York: Oceana Publications Inc., New Series, Release 86-2, issued September 1986, J. 24, pp. 3-14; William L. Sullivan, Jr., "Special Problems Concerning Fishing," in *United States Law of the Sea Policy: Options for the Future*, Ocean Policy Study Series, No. 6, 1985, pp. 255-258, 260-261.

Oregon Law Review: William T. Burke, "The Law of the Sea Convention Provisions on Conditions of Access to Fisheries Subject to National Jurisdiction," *Oregon Law Review*, Vol. 63(1984), pp. 78-79, 84-85, 87-89. Copyright 1984 by University of Oregon. Reprinted by permission also of the author.

In the 1980 edition of this casebook published by Claitor's Law Books & Publishing Division, *McGill Law Journal*, granted permission to reprint E. J. Cosford, "Continental Shelf 1910-1945," *McGill Law Journal*, Vol. 4 (1958), pp. 245, 246-253. However, with the revision of the copyright law, Julia E. Hanigsberg, Editor-in-Chief of the MLJ informed me in a letter dated July 16, 1990 that the MLJ no longer holds the copyright for that article and that permission must be requested from the author. However, the MLJ was unable to provide an address of the author to me. I have made reasonable efforts to locate the author but without avail. I think that inclusion of approximately 3 pages of this article in this casebook is consistent with the "fair use" principle of the copyright law. Similarly, I have been unable to locate Michael R. Molitor to get his permission to reprint 3 pages from Hugo Caminos and Michael R. Molitor, "Progressive Development of International Law and the Package Deal," *American Journal of International Law*, Vol. 79 (1985), pp. 879, 887-889. Since one of the authors has granted me permission to reprint that article, I think that inclusion of 3 pages of this article in this casebook is consistent with the "fair use" principle of the copyright law. I am also prepared, if necessary, to pay a reasonable fee to each of these two authors for reprinting those pages of their articles in this casebook, as soon as they have been located.

HUNGDAH CHIU
January 21, 1991

FOREWORD

This collection of materials prepared by Gary Knight and Hungdah Chiu illustrates the fact that since 1945 international law of the sea has been developing at a rapid pace, becoming one of the most important areas of public international law. Its 1982 codification in the form of the United Nations Convention on the Law of the Sea contains more than 400 articles in its text and substantive annexes, and its printed version is a sizable book of more than 200 pages. And this is only the beginning! There are in addition more than a hundred of additional treaties, conventions and protocols dealing with various aspects of the law of the sea.

The authors of this casebook have made a valiant attempt to bring order into this chaos, using a variety of materials to introduce the reader to fifteen principal aspects of the law of the sea. The first three chapters provide a general introduction to the subject--on the variety of the ocean spaces and jurisdictional zones, on the history of the subject from the Greeks and the Romans to the protracted negotiations that resulted in the 1982 Convention, and on special problems facing an international lawyer trying to determine whether there is a rule on the subject that interests his/her client. Two chapters deal with the many disputes relating to the delimitation of jurisdictional zones in the ocean. The next four chapters consider the consequences of this delimitation in the centuries old struggle between coastal states trying to extend their jurisdiction as far as possible into the sea and the seafaring states insisting on as complete freedom of navigation as possible not only on the high seas but also in the areas close to the coast. Four other chapters deal with problems which became specially acute in recent years--fishing, marine pollution, oceanic scientific research, and exploitation of mineral resources of the seabed (especially manganese nodules). The final two chapters consider the two methods for settling international maritime disputes--by peaceful means or naval warfare.

The sources of international law of the sea used by the authors consist largely of the provisions of the 1982 Law of the Sea Convention, a few relatively long and many short excerpts from judicial decisions, a large number of excerpts from books and articles, and some excerpts from various reports relating to the draft history of the various treaty articles. The authors take also into account United States laws and regulations on the subject. There are many notes providing additional information, as well as numerous lists of "references," containing well-arranged bibliographical information.

Since its first edition by Professor Knight in 1969, many additions have been made to the original materials, and Professor Chiu in this new edition has added another large amount of documentation relating to the 1982 Convention which was adopted after the last Knight edition. By now it is a real treasure trove of materials on the subject.

The interest in the law of the sea has not been diminished by the United States' refusal to ratify the Law of the Sea Convention, as the Reagan Administration had in fact accepted most of it as a crystallization of customary international law. Even the subject of deep seabed mining has become more acceptable after the international consortia, in which several United States companies participate, obtained from the United Nations Preparatory Commission, with the help of several foreign allies, a guarantee to be treated as pioneer investors with the privilege to explore and exploit specified areas of the North Pacific when the Convention comes into force. By a series of exchanges of notes the United States accepted these complex arrangements.

Consequently, the United States will soon need a generation of international lawyers that will be familiar with the law of the sea; law schools will have to start teaching it more thoroughly; and books like this one will provide the necessary guides to this complicated subject.

Athens, Georgia
January 1. 1991

LOUIS B. SOHN
Woodruff Professor of International Law,
University of Georgia, School of Law;
Bemis Professor of International Law,
Emeritus, Harvard Law School

THE INTERNATIONAL LAW OF THE SEA: CASES, DOCUMENTS AND READINGS

Gary Knight and Hungdah Chiu

SUMMARY OF CONTENTS

DETAILED TABLE OF CONTENTS

CHAPTER VI THE INTERNAL WATERS, TERRITORIAL SEA, STRAIT AND CONTIGUOUS ZONE

CHAPTER VII   THE HIGH SEAS

CHAPTER VIII   CONTINENTAL SHELF

CHAPTER IX   EXCLUSIVE ECONOMIC ZONE

**CHAPTER X   EXPLOITATION AND USE OF THE SEABED
                BEYOND NATIONAL JURISDICTION**

CHAPTER XI   INTERNATIONAL FISHERY MANAGEMENT AND PROTECTION OF MARINE MAMMALS

CHAPTER XII   MARINE POLLUTION

CHAPTER XIII   MARINE SCIENTIFIC RESEARCH AND
                     TRANSFER OF MARINE TECHNOLOGY

CHAPTER I

THE NATURE OF OCEANS AND SEAS
AND THEIR JURISDICTIONAL ZONES

A. OCEANS AND SEAS IN GENERAL

"Oceans and Seas," *Encyclopaedia Britannica*, Macropaedia, Vol. 13, Chicago et al.: Encyclopaedia Britannica, Inc., 15th ed., 1974, 1982 reprint, pp. 482-484. Reprinted by permission of Encyclopaedia Britannica, Inc.

The oceans and seas cover about 71 percent of the Earth's surface and constitute its most conspicuous feature. These waters, together with the relatively small amount that occurs in the form of rivers, lakes, ice, and ground water, are called the Earth's hydrosphere. The other physical spheres of the Earth are the atmosphere and the lithosphere (the rock sphere of the Earth).

The oceans and seas form an integrated unit and together may properly be called the World Ocean. The Caspian Sea and the Dead Sea, however, are generally considered to be salty lakes. The exact boundaries between the various seas and oceans are arbitrarily defined and have been fixed by convention.

For many years, five oceans were accepted, namely the Atlantic, Pacific, Indian, Arctic, and Antarctic oceans. After the work of Otto Krümmel (*Handbuch der Ozeanographie 1897*), however, it became common practice to recognize only three oceans, the Atlantic, Pacific and Indian. The Arctic Ocean is now regarded as belonging to the Atlantic Ocean; this is a not unreasonable view, because it is a marginal sea of the Atlantic. The Bering Strait, which divides the Arctic from the Pacific Ocean, is only 58 kilometers (36 miles) wide and 58 meters (190 feet) deep.

The great Southern Ocean, as it is sometimes called, is one continuous stretch of water encircling the Antarctic continent. By convention, it has been divided into three portions, one for each of the three principal oceans. The dividing line between the Atlantic and the Indian oceans is the meridian through Cape Agulhas, South Africa (20° E). The Atlantic is divided from the Pacific Ocean by a line extending from Cape Horn at the southern tip of South America to the South Shetland Islands, off the tip of the Antarctic continent, in the Falkland Islands dependency; in the north, the separation consists of the narrowest part of the Bering Strait, separating Alaska and western Siberia. The dividing line between the Indian Ocean and the Pacific extends from the Malay Peninsula through Sumatra, Java, Timor, and Cape Londonderry in Australia to Tasmania and thence continuing along the meridian of 147° E, directly south to Antarctica. Notwithstanding these conventional divisions, the great marine area in the far south, the Southern Ocean, exhibits global continuity and marked oceanographic and meteorological features that distinguish it as a physical entity. One outstanding feature is the predominance of west winds, which give rise to the powerful West Wind Drift, a broad, closed west-east current in the upper water layers.

The oceans predominate over land areas in the Southern Hemisphere far more than they do in the Northern Hemisphere; the ratio of water to land area is roughly 4:1, 81:19 in the Southern Hemisphere and roughly 3:2, 61:39 in the Northern. Considering zones, or belts, on the earth's surface at intervals of five degrees, latitude, land predominates only between 45° and 70°N, where the Eurasian continent lies, and between 70° and 90° S, which is the location of Antarctica.

Everywhere else the oceans predominate; indeed, between about 84° and 90° N there is no known land at all, and from 45° to 66° S only a very small fraction of the surface is land. The areas of the Atlantic, the Indian, and the Pacific oceans, including their marginal seas, are roughly in the proportion of 10:7:17, respectively. . . .

In shape, the Atlantic Ocean is distinctly oblong in a north-south direction and is much more irregular than the other two oceans. It narrows between the eastern tip of Brazil and the western bulges of Africa, and this aspect of its shape is striking. On both sides of the North Atlantic but especially on the eastern side, large marginal seas and bays occur; the Mediterranean and Black Sea, the Bay of Biscay, the North Sea, the Baltic Sea, all on the eastern side, Baffin Bay, Hudson Bay, the Gulf of Mexico, and the Caribbean Sea on the western side are examples. By contrast, the configuration of the South Atlantic is much smoother, as is the eastern littoral (coastal region) of the Pacific Ocean from north to south. The western border of the Pacific, however, is indented considerably by adjacent seas such as the Sea of Okhotsk, the Sea of Japan, the East China Sea, the Yellow Sea, the South China Sea, and the seas of the Indonesian archipelago. Finally, in the Indian Ocean, only a few seas of significance occur along its northern margin, namely the Red Sea, the Persian Gulf, the Arabian Sea, and the Bay of Bengal.

The Atlantic Ocean has the greatest length of coastline because of its irregular shape; the length is greater than that of the Indian and Pacific oceans combined. Another distinctive feature of the Atlantic Ocean is that the major continental rivers discharge into it. Because navigation has played an important part in the history of civilization, the presence of irregular coastlines with many marginal seas, shielded bays, and river mouths, which provide excellent natural harbours, has contributed to the development and spread of culture. The lands bordering the Mediterranean Sea and western Europe and the coastal regions of India, China, and Japan have been so favoured. . . .

The average depth of all the seas has been estimated at 3,790 meters (12,430 feet), a figure considerably larger than that of the average elevation of the land above the sea level, which is 840 meters (2,760 feet). If the average depth is multiplied by its respective surface area, the volume of the World Ocean is 11 times the volume of the land above sea level. The maximum depth of the ocean, 10,850 meters (35,597 feet), occurs in the Mariana Trench, halfway between the islands of Guam and Yap in the Pacific Ocean. This depth exceeds the height of Mt. Everest, which is 8,848 meters (29,028 feet).

. . . . Because the 0-200 meter (660-foot) depth zone corresponds to the continental shelf, it covers almost as large an area as the zone with depths of 200-2,000 meters, which is the region of occurrence of the far steeper continental slope; on the other hand, depths of more than 6,000 meters cover only a very small part of the ocean bottom, in contrast to 3,000-6,000 meter depths. . . .

The relatively shallow, submerged platform bordering the continents, called the continental shelf, slopes gently seaward to the shelf break, where an increase in gradient leads to the continental slope. Conventionally, the edge of the shelf has been placed at the 100-fathom (180-meter; about 600-foot) depth line, although the water depth at the shelf break is more nearly 85 fathoms. The width of the continental shelf varies enormously, from nearly zero along parts of the west coast of North and South America to more than 1,000 kilometers (620 miles) off the north coast of Siberia. The average width is 75 kilometers (47 miles), and the average slope is 1.7 meters per kilometer (0.1°). The continental slope extends downward to a depth of about 4,000 meters (13,000 feet). Its average slope near the shelf is some 70 meters per kilometer (4°) over a width of 20-100 kilometers, and farther out to sea it gradually becomes gentler. The third zone, which may vary in width from 0 to 600 kilometers (400 miles), is called the continental rise. It merges with the deep-sea abyssal plain at an average depth of about 4,000 meters (13,100 feet).

An extraordinary feature of the continental slope is that at many places it is intersected by chasms with steep irregular sides, called submarine canyons, which extend from the continental margin to the ocean floors....

A rise is a long, broad elevation coming gently and smoothly from the sea floor. A ridge is a long, narrow elevation of the sea floor with steep sides and topography more irregular than that of a rise. Sometimes, the highest parts of a ridge project as islands above the sea, as is the case with the Azores, on the Mid-Atlantic Ridge. A sill is a ridge or rise separating a partially closed basin, trough, or trench from another basin or from the adjacent sea floor. The greatest water depth over a sill is called the sill depth. A plateau is the upper surface of a comparatively flat-topped, extensive elevation of the sea floor, normally rising more than 100 fathoms on all sides. A bank is an elevation of the sea floor that is located on a continental shelf or an island shelf and over which the depth of water is relatively shallow but sufficient for surface navigation. A basin is a large depression of the sea floor that is more or less equidimensional in form. When the length of a depression is considerably greater than the width, and the slope of the sides is fairly gentle, the feature is called a trough. A trench is a long, narrow depression of the deep-sea floor having relatively steep sides and generally greater depths than those occurring in troughs.

B. OCEAN/SEA SPACE STRATA AND THEIR USES/VALUES FOR MANKIND

A cross section of ocean space, such as that seen in Figure 1-2, indicates that there are five basic strata, each of which has particular uses or values for man.

The *atmosphere* has obvious value as a medium for flight. Although "air law" is a distinct subject from "law of the sea," there are aspects of ocean overflight which are of importance to the material in this book. For example, questions of passage through straits used for international navigation involve overflight of such straits as well as navigation through them. Further, in the chapter on special contiguous zones, mention is made of the United States Air Defense Identification Zone system among other examples of contiguous zone jurisdiction. Finally, though weather modification is not yet a branch of law of the sea, Figure 1-1 recognizes that the atmosphere-ocean interaction is a critical component in weather determination.

The *surface* of the sea has as its most obvious and important use the navigation of ships. Transportation of goods by merchant shipping still ranks number one among uses of ocean space in terms of gross annual product. Naval forces are, of course, essential to national security in most coastal nations. Navigation is also a necessary component of virtually every other use of the water column, seabed, and subsoil--fishing is dependent on surface navigation, but so is the development of offshore petroleum and natural gas deposits (for vessels must tow the structures to their oceanic locations before drilling can begin); further, installations for the extraction of petroleum, natural gas, and sulfur from submerged lands must also occupy a portion of the surface of the sea. This area is also the site of several of the newer and more exotic uses of the ocean, including offshore deep draft harbor facilities ("superports"), buoyant power generating plants, floating cities and airports, and multipurpose artificial sea islands.

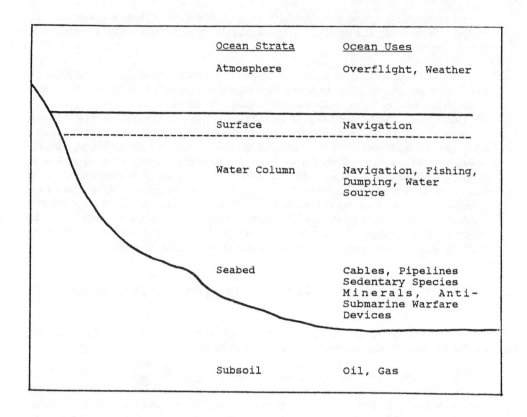

Ocean Space: Strata and Uses
Figure 1-1

The *water column* is the repository of vast quantities of living marine resources. The world fishery is second only to transportation in gross annual economic value. Submarines, an integral part of national defense systems, navigate through the water column as well as on the surface. The water column also accepts waste products dumped into the ocean. Finally, seawater can be converted into fresh water by the process of desalination. A more exotic use of the water column is the use of temperature differentials to generate electrical power through ocean thermal energy conversion devices.

The earliest use of the *seabed* was the exploitation of sedentary species of living resources. Later, submarine cables for intercontinental communication were laid on the bed of the sea. More recently, pipelines have been situated there to transport fossil fuels to shore from their continental shelf sources. Hard minerals are now being mined from the deep ocean floor and anti-submarine warfare (ASW) tracking and detection devices have been implanted on continental shelves and slopes the world over.

The *subsoil* holds substantial quantities of minerals such as oil, gas, and sulfur, the extraction of which places them behind only transportation and fisheries in gross annual value.

C. JURISDICTIONAL ZONES IN OCEANS/SEAS

The seabed and subsoil are not smooth, plain features. They are constituted of complex geological phenomena, some as yet not perfectly understood. Figure 1-2 identifies the major geomorphological features of the sea floor in a typical coastal area. The most important point to bear in mind at this stage is that legal concepts and zones in the ocean seldom bear direct relationships to geologic or scientific facts. For example, the 12, 50, and 200 mile limits for fishery jurisdiction hardly ever coincide with the actual migratory patterns of fish.

Figures 1-3 and 1-4 illustrate the basic zones of ocean/sea jurisdiction under the four 1958 Geneva Conventions on the Law of the Sea and the 1982 United Nations Convention on the Law of the Sea.

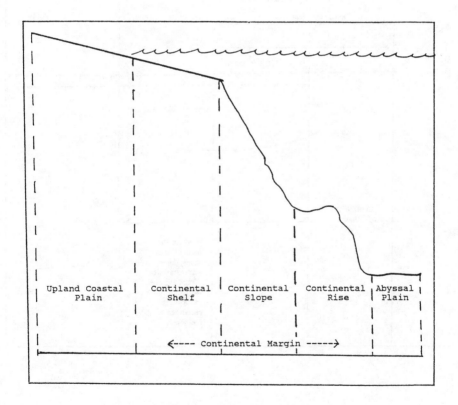

Geology of Seabed and Subsoil
Figure 1-2

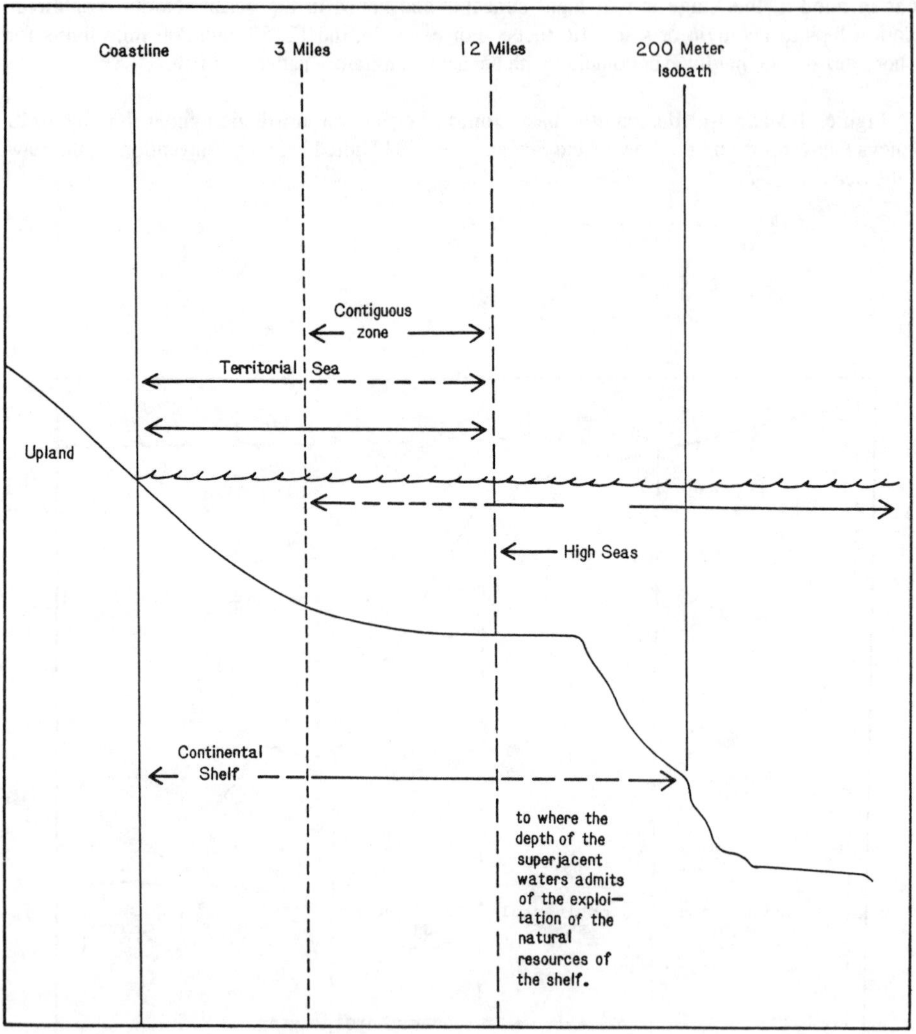

Basic Zones of Ocean/Sea Jurisdiction Under the 1958
Geneva Conventions on the Law of the Sea
Figure 1-3

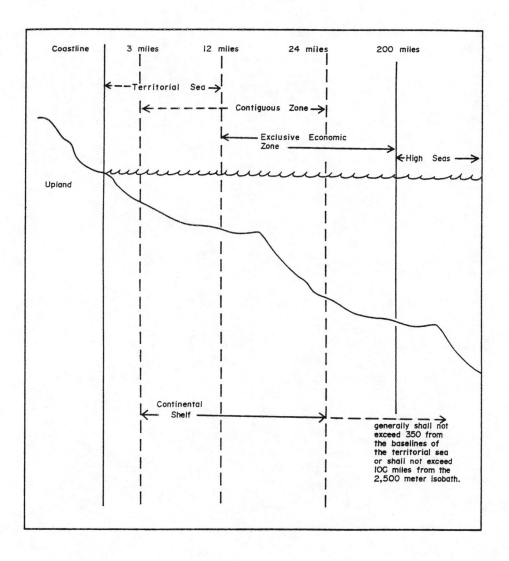

Basic Zones of Ocean/Sea Jurisdiction Under the 1982
United Nations Convention on the Law of the Sea
Figure 1-4

CHAPTER II

THE HISTORY OF THE LAW OF THE SEA

A. INTRODUCTION

D.P. O'Connell, *The International Law of the Sea*, edited by I.A. Shearer, Vol. 1, New York: Oxford University Press, 1982, p. 1. Reprinted by permission of Oxford University Press.

The history of the law of the sea has been dominated by a central and persistent theme: the competition between the exercise of governmental authority over the sea and the idea of the freedom of the seas. The tension between these has waxed and waned through the centuries, and has reflected the political, strategic, and economic circumstances of each particular age. When one or two great commercial powers have been dominant or have achieved parity of power, the emphasis in practice has lain upon the liberty of navigation and the immunity of shipping from local control; in such ages the seas have been viewed more as strategic than as economic areas of competition. When, on the other hand, great powers have been in decline or have been unable to impose their wills upon smaller States, or when an equilibrium of power has been attained between a multiplicity of States, the emphasis has lain upon the protection and reservation of maritime resources, and consequently upon the assertion of local authority over the sea. That was the case in the first half of the seventeenth century, when the Habsburg Empire was in decline and new local forces were asserting themselves, notably England and Sweden; at that time there was much talk about marine resources being exhaustible and in need of conservation; and that is the case again today, when the maritime powers coexist in equilibrium upon the pivot of mutual deterrence and cannot prevail over the host of small States that have tended to usurp their authority. After three hundred years, the talk is again of the exhaustibility of resources.

REFERENCES

There are numerous articles or books relating to the history of the law of the sea; it is neither possible nor necessary to list many of them here. Therefore, for Sections A to E of this Chapter, one should read the appropriate parts of the following works (and the literature cited there) for detailed information on the period in which one has an interest: C. John Colombos, *The International Law of the Sea*, 6th rev. ed., London: Longmans, 1967, pp. 7-46; R.P. Anand, *Origin and Development of the Law of the Sea, History of International Law Revisited*, The Hague: Martinus Nijhoff Publishers, 1982; D.P. O'Connell, *The International Law of the Sea*, edited by I.A. Shearer, Vol. 1, New York: Oxford University Press, 1982, pp. 1-21.

On development of the law of the sea in different regions or countries, *see* F.V. Garcia Amador, *Latin America and the Law of the Sea*, Law of the Sea Institute, University of Rhode Island, Occasional Paper No. 14, 1972; W.E. Butler, *The Soviet Union and the Law of the Sea*, Baltimore: Johns Hopkins University Press, 1971; A.A. el-Hakim, *The Middle Eastern States and the Law of the Sea*, Manchester: Manchester University Press, 1979, J. Greenfield, *China and the Law of the Sea, Air and Environment*, Alphen aan den Rijn, The Netherlands: Sijthoff & Noordhoff, 1979; A.L. Hollick, *U.S. Foreign Policy and the Law of the Sea*, Princeton, N.J.: Princeton University Press, 1981; Charles G. MacDonald, *Iran, Saudi Arabia, and the Law of the Sea, Political Interaction and Legal Development in the Persian Gulf*, Westport, Conn: Greenwood Press, 1980; N.S. Rembe, *Africa and the International Law of the Sea*, The Hague: Sijthoff & Noordhoff, 1980.

B. THE GREEK AND ROMAN PERIOD

> Coleman Phillipson, *The International Law and Custom of Ancient Greece and Rome*, London: Macmillan and Co., Ltd., 1911, pp. 376-378. Reprinted by permission of Macmillan Publishers, Ltd.

[In Ancient Greece] [p]roperty in the sea was considered possible, not merely in the territorial waters, but in regions extending far beyond these limits. The maritime ascendency of this or that conquering nation was not regarded from a merely comparative point of view as to the predominance of interests, but was asserted and exercised rather in the sense of absolute proprietorship. Herodotus refers to Minos the Cnossian as having obtained the empire of the sea . . . . In the provisions of alliances are sometimes found such expressions as . . . "to rule the sea," . . . "to be lord or master". . . . "to become lord of the sea," . . . "to have command of the sea;" but such terms have different shades of meaning according to the circumstances of time and place, and are seldom used in the literal sense of complete ownership; for the most part they designate temporary supremacy, or predominating influence . . . .

Most of the leading maritime States of antiquity claimed such sovereignty at one time or another. The policy of Athens was, in this respect, often avowed openly; and to attain this supremacy she was ready to wage war against Sparta or Philip, as the case might be . . . . But the Athenians refrained from exercising tyrannical power over the seas. They welcomed all commercial relationships . . . . Indeed, the Athenians were in favour of the freedom of the sea.

> Pitman Benjamin Potter, *The Freedom of the Sea in History, Law and Politics*, New York and London: Longmans, Green & Co., 1924, pp. 27, 30-35. Reprinted by permission of Longmans Group.

When we turn to state practice in the Roman period, on the other hand, we find phenomena almost identical with those observed among the Greek states. Carthage, the Italian states preceding Rome, and Rome herself, all attempted to secure, and definitely claimed, maritime dominion as clearly as, if not more clearly than, had Athens and Crete in their day.

What, now, shall be said of the value and significance of this evidence of Roman maritime dominion, and how to reconcile the doctrine of the jurists with the practice of the Roman state?

In the first place, it is notable that Rome was dealing here not with local or limited bodies of water merely, such as the Aegean Sea or the coastal waters of Greece or Italy, but the whole Mediterranean, an inland sea in one sense, but the open sea as the Romans knew it. On the other hand, it is noticeable that the Roman policy and claim was applied to the Mediterranean chiefly as it became a lake surrounded entirely by Roman territory, and not -- except by extremists -- to the Atlantic Ocean although the Romans were fully acquainted with the latter.

Even as applied solely to the Mediterranean, however, the state policy of Rome seems to conflict directly with the principles of the Institutes and the Digest and, in view of the importance which has been attached to those principles in the history of the controversy over the freedom of the sea, it will be necessary to examine the matter with some care.

. . . .

The rules in the Institutes and in the Digest refer merely to the free use, common use, public use, of the sea by all members of the Roman state. They relate to the rights of individuals toward one another in a single national society. They are not rules of interstate or international law at all. Antoninus spoke not of a law of nations but of Roman public law alone. This appears to be evident on the surface, but, if any further proof were needed, the use of the term "public," which meant common to all Roman citizens, would be conclusive. The limitation upon individual use, under the general right of public enjoyment, in the interests of preserving that public enjoyment, is further evidence to the same conclusion. Likewise, the shores, which fell under the principle of public use, were specifically declared to belong "to the Roman people."

Granting then, that the law of the Institutes and Digest does not itself disprove the existence of Roman maritime dominion as against other states -- and perhaps even reenforces it by implying a Roman state dominion in the sea for the enjoyment of all Roman citizens -- can the theory of that law be recast or transposed to apply in the international sphere? . . .

Again in this period, as in the period of Athenian supremacy, the condition of international law presents a bar to the sure conclusion that Rome possessed a maritime dominion recognized by a law of nations. Now more than ever before was a true international law impossible. Rome had swallowed up the independent states of the Mediterranean basin. She claimed a maritime dominion, took control by her naval power, and exercised it freely and fully. But not with the free consent of free states. As a result of her conquests her sea dominion became a matter of imperial constitutional law and practice. As in Greek times, so here, we find practially no recognition of Roman maritime dominion among the many treaties concluded by Rome with other powers. Rome held more physical power over the sea than any state in antiquity; less than in the days of Pericles, however, could it be said that there existed a freely recognized maritime dominion under freely accepted international law.

. . . .

In sum, it cannot be said that either Athens or Rome held a maritime dominion recognized by a law among independent states as legally valid, in spite of their naval supremacy, their success in suppressing piracy, and the ideas and feelings of historians and poets regarding their position in general. The freedom of the seas was a great problem of interstate politics and diplomacy in this age, but not one which had yet become a matter of formal international law.

C. DEVELOPMENTS IN THE MIDDLE AGES

Thomas Wemyss Fulton, *The Sovereignty of the Sea*, Edinburgh and London: W. Blackwood and Sons, 1911, pp. 3-6.   Reprinted by permission of Blackwood Pillan & Wilson Co.

Although according to the Roman law the sea was common and free to all, in the middle ages many seas had become more or less effectively appropriated, and civilian writers began to assign to maritime states, as a principle of law, a certain jurisdiction in the waters adjacent to their coasts. The distance to which such jurisdiction was allowed by those writers was variously stated. Very commonly it extended to sixty or one hundred miles from the land, and thus included all the bordering sea within which navigation was practically confined.   Sometimes the principle governing the ownership of rivers was transferred in theory to the sea, the possession of the opposite shores by the same state being held to entitle that state to the sovereignty over the intervening water; or, if it possessed only one shore, to the same right as far as the mid-line. In most cases, however, the appropriation of the sea was effected by force and legalized afterwards, if legalized at all, and the disputes on the subject between different nations not infrequently led to

legalized at all, and the disputes on the subject between different nations not infrequently led to sanguinary wars.

The most notable instances are to be found among the early Italian Republics. Long before the end of the thirteenth century Venice, eminent for her commerce, wealth, and maritime power, assumed the sovereignty over the whole of the Adriatic, though she was not in possession of both the shores, and after repeated appeals to the sword she was able to enforce the right to levy tribute on the ships of other peoples which navigated the Gulf, or to prohibit their passage altogether. The neighboring cities and commonwealths were soon compelled to agree to her claim, which was eventually recognized by other Powers of Europe and by the Pope. The right of Venice to the dominion of the Adriatic, arising in this way by force, became firmly established by custom and treaty; and even after she had fallen from her greatness and was hardly able to sustain her claim by the sword, it was still for a time admitted by other nations, who looked upon the Republic as forming a useful barrier to the farther extension of the Turk in Europe and as a scourge to the Saracen pirates. On the other side of the Italian peninsula, the Republic of Genoa advanced a similar claim to the dominion of the Ligurian Sea, and some of the other Mediterranean states followed the sample in the waters with which they were most immediately concerned.

Then in the north of Europe, Denmark and Sweden, and later Poland, contended for or shared in the dominion of the Baltic. The Sound and the Belts fell into the possession of Denmark, the Bothnian Gulf passed under the rule of Sweden; and all the northern seas between Norway on the one hand, and the Shetland Isles, Iceland, Greenland, and Spitzbergen on the other, were claimed by Norway and later by Denmark, on the principle referred to above, that possession was held of the opposite shores. The Scandinavian claims to maritime dominion are probably indeed the most important in history. They led to several wars; they were the cause of many international treaties and of innumerable disputes about fishery, trading, and navigation; they were the last to be abandoned. Until about half a century ago Denmark still exacted a toll from ships passing through the Sound, -- a tribute which at one time was a heavy burden on the trade to and from the Baltic.

D.P. O'Connell, *The International Law of the Sea*, edited by I.A. Shearer, Vol. 1, New York: Oxford University Press, 1982, pp. 2-3. Notes omitted. Reprinted by permission of Oxford University Press.

The celebrated Bull of Pope Alexander VI, given legal effect in the Treaty of Tordesillas in 1494, was issued as a result of the discoveries of Columbus, which were at that time thought to have encroached on the areas of Portuguese discovery to the east. It drew a line down a meridian of longitude through Brazil. East of that line would be the area of Portuguese expansion and westward would be that of Spain. The Pope's role arose because of the question raised in canon law of the jurisdiction of the religious orders which sent out missions in the wake of the discoveries. It was not intended as a reservation of the seas to Spain and Portugal, but it was later thought that it had that effect when both countries forbade trade within their respective areas. It was, in fact, to counter the supposed pretension of the Portuguese in the East Indies that Grotius wrote on the freedom of the seas early in the seventeenth century.

The doctrine of the sovereignty of the seas, as a general concept, really dates from the publication of Bodin's treatise on sovereignty in 1582, when he wrongly ascribed to Baldus the idea that governmental power was exercisable over shipping within sixty miles from the coast. That appeared at the time to vindicate a rather vague notion that the Italian maritime cities had traditionally exercised such a jurisdiction. Certainly it propagated the notion at a time when governments were susceptible and the political circumstances favorable to it. By 1600, the idea of sovereignty itself had gained a firm grip on political and legal theory, and the formulation of the sovereignty of the seas during the following two decades was a plausible corollary to it. To that extent, the doctrine can be regarded as a Renaissance artefact.

Apart from the shadowy instance of Venice in the Adriatic, which was defended by Pacius in 1619, the two notable claims to sovereignty of the seas, out of which the controversy leading to the modern law of the sea arose, were those of England and Sweden. The latter's claim to sovereignty over the Baltic, which was a feature of the expansionist policy of Gustavus Adolphus, was really a claim to a closed sea from which non-Baltic Powers were to be excluded in their commercial activity except upon payment of tolls. It was thus different in character as well as in geographical scope from the claims of England.

James I brought with him to England the Scottish notion of land-kenning, according to which the King of Scotland was deemed to possess whatever lay within the range of vision of a ship in sight of the coast. That was probably not a doctrine peculiar to Scotland, but one common to the northern countries. At all events, it is likely to have influenced James I's policy of claiming sovereignty over the British seas [in 1609] . . . .

D . FROM THE SEVENTEENTH CENTURY TO THE LATE NINETEENTH CENTURY

> D.P. O'Connell, *International Law*, Vol. 1, London: Stevens & Sons, 1970, pp. 455-459. Notes omitted. Reprinted with the permission of Sweet & Maxwell.

(a)   The Seventeenth Century

The Roman lawyers characterized the sea as *res communis*, by which they meant that it was beyond appropriation. They were thinking, of course, in terms of appropriation by private persons, and the problem of appropriation by the State could not have occurred within the context of the Roman Empire. Nonetheless, their characterization was to influence the outcome of the passionate debate in the seventeenth century on the freedom of the sea which began in earnest when James I of England, who had inherited a developed doctrine of the rights of the King of Scotland in the sea, issued in 1609 a proclamation excluding Dutch fishermen from operating off the shores of England. By coincidence the same year saw the publication of Grotius' treatise *Mare Liberum* which was a counterblast, not to James' pretensions, but to those of the Portuguese. Just as today, fisheries in the seventeenth century were vital national interests, and the collision of these interests between Holland and England prompted a reply to Grotius on the part of several English lawyers. Actually Grotius had written on the freedom of navigation, but Welwood, a Scottish lawyer in 1613 attacked him on the ground that *mare liberum* would leave England's fisheries to the mercy of every comer. Grotius was stimulated to a retort, later embodied in *De jure belli ac pacis*. In turn the challenge was taken up by Callis, Boroughs and Selden.

At this point, then, the question of fishery became inextricably entangled with the question of the extent of national territory. What Grotius meant when he said that "no part of the sea can be counted in the territory of any people" is not clear, for elsewhere he said that the controversy was not over gulfs or straits "nor indeed of all that which is visible from the shore." Welwood seized on this exception and used it to rationalize the proclamation of James I, which moved Grotius to shift his ground and conclude that if the sea is common to all men "therefore no man should be prohibited from fishing in the sea." Whether Grotius thus excluded the conception of the territorial sea we cannot exactly tell, but his fellow-countryman Pontanus proposed that the Grotian rule be valid only outside an area of coastal waters which the coastal State might appropriate. Pontanus thus appears to be the originator of the modern doctrine of territorial waters. He was followed in England by Meadows at a time when that country's more exaggerated claims were in process of evaporation. Out of the controversy evolved the two conceptions, each the corollary of the other, of the freedom of the seas and the territorial sea.

(b)   The Eighteenth Century

It is probable that England's claims were altogether abandoned by 1700, and that the maritime boundary did not retreat to the three-mile limit but to the low-water mark, with an advance to a marine league at a later stage. The eighteenth century, then, is the period when the new conception of the territorial sea was in process of crystallization. In 1704 Bynkershoek, discarding Grotius' distinction between *imperium* and *dominium*, proposed that sovereignty should be exercised as far as authority extends by force of arms. Vattel to some extent put the question back in the melting pot by advancing an argument anticipating those in favor of the continental shelf of today, but most of his contemporaries settled for Bynkershoek's principle, which came to be known as the cannon-shot rule from the notion that he who can dominate the sea with artillery placed on the coast satisfies the criterion of effective control.

The same criterion was adopted when neutrality questions became prominent in the American War of Independence, and Galiani is credited with the proposal that war could not be waged within three miles of a neutral coast, three miles being, supposedly, the ultimate range of artillery at that time. Whether the three-mile rule was ever regarded as a mere fixing of the limits of the cannon-shot is disputable. In fact all through the eighteenth century, for one purpose or another, varying distances were adopted in the exercise of maritime jurisdiction. For example, in the first English Acts of Parliament dealing with smuggling varying limits were set to customs jurisdiction, apparently on the assumption that international law placed no precise limit on the extent of jurisdiction to protect the revenue. Later the revenue jurisdiction over foreign ships was restricted to three miles.

Sometime during the French Revolutionary period disparate jurisdictions such as fishing, police, revenue and neutrality, each claiming the privilege of the cannon-shot rule, came to be fused in British and American practice under the comprehensive notion of the territorial sea. In 1794 the extent of this sea was fixed for neutrality purposes by the United States at a marine league, and doubtless this influenced the English prize courts in their development of the three mile rule during the Napoleonic Wars. Actually, the United States, except for neutrality purposes, at that time favored a three-league territorial sea, and it seems to have been British pressure that consolidated the three-mile rule and brought fishery jurisdiction within it.

(c)   The Nineteenth Century

While the neutrality and fishery jurisdictions stabilized in Anglo-American practice at three miles, the revenue jurisdiction was gradually disengaged, until sometime in the middle of the nineteenth century the notion of a contiguous zone outside the territorial sea and within the high seas emerged, within which zone the customs authorities might take action against foreign smuggling vessels.

During the whole of the nineteenth century the three-mile rule for fishery remained one of controversy. Spain, in deference to England's wishes, experimented with it in the 1820's and returned to a six-mile limit. Scandinavian countries maintained a four-mile rule established in

1812. Denmark adopted the three-mile rule in 1882. In 1837 a mixed Anglo-French commission was set up to deal with the fishery question in the Channel. The result was the Fishery Convention of 1839 which reserved oyster beds in Granville Bay to France and applied the three-mile rule to other fisheries. This limit was thought sufficient to protect breeding. In 1849 a dispute developed with Belgium over the right of Belgian fishermen to fish within three miles of the coast of England, and in 1852 it was settled on the most-favored-nation principle. Belgium had adopted the three-mile rule in 1832 and Holland followed in 1883. Greece also adopted three miles in 1869. Following the *Franconia* case in 1876 there was an exchange of correspondence with Germany in which the latter asserted that there was no legal limit to territorial waters. In fact Great Britain was careful not to commit herself to three miles, and studiously omitted all reference to it from the Territorial Waters Jurisdiction Act 1878. In the 1880's negotiations were instituted for joint conservation measures in the North Sea, and curiously it was Great Britain that did not want to specify a limit to territorial waters and France that urged the three-mile rule. In the outcome the North Sea Fishery Convention 1882 adopted a three-mile limit but reserved the Zuider Zee, the Skagerrak and certain shoal water off the Elbe.

(d)   The Arbitrations

This was the era of the great arbitrations which settled the freedom of the sea. The *Costa Rica Packet* arbitration in 1897 distinguished jurisdictions on the high seas from those within "the range of cannon." In the *Behring Sea Fur Seal* arbitration of 1895:

> British subjects were engaged in taking fur seals in the Behring Sea beyond American territorial waters. This had the effect of diminishing the stock which was accustomed to breed in American territory. United States officers seized British sealers on the high seas and the resultant dispute was referred to arbitration. Among the arguments canvassed by the United States were the necessity for fishery conservation and the exclusion of fur seals from the category of "fish" for the purposes of formulating the freedom to fish; an effort was made to assimilate seals to domesticated animals. The arbitrators held that:

> "The United States has not any right of protection or property in the fur seals frequenting the islands of the United States in Behring Sea when such seals are found outside the ordinary three-mile limit."

The three-mile limit in question was that of the United States and the award is not relevant to the general issue of the extent of territorial waters. Regulations were proposed to the two States for agreement and these offered a satisfactory basis of conservation.

This was followed by an arbitration between Russia and the United States in the cases of the *Cape Horn Pigeon*, *Kate and Anna*, *James Hamilton Lewis* and *C.H. White* in which the seizure by Russia of American fishing vessels outside territorial waters was held to be illegal. Then in 1909 there was the award of the Permanent Court of Arbitration in the *North Atlantic Coast Fisheries* arbitration.

This was concerned with the interpretation of the Anglo-American Fishery Convention of 1818, particularly with the question from where sould be measured the "three marine miles of any of the coasts, bays, creeks, or harbors" within which the United States had renounced the right of fishing. The arbitrators found that in 1818 the negotiators had intended a geographical conception, and that the measurement should be from a straight line across water at the point where it ceased to have the configuration of a bay. In part the award was an interpretation and in part a recommendation, and though it is of little direct interest in international law various observations were made during the hearing and in the award which illuminate several questions of international law.

LE LOUIS
2 Dodson 210, 165 Eng. Rpts. 1464 (1817)

This was the case of a French vessel which sailed from Martinique on the 30th of January 1816, destined on a voyage to the coast of Africa and back, and was captured ten or twelve leagues to the southward of Cape Mesurada, by the "Queen Charlotte" cutter, on the 11th of March in the same year, and carried to Sierra Leone. She was proceeded against in the Vice-Admiralty Court of that colony, and the information pleaded, -- 1st, that the seizors were duly and legally commissioned to make captures and seizures. 2d, That the seizure was within the jurisdiction of the Court. 3d, That the vessel belonged to French subjects or others, and was fitted out, manned, and navigated for the purpose of carrying on the African slave trade, after that trade had been abolished by the internal laws of France, and by the treaty between Great Britain and France. 4th, That the vessel had bargained for twelve slaves at Mesurada, and was prevented by the capture alone from taking them on board. 5th, That the brig being engaged in the slave trade, contrary to the laws of France, and the law of nations, was liable to condemnation, and could derive no protection from the French or any other flag. 6th, That the crew of the brig resisted the "Queen Charlotte," and piratically killed eight of her crew, and wounded twelve others. 7th, That the vessel being engaged in this illegal traffic, resisted the King's duly commissioned cruisers, and did not allow of search until overpowered by numbers. And 8th, That by reason of the circumstances stated, the vessel was out of the protection of any law, and liable to condemnation. The ship was condemned to His Majesty in the Vice-Admiralty Court at Sierra Leone, and from this decision an appeal was made to this Court.

[After noting that the evidence showed that the French ship was engaged in the slave trade and that she "resisted by force the King of England's commissioned cruiser," Justice Scott stated:]

Assuming the fact . . . that there was a demand, and a resistance producing the deplorable results here described, I think that the natural order of things compels me to enquire first, whether the party who demanded had a right to search; for if not, then not only was the resistance to it lawful, but likewise the very fact on which the ground of condemnation rests is totally removed. . . .

Upon the first question, whether the right of search exists in time of peace, I have to observe, that two principles of public law are generally recognized as fundamental. One is the perfect equality and entire independence of all distinct states . . . . The second is, that all nations being equal, all have an equal right to the uninterrupted use of the unappropriated parts of the ocean for their navigation. In places where no local authority exists, where the subjects of all states meet upon a footing of entire equality and independence, no one state, or any of its subjects, has a right to assume or exercise authority over the subjects of another. I can find no authority that gives the right of interruption to the navigation of states in amity upon the high seas, excepting that which the rights of war give to both belligerents against neutrals. This right, incommodious as its exercise may occasionally be to those who are subjected to it, has been fully established in the legal practice of nations, having for its foundation the necessities of self-defense, in preventing the enemy from being supplied with the instruments of war, and from having his means of annoyance augmented by the advantages of maritime commerce. . . .

With professed pirates there is no state of peace. They are the enemies of every country, and at all times; and therefore are universally subject to the extreme rights of war . . . But at present, under the law, as now generally understood and practiced, no nation can exercise a right of visitation and search upon the common and unappropriated parts of the sea, save only on the belligerent claim . . . . It is true, that wild claims (alluded to in the argument) have been occasionally set up by nations, particularly those of Spain and Portugal, in the East and West Indian seas: but these are claims of a nature quite foreign to the present question, being claims not of a general right of visitation and search upon the high seas unappropriated, but extravagant claims to the appropriation of particular seas, founded upon some grants of a pretended authority, or upon some ancient exclusive usurpation. Upon a principle much more just in itself and more temperately applied, maritime states have claimed a right of visitation and enquiry within those parts of the ocean adjoining to their shores, which the common courtesy of nations has for their common convenience allowed to be considered as parts, of their dominions for various domestic purposes, and particularly for fiscal or defensive regulations more immediately affecting their safety and welfare. This has nothing in common with a right of visitation and search upon the unappropriated parts of the ocean.

[Justice Scott then observed that the only way in which the seizure could be justified was to characterize the French ship as a pirate, which he refused to do. Other grounds were likewise rejected and the seizure was held unlawful.]

THE MARIANNA FLORA
11 Wheat. (24 U.S.) 1 (1826)

[The *Marianna Flora*, a Portuguese vessel, apparently without cause fired upon an armed American schooner, the *Alligator*, in an area of the high seas approximately nine miles off the coast of the United States. The *Alligator* was at the time engaged in approaching the Portuguese ship for observational purposes. After a sea battle of modest proportions, the *Alligator* captured the *Marianna Flora*, at which time the Portuguese captain explained that he mistook the *Alligator* (which had hoisted the American flag and pendant when fired upon) for a pirate ship. The *Marianna Flora* was brought to port and subsequently libelled by the United States. Judgment was in favor of the *Marianna Flora*, awarding damages for the illegal seizure and detention. The circuit court reversed the award for damages, although sustaining the illegality of the seizure to which judgment the Portuguese excepted. On appeal to the United States Supreme Court the decision of the circuit court was affirmed, no damages being awarded. The court concluded that the *Alligator* did not initiate the conflict and although in the wrong in seizing the *Marianna Flora*, nonetheless should not pay damages.]

In considering the circumstances, the court has no difficulty in deciding, that this is not a case of piratical aggression, in the sense of the act of congress. The Portuguese ship, though armed, was so for a purely defensive mercantile purpose. She was bound homewards, with a valuable cargo on board, and could have no motive to engage in any piratical act or enterprise. It is true, that she made a meditated, and, in a sense, a hostile attack, upon the *Alligator*, with the avowed intention of repelling her approach, or of crippling or destroying her. But there is no reason to doubt, that this attack was not made with a piratical or felonious intent, or for the purpose of wanton plunder, or malicious destruction of property. It was done upon a mistake of the facts, under the notion of just self-defense, against what the master very imprudently deemed a piratical cruiser. The combat was, therefore, a combat on mutual misapprehension; and it ended, without any of those calamitous consequences to life, which might have brought very painful considerations before the court . . .

. . . .

In considering these points [that the conduct of the *Alligator* in the approach and seizure of the *Marianna Flora* was unjustifiable, and that the subsequent sending her in for adjudication was without reasonable cause], it is necessary to ascertain, what are the rights and duties of armed, and other ships, navigating the ocean, in time of peace. It is admitted, that the right of visitation and search does not, under such circumstances, belong to the public ships of any nation. This right is strictly a belligerent right, allowed by the general consent of nations, in time of war, and limited to those occasions. . . .

Upon the ocean, then, in time of peace, all possess an entire equality. It is the common highway of all, appropriated to the use of all; and no one can vindicate to himself a superior or exclusive prerogative there. Every ship sails there with the unquestionable right of pursuing her own lawful business, without interruption; but whatever may be that business, she is bound to pursue it in such a manner as not to violate the rights of others. The general maxim in such cases is, *sic utere tuo, ut non alienum laedas*.

It has been argued, that no ship has a right to approach another at sea; and that every ship has a right to draw round her a line of jurisdiction, within which no other is at liberty to intrude. In short, that she may appropriate so much of the ocean as she may deem necessary for her protection, and prevent any nearer approach. This doctrine appears to us novel, and is not supported by any authority. It goes to establish upon the ocean a territorial jurisdiction, like that which is claimed by all nations, within cannon-shot of their shores, in virtue of their general sovereignty. But the latter right is founded upon the principle of sovereign and permanent appropriation, and has never been successfully asserted beyond it. Every vessel, undoubtedly, has a right to the use of so much of the ocean as she occupies, and as is essential to her own movements. Beyond this, no exclusive right has ever yet been recognized, and we see no reason for admitting its existence.

E. CODIFICATION EFFORTS BEFORE 1945

D.P. O'Connell, *The International Law of the Sea*, edited by I.A. Shearer, Vol. 1, New York: Oxford University Press, 1982, pp. 20-21. Notes omitted. Reprinted by permission of Oxford University Press.

The stability attained in the law of the sea in the second half of the nineteenth century warranted the codifiction of its rules. This was because there were implications to be drawn in the field of the conflict of laws from the operation of the rules of public international law, especially in matters such as collisions at sea. To this task the Institut de Droit International devoted itself during the 1880s and 1890s. Its programme was modest--to establish the geographical areas for the choice of maritime laws--but it ran into difficulties on the questions both of the extent and the nature of territorial waters. So far as extent was concerned, the difficulty was that the increasing range of cannon was invalidating the criterion thought to underlie the three-mile limit, and raising new questions of strategic importance for naval operations in time of war. These new questions came out into the open in the drafting of the Convention on Automatic Contact Mines at the Hague Peace Conference in 1907, and at the London Naval Conference in 1909. Inshore strategic measures would henceforth not only be dangerous but also ineffective, and distant blockade presaged contradictions of the freedom of the seas which many nations found unacceptable. This was to complicate Great Britain's naval planning in 1914 and 1915.

The establishment of the League of Nations seemed auspicious for a final codification of the law of the sea. Various bodies in the 1920s essayed their own codes, and reached a surprising degree of unanimity. They were the Institut de Droit International, the International Law Association, the German and Japanese Societies of International Law and the American Institute of International Law. In addition, two private codifications were attempted, one by Strupp in a celebratory volume dedicated to the Reichsgericht, and another by Harvard Law School. All of these were preambular to the Hague Codification Conference of 1930, which was called by the Assembly of the League to codify, among other things, the law relating to territorial waters. The Conference was planned over several years. A Preparatory Committee was set up to draft Articles for submission to the Conference. It had as rapporteurs, Schücking, assisted by Wickersham and Barbosa de Magalhaes. Their draft was prepared on the basis of a questionnaire sent to governments, whose answers were then commented upon. The whole procedure was directed to establishing what the rules of international law then were, not what they might become. To that extent, the emphasis at the Conference was more legal than political, and delegations included prominent legal experts.

Yet the Hague Conference failed for a political reason, namely the fact that insufficient countries were prepared to commit themselves indefinitely to a three-mile limit for fisheries. Already the issue of fishery conservation had become politically significant. At the fisheries conferences from the 1890s, attention had been drawn to the dangers of over-fishing, and to the need for legal controls, and these had ushered in recurrent demands for coastal State fishing jurisdiction beyond the limit of three miles. If, because of the freedom of the seas, this could not be achieved outside territorial waters, then let the limit of these waters be extended.

F. THE 1958 GENEVA CONVENTIONS ON THE LAW OF THE SEA

D.P. O'Connell, *The International Law of the Sea*, edited by I.A. Shearer, Vol. 1, New York: Oxford University Press, 1982, pp. 21-22. Notes omitted. Reprinted by permission of Oxford University Press.

When the [1930] Hague Conference reported to the League of Nations that it was unable to reach agreement on the extent of the territorial sea, the intention was to explore the question further after a time and reconvene the Conference. The crises of the 1930s and World War II prevented the realization of this design, and it was not until the United Nations was set up that it proved possible to return to the codification of the law of the sea. That was one of the first tasks undertaken by the International Law Commission, which began its work on the subject in 1950. The emphasis of the Commission necessarily differed from that of Schücking in the Preparatory Committee of the Hague Codification Conference, because the Commission's mandate was not only the codification of international law but also its progressive development. That obscured the distinction between the recording of law and the enunciation of proposals. Since the Draft Articles which the commission prepared were preemptory in character, they could not of themselves indicate on which side of the distinction they fell. That could only be determined from the commentaries which the Commission attached to the Draft Articles, or from the debates in the Commission about them.

D.P. O'Connell, *International Law*, Vol. 1, London: Stevens & Sons, 1970, pp. 459-461. Notes omitted. Reprinted with the permission of Sweet & Maxwell.

Between the Conferences of 1930 and 1958 great changes in the practice of States concerning the maritime domain had occurred. In the first place the continental shelf doctrine had emerged and had to be rationalized in terms of the freedom of the seas. Secondly, there was strong pressure in favor of a much wider area of territorial sea. Thirdly, the decision of the International Court of Justice in the *Anglo-Norwegian Fisheries* case had added new considerations to the law. Fourthly, a large number of new States had emerged which were uncommitted to any traditional doctrine and had varying economic interest in the exploitation of the sea and in conservation of its resources. To some it was a matter of interest to sacrifice one's own maritime domain in order to exploit another's; in other cases local interests predominated. The neutrality limit had ceased to be a matter of great moment and there was general agreement on the extent of revenue, police and sanitary measures. It was fishery that was critical. In short, the emphasis in this century has shifted from the sea as a highway to the sea as a reservoir of economic resources.

The International Law Commission's report was debated during the 1957 session of the General Assembly of the United Nations and in the Sixth Committee. Drafts of proposals were distributed to governments and their comments taken into account in the several revisions. The *Geneva Conference* of 1958 was intended in part to explore the possibility of finding agreement on the existing law, and in part to formulate certain proposals to be embodied in draft conventions. A two-third voting rule was adopted. The result, where agreement was reached, was in part declaratory of the law and in part legislative. No agreement was reached at this or a subsequent [second] conference in 1960 on the extent of the territorial sea, but conventions were adopted on most other aspects of jurisdiction on the high seas and in territorial waters. The formulations will be discussed each in its proper context, but some guidance is required on the question to what extent they are *de lege ferenda* and to what extent *de lege lata*. *The Convention on the Territorial Sea and the Contiguous Zone* makes no attempt to clarify the relation between the rules it lays down and the customary law. The failure is the more regrettable in that no hint is given as to the possibility of reservations, and the boundary within which States may contract out of the rules is not even indicated. *The Convention on the High Seas* is expressed to be declaratory of customary law, though some of its formulations, for example, the immunity from arrest of a ship in innocent passage, are not beyond controversy. It is also silent on the question of reservations, possibly because it is intended as a codification of existing law. *The Convention on Fishing and Conservation of the Living Resources of the High Seas* is clearly not a formulation of customary law. Reservations are allowed for all except Articles 6, 7, 9, 10, 11 and 12. The *Convention on the Continental Shelf* avoids committing itself to the question of its relation to customary law, but allows reservations for all the articles which formulate the duties of the coastal State and excludes them from those which allow their rights. It is, perhaps, important to realize that most of the debate at the Conference on this Convention was directed to doctrinal issues, and there was little political objection to the shelf conception as one of law.

The Geneva Conventions may have been premature in two respects: technological development in the exploitation of marine resources was insufficiently developed to reveal the trend of economic interests of the future; and, since decolonization was just beginning, insufficient account was taken of the interests of developing countries. Owing to the hazards of the voting procedures at Geneva the Conventions are in some respects ambiguous and inconsistent, and the selective ratification of some but not all of the Conventions has distorted the total scheme. For example, the Convention on Fishing was intended to mitigate the stringency of the Convention on the High Seas, yet it has not been widely ratified by the exploiting nations, whose highly capitalized fishing industries claim the unrestricted advantages of the freedom of the seas. Since the Conventions tend to put excessive constraints on technological progress it is unlikely that they will become a universal system, and it is likely that parties to them will exploit the loopholes to escape as far as possible from these constraints. It is likely that customary international law will alter under the impact of practices of the non-ratifying nations, so that a disparity between them and the ratifying ones will become increasingly obvious.

D.P. O'Connell, *The International Law of the Sea*, edited by I.A. Shearer, Vol. 1, New York: Oxford University Press, 1982, pp. 23-24. Notes omitted. Reprinted by permission of Oxford University Press.

What is now clear is that the Geneva Conventions cannot be regarded as a 'package' all of the provisions of which are incumbent without regard to their genesis or character. For parties they are such a package, but for non-parties their rules apply only inasmuch as they are customary rules. This has led to a spectrum of situations. There are 56 parties to the High Seas Convention, 45 to the Convention on the Territorial Sea and Contiguous Zone, 53 to the Convention on the Continental Shelf, and 35 to the Convention on the Conservation of Fisheries. Only a minority of States are, therefore, bound by the package. Others are bound in varying degress by the Geneva rules to the extent that these are customary law. As to that, the Conventions themselves give only slight indication.

The character of the Geneva Conventions, at least for parties to them, became controversial when in 1971 Senegal denounced the Convention on the Territorial Sea and Contiguous Zone, and the Convention on Fishing and Conservation of the Living Resources of the High Seas. The Secretary-General of the United Nations declined to accept the denunciation because the Geneva Conventions do not provide for denunciation. That gave rise to an issue between him and Senegal respecting the scope of his depositary functions, and he referred the question to parties to the Convention. Only one Government replied, the United Kingdom, which said that in its view the Geneva Conventions are not snilateral denunciation, and that therefore the validity or effectiveness of the Senegal denunciations could not be accepted. The United Kingdom would continue to regard Senegal as bound by the Conventions.

In the *Channel Continental Shelf Case,* France contended that the Geneva Conventions had been rendered obsolete by the evolution of customary law stimulated by the work of the Third Law of the Sea Conference, at which, it argued, a consensus had been reached regarding the right of a coastal State to a 200-mile economic zone; this development was not compatible with the continuance in force of the Geneva Conventions. The Court of Arbitration said that "only the most conclusive indications of the intention of the parties to the 1958 Convention to regard it as terminated could warrant this Court in treating it as obsolete and inapplicable." In the Court's opinion, neither the records of the Third Law of the Sea Conference nor the practice of States provided any such conclusive indications.

The Geneva Conventions, if not altogether codificatory in character, did at the time they were adopted embody a high degree of agreement because of the two-third majority voting rule of procedure at the Conference. Each Article attracted that majority. However, the implications of this relative unanimity were quickly dispelled by the proliferation of States which occurred in the years immediately following the Conference. Some new States acknowledged succession to the Conventions which the imperial powers had ratified, while others did not. But most escaped the issue of succession altogether because they attained independence between the date of the Conference and the date of the ratifications. The result was to upset the balance between affirmation and non-affirmation attained at the Conference. Some new States had legitimate grievances at despoliation of neighboring fisheries which the Geneva Conventions did not permit them, they believed, to resist. But others, inspired more by emotion than legal analysis, purported to find their hands tied by the Conventions in the interests of the great powers, and were disposed to overthrow the whole Geneva system as having been contrived without their consent and against their interests. So the Geneva Conventions had barely come into force before their psychological basis became threatened by the political changes of the 1960s.

REFERENCES

(First Conference and the Geneva Conventions)

P.C. Jessup, "Geneva Conference on the Law of the Sea: A Study in International Law-Making," *American Journal of International Law*, Vol. 52 (1958), pp. 730-733; M.S. McDougal & W.T. Burke, "Crisis in the Law of the Sea: Community Perspectives versus National Egoism," *Yale Law Journal*, Vol. 67 (1958), pp. 539-589; M. Sorensen, "Law of the Sea," *International Conciliation* 210, 520 (1958), pp. 195-255; C. Swan, C. & J. Veberhorst, "The Conference on the Law of the Sea: A Report," *Michigan Law Review*, Vol. 56 (1958), pp. 1132-1141; W.T. Burke, "Some Comments on the 1958 Conventions," *Proceedings of the American Society of International Law*, 53rd Annual meeting, (1959), pp. 197-206; D. Chappell, "Conference on the Law of the Sea," Tasmanian University Law Review, Vol. 1 (1959), pp. 323-333; A.H. Dean, "Achievements at the Law of the Sea Conference," 53 *Proceedings of the American Society of International Law*, 53rd Annual meeting (1959), pp. 186-197; P.C. Jessup, "United Nations Conference on the Law of the Sea," 59 *Columbia Law Review*, Vol. 59 (1959), pp. 234-268; D.H.N. Johnson, "The Geneva Conference on the Law of the Sea," *Yearbook of World Affairs*, Vol. 13 (1959), pp. 68-94; D.H.N. Johnson, "The Preparation of the 1958 Geneva Conference on the Law of the Sea," *International and Comparative Law Quarterly*, Vol. 8 (1959), pp. 122-145; Shigeru Oda, "Japan and the United Nations Conference on the Law of the Sea," *Japanese Annual of International Law*, No. 3 (1959), pp. 65-86; C.M. Franklin, *The Law of the Sea: Some Recent Developments (with Particular Reference to the United Nations Conference on 1958)*, Vol. 52 of Naval War College, *International Law Studies*, 1959-1960, NAVPERS 15031. Washington, D.C.: U.S. Government Printing Office, 1961; C.M. Franklin, "The Law of the Sea: Some Recent Developments," 33 *Southern California Law Review*, Vol. 33 (1960), pp. 357-369; R.H. Manley, "The Geneva Conferences on the Law of the Sea as a Step in the International Law-Making Process," 25 *Albany Law Review*, Vol. 25 (1961), pp. 17-38; Yuen-Li Liang, "The Codification of the Law of the Sea Under the Auspices of the United Nations," 1 *Annales of the Chinese Society of International Law (Taipei)*, Vol. 1, (1964), pp. 3-23; R.L. Friedheim, "The "Satisfied" and "Dissatisfied" States Negotiate International Law: A Case Study," 18 *World Politics*, Vol. 18 (1965), pp. 20-41; A.H. Dean, "The Law of the Sea Conference, 1958-1960, and Its Aftermath," in Lewis M. Alexander, ed., *The Law of the Sea: Offshore Boundaries and Zones* (Proceedings of the First Annual Conference of the Law of the Sea Institute, June 27-July 1, 1966), Columbus, Ohio: Ohio State University, 1967, pp. 244-264; W.R. Neblett, "The 1958 Conference on the Law of the Sea: What Was Accomplished," in *ibid.*, pp. 36-46; "A Symposium on the Geneva Conventions and the Need for Future Modifications," in *ibid.*, pp. 265-298; M.S. McDougal, "Revision of the Geneva Conventions on the Law of the Sea - The Views of a Commentator," *Natural Resources Lawyer*, Vol. 1, No. 1 (1968), pp. 19-28; Shigeru Oda, "The Geneva Conventions on the Law of the Sea: Some Suggestions for their Revision," *Natural Resources Lawyer*, Vol. 1, No. 2 (1968), pp. 103-113.

(Second Geneva Conference, 1960)

D.W. Bowett, "The Second United Nations Conference on the Law of the Sea," *International and Comparative Law Quarterly*, Vol. 9 (1960), pp. 415-435; A.H. Dean, "The Second Geneva Conference on the Law of the Sea; The Fight for Freedom of the Sea," *American Journal of International Law*, Vol. 54 (1960), pp. 751-789; A.H. Dean, "The Second United Nations Conference on the Law of the Sea, Response," *American Journal of International Law*, Vol. 55 (1961), pp. 675-680; Robles A. Garcia, "Second U.N. Conference on the Law of the Sea," *American Journal of International Law*, Vol. 55 (1961), pp. 669-675; F.V. Garcia Amador, *Addendum on the Second United Nations Conference on the Law of the Sea*, (Addendum to the *Exploitation and Conservation of the Resources of the Sea*), Leyden, The Netherlands: A.W. Sijthoff, 1963.

(Documents)

United Nations Conference on the Law of the Sea, Geneva, 24 February - 27 April 1958, Official Records, [7 Vols., Vol. I: Preparatory Documents; Vol. II: Plenary Meetings; Vol. III: First Committee (Territorial Sea and Contiguous Zone); Vol. IV: Second Committee (High Seas: General Regime); Vol. V: Third Committee (High Seas: Fishing, Conservation of Living Resources); Vol. VI: Fourth Committee (Continental Shelf); Vol. VII: Fifth Committee (Questions of Free Access to the Sea of Landlocked Countries)]; *Second United Nations Conference on the Law of the Sea; Geneva, 17 March - 26 April 1960, Official Records*.

G. THE 1982 UNITED NATIONS CONVENTION ON THE LAW OF THE SEA

Bernardo Zuleta, "Introduction," in *The Law of the Sea*, New York: The United Nations, 1983, pp. xix-xxviii.

On 10 December 1982 the United Nations Convention on the Law of the Sea was opened for signature in Montego Bay, Jamaica. This marked the culmination of over 14 years of work involving participation by more than 150 countries representing all regions of the world, all legal and political systems, all degrees of socio-economic development, countries with various dispositions regarding the kinds of minerals that can be found in the sea-bed, coastal States, States described as geographically disadvantaged with regard to ocean space, archipelagic States, island States and land-locked States. These countries convened for the purpose of establishing a comprehensive regime "dealing with all matters relating to the law of the sea, . . . bearing in mind that the problems of ocean space are closely interrelated and need to be considered as a whole." The fruits of their labors are embodied in the United Nations Convention on the Law of the Sea.

The Convention is multi-faceted and represents a monument to international cooperation in the treaty-making process: the need to elaborate a new and comprehensive regime for the law of the sea was perceived, and the international community expressed its collective will to cooperate in this effort on a scale the magnitude of which was unprecedented in treaty history. The elaboration of the Convention represents an attempt to establish true universality in the effort to achieve a "just and equitable international economic order" governing ocean space.

. . . It comprises 320 articles and nine annexes, governing all aspects of ocean space . . . . An examination of the character of the individual provisions reveals that the Convention represents not only the codification of customary norms, but also and more significantly the progressive development of international law, and contains the constituent instruments of two major new

development of international law, and contains the constituent instruments of two major new international organizations.

It is, however, the conceptual underpinnings of the Convention as a "package" which is its most significant quality, and has contributed most distinctly to the remarkable achievement of the Convention. Its quality as a package is a result of the singular nature of the circumstances from which it emerged, which factors included the close interrelationship of the many different issues involved, the large number of participating States, and the vast number of often conflicting interests which frequently cut across the traditional lines of negotiation by region. In addition, the strong desire that the Convention allows for flexibility of practice in order to ensure durability over time, and so as not to encroach upon the sovereignty of States, was recognized as another important consideration. All of these factors necessitated that every individual provision of the text be weighed within the context of the whole, producing an intricately balanced text to provide a basis for universality.

The concept of the package pervaded all work on the elaboration of the Convention and was not limited to consideration of substance alone. It became the *leit-motiv* of the Conference and in fact permeates the law of the seas as its exists today.

THE HISTORY OF THE CONVENTION

The mammoth task of elaborating this new regime began in 1967, when the concept of the Common Heritage of Mankind was first discussed by the General Assembly in the context of the question of preservation of the sea-bed and ocean floor exclusively for peaceful purposes. The common heritage concept was not a new one (it dates back to the 19th century, and was referred to by the President of the first Law of the Sea Conference in his opening speech in 1958) but it had never before been discussed in an international forum. It is of particular relevance to note that the discussion took place in the First Committee of the General Assembly as the item was perceived from the very beginning as being of primarily political significance, and not limited to strictly legal or economic concern. This conclusion was based on the same rationale which is the foundation of the package concept, and is the reason that the work of the Third United Nations Conference was not based on draft articles prepared by the International Law Commission, as was the work of the 1958 Conference.

The General Assembly established an *Ad Hoc* Committee to study the Peaceful Uses of the Sea-Bed and the Ocean Floor beyond the Limits of National Jurisdiction, and subsequently created a standing committee, the Committee on the Peaceful Uses of the Sea-Bed and Ocean Floor beyond the Limits of National Jurisdiction (Sea-Bed Committee), for the purpose of shaping and refining the ideas and concepts which were to form the basis of the new international regime. These committees, cognizant of the concerns which were to develop into the concept of the package, worked on the basis of consensus.

In 1970 the General Assembly adopted a Declaration of Principles (General Assembly resolution 2749 (XXV)), following upon negotiations which took place in the Sea-Bed Committee, which resolution solemnly declared that "The sea-bed and ocean floor, and the subsoil thereof, beyond the limits of national jurisdiction . . . as well as the resources of the area, are the common heritage of mankind" and "shall not be subject to appropriation by any means by States or persons." In addition, it was declared that this area "shall be open to use exclusively for peaceful purposes by all States . . . without discrimination." Thus, the common heritage was formally spelled out.

The General Assembly at the same time adopted a related three-part resolution, the preambular paragraphs of which reiterated the recognition of need for a reformed regime and mandated its consideration as a package as follows:

Conscious that the problems of ocean space are closely interrelated and need to be considered as a whole,

Noting that the political and economic realities, scientific development and rapid technological advances of the last decade have accentuated the need for early and progressive development of the law of the sea in a framework of close international cooperation,

Having regard to the fact that many of the present States Members of the United Nations did not take part in the previous United Nations Conferences on the law of the sea, ...

The resolution continued, calling upon the Sea-Bed Committee to act as a preparatory committee for the future conference . . .

In late 1973 the Third United Nations Conference on the Law of the Sea was convened in accordance with General Assembly resolution 3067 (XXVIII), and set about its task with an organizational session. The first order of business was the question of procedure; procedural practices had to be developed which would foster the cohesiveness of the "package" of law of the sea. . . .

As a consequence of the deliberations, the Conference adopted its Rules of Procedure (A/CONF.62/30/Rev.3). Since the earlier committees had worked on the basis of consensus, and due to the widely divergent interests on issues of such paramount importance, it was recognized that resort to traditional voting rules would be unsatisfactory as a method for achieving the desired goals. Consensus was therefore adopted as the principal means by which decisions were to be taken. This notion was embodied in the Declaration incorporating the Gentleman's Agreement, appended to the Rules of Procedure, and provided the context in which the rules themselves were framed. For example, the rules on decision-making require that the Conference in the first instance decide that it has exhausted all efforts to reach consensus before any voting on questions of substance can take place. In order to ensure that this decision is not taken lightly, the rules allow various deferment or "cooling-off" periods before the actual voting may begin. By delaying the voting as long as possible, it was hoped that the divergent positions might be reconciled in the interim, thus obviating the need to vote at all.

The Conference realized at an early stage that negotiations could not be effectively carried out in formal proceedings, and that because of the large number of participants and sensitive issues involved, working groups would be more efficient than plenary meetings. Indeed, much of the elaboration process took place in smaller or more informal meetings, but always on an *ad referendum* basis of consensus. The working or negotiating groups were generally established on the basis of interest in a particular issue. In this respect States did not coalesce within traditional regional or political alignments. Rather, they grouped themselves to face specific issues and to protect clearly identifiable interests. For example, coastal States wanted a legal regime that would allow them to manage and conserve the biological and mineral resources within their national jurisdiction; archipelagic States wanted to obtain recognition for the new regime of archipelagic waters; landlocked States were seeking general rules of international law that would grant them transit to and from the sea and rights of access to the living resources of their neighboring States;

some industrialized nations wanted to have guaranteed access to the sea-bed mineral resources beyond national jurisdiction within a predictable legal framework; countries that produced the same minerals in their territories wanted assurances that the sea-bed production of these minerals would not undermine their economies or result in a "de facto" monopoly; developing countries wanted to be more than silent witnesses to the acquisition of new knowledge of the oceans so that marine science and technology could be put at the service of all and not only of a limited number of very wealthy countries; States bordering straits wanted to ensure that free passage would not result in damage to their marine environment or threats to their national security; practically all nations wanted to preserve the freedoms of navigation, commerce and communication; and finally, mankind as a whole needed to ensure that a new legal regime would safeguard the marine environment against depredation or irrational use of non-renewable resources, the discharge or dumping of noxious substances into the oceans or the so-called scientific tests that could affect the delicate balance of marine life. These are only a few of the multitude of particular interests which needed consideration at the Conference. Any individual State could fall into any number of different interest groups, depending upon its individual national concerns and the texture of the negotiations on the overall package. The interest groups did not, however, replace regional group consultations, which also took place, thereby enhancing the flow of information and compounding the number of considerations which had to be weighed with respect to any given issue at any given time. . . .

. . . .

A significant procedural step . . . took place in 1977, at the seventh session of the Conference, when the program of work contained in document A/CONF.62/62 was adopted. This document followed upon the consolidation, at the end of the sixth session of the various parts of the text into a single working paper, the Informal Composite Negotiating Text. . . .

The emergence of the Informal Composite Negotiating Text denotes that the negotiations had proceeded to a very delicate stage, and threw into relief the remaining "hard-core" issues which required resolution. Document A/CONF.62/62 acknowledged this situation and mandated the institutionalization of various previously utilized Informal Conference practices to promote agreement. One such practice was the establishment of issue-specific negotiating groups. Another was the formal institution of the President's "Colloquium," the body of principal officers of the Conference which acted in an advisory capacity to the President. It had been the principal officers who had informally prepared and revised the negotiating texts upon which the work of the Conference had been focused all along. However, the program of work now established stringent standards to direct the Colloquium in its work: it mandated that no revision could be made without prior presentation of the proposed change to the Plenary, wherein it must have received "widespread and substantial support," indicating that it offered a "substantially improved prospect of consensus." By these procedural devices the Conference was able to ensure that the package remained cohesive until such time as all of the pieces fell into place.

Another of the peculiarities of the law of the sea treaty is that it is a major instrument which has equally authentic Arabic, Chinese, English, French, Russian and Spanish texts. Indeed, if the object of the package is to have a Convention which is universally acceptable, then it follows that it must be acceptable in each and every of the six languages to which a State may refer. The achievement of this goal required another innovation in the treaty-making process as applied to the Drafting Committee.

The Drafting Committee of the Conference undertook its work in two stages. The first stage involved the harmonization of recurring words and phrases so as to ensure a sense of a whole, unified text, and to avoid misinterpretation and confusion in instances when an identical meaning was intended by phraseology which was varied. Such discrepancies had arisen because the different parts of the text had been drafted in different committees, with reference to varied existing treaty sources, thus necessitating this first stage. The second stage of the work involved the article-by-article reading of the text for the purpose of ensuring that each provision was identical in meaning in each of the languages.

To facilitate its work in the light of the desired goals, and because the Drafting Committee was the only committee of limited representation in the Conference, it was necessary to devise a procedure to ensure universality of participation in the work of the Committee. The informal language groups of the Conference accordingly developed. These were open-ended groups which grappled with Drafting Committee issues and their coordination, and then reported back to the Committee. The role of the Committee itself was reserved to policy and decision-making, with little of the actual deliberations taking place in that forum.

At the close of the tenth session in 1981, the Conference decided to revise the informal text, offically producing a Draft Convention (A/CONF.62/L.78). Virtually all the parts of the package had by now fallen into place--only the most seemingly intractable political questions remained. The shape of the comprehensive package on the law of the sea, as comprising the Convention itself plus a number of resolutions, could by now be foreseen. In conjunction with the issuance of the Draft Convention, the Conference adopted a timetable calling for the final decision-making session to be held in 1982. The five-week plan allowed time for negotiation of the remaining points to be resolved; these points included the mandate of the Preparatory Commission and the rules governing pioneer investors in the sea-bed Area prior to the entry into force of the Convention, that is, questions of the work to succeed the Conference.

After long deliberations marking the culmination of over ninety weeks of work, on 23 April 1982, the Conference, in accordance with its Rules of Procedure, determined that all efforts to reach a consensus had been exhausted. Thus, the machinery for the final decision-making was set in motion. The Draft Convention and the four Resolutions that were before the Conference on 30 April 1982 did not include any texts which had not undergone an elaborate structure of negotiations devised by the Conference in order to ensure that all provisions could command widespread and substantial support. On that day the Conference, at the request of one delegation, had to resort to voting on the question of adoption of the whole of the package on the law of the sea. The results of that vote (130 in favor, 4 against, with 17 abstentions) represented the overwhelming reaffirmation of support for the ideals, principles and goals of a new international order for the seas as embodied in the package of the Convention on the Law of the Sea. This reaffirmation of support is further strengthened by the fact that the majority of States which abstained in the voting later became signatories to the Convention.

The final meetings of the Conference were held in Montego Bay, Jamaica from 6 December to 10 December 1982. The Conference heard closing statements by delegations (*see* A/CONF.62/PV.185-193), after which the Final Act was signed. . . . The Convention was opened for signature in Jamaica on 10 December. On tl.at first day, signatures from 119 delegations comprising 117 States, the Cook Islands (a self-governing associated State) and the United Nations Council for Namibia, were appended to the Convention. In addition, one ratification, that of Fiji, was deposited that day. Never before has such overwhelming support been demonstrated so concretely on the first day that a treaty has been open for signature. The Convention's first achievement in its own right was unprecedented in the history of treaty law.

THE TEXT ITSELF: SOME HIGHLIGHTS

The Convention itself establishes a comprehensive framework for the regulation of all ocean space. It is divided into 17 parts and nine annexes, and contains provisions governing, *inter alia*, the limits of national jurisdiction over ocean space, access to the seas, navigation, protection and preservation of the marine environment, exploitation of living resources and conservation, scientific research, sea-bed mining and other exploitation of non-living resources, and the settlement of disputes. In addition, it establishes new international bodies to carry out functions for the realization of specific objectives.

The touchstone of the package of the Convention is the notion that the enjoyment of rights and benefits involves the concomitant undertaking of duties and obligations, so that an overall equitable order may be created. The paramount duty of all States Parties is to respect the rights of others; however, some duties may entail more executory acts. The duty to give due notice of hazards would be an example of the latter kind of duty. This onmipresent concept of the balance of rights and duties is emphasized by article 300 of the Convention, which mandates good faith in the fulfillment of obligations and proscribes the abuse of rights.

The first six parts of the Convention deal generally with the question of areas of national jurisdiction. The General Assembly Declaration of Principles (resolution 2749 (XXV)) established that the Common Heritage of Mankind comprises the area of sea-bed and ocean floor beyond the limits of national jurisdiction, "the precise limits of which are yet to be determined." It is the Convention which sets out the guideines for the determination of those limits.

The Convention allows for the establishment of a territorial sea of up to 12 nautical miles in breadth, providing various methods for determining baselines and for distinguishing between territorial waters and internal waters. The traditional right of innocent passage through territorial waters is recognized, and some specifically as to what kinds of activities will contravene innocence of passage is included. In the case of the waters of States bordering straits, the concept of transit passage is introduced, which draws more from the concept of necessity than does innocent passage and is somewhat more liberal. The concept of archipelagic waters is introduced for the case of archipelagoes, whereby sovereignty may be recognized over the waters within an island group, and the conditions and modalities for establishment of baselines in such cases are specified. Archipelagic sea-lanes passage is also provided.

Beyond territorial waters, the Convention allows the creation of an exclusive economic zone of up to 200 nautical miles. Traditionally, all areas beyond territorial waters comprised the high seas. In order for coastal States to gain economic benefit from areas further off their shores, it was necessary for them to extend their territorial waters, thus eliminating all freedoms of the high seas in the annexed areas. This imposed upon the interest of other maritime States, which insisted that customary law permitted a territorial sea of only three miles breadth, and that anything beyond that entailed abridgment of their freedoms. This disagreement was one of the major issues facing the Conference when it began its work.

The provisions pertaining to the exclusive economic zone are the manifestation of one of the first "mini-packages" of delicately balanced compromises to emerge from the negotiations. The ubiquitous concept of the balance of rights and duties can be most clearly illustrated in this context. The Convention allows the coastal state certain rights in the exclusive economic zone for the purpose of economic advantage, notably rights over fishing and exploitation of non-living resources, as well as concomitant limited jurisdiction in order to realize those rights. At the same time, however, neighboring land-locked and geographically disadvantaged States must be allowed access to those resources of the zone that the coastal state does not exploit, and, further, the traditional freedoms of the high seas are to be maintained in this area. The recognition of the rights of others in the zone is, however, without prejudice to the rights of the coastal State. In order to safeguard the protection of so many different interests in the zone, all States must undertake to respect and accommodate the rights and legitimate uses of other States in the zone. The Convention lays a broad framework for the peaceful accomplishment of this purpose.

Beyond the limits of the exclusive economic zone, the determination of which provisions of the Convention are applicable to a given activity depends upon the site of the activity involved. Activities on the surface and in the water column are governed by the provisions on the high seas. These generally follow customary international law allowing the freedoms of the high seas, but augment the law in several important respects, notably with regard to pollution and safety regulations, scientific research, conservation, and prevention of illicit traffic in drugs and psychotropic substances. Activities on the sea-bed and in the subsoil of the continental shelf may fall within the national jurisdiction of the coastal state if the formation of the continental shelf meets specific criteria. The Convention provides for the establishment of a Commission of experts to advise on the delineation of the outer edge of the continental margin, that is, the limit of national jurisdiction over the continental shelf.

Having provided the guidelines for the determination of the limits of national jurisdiction, the Convention then sets out the principles and regulations governing the sea-bed and ocean floor beyond those limits, the common heritage of mankind. The formulation of these provisions was especially difficult since it wholly represents the progressive development of law, and was therefore unaided by the guidance of precedent. The very delicate balance of compromises which emerged represented another "mini-package" within the package, and cannot be divorced from the provisions of resolutions I and II.

The body empowered to administer the common heritage of mankind and to regulate its exploration and exploitation will be the International Sea-Bed Authority, an international organization open to membership by all States as well as international organizations and other entities meeting specified criteria (parties to the Convention are *ipso facto* members of the Authority, article 156). The Authority will have an Assembly, which will be the supreme body and will reflect the balance between the sovereign equality of all States, and a Council with limited representation. The Council will have primary responsibility over sea-bed mining activities, and will be advised by specialized commissions.

It is not the structure but the functions of the International Sea-Bed Authority which make it a forerunner in the development of the law of international organizations. Not only will it be entrusted with the power to directly regulate purely commercial activities, but it will also be empowered to engage in sea-bed mining in its own right, through its commecial arm, the Enterprise. This is the essence of the "parallel system," a concept arrived at as a compromise in 1976 after arduous negotiations. The conditions and modalities for financing the Enterprise and for ensuring that it is technologically equipped to carry out activities form an integral part of the package. The Convention also delineates specific provisions regarding how the Authority must go about selecting among applicants for sea-bed mining and on what basis, how much production from the resources of the Area will be allowed in a specified period, and other technical apsects of application, authorization and the conduct of sea-bed activities.

Resolution 1 creates the Preparatory Commission, the body which will make the arrangements enabling the Authority (and the International Tribunal for the Law of the Sea) to be set up and to operate. The Commission will draft the specific rules, regulations and procedures of the Authority to govern activities in the Area so that the system of sea-bed mining under the Convention can commence. The shape these rules and regulations take may well determine the viability of the system as a whole, and therefore the significance of this task and its place within the overall package cannot be underestimated.

The Preparatory Commission will also be entrusted to carry out functions under resolution II, which governs preparatory investment in pioneer activities. Under this resolution, certain protections are granted to qualifying sea-bed miners who apply to the Commis-sion and are registered by it to conduct exploratory activities. It is the Commission which will be empowered to fulfill certain functions on behalf of the international community as a whole, on the "other" side of the parallel system, prior to the entry into operation of the Authority.

In addition to the enunciation of regimes on a spatial basis, the Convention deals with certain other matters of global concern. Among these are ecological and environmental issues. The general principles and policies governing prevention, reduction and control of pollution throughout the marine environment are established, as are the specific rights and duties of States concerned for the realization of their environmental and ecological goals. The allocation of the rights and the burden of the duties would vary depending upon the location and/or the type of pollution involved, and specific safeguard and enforcement provisions are included. The Convention is intended to be compatible with existing treaties on this question and to provide a broad framework for the conclusion of future, more specific agreements.

The Convention also includes provisions intended to foster the development and facilitate the transfer of all kinds of marine technology, and to encourage the conduct of marine scientific research. The inclusion of such provisions was dependent upon the establishment of adequate safeguards for the holders of rights concerned.

The elaboration of the international regime comes full circle with the stipulation of a comprehensive set of provisions governing the settlement of disputes. It could be foreseen that the effective implementation of the complex new international order under the Convention would be greatly hindered without the creation of an obligation to settle disputes and the designation of means for doing so.

The Convention obliges parties to settle their disputes peacefully, and provides a selection of methods for doing so in the event that they are otherwise unable to reach agreement even with third party intervention. The system under the Convention is a compulsory and binding one in that, with limited exceptions, a party has no choice but to submit to a settlement procedure if requested to do so by the other disputant, and is bound to abide by the findings of the body to which the dispute is submitted. States may make a prior determination of which fora they would be amenable to, and for this purpose the Convention allows a choice from among the International Court of Justice, arbitration, or the International Tribunal for the Law of the Sea, a new and autonomous specialized tribunal established by the Convention. In certain cases where the Convention does not call for a binding method of settlement, the parties are enjoined to submit their dispute to conciliation.

The International Tribunal for the Law of the Sea will have shared competence over all law of the sea matters, but it is its specialized chamber, the Sea-Bed Disputes Chamber, that will have exclusive competence over all disputes involving the international sea-bed area, even as against the rest of the Tribunal. That is, the Sea-Bed Disputes Chamber alone will have competence to the exclusion of all other fora over sea-bed mining and related activities.

The creation of the International Tribunal for the Law of the Sea marks an advance in the evolution of the law of international institutions of its kind not only because of the structural autonomy of the Sea-Bed Disputes Chamber and the fact that the Chamber has exclusive jurisdiction over sea-bed matters, but also because private and juridical persons will have direct access to the Chamber on an equal footing with States, since these persons will be the ones directly involved in the activities over which the disputes may arise. . . .

The Convention is due to enter into force twelve months after the deposit of the sixtieth instrument of ratification or accession . . . .

REFERENCES

There are numerous writings on the Third United Nations Conference on the Law of the Sea [1973-1982] and the Convention it adopted; it is neither possible nor necessary to list most of them here. Therefore, only a few articles reviewing the work of the sessions of the Conference, its negotiation process and the official records of the Conference are listed here.

(Reviewing the Work of Sessions of the Conference)

J.R. Stevenson & B.H. Oxman, "The Preparation for the Law of the Sea Conference," *American Journal of International Law*, Vol. 68 (1974), pp. 1-32; "Caracas Session of the Third U.N. Conference on the Law of the Sea," *U.S. Department of State Bulletin*, Vol. 71, No. 1839, (September 23, 1974), pp. 389-422; "Law of the Sea: From Caracas to Geneva - A Time for Decision," *Columbia Journal of International Law*, Vol. 14 (1975) - Special Issue; Shigeru Oda, "The Caracas Session of the Third Law of the Sea Conference," *Journal of International Law and Diplomacy*, Vol. 73 (1975), pp. 1-35; J.R. Stevenson & B.H. Oxman, "The Third United Nations Conference on the Law of the Sea: The 1974 Caracas Session," *American Journal of International Law*, Vol. 69 (1975), pp. 1-30; J.R. Stevenson & B.H. Oxman, "The Third United Nations Conference on the Law of the Sea: The 1975 Geneva Session," *American Journal of International Law*, Vol. 69 (1975), pp. 763-797; "The Law of the Sea Conference and its Aftermath," in *Proceedings of the American Society of International Law*, 71st Annual Meeting (1977), pp. 107-128; B.H. Oxman, "The Third United Nations Conference on the Law of the Sea: The 1976 New York Sessions," *American Journal of International Law*, Vol. 71 (1977), pp. 247-269; B.H. Oxman, "The Third United Nations Conference on the Law of the Sea: The 1977 New York Session," *American Journal of International Law*, Vol. 72 (1978), pp. 57-83; G.W. Haight *et al.*, "The United Nations Conference on the Law of the Sea," *International Lawyer*, Vol. 12 (1978), pp. 21-62; B.H. Oxman, "The Third United Nations Conference on the Law of the Sea: The Seventh Session (1978)," *American Journal of International Law*, Vol. 73 (1979), pp. 1-41; B.H. Oxman, "The Third United Nations Conference on the Law of the Sea: The Eighth Session (1979)," *American Journal of International Law*, Vol. 74 (1980), pp. 1-47; B.H. Oxman, "The Third United Nations Conference on the Law of the Sea: The Ninth Session (1980)," *American Journal of International Law*, Vol. 75 (1981), pp. 211-256; B.H. Oxman, "The Third United Nations Conference on the Law of the Sea: The Tenth Session (1981)," *American Journal of International Law*, Vol. 76 (1982), pp. 1-23; E.L. Richardson et al., "The United Nations Conference on the Law of the Sea," *Proceedings of the American Society of International Law*, 76th Annual Meeting (1982), pp. 107-120; B.H. Oxman et al., "Law of the Sea," in *Proceedings of the American Society of International Law, 77th Annual Meeting* (1983), pp. 150-168; Arvid Pardo, "The Convention on the Law of the Sea: A Preliminary Appraisal," *San Diego Law*

Review, Vol. 20 (1983), pp. 489-503; E.L. Richardson, "The United States Posture Toward the Law of the Sea Convention: Awkward But Not Irreparable," *San Diego Law Review*, Vol. 20 (1983), pp. 505-519; Tommy T.B. Koh, "The Origins of the 1982 Convention on the Law of the Sea," *Malaya Law Review*, Vol. 29 (1987), pp. 1-17.

(Negotiation and the Conference Procedure)

B. Buzan, "Negotiating by Consensus: Developments in Technique at the United Nations Conference on the Law of the Sea," *American Journal of International Law*, Vol. 75 (1981), pp. 324-348; M.H. Nordquist and Choon-ho Park, eds., *Reports of the United States Delegation to the Third United Nations Conference on the Law of the Sea*, Honolulu: Law of the Sea Institute, University of Hawaii, Occasional Paper No. 33, 1983; James K. Sebenius, *Negotiating the Law of the Sea*, Cambridge, Mass.: Harvard University Press, 1984.

(Documents)

Third United Nations Conference on the Law of the Sea, 1973-1982, Official Records [17 Vols., Vol. I, First/Second Session; Vol. II, Second Session; Vol. III, Documents of the Conference, First/Second Session; Vol. IV, Third Session; Vol. V, Fourth Session; Vol. VI, Fifth Session; Vol. VII, Sixth Session; Vol. VIII, Informal Composite Negotiating Text; Vol. IX, Seventh and Resumed Session; Vol. X, Reports of the Committees and Negotiating Groups; Vol. XI, Eighth Session; Vol. XII, Resumed Eighth Session; Vol. XIII, Ninth Session; Vol. XIV, Resumed Ninth Session; Vol. XV, Tenth and Resumed Session; Vol. XVI, Eleventh Session; Vol. XVII, Resumed Eleventh Session and Final Part of the Eleventh Session and Conclusion of the Conference]; Renate Platzoder, ed., *Third United Nations Conference on the Law of the Sea: Documents*, 18 Vols., Dobbs Ferry, New York: Oceana, 1982-1988.

CHAPTER III

THE SOURCES OF THE INTERNATIONAL LAW OF THE SEA

A. SOURCES OF INTERNATIONAL LAW IN GENERAL

STATUTE OF THE INTERNATIONAL COURT OF JUSTICE .
Signed at San Francisco on June 26, 1945 and entered into force on
October 24, 1945, 59 Stat. 1055; T.S. 993, 3 Bevans 1179.

Article 38

1. The Court, whose function is to decide in accordance with international law such disputes
as are submitted to it, shall apply:

a. international conventions, whether general or particular, establishing rules
expressly recognized by the contesting states;

b. international custom, as evidence of a general practice accepted as law;

c. the general principles of law recognized by civilized nations;

d. subject to the provisions of Article 59, judicial decisions and the teachings of the
most highly qualified publicists of the various nations, as subsidiary means for the determination
of rules of law.

2. This provision shall not prejudice the power of the Court to decide a case *ex aequo et
bono*, if the parties agree thereto.

Restatement of the Foreign Relations Law of the United States, 3rd
revision, Vol. 1, St. Paul, Minn.: American Law Institute, 1987, pp.
24-29, 35-36, 38-39. Copyright by the American Law Institute.
Reprinted with the permission of The American Law Institute.

§ 102. Sources of International Law

(1) A rule of international law is one that has been accepted as such by the international
community of states

(a) in the form of customary law;

(b) by international agreement; or

(c) by derivation from general principles common to the major legal systems of the
world.

(2) Customary international law results from a general and consistent practice of states
followed by them from a sense of legal obligation.

(3) International agreements create law for the states parties thereto and may lead to the creation of customary international law when such agreements are intended for adherence by states generally and are in fact widely accepted.

(4) General principles common to the major legal systems, even if not incorporated or reflected in customary law or international agreement, may be invoked as supplementary rules of international law where appropriate.

Comment:

a. Sources and evidence of international law distinguished. This section indicates the ways in which rules or principles become international law. The means for proving that a rule or principle has in fact become international law in one of the ways indicated in this section is dealt with in § 103.

b. Practice as customary law. "Practice of states," Subsection (2), includes diplomatic acts and instructions as well as public measures and other governmental acts and official statements of policy, whether they are unilateral or undertaken in cooperation with other states, for example in organizations such as the Organization for Economic Cooperation and Development (OECD). Inaction may constitute state practice, as when a state acquiesces in acts of another state that affect its legal rights. The practice necessary to create customary law may be of comparatively short duration, but under Subsection (2) it must be "general and consistent." A practice can be general even if it is not universally followed; there is no precise formula to indicate how widespread a practice must be, but it should reflect wide acceptance among the states particularly involved in the relevant activity. Failure of a significant number of important states to adopt a practice can prevent a principle from becoming general customary law though it might become "particular customary law" for the participating states. See Comment e. A principle of customary law is not binding on a state that declares its dissent from the principle during its development. See Comment d.

c. Opinio juris. For a practice of states to become a rule of customary international law it must appear that the states follow the practice from a sense of legal obligation (*opinio juris sive necessitatis*); a practice that is generally followed but which states feel legally free to disregard does not contribute to customary law. A practice initially followed by states as a matter of courtesy or habit may become law when states generally come to believe that they are under a legal obligation to comply with it. It is often difficult to determine when that transformation into law has taken place. Explicit evidence of a sense of legal obligation (e.g., by official statements) is not necessary; *opinio juris* may be inferred from acts or omissions.

d. Dissenting views and new states. Although customary law may be built by the acquiescence as well as by the actions of states (Comment b) and become generally binding on all states, in principle a state that indicates its dissent from a practice while the law is still in the process of development is not bound by that rule even after it matures. Historically, such dissent and consequent exemption from a principle that became general customary law has been rare. See Reporters' Note 2. As to the possibility of dissent from peremptory norms (*jus cogens*), see Comment k. A state that enters the international system after a practice has ripened into a rule of international law is bound by that rule.

e. General and special custom. The practice of states in a regional or other special grouping may create "regional," "special," or "particular" customary law for those states *inter se*. It must be shown that the state alleged to be bound has accepted or acquiesced in the custom as a matter of legal obligation, "not merely for reasons of political expediency." Asylum Case (Colombia v. Peru), [1950] I.C.J. Rep. 266, 277. Such special customary law may be seen as essentially the result of tacit agreement among the parties.

f. International agreement as source of law. An international agreement creates obligations binding between the parties under international law. See § 321. Ordinarily, an agreement between states is a source of law only in the sense that a private contract may be said to make law for the parties under the domestic law of contracts. Multilateral agreements open to all states, however, are increasingly used for general legislation, whether to make new law, as in human rights . . . , or for codifying and developing customary law, as in the Vienna Convention on the Law of Treaties. . . .

g. Binding resolutions of international organizations. Some international agreements that are constitutions or charters of international organizations confer power on those organizations to impose binding obligations on their members by resolution, usually by qualified majorities. Such obligations derive their authority from the international agreement constituting the organization, and resolutions so adopted by the organization can be seen as "secondary sources" of international law for its members. For example, the International Monetary Fund may prescribe rules concerning maintenance or change of exchange rates or depreciation of currencies. . . . The International Civil Aviation Organization may set binding standards for navigation or qualifications for flight crews in aviation over the high seas.

For resolutions of international organizations that are not binding but purport to state the international law on a particular subject, see § 103 [Editors' Note 2].

h. The United Nations Charter. The Charter of the United Nations has been adhered to by virtually all states. Even the few remaining non-member states have acquiesced in the principles it established. The Charter provisions prohibiting the use of force have become rules of international law binding on all states. Compare Article 2(6). . . .

Article 103 of the Charter provides:

> In the event of a conflict between the obligations of the Members of the
> United Nations under the present Charter and their obligations under any
> other international agreement, their obligations under the present
> Charter shall prevail.

Members seem to have read this article as barring them from making agreements inconsistent with the Charter, and have refrained from making such agreements. See, *e.g.*, Article 7 of the North Atlantic Treaty, 1949, 63 Stat. 2241, T.I.A.S. No. 1964, 34 U.N.T.S. 243; Article 102 of the Charter of the Organization of American States, 1948, 2 U.S.T. 2394, T.I.A.S. No. 2361, 119 U.N.T.S. 3. And see Comment k.

i. International agreements codifying or contributing to customary law. International agreements constitute practice of states and as such can contribute to the growth of customary law under Subsection (2). See North Sea Continental Shelf Cases (Federal Republic of Germany v. Denmark & Netherlands), [1969] I.C.J. Rep. 3, 28-29, 37-43. Some multilateral agreements may come to be law for non-parties that do not actively dissent. That may be the effect where the multilateral agreement is designed for adherence by states generally, is widely accepted, and is not rejected by a significant number of important states. A wide network of similar bilateral arrangements on a subject may constitute practice and also result in customary law. If an international agreement is declaratory of, or contributes to, customary law, its termination by the parties does not of itself affect the continuing force of those rules as international law. However, the widespread repudiation of the obligations of an international agreement may be seen as state practice adverse to the continuing force of the obligations. See Comment j.

j. Conflict between international agreement and customary law. Customary law and law made by international agreement have equal authority as international law. Unless the parties evince a contrary intention, a rule established by agreement supersedes for them a prior inconsistent rule of customary international law. However, an agreement will not supersede a prior rule of customary law that is a peremptory norm of international law; and an agreement will not supersede customary law if the agreement is invalid because it violates such a peremptory norm. See Comment k. A new rule of customary law will supersede inconsistent obligations created by earlier agreement if the parties so intend and the intention is clearly manifested. Thus, the United States and many other states party to the 1958 Law of the Sea Conventions accept that some of the provisions of those conventions have been superseded by supervening customary law.

k. Peremptory norms of international law (*jus cogens*). Some rules of international law are recognized by the international community of states as peremptory, permitting no derogation. These rules prevail over and invalidate international agreements and other rules of international law in conflict with them. Such a peremptory norm is subject to modification only by a subsequent norm of international law having the same character. It is generally accepted that the principles of the United Nations Charter prohibiting the use of force (Comment h) have the character of *jus cogens*. . . .

1. General principles as secondary source of law. Much of international law, whether customary or constituted by agreement, reflects principles analogous to those found in the major legal systems of the world, and historically may derive from them or from a more remote common origin. General principles common to systems of national law may be resorted to as an independent source of law. That source of law may be important when there has not been practice by states sufficient to give the particular principle status as customary law and the principle has not been legislated by general international agreement.

General principles are a secondary source of international law, resorted to for developing international law interstitially in special circumstances. For example, the passage of time as a defense to an international claim by a state on behalf of a national may not have had sufficient application in practice to be accepted as a rule of customary law. Nonetheless, it may be invoked as a rule of international law, at least in claims based on injury to persons . . . because it is a general principle common to the major legal systems of the world and is not inappropriate for international claims. Other rules that have been drawn from general principles includes rules relating to the administration of justice, such as the rule that no one may be judge in his own cause; *res judicata*; and rules of fair procedure generally. General principles may also provide "rules of reason" of a general character, such as acquiescence and estoppel, the principle that rights must not be abused, and the obligation to repair a wrong. International practice may sometimes convert such a principle into a rule of customary law.

m. Equity as general principle. Reference to principles of equity, in the sense of what is fair and just, is common to major legal systems, and equity has been accepted as a principle of international law in several contexts. . . . That principle is not to be confused with references to "equity," and distinctions between law and equity as separate bodies of law, in traditional Anglo-American jurisprudence. Reference to equity as a principle incorporated into international law is also to be distinguished from the power, conferred on the International Court of Justice in Article 38(2) of the Statute (and on other tribunals in numerous arbitration agreements), to decide cases *ex aequo et bono* if the parties agree thereto, which permits the Court to settle a case without being confined to principles of law. . . .

§ 103. Evidence of International Law

(1) Whether a rule has become international law is determined by evidence appropriate to the particular source from which that rule is alleged to derive (§ 102).

(2) In determining whether a rule has become international law, substantial weight is accorded to

(a) judgments and opinions of international judicial and arbitral tribunals;

(b) judgments and opinions of national judicial tribunals;

(c) the writings of scholars;

(d) pronouncements by states that undertake to state a rule of international law, when such pronouncements are not seriously challenged by other states.

Comment:

a. Primary and secondary evidence of international law. . . . for customary law the "best evidence" is proof of state practice, ordinarily by reference to official documents and other indications of governmental action. (Similar forms of proof would be adduced as evidence that a state is not bound by a principle of law because it had dissented, § 102, Comment d). Law made by international agreement is proved by reference to the text of the agreement, but appropriate supplementary means to its interpretation are not excluded. See § 325. Subsection (2) refers to secondary evidence indicating what the law has been found to be by authoritative reporters and interpreters; the order of the clauses is not meant to indicate their relative importance. Such evidence may be negated by primary evidence, for example, as to customary law, by proof as to what state practice is in fact.

A determination as to whether a customary rule has developed is likely to be influenced by assessment as to whether the rule will contribute to international order. . . .

REPORTERS' NOTE

. . . .

2. Declaratory resolutions of international organizations. Article 38(1)(d) of the Statute of the International Court of Justice, § 102, Reporters' Note 1, does not include resolutions of international organizations among the "subsidiary means for the determination of rules of law." However, the Statute was drafted before the growth and proliferation of international organizations following the Second World War. Given the universal character of many of those organizations and the forum they provide for the expression by states of their views regarding legal principles, such resolutions sometimes provide important evidence of law. A resolution purporting to state the law on a subject is some evidence of what the states voting for the resolution regard the law to be, although what states do is more weighty evidence than their declarations or the resolutions they

vote for. The evidentiary value of such a resolution is high if it is adopted by consensus or by virtually unanimous vote of an organization of universal membership such as the United Nations or its Specialized Agencies. On the other hand, majorities may be tempted to declare as existing law what they would like the law to be, and less weight must be given to such a resolution when it declares law in the interest of the majority and against the interest of a strongly dissenting minority. See, *e.g.*, the General Assembly resolution declaring that the use of nuclear weapons is a violation of international law (G.A. Res. 1653, U.N. GAOR, Supp. No. 17 at 4), and the "Moratorium Resolution" declaring that no one may mine for resources in the deep-sea bed until there is an agreed international regime and only in accordance with its terms (G.A. Res. 2574(D), 24 U.N. GAOR, Supp. No. 30, at 11), both of which were challenged by the United States, a principal power immediately affected by those resolutions. See § 523, Reporters' Note 2. Even a unanimous resolution may be questioned when the record shows that those voting for it considered it merely a recommendation or a political expression, or that serious consideration was not given to its legal basis. A resolution is entitled to little weight if it is contradicted by state practice, Comment a, or is rejected by international courts or tribunals. On the other hand, a declaratory resolution that was less than unanimous may be evidence of customary law if it is supported by thorough study by the International Law Commission or other serious legal examination. See, for example, the reliance on one United Nations General Assembly resolution but deprecation of another resolution by the arbitrator in Texas Overseas Petroleum Co. v. Libyan Arab Republic (1977), 17 Int'l Leg. Mat. 1 (1978).

Resolutions by a principal organ of an organization interpreting the character of the organization may be entitled to greater weight. In some instances, such an interpretation may, by the terms of the charter, be binding on the parties, for example, those of the Council of the International Coffee Organization. See Charter of the International Coffee Organization, 469 U.N.T.S. 169. Declarations interpreting a charter are entitled to considerable weight if they are unanimous or nearly unanimous and have the support of all the principal members.

NOTE

For a more comprehensive discussion and analysis on the sources and evidence of international law, see Louis Henkin, Richard C. Pugh, Oscar Schachter and Hans Smit, *International Law, Cases and Materials*, 2nd ed., St. Paul, Minn.: West Publishing Co., 1987, pp. 35-136 and the literature cited therein.

B. SPECIAL PROBLEMS CONCERNING THE SOURCES OF THE INTERNATIONAL LAW OF THE SEA

> D. P. O'Connell, *The International Law of the Sea*, edited by I. A. Shearer, Vol. 1, New York: Oxford University Press, 1982, pp. 29, 31, 32-34, 36-42, 46-47, 57-58. Notes omitted. Reprinted by permission of Oxford University Press.

. . . the law of the sea has manifested, more directly and more obviously than any other branch of international law, the tensions between stability and change, and between rules and actions that are part of the processes of history. So much of the law of the sea is of its essence pragmatic, that no plausible conclusions respecting its content could easily be drawn from speculation about the nature of man or the nature of society, as in other fields of international law. Because of this pragmatic character, the law of the sea is readily susceptible to the influence of unilateral acts:

whether the extent of the territorial sea is to be three miles, twelve miles, or 200 miles is not a question to which philosophy can give an answer. The answer is furnished by state practice in the most elementary sense of that expression. . . .

1. Unilateral Action

One cannot complain that this is an illicit process in any way, for the technological changes of the time, and the disturbances that have resulted in environmental and social matters, require that there be changes in the law. It is not a matter of recording old rules, but one of making new ones, and there are no other ways of doing this than by agreement or unilateral action; and when agreement is not forthcoming then by unilateral action alone.

It has always been the case that claims to the sea have been made unilaterally, but since 1945 there has been a fundamental change in the way they have been vindicated. Previously, they were defined as consistent with the existing law, because its rules were said to be unclear or flexible. Ambiguity was exploited. Today they tend increasingly to be justified only on the hypothesis that change is necessary. It is this alteration in emphasis that so seriously affects the methodology of international law, for there is no discernible criterion for determining, in a condition of incoherence, what rule the practice of States supports. Certainly a prime condition of authentic legal reasoning is that it supports the old rule until the new one takes its place, but it is often difficult to say, from the mere enumeration of subscribers to the one or the other point of view, when the substitution has taken place. . . .

The evolution of the law relating to adjacent fishing zones, and eventually the EEZ [Exclusive Economic Zone], is the most striking illustration of the cumulative effect of unilateral acts. In the *Fisheries Jurisdiction Case*, the International Court conceded this effect. The diplomatic modalities whereby the effect was produced, however, make it clear that unilateralism of itself is insufficient. These involved step by step acknowledgements of the claims made in the course of negotiations in which trades-off and phasing-out agreements were reached, so that gradually a net of bilateral links was woven. By 1967, enough such nets had come into existence to warrant the view that in the case of twelve-mile fishery limits, international law had endorsed the changes vis-a-vis governments other than the parties to these agreements.

For many years, the 200-mile limit failed to gain such general approbation as the twelve-mile limit. It was restricted geographically and to a small number of States; it had an authentic scientific basis in the cases of only three of these. It had been diplomatically resisted, with varying success, by those to whom it was in practice opposed. But in 1976 there came a change. The Third Law of the Sea Conference had made it clear that there was now general approbation of the concept of the EEZ; preserves in many countries had been built up which made political action in many areas of the world imperative; and, following the enactment of legislation by the United States, every North Atlantic country followed suit. This was a triumph of unilateralism, but it was not merely unilateralism: it was an engineered process when the conditions for a change in the law existed.

2. The Custom of the Sea and Unilateral Acts

Because the freedom of the seas is axiomatic, it follows that, as the International Court said in the *Anglo-Norwegian Fisheries Case*, "the delimitation of sea areas always has an international aspect and cannot be dependent merely upon the will of the coastal States as expressed in its municipal law." The *opinio juris* must presuppose this fundamental rule of the law of the sea.

The traditional doctrine concerning *opinio juris* received its classical, and perhaps ultimate, exposition in the *North Sea Continental Shelf Case*. The International Court said that for actions of States to constitute *opinio juris*, two conditions must be fulfilled:

> Not only must be acts concerned amount to a settled practice, but they must also be such, or be carried out in such a way, as to be evidence of a belief that this practice is rendered obligatory by the existence of the rule of law requiring it. The need of such a belief, i.e., the existence of a subjective element, is implicit in the very notion of the *opinio juris sive necessitatis*. The States concerned must therefore feel that they are conforming to what amounts to a legal obligation. The frequency, or even habitual character of the acts is not in itself enough. There are many international acts, e.g. in the field of ceremonial and protocol, which are performed almost invariably, but which are motivated only by considerations of courtesy, convenience, or tradition, and not by any sense of legal duty.

Only five years later the same Court found it impossible to reiterate this, because in the meanwhile it had become clear that one could not explain the legal process by assuming that the only relevant State conduct is that which is prompted by a sense of "conforming to what amounts to a legal obligation"; and because the Court's way of putting it would not only make change impossible but would also make the initiation of a rule impossible: for, it is manifestly question-begging to say that a customary rule can come into existence only because of an erroneous belief that it exists already.

Accordingly, in the *Fisheries Jurisdiction Case* the Court discarded the apparatus of *opinio juris* and phrased the position in a more contemporary and more plausible, if in a less reassuring way: it said that after the Law of the Sea Conference of 1958 "the law evolved through the practice of States on the basis of the debates and near agreements at the Conference." State practice, it said, revealed an increasing and widespread acceptance of the concept of preferential rights for coastal States. Various steps taken in the Conference were approved by a large majority, "thus showing overwhelming support for that idea that in certain special situations it was fair to recognize that the coastal State had preferential fishing rights. After these Conferences, the preferential rights of the coastal State were recognized in various bilateral and multilateral international agreements." What the court was doing here was yielding to the normative force of fact.

But the question is, which facts have this force and which do not? The difficulty in making any choice is evident from the division of opinion of the Court itself: whereas the majority said that the pressures exerted in the direction of changes in the law at the Third Law of the Sea Conference were to be regarded as only "manifestations of the views and opinions of individual States and as vehicles of their aspirations, rather than as expressing principles of existing law," half of that majority in a joint separate opinion said that it was not possible thus to "brush aside entirely these pronouncements of States and consider them devoid of all legal significance." In a situation of great uncertainty, these judges said, the impact of such pronouncements "must undoubtedly have an unsettling effect on the crystallization of a still evolving customary law on the subject." They were to be regarded as "of significance to determine the views of those States as to the law on fisheries jurisdiction, and their *opinio juris* on a subject regulated by customary law." . . .

. . . the difficulty lies in the circumstance that practice may not be concurrent or congruent, and yet something more than adding up numbers is needed before the relevant factual judgments can be validly made. While unanimity is not a requirement in fact, neither is there special significance in the notion of "widespread support," for, although all States may be equal legislators, not all are equal actors, and a rule may be more dependent upon the conduct of a small group of States than upon the proclamations of the great majority. For example, it would not matter if a hundred non-shipping countries enacted legislation to exercise jurisdiction over ships, if all the shipping countries resisted. Qualitative as well as quantitative judgments are essential.

If the one hundred countries, however, manage to enforce their jurisdiction the situation must be adjudged differently, for now their legislation has been made effective. While it is untrue to suggest that the doctrine of effectiveness has become a substitute for the traditional doctrine of *opinio juris*--for that would involve treating facts as normative merely because they are made facts by acts of force--that doctrine has assumed greater prominence in the processes of empirical judgment. It was given classical expression by Judge Read in the *Anglo-Norwegian Fisheries Case*, when he said that "the only convincing evidence of State practice is to be found in seizures, where the coastal State asserts its sovereignty over the waters in question." Mere claim, even if embodied in legislation, is insufficient, according to this view, to bring about changes in the law which do not have widespread support at first, but actual enforcement, even if it amounts at the time to breach of the law, can bring about such changes because it induces widespread acquiescence. If a claim can be vindicated by action, then, it is apt to consolidate itself, either as a contribution to global action to change customary law, or as an historic derogation from the standard rules.

There are, in fact, two views about effectiveness which are mutually incompatible. One view is that a legal regime must be made effective in fact in order to become an institution of international law; and the supposition behind the question, how can one speak seriously of effective, meaning continuing, control over hundreds of miles of ocean, is that a regime can only become such an institution when all States in the relevant circumstances can, in a practical sense, administer what they claim--which, in the case of the EEZ is evidently beyond the resources of most claimants. The other view accords to effectiveness a role in tacit consent: that is, if governments tolerate spasmodic enforcement, a mood of widespread acceptance is generated which is sufficient to establish an institution. The processes of making judgments, as well as the practical politics of the matter, vindicate the second view even if it is anomalous in both political theory and legal history, that States may have rights over geographical areas which they cannot practically administer. The reason for the acquiescence in this type of case is that possession has economic advantages, for fishing rights can be sold even if they cannot be enforced.

3. The Methodology of the Law of the Sea

In a time of political, social, and economic stability, the rules of law are apt to be relatively stable, whereas in a time of rapid changes, they are apt to become unstable. That does not mean that all legal certainty is excluded. There will be stable rules, to which the traditional methodology of *opinio juris* remains authentic and appropriate; there will be new rules which can be vindicated by reference to the doctrine of effectiveness; and there will be rules in treaties which are susceptible of the usual canons of construction. It is a matter of legal technique to determine into which category any particular question falls, and the scrutiny of factors is traditional to the skills of the international jurist.

However, except perhaps in the construction of hard and fast rules of treaty law, the enunciation of a rule of customary law, especially of the unstable variety, cannot be exclusively a matter of counting the number of acting and approving States, or restating a number of facts about actions and counter-actions, for the process is not of establishing the record but of discerning the emergence and operation of a principle of conduct. Nor is that discernment independent of the juristic antecedents. For this reason, the historical method of investigating the law of the sea is the only valid one. It is impossible to evaluate a situation of action and inaction isolated in time and space: the situation is a product, not only of historical forces, but also of the history of the law. . . .

4. The Significance of Protest in the Law of the Sea

. . . .

The common element in protests is that they deny the validity of claims made. But if the claims seek to invoke history as well as changing circumstances or special considerations as their basis, the draftsman of a protest may have had in mind either to deny the acquiescence which is sometimes thought to be essential to the creation of a regime in derogation of international law, or to withhold consent in an effort to arrest the growth of a customary rule of law, based on State practice, which might validate a claim as an instance of the law, rather than as an exception to it. The nature of the protest may well vary, depending upon whether it aims to reserve existing rights from invasion and so prevent an historic claim from maturing, or, by denying to the claimant State the benefit of the element of general consent of nations, to inhibit custom.

The difference between the two roles played by protest has not always been recognized, and has not often been closely examined, so that doctrine remains unclear. It seems obvious that the scope of acquiescence is different in respect of the growth of custom, from what it is in respect of the consolidation of an historic right. The withholding of consent by one State has never been decisive in the translation of *lex ferenda* into *lex lata*, for State practice is not a matter of counting heads but of juristic evaluation of the factors that tend to legitimize action by individual States. The number of protests, the vehemence of the protests, the subsequent actions of all parties, the importance of the interests affected, and the effluxion of time are all factors for evaluation in a contest about an alleged rule of customary law, or a change in the content of that rule.

In the case of historic claims in derogation from the law, however, protest, as a withholding of acquiescence, plays a more significant role. Here the claimant State has a much greater burden of proof thrust upon it than is required in the case of a rule of customary law, where, as the *Lotus Case* and the *Anglo-Norwegian Fisheries Case* both show, the advantage lies with the party which acts and the disadvantage with the party which must demonstrate that the action is illegal. In the case of historic waters, what has to be established is the virtually total toleration of those nations whose interests are clearly affected, because the situation, having its origins in an illegal act which time and an absence of opposition alone can validate, is analogous to the subversion of a neighbouring title on land by adverse occupation. Protest in this case is the opposite of that mere inaction which could lead a tribunal at some future date to presume toleration sufficient for an exceptional title to be vindicated. It is undisputed that a claim which encounters no opposition is readily legitimized, however irregular its origins, and that, it seems, within a relatively short period of time. . . .

. . . the tendency is to regard diplomatic protests as of limited significance, and certainly not as the principal, let alone the sole, method of interrupting the consolidation of a pretense into a right. Protest will not preserve rights indefinitely unless in the circumstances it is the only lawful means available to the State concerned. It must, at the very least, be repeated; it must be supported by conduct which opposes the pretensions of the claimant State; and if such conduct is impossible for reasons of disparity in the power to influence events, it must be followed up by every available diplomatic means. Proposals for negotiations or settlement, if rejected or ignored, add to the intrinsic value of the protest, and assist the protest to retain that value over a longer period of time.

Protest, in fact, is the obverse of effectiveness. While it is true that States are obliged to respect the rights of other States, an effective interruption of those rights can result in a change in the legal situation to an extent not contemplated by municipal law. This is specially so with respect to unilateral acts, for these are covered by a presumption that the acting State did not contemplate a result incompatible with customary international law. Maritime claims are rarely validated while they remain paper claims. . . .

A protest will often give rise to a reply from the claimant State making it clear that further protests will in no way alter the situation. Repeated protests in these circumstances can have little cumulative effect, and if the issue is to be resolved one way or the other the protesting State should be prepared to make use of the adjudicatory machinery at its disposal. It can propose that the matter be submitted to the International Court or to arbitration if the relevant States are not parties to the Optional Clause or to the Optional Protocol to the Geneva Convention, or to other treaties providing for arbitration; and if the proposal is rejected by the claimant State the protest gains weight. If judicial machinery is available on unilateral application, failure to utilize it might reduce the significance of protest quite seriously. . . .

It is, of course, not unilateral action alone that creates law or transforms an illegal situation into a legal one, but the whole context; and in maritime claims the context will be geographical, geophysical, sociological and economic as well as political. Claimant States are usually sufficiently astute to avoid direct confrontation with protesting States in making their claims effective, and will rely on probing to ascertain how far they can go in practice without exacerbating the diplomatic situation beyond what is necessary and proportionate in the circumstances. By a series of successful steps, the claim can be consolidated in fact, and the protests directed towards it can be undermined by a series of retreats on the part of protesting States. . . .

The value of the protest should also be measured against the totality of the relations between the two States as well as in the context of the international community and its reaction to the alleged evolving custom. It is clear that one State by protesting cannot stand out in perpetuity against the *opinio juris* of the majority of States, and what the protesting State would be seeking to protect would no longer be rights but only interests. It would seem that the only safe course of conduct for a State is to follow up a protest by every available action. . . .

6. The Relationship Between Treaties and Customary Law

It is a fundamental rule of international law that in treaties the parties make their own law: *lex specialis derogat lege generali.* A rule of customary law is overridden by a rule of treaty law, and since treaties can only fall into desuetude if the parties so intend, a rule of the Law of the Sea which is set forth in a treaty is not easily subverted by the progress of customary law. But that it can be modified, especially where its stability is a matter of inference rather than of textual prescription, has been made clear in the *Fisheries Jurisdiction Case*. Article 1 of the High Seas Convention proclaims fishing to be among the freedoms of the high seas, and the high seas are defined as those outside of the territorial sea. Yet the International Court held that the extension of an "exclusive fishery jurisdiction independently of its territorial sea" up to a limit of twelve miles had become a right "generally accepted"; and similarly that the concept of preferential rights in additional adjacent waters had also become established. So, at the very least, custom had put a gloss upon the Convention: in fact it altered the literal interpretation of it. . . .

9. The Concept of Reasonable Use

One common thread running through the formulation of the various jurisdictional zones in the contemporary law of the sea is the idea of accommodation of interests, or a balancing of rights and duties, which can be summed up in the concept of "reasonable use." The result is that there is little absolutism in the rights of States with respect to the sea.

The International Law Commission gave marked impetus to the concept during the history of the Geneva Conventions. The Special Rapporteur, François, approached the novel question of the continental shelf from that point of view. He argued that the interests of navigation and fishing would have to yield to the larger interests of a new industry, and could not enjoy any preference. It was, he said, a question of balance of interests. The approach was reflected in the Commission's commentary, which said that "the progressive development of international law, which takes place against the background of established rules, must often result in the modification of those rules by reference to new interests or needs." It then went on to speak of "reasonably conceived requirements". . . .

However plausible the concept of reasonable use may be, it is essentially relativistic and hence susceptible of subjective evaluation. From it diametrically opposite inferences can be drawn, as occurred in the case of the debate over nuclear testing at sea. The concept is, therefore, not capable of resolving specific questions: all that it is capable of is the exclusion of their automatic resolution according to rigid rules, and the requirement that resolution be based upon appraisal as distinct from mandate.

REFERENCES

Chapter I, "The Sources and Development of the International Law of the Sea," C. John Colombos, *The International Law of the Sea*, 6th ed., London: Longman, 1967, pp. 7-46; Rudolf Bernhardt, "Custom and Treaty in the Law of the Sea," *Recueil des Cours* (Hague Academy of International Law), Vol. 205 (5) (1987), pp. 247-330; Chapter I, "The Concept, Sources and Principles of the International Law of the Sea," of I. P. Blishchenko, ed., *The International Law of the Sea*, Moscow: Progress Publishers, 1988, pp. 8-25.

Myres S. McDougal, "The Hydrogen Bomb Tests and the International Law of the Sea," *American Journal of International Law*, Vol. 49 (1955), pp. 356-359. Some footnotes omitted or renumbered. Reprinted with the permission of The American Society of International Law and the author.

From the perspective of realistic description, the international law of the sea is not a mere static body of rules but is rather a whole decision-making process, a public order which includes a structure of authorized decision-makers as well as a body of highly flexible, inherited prescriptions. It is, in other words, a process of continuous interaction, of continuous demand and response, in which the decision-makers of particular nation states unilaterally put forward claims of the most diverse and conflicting character to the use of the world's seas, and in which other decision-makers, external to the demanding state and including both national and international officials, weigh and appraise these competing claims in terms of the interests of the world community and of the rival claimants, and ultimately accept or reject them. As such a process, it is a living, growing law, grounded in the practices and sanctioning expectations of nation-state officials, and changing as their demands and expectations are changed by the exigencies of new interests and technology and by other continually evolving conditions in the world arena.

The factual claims asserted by nation state decision-makers to the use of the world's seas, the events to which the "regime of the high seas" is authoritative response, vary enormously in the comprehensiveness and particularity of the interests sought to be secured, in the location and size of the area affected, in the duration of claim, and in the degree of interference with others. Such claims range, in rough categorization, from the comprehensive and continuous claim to practically all competence in the "territorial sea" through the continuous but limited claims to navigation, fishing, and cable-laying upon the "high seas," to the relatively temporary and limited claims to exercise authority and control beyond territorial boundaries for a vast array of national purposes, such as security and self-defense, enforcement of health, neutrality and customs regulations, conservation or monopolization of fisheries, exploitation of the sedentary fisheries and mineral resources of the sea bed and continental shelf, the conducting of naval maneuvers and other military exercises, and so on. It may be observed, however, that, despite their variety in institutional nuance, all these claims share certain common characteristics: they are all unilateral assertions of demands by particular claimants to the individual use of a great common resource and all are affected in equal degree--navigation and fishing no more and no less than the others--with a community interest in fullest utilization and conservation and with specific national interest, which, though varying in particular instances with geographic propinquity, is in the sum of all instances common to all claimants.

The authoritative decision-makers put forward by the public order of the high seas to resolve all these competing claims include, of course, not merely judges of international courts and other international officials, but also those same nation-state officials who on other occasions are themselves claimants. This duality in function ("*dédoublement fonctionnel*"), or fact that the same nation-state officials are alternately, in a process of reciprocal interaction, both claimants and external decision-makers passing upon the claims of others, need not, however, cause confusion: it merely reflects the present lack of specialization and centralization of policy functions in international law generally. Similarly, it may be further observed, without deprecating the authority of international law, that these authoritative decision-makers projected by nation states for creating and applying a common public order, honor each other's unilateral claims to the use of the world's seas not merely by explicit agreements but also by mutual tolerances--expressed in countless decisions in foreign offices, national courts, and national legislatures--which create expectations that effective power will be restrained and exercised in certain uniformities of pattern. This process of reciprocal tolerance of unilateral claim is, too, but that by which in the present state of world organization most decisions about jurisdiction in public and private international law are, and must be, taken.[1]

The overriding policy which has in the past infused this whole decision-making process, and which from the perspective of rational preference should continue to infuse it, is not the negation,

[1]It is not of course the unilateral claims but rather the reciprocal tolerances of the external decision-makers which create the expectations of pattern and uniformity in decision, of practice in accord with rule, commonly regarded as law.

The great bulk of claims to authority and control upon the high seas are honored and protected, it may be emphasized, not by explicit bilateral or multilateral agreement, but by this process of mutual tolerance. . . .

but rather the encouragement, of use. The major policy purpose inspiring the regime of the high seas has been not merely the negation of unnecessary restrictions upon navigation and fishing, but also the effective promotion of the fullest, peaceful, and conserving use and development by all peoples of a great common resource, covering two thirds of the world's surface, for all contemporary values. The concept of a common and reciprocal interest in fullest utilization has underlain, and should continue to underlie, the whole flow of decision.

For implementing this overriding policy of fullest, peaceful utilization in resolving the conflicting claims which confront them, the authoritative decision-makers of the world community have elaborated a comprehensive body of technical doctrine, "the regime of the high seas," composed of two complementary sets of prescriptions. The one set of these prescriptions, that generally referred to under the label of "freedom of the seas," was formulated, and is invoked, to honor unilateral claims to navigation, fishing, cable-laying, and other similar uses. The other set, that which includes the prescriptions summed up in a wide range of technical terms such as "territorial sea," "contiguous zones," "jurisdiction," and "continental shelf," was formulated, and is invoked, to honor all the great variety of claims, both comprehensive and particular, which may interfere, in greater or less degree, with navigation and fishing. To the initiated, these prescriptions and technical terms are not absolute, inelastic dogmas but rather flexible policy preferences, permitting decision-makers a very broad discretion for adjusting particular controversies in terms of the multiple variables peculiar to each controversy and for promoting major policies. For all types of controversies the one test that decision-makers have in fact invoked and applied is that simple and ubiquitous, but indispensable, standard of what, considering all relevant policies and variables in context, is *reasonable* as between the parties; and for clarification of detailed policies in ascribing meaning to particular prescriptions and terms, such decision-makers have habitually turned to all those sources authorized for the International Court of Justice, including not only "international conventions, whether general or particular" but also "international custom, as evidence of a general practice accepted as law," "the general principles of law recognized by civilized nations," "judicial decisions and the teachings of the most qualified publicists," and considerations "*ex aequo et bono.*"[2]

---

[2]Stat. I.C.J., Art. 38. A decision-maker is thus not confined, in determination of lawfulness, to explicit agreements or inferences from prior customary behavior, but may draw creatively upon a great variety of principles, precedents, analogies, and considerations of fairness. An excellent example of this process by which external decision-makers appraise unilateral claims is offered by the Anglo-Norwegian Fisheries Case, Judgment of Dec. 18, 1951, [1951] I.C.J. Rep. 116. In this case Norway asserted claims which could not be justified by reference to either explicit agreement or widely accepted custom, and which had been protested by other nation states, but by drawing upon all relevant sources of policy and a great variety of considerations in the context, the Court concluded that Norway's claims were lawful. . . .

C. THE UNITED STATES AND THE 1982 UNITED NATIONS CONVENTION ON THE LAW OF THE SEA

"Introductory Note to Part V, The Law of the Sea," *Restatement on Foreign Relations Law of the United States*, Vol. 2, 3rd revised ed., St. Paul, Minn.: American Law Institute, 1987, pp. 5-6. Some notes omitted. Copyright by The American Law Institute. Reprinted with the permission of The American Law Institute.

As of 1987, the Convention was not yet in force, and, after its entry into force, it will apply as such to the United States only if the United States becomes a party to it.

For purposes of this Restatement, therefore, the Convention as such is not [the] law of the United States. However, many of the provisions of the Convention follow closely provisions in the 1958 conventions to which the United States is a party and which largely restated customary law as of that time. Other provisions in the LOS Convention set forth rules that, if not law in 1958, became customary law since that time, as they were accepted at the Conference by consensus and have influenced, and came to reflect, the practice of states. . . . In particular, in March 1983 President Reagan proclaimed a 200-nautical-mile exclusive economic zone for the United States and issued a policy statement in which the United States in effect agreed to accept the substantive provisions of the Convention, other than those dealing with deep sea-bed mining, in relation to all states that do so with respect to the United States. Thus, by express or tacit agreement accompanied by consistent practice, the United States, and states generally, have accepted the substantive provisions of the Convention, other than those addressing deep sea-bed mining, as statements of customary law binding upon them apart from the Convention. See Case concerning Delimitation of the Maritime Boundary of the Gulf of Maine (Canada/United States), [1984] I.C.J. Rep. 246, 294 (the provisions of the LOS Convention concerning the continental shelf and the exclusive economic zone "were adopted without any objections" and may "be regarded as consonant at present with general international law on the question"). In a few instances, however, there is disagreement whether a provision of the Convention reflects customary law. . . . Some provisions of the Convention notably those accepting particular arrangements for settling disputes, clearly are not customary law and have not been accepted by express or tacit agreement.[1]

---

[1]Some provisions of the LOS Convention either would have no application to the United States or their applicability is in doubt. See, e.g., the following Comments and Reporters' Notes:

Substantive provisions:

Section 514, Reporters' Note 4. Special rules apply to fishing for certain stocks and species of fish and to marine mammals. There is some disagreement whether all the details of these provisions are customary law. (Arts. 64-67.)

Section 515, Comments a, b. Parties to the Convention that exploit non-living resources of the continental shelf beyond 200 miles will have to make payments to the International Sea-Bed Authority. (Art. 82.)

Section 515, Reporters' Note 1. On the basis of the 1958 Convention on the Continental Shelf, some states have claimed as continental shelf sea-bed areas extending beyond 200 miles. Some developing countries have taken the view that the consensus on the definition of the continental shelf is contingent on payments to the international fund from the area beyond 200 miles. Thus, whether as a matter of customary law a state can claim such an area as

REFERENCES

Louis B. Sohn, "Thoughts on Customary International Law," *Rusk Center Newsletter*, Vol. 1, No. 2 (January 1984), pp. 1-3; David Lawrence Treat, "The United States' Claims of Customary Legal Rights Under the Law of the Sea Convention," *Washington and Lee Law Review*, Vol. 41 (1984), pp. 253-273.

NOTE

Although the United States Department of State has still listed the four 1958 Geneva Conventions on the Law of the Sea in its annual *Treaties in Force* (*e.g.*, *see Treaties in Force 1989*, Washington, D.C.: U.S. Government Printing Office, 1989, pp. 309 (Fishery), 336-337 (High Sea, Continental Shelf and Territorial Sea)), the *Restatement of Foreign Relations Law of the United States*, third revision, Section 115, Comment d states:

> It has also not been authoritatively determined whether a rule of customary international law that developed after, and is inconsistent with, an earlier statute or international agreement of the United States should be given effect as the law of the United States. In regard to the

miles. Thus, whether as a matter of customary law a state can claim such an area as continental shelf without making such payments is in dispute. (Arts. 76, 82.)

Section 523. This section departs from Part XI of the LOS Convention, which establishes a regime for deep sea-bed exploration and exploitation, much of which is not customary law.

Institutions and Procedures:

The provisions of the LOS Convention establishing new institutions and a system for the settlement of disputes arising under the Convention are not customary international law and will not become law for the United States unless the United States becomes a party to the Convention. See, e.g.:

. . . Where a state suffers a loss due to the failure of the flag state to exercise proper control, a special dispute settlement mechanism is provided in Part XV of the Convention.

. . . A special procedure to resolve continental shelf issues is to be established. (Art. 76(8).)

. . . Under the Convention there will be a special procedure for settling certain disputes between coastal and other states as to their respective rights and duties in the exclusive economic zone. (Art. 297.)

. . . The Convention provides for submission of certain maritime boundary disputes to a conciliation commission. (Art. 298(91)(a).)

In addition to effecting changes in the substantive rules governing mining in the deep sea-bed, the Convention would establish institutions and procedures that are binding only on parties to the Convention. . . .

law of the sea, the United States has accepted customary law that modifies earlier treaties as well as United States statutes.

Restatement of Foreign Relations Law of the United States, Vol. 1, 3rd ed., St. Paul, Minn.: American Law Institute, 1987, pp. 65-66.

STATEMENT OF PRESIDENT T. T. KOH OF THE THIRD UNITED NATIONS CONFERENCE ON THE LAW OF THE SEA AT THE CLOSING SESSION OF THE CONFERENCE, DECEMBER 10, 1982. *Third United Nations Conference on the Law of the Sea, Official Record*, Vol. XVII, pp. 135-136.

45. During the last four days I have sat here and listened attentively to the statements made by 121 delegations. I should like to highlight the major themes which I have found in those statements. . . .

47. The second theme which has emerged from the statements is that the provisions of the Convention are closely interrelated and form an integral package. Thus it is not possible for a State to pick what it likes and to disregard what it does not like. It was also said that rights and obligations go hand in hand and it is not permissible to claim rights under the Convention without being willing to shoulder the corresponding obligations.

48. The third theme I have heard is that this Convention is not a codification convention. The argument that, except for Part XI, the Convention codifies customary law or reflects existing international practice is factually incorrect and legally insupportable. The regime of transit passage through straits used for international navigation and the regime of archipelagic sea lanes passage are only two examples of the many new concepts in the Convention. Even in the case of article 76, on the continental shelf, the article contains new law in that it has expanded the concept of the continental shelf to include the continental slope and the continental rise. This concession to the broad-margin States was in return for their agreement to revenue-sharing on the continental shelf beyond 200 miles. It is therefore my view that a State which is not a party to this Convention cannot invoke the benefits of article 76.

49. The fourth theme relates to the lawfulness of any attempt to mine the resources of the international area of the sea-bed and ocean floor. Speakers from every regional and interest group expressed the view that the doctrine of the freedom of the high seas can provide no legal basis for the grant by any State of exclusive title to a specific mine site in the international area of the sea-bed. Many are of the view that article 137 of the Convention has become as much a part of customary international law as the freedom of navigation. Any attempt by any State to mine the resources of the deep sea-bed outside the Convention will therefore earn the universal condemnation of the international community and will incur grave political and legal consequences. All speakers have addressed an earnest appeal to the United States to reconsider its position. The United States is a country which has throughout its history supported the progressive development of international law and has fought for the rule of law in relations between States. The present position of the United States Government towards this Convention is therefore inexplicable in the light of its history, in the light of its specific law-of-the-sea interests and in the light of the leading role which it has played in negotiating the many compromises that have made this Convention possible.

Hugo Caminos and Michael R. Molitor, "Progressive Development of International Law and the Package Deal," *American Journal of International Law*, Vol. 79 (1985), pp. 879, 887-889. Notes omitted. Reprinted with the permission of The American Society of International Law and Hugo Caminos.

To understand how the package deal may have affected the traditional treaty-custom relationships, it is necessary first to survey the conventional rules. Article 34 of the 1969 Vienna Convention on the Law of Treaties provides: "A treaty does not create either obligations or rights for a third State without its consent," i.e., the familiar maxim, *pacta tertiis nec nocent nec prosunt*. This general rule, of course, is modified by Article 38: "Nothing in articles 34 to 37 precludes a rule set forth in a treaty from becoming binding upon a third State as a customary rule of international law." Article 38 appears to suggest that provisions of multilateral treaties that reflect customary norms can be invoked *against* as well as *by* third states. Such provisions would operate between states parties on the basis of treaty law and between any other combination of parties and nonparties on the basis that they reflect customary law. As noted early on by the International Law Commission (ILC):

> A principle or rule of customary international law may be embodied in a bipartite or multipartite agreement so as to have, within the stated limits, conventional force for the States parties to the agreement so long as the agreement is in force; yet it would continue to be binding as a principle or rule of customary international law for other States. . . .

V. THE LIMITATIONS OF THE PACKAGE DEAL

The legal effect of the package deal, albeit a significant departure from the traditional treaty-custom rules, is not without its limitations. The door has not been completely closed on the ability of the 1982 Convention to reflect customary rights and obligations binding upon third states. The limitations apply to two categories of customary norms. First, and most important, the package deal cannot affect those provisions of the Convention which were carried over directly from the 1958 Conventions and which reflected customary law prior to UNCLOS III. Such provisions, irrespective of their place within the 1982 package, continue to be exercisable by, and binding upon, third states. However, where established customary rules appearing in the 1982 Convention have been changed, it must not be presumed that such modifications have acquired similar status. In fact, significant changes have been made in the majority of such articles in the 1982 Convention.

The other group of provisions that remain unaffected by the package deal includes all of the innovative provisions of the 1982 Convention that achieved customary status while the negotiations were being held, that is, after the conference began in 1973 and before the adoption of the treaty on April 30, 1982. This exception holds true only because the package deal could not have crystallized all of the provisions of the Convention into an indivisible whole before the treaty was adopted. As the President of the conference noted:

> [T]he very nature of the concept of a package deal must mean that no delegation's position on a particular issue would be treated as irrevocable until at least all the elements of the "package" as contemplated had formed the subject of agreement. Every delegation, therefore, had the right to reserve its position on any particular issue

until it had received satisfaction on other issues which it considered to
be of vital importance to it.

It appears, therefore, that the package could not have been definitively "sealed" while the
negotiations were still under way and that such a process could only have occurred when the 1982
Convention was formally adopted.

The innovative provisions of the Convention that achieved customary status before the
package had crystallized are surely excluded from the effect of the package deal. Therefore, such
provisions may continue to reflect rights and obligations for both parties and nonparties. A good
example is part V of the Convention on the exclusive economic zone (EEZ). State practice in
establishing 200-mile resource zones suggests that the EEZ concept had achieved customary status
prior to the adoption of the 1982 Convention. It must be emphasized that the customary rule does
not derive from the EEZ provisions of the Convention but rather from the practice of states
reflected in the combined effect of the numerous municipal laws establishing such zones and the
numerous bilateral fisheries agreements concluded during the last 10 years. Clearly, exclusive
economic zones as they now exist under customary international law may not resemble in all
respects the EEZ regime embodied in the 1982 Convention.

The final category of provisions that require comment includes those which, as of April 30,
1982, had failed to achieve customary law status. If one assumes that the package deal was
solidified at the time that the Convention was formally adopted, then those of its provisions that
had not attained customary status by that date may have been precluded from ever doing so.
Certainly, through time, certain third states may possibly begin to acquire rights reflected in the
1982 Convention vis-à-vis other third states, as well as states parties, through the acquiescence of
uniform and widespread state practice. Such an outcome, however, cannot lightly be presumed to
transfer the multitude of innovative provisions of the 1982 Convention into the general corpus of
international law. Furthermore, such a process represents a two-edged sword in that it may make
equally applicable to third states the innovative obligations in the Convention.

The full thrust of the legal effect of the package deal, therefore, applies to this third category
of provisions. They constitute the major part of the Convention and include, most notably, Part
III, Section II: Transit Passage, and most of Part XI: The Area. More than 150 states agreed to
the consensus and package deal negotiating procedures that juridically bound this final category of
provisions to the entire Convention package. For this reason, third states may find it
tremendously difficult to invoke such provisions under the traditional rules by which multilateral
conventions provide the impetus for creating new customary norms.

Finally, to conclude, something should be said about the notion of the instant crystallization
of customary international law and its application to the 1982 Convention. There are those who
argue that, as nearly all the members of the international community had gathered at UNCLOS III,
and through their collective efforts they adopted many provisions by consensus, the resulting
articles automatically entered into customary international law. Those who hold this view
maintain that the requirements of time and *opinio juris* must be discounted because the entire
international community acted collectively and swiftly to indicate its consent to these norms.

This proposition is indeed difficult to accept for two important reasons. First, an individual
state not formally objecting to a particular provision may not, in every instance, be indicating its
consent to be bound, regardless of whether or not the entire international community is
participating in the consensus. Moreover, the true test for the existence of a customary norm of
international law is state practice. The legal relations arising from instruments concluded in

international law is state practice. The legal relations arising from instruments concluded in multilateral negotiations are not customary in nature but rather contractual.

State practice, therefore, remains the exclusive means of identifying customary norms. In the case of the 1982 Convention, the package deal has created serious implications for the straight-forward application of that test inasmuch as many provisions may be precluded from achieving customary status. The extent to which the future states parties feel bound to the package deal, and act accordingly in not acquiescing in the creation of customary norms, will determine which, if any, of the majority of the innovative provisions in the 1982 Convention will enter into the general corpus of international law. The future of the package deal therefore lies in the hands of the future states parties and in their commitment to its continuing effect.

REFERENCES

David L. Larson, "The Reagan Rejection of the U.N. Convention," *Ocean Development and International Law*, Vol. 14 (1984-85), pp. 337-361; Finn Laursen, *Superpower at Sea: U.S. Ocean Policy*, New York: Praeger, 1983; James L. Malone, "The United States and the Law of the Sea After UNCLOS III," *Law and Contemporary Problems*, Vol. 46 (1983), pp. 29-63; James L. Malone, "The United States and the Law of the Sea," *Virginia Journal of International Law*, Vol. 24 (1983-84), pp. 785-807; James L. Malone, "Who Needs the Sea Treaty?," *Foreign Policy*, Vol. 54 (1984), pp. 44-63; Carlyle E. Maw, ed., *What Law Now for the Seas?*, Washington, D.C.: American Bar Association, 1984; Bernard H. Oxman, David D. Caron and Charles L. L. Buderi, ed., *Law of the Sea: U.S. Policy Dilemma*, San Francisco: Institute for Contemporary Studies, 1984; Jon M. Van Dyke, ed., *Consensus and Confrontation: The United States and the Law of the Sea Convention*, Honolulu: Law of the Sea Institute, University of Hawaii, 1985.

CHAPTER IV

THE BASELINE

A. INTRODUCTION

The majority of ocean space zones are delimited on the basis of a fixed distance from the coastline. As will be seen, the coastline has been defined in an international agreement as the "baseline" and it is from the baseline that those zones of ocean space are delimited. The baseline has another critical function. Waters on the landward side of it are denominated as "internal" or "inland" waters, while waters on the seaward side are "territorial" waters. There is, as you will learn, a significant difference in the legal regime between internal and territorial waters. By claiming an area as internal waters, the coastal state obviates the need for arguing the niceties of the juridical content of the territorial sea, fisheries zones, and areas of continental shelf. It has absolute jurisdiction over resources in internal waters or the seabed below them. Thus, it should not be surprising to find that many attempts have been made to delimit the baseline in such a manner as to avoid the question of the proper breadth of territorial waters or a fisheries zone.

Thus, much of the material in this chapter concerning baselines, bays, historic waters, and the like, has an important bearing on the nature of coastal state jurisdiction over off-shore resources. You will learn the detailed nature of that jurisdiction in subsequent parts of this book.

FISHERIES CASE (UNITED KINGDOM v. NORWAY)
Judgment of December 18, 1951
I.C.J. Reports, 1951, p. 116, at p. 132.

The delimitation of sea areas has always an international aspect; it cannot be dependent merely upon the will of the coastal State as expressed in its municipal law. Although it is true that the act of delimitation is necessarily a unilateral act, because only the coastal State is competent to undertake it, the validity of the delimitation with regard to other States depends upon international law.

Myres S. McDougal and William T. Burke, *The Public Order of the Oceans*, New Haven, Connecticut and London: Yale University Press, 1962, pp. 306-308. Reprinted by permission of the authors.

. . . [C]ritical differences in the competences accorded coastal states are effected by the location of the baseline delimiting internal waters from the territorial sea because, by fixing the point from which measurement of the width of the territorial sea begins, such location determines also whether adjacent waters are within or beyond the territorial sea. Whatever the width of the territorial sea, the movement of the baseline further seaward at the same time projects the outer limit of the territorial sea further seaward. . . .

That there is a special problem about determining what areas are within internal waters, or within the territorial sea, or outside both as high seas, is primarily a function of two sets of interrelated factors, one geographical and the other predispositional. The geographical factors embrace all the varying configurations of the coasts of the world. The predispositional factors are comprised of the distinctive perspectives--demands, identification, and expectations--sometimes achieved by coastal inhabitants.

With respect to geography, if all coasts were nicely formed of straight, or gently rounded, lines and the immediately adjacent waters bare of distinctive physical features, the question of where to begin in measuring the width of the territorial sea would perhaps admit of easy answer. Unfortunately, however, geography does not so conveniently conform to wishes for simplicity. Some coastal areas do appear to be without any distinctive or special configuration and are characterized by relatively uncomplicated contours, but these are more the exception than the rule. Other coasts display a great variety of configurations, such as indentations that vary in size, shape, general usage, and relationship to other physical features. An indentation may represent merely a small intrusion of the ocean into the land mass or mark the point at which a great watercourse empties a drainage area, perhaps as large as a continent, into the ocean. In further complexity, the coastal zone may be spotted with islands of various sizes, shapes, and relationships with each other and with other physical features of the coastal area. In some instances these islands may be found in great clusters, extending along the coast for great distances. Some of these so-called islands may actually be bits of ocean floor that appear above the surface only at certain stages of the tide.

All these features--the indentations, rivers, islands, groups of islands, and rocks--may occur in simultaneous abundance along the same stretch of coastline. And in addition to these natural features, man-made features including harborworks, buoys, artificial islands, and other artificial structures of various sorts built in the sea may also be found on and near the same coastal areas.

The perspectives of coastal inhabitants which may significantly affect community policies in delimiting areas of internal waters, territorial sea, and high seas are no less varied. The people in regions near the ocean, and sometimes of whole states, must on occasion rely for sustenance and general livelihood upon the produce of the ocean waters, and sometimes in otherwise nonproductive regions, these peoples come to be highly dependent upon ocean areas immediately adjacent to them. The result over a period of time may be the emergence of strong identifications with the proximate geographic areas and the formation of attitudes that outside groups must not intrude into such areas unless invited or forced to do so. Again, this attitude of exclusivity may ensue, not from historical patterns of life, but from emerging and anticipated conceptions of new needs, caused by changes in technology and customs, whose satisfaction is expected to be partially derived from uses of maritime resources. In sum, the circumstance of complex coastal configurations abutting on waters which can afford sustenance and gainful employment, coupled with a relative lack of other resources useful for these purposes, may lead to unusual expansion of exclusive claims over the adjacent water areas.

The important point is that while the occurrence of particular configurations may on occasion give rise, without reference to other features of the context, to unique, exclusive claims about the delimitation of internal waters, territorial seas, or high seas, full understanding of what is at stake in controversies about these claims calls for reference to the types and patterns of activities on land as well as to the activities of seafarers. The mere occurrence of an island or group of islands or a coastal indentation almost never accounts for the differing claims to delimit the varying water areas, over which coastal competence so greatly varies. It is completely clear, in any event, that desirable community policy can seldom rest solely upon the presence of certain geographic features as justification for particular delimitations, if these features are divorced from the social processes by which people exploit them. . . .

G.E. Pearcy, "Geographical Aspects of the Law of the Sea," *Annals of the Association of American Geographers*, Vol. 49 (1959), p. 5. Reprinted by permission of the Association of the American Geographers.

Key to all zonation of water and seabed off the coast of a state is the *baseline*. It forms the inner limit of the territorial sea, and from it is measured the outer limit. The same baseline forms the maximum seaward margin of a state's internal waters, such as bays, inlets, estuaries and other bodies of water associated with the shoreline. In addition . . . the baseline serves indirectly as a point of departure for determining both the inner and outer limits of the contiguous zone and the inner limits of the continental shelf and the high seas.

The specific placement of a baseline, therefore, is fundamental in ascertaining just how far seaward a state may exercise any given form of jurisdiction, whether it be complete sovereignty or only exercise of control to prevent infringement of regulations over such matters as customs, immigration, and sanitation. . . .

REFERENCES

T. Gihl, "The Baseline of the Territorial Sea," *Scandinavian Studies in Law*, Vol. 11 (1967), pp. 119-174; P.B. Beazley, *Maritime Limits and Baseline*, Hydrographic Society, Special Publication No. 2, 2nd ed., 1978; Lewis M. Alexander, "Baseline Delimitations and Maritime Boundary," *Virginia Journal of International Law*, Vol. 23 (1983), pp. 503-536; I. Aurrecoechea and J.S. Pethick, "The Coastline, Its Physical and Legal Definition," *International Journal of Estuarine and Coastal Law*, Vol. 1 (1986), pp. 29-42; Victor Prescott, "Delimitation of Marine Boundaries by Baseline," *Marine Policy Report*, Vol. 8 (1986), No. 3, pp. 1-5; Office for Ocean Affairs and the Law of the Sea, United Nations, *The Law of the Sea Baselines: An Examination of the Relevant Provisions of the United Nations Convention on the Law of the Sea*, New York: The United Nations, 1989.

B. NORMAL BASELINE

1. Mainland Areas

FISHERIES CASE (UNITED KINGDOM v. NORWAY)
Judgment of December 18, 1951
I.C.J. Reports, 1951, p. 116, at p. 128.

The Court has no difficulty in finding that, for the purpose of measuring the breadth of the territorial sea, it is the low-water mark as opposed to the high-water mark, or the mean between the two tides, which has generally been adopted in the practice of States. This criterion is the most favourable to the coastal State and clearly shows the character of territorial waters as appurtenant to the land territory.

1958 CONVENTION ON THE TERRITORIAL
SEA AND THE CONTIGUOUS ZONE

Article 3

Except where otherwise provided in these articles, the normal baseline for measuring the breadth of the territorial sea is the low-water line along the coast as marked on large-scale charts officially recognized by the coastal State.

[Article 5 of the 1982 United Nations Convention on the Law of the Sea is identical with this article on the normal baseline, except "these articles" are changed to "this Convention."]

INTERNATIONAL LAW COMMISSION
1956 Commentary, Draft Article 4
Yearbook of the International Law Commission 1956,
Vol. II, pp. 266-267.

(1) The Commission was of the opinion that, according to the international law in force, the extent of the territorial sea is measured either from the low-water line along the coast, or, in the circumstances envisaged in article 5, from straight baselines independent of the low-water mark. This is how the Commission interprets the judgment of the International Court of Justice rendered on 10 December 1951 in the Fisheries Case between the United Kingdom and Norway.

(2) The traditional expression "low-water mark" may have different meanings; there is no uniform standard by which States in practice determine this line. The Commission considers that it is permissible to adopt as the base line the low-water mark as indicated on large-scale charts officially recognized by the coastal State. The Commission is of the opinion that the omission of detailed provisions such as were prepared by the 1930 Codification Conference is hardly likely to induce Governments to shift the low-water lines on their charts unreasonably.

INTERNATIONAL LAW COMMISSION
1955 Commentary, Ch. III, Draft Article 4
Yearbook of the International Law Commission 1955,
Vol. II, p. 35.

The final sentence of the article adopted in 1954 read: "If no detailed charts of the area have been drawn which show the low-water line, the shore-line (high-water line) shall be used." This sentence might lead to confusion, since it could be interpreted as meaning that not only a ship on the high seas but also the coastal State must take the high-water line as baseline in the absence of detailed charts, which was not the Commission's intention. The Commission therefore decided to delete it.

W. L. Griffin, "The Emerging Law of Ocean Space," *International Lawyer*, Vol. 1 (1969), pp. 556-560. Reprinted by permission of the American Bar Association.

The normal baseline for measuring the breadth of the territorial sea is the low-water line as marked on large scale charts. "Large scale" may be defined as scale ratios of 1/80,000 or larger.

All of the Atlantic and Gulf coastline of the United States is covered by 1/80,000 scale charts. Most of the Pacific coastline of the country is covered by a series of charts at scales ranging from about 1/200,000 to 1/300,000. Only comparatively small sections of the Pacific coast are covered at larger scales and some of the Alaska coastline is covered only by small scale charts.

> A. L. Shalowitz, *Shore and Sea Boundaries*, Vol. 1, Washington, D.C.:
> U. S. Government Printing Office, 1962, p. 274.

Although "large-scale" is a relative term and is not defined in the convention, a scale of 1/80,000 (approximately 1 nautical mile to the inch) would probably be the upper limit of such classification.

> A. L. Shalowitz, *Shore and Sea Boundaries*, Vol. 2, Washington, D.C.:
> U. S. Government Printing Office, 1964, p. 105.

Insofar as Coast [and Geodetic] Survey usage is concerned, scales up to and including 1/20,000 would be considered *large* scales, those between 1/20,000 and 1/80,000 would be classed as *intermediate* scales, and scales smaller than 1/80,000 would fall into the category of *small* scales.

REFERENCES

Henry S. Frazer, "The Extent and Delimitation of Territorial Waters," *Cornell Law Quarterly*, Vol. II (1926), pp. 455-481; S. W. Boggs, "Delimitation of Seaward Areas Under National Jurisdiction," *American Journal of International Law*, Vol. 45 (1951), pp. 240-260; Burdick H. Brittin, "Article 3, Regime of the Territorial Sea," *American Journal of International Law*, Vol. 50 (1956), pp. 934-941; G. E. Pearcy, "Measurement of the U.S. Territorial Sea," *U. S. Department of State Bulletin*, Vol. 40, No. 1045 (June 29, 1959), pp. 963-971; L. A. Teclaff, "Shrinking the High Seas by Technical Methods--From the 1930 Hague Convention to the 1958 Geneva Conference," *University of Detroit Law Journal*, Vol. 39 (1962), pp. 660-684; P. K. Nunez, "Fluctuating Shorelines and Tidal Boundaries: An Unresolved Problem," *San Diego Law Review*, Vol. 6 (1969), pp. 447-469.

> Harold W. Dubach and Robert W. Taber, *Questions About the Oceans*,
> Washington, D.C.: U.S. Government Printing Office, 3rd printing,
> 1969, pp. 33-34.

31. What causes the tides?

Tides are caused by gravitational forces of the moon, the sun, and various other celestial bodies. The moon, being nearest, has the greatest effect. The sun, despite its greater mass, exerts only a secondary effect, less than half that of the moon.

High tides are generated on the sides of the earth nearest to and farthest from the moon. At times of new moon and full moon, the sun's attraction reinforces that of the moon, producing higher (spring) tides. Halfway between new and full moon, solar attraction does not coincide with lunar attraction and therefore the difference between high and low tides is less; these lesser tides are called neap tides.

When the moon is over the Equator as the earth rotates, a point on the earth passes through two high and two low areas each day. When the moon is north or south of the Equator, the two highs are unequal in height or there may be only one high tide.

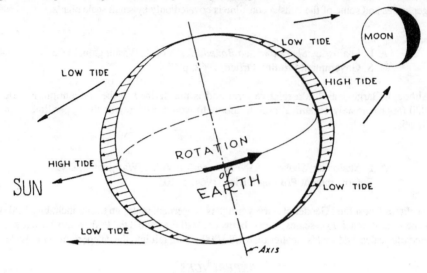

Sun, Earth, Moon and Tide
Fig. 4-1

32. Why do tide ranges in the same geographical areas of the world differ so greatly?

In addition to effects of the moon and sun, tide ranges are affected by shape and dimension of the coastline and sea floor. In some restricted water areas (bays, channels, etc.), heights may build up to 50 feet and tidal currents of as much as 10 knots occur.

Tides moving upstream in an estuary are slowed down by bottom friction, and the following water piles up. The water rises more rapidly than it falls, and the flood stream has higher velocity than the ebb.

Some areas of great tidal ranges are the Bay of Fundy, Bristol Channel, and the Sea of Okhotsk. The famous Bay of Fundy tidal bore moves more than 100 billion tons of water a day.

There are also areas in the world that are almost tideless; among these are the Mediterranean, Baltic, and Adriatic Seas, and the Gulf of Mexico.

A. L. Shalowitz, *Shore and Sea Boundaries*, Vol. 1, Washington, D.C.:
U.S. Government Printing Office, 1962, pp. 84-90.

62. Aspects of the Tide

. . . .The phenomenon of the tide is far from being a simple one. The tidal effect of sun and moon upon the waters of the earth depends upon the relative positions of the three bodies at a particular time and a particular place. Considering then that the earth revolves on its axis once every 24 hours, and its journey around the sun takes 1 year; that the moon revolves around the earth once every 29´ days, and its orbit is inclined on the average 23´° to the earth's equator; that every body of water has its own period of oscillation, and responds differently to the tide-producing forces; and that all of these factors, together with the configuration of the land bordering the water areas, enter into the formation of the tide, there is present an almost limitless number of possible combinations into which these factors can unite to produce both differences at the same time at different places and differences at the same place at different times.

621 [sic]. Diurnal Inequality

. . . .the mixed type of tide is the predominant one--two high and two low waters occur each tidal day, with marked differences between the morning and afternoon tides. This difference is called *diurnal inequality* and varies with the changing declination of the moon during a lunar month. In general, the inequality tends to increase with an increasing declination, either north or south, and to diminish as the moon approaches the equator.

The existence of diurnal inequality is an important factor in the determinations of the various vertical datums based on tidal definition, and makes necessary the distinction between the two high waters and between the two low waters of a day. Thus, of the former the higher is called the "higher high water" and the lower the "lower high water." Similarly, of the two low waters, the lower is called "lower low water" and the higher the "higher low water."

622 [sic]. Spring and Neap Tides

Another variation in the rise and fall of the tide is related to the different phases through which the moon passes during a lunar, or synodic, month of approximately 29´ days. At new moon the sun and moon are in line and on the same side of the earth. The tidal forces are then in the same phase and work in conjunction to strengthen each other and bring about the large tides which have been designated "spring tides." At such times high water rises higher and low water falls lower than at other times. At the end of 7´ days the moon has passed through one-quarter of its journey and has reached quadrature. The tidal forces of sun and moon then act at right angles on the waters of the earth and are in opposition to each other, or in opposite phase. Each force tends to minimize the force of the other body. The tide therefore does not rise as high nor fall as low as on the average. Because of their small range they have been designated as "neap tides."

After another 7´ days, the sun and moon are again in line but on opposite sides of the earth. The moon is then in its "full" phase and the tidal forces act the same as during new moon and spring tides again occur. At the end of another period of 7´ days, the moon has arrived at the third quarter of its course and is again in quadrature. The tidal forces again act in opposition as in the first quarter and neap tides result. At the end of a further period of 7´ days, the sun and moon are again in line and on the same side of the earth and another cycle begins. . . .

64. Demarcation of Tidal Boundaries

Boundaries determined by the course of the tides involve two engineering aspects: a vertical one, predicated on the height reached by the tide during its vertical rise and fall, and constituting a tidal plane or datum, such as mean high water, mean low water, etc.; and a horizontal one, related to the line where the tidal plane intersects the shore to form the tidal boundary desired, for example, mean high-water mark, mean low-water mark. The first is derived from tidal observations alone, and, once derived (on the basis of long-term observations), is for all practical purposes a permanent one. The second is dependent on the first, but is also affected by the natural processes of erosion and accretion, and the artificial changes made by man. A water boundary determined by tidal definition is thus not a fixed, visible mark on the ground, such as a roadway or fence, but represents a condition at the water's edge during a particular instant of the tidal cycle.

BORAX CONSOLIDATED v. CITY OF LOS ANGELES,
296 U.S. 10 (1935)

[This case involved an action to quiet title to tidelands in Los Angeles harbor brought by the City of Los Angeles against Borax Consolidated. One of the issues presented to the Court was the question of how the boundary between state-owned tidelands and privately-owned upland areas was to be determined. The excerpt which follows contains the Court's pronouncements on the point, a decision implemented in all tidal datum work to the present day.]

There remains for our consideration, however, the ruling of the Court of Appeals in instructing the District Court to ascertain as the boundary "the mean high-tide line" and in thus rejecting the line of "neap tides."

Petitioners claim under a federal patent which, according to the plat, purported to convey land bordering on the Pacific Ocean. There is no question that the United States was free to convey the upland, and the patent affords no ground for holding that it did not convey all the title that the United States had in the premises. The question as to the extent of this federal grant, that is, as to the limit of the land conveyed, or the boundary between the upland and the tideland, is necessarily a federal question. It is a question which concerns the validity and effect of an act done by the United States; it involves the ascertainment of the essential basis of a right asserted under federal law. . . .

The tideland extends to the highwater mark. . . .This does not mean, as petitioners contend, a physical mark made upon the ground by the waters; it means the line of high water as determined by the course of the tides. By the civil law, the shore extends as far as the highest waves reach in winter. . . . But by the common law, the shore "is confined to the flux and reflux of the sea at ordinary tides." . . . It is the land "between ordinary high and low water mark, the land over which the daily tides ebb and flow. When, therefore, the sea or a bay, is named as a boundary, the line of ordinary high-water mark is always intended where the common law prevails." . . .

The range of the tide at any given place varies from day to day, and the question is: How is the line of "ordinary" high water to be determined? The range of the tide at times of new moon and full moon "is greater than the average," as "high water then rises higher and low water falls lower than usual." The tides at such times are called "spring tides." When the moon is in its first and third quarters, "the tide does not rise as high nor fall as low as on the average." At such times the tides are known as "neap tides." . . . The view that "neap tides" should be taken as the ordinary tides had its origin in the statement of Lord Hale. . . .In his classification, there are "three sorts of shores, or littora marina, according to the various tides": (1) "The high spring tides, which are the fluxes of the sea at those tides that happen at the two equinoxials." (2) "The spring tides, which happen twice every month at full and change of the moon." And (3) "ordinary tides, or neap tides, which happen between the full and change of the moon." The last kind of shore, said Lord Hale, "is that which is properly littus maris." He thus excluded the "spring tides" of the month, assigning as the reason that "for the most part the lands covered with these fluxes are dry and maniorable," that is, not reached by the tides.

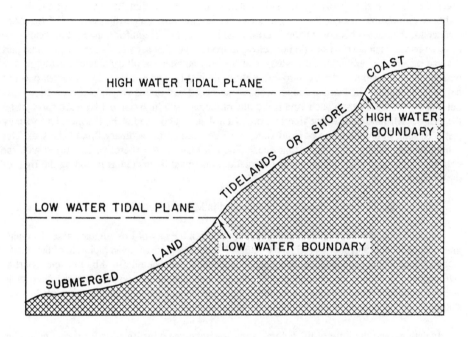

High/Low Water Tidal Plane
Fig. 4-2

Source: A. L. Shalowitz, *Shore and Sea Boundaries*, Vol. 1, Washington, D.C., U. S.
Government Printing Office, 1962, p. 90.

The subject was thoroughly considered in the case of *Attorney General v. Chambers*, 4 De G.
M. & G. 206. In that case Lord Chancellor Cranworth invited Mr. Baron Alderson and Mr. Justice
Maule to assist in the determination of the question as to "the extent of the right of the Crown to
the seashore." Those judges gave as their opinion that the average of the "medium tides in each
quarter of a lunar revolution during the year: fixed the limit of the shore. Adverting to the
statement of Lord Hale, they thought that the reason he gave would be a guide to the proper
determination. "What," they asked, are "the lands which for the most part of the year are reached
and covered by the tides?" They found that the same reason that excluded the highest tides of the
month, the spring tides, also excluded the lowest high tides, the neaps, for "the highest or spring-
tides and the lowest high tides (those at the neaps) happen as often as each other." Accordingly,
the judges thought that "the medium tides of each quarter of the tidal period" afforded the best
criterion. They said: "It is true of the limit of the shore reached by these tides that it is more
frequently reached and covered by the tide than left uncovered by it. For about three days it is

exceeded, and for about three days it is left short, and on one day it is reached. This point of the shore therefore is about four days in every week, i.e., for the most part of the year, reached and covered by the tides." . . .

Having received this opinion, the Lord Chancellor stated his own. He thought that the authorities had left the question "very much at large." Looking at "the principle of the rule which gives the shore to the Crown," and finding that principle to be that "it is land not capable of ordinary cultivation or occupation, and so is in the nature of unappropriated soil," the Lord Chancellor thus stated his conclusion: "Lord Hale gives as his reason for thinking that lands only covered by the high spring-tides do not belong to the Crown, that such lands are for the most part dry and maniorable; and taking this passage as the only authority at all capable of guiding us, the reasonable conclusion is that the Crown's right is limited to land which is for the most part not dry or maniorable. The learned Judges whose assistance I had in this very obscure question point out that the limit indicating such land is the line of the medium high tide between the springs and the neaps. All land below that line is more often than not covered at high water, and so may justly be said, in the language of Lord Hale, to be covered by the ordinary flux of the sea. This cannot be said of any land above that line." The Lord Chancellor therefore concurred with the opinion of the judges "in thinking that the medium line must be treated as bounding the right of the Crown." . . .

This conclusion appears to have been approved in Massachusetts. . . .

In California, the Acts of 1911 and 1917, upon which the city of Los Angeles bases its claim, grant the "tidelands and submerged lands" situated "below the line of mean high tide of the Pacific Ocean." Petitioners urge that "ordinary high-water mark" has been defined by the state court as referring to the line of the neap tides. We find it unnecessary to review the cases cited or to attempt to determine whether they record a final judgment as to the construction of the state statute, which, of course, is a question for the state courts.

In determining the limit of the federal grant, we perceive no justification for taking neap high tides, or the mean of those tides, as the boundary between upland and tideland, and for thus excluding from the shore the land which is actually covered by the tides most of the time. In order to include the land that is thus covered, it is necessary to take the mean high-tide line which, as the Court of Appeals said, is neither the spring tide nor the neap tide, but a mean of all the high tides.

In view of the definition of the mean high tide, as given by the United States Coast and Geodetic Survey, that "Mean high water at any place is the average height of all the high waters at that place over a considerable period of time," and the further observation that "from theoretical considerations of an astronomical character" there should be "a periodic variation in the rise of water above sea level having a period of 18.6 years," the Court of Appeals directed that in order to ascertain the mean high-tide line with requisite certainty in fixing the boundary of valuable tidelands, such as those here in question appear to be, "an average of 18.6 years should be determined as near as possible." We find no error in that instruction.

The decree of the Court of Appeals is affirmed.

REFERENCES

A. L. Shalowitz, "Boundary Problems Raised by the Submerged Lands Act," *Columbia Law Review*, Vol. 54 (1954), pp. 1038-42; A. Defant, *Ebb and Flow: The Tides of Earth, Air, and Water*, Ann Arbor, Michigan: n.p., 1958; J. H. Williams, *Oceanography, An Introduction to the*

Marine Sciences, Boston: Little Brown, 1962, pp. 196-209; C. A. M. King, *An Introduction to Oceanography*, New York: McGraw Hill, 1963, pp. 157-195; W. Bascom, *Waves and Beaches*, Garden City, N.J.:   Anchor Books, 1964; P. K. Nunez, "Fluctuating Shorelines and Tidal Boundaries: An Unresolved Problem," *San Diego Law Review*, Vol. 6 (1969), pp. 447-469; Orlin, "Verticle Datum for Boundary Determination," in Lewis M. Alexander, editor, *The Law of the Sea: National Policy Recommendations. Proceedings of the Fourth Annual Conference of the Law of the Sea Institute*, Kingston, Rhode Island: The University of Rhode Island, 1970, p. 416; R. H. Houlder, "Establishing Marine Boundaries--A New Federal Effort," *Sea Technology*, Vol. 17, No. 12 (1976), pp. 33-35.

2.   Islands

a. What is an Island?

1958 CONVENTION ON THE TERRITORIAL
SEA AND THE CONTIGUOUS ZONE

Article 10(1)

An island is a naturally formed area of land, surrounded by water, which is above water at high tide.

[Article 121(1) of the 1982 United Nations Convention on the Law of the Sea is identical.]

INTERNATIONAL LAW COMMISSION
1956 Commentary, Draft Article 10
Yearbook of the International Law Commission 1956,
Vol. II, p. 270

(2) An island is understood to be any area of land surrounded by water which, except in abnormal circumstances, is permanently above high-water mark. Consequently, the following are not considered islands and have no territorial sea:

(i) Elevations which are above water at low tide only. Even if an installation is built on such an elevation and is itself permanently above water--a lighthouse, for example--the elevation is not an "island" as understood in this article;

(ii) Technical installations built on the seabed, such as installations used for the exploitation of the continental shelf (see article 71). The Commission nevertheless proposed that a safety zone around such installations should be recognized in view of their extreme vulnerability. It does not consider that a similar measure is required in the case of lighthouses.

R. D. Hodgson, *Islands: Normal and Special Circumstances*, Washington, D.C.: Bureau of Intelligence and Research, U.S. Department of State, Dec. 10, 1973, pp. 4, 6-7, 13-15, 69-71.

Smaller in size than continents but situated above mean high water at all times are more than one-half million pieces of distinctly subcontinental land territory defined generically as islands. With a combined area exceeding 3,823,000 square miles, islands range in size from mere dots or pinnacles, virtually without measurable surface, to such extensive masses as Greenland, which possesses an area of more than 840,000 square miles, greater in size than all but 11 countries of the world. In fact, 62 islands have areas in excess of 4,000 square miles; at least 126 are larger in area than 1,000 square miles.

. . . .

Approximately 7 percent of the land area of the earth is encompassed by oceanic islands. (The figure would be greater if it included islands in lakes and rivers, but these are essentially beyond the scope of this paper.) Almost every coastal country possesses islands, to a greater or lesser degree, and many countries are totally insular in geography.

Islands are situated in all manners and patterns. Some perch immediately adjacent to continental masses; some are dispersed in mid-ocean. They are found in singular isolation or grouped by dozens, hundreds, or even thousands. Many are arranged in quasi-geometric patterns-- arcs, quadrangles, triangles, polyhedrons, etc.; others are strewn randomly across the water surface. . . .

. . . .

[Article 10(1) of the Convention on the Territorial Sea and the Contiguous Zone] suggests no size criterion, locational requirement in relation to mainland, or other particular geographical or special condition. It specifies, however, that the island must be *naturally formed*.

The use of "formed" rather than "created" raises distinct or potential questions of interpretation. Obviously, the island must be composed of land-dirt, rock, organic matter, or a combination thereof. Its formation may be assisted, however, by man's efforts. To maintain navigation channels, states and individuals dredge certain earth materials from the subsoil of rivers, harbors, and other coastal areas. Such material, or spoil, creates problems of disposal; and dredgers, motivated by cost factors, seek a local place in which to dump the spoil. Nearby shallow waters often furnish the site.

Currents, tides, and other natural forces act upon these manmade dumps of earth. When dumping ceases, most often they disappear, transported and redistributed by the restless environ- ment of coastal waters over the bottom from which they were dredged. Occasionally these spoil dumps remain above sea level, but their external shapes and dimensions are altered markedly or "formed" by the actions of tides, waves, currents, and wind. Thus, a "naturally formed island" is born. Should it be considered an island under the terms of the Convention?

The language of the Convention and the labors of the legal and technical experts who assisted in its preliminary drafts emphasize chart representation of geographic features--the external, two-dimensional forms. Genesis of landforms, difficult and expensive to establish or prove, was not a major factor in the proceedings. Charted forms dominate in the geographic-legal definitions of bays, river mouths, etc. As a consequence, man-created spoil banks may become, through the forces of nature, islands in the legal-political, as well as geographical, sense of the Convention. It should be noted, however, that the effects of such islands on the extension of the territorial sea normally are limited since the islands, to survive, must be in relatively shallow water close to land.

However, if dumping of spoil at a site continues, the artificial nature of the spoil bank will be maintained. The shape of the "island" will continue to be artificially formed and the definition in the Convention will be negated. This fact would be reinforced if the coastal state continued to mark the "island" as "spoil" on official charts. The "island" would then remain "an artificially formed" node above sea level and should have no effect on the extension of the territorial sea. Geographically an island, the spoil bank would not exist legally as a basepoint.

Times and technology, however, have changed and will continue to change. The rate of change, in fact, accelerates. Consequently, a revised or new convention must face novel uses, not necessarily related to the seabed, which may or may not require sovereignty or sovereign rights:

1)   offshore loading and unloading ports;

2)   floating airports;

3)   atomic power plants situated offshore to minimize environmental damage;

4)   permanent storage structures for gas, petroleum, and other products, etc.

. . . .

REFERENCES

M. S. McDougal and W. T. Burke, *The Public Order of the Oceans: A Contemporary International Law of the Sea*, New Haven and London: Yale University Press, 1962, pp. 387-398; *U. S. v. Ray*, 423 F.2d 16 (5 Cir. 1970); R. D. Hodgson, "Islands: Normal and Special Circumstances"; J. K. Gamble and G. Pontecorvo, editors, *The Law of the Sea: The Emerging Regime of the Oceans*, Kingston, R.I.: The University of Rhode Island, 1974, pp. 137-199; D. W. Bowett, *The Legal Regime of Islands in International Law*, Dobbs Ferry, New York: Oceana Publications, 1979; Andreas J. Jacovides, "Three Aspects of the Law of the Sea: Islands, Delimitation and Dispute Settlement," *Marine Policy*, Vol. 3 (1979), No. 4, pp. 278-288; Clive Ralph Symmons, *The Maritime Zones of Islands in International Law*, The Hague/Boston: Martinus Nijhoff, 1979; Jon M. Van Dyke and Robert A. Brooks, "Uninhabited Islands: Their Impact on the Ownership of the Oceans' Resources," *Ocean Development and International Law*, Vol. 12 (1983), pp. 265-300; M. Habibur Rahman, "The Impact of the Law of the Sea Convention on the Regime for Island: Problems for the Coastal State in Asserting Claims to 'New-Born' Islands in Maritime Zone," *International and Comparative Law Quarterly*, Vol. 34 (1985), pp. 368-376; Janusz Symnides, "The Legal Status of Islands in the New Law of the Sea," *Revue de Droit International, de Sceinces Diplomatiques et Politiques*, Vol. 65 (1987), No. 3, pp. 161-180.

R.R. Churchill and A.V. Lowe, *The Law of the Sea*, 2nd ed.,
Manchester: Manchester University Press, 1988, pp. 42-43. Reprinted
by permission.

Artificial islands. The definition in the Conventions of an island as being "naturally-formed" excludes artificial islands, although the distinction between a "naturally-formed" and an "artificial" island may not always be easy to make in practice: e.g. if a State constructs some kind of barrier in the sea so that sand being moved by currents piles up against it, with the result that eventually an island is formed, is this a "naturally-formed" or an artificial island? The only provision on artificial islands in the 1958 Geneva Conventions is article 5(4) of the Continental Shelf

Convention, which provides that installations connected with the exploration and exploitation of the shelf's natural resources and located on the continental shelf have no territorial sea nor do they affect its delimitation. The implication would seem to be that no artificial island is entitled to a territorial sea or, therefore, to serve as a basepoint. The Law of the Sea Convention reinforces this conclusion. First, article 11 provides . . . that "offshore installations and artificial islands shall not be considered as permanent harbour works" and therefore do not, *qua* harbour works, form part of the baseline. Secondly, articles 60(8) and 80 provide that artificial islands and installations constructed in the EEZ or on the continental shelf have no territorial sea of their own nor does their presence affect the delimitation of the territorial sea, EEZ or continental shelf. Thirdly, even though the construction of artificial islands on the high seas is now recognised as a freedom of the high seas (LOSC, art. 87), the prohibition on States from subjecting any part of the high seas to their sovereignty (LOSC, art. 89) prevents the establishment of any maritime zones around artificial islands on the high seas. This principle is spelt out for that part of the high seas overlying the International Sea Bed Area. Under article 147(2) stationary installations used for the conduct of activities in the Area have no territorial sea of their own, nor do they affect the delimitation of the territorial sea, EEZ or continental shelf.

NOTE

For the status of ice on the high seas, see Jorgen Molde, "The Status of Ice in International Law," *Nordisk Tidsskrift for International Ret. Acta Scandinavica Juris Gentium* (Copenhagen), Vol. 51 (1982), Nos. 3/4, pp. 164-178.

b.   Do Islands Have Territorial Sea, Continental Shelf or Exclusive Economic Zone?

1958 CONVENTION ON THE TERRITORIAL SEA AND THE CONTIGUOUS ZONE

Article 10(2)

The territorial sea of an island is measured in accordance with the provisions of these articles.

INTERNATIONAL LAW COMMISSION
1956 Commentary, Draft Article 10
Yearbook of the International Law Commission, 1956,
Vol. II, p. 270.

(1) This article applies both to islands situated in the high seas and to islands situated in the territorial sea. In the case of the latter, their own territorial sea will partly coincide with the territorial sea of the mainland. The presence of the island will create a bulge in the outer limit of the territorial sea of the mainland. The same idea can be expressed in the following form: islands, wholly or partly situated in the territorial sea, shall be taken into consideration in determining the outer limit of the territorial sea.

1958 CONVENTION ON THE CONTINENTAL SHELF

Article 5(2), (4)

2. . . . the coastal state is entitled to construct and maintain or operate on the continental shelf installations and other devices necessary for its exploration and the exploitation of its natural resources. . . .

. . . .

4. Such installations and devices, though under the jurisdiction of the coastal State, do not possess the status of islands. They have no territorial sea of their own, and their presence does not affect the delimitation of the territorial sea of the coastal State.

INTERNATIONAL LAW COMMISSION
1956 Commentary, Draft Article 71
Yearbook of the International Law Commission, 1956,
Vol. II, pp. 299-300.

(6) With regard to the general status of installations, it has been thought useful to lay down expressly that they do not possess the status of islands and that the coastal State is not entitled to claim for installations any territorial waters of their own or treat them as relevant for the delimitation of territorial waters. In particular, they cannot be taken into consideration for the purpose of determining the baseline. On the other hand, the installations are under the jurisdiction of the coastal State for the purposes of maintaining order and of the civil and criminal competence of its courts.

THE ANNA
5 C. Rob 373 (1805)
165 Eng. Rep. 809

[This case involved the seizure of an American ship near the mouth of the Mississippi River, within the claimed three mile territorial sea limit of the United States adjacent to a "mud island" but more than three miles from firm land. Among the questions considered by the English court was whether the territorial sea of the United States could properly be measured from such insubstantial islands.]

When the ship was brought into this country, a claim was given of a grave nature, alleging a violation of the territory of the United States of America. This great leading fact has very properly been made a matter of much discussion, and charts have been laid before the Court to show the place of capture, though with different representations from the adverse parties. The capture was made, it seems, at the mouth of the River Mississippi, and, as it is contended in the claim, within the boundaries of the United States. We all know that the rule of law on this subject is "*terrae dominium finitur, ubi finitur armorum vis* [territorial command extends as far as the power of arms carries]," and since the introduction of fire-arms, that distance has usually been recognised to be about three miles from the shore. But it so happens in this case, that a question arises as to what is to be deemed the shore, since there are a number of little mud islands composed of earth and trees drifted down by the river, which form a kind of portico to the mainland. It is contended that these are not to be considered as any part of the territory of America, that they are a sort of "*no man's land*," not of consistency enough to support the purposes of life, uninhabited, and resorted to, only, for shooting and taking birds' nests. It is argued that the line of territory is to be taken only from the Balise, which as a fort raised on made land by the former Spanish possessors. I am of a different opinion; I think that the protection of territory is to be reckoned from these islands; and that they are the natural appendages of the coast on which they border, and from which indeed they are formed. Their elements are derived immediately from the territory, and on the principle of alluvium and increment, on which so much is to be found in the books of law, *Quod vis fluminis de tuo proedio detraxerit, & vicino proedio attulerit, palam tuum remanet*, (a) even if it had been carried over to an adjoining territory. Consider what the consequence would be if lands of this description were not considered as appendant to the mainland, and as comprised within the bounds of territory. If they do not belong to the United States of America, any other power might occupy them; they might be embanked and fortified. What a thorn would this be in the side of America! It is physically possible at least that they might be so occupied by European nations, and then the command of the river would be no longer in America, but in such settlements. The possibility of such a consequence is enough to expose the fallacy of any arguments that are addressed to show that these islands are not to be considered as part of the territory of America. Whether they are composed of earth or solid rock, will not vary the right of dominion, for the right of dominion does not depend upon the texture of the soil.

I am of opinion that the right of territory is to be reckoned from those islands. That being established, it is not denied that the actual capture took place within the distance of three miles from the islands, and at the very threshold of the river.

REFERENCE

M.S. McDougal & W.T. Burke, *The Public Order of the Oceans: A Contemporary Law of the Sea*, New Haven and London: Yale University Press, 1962, pp. 373-387; D.W. Bowett, *The Legal Regime of Islands in International Law*, Dobbs Ferry, New York: Oceana Publications, 1979, Chapter 1.

1982 UNITED NATIONS CONVENTION ON THE LAW OF THE SEA

Article 121
Regime of Islands

. . . .

2. Except as provided for in paragraph 3, the territorial sea, the contiguous zone, the exclusive economic zone and the continental shelf of an island are determined in accordance with the provisions of this Convention applicable to other land territory.

3. Rocks which cannot sustain human habitation or economic life of their own shall have no exclusive economic zone or continental shelf.

R.R. Churchill and A.V. Lowe, 2nd ed., *The Law of the Sea*, Manchester University Press, 1988, pp. 43-44. Reprinted by permission.

The coral reefs of atolls present a problem in that they may be continuously submerged or, if exposed at low tide, may be situated from the islands of the atoll at a distance greater than the breadth of the territorial sea: in neither case, therefore, under the rules so far considered could such reefs serve as the baseline. And yet it is desirable for a variety of reasons, principally ecological, that the territorial sea should be measured from the outer limit of the reef so that the lagoon inside the reef has the status of internal waters. The problem of coral reefs was recognized and discussed by the ILC in the earlier stages of its work but no provision on the subject was contained in its final draft, nor does the matter appear to have been discussed at UNCLOS I. With the emergence into independence since 1958 of many States formed of atolls in the Caribbean and Indian and Pacific Oceans, such as the Bahamas, the Maldives and Nauru, there has come greater political impetus for a specific rule for coral reefs, and such a rule is now contained in the Law of the Sea Convention. Article 6 provides that:

> In the case of islands situated on atolls or of islands having fringing reefs, the baseline for measuring the breadth of the territorial sea is the seaward low-water line of the reef, as shown by the appropriate symbol on charts officially recognized by the coastal State.

A number of points may be noted about this provision. First, it is not limited in its application to atolls or coral reefs (unlike an early draft provision in the ILC) Secondly, it suggests that only reefs exposed at low tide, and not wholly submerged reefs, may be used as baselines (again unlike the early ILC draft, which had provided that "the edge of the reef as marked on . . . charts, should be accepted as the low-water line"). Thirdly, it is not clear how far from the island the fringing reef may lie before it ceases to be eligible to serve as the baseline. It may be that "fringing reef" is used in its technical geographical sense as meaning a reef extending outwards from the shore, from which it is not separated by a channel (as opposed to a barrier reef, which lies at some distance from the shore). On the other hand, a literal reading of article 6 would suggest that it could apply to the Great Barrier Reef, which can be said to fringe the island of Australia; yet the reef is at points 150 miles from the coast. It must be assumed that article 6 is not intended to apply to this situation, and it therefore seems desirable that, if the term is not used in its technical geographical sense, some limit should be placed on the distance a fringing reef which is to serve as a baseline may lie from the coast of an island. A further problem is that article 6 does not specify what is to happen where there is a gap in the fringing reef. The obvious solution is to draw a straight line across the gap, and this appears to be the growing practice of States; see, for example, the legislation of Nauru and of New Zealand in respect of the Tokelau Islands. Finally, many atolls form part of archipelagos. In such cases it will often be simpler and more advantageous for the archipelagic State to use archipelagic baselines as the baseline. . . . than to construct baselines in accordance with the provisions of article 6.

REFERENCES

Maria Silvana, "The Legal Regime of Uninhabited 'Rocks' Lacking an Economic Life of Their Own," *Italian Yearbook of International Law*, Vol. 4 (1978-79), pp. 47-58; Jon M. Van Dyke and Robert A. Brooks, "Uninhabited Islands: Their Impact on the Ownership of the Oceans' Resources.," *Ocean Development and International Law*, Vol. 12 (1983), pp. 265-300; Office for Ocean Affairs and the Law of the Sea, *The Law of the Sea, Regime of Isnands, Legislative History of Part VIII (Article 121) of the United Nations Convention of the Law of the Sea*, New York: The United Nations, 1987.

C. PERMISSIBLE DEVIATIONS FROM THE NORMAL BASELINE

1982 UNITED NATIONS CONVENTION ON THE LAW OF THE SEA

Article 14
Combination of methods for determining baselines

The coastal State may determine baselines in turn by any of the methods provided for in the foregoing articles to suit different conditions. [The "foregoing articles" deal with low-tide elevations, roadsteads, ports, bays, mouths of rivers, straight baselines, and reefs.]

1.   Straight Baselines

a.   Coastal Areas

> L.A. Teclaff," Shrinking the High Seas by Technical Methods--From the 1930 Hague Convention to the 1958 Geneva Conference," *University of Detroit Law Journal*, Vol. 39 (1962), pp. 661-663. Reprinted by permission.

There are two methods of tracing the baseline. According to one, it should be drawn from headland to headland of the coast; according to another, it should run parallel to the contours of the land at some sea level. Of the two, the headline method served in the past and again serves to claim large stretches of the sea as national domain.

. . . .

The Headland-to-Headland Baseline

The headland method goes back at least to 1604, when King James of England decreed that imaginary lines be drawn from headland to headland on the English coast and proclaimed the waters landward from these lines to be "king's domain" or "king's chambers." The doctrine of "King's chambers" was expressly rejected in the 1854 award in the arbitration between the United States and Great Britain concerning the ship *Washington*. It has been used by Norway at least since the Royal Decree of 1812; it was also advocated by Kent for the delimitation of the United States territorial sea. Kent proposed to draw a straight line from Cape Ann to Cape Cod, from Nantucket to Montauk Point, thence to the Capes of Delaware, and from the South Cape of Florida to the Mississippi.

The Baseline Following Sinuosities of the Coast

The baseline following sinuosities of the coast seems to have had more adherents, though there was little agreement at first as to where this line should begin. Some proposed a line above high tide, because this was the most seaward line from which control could be exercised over the territorial sea at all times; others considered that the territorial sea should be measured from the line at which the sea becomes navigable. However, the low-tide line was adopted by the North Sea Fisheries Convention of 1882 between Great Britain, Germany, Belgium, Denmark, France and The Netherlands, and, earlier, by the treaty of 1825 between Great Britain and Russia concerning Alaska, the shore of which is not unlike that of Norway.

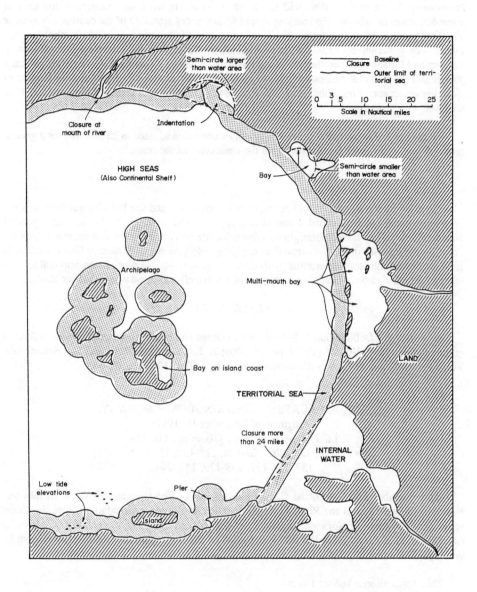

Various Baselines under the 1958 Geneva
Conventions on the Law of the Sea
Figure 4-3

Source: Sovereignty of the Sea, rev. ed., Washington, D.C.: Geographic Bulletin No. 3,
Department of State, October, 1969.

. . . .

In view of the divergent practice of states and the divergent opinions of writers, the Preparatory Committee of the 1930 Conference began its work by examining opinions of interested states on whether the baseline should follow every sinuosity of the coast at low tide, or whether it should be drawn from certain salient points of the coast, or in some other manner. Twenty-one governments expressed their opinions on the subject and all except three (Norway, Sweden and Poland) favored the line along the coast. Germany's opinion is interesting in that it pointed out the different methods employed by states to fix the low-tide level, such as the line of mean low-water spring tides, the spring-tide low water during the equinoxes, mean water, and mean sea level.

On the basis of these opinions the Preparatory Committee adopted as its proposal for a general rule: "A low-water-mark line following all the sinuosities of the coast."

. . . .

The Conference adjourned without signing a convention and the baseline question was not even mentioned in the Second Committee's report. The matter rested with the report of Subcommittee II, in which the straight baseline principle was not included, and the majority of the Sub-Committee considered the method as applying solely to bays. Professor Gidel, writing in 1934, criticized the straight baseline method on the grounds that it was almost impossible for a sailor to determine from a chart, in the absence of pre-established rules, where that line started.

REFERENCES

S. W. Boggs, "Delimitation of Seaward Areas Under National Jurisdiction," *American Journal of International Law*, Vol. 45 (1951), pp. 240-260; A. L. Shalowitz, *Shore and Sea Boundaries*, Vol. 1, Washington, D.C.: U.S. Government Printing Office, 1962, pp. 27-30.

FISHERIES CASE (UNITED KINGDOM v. NORWAY)
Judgment of December 18, 1951
I.C.J. Reports 1951, p. 116, at pp. 118-119,
124, 125, 126, 127-128, 129-130, 131-132,
133, 136-137, 138-139, 143, 144.

On September 28th, 1949, the Government of the United Kingdom of Great Britain and Northern Ireland filed in the Registry an Application instituting proceedings before the Court against the Kingdom of Norway, the subject of the proceedings being the validity or otherwise under international law, of the lines of delimitation of the Norwegian fisheries zone laid down by the Royal Decree of July 12th, 1935, as amended. . . .

This Application asked the Court

"(a) to declare the principles of international law to be applied in defining the baselines, by reference to which the Norwegian Government is entitled to delimit a fisheries zone, extending to seaward 4 sea miles from those lines and exclusively reserved for its own nationals, and to define the said baselines in so far as it appears necessary, in the light of the arguments of the Parties, in order to avoid further legal differences between them;

(b) to award damages to the Government of the United Kingdom in respect of all interferences by the Norwegian authorities with British fishing vessels outside the zone which, in accordance with the Court's decision under (a), the Norwegian Government is entitled to reserve for its nationals."

. . . .

The historical facts laid before the Court establish that as the result of complaints from the King of Denmark and of Norway, at the beginning of the seventeenth century, British fishermen refrained from fishing in Norwegian coastal waters for a long period, from 1616-1618 until 1906.

In 1906 a few British fishing vessels appeared off the coasts of Eastern Finnmark. From 1903 onwards they returned in greater numbers. These were trawlers equipped with improved and powerful gear. The local population became perturbed, and measures were taken by the Norwegian Government with a view to specifying the limits within which fishing was prohibited to foreigners.

The first incident occurred in 1911 when a British trawler was seized and condemned for having violated these measures. Negotiations ensued between the two Governments. These were interrupted by the war of 1914. From 1922 onwards incidents recurred. Further conversations were initiated in 1924. In 1932, British trawlers, extending the range of their activities, appeared in the sectors off the Norwegian coast west of the North Cape, and the number of warnings and arrests increased. On July 27th, 1933, the United Kingdom Government sent a memorandum to the Norwegian Government complaining that in delimiting the territorial sea the Norwegian authorities had made use of unjustifiable baselines. On July 12th, 1935, a Norwegian Royal Decree was enacted delimiting the Norwegian fisheries zone north of 66°28.8' North latitude.

. . . .

The Norwegian Royal Decree of July 12th, 1935, concerning the delimitation of the Norwegian fisheries zone sets out in the preamble the considerations on which its provisions are based. In this connection it refers to "well-established national titles of right," "the geographical conditions prevailing on the Norwegian coasts,"" the safeguard of the vital interests of the inhabitants of the northern-most parts of the country"; it further relies on the Royal Decrees of February 22nd, 1812, October 16th, 1869, January 5th 1881, and September 9th, 1889.

The Decree provides that "lines of delimitation towards the high sea of the Norwegian fisheries zone as regards that part of Norway which is situated northward of 66°28.8' North latitude . . . shall run parallel with straight baselines drawn between fixed points on the mainland, on islands or rocks, starting from the final point of the boundary line of the Realm in the easternmost part of the Varangerfjord and going as far as Traena in the County of Nordland." An appended schedule indicates the fixed points between which the baselines are drawn.

The subject of the dispute is clearly indicated under point 8 of the Application instituting proceedings: "The subject of the dispute is the validity or otherwise under international law of the lines of delimitation of the Norwegian fisheries zone laid down by the Royal Decree of 1935 for that part of Norway which is situated northward of 66°28.8' North latitude." And further on: ". . . . the question at issue between the two governments is whether the lines prescribed by the Royal Decree of 1935 as the baselines for delimitation of the fisheries zone have or have not been drawn in accordance with the applicable rules of international law."

Although the Decree of July 12th, 1935 refers to the Norwegian fisheries zone and does not specifically mention the territorial sea, there can be no doubt that the zone delimited by this Decree is none other than the sea area which Norway considers to be her territorial sea. That is how the Parties argued the question and that is the way in which they submitted it to the Court for decision.

. . . .

The claim of the United Kingdom Government is founded on what it regards as the general international law applicable to the delimitation of the Norwegian fisheries zone.

The Norwegian Government does not deny that there exist rules of international law to which this delimitation must conform. It contends that the propositions formulated by the United Kingdom Government in its "Conclusions" do not possess the character attributed to them by that Government. It further relies on its own system of delimitation which it asserts to be in every respect in conformity with the requirements of international law.

. . . .

The coastal zone concerned in the dispute is of considerable length. It lies north of latitude 66°28.8' N., that is to say, north of the Arctic Circle, and it includes the coast of the mainland of Norway and all the islands, islets, rocks and reefs, known by the name of "skjaergaard" (literally, rock rampart), together with all Norwegian internal and territorial waters. The coast of the mainland, which, without taking any account of fjords, bays, and minor indentations, is over 1,500 kilometers in length, is of a very distinctive configuration. Very broken along its whole length, it constantly opens out into indentations often penetrating for great distances inland: the Porsangerfjord, for instance, penetrates 75 sea miles inland. To the west, the land configuration stretches out into the sea: the large and small islands, mountainous in character, the islets, rocks and reefs, some always above water, others emerging only at low tide, are in truth but an extension of the Norwegian mainland. The number of insular formations, large and small, which make up the "skjaergaard," is estimated by the Norwegian Government to be one hundred and twenty thousand. From the southern extremity of the disputed area to the North Cape, the "skjaergaard" lies along the whole of the coast of the mainland; east of the North Cape, the "skjaergaard" ends, but the coast line continues to be broken by large and deeply indented fjords.

Within the "skjaergaard," almost every island has its large and its small bays; countless arms of the sea, straits, channels and mere waterways serve as a means of communication for the local populations which inhabits the islands as it does the mainland. The coast of the mainland does not constitute, as it does in practically all other countries, a clear dividing line between land and sea. What matters, what really constitutes the Norwegian coast line, is the outer line of the "skjaergaard."

The whole of this region is mountainous. The North Cape, a sheer rock little more than 300 meters high, can be seen from a considerable distance; there are other summits rising to over a thousand meters, so that the Norwegian coast, mainland and "skjaergaard," is visible from far off.

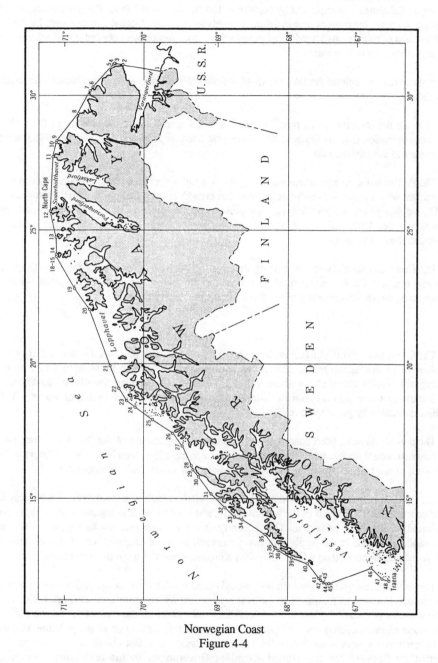

Norwegian Coast
Figure 4-4

Source: A. L. Shalowitz, *Shore and Sea Boundaries*, Vol. 1, Washington D.C.: U.S. Government Printing Office, 1962, p. 69.

Along the coast are situated comparatively shallow banks, veritable under-water terraces which constitute fishing grounds where fish are particularly abundant; these grounds were known to Norwegian fishermen and exploited by them from time immemorial. Since these banks lay within the range of vision, the most desirable fishing grounds were always located and identified by means of the method of alignments ("meds"), at points where two lines drawn between points selected on the coast or on islands intersected.

In these barren regions the inhabitants of the coastal zone derive their livelihood essentially from fishing.

Such are the realities which must be borne in mind in appraising the validity of the United Kingdom contention that the limits of the Norwegian fisheries zone laid down at the 1935 Decree are contrary to international law.

The Parties being in agreement on the figure of 4 miles for the breadth of the territorial sea, the problem which arises is from what baseline this breadth is to be reckoned. The Conclusions of the United Kingdom are explicit on this point: the baseline must be low-water mark on permanently dry land which is a part of Norwegian territory, or the proper closing line of Norwegian internal waters.

The Court has no difficulty in finding that, for the purpose of measuring the breadth of the territorial sea, it is the low-water mark as opposed to the high-water mark, or the mean between the two tides, which has generally been adopted in the practice of States.

. . . .

The Court finds itself obliged to decide whether the relevant low-water mark is that of the mainland or of the "skjaergaard." Since the mainland is bordered in its western sector by the "skjaergaard," which constitutes a whole with the mainland, it is the outer line of the "skjaergaard" which must be taken into account in delimiting the belt of Norwegian territorial waters. This solution is dictated by geographic realities.

Three methods have been contemplated to effect the application of the low-water mark rule. The simplest would appear to be the method of the *trace parallele*, which consists of drawing the outer limit of the belt of territorial waters by following the coast in all its sinousities. . . .

. . . .In the present case this method of *trace parallele*, which was invoked against Norway in the Memorial, was abandoned in the written Reply, and later in the oral argument of the Agent of the United Kingdom Government. Consequently, it is no longer relevant to the case. "On the other hand," it is said in the Reply, the *courbe tangente*--or, in English, "envelopes of 'arcs of circles'--method is the method which the United Kingdom considers to be the correct one."

The arcs of circles method, which is constantly used for determining the position of a point or object at sea, is a new technique in so far as it is a method for delimiting the territorial sea. This technique was proposed by the United Kingdom delegation at the 1930 Conference for the codification of international law. Its purpose is to secure the application of the principle that the belt of territorial waters must follow the line of the coast. It is not obligatory by law, as was admitted by Counsel for the United Kingdom Government in his oral reply. In these circumstances, and although certain of the Conclusions of the United Kingdom are founded on the application of the arcs of circles method, the Court considers that it need not deal with these Conclusions in so far as they are based upon this method.

The principle that the belt of territorial waters must follow the general direction of the coast makes it possible to fix certain criteria valid for any delimitation of the territorial sea; these criteria will be elucidated later. The Court will confine itself at this stage to noting that, in order to apply this principle, several States have deemed it necessary to follow the straight baselines method and that they have not encountered objections of principle by other States. This method consists of selecting appropriate points on the low-water mark and drawing straight lines between them. This has been done, not only in the case of well-defined bays, but also in cases of minor curvatures of the coast line where it was solely a question of giving a simpler form to the belt of territorial waters.

. . . .

The Court now comes to the question of the length of the baselines drawn across the waters lying between the various formations of the "skjaergaard." Basing itself on the analogy with the alleged general rule of ten miles relating to bays, the United Kingdom Government still maintains on this point that the length of straight lines must not exceed ten miles.

In this connection, the practice of States does not justify the formulation of any general rule of law. The attempts that have been made to subject groups of islands or coastal archipelagoes to conditions analogous to the limitations concerning bays (distance between the islands not exceeding twice the breadth of the territorial waters, or ten or twelve sea miles), have not got beyond the stage of proposals.

Furthermore, apart from any question of limiting the lines to ten miles, it may be that several lines can be envisaged. In such cases the coastal State would seem to be in the best position to appraise the local conditions dictating the selection.

Consequently, the Court is unable to share the view of the United Kingdom Government, that "Norway, in the matter of baselines, now claims recognition of an exceptional system." As will be shown later, all that the Court can see therein is the application of general international law to a specific case.

The Conclusions of the United Kingdom, points 5 and 9 to 11, refer to waters situated between the baselines and the Norwegian mainland. The Court is asked to hold that on historic grounds these waters belong to Norway, but that they are divided into two categories: territorial and internal waters, in accordance with two criteria which the Conclusions regard as well founded in international law, the waters falling within the conception of a bay being deemed to be internal waters, and those having the character of legal straits being deemed to be territorial waters.

As has been conceded by the United Kingdom, the "skjaergaard" constitutes a whole with the Norwegian mainland; the waters between the baselines of the belt of territorial waters and the mainland are internal water. However, according to the argument of the United Kingdom a portion of these waters constitutes territorial waters. These are *inter alia* the waters followed by the navigational route known as the Indreleia. It is contended that since these waters have this character, certain consequences arise with regard to the determination of the territorial waters at the end of this waterway considered as a maritime strait.

The Court is bound to observe that the Indreleia is not a strait at all, but rather a navigational route prepared as such by means of artificial aids to navigation provided by Norway. In these circumstances the Court is unable to accept the view that the Indreleia, for the purposes of the present case, has a status different from that of the other waters included in the "skjaergaard."

Thus the Court, confining itself for the moment to the Conclusions of the United Kingdom, finds that the Norwegian Government in fixing the baselines for the delimitation of the Norwegian fisheries zone by the 1935 Decree has not violated international law.

It does not at all follow that, in absence of rules having the technically precise character alleged by the United Kingdom Government, the delimitation undertaken by the Norwegian Government in 1935 is not subject to certain principles which make it possible to judge as to its validity under international law. The delimitation of sea areas has always an international aspect; it cannot be dependent merely upon the will of the coastal State as expressed in its municipal law. Although it is true that the act of delimitation is necessarily a unilateral act, because only the coastal State is competent to undertake it, the validity of the delimitation with regard to other States depends upon international law.

In this connection, certain basic considerations inherent in the nature of the territorial sea, bring to light certain criteria which, though not entirely precise, can provide courts with an adequate basis for their decisions, which can be adapted to the diverse facts in question.

Among these considerations, some reference must be made to the close dependence on the territorial sea upon the land domain. It is the land which confers upon the coastal State a right to the waters off its coast. It follows that while such a State must be allowed the latitude necessary in order to be able to adapt its delimitation to practical needs and local requirements, the drawing of baselines must not depart to any appreciable extent from the general direction of the coast.

Another fundamental consideration, of particular importance in this case, is the more or less close relationship existing between certain sea areas and the land formations which divide or surround them. The real question raised in the choice of baselines is in effect whether certain sea areas lying within these lines are sufficiently closely linked to the land domain to be subject to the regime of internal waters. This idea, which is at the basis of the determination of the rules relating to bays, should be liberally applied in the case of a coast, the geographical configuration of which is as unusual as that of Norway.

Finally, there is one consideration not to be overlooked, the scope of which extends beyond purely geographical factors: that of certain economic interests peculiar to a region, the reality and importance of which are clearly evidenced by a long usage.

. . . .

The Court, having . . . established the existence and the constituent elements of the Norwegian system of delimitation, further finds that this system was consistently applied by Norwegian authorities and that it encountered no opposition on the part of other States.

. . . .

In the light of these considerations, and in the absence of convincing evidence to the contrary, the Court is bound to hold that the Norwegian authorities applied their system of delimitation consistently and uninterruptedly from 1869 until the time when the dispute arose.

From the standpoint of international law, it is now necessary to consider whether the application of the Norwegian system encountered any opposition from foreign States.

. . . .

The general toleration of foreign States with regard to the Norwegian practice is an unchallenged fact. For a period of more than sixty years the United Kingdom Government itself in no way contested it. . . .

The United Kingdom Government has argued that the Norwegian system of delimitation was not known to it and that the system therefore lacked the notoriety essential to provide the basis of an historic title enforceable against it. The Court is unable to accept this view. As a coastal State on the North Sea, greatly interested in the fisheries in this areas, as a maritime Power traditionally concerned with the law of the sea and concerned particularly to defend the freedom of the seas, the United Kingdom could not have been ignorant of the Decree of 1869 which had at once provoked a request for explanations by the French Government. Nor, knowing of it, could it have been under any misapprehension as to the significance of its terms, which clearly described it as constituting the application of a system. . . .

. . . .

The Court is thus led to conclude that the method of straight lines, established in the Norwegian system, was imposed by the peculiar geography of the Norwegian coast; that even before the dispute arose, this method had been consolidated by a constant and sufficiently long practice, in the face of which the attitude of governments bears witness to the fact that they did not consider it to be contrary to international law.

. . . .

For these reasons, the Court, rejecting all submissions to the contrary, finds by ten votes to two, that the method employed for the delimitation of the fisheries zone by the Royal Norwegian Decree of July 12th, 1935, is not contrary to international law; and by eight votes to four, that the baselines fixed by the said Decree in application of this method are not contrary to international law.

. . . .

Judge Hackworth declares that he concurs in the operative part of the Judgment but desires to emphasize that he does so for the reasons that he considers that the Norwegian Government has proved the existence of a historic title to the disputed areas of water.

Judge Alvarez and Hsu Mo, availing themselves of the right conferred on them by Article 57 of the Statute, append to the Judgment of the Court statements of their separate opinions.

Judges Sir Arnold MacNair and Read, availing themselves of the right conferred on them by Article 57 of the Statute, append to the Judgment statements of their dissenting opinions.

REFERENCES

C. H. M. Waldock," The Anglo-Norwegian Fisheries Case," *British Yearbook of International Law*, Vol. 28 (1951), pp. 114-171; J. Evensen, "The Anglo-Norwegian Fisheries Case and its Legal Consequences," *American Journal of International Law*, Vol. 46 (1952), pp. 609-630; D. H. N. Johnson, "The Anglo-Norwegian Fisheries Case," *International and Comparative Law Quarterly*, Vol. 1 (1952), pp. 145-180; R. Young, "The Anglo-Norwegian Fisheries Case," *American Bar Association Journal*, Vol. 38 (1952), pp. 145-180; L. G. Green, "The Anglo-Norwegian Fisheries Case," *Modern Law Review*, Vol. 15 (1952), pp. 373-377; H. A. Smith, "The Anglo-Norwegian Fisheries Case," *Yearbook of World Affairs*, Vol. 7 (1953), pp 283-308; R.O. Wilberforce, "Some Aspects of the Anglo-Norwegian Fisheries Case," *Transactions of the Grotian Society*, Vol. 38 (1953), pp. 151-168; Sir Gerald Fitzmaurice, "The Law and Procedure of the International Court of Justice, 1951-54: Substantive Law, Part I," *British Yearbook of International Law*, Vol. 31 (1954), pp. 371-429; L.F.E. Goldie, "Legal Pluralism and 'No-Law' Sectors," *Australian Law Journal*, Vol. 32 (1958), pp. 220-227; T. Kobayaski, *The Anglo-Norwegian Fisheries Case of 1951 and the Changing Law of Territorial Sea*, University of Florida Monographs, Social Sciences, No. 26, 1965.

1958 CONVENTION ON THE TERRITORIAL SEA
AND THE CONTIGUOUS ZONE
Article 4

1. In localities where the coastline is deeply indented and cut into, or if there is a fringe of islands along the coast in its immediate vicinity, the method of straight baselines joining appropriate points may be employed in drawing the baseline from which the breadth of the territorial sea is measured.

2. The drawing of such baselines must not depart to any appreciable extent from the general direction of the coast, and the sea areas lying within the lines must be sufficiently closely linked to the land domain to be subject to the regime of internal waters.

3. Baselines shall not be drawn to and from low-tide elevations, unless lighthouses or similar installations which are permanently above sea level have been built on them.

4. Where the method of straight baselines is applicable under the provisions of paragraph 1, account may be taken, in determining particular baselines, of economic interests peculiar to the region concerned, the reality and the importance of which are clearly evidenced by a long usage.

5. The system of straight baselines may not be applied by a State in such a manner as to cut off from the high seas the territorial sea of another State.

6. The coastal State must clearly indicate straight baselines on charts, to which due publicity must be given.

Article 5

1. Waters on the landward side of the baseline of the territorial sea form part of the internal waters of the State.

2. Where the establishment of a straight baseline in accordance with article 4 has the effect of enclosing as internal waters areas which previously had been considered as part of the territorial sea or of the high seas, a right of innocent passage, as provided in articles 14 to 23, shall exist in those waters.

INTERNATIONAL LAW COMMISSION
1956 Commentary, Draft Article 5
Yearbook of the International Law Commission 1956,
Vol. II, pp. 267-268.

(1) The International Court of Justice, in its decision regarding the Fisheries Case between the United Kingdom and Norway, considered that where the coast is deeply indented or cut into, or where it is bordered by an insular formation such as the Skjaergaard in Norway, the baseline becomes independent of the low-water mark and can only be determined by means of a geometric construction. The Court said:

> "[In such circumstances the line of the low-water mark can no longer be put forward as a rule requiring the coastline to be followed in all its sinuosities. Nor can one characterize as exceptions to the rule the very many derogations which would be necessitated by such a rugged coast; the rule would disappear under the exceptions. Such a coast, viewed as a whole, calls for the application of a different method; that is, the method of the base-lines which, within reasonable limits, may depart from the physical line of the coast]. . . .
>
> "The principle that the belt of territorial waters must follow the general direction of the coast makes it possible to fix certain criteria valid for any delimitation of the territorial sea; these criteria will be elucidated later. The Court will confine itself at this stage to noting that, in order to apply this principle, several States have deemed it necessary to follow the straight baselines method and that they have not encountered objections of principle by other States. This method consists of selecting appropriate points on the low-water mark and drawing straight lines between them. This has been done, not only in the case of well-defined bays, but also in cases of minor curvatures of the coast line where it was solely a question of giving a simpler form to the belt of territorial waters."

(2) The Commission interpreted the Court's judgment, which was delivered on the point in question by a majority of 10 votes to 2, as expressing the law in force; it accordingly drafted the article on the basis of this judgment. It felt, however, that certain rules advocated by the group of experts who met at The Hague in 1953 (see introduction to chapter II, paragraph 17 above) might serve to round off the criteria adopted by the Court. Consequently, at its sixth session, it inserted the following supplementary rules in paragraph 2 of the article:

> "As a general rule, the maximum permissible length for a straight baseline shall be ten miles. Such baselines may be drawn, when justified according to paragraph 1, between headlands of the coastline or between any such headland and an island less than five miles from the

coast, or between such islands. Longer straight baselines may, however, be drawn provided that no point on such lines is more than five miles from the coast. Baselines shall not be drawn to and from drying rocks and shoals."

(3) Some Governments raised objections to this paragraph 2, arguing that the maximum length of ten miles for baselines and the maximum distance from the coast of five miles seemed arbitrary and, moreover, not in conformity with the Court's decision. Against this certain members of the Commission pointed out that the Commission had drafted these provisions for application "as a general rule" and that it would always be possible to depart from them if special circumstances justified doing so. In the opinion of those members, the criteria laid down by the Court was not sufficiently precise for general application. However, at its seventh session in 1955, after further study of the question the Commission decided, by a majority, that paragraph 2 should be deleted so as not to make the provisions of paragraph 1 too mechanical. Only the final sentence was kept and added to paragraph 1.

(4) At this same session, the Commission made a number of changes designed to bring the text even more closely into line with the Court's judgment in the above-mentioned Fisheries Case. In particular it inserted in the first sentence the words: "or where this is justified by economic interests peculiar to a region, the reality and importance of which are clearly evidenced by a long usage." Some Governments stated in their comments on the 1955 text that they could not support the insertion of "economic interests" in the first sentence of the article. In their opinion, this reference to economic interests was based on a misinterpretation of the Court's judgment. The interests taken into account in the judgment were considered solely in the light of the historical and geographical factors involved and should not constitute a justification in themselves. The application of the straight baseline system should be justified in principle on other grounds before purely local economic considerations could justify a particular way of drawing the lines.

(5) Although this interpretation of the judgment was not supported by all the members, the great majority of the Commission endorsed this view at the eighth session, and the article was recast in that sense.

(6) The question arose whether in waters which become internal waters when the straight baseline system is applied the right of passage should not be granted in the same way as in the territorial sea. Stated in such general terms, this argument was not approved by the majority of the Commission. The Commission was, however, prepared to recognize that if a State wished to make a fresh delimitation of its territorial sea according to the straight baseline principle, thus including in its internal waters parts of the high seas or of the territorial sea that had previously been waters through which international traffic passed, other nations could not be deprived of the right of passage in those waters. Paragraph 3 of the article is designed to safeguard that right.

(7) Straight baselines may be drawn only between points situated on the territory of a single State. An agreement between two States under which such baselines were drawn along the coast and connecting points situated on the territories of different States, would not be enforceable against other States.

(8) Straight baselines may be drawn to islands situated in the immediate vicinity of the coast, but not to drying rocks and drying shoals. Only rocks or shoals permanently above sea level may be used for this purpose. Otherwise the distance between the baselines and the coast might be extended more than [is] required to fulfill the purpose for which the straight baseline method is applied, and, in addition, it would not be possible at high tide to sight the points of departure of

applied, and, in addition, it would not be possible at high tide to sight the points of departure of the baselines.

R.D. Hodgson, *Islands: Normal and Special Circumstances*, Washington, D.C.: Bureau of Intelligence and Research, U.S. Department of State, Dec. 10, 1973, pp. 21-23.

Probably no other article of the Convention, based on islands, has been so used and perhaps misused by the states of the world. More than 60 coastal nations have employed straight baselines or have enabling legislation which permits their use. National practice varies from the very conservative Finnish model, in which no baseline segment exceeds twice the breadth of the territorial sea claim of 4 miles, to extreme and indefensible violations of the intent of the Convention. Many states have segments which measure more than 100 nautical miles in length. The Burmese example contains a line segment measuring over 222 miles in length. While a restriction of segment length, in general, could be the most important factor to prevent abuses of the system inherent to the article's vague language, length alone is insufficient.

[T]he salient factors, which have been demonstrated to determine the applicability of a system, are as follows:

1. General Direction of the Coast

Single segments of a straight baseline system should not depart more than 15° from the general direction of the coastline. The latter should be determined, for a reasonably extensive coastal length, by an analysis of small-scale charts, i.e., c. 1:1,000,000. Should local departure from the norm be dictated by special conditions, large-scale charts of the locality should be consulted. However, the concept of the "outermost points of the outermost island," as a determinant of the general direction of the coast, is patently ridiculous. By this criterion, any line connecting any two islands would follow the general direction of the coast. One need only examine certain national systems to see the abuses to which such a criterion may lead.

2. Length of Line

While not specified in the Convention, the maximum length-of-line concept becomes essential. Generally speaking, the longer the length, the greater the chance for manifest abuse. In the *Anglo-Norwegian Fisheries Case*, the longest geographical line measured slightly more than 40 nautical miles. In the Lopphavet sector, where historic-economic factors were determinants, the length of line was greater--45 miles. Except for these isolated instances, provisions should be made to limit the length in relation to its distance from enclosed islands on the mainland. For example, a 100-mile-long line segment which "skims" a fringe of islands at distances of a few miles would be far more acceptable, within the provisions of the Fisheries Case, than a line of 60 miles in length which, in certain areas, is tens of miles from the nearest, intervening basepoint.

3. Fringing Islands

Next to length of line, the concept of "fringing islands" has been the factor most subject to abuse. In certain national systems a small island every 20 or 30 miles has been deemed "fringing." In others, reefs and shoals, both submerged or drying features, have been utilized in national law as parts of the system. In contrast, in the Norwegian example, islands masked, on the average, nearly two-thirds of the length of the coastline. In many areas, the mainland was totally obscured from the sea by continuous and overlapping lines of islands. The Norwegian guide should be paramount. Furthermore, where fringing islands cease to exist, the system of straight baselines, in the absence of a deeply indented coastline, should return to the mainland and terminate. A second system obviously may be established when proper conditions again dominate.

4. Subject to the Regime of Internal Waters.

Because of the complexity of potential land/water relationships (i.e., islands may be situated in numberless arrangements), an ideal measurement relates to the land/water ratio contained within the straight baseline system and the normal baseline of the coastline. The Norwegian ratio was determined to be 1/3.5. In combination with length of line, the ratio forms the best basis for evaluating a system of straight baselines to determine its conformity with the spirit of the Convention's Article 4 and the Norwegian example.

These determinants, of course, mark norms. States may establish more restricted systems which meet their national demands for security and for the protection of economic, historic, environmental, and social interests. The entire Article, in fact, is not self-executing; the coastal State need not employ straight baselines even where favorable geographic conditions occur.

1982 UNITED NATIONS CONVENTION ON THE LAW OF THE SEA

Article 7
Straight baselines

1. In localities where the coastline is deeply indented and cut into, or if there is a fringe of islands along the coast in its immediate vicinity, the method of straight baselines joining appropriate points may be employed in drawing the baseline from which the breadth of the territorial sea is measured.

2. Where because of the presence of a delta and other natural conditions the coastline is highly unstable, the appropriate points may be selected along the furthest seaward extent of the low-water line, and, notwithstanding subsequent regression of the low-water line, the straight baselines shall remain effective until changed by the coastal State in accordance with this Convention.

3. The drawing of straight baselines must not depart to any appreciable extent from the general direction of the coast, and the sea areas lying within the lines must be sufficiently closely linked to the land domain to be subject to the regime of internal waters.

4. Straight baselines shall not be drawn to and from low-tide elevations, unless lighthouses or similar installations which are permanently above sea level have been built on them or except in instances where the drawing of baselines to and from such elevations has received general international recognition.

5. Where the method of straight baselines is applicable under paragraph 1, account may be taken, in determining particular baselines, of economic interests peculiar to the region concerned, the reality and the importance of which are clearly evidenced by long usage.

6. The system of straight baselines may not be applied by a State in such a manner as to cut off the territorial sea of another State from the high seas or an exclusive economic zone.

[Article 7 is identical with Article 4 of the 1958 Convention on the Territorial Sea and the Contiguous Zone with two exceptions. First, Article 4(3) has been modified by adding "or except in instances where the drawing of baseline to and from such elevations has received general international recognition. Second, Article 7(2) of the 1982 Convention is a new paragraph.]

Article 8
Internal Waters

1. Except as provided in Part IV, waters on the landward side of the baseline of the territorial sea form part of the internal waters of the State.

2. Where the establishment of a straight baseline in accordance with the method set forth in article 7 has the effect of enclosing as internal waters areas which had not previously been considered as such, a right of innocent passage as provided in the Convention shall exist in those waters.

NOTE

In the United States, litigation between the Federal Government and the coastal states of the Nation concerning jurisdiction over offshore resources led to a consideration of the rules governing the line from which the Federal-state offshore boundary line would be measured. The United States Supreme Court held that the rules concerning the location of the baseline set forth in the Convention on the Territorial Sea and the Contiguous Zone, to which the United States was a party, would be applicable to the dispute. The following excerpts from two of the submerged lands cases indicate the court's viewpoint on the question of straight baselines.

Normal Baseline

The Role of Straight Baselines in
Simplifying Territorial Sea Boundaries

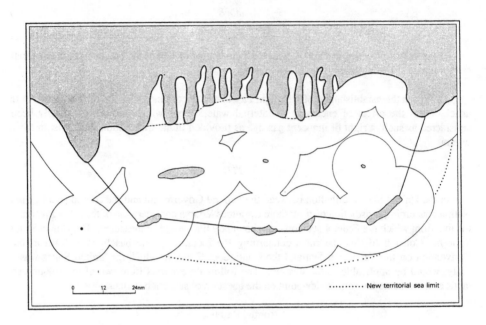

Deeply Indented/Complex Coasts and Straight Baseline
Figure 4-5

Source: Office for Ocean Affairs and the Law of the Sea, United Nations, *The Law of the
Sea, Baselines: An Examination of the Relevant Provisions of the United
Nations Convention on the Law of the Sea*, New York: The United Nations,
1989, pp. 18-19.

UNITED STATES v. CALIFORNIA
381 U.S. 139, 167-169 (1964)

California argues that because the Convention permits a nation to use the straight baseline
method for determining its seaward boundaries if its "coastline is deeply indented and cut into, or if
there is a fringe of islands along the coast in its immediate vicinity," California is therefore free to
use such boundary lines across the openings of its bays and around its islands. We agree with the
United States that the Convention recognizes the validity of straight-baselines used by other
countries, Norway for instance, and would *permit* the United States to use such base lines if it
chose, but that California may not use such base lines to extend our international boundaries

beyond their traditional international limits against the expressed opposition of the United States. The national responsibility for conducting our international regulations obviously must be accommodated with the legitimate interest of the States in the territory over which they are sovereign. Thus a contraction of a State's recognized territory imposed by the Federal Government in the name of foreign policy would be highly questionable. But an extension of states sovereignty to an international area by claiming it as inland water would necessarily also extend national sovereignty, and unless the Federal Government's responsibility for questions of external sovereignty is hollow, it must have the power to prevent States from so enlarging themselves. We conclude that the choice under the Convention to use the straight-baseline method for determining inland waters claimed against other nations is one that rests with the Federal Government, and not with the individual States.

California relies upon *Manchester v. Massachusetts*, 139 U.S. 240, for the proposition that a State may draw its boundaries as it pleases within limits recognized by the law of nations regardless of the position taken by the United States. Although some dicta in the case may be read to support that view, we do not so interpret the opinion. The case involved neither an expansion of our traditional international boundary nor opposition by the United States to the position taken by the State.

UNITED STATES v. LOUISIANA
394 U.S. 11, 72-73 (1969)

In United States v. California . . . we held that "the choice under the Convention to use the straight-baseline method for determining inland waters claimed against other nations is one that rests with the Federal Government, and not with the individual States." Since the United States asserts that it has not drawn and does not want to draw straight baselines along the Louisiana coast, that disclaimer would, under the *California* decision, be conclusive of the matter. Louisiana argues, however, that because the Louisiana coast is so perfectly suited to the straight baseline method, and because it is clear that the United States would employ it in the conduct of its international affairs were it not for this lawsuit, the Court should reconsider its holding in *California* and itself draw appropriate baselines. While we agree that the straight base line method was designed for precisely such coasts as the Mississippi River Delta area, we adhere to the position that the selection of this optional method of establishing boundaries should be left to the branches of Government responsible for the formulation and implementation of foreign policy. It would be inappropriate for this Court to review or overturn the considered decision of the United States, albeit partially motivated by a domestic concern, not to extend its borders to the furthest extent consonant with international law.

QUESTION

Why would the United States Government not wish to promulgate straight baselines in areas along the coast of the United States which would obviously meet the criteria of Article 4 of the Convention on the Territorial Sea and the Contiguous Zone (e.g., the Aleutian Islands, the Mississippi River Delta, the New England coast)?

REFERENCES

Mark B. Feldman and David Colson, "The Maritime Boundaries of the United States," *American Journal of International Law*, Vol. 75 (1981), pp. 729-763; Edward Collins, Jr. and Martin A. Rogoff, "The International Law of Maritime Boundary Delimitation," *Maine Law*

Review, Vol. 34 (1982), pp. 1-62; R. R. Churchill, "Maritime Delimitation in the Jan Mayen Area," *Marine Policy*, Vol. 9 (1985), pp. 16-38; Stephen W. Aronson, "Baselines Configure the Atlantic Coastline of the United States: United States v. Seward," *Connecticut Journal of International Law*, Vol. 1 (1985-86), pp. 185-216; D. J. Devine," Bays, Baselines, Passage and Pollution in the South African Waters," *The Comparative and International Law Journal of Southern Africa*, Vol. 19 (1986), pp. 85-98; Jonathan I. Charney, "The Delimitation of Ocean Boundaries," *Ocean Development and International Law*, Vol. 18 (1987), pp. 497-531.

REPUBLIC OF ECUADOR, SUPREME DECREE NO. 959-A
JOSE MARIA VELASCO IBARRA, PRESIDENT OF THE REPUBLIC
June 28, 1971, *Official Register* No. 265; July 13, 1971

WHEREAS, Article 628 of the Civil Code establishes that the Ecuadorean territorial sea shall be measured, in both the continental territory of the Republic and the Galapagos Islands, from the straight baselines which will be determined for this purpose under an Executive Decree; and

WHEREAS, a Commission composed of representatives of the Ministry of Foreign Relations, the Navy and the Military Geographic Institute has studied the plotting of such lines and determined their trajectory; and

Whereas, such study has been approved by the Ministry of Foreign Relations and the Ministry of National Defense on the grounds that it is in the national interest and fully conforms to the rules of international law which are in force on the matter,

It is Decreed:

Article 1. The straight baselines from which the width of the territorial sea of the Republic shall be measured will be constituted by the following-described traverses:

I. ON THE CONTINENT

(a) The line will start from the point of intersection of the maritime border with Columbia with the straight line Punta Manglares (Colombia)--Punta Galea (Ecuador);

(b) From this point a straight line passing through Punta Galea and meeting the northernmost point of Isla de la Plata;

(c) From this point a straight line to Puntilla de Santa Elena;

(d) A straight line from Puntilla de Santa Elena in the direction of Cabo Blanco (Peru) to the intersection with the geographic parallel constituting the maritime border with Peru.

. . . .

Article 2. The sea areas lying between the lines described in Article 1 (I) and the coast line on the Continent . . . constitute interior waters.

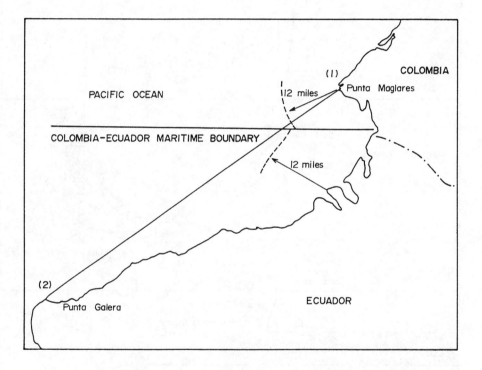

Ecuadorean Baseline (1)
Figure 4-6

Source: U.S. Department of State, The Georgrapher, Limits in the Seas, No. 88, Maritime Boundary: Ecuador-Peru, October 2, 1979.

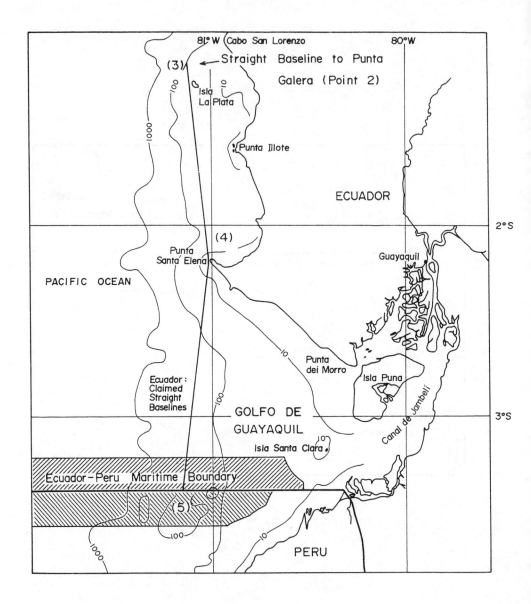

Ecuadorean Baseline (2)
Figure 4-7

Source: U.S. Department of State, The Geographer, *Limits in the Seas*, No. 88,
Maritime Boundary: Ecuador-Peru, October 2, 1979.

International Boundary Study, No. 42, *Straight Baselines, Ecuador*, Washington, D.C.:   Bureau of Intelligence and Research, U.S. Department of State, May 23, 1972.

Straight Baselines, 1971

The straight baseline system consists of 13 points: 5 on or near the mainland, and 8 around the Galapagos Islands. The total length of all the straight baselines is 897 nautical miles. The longest segment, 136 nautical miles, connects Punta Galera (Point 2) and Isla de la Plata (Point 3). The shortest baseline, 37 nautical miles, connects Isla Isabela (Point 12) and Isla Fernandina (Point 13). The average length of the straight baseline segments is 74.8 nautical miles.

The following point-by-point analysis of the straight baselines utilizes Chart N.O. 21036 (H.O. 5743), 2nd Edition, Feb. 1952; revised 1/12/70, published by the U.S. Navy Oceanographic Office.

Segment	Distance (n.m.)	Comments
1-2	81	Closes Bahia Ancon de Sardinas, which is neither a historical nor juridical bay, by connecting Cabo Manglares, Colombia (1) and Punta Galera, Ecuador (2). Bay closing lines are applicable only to bays which are in a single State; therefore the selection of Point 1 and the resulting baseline would not be acceptable under customary international law.
2-3	136	Connects Punta Galera (2), on the mainland, with Isla de la Plata (3). This is the longest segment of the baseline system. The extent of this section is questionable as more relevant coastal basepoints were ignored in favor of an offshore island in the construction of the baseline. Further, Isla de la Plata would be ruled out as a basepoint as it is not one of "a fringe of islands along the coast in its vicinity. . . ."
3-4	56	Connects Isla de la Plata (3) with Puntilla de Santa Elena (4). The use of the island basepoint is unacceptable as the island is not one of "a fringe of islands along the coast in its immediate vicinity. . . ."
4-5	72	Connects Puntilla de Santa Elena (4) with a point on the Ecuador-Peru Maritime Boundary (5). Point 5 marks the site where the line connecting Puntilla de Santa Elena, Ecuador and Cabo Blanco, Peru intersects the maritime boundary. Point 5 is 46 n.m. from the nearest Ecuadorean territory, Islan de Santa Clara. Point 5 is not an acceptable basepoint because it is not a high-tide elevation or a low-tide elevation with a permanent facility which is above high tide.

. . . .

Baselines-Mainland

The mainland portion of the Ecuadorean baseline system brings for issues of the acceptability of the system. Article 4 (1) of the 1958 Geneva Convention on the Territorial Sea and Contiguous Zone states that:

> 1. In localities where the coastline is deeply indented and cut into, or if there is a fringe of islands along the coast in its immediate vicinity, the method of straight baselines joining appropriate points may be employed in drawing the baseline from which the breadth of the territorial sea is measured.

The Ecuadorean coastline can hardly be construed to be representative of a coastline which is "deeply indented and cut into." Therefore, the question arises as to Ecuador's right, under customary international law, to construct baselines along its rather regular coastline.

Even if it is agreed that Ecuador has the right to construct straight baselines along its regular coastline, the basepoints that have been used along the mainland are not reasonable given the configuration of the coast.

If the mainland baselines are to conform to the 1958 Geneva Convention of the Territorial Sea and Contiguous Zone, then, Article 4 (2) requires that:

> 2. The drawing of such baselines must not depart to any appreciable extent from the general direction of the coast. . . .

All segments of the mainland portion of the baseline system deviate, to some degree, from the general direction of the coast because basepoints that relate more to the general configuration of the coastline have not been used to delimit the baselines. Therefore, the result is inordinately long baselines in areas where shorter segments would be much more reasonable. . . .

Summary

. . . .

Of the 12 segments of the Ecuadorean straight baselines, all but one exceed the length of the longest baseline approved by the International Court of Justice (ICJ) in the *Anglo-Norwegian Fisheries Case*. The ICJ, on December 18, 1951, approved a Norwegian straight baseline 44 nautical miles in length. However, the length of the Norwegian baselines was directly related to the decision that much of the water enclosed by the baselines was indeed Norwegian historic waters. The issue of historic waters is irrelevant when considering the Ecuadorean straight baselines, as the coastal waters are not viewed to be historically within the domain of Ecuador because of long usage of the coastal regime.

QUESTIONS

As Ecuador is not a party to the Convention on the Territorial Sea and the Contiguous Zone, how can the United States Government criticize the Ecuadorean straight baseline system on the basis of that convention? What are the "accepted international legal practices" to which the United States Government refers in the summary?

BANGLADESH MINISTRY OF FOREIGN AFFAIRS ORDER
April 13, 1974

No. LT-I/3/74 -- 3. The baselines from which territorial waters shall be measured seaward are the straight lines linking successively the baseline points set out below:

Baseline Point	Geographical Co-ordinates baseline point	
	Latitude	Longitude
No. 1	21°12'00" N.	89°06'45" E.
No. 2	21°15'00" N.	89°16'00" E.
No. 3	21°29'00" N.	89°36'00" E.
No. 4	21°21'00" N.	89°55'00" E.
No. 5	21°11'00" N.	90°33'00" E.
No. 6	21°07'30" N.	91°06'00" E.
No. 7	21°10'00" N.	91°56'00" E.
No. 8	20°21'45" N.	92°17'30" E.

NOTE

All of the points on the Bangladesh baseline are located at substantial distances from the coast and appear in fact to be based on an isobath line [See Figure 4-8] rather than the coastline as required by Article 4 of the 1958 Convention on the Territorial Sea and Contiguous Zone and Article 7 of the 1982 United Nations Convention of the Law of the Sea. Bangladesh is, however, not a party to the 1958 Convention.

REFERENCES

(1) One of the best collections of national laws concerning delimitation of straight baselines is the *Limits in the Seas* series published by the U.S. Department of State (Bureau of Intelligence and Research). The excerpt from pamphlet No. 42 (Ecuador) in the series is typical of the work product.

(2) M. S. McDougal and W. T. Burke, *The Public Order of the Oceans: A Contemporary International Law of the Sea*. New Haven and London: Yale University Press, 1962, pp. 398-411; T. Gihl, "The Baseline of the Territorial Sea," *Scandinavian Studies in Law*, Vol. 11, (1967), pp. 119-174; W. E. Butler, "New Soviet Legislation On Straight Baselines," *International and Comparative Law Quarterly*, Vol. 29 (1971), pp. 750-752; R. D. Hodgson and Lewis Alexander, "Toward an Objective Analysis of Special Circumstances: Bays, Rivers, Coastal and Oceanic Archipelagos and Atolls," Law of the Sea Institute, Kingston: University of Rhode Island Occasional Paper No. 13 (1972), pp. 23-44; G. Marston, "Low-Tide Elevations and Straight Baselines," *British Yearbook of International Law*, Vol. 46 (1972-73), pp. 405-423.

NOTE

In 1988, about 82 countries claimed straight baselines with about 70 straight baseline systems being implemented with the publication of geographical coordinates for the baseline turning points. Robert W. Smith, "Global Maritime Claims," *Ocean Development and International Law*, Vol. 20 (1989), p. 87. See also *Law of the Sea: Baselines-National Legislation with Illustrative Maps*, New York: The United Nations, 1989.

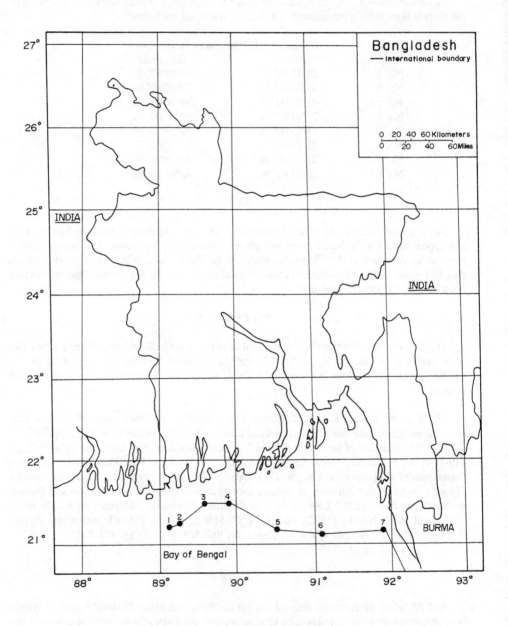

Baseline of Bangladesh
Figure 4-8

b.   Outlying Archipelagos

> Jen Evensen, "Certain Legal Aspects Concerning the Delimitation of
> the Territorial Waters of Archipelagoes," [First] United Nations
> Conference on the Law of the Sea, *Official Records*, Vol. I, *Preparatory
> Documents*, p. 290.

C. As a starting point the following definition of the term archipelago may be laid down; an archipelago is a formation of two or more islands (islets or rocks) which geographically may be considered as a whole.

One glance at the map is sufficient to show that the geographical characteristics of archipelagos vary widely. They very as to the number and size of the islands and islets as well as with regard to the size, shape and position of the archipelagoes. In some archipelagos the islands and islets are clustered together in a compact group while others are spread out over great areas of water. Sometimes they consist of a string of islands, islets and rocks forming a fence or rampart for the mainland against the ocean. In other cases they protrude from the mainland out into the sea like a peninsula or a cape, like the Cuban Cays or the Keys of Florida.

Geographically these many variations may be termed archipelagos. Quite another question is whether the same rules of international law will apply to these highly different geographical formations where the question of the delimitations of their territorial waters is concerned. For the problems here involved it may prove helpful to distinguish between two basic types of archipelagos, namely:

1. Coastal Archipelagos

2. Outlying (or mid-ocean) archipelagos.

Coastal Archipelagos are those situated so close to a mainland that they may reasonably be considered part and parcel thereof, forming more or less an outer coastline from which it is natural to measure the marginal seas. The most typical example of such coastal archipelagos is the Norwegian "Skjaergaard" stretching out almost all along the coast of Norway forming a fence-- marked outer coastline--toward the sea. Other typical examples of such coastline archipelagos are offered by the coasts of Finland, Greenland, Iceland, Sweden, Yugoslavia, and certain stretches on the coasts of Alaska and Canada, just to mention a few of many examples.

Outlying (mid-ocean) archipelagos are groups of islands situated out in the ocean at such a distance from the coasts of a firm land as to be considered as an independent whole rather than forming part of or outer coastline of the mainland. A few examples suffice in this connexion: The Faeroes, Fiji Islands, Galapagos, Hawaiian Islands, Indonesia, Japan, Philippines, Solomon Islands, the Svalbard Archipelago.

> Hungdah Chiu, "Some Problems Concerning the Delimitation of
> Maritime Boundary Between the Republic of China and the
> Philippines," *Chinese Yearbook of International Law and Affairs*, Vol.
> 3 (1983), pp. 10-12. Notes Omitted. Reprinted by permission of the
> Chinese Society of International Law.

Until recently few international law scholars and few countries have paid much attention to the special legal problems concerning mid-ocean archipelagos. The question of whether a group of islands can be considered as a unit in delimiting a territorial sea has, according to most authorities, been adequately solved by general rules concerning the delimitation of the territorial sea of the mainland or island. The 1929 Harvard Draft on the Law of the Territorial Sea contains no provision relating to groups of islands or archipelagos. Article 7 of the Draft provides that the territorial sea of islands should be measured in a similar way to that of the mainland. It is a contention of this article that no different rule should be established for groups of islands or archipelagos, except that, if the outer fringe of islands is sufficiently close to form one complete belt of marginal sea, then the waters within such belt should be considered as territorial waters.

At the Hague Codification Conference, convened by the League of Nations in 1930, the question of archipelagos was raised by Portugal, which submitted the following proposal as a basis of discussion:

> In the case of an archipelago, the islands forming the archipelago shall be deemed to be a unit and the breadth of the territorial sea shall be measured from the islands most distant from the centre of the archipelago.

The United States proposed the total deletion of the archipelago concept. After discussion, the Conference did not attempt to draft an article on this subject. Only a few writers discussed this problem after the Conference, and, with the exception of Munch, none of them made any concrete proposal.

When the United Nations International Law Commission (ILC) began to draft its text on the law of the sea, only cursory attention was paid to the question of archipelagos.

In J. P. A. Francois's Third Report on the Regime of the Territorial Sea to the United Nations International Law Commission he included a draft article on the "groups of islands" as follows:

> 1. The term "groups of islands" in the juridical sense, shall be determined to mean three or more islands enclosing a portion of the sea when joined by straight lines not exceeding five miles in length except that one such line may extend to a maximum of ten miles.

> 2. The straight lines specified in the preceding paragraph shall be the baseline for measuring the territorial sea. Waters lying within the area bounded by such lines and the islands themselves shall be considered as inland waters.

Because of the divergent views expressed by several members of the Commission and the press of time, in 1956 Francois suggested leaving the matter to the diplomatic conference to be convened. His suggestion was adopted by the Commission and the matter was shelved. The Draft Articles on the Law of the Sea submitted to the 1958 UNCLOS I at Geneva contain no provision on archipelagos at all. At the conference, only two countries--the Philippines and Yugoslavia--raised the question of archipelagos, and the Convention on the Territorial Sea and Contiguous Zone, which was adopted by the 1958 Conference, is silent on the problem.

At the UNCLOS II in 1960 the Philippines again raised the archipelago question, but the Conference did not take any action on it. It was not until the early 1960s that scholars of international law began to pay attention to the special problems of the archipelagos. In the meantime a number of former archipelago colonies had become independent. They are likely to make archipelago claims to protect or expand their maritime interests.

At UNCLOS III, Part VII of the Informal Single Negotiating Text, issued in 1975 and entitled "Archipelagos," contains two sections, the first of which relates to archipelagic states, i.e., states constituted wholly by one or more archipelagos which may include other islands, and the second to oceanic archipelagos belonging to continental states. Section one contains 14 articles (117-130), while section two contains only one article (131), which provides that "the provisions of section 1 are without prejudice to the status of oceanic archipelagos forming an integral part of the territory of a continental state." In other words, continental states' archipelagos can also apply the so-called archipelagic principle to their archipelagos in delimiting maritime boundaries. The benefit of this method of delimitation is obvious. A state can draw straight baselines joining the outermost points of the outermost islands and drying reefs of the archipelago. After discussion at the Fourth Session of the Conference, held between March 15 and May 7, 1976, the informal text was revised and distributed on May 6, 1976. In the revised text, Part VII became Chapter VII and was renamed "Archipelagic States." The revised text contains no article on oceanic archipelagos of a continental state. In other words, a continental state cannot apply the archipelagic principle in delimiting its oceanic archipelagos. This approach was later formally adopted in the 1982 Convention. The UNCLOS official records and press releases do not disclose why continental states with archipelagos agreed to such an arrangement.

c. Archipelagic States

1982 UNITED NATIONS CONVENTION ON THE LAW OF THE SEA
PART IV
ARCHIPELAGIC STATES

Article 46
Use of Terms

For the purposes of this Convention:

(a)   "archipelagic State" means a State constituted wholly by one or more archipelagos and may include other islands;

(b)   "archipelago" means a group of islands, including parts of islands, interconnected waters and other natural features which are so closely interrelated that such islands, waters and other natural features form an intrinsic geographical, economic and political entity, or which historically have been regarded as such.

Article 47
Archipelagic baselines

1. An archipelagic State may draw straight archipelagic baselines joining the outermost points of the outermost islands and drying reefs of the archipelago provided that within such baselines are included the main islands and an area in which the ratio of the area of the water to the area of the land, including atolls, is between 1 to 1 and 9 to 1

2. The length of such baselines shall not exceed 100 nautical miles, except that up to 3 per cent of the total number of baselines enclosing any archipelago may exceed that length, up to a maximum length of 125 nautical miles.

3. The drawing of such baselines shall not depart to any appreciable extent from the general configuration of the archipelago.

4. Such baselines shall not be drawn to and from low-tide elevations, unless lighthouses or similar installations which are permanently above sea level have been built on them or where a low-tide elevation is situated wholly or partly at a distance not exceeding the breadth of the territorial sea from the nearest island.

5. The system of such baselines shall not be applied by an archipelagic State in such a manner as to cut off from the high seas or the exclusive economic zone the territorial sea of another State.

6. If a part of the archipelagic waters of an archipelagic State lies between two parts of an immediately adjacent neighboring State, existing rights and all other legitimate interests which the latter State has traditionally exercised in such waters and all rights stipulated by agreement between those States shall continue and be respected.

7. For the purpose of computing the ratio of water to land under paragraph 1, land areas may include waters lying within the fringing reefs of islands and atolls, including that part of a steep-sided oceanic plateau which is enclosed or nearly enclosed by a chain of limestone islands and drying reefs lying on the perimeter of the plateau.

8. The baselines drawn in accordance with this article shall be shown on charts of a scale or scales adequate for ascertaining their position. Alternatively, lists of geographical co-ordinates of points, specifying the geodetic datum, may be substituted.

9. The archipelagic State shall give due publicity to such charts or lists of geographical co-ordinates and shall deposit a copy of each such chart or list with the Secretary-General of the United Nations.

Article 48
Measurement of the breadth of the territorial sea, the
contiguous zone, the exclusive economic zone
and the continental shelf

The breadth of the territorial sea, the contiguous zone, the exclusive economic zone and the continental shelf shall be measured from archipelagic baselines drawn in accordance with article 47.

Article 49
Legal status of archipelagic waters, of the air space
over archipelagic waters and of their bed and subsoil

1. The sovereignty of an archipelagic State extends to the waters enclosed by the archipelagic baselines drawn in accordance with article 47, described as archipelagic waters, regardless of their depth or distance from the coast.

2. This sovereignty extends to the air space over the archipelagic waters, as well as to their bed and subsoil, and the resources contained therein.

3. This sovereignty is exercised subject to this Part.

4. The regime of archipelagic sea lanes passage established in this Part shall not in other respects affect the status of the archipelagic waters, including the sea lanes, or the exercise by the archipelagic State of its sovereignty over such waters and their air space, bed and subsoil, and the resources contained therein.

Article 50
Delimitation of internal waters

Within its archipelagic waters, the archipelagic State may draw closing lines for the delimitation of internal waters, in accordance with articles 9, 10 and 11.

Article 51
Existing agreements, traditional fishing rights
and existing submarine cables.

1. Without prejudice to article 49, the archipelagic State shall respect existing agreements with other States and shall recognize traditional fishing rights and other legitimate activities of the immediate adjacent neighboring States in certain areas falling within archipelagic waters. The terms and conditions for the exercise of such rights and activities, including the nature, the extent and the areas to which they apply, shall, at the request of any of the States concerned, be regulated by bilateral agreements between them. Such rights shall not be transferred to or shared with third States or their nationals.

2. An archipelagic State shall respect existing submarine cables laid by other States and passing through its waters without making a landfall. An archipelagic State shall permit the maintenance and replacement of such cables upon receiving due notice of their location and the intention to repair or replace them.

Article 52
Right of innocent passage

1. Subject to article 53 and without prejudice to article 50, ships of all States enjoy the right of innocent passage through archipelagic waters, in accordance with Part II, section 3.

2. The archipelagic State may, without discrimination in form or in fact among foreign ships, suspend temporarily in specified areas of its archipelagic waters the innocent passage of foreign ships if such suspension is essential for the protection of its security. Such suspension shall take effect only after having been duly published.

Article 53
Right of archipelagic sea lanes passage

1. An archipelagic State may designate sea lanes and air routes thereabove, suitable for the continuous and expeditious passage of foreign ships and aircraft through or over its archipelagic waters and the adjacent territorial sea.

2. All ships and aircraft enjoy the right of archipelagic sea lanes passage in such sea lanes and air routes.

3. Archipelagic sea lanes passage means the exercise in accordance with this Convention of the rights of navigation and overflight in the normal mode solely for the purpose of continuous, expeditious and unobstructed transit between one part of the high seas or an exclusive economic zone and another part of the high seas or an exclusive economic zone.

4. Such sea lanes and air routes shall traverse the archipelagic waters and the adjacent territorial sea and shall include all normal passage routes used as routes for international navigation or overflight through or over archipelagic waters and, within such routes, so far as ships are concerned, all normal navigational channels, provided that duplication of routes of similar convenience between the same entry and exit points shall not be necessary.

5. Such sea lanes and air routes shall be defined by a series of continuous axis lines from the entry points of passage routes to the exit points. Ships and aircraft in archipelagic sea lanes passage shall not deviate more than 25 nautical miles to either side of such axis lines during passage, provided that such ships and aircraft shall not navigate closer to the coast than 10 per cent of the distance between the nearest points on islands bordering the sea lane.

6. An archipelagic State which designates sea lanes under this article may also prescribe traffic separation schemes for the safe passage of ships through narrow channels in such sea lanes.

7. An archipelagic State may, where circumstances require, after giving due publicity thereto, substitute other sea lanes or traffic separation schemes for any sea lanes or traffic separation schemes previously designated or prescribed by it.

8. Such sea lanes and traffic separation schemes shall conform to generally accepted international regulations.

9. In designating or substituting sea lanes or prescribing or substituting traffic separation schemes, an archipelagic State shall refer proposals to the competent international organization with a view to their adoption. The organization may adopt only such sea lanes and traffic separation schemes as may be agreed with the archipelagic State, after which the archipelagic State may designate, prescribe or substitute them.

10. The archipelagic State shall clearly indicate the axis of the sea lanes and the traffic separation schemes designated or prescribed by it on charts to which due publicity shall be given.

11. Ships in archipelagic sea lanes passage shall respect applicable sea lanes and traffic separation schemes established in accordance with this article.

12. If an archipelagic State does not designate sea lanes or air routes, the right of archipelagic sea lanes passage may be exercised through the routes normally used for international navigation.

Article 54
Duties of ships and aircraft during their passage, research and survey activities,
duties of the archipelagic State and laws and regulations of the archipelagic
State relating to archipelagic sea lanes passage

Articles 39, 40, 42 and 44 apply *mutatis mutandis* to archipelagic sea lanes passage. [These articles refer to duties of ships and aircraft during transit passage of strait, research and survey activities during strait passage, laws and regulations of States bordering straits relating to transit passage and duties of States bordering straits.]

REFERENCES

M. S. McDougal and W. T. Burke, *The Public Order of the Oceans: A Contemporary International Law of the Sea*, New Haven and London: Yale University Press, 1962, pp. 398-411; Brock, "Archipelago Concept of Limits of Territorial Seas," *Naval War College Review*, Vol. 19, No. 4 (1966), pp. 36-   ; C. B. Klein, "The Territorial Waters of Archipelagos," *Federal Bar Journal*, Vol. 26 (1966), pp. 317-323; J. W. Dellapenna, "The Philippines Territorial Water Claim in International Law," *Journal of Law and Economic Development*, Vol. 5 (1970), pp. 45-61; W. H. McConnell, "The Legal Regime of Archipelagos," *Saskatchewan Law Review*, Vol. 35(2) (1970), pp. 121-145; Estelito P. Mendoza, "The Baselines of the Philippine Archipelago," *Philippine Law Journal*, Vol. 46 (1971), pp. 628-638; D. P. O'Connell, "Mid-Ocean Archipelagos in International Law," *British Yearbook of International Law*, Vol. 45 (1971), pp. 1-77; Mochtar Kusamaatmadja, "The Legal Regime of Archipelagos; Problems and Issues," in Lewis M. Alexander, ed., *The Law of the Sea: Needs and Interests of Developing Countries*, Kingston, R. I.: University of Rhode Island, 1973, pp. 166-172; Michael A. Leverson," The Problems of Delimitations of Base Lines for Outlying Archipelagos," *San Diego Law Review*, Vol. 9 (1972), pp. 733-746; H. P. Rajan, "Towards Codification of Archipelagos in International Law," *Indian Journal of International Law*, Vol. 13 (1973), pp. 468-480; J. J. G. Syatauw, "Revisiting the Archipelago: An Old Concept Gains New Respectability," *Indian Quarterly*, Vol. 29 (1973), pp. 104-119; C. F. Amerasinghe, "The Problem of Archipelagoes in the International Law of the Sea," *International and Comparative Law Quarterly*, Vol. 23 (1974), pp. 539-575; L. F. Ballah, "Applicability of the Archipelagoes and Mare Clausum Concepts to the Caribbean Sea," in *Caribbean Study and Dialogue*, Malta: University Press, 1974, pp. 276-304; K. D. Hodgson, "Islands: Normal and Special Circumstances," in J. K. Gamble and G. Pontecorvo, *The Law of the Sea: The Emerging Regime of the Oceans*, Kingston, R.I.: The University of Rhode Island, 1974, pp. 137-199; H. C. Lee, "Archipelagic Claims for Papua New Guinea," *Melanesian Law Journal*, Vol. 2 (1974), pp. 91-107; H. P. Rajan, "The 1973 Articles on Archipelagoes by Fiji, Indonesia, Mauritius and the Philippines Analyzed," *Indian Journal of International Law*, Vol. 14 (1974), pp. 230-244; M. D. Sanitago, "The Archipelago Concept in the Law of the Sea: Problems and Perspectives," *Philippine Law Journal*, Vol. 49 (1974), pp. 315-386; B. H. Dubner, "A Proposal for Accommodating the Interests of Archipelagic and Maritime States," *New York University Journal of International Law and Politics*, Vol. 8 (1975), pp. 39-61; R.G. Schmitt, et. al., *The Hawaiian Archipelago: Defining the Boundaries of the State*, Honolulu: University of Hawaii Sea Grant Program, Working Paper No. 16 (1975); A. Demirali, "The Third United Nations Conference on the Law of the Sea and Archipelagic Regime," *San Diego Law Review*, Vol. 13 (1976), pp. 742-764; B. H. Dubner, *The Law of Territorial Waters of Mid-Ocean Archipelagos and Archipelagic States*, The Hague: Martinus Nijhoff, 1976; J. A. Draper, "The Indonesian Archipelagic State Doctrine and Law of the Sea: 'Territorial Grab' or Justifiable Necessity?," *The International Lawyer*, Vol. 11 (1977), pp. 143-162; A. D. Pharand, "International Straits," Thessaloniki: Thesaurus Acroasium: The Law of the Sea, Vol. VII (1977), pp. 59-100; D. Andrew, "Archipelagoes and the Law of the Sea; Islands Straits States or Islands--Studded Sea Space?," *Marine Policy*, Vol. 2 (1978), pp. 46-64; D. W. Bowett, *The Legal Regime of Islands in International Law*, Dobbs Ferry, New York: Oceana Publications 1978, Chapter 4; Ram Prakash Anand, "Mid-ocean Archipelagos in International Law: Theory and Practice," *Indian Journal of International Law*, Vol. 19 (1979), pp. 228-256; Jorge R. Coquia, "Analysis of the Archipelagic Doctrine in the New Convention on the Law of the Sea," *Philippine Yearbook of International Law*, Vol. 8 (1982), pp. 24-38; Mochtar Kusumaatmadja, "The Concept of the Indonesian Archipelago," *Indonesian Quarterly*, Vol. 10, No. 4 (October 1982), pp. 12-26; Phiphat Tangsubkul and Daniel J. Dzurek, "The Emerging Concept of Mid-ocean Archipelagos," *Ocean Yearbook*, Vol. 3 (1982), pp. 386-404; Jorge R. Coquia, "Development of the Archipelagic

Doctrine as a Recognized Principle of International Law," *Philippine Law Journal*, Vol. 58 (1983), pp. 13-41; B. A. Hamzah," Indonesia's Archipelagic Regime, Implications for Malaysia," *Marine Policy*, Vol. 8 (1984), No. 1, pp. 30-43; Arturo M. Tolentino, "Archipelagoes under the Convention on the Law of the Sea," *Far Eastern Law Review*, Vol. 28 (1984), pp. 1-9; L. L. Herman, "The Modern Concept of the Off-lying Archipelago in International Law," *Canadian Yearbook of International Law*, Vol. 23 (1985), pp. 172-200; H. P. Rajan, "The Legal Regime of Archipelagos," *German Yearbook of International Law*, Vol. 29 (1986), pp. 137-153; David L. Larson, "Innocent, Transit, and Archipelagic Sea Lane Passage," *Ocean Development and International Law*, Vol. 18 (1987), pp. 411-444; *Law of the Sea Studies, Analytical Studies on the Law of the Sea Convention - Archpelagic States*, New York: The United Nations, 1990.

NOTE

Up to 1988, about 11 countries claimed archipelagic status, with nine of them having published geographical coordinates of the straight baseline. Robert W. Smith, "Global Maritime Claims," *Ocean Development and International Law*, Vol. 20 (1989), p. 92.

2. Bays

a. General Situation

A. L. Shalowitz, *Shore and Sea Boundaries*, Vol. 1, Washington, D.C.:
U.S. Government Printing Office, 1962, pp. 31-34.

41. Boundary at Bays

411. North Atlantic Coast Fisheries Arbitration

Probably the most cogent available evidence on the question of the boundary at bays, and what constitutes a "true" bay, is the exhaustive study made by the North Atlantic Coast Fisheries Tribunal in 1910, in the famous arbitration between Great Britain and the United States over the interpretation of Article I in the Convention of October 20, 1818, in which the United States renounced the right of its nationals to fish within "three marine miles of any of the coasts, bays, creeks, or harbours" of the British dominions in America. Seven questions were referred to a tribunal selected from the panel of the Permanent Court of Arbitration at The Hague, the fifth one raising directly the problem of how the 3-mile distance was to be measured at bays. Great Britain interpreted the provision to exclude American fishermen from all bays, regardless of size, contending that the word "bays" was used in a geographical sense and therefore included all the great bodies of water marked on maps and generally known as bays. In other words, in the case of such bodies of water the 3-mile distance was to be measured from a headland-to-headland line. The United States took the position that the word "bays" in the treaty meant those smaller indentations which would naturally be classed with creeks and harbors, contending that only bays not more than 6 miles wide at the entrance (twice the 3-mile marginal belt) should be excluded. In its view, the renunciation in the Treaty of 1818 was a renunciation of a right to fish in British territorial waters and no more. Bays more than 6 miles wide, not being "territorial" waters, it contended, were not within the renunciation clause and American fishermen therefore had the right to fish in such waters.

After an elaborate presentation by both parties, the tribunal rejected the United States position and made the following award:

In case of bays, the three marine miles are to be measured from a straight line drawn across the body of water at the place where it ceases to have the configuration and characteristics of a bay. At all other places the three marine miles are to be measured following the sinousities of the coast.

The tribunal recognized that the decision, though correct in principle, and in its opinion "the only one possible in view of the want of sufficient basis for a more concrete answer," was not entirely satisfactory as to its practical applicability. It therefore adjoined to the decision, as it was empowered to do under a special agreement, the following recommendation:

In every bay not hereinafter specifically provided for the limits of exclusion shall be drawn three miles seaward from a straight line across the bay in the part nearest the entrance at the first point where the width does not exceed ten miles.

With regard to the special character of bays and their exclusion from the rule of the tidemark, the tribunal said: "admittedly the geographical character of a bay contains conditions which concern the interests of the territorial sovereign to a more intimate and important extent than do those connected with the open coast. Thus conditions of national and territorial integrity, of defence, of commerce and of industry are all vitally concerned with the control of the bays penetrating the national coast line. This interest varies, speaking generally, in proportion to the penetration inland of the bay."

The award and recommendations of the tribunal were substantially accepted by the two countries in the Treaty of July 20, 1912 (37 Stat. 1634). For the United States, it represented a recession from its position that inland waters were limited by the 3-mile rule to bays 6 miles wide, but it was accepted as a proper limitation on the sweeping headland-to-headland doctrine advocated by Great Britain.

The net effect of the tribunal's recommendations was to limit inland waters to a 10-mile distance where the indentation is wider than 10 lines at the entrance. There was no provision as to the nature of the indentation other than that contained in the award regarding the "configuration and characteristics of a bay." This left unsettled the important question of the kind of indentations that possess the configuration and characteristics to bring them into the category of inland waters over which a nation could exercise exclusive jurisdiction. This remained for future technicians to grapple with.

42. Concept of a Bay as Inland Waters

The difficulty that would be encountered in the practical application of the principle laid down by the North Atlantic Tribunal in 1910 is illustrated by a consideration of the California coastline. Undoubtedly, indentations such as San Francisco Bay and San Diego Bay would possess the "configuration and characteristics" contemplated by the tribunal and would be inland waters. But would the same apply to Halfmoon Bay, to Monterey Bay, to Estero Bay, and to Santa Monica Bay? And if no, then where is the dividing line?

The term "bay," as actually applied in common usage, is so indefinite as not to be susceptible of precise definition which is at once inclusive and exclusive. A bay is a subordinate adjunct to a larger body of water; a penetration of that larger body into the land; a body of water between and inside of two headlands. The mere fact that a body of water is called a bay does not make it so in a geometric sense.

In theory, the question whether a bay is intraterritorial--that is, whether inland waters or open sea--would seem to depend upon the extent to which the waters penetrate into the land, or, more precisely, upon the ratio of that penetration to the dimension of the entrance. This was recognized by the tribunal, but it perceived no formula for its determination. Can that ratio be expressed satisfactorily in mathematical terms?

REFERENCES

On the North Atlantic Coast Fisheries Arbitration, see Philip C. Jessup, *The Law of Territorial Waters and Maritime Jurisdiction*, New York: G. A. Jennings Co., 1927, pp. 363-382; E. M. Borchard, "The North Atlantic Coast Fisheries Arbitration," *Columbia Law Review*, Vol. 11 (1911), pp. 1-23; R. Lansing, "The North Atlantic Coast Fisheries Arbitration," *American Journal of International Law*, Vol. 5 (1911), pp. 1-31; C. P. Anderson, "The Final Outcome of the Fisheries Arbitration," *American Journal of International Law*, Vol. 7 (1913), pp. 1-16.

CONFERENCE FOR THE CODIFICATION
OF INTERNATIONAL LAW
[The Hague, March-April, 1930]
Report of the Second Committee (Territorial Sea)
Annex I ("The Legal Status of the Territorial Sea"), *American Journal of International Law*, Vol. 24 (1930), Supplement, pp. 248-250. Reprinted with the permission of The American Society of International Law.

Bays

In the case of bays the coasts of which belong to a single State, the belt of territorial waters shall be measured from a straight line drawn across the opening of the bay. If the opening of the bay is more than ten miles wide, the line shall be drawn at the nearest point to the entrance at which the opening does not exceed ten miles.

Observations

It is admitted that the base line provided by the sinousities of the coast should not be maintained under all circumstances. In the case of an indentation which is not very broad at its opening, such a bay should be regarded as forming part of the inland waters. Opinions were divided as to the breadth at which this opening should be fixed. Several Delegations were of opinion that bays, the openings of which did not exceed ten miles, should be regarded as inland waters; an imaginary line should be traced across the bay between the two points jutting out furthest, and this line would serve as a basis for determining the breadth of the territorial waters. If the opening of the bay exceeds ten miles, this imaginary line will have to be drawn at the first place, starting from the opening, at which the width of the bay does not exceed ten miles. This is the system adopted i.a. in the North Sea Fisheries Convention of May 6th, 1882. Other Delegations were only prepared to regard the waters of a bay as inland waters if the two zones of territorial sea met at the opening of the bay, in other words, if the opening did not exceed twice the breadth of the territorial sea. States which were in favour of a territorial belt of three miles held that the opening should therefore not exceed six miles. Those who supported this opinion were afraid that the adoption of a greater width for the imaginary lines traced across the bays might undermine the principle enunciated in the preceding article as long as the conditions which an indentation has to fulfill in order to be regarded as a bay remained undefined. Most Delegations agreed to a width of ten miles, provided a system were simultaneously adopted under which slight indentations would not be treated as bays.

However, these systems could only be applied in practice if the Coastal States enabled sailors to know how they should treat the various indentations of the coast.

Two systems were proposed; these have been set out as annexes to the observations on this article. The Sub-Committee gave no opinion regarding these systems, desiring to reserve the possibility of considering other systems or modifications of either of the above systems.

Appendix A

Proposal of the Delegation
of the United States of America

In the case of a bay or estuary the coasts of which belong to a single State, or two or more States which have agreed upon a division of the waters thereof, the determination of the status of the waters of the bay or estuary shall be made in the following number:

(1) On a chart or map a straight line not to exceed ten nautical miles in length shall be drawn across the bay or estuary as follows: The line shall be drawn between two headlands or pronounced convexities on the coast which embrace the pronounced indentation or concavity comprising the bay or estuary if the distance between the two headlands does not exceed ten nautical miles; otherwise the line shall be drawn through the point nearest to the entrance at which the width does not exceed ten nautical miles;

(2) The envelope of all arcs of circles having a radius equal to one-fourth the length of the straight line across the bay or estuary shall then be drawn from all points on the coast of the mainland (at whatever line of sea-level is adopted on the charts of the coastal State) but such arcs of circles shall not be drawn around islands in connection with the process which is next described;

(3) If the area enclosed within the straight line and the envelope of the arcs of circles exceeds the area of a semi-circle whose diameter is equal to one-half the length of the straight line across the bay or estuary, the waters of the bay or estuary inside of the straight line shall be regarded, for the purposes of this convention, as interior water; otherwise they shall not be so regarded.

When the determination of the status of the waters of a bay or estuary has been made in the manner described above, the delimitation of the territorial waters shall be made as follows:

(1) If the waters of the bay or estuary are found to be interior waters, the straight line across the entrance or across the bay or estuary shall be regarded as the boundary between interior waters and territorial waters, and the three-mile belt of territorial waters shall be measured outward from that line in the same manner as if it were a portion of the coast;

(2) Otherwise the belt of territorial waters shall be measured outward from all points on the coast line;

(3) In either case arcs of circles of three mile radius shall be drawn around the coasts of islands (if there be any) in accordance with provisions for delimiting territorial waters around islands.

Appendix B

Compromise-Proposal of the French Delegation

In the case of indentations where there is only one Coastal State, the breadth of the territorial sea may be measured from a straight line drawn across the opening of the indentation provided that the length of this line does not exceed ten miles and that the indentation may properly be termed a bay.

In order that an indentation may be properly termed a bay, the area comprised between the curve of the coast and its chord must be equal to or greater than the area of the segment of the circle the centre of which is situated on the perpendicular to the chord in its middle, at a distance from the chord equal to one half of the length of this chord and of which the radius is equal to the distance which separates this point from one end of the curve.

REFERENCES

L. A. Teclaff, "Shrinking the High Seas by Technical Methods--From the 1930 Hague Conference to the 1958 Geneva Conference," *University of Detroit Law Journal*, Vol. 39 (1962), pp. 660-684; S. W. Boggs, "Delimitation of the Territorial Sea," *American Journal of International Law*, Vol. 24 (1930), pp. 541-555.

1958 CONVENTION ON THE TERRITORIAL SEA AND THE CONTIGUOUS ZONE

Article 7

1. This article relates only to bays the coasts of which belong to a single State.

2. For the purpose of these articles, a bay is a well-marked indentation whose penetration is in such proportion to the width of its mouth as to contain landlocked waters and constitute more than a mere curvature of the coast. An indentation shall not, however, be regarded as a bay unless its area is as large as, or larger than, that of the semi-circle whose diameter is a line drawn across the mouth of that indentation.

3. For the purpose of measurement, the area of an indentation is that lying between the low-water mark around the shore of the indentation and a line joining the low-water mark of its natural entrance points. Where, because of the presence of islands, an indentation has more than one mouth, the semi-circle shall be drawn on a line as long as the sum total of the lengths of the lines across the different mouths. Islands within an indentation shall be included as if they were part of the water area of the indentation.

4. If the distance between the low-water marks of the natural entrance points of a bay does not exceed twenty-four miles, a closing line may be drawn between these low-water marks, and the waters enclosed thereby shall be considered as internal waters.

5. Where the distance between the low-water marks of the natural entrance points of a bay exceeds twenty-four miles, a straight baseline of twenty-four miles shall be drawn within the bay in such a manner as to enclose the maximum area of water that is possible with a line of that length.

6. The foregoing provisions shall not apply to so-called "historic" bays, or in any case where the straight baseline system provided for in article 4 is applied.

INTERNATIONAL LAW COMMISSION
1956 Commentary, Draft Article 7
Yearbook of the International Law Commission 1956,
Vol. II, p. 269.

(1) Paragraph 1 . . . lays down the conditions that must be satisfied by an indentation or curve in order to be regarded as a bay. In adopting this provision, the Commission repaired the omission to which attention had already been drawn by The Hague Codification Conference of 1930 and which the International Court of Justice again pointed out in its judgement in the Fisheries Case. Such an explanation was necessary in order to prevent the system of straight baselines from being applied to coasts whose configuration does not justify it, on the pretext of applying the rules for bays.

(2) If, as a result of the presence of islands, an indentation whose features as a "bay" have to be established has more than one mouth, the total length of the lines drawn across all the different mouths will be regarded as the width of the bay. Here, the Commission's intention was to indicate that the presence of islands at the mouth of an indentation tends to link it more closely to the mainland, and this consideration may justify some alteration in the ratio between the width and the penetration of the indentation. In such a case an indentation which, if it had no islands at its mouth, would not fulfill the necessary conditions, is to be recognized as a bay. Nevertheless, islands at the mouth of a bay cannot be considered as "closing" the bay if the ordinary sea route passes between them and the coast.

(3) The Commission discussed at length the question of the conditions under which the waters of a bay can be regarded as internal waters. The majority considered that it was not sufficient to lay down that the waters must be closely linked to the land domain by reason of the depth of penetration of the bay into the mainland, or otherwise by its configuration, or by reason of the utility the bay might have from the point of view of the economic needs of the country. These criteria lack legal precision.

(4) The majority of the Commission took the view that the maximum length of the closing line must be stated in figures and that a limitation based on geographical or other considerations, which would necessarily be vague, would not suffice. It considered, however, that the limit should be more than ten miles. Although not prepared to establish a direct relationship between the length of the closing line and the breadth of the territorial sea--such a relationship was formally denied by certain members of the Commission--it felt bound to take some account of tendencies to extend the breadth of the territorial sea by lengthening the closing line of bays. As an experiment the Commission suggested, at its seventh session, a distance of twenty-five miles. . . . Since, firstly, historic bays, some of which are wider than twenty-five miles, would not come under the article and since, secondly, the provision contained in paragraph 1 of the article concerning the characteristics of a bay was calculated to prevent abuse, it seemed not unlikely that some extension of the closing line would be more readily accepted than an extension of the breadth of the territorial sea in general. At the seventh session, the majority of the Commission rejected a proposal that the length of the closing line should be set at twice the breadth of the territorial sea, primarily because it considered such a delimitation unacceptable to States that have adopted a breadth of three or four miles for their territorial sea. At its eighth session the Commission again examined this question in the light of replies from Governments. The proposal to extend the closing line to

twenty-five miles had found little support; a number of Governments stated that, in their view, such an extension was excessive. By a majority, the Commission decided to reduce the twenty-five miles figure, proposed in 1955, to fifteen miles. While appreciating that a line of ten miles had been recognized by several Governments and established by international conventions, the Commission took account of the fact that the origin of the ten-mile line dates back to a time when the breadth of the territorial sea was much more commonly fixed at three miles than it is now. In view of the tendency to increase the breadth of the territorial sea, the majority in the Commission thought that an extension of the closing line to fifteen miles would be justified and sufficient.

(5) If the mouth of a bay is more than fifteen miles wide, the closing line will be drawn within the bay at the point nearest to the sea where the width does not exceed that distance. Where more than one line of fifteen miles in length can be drawn, the closing line will be so selected as to enclose the maximum water area within the bay. The Commission believes that other methods proposed for drawing this line will give rise [to] uncertainties that will be avoided by adopting the above method, which is that proposed by the above-mentioned committee of experts.

(6) Paragraph [6] states that the foregoing provisions shall not apply to "historic" bays.

(7) The Commission felt bound to propose only rules applicable to bays the coasts of which belong to a single State. As regards other bays, the Commission has not sufficient data at its disposal concerning the number of cases involved or the regulations at present applicable to them.

UNITED STATES v. LOUISIANA
394 U.S. 11, 48-68 (1969). Notes Omitted.

[This decision of the United States Supreme Court is another in the chain of cases concerning the submerged lands dispute between the federal government and the several coastal states. At issue in the excerpts presented here and elsewhere in this chapter is the location of the baseline from which the three mile wide band of submerged lands granted to the State of Louisiana by the Submerged Lands Act of 1953 is to be measured. Although the question of the precise location of that baseline was tendered to a Special Master, the Court did issue several guidelines and passed on some substantive questions of law relating to the effect of bays on the location of the baseline.]

3. *The Semi-circle test.*

. . . .

(a) In several areas along the Louisiana coast the parties raise the problem of whether and to what extent indentations within or tributary to another indentation can be included in the area of the latter for purposes of the semi-circle test [see Figure 4-9]. Louisiana argues that a closing line should be drawn across what it calls "Outer Vermilion Bay" from Tigre Point to Shell Keys [see Figure 4-10a]. That body of water does not meet the semi-circle test unless the area of Vermilion Bay, joined to "Outer Vermilion Bay" only by a channel between the mainland and Marsh Island, is included. Similarly Louisiana contends that "Ascension Bay," whose headlands are said to be the jetties at Belle Pass on the west and Southwest Pass on the east, is a bay under Article 7(2) [of the 1958 Convention] [see Figure 4-10b]. Again, however, its area will satisfy the semi-circle test only if deemed to include the waters of the Barataria Bay-Caminada Bay complex, which are separated from the outer indentation by a string of islands.

Louisiana argues that the area of tributary bays or other indentations must be included within that of the primary indentation. Article 7(3) provides that "for the purpose of measurement, the area of an indentation is that lying between *the low-water mark around the shore* of the indentation and a line joining the low-water marks of its natural entrance points." (Emphasis supplied.) The [italicized] phrase, it is said, constitutes a direction to follow the low-water line wherever it goes, including into other indentations, in drawing the perimeter of the primary bay. The general rule is well-recognized, Louisiana argues, by the United States Department of State among others, that the area of bays within bays is included in calculating the semi-circle test.

The United States does not reject the notion that some indentations which would qualify independently as bays may nonetheless be considered as part of larger indentations for purposes of the semi-circle test; but it denies the existence of any rule that all tributary waters are so includible. Article 7(2), it emphasized, refers to "that indentation." The inner bays can be included, therefore, only if they can reasonably be considered part of the single, outer indentation. And that cannot be said of inland waters which, like Vermilion Bay and Barataria Bay-Caminada Bay, are wholly separate from the outer body of water and linked only by narrow passages or channels.

For purposes of this lawsuit, we find it unnecessary to provide a complete answer to the questions posed by the parties. "Outer Vermilion Bay," if it is to qualify under the semi-circle test, must include the waters of Vermilion Bay. Yet Vermilion Bay is itself a part of the much larger indentation which includes West and East Cote Blanche Bays and Atchafalaya Bay and which opens to the sea between Marsh Island and Point au Fer. Recognition of the unitary nature of this larger indentation follows from Louisiana's insistence that the low-water mark must be followed around the entire indentation. If, as Louisiana posits, the western headland of the indentation is at Tigre Point, then a closing line across its mouth to Point au Fer far exceeds the 24-mile limit imposed by Article 7(4). It follows that "Outer Vermilion Bay" is neither itself a bay nor part of a larger bay under the Convention on the Territorial Sea and the Contiguous Zone.

We have concluded, on the other hand, that the area of "Ascension Bay" does include the Barataria Bay-Caminada Bay complex and therefore meets the semi-circle test. Those inner bays are separated from the larger "Ascension Bay" only by the string of islands across their entrances. If those islands are ignored, the entrance to Barataria and Caminada Bay is sufficiently wide that those bays and "Ascension Bay" can reasonably be deemed a single large indentation even under the United States approach. Article 7(3) provides that for the purposes of calculating the semi-circle test, "[i]slands within an indentation shall be included as if they were part of the water area of the indentation." The clear purpose of the Convention is not to permit islands to defeat the semi-circle test by consuming areas of the indentation. We think it consistent with that purpose that islands should not be permitted to defeat the semi-circle test by sealing off one part of the indentation from the rest. Treating the string of islands "as if they were part of the water area" of the single large indentation within which they lie, "Ascension Bay" does meet the semi-circle test.

(b) Another issue involving the semi-circle test arises in East Bay in the Mississippi River Delta. Since East Bay does not meet the semi-circle test on a closing line between its seawardmost headlands--the tip of the jetty at Southwest Pass and the southern end of South Pass-- it does not qualify as a bay under Article 7 of the Convention on the Territorial Sea and the Contiguous Zone. There is a line which can be drawn within East Bay, however, so as to satisfy the semi-circle test. Louisiana argues that, just as under Article 7(5) a 24-mile line can be drawn within a bay whose mouth is more than 24 miles wide, so also can a line which satisfies the semi-circle test be drawn within a bay whose mouth is too wide to meet that test.

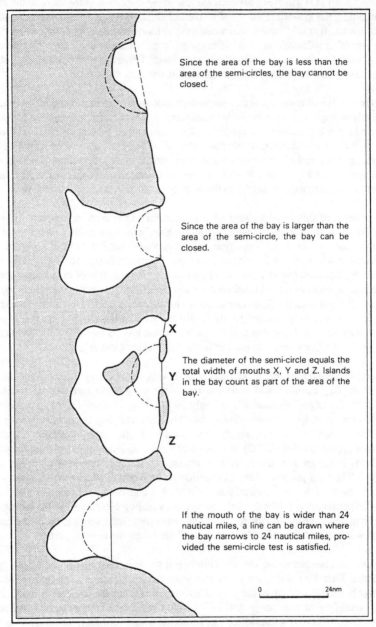

Since the area of the bay is less than the area of the semi-circles, the bay cannot be closed.

Since the area of the bay is larger than the area of the semi-circle, the bay can be closed.

The diameter of the semi-circle equals the total width of mouths X, Y and Z. Islands in the bay count as part of the area of the bay.

If the mouth of the bay is wider than 24 nautical miles, a line can be drawn where the bay narrows to 24 nautical miles, provided the semi-circle test is satisfied.

0   24nm

Rules for Closing Juridical Bays
Figure 4-9

Source: Office for Ocean Affairs and the Law of the Sea, United Nations, *The Law of the Sea, Baselines: An Examination of the Relevant Provisions of the United Nations Convention on teh Law of the Sea,* New York: The United Nations, 1989, p. 29.

The analogy is unsound. A bay whose mouth is wider than 24 miles is nevertheless a bay. But an indentation that does not meet the semi-circle test is not a bay but open sea. If an indentation which satisfies the semi-circle test is a true bay, therefore, it cannot be on the theory that the closing line carves out a portion of a larger bay. The enclosed indentation must by its own features qualify as a bay.

The United States argues that the area within East Bay enclosed by Louisiana's proposed line does not constitute a bay because there is no "well-marked indentation" with identifiable headlands which encloses "landlocked" waters. Indeed, it is said, there is not the slightest curvature of the coast at either asserted entrance point. We do not now decide whether the designated portion of East Bay meets these criteria, but hold only that they must be met. We cannot accept Louisiana's argument that an indentation which satisfies the semi-circle test *ipso facto* qualifies as a bay under the Convention. Such a construction would fly in the face of Article 7(2), which plainly treats the semi-circle test as a minimum requirement. And we have found nothing in the history of the Convention which would support so awkward a construction.

4. Islands at the mouth of a bay.

. . . .

While the only stated relevance of such islands is to the semi-circle test, it is clear that the lines across the various mouths are to be the baselines for all purposes. The application of this provision to the string of islands across the openings to the Lake Pelto-Terrebone Bay-Timbalier Bay complex has raised the following questions: (a) between what points on the islands are the closing lines to be drawn, and (b) whether the lines should be drawn landward of a direct line between the entrance points on the mainland.

(a) It is Louisiana's primary contention that when islands appear in the mouth of a bay, the lines closing the bay and separating inland from territorial waters should be drawn between the mainland headlands and the *seaward-most* points on the islands. This position, however, if refuted by the language of Article 7(3), which provides for the drawing of baselines "across the different *mouths*" (emphasis supplied), not across the most seaward tips of the islands. There is no suggestion in the Convention that a mouth caused by islands is to be located in a manner any different from a mouth between points on the mainland--that is, by "a line joining the low-water marks of [the bay's] natural entrance points." The "natural entrance points" may, and in some instances in the Lake Pelto-Terrebone Bay-Timbalier Bay complex [see Figure 4-10c] do, coincide with the outermost edges of the islands. But there is no automatic correlation, and the headlands must be selected according to the same principles that govern the location of entrance points on the mainland.

(b) Louisiana argues in the alternative that even if the closing lines should not necessarily connect the most seaward points on the islands, in no event should they be drawn landward of a direct line between the entrance points on the mainland. The purpose of Article 7(3) is expressed in the following passage from the Commentary of the International Law Commission:

> "Here, the Commission's intention was to indicate that the presence of
> islands at the mouth of an indentation tends to link it more closely to
> the mainland, and this consideration may justify some alteration in the
> ratio between the width and the penetration of the indentation."

It is evident, Louisiana argues, that Article 7(3) was designed to enlarge rather than contract the area of island waters; and that this policy would not be served by permitting islands intersected by a direct closing line between the mainland headlands to pull that line inward, particularly when the indentation would qualify as a bay even in the absence of the islands. Rather, the line should be selected which will enclose the maximum area of inland waters.

Louisiana's argument is undermined, however, by the natural effect of islands at the mouth of an indentation described in the International Law Commission Commentary. Just as the "presence of islands at the mouth of an indentation tends to link it more closely with the mainland," so also do the islands tend to separate the waters within from those without the entrances to the bay. Even waters which would be considered within the bay and therefore "landlocked" in the absence of the islands are physically excluded from the indentation if they lie seaward of the mouths between the islands. It would be anomalous indeed to say that waters are part of a bay even though they lie outside its natural entrance points. No doubt there could be islands which would not, whether because of their size, shape, or relationship to the mainland, be said to create more than one mouth to the bay. But where, as in the Lake Pelto-Terrebone Bay-Timbalier Bay complex, a string of islands covers a large percentage of the distance between the mainland entrance points, the openings between the islands are distinct mouths outside of which the waters cannot sensibly be called "inland."

Louisiana purports to find support for its position in the provision of Article 7(3) that "islands within an indentation shall be included as if they were part of the water area of the indentation." This provision would preclude drawing lines to an island wholly within the indentation, Louisiana argues, and it should therefore also preclude drawing closing lines to any part of an island landward of a straight line between the mainland headlands. We cannot, however, accept this construction of the Convention. An island which is intersected by a direct mainland-to-mainland closing line is not "within the indentation." Nor can an island which forms the mouth of an indentation be "within" it. Article 7(3) clearly distinguishes between islands which, by creating multiple mouths, form a part of the perimeter of the bay and those which, by their presence wholly "within" the bay, are treated as part of its water area.

In sum, we hold that where islands intersected by a direct closing line between the mainland headlands create multiple mouths to a bay, the bay should be closed by lines between the natural entrance points on the islands, even if those points are landward of the direct line between the mainland entrance points.

5. *Islands as headlands of bays.* With respect to many of the bays on the Louisiana coast the question is presented whether a headland of an indentation can be located on an island. The United States argues that the Convention on the Territorial Sea and the Contiguous Zone flatly prohibits the drawing of bay-closing lines to islands. A true bay, it is said, is an "indentation" within the mainland, and it cannot be created by the "projection" of an island or islands from the coast. Moreover, the rule of Article 7(3) that the area of an indentation lies between the closing line and the "low-water mark around the shore on the indentation" contemplated a perimeter or day land unbroken by any opening other than the bay's entrance. Finally, the United States argues, such an opening between the island and the mainland would deprive the enclosed waters of the "landlocked" quality required in a true bay.

We do not agree that the face of the Convention clearly concludes the question. No language in Article 7 or elsewhere positively excludes all islands from the meaning of the "natural entrance points" to a bay. Water within an indentation which are "land-locked" despite the bay's wide entrance surely would not lose that characteristic on account of an additional narrow opening to the sea. That the area of a bay is delimited by the "low-water mark around the shore" does not necessarily mean that the low-water mark must be continuous.

Moreover, there is nothing in the history of the Convention or of the international law of bays which establishes that a piece of land which is technically an island can never be the headland of a bay. Of course, the general understanding has been--and under the Convention certainly remains--that bays are indentations in the *mainland*, and that islands off the shore are not headlands but at the most create multiple mouths to the bay. In most instances and on most coasts it is no doubt true that islands would play only that restricted role in the delimitation of bays. But much of the Louisiana coast does not fit the usual mold. It is marshy, insubstantial, riddled with canals and other waterways, and in places consists of numerous small clumps of land which are entirely surrounded by water and therefore technically islands. With respect to some spots along the Louisiana coast even the United States had receded from its rigid position and recognized that these configurations are really "part of the mainland." The western shore of the Lake Pelto-Terrebone Bay-Timbalier Bay indentation is such a formation, and is treated by the United States as part of the coast.

This Court too has in the past adopted this realistic approach to similar land formations. In *Louisiana v. Mississippi*, 202 U.S. 1, 45-46, 26 S.Ct. 408, 420, 50 L.Ed. 913, we wrote:

> "Mississippi denies that the peninsula of St. Bernard and the Louisiana marshes constitute a peninsula in the true sense of the word, but insists that they constitute an archipelago of islands. Certainly there are in the body of the Louisiana marshes or St. Bernard peninsula portions of sea marsh which might technically be called islands, because they are land entirely surrounded by water, but they are not true islands. They are rather, as the Commissioner of the General Land Office wrote the Mississippi land commissioner in 1904, 'in fact, hummocks of land surrounded by the marsh and swamp in said townships. . . '

> "And when the Louisiana act used the words: 'thence bounded by the said gulf to the place of beginning including all islands within three leagues of the coast', the coast referred to is the whole coast of the state, and the peninsula of St. Bernard formed an integral part of it."

Naturally this common-sense approach extends to the coastal formations where there are only a few islands, or even a single island, as well as to those where there are many. Such has been the view of other courts and of the textwriters. Much of the Louisiana coast on or near the Mississippi River Delta is of the same general consistency as the western shore of the Lake Pelto-Terrebone Bay-Timbalier Bay complex, and some of the islands may be so closely linked to the mainland as realistically to be assimilated to it. While there is little objective guidance on this question to be found in international law, the question whether a particular island is to be treated as part of the mainland would depend on such factors as its size, its distance from the mainland, the depth and utility of the intervening waters, the shape of the island, and its relationship to the configuration or curvature of the coast. We leave to the Special Master the task of determining in the first instance--in the light of these and any other relevant criteria and any evidence he finds it helpful to consider--whether the islands which Louisiana has designated as headlands of bays are so integrally related to the mainland that they are realistically parts of the "coast" within the meaning of the Convention on the Territorial Sea and the Contiguous Zone.

6. *Fringes of islands.* At several places the question is raised whether areas between the mainland and fringes or chains of islands along the coast are inland waters. The parties agree that no article of the Convention specifically provides that such areas are inland waters. Louisiana argues that they are inland waters, under any one of several theories: that such island fringes form the perimeter of bays under Article 7, that straight baselines must be drawn along the islands under Article 4, or that the waters should be deemed "inland" under general principles of international law which antedate and supplement the Convention on the Territorial Sea and the Contiguous Zone. The position of the United States is that such island chains can be taken into account as enclosing inland waters only by drawing straight baselines; yet the decision whether to draw such baselines is within the sole discretion of the Federal Government, and the United States has not chosen to do so.

We have concluded that Article 7 does not encompass bays formed in part by islands which cannot realistically be considered part of the mainland. Article 7 defines bays as indentations in the "coast," a term which is used in contrast with "islands" throughout the Convention. Moreover, it is apparent from the face and the history of the Convention that such insular formations were intended to be governed solely by the provision in Article 4 for straight baselines.

QUESTIONS

(1) Is there a 24 mile maximum on the length of closing lines in multi-mouth bays? See A. L. Shalowitz, *Shore and Sea Boundaries*, Vol. 1, Washington, D.C.: U.S. Government Printing Office, 1962, pp. 220-222; G. E. Pearcy, "Geographical Aspects of the Law of the Sea," *Annals of the Association of American Geographers*, Vol. 49(1) (March 1959), pp. 7-8; International Law Commission, Commentary (2) to Draft Article 7, *Yearbook of the International Law Commission 1956*, Vol. II, p. 269; United States v. Louisiana, 394 U.S. 1, 55 (fn.74) (1969).

(2) Must the semi-circle test be applied again in the situation where a twenty-four mile closing line is drawn inside the natural entrance points in accordance with Article 7, paragraph 5 of the Convention on the Territorial Sea and the Contiguous Zone? According to A.L. Shalowitz, "the portion of indentation enclosed by the closing line must satisfy the semi-circle test . . . [this is because] where an indentation has a greater width at the entrance than the permissible closing line, the question of its status does not arise until the limiting is drawn." See his *Shore and Sea Boundaries*, Vol. 1, Washington, D.C.: U. S. Government Printing Office, 1962, p. 223. Is Shalowitz's argument sound? Other scholars do not seem to have discussed this issue.

(3) May the closing line be moved landward of the natural entrance points of the bay where the distance between such points is less than twenty-four miles solely for purposes of meeting the semicircle test? See *United States v. Louisiana*, 89 S. Ct. 773, 797 (1969).

(4) Where islands intersect or are near to the line connecting the natural entrance points of a bay, what rules determine whether the closing line is to deviate to include all or a portion of such islands, or whether the closing line is to be drawn around the seaward or landward side of such islands? See *United States v. Louisiana*, 89 S. Ct. 773, 797 *et seq.* (1969); cf. A. L. Shalowitz, *Shore and Sea Boundaries*, Vol. 1, Washington, D.C.: U. S. Government Printing Office, 1962, p. 225.

NOTE

Article 10 of the 1982 United Nations Convention on the Law of the Sea is identical with Article 7 of the 1958 Convention on the Territorial Sea and the Contiguous Zone concerning bays.

REFERENCES

Sir Cecil Hurst, "The Territoriality of Bays," *British Yearbook of International Law*, Vol. 3 (1922-23), p. 42; P. C. Jessup, *The Law of Territorial Waters and Maritime Jurisdiction*, New York: G. A. Jennings Co., 1927, ch. VIII; A. L. Shalowitz, "The Concept of a Bay as Island Waters," *Surveying and Mapping*, Vol. 13(4) (1953), pp. 432-440; A. L. Shalowitz, "Boundary Problems Raised by the Submerged Lands Act," *Columbia Law Review*, Vol. 54 (1954), pp. 1021, 1028-1035; M. S. McDougal & W. T. Burke, *The Public Order of the Oceans: A Contemporary International Law of the Sea*, New Haven and London: Yale University Press, 1962, pp. 327-373; A. L. Shalowitz, *Shore and Sea Boundaries: Boundary Problems Associated with the Submerged Lands Act*, Vol. I, Washington D.C.: U.S. Government Printing Office, 1962, pp. 31-47, 218-225; M. P. Strohl, *The International Law of Bays*, The Hague: Nijhoff, 1963; L. J. Bouchez, *The Regime of Bays in International Law*, The Hague: Nijhoff, 1964; C. J. Colombos, *The International Law of the Sea*, (6th rev. ed.) London: Longmans, 1967, ch. IV; G. T. Yates, "International Law and the Delimitation of Bays," *North Carolina Law Review*, Vol. 49 (1971), pp. 943-963; R. D. Hodgson and Lewis Alexander, *Toward an Objective Analysis of Special Circumstances: Bays, Rivers, Coastal and Oceanic Archipelagos and Atolls*, Kingston, R.I.: University of Rhode Island, Law of the Sea Institute, Occasional Paper No. 13 (1972), pp. 3-22; K. L. Walz," The United States Supreme Court and Article 7 of the 1958 Convention on the Territorial Sea and Contiguous Zone," *University of San Francisco Law Review*, Vol. 11 (1976), pp. 1-51; Gayl S. Westerman, *The Juridical Bay*, New York: Oxford University Press, 1987; Tuillo Scovazzi, "Bays and Straight Baselines in the Mediterranean," *Ocean Development and International Law*, Vol. 19 (1988), pp. 401-420.

b.   Historic Bays

Nations may perceive vital interests in bodies of waters known as "bays" but which do not meet the criteria of Article 7 of the Convention on the Territorial Sea and the Contiguous Zone. Paragraph 6 of that Article specifically provided that its other provisions "shall not apply to so-called historic bays." This provides some evidence of international community recognition of the basic concept of historic bays, albeit without any definition of the phenomenon. Unless there are constraints on the authority of a coastal state to claim designated waters as "historic" bays (and therefore treat them as internal waters), vast areas of high seas could be subjected, unilaterally, to absolute coastal state control. Unfortunately, there have been no international adjudications on the point so that criteria have to be gleaned from text writers, studies, and the court decisions in the state-federal disputes over title to resources in submerged lands in the United States. The materials in this subsection are examples of the presumed state of knowledge on the question of historic bays.

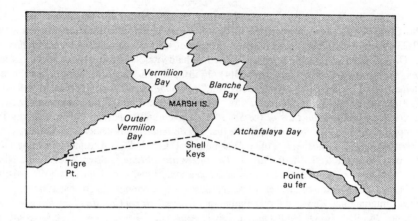

Figure 4-10a

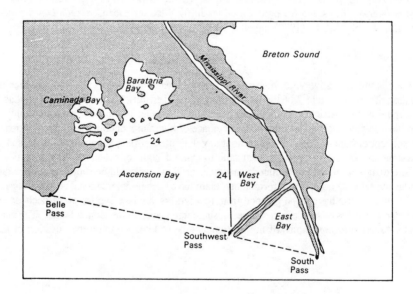

Figure 4-10b

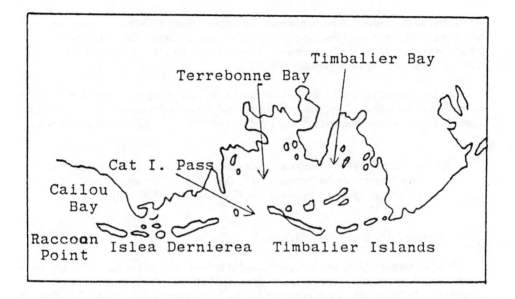

Selected Bays in Louisiana
Figure 4-10c

Source: Figures 10-a and 4-10b are reproduced from D. P. O'Connell, *The International Law of the Sea*, I. A. Shearer, ed., Vol. I, New York: Oxford University Press, 1982, p. 401. Reprinted by permission of Oxford University Press. Figure 4-10c is drawn by Hungdah Chiu.

L. J. Bouchez, *The Regime of Bays in International Law*, The Hague: Martinus Nijhoff, 1964, p. 281.

[T]he following requirements for the existence of historic bays may be gathered:

(1) The claimed water area ought to be adjacent to the coast of the claimant State. . . .

(2) The waters must be claimed by the coastal State *a titre de souverain*. . . .

(3) The pretended sovereignty has to be exercised effectively and for a sufficiently long period.

. . .

(4) The so created situation ought to be a matter of common knowledge, at least for the directly interested States. . . .

(5) The international community of States, and certainly the directly interested nations must have acquiesced in the pretended territorial rights. . . .

Therefore the concept of "historic waters" can best be defined as follows: *Historic waters are waters over which the coastal State, contrary to the generally applicable rules of international law, clearly, effectively, continuously, and over a substantial period of time, exercises sovereign rights with the acquiescence of the community of States.*

The main consequence of the existence of historic bays is that the waters no longer fall under the regime of the high seas, but belong to the internal waters of the coastal State(s). Even the right of innocent passage is absent, because the waters do not possess the status of territorial sea.

JURIDICAL REGIME OF HISTORIC WATERS, INCLUDING HISTORIC BAYS.
Study Prepared by the Secretariat, U.N. Doc A/CN.4/143, March 9, 1962.
Yearbook of the International Law Commission, 1962, Vol. II, p. 1.

C. Elements of Title to "Historic Waters"

There seems to be fairly general agreement that at least three factors have to be taken into consideration in determining whether a State has acquired a historic title to a maritime area. These factors are: (1) the exercise of authority over the area by the State claiming the historic right; (2) the continuity of this exercise of authority; (3) the attitude of foreign States. First, the State must exercise authority over the area in question in order to acquire a historic title to it. Secondly, such exercise of authority must have continued for a considerable time; indeed it must have developed into a usage. More controversial is the third factor, the position which the foreign States may have taken towards this exercise of authority. Some writers assert that the acquiescence of other States is required for the emergence of an historic title; others think that absence of opposition by these States is sufficient.

Besides the three factors just referred to, a fourth is sometimes mentioned. It has been suggested that attention should also be given to the question whether the claim can be justified on the basis of economic necessity, national security, vital interest or a similar ground. According to one view, such grounds should even be considered to form the fundamental basis for a right to "historic waters," so that they would be sufficient to sustain the right even if the historic element were lacking.

. . . .

1. *Exercise of authority over the area claimed.*

Various expressions are used in theory and practice to indicate the authority which a State must continuously exercise over a maritime area in order to be able to validly claim the area on the basis of an historic title. As examples may be mentioned: "exclusive authority," "jurisdiction," "dominion," "sovereign ownership," "sovereignty." The abundance of terminology does not, however, mean that there is a great and confusing divergence of opinion regarding the requirements which this exercise of authority would have to fulfill. On the contrary there seems to be rather general agreement as to the three main questions involved, namely, the scope of the authority, the acts by which it can be exercised and its effectiveness.

(a) Scope of the authority exercised

There can hardly be any doubt that the authority which a State must continuously exercise over a maritime area in order to be able to claim it validly as "historic waters" is sovereignty. An authority more limited in scope than sovereignty would not be sufficient to form a basis for a title to such waters. This view, which does not seem to be seriously disputed, is based on the assumption that a claim to an area as "historic waters" means a claim to the area as part of the maritime domain of the State. It is logical that the scope of the authority required to form a basis for a claim to "historic waters" will depend on the scope of the claim itself. If, therefore, as is the generally accepted view, a claim to "historic waters" means a claim to a maritime area as part of the national domain, i.e., if the claim to "historic waters" is a claim to sovereignty over the area, than the authority exercised, which is a basis for the claim, must also be sovereignty.

(b) Acts by which the authority is exercised

. . . .

. . . .In the first place the acts must emanate from the State or its organs. Acts of private individuals would not be sufficient--unless, in exceptional circumstances, they might be considered as ultimately expressing the authority of the State. As Sir Arnold McNair said in his dissenting opinion in the *Fisheries* case:

> "Another rule of law that appears to me to be relevant to the question of historic title is that some proof is usually required of the exercise of State jurisdiction, and that the independent activity of private individuals is of little value unless it can be shown that they have acted in pursuance of a license or some other authority received from their Governments or that in some other way their Governments have asserted jurisdiction through them."

Furthermore, the acts must be public; they must be acts by which the State openly manifests its will to exercise authority over the territory. The acts must have the notoriety which is normal for acts of State. Secret acts could not form the basis of a historic title; the other State must have at least the opportunity of knowing what is going on.

Another important requirement is that the acts must be such as to ensure that the exercise of authority is effective.

(c) Effectiveness of authority exercised

On this point there is full agreement in theory and practice. Bourquin expresses the general opinion in these words:

> "Sovereignty must be effectively exercised; the intent of the State must be expressed by deeds and not merely by proclamations."

This does not, however, imply that the State necessarily must have undertaken concrete action to enforce its relevant laws and regulations within or with respect to the area claimed. It is not impossible that these laws and regulations were respected without the State having to resort to particular acts of enforcement. It is, however, essential that, to the extent that action on the part of the State and its organs was necessary to maintain authority over the area, such action was undertaken.

The first requirement to be fulfilled in order to establish a basis for a title to "historic waters" can therefore be described as the effective exercise of sovereignty over the area by appropriate action on the part of the claiming State. We can now proceed to the second requirement, namely, that this exercise of sovereignty continued for a time sufficient to confer upon it the quality of usage.

2. *Continuity of the exercise of authority: usage*

A Study of the extensive material included in the Secretariat memorandum on "historic bays" (A/CONF.13/1) and drawn from State practice, arbitral and judicial cases, codification projects and opinions of learned authors, provides ample proof of the dominant view that usage is required for the establishment of title to "historic waters." This view seems natural and logical considering that the title to the area is a *historic* title. . . .

The term "usage" is not wholly unambiguous. On the one hand it can mean a generalized pattern of behavior, i.e., the fact that many persons behave in the same (or a similar) way. On the other hand it can mean the repetition by the same person of the same (or a similar) activity. It is important to distinguish between these two meanings of "usage," for while usage in the former sense may form the basis of a general rule of customary law, only usage in the latter sense can give rise to a historic title.

As was established above, a historic title to a maritime area must be based on the effective exercise of sovereignty over the area by the particular State claiming it. The activity from which the required usage must emerge is consequently a repeated or continued activity of the same State. The passage of time is therefore essential; the State must have kept up its exercise of sovereignty over the area for a considerable time.

On the other hand, no precise length of time can be indicated as necessary to build the usage on which the historic title must be based. It must remain a matter of judgment when sufficient time has elapsed for the usage to emerge. The addition of the adjective "immemorial" is of little assistance in this respect. Taken literally "immemorial" would be a wholly impractical notion; the term "immemorial" could, therefore, at the utmost be understood as emphasizing, in a vague manner, the time-element contained in the concept of "usage." It will anyhow be a question of evaluation whether, considering the circumstances of the particular case, time has given rise to a usage.

Usage, in terms of a continued and effective exercise of sovereignty over the area by that State. But is usage in this sense also sufficient? There seems to be practically general agreement that besides this national usage, consideration must also be given to the international reaction to the said exercise of sovereignty. It is sometimes said that the national usage has to develop into an "international usage." This may be a way of underlining the importance of the attitude of foreign States in the creation of a historic title; in any case, a full understanding of the matter requires an analysis of the question how and to what extent the reaction of foreign States influences the growth of such a title.

3. *Attitude of Foreign States*

In essence, this is the problem of the so-called acquiescence of foreign States. As was indicated above according to a widely held opinion, acquiescence in the exercise of sovereignty by the coastal State over the area claimed is necessary for the emergence of an historic title to the area. The connexion between this requirement of acquiescence and the opinion that "historic waters" are an exception to the general rules of international law governing the delimitation of maritime areas was also pointed out above. It might be recalled that the argument was on the following lines. The State which claims "historic waters" in effect claims a maritime area which according to general international law belongs to the high seas. As the high seas are *res communis omnium* and not *res nullis*, title to the area cannot be obtained by occupation. The acquisition by historic title is "adverse acquisition," akin to acquisition by prescription, in other words, title to "historic waters" is obtained by a process through which the originally lawful owners, the community of States, are replaced by the coastal State. Title to "historic waters," therefore has its origin in an illegal situation which was subsequently validated. This validation could not take place by the mere passage of time; it must be consummated by the acquiescence of the rightful owners.

. . . .

Assuming now that the time necessary for the formation of a historic title has begun to run, sufficient opposition to block the title may not be forthcoming immediately. One or two States may protest, but still the over-all situation may be one of general toleration on the part of the foreign States. Opposition may build up successively and finally reach a stage where it no longer can be said that the exercise of sovereignty of the coastal State over the area is generally tolerated. Thereby the emergence of the historical title will be prevented, providing that this stage is not reached too late, i.e., at a time when the title has already come into existence because sufficient time under the condition of general toleration has already elapsed. There would therefore be a kind of race taking place between the lapse of time and the building up of the opposition. The outcome of the race is necessarily a matter of judgment as there are no precise criteria to be applied to either of the two competing factors. There is no precise time limit for the lapse of time necessary to allow the emergence of the historic right, and there is no precise measure for the amount of opposition which is necessary to exclude "general toleration." . . .

III. Conclusions

. . . .

The burden of proof of title to "historic waters" is on the State claiming such title, in the sense that if the State is unable to prove to the satisfaction of whoever has to decide the matter that the requirements necessary for the title have been fulfilled, its claim to the title will be disallowed. In a dispute both parties will most probably allege facts in support of their respective contentions, and in accordance with general procedural rules each party has the burden of proof with respect to the facts on which he relies. It is therefore doubtful whether the general statement that the burden of proof on the State claiming title to "historic waters," although widely accepted, is really useful as a definite criterion.

The legal status of "historic waters," i.e., the question whether they are to be considered as internal waters or as part of the territorial sea, would in principle depend on whether the sovereignty exercised in the particular case over the area by the claiming State and forming a basis for the claim, was sovereignty as over internal waters or sovereignty as over the territorial sea. It seems logical that the sovereignty to be acquired should be commensurate with the sovereignty

seems logical that the sovereignty to be acquired should be commensurate with the sovereignty actually exercised.

The idea of establishing a definite list of "historic waters" in order to diminish the uncertainty which claims to such waters might cause has serious drawbacks. An attempt to establish such a list might induce States to overstate both their claims and their opposition to the claims of other States, and so give rise to unnecessary disputes. Moreover, it would in any case be extremely difficult, not to say impossible, to arrive at a list which would be really final.

On the other hand, it would be desirable to establish a procedure for the obligatory settlement of disputes regarding claims to "historic waters." As a pattern for such a procedure one might use the relevant provisions of the 1958 Geneva Convention on Fishing and Conservation of the Living Resources of the High Seas; in that case disputes would be referred to a special commission, unless the parties agreed on another method of peaceful settlement. Or one could follow the optional protocols adopted at the 1958 Geneva Conference on the Law of the Sea and the 1961 Vienna Conference on Diplomatic Intercourse and Immunities; disputes would then lie within the compulsory jurisdiction of the International Court of Justice, subject to the possibility of having recourse also to a conciliation procedure or to arbitration.

For practical reasons, an agreement on the settlement of disputes might preferably be included in a protocol separate from any instrument containing substantive rules on "historic water." In that way, States which would be unwilling to subscribe to a procedure for the compulsory settlement of disputes could adhere to the substantive rules agreed upon.

UNITED STATES POSITION
ON HISTORIC BAYS
Department of State File No. POL 33-26
(September 17, 1973)

With respect to historic bays, the U.S. position has been as follows. To meet the international standard for establishing such claims, a State must show: A) open, notorious and effective exercise of authority over the bay by the coastal nation; B) continuous exercise of that authority; C) acquiescence by foreign nations in the exercise of that authority. . . .

(A) On the first factor, the United State's position is that a State must indicate its intent to act as sovereign. To do this, acts of authority must be exercised in opposition to the rights which foreign nations could exercise in the absence of a claim. Although the intent to exercise authority may be expressed by local legislation or proclamation, authority must also be effectively exercised by deeds undertaken in the area of the claim. To the extent that action on the part of the State is necessary to maintain its sovereignty over the area, such action must be taken. (Cook Inlet post-trial brief.) Based on the United Nations Secretariat Study, *Judicial Regime of Historic Waters, Including Historic Bays* (A/CH.4/143) (1962), the United States has contended that the scope of the claim is established by the scope of the authority exercised.

(B) The exercise of authority must have been exercised continuously over a sufficiently long period of time to have developed into a usage. . . . The passage of a considerable amount of time is required. This is a factual question and depends upon the circumstances of the particular case. (*Juridicial Regime*).

(C) On the third factor (attitude of foreign nations) there has been question whether a showing of acquiescence is required or whether the mere absence of opposition is sufficient. The U.S. has taken the position that an actual showing of acquiescence is required. . . . This position is reflected in a U.S. note of March 6, 1958 to the U.S.S.R. regarding Peter the Great Bay. That note states a requirement of a degree of acceptance on the part of the rest of the world to justify the U.S.S.R. claim. In order to receive the required acceptance by other nations, the coastal State's acts of sovereignty must be known to foreign nations. In the Alaska case we have contended that foreign fishing activity in the area is proof of lack of acquiescence. We have also contended that the consent or opposition of some States (i.e., neighboring or interested States) may be more important in establishing acquiescence than the actions of uninterested States.

REFERENCES

Cecil Hurst, "The Territoriality of Bays," *British Yearbook of International Law*, Vol. 3 (1922-23), pp. 42-54; "Historical Bays," Memorandum by the Secretariat of the United Nations, U.N. Doc. A/ CONF.13/1; in Official Records: United Nations Conference on the Law of the Sea, Doc. A/CONF. 13/37 at 1 (1957); A. N. Nikolaev, "Peter the Great Bay," *International Affairs* (Moscow) 1958, No. 2, pp. 38-43; Z. Ohira, "Fishery Problems between Soviet Russia and Japan," *Japanese Annual of International Law*, Vol. 2 (1958), pp. 13-18; M. S. McDougal and W. T. Burke, *The Public Order of the Oceans: A Contemporary International Law of the Sea*; New Haven and London: Yale University Press, 1962, pp. 358-368; Y. Z. Blum, *Historic Titles in International Law*, The Hague: Martinus Nijhoff, 1965; W. R. Edeson, "Australian Bays," *Australian Yearbook of International Law*, Vol. 5 (1968-69), pp. 5-54; Z. Hashem," Rationale of the Theory of Historic Bays with Special Reference to the International Status of the Gulf of Aqaba," *Revue Egyptienne de Droit International*, Vol. 25 (1969), pp. 1-65; G. N. Barrie, "Historical Bays," *The Comparative and International Law Journal of Southern Africa*, Vol. 6 (1973), pp. 39-62; W. R. Edeson "Validity of Australia's Possible Maritime Historical Claims in International Law," *Australian Law Journal*, Vol. 48 (1974), pp. 295-305; "Recent Developments: Law of the Sea--Submerged Land--A State Must Exercise Substantial, Continuous, and Recognized Authority to Establish a Body of Water as a Historic Bay," *Georgia Journal of International and Comparative Law*, Vol. 6 (1976), pp. 309-322; L. F. E. Goldie, "Historic Bays in International Law: An Impressionistic Overview," *Syracuse Journal of International Law and Commerce*, Vol. 11 (1984), pp. 211-273; "Historical Bays of the Mediterranean," *Syracuse Journal of International Law and Commerce*, Vol. 11 (1984), No. 2, pp. 205-415; Natalino Ronzitti, "New Criticism on the Gulf of Taranto Closing Line: A Restatement of a Different View," *Syracuse Journal of International Law and Commerce*, Vol. 12 (1986), pp. 465-472; James Michael Zimmerman, "The Doctrine of Historic Bays: Applying An Anachronism in the Alabama and Mississippi Boundary Case," *San Diego Law Review*, Vol. 23 (1986), pp. 763-790.

CLAIM OF LIBYA OVER GULF OF SIRTE [SIDRA]
"Navigation Rights and the Gulf of Sidra," *Department of State Bulletin*,
Vol. 87, No. 2119 (February 1987), pp. 69-70.

Background

In October 1973, Libya announced that it considered all water in the Gulf of Sidra south of a straight baseline drawn at 32°30' north latitude to be internal Libyan waters because of the gulf's geographic location and Libya's historic control over it. The United States and other countries, including the U.S.S.R., protested Libya's claim as lacking any historic or legal justification and as illegally restricting freedom of navigation on the high seas. Further, the U.S. Navy has conducted many operations within the gulf during the past 12 years to protest the Libyan claim. These exercises have resulted in two shooting incidents between Libya and U.S. forces. The first was in 1981, when two Libyan aircraft fired on U.S. aircraft and were shot down in air-to-air combat, and the second in March 1986, when the Libyans fired several missiles at U.S. forces and the United States responded by attacking Libyan radar installations and patrol boats.

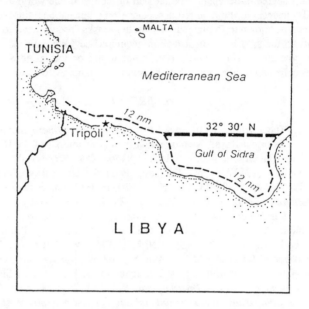

The Gulf of Sidra (Sirte)
Figure 4-11

Barbary Coast History

This is not the first time that the United States had contended with navigational hindrances imposed by North African states. After the American Revolution, the United States adhered to the then common practice of paying tribute to the Barbary Coast states to ensure safe passage of U.S. merchant vessels. In 1796, the United States paid a one-time sum (equal to one-third of its defense budget) to Algiers, with guarantees of further annual payments. In 1801, the United States refused to conclude a similar agreement with Tripoli, and the Pasha of Tripoli declared war on the United States. After negotiations failed, the United States blockaded Tripoli; in the autumn of 1803 Commodore Edward Preble led a squadron, including the U.S.S. *Constitution* ("Old Ironsides"), to the Mediterranean to continue the blockade. Shortly after the squadron arrived off Tripoli, a U.S. frigate, the *Philadelphia*, ran aground and was captured. Lt. Stephen Decatur led a team into Tripoli harbor and successfully burned the *Philadelphia*. In June 1805, the Pasha agreed to terms following a ground assault led by U.S. Marines that captured a port near Tripoli. In 1810 Algiers and Tripoli renewed raids against U.S. shipping, and in 1815, Commodore Decatur's squadron caught the Algerian fleet at sea and forced the Dey of Algiers to agree to terms favorable to the United States. Decatur then proceeded to Tunis and Tripoli and obtained their consent to similar treaties. A U.S. squadron remained in the Mediterranean for several years to ensure compliance with the treaties.

Current Law and Custom

By custom, nations may lay historic claim to those bays and gulfs over which they have exhibited such a degree of open, notorious, continuous, and unchallenged control for an extended period of time as to preclude traditional high seas freedoms within such waters. Those waters (closed off by straight baselines) are treated as if they were part of the nation's land mass, and the navigation of foreign vessels is generally subject to complete control by the nation. Beyond lawfully closed-off bays and other areas along their coasts, nations may claim a "territorial sea" of no more than 12 nautical miles in breadth (measured 12 miles out from the coast's low water line-- or legal straight baseline) within which foreign vessels enjoy the limited navigational "right of innocent passage." Beyond the territorial sea, vessels and aircraft of all nations enjoy freedom of navigation and overflight.

Since Libya cannot make a valid historic waters claim and meets no other international law criteria for enclosing the Gulf of Sidra, it may validly claim a 12-nautical mile territorial sea as measured from the normal low-water line along its coast [see Figure 4-11]. Libya also may claim up to a 200-nautical-mile exclusive economic zone in which it may exercise resource jurisdiction, but such a claim would not affect freedom of navigation and overflight. (The United States has confined its exercises to areas beyond 12 miles from Libya's coast.)

U.S. Position

The United States supports and seeks to uphold the customary law outlined above, and it has an ongoing global program of protecting traditional navigation rights and freedoms from encroachment by illegal maritime claims. This program includes diplomatic protests (delivered to more than 50 countries since 1975) and ship and aircraft operations to preserve those navigation rights. Illegal maritime claims to which the United States responds include:

. Excessive territorial sea claims;

. Improperly drawn baselines for measuring maritime claims; and

.Attempts to require notification or permission before foreign vessels can transit a nation's territorial sea under the right of innocent passage.

Thus Libya has not been singled out for special consideration but represents simply one instance in the continuing U.S. effort to preserve worldwide navigational rights and freedoms. The fact that Libya chose to respond militarily to the U.S. exercise of traditional navigation rights was regrettable and without any basis in international law.

U.S. Intentions

The United States will pursue actively its efforts to preserve traditional navigational rights and freedoms that are equally guaranteed to all nations. The preservation of rights is essential to maritime commerce and global naval and air mobility and is imperative if all nations are to share equally in the benefits of the world's oceans. As always, the United States will exercise its rights and freedoms fully in accord with international law and hopes to avoid further military confrontations, but it will not acquiesce in unlawful maritime claims and is prepared to defend itself if circumstances so require.

REFERENCES

Francesco Francioni, "The Gulf of Sirte Incident (United States v. Libya) and International Law," *Italian Yearbook of International Law*, Vol. 5 (1980/81), pp. 85-109; Bridget Bolcik, "The Legality of Libya's Claim to the Gulf of Sidra as a Historical Gulf," *Towson State Journal of International Affairs*, Vol. 18, No. 2 (Spring 1984), pp. 44-64; Francesco Francioni, "The Status of the Gulf of Sirte in International Law," *Syracuse Journal of International Law and Commerce*, Vol. 11 (1984), pp. 311-326; Steven R. Ratner, "The Gulf of Sidra Incident of 1981: A Study of the Lawfulness of Peacetime Aerial Engagements," *Yale Journal of International Law*, Vol. 10 (1984), pp. 59-77; Yehuda Z. Blum, "The Gulf of Sidra Incident," *American Journal of International Law*, Vol. 80 (1986), pp. 668-677.

UNITED STATES v. ALASKA
422 U.S. 184 (1975)

The issue here is whether the body of water known as Cook Inlet is a historic bay . . . .

I

In early 1967 the State of Alaska offered 2,500 acres of submerged lands in lower Cook Inlet for a competitive oil and gas lease sale. The tract in question is more than three geographical miles from the shore of the inlet and is seaward more than three miles from a line across the inlet at Kalgin Island, where the headlands are about 24 miles apart, as contrasted with 47 miles at the natural entrance at Cape Douglas. In the view of the United States, the Kalgin Island line marks the limit of the portion of the inlet that qualifies as inland waters. The United States, contending that the lower inlet constitutes high seas, brought suit in the United States District Court for the District of Alaska to quiet title and for injunctive relief against the State. Alaska defended on the ground that the inlet, in its entirety, was within the accepted definition of a "historic bay" and thus constituted inland waters properly subject to state sovereignty. Alaska prevailed in the District Court. 352 F.Supp. 815 (1972). The United States Court of Appeals for the Ninth Circuit affirmed with a *per curiam* opinion. 497 F.2d 1155 (1974). We granted certiorari because of the importance of the litigation and because the case presented a substantial question concerning the proof necessary to establish a body of water as a historic bay. 419 U.S. 1045 (1974).

II

. . . Since the distance between the natural entrance points to Cook Inlet is greatly in excess of 24 miles, the parties agree that Alaska must demonstrate that the inlet is a historic bay in order to successfully claim sovereignty over its lower waters and the land beneath those waters.

The term "historic bay" is not defined in the Convention. The Court, however, has stated that in order to establish that a body of water is a historic bay, a coastal nation must have "traditionally asserted and maintained dominion with the acquiescence of foreign nations." *United States v. California*, 381 U.S., at 172. Furthermore, the Court appears to have accepted the general view that at least three factors are significant in the determination of historic bay status: (1) the claiming nation must have exercised authority over the area; (2) that exercise must have been continuous; and (3) foreign states must have acquiesced in the exercise of authority. *Louisiana Boundary Case*, 394 U.S., at 75 and 23-24, n. 27. These were the general guidelines for the District Court and for the Court of Appeals in the present case.

III

The District Court divided its findings on the exercise of authority over lower Cook Inlet into three time periods, namely, that of Russian sovereignty, that of United States sovereignty, and that of Alaskan statehood. We discuss these in turn.

A

The evidence that Russia exercised authority over lower Cook Inlet as inland waters is understandably sparse. The District Court, nonetheless, concluded that "Russia exercised sovereignty over the disputed area of Cook Inlet." The court based this conclusion on three findings. First, by the early 1800's there were four Russian settlements on the shores of Cook Inlet. Second, about 1786, an attempt by an English vessel to enter the inlet drew a volley of cannon fire from a Russian fur trader in the vicinity of Port Graham. Third, in 1821, Tsar Alexander I issued a ukase that purported to exclude all foreign vessels from the waters within 100 miles of the Alaska coast . . .

We feel that none of these facts, as found by the District Court, demonstrate the exercise of authority essential to the establishment of a historic bay. The presence of early Russian settlements on the shores of Cook Inlet certainly demonstrates the existence of a claim to the land, but it gives little indication of the authority Russia may have exerted over the vast expanse of waters that constitutes the inlet. The incident of the fur trader's firing on an English vessel near Port Graham might be some evidence of a claim of sovereignty over the waters involved, but the act appears to be that of a private citizen rather than of a government official. In the absence of some evidence that the trader was acting with governmental authority, the incident is entitled to little legal significance. Moreover, under the then-common Cannon Shot Rule, the firing of a cannon from shore was wholly consistent with the present position of the United States that the inland waters of Alaska near Port Graham are to be measured by the three-mile limit. Finally, the imperial ukase of 1821 is clearly inadequate as a demonstration of Russian authority over the waters of Cook Inlet because shortly after it had been issued the ukase was unequivocally withdrawn in the face of vigorous protests from the United States and England.

B

In reviewing the period of United States sovereignty over the territory of Alaska, the District Court found that there had been five separate instances in which the Federal Government had exercised authority over all the waters of Cook Inlet. [The Court then reviewed the facts pertaining to the five instances]. . . .

Based on the facts summarized above, the District Court concluded that the United States had exercised authority over the waters of lower Cook Inlet continuously from the Treaty of Cession in 1867 until Alaska statehood. The District Court, of course, was clearly correct insofar as it found that the United States had exercised jurisdiction over lower Cook Inlet during the territorial period *for the purpose of fish and wildlife management*. It is far from clear, however, that the District Court was correct in concluding that the fact of enforcement of fish and wildlife regulations was legally sufficient to demonstrate the type of authority that must be exercised to establish title to a historic bay.

In determining whether the enforcement of fishery and wildlife management regulations in Cook Inlet was an exercise of authority sufficient to establish title to that body of water as a historic bay, it is necessary to recall the threefold division of the sea recognized in international

Cook Inlet was an exercise of authority sufficient to establish title to that body of water as a historic bay, it is necessary to recall the threefold division of the sea recognized in international law. As the Court stated in the *Louisiana Boundary Case*:

> "Under generally accepted principles of international law, the navigable sea is divided into three zones, distinguished by the nature of the control which the contiguous nation can exercise over them. Nearest to the nation's shores are its inland, or internal waters. These are subject to the complete sovereignty of the nation, as much as if they were a part of its land territory, and the coastal nation has the privilege even to exclude foreign vessels altogether. Beyond the inland waters, and measured from their seaward edge, is a belt known as the marginal, or territorial, sea. Within it the coastal nation may exercise extensive control but cannot deny the right of innocent passage to foreign nations. Outside the territorial sea are the high seas, which are international waters not subject to the dominion of any single nation."
> 394 U.S., at 22-23 (footnotes omitted).

We also recognize in the *Louisiana Boundary Case* that the exercise of authority necessary to establish historic title must be commensurate in scope with the nature of the title claimed. There the State of Louisiana argued that the exercise of jurisdiction over certain coastal waters for purposes of regulating navigation had given rise to historic title over the waters in question as inland waters. Since the navigation rules in question had allowed the innocent passage of foreign vessels, a characteristic of territorial seas rather than of inland waters, the Court concluded that the exercise of authority was not sufficient in scope to establish historic title over the area as inland waters.

As has been noted, and as the parties agree, Alaska, in order to prevail in this case, must establish historic title to Cook Inlet as inland waters. For this showing, the exercise of sovereignty must have been, historically, an assertion of power to exclude all foreign vessels and navigation. The enforcement of fishing and wildlife regulations, as found and relied upon by the District Court, was patently insufficient in scope to establish historic title to Cook Inlet as inland waters.

Only one of the fishing regulations relied upon by the court, the Alien Fishing Act, treated foreign vessels any differently than it did the American vessels. That Act, however, did not purport to apply beyond the three-mile limit in Cook Inlet. It simply applied to "the waters of Alaska under the jurisdiction of the United States." . . . The meaning of that general statutory phrase, as applied to Cook Inlet, can only be surmised, since there was not a single instance of enforcement to suggest that the Act was applicable to foreign vessels in the waters beyond the three-mile limit in lower Cook Inlet. The remainder of the fish and wildlife regulations relied upon by the District Court clearly were enforced throughout lower Cook Inlet for at least much of the territorial period, but these regulations were not commensurate in scope with the claim of exclusive dominion essential to historic title over inland waters. Each afforded foreign vessels the same rights as were enjoyed by American ships. To be sure, there were instances of enforcement in the lower inlet, but in each case the vessels involved were American. These incidents prove very little, for the United States can and does enforce fishing and wildlife regulations against its own nationals, even on the high seas. . . .

Our conclusion that the fact of enforcement of game and fish regulations in Cook Inlet is inadequate, as a matter of law, to establish historic title to the inlet as inland waters is not based on mere technicality. The assertion of national jurisdiction over coastal waters for purposes of fisheries management frequently differs in geographic extent from the boundaries claimed as inland or even territorial waters. . . . This limited circumscription of the traditional freedom of fishing on the high seas is based, in part, on a recognition of the special interest that a coastal state has in the presevation of the living resources in the high seas adjacent to its territorial sea. . . .

Even a casual examination of the facts relied upon by the District Court in this case reveals that the geographic scope of the fish and wildlife enforcement efforts was determined primarily, if not exclusively, by the needs of effective management of the fish and game population involved. . . .

Even if we could agree that the boundaries selected for purposes of enforcing fish and wildlife regulations coincided with an intended assertion of territorial sovereignty over Cook Inlet as inland waters, we still would disagree with the District Court's conclusion that historic title was established in the territorial period. The court found that the third essential element of historic title, acquiescence by foreign nations, was satisfied by the failure of any foreign nation to protest. Scholarly comment is divided over whether the mere absence of opposition suffices to establish title. . . . In this case, we feel that something more than the mere failure to object must be shown. The failure of other countries to protest is meaningless unless it is shown that the governments of those countries knew or reasonably should have known of the authority being asserted. Many assertions of authority are such clear expressions of exclusive sovereignty that they cannot be mistaken by other governments. Other assertions of authority, however, may not be so clear. One scholar notes: "Thus, the placing of lights or beacons may sometimes appear to be an act of sovereignty, while in other circumstances it may have no such significance." . . . We believe that the routine enforcement of domestic game and fish regulations in Cook Inlet in the territorial period failed to inform foreign governments of any claim of dominion. In the absence of any awareness on the part of foreign governments of a claimed territorial sovereignty over lower Cook Inlet, the failure of those governments to protest is inadequate proof of the acquiescence essential to historic title.

C

The District Court stresses two facts as evidence that Alaska had exercised sovereignty over all the waters of Cook Inlet in the recent period of Alaska statehood. First, the court found that since statehood Alaska had enforced fishing regulations in basically the same fashion as had the United States during the territorial period. Second, the court found that in 1962 Alaska had arrested two vessels of a Japanese fishing fleet in the Shelikof Strait. Since we have concluded that the general enforcement of fishing regulations by the United States in the territorial period was insufficient to demonstrate sovereignty over Cook Inlet as inland waters, we also must conclude that Alaska's following the same basic pattern of enforcement is insufficient to give rise to the historic title now claimed. The Shelikof Strait incident, however, deserves scrutiny because the seizure of a foreign vessel more than three miles from the shore manifests an assertion of sovereignty to exclude foreign vessels altogether.

The facts of the incident, for the most part, are undisputed. In early 1962 a private commercial fishing enterprise in Japan, Eastern Pacific Fisheries Company, publicly announced its intention to send a fishing fleet into the waters of Cook Inlet and the Shelikof Strait. Alaska officials learned of the plan through newspaper accounts and requested action by the Federal Government to prevent entry of the fleet into the inlet and the strait. The Federal Government, although thus forewarned of the intrusion, significantly took no action. In March 1962, the mothership, *Banshu Maru 31*, and five other vessels arrived at the Kodiak fishing grounds. On

April 5, the six vessels sailed north of the Barren Islands into the lower portion of Cook Inlet. The vessels left the inlet the next day without incident and sailed southwest into the Shelikof Strait. The vessels fished in the strait for approximately 10 days undisturbed. Then, on April 15, Alaska law enforcement officials boarded two of the vessels in the Shelikof Strait. At the time, at least one of the ships was more than three miles from shore. The officials arrested three of the fleet's captains and charged them with violating the state fishing regulations applicable to the strait. On April 19, Eastern Pacific Fisheries Company and the State of Alaska entered into an agreement whereby the State released the company's employees and ships in return for a promise from the company that it would not fish in the inlet or in the strait pending judicial resolution of the State's jurisdiction to enforce fishing regulations therein. . . . The Japanese Government did not participate in, or approve of, the agreement between the company and Alaska. Instead, shortly after the agreement was executed, Japan formally protested to the United States government. Our Government declined to take an official position on the matter pending completion of the judicial proceedings. Ultimately, the judicial proceedings were dismissed without reaching any conclusion on the extent of Alaskan jurisdiction over the strait. The Federal Government took no formal position on the issue after the dismissal of the proceedings.

To the extent that the Shelikof Strait incident reveals a determination on the part of Alaska to exclude all foreign vessels, it must be viewed, to be sure, as an exercise of authority over the waters in question as inland waters. Nevertheless, for several reasons, we find the incident inadequate to establish historic title to Cook Inlet as inland waters. First, the incident was an exercise of sovereignty, if at all, only over the waters of Shelikof Strait. The vessels were boarded in the strait, some 75 miles southwest from the nearest portion of the inlet. Although Alaska officials knew of the fleet's earlier entry into Cook Inlet, no action was taken to force the vessels to leave the inlet and no charges were filed for the intrusion into those waters. Second, even if the events in Shelikof Strait could constitute an assertion of authority over the waters of Cook Inlet as well as those of the strait, we are not satisfied that the exercise of authority was sufficiently unambiguous to serve as the basis of historic title to inland waters. The adequacy of a claim to historic title, even in a dispute between a State and the United States, is measured primarily as an international, rather than a purely domestic, claim . . . Viewed from the standpoint of the Japanese government, the import of the incident in the strait is far from clear. Alaska clearly claimed the waters in question as inland waters, but the United States neither supported nor disclaimed the State's position. Given the ambiguity of the Federal Government's position, we cannot agree that the assertion of sovereignty possessed the clarity essential to a claim of historic title over inland waters. Finally, regardless of how one views the Shelikof Strait incident, it is impossible to conclude that the exercise of sovereignty was acquiesced to by the Japanese Government. Japan immediately protested the incident and has never acceded to the position taken by Alaska. Admittedly, the Eastern Pacific Fisheries Company formally and tentatively agreed to respect the jurisdiction claimed by Alaska, but, as we have already noted, the acts of a private citizen cannot be considered representative of a government's position in the absence of some official license or other government authority.

In sum, we hold that the District Court's conclusion that Cook Inlet is a historic bay was based on an erroneous assessment of the legal significance of the facts it had found. The judgment of the Court of Appeals, accordingly, is reversed and the case is remanded for further proceedings consistent with this opinion.

c. Bays Bounded by Two or More States

L. Oppenheim, *International Law*, Vol. 1, 8th ed. by H. Lauterpacht,
London: Longmans, Green and Co., 1955, pp. 508-509. Reprinted
with the permission of the Longman Group.

[A]ll gulfs and bays enclosed by the land of more than one littoral State, however narrow their entrance may be, are non-territorial. They are parts of the open sea, the marginal belt inside the gulfs and bays excepted. They can never be appropriated; they are in time of peace and war open to vessels of all nations, including men-of-war, and foreign fishing vessels cannot therefore be compelled to comply with municipal regulations of the littoral State concerning the mode of fishing.

L. J. Bouchez, *The Regime of Bays in International Law*, The Hague:
Martinus Nijhoff, 1964, pp. 116-17, 198. Reprinted with the
permission of Kluwer Academic Publishers Group.

The primary question in dealing with bays enclosed by more than one State is not *within which limits*, but *whether* the water area comprised by the ball will be assigned to the coastal States. In this respect, it is once more of great interest to distinguish between two possibilities. To the first category belong those bays which ir they were enclosed by a single State would fall automatically under the sovereignty of the coastal State. In addition, the second category of bays consists of historic bays. It is self-evidence that the problem of historic bays is not restricted to bays enclosed by a single State, but also plays a role if there are more than one coastal State. In this respect the Gulf of Fonseca is an example.

If one takes the view that bays enclosed by more than one coastal State fall under the sovereignty of those States all kinds of problems may arise, such as: does there exist joint sovereignty of the coastal States, or will the water area be divided in several parts? Starting from the latter view, in which way is the water area to be divided? In order to give a relevant answer to these questions we have to take into account the local circumstances. In this case it is impossible to establish generally applicable rules. Accordingly, a careful approach to the problem of bays enclosed by more than one State is necessary. The guiding principle in solving the problem of bays enclosed by more than one State has to consist not in the development of generally applicable rules, but in the application of special regulations in accordance with the prevailing circumstances.

. . . .

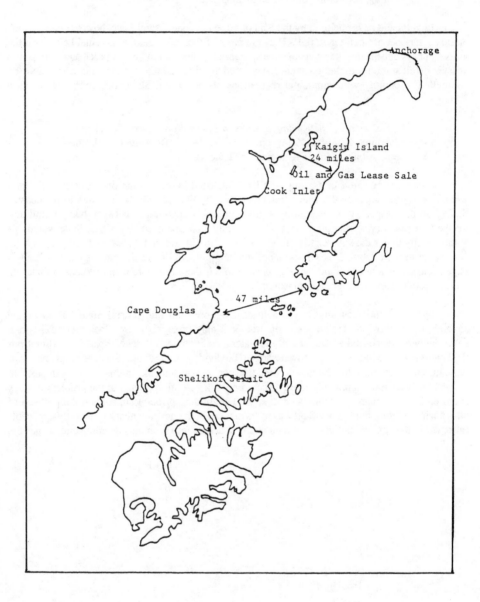

The Cook Inlet
Figure 4-12

(1) There are no general rules of positive international law governing the problem of bays enclosed by more than one State. (2) In this case sovereignty must be recognized to the coastal States within the same limits in which it is generally permitted to claim bays enclosed by a single State. In addition, the coastal States are entitled to exercise sovereign rights over bays of a larger size, if these water areas fall under the concept of historic waters. (3) In applying the doctrine of recognition of sovereign rights *freedom of communication* between all coastal States and the high seas must be safeguarded. Direct and free communication is safeguarded: (a) if suitable boundaries are fixed and (b) if the coastal States exercise joint sovereignty over the bay (*condominium*). If in consequence of the apportionment of the waters, one of the coastal States does not exercise sovereignty over part of the entrance, free communication can be guaranteed (a) by analogous application of Article 5 of the Geneva Convention on the Territorial Sea and Contiguous Zone, (b) by the establishment of a servitude of transit on behalf of the State not situated at the entrance, and (c) by lending the status of territorial sea to the waters comprised by the bay. (4) The waters of the bay fall under joint sovereignty or are divided among the coastal States. The geographical situation and the functional significance of the waters are the determining factors in fixing the boundary or boundaries in the waters comprised by the bay.

REFERENCE

J. D. Ewen, "The United States and Canada in Passamaquoddy Bay: Internal Waters and the Right of Passage to a Foreign Port," *Syracuse Journal of International Law and Commerce*, Vol. 4 (1976), pp. 167-188.

NOTES

(1) M. S. McDougal and W. T. Burke, *The Public Order of the Oceans: A Contemporary International Law of the Sea*, New Haven and London: Yale University Press, 1962, pp. 427-428, 437-445.

(2) In response to the International Law Commission's observation that it did not have sufficient data at its disposal concerning the frequency of multi-nation bays or the regulations applicable to them, Commander R. H. Kennedy prepared a paper at the request of the Secretariat of the United Nations entitled "A Brief Geographical and Hydrographical Study of Bays and Estuaries the Coasts of Which Belong to Different States," (A/CONF.13/15, United Nations Conference on the Law of the Sea, Geneva, February 24-April 27, 1958, *Official Records*, Vol. 1, pp. 198-249. The paper lists forty-eight such bays and estuaries the better known of which include the Gulf of Fonseca, the Gulf of Paria, the Gulf of Aqaba, the Hong Kong Area, and the Gulf of Trieste. Strohl adds the Bay of Fundy and the Bay of Gibraltar to Kennedy's forty-eight, which list does not purport to be exhaustive. Within this category of bay there is also a sub-category, viz., the situation where a state has a port in the bay or estuary but does not have possession of the shores at the point where the bay connects with the open sea. Strohl gives the following examples of this anomaly--The Tana Lagoon, shared by Ghana and the Ivory Coast, with the latter controlling the headlands; the Gulf of Fonseca, shared by El Salvador, Nicaragua and Honduras, with the first two possessing the headlands; Chetumal Bay in Central America with British Honduras controlling the headlands and sharing the bay with Mexico; and the gulf of Aqaba, shared by Egypt, Israel, Jordan and Saudi Arabia, with Egypt and Saudi Arabia controlling the headlands.

(3) The situation in the Gulf of Fonseca [see Figure 4-13] gave rise to litigation in the Central American Court of Justice (*Republic of El Salvador v. Republic of Nicaragua*, March 9, 1917), reported in "Judicial Decisions Involving Questions of International Law," *American Journal of International Law*, Vol. 11 (1917), pp. 674-730. The case is unique in international

law in its holding that the Gulf was, by virtue of its being a historic bay, jointly held by the three bordering states, contrary to the general rule enunciated by Oppenheim, *supra*. On December 11, 1986, El Salvador and Honduras submitted their maritime boundary delimitation dispute to the International Court of Justice for adjudication. *Law of the Sea Bulletin*, No. 9 (April 1987), p. 65.

(4) The question of right of access to the high seas through the gulf of Aqaba [see Figure 4-14] has, of course, been an important element in the Arab-Israeli dispute of the past twenty-five years. Israel claims the right to freely navigate in the Gulf and through the Straits of Tiran, while the Arab states regard the Gulf historically as an "Arab lake" and deny to Israel the right of passage through the Straits of Tiran on the ground that the entrance consists of territorial waters, innocent passage not being applicable. The literature on the Aqaba question is voluminous. See L. M. Bloomfield, *Egypt, Israel, and the Gulf of Aqaba in International Law*, Toronto, 1957; "The Aqaba Question and International Law," *Revue Egyptienne de Droit International*, Vol. 13 (1957), pp. 86-94; C. B. Selak, "A Consideration of the Legal Status of the Gulf of Aqaba," *American Journal of International Law*, Vol. 52 (1958), pp. 660-698; L. M. Gross, "The Geneva Conference on the Law of the Sea and the Right of Innocent Passage Through the Gulf of Aqaba," *American Journal of International Law*, Vol. 53 (1959), pp. 564-594; M. B. W. Hammad, "The Right of Passage in the Gulf of Aqaba," *Revue Egyptienne de Droit International*, Vol. 15 (1959), pp. 118-151; A. Melamid, "Legal Status of the Gulf of Aqaba," *American Journal of International Law*, Vol. 53 (1959), pp. 412-413; R.R. Baxter, *The Law of International Waterways*, Cambridge: Harvard University Press, 1964, pp. 160-162, 209 *et seq.*; Y. Z. Blum, *Historic Titles in International Law*, The Hague: Martinus Nijhoff, 1965, pp. 272-277; B. S. N. Murty, "The Legal Status of the Gulf of Aqaba," *Indian Journal of International Law*, Vol. 7 (1967), p. 201-206; Anthony S. Reyner, "The Strait of Tiran and the Sovereignty of the Sea," *Middle East Journal*, Vol. 21 (1967), pp. 403-408; L. M. Gross, "Passage Though the Strait of Tiran and in the Gulf of Aqaba," *Law and Contemporary Problems*, Vol. 33 (1968), pp. 125-146; R. J. Eckert, "Straits of Tiran: Innocent Passage or an Endless War?," *University of Miami Law Review*, Vol. 22 (1968), pp. 873-883; D. H. N. Johnson, "Some Legal Problems of International Waterways, With Particular Reference to the Straits of Tiran and the Suez Canal," *Modern Law Review*, Vol. 31 (1968), pp. 153-164; Salans, "Gulf of Aqaba and Strait of Tiran: Troubled Waters," *U. S. Naval Institute Proceedings*, Vol. 94, No. 12 (1968), pp. 54-62; Z. Hashem, "Rationale of the Theory of Historic Bays with Special Reference to the International Status of the Gulf of Aqaba," *Revue Egyptienne de Droit International*, Vol. 25 (1969), pp. 1-65; Ann Ellen Danseyar, "Legal Status of the Gulf of Aqaba and the Strait of Tiran: From Customary International Law to the 1979 Egyptian-Israel Peace Treaty," *Boston College International and Comparative Law Review*, Vol. 5 (1982), pp. 127-174.

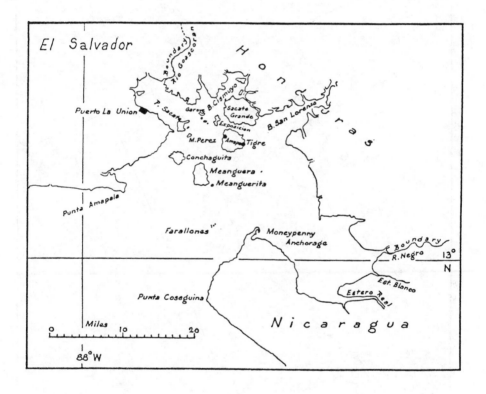

Gulf of Fonesca
Figure 4-13

Source: [First] United Nations Conference on the Law of the Sea, *Official Records*, Vol.
I, *Preparatory Documents*, p. 226.

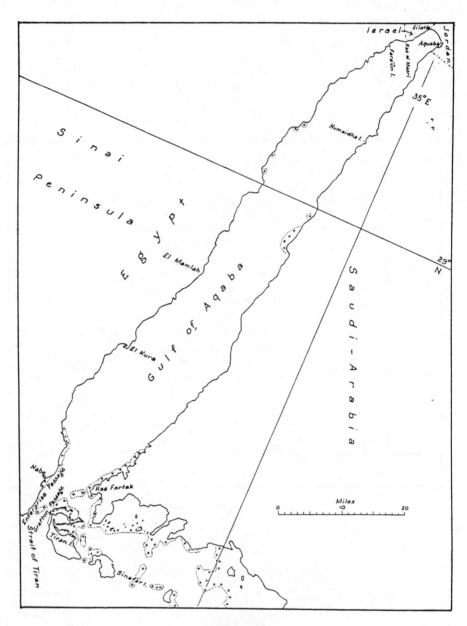

Gulf of Aqaba
Figure 4-14

Source: [First] United Nations Conference on the Law of the Sea, *Official Records*, Vol.
I, *Preparatory Documents*, p. 232.

3. Permanent Harbor Works

1958 CONVENTION OF THE TERRITORIAL SEA
AND THE CONTIGUOUS ZONE

Article 8

For the purpose of delimiting the territorial sea, the outermost permanent harbour works which form an integral part of the harbour system shall be regarded as forming part of the coast.

INTERNATIONAL LAW COMMISSION
1956 Commentary, Draft Article 8
Yearbook of the International Law Commission 1956,
Vol. II, p. 270.

(1) The waters of a port up to a line drawn between the outermost installations form part of the internal waters of the coastal State. No rules for ports have been included in this draft, which is exclusively concerned with the territorial sea and the high seas.

(2) Permanent structures erected on the coast and jutting out to sea (such as jetties and coast protective works) are assimilated to harbour works.

(3) Where such structures are of excessive length (for instance, a jetty extending several kilometers into the sea), it may be asked whether this article could still be applied or whether it would not be necessary, in such cases, to adopt the system of safety zones provided for in article 71 for installations on the continental shelf. As such cases are very rare, the Commission, while wishing to draw attention to the matter, did not deem it necessary to state an opinion.

. . . .

UNITED STATES v. CALIFORNIA
381 U.S. 139, 175 (1965)

The parties disagree as to whether inland waters should encompass anchorages beyond the outer harborworks of harbors. The Convention on the Territorial Sea and the Contiguous Zone (Art. 8) states without qualification that "the outermost permanent harbour works which form an integral part of the harbour system shall be regarded as forming part of the coast." We take that to be the line incorporated in the Submerged Lands Act.

QUESTION

In view of Article 8 of the Convention, is there any reason why a state may not authorize the construction of extensive harborworks for the primary purpose of extending its territorial sea?

What about the same situation for states of the United States? In 33 U.S.C. §403 it is provided that, in the absence of affirmative authorization by Congress, no "wharf, pier, dolphin, boom, weir, breakwater, bulkhead, jetty or other structure" may be constructed in waters of the United States, nor may any excavation, fill or other modification of navigable waters of the United States be undertaken, without prior approval of plans therefor by the Chief of Engineers and authorization by the Secretary of the Army. In *United States v. California*, 381 U.S. 139 (1965)

authorization by the Secretary of the Army. In *United States v. California*, 381 U.S. 139 (1965) Justice Halan, speaking for the majority, observed in this regard that:

"Arguments based on the inequity to the United States of allowing California to effect changes in the boundary between federal and state submerged lands by making future artificial changes in the coastline are met. . . . by the ability of the United States to protect itself through its power over navigable waters." At 177.

UNITED STATES v. LOUISIANA
394 U.S. 11, 36-38 (1969). Notes Renumbered.

1. *Dredged channels.* A recurring question in the application of the Convention to the Louisiana coast is whether dredged channels in the Gulf leading to inland harbors comprise inland waters. In support of its contention that dredged channels, as such, are inland waters, Louisiana relies principally on Article 8 of the Convention:

"For the purpose of delimiting the territorial sea, the outermost permanent harbour works which form an integral part of the harbour system shall be regarded as forming part of the coast."

Incontestably, Louisiana argues, the channels "form an integral part of the harbour system"; that they are "harbour works" as well should also be obvious in light of the enormous cost and effort which the United States has expended in dredging and maintaining them.

The United States argues more convincingly, however, that Article 8 applies only to raised structures. The discussions of the Article by the 1958 Geneva Conference and the International Law Commission reveal that the term "harbour works" connoted "structures" and "installations" which were "part of the land" and which in some sense enclosed and sheltered the waters within.[1]

[1]A member of the International Law Commission gave the following explanation:

"The Commission's rule that jetties and piers be treated as part of the coastline [was] based on the assumption that those installations would be of such a type as to constitute a physical part of such coastline; it would indeed have been inconvenient to treat that kind of installation otherwise than in the manner advocated by the Commission." [1955] 1 Y.B. Int'l L. Comm'n 174.

See also [1956] 1 Y.B. Int'l L. Comm'n 193: [1954] 1 Y.B. Int'l L. Comm'n 88-89.

The same understanding is reflected in the discussions at the 1958 Geneva Conference:

"4. Mr. Carmona (Venezuela) stressed that the International Law Commission had approved the text of article 8 only after the most exhaustive study. The construction of harbour works being of vital importance not only to the coastal State but also to the ships of all nations, no doubt should be allowed to subsist regarding the status of such works. Governments which had made heavy economic sacrifices to secure their port facilities against the elements had always acted on the assumption that the legal position was precisely as stated in the Commission's text. In those circumstances, any interference with that text might have very serious consequences." United Nations Conference on the Law of the Sea, Official Records, Vol. III: First Committee (Territorial Sea and Contiguous Zone), Summary Records of Meetings and Annexes, U.N. Doc. A/CONF.13/39, p. 142.

It is not enough that the dredged channels may be an "integral part of the harbour system"; even raised structures which fit that description, such as lighthouses, are not considered "harbour works" unless they are "connected with the coast." Thus, Article 8 provides that "harbour works . . . shall be regarded as forming part of the *coast*" (emphasis supplied), a description which hardly fits underwater channels. As part of the "coast," the breadth of the territorial sea is measured from the harbour works' low-water lines, attributes not possessed by dredged channels.[2] We must therefore conclude that Article 8 does not establish dredged channels as inland waters.

REFERENCES

M. S. McDougal and W. T. Burke, *The Public Order of the Oceans: A Contemporary International Law of the Sea*, New Haven and London: Yale University Press, 1962, pp. 419-427; M. M. Whiteman, *Digest of International Law*, Vol. 4 (1965), pp. 258-273.

1982 UNITED NATIONS CONVENTION OF THE LAW OF THE SEA

Article 11
Ports

For the purpose of delimiting the territorial sea, the outermost permanent harbour works which form an integral part of the harbour system are regarded as forming part of the coast. Off-shore installations and artificial islands shall not be considered as permanent harbour works.

And this view comports with generally accepted definitions of the terms "harbour' and "harbour works." See e. g., 1 [A.] Shalowitz, [Shore and Sea Boundaries 292 (1962)]:

"Harbourworks.--Structures erected along the seacoast at inlets or rivers for protective purposes, or for enclosing sea areas adjacent to the coast to provide anchorage and shelter."

See also id., at 60, n. 65; [M.] Strohl [The International Law of Bays 71-72 (1963)].

[2]Article 3 provides as follows:

"Except where otherwise provided in these articles, the normal baseline for measuring the breadth of the territorial sea is the low-water line along the coast as marked on large-scale charts officially recognized by the coastal state." Louisiana argues that, in view of the proviso "except as otherwise provided in these articles," the United States cannot maintain that a dredged channel is not a baseline just because it has no low-water line. Article 8, it is said, is one of the provisions covered by the exception in Article 3. This argument, however, founders on the language of Articles 3 and 8. The exception in Article 3 refers to methods of determining the baseline other than by the low-water mark along the coast. Article 8 does not provide such an alternative method, but merely identifies certain structures which are to be considered part of the coast.

In this regard, the United States points out that if dredged channels were really "part of the coast" within Article 8, their seawardmost extensions could also serve as headlands from which lines closing indentations could be drawn. As the International Law Commission Commentary explained, "[t]he waters of a port up to a line drawn between the outermost installations form part of the internal waters of the coastal State." [1956] 1 Y.B. Int'l Comm'n 270. Yet even Louisiana has recognized the inappropriateness of using the ends of such channels as headlands of bays.

4. Roadsteads

1958 CONVENTION ON THE TERRITORIAL
SEA AND THE CONTIGUOUS ZONE

Article 9

Roadsteads which are normally used for the loading, unloading and anchoring of ships, and which would otherwise be situated wholly or partly outside the outer limit of the territorial sea, are included in the territorial sea. The coastal State must clearly demarcate such roadsteads and indicate them on charts together with their boundaries, to which due publicity must be given.

INTERNATIONAL LAW COMMISSION
1956 Commentary, Draft Article 9
Yearbook of the International Law Commission 1956,
Vol. II, p. 270.

In substance, this article is based on the 1930 Codification Conference text. With some dissenting opinions, the Commission considered that roadsteads situated outside the territorial sea should not be treated as internal waters. While appreciating that the coastal State must be able to exercise special supervisory and police rights in such roadsteads, the Commission thought it would be going too far to treat them as internal waters, since innocent passage through them might then be prohibited. It considered that the rights of the coastal State were sufficiently safeguarded by the recognition of such waters as territorial sea.

CONFERENCE FOR THE CODIFICATION OF INTERNATIONAL LAW
THE HAGUE, MARCH-APRIL, 1930
REPORT OF THE SECOND COMMITTEE (TERRITORIAL SEA)
ANNEX I ["The Legal Status of the Territorial Sea,"]
American Journal of International Law, Vol. 24 (1930),
Supplement, pp. 234, 250-251].

Roadsteads

Roadsteads used for the loading, unloading and anchoring of vessels, the limits of which have been fixed for that purpose by the Coastal State, are included in the territorial sea of that State, although they may be situated partly outside the general belt of territorial sea. The Coastal State must indicate the roadsteads actually so employed and the limits thereof.

1982 UNITED NATIONS CONVENTION OF THE LAW OF THE SEA

Article 12
Roadsteads

Roadsteads which are normally used for the loading, unloading, and anchoring of ships, and which would otherwise be situated wholly or partly outside the outer limit of the territorial sea, are included in the territorial sea.

NOTE

The question of superport will be discussed in Chapter VI.

5. Low Tide Elevations

1958 CONVENTION ON THE TERRITORIAL SEA
AND THE CONTIGUOUS ZONE

Article 11

1. A low-tide elevation is a naturally formed area of land which is surrounded by and above water at low-tide but submerged at high tide. Where a low-tide elevation is situated wholly or partly at a distance not exceeding the breadth of the territorial sea from the mainland or an island, the low-water line on that elevation may be used as the baseline for measuring the breadth of the territorial sea.

2. Where a low-tide elevation is wholly situated at a distance exceeding the breadth of the territorial sea from the mainland or an island, it has no territorial sea of its own.

INTERNATIONAL LAW COMMISSION
1956 Commentary, Draft Article 1
Yearbook of the International Law Commission 1956,
Vol. II, pp. 270-271.

(1) Drying rocks and shoals situated wholly or partly in the territorial sea are treated in the same way as islands. The limit of the territorial sea will make allowance for the presence of such drying rocks and will show bulges accordingly. On the other hand, drying rocks and shoals situated outside the territorial sea, as measured from the mainland or an island, have no territorial sea of their own.

(2) It was suggested that the terms of article 5 (under which straight baselines are not drawn to or from drying rocks or shoals) might be incompatible with the present article. The Commission sees no incompatibility. The fact that for the purpose of determining the breadth of the territorial sea drying rocks and shoals are assimilated to islands does not imply that such rocks and shoals are treated as islands in every respect. In the comment to article 5 it has already been pointed out that if they were so treated, then, where straight baselines are drawn, and particularly in the case of shallow waters off the coast, the distance between the baseline and the coast might be far greater than that required to fulfill the purpose for which the straight baseline method was designed.

R. v. KENT JUSTICES
[1967] 1. All E.R. 560 (Q.B.)

Since September, 1965, the appellant company (a company registered in the United Kingdom), of whom the applicants L. and A. were directors, had been broadcasting from Red Sands Tower, an old disused fort some 4.9 nautical miles from low-water mark off the Kent coast. Red

Sands Tower lay less than three miles from a sand bank, Middle Sand, which was itself within three nautical miles of the low-water mark off the Kent coast and was a low-tide elevation within the meaning of art. 5(2) of the Territorial Waters Order in Council 1964 (implementing the Convention on the Territorial Sea and the Contiguous Zone, 1958), which laid down base lines from which the three nautical miles could be measured. The applicants were convicted before the Kent justices of unlawfully using apparatus for wireless telegraphy, namely, a transmitter, without a license issued by the Postmaster General, contrary to s. 1(1) of the Wireless Telegraphy Act, 1949, the justices being of the opinion that Red Sands Tower lay in territorial waters within the meaning of s.6(1)(a) of the Act of 1949 and that, accordingly, they had jurisdiction to try the case.
. . .

. . . .

. . . .The foundation of counsel for the applicants' argument before us, as I understand it, is that, at any rate at the time of the passing of the Wireless Telegraphy Act, 1949, it was the law of nations, by which I mean the consensus of nations, one of which was this country, that no jurisdiction could be exercised by any nation over the open seas except within three nautical miles from low-water mark, and that that law of nations had been incorporated into the municipal law of this country by the Territorial Waters Jurisdiction Act of 1878. . . .

The prosecution, on the other hand, relied on an Order in Council (1) issued under the royal prerogative on Sept. 25, 1964, which was clearly intended to implement, as it were, a convention signed at Geneva on Apr. 29, 1958, which was ratified by the United Kingdom on Mar. 14, 1960, and came into force on Sept. 10, 1964, some fourteen days before the order in council. The convention and the order in council laid down base lines, as they are called, from which the three nautical miles could be measured, and in particular provided that it could be measured from what is called any "low-tide elevation" which itself was within the three mile limit. "Low-tide elevation" was defined in art. 5(2) of the order in these terms:

"the expression 'low-tide elevation' means a naturally formed area of drying land surrounded by water which is below water at mean high water spring tides."

It was claimed by the prosecution that an elevation known as Middle Sand which was within three nautical miles of the low-water mark off the Kent coast was such an elevation, and it is conceded that there was evidence before the justices which entitled them to hold that Middle Sand was a low-tide elevation. It is further conceded that the Red Sands Tower is less than three nautical miles from Middle Sand and, therefore, within territorial waters as measured under the terms of the order in council.

The answer made by the applicants quite generally is that such an order was *ultra vires*, since the Crown must be taken to have abrogated the exercise of the prerogative powers within this field in entrusting to Parliament by the Act of 1878 the right to define territorial waters. . . .

For my part, I think that the proper approach to this question is to look first at the Wireless Telegraphy Act, 1949. The real issue, as it seems to me, in the present case is what Parliament meant by the expression "territorial waters" in that Act. Does it mean "territorial waters" as, to put it quite generally, accepted by this country at that time, or does it mean territorial waters from time to time according to international law, or according to the exercise of sovereignty by the Crown? In the absence of a definition, and there is none in the Act of 1949, I have come to the conclusion that the expression "territorial waters" must mean waters over which from time to time the Crown may declare sovereignty. No doubt any declaration of sovereignty will in general, if not always, be made within the international law current at the time, though if the Crown did exercise sovereignty over a greater area, these courts would have to enforce it; but in general the exercise by the Sovereign will not be over an area greater than is permitted under international law. I have come to that conclusion in the first place because, as it seems to me, if it was intended that the expression "territorial waters" was to be confined to a precise limit, then known, it would have been perfectly easy to provide, as indeed was provided in the Act of 1878, for an express limitation of territorial waters. There is no such limitation. Secondly, as it seems to me, although as I have said it is open to the Sovereign to declare sovereignty over an area greater than is strictly permitted by international law, international law will be the framework within which that declaration of sovereignty will in general be made, and it is well known that international law on this matter has been throughout in a state of flux. This country has in general proceeded on the basis that territorial waters are limited to three nautical miles from low-water mark, but other countries have taken different views. Indeed, as I understand it, this country itself has on a number of occasions not limited territorial waters to three nautical miles from low-water mark. Accordingly, the boundaries of territorial waters must inevitably have been expected to change from time to time, and may do so in the future, although at the moment they are crystallized by the Convention of 1958 to which I have referred. Thirdly, as it seems to me, this is a matter of sovereignty; it is a matter of an extension of sovereignty over the open seas, and as such is peculiarly a matter for the Crown from time to time under their prerogative to determine. One would expect that to be done from time to time without the need for specific legislation.

[Convictions confirmed.]

NOTE

In accord was the subsequent English decision in *Post Office v. Estuary Radio, Ltd.*, [1967] 3 All E.R. 663 (C.A.). *See* Note on *R. v. Kent Justices* in Robert S. Marguis, "Territorial Waters-Baselines-British Courts Have Jurisdiction Over Private Radio Station," *Texas International Law Forum*, Vol. 4 (1968), pp. 239-249.

UNITED STATES v. LOUISIANA
394 U.S. 11, 40-47 (1969)
Notes Renumbered.

2. *The territorial sea of low-tide elevations.* Article 11 of the Convention on the Territorial Sea and the Contiguous Zone deals with the subject of low-tide elevations. . . .

The question presented by the application of this provision to the Louisiana coast is whether the territorial sea--or, for purposes of this case, the three mile grant to Louisiana under the Submerged Lands Act--is to be measured from low-tide elevations which lie within three miles of the baseline across the mouth of a bay but more than three miles from any point on the mainland or an island.

The United States argues that the phrase "at a distance not exceeding the breadth of the territorial sea from the mainland" does not refer to the territorial sea as a *situs*. Rather it uses the width of the territorial sea only as a measurement of distance --a circumlocution made necessary by the failure of the 1958 Geneva Conference to agree upon a uniform width. And that distance--three miles in this case--is to be measured from the "mainland," a term which does not comprise baselines across bodies of water but is limited to the low-water mark on dry land. Louisiana, on the other hand, interprets the Article as covering all low-tide elevations situated anywhere within the territorial sea. And the drawing of baselines across the mouths of bays is an integral step in the determination of the area of the territorial sea. Moreover, Louisiana argues, the term "mainland' does include inland waters. The theory of the Convention, it is argued, reflects a long-standing principle of international law--that bays and other inland waters are practically assimilated to the dry land and treated for all legal purposes as if they were a part of it.

The parties agree that Article 11 on its face is not wholly dispositive of the issue, and that the language does not preclude either construction. Each party, therefore, relies on the origins of the Article and the statements of its drafters. When the provision was first proposed to the International Law Commission in 1952, it read as follows:

> "Elevations of the sea bed *situated within the territorial sea*, though only above water at low tide, are taken into consideration for the determination of the base line of the territorial sea." (Emphasis supplied.)

After several amendments to the rapporteur's draft, the Commission in 1954 adopted a version with substantially the same meaning.

> "Drying rocks and shoals *which are wholly or partly within the territorial sea* may be taken as points of departure for delimiting the territorial sea." (Emphasis supplied).

As the discussion made clear, both drafts of the Article covered *all* low-tide elevations within the territorial sea, however measured. Moreover, the provision was thought to embody long-standing principles of international law.

The draft encountered a serious objection, however, which led to its further amendment by the International Law Commission. If every low-tide elevation "within the territorial sea" was to have a territorial sea of its own, then

> "a country like Holland might extend its territorial sea very considerably by advancing from one shoal to another, claiming that a shoal situated within the territorial sea of another shoal had itself a territorial sea."

To avoid this undue extension of the territorial sea, the final draft of the Commission was revised to read as follows:

> "Drying rocks and shoals which are wholly or partly within the territorial sea, *as measured from the mainland or an island*, may be taken as points of departure for measuring the extension of the territorial sea." (Emphasis supplied.)

It is clear that under the International Law Commission version of Article 11, the "territorial sea as measured from the mainland" included those portions which extended from baselines enclosing bays.[1] The sole purpose of the amendment to the initial proposals was to indicate that "drying

---

[1] The United States argues that its construction of Article 11 is supported by the failure of the International Law Commission to adopt a proposal of the United Kingdom to insert after the words "territorial sea" the phrase "as measured from the low-water mark or from a baseline." Report of the International Law Commission Covering the Work of its Seventh Session, [1955] 2 Y.B. Int'l L. Comm'n 58, U.N. Doc.A/CN.4/94 (1955). The preference of the Commission for the phrase "as measured from the mainland" to the British terminology, however, is consistent with the view

rocks and drying shoals could be used once as points of departure for extending the territorial sea and that the process could not be repeated by leap-frogging, as it were, from one rock to another."

The United States contends that by changing the language of the International Law Commission draft to its present form in the Convention, the Geneva Conference intended also to change its meaning. Precisely the opposite conclusion, however, flows from an inspection of the history of the Convention. The amendment was advanced by the United States; yet its explanation for the proposal contained not the slightest indication that any change in the basic meaning of the Article was intended. Surely there would have been some discussion of the reference to the territorial sea as a measure of distance rather than as a situs had it been the purpose of the United States or the Conference to alter so significantly the meaning of prior drafts and the existing international consensus.[2] Instead, the expert to the Secretariat of the Conference explained "that all the proposals on Article 11 corresponded entirely to the intentions of the International Law Commission." We therefore conclude that the low-tide elevations situated in the territorial sea as measured from bay-closing lines are part of the coastline from which the three-mile grant of the Submerged Lands Act extends.

MESSAGE FROM THE PRESIDENT OF THE UNITED STATES TRANSMITTING
THE TREATY BETWEEN THE UNITED STATES AND COLOMBIA CONCERNING
THE STATUS OF QUITA SUENO, RONCADOR, AND SERRANA
Signed at Bogota on September 8, 1972
(93d Cong., 1st Sess., Executive A)

. . . .

Of the three original guano islands in the group, only two, Roncador and Serrana, contain cays which qualify as islands under international law. Quita Sueno Bank is now totally submerged at high tide and . . . must be regarded as a part of the high seas and thus beyond the exercise of sovereignty by any state.

. . . .

Exchange of Notes
Concerning Legal Positions

[T]he Government of the United States wishes to reaffirm to the Government of the Republic of Colombia its legal position respecting Article 1 of that Treaty. That legal position is as follows:

---

that the phrases were thought to have the same meaning.

[2]The United States argues that the meaning of its proposal must have been clear to all, since only three days earlier it had submitted a proposed amendment to another article, introducing the word "mainland" for the expressed purpose of excluding water crossings from its scope. See id., at 236. But at the time of the United States proposal the word "mainland" already appeared in the Conference draft of Article 11 in a context which made clear that measurement of the territorial sea from bay-closing lines was not excluded. Moreover, if the United States had in fact intended its amendment to Article 11 to exclude water crossings, it seems likely that the United States would have spelled out that intention as it had done with respect to the proposal to amend the other article three days before.

Quita Sueno, being permanently submerged at high tide, is at the present time not subject to the exercise of sovereignty. The Government of the United States notes that the 1928 Treaty and Protocol between the Government of the Republic of Colombia and the Government of the Republic of Nicaragua specifically provide that the Treaty does not apply to Quita Sueno, Roncador and Serrana, sovereignty over which was recognized as being in dispute between the United States and Colombia. The Government of the United States further notes that under the terms of its exchange of notes with the Government of the Republic of Colombia of April 10, 1928, it was recognized at that time that sovereignty over Quita Sueno was claimed by both the United States and Colombia and it was agreed that the status quo in respect of the matter should be maintained.

The government of the United States understands the legal position of the Government of the Republic of Colombia to be as follows:

The physical status of Quita Sueno is not incompatible with the exercise of sovereignty. In the view of the Government of the Republic of Colombia, the stipulations of the Treaty between Colombia and Nicaragua of March 24, 1928 and the protocol of exchange of ratifications of May 10, 1930 recognized Colombia's sovereignty over the islands, islets and cays that make up the archipelago of San Andres and Providencia east of the 82 meridian of Greenwich, with the exception of the cays of Roncador, Quita Sueno and Serrana, the sovereignty of which was in dispute between the United States and the Republic of Colombia.

Therefore, with the renunciation of sovereignty by the United States over Quita Sueno, Roncador and Serrana, the Republic of Colombia is the only legitimate title holder on these banks or cays, in accordance with the aforementioned instruments and international law.

REFERENCES

Aaron L. Shalowitz, "Boundary Problems Raised by the Submerged Lands Act," *Columbia Law Review*, Vol. 54 (1954), pp. 1021, 1035-1037; Sir Gerald Fitzmaurice, "Some Results of the Geneva Conference on the Law of the Sea," *International and Comparative Law Quarterly*, Vol. 8 (1959), pp. 86-87; Aaron L. Shalowitz, *Shore and Sea Boundaries: Boundary Problems Associated with the Submerged Lands Act*, Vol. I, Washington, D.C.: U.S. Government Printing Office, 1962, pp. 66-81, 225-229; G. Marston, "Low-Tide Elevations and Straight Baselines," *British Yearbook of International Law*, Vol. 46 (1972-73), pp. 405-423.

NOTE

Article 13 of the 1982 United Nations Convention of the Law of the Sea is identical with Article 11 of the 1958 Convention on the Territorial Sea and the Contiguous Zone concerning low-tide elevations.

6.   Rivers Emptying Into the Sea

1958 CONVENTION OF THE TERRITORIAL SEA AND THE CONTIGUOUS ZONE

Article 13

If a river flows directly into the sea, the baseline shall be a straight line across the mouth of the river between points on the low-tide line of its banks.

INTERNATIONAL LAW COMMISSION
1956 Commentary, Draft Article 13
Yearbook of the International Law Commission 1956,
Vol. II, pp. 271-272.

The substance of this article is taken from the Report of Sub-Committee II of the Second Committee of The Hague Conference of 1930 for the Codification of International Law. So far as paragraph 2 is concerned, the Commission has not the necessary geographical data at its disposal to decide whether this provision is applicable to all existing estuaries.

> R. D. Hodgson and Lewis Alexander, *Toward an Objective Analysis of Special Circumstances: Bays, Rivers, Coastal and Oceanic Archipelagos and Atolls*, Kingston: University of Rhode Island, Law of the Sea Institute, Occasional Paper No. 13 (1972), p. 3. Reprinted by permission.

The Geneva Convention on the Territorial Sea and the Contiguous Zone provides in Articles 7 and 13 for the automatic, i.e., self-executing, closure of bays and rivers for their determination of the baseline from which the breadth of the territorial sea is measured. In contrast, Article 4 requires that straight baselines be plotted on official charts to which due publicity must be given. The configuration of bays is generally delimited in both shape and size while the rivers must rely on the general understanding of their nature. No specific dimensions of configurations are noted in the convention with respect to rivers except that they must flow directly into the sea, i.e., not through a bay or an estuary. While certain other features may presumably be confused with rivers, the problems obviously did not trouble the negotiators and need not be deemed serious. Article 13 states simply "If a river flows directly into the sea, the baseline shall be a straight line across the mouth of the river between points on the low-tide line of its banks." No width maximum is noted and, for major rivers such as the St. Lawrence or the Amazon, the length of line could presumably exceed the maximum limit specified for a bay-closing line.

A major problem remains without guidance: if these features are enclosed automatically by baselines into the internal waters of a coastal state without the need for enactment into public law and without the need to be published on official, publicized charts of the state, how may a mariner know, without question, the precise position of the closing line? A glance at any chart will show a multiple choice for closure and the selection of the wrong line could result in the violation of the territorial sea of the coastal state. There is no doubt, as a result, that objective criteria must be established for the proper selection of the sole, correct closing line or the Convention must be changed to require the lines to be charted by the coastal state.

"Contemporary Practice of the United States Relating to International Law," *American Journal of International Law*, Vol. 57 (1963), pp. 403-404. Reprinted with the permission of The American Society of International Law.

The Department of State instructed the American Embassy, Montevideo, Uruguay, to communicate to the Foreign Office the position of the United States regarding the declaration signed on January 30, 1961, between the Ministry of Foreign Affairs and the Argentine Ambassador. The Department of State instruction stated in part:

"The Declaration signed on January 30, 1961, between the Ministry of Foreign Affairs and the Argentine Ambassador purports to lay down the exterior limit of the River Plate dividing it from the Atlantic Ocean. The dividing line as defined in paragraph 1 of the Declaration is an imaginary straight line which unites Punta del Este in Uruguay with Punta Rasa of the Cabo San Antonio in Argentina.

"Paragraph 2 of the Declaration provides that the dividing line will also be the baseline from which the territorial sea is measured.

"The effect of these provisions if valid would be to reduce all of the waters of the River Plate estuary landward of the dividing line to the status of internal waters seaward of which would be the territorial sea belt.

"The Government of the United States considers that these provisions are contrary to international law as understood by it and as reflected in the Convention on the Territorial Sea and the Contiguous Zone adopted at the First Law of the Sea Conference at Geneva in 1958. Article 7 of that Convention sets forth the principles governing the status of bays, the coasts of which belong to a single State. By the provisions of Article 7 closing lines for such bays must not exceed twenty-four miles. With the exception of bays whose coasts belong to a single State there is no known basis in international law for coastal States claiming the waters of a bay (or estuary) beyond the limit of the territorial sea measured from low-water mark on the coast as the baseline. Thus, in the case of a multi-national bay the waters of the bay outside the territorial sea along the coasts must be regarded as high seas. Agreements between the coastal States of a multi-national bay cannot be considered to be binding on others than the parties to such agreements or to affect the rights of non-parties under international law."

It is noted that the parties to the Declaration of January 30, 1961 purport to base their action on Article 13 of the above Convention on the Territorial Sea and the Contiguous Zone. However, the Article relates to rivers which flow directly into the sea which is not the situation of the River Plate which flows into an estuary or bay. Furthermore, it is the view of the United States Government that the provisions of Article 13 relate only to rivers which flow directly into the sea from the territory of a single State and not to rivers whose coasts belong to two or more different States.

For the reasons indicated above, it is the opinion of the United States Government that the provisions of the Declaration of January 30, 1961 so far as they purport to be applicable to others than the parties to the Declaration are inconsistent with general principles of international law and are not supported by the provisions of Article 13 of the Geneva Convention referred to. Accordingly, the Government of the United States reserves its position on the Declaration and does not regard it as affecting in any way its rights and those of its nationals under international law. (Unclassified air-gram A-46, December 14, 1962.)

REFERENCES

International Boundary Study, Series A, *Limits in the Seas, Straight Baselines*, Argentina (No. 44, August 10, 1972) (U.S. Department of State.)

NOTE

Article 9 of the 1982 United Nations Convention On the Law of the Sea is identical with Article 13 of the Convention on the Territorial Sea and the Contiguous Zone concerning mouths of rivers.

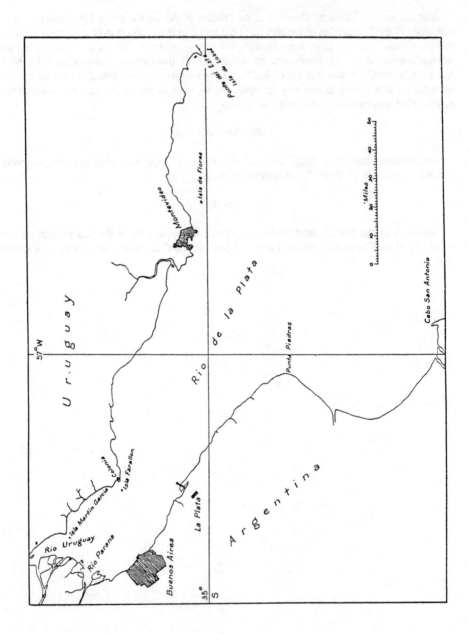

Mouth of Rio de la Plata
Figure 4-15

Source: [First] United Nations Conference on the Law of the Sea, *Official Records*, Vol.
I, *Preparatory Documents*, p. 230.

CHAPTER V

DELIMITATION AND APPORTIONMENT

A.   DELIMITATION OF OCEAN BOUNDARIES

1958 CONVENTION OF THE TERRITORIAL SEA
AND THE CONTIGUOUS ZONE

Article 6

The outer limit of the territorial sea is the line every point of which is at a distance from the nearest point of the baseline equal to the breadth of the territorial sea. [Article 4 of the 1982 United Nations Convention on the Law of the Sea is identical to this article.]

INTERNATIONAL LAW COMMISSION
1956 Commentary, Draft Article 6
Yearbook of the International Law Commission 1956
Vol. II, p. 268.

(1) According to the committee of experts . . . this method of determining the outer limit has already been in use for a long time. In the case of deeply indented coasts the line it gives departs from the line which follows the sinuosities of the coast. It is undeniable that the latter line would often be so tortuous as to be unusable for purposes of navigation.

(2) The line all the points of which are at a distance of T miles from the nearest point on the coast (T being the breadth of the territorial sea) may be obtained by means of a continuous series of arcs of circles drawn with a radius of T miles from all points on the coast line. The outer limit of the territorial sea is formed by the most seaward arcs. In the case of the rugged coast, this line, although undulating, will be less of a zigzag than if it followed all the sinuosities of the coast, because circles drawn from those points on the coast where it is most deeply indented will not usually affect the outer limit of the seaward arcs. In the case of the straight coast, or if the straight baseline method is followed, the arcs of circles method produces the same results as the strictly parallel line.

(3) The Commission considers that the arcs of circles method is to be recommended because it is likely to facilitate navigation. In any case, the Commission feels that States should be free to use this method without running the risk of being charged with a breach of international law on the ground that the line does not follow all the sinuosities of the coast.

Aaron L. Shalowitz, *Shore and Sea Boundaries*, Vol. 1, Washington
D.C.: U.S. Government Printing Office, 1962, pp. 169-172.

Basically, the concept of a marginal sea is that of a belt of water of a fixed breadth throughout its extent. In the United States, this belt is considered to be 3 nautical miles wide. But this does not mean that the belt runs like a ribbon along the coast, of even width throughout every sinuosity. It does mean that all the water which is within the fixed distance from the baseline (the low-water line, subject to exceptions) is part of the marginal sea. Three processes of drawing these exterior boundaries have been mentioned in the literature: (a) a replica line, (b) a conventional line, and (c) an envelope line. In front of straight coastlines, all three procedures would produce the same result.

(a) *A Replica Line*. --This line (often called the *trace parallele*) results from lifting the low-water line bodily from its existing position, moving it seaward a distance equal to the width of the marginal sea, and laying it down parallel to its former position. Such a line will usually be extremely irregular, following all the sinuosities presented by the low-water line. This procedure has never been seriously advocated by geographers or cartographers. The reasons are obvious: it requires an actual charting of the line to be of value to the user; it must be drawn parallel to the general trend of the coast, which opens the door to diverse interpretations; it introduces refinements not justified by a seaward boundary 3 or more miles from shore; and, surprisingly, it only partially preserves the concept of a fixed distance from the low-water line.

(b) *A Conventional Line*. --This may be any one of a number of lines. It is usually associated with straight lines, but may be a combination of lines: straight lines along a concave coast and curved lines (the *trace parallele* or the "envelope line") along a convex coast, for example. A conventional line may also encompass a series of connected straight-line segments related to major or minor headlands along a coast without regard to the adopted baseline for the seaward limits on inland waters. In the case of any conventional line, the actual delineation of the line based on any principles adopted becomes a matter of individual judgment, and considerable differences in the results may be obtained by even two experts. Probably the greatest value inherent in the conventional line is in the opportunity it affords for reaching a compromise between conflicting national interests. On the other hand, because of the wide choice of such lines along a given coast, one of its great drawbacks is that an actual charting of the seaward boundary is necessary to make the line of value to the user.

(c) *An Envelope Line*. --The preferred method of delimiting the exterior boundary of the marginal sea is by means of an envelope line. It is defined as a line every point of which is at a distance from the nearest point of the baseline equal to the breadth of the marginal sea. It is not a true envelope in a geometric sense, but is so named because it forms a continuous series of intersecting arcs which are farthest seaward of all the possible arcs that can be drawn from the baseline with the same radius, and thus envelops, so to speak, all arcs that fall short of the most seaward arcs. . . . The result is that minor sinuosities in the baseline are not reproduced in the envelope line because by definition every point on such line must be a fixed distance from the *nearest* point on the baseline and at least that distance away from *every* point on the baseline. If the baseline is straight or a smooth curve, the envelope line will be of the same character; if the baseline consists of indentations with projecting points, the envelope line will not form a smooth curve but will consist of a number of intersecting arcs.

Geometrically, the envelope line is the locus of the center of a circle the circumference of which is always in contact with the coastline, that is, with the low-water line or the seaward limits of the inland waters. Although often referred to as the "arcs-of-circles method", because of the manner in which the line can be drawn (by swinging arcs from points along the coastline), it will occasion less confusion if thought of in its geometric sense, that is, as a derivative of the coastline.

The principle of the envelope line is so definite and conclusive that under it only one line can possibly be drawn from a given coastline. And even though no actual line is charted, a navigator would fine no difficulty in determining whether he is within or without the marginal sea. Having plotted his position on his chart, he describes an arc to landward with a radius equal to the width of the marginal sea -- if the arc cuts land (the low-water line) or inland waters, he is in the marginal sea; if it just touches such features, he is exactly on the boundary between the marginal sea and the high seas; and if it fails to touch at all, he is outside the marginal sea.

These practical advantages of the envelope line are so overriding as to more than offset the departures of the line from strict parallelism to the sinuosities of the coast. The envelope line adheres in essence to the rule of the tidemark because every point on it is a fixed distance from some point on the low-water line, even though *every* point on the low-water line is not a fixed distance from the envelope line.

NOTE

The outer limit of the continental shelf and the exclusive economic zone will be discussed in Chapter 8 and 9 respectively.

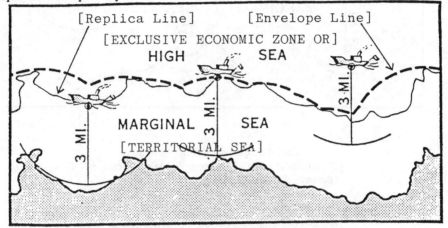

Replica Line (Trace Parallel)/Envelope Line (Arcs of Circles)
5-1a

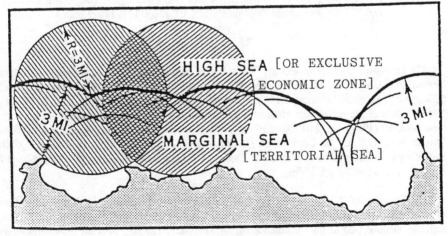

How to Draw Envelope Line
(The envelope line is the locus of the center of a circle rolled
along the coastline with circumference always in contact with it.)
5-1b

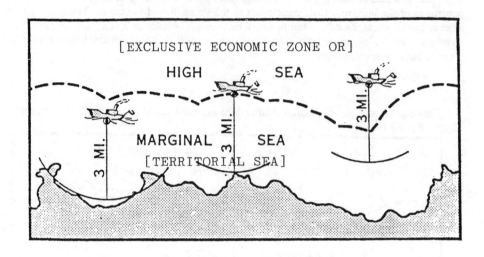

The Envelope Line and the Navigator
(The navigator can readily determine his relationship to
the envelope line without such line being charted.)
5-1c

Methods of Delimiting Outer Limit of Territorrial Sea
Figure 5-1

Source: Revised from A.L. Shalowitz, *Shore and Sea Boundaries*, Vol. 1, Washington,
D.C.: U.S. Government Printing Office, 1962, pp. 171, 172 (Figures 27-28).

REFERENCES

(1) Territorial Sea: S. W. Boggs, "Delimitation of the Territorial Sea," *American Journal of
International Law*, Vol. 24 (1930), pp. 541-555 [discussing the United States' proposal on
delimitation of the territorial sea made at the 1930 Hague Codification Conference]; S. W. Boggs,
"Delimitation of Seaward Areas Under National Jurisdiction," *American Journal of International
Law*, Vol. 45 (1951), pp. 240, 247-250; M. M. Whiteman, *Digest of International Law*, Vol. 4,
Washington, D.C.:U. S. Government Printing Office, pp. 195-207; H. Orlin, "Offshore
Boundaries: Engineering and Economic Aspects," *Ocean Development and International Law
Journal*, Vol. 3 (1975), pp. 87-96.

(2) Continental Shelf: M. D. Blecher, "Equitabie Delimitation of Continental Shelf."
American Journal of International Law, Vol. 73 (1979), pp. 60-88; S. H. Amin, "Customary
Rules of Delimitation of the Continental Shelf: The Gulf Practice," *Journal of Maritime Law &
Commerce*, Vol. 11 (1980), pp. 509-526; S. H. Amin, "Law of the Continental Shelf
Delimitation: The Gulf Example," *Netherlands International Law Review*, Vol. 27 (1980), pp.
335-346; Stephen Beaglehole, "The Equitable Delimitation of the Continental Shelf," *Victoria
University of Wellington Law Review*, Vol. 14 (1984), pp. 415-442; D. N. Hutchinson, "The
Concept of Natural Prolongation in the Jurisprudence Concerning Delimitation of Continental

Shelf Areas," *British Yearbook of International Law*, Vol. 55 (1984), pp. 133-187; D. N. Hutchinson, "The Seaward Limit to Continental Shelf Jurisdiction on Customary International Law," *British Yearbook of International Law*, Vol. 56 (1985), pp. 111-188; Duncan J. McMillan, "The Extent of the Continental Shelf. Factors Affecting the Accuracy of A Continental Margin Boundary," *Baden-Wurttembergische Versaltungspraxis* (West Germany), Vol. 9 (1985), No. 2, pp. 148-156; Wijnand Langeraar, "Delimitation of Continental Shelf Areas: A New Approach," *Journal of Maritime Law & Commerce*, Vol. 17 (1986), pp. 389-406; Umberto Leanza and Luigi Sico, eds., *Mediterranean Continental Shelf; Delimitations and Regimes*, 2 Vols. in 4 books, Dobbs Ferry, New York: Oceana, 1988.

(3) Maritime/Ocean Boundary: L. D. M. Nelson, "Equity and the Delimitation of Maritime Boundaries," *Revue Iranienne Des Relations Internationales*, No. 11/12 (Spring 1978), pp. 197-218; Hollis D. Hedberg, "Ocean Floor Boundaries: The Base-Of-Slope Boundaries Zone Formula Gives the Most Acceptable Jurisdictional Limit for Mineral Resources," *Science*, No. 204 (1979), pp. 135-144; Robert D. Hodgson and Robert W. Smith, "Boundary Issues Created by Extended National Marine Jurisdiction," *Geographical Review*, Vol. 69 (1979), pp. 423-433; "The Frontier of the Seas: The Problems of Delimitation," in *Proceedings of the 5th International Ocean Symposium, Tokyo, November 26-27, 1980*, Tokyo,: Japan Shipping Club/Ocean Association of Japan, 1981,, xiii, 82 pp.; E. D. Brown, "Delimitation of Offshore Areas: Hard Labour and Bitter Fruits at UNCLOS III," *Marine Policy*, Vol. 5 (1981), No. 3, pp. 172-184; Edward J. Collins and Martin Rogoff, "The International Law of Maritime Boundary Delimitation." *Maine Law Review*, Vol. 34 (1982), pp. 1-62; Robert W. Smith, "A Geographical Primer to Maritime Boundary-Making." *Ocean Development and International Law*, Vol. 12 (1982), pp. 1-22; Richard T. S. Hsu, "A Rational Approach to Maritime Boundary Delimitation," *Ocean Development and International Law*, Vol. 13 (1983), pp. 103-113; Jonathan I. Charney, "Ocean Boundaries Between Nations: A Theory for Progress," *American Journal of International Law*, Vol. 78 (1984) pp. 582-606; Janusz Symonides, "Delimitation of Maritime Areas Between the States with Opposite or Adjacent Coasts," *Polish Yearbook of International Law*, Vol. 13 (1984), pp. 19-46; Marvin A. Fentress, "Maritime Boundary Dispute Settlement: The Nonemergence of Guiding Principles," *Georgia Journal of International & Comparative Law*, Vol. 15, (1985), pp. 591-625; D. C. Kappor and Adam J. Kerr, *A Guide to Maritime Boundary Delimitation*, Toronto: Carswell, 1986; Wijnand Langeraar, "Maritime Delimitation: The Equiratio Method--A New Approach," *Marine Policy*, Vol. 10 (1986), No. 1, pp. 3-18; L. A. Willis, "From Precedent to Precedent: The Triumph of Pragmatism in the Law of Maritime Boundaries." *Canadian Yearbook of International Law*, Vol. 24 (1986), pp. 3-60; Jonathan I. Charney, "The Delimitation of Ocean Boundaries," *Ocean Development and International Law*, Vol. 18 (1987), pp. 497-531; Barbara Kwiatkowska, "Equitable Maritime Boundary Delimitation: A Legal Perspective," *International Journal of Estuarine and Coastal Law*, Vol. 3, No. 4 (November 1988), pp. 287-304; Dorinda G. Dalkmeyer and Louis DeVorsey, Jr., eds., *Rights to Oceanic Resources: Deciding and Drawing Maritime Boundaries*, Dordrecht, Boston, London: Martinus Nijhoff Publishers, 1989; Malcolm D. Evans, *Relevant Circumstances and Maritime Delimitation*, New York: Oxford University Press, 1989; Douglas M. Johnston, *The Theory and History of Ocean Boundary-Making*, Kingston and Montreal: McGill Queen's University Press, 1989; Prosper Weil, *The Law of Maritime Delimitations-Reflections*, Cambridge, United Kingdom: Grotius Publications, 1989.

(4) Domestic Maritime Boundary: Jonathan I. Charney, "The Delimitation of Lateral Seaward Boundaries Between States in a Domestic Context," *American Journal of International Law*, Vol. 75 (1981), pp. 28-68;1 Donna R. Christie, "Coastal Energy Impact Program Boundaries on the Atlantic Coast: A Case Study of the Law Applicable to Lateral Seaward Boundaries," *Virginia Journal of International Law*, Vol. 19 (1979), pp. 841-882.

B. DELIMITATION OF TERRITORIAL SEA BETWEEN STATES WITH ADJACENT OR OPPOSITE COAST

1958 CONVENTION OF THE TERRITORIAL SEA AND THE CONTIGUOUS ZONE

Article 12

1. Where the coasts of two States are opposite or adjacent to each other, neither of the two States is entitled, failing agreement between them to the contrary, to extend its territorial sea beyond the median line every point of which is equidistant from the nearest points on the baselines from which the breadth of the territorial seas of each of the two States is measured. The provisions of this paragraph shall not apply, however, where it is necessary by reason of historical title or other special circumstances to delimit the territorial seas of the two States in a way which is at variance with this provision.

2. This line of delimitation between the territorial seas of two States lying opposite to each other or adjacent to each other shall be marked on large-scale charts officially recognized by the coastal States.

INTERNATIONAL LAW COMMISSION
1956 Commentary, Draft Article 12
Yearbook of the International Law Commission, 1956,
Vol II, p. 271.

(1) The 1955 draft contained an article (12) entitled "Delimitation of the territorial sea in straits," and another (14) entitled "Delimitation of the territorial sea of two States, the coasts of which are opposite each other." It was correctly pointed out that the text could be simplified by combining these two articles, since the delimitation of the territorial sea in straits did not present any different problem from that of the opposite coasts of two States generally. It is only the right of passage in straits that calls for special attention. The Commission has dealt with this in article 17, paragraph 4.

(2) The delimitation in case of disagreement between those States, of the territorial seas between two States the coasts of which are opposite each other, was one of the main tasks of the committee of experts which met at The Hague in April 1953 at the Commission's request. The Commission approved the experts' proposals (A/CN.4/61/Add.1) and took them as a basis for this article. It considered, however, that it would be wrong to go into too much detail and that the rule should be fairly flexible. Consequently, it did not adopt certain points of detail laid down by the experts. Although the Commission noted that special circumstances would probably necessitate frequent departures from the mathematical median line, it thought it advisable to adopt, as a general rule, the system of the median line as a basis for delimitation.

(3) Under the term "baselines" at the end of paragraph 1 the Commission includes both normal baselines and those applied under any straight baseline system adopted for the coast in question.

. . . .

(6) The Commission is aware that the rules it has formulated in paragraphs 2 and 3 cannot be applied in all circumstances. Cases may arise in which, either by reason of differences in

customary law or by reason of international conventions, it is necessary to apply a different rule to the sea between the two coasts. It is not impossible that the area of sea between two coasts of the same State may have the character of an internal sea subject to special rules. The Commission cannot undertake to study these special cases; it must confine itself to stating the principles which, in general, could serve as a point of departure for determining the legal status of the areas in question.

(7) The rule established by the present article does not provide any solution for cases in which the States opposite each other have adopted different breadths for their territorial seas. As long as no agreement is reached on the breadth of the territorial sea, disputes of this kind cannot be settled on the basis of legal rules; they must be settled by agreement between the parties.

INTERNATIONAL LAW COMMISSION
1956 Commentary, Draft Article 14
Yearbook of the International Law Commission, 1956,
Vol. II, p. 272

(1) The situation (of adjacent states) can be regulated in various ways.

(2) First, it would be possible to consider extending the land frontier out to sea as far as the outer limit of the territorial sea. This line can only be used if the land frontier meets the coast at a right angle; if the angle is acute, the result is impracticable.

(3) A second solution would be to draw a line at right angles to the coast at the point where the land frontier reaches the sea. This method is open to criticism if the coastline curves in the vicinity of the point in question; for in that case the line drawn at right angles may meet the coast again at another point.

(4) A third solution would be to adopt as the demarcation line the geographical parallel passing through the point at which the land frontier meets the coast. This solution is not applicable to all cases either.

(5) A fourth solution would be to draw a line at right angles to the general direction of the coastline. The Norwegian and Swedish Governments drew attention to the arbitral award of 23 October 1909 in a dispute between Norway and Sweden, of which the statement of reasons contains the following sentence:

> "The delimitation shall be made by tracing a line perpendicularly to the general direction of the coast." (A/CN.4/71, p. 14 and A/CN.4/71/Add.1,p. 3)

(6) The group of experts, mentioned above, was unable to support this last method of drawing the boundary line. It was of opinion that it was often impracticable to establish any "general direction of the coast"; the result would depend on the "scale of charts used for the purpose and . . . how much coast shall be utilized in attempting to determine any general direction whatever." Consequently, since the method of drawing a line at right angles to the general direction of the coastline is too vague for purposes of law, the best solution seems to be the median line which the group of experts suggested. Such a line should be drawn according to the principle of equidistance from the respective coastlines. Where the coast is straight, a line drawn according to this method will coincide with one drawn at right angles to the coast at the

intersection of the land frontier and the coastline. If, however, the coast is curved or irregular, the line takes the contour into account, whole avoiding the difficulties of the problem of the general direction of the coast.

(7) The Commission agreed with the view taken by the group of experts. As in the case dealt with by the preceding article, however, it considers that the rule should be very flexibly applied.

REFERENCES

(1) On techniques involved in such delimitation, see S. W. Boggs, "Delimitation of the Seaward Areas Under National Jurisdiction," *American Journal of International Law*, Vol. 45 (1951), pp. 240, 256-263; G. E. Pearcy, "Geographical Aspects of the Law of the Sea," *Annals of the Association of American Geographers*, Vol. 49 (March 1959), pp. 14-20.

(2) The U. S. Department of State publishes, in its *Limits in the Sea* series, maps and descriptions of all territorial sea boundaries agreed to by the affected states. These pamphlets can be obtained from the Office of the Geographer. The series also covers continental shelf apportionment agreements, descriptions of important international straits, and the delimitation of straight baselines by coastal states.

Aaron L. Shalowitz, *Shore and Sea Boundaries*, Vol. 1 Washington D. C.: U. S. Government Printing Office, 1962, pp. 232-235.

A. Construction of a Median Line

The precise median line or the median-line principle can be applied in a large variety of geographic situations to delimit the sea boundary between coastal States in an equitable manner. Among these may be found cases where States are opposite each other, adjacent to each other, opposite and adjacent, or where islands exist in the vicinity of the boundary line. Only the methods applicable to the first two will be described.

In constructing a true median-line boundary, it is essential to keep in mind that every point on such a boundary must always be equidistant from the nearest point on the baselines from which the territorial sea is drawn. Unless this geometric principle is satisfied the resulting boundary will not be a true median line. And for purposes of drawing median lines, the baselines from which equal distances are measured may be the low-water lines, closing lines of bays, or straight baselines. The technical construction for the two cases is somewhat different and will be treated separately.

(a) *Where the Coasts Are Opposite Each Other*.--In figure [5-2] a point on the true median line must first be established. This can be a trial-and-error method, or it may be a direct method as follows: Center the dividers on a prominent point of the coast of State A and swing an arc until a point on the coast of State B nearest to this center is found. With the same radius, center the dividers on the point on the coast of State B and verify that the original point on State A is the nearest to it. (This is not necessarily always so and is dependent upon the particular shapes of the coastlines.) If the selected points are not the nearest to each other *from both coasts*, two other points must be found that are. The initial point on the median line is the midpoint of the line joining these two points. In the figure, *a* and *b* are the points nearest to each other and *m* is a point on the median line. Having established the initial point, other points on the median line are derived as follows:

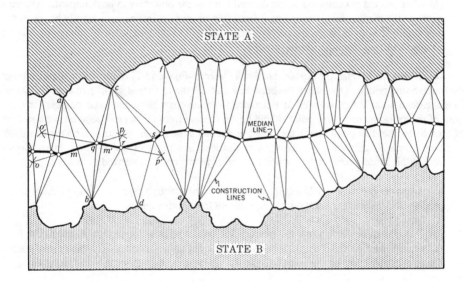

Median Line of Opposite States
Figure 5-2
Source: Aaron L. Shalowitz, *Shore and Sea Boundaries*, Vol. 1, Washington, D.C.: U.
S. Government Printing Office, 1962, p. 233.

(1) Draw a perpendicular *omp* to the line *ab* at point *m*. This will be the median line, since
from the geometric construction every point on this line is equidistant from both *a* and *b*.

(2) A point *q* is next found by trial and error in the line *mp* that is equidistant from the nearest
point on the coast of either State and from points *a* and *b*. Let this point be *c* on the coast of
State *1 A*. Hence, at *q*, the relationship *qa=qb=qc* exists, and there are no points on the
coastline of either State nearer to the median line than points *a*, *b*, and *c*.

(3) A perpendicular bisector *o'm'p'* is next drawn to line *bc* (this must pass through point *q*
since *qb* is equal to *qc*), and a point *r* found on this bisector that is equidistant from *b* and *c* and
from the nearest point on the coast of either State. Let this point be *d* on the coast of State *B*.

(4) A perpendicular bisector is next drawn to line cd , and a point s is found on this bisector that is equidistant from c and d and from the nearest point on the coast of either State. Let this point be e on the coast of State B.

(5) A perpendicular bisector is next drawn to line ce, and a point t found on this bisector that is equidistant from $c1$ and e and from the nearest point of the coast of either State. Let this point be f on the coas1t of State A.

(6) This process is continued to the desired limit of the boundary to be delimited. [Where a point on the median line is equidistant from four or more points as occasionally happens, the median line continues along the perpendicular bisector of the two points on the opposite coast furthest removed from the starting point.]

(b) *Where the Coasts Are Adjacent to Each Other*. --Figure [5-2] illustrates an application of the median-line principle to delimit the boundary through the territorial sea of two adjacent States. In this case, a point is first selected at a distance from the coast sufficient to encompass the outer limit of the territorial sea. This point should be equidistant from the nearest point on the coastline of each State. Let this point be t in the figure and a and b the nearest points to it on the coastlines of State A and B, respectively. This, by definition, is a point on the median line. Having established this initial point on the median line, other points on it are derived as follows:

(1) Draw a perpendicular bisector otp to the line ab through point t. This bisector is the median line since every point on it is equidistant from both a and b.

(2) Proceed shorewards along the median line until a point is found that is equidistant from the nearest point on the coast of either State and from points a and b. Let this point be u and the nearest point be c on the coast of State A. Hence at u, the relationship $ua=ub=uc$ exists.

(3) Draw a perpendicular bisector through u to the line cb and proceed along this bisector shorewards until a point is reached that is equidistant from points b and c and the nearest point on the coast of either State. Let this point be v and the nearest point be d on the coast of State A.

(4) Draw a perpendicular bisector through v to the line db and proceed along this bisector shorewards until a point is reached that is equidistant from points d and b and the nearest point on the coast of either State. Let this point be w and the nearest point be e on the coast of State B.

(5) Draw a perpendicular bisector through w to the line de and proceed along this bisector shorewards until a point is reached that is equidistant from points d and e and the nearest point on the coast of either State. Let this point be x and the nearest point be f on the coast of State A.

(6) This process is continued, always taking the perpendicular bisector from a point on the median line to the nearest points on the coasts of States A and B, until the boundary at the coast is reached.

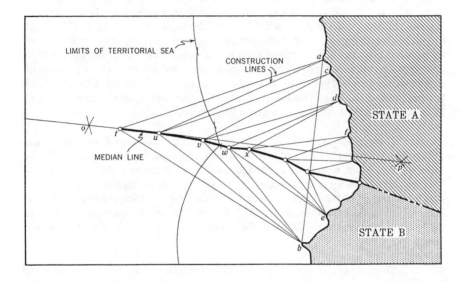

Median Line of Adjacent States
Figure 5-3

Source: Aaron L. Shalowitz, *Shore and Sea Boundaries*, Vol. 1, Washington D.C.: U.S. Government Printing Office, 1962, p. 235.

International Boundary Study, Series A, Limits in the Seas, No. 45, *Maritime Boundary: Mexico-United States*.

On November 23, 1970, the Governments of Mexico and the United States signed a treaty [Treaty to Resolve Pending Boundary Differences and Maintain the Rio Grande and Colorado River as the International Boundary, 23 U.S.T. 371; TIAS7313] for the clarification of the Rio Grande boundary and the creation of maritime boundaries between the claimed 12-nautical-mile Mexican territorial sea and the territorial sea and contiguous zone of the United States. The treaty delimits, in principle, the lines of separation in the Gulf of Mexico and the Pacific Ocean. The two governments then established the final lines which were represented, at reduced scales, on two maps affixed to the treaty....

Article V of the treaty, which delimited the maritime boundaries, states:

Article V

The Contracting States agree to establish and recognize their maritime boundaries in the Gulf of Mexico and in the Pacific Ocean in accordance with the following provisions:

A. The international maritime boundary in the Gulf of Mexico shall begin at the center of the mouth of the Rio Grande, wherever it may be located; from there it shall run in a straight line to a fixed point, at 25°57'22.18" North latitude, and 97°8'19.76" West longitude, situated approximately 2,000 feet seaward from the coast; from this fixed point the maritime boundary shall continue seaward in a straight line the delineation of which represents a practical simplification of the line drawn in accordance with the principle of equidistance established in Articles 12 and 24 of the Geneva Convention on the Territorial Sea and Contiguous Zone. This line shall extend into the Gulf of Mexico to a distance of 12 nautical miles from the baseline used for its delineation....

B. The international maritime boundary in the Pacific Ocean shall begin at the westernmost point on the mainland boundary; from there it shall run seaward on a line the delineation of which represents a practical simplification, through a series of straight lines, on the line drawn in accordance with the principle of equidistance established in Articles 12 and 24 of the Geneva Convention on the Territorial Sea and the Contiguous Zone. This line shall extend seaward to a distance of 12 nautical miles from the baselines used for its delineation along the coast of the mainland and the islands of the Contracting States. . . .

C. These maritime boundaries. . . shall permanently represent the maritime boundaries between the two Contracting States; on the south side of these boundaries the United States shall not, and on the north side of them Mexico shall not, for any purpose claim or exercise sovereignty, sovereign rights or jurisdiction over the waters, air space, or seabed and subsoil. . . .

The treaty has been ratified by both states and ratifications were exchanged in Washington, D.C. April 18, 1972.

Analysis

The Gulf of Mexico sector of the maritime boundary offers a unique solution to the problem of maritime boundaries tied to ambulatory features. The Mexico-United States terrestrial boundary reaches the sea in the Rio Grande. The river, which is subject to wide fluctuations in level and in course, is particularly susceptible to changes at its mouth. Seeking a relative degree of permanence in the maritime boundary, the two countries agreed that the point of origin would be the center of the mouth of the river, wherever it may be. The second point would be situated 2,000 feet due east of the midpoint of the river mouth at the time of the treaty (in effect at the time of the mapping of the river immediately after the signature of the document). Point one may meander with the mouth but point two will remain constant as a hinge. As a consequence, the stability of most of the boundary is assured. Finally, an equidistance boundary was constructed from the mouth of the river to the twelve-nautical mile limit measured from the respective low-water baselines and this point of intersection was chosen as the terminal point of the maritime boundary. In fact, the equidistance line did not vary to a great degree from the straight line

boundary. In fact, the equidistance line did not vary to a great degree from the straight line segment between points two and three.

The two governments, however, sought a simple limit which would be practical to administer and which would not cause difficulties for fishing craft operating with unsophisticated navigational gear. Provisions exist to establish two markers on the ground, one in each state, to assist in the visual determination of position relative to the maritime boundary. The final segment of the boundary is formed by the great circle connecting the two points. The values of the points, on the North American datum, are given on the attached maps of the boundary. The very nature of the coastline, which is smooth and gently arcuate, favored the simplification of the boundary.

The maritime boundary in the Pacific also followed the principle of equidistance but with a measure of simplification particularly near the continental shore. Full value, as basepoint, was given to the Mexican Islas los Coronados which were situated to the south of the terrestrial boundary. The maritime limit from the shore to the point where the islands began to affect the equidistant line was simplified by an equal exchange of territory. The recalculation of a "terminal" point on the line affected by the Coronados, i.e., the first point after leaving the land terminus, involved a transfer of 608,141 square meters from Mexico to the United States and 608,139 square meters from the United States to Mexico. The difference in transfers were a mere 2 square meters. (Note: The transfers, of course, apply only to the difference between the practical lateral line and the "simplified" line agreed upon in the treaty.)

The final segments of the boundary were constructed by equidistance on specially constructed large-scale charts and verified by "computer" calculations to eliminate problems due to projections and to mechanical deficiencies, e.g., width of line of chart, distortion due to instability of base map, if any, etc.

As in the Gulf of Mexico, the segments between turning points relate to the great circles which connect the points. The final point of the maritime boundary is precisely 12 nautical miles from a cape on the western side of Point Loma (California) and one on the northwest shore of the northern island of Los Coronados.

REFERENCES

(1) On the United States-Mexico treaty, see "Message from the President of the United States Transmitting the Treaty to Resolve Pending Boundary Differences and Maintain the Rio Grande and Colorado River as the International Boundary between the United States of America and the Mexican States Signed at Mexico City on November 23, 1970," 92d Cong., 1st Sess., Executive B; *Report on Treaty with Mexico Resolving Boundary Differences*, 92d Cong., 1st Sess., Executive Rept. No. 92-11 (November 19, 1971); "Boundary Treaty with Mexico Enters Into Force," *Department of State Bulletin*, Vol. 66, No. 1715 (May 8, 1972), pp. 679-680.

(2) On the subject of international lateral boundaries of the United States, see W. L. Griffin, "The Emerging Law of Ocean Space," *International Lawyer*, Vol. 1 (1967), pp. 548, 562-564; W. L. Griffin, "Delimitation of Ocean Space Boundaries between Adjacent Coastal States of the United States," in L. M. Alexander (ed.), *The Law of the Sea: International Rules and Organization for the Sea*, Kingston, R.I.: University of Rhode Island, 1969, pp. 142-155.

(3) For a historical treatment of territorial sea boundary problems, see *The Grisbadarna Case* (Norway/Sweden, 1909), *Reports of International Arbitral Awards*, Vol. 11, pp. 147-166; for a current problem, see A. M. Birken, "Gulf of Venezuela: Border Dispute," *Lawyer of the Americas*,

Vol. 6 (1974), pp. 52-68; See also M. S. McDougal & W. T. Burke, *The Public Order of the Oceans: A Contemporary International Law of the Sea*, New Haven and London: Yale University Press, 1962, pp. 428-437.

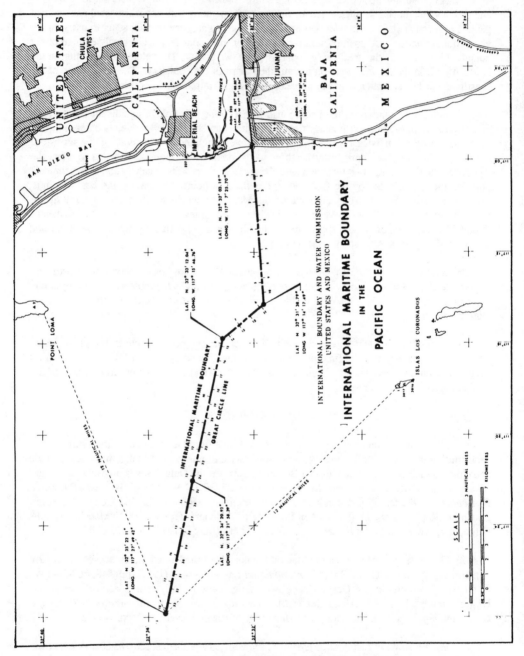

U.S.-Mexico Maritime Boundary in the Pacific Ocean
Figure 5-4

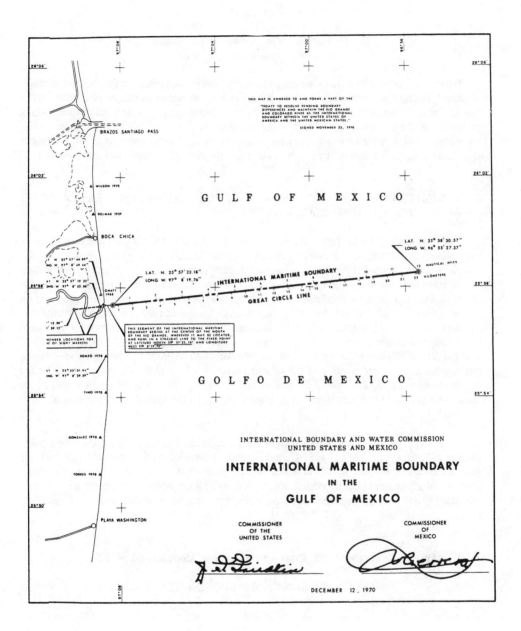

U.S.-Mexico Maritime Boundary in the Gulf of Mexico
Figure 5-5

1982 UNITED NATIONS CONVENTION ON THE LAW OF THE SEA

Article 15

Delimitation of the territorial sea between
States with opposite or adjacent coasts

Where the coasts of two states are opposite or adjacent to each other, neither of the two states is entitled, failing agreement between them to the contrary, to extend its territorial sea beyond the median line every point of which is equidistant from the nearest point on the baselines from which the breadth of the territorial seas of each of the two states is measured. The above provision does not apply, however, where it is necessary by reason of historic title or other special circumstances to delimit the territorial seas of the two states in a way which is at variance with this therewith.

C. DELIMITATION OF CONTINENTAL SHELF BETWEEN STATES WITH ADJACENT OR OPPOSITE COASTS

Some students and instructors may prefer to omit this section at this time and incorporate it when the substantive issues involved in the continental shelf are taken up in Chapter 9. If the material is to be covered at this point, a few introductory comments are in order. Under existing conventional and customary international law, coastal states possess exclusive rights to explore for and exploit the non-living natural resources (and sedentary species of living resources) located on and in the continental shelves adjacent to their coasts. Such states are entitled to erect artificial structures on their continental shelves for such purposes. The *seaward limit* of such national jurisdiction was originally provided in Article 1 of the 1958 Convention on the Continental Shelf as extending to 200 meter (about 600 feet) isobath "or. . . to where the depth of the superjacent waters admits of the exploitation of the natural resources of the said areas." The 1982 United Nations Convention on the Law of the Sea provides in Article 76 that the maximum limit of the continental shelf is 350 miles from the baseline from which the breadth of the territorial sea is measured.

Except for "rocks which cannot sustain human habitation or economic life of their own" (Article 121, paragraph 3 of the 1982 United Nations Convention on the Law of the Sea) islands generate continental shelf jurisdiction just as mainland areas do. Obviously, some difficult problems of allocation of continental shelf jurisdiction can arise where states are situated in close proximity to one another, or where an island owned by one state is situated close to the coast of another.

1.   Article 6 of the 1958 Convention on the Continental Shelf

1958 CONVENTION ON THE CONTINENTAL SHELF

Article 6

1. Where the same continental shelf is adjacent to the territories of two or more States whose coasts are opposite each other, the boundary of the continental shelf appertaining to such States shall be determined by agreement between them. In the absence of agreement, and unless another boundary line is justified buy special circumstances, the boundary is the median line, every point of which is equidistant from the nearest points of the baselines from which the breadth of the

of which is equidistant from the nearest points of the baselines from which the breadth of the territorial sea of each State is measured.

2. Where the same continental shelf is adjacent to the territories of two adjacent States, the boundary of the continental shelf shall be determined by agreement between them. In the absence of agreement, and unless another boundary line is justified by special circumstances, the boundary shall be determined by application of the principle of equidistance from the nearest points of the baselines from which the breadth of the territorial sea of each State is measured.

3. In delimiting the boundaries of the continental shelf, any lines which are drawn in accordance with the principles set out in paragraphs 1 and 2 of this article should be defined with reference to charts and geographical features as they exist at a particular date, and reference should be made to fixed permanent identifiable points of land.

INTERNATIONAL LAW COMMISSION
1956 Commentary, Draft Article 72
Yearbook of the International Law Commission,
1956, Vol. II, p. 300

(1) For the determination of the limits of the continental shelf the Commission adopted the same principles as for the articles 12 and 14 concerning the delimitation of the territorial sea. As in the case of the boundaries of their territorial sea, provision must be made for departures necessitated by any exceptional configuration of the coast, as well as the presence of islands or of navigable channels. This case may arise fairly often, so that the rule adopted is fairly elastic.

(2) There would be certain advantages in having the boundary lines marked on official large-scale charts. But as it is less important to users of such charts to have this information than to know the boundary of the territorial sea, the Commission refrained from imposing any obligation in the matter.

REFERENCES

M. M. Whiteman, "Conference on the Law of the Sea: Convention on the Continental Shelf," *American Journal of International Law,* Vol. 52 (1958), pp. 629, 648-654; J. A. C. Gutteridge, "The 1958 Geneva Convention on the Continental Shelf," *British Yearbook of International Law,* Vol. 35 (1959), pp. 102, 119-120; D. J. Padwa, "Submarine Boundaries," *International and Comparative Law Quarterly,* Vol. 9 (1960), pp. 628-653; M. M. Whiteman, *Digest of International Law,* Vol. IV, Washington D.C: U. S. Government Printing Office, 1965, pp. 903-917.

a. The 1969 North Sea Continental Shelf Cases

NORTH SEA CONTINENTAL SHELF CASES
(FEDERAL REPUBLIC OF GERMANY v. DENMARK;
FEDERAL REPUBLIC OF GERMAN v. THE NETHERLANDS)
Judgement of February 20, 1969
I.C.J. Reports, 1969, p. 3.

[Being unable to arrive at a negotiated settlement concerning their continental shelf boundaries, the nations of West Germany, Denmark, and the Netherlands agreed to submit the dispute to the International Court of Justice for guidance concerning appropriate delimitation procedures. Figure 5-6 indicates the nature of the dispute, arising principally from the concave construction of West Germany's coastline. Relevant excerpts from the Court's opinion appear below.]

5. In addition to the partial boundary lines Federal Republic/Denmark and Federal Republic/Netherlands, which. . . were respectively established by the agreements of 9 June 1965 and 1 December 1964, and which are shown as lines A-B and C-D on [Figure 5-6], another line has been drawn in this area, namely that represented by the line E-F on that map. This line, which divides areas respectively claimed (to the north of it) by Denmark, and (to the south of it) by the Netherlands, is the outcome of an agreement between those two countries dated 31 March 1966, reflecting the view taken by them as to what are the correct boundary lines between their respective continental shelf areas and that of the Federal Republic, beyond the partial boundaries A-B and C-D already drawn. These further and unagreed boundaries to seaward, are shown on [Figure 5-6] by means of the dotted lines B-E and D-E. They are the lines, the correctness of which in law the Court is in effect, though indirectly, called upon to determine. Also shown on [Figure 5-6] are the two pecked lines B-F and D-F, representing approximately the boundaries which the Federal Republic would have wished to obtain in the course of the negotiations that took place between the Federal Republic and the other two Parties prior to the submission of the matter to the Court. . . .

[The Court then held that Article 6 of the Convention on the Continental Shelf was *per se* inapplicable to the controversy because West Germany had never ratified it. Finding also that Article 6 did not reflect a customary law rule on the subject, the Court then elaborated the principles which it felt were applicable to the situation.]

42. There seems in consequence to be no necessary, and certainly no complete, identity between the notions of adjacency and proximity; and therefore, the question of which parts of the continental shelf "adjacent to" a coastline bordering more than one State fall within the appurtenance of which of them, remains to this extent an open one, not to be determined on a basis exclusively of proximity. Even if proximity may afford one of the tests to be applied and an important one in the right conditions, it may not necessarily be the only, nor in all circumstances, the most appropriate one. Hence it would seem that the notion of adjacency so constantly employed in continental shelf doctrine from the start, only implies proximity in a general sense, and does not imply any fundamental or inherent rule the ultimate effect of which would be to prohibit any State (otherwise than by agreement) from exercising continental shelf rights in respect of areas closer to the coast of another State.

43. More fundamental than the notion of proximity appears to be the principle--constantly relied upon by all the Parties - of the natural prolongation or continuation of the land territory or domain, or land sovereignty of the coastal State into and under the high seas via the bed of its territorial sea which is under the full sovereignty of that State. There are various ways of formulating this principle, but the underlying idea, namely of an extension of something already possessed, is the same, and it is this idea of extension which is, in the Court's opinion, determinant. Submarine areas do not really appertain to the coastal State because--or not only because-- they are near it. They are near it of course; but this would not suffice to confer title, any more than, according to a well-established principle of law recognized by both sides in the present case, mere proximity confers *per se* title to land territory. What confers the *ipso jure* title which international law attributes to the coastal State in respect of its continental shelf, is the fact that the submarine areas concerned may be deemed to be actually part of the territory over which the coastal State already has dominion--in the sense that, although covered with water, they are a

prolongation or continuation of that territory, an extension of it under the sea. From this it would follow that whenever a given submarine area does not constitute a natural--or the most natural-- extension of the land territory of a coastal State, even though that area may be closer to it than it is to the territory of any other State, it cannot be regarded as appertaining to that State; or at least it cannot be so regarded in the face of a competing claim by a State of whose land territory the submarine area concerned is to be regarded as a natural extension, even if it is less close to it . . . .

85. It emerges from the history of the development of the legal regime of the continental shelf, which has been reviewed earlier, that the essential reason why the equidistance method is not to be regarded as a rule of law is that, if it were to be compulsorily applied in all situations, this would not be consonant with certain basic legal notions which . . . have from the beginning reflected the *opinio juris* in the matter of delimitation; those principles being that the delimitation must be the object of agreement between the States concerned, and that such agreement must be arrived at in accordance with equitable principles. On a foundation of very general precepts of justice and good faith, actual rules of law are here involved which govern the delimitation of adjacent continental shelves--that is to say, rules binding upon States for all delimitations--in short, it is not a question of applying equity simply as a matter of abstract justice, but of applying a rule of law which itself requires the application of equitable principles, in accordance with the ideas which have always underlain the development of the legal regime of the continental shelf in this field, namely:

(a) the parties are under an obligation to enter into negotiations with a view towards arriving at an agreement and not merely to go through a formal process of negotiation as a sort of certain pre- condition for the automatic application of a certain method of delimitation in the absence of agreement; they are under an obligation to conduct themselves so that the negotiations are meaningful, which will not be the case when either of them insists upon its own position without contemplating any modification of it;

(b) the parties are under an obligation to act in such a way that, in the particular case, and taking all the circumstances into account, equitable principles are applied--for this purpose the equidistance method can be used, but other methods exist and may be employed, alone or in combination, according to the areas involved;

(c) for the reasons given in paragraphs 43 and 44, the continental shelf of any State must be the natural prolongation of its land territory and must not encroach upon what is the natural prolongation of the territory of another State.

. . . .

101. For these reasons,

THE COURT,

by eleven votes to six,

finds that, in each case,

(A) the use of the equidistance method of delimitation not being obligatory as between the Parties; and

(B) there being no other single method of delimitation the use of which is in all circumstances obligatory;

(C) the principles and rules of international law applicable to the delimitation as between the Parties of the areas of the continental shelf in the North Sea which appertain to each of them beyond the partial boundary determined by the agreements of 1 December 1964 and 9 June 1965 respectively, are as follows:

(1) delimitation is to be effected by agreement in accordance with equitable principles, and taking account of all the relevant circumstances, in such a way as to leave as much as possible to each Party all those parts of the continental shelf that constitute a natural prolongation of its land territory into and under the sea, without encroachment on the natural prolongation of the land territory of the other;

(2) if, in the application of the preceding subparagraph, the delimitation leaves to the Parties areas that overlap, these are to be divided between them in agreed proportions or, failing agreement, equally, unless they decide on a regime of joint jurisdiction, user, or exploitation of the zones of overlap or any part of them;

(D) in the course of the negotiations, the factors to be taken into account are to include:

(1) the general configuration of the coasts of the Parties, as well as the presence of any special or unusual features;

(2) so far as known or readily ascertainable, the physical and geological structure, and natural resources, of the continental shelf areas involved;

(3) the element of a reasonable degree of proportionality, which a delimitations carried out in accordance with equitable principles ought to bring about between the extent of the continental shelf areas appertaining to the coastal State and the length of its coast measured in the general direction of the coastline, account being taken for this purpose of the effects, actual or prospective, of any other continental shelf delimitations between adjacent States in the same region.

REFERENCES

J. Andrassy, "Application of the Geneva Convention, 1958, in Delimiting the Continental Shelf of the North Sea Area," *Revue Egyptienne de Droit International*, Vol. 23-24 (1967-1968), pp. 1-19; L. F. E. Goldie, "Sedentary Fisheries and the North Sea Continental Shelf Cases," *American Journal of International Law*, Vol. 63 (1969), p. 536; D. H. N. Johnson, "The North Sea Continental Shelf Cases," *International Relations* (London), Vol. 3 (1969), pp. 522-540; R. Y. Jennings, "The Limits of the Continental Shelf Jurisdiction: Some Possible Implications of the North Sea Case Judgement," *International and Comparative Law Quarterly*, Vol. 18 (1969), pp. 819-832; E. D. Brown, "The North Sea Continental Shelf Cases," *Current Legal Problems*, Vol. 23 (1970), pp. 187-215; A. D'Amato, "Manifest Intent and the Generation Treaty of Customary Rules of International Law," *American Journal of International Law*, Vol. 64 (1970), p. 892; L. F. E. Goldie, "North Sea Continental Shelf Cases - A Ray of Hope for the International Court," *New York Law Forum*, Vol. 16 (1970), pp. 325-377; E. Grisel, "The Lateral Boundaries of the Continental Shelf and the Judgement of the International Court of Justice in the North Sea Continental Shelf Cases," *American Journal of International Law*, Vol. 64 (1970), pp. 562-593; S. J. Murray, "A Discussion of the World Court's North Sea Judgment," *American University*

Law Review, Vol. 19 (1970), pp. 470-493; L. F. E. Goldie, "A Lexicographical Controversy - The Word 'Adjacent' in Article 1 of the Continental Shelf Convention," *American Journal of International Law*, Vol. 66 (1972), pp. 829-835; L. F. E. Goldie, "North Sea Continental Shelf Cases: A Postscript," *New York Law Forum*, Vol. 18(2) (Fall 1972), pp. 411-434; L. D. M. Nelson, "The North Sea Continental Shelf Cases and Law Making Conventions," *Modern Law Review*, Vol. 35 (1972), pp. 52-56; T. Rothpfeffer, "Equity in the North Sea Continental Shelf Cases; A Case Study in the Legal Reasoning of the International Court of Justice," *Nordisk Tidsskrift for International Ret*, Vol. 42 (1972), pp. 81-137; S. C. Chaturvedi, "The North Sea Continental Shelf Cases Analyzed," *Indian Journal of International Law*, Vol. 13 (1973), pp. 481-493; M. K. Nawaz," The North Sea Continental Shelf Cases Revisited," *Indian Journal of International Law*, Vol. 15 (1975), pp. 506-520: C. M. Mason (ed.), *The Effective Management of Resources: The International Politics of the North Sea*, New York: Nichols, 1979.

NOTE

Following this decision, the affected nations resumed negotiations and ultimately reached a settlement depicted by the map in Figure 5-7. See Exchange of Notes Constituting an Agreement between the Netherlands and the Federal Republic of Germany, Copenhagen, January 28, 1971 and Agreement Between the Federal Republic of Germany and Denmark Concerning the Delimitation of the Continental Shelf under the North Sea, Copenhagen, January 28, 1971, both texts in *National Legislation and Treaties Relating to the Law of the Sea*, UN Legislative Series. ST/LEG/SER.B/16, New York: The United Nations, 1974, pp. 422-424 (The Netherlands), 424-428 (Denmark).

QUESTION

Assuming that there are significant deposits of natural gas at points "A" and "B", and that the "panhandle" area is likely devoid of natural resources, why would the Federal Republic of Germany opt for the panhandle, giving Denmark and the Netherlands exclusive access to the resource deposits?

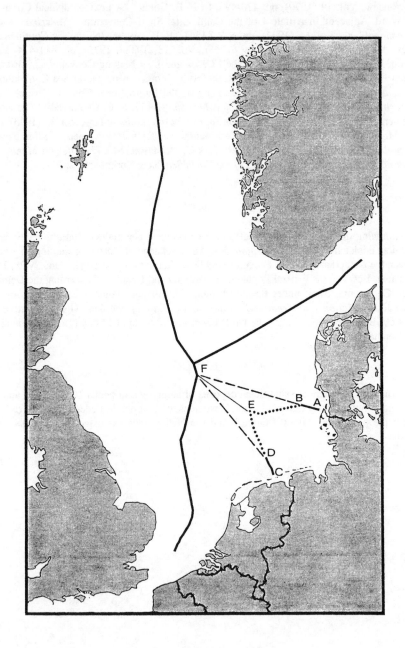

Continental Shelf Claims in North Sea
Figure 5-6

Source: *I.C.J. Reports, 1969*, p. 16.

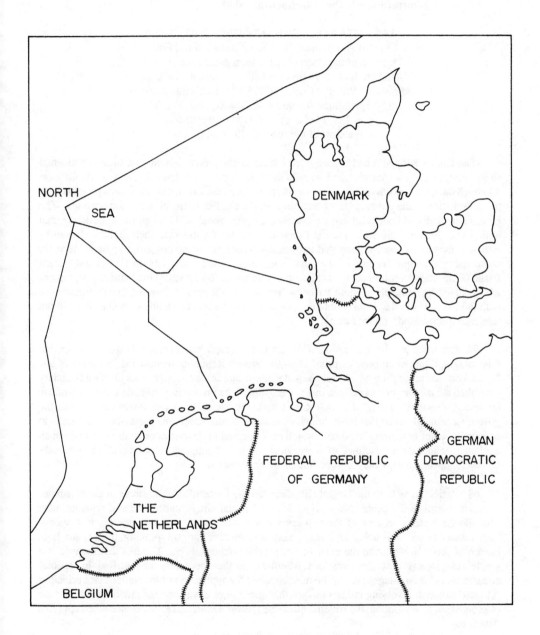

North Sea Continental Shelf Boundaries Following German-Denmark-Netherlands Settlement
Figure 5-7

Source: Based on a map drawn by The Office of the Geographer, U.S. Department of
State.

b.   **The 1977 Arbitration between the United Kingdom and France on the Delimitation of the Continental Shelf**

DELIMITATION OF THE CONTINENTAL SHELF
Court of Arbitration: The United Kingdom and France
Decision of the Court of Arbitration dated June 30, 1977
and March 14, 1978 (Interpretation). *International Legal
Materials*, Vol. 18 (1979), pp. 395-462 (Decision), 462-494
(Interpretation); *International Law Reports*, Vol. 54,
pp. 6-138 (Decision), 139-213 (Interpretation).
Excerpts of the June 30, 1977 Decision.

[The United Kingdom and France were unable to agree on a delimitation of the continental shelf between the two nations and so submitted the issue to a special Court of Arbitration. Although the Court addressed several issues in its decision, the excerpt below relates principally to the delimitation in the Atlantic Ocean area, beyond the English Channel and in the open sea. The United Kingdom had contended that the *equidistance* principle should be applied, considering that both it and France were parties to the Convention on the Continental Shelf and thus bound by Article 6 thereof. France argued that an inequity would be worked by strict application of the equidistance principle because of the relative locations of the Scilly Islands (U.K.) and Ushant Island (Fr.). The Court ultimately decided upon a variation from a strict equidistance line, but one which did use the principle of equidistance by "splitting the difference" between an equidistance line with the two sets of islands taken into consideration, on the one hand, and a similar line without reference to the islands, on the other.]

67. [I]n invoking the application of Article 6, paragraph 1, the United Kingdom claims that this paragraph places an onus of proof upon the French Republic to show the existence of any "special circumstances" on which it relies and to show that these circumstances justify a boundary other than the median line as defined by the paragraph. The French Republic, on the other hand, in contesting the applicability of Article 6 and invoking the rules of customary law, claims the governing principle to be that the delimitation must be equitable and the equidistance principle to be merely one of numerous "methods" which may in certain circumstances be used to produce an equitable delimitation. Neither of these views of the equidistance "principle" or "method," however, appears to the Court to place it in its true perspective.

68. Article 6, as both the United Kingdom and the French Republic stress in the pleadings, does not formulate the equidistance principle and "special circumstances" as two separate rules. The rule there stated in each of the two cases is a single one, a combined equidistance-special circumstances rule. This being so, it may be doubted whether, strictly speaking, there is any legal burden of proof in regard to the existence of special circumstances. The fact that the rule is a single rule means that the questions whether "another boundary is justified by special circumstances" is an integral part of the rule providing for application of the equidistance principle. As such, although involving matters of fact, that question is, always one of law of which, in case of submission to arbitration, the tribunal must itself, *propio motu*, take cognisance when applying Article 6.

69. It also follows that the relevance of "special circumstances" in the application of Article 6 does not depend on a claim to invoke special circumstances having been advanced by the interested State when ratifying or acceding to the Convention. . . . Clearly this feature of Article 6 further underlines the full liberty of the Court in appreciating the geographical and other circumstances relevant to the determination of the continental shelf boundary, and at the same time reduces the

possibility of any difference in the appreciation of these circumstances under Article 6 and customary law.

70. The Court does not overlook that under Article 6 the equidistance principle ultimately possesses an obligatory force which it does not have in the same measure under the rules of customary law; for Article 6 makes the application of the equidistance principle a matter of treaty obligation for Parties to the Convention. But the combined character of the equidistance-special circumstances rule means that the obligation to apply the equidistance principle is always one qualified by the condition "unless another boundary line is justified by special circum-stances." Moreover, the *travaux preparatoires* of Article 6, in the International Law Commission and at the Geneva Conference of 1958, show that this condition was introduced into paragraphs 1 and 2 of the Article because it was recognized that, owing to particular geographical features or configurations, application of the equidistance principle might not infrequently result in an unreasonable or inequitable delimitation of the continental shelf. In short, the role of the "special circumstances" condition in Article 6 is to ensure an equitable delimitation; and the combined "equidistance-special circumstances rule," in effect, gives particular expression to a general norm that, failing agreement, the boundary between States abutting on the same continental shelf is to be determined on equitable principles. In addition, Article 6 neither defines "special circumstances" nor lays down the criterion by which it is to be assessed whether any given circumstances justify a boundary line other than the equidistance line. Consequently, even under Article 6 the question whether the use of the equidistance principle or some other method is appropriate for achieving an equitable delimitation is very much a matter of appreciation in the light of the geographical and other circumstances. In other words, even under Article 6 it is the geographical and other circumstances of any given case which indicate and justify the use of the equidistance method as the means of achieving an equitable solution rather than the inherent quality of the method as a legal norm of delimitation.

. . . .

75. [T]he Court considers that Article 6 is applicable, in principle, to the delimitation of the continental shelf as between the Parties under the Arbitration Agreement. This does not, however, mean that the Court considers the rules of customary law discussed in the judgment in the *North Sea Continental Shelf* cases to be inapplicable in the present case. As already pointed out, the provisions of Article 6 do not define the conditions for the application of the equidistance-special circumstances rule and the rules of customary law have the same object -- the delimitation of the boundary in accordance with equitable principles. In the view of this Court, therefore, the rules of customary law are a relevant and even essential means both for interpreting and completing the provisions of Article 6. Indeed, the Court observes that in the present case, whether discussing the application of Article 6 or the position under customary law, both parties have had free recourse to pronouncements of the International Court of Justice regarding the rules of customary law applicable in the matter. . .

. . . .

239. In the situation where the coasts of the two states are opposite each other, the median line will normally affect a broadly equal and equitable delimitation. But this is simply because of the geometrical effects of applying the equidistance principle to an area of continental shelf which, in fact, lies between coasts that face each other across that continental shelf. In short, the equitable character of the delimitation results not from the *legal* designation of the situation as one of "opposite" States *but from its actual geographical character as such.* Similarly, in the case of "adjacent" states it is the lateral geographical relationship of the two coasts, when combined with a large extension of the continental shelf seawards from those coasts, which makes individual geographical features on either coast more prone to render the geometrical effects of applying the

equi-distance principle inequitable than in the case of "opposite" States. The greater risk in these cases that the equidistance method may produce an inequitable delimitation thus also results not from the *legal* designation of the situation as one of "adjacent" States but *from its actual geographical character as one involving laterally related coasts.*

. . . .

244. The projection of the Cornish peninsula and the Isles of Scilly, further seawards into the Atlantic Ocean than the Brittany peninsula and the island of Ushant, is a geographical fact, a fact of nature; and, as was observed in the *North Sea Continental Shelf* cases, there is no question of equity "completely refashioning nature" or "totally refashioning geography." It may also be urged that the very fact of the projection of the United Kingdom land mass further into the Atlantic Ocean region has the natural consequence of rendering greater areas of continental shelf appurtenant to it. Nevertheless, when account is taken of the fact that in other respects the two States abut on the same continental shelf with coasts not markedly different in extent and broadly similar in their relation to that shelf, a question arises as to whether giving full effect to the Scilly Isles in delimiting an equidistance boundary out to the 1,000-meter isobath may not distort the boundary and have disproportionate effects as between the two States. In the view of the Court, the further projection westwards of the Scilly Isles, when superadded to the greater projection of the Cornish mainland westwards beyond Finistere, is of much the same nature for present purposes, and has much the same tendency to distortion of the equidistance line, as the projection of an exceptionally promontory, which is generally recognized to be one of the potential forms of "special circumstances." In the present instance, the Court considers that the additional projection of the Scilly Isles into the Atlantic region does constitute an element of distortion which is material enough to justify the delimitation of a boundary other than the strict median line envisaged in Article 6, paragraph 1, of the Convention.

245. The Court thus recognized that the position of the Scilly Isles west-south-west of the Cornish peninsula constitutes a "special circumstance" justifying a boundary other than the strict median line. It does not, however, consider that the existence of this "special circumstance" in the Atlantic region gives it carte blanche to employ any method that it chooses in order to effect an equitable delimitation of the continental shelf. The French Republic, it is true, has impressed upon this Court certain observations in the Judgement in the *North Sea Continental Shelf* cases to the effect that, in order to achieve an equitable solution, "it is necessary to seek, not one method of delimitation but one goal," and that "there is no legal limit to the considerations which States may take account of for the purpose of making sure that they apply equitable procedures." But in those cases the Parties had retained the actual delimitation of the boundary in their own hands for further negotiation in the light of the principles and rules to be stated by the International Court of Justice; and in any event the observations invoked by the French Republic have to be read in the light of certain other observations of the International Court in the same Judgment. In these other observations, it was stressed that any recourse to equitable considerations must be to considerations "lying not outside but within the rules" of law, and that there is no question of any decision that *ex aequo et bono*; and, as already noted, it was also stressed that "there can never be any question of completely refashioning nature." Furthermore, at the outset of the Judgment it was underlined that delimitation of the continental shelf is not a process of dividing it up into equitable "shares" but of delimiting a boundary in areas which, in principle, already appurtenant to one or other State; and that the notion of "the just and equitable share" is wholly at variance with the fundamental principle that the continental shelf appertains to the coastal State as the natural prolongation of its land territory.

246. The "equitable" method of delimitation which is advocated by the French Republic, and which invokes a median line delimited by reference to prolongation of the general directions of the

Channel coasts of the two countries, does not appear to the Court to be one that is compatible with the legal regime of the continental shelf. It detaches the delimitation almost completely from the coasts which actually abut on the continental shelf of the Atlantic region, and is thus not easily reconciled with the fundamental principle that the continental shelf constitutes the natural prolongation of a State's territory under the sea. In so far as that method may have relation to the respective land masses of the Parties, it is not apparent why the general directions of their Channel coasts alone should be considered to represent either the totality or any particular part of their land masses. In addition, there appears to be a radical inconsistency in the French Republic's recourse to the general directions of the two Channel coasts as the criterion for delimiting the continental shelf of the Atlantic region. In the pleadings, the French Republic has insisted that the coasts of the two countries within the Channel are irrelevant for the purpose of determining whether the situation in the Atlantic region is one of "opposite" States, for which a median line delimitation is indicated both by Article 6, paragraph 1 of the Convention and by customary law unless another boundary is justified by special circumstances. It is not, therefore, obvious how or why the coasts within the Channel should, on the contrary, acquire an absolute relevance in determining the course of the boundary itself in the Atlantic region. Nor is this inconsistency removed by invoking an alleged principle of proportionality by reference to length of coastlines; for use of the Channel, rather than the Atlantic, coastlines is still left unexplained. Moreover, as the Court has already stated in paragraphs 95-98, "proportionality" is not in itself a source of title to the continental shelf, but rather a criterion for evaluating the equities of certain geographical situations.

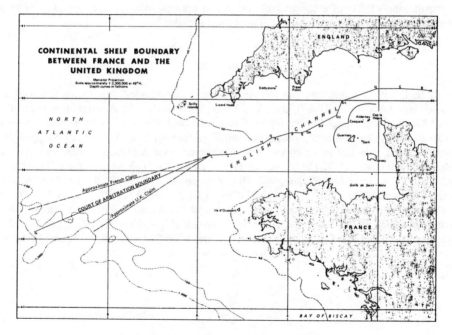

Anglo-French Continental Shelf Boundaries
Figure 5-8

Source: L.A. Willis, "From Precedent to Precedent: The Triumph of Pragmatism in the Law of Maritime Boundaries," *Canadian Yearbook of International Law*, Vol. XXIV (1986), p. 11. Reprinted by permission of the University of British Columbia Press and Professor C.B. Bourne, Editor-in-Chief of the *Yearbook*.

247. The Court, for the above reasons, finds itself unable to accept the prolongations of the general directions of the Channel coasts of the two countries as a relevant basis for determining the course of the boundary in the Atlantic region. . . .

. . . .

249. The Court notes that in a large proportion of the delimitations known to it, where a particular geographical feature has influenced the course of a continental shelf boundary, the method of delimitation adopted has been some modification or variant of the equidistance principle rather than its total rejection. In the present instance, the problem also arises precisely from the distorting effect of a geographical feature in circumstances in which the line equidistant from the coasts of the two States would otherwise constitute the appropriate boundary. Consequently, it seems to the Court to be in accord not only with legal rules governing the continental shelf but also with State practice to seek the solution in a method modifying or varying the equidistance method rather than to have recourse to a wholly different criterion of delimitation. The appropriate method, in the opinion of the Court, is to take account of the Scilly Isles as part of the coastline of the United Kingdom but to give them less than their full effect in applying the equidistance method. Just as it is not the function of the equity in the delimitation of the continental shelf completely to refashion geography, so it is also not the function of equity to create a situation of complete equity where nature and geography have established an inequity. Equity does not, therefore call for coasts, the relation of which to the continental shelf is not equal, to be treated as having completely equal effects. What equity calls for is an appropriate abatement of the disproportionate effects of a considerable projection onto the Atlantic continental shelf of a somewhat attenuated portion of the coast of the United Kingdom.

. . . .

REFERENCES

K. B. Berry, "Delimitation and the Anglo-French Arbitration," *Australian Yearbook of International Law*, Vol. 6 (1987), pp. 139-152; D. W. Bowett, "The Arbitration between the United Kingdom and France Concerning the Continental Shelf Boundary in the English Channel and South-Western Approaches," *British Yearbook of International Law*, Vol. 49 (1978), pp. 1-29; David A Colson, "The United Kingdom-France Continental Shelf Arbitration," *American Journal of International Law*, Vol. 72 (1978), pp. 95-112; E. D. Brown, "The Anglo-French Continental Shelf Case," *San Diego Law Review*, Vol. 16 (1979), pp. 461-530; E. D. Brown, "The Anglo-French Continental Shelf Case," *Yearbook of World Affairs*, Vol. 33 (1979), pp. 304-327; David A. Colson, "The United Kingdom-France Continental Shelf Case Arbitration: Interpretive Decision of March, 1978," *American Journal of International Law*, Vol. 73 (1979), pp. 112-120; J. G. Merrills, "The United Kingdom-France Continental Shelf Arbitration," *California Western International Law Journal*, Vol. 10 (1980), pp. 314-364.

2.   **Article 83, Paragraph 1, of the 1982 United Nations Convention on the Law of the Sea**

a. **Legislative History of Article 83, Paragraph 1**

Hungdah Chiu, "Some Problems Concerning the Application of the Maritime Boundary Delimitation Provisions of the 1982 United Nations Convention on the Law of the Sea Between Adjacent or Opposite States," *Maryland Journal of International Law and Trade*, Vol. 9 (1985), pp. 4-6. Notes omitted. Reprinted by permission.

Articles 74 and 83 . . . were subject to lengthy debate at UN CLOS III. The Conference ultimately took the position that these articles' principles for delimitation of the continental shelf and exclusive economic zone (EEZ) should be the same. One group of countries had favored drawing the line equidistant from the two shorelines in question, although many of these countries contended that "special circumstances" might justify another method. Another group had wished to emphasize "equitable principles" and "relevant circumstances." The Draft Conventions on the Law of the Sea (Informal Text) issued by the President of the Conference on September 22, 1980 provides that the delimitation of maritime boundaries of the economic zone and the continental shelf between adjacent or opposite countries "shall be effected by agreement in conformity with international Law" and "such an agreement shall be in accordance with equitable principles, employing the median or equidistance line, where appropriate, and taking account of all circumstances prevailing in the area concerned."

Among the countries that favored the 1980 draft arrangement were Canada, Costa Rica, Cyprus, Democratic Yemen, Denmark, the Dominican Republic, Ethiopia, Greece, Ireland, Italy, Japan, Malaysia, Nigeria, Norway, Oman, Portugal, the Republic of Korea, Sao Tome and Principe, Spain, Sweden, the USSR, the United Arab Emirates and the United Kingdom. New Zealand favored an earlier formula presented at the informal negotiation referring to equitable principles and citing the median line as one method to be employed in appropriate cases. Kuwait and Peru also endorsed the equidistance principle.

Some of those states emphasizing "equitable principles" regarded the 1980 draft provision on delimitation as unacceptable. Among them were Algeria, Argentina, the People's Republic of China, Democratic Kampuchea, Ireland, Kenya, Libya, Mali, Morocco, Nicaragua, Poland, Romania, Senegal, Somalia, Surinam, Syria, Turkey, and Venezuela. They argued that delimitation should be based on agreement between the states concerned and the application of equitable principles, taking into account all circumstances, and without prejudicing the methods to be utilized. Some of them added first, that the text in the draft convention used terms such as "relevant circumstances" that were open to misunderstanding and would not help to avoid disputes, and secondly, that it was legally invalid, since delimitation criteria already existed in international law. Also favoring an emphasis on equitable principles were Bangladesh, Dominica, the Ivory Coast, Mozambique, Vietnam and Zaire.

In an effort to remove the deadlock over the question, the President of the Conference, Tommy T. K. Koh of Singapore, submitted a new compromise proposal at the Resumed Tenth Session in August 1981 which was finally accepted by the Conference and became articles 74 and 83 of the Convention. Article 74 provides:

The delimitation of the exclusive economic zone between states with opposite or adjacent coasts shall be effected by agreement on the basis of international law, as referred to in

Article 38 of the Statute of the International Court of Justice, in order to achieve an equitable solution.

Article 83 uses the same language as article 74 to deal with the delimitation of "continental shelves."

This compromise proposal was acceptable to the group in favor of subscribing to "equitable principles" in resolving maritime boundary disputes because it omitted the reference to the equidistance or median rule in the text. According to this group, in the 1969 *North Sea Continental Shelf* cases, the International Court of Justice (ICJ) referred to "equitable principles" as the rule for delimitation. Thus, the reference to article 38 of the Statute of the International Court of Justice appears to support this group's view because the Court's decision is at least a subsidiary means for the determination of rules of international law. On the other hand, the text only referred to the broad phrase "equitable solution" and not to "equitable principles" so that it is also acceptable to the group in favor of the equidistance or median rule. . . the need to compromise by adopting these two general articles relating to maritime boundary delimitation resulted in insufficiently clear guidelines for resolving various delimitation issues.

REFERENCES

Hollis D. Hedberg, "A Critique of Boundary Provisions on the Law of the Sea," *Ocean Development and International Law*, Vol. 12 (1983), pp. 337-342; Paul Bravender-Coyle, "The Emerging Legal Principles and Equitable Criteria Governing the Delimitation of Maritime Boundaries Between States," *Ocean Development and International Law*, Vol. 19 (1988), pp. 171-228; Malcolm D. Evans, *Relevant Circumstances and Maritime Delimitation*, New York: Oxford University Press, 1989.

b.   1982 Case Concerning the Continental Shelf between Tunisia and Libya and 1985 Interpretation

CASE CONCERNING THE CONTINENTAL SHELF
(TUNISIA/LIBYAN ARAB JAMAHIRIYA)
JUDGMENT of February 24, 1982
I.C.J. Reports, 1982, p. 18.

[Under a Special Agreement concluded on June 10, 1977 between Tunisia and Libya, the Court was requested to declare what principles and rules of international law might be applied for the delimitation of each Party's continental shelf and to clarify the practical method of their application. Article 1, paragraph 1 of the Agreement specifically requests the Court, in rendering its decision, to take account of the following three factors: (a) equitable principles; (b) the relevant circumstances which characterize the area; and (c) new accepted trends in the Third United Nations Conference on the Law of the Sea.]

19. The Republic of Tunisia (hereinafter called "Tunisia") and the Socialist People's Libyan Arab Jamahiriya (hereinafter called "Libya") are both situated on the northern coastline of the African continent, fronting on the Mediterranean Sea. The more westerly of the two States is Tunisia, lying approximately between 30°N and 38°N and between 7°E and 12°E. To the east and south-east of it lies Libya, approximately between 19°N and 34°N and between 9°E and 25°E. The eastern coast of Tunisia more or less coincides with the western end of a roughly rectangular indentation, longer from west to east than its depth from north to south, in the northern coastline

of Africa, the eastern end of which is constituted by the Gulf of Sirt on the Libyan coast. Thus not far west of the point (Ras Ajdir) at which the land frontier between Libya and Tunisia commences on the sea coast, there is a change in the direction of the coastline. If one follows the coast of Libya towards Tunisia, for some distance before and after the frontier point, the general line of the coast is somewhat north of west; beyond the frontier point, after passing the island of Jerba, one enters the concavity of the Gulf of Gabes, which leads round to a length of coastline running roughly north-east to Ras Kaboudia. Then follows the Gulf of Hammamet, the protrusion (roughly north-eastwards) of Cape of Bon, and the Gulf of Tunis, before the final section of the Tunisian coast, which runs again somewhat north of west, though some four degrees of latitude further to the north than the coast on each side of Ras Ajdir. . . .

44. Both parties to the present case have in effect based their argument upon the idea that because a delimitation should, in accordance with the Judgment in the *North Sea Continental Shelf* cases, leave to each Party "all those parts of the continental shelf that constitute a natural prolongation of its land territory into and under the sea" (I. C. J. Reports 1969, p. 53, para. 101(c) (I)), therefore the determination of what constitutes such natural prolongation will produce a correct delimitation. The Court in 1969 did not regard an equitable delimitation and a determination of the limits of "natural prolongation" as synonymous, since in the operative clause of its Judgment, just quoted, it referred only to the delimitation being affected in such a way as to leave "as much as possible" to each Party the shelf areas constituting its natural prolongation. The Court also clearly distinguished between a principle which affords the justification for the appurtenance of an area to a State and a rule for determining the extent and limits of such area: "the appurtenance of a given area, considered as an entity, in no way governs the precise delimitation of its boundaries" (I. C. J. Reports 1969,p. 32, para. 46). The Court is therefore unable to accept the contention of Libya that "once the natural prolongation of a State is determined, delimitation becomes a simple matter of complying with the dictates of nature". It would be a mistake to suppose that it will in all cases, or even in the majority of them, be possible or appropriate to establish that the natural prolongation of one State extends, in relation to the natural prolongation of another State, just so far and no farther, so that the two prolongations meet along an easily defined line. Nor can the Court approve the argument of Tunisia that the satisfying of equitable principles in a particular geographical situation is just as much a part of the process of the identification of the natural prolongation as the identification of the natural prolongation is necessary to satisfy equitable principles. The satisfaction of equitable principles is, in the delimitation process, of cardinal importance, as the Court will show later in the Judgment, and identification of natural prolongation may, where the geographical circumstances are appropriate, have an important role to play in defining an equitable delimitation, in view of its significance as the justification of continental shelf rights in some cases; but the two considerations--the satisfying of equitable principles and the identification of the natural prolongation--are not to be placed on a plane of equality. . . .

45. Since the Court gave judgment in the *North Sea Continental Shelf* cases, a period has elapsed during which there has been much State practice in this field of international law, and it has been under very close review, particularly in the context of the Third United Nations Conference on the Law of the Sea. The term "natural prolongation" has now made its appearance in Article 76 of the draft convention on the Law of the Sea. At this point, the Court must thus turn to the question whether principles and rules of international law applicable to the delimitation may be derived from, or may be affected by the "new accepted trends" which have emerged at the Third United Nations Conference on the Law of the Sea. . . .

47. Article 76 and Article 83 of the draft convention are the provisions of the draft convention prepared by the Conference which may be relevant as incorporating new accepted trends to be taken

prepared by the Conference which may be relevant as incorporating new accepted trends to be taken into account in the present case. According to Article 76, paragraph 1,

> "the continental shelf of a coastal State comprises the sea-bed and subsoil of the submarine areas that extend beyond its territorial sea throughout the natural prolongation of its land territory to the outer edge of the continental margin, or to a distance of 200 nautical miles from the baselines from which the breadth of the territorial sea is measured where the outer edge of the continental margin does not extend up to that distance."

Paragraphs 2 to 9 of the Article, which deal with details of the outer limits of the continental shelf, can be disregarded for the purposes of the present Judgment. While paragraph 10 states that the provisions of the Article "are without prejudice to the question of delimitation of the continental shelf between States with opposite or adjacent coasts", the definition given in paragraph 1 cannot be ignored. That definition consists of two parts, employing different criteria. According to the first part of paragraph 1 the natural prolongation of the land territory is the main criterion. In the second part of the paragraph, the distance of 200 nautical miles is in certain circumstances the basis of the title of a coastal State. The legal concept of the continental shelf as based on the "species of platform" has thus been modified by this criterion. The definition of Article 76, paragraph 1, also discards the exploitability test which is an element in the definition of the Geneva Convention of 1958.

48. The principle that the natural prolongation of the coastal State is a basis of its legal title to continental shelf rights does not in the present case . . . necessarily provide criteria applicable to the delimitation of the areas appertaining to adjacent States. In so far as Article 76, paragraph 1, of the draft convention repeats this principle, it introduces no new element and does not therefore call for further consideration. In so far however as the paragraph provides that in certain circumstances the distance from the baseline, measured on the surface of the sea, is the basis for the title of the coastal State, it departs from the principle that natural prolongation is the sole basis of the title. The question therefore arises whether the concept of the continental shelf as contained in the second part of the definition is relevant to the decision of the present case. It is only the legal basis of the title to continental shelf rights - the mere distance from the coast - which can be taken into account as possibly having consequences for the claims of the Parties. Both Parties rely on the principle of natural prolongation: they have not advanced any argument based on the "trend" towards the distance principle. The definition in Article 76, paragraph 1, therefore affords no criterion for delimitation in the present case.

49. With regard to the delimitation of the continental shelf between States with opposite or adjacent coasts, Article 83, paragraph 1, of the Informal Composite Negotiating Test of the Third United Nations Conference on the Law of the Sea (A/CONF.62/ WP.10/Rev.2) provided that:

> "The delimitation of the continental shelf between States with opposite or adjacent coasts shall be effected by agreement in conformity with international law. Such an agreement shall be in accordance with equitable principles, employing the median line or equidistance line, where appropriate, and taking account of all circumstances prevailing in the area concerned."

But, on 28 August 1981, the President of the Conference presented to the Conference in Geneva the following proposal to replace Article 83, paragraph 1:

"The delimitation of the continental shelf between States with opposite or adjacent coasts shall be effected by agreement on the basis of international law, as referred to in Article 38 of the Statute of the International Court of Justice, in order to achieve an equitable solution."

In accordance with the decision taken by the Conference, this proposal has now acquired the status of part of the official draft convention before the Conference.

50. In the new text, any indication of a specific criterion which could give guidance to the interested States in their effort to achieve an equitable solution has been excluded. Emphasis is placed on the equitable solution which has to be achieved. The principles and rules applicable to the delimitation of continental shelf areas are those which are appropriate to bring about an equitable result; this is a matter which the Court will have to consider further at a later stage. For the present, the Court notes that the new text does not affect the role of the concept of natural prolongation in this domain. . . .

67. The submarine area of the Pelagian Block which constitutes the natural prolongation of Libya substantially coincides with an area which constitutes the natural submarine extension of Tunisia. Which parts of the submarine area appertain to Libya and which to Tunisia can therefore not be determined by criteria provided by a determination of how far the natural prolongation of one of the Parties extends in relation to the natural prolongation of the other. In the present case, in which Libya and Tunisia both derive continental shelf title from a natural prolongation common to both territories the ascertainment of the extent of the areas of shelf appertaining to each State must be governed by criteria of international law other than those taken from physical features. . .
.

75. Nevertheless, for the purpose of shelf delimitation between the Parties, it is not the whole of the coast of each Party which can be taken into account; the submarine extension of any part of the coast of one Party, which, because of its geographic situation, cannot overlap with the extension of the coast of the other, is to be excluded from further consideration by the Court. It is clear from the map that there comes a point on the coast of each of the two Parties beyond which the coast in question no longer has a relationship with the coast of the other Party relevant for submarine delimitation. The sea-bed areas off the coast beyond that point cannot therefore constitute an area of overlap of the extensions of the territories of the two Parties, and are therefore not relevant to the delimitation. In the view of the Court, in the present context that point on the Tunisian coast is Ras Kaboudia; on the Libyan coast it is Ras Tajoura. The Court cannot, therefore, take into consideration such parts of the sea-bed of the Pelagian Block as lie beyond those points. As for the boundaries to seaward of the area relevant for the delimitation, these are not at present material and will be considered only in relation to the criterion of proportionality, for the purposes of which such boundaries will have to be defined. The conclusion that these areas are not legally relevant to the delimitation between the Parties does not however lead to the conclusion by way of corollary that the whole area bounded by the coasts of both countries and by such seaward boundaries is reserved in its entirety for division between Libya and Tunisia. As mentioned above, the rights of other States bordering on the Pelagian Sea which may be claimed in the northern and north-eastern parts of that area must not be prejudged by the decision in the present case. . . .

81. The "relevant circumstances which characterize the area" are not limited to the facts of geography or geomorphology, either as a matter of interpretation of the Special Agreement or in application of the equitable principle requiring all relevant circumstances to be taken into account.

Apart from the circumstances of the existence and interests of other States in the area, and the existing or potential delimitation between each of the Parties and such States, there is also the position of the land frontier, or more precisely the position of its intersection with the coastline, to be taken into account. . . .

104. In the circumstances of the present case, the Court is not convinced by the Tunisian contention that the areas of internal and territorial waters must be excluded from consideration; but in so finding it is not making any ruling as to the validity or opposability to Libya of the straight baselines. It should be reaffirmed that the continental shelf, in the legal sense, does not include the sea-bed areas below territorial and internal waters, but the question is not one of definition, but of proportionality as a function of equity. The fact that a given area is territorial sea or internal waters does not mean that the coastal State does not enjoy "sovereign rights for the purpose of exploring it and exploiting its natural resources"; it enjoys those rights and more, by virtue of its full sovereignty over that area. Furthermore, the element of proportionality is related to lengths of the coasts of the States concerned, not to straight baselines drawn round those coasts. The question raised by Tunisia: "how could the equitable character of delimitation of the continental shelf be determined by reference to the degree of proportionality between areas which are not the subject of that delimitation?" is beside the point; since it is a question of proportionality, the only absolute requirement of equity is that one should compare like with like. If the shelf areas below the low-water mark of the relevant coasts of Libya are compared with those around the relevant coasts of Tunisia, the resultant comparison will, in the view of the Court, make it possible to determine the equitable character of a line of delimitation. . . .

106. In their pleadings, as well as in their oral arguments, both Parties appear to have set so much store by economic factors in the delimitation process that the Court considers it necessary here to comment on the subject. Tunisia seems to have invoked economic considerations in two ways: firstly, by drawing attention to its relative poverty vis-a-vis Libya in terms of absence of natural resources like agriculture and minerals, compared with relative abundance in Libya, especially of oil and gas wealth as well as agricultural resources; secondly, by pointing out that fishing resources derived from its claimed "historic rights" and "historic waters" areas must necessarily be taken into account as supplementing its national economy in eking out its survival as a country. For its part, Libya strenuously argues that, in view of its invocation of geology as an indispensable attribute of its view of "natural prolongation", the presence or absence of oil or gas in the oil-wells in the continental shelf areas appertaining to either Party should play an important part in the delimitation process. Otherwise, Libya dismisses as irrelevant Tunisia's argument in favor of economic poverty as a factor of delimitation on any other grounds.

107. The Court is, however, of the view that these economic considerations cannot be taken into account for the delimitation of the continental shelf areas appertaining to each Party. They are virtually extraneous factors since they are variables which unpredictable national fortune or calamity, as the case may be, might at any time cause to tilt the scale one way or the other. A country might be poor today and become rich tomorrow as a result of an event such as the discovery of a valuable economic resource. As to the presence of oil-wells in an area to be delimited, it may, depending on the facts, be an element to be taken into account in the process of weighing all relevant factors to achieve an equitable result. . . .

110. Nor does the Court consider that it is in the present case required, as a first step, to examine the effects of a delimitation by application of the equidistance method, and to reject that method in favor of some other only if it considers the results of an equidistance line to be inequitable. A finding by the Court in favor of a delimitation by an equidistance line could only be based on considerations derived from an evaluation and balancing up of all relevant

circumstances, since equidistance is not, in the view of the Court, either a mandatory legal principle, or a method having some privileged status in relation to other methods. It is to be noted that in the present case Tunisia, having previously argued in favor of a delimitation by the equidistance method for at least some of the area in dispute, contended in its Memorial that the result of using that method would be inequitable to Tunisia; and that Libya has made a formal submission to the effect that in the present case the equidistance method would result in an inequitable delimitation. The Court must take this firmly expressed view of the Parties into account. If however the Court were to arrive at the conclusion, after having evaluated all relevant circumstances, that an equidistance line would bring about an equitable solution of the dispute, there would be nothing to prevent it from so finding even though the Parties have discarded the equidistance method. But if that evaluation leads the Court to an equitable delimitation on a different basis, there is no need for it to give any further consideration to equidistance.

111. The Parties recognize that in international law there is no single obligatory method of delimitation and that several methods may be applied to one and the same delimitation. . . .

122. The most evident geographical feature of the coastlines fronting on the area of the shelf relevant for the delimitation is the radical change in the general direction of the Tunisian coastline marked by the Gulf of Gabes; and clearly no delimitation of the continental shelf in front of the coasts of the Parties could be regarded as equitable which failed to take account of that feature. . . .

128. The general change in direction of the Tunisian coast may, in the view of the Court, be regarded as expressed in a line drawn from the most westerly point of the Gulf of Gabes. . . . to Ras Kaboudia, and the Court notes that the bearing of this line is approximately 42° to the meridian. To the east of this line, however, lie the Kerkennah Islands, surrounded by islets and low-tide elevations, and constituting by their size and position a circumstance relevant for the delimitation, and to which the Court must therefore attribute some effect. The area of the islands is some 180 square kilometers; they lie some 11 miles east of the town of Sfax, separated from the mainland by an area in which the water reaches a depth of more than four metres only in certain channels and trenches. Shoals and low-tide elevations also extend on the seaward side of the islands themselves, which are surrounded by a belt of them varying from 9 to 27 kilometers in width. In these geographical circumstances, the Court has to take into account not only the islands, but also the low-tide elevations which, while they do not, as do islands, have any continental shelf of their own, do enjoy some recognition in international law for certain purposes, as is shown by the 1958 Geneva Conventions as well as the draft convention on the Law of the Sea. It is not easy to define what would be the inclination of a line drawn from the most westerly point of the Gulf of Gabes to seaward of the Kerkennah Islands so as to take account of the low-tide elevations to seaward of them; but a line drawn from that point along the seaward coast of the actual islands would clearly run a bearing of approximately 62° to the meridian. However, the Court considers that to cause the delimitation line to veer even as far as to 62°, to run parallel to the island coastline would, in the circumstances of the case, amount to giving excessive weight to the Kerkennahs.

129. The Court would recall however that a number of examples are to be found in State practice of delimitations in which only partial effect has been given to islands situated close to the coast; the method adopted has varied in response to the varying geographical and other circumstances of the particular case. One possible technique for this purpose, in the context of a geometrical method of delimitation", is that of the "half-effect" or "half-angle". Briefly, the technique involves drawing two delimitation lines, one giving to the island the full effect attributed to it by the delimitation method in use, and the other disregarding the island totally, as though it did not exist. The delimitation line actually adopted is then drawn between the first two lines,

either in such a way as to divide equally the area between them, or as bisector of the angle which they make with each other, or possibly by treating the island as displaced toward the mainland by half its actual distance therefrom. Taking into account the position of the Kerkennah Islands, and the low-tide elevations around them, the Court considers that it should go so far as to attribute to the Islands a "half-effect" of a similar kind. On this basis the delimitation line, seawards of the parallel of the most westerly point of the Gulf of Gabes, is to be parallel to a line drawn from that point bisecting the angle between the line of the Tunisian coast (42°) and the line along the seaward coast of the Kerkennah Islands (62°), that is to say at an angle of 52° to the meridian. For illustrative purposes only, and without prejudice to the role of the experts in determining the line with exactness, [Figure 5-10] is attached, which reflects the Court's approach. . . .

131. The Court notes that the length of the coast of Libya from Ras Tajourna to Ras Ajdir, measured along the coastline without taking account of small inlets, creeks, and lagoons, is approximately 185 kilometres, the length of the coast of Tunisia from Ras Adjir to Ras Kabouria, measured in a similar way, and treating the island of Jerba as though it were a promontory, is approximately 420 kilometers. Thus the relevant coastline of Libya stands in the proportion of approximately 31:69 to the relevant coastline of Tunisia. It notes further that the coastal front of Libya represented by a straight line drawn from Ras Tajourna to Ras Ajdir, stands in the proportion of approximately 34:66 to the sum of the two Tunisian coastal fronts represented by a straight line drawn from the Ras Kaboudia to the most westerly point of the Gulf of Gabes, and a second straight line from that point to Ras Ajdir. With regard to sea-bed areas, it notes that the areas of shelf below low-water mark within the area relevant for delimitation appertaining to each State following the method indicated by the Court stand to each other in approximately the proportion: Libya 40; Tunisia 60. This result, taking into account all the relevant circumstances, seems to the Court to meet the requirements of the test of proportionality as an aspect of equity.

NOTE

On July 27, 1984, Tunisia submitted to the International Court of Justice an Application for the revision and interpretation of the Judgment of February 24, 1982. The Court rendered its judgment on December 10, 1985. The opinion of the Court does not affect the international law principles stated in the 1982 Court's Judgement. See Application for Revision and Interpretation of the Judgement of 24 February 1982 in the Case concerning the Continental Shelf (Tunisia/Libyan Arab Jamahiriya), Judgment, I. C. J. Reports 1985, p. 192.

REFERENCES

Mark B. Feldman, "The Tunisia-Libya Continental Shelf Case: Geographic Justice or Judicial Compromise?" *American Journal of International Law*, Vol. 77 (1983), pp. 219-238; E. D. Brown, "The Tunisia-Libya Continental Shelf Case: A Missed Opportunity," *Marine Policy*, Vol. 7 (1983), No. 3, pp. 142-162; Donna R. Christie, "From the Shoals of Ras Kaboudia to the Shores of Tripoli: The Tunisia-Libya Continental Shelf Boundary Delimita-tion," *Georgia Journal of International and Comparative Law*, Vol. 13 (1983), pp. 1-30; Lawrence L. Herman, "The Court Giveth and the Court Taketh Away: An Analysis of the Tunisia-Libya Continental Shelf Case", *International and Comparative Law Quarterly*, Vol. 33 (1984), pp. 825-858; *Case Western Reserve Journal of International Law*, Vol. 16 (1984), pp. 1-37.

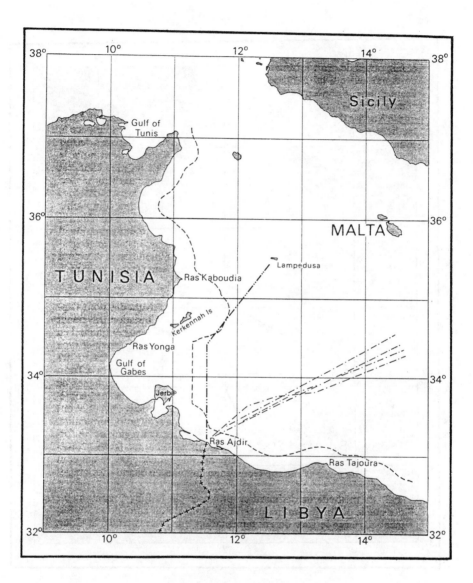

Tunisia/Libya Maritime Boundary Claims
Figure 5-9

_____ Limit of territorial waters claimed by each Party
_.._.._ Line resulting from Libyan method of delimitation
_._._._ Sheaf of lines resulting from Tunisian methods of delimitation

Source: I.C.J. Reports, 1982, p. 81.

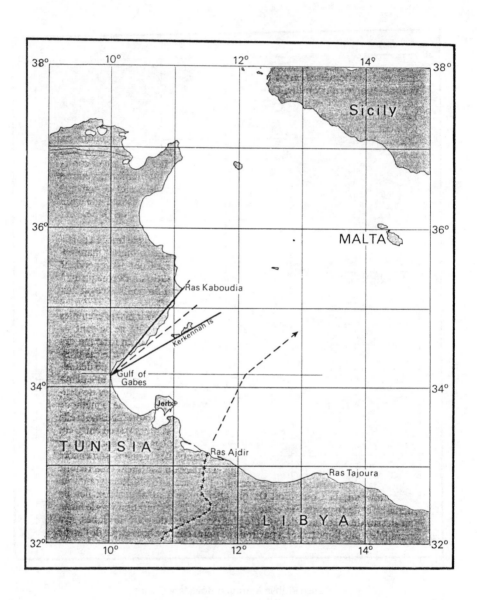

Tunisia/Libya Continental Shelf Boundaries
Figure 5-10

Source: *I.C.J. Reports, 1982*, p. 90.

c.   1985   Case   Concerning   the   Continental   Shelf   between   Libya   and   Malta

CONTINENTAL SHELF (LIBYAN ARAB JAMAHIRIYA/MALTA)
Judgment of June 3, 1985
I.C.J. Reports 1985, p. 13.

[By a Special Agreement concluded on May 23, 1976 and ratification exchanged on March 20, 1982, Libya and Malta submitted their dispute with respect to the delimitation of continental shelf to the International Court of Justice.]

33. In the view of the Court, even though the present case relates only to the delimitation of the continental shelf and not to that of the exclusive economic zone, the principles and rules underlying the latter concept cannot be left out of consideration. As the 1982 Convention demonstrates, the two institutions - continental shelf and exclusive economic zone - are linked together in modern law. Since the rights enjoyed by a State over its continental shelf would also be possessed by it over the sea-bed and subsoil of any exclusive economic zone which it might proclaim, one of the relevant circumstances to be taken into account for the delimitation of the continental shelf of a State is the legally permissible extent of the exclusive economic zone appertaining to that same State. This does not mean that the concept of the continental shelf has been absorbed by that of the exclusive economic zone; it does, however, signify that greater importance must be attributed to elements, such as distance from the coast, which are common to both concepts.

34. . . . . Although the institutions of the continental shelf and the exclusive economic zone are different and distinct, the rights which the exclusive economic zone entails over the sea-bed of the zone are defined by reference to the regime laid down for the continental shelf. Although there can be a continental shelf where there is no exclusive economic zone, there cannot be an exclusive economic zone without a corresponding continental shelf. It follows that, for juridical and practical reasons, the distance criterion must now apply to the continental shelf as well as to the exclusive economic zone; and this quite apart from the provision as to distance in paragraph 1 of Article 76. This is not to suggest that the idea of natural prolongation is now superseded by that of distance. What it does mean is that where the continental margin does not extend as far as 200 miles from the shore, natural prolongation, which in spite of its physical origins has throughout its history become more and more a complex and juridical concept, is in part defined by distance from the shore, irrespective of the physical nature of the intervening sea-bed and subsoil. The concepts of natural prolongation and distance are therefore not opposed but complimentary; and both remain essential elements in the juridical concept of the continental shelf. As the Court has observed, the legal basis of that which is to be delimited cannot be other than pertinent to the delimitation; the Court is thus unable to accept the Libyan contention that distance from the coast is not a relevant element for the decision of the present case. . . .

36. . . . . For Libya, as a first step each Party has to prove that the physical natural prolongation of its land territory extends into the area in which the delimitation is to be affected; if there exists a fundamental discontinuity between the shelf area adjacent to one Party and the shelf area adjacent to the other, than the boundary , it is contended, should lie along the general line of that fundamental discontinuity. The delimitation of continental shelf between Libya and Malta must therefore respect the alleged existence of a fundamental discontinuity which, according to Libya, divides the areas of physical continental shelf appertaining to each of the Parties. The argument is thus that there is no problem of overlapping shelves, but that, on the contrary, two distinct continental shelves are separated by what Libya calls the "rift zone". . . .

39. The Court, however, considers that since the development of the law enables a State to claim that the continental shelf appertaining to it extends up to as far as 200 miles from its coast, whatever the geological characteristics of the corresponding sea-bed and subsoil, there is no reason to ascribe any role to geological or geophysical factors within that distance either in verifying the legal title of the States concerned or in proceeding to a delimitation as between their claims. This is especially clear where verification of the validity of title is concerned, since, at least in so far as those areas are situated at a distance of under 200 miles from the coasts in question, title depends solely on the distance from the coasts of the Claimant States of any areas of sea-bed claimed by way of continental shelf, and the geological or geomorphological characteristics of those areas are completely immaterial. It follows that, since the distance between the coasts of the Parties is less than 400 miles, so that no geophysical feature can lie more than 200 miles from each coast, the feature referred to as the "rift zone" cannot constitute a fundamental discontinuity terminating the southward extension of the Maltese shelf and the northward extension of the Libyan as if it were some natural boundary. . . .

42. Neither, however, is the Court able to accept the argument of Malta--almost diametrically opposed to the Libyan rift-zone argument--that the new importance of the idea of distance from the coast has, at any rate for delimitation between opposite coasts, in turn conferred a primacy on the method of equidistance. . . .

43. The Court is unable to accept that, even as a prelimin-ary and provisional step towards the drawing of a delimitation line, the equidistance method is one which must be used, or that the Court is "required, as a first step, to examine the effects of a delimitation by application of the equidistance method" (*I.C.J. Reports 1928*, p. 79, para. 110). Such a rule would come near to an espousal of the idea of "absolute proximity": which was rejected by the Court in 1969 (See *I.C.J. Reports 1969*, p. 30, para. 41), and which has since, moreover, failed of acceptance at the Third United Nations Conference on the Law of the Sea. That a coastal State may be entitled to continental shelf rights by reason of distance from the coast, and irrespective of the physical characteristics of the intervening sea-bed and subsoil, does not entail that equidistance is the only appropriate method of delimitation, even between opposite or quasi-opposite coasts, nor even the only permissible point of departure. The application of equitable principles in the particular relevant circumstances may still require the adoption of another method, or combination of methods, of delimitation, even from the outset.

44. In this connection, something may be said on the subject of the practice of States in the field of continental shelf delimitation. . . . The Court for its part has no doubt about the importance of State practice in this matter. Yet that practice, however interpreted, falls short of proving the existence of a rule prescribing the use of equidistance, or indeed of any method, as obligatory. Even the existence of such a rule as is contended for by Malta, requiring equidistance simply to be used as a first stage in any delimitation, but subject to correction, cannot be supported solely by the production of numerous examples of delimitations using equidistance or modified equidistance, though it is impressive evidence that the equidistance method can in many different situations yield an equitable result.

[Paras. 45-47. The parties agree that the delimitation of the continental shelf must be effected by the application of equitable principles in all the relevant circumstances in order to achieve an equitable result. The Court lists some of these principles: the principle that there is to be no question of refashioning geography; the principle of non-encroachment by one Party on areas appertaining to the other; the principle of the respect due to all relevant circumstances; the principle that "equity does not necessarily imply equality" and that there can be no question of distributive justice.]

51. Malta contends that the "equitable consideration" of security and defense interests confirms the equidistance method of delimitation, which gives each party a comparable lateral control from its coast. Security considerations are of course not unrelated to the concept of the continental shelf. . . . However, in the present case neither Party has raised the question whether the law at present attributes to the coastal State particular competences in the military field over its continental shelf, including competences over the placing of military devices. In any event, the delimitation which will result from the application of the present Judgement is not so near to the coast of either Party as to make questions of security a particular consideration in the present case.
. . .

54. Malta has . . . invoked the principle of sovereign equality of States as an argument in favor of the equidistance method pure and simple, and as an objection to any adjustment based on length of coasts or proportionality considerations. It has observed that since all States are equal and equally sovereign, the maritime extensions generated by the sovereignty of each State must be of equal juridical value, whether or not the coasts of one State are longer than those of the other. The first question is whether the use of the equidistance method or recourse to proportionality considerations derive from legal rules accepted by States. If, for example, States had adopted a principle of apportionment of shelf on a basis of strict proportionality of coastal lengths (which the Court does not consider to be the case), their consent to that rule would be no breach of the principle of sovereign equality between them. Secondly, it is evident that the existence of equal entitlement, *ipso jure* and *ab initio*, of coastal States, does not imply an equality of extent of shelf, whatever the circumstances of the area; thus reference to the length of the coasts as a relevant circumstance cannot be excluded *a priori*. The principle of equality of States has therefore no particular role to play in the applicable law. . . .

58. . . . .to use the ratio of coastal lengths as of itself determinative of the seaward reach and area of continental shelf proper to each Party, is to go far beyond the use of proportionality as a test of equity, and as a corrective of the unjustifiable difference of treatment resulting from some method of drawing the boundary line. If such a use of proportionality were right, it is difficult indeed to see what room would be left for any other consideration; for it would be at once the principle of entitlement to continental shelf rights and also the method of putting that principle into operation. Its weakness as a basis of argument, however, is that the use of proportionality as a method in its own right is wanting of support in the practice of States, in the public expression of their views at (in particular) the Third United Nations Conference on the Law of the Sea, or in the jurisprudence. It is not possible for the Court to endorse a proposal at once so far-reaching and so novel. That does not however mean that the "significant difference in lengths of the respective coastlines" is not an element which may be taken into account at a certain stage in the delimitation process; this aspect of the matter will be returned to at the appropriate stage in the further reasoning of the Court. . . .

60. In applying the equitable principles and in the light of the relevant circumstances, the Court intends to proceed by stages; thus, it will first make a provisional delimitation by using a criterion and a method both of which are clearly destined to play an important role in producing the final result; it will then examine this provisional solution in the light of the requirements derived from other criteria, which may call for a correction of this initial result.

61. The Court has little doubt which criterion and method it must employ at the outset in order to achieve a provisional position in the present dispute. The criterion is linked with the law relating to a State's legal title to the continental shelf. The law applicable to the present dispute, that is, to claims relating to continental shelves located less that 200 miles from the coasts of the States in question, is based not on geological or geomorphological criteria, but on a criterion of

distance from the coast or, to use the traditional term, on the principle of adjacency as measured by distance. It therefore seems logical to the Court that the choice of the criterion and the method which it is to employ in the first place to arrive at a provisional result should be made in a manner consistent with the concepts underlying the attribution of legal title. . . .

63. The median line drawn in this way is thus only provisional. . .Under existing law, it must be demonstrated that the equidistance method leads to an equitable result in the case in question. To achieve this purpose, the result to which the distance criterion leads must be examined in the context of applying equitable principles to the relevant circumstances.

64. An immediate qualification of the median line which the Court considers must be made concerns the basepoints from which it is to be constructed. The line put forward by Malta was constructed from the low-water mark of the Libyan coast, but with regard to the Maltese coast from straight baselines (inter alia) connecting the island of Malta to the uninhabited islet of Filfla. The Court does not express any opinion on whether the inclusion of Filfla in the Maltese baselines was legally justified; but in any event the baselines as determined by coastal States are not *per se* identical with the points chosen on a coast to make it possible to calculate the area of continental shelf appertaining to that State. In this case, the equitableness of an equidistance line depends on whether the precaution is taken of eliminating the disproportional effect of certain "islets, rocks and minor coastal projections", to use the language of the Court in its 1969 Judgement, quoted above. The Court thus finds it equitable not to take account of Filfla in the calculation of the provisional median line between Malta and Libya. Having established such a provisional median line, the Court still has to consider whether other considerations, including the factor of proportionality, should lead to an adjustment of that line being made. . . .

68. On the Libyan side, Ras Ajdir, the terminus of the frontier with Tunisia, must clearly be the starting point; the meridian 15° 10'E which has been found by the Court to define the limits of the area in which the Judgment can operate crosses the coast of Libya not far from Ras Zarruq, which is regarded by Libya as the limit of the extent of its relevant coast. If the coasts of Malta and the coast of Libya from Ras Ajdir to Ras Zarruq are compared, it is evident that there is a considerable disparity between their lengths, to a degree which, in the view of the Court, constitutes a relevant circumstance which should be reflected in the drawing of the delimitation line. The coast of Libya from Ras Ajdir to Ras Zarruq, measured following its general direction, is 192 miles long, and the coast of Malta from Ras il-Wardija to Delimara Point, following straight baselines but excluding the islet of Filfla, is 24 miles long. In the view of the Court, this difference is so great as to justify the adjustment of the median line so as to attribute a larger shelf area to Libya; the degree of such adjustment does not depend upon a mathematical operation and remains to be examined.

[Paras. 69-71. A further geographical feature must be taken into consideration as a relevant circumstance; this is the southern location of the coasts of the Maltese islands, within the general geographical context in which the delimitation is to be offered. The Court points to a further reason for not accepting the median line, without adjustment, as an equitable boundary; namely that this line is to all intents and purposes controlled on each side, in its entirety, by a handful of salient points concentrated immediately east of Ras Tadjoura for Libya. The Court therefore finds it necessary that the delimitation line be adjusted so as to lie closer to the coasts of Malta. The coasts of the Parties being opposite to each other, and the equidistance line lying broadly west to east, this adjustment can be satisfactorily and simply achieved by transposing it in an exactly northward direction.]

72. Once it is contemplated that the boundary requires to be shifted northward on the median line between Libya and Malta, it seems appropriate first to establish what might be the extreme limit of such a shift. This is easily done and indeed the calculation is, in broad terms, apparent from any map of the area as a whole, showing the wider geographical context which the Court has found to be relevant. Let it be supposed, for the sake of argument, that the Maltese islands were part of Italian territory, and that there was a question of the delimitation of the continental shelf between Libya and Italy, within the area to which this Judgment relates. Again, between opposite coasts, with a large, clear area between them, that boundary would not then be the median line, based solely upon the coasts of Libya to the south and Sicily to the north. At least some account would be taken of the islands of Malta; and even if the minimum account were taken, the continental shelf boundary between Italy and Libya would be somewhat south of the median line between the Sicilian and Libyan coasts. Since Malta is not part of Italy, but is an independent State, it cannot be the case that, as regards continental shelf rights, it will be in a worse position because of its independence. Therefore, it is reasonable to assume that an equitable boundary between Libya and Malta must be to the south of a notional median line between Libya and Sicily; for that is the line, as we have seen, which allows no effect at all to the islands of Malta. The position of such a median line, employing the baselines of the coasts of Sicily established by the Italian Government, may be defined for present purposes, by its intersection with the meridian 15° 10'E; according to the information supplied to the Court, this intersection is at about latitude 34°36'N. The course of that line evidently does not run parallel to that of the median line between Malta and Libya, but its form is, it is understood, not greatly different. The equidistance line drawn between Malta and Libya (excluding as basepoint the islet of Filfla), according to the information available to the Court, intersects that same meridian 15°10'E at approximately 34°12'N. A transposition north-wards through 24' of latitude of the Malta-Libya median line would therefore be the extreme limit of such northward adjustment.

73. . . .the Court has concluded that a boundary line that represents a shift around three-quarters of the distance between the two outer parameters--that is to say between the median line and the line 24' north of it--achieves an equitable result in all the circumstances. It has therefore decided that the equitable boundary line is a line produced by transposing the median line northwards through 18' of latitude. By "transposing" is meant the operation whereby to every point on the median line there will correspond a point on the line of delimitation, lying on the same meridian of longitude but 18' further to the north. Since the median line intersects the meridian 15°10' E at 34°12'N approximately, the delimitation line will intersect the meridian at 34°30' approximately. . . .

[Paras 74-75. While considering that there is no reason of principle why a test of proportionality, based on the ratio between the lengths of the relevant coasts and the areas of shelf attributed, should not be employed to verify the equity of the result, the Court states that there may be certain practical difficulties which render this test inappropriate. They are particularly evident in the present case, *inter alia*, because the area to which judgment would apply is limited by reason of the existence of claims of third States, and to apply the proportionality test simply to the areas within these limits would be unrealistic. However, it seems to the Court that it can make a broad assessment of the equity of the result without attempting to express it in figures. It concludes that there is certainly no manifest disproportion between areas of shelf attributed to each of the Parties, such that it might be claimed that the requirements of the test of proportionality as an aspect of equity are not satisfied.]

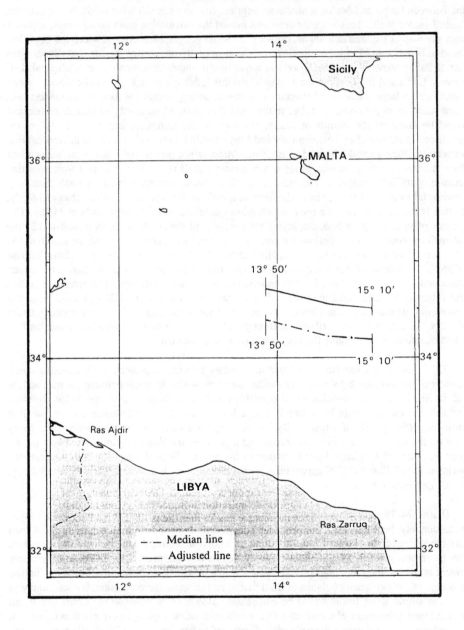

Libya/Malta Continental Shelf Boundaries
Figure 5-11

Source: *I.C.J. Reports, 1985*, p. 54.

REFERENCE

Ted L. McDorman, "The Libya-Malta Case: Opposite States Confront the Court," *Canadian Yearbook of International Law*, Vol. 24 (1986), pp. 335-367.

3. Interim Arrangement and Bilateral Agreement

1982 UNITED NATIONS CONVENTION ON THE LAW OF THE SEA

Article 83
Delimitation of the continental shelf between States with
opposite or adjacent coasts

1. The delimitation of the continental shelf between States with opposite or adjacent coasts shall be effected by agreement on the basis of international law, as referred to in Article 38 of the Statute on the International Court of Justice, in order to achieve an equitable solution.

2. If no agreement can be reached within a reasonable period of time, the States concerned shall resort to the procedures provided for in Part XV.

3. Pending agreement as provided for in paragraph 1, the States concerned in a spirit of understanding and co-operation, shall make every effort to enter into provisional arrangements on a practical nature and, during this transitional period, not to jeopardize or hamper the reaching of the final agreement. Such arrangements shall be without prejudice to the final delimitation.

4. Where there is an agreement in force between the States concerned, questions relating to the delimitation of the continental shelf shall be determined in accordance with the provisions of that agreement.

D. DELIMITATION OF EXCLUSIVE ECONOMIC ZONE BETWEEN STATES WITH ADJACENT OR OPPOSITE COASTS AND THE QUESTION OF SINGLE BOUNDARY FOR DIFFERENT MARITIME ZONES

1. Article 74, paragraph 1, of the 1982 United Nations Convention on the Law of the Sea

a. Legislative History of Article 74, Paragraph 1

See Section C. Subsection 2, a [pp. 179-180].

REFERENCE

Francisco Orrego Vicuna, "The Contribution of the Exclusive Economic Zone to the Law of Maritime Delimitation," *German Yearbook of International Law*, Vol. 31 (1988), pp. 120-137.

b. 1984 Delimitation of the Maritime Boundary in the Gulf of Maine Area Case

DELIMITATION OF THE MARITIME BOUNDARY
IN THE GULF OF MAINE AREA,
(CANADA/UNITED STATES OF AMERICA)
Judgement of October 12, 1984
Given by the Chamber Constituted By the Order
Made by the Court on January 20, 1982
I.C.J. Reports 1984, p. 246.

[In accordance with a Special Agreement between the United States and Canada concluded on March 29, 1979, and entered into force on November 20, 1981, both countries submitted, on November 25, 1981, to a chamber of the International Court Justice a question as to the course of the maritime boundary dividing the continental shelf and fisheries zones of the two Parties in the Gulf of Maine area. A five-member Chamber was constituted after consultation with the Parties, pursuant to Article 26, paragraph 2, and Article 31 of the Statute of the Court.]

[In paras. 97-111, the Chamber rejects the Canadian argument from geographical adjacency to the effect that a rule exists whereby a State any part of whose coasts is less distant from the zones to be attributed that those of the other State concerned would be entitled to have the zones recognized as its own. It also finds unacceptable the distinction made by the United States between "primary" and "secondary" coasts and the consequent preferential relationship said to exist between the "principal" coasts and the maritime and submarine areas situated frontally before them.]

112. . . . What general international law prescribes in every maritime delimitation between neighboring States could be defined as follows:

(1) No maritime delimitation between States with opposite or adjacent coasts may be effected unilaterally by one of those States. Such delimitation must be sought and effected by means of an agreement, following negotiations conducted in good faith and with the genuine intention of achieving a positive result. Where, however, such agreement cannot be achieved, delimitation should be effected by course to a third party possessing the necessary competence.

(2) In either case, delimitation is to be effected by the application of equitable criteria and by the use of practical methods capable of ensuring, with regard to the geographical configuration of the area and other relevant circumstances, an equitable result.

194. In reality, a delimitation by a single line, such as that which has to be carried out in the present case, i.e., a delimitation which has to apply at one and the same time to the continental shelf and to the superjacent water column can only be carried out by the application of a criterion, or combination of criteria, which does not give preferential treatment to one of these two objects to the detriment of the other, and at the same time is such as to be equally suitable to the division of either of them. In that regard, moreover, it can be foreseen that with the gradual adoption by the majority of maritime States of the exclusive economic zone and, consequently, an increasingly general demand for single delimitation, so as to avoid as far as possible the disadvantages inherent in a plurality of separate delimita-tions, preference will henceforth inevitably be given to criteria that, because of their more neutral character, are best suited for use in a multi-purpose delimitation.

195. To return to the immediate concerns of the Chamber, it is, accordingly, towards an application to the present case of criteria more especially derived from geography that it feels bound to turn. What is here understood by geography is of course mainly the geography of the coasts, which has primarily a physical aspect, to which it may be added, in the second place, a political aspect. Within this framework, it is inevitable that the Chamber's basic choice should favor a criterion long held to be as equitable as it is simple, namely that in principle, while having regard to the special circumstances of the case, one should aim at an equal division of areas where the maritime projections of the coasts of the States between which delimitation is to be effected converge and overlap.

196. Nevertheless, it is not always the case that the choice of this basic criterion appears truly equitable when it, and it alone, is exclusively applied to the particular situation. The multiplicity and diversity of geographical situations frequently call for this criterion to be adjusted or flexibly applied to make it genuinely equitable, not in the abstract, but in relation to the varying requirements of a reality that takes many shapes and forms. To mention only the situation involved in the present proceedings, it is a fact, that the Parties, and one of them in particular, with the aid of comparisons with situations considered in previous cases, persistently emphasized the importance they attached to one concrete aspect or another of the geographical situation in the present case. The Chamber cannot but recognize, to a certain extent, that the concerns thus expressed were not wholly unfounded. It does not here intend to enter into detailed considerations, for it will be sufficient to note in general at this stage that, in the present case, the situation arising out of the physical and political geography of the delimitation area does not present ideal conditions for the full, exclusive application of the criterion specified at the end of the previous paragraph. Some corrections must be made to certain effects of the application that might be unreasonable, so that the concurrent use of auxiliary criteria may appear indispensable. Having regard to the special characteristics of the area, the auxiliary criterion of weight should be given to a by no means negligible difference within the delimitation area between the lengths of the respective coastlines of the countries concerned. It also has in mind the likewise auxiliary criterion whereby it is held equitable partially to correct any effect of applying the basic criterion that would result in cutting off one coastline, or part of it, from its appropriate projection across the maritime expanses to be divided, or then again the criterion - it too being of an auxiliary nature - involving the necessity of granting some effect, however limited, to the presence of a geographical feature such as an island or group of islands lying off a coast, when strict application of the basic criterion might entail giving then full effect or, alternatively, no effect.

197. At this point, accordingly, the Chamber finds that is must finally confirm its choice, which is to take as its starting-point the above-mentioned criterion of the division--in principle, equal division--of the areas of convergence and overlapping of the maritime projections of the coastlines of the States concerned in the delimitation, a criterion which need only be stated to be seen as intrinsically equitable. However, in the Chamber's view, the adoption of the appropriate auxiliary criteria in so far as it is apparent that this combination is necessitated by the relevant circumstances of the area concerned, and provided they are used only to the extent actually dictated by this necessity. By this approach the Chamber seeks to ensure the most correct application in the present case of the fundamental rule of international law here applicable, which requires that any maritime delimitation between States would be carried out in accordance with criteria that are equitable and are found more specifically to be so in relation to the particular aspects of the case under consideration. . . .

201. In this connection, the Chamber would emphasize the necessity of not allowing oneself to be too easily swayed by the perfection which is apparent *a pioiro*, from the viewpoint of equally dividing a disputed area, in a line drawn in strict compliance with the canons of geometry, i.e., a

line so constructed that each point in it is equidistant from the most salient points on the respective coastlines of the parties concerned. In an apposite passage of the 1969 Judgment on the *North Sea Continental Shelf* cases, (*I.C.J. Reports 1969*, p. 36, para. 57), the Court showed how, in determining the course of a delimitation line intended to "effect an equal division of the particular area involved" between two coasts, no account need be taken of the presence of "islets, rocks, and minor coastal projections, the disproportionally distorting effect of which can be eliminated by other means". In pursuance of this remark, the Chamber likewise would point out the potential disadvantages inherent in any method which takes tiny islands, uninhabited rocks or low-tide elevations, sometimes lying at a considerable distance from terra firma, as a basepoint for the drawing of a line intended to affect an equal division of a given area. If any of these geographical features possess some degree of importance, there is nothing to prevent their subsequently being assigned whatever limited corrective effect may equitably be ascribed to them, but that is an altogether different operation from making a series of such minor features the very basis for the determination of the dividing line, or from transforming them into a succession of basepoints for the geometrical construction of the entire line. It is very doubtful whether a line so constructed could, in many concrete situations, constitute a line genuinely given effect to the criterion of equal division of the area in question, especially when it is not only a terrestrial area beneath the sea which has to be divided but also a maritime expanse in the proper sense of the term, since in the latter case the result may be even more debatable.

202. Furthermore, a line which, on account of the refinements in the technical method used to determine its course, follows a complicated or even a zigzag path, made up of a succession of segments of different bearings, might, if need be, seem acceptable as a boundary dividing the sea-bed along, i.e., a boundary to be observed in the exploration and exploitation of the resources located in given areas of the subsoil. But there would seem to be far less justification for adopting such a line as a limit appropriate to maritime fishery zones, i.e., areas whose exploitable resources are not, for the most part, resources attached to the soil. Exploitation of the sea's fishery resources calls for the existence of clear boundaries of a constant course that do not compel those engaging in such activity to keep checking their position in relation to the complicated path of the line to be respected.

203. In sum, just like the criteria to be applied to the delimitation, the methods to be used for the purpose of putting those criteria into practice cannot fail to be influenced by the special characteristics and requirements pertaining to the delimitation by a single boundary of both the continental shelf and the superjacent water column which, far from being a genuine column of definite shape, is in reality a volume of liquid in movement, forming the habitat of mobile fauna. Undeniably, a degree of simplification is an elementary requisite to the drawing of any delimitation line in such an environment. . . .

[The remaining parts of the judgment (paras. 204-241) deal with the lines resulting from the application of the criteria and methods of delimitation discussed above and the verification of the equitable character of the result of the delimitation. The following summary is taken from International Court of Justice, *Yearbook 1984-1985* (No. 39), The Hague: I. C. J. 1985, pp. 169-170:

Turning to the concrete choice of the methods it considers appropriate for implementing the equitable criteria it has decided to apply, the Chamber notes that the coastal configuration of the Gulf of Maine excludes any possibility of the boundary's being formed by a basically unidirectional line, given the change of situation noted in the geography of the Gulf. It is only in the northeastern sector of the Gulf that the prevailing relationship of the coasts of the United States and Canada is one of lateral adjacency. In the sector closest to the closing line, it is one of oppositeness. In the Chamber's view it is therefore obvious that, between point A and the line from Nantucket to Cape Sable, i.e., within the limits of the Gulf of Maine proper, the delimitation line must comprise two segments.

In the case of the first segment, the one closest to the international boundary terminus, there is no special circumstances to militate against the division into, as far as possible, equal parts of the overlapping created by the lateral superimposition of the maritime projections of the two States' coasts. Rejecting the employment of the lateral equidistance line on account of the disadvantages it is found to entail, the Chamber follows the method of drawing, from Point A, two perpendiculars to the two basic coastal lines, namely the line from Cape Elizabeth to the international boundary terminus and the line running thence to Cape Sable. At Point A, those two perpendiculars form an acute angle of 278°. It is the bisector of this angle which is prescribed for the first sector of the delimitation line (Figure 5-13).

In turning to the second segment, the Chamber proceeds by two stages. First, it decides the method to be employed in view of the quasi-parallelism between the coasts of Nova Scotia and Massachusetts. As these are opposite coasts, the application of a geometrical method can only result in the drawing of a median delimitation line approximately parallel to them. The Chamber finds, however, that while a median line would be perfectly legitimate if the international boundary ended in the very middle of the coast at the back of the Gulf, in the actual circumstances where it is situated at the northeastern corner of the rectangle which geometrically represents the shape of the Gulf, in the actual circumstances where it is situated at the northeastern corner of the rectangle which geometrically represents the shape of the Gulf, the use of a median line would result in an unreasonable effect, in that it would give Canada the same overall maritime projection in the delimitation area as if the entire eastern coast of Maine belonged to Canada instead of the United States. That being so, the Chamber finds a second stage necessary, in which it corrects the median line to take account of the undeniably important circumstances of the difference in length between the two States' coastlines abutting on the delimitation area. As the total length of the United States coastlines on the Gulf of Maine is approximately 284 nautical miles, and that of the Canadian coasts (including part of the coast of the Bay of Fundy) is approximately 206 nautical miles, the ratio of the coastlines is 1.38 to 1. However, a further correction is necessitated by the presence of Seal Island off Nova Scotia. The Chamber considers that it would be excessive to consider the coastline of Nova Scotia as displaced in a southwesterly direction by the entire distance between Seal Island and that coast, and therefore considers it appropriate to attribute half effect to the island. Taking that into account, the ratio to be applied to determine the position of the corrected median line on a line across the Gulf between the points where the coasts of Nova Scotia and Massachusetts are closest (i.e., a line from the tip of Cape Cod to Chebogue Point) becomes 1.32 to 1. The second segment of the delimitation will therefore correspond to the median line as thus corrected, from its intersection with the bisector drawn from point A (first segment) to the point where it reaches the closing line of the Gulf (Figure 5-13).

As for the third segment of the delimitation, relating to that part of the delimitation area lying outside the Gulf of Maine, this portion of the line is situated throughout its length into open ocean. It appears obvious that the most appropriate geometrical method for this segment if the drawing of a perpendicular to the closing line of the Gulf. One advantage of this method is to give the final segment of the line practically the same orientation as that given by both Parties to the final portion of the respective lines they envisaged. As for the exact point on the closing line from which the perpendicular should be drawn seawards, it will coincide with the intersection of that line with the corrected median line. Starting from that point, the third segment crosses Georges Banks between points on the 100-fathom depth line with the following co-ordinates:

42°10'.8N, 67°11'.0W
41°10'.1N, 66°17'.9W

The terminus of this final segment will be situated within the triangle defined by the Special Agreement and coincide with the last point it reaches within the overlapping of the respective 200-mile zones claimed by the two states.

Having drawn the delimitation line requested by the Parties, the final task of the Chamber is to verify whether the result obtained can be considered as intrinsically equitable in the light of all the circumstances. While such verification is not absolutely necessary where the first two segments of the line are concerned, since the Chamber's guiding parameters were provided by geography, the situation is different as regards the third segment, which is the one of greatest concern to the Parties on account of the presence in the area it traverses of Georges Bank, the principle stake in the proceedings on account of the potential resources of its subsoil and the economic importance of its fisheries.

In the eyes of the United States, the decisive factor lies in the fishing carried on by the United States and its nationals ever since the country's independence and ever before, activities which they are held to have been alone in pursuing over the greater part of that period, and which were accompanied by other maritime activities concerning navigational assistance, rescue, research, defence, etc. Canada laid greater emphasis on the socio-economic aspects, concentrating on the recent past, especially the last 15 years, and presenting as an equitable principle the idea that a single maritime boundary should ensure the maintenance of the existing structures of fishing which, according to it, were of vital importance to the coastal communities of the area.

The Chamber explains why it cannot subscribe to these conten-tions and finds that it is clearly out of the question to consider the respective scale of activities in the domain of fishing or petroleum exploitation as an equitable criterion to be applied in determining the delimitation line. What the Chamber would regard as a legitimate scruple lies rather in concern lest, unexpectedly, the overall result should appear radically inequitable as entailing disastrous repercussions on the subsistence and economic develop-ment of the populations concerned. It considers that there is no reason to fear any such danger in the present case on account of the Chamber's choice of delimitation line or, more especially, the course of its third segment, and concludes that the overall result of the delimitation is equitable. Noting the long tradition of friendly and fruitful co-operation in maritime matters between Canada and the United States, the Chamber considers that the Parties will be able to surmount any difficulties and take the right steps to ensure the positive development of their activities in the important domains concerned.]

LEGEND

———————— Canadian Claim (1979)
— — — — — — United States Claim (1982)
⊶ — — — — ⊶— 200 - mile Fishing Zone
—·——·——·——·— Boundary Drawn by the Chamber

Map Showing Claims of 1979 and 1982 and the Boundary Drawn
by the I. C. J. Chamber in the Gulf of Maine

Figure 5-12

Source: John Copper, Delimitation of the Maritime Boundary in the Gulf of Maine
Area," *Ocean Development and International Law*, Vol. 16 (1986), p. 77.
Reprinted by permission of the Hemisphere Publishing Corporation.

REFERENCES

"Boundary Delimitation in the Economic Zone: The Gulf of Maine Dispute," *Maine Law Review*, Vol. 30 (1978-1979), pp. 207-245; Donald M. McRae, "Adjudication of the Maritime Boundary in the Gulf of Maine," *Canadian Yearbook of International Law*, Vol. 17 (1979), pp. 292-303; Daniel P. Finn, "Georges Bank: The Legal Issue," *Oceanus* (Boston), vol.23, No. 2 (Summer 1980), 00. 28-38; Donald M. McRae, "Proportionality and the Gulf of Maine Maritime Boundary Dispute," *Canadian Yearbook of International Law*, Vol. 19 (1981), pp. 287-302; Sang-Myon Rhee, "Equitable Solutions to the Maritime Boundary Dispute between the United States and Canada in the Gulf of Maine," *American Journal of International Law*, Vol. 75 (1981), pp. 591-628; Donald M. McRae, "The Gulf of Maine Case: The Written Proceedings," *Canadian Yearbook of International Law*, Vol. 21 (1983), pp. 266-283; L. H. Legault and Donald M. McRae, "The Gulf of Maine Case," *Canadian Yearbook of International Law*, Vol. 22 (1984), pp. 267-290; Paul D. McHugh, "International Law--Delimitation of Maritime Boundaries [Casenotes of the Gulf of Maine Case]," *Natural Resources Journal*, Vol. 25 (1985), pp. 1025-1038; Levi E. Clain, "Gulf of Maine--A Disappointing First in the Delimitation of A Single Maritime Boundary," *Virginia Journal of International Law*, Vol. 25 (1985), pp. 521-620; L. H. Legault, "A Line for All Uses: The Gulf of Maine Boundary Revisited," *International Journal* (Toronto), Vol. 40 (1985), pp. 461-477; L. H. Legault and Blair Hankey, "From Sea to Seabed: The Single Maritime Boundary in the Gulf of Maine Case," *American Journal of International Law*, Vol. 79 (1985), pp. 961-991; Ted L. McDorman, Phillip M. Saunders and David L. VanderZwaag," The Gulf of Maine Boundary, Dropping Anchor or Selling a Course?," *Marine Policy*, Vol. 9 (1985), pp. 90-107; Donat Pharand, "Delimitation of Maritime Boundaries, Continental Shelf and Exclusive Economic Zone in Light of the Gulf of Maine Case, Canada v. USA (1984)," *Revue General De Droit* (Ottawa), Vol. 16 (1985), pp. 263-286; David R. Robinson, David A. Colson and Bruce C. Rashkow, "Some Perspectives on Adjudicating before the World Court: The Gulf of Maine Case," *American Journal of International Law*, Vol. 79(1985), pp. 578-597; Jan Schneider, "The Gulf of Maine Case: The Nature of An Equitable Result," *American Journal of International Law*, Vol. 79 (1985), pp. 539-5477; Nora T. Terres, "The United States/Canada Gulf of Maine Maritime Boundary Delimitation," *Maryland Journal of International Law*, Vol. 9 (1985), pp. 135-180; Edward Collins, Jr. and Martin A. Rogolf, The Gulf of Maine Case and the Future of Ocean Boundary Delimitation" *Maine Law Review*, Vol, 38 (1986), pp. 1-48; John Copper, "Delimitation of the Maritime Boundary in the Gulf of Maine Area," *Ocean Development and International Law*, Vol. 16 (1986), pp. 59-90; Louis de Vorsey and Megan C. Vorsey, "The World Court Decision in the Canada-United States Gulf of Maine Seaward Boundary Dispute: A Perspective from Historical Geography," *Case Western Reserve Journal of International Law*, Vol. 18 (1986), pp. 415-442.

c.   1985 Arbitral Award on the Maritime Delimitation Between Guinea and Guinea-Bissau

AWARD BY THE ARBITRAL TRIBUNAL ON THE MARITIME DELIMITATION
(GUINEA/GUINEA-BISSAU)
February 14, 1985
International Legal Materials, Vol. 25 (1986), p. 252-307;
International Law Reports, Vol. 77, pp. 635-692.

[The neighboring countries of Guinea and Guinea-Bissau, before gaining independence, were colonies of France and Portugal respectively. The final paragraph of Article 1 of the Convention of 12 May 1886 between France and Portugal for the delimitation of their respective possessions in West Africa states that:

Portugal will possess all the islands included between the meridian of Cape Roxo, the coast and the southern limit formed by a line following the thalweg of the Cajet River, and afterwards turning towards the south-west across Pilots Passage, where it reaches 10°14' north latitude, and follows it as far as the meridian of Cape Roxo.

The provision applied mainly to the islands of the Bijagos archipelago. Its implementation caused no difficulty until 1958. At that time, Portugal granted an oil concession. Like Guinea and Guinea-Bissau which had now become independent, Portugal also proceeded to issue laws and decrees defining its territorial waters. The effect of these various definitions was that the maritime areas over which these countries claimed to exercise jurisdiction overlapped. Negotiations then took place during which, in January 1978, it transpired that a legal dispute existed between Guinea and Guinea-Bissau concerning the delimitation of their maritime territories.

On February 18, 1983, these two States decided to seek arbitration of the matter through an Arbitral Tribunal which was established on October 14, 1983 and is independent of the International Court of Justice, although its three Members are also Members of the latter court. The arbitral award was rendered on February 14, 1985.

The Tribunal concludes, in the light of the preparatory work and of the circumstances prevailing at the time, that the 1886 Convention did not fix any maritime boundary between the French and Portuguese possessions in Guinea. It then proceeds to determine the course of the single line delimiting the territorial waters, the exclusive economic zones and the continental shelves between the two countries.]

92. In order for any delimitation to be made on an equitable and objective basis, it is necessary to ensure that, as far as possible, each State controls the maritime territories opposite its coasts and in their vicinity. First of all, therefore, it is necessary to define the coastline concerned with a view to delimitation. In this particular case, the coastline is continuous, although fairly irregular, from Cape Roxo in the north to the region of Sallatouk Point in the south. . . .

95. The coastline to be considered. . .is marked by the presence of numerous islands. In order to determine the extent to which these should be taken into account for delimitation purposes, it is necessary to distinguish three types of islands:

a) The coastal islands, which are separated from the continent by narrow sea channels or narrow watercourses and are often joined to it at low tide, must be considered as forming an integral part of the continent.

b) The Bijagos Islands, the nearest of which is two nautical miles from the continent and the furthest 37 miles, and no two of which are further apart than five miles, can be considered, if the 12-mile rule accepted by the Parties is applied, as being in the same territorial waters as each other and as being linked to those of the continent.

c) There are also the more southerly islands scattered over shallow areas (Poilao, Samba, Sene, Alcatraz), some of which may be taken into account for the establishment of baselines and be included in the territorial waters.

Although it cannot be denied that, somehow or other, the delimitation must leave to each State the islands over which it has sovereignty, it nevertheless remains that, in the search for the general criteria to be applied, it is above all the islands in categories (a) and (b) that are considered as

islands over which it has sovereignty, it nevertheless remains that, in the search for the general criteria to be applied, it is above all the islands in categories (a) and (b) that are considered as relevant. . . .

97. . . .In the present case, the Tribunal considers that account should be taken of the coastal islands and the Bijagos Archipelago as they are define in paragraphs 95 (a) and (b) above but not of the scattered islands referred to in paragraph 95 (c). Furthermore, the relevant islands must not be taken into account in the form of the total obtained by adding together the perimeters of each of them, but as elements determining the general direction of the entire coastline of the country considered. For Guinea-Bissau, this gives a broken line which, starting from the Cape Roxo, would be at a tangent to the islands of Unhocomo and Orange and would end at the thalweg of the Cajet River. For Guinea, there would be a straight line from the mouth of the Cajet River to Sallatouk Point. Using this method of evaluation, each country's coastline is about 154 miles long. If the Bijagos Islands were not taken into account, the coastline of Guinea-Bissau would be only 128 miles long. This State's coastline is therefore affected by a coefficient of 20%, which equitably brings out the importance of the islands in this case. The Parties must therefore be considered by the Tribunal as having, in its opinion, coastlines of the same length. . . .

103. If the coasts of each country are examined separately, it can be seen that the Guinea-Bissau coastline is convex, when the Bijagos are taken into account, and that that of Guinea is concave. However, if they are considered together, it can be seen that the coastline of both countries is concave and this characteristic is accentuated if we consider the presence of Sierra Leone further south. What are the effects of such a circumstance? Between two adjacent countries, whatever method of delimitation is chosen, the likelihood is that both will lose certain maritime areas which are unquestionably situated opposite and in the vicinity of their coasts. This is the cut-off effect. Where equidistance is concerned, the Tribunal, which as we have seen is confronted here with two lines of equidistance, is forced to accept that both would have serious drawbacks in the present case. In the vicinity of the coast, they would give exaggerated importance to certain insignificant features of the coastline, producing a cut-off effect which would satisfy no equitable principle and which the Tribunal could not approve. In one case, this would be to the detriment of Guinea-Bissau and, in the other, to the detriment of Guinea, with the island of Alcatraz being "on the wrong side". In the latter case, Guinea-Bissau has put forward several propositions to correct this situation and finally, in its conclusion, offers to leave this island with a 2-mile enclave measured from the low-water mark.

104. When in fact--as is the case here, if Sierra Leone is taken into consideration--there are three adjacent States along a concave coastline, the equidistance method has the other drawback of resulting in the middle country being enclaved by the other two and thus prevented from extending its maritime territory as far seaward as international law permits. In the present case, this is what would happen to Guinea, which is situated between Guinea-Bissau and Sierra Leone. Both the equidistance lines envisaged arrive too soon at the parallel of latitude drawn from the land boundary between Guinea and Sierra Leone which Guinea has unilaterally taken as its maritime boundary.

105. This being said, the Tribunal must now consider whether the "southern limit" referred to in the final paragraph of Article I of the 1886 Convention, and claimed by Guinea as a line of delimitation, is of a more equitable character that a line of equidistance. . . . The "southern limit" coincides. . . with a short segment of the land boundary, i.e., that which passes between the coastal islands; that from this point, it runs for about twenty miles along the Pilots' Pass, which is the geographical prolongation of the land boundary and more or less follows the same direction, being roughly perpendicular to the coast at this point. . . . The said limit then follows the parallel of 10°40' north latitude and passes 2.25 nautical miles north of the island of Alcatraz, which is the

most western possession of Guinea. . . . The Tribunal believes itself justified in considering the "southern limit", until it draws abreast of Alcatraz, as a factor it should take into account with a view to a delimitation tending to achieve an equitable result. . . .

108. In the Tribunal's view, a valid method consists of looking at the whole of West Africa and of seeking a solution which would take overall account of the shape of its coastline. This would mean no longer restricting considerations to a *short coastline* but to a *long coastline*. However, while the continuous coastline of the two Guineas--or of the three countries when Sierra Leone is included--is generally concave, that of West Africa in general is undoubtedly convex. With this in mind, the Tribunal considers that the delimitation of maritime territories to be attributed to coastal States could be made following one of the directions which takes this circumstance into account. These directions would be approximately divergent. This idea, which in the present case would seem to offer an equitable result, automatically condemns the system of parallels of latitude defended by Guinea and of which the limit represented by the parallel of 10°40' north latitude would have been just one example. However, it also condemns the equidistance method as seen by Guinea-Bissau. It leads toward a delimitation which is integrated into the present or future delimitations of the region as a whole.

109. In order for the delimitation between the two Guineas to be suitable for equitable integration into the existing delimitations of the West Africa region, as well as into future delimitations which would be reasonable to imagine from a consideration of equitable principles and the most likely assumptions, it is necessary to consider how all these delimitations fit in with the general configuration of the West Africa coastline, and what deductions should be drawn from this in relation to the precise area concerned in the present delimitation. To this end, the configuration of the coastline should be interpreted in a simple manner. In practice, two systems are presented and from them the Tribunal must find a solution likely to provide an equitable result. A first system would be based on the outer perimeter of the coasts and their islands. Without going so far as to select an arc of a circle passing through Almadies Point (Senegal), Cape Roxo and the southern extremity of Liberia, this being too distant from the coast, the Tribunal could envisage a polygon with protruding angles, which would include every part of the coast. This polygon would join the following points: Almadies Point--Cape Roxo--Unhocomo Island--Tortue Island (Sierra Leone). A variation of this system would consist of using a polygon with re-entering angles. This would have the advantage of enabling the selection of line segments which do not touch any third State, e.g., Orango Island--Sallatouk POint or Orango Island--Cape Verga. However, this would restrict the coastline to limits which would be too narrow. . . .

110. A second system would consist of using the maritime facade and, for this purpose, selecting a straight line joining two coastal points on the continent. This would have the advantage of giving more weight to the general direction of the coastline, at the risk of starting from a line crossing through islands and even encroaching on the continent. There would be two possible facades: one would be a line joining Cape Roxo and Sallatouk Point and would concern only the two Guineas; the other would be a line joining Almadies Point (Senegal) and Cape Shilling (Sierra Leone) and would thus involve two third States. The second system is better suited to the circumstances chosen by the Tribunal, i.e., the overall configuration of the West African coastline, and the Almadies Point-Cape Shilling line reflects this circumstance more faithfully.

111. This opens the possibility of an equitable delimitation which would consist of:

a) first following the "southern limit" of the 1886 Convention, i.e., the Pilots' Pass from the mouth of the Cajet River and the parallel of 10°40' north latitude, as far as the island of Alcatraz. Because , in this way, the island in question would have only 2.25 nautical miles of territorial waters to the north--and there is even less reason to grant more in this direction in that the "southern limit" marked the maximum claim by Guinea in its conclusions--the Tribunal would consider it equitable to grant it, at least towards the west, the 12 nautical miles provided for in the 1982 Law of the Sea Convention, without however taking into account any reefs. The "southern limit" could therefore be adopted as far as 12 miles west of Alcatraz.

b) The line would then go in a southwesterly direction, being *grosso modo* perpendicular to the line joining Almadies Point and Cape Shilling. This would give just one straight line bearing 236°. The Tribunal considers that such a line would reduce the risk of enclavement to a minimum and, in this respect, would be more satisfactory than any line drawn perpendicular to the other lines envisaged in paragraphs 109 and 110 above.

112. The Parties have invoked several other circumstances, while according them unequal importance. By referring to circumstances which it considers relevant in the present case, the Tribunal considers that it has already determined a line offering an equitable delimitation. It is now necessary, by considering other circumstances, to establish whether the chosen line effectively leads to an equitable result.

113. The first of these other circumstances is the structure and nature of the continental shelf.
. . .

116. . . . In any event, however, the rule of natural prolongation can be effectively invoked for purposes of delimitation only where there is a separation of continental shelves. In the present case, both Parties have been obliged to recognize that the continental shelf formed by the prolongation of their respective coasts is one and the same (see paragraph 19 above). This is the same shelf, with the same geological history and, generally speaking, with the same physical characteristics. It is an extension of all the territories of both States. It matters little how the structure was formed. What does matter is its present state and unity. None of the physical characteristics invoked by Guinea-Bissau, and which Guinea-Bissau itself has described as "secondary", appear to the Tribunal to be sufficiently important to be taken as constituting a separation of the natural prolongations of the two States concerned. . . .

117. . . . .The characteristics of a continental shelf may serve to demonstrate the existence of a break in the continuity of the shelf or in the prolongation of territories of the States which are parties to a delimitation. However, if the continental shelf is assumed to be continuous, in the present state of international law no characteristic could validly be invoked to support an argument based on the rule of natural prolongation and designed to justify a delimitation establishing a natural separation.

118. The proportionality between the surface areas of maritime zones to be attributed is another circumstance which the Tribunal has to examine. The parties have argued this question from two aspects: proportionality in relation to the land mass of each State and proportionality in relation to the length of their coastlines. As far as the Tribunal is concerned, proportionality must be considered in the assessment of factors which enter into the equation leading to an equitable result. Combined with all the other factors, it enables the States concerned to be dealt with on an equal footing. However, this does not concern mathematical equality, but rather legal equality.

119. As for proportionality with relation to the land mass of each State, the Tribunal considers that this does not constitute a relevant factor in this case. The rights which a State may

claim to have over the sea are not related to the extent of the territory behind its coasts, but to the coasts themselves and to the manner in which they border this territory. A State with a fairly small land area may well be justified in claiming a much more extensive maritime territory than an larger country. Everything depends on their respective maritime facades and their formations.

120. The only relevant proportionality is that between the length of the coastline and the surface area of the zone to be attributed to each State. However, this circumstance must not be exaggerated. The delimitation, which the International Court of Justice said in the *North Sea Continental Shelf* cases (*I.C.J. Reports 1969*, p. 22, paragraph 20) must not be a mere apportionment, cannot be effected by simply dividing the maritime zones equally between the two States in proportion to the lengths of their coastlines. A delimitation is a legal operation. In order to effect a delimitation, it is certainly necessary to refer to circumstances which may have physical characteristics, but these circumstances must nevertheless be based on considerations of law. Furthermore, the rule of proportionality is not a mechanical rule based only in figures reflecting the length of the coastline. It must be used in a reasonable way, with due account being given to other circumstances in the case (see, in particular, *North Sea Continental Shelf* cases, *I.C.J. Reports 1969*, p. 54, paragraph 101, *Tunisia/Libya* case, *I.C.J. Reports 1982*, p. 93, paragraph 133). More precisely, in the present case, the fact of taking the islands into account results in the coastlines of the two States being considered by the Tribunal as having the same length. Where proportionality is concerned, therefore, neither of the two Parties can claim any additional advantage.

121. The Parties have invoked economic circumstances. . . However, this Tribunal has not, any more than the International Court of Justice in the *Tunisia/Libya* case (*I.C.J. Reports 1982*, pp. 77-78, paragraph 107) acquired the conviction that economic problems constitute permanent circumstances to be taken into account for the purposes of delimitation. . . .

123. Some States may have been treated by nature in a way that favors their boundaries or their economic development; others may be disadvantaged. The boundaries fixed by man must not be designed to increase the difficulties of States or to complicate their economic life. The fact is that the Tribunal does not have the power to compensate for the economic inequalities of the States concerned by modifying a delimitation which it considers is called for by objective and certain circumstances. . . .

124. To the economic circumstances, the Parties linked a circumstance concerned with security. This is not without interest, but it must be emphasized that neither the exclusive economic zone nor the continental shelf are zones of sovereignty. However, the implications that this circumstance might have had were avoided by the fact that, in its proposed solution, the Tribunal has taken care to ensure that each State controls the maritime territories situated opposite its coasts and in their vicinity. The Tribunal has constantly been guided by its concern to find an equitable solution. Its prime objective had been to avoid that either Party, for one reason or another, should see rights exercised opposite its coast or in the immediate vicinity thereof, which could prevent the exercise of its own right to development or compromise its security.

130. For this reason,

The Tribunal
has unanimously
decided that:

1) the Convention of 12 May 1886 between France and Portugal did not determine a maritime boundary between the respective possessions of those two States in West Africa;

2) the protocols and documents annexed to the 1886 Convention have an important role to play in the legal interpretation of the said Convention;

3) the line delimiting the respective maritime territories of the Republic or Guinea-Bissau and the Republic of Guinea:

a) starts form the intersection of the thalweg of the Cajet River and the meridian of 15°06'30" west longitude;

b) joins by loxodromic segments the following points:

	Latitude North	Longitude West
A	10°50'00"	15°09"00"
B	10°40'00"	15°20'30"
C	10°40'00"	15°34'15"

c) follows a loxodromic line on an azimuth of 236° from point C above to the outer limit of the maritime territories of each State as recognized under general international law.

REFERENCES

Kathleen A. McLlarky, "Guinea/Guinea-Bissau: Dispute Concerning Delimitation of Maritime Boundary, February 14, 1985," *Maryland Journal of International Law and Trade*, Vol. 11 (1987), pp. 93-121.

NOTE

On August 16, 1988, Denmark filed a case against Norway before the International Court of Justice, requesting the court "to decide, in accordance with the international law, where a single line of delimitation shall be drawn between Denmark's and Norway's fishing zones and continental shelf areas in the waters between Greenland and Jan Mayan." *Law of the Sea Bulletin*, No. 12 (December 1988), p. 76.

2.   The Delimitation of Economic Zones and its Relation to the Delimitation of the Continental Shelf

If, between two opposite states, one declares an exclusive economic zone and one does not, how should the maritime boundary between them be delimited? This is a question which has not been discussed within the extensive literature on maritime boundary delimitation or in any international cases. Since the regime of the continental shelf emerged earlier than that of the exclusive economic zone, and under Article 2, paragraph 3 of the 1958 Convention on the Continental Shelf and Article 72, paragraph 3 on the Law of the Sea, the 1982 United Nations Convention , "the rights of the coastal State over the continental shelf do not depend on occupation, effective or national, or on any express proclamation," it is unlikely that a coastal state would give up its claim to continental shelf beyond the median line of two states with opposite coasts.

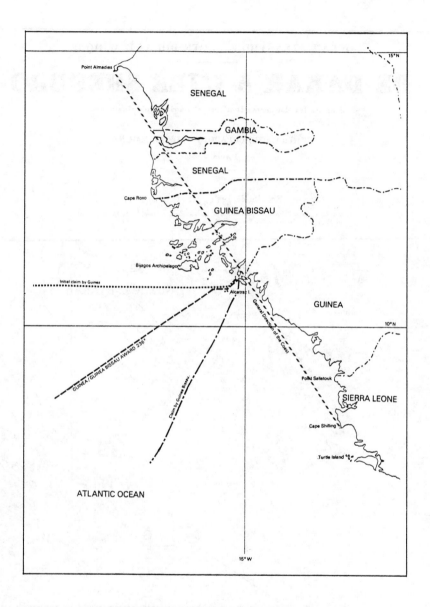

Guinea-Bissau-Guinea Maritime Boundary Claims
Figure 5-13

Source: L.A. Willis, "From Precedent to Precedent: The Triumph of Pragmatism in the
Law of Maritime Boundaries," *Canadian Yearbook of International Law*, Vol.
XXIV (1986), p. 26. Reprinted by permission of the University of British
Columbia Press and Professor C.B. Bourne, Editor-in-Chief of the Yearbook.

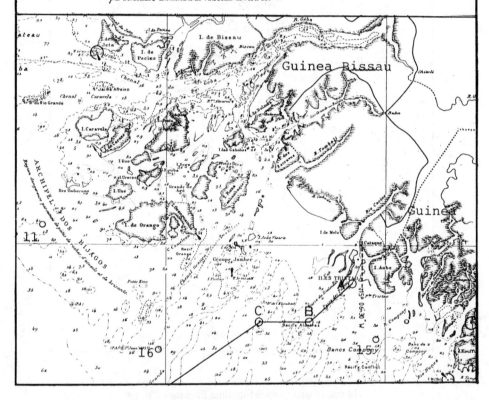

Guinea-Bissau/Guinea Maritime Boundary
Figure 5-14

Source: *International Legal Materials*, Vol. 25 (1986), pp. 306-307. Reprinted by permission of The American Society of International Law.

On the other hand, under Article 56, paragraph 1, of the 1982 Convention, a coastal state has "sovereign rights for the purpose of exploring and exploiting, conserving and managing the natural resources, whether living or non-living, of the waters superjacent to the seabed and of the seabed and its subsoil. . . ," up to 200 miles from its coast so it is unlikely that a state would allow an opposite state to claim the continental shelf under its exclusive economic zone.

One possible solution is to absorb the regime of continental shelf within 200 miles into the exclusive economic zone. Thus, if the distance between two states of opposite coasts is within 400 miles, then the exclusive economic zone should be delimited regardless of the continental shelf between them. Professor Shigeru Oda of Japan appears to favor this view.[1]

However, a state with a broad shelf vis-a-vis an opposite state is likely to oppose this view. Under such circumstances, it is possible for that state not to declare an exclusive economic zone, but to base its claim on the doctrine of the continental shelf. Moreover, even if a state makes a declaration on an exclusive economic zone, it can still assert its rights on a continental shelf based on conventional and customary rules of international law. For instance, when the Chinese government at Taipei made a declaration of its economic zone on September 6, 1979, it specifically pointed out:

> The sovereign rights enjoyed by the Republic of China over the continental shelf contiguous to its coast as recognized by the Convention on the Continental Shelf of 1958 and the general principles of international law shall not be prejudiced in any manner by the proclamation of the present exclusive economic zone or the establishment of such zones, by any other state.[2]

Another solution is to have different maritime boundary lines for the exclusive economic zone and the continental shelf. For instance, in the *Case Concerning the Continental Shelf* (Tunisia/Libya), Libya expressed the following view at a hearing held on October 9, 1981:

> Libya considers that, as between States with opposite or adjacent coasts, the delimitation of their respective continental shelf areas and of their economic zones ought not, in the majority of cases, to be different. Nevertheless, there may be factors relevant to fishing, such as established fishing practices, which have no relevance to shelf resources; and, conversely, there may be factors relevant to shelf resources--such as geological features controlling the extent of a natural prolongation--of no relevance to fishing. *It therefore follows that the two boundaries need not necessarily coincide.* [Emphasis added].[3]

In actual cases of delimitation, a few states do agree to have two different maritime boundary lines

---

[1]Shigeru Oda, *International Law of the Resources of the Sea*, Alphen aan den Rijn; Germantown, MD: Sijthoff & Noordhoff, 1979, p. 93.

[2]Cited from *Chinese Yearbook of International Law and Affairs*, Vol. 1 (1981), p. 152.

[3]Cited from 1982 *I. C. J. Reports*, p. 232.

for different purposes. For instance, in the Treaty between Papua New Guinea and Australia concluded on December 8, 1978, the fisheries-jurisdiction line does not correspond to the seabed and subsoil (continental shelf) boundary.[4]

Since the 1982 Convention on the Law of the Sea has made it clear in Article 74, paragraph 1, and Article 83, paragraph 1, that the purpose of delimitation is "to achieve an equitable solution" and if a single boundary approach to the delimitation between the continental shelf and the exclusive economic zone is unlikely to achieve that purpose, then a two boundary line approach would do justice to both countries of opposite coasts.

On the other hand, if opposite states agreed to have a single maritime boundary between one's continental shelf and the other's exclusive economic zone, an approach similar to that of 1985 *Malta/Libya Continental Shelf Case* may be adopted to delimit that line through the following stages: (1) delimit a continental shelf line between them in accordance with applicable rules of international law; discussed earlier; (2) delimit an exclusive economic zone between them in accordance with applicable rules of international law; and (3) use the median line between those two lines as the single maritime boundary line between these opposite states. This approach would do justice to both countries since one effectively has traded part of its continental shelf for a shorter distance of the exclusive economic zone of the other and vice versa.

A scholar expressed the view that within 200 miles of the coast, the natural prolongation principle of the continental shelf should be absorbed by the distance principle of the exclusive economic zone.[5]

3. The Problem of Islands

David Attard, *The Exclusive Economic Zone in International Law*, New
York: Oxford University Press, 1987, pp. 259-264. Notes Omitted.
Reprinted by permission of Oxford University Press.

The presence of islands may create two problems: (a) one relating to their entitlement to an EEZ, (b) one relating to their effect on EEZ delimitations.

The question of whether all islands, irrespective of their size and condition, generate an EEZ has been controversial throughout UNCLOS III. The importance of this issue becomes clearer when one considers that a small island like Amsterdam in the Indian Ocean, which can sustain habitation, can generate an EEZ larger that that of Belgium, Netherlands, and the Federal Republic of Germany put together.

Article I(b) of the 1958 Shelf Convention, considered by the International Court to reflect customary law, makes no distinction and recognizes that all islands generate a shelf. The definition of an island found in Article 10 (I) of the Territorial Sea Convention was assumed also to apply to the Shelf Convention. This definition is also reproduced in the 1982 Convention. However, whilst islands generate an EEZ and a shelf, rocks "which cannot sustain human habitation or economic life of their own" do not. The words "of their own" ensure that no State

---

[4]*International Legal Material*, Vol. 18 (1979), pp. 291-331.

[5]See Surya P. Sharma, "The Single Maritime Boundary Regime and the Relationship Between the Continental Shelf and the Exclusive Economic Zone," *International Journal of Estuarine and Coastal Law*, Vol. 2, No. 4 (November 1987), pp. 203-226.

may artificially create the necessary conditions. Nor may States artificially extend the rocks for the purpose of delimitation; for under Article 60, artificial islands may not have a territorial sea or even affect the EEZ's delimitation. The proposed qualifications present problems of interpretation. Are both qualifications necessary, or is the absence of one sufficient to prevent the "rock" from generating an EEZ? Does "sustain" refer to natural resources or to geographic conditions?

Only a few States--Mexico is an example--prevent "islands which cannot be kept inhabited or which do not have an economic life of their own" from generating an EEZ. Most States do not adopt the 1982 [UN]CLOS distinction, and claim an EEZ for all their islands. Democratic Yemen, for example, explicitly states that all its islands generate an EEZ. The position seems to be the same with regard to the shelf: "In practice States. . . .whether 'island-States' or continental States with offshore islands, have asserted rights to a continental shelf for their islands."

Furthermore, whilst there are cases where States by agreement have allocated restricted shelves to rocks, it is difficult to find a general practice denying them any entitlement. Aves Island was given full effect by the US/Venezuela Maritime Boundary Agreement despite its very small size and lack of habitation. Iceland and Denmark have protested on the basis of Article 121(3) against British claims that Rockall generates a 200-n.m. EZ. Professor Brownlie states that Rockall is "only marginally" an island; however, State practice contains many marginal applications, and many problems would arise if the simple geographical definition of what is an island were changed. It is therefore difficult to see how Article 121(3) reflects customary law.

Professor Bowett rightly states that Article 121(3) would seem not to apply in cases where rocks form part of the baseline from which the EEZ boundary is measured. This view is compatible with the general practice of using rocks as turning-points for baselines. New Zealand defines a "baseline", from which its EEZ is measured, as the low-water mark along the coast. . . .including the coasts of all islands." This includes uninhabited islands such as Auckland and Bounty islands. Burma, Canada, Cuba, Iceland, and Brazil adopted a similar approach.

The presence of islands is possibly the major issue which is likely to cause complications in boundary negotiations. Generally, there are three approaches to solving the presence of islands in EEZ delimitations. The first would be to draw a boundary ignoring the existence of islands; the second would give full effect to islands; and the third would give effect to islands depending on relevant factors such as distance from the coast, size, population, and economic and political development. The question here arises of whether shelf-delimitation principles on the role of islands could also apply to EZ delimitation. If one accepts that islands have an EZ and a shelf than it is difficult to see how certain principles are not applicable. In the case of adjacent coasts, the 1969 Judgment recognized that the use of equidistance could produce a distorting effect, under certain conditions of coastal configuration, in the delimitation of both the territorial sea and the shelf. The presence of offshore islands could produce a concave coastline similar to that considered by the International Court. In the case of opposite States, the Court held that the "presence of islets, rocks and minor coastal projections: could create a "disproportionately distorted effect" on the use of the median line. This effect should, however, not be allowed to affect the use of the median line, for it could be eliminated by other means.

The question of whether islands should be ignored, given full effect, or given a limited effect, depends ultimately on the extent to which they are factors of inequity. Prima Facie it would not seem difficult to include islands within the "relevant circumstances" concept. The weight they receive would depend on their own characteristics and other prevailing circumstances. It is noteworthy that because certain factors are relevant only to shelf delimitations or EEZ delimitations, the effect of islands in the balancing of factors may depend on the boundary in

delimitations, the effect of islands in the balancing of factors may depend on the boundary in question.

In the *Channel* Dispute, the Court of Arbitration recognized that the relevance of islands' size and importance "may properly be taken into account in balancing the equities." It also considers other circumstances: the limits of the territorial seas and coastal fisheries, the islands' political status, and their geographical location. It rejected the French arguments, based on the "equality of States" justifying a curtailment of an island's shelf as not constituting an equitable ground. In the final analysis it found that, because the Channel Islands were "on the wrong side" of the median line between States with "almost equal coastlines", "close to the French coast", and "wholly detached geographically" from Britain to divert the mid-channel median line would effect a 'radical distortion of the boundary creative of inequality". It therefore enclaved the Channel Islands in a 12-n.m. shelf zone, within the French shelf, and retained the median line between the two States. It pointed out that this case was "quite different from that of small islands on the right side or closer to the median line, and also quite different from the case where numerous islands stretch out one after another long distances from the mainland."

Reference was made to the Case of *St. Pierre et Miquelon* which, whilst presenting analogies, also had important differences. France and Canada were not, it held, opposite States in equal relationship. The open waters to the east allowed more scope for "redressing inequities" than the Channel's narrow waters. This seems to imply that the use of enclaves should be restricted to cases of narrow waters. The Court even referred to the 1972 Releve de Conclusions which allotted only a 12-n.m. territorial sea. It is interesting, however, that under its 1977 EEZ Legislation France claimed an EEZ beyond 12-n.m. The Court found that the Scilly archipelago was a "special circumstance" on the "right side" of the median line, which, in the light of all the pertinent geographical circumstances, amounted to an inequitable distortion of the equidistance line.

In the *Tunisia/Libya* Case, the International Court considered the Kerkennah Islands, in view of their size and position, a relevant circumstance to which it had to attribute some effect. It was not, however, willing to give any weight to Jerba Island, as in the "area to be delimited in which the island . . . would be relevant, there are other circumstances which prevail over the effects of its presence." The treatment of the Island (690 sq. kilometers in area, surrounded by stationary fishing gear) suggests that an island's relevance may be disregarded if counterbalanced by other factors.

Should island States in EEZ delimitations be treated differently from dependent islands? Neither the 1958 conventions nor the UNCLOS III tests considered this specific question. The issue was discussed in the *Channel Dispute* in which France contended that international law does not contemplate a single concept of "islands' and that any legal classification may have to take into account political circumstances. It insisted that the Channel Islands, not themselves directly responsible for their foreign relations, were distant from the island States. Britain replied that they were direct dependencies of the Crown, with their own legislative assemblies, fiscal and legal systems, and courts of law, as well as their own coinage and postal services. Thus whilst Britain was responsible for the Islands's foreign relations, they enjoyed "an important degree of political, legislative, administrative and economic independence of ancient foundation." It was therefore a question of delimiting the Islands' boundary with France. The Court accepted the view that the Islands should be differentiated from rocks or small islands, as they possessed, *inter alia*, "a very large measure of political, legislative, administrative, and economic autonomy". However, it refused to treat them as independent or semi-independent States and considered them as separate islands of the United Kingdom. Thus, whilst it was prepared to recognize a 12-n.m. shelf for the Islands, in effect this meant that they received no more than if they had claimed a 12-n.m.

Islands, in effect this meant that they received no more than if they had claimed a 12-n.m. territorial sea.

This solution contrasts with the "semi-enclave" approach found in the 1971 Italy/Tunisia Agreement whereby a 1-n.m. shelf boundary beyond Italy's 12-n.m. territorial sea was given to Pantelleia, Lampedusa, and Linosa. The US-Cook Islands maritime boundary indicates that States may be prepared to recognize political entities as generating a 200-n.m. even though the Islands' foreign relations are conducted in conjunction with New Zealand. Like the Channel Islands, they are internally self-governing.

It is submitted that any distinction between island States and coastal States would be contrary to the general principles of international law relating to sovereignty and equality of States. The very use of such terms as "sovereign rights" and "jurisdiction" reflects the relationship between States' sovereignty and maritime control. State practice and the UNCLOS III debates confirm that there is no support for such a distinction. Some twenty-nine island States have established an EEZ. Furthermore, there are numerous examples of these claims having been recognized by coastal States. The 1976 India/Sri Lanka Agreement, for example, does not discriminate against Sri Lanka.

REFERENCES

N. Ely, "Seabed Boundaries Between Coastal States: The Effect to be Given Islets as 'Special Circumstances'," *International Lawyer*, Vol. 6 (1972), pp. 219-236; J. D. Gass, "The French Claim to the Eastern North American Continental Shelf," *JAG Journal*, Vol. 27 (1973), Washington D.C.: Office of the Judge Advocate General of the U. S. Navy, pp. 367-391; L. F. E. Goldie, "The International Court of Justice's 'Natural Prolongation' and the Continental Shelf Problem of Islands," *Netherlands Yearbook of International Law*, Vol. 4 (1973), pp. 237-261; D. E. Karl, "Islands and the Delimitation of the Continental Shelf: A Framework for Analysis," *American Journal of International Law*, Vol. 71 (1977), pp. 642-673; Jimmy L. Verner, Jr., "Legal Claims to Newly Emerged Islands," *San Diego Law Review*, Vol. 15 (1978), pp. 525-545.; D. W. Bowett, *The Legal Regime of Islands in International Law*, Dobbs Ferry, New York: Oceana, 1979; Andreas J. Jacovide, "Three Aspects of the Law of the Sea: Islands, Delimitation and Dispute Settlement," *Marine Policy*, Vol. 3 (1979), No. 4, pp. 278-288; C. R. Symmons, *The Maritime Zones of Islands in International Law*, The Hague: Martinus Nijhoff, 1979; Emmanuel Gounaris, "The Delimitation of the Continental Shelf of Islands: Some Observations," *Revue Hellenique De Droit International*, Vol. 33 (1980), No. 1, pp. 111-119; Efthalia Papakosta, "The Question of the Continental Shelf of Islands: The Case of the Aegean Sea Island," *Revue Hellenique de Droit International*, Vols. 38/39 (1985/1986), pp. 177-204; Kilaparti Ramakrishna, Robert E. Bowen and Jack H. Archer, "Outer Limits of Continental Shelf: A Legal Analysis of Chilean and Ecuadorian Island Claims and US Response," *Marine Policy*, Vol. 11 (1987), No. 1, pp. 58-68; *The Law of the Sea. Regime of Islands. Legislative History of Part VIII (Article 121) of the United Nations Convention on the Law of the Sea*, New York: The United Nations, 1987; John Briscoe, "Islands in Maritime Boundary Delimitation," *Ocean Yearbook*, Vol. 7 (1988), pp. 14-41; Walter Van Overbeek, "Article 121(3) LOSC in Mexican State Practice in the Pacific," *International Journal of Estuarine and Coastal Law*, Vol. 4, No. 4 (November 1989), pp. 252-267.

NOTE ON CERTAIN ISLAND DISPUTES

(1) *East China Sea:* The T'iao-yu Tai Islets or Senkaku Gunto are claimed both by China (Mainland and Taiwan) and Japan. Their location in the East China Sea is critical in determining the allocation of the continental shelf or economic zone between the two countries. See T.

Okuhara, "The Territorial Sovereignty Over the Senkaku Island and the Problem on the Surrounding Continental Shelf," *Japanese Annual of International Law*, No. 15 (1971), pp. 97-106; Determining R. Allen and P.H. Mitchell, "The Legal Status of the Continental Shelf of the East China Sea," *Oregon Law Review*, Vol. 51 (1972), pp. 789-812; T.R. Ragland, "A Harbinger: The Senkaku Islands," *San Diego Law Review*, Vol. 10 (1973), pp. 664-691; T. Cheng, "The Sino-Japanese Dispute Over the Senkaku Islands and the Law of Territorial Acquisition," *Virginia Journal of International Law*, Vol. 14 (1974), pp. 221-266; Hungdah Chiu, "Island Disputes in the Far East," in R. Bernardt, ed., *Encyclopedia of Public International Law*, Vol. 6 (1983), pp. 233-236.

(2) *South China Sea*: China (Mainland and Taiwan), Vietnam, the Philippines and Malaysia have been in dispute over Paracel Islands and Spratly Islands for many years. These islands are of critical importance in delimiting the continental shelves and exclusion zones in the South China Sea. See Hungdah Chiu and Choon-ho Park, "Legal Status of the Paracel and Spratly Islands," *Ocean Development and International Law*, Vol. 3 (1975), pp. 1-28; Dieter Heinzig, *Disputes Islands in the South China Sea*, Hamburg: Institute of Asian Affairs, 1976; Hungdah Chiu, "South China Sea Islands--Implication for Delimiting Seabed and Future Shipping Route," *The China Quarterly*, No. 72 (1978), pp. 743-765; M.S. Samuels, *Contest for the South China Sea*, London and New York: Methuen, 1982; J.R.V. Prescott, *The Maritime Political Boundaries of the World*, London and New York: Methuen, 1985, pp. 209-233.

(3) *The Aegean Sea*: Greece and Turkey have been in dispute over the proper delimitation of continental shelf in the Aegean Sea. Greece claims that its archipelagic islands are entitled, in accordance with the provisions of the 1958 Convention on the Continental Shelf, to generate continental shelf the same as mainland areas. Turkey, which has not ratified the 1958 Convention, opposes the Greek position as it would effectively eliminate Turkey from all continental shelf in the Aegean Sea. See A. Phylactopoulos, "Mediterranean Discord: Conflicting Greek-Turkish Claims on the Aegean Seabed," *International Lawyer*, Vol. 8 (1974), pp. 431-441; C.L. Rozakis, *The Greek-Turkish Dispute Over the Aegean Continental Shelf*, Kingston, Rhode Island: University of Rhode Island Law of the Sea Institute, Occasional Paper No. 27 (1975); L. Gross, "The Dispute Between Greece and Turkey Concerning the Continental Shelf in e Aegean," *American Journal of International Law*, Vol. 71 (1977), pp. 31-59; Efthalia Papakosta, "The Question of the Continental Shelf of Islands: The Case of the Aegean Sea Islands," *Revenue Hellenique de Droit International*, Vols. 38/39 (1985/1986), pp. 177-204.

(4) *Rockall*: This British owned tiny rock in the North Atlantic Ocean cuts significantly into Irish continental shelf and thus becomes a dispute between the two countries. See E.DETERMINING. Brown, "Rockall and the Limits of National Jurisdiction of the United Kingdom," *Marine Policy*, Vol. 2 (1978), pp. 181-211, 275-302.

4. Interim Arrangement and Bilateral Agreement

1982 UNITED NATIONS CONVENTION ON THE LAW OF THE SEA

Article 74
Delimitation of the exclusive economic zone between States
with opposite or adjacent coasts

1. The delimitation of the exclusive economic zone between States with opposite or adjacent coasts shall be effected by agreement on the basis of international law as referred to in Article 38 of the Statute of the International Court of Justice, in order to achieve an equitable solution.

2. If no agreement can be reached within a reasonable period of time, the States concerned shall resort to the procedures provided for in Part XV.

3. Pending agreement as provided for in paragraph 1, the States concerned, in a spirit of understanding and co-operation, shall make every effort to enter into provisional arrangements of a practical nature and, during this transitional period, not to jeopardize or hamper the reaching of the final agreement Such arrangements shall be without prejudice to the final delimitation.

4. Where there is an agreement in force between the States concerned, questions relating to the delimitation of the exclusive economic zone shall be determined in accordance with the provisions of that agreement.

E. BILATERAL AGREEMENTS ON MARITIME BOUNDARY

1. Tunisia-Italy Continental Shelf Boundary

AGREEMENT BETWEEN THE GOVERNMENT OF THE REPUBLIC OF TUNISIA AND THE GOVERNMENT OF THE ITALIAN REPUBLIC CONCERNING THE DELIMITATION OF THE CONTINENTAL SHELF BETWEEN THE TWO COUNTRIES, August 20, 1971, Office for Ocean Affairs and the Law of the Sea, *The Law of the Sea, Maritime Boundary Agreements (1970-1984)*, New York: The United Nations 1987, pp. 174-180.

ARTICLE I

The boundary line of the continental shelf between the two countries shall be the median line every point of which is equidistant from the nearest points on the baselines from which the breadth of the territorial seas of Tunisia and Italy is measured, taking into account islands, islets, and uncovered shoals, except Lampione, Lamdedusa, Linosa and Pantelleria.

ARTICLE II

With regard to the islands referred to in Article I, the boundary line of the continental shelf is defined by the following provisions:

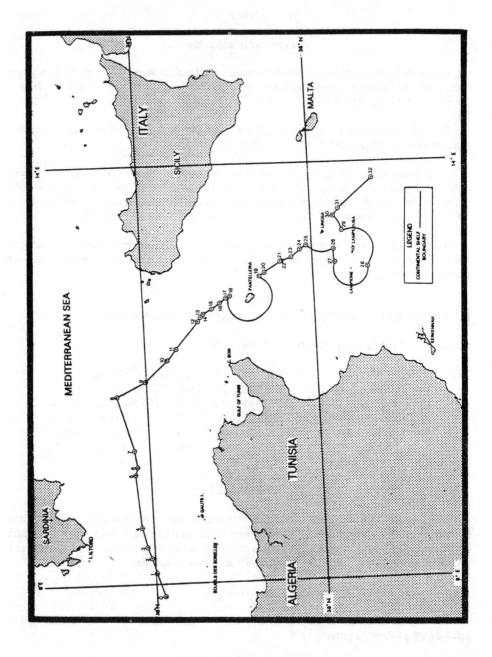

Tunisia/Italy Maritime Boundary
Figure 5-15

(a) Around Pantelleria, the boundary line towards Tunisia shall be made up of the curve forming the envelope of the circles having a radius of 13 nautical miles and having their centers on the coastline of this island, as far as the intersection of this envelope with the median line defined in article I.

(b) Around Lampoine, the boundary line towards Tunisia shall be made up of the curve forming the envelope of the circles having a radius of 12 nautical miles and having their centers on the coastline of this island, as far as the intersection of this envelope with the one relating the Lampedusa as defined in subparagraph (c) below

(c) Around Lampedusa, the boundary line towards Tunisia shall be made up of the sections of the curve forming the envelope of the circles having a radius of 13 nautical miles and having their centers on the coastline of this island, these sections being included between the intersections of this envelope, on the one hand, with that of Lampione as defined in subparagraph (b) above, and, on the other hand, with the envelope relating to Linosa, as defined in subparagraph (d) below.

(d) Around Linosa, the boundary line towards Tunisia shall be made up of the sections of the curve forming the envelope of the circles having a radius of 13 nautical miles and having their centers on the coastline of this island, these sections being included between the intersections of this envelope, on the one hand, with that of Lampedusa as defined in subparagraph (c) above and, on the other hand, with the median line defined in article I.

. . . .

2.   American Samoa--Tokelau Maritime Boundary

TREATY BETWEEN THE UNITED STATES OF AMERICA AND NEW ZEALAND ON THE DELIMITATION OF THE MARITIME BOUNDARY BETWEEN TOKELAU AND THE UNITED STATES OF AMERICA, December 2, 1980, Office for Ocean Affairs and the Law of the Sea, *The Law of the Sea, Maritime Boundary Agreements (1979-1984)*, New York: The United Nations, 1987, pp. 290-293.

The Two Governments,

Recalling the responsibilities exercised by New Zealand in respect to Tokelau pending the exercise by the people of Tokelau of their right to self-determination in accordance with the Untied Nations Declaration on the Granting of Independence to Colonial Countries and Peoples. . . .

Noting that the United States of America has maintained a claim to sovereignty over the islands of Atafu Nukunonu, and Fakaofo and that this claim has not been recognized by New Zealand or the people of Tokelau; . . . .

Have agreed, with the concurrence of the people of Tokelau, as follows:

Article I

The maritime boundary between Tokelau and the United States shall be determined by the geodetic lines connecting the following coordinates:

Latitude (South)	Longitude (West)
10°01'26"	168°31'25"
10°07'52"	169°46'50"
10°10'18"	170°16'10"
10°15'17"	171°15'32"
10°17'50"	171°50'58"
10°25'26"	172°11'01"
10°46'15"	173°03'53"
11°02'17"	173°44'48"

Article II

The geodetic and computational bases used for determining the coordinate values in Article I are the World Geodetic System, 1972 (WGS 72) and the following charts and aerial plans:

- Charts published by the National Ocean Survey of the United States of America;
  NOS No. 83484, 6th edition, March 26, 1977;

- Charts published by the Defense Mapping Agency of the United States of American;
  DMAHTC No. 83478, 7th Edition, May 3, 1976;

- Aerial Plans published by the Department of Lands and Survey of New Zealand;
  No. 1036/7C, 1974; No. 1036/7B2, 1974; No. 1036/8d, 1975.

Article III

On the side of the maritime boundary adjacent to Tokelau, the United States of America shall not claim or exercise for any purpose sovereign rights or jurisdiction over the waters or seabed and subsoil. On the side of the maritime boundary adjacent to American Samoa there shall not be claimed or exercised for any purpose in respect to Tokelau sovereign rights or jurisdiction over the waters or seabed and subsoil.

Article IV

The maritime boundary established by this Treaty shall not affect or prejudice in any manner either Government's position with respect to the rules of international law concerned with the exercise of jurisdiction over the waters or seabed and subsoil or any other matter relating to the Law of the Sea.

Article V

The United States recognizes that sovereignty over the islands of Atafu, Nukunonu and Fakaofo, together comprising Tokelau is vested in the people of Tokelau and is exercised on their behalf by the Government of New Zealand pending an act of self-determination in accordance with the Charter of the United Nations.

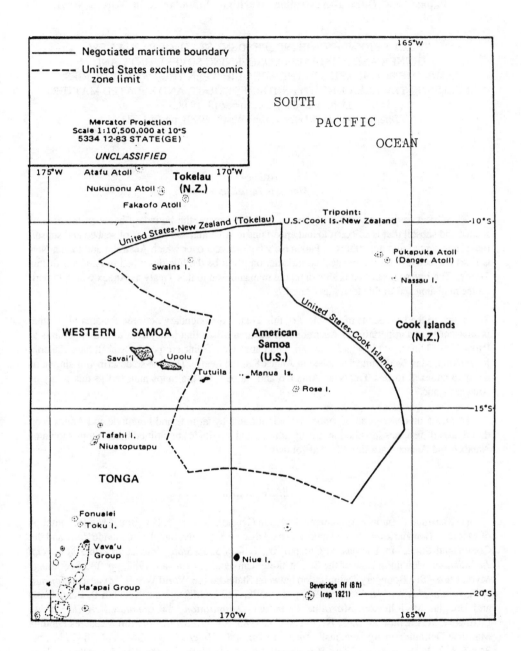

U.S. / Tokelau Maritime Boundary
Figure 5-16

3.   **Papua New Guinea--Australian Maritime Boundaries in Torres Strait**

TREATY BETWEEN THE INDEPENDENT STATE OF PAPUA NEW
GUINEA AND AUSTRALIA CONCERNING SOVEREIGNTY AND
MARITIME BOUNDARIES IN THE AREA BETWEEN THE TWO COUNTRIES,
INCLUDING THE AREA KNOWN AS TORRES STRAIT, AND RELATED MATTERS
Done at Sydney, December 18, 1978,.[1]
International Legal Materials, Vol. 18 (1979), pp. 291-331.

. . . .

Article 4
Maritime Jurisdiction

1.   Subject to the provisions of Article 2 of this Treaty, the boundary between the area of
seabed and subsoil that is adjacent to and appertains to Australia and the area of seabed and subsoil
that is adjacent to and appertains to Papua New Guinea, and over which Australia and Papua New
Guinea respectively shall have seabed jurisdiction, shall be the line described in Annex 5 of this
Treaty. The line so described is shown on the map annexed to this Treaty as Annex 6 and, in part,
on the map annexed to this treaty as Annex 7.

2.   Subject to the provisions of Article 2 of this Treaty, the boundary between the area of sea that
is adjacent to and appertains to Australia and the area of sea that is adjacent to and appertains to
Papua New Guinea, and in which Australia and Papua New Guinea respectively shall have fisheries
jurisdiction, shall be the line described in Annex 8 to the treaty. The line so described is shown on
the map annexed to this Treaty as Annex 6 and, in part, on the maps annexed to this treaty as
Annexes 2 and 7.

. . . .

[Annex 5 on description of seabed jurisdiction line by latitude and longitude and Annex 8 on
description of fisheries jurisdiction line by latitude and longitude are omitted here. Maps shown on
Annex 6 and Annex 7 are simplified as follows:]

REFERENCES

(1) Maritime Boundary Agreements/Issues in General: Robert D. Hodgson, "The Delimitation
of Maritime Boundaries Between Opposite and Adjacent States through the Economic Zone and the
Continental Shelf," in Thomas A. Clingan, Jr., *Law of Sea: State Practice in Zones of Special
Jurisdiction*: Honolulu: Law of the Sea Institute, University of Hawaii, 1982, pp. 280-316; Sang-
Myon Rhee, "Sea Boundary Delimitation between States before World War II," *American Journal
of International Law*,. Vol. 76 (1982), pp. 555-588; Ted L. McDorman, Kenneth P. Beauchamp
and Douglas M. Johnston, *Maritime Boundary Delimitation, An Annotated Bibliography*,
Lexington, Massachusetts: D. C. Heath and Co., 1983; Rainer Lagoni, "Interim Measures Pending
Maritime Delimitation Agreements," *American Journal of International Law*, Vol. 78 (1984), pp.
345-368; J. R. V. Prescott, *The Maritime Political Boundaries of the World*, London & New
York, Methuen, 1985; Office for Ocean Affairs and the Law of the Sea, *The Law of the Sea*,

---

[1]This Treaty is analyzed in H. Burmester, "The Torres Strait Treaty: Ocean Boundary Delimitation
by Agreement," *American Journal of International Law*, Vol. 76 (1982), pp. 321-349.

Maritime Boundary Agreements (1979-1984), New York: The United Nations, 1987; Hans J. Buchholz, *Law of the Sea Zones in the Pacific Ocean*, Singapore: Institute of South Asian Studies, 1987; Douglas M. Johnston and Philip M. Saunders, *Ocean Boundary Making: Regional Issues and Developments*, London/New York/Sydney: Croom Helm, 1988.

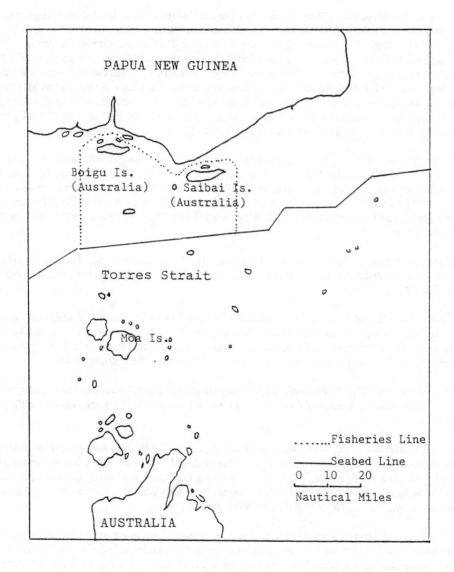

Australia/Papua New Guinea Maritime Boundary
Figure 5-17

(2) United States and Neighboring Countries: (General) Mark B. Feldman and David A. Colson, "The Maritime Boundaries of the United States," *American Journal of International Law*, Vol. 75 (1981), pp. 729-763; Robert W. Smith, "The Maritime Boundaries of the United States," *Geographical Review*. Vol. 71, No. 4 (October 1981), pp. 395-410; Donna Darm, "The Outward Limits of the Department of Interior's Authority Over Submerged Lands--the Effect of Customary International Law on the Outer Continental Shelf Lands Act," *Washington Law Review*, Vol.60 (1985), pp. 673-696.

(Canada) San-Myon Rhee, "The Application of Equitable Principles to Resolve the United States-Canada Dispute over East Coast Fisheries," *Harvard International Law Journal*, Vol. 21 (1980), pp. 667-683; Karin L. Lawson, "Delimiting Continental Shelf Boundaries in the Arctic: The United States-Canada Beaufort Sea Boundary," *Virginia Journal of International Law*, Vol.22 (1981), pp. 221-246; Robert E. Bowen and Timothy Hennessey, "Adjacent State Issues for the United States in Establishing an Exclusive Economic Zone: The Cases of Canada and Mexico," *Ocean Development and International Law*, Vol. 15 (1985), pp. 353-375; Willy Streng, "Delimitation Arrangements in Arctic Seas. Cases of Precedence or Security of Strategic/Economic Interests?" *Marine Policy*, Vol. 10 (1986), No. 2, pp. 132-154.

(Mexico) Hollis D. Hedberg, "Evaluation of U.S.-Mexico Draft Treaty on Boundaries in the Gulf of Mexico," *Marine Technology Society Journal*, Vol. 14 (1980), pp. 32-37; Karl M. Schmitt, "The Problem of Maritime Boundaries in U.S.-Mexican Relations," *Natural Resources Journal*, Vol. 22 (1982), pp. 139-153; Alberto Szekely, "A Comment with the Mexican View on the Problem of Maritime Boundaries in U. S.-Mexican Relations," *Natural Resources Journal*, Vol. 22 (1982), pp. 155-159.

(Bahamas) Philip A. Allen, "III Law of the Sea: The Delimitation of the Maritime Boundary Between the United States and the Bahamas," *University of Florida Law Review*, Vol. 33 (1981), pp. 207-239.

(Soviet Union-Bering Sea) Hollis D. Hedberg, "Ocean Floor Jurisdictional Boundaries for the Bering Sea," *Marine Technology Society Journal*, Vol. 14 (1980-1981), pp. 47-53; Camille M. Antinori, "The Bering Sea: A Maritime Delimitation Dispute between the United States and the Soviet Union," *Ocean Development and International Law*, Vol. 18 (1987), pp. 1-47.

(Central America) David Freestone, "El Salvador/Honduras: Land, Island and Maritime Frontier Case," *International Journal of Estuarine and Coastal Law*, Vol. 3, No. 4 (November 1988), pp. 342-344.

(3) Mediterranean Sea: Umberto Leanza and Luigi Sico, *The Mediterranean Continental Shelf: Delimitation and Regime, International and National Legal Sources*, 4 Vols., Dobbs Ferry, New York: Oceana Publications, 1988; Gaetano Arangio-Ruiz, "The Italian Continental Shelf Delimitation Agreements and the General Law on Shelf Delimitation," *Rivista Di Studi Politici Internationali*, Vol. 56, No. 2 (April-June 1989), pp. 245-265.

(4) Asia-Oceania: Hungdah Chiu, "Some Problems Concerning the Delimitation of the Maritime Boundary Between the Republic of China and the Philippines," *Chinese Yearbook of International Law and Affairs*, Vol. 3 (1983), pp. 1-21; C. Cook, "Filling the Gap: Delimiting the Australia-Indonesia Maritime Boundary," *Australia Yearbook of International Law*, Vol. 10 (1987), pp. 131-175; Kriangsak Kittichaisaree, *The Law of the Sea and Maritime Boundary Delimitation in South-East Asia*, New York and Singapore: Oxford University Press, 1987.

(5) Europe: Erik Franckx, "The 1989 Maritime Boundary Delimitation Agreement between the German Democratic Republic and Poland," *International Journal of Estuarine and Coastal Law*, Vol. 4, No. 4 (November 1989), pp. 237-251; Hugo Tiberg, "New Sea Boundaries in A Swedish Perspective," *Michigan Journal of International Law* , Vol. 10 (1989), pp. 686-697.

CHAPTER VI

THE INTERNAL WATERS, TERRITORIAL SEA, STRAIT AND CONTIGUOUS ZONE

A. INTRODUCTION

In this chapter the legal rules applicable to internal waters, the territorial sea and contiguous zone will be presented. The matter of internal waters presents little difficulty, save for the question of the location of the baseline, a subject previously discussed (Chapter IV). There is likewise little debate over the juridical content of the territorial sea, save for questions relating to innocent passage.

More troublesome are the questions of the maximum legitimate breadth of the territorial sea, and the matter of passage through international straits constituted of territorial sea. In reading and discussing these materials, the relationship between the territorial sea and other law of the sea issues should be borne in mind. For instance, if an exclusive economic zone of 200 miles breadth accords the coastal state all the competence it seeks over living and non-living resources of the adjacent ocean, what functions are served by the territorial sea? Is there any need for the concept at all under such conditions?

What are the interests which coastal states perceive in their territorial waters? How can those interests best be protected -- through a complex of functionally limited special contiguous zones, or through a broad territorial sea? What interests of the international community at large are involved in the delimitation of the territorial sea? Are or should coastal state interests be predominant in the policy making process?

REFERENCES

W.T. Burke, "Who Goes Where, When, and How: International Law of the Sea for Transportation," *International Organization*, Vol. 31 (2) (1977), pp. 267-290; D. Shelton and G. Rose, "Freedom of Navigation: The Emerging International Regime," *Santa Clara Law Review*, Vol. 17 (1977), pp. 523-558.

B. THE LEGAL REGIME OF INTERNAL WATERS

This section describes the international legal effects attributable to occurrences taking place *landward* of the baseline. The rules are fairly simple and straightforward and should be easily digested. One caveat--the terms "internal waters" and "inland waters" are synonymous, the latter being used in the 1953 Submerged Lands Act, 67 Stat. 29, and in conjunction with state-Federal litigation in the United States over title to resources in submerged lands.

1958 CONVENTION ON THE TERRITORIAL SEA AND THE CONTIGUOUS ZONE

Article 5

1.   Waters on the landward side of the baseline of the territorial sea form part of the internal waters of the State.

2.   Where the establishment of a straight baseline in accordance with article 4 has the effect of enclosing as internal waters areas which previously had been considered as part of the territorial sea or of the high seas, a right of innocent passage, as provided in articles 14-23, shall exist in those waters.

NOTE

Internal waters are also subject to the right of entry in distress (see Section C, 5 of this chapter.)

1982 UNITED NATIONS CONVENTION ON THE LAW OF THE SEA

Article 8
Internal waters

1. Except as provided in Part IV, waters on the landward side of the baseline of the territorial sea form part of the internal waters of the State.

2. Where the establishment of a straight baseline in accordance with the method set forth in article 7 has the effect of enclosing as internal waters areas which had not previously been considered as such, a right of innocent passage as provided in this Convention shall exist in those waters.

NOTE

Part IV refers to Archipelagic States (see Chapter IV, Section 3, Subsection a, iii), and Article 7 refers to straight baseline (see Chapter IV, Section 3, Subsection a, i).

The common legal feature of all inland waters is the complete sovereignty which a nation exercises over them, the same as it exercises over its land territory. This sovereignty includes the right of exclusion of foreign vessels. A. L. Shalowitz, *Shore and Sea Boundaries*, Vol. 1, Washington, D.C.: U.S. Government Printing Office, 1962, p. 23.

TREATY OF FRIENDSHIP, COMMERCE AND NAVIGATION BETWEEN THE UNITED STATES OF AMERICA AND THE FEDERAL REPUBLIC OF GERMANY
Signed October 29, 1954; entered into force July 14, 1956
T.I.A.S. No. 3593; 7 U.S.T. 1839; 273 U.N.T.S. 3.

Art. XX

1. Vessels of either Party shall have liberty, on equal terms with vessels of the other Party and on equal terms with vessels of any third country, to come with their cargoes to all ports, places and waters of such other Party open to foreign commerce and navigation. Such vessels and cargoes shall in the ports, places and waters of such other Party be accorded in all respects national treatment and most-favored-nation treatment.

. . . .

5. The provisions of the present Article shall not apply to fishing vessels.

. . . .

Art. XXIV

1. The present Treaty shall not preclude the application by either Party of measures:

. . . .

(d) necessary to fulfill its obligations for the maintenance or restoration of international peace and security, or necessary to protect its essential security interests . . . .

NOTE

See Executive Order 10173 (October 18, 1950), for an example of the security measures which the United States has taken with respect to internal waters and port facilities. See also A.V. Lowe, "The Right of Entry into Maritime Ports in International Law," *San Diego Law Review*, Vol. 14 (1977), pp. 597-622.

WILDENHUS'S CASE
120 U.S. 1 (1886)

[In this case a Belgian crewman killed another crewman on a Belgian ship anchored in New Jersey, within the internal waters of the United States. A question arose over which nation--Belgium or the United States--had jurisdiction over the case.]

It is part of the law of civilized nations that when a merchant vessel of one country enters the ports of another for the purposes of trade, it subjects itself to the law of the place to which it goes, unless by treaty or otherwise the two countries have come to some different understanding or agreement. . . .

From experience, however, it was found long ago that it would be beneficial to commerce if the local government would abstain from interfering with the internal discipline of the ship, and the general regulation of the rights and duties of the officers and crew towards the vessel or among themselves. And so by comity it came to be generally understood among civilized nations that all matters of discipline and all things done on board which affected only the vessel or those belonging to her, and did not involve the pace or dignity of the country, or the tranquility of the port, should be left by the local government to be dealt with by the authorities of the nation to which the vessel belonged as the laws of that nation or the interests of its commerce should require. But if crimes are committed on board of a character to disturb the place and tranquility of the country to which the vessel has been brought, the offenders have never by comity or usage been entitled to any exemption from the operation of the local laws for their punishment, if the local tribunals see fit to assert their authority.

. . . .

This being the case, the only important question left for our determination is whether the thing which has been done--the disorder that has arisen--on board this vessel is of a nature to disturb the public peace, or, as some writers term it, the "public repose" of the people who look to the State of New Jersey for their protection. If the thing done--"the disorder," as it is called in the treaty--is of a character to affect those on shore or in the port when it becomes known, the fact that only those on the ship saw it when it was done is a matter of no moment. Those who are not on the vessel pay no special attention to the mere disputes or quarrels of the seamen while on board, whether they occur under deck or above. Neither do they as a rule care for anything done on board which relates only to the discipline of the ship, or to the preservation of order and authority. Not so, however, with crimes which from their gravity awaken a public interest as soon as they become known, and especially those of a character which every civilized nation considers itself bound to provide a severe punishment for when committed within its own jurisdiction. In such cases inquiry is certain to be instituted at once to ascertain how or why the thing was done, and the popular excitement rises or falls as the news spreads and the facts become known. It is not alone the publicity of the act, or the noise and clamor which attends it, that fixes the nature of the crime, but the act itself. If that is of a character to awaken public interest when it becomes known, it is a "disorder" the nature of which is to affect the community at large, and consequently to invoke the power of the local government whose people have been disturbed by what was done. The very nature of such an act is to disturb the quiet of a peaceful community, and to create, in the language of the treaty, a "disorder" which will "disturb tranquility and public order on shore or in the port." The principle which governs the whole matter is this: Disorders which disturb only the peace of the ship or those on board are to be dealt with exclusively by the sovereignty of the home of the ship, but those which disturb the public peace may be suppressed, and, if need be, the offenders punished by the proper authorities of the local jurisdiction. It may not be easy at all times to determine to which of the two jurisdictions a particular act of disorder belongs. Much will undoubtedly depend on the attending circumstances of the particular case, but all must concede that felonious homicide is a subject for the local jurisdiction, and that if the proper authorities are proceeding with the case in a regular way, the consul has no right to interfere to prevent it. . . .

CODE OF FEDERAL REGULATIONS
TITLE 22
(Revised as of 1 April 1979)

Chapter 1. Department of State
Subchapter I. Shipping and Seamen
Part 83. Protests, Disputes and Offenses.

. . . .

§83.8 Jurisdiction over offenses committed in port or territorial waters.

(a) *Offenses involving the peace of the port.* When an offense is committed aboard a merchant vessel in the port or territorial waters of a nation other than the nation of registry, and when the offense involves the peace of the port, the nation in whose waters the offense is committed has jurisdiction under an accepted principle of international law.

(b) *Offenses not involving the peace of the port*. When an offense is committed aboard a merchant vessel in the port or territorial waters of a nation other than the nation of registry, but does not involve the peace of the port, such offense is usually left by local governments to be adjusted by officers of the vessel and the diplomatic or consular representatives of the nation of registry. In the case of vessels of the United States, the right to protection against intervention by a foreign government in this class of cases is safeguarded in many areas by a treaty of friendship, commerce and navigation or by a consular convention between the United States and the foreign government concerned. Even where no treaty or convention exists, the local foreign government will usually refrain from intervening in such cases on the basis of comity between nations.

NOTE

It has often been asserted that a ship is a piece of "floating territory" of the nation whose flag it flies. Though support for this principle can be inferred from the case of *The Lotus*, P.C.I.J., Ser. A, No. 10 (1927), it is virtually agreed today that a ship is not floating territory but is only subject to the special maritime jurisdiction of the nation in which it is registered. In the case of *Maksymillian K.* (Poland, Supreme Court, February 20, 1964), it was held that leaving a Polish ship in a foreign port did not constitute commission of the Polish offense of crossing the national boundary without authorization. A Polish ship, the Court held, when outside Polish territory, is not part of that territory, *International Law Reports*, Vol. 47, p. 118.

REFERENCES

Jeffrey D. Ewen, "The United States and Canada in Passamaquoddy Bay: Internal Waters and the Right of Passage to a Foreign Port," *Syracuse Journal of International Law & Commerce*, Vol. 4 (1976), pp. 167-188; P. Naskou, "Some Legal Facts about Internal Waters," *Thesaurus Acroasium: The Law of the Sea*, Vol. 7 (1977), pp. 483-488; Dennis K. Yamase, "State-Federal Jurisdictional Conflict over the Internal Waters and Submerged Lands of the Northwestern Hawaiian Islands," *University of Hawaii Law Review*, Vol. 4 (1982), pp. 139-180; V.D. Degan, "Internal Waters," *Netherlands Yearbook of International Law*, Vol. 17 (1986), pp. 3-44.

C. THE LEGAL REGIME OF TERRITORIAL SEA

1.   **The Origin and Development of the Regime of Territorial Sea**

P.C. Jessup, *The Law of Territorial Waters and Maritime Jurisdiction*, New York: G.A. Jennings Co., 1927, pp. 3-5. Reprinted by permission of Philip Caryl Jessup, Jr., heir and executor of P.C. Jessup.

It is not possible to divorce territorial waters and high seas; scarcely can one secure a separation. Not until the seventeenth and eighteenth centuries did national pretensions to vast expanses of ocean meet with violent objections and ultimate abandonment. Yet for two or three hundred previous years nations were familiar with the idea that a littoral state might properly claim a special interest in the waters adjacent to its shores. . . .

. . . .

The general development was thus summed up by one of the greatest statesmen of modern times [Elihu Root]:

These vague and unfounded claims [of the 18th, 17th, and earlier centuries] disappeared entirely, and there was nothing of them left. . . . The sea became, in general, as free internationally as it was under the Roman law. But the new principle of freedom, when it approached the shore, met with another principle, the principle of protection, not a residuum of the old claim, but a new independent basis and reason for modification, near the shore, of the principle of freedom. The sovereign of the land washed by the sea asserted a new right to protect his subjects and citizens against attack, against invasion, against interference and injury, to protect them against attack threatening their peace, to protect their revenues, to protect their health, to protect their industries. This is the basis and sole basis on which is established the territorial zone that is recognized in the international law of today. Warships may not pass without consent into this zone, because they threaten. Merchant ships may pass and repass because they do not threaten.

NOTES

1. See P.T. Fenn, "Origins of the Theory of Territorial Waters," *American Journal of International Law*, Vol. 20 (1926), pp. 465-482 for an analysis of the Roman law origins of claims to sovereignty over coastal sea areas, the feudal influence on development of the concept, and the effect of 17th and 18th century legal scholars. See also Bram Thompson, "The Territorial Water Belt," *Canadian Law Times*, Vol. 40 (1920), pp. 470-490 [emphasizing the development of the territorial sea concept in England and Canada]; H.S.K. Kent, "Historical Origins of the Three-Mile Limit," *American Journal of International Law*, Vol. 48 (1954), pp. 537-553.

2. Approving the theory that the territorial sea is merely a residuum of earlier pretentious claims to sovereignty over sea areas, see H.M. Cleminson, "Laws of Maritime Jurisdiction in Time of Peace with Special Reference to Territorial Waters," *British Yearbook of International Law*, Vol. 6 (1925) p. 144, 146 and E.D. Dickinson, "Jurisdiction at the Maritime Frontier," *Harvard Law Review*, Vol. 40 (1926), pp. 1-20.

> Cornelius van Bynkershoek, *De Dominio Maris Dissertatio*, translation of 1737 text by Ralph Van Deman Magoflin, London and New York: Oxford University Press, 1923, pp. 41-45. [Bynkershoek was a Dutchman and held the office of Judge in the Supreme Court of Appeal of Holland, Zealand, and West Friesland.] Reprinted by permission.

Chapter II

Whether a Maritime Belt Can Be Occupied and Held Under Sovereignty, and If So, in What Way It May Be Done

. . . .

But indeed since by the law of nations we do not recognize ownership without possession, we must examine how far the ownership of a maritime belt seems to have extended. I for my part say, in accordance with a passage of the Digest, that when part of an estate is possessed, the whole of it is possessed all the way to its boundary, provided that is the intent of the possessor; but if there is no definite boundary, and the part held is thus indefinite, there is no acquisition of possession. Here, however, if you look at the "boundless" sea, there was either no definite boundary at all, or at any rate it was unknown. Nay, if you cared to set down some such boundary, and were able to do so, we should have to consider that it was not a matter of the mere

boundary, and were able to do so, we should have to consider that it was not a matter of the mere law of nations, as the Digest says.

For according to that law, possession is not acquired, unless the entire "res" in question is brought under control of the man who wishes to possess it, as we said in the preceding chapter. And in fact by the mere law of nations that matter cannot be explained in any other way; for otherwise each single individual would have occupied the universe.

Since, therefore, by the law of nations the lords of the lands cannot rule the sea, except where they are in possession of it, and since when possession is lost, ownership also is lost, the situation requires us to go on and examine how far a people, or the ruler of a state into which individuals have united themselves, may seem to hold a maritime belt by perpetual possession; as for the outer seas, we shall treat them later on. Of course, the literal consequence of what I have just maintained is that the sea should be understood as possessed only so far as it is navigated, and navigated perpetually. But who could navigate perpetually, and be always skirting the shores? Who could navigate with intent of ownership always, and always at the same interval from the land? That is hardly to be admitted, except in a very broad sense.

I should think, therefore, that the possession of a maritime belt ought to be regarded as extending just as far as it can be held in subjection to the mainland; for in that way, although it is not navigated perpetually, still the possession acquired by law is properly defended and maintained; for there can be no question that he possesses a thing continuously who so holds it that another cannot hold it against his will. Hence, we do not concede ownership of a maritime belt any farther out than it can be ruled from the land, and yet we do concede it that far; for there can be no reason for saying that the sea which is under some one man's command and control is any less his than a ditch in his territory.

. . .

Wherefore on the whole it seems a better rule that the control of the land [over the sea] extends as far as cannon will carry; for that is as far as we seem to have both command and possession. I am speaking, however, of our own times, in which we use those engines of war; otherwise I should have to say in general terms that the control from the land ends where the power of men's weapons ends; for it is this, as we have said, that guarantees possession. This seems to have been the opinion followed by the Estates of the Belgic Confederation who decreed on the third of January, 1671, that the commanders of vessels off the coast of foreign princes should salute at sea as far out as cannon will carry from their cities and forts, according as the prince of the shore in question might prescribe; as for his caring to return the salute, that must be left to him to decide. And they said further that every man is an absolute lord in his own domain, and every foreigner subject unto him. And they were right, in my judgment, though other princes have been wrong in this particular matter. . . .

NOTE

1.   Commenting upon Bynkershoek's contribution, Fulton says:

"[T]he merit of Bynkershoek's doctrine was, that it transferred in theory to all parts of a coast this decisive property of compulsion and dominion which, strictly speaking, only existed where forts or batteries were placed. The doctrine, justly enough, has been called fictitious, because there are various coasts and districts where it would be impracticable to maintain dominion over the territorial sea by means of artillery on shore; and because in point of fact such dominion, unless in the neighborhood of forts, is actually maintained by other means, as by coastguards and naval vessels. Nevertheless the principle, though resting largely on hypothesis, had much to recommend it, and it gradually became incorporated into international law as the rule for fixing the boundary of the territorial waters.   Apart from its intrinsic merits, its acceptance was perhaps not a little facilitated by the felicity with which it was expressed. Bynkershoek gave it the form almost of an aphorism, and the phrase, *terrae dominium finitur ubi finitur armorum vis*, had been quoted by almost all later writers." T.W. Fulton, *Sovereignty of the Seas: An Historical Account of the Claims of England to the Dominion of the British Seas*, Edinburgh and London: W. Blackwood and Sons, 1911, p. 558.

2. Jessup has a similar observation:

"The truth seems to be that the value of Bynkershoek's maxim lay in the fact that it denied the ancient theory that the sea was incapable of appropriation without countenancing the excessively wide claims which had led to the famous Grotious-Selden controversy. The nations were unwilling to say that the free and common seas touched their very shores, and on the other hand they found it impracticable to claim dominion over vast oceans. Bynkershoek supplied the happy medium on a theoretical basis which appealed to the spirit of the times. His norm of cannon range was adopted and accepted for nearly a century before Jefferson started the fashion of using three miles, or a marine league, as the alternative. It was then approximately an exact equivalent, and to this its introduction was no doubt due, but once introduced it remained because the nations found it a convenient compromise between conflicting interests. When it ceases to be generally convenient, it will probably be changed by general convention." P.C. Jessup, *The Law of Territorial Waters and Maritime Jurisdiction*, New York: G.A. Jennings Co., 1927, p. 7.

Wyndham L. Walker, "Territorial Waters: The Cannon Shot Rule," *British Yearbook of International Law*, Vol. 22 (1945), pp. 210, 230-231. Reprinted by permission of Fred. B. Rothman and Co.

It thus appears that though Bynkershoek was apparently the earliest jurist to record in a treatise upon questions of international law the existence of the cannon shot rule, he was by no means its originator. That rule was already well known and appealed to as law by diplomatists before Bynkershoek wrote. Bynkershoek restated the rule and accepted it as a general principle, applicable not merely to questions of neutrality in time of war. In this extension of the more generally received scope of the rule he may not have been entirely original--there are traces that in Holland at any rate attempts so to apply it had already been made. But the instances recorded in practice in which the cannon range principle was invoked are nevertheless almost all cases of alleged violation of neutral waters in time of war. It is questionable whether the doctrine which Bynkershoek himself approved differed essentially or was any more extensive than that supported in practice by the Governments of France and other States. His words are consistent with the French Doctrine that an actual cannon posted on the shore was necessary--where there was no cannon there was no "armorum vis." The result of that doctrine is not the creation of a general principle that a State has jurisdiction over a maritime belt extending seawards from its shore up to the extreme range of any known cannon, but the recognition of a right of protection in a series of fortress areas or zones covered by the actual guns of forts on shore.

The old cannon shot rule thus differs radically from its successor, the three mile limit rule. In the time of Bynkershoek cannon range was considerably less than three miles. Whether it had even reached that extent in 1782, when Galiani suggested a uniform belt of three miles as a substitute for cannon shot, is doubtful. The three mile rule does not make its appearance in the literature of international law until 1782, and within a few years of that date cannon shot and three miles were being widely treated as equivalents. This may mean that during the closing twenty years of the eighteenth century the cannon shot rule obtained general acceptance, but was converted into a measured distance of three miles, which is the view which has hitherto received the wider acceptance. However, the two rules were very distinct in their nature, and may well have been equally distinct both in origin and development.

In the eighteenth century the cannon shot rule was the one which prevailed in matters relating to maritime neutrality in France, Spain and Southern Europe, but the Northern Maritime Powers had never accepted so narrow a limit to their jurisdiction. A generation before the three mile limit makes its entry into the works of international publicists in Southern Europe, the Scandinavian Powers were already claiming jurisdiction over a maritime belt to the extent of one marine league-- reckoned at about four miles--from the shore. Even outside Scandinavia, customs, sanitary and fishery control regulations tended to claim jurisdiction over areas measured in leagues from the shore. The question may fairly be asked: Was the three mile limit merely cannon shot range converted into mileage, or is its origin more truly to be sought in the practice of States in Northern Europe, or elsewhere? The historical identification of cannon range with the three mile limit does not carry complete conviction. May not that identification have been little more than a fiction of eighteenth-century jurists striving to combine, reconcile and explain divergent practices, and to secure for the future a more practical working rule? In its nature the three mile rule looks like a wholly independent growth from the cannon range, the old war rule of the eighteenth century, though living on in the maritime ordinances of certain Powers, in the early years of the nineteenth century gave way to a rule springing more directly from pacific and economic roots; and the maritime belt of three marine miles took its present place on the statute book of the modern maritime world.

REFERENCES

H. S. K. Kent, "Historical Origins of the Three-Mile Limit," *American Journal of International Law*, Vol. 48 (1954), pp. 537-553; D. Wilkes, "Use of World Resources Without Conflict: Myths about the Territorial Sea," *Wayne Law Review*, Vol. 14 (1968), pp. 441-470.

NOTE FROM SECRETARY OF STATE THOMAS JEFFERSON
TO THE BRITISH MINISTER, MR. HAMMOND, NOVEMBER 8, 1793
J.B. Moore, *International Law Digest*,
Vol. 1, Washington, D.C.: U.S. Government
Printing Office, 1906, pp. 702-703.

The President of the United States, thinking that, before it shall be finally decided to what distance from our seashores the territorial protection of the United States shall be exercised, it will be proper to enter into friendly conferences and explanations with the powers chiefly interested in the navigation of the seas on our coasts, and relying that convenient occasions may be taken for these hereafter, finds it necessary in the meantime to fix provisionally on some distance for the present government of these questions. You are sensible that very different opinions and claims have been heretofore advanced on this subject. The greatest distance to which any respectable assent among nations has been at any time given, has been the extent of the human sight, estimated at upwards of twenty miles, and the smallest distance, I believe, claimed by any nation whatever, *is the utmost range of a cannon ball*, usually stated at one sea league. Some intermediate distances have also been insisted on, and that of three sea leagues has some authority in its favor. The character of our coast, remarkable in considerable parts of it for admitting no vessels of size to pass near the shores, would entitle us, in reason, to as broad a margin of protected navigation as any nation whatever. Reserving, however, the ultimate extent of this for future deliberation, the President gives instructions to the officers acting under his authority to consider those heretofore given them as restrained for the present to the distance of one sea league or three geographical miles from the seashores. This distance can admit of no opposition, as it is recognized by treaties between some of the power with whom we are connected in commerce and navigation, and is as little, or less, than is claimed by any of them on their own coasts.

For the jurisdiction of the rivers and bays of the United States, the laws of the several States are understood to have made provision, and they are, moreover, as being landlocked, within the body of the United States.

CUNARD S.S. CO. v. MELLON
262 U.S. 101, at 119, 120-121,
122-124, 125-126 (1923)

These are suits by steamship companies operating passenger ships between United States ports and foreign ports to enjoin threatened application to them and their ships of certain provisions of the National Prohibition Act. The defendants are officers of the United States charged with the act's enforcement. In the first ten cases the plaintiffs are foreign corporations and their ships are of foreign registry, while in the remaining two the plaintiffs are domestic corporations and their ships are of United States registry. All the ships have long carried and now carry, as part of their sea stores, intoxicating liquors intended to be sold or dispensed to their passengers and crews at meals and otherwise for beverage purposes. Many of the passengers and crews are accustomed to using such beverages and insist that the ships carry and supply liquors for such purposes. By the laws of all the foreign ports at which the ships touch this is permitted and by the laws of some it is required. The liquors are purchased for the ships and taken on board in the foreign ports and are sold or dispensed in the course of all voyages, whether from or to those ports. . . .

On October 6, 1922, the Attorney General, in answer to an inquiry by the Secretary of the Treasury, gave an opinion to the effect that the National Prohibition Act, construed in connection with the Eighteenth Amendment to the Constitution, makes it unlawful (a) for any ship, whether domestic or foreign, to bring into territorial waters of the United States, or to carry while within such waters, intoxicating liquors intended for beverage purposes, whether as sea stores or cargo, and (b) for any domestic ship even when without those waters to carry such liquors for such purposes either as cargo or sea stores. The President thereupon directed the preparation, promulgation and application of new instructions conforming to that construction of the act. Being advised of this and that under the new instructions the defendants would seize all liquors carried in contravention of the act as so construed and would proceed to subject the plaintiffs and their ships to penalties provided in the act, the plaintiffs brought these suits. . . .

Various meanings are sought to be attributed to the term "territory" in the phrase "the United States and all territory subject to the jurisdiction thereof." We are of opinion that it means the regional areas--of land and adjacent waters--over which the United States claims and exercises dominion and control as a sovereign power. The immediate context and the purport of the entire section show that the term is used in a physical and not a metaphorical sense--that it refers to areas or districts having fixity of location and recognized boundaries. See *United States v. Bevans*, 3 Wheat, 336, 390.

It is now settled in the United States and recognized elsewhere that the territory subject to its jurisdiction includes the land areas under its dominion and control, the ports, harbors, bays and other enclosed arms of the sea along its coast and a marginal belt of the sea extending from the coast line outward a marine league, or three geographic miles. *Church v. Hubbart*, 2 Cranch 187, 234; *The Ann*, 1 Fed. Cas., p. 926; *United States v. Smiley*, 27 Fed. Cas., p. 1132; *Manchester v. Massachusetts*, 139 U.S. 240, 257-258; *Louisiana v. Mississippi*, 202 U.S. 1, 52; 1 Kent's Com., 12th ed., 29; 1 Moore International Law Digest, § 145; 1 Hyde International Law, §§ 141, 142, 154; Wilson International Law, 8th ed., § 54; Westlake International Law, 2d ed., p. 187 *et seq.*; Wheaton International Law, 5th Eng. ed. (Phillipson), p. 282; 1 Oppenheim International Law, 3d ed., §§ 185-189, 252. This, we hold, is the territory which the Amendment designates as its field of operation; and the designation is not of a part of this territory but of "all" of it.

The defendants contend that the Amendment also covers domestic merchant ships outside the waters of the United States, whether on the high seas or in foreign waters. But it does not say so, and what it does say shows, as we have indicated, that it is confined to the physical territory of the United States. In support of their contention the defendants refer to the statement sometimes made that a merchant ship is a part of the territory of the country whose flag she flies. But this, as has been aptly observed, is a figure of speech, a metaphor. . . . The jurisdiction which it is intended to describe arises out of the nationality of the ship, as established by her domicile, registry and use of the flag, and partakes more of the characteristics of personal than of territorial sovereignty. . . . It is chiefly applicable to ships on the high seas, where there is no territorial sovereign; and as respects ships in foreign territorial waters it has little application beyond what is affirmatively or tacitly permitted by the local sovereign. . . .

The defendants further contend that the Amendment covers foreign merchant ships when within the territorial waters of the United States. Of course, if it were true that a ship is a part of the territory of the country whose flag she carries, the contention would fail. But, as that is a fiction, we think the contention is right.

A merchant ship of one country voluntarily entering the territorial limits of another subjects herself to the jurisdiction of the latter. The jurisdiction attaches in virtue of her presence, just as with other objects within those limits. During her stay she is entitled to the protection of the laws of that place and correlatively is bound to yield obedience to them. Of course, the local sovereign may out of considerations of public policy choose to forego the exertion of its jurisdiction or to exert the same in only a limited way, but this is a matter resting solely in its discretion . . . .

In principle, therefore, it is settled that the Amendment could be made to cover both domestic and foreign merchant ships when within the territorial waters of the United States. And we think it has been made to cover both when within those limits . . . . [Dismissals affirmed in part and reversed in part.]

REFERENCES

Edwin D. Dickinson, "Jurisdiction at the Maritime Frontier," *Harvard Law Review*, Vol. 40 (1926), pp. 1-29; Joseph Whitla Stinson, "Marshall on the Jurisdiction of the Littoral Sovereign Over Territorial Waters," *American Law Review*, Vol. 57 (1923), pp. 567-578.

CONVENTION BETWEEN THE UNITED STATES AND GREAT BRITAIN
FOR PREVENTION OF SMUGGLING OF INTOXICATING LIQUORS
Signed January 23, 1924; entered into force May 22, 1924
43 Stat. 1761; U.S.T.S. 685; IV Trenwith, Treaties, etc.
(1938) 4225; 27 L.N.T.S. 182.

Article I

The High Contracting Parties declare that it is their firm intention to uphold the principle that three marine miles extending from the coastline outwards and measured from low-water mark constitute the proper limits of territorial waters.

> Bernard G. Heinzen, "The Three-Mile Limit: Preserving the Freedom of the Seas," *Stanford Law Review*, Vol. 11 (1959), pp. 629-634, 641-651. Notes omitted. Copyright 1959 by the Board of Trustees of the Leland Stanford Junior University. Reprinted by permission of the copyright holder and Fred B. Rothman & Co.

Establishment of Three-Mile Limit as International Custom

During the first half of the nineteenth century, the three-mile or one-league limit had considerable support in state practice. Although a few states claimed a more extended general or exclusive jurisdiction over legitimate navigation, those claims were generally much more limited than the claims to plenary jurisdiction in a one-league territorial sea. Moreover, other states successfully opposed these more extensive claims, and only Spain attempted to claim more than one league of general jurisdiction for as much as twenty years during the first half of the century.

During the second half of the nineteenth century some states attempted to assert a general jurisdiction beyond one league at various times, but all such claims were vigorously opposed. Not even the Danes were able to maintain their historic four-mile league against the opposition of France, England, and Germany, who asserted the right of their nationals to fish three miles from the coasts of Denmark and Iceland.

Aside from those Scandinavian states which claimed a four-mile league on a historical basis, Spain was the only country which claimed more than three miles of either general jurisdiction or territorial sea during a substantial portion of the nineteenth century. Spain seems to have asserted jurisdiction over vessels situated beyond three miles from its coast only in connection with its customs or antismuggling legislation, and the Spaniards appear to have taken concrete action to enforce this claim on relatively few occasions. Nevertheless, these acts were always vigorously opposed, particularly by England and the United States, and Spain finally, around 1880, seems to have abandoned attempts at enforcement.

In 1906 Spain, for the first time, enacted legislation prohibiting all foreigners from fishing within six miles of its shores. However, Spain seems to have tolerated British fishing up to three miles off the coast during the first part of the twentieth century. The same toleration was probably extended to French and German fishermen. Since at least some of this restraint appears to have been due to pressure from other governments, it seems reasonable to conclude that Spain consciously refrained from taking any practical steps to enforce plenary or territorial jurisdiction beyond three miles.

During the nineteenth century, some important users of the sea had reservations about consenting to a coastal state's assertion of proprietary rights or plenary jurisdiction over as much as three miles of territorial sea. Thus between 1848 and 1852 Belgium opposed English enforcement of its three-mile limit against Belgian fishing vessels. As late as 1879, Germany asked England to reconsider the principle, asserted in the Territorial Jurisdiction Act of 1878, that the coastal state is entitled to assert complete criminal jurisdiction over all acts committed within three miles of its coast, and France refused to recognize the right of England to punish French fishing boats for violating the three-mile fishing limit. By the end of the nineteenth century, however, these powers and the other important users of the sea had adopted the three-mile limit, and thereby consented to this derogation from the freedom of the seas and the *res communis* of the high seas.

By 1900 the three-mile or one-league limit had been positively adopted or acknowledged as law by twenty of the twenty-one states which claimed or acknowledged a territorial sea at that time. The twenty states claiming a maximum of one league were Argentina, Austria-Hungary, Belgium, Brazil, Chile, Denmark, Ecuador, El Salvador, France, Germany, Great Britain, Greece, Honduras, Italy, Netherlands, Norway, Russia, Sweden, Turkey, and the United States. The twenty-first state, Spain, at times claimed six miles of a general jurisdiction over legitimate navigation, rather than a strictly limited preventive jurisdiction, under its antismuggling legislation.

Although some allege a concentration of three-mile jurisdictions in Europe or among a few sea powers, many non-European coastal states, particularly in Latin America, and many states not then major sea powers, practiced the three-mile limit by 1900. Since the three-mile or one-league limit had the consent of virtually all coastal states claiming a territorial sea, it may therefore be said that it was, at the turn of the present century, generaly accepted as a customary rule of international law.

. . . .

The Legal Situation at the Opening of the 1958 Geneva Conference

On the basis of state practice in early 1958, just prior to the Geneva Conference on the Law of the Sea, it was clear that the three-mile or one-league limit was still the maximum breadth of the territorial sea cognizable under customary international law.

No more than twenty-seven of seventy-three coastal states claimed a specific breadth of territorial sea in excess of three miles or one league. The claims of these states were as follows:

Six miles: Ceylon, Greece, Haiti, India, Iran, Israel, Italy, Libya, Spain, Yugoslavia.

Nine miles: Mexico.

Ten miles: Albania.

Twelve miles: Bulgaria, Colombia, Ethiopia, Guatemala, Indonesia, Rumania, Saudi Arabia, Union of Soviet Socialist Republics, United Arab Republic, Venezuela.

Zones up to 200 miles: Chile, Ecuador, El Salvador, Korea, Peru.

No more than one or two of the claims to an extensive jurisdiction beyond twelve miles, however, even approximates a claim to plenary or territorial jurisdiction in the zone specified. The claim most closely resembling a claim to a modern territorial sea is that of El Salvador which states that it does "not affect freedom of navigation in accordance with principles accepted by International Law." This is clearly more than a concession of the right of innocent passage through territorial waters, and is totally inconsistent with the accompanying claim to a 200 mile territorial sea. The extent of the territorial sea claimed by most of these five powers is unknown or uncertain.

The claims of six other states: Honduras, Lebanon, Portugal, Thailand, Uruguay, and Yemen, were either uncertain or unknown.

In summary, although up to twenty-seven states claimed limits for their territorial seas from six to 200 miles, the two groups of ten states, claiming six and twelve miles respectively, constituted the largest groups of non-three or four-mile jurisdictions. Moreover, only three or four of the seven other states asserting claims over zones varying from nine to 200 miles were known to have claimed a specific breadth of territorial sea extending beyond one league.

In contrast, at least forty coastal states, or an absolute majority of the seventy-three coastal states, in early 1958 still claimed no more than one league as the breadth of their territorial seas. These states were Argentina, Australia, Belgium, Brazil, Burma, Cambodia, Canada, China, Costa Rica, Cuba, Denmark, Dominican Republic, Finland, France, Germany, Ghana, Iceland, Iraq, Ireland, Japan, Jordan, Liberia, Malaya, Morocco, Netherlands, New Zealand, Nicaragua, Norway, Pakistan, Panama, Philippines, Poland, Sudan, Sweden, Tunisia, Turkey, Union of South Africa, United Kingdom, United States, and Vietnam.

In addition, almost all of the principal users of the sea were still firm advocates of the three-mile or one league limit and the freedom of the seas. As of July 1957, just under eighty-seven percent of the world's merchant tonnage was registered in countries claiming no more than one league of territorial sea. All of the ten ranking maritime countries except Italy practiced the one-league limit.

Thus there was, in early 1958, no basis in state practice to support a contention that any fixed limit other than the three-mile or one-league limit was the maximum breadth of the territorial sea under international law.

Nevertheless, a minority of governments contended that the three-mile or one-league limit had been superseded by some other rule of international law. There was no general agreement, however, as to what the governing rule was. The diversity among the unilateral extensions of the territorial sea itself precluded any limit other than three miles or one league from having the general consent of other states.

Since a rule of customary international law derives from the consent of states, once it is established it can be superseded only by the consent of states. Almost all of the main users of the sea have constantly invoked the three-mile or one-league limit in opposition to all pretensions beyond that distance, and that limit was still, in February 1958, practiced by a majority of coastal states. The three-mile or one-league limit, therefore must still be regarded as having been, in early 1958, the maximum limit of the territorial sea under international law.

REFERENCES

"The Three Mile Limit as a Rule of International Law," *Columbia Law Review*, Vol. 23 (1923), pp. 472-476; Shigeru Oda, "The Territorial Sea and Natural Resources," *International and*

Comparative Law Quarterly, Vol. 4 (1955), pp. 415-425. L. Becker, "The Breadth of the Territorial Sea and Fisheries Jurisdiction," *Department of State Bulletin*, Vol. 40 No. 1019 (January 5, 1959), pp. 369-374; M.S. McDougal & W.T. Burke, "The Community Interest in a Narrow Territorial Sea: Inclusive Versus Exclusive Competence Over the Oceans," *Cornell Law Quarterly*, Vol. 45 (1960), pp. 171-253; G.E. Carlisle, "Three-Mile-Limit--Obsolete Concept?," *U.S. Naval Institute Proceedings*, Vol. 93 (1967), pp. 24-34; James F. Meade, "The Great Territorial Sea Squabble," *U.S. Naval Institute Proceedings*, Vol. 95 (4) (1969), pp. 45-53; B.L. Florsheim, "Territorial Sea, 3000 Year Old Question," *Journal of Air Law and Commerce*, Vol. 36 (1970), pp. 73-104. For an excellent, thorough analysis of the question see D.P. O'Connell, "The Juridical Nature of the Territorial Sea," *British Yearbook of International Law*, Vol. 45 (1971), pp. 303-383; Tommy T.B. Koh, "The Territorial Sea, Contiguous Zone, Straits and Archipelagos Under the 1982 Convention on the Law of the Sea," *Malaya Law Review*, Vol. 29 (1987), pp. 163-199.

2. The Juridical Content of the Territorial Sea

1958 CONVENTION ON THE TERRITORIAL SEA AND THE CONTIGUOUS ZONE

Article 1

1.   The sovereignty of a State extends, beyond its land territory and its internal waters, to a belt of sea adjacent to its coast, described as the territorial sea.

2.   This sovereignty is exercised subject to the provisions of these articles and to other rules of international law.

Article 2

The sovereignty of a coastal State extends to the air space over the territorial sea as well as to its bed and subsoil.

INTERNATIONAL LAW COMMISSION
1956 Commentary, Draft Article 1
Yearbook of the International Law Commission 1956
Vol. II, p. 265

(1) Paragraph 1 brings out the fact that the rights of the coastal State over the territorial sea do not differ in nature from the rights of sovereignty which the State exercises over other parts of its territory. There is an essential difference between the regime of the territorial sea and that of the high seas since the latter is based on the principle of free use by all nations. The replies from Governments in connection with The Hague Codification Conference of 1930 and the report of the Conference's Committee on the subject confirmed that this view, which is almost unanimously held, is in accordance with existing law. It is also the principle underlying a number of multilateral conventions--such as the Air Navigation Convention of 1919 and the International Civil Aviation Convention of 1944--which treat the territorial sea in the same way as other parts of State territory.

(2) The Commission preferred the term "territorial sea" to "territorial waters." It was of the opinion that the term "territorial waters" might lead to confusion, since it is used to describe both

internal waters only, and internal waters and the territorial sea combined. For the same reason, the Codification Conference also expressed a preference for the term "territorial sea." Although not yet universally accepted, this term is becoming more and more prevalent.

(3) Clearly, sovereignty over the territorial sea cannot be exercised otherwise than in conformity with the provisions of international law.

(4) Some of the limitations imposed by international law on the exercise of sovereignty in the territorial sea are set forth in the present articles which cannot, however, be regarded as exhaustive. Incidents in the territorial sea raising legal questions are also governed by the general rules of international law, and these cannot be specially codified in the present draft for the purposes of their application to the territorial sea. That is why "other rules of international law" are mentioned in addition to the provisions contained in the present articles.

(5) It may happen that, by reason of some special relationship, geographical or other, between two States, rights in the territorial sea of one of them are granted to the other in excess of the rights recognized in the present draft. It is not the Commission's intention to limit in any way any more extensive right of passage or other right enjoyed by States by custom or treaty.

REFERENCES

For an excellent, thorough analysis of the question, see D.P. O'Connell, "The Juridical Nature of the Territorial Sea," *British Yearbook of International Law*, Vol. 45 (1971), pp. 303-383. See also the decision in *Cunard S.S. Co. v. Mellon*, 262 U.S. 101 (1923); R. Lapidoth, "Freedom of Navigation and the New Law of the Sea," *Israel Law Review*, Vol. 10 (1975), pp. 456-502; John Gibson, "The Owernship of the Sea Bed under British Territorial Waters," *International Relations* (London), Vol. 6 (1978), pp. 474-499.

JOHNSON v. MEXICO ("THE DAYLIGHT")
(U.S.-MEXICAN CLAIMS COMMISSION; APRIL 15, 1927)
American Journal of International Law, Vol. 21 (1927), pp. 794-95.
Reprinted with the permission of The American Society of International Law.

[This claim involved damage to a United States flag vessel at anchor outside Tampico, Mexico, but located within the territorial sea of Mexico. One of the issues concerned the applicable law, and the Commission commented as follows.]

The United States contends that [the applicable principles of law] are recognized by universal maritime law, and should be applied by this Commission which is bound to decide in accordance with the principles of international law, justice and equity. Mexico, on the other hand, asserts that, as the collision occurred in Mexican waters, Mexican law is applicable. . . . There would seem to be no doubt but that with reference to the present collision the law of Mexico is applicable. In the *Sidra* case the British-American arbitral tribunal held that "according to the well settled rule of international law, the collision having occurred in the territorial waters of the United States, the law applicable to the liabilitiy is the law of the United States" (Nielsen's Report, 457; *see* the *Canadienne* case, Nielsen's Report, 430). In 1888, at its session of Lausanne, the *Institut de droit International* considering the problem of collisions both from the viewpoint of existing law and from that of a future uniform law, resolved in its drafts covering both viewpoints (under the guidance of such experts as Messrs. Lyon-Caen and Renault from Paris) that the law applicable is the law of the land where the collision took place--a solution qualified by Mr. Renault as required even by *"ordre public"*--and the Institute identified collisions within territorial waters with collisions in the interior of a country. If Mexican law in this matter were in open conflict with a universally recognized provision of international law the Commission should take such conflict into account. . . .

SNYDER v. MOTORISTS MUTUAL INS. CO.
2 Ohio App.2d 19, 206 N.E.2d 227 (1965)
Notes omitted.

DOYLE, J. In this action commenced in the Court of Common Pleas of Summit County for damages based upon a policy of insurance, a judgment was entered on the verdict of a jury in favor of the boat owner, Harvey J. Snyder (plaintiff-appellee), and against the Motorists Mutual Insurance Company (defendant-appellant), which company had issued its policy of insurance covering damage to the boat and loss to the owner occurring "within the limits of the continental United States of America. . . ."

The main issue before this court is whether the trial court erred in charging the jury, as a matter of law, that the loss in damages to the sunken boat occurred within the limits of the continental United States of America.

It appears from the evidence that on March 8, 1960, Snyder was engaged in the sport of fishing from his boat in the Atlantic Ocean off the Florida Keys, when the craft capsized. The geographical point of mishap was located as being approximately four nautical miles from the center of Bahia Honda bridge, and three and six-tenths miles from the nearest shore line, and in a part of the ocean having a water depth of approximately thirty-one feet.

. . . .

The Insurance Company claims that a point in the ocean beyond three nautical miles from the coast line is not within the continental limits of the United States, as that language is used in the policy of insurance.

In our research of the questions in this case, we have been unable to find a reported decision of any reviewing court in the country defining the contract limitation provision before us, although the limitation of risk as to place appears in a number of standard contract forms.

From decided cases in this state, and elsewhere, however, the following general rules governing the interpretation of insurance contracts may be deduced:

1. A contract of marine insurance must be given a fair and reasonable interpretation to cover the risks anticipated by the parties;

2. The contract is strictly construed against the insurer and favorable to the insured;

3. Where several interpretations are reasonably possible, that which will favor the insured will be adopted;

4. Ambiguities in the policy will be resolved against the insurance company, so as to give effect to the dominant purpose of the contract; and

5. If an insurance company, in issuing a marine policy, desires to limit or restrict the operation of the general provisions of its contract by limiting its risk as to place, it should do so in clear and unmistakable language.

From early times, it has been recognized that the sovereignty of nations bordering the seas does not stop at the shoreline, but that for some distance it extends over and under the ocean. . . . [Citing Grotius, Bynkershoek and others.]

While generally adhering to the doctrine of the freedom of the seas beyond the three-mile limit, the United States has, on numerous occasions, exercised authority beyond the limit, in the fields of law enforcement and national security. Congress has authorized federal officers to board vessels bound for the United States ports when within four leagues, or four nautical miles, of the coast for the purpose of determining the character of the cargo. Similar laws were enacted to enforce national prohibition.

The principle underlying the three-mile limit rule appears to be the attempted establishment of a "freedom of the seas" doctrine, the right of free navigation, and the right of free fishing on the high seas, which are recognized by some nations, including the United States, as rights belonging to all of the peoples of the world.

Furthermore, it has been American policy to establish national dominion over a definite marginal zone (the three-mile limit) to protect our neutrality against foreign nations.

The foregoing statement of governmental policy does not define limits of the continental United States, any more than do the various decisions of the Supreme Court of the United States in ruling upon the rights of states, as against the rights of the federal government, to oil and minerals under the waters of the ocean within and beyond the three-mile limit; or the various laws enacted by the Congress of the United States known as the Submerged Lands Act, and the Outer Continental Shelf Lands Act. (Under the latter Act, the United States claims the right to oil beneath the continental shelf and beyond the three-mile limit.)

Every continent rests on a submarine base which extends seaward from the shore. This underwater extension on the part of the continent above sea level is called the "continental shelf." It has been defined as the submerged portion of a continent which slopes gently seaward from the low water line to a point under the sea where a substantial break in grade occurs, at which point the bottom slopes steeply until the great ocean depths are reached. The point or line of break defines the edge of the shelf.

It is common knowledge to the people of the United States that during the years of operation of the Submerged Lands Act, and the Outer Continental Shelf Lands Act, the government of the United States has received millions of dollars from leases of submerged lands beyond this three-mile limit on the continental shelf adjacent to the shore line of the United States.

It thus appears that the place where the boating accident in the instant lawsuit occurred, although a short distance beyond the three-mile limit, was above the continental shelf of the United States, and over lands which the 83rd Congrss of the United States (Public Law 212, 67 Stats. at L.462) declared subject to "the Constitution and laws and civil and political jurisdiction of the United States" for the purpose of "exploring for, developing, removing, and transporting resources therefrom, to the same extent as if the outer Continental Shelf were an area of exclusive Federal jurisdiction located within a State. . . ."

It is our view that the language of the policy limiting the risk as to place as one occurring "within the Continental limits of the United States" is fraught with so much ambiguity that it is beyond reasonable definition. In the context in which it is employed, it could mean (1) within the three-mile limit; or, it could mean (2) beyond the three-mile limit, and over the "continental shelf" (and perhaps at numerous other places unnecessary to explore here).

Therefore, first: resolving the ambiguous language against the insurance company to give effect to the dominant purpose of the policy, and, second: adopting one reasonable interpretation of the "continental shelf" theory which will give effect to the policy; and, third: strictly construing the policy against the insurer, and in favor of the insured; this court orders a judgment of affirmance.

We find no error committed by the trial court prejudicial to the rights of the appellant, the Motorists Mutual Insurance Company.

Judgment affirmed.

EMPLOYERS MUTUAL CASUALTY COMPANY v. SAMUELS
407 S.W.2d 839 (Tex. Civ. App. 1966)
Notes omitted.

[This case involved a claim against an insurance company by a surviving spouse for a death occurring as the result of an aircraft crash twenty-one miles off the coast of Texas. The insurance policy coverage was limited to "injury or death sustained in the United States of America, its territories or possessions, or Canada." Appellant insurance company contended that the trial court erred in finding for plaintiff, on the ground that the death did not occur within the area stipulated in the policy.]

While there is not universal agreement on the extent of a nation's territorial waters, the United States, along with Great Britain and other countries, has consistently adopted the three-mile limit.
. . .

Under these traditional concepts relating to national jurisdiction and sovereignty, it would follow that the fatal accident with which we are now concerned did not occur in the United States, its territories or possessions. However, appellee contends that, because of recent developments and claims advanced by various nations, including the United States, with reference to the so-called continental shelf, this accident, which occurred on the waters above such shelf, must be considered as having occurred within the United States, its territories or possessions.

The Submerged Lands Act recognizes the rights of each coastal State in the natural resources of the submerged lands off its shores out to its offshore boundary, subject to the constitutional powers of the United States in the fields of commerce, navigation, defense and international affairs. Under this statute, the seaward boundary of Texas, insofar as title to natural resources is concerned, is three marine leagues, or nine nautical miles, from the Texas coast line. . . .

The Outer Continental Shelf Lands Act, insofar as pertinent here, is an assertion of Federal sovereignty. The Act first declares the policy of the United States to be that "the subsoil and seabed of the outer Continental Shelf appertain to the United States and are subject to its jurisdiction, control, and power of disposition" as provided in the Act. 43 U.S.C.A., §1332(a). Section 1333(a)(1) provides that the "Constitution and laws and civil and political jurisdiction of the United States are extended to the subsoil and seabed of the outer Continental Shelf and to all artificial islands and fixed structures which may be erected thereon . . . to the same extent as if the outer Continental Shelf were an area of exclusive Federal jurisdiction located within a State. . . ."

Since the accident occurred twenty-one miles seaward from the Texas coast, it is apparent that it did not occur within the boundaries of the State of Texas. Those boundaries are established under the Submerged Lands Act at a point nine nautical miles, or 10.359 statute miles, seaward from the Texas coast. We conclude, further, that the death did not occur within the United States, its territories or possessions.

While the language of the Outer Continental Shelf Lands Act expressly amounts to an assertion of jurisdiction, the words make manifest that federal jurisdiction and control are extended only to the subsoil and seabed of the shelf, and to all artificial islands and fixed structures which may be erected thereon. The enactment explicitly disclaims, as did the Presidential Proclamation of 1945, any intention to affect the "character as high seas" of the waters above the shelf. 43 U.S.C.A. §1333(a)(3).

If, as the Presidential Proclamation and the Outer Continental Shelf Lands Act expressly recognize, these unilateral declarations of the United States concerning the subsoil and seabed of the shelf do not affect the status of the superjacent waters as "high seas," then it follows that the crash which took the life of Mr. Samuels occurred in an area which is the territory of no nation.

. . . .

Our conclusion finds support in the provisions of the Convention on the Continental Shelf (U.N. Doc. A/CONF.13/L.55), adopted by the United Nations Conference on the Law of the Sea, April 29, 1958, and acceded to by the United States on April 12, 1961. Broadly speaking, this document recognizes and gives effect to the doctrine underlying the unilateral declarations by the United States and other nations asserting jurisdiction and control over the continntal shelf and associated offshore areas, but its provisions stop short of acknowledging any unlimited jurisdiction by a littoral nation over shelf waters. While Article 2 of the Convention confers "sovereign rights" to the coastal nation over the continental shelf, it does so only "for the purpose of exploring it and exploiting its mineral resources." Article 3 declares that the rights of the littoral nation over the continental shelf "do not affect the status of the superjacent waters as high seas, or that of the air space above such waters."

. . . .

It is true that the United States Coast Guard is authorized to make and enforce safety regulations concerning the structures and "waters adjacent thereto." 43 U.S.C.A. §1333(a)(3)(e)(1), (2). But this is a far cry from that assertion of exclusive jurisdiction which would have the effect of making the waters over the shelf a "territory" or "possession" of the United States.

. . . .

We do not believe that the geographical limitation on coverage contained in the policy under which appellee claims is so worded as to create ambiguity, when an effort is made to apply it to an accident which occurred twenty-one miles off the Texas coast. *Cf. Snyder v. Motorists Mutual Ins. Co.*, 2 Ohio App.2d 19, 206 N.E.2d 227.

[Judgement reversed.]

QUESTIONS

Are there any distinguishing facts in *Snyder* and *Samuels* cases which warrant the contradictory holdings? Were the decisions based on principles of insurance contract interpretation or on principles of law of the sea?

REFERENCES

See *Gokuldas Khimji Hindoo v. Regina*, Zanzibar Eastern Africa Court of Appeal, November 6, 1957, *International Law Reports*, Vol. 27, pp. 98-102, in which defendant's conviction for illegally importing gold into Zanzibar was reversed by the Eastern African Court of Appeal where it was found that the gold came into defendant's possession after the inbound vessel on which he was a passenger had entered Zanzibar's territorial waters. The court's interpretation of the applicable legal principle was that property is imported into a state at the moment when the ship comes within the territorial waters of that state and thus, in the instant case, defendant could not properly be said to have "imported" the property in question. The earlier opinion of the High Court of Zanzibar, May 31, 1957 is reported in *International Law Reports*, Vol. 24 (1957), pp. 142-145.

1982 UNITED NATIONS CONVENTION ON THE LAW OF THE SEA

Article 2

*Juridical status of the territorial sea, of the air space
over the territorial sea and of its bed and subsoil*

1. The sovereignty of a coastal State extends beyond its land territory and internal waters, and in the case of an archipelagic State, its archipelagic waters, over an adjacent belt of sea described as the territorial sea.

2. This sovereignty extends to the air space over the territorial sea as well as to its bed and subsoil.

3. The sovereignty over the territorial sea is exercised subject to this Convention and to other rules of international law.

3. The Breadth of the Territorial Sea

The question of the permissible breadth of the territorial sea has been one of the most contentious issues in the development of the law of the sea. Much of the problem has been bound up with fisheries, a topic not discussed in detail until later in this book. However, it must be realized that territorial seas were developed initially in response to two principal perceived needs of coastal states--(1) exclusive access to fishery resources, and (2) protection from military incursions. In reviewing the materials in this section, then, the reader must bear in mind that the territorial sea has meant different things to different nations throughout history, and that the issues involved cut across the entire range of law of the sea problems.

a.   Authority to Establish Breadth

ANGLO-NORWEGIAN FISHERIES CASE
(UNITED KINGDOM v. NORWAY)
Judgment of December 18, 1951
I.C.J. Reports 1951, p. 116, at p. 132.

The delimitation of sea areas has always an international aspect; it cannot be dependent merely upon the will of the coastal State as expressed in its municipal law. Although it is true that the act of delimitation is necessarily a unilateral act, because only the coastal State is competent to undertake it, the validity of the delimitation with regard to other States depends upon international law.

NOTE

Assertions have been made on several occasions, both prior to and after the First U.N. Conference on the Law of the Sea, that coastal states ought to be the sole arbiters of the extent of their territorial seas. This view is commonly held among Latin American nations and is usually related to their desire to secure jurisdiction over living resources located beyond a generally accepted 12-mile exclusive fishery zone. The question of extending territorial sea beyond 12-mile limit has been removed by acceptance of the 200 miles exclusive economic zone at the 1982 United Nations Convention on the Law of the Sea.

b.   Interest Involved

Shigeru Oda, "International Law of the Resources of the Sea," *Hague Recueil des Cours*, Vol. 127 (1970) pp. 384-387. Reprinted with the permission of the Kluwer Academic Publishers Group.

National Interests and the Extent of the Territorial Sea

(i) Guarantee of Free Navigation

First, those maritime States which maintain large merchant fleets understandably oppose any extension of the territorial sea, since freedom of navigation is assured only on the high seas. But since the right of innocent passage is granted to foreign vessels on the territorial sea, the passage of merchant vessels is of little relevance to the width of this stretch of water. Although the right of innocent passage of merchant ships through the territorial sea is not precisely comparable to free passage on the high seas, it is hardly likely that the distinction between the two concepts can have a bearing on the final determination of the extent of the territorial sea.

(ii) Security Considerations

Security considerations are sometimes raised in support of a completely opposite policy on the extent of the territorial sea. And, indeed, there seem to be valid grounds for claiming a broader territorial sea as a means of maintaining the security of the coastal State. It is no secret that certain developing States are apprehensive about the foreign warships which approach their off-shore areas, and new States have displayed considerable irritation, but from a somewhat different point of view, over the maneuvers of foreign fleets conducted off their coasts.

The real concern of the United States was clearly outlined by Arthur Dean, President of the United States delegation in both 1958 and 1960, in articles which he published after the first Geneva Conference. First, he was quite frank about the danger of Russian submarines equipped with missiles. He stated:

> . . . if the territorial sea were extended to 12 miles, an enemy submarine (particularly a nuclear submarine which could operate silently for long periods without surfacing) would be able to move about undetected in a neutral State's territorial sea, whereas our surface ships would not operate there without violating the State's neutrality.

Secondly, he found it unacceptable that the territorial sea might be so extended as to limit the maneuvers of the United States fleet. His statement on 20 January 1960 before the United States Senate Committee on Foreign Relations clearly reflects this position:

> Our Navy would like to see as narrow a territorial sea as possible in order to preserve the maximum possibility of deployment, transit, and maneuverability on and over the high seas, free from the jurisdictional control of individual States. . . .

(iii) Fishery Interests

As already indicated, there was, in the course of discussions at the 1958 and 1960 Geneva Conferences, an attempt to compromise on a narrower territorial sea by treating fishery interests independently of the regime of the territorial sea.

Many of the delegates considered these interests of overriding importance in the delimitation of the territorial sea. In order to secure a greater advantage in this respect, a large number of States favored a wider extension of the territorial sea which would serve to exclude foreign fishing from the coastal areas. Those States boasting advanced skills in fishing, however, were very much concerned with the right to fish in off-shore areas of *other* States. Certain statements made at the Geneva Conferences by delegates of advanced fishing States clearly indicated that any extension of the territorial sea would represent an intolerable blow to their fishery interests. "Fishery interests" was used to support both a wider and a narrower territorial sea. . . .

REFERENCES

M.S. McDougal & W.T. Burke, *The Public Order of the Oceans: A Contemporary Law of the Sea*, New Haven and London: Yale University Press, 1962, pp. 453-486; C.J. Colombos, *The International Law of the Sea*, (6th rev. ed.) London: Longmans, 1967, p. 87; B.L. Florsheim, "Territorial Sea, 3000 Year Old Question," *Journal of Air Law and Commerce*, Vol. 36 (1970), pp. 98-103.

c.   The 1958-60 First and Second Conferences on the Law of the Sea

1958 CONVENTION ON THE TERRITORIAL SEA
AND THE CONTIGUOUS ZONE

Article 6

The outer limit of the territorial sea is the line every point of which is at a distance from the nearest point of the baseline equal to the breadth of the territorial sea.

Bernard G. Heinzen, "The Three-Mile Limit: Preserving the Freedom of the Seas," *Stanford Law Review*, Vol. 11 (1959), pp. 652-655. Copyright by the Board of Trustees of the Leland Stanford Junior University. Reprinted by permission also of Fred B. Rothman Co.

The United States and many other governments strongly supported the codification of the three-mile or one-league limit as an existing rule of international law during the early stages of the Geneva Conference. But insofar as the breadth of the territorial sea was concerned, many delegations had little or no inclination to discuss or consider the merits of various proposals as principles of international law or as methods for meeting new needs within the existing framework of customary international law. In other words, there was far too little tendency to consider either the extent to which the original reasons for the freedom of the seas still prevail or whether there is a rational basis for changing the customary breadth of the territorial sea. Moreover, the practice of bloc voting was another factor which tended to discourage states from supporting the three-mile or one-league limit.

In general, there were at least four approaches to the problem on the part of nations who urged a rule other than the three-mile or one-league limit.

First, the Soviet or Iron-Curtain bloc of ten nations supported the twelve-mile limit in order to advance their "Cold-War" interests.

Second, the entire Arab bloc of ten votes was also committed to support the twelve-mile limit in the hope that this might enhance their ability legally to close off the Gulf of Aqaba which is less than twenty-four miles in breadth at its widest point.

The Soviet and Arab blocs, with a combined total of twenty votes at their disposal, were unalterably opposed to any proposal for less than twelve miles of territorial sea. Since there were eighty-six votes to be cast, this Arab-Soviet position meant that any nation or group of nations endeavoring to harmonize their positions with the undercurrent of compromise motivating many non-Soviet and non-Arab delegations could afford to lose only eight of the remaining sixty-six votes, which included other bloc votes.

The third group, composed mostly of Latin-American nations, tended to favor either an extension of the territorial sea or a contiguous zone for exclusive fishing control because of the desire of these states to assure either the conservation or the unilateral control of fish resources in areas adjacent to their coasts.

Fourth, many newly independent states, primarily members of the Afro-Asian bloc, opposed the retention of the three-mile limit on the grounds that it had been adopted by the major maritime powers before the new states had come into existence. In many ways, this was the least objective approach to the problem, since these nations, who have a real stake in promoting world commerce and economic development, felt almost duty-bound to oppose the three-mile or one-league limit irrespective of any compromise offer to meet their real or potential economic needs by devices other than an extension of the territorial sea.

The most significant of the considerations which motivated opposition to the three-mile or one-league limit was the concern of many nations that they should have exclusive control over fishing off their own coasts. On the other hand, the economy of other nations depends, to a substantial extent, on continued fishing in long established fisheries off foreign coasts.

In the later stages of the Conference, it became evident that agreement on the breadth of the territorial sea was impossible unless at least some of the various differences could be resolved. Many nations came to the Conference with a genuine desire to reach agreement, but there was a growing tendency upon the part of some to support a proposal which, from the viewpont of those desiring to preserve the maximum freedom of the seas and *res communis*, was a compromise in name only. This was the proposal originally introduced by India and Mexico which would have given each state the right to fix its territorial sea at any distance up to twelve miles. Such action would have been tantamount to the adoption of the twelve-mile limit.

After studying the various conflicting interests, the United States ultimately put forward a proposal which it hoped would serve to reconcile these conflicting interests to the extent necessary to achieve general agreement. This proposal would have permitted a territorial sea of up to six miles plus exclusive fishing rights in a zone extending up to twelve miles from the coast. A coastal state, however, could not exclude from the outer six miles of its fishery zone the fishing vessels of states whose vessels had fished within those waters in the past five years, provided that such vessels observed any reasonable conservation measures imposed by the coastal state.

Although the United States proposal did not attain the two-thirds majority necessary for adoption by the conference, it did gain the only absolute majority of any of those proposals voted upon in plenary session. Thus the vote on the United States proposal was forty-five in favor to thirty-three against with seven abstentions. The flexible three-to twelve-mile proposal sponsored by Mexico and seven other powers obtained only thirty-nine votes in favor with thirty-eight against and eight abstentions, while a Soviet proposal for a territorial sea of at least twelve miles in breadth was soundly defeated by a vote of forty-seven against, twenty-one in favor and seventeen abstentions. A Canadian proposal for a twelve-mile exclusive fishing zone received a vote of only thirty-five in favor with thirty against and twenty abstentions.

Thus, because of a variety of political and other considerations, the Conference never seriously considered the question of the maximum breadth of the territorial sea cognizable under international law. . . .

REFERENCES

In addition to the articles of the 1958 Conference cited in Chapter II, *see also* L. Becker, "The Breadth of the Territorial Sea and Fisheries Jurisdiction," *U.S. Department of State Bulletin*, Vol. 40, No. 1019 (January 5, 1959), pp. 369-374; R.J. Yalem, "The International Legal Status of the Territorial Sea," *Villanova Law Review*, Vol. 5 (1959), p. 206-214; W.P. Gormley, "The Unilateral Extension of Territorial Waters: The Failure of the United Nations to Protect Freedom of the Seas," *University of Detroit Law Journal*, Vol. 43 (1966), pp. 695, 706-718.

> Arthur H. Dean, "The Second Geneva Conference on the Law of the Sea: The Fight for Freedom of the Seas," *American Journal of International Law*, Vol. 54 (1960), pp. 772-773, 775-776. Reprinted with the permission of The American Society of International Law and the author.

The second Conference, like the first Conference, was governed by procedural rules adopted at the Conference and resembling United Nations rules in voting procedure. A Committee of the Whole was formed by all the states present for the purpose of discussing and debating the various proposals on the territorial sea and contiguous fishing zone. This committee by a simple majority vote could adopt a report which would include proposals to the Plenary Session of the Conference, where an official convention could be adopted by the same delegates upon the affirmative votes of two-thirds of the states present and voting and not abstaining. . . .

The U.S.-Canadian compromise "joint proposal" was sincerely designed to find a rule acceptable to the Conference, though admittedly at considerable expense to U.S. fishing interests. In the absence of treaty rights, it would necessitate immediately giving up the right to fish off foreign coasts within 6 miles, and between 6 and 12 miles except where the practice of fishing during the 5-year base period could be proved; it would necessitate giving up such fishing rights within 12 miles everywhere after 10 years unless bilateral treaties with respect to such rights could be negotiated in the interim. *Per contra*, in the absence of any agreement, as nations unilaterally extend the breadths of their territorial seas and attempt to prevent foreign fishing therein, the fishing rights of American vessels might gradually be whittled away so that continued operation would be uneconomic. The sacrifice inherent in the joint proposal was offered in the hope of achieving agreement at the Conference on a territorial sea limited to 6 miles without increasing the contiguous fishing zone beyond 12 miles, while protecting American fishing vessels against unilateral claims for at least 10 years. Thus, it is not correct to say that security interests overrode all consideration of American fishing interests; it was a question of timing and of balance.

This joint proposal was favorably received in the Committee of the Whole and was adopted by a vote of 43 in favor to 33 against, with 12 abstentions, out of a total of 76 nations voting. The proposal thus obtained more than the simple majority of votes required in the Committee of the Whole and became its proposal in its Report to the Plenary Session. Subsequently, this U.S.-Canadian joint proposal, embodied in the Report of the Committee of the Whole, after being amended, received support in the Plenary Session from 54 nations in favor, to 28 against, with a total of 82 nations voting and 5 abstentions. Thus, this proposal was only one negative vote short of a two-thirds' majority as required in Plenary Session under the rules adopted by the Conference. . . .

REFERENCES

D.W. Bowett, "The Second United Nations Conference on the Law of the Sea," *International and Comparative Law Quarterly*, Vol. 9 (1960), pp. 415-435; C.M. Franklin, "The Law of the Sea: Some Recent Developments," *Southern California Law Review*, Vol. 33 (1960), pp. 357-369; P.C. Jessup, "The Law of the Sea Around Us," *American Journal of International Law*, Vol. 55 (1961), pp. 104-109; and reply and response to reply in *American Journal of International Law*, Vol. 55 (1961), pp. 669 and 675; R.H. Manley, "The Geneva Conferences on the Law of the Sea as a Step in the International Law-Making Process," *Albany Law Review*, Vol. 25 (1961), pp. 17-38; R.D. Powers and L.R. Hardy, "How Wide the Territorial Sea," *U.S. Naval Institute Proceedings*, Vol. 87(2) (1961), pp. 68-71; Shigeru Oda, "The Extent of the Territorial Sea--Some Analysis of the Geneva Conferences and Recent Developments," *Japanese Annual of International Law*, Vol. 6 (1962), pp. 7-38; W.P. Gormley, "The Unilateral Extension of Territorial Waters: The Failure of the United Nations to Protect Freedom of the Seas," *University of Detroit Law Journal*, Vol. 43 (1966), pp. 695, 718-722; Inter-American Juridical Committee, *Opinion on the Breadth of the Territorial Sea*, Washington, D.C.: Pan American Union, 1966, pp. 82-89; R.L. Friedheim, "Factor Analysis as a Tool in Studying the Law of the Sea," in Lewis A. Alexander, ed., *The Law of the Sea: Offshore Boundaries and Zones*, Columbus, Ohio: Ohio State University Press, 1967, pp. 47-70.

d. The Third United Nations Conference on the Law of the Sea

1982 UNITED NATIONS CONVENTION ON THE LAW OF THE SEA

Article 3
Breadth of the territorial sea

Every State has the right to establish the breadth of its territorial sea up to a limit not exceeding 12 nautical miles, measured from baselines determined in accordance with this Convention.

Article 4
Outer limit of the territorial sea

The outer limit of the territorial sea is the line every point of which is at a distance from the nearest point of the baseline equal to the breadth of the territorial sea.

REFERENCES

Shigeru Oda, "The Territorial Sea and Natural Resources," *International and Comparative Law Quarterly*, Vol. 4 (1955), pp. 415-425; M.S. McDougal and W.T. Burke, "The Community Interest in a Narrow Territorial Sea: Inclusive versus Exclusive Competence Over the Oceans," *Cornell Law Quarterly*, Vol. 45 (1960), pp. 171-253; Shigeru Oda, "The Extent of the Territorial Sea--Some Analysis of the Geneva Conferences and Recent Developments," *Japanese Annual of International Law*, Vol. 6 (1962), pp. 7-38; O. Svarlien, "The Territorial Sea: A Question for Uniformity," *University of Florida Law Review*, Vol. 15 (1962), pp. 333-351; W.P. Gormley, "The Unilateral Extension of Territorial Waters: The Failure of the United Nations to Protect Freedom of the Seas," *University of Detroit Law Journal*, Vol. 43 (1966), pp. 695-730; G.E. Carlisle, "Three-Mile-Limit--Obsolete Concept?" *U.S. Naval Institute Proceedings*, Vol. 13 (1967), pp. 24-34; Meade, "The Great Territorial Sea Squabble," *U.S. Naval Institute Proceedings*, Vol. 95 (April, 1969), p. 45; B.L. Florsheim, "Territorial Sea, 3000 Year Old Question," *Journal of Air Law and Commerce*, Vol. 36 (1970), pp. 73-104; B.A. Brickell, "National Sovereignty and the Two Hundred Mile Limit: The Case for the Littoral State," *American University Law Review*, Vol. 21 (1972), pp. 593-608; H.G. Knight, "The 1971 U.S. Proposals on the Breadth of the Territorial Sea and Passage Through International Straits," *Oregon Law Review*, Vol. 51 (1972), pp. 759-785; R.O. Freeman, "Possible Solutions to the 200-Mile Territorial Limit," *International Lawyer*, Vol. 7 (1973), pp. 387-395; "The Three Mile Limit as a Rule of International Law," *Columbia Law Review*, Vol. 23 (1973), pp. 472-476; A. Akinsanya, "The Nigerian Territorial Waters Decrees of 1967 and 1971," *Indian Journal of International Law*, Vol. 16 (1976), pp. 276-286; H.G. de Jong, "Extension of the Territorial Sea of the Kingdom of the Netherlands," *Netherlands International Law Review*, Vol. 30 (1983), No. 2, pp. 129-145; Vladimir Kopal, "Breadth of the Territorial Sea. Evolution of the Question, Present State and Prospects," *Studiez Mesinarodniho Prava*, (Prague, Czechoslovakia), Vol. 17 (1983), pp. 43-68.

e. Current Status

According to the United Nations Office for Ocean Affairs and the Law of the Sea, the following number of countries claimed the specified breadths of territorial sea:

Breadth	Number of Countries	Breadth	Number of Countries	Breadth	Number of Countries
3 miles	10	4 miles	2	6 miles	4
12 miles	110	(Note: The Republic of China on Taiwan also claims a 12 mile territorial sea.)			
20 miles	1	30 miles	2	35 miles	1
50 miles	1	200 miles	12		

(*Law of the Sea Bulletin*, No. 15 (May 1990), p. 39.)

UNITED STATES: PRESIDENTIAL PROCLAMATION ON THE
TERRITORIAL SEA OF THE UNITED STATES
December 27, 1988
International Legal Materials,
Vol. 28 (1989), p. 284.

International Law recognizes that coastal nations may exercise sovereignty and jurisdiction over their territorial seas.

The territorial sea of the United States is a maritime zone extending beyond the land territory and internal waters of the United States over which the United States exercises sovereignty and jurisdiction, a sovereignty and jurisdiction that extend to the airspace over the territorial sea, as well as to its bed and subsoil.

Extension of the territorial sea by the United States to the limits permitted by international law will advance the national security and other significant interests of the United States.

Now, therefore, I, Ronald Reagan, by the authority vested in me as President by the Constitution of the United States of America, and in accordance with international law, do hereby proclaim the extension of the territorial sea of the United States of America, the Commonwealth of Puerto Rico, Guam, American Samoa, the United States Virgin Islands, the Commonwealth of the Northern Mariana Islands, and any other territory or possession over which the United States exercises sovereignty.

The territorial sea of the United States henceforth extends to 12 nautical miles from the baselines of the United States determined in accordance with international law.

In accordance with international law, as reflected in the applicable provisions of the 1982 United Nations Convention on the Law of the Sea, within the territorial sea of the United States, the ships of all countries enjoy the right of innocent passage and the ships and aircraft of all countries enjoy the right of transit passage through international straits.

Nothing in this Proclamation:

(a) extends or otherwise alters existing Federal or State law or any jurisdiction, rights, legal interests, or obligations derived therefrom; or

(b) impairs the determination, in accordance with international law, of any maritime boundary of the United States with a foreign jurisdiction.

In witness whereof, I have hereunto set my hand this twenty-seventh day of December, in the year of our Lord nineteen hundred and eighty-eight, and of the Independence of the United States of America the two hundred and thirteenth.

/s/ **Ronald Reagan**

NOTE

It is reported that the U.S. extension of its territorial sea was "motivated in part by a desire to keep Soviet intelligence gathering vessels farther from the shoreline . . . and the Navy and intelligence officials had been pressing for such a move for some time." Andrew Rosenthal, "Reagan Extends Territorial Waters to 12 Miles," *New York Times*, December 29, 1988, p. 17. For a discussion on why the U.S. was previously reluctant to extend its territorial sea to 12 miles, *see* Robert W. Knecht and William E. Westermeyer, "State vs. National Interests in an Expanded Territorial Sea," *Coastal Zone Management Journal*, Vol. 11 (1983-1984), pp. 317-333; Richard K. Littleton, "Coastal State, and A 12-mile Territorial Sea," *Journal of Maritime Law & Commerce*, Vol. 17 (1986), pp. 539-565; Bruce E. Alexander, "The Territorial Sea of the United States: Is It Twelve Miles or Not," *Journal of Maritime Law and Commerce*, Vol. 20 (1989), pp. 449-488; Henry M. Arruda, "The Extension of the United States Territorial Sea: Reasons and Effects," *Connecticut Journal of International Law*, Vol. 4 (1989), pp. 697-727.

On October 1, 1987, the United Kingdom extended its territorial sea to twelve miles, see U.K. *Territorial Sea Act of 1987*, in *Law of the Sea Bulletin*, No. 10 (November 1987), pp. 12-20.

4.   Innocent Passage

a.   Concept and Meaning

1982 UNITED NATIONS CONVENTION ON THE LAW OF THE SEA

Article 17
Right of innocent passage

Subject to this Convention, ships of all States, whether coastal or land-locked, enjoy the right of innocent passage through the territorial sea.

Article 18
Meaning of passage

1. Passage means navigation through the territorial sea for the purpose of:

(a)   traversing that sea without entering internal waters or calling at a roadstead or port facility outside internal waters; or

(b)   proceeding to or from internal waters or a call at such roadstead or port facility.

2. Passage shall be continuous and expeditious. However, passage includes stopping and anchoring, but only in so far as the same are incidental to ordinary navigation or are rendered necessary by *force majeure* or distress or for the purpose of rendering assistance to persons, ships or aircraft in danger or distress.

Article 19
Meaning of innocent passage

1. Passage is innocent so long as it is not prejudicial to the peace, good order or security of the coastal State. Such passage shall take place in conformity with this Convention and with other rules of international law.

2. Passage of a foreign ship shall be considered to be prejudicial to the peace, good order or security of the coastal State if in the territorial sea it engages in any of the following activities:

(a)   any threat or use of force against the sovereignty, territorial integrity or political independence of the coastal State, or in any other manner in violation of the principles of international law embodied in the Charter of the United Nations;

(b)   any exercise or practice with weapons of any kind;

(c)   any act aimed at collecting information to the prejudice of the defense or security of the coastal State;

(d)   any act of propaganda aimed at affecting the defense or security of the coastal State;

(e)   the launching, landing or taking on board of any aircraft;

(f)   the launching, landing or taking on board of any military device;

(g)   the loading or unloading of any commodity, currency or person contrary to the customs, fiscal, immigration or sanitary laws and regulations of the coastal State;

(h)   any act of willful and serious pollution contrary to this Convention;

(i)   any fishing activities;

(j)   the carrying out of research or survey activities;

(k)   any act aimed at interfering with any systems of communication or any other facilities or installations of the coastal State;

(l)   any other activity not having a direct bearing on passage.

NOTE

Article 14, paragraph 1 of the 1958 Convention on the Territorial Sea and Contiguous is essentially the same as Article 17 of the 1982 Convention. Article 14, paragraphs 2 and 3 of the

1958 Convention is essentially the same as Article 18 of the 1982 Convention. Article 14, paragraphs 4 and 5 of the 1958 Convention are essentially the same as Article 19, paragraphs 1 and 2 (first part) of the 1982 Convention. Article 19, paragraph 2, sub-paragraphs (a) to (1) are new.

> *Restatement of the Foreign Relations Law of the United States*, 3rd Revision, Vol. 2, St. Paul, Minn.: American Law Institute, 1987, pp. 50, 55. Copyright by The American Law Institute. Reprinted with the permission of The American Law Institute.

Section 513, Comment i.

> *i. No right of innocent passage in airspace above territorial sea.* The sovereignty of the coastal state in the airspace above its territorial sea is not subject to any right of innocent passage except as provided by international agreement. See Chicago Convention on International Civil Aviation of December 7, 1944, Articles 1-2, 61 Stat. 1180, T.I.A.S. No. 1591, 15 U.N.T.S. 295.

> . . . .

Editors' Note 6.

6. *Right to overfly the territorial sea.* Most coastal states have granted rights to overfly their territorial sea as part of an agreement to overfly their territory generally. See Chicago International Air Services Transit Agreement of December 7, 1944, 59 Stat. 1693, E.A.S. 487, 3 Bevans 916, 84 U.N.T.S. 389. For a comment by the International Civil Aviation Organization, see 1 UNCLOS I, Off. Rec. 336 (1958). See generally, Lowenfeld, Aviation Law: Cases and Materials, Chapt. 2 (2d ed. 1981). Military and other state aircraft are not covered by these agreements and enjoy overflight or landing rights only by special agreement.

After a Korean passenger plane was shot down by a Soviet plane near Sakhalin Island in September 1983, the ICAO Assembly adopted in May 1984 an amendment to the 1944 Convention on International Civil Aviation obligating every state to "refrain from resorting to the use of weapons against civil aircraft in flight," and recognizing that "the lives of persons on board and the safety of aircraft must not be endangered." 39 ICAO Bull., No. 6, at 10-11 (1984).

b.   General Rules

1958 CONVENTION ON THE TERRITORIAL SEA AND CONTIGUOUS ZONE

Article 14

6. Submarines are required to navigate on the surface and to show their flag.

Article 15

1. The coastal State must not hamper innocent passage through the territorial sea.

2. The coastal State is required to give appropriate publicity to any dangers to navigation, of which it has knowledge, within its territorial sea.

Article 16

1. The coastal State may take the necessary steps in its territorial sea to prevent passage which is not innocent.

2. In the case of ships proceeding to internal waters, the coastal State shall also have the right to take the necessary steps to prevent any breach of the conditions to which admission of those ships to those waters is subject.

3. Subject to the provisions of paragraph 4, the coastal State may, without discrimination amongst foreign ships, suspend temporarily in specified areas of its territorial sea the innocent passage of foreign ships if such suspension is essential for the protection of its security. Such suspensions shall take effect only after having been duly published.

4. There shall be no suspension of the innocent passage of foreign ships through straits which are used for international navigation between one part of the high seas and another part of the high seas or the territorial sea of a foreign State.

Article 17

Foreign ships exercising the right of innocent passage shall comply with the laws and regulations enacted by the coastal State in conformity with these articles and other rules of international law and, in particular, with such laws and regulations relating to transport and navigation.

Article 18

1. No charge may be levied upon foreign ships by reason only of their passage through the territorial sea.

2. Charges may be levied upon a foreign ship passing through the territorial sea as payment only for specific services rendered to the ship. These charges shall be levied without discrimination.

1982 UNITED NATIONS CONVENTION ON THE LAW OF THE SEA

Article 20
Submarines and other underwater vehicles

In the territorial sea, submarines and other underwater vehicles are required to navigate on the surface and to show their flag.

Article 21
Laws and regulations of the coastal State relating to innocent passage

1. The coastal State may adopt laws and regulations, in conformity with the provisions of this Convention and other rules of international law, relating to innocent passage through the territorial sea, in respect of all or any of the following:

(a)   the safety of navigation and the regulation of maritime traffic;

(b)   the protection of navigational aids and facilities and other facilities or installations;

(c)   the protection of cables and pipelines;

(d)   the conservation of the living resources of the sea;

(e)   the prevention of infringement of the fisheries laws and regulations of the coastal State;

(f)   the preservation of the environment of the coastal State and the prevention, reduction and control of pollution thereof;

(g)   marine scientific research and hydrographic surveys;

(h)   the prevention of infringement of the customs, fiscal, immigration or sanitary laws and regulations of the coastal State.

2.   Such laws and regulations shall not apply to the design, construction, manning or equipment of foreign ships unless they are giving effect to generally accepted international rules or standards.

3. The coastal State shall give due publicity to all such laws and regulations.

4. Foreign ships exercising the right of innocent passage through the territorial sea shall comply with all such laws and regulations and all generally accepted international regulations relating to the prevention of collisions at sea.

Article 22
Sea lanes and traffic separation schemes in the territorial sea

1. The coastal State may, where necessary having regard to the safety of navigation, require foreign ships exercising the right of innocent passage through its territorial sea to use such sea lanes and traffic separation schemes as it may designate or prescribe for the regulation of the passage of ships.

2. In particular, tankers, nuclear-powered ships and ships carrying nuclear or other inherently dangerous or noxious substances or materials may be required to confine their passage to such sea lanes.

3. In the designation of sea lanes and the prescription of traffic separation schemes under this article, the coastal State shall take into account:

(a)   the recommendations of the competent international organization;

(b)   any channels customarily used for international navigation;

(c)   the special characteristics of particular ships and channels; and

(d)   the density of traffic.

4. The coastal State shall clearly indicate such sea lanes and traffic separation schemes on charts to which due publicity shall be given.

. . . .

Article 24
Duties of the coastal State

1. The coastal State shall not hamper the innocent passage of foreign ships through the territorial sea except in accordance with this Convention. In particular, in the application of this Convention or of any laws or regulations adopted in conformity with this Convention, the coastal State shall not:

(a)   impose requirements on foreign ships which have the practical effect of denying or impairing the right of innocent passage; or

(b)   discriminate in form or in fact against the ships of any State or against ships carrying cargoes to, from or on behalf of any State.

2. The coastal State shall give appropriate publicity to any danger to navigation, of which it has knowledge, within its territorial sea.

Article 25
Rights of protection of the coastal State

1. The coastal State may take the necessary steps in its territorial sea to prevent passage which is not innocent.

2. In the case of ships proceeding to internal waters or a call at a port facility outside internal waters, the coastal State also has the right to take the necessary steps to prevent any breach of the conditions to which admission of those ships to internal waters or such a call is subject.

3. The coastal State may, without discrimination in form or in fact among foreign ships, suspend temporarily in specified areas of its territorial sea the innocent passage of foreign ships if such suspension is essential for the protection of its security, including weapons exercises. Such suspension shall take effect only after having been duly published.

Article 26
Charges which may be levied upon foreign ships

1. No charge may be levied upon foreign ships by reason only of their passage through the territorial sea.

2. Charges may be levied upon a foreign ship passing through the territorial sea as payment only for specific services rendered to the ship. These charges shall be levied without discrimination.

U.S. TEMPORARY SUSPENSION OF RIGHT
OF INNOCENT PASSAGE NEAR AMCHITKA
Department of State Bulletin, Vol. 65,
No. 1691 (November 22, 1971), p. 599

Following are notices by the Government of the United States of temporary suspension of right of innocent passage through territorial waters surrounding Amchitka Island.

FIRST NOTICE, NOVEMBER 1
Press release 252 dated November 1

Pursuant to Article 16[1] of the 1958 Geneva Convention on the Territorial Sea and the Contiguous Zone, the right of innocent passage within three nautical miles of Amchitka Island (51 Degrees 25 Minutes N, 179 Degrees 10 Minutes E) is suspended temporarily from 0001X November 2, 1971 to 2400X November 4, 1971, inclusive, Bering Sea Daylight Time due to U.S. Atomic Energy Commission experiment.

SECOND NOTICE, NOVEMBER 4
Press release 255 dated November 4

Pursuant to Article 16 of the 1958 Geneva Convention on the Territorial Sea and the Contiguous Zone, the right of innocent passage within three nautical miles of Amchitka Island (51 Degrees 25 Minutes N, 179 Degrees 10 Minutes E) is suspended temporarily from 0001X November 5, 1971, to 2400X November 7, 1971, inclusive, Bering Sea Daylight Time due to U.S. Atomic Energy Commission experiment.

NIGERIAN PORTS AUTHORITY
HARBOUR MASTER'S NOTICE NO. 124 OF 1967
NOTICE OF PROHIBITED ZONE
International Legal Materials, Vol. 6 (1967), p. 682

Notice is hereby given that a Prohibited zone to all shipping including fishing boats has been established as follows:

> East of a line Cape Formosa and position Latitude 04° 04' North Longitude 06° 05.5' East and a line parallel at a distance of twelve nautical miles from the coast of Nigeria until the international waters of the Republic of Cameron are reached off the Calabar River.

AUTHORITY: Federal Ministry of Transport, Lagos.
DATE: 30th May, 1967

---

[1]Article 16, paragraph 3, provides: ". . . the coastal State may, without discrimination amongst foreign ships, suspend temporarily in specified areas of its territorial sea the innocent passage of foreign ships if such suspension is essential for the protection of its security. Such suspension shall take effect only after having been duly published." Article 25, paragraph 3 of the 1982 United Nations Convention on the Law of the Sea is identical.

VIETNAM DECREE ON SEA SURVEILLANCE COMMUNIQUE
OF THE MINISTRY OF FOREIGN AFFAIRS
REPUBLIC OF VIETNAM, APRIL 27, 1965
International Legal Materials, Vol. 4 (1965), p. 461

Due to the fact of a constant and increasing infiltration by sea into the Republic of Vietnam of Viet Cong personnel, arms, ammunition and various war supplies, the Prime Minister has signed Decree No. 81/NG of the 27th of April 1965, by which the following measures have been decided upon to ensure the security and the defense of the territorial waters of Vietnam:

I. - The territorial waters up to the three mile limit is declared a defensive sea area. The passage of vessels through the territorial sea of the Republic of Vietnam which is prejudicial to the peace, good order or security of the Republic of Vietnam is not considered as innocent passage and is forbidden by the law of the Republic of Vietnam. Ships of any country operating within the territorial sea of the Republic of Vietnam which are not clearly engaged in innocent passage are subject to visit and search, and may be subject to arrest and disposition, as provided by the law of the Republic of Vietnam in conformity with accepted principles of international law.

Cargoes will be considered suspect unless it can be clearly established that they are destined for a port outside the Republic of Vietnam or a legitimate recipient in the Republic of Vietnam. Cargoes will be considered particularly suspect if containing any of the items listed below.

1) Weapons, ammunition, electrical and communications equipment.

2) Primer, mine, gunpowder and other explosives.

3) Chemical products which can serve military purposes. . . .

4) Medical supplies of Communist North Vietnam, Communist China or Soviet Bloc origin.

5) Foodstuffs of Communist North Vietnam, Communist China or Soviet Bloc origin.

. . . .

QUESTIONS

What gave rise in each of these three cases for the need to suspend innocent passage? Are any or all of the suspensions sanctioned by Article 16(3) of the Convention?

Is the "innocence" criterion entirely subjective? Could innocence depend on factors such as a ship's cargo or its destination?

What entity makes the final decision as to whether a given act of passage is or is not innocent? Can you envision a situation in which a coastal state would be tempted to declare a passage not innocent for reasons totally unrelated to law of the sea issues?

REFERENCES

P.C. Jessup, "Civil Jurisdiction over Ships in Innocent Passage," *American Journal of International Law*, Vol. 27 (1933), pp. 747-750; C.B. Selak, "Fishing Vessels and the Principle of Innocent Passage," *American Journal of International Law*, Vol. 48 (1954), pp. 627-635; R.B.

Lillich, "The Geneva Conference on the Law of the Sea and the Immunity of Foreign State-Owned Commercial Vessels," *George Washington Law Review*, Vol. 28 (1960), pp. 408-420; L.T. Lee, "Jurisdiction over Foreign Merchant Ships in the Territorial Sea: An Analysis of the Geneva Convention on the Law of the Sea," *American Journal of International Law*, Vol. 55 (1961), pp. 77-96; M.S. McDougal & W.T. Burke, *The Public Order of the Oceans: A Contemporary International Law of the Sea*, New Haven and London: Yale University Press, 1962, pp. 214-269; W.E. Butler, "Soviet Concepts of Innocent Passage," *Harvard International Law Club Journal*, Vol. 7 (1965), pp. 113-130, A.D. Pharand, "Innocent Passage in the Arctic," *Canadian Yearbook of International Law*, Vol. 6 (1968), pp. 3-60; Walker, "What is Innocent Passage?," *U.S. Naval War College Review*, Vol. 21 (No. 5) (1969), p. 53; O.G. deVaries Reilingh, "Warships in Territorial Waters: Their Right of Innocent Passage," *Netherlands Yearbook of International Law*, Vol. 2 (1971), pp. 29-67; G.P. Smith, "Politics of Lawmaking: Problems in International Maritime Regulation--Innocent Passage v. Free Transit," *University of Pittsburgh Law Review*, Vol. 37 (1976), pp. 487-550; Shekhar Gosh, "The Legal Regime of Innocent Passage Through the Territorial Sea," *Indian Journal of International Law*, Vol. 20 (1980), pp. 216-242; Brian Smith, "Innocent Passage as a Rule of Decision: Navigation Versus Environmental Protection," *Columbia Journal of Transnational Law*, Vol. 21 (1982), pp. 49-102; Karin M. Burke and Deborah A. DeLeo, "Innocent Passage and Transit Passage in the United Nations Convention on the Law of the Sea," *Yale Studies in World Public Order*, Vol. 9 (1983), pp. 389-408; M. Ye Volosov, "The International Legal Status of Nuclear-Powered Merchant Ships in Foreign Territorial Waters," *Soviet Yearbook of Maritime Law*, 1984, pp. 83-89; D.J. Devine, "Sea Passage in South African Maritime Zones: Actualities and Possibilities," *Acta Juridica* (Cape Town), 1986, pp. 203-226; W.E. Butler, "Innocent Passage and the 1982 Convention: The Influence of Soviet Law and Policy," *American Journal of International Law*, Vol. 81 (1987), pp. 331-347.

NOTE

THE MAYAGUEZ INCIDENT

In May, 1975, the United States flag merchant vessel *Mayaguez* was stopped, boarded, and seized by regular military forces of the Communist Government of Cambodia at a point generally agreed to have been approximately 6 miles from the Wai Islands in the Gulf of Thailand. Although Cambodian forces occupied the islands, title to them was disputed at the time among Thailand, Vietnam, and Cambodia. Cambodia alleged that the vessel was within claimed Cambodian territorial waters (12 nautical miles) while the United States urged that (1) the vessel was on the high seas since it recognizes only a three mile territorial sea limit, and (2) even if the vessel were within Cambodia's territorial sea it was entitled to the right of innocent passage and the seizure and detention of the crew were therefore unlawful. Relying on the international law of reprisal (an international wrong, an unsatisfied demand for redress, application of reasonable force), armed forces of the United States raided a Cambodian island where the crew was thought to be held and also bombed the Cambodian mainland. The crew was released unharmed. For details of the incident, see *Hearings on Seizure of the Mayaguez before the Subcommittee on International Political and Military Affairs of the House Committee on International Relations* (94th Cong., 1st Sess., May 14, 15, June 19, 25, July 25, 1975), Parts I & II; *Time Magazine*, May 26, 1975, p. 9; *Newsweek*, May 26, 1975, p. 16. Selected official communications appear in "U.S. Recovers Merchant Ship Seized by Cambodian Navy," *Department of State Bulletin*, Vol. 72, No. 1875 (June 2, 1975), pp. 719-722. See also, J.J. Paust, "Seizure and Recovery of the Mayaguez," *Yale Law Journal*, Vol. 85 (1976), pp. 774-806; J.J. Paust, "Correspondence: Mayaguez--Reply," *Yale Law Journal*, Vol. 86 (1976), pp. 207-213; M.D. Sandler, "Correspondence: Mayaguez," *Yale Law Journal*, Vol. 86 (1976), pp. 203-207; R.E. Ward, "The Mayaguez: The Right of Innocent

Passage and the Legality of Reprisal," *San Diego Law Review*, Vol. 13 (1976), pp. 765-778; "'Mayaguez' Rescue and Vietnam Evacuation: Violations of Statutory Law?" *Congressional Record*, May 12, 1976, p. S7019, *et seq.*; S.B. Finch, "Pueblo and Mayaguez: A Legal Analysis," *Case Western Reserve Journal of International Law*, Vol. 9 (1977), pp. 79-116; R.A. Friedlander, "The Mayaguez in Retrospect: Humanitarian Intervention or Showing the Flag?," *St. Louis University Law Journal*, Vol. 22 (1978), pp. 601-613; Robert Simmons, *The Pueblo, EC-121, and Mayaguez Incidents: Some Continuities and Changes*, Baltimore: University of Maryland Law School Occasional Papers/Reprints Series in Contemporary Asian Studies, No. 8-1978 (20); Thomas E. Behuniak, "The Seizure and Recovery of the S.S. Mayaguez: A Legal Analysis of United States Claims," *Military Law Review*, Vol. 83 (1978), pp. 41-170 and Vol. 83 (1979), pp. 59-129.

c.   **Nuclear-Powered Ships or Ships Carrying Nuclear or Noxious Substances**

1982 UNITED NATIONS CONVENTION ON THE LAW OF THE SEA

Article 23
Foreign nuclear-powered ships and ships carrying nuclear
or other inherently dangerous or noxious substances

Foreign nuclear-powered ships and ships carrying nuclear or other inherently dangerous or noxious substances shall, when exercising the right of innocent passage through the territorial sea, carry documents and observe special precautionary measures established for such ships by international agreements.

NOTE

Article 22, paragraph 2 of the 1982 Convention specifically authorizes a coastal state to confine nuclear-powered ships or ships carrying nuclear or noxious substances to confine their passage to any sea lanes which it might have designated in its territorial seas.

The Spanish Act No. 25/64 of 29 April 1964 Concerning Nuclear Energy provides in Article 7 that "[t]he passage through territorial waters of nuclear ships . . . shall be considered exception to the right of 'innocent passage.'" Article 71 provides that "[t]he government of the country in which the nuclear ship . . . is registered and by which the operator thereof is licensed shall: . . . (c) Guarantee, in a form deemed sufficient, coverage for any civil liability which may ensure from nuclear damage a nuclear accident." *National Legislation and Treaties Relating to the Law of the Sea*, United Nations Legislative Series ST/LEG/SER.B/16, New York: The United Nations, 1974, p. 46.

Before the United States nuclear-powered ship N.S. Savannah visited the United Kingdom in 1964, an elaborate agreement had been concluded between the two countries, whereby the United States assumed strict liability for all damage arising out of a nuclear incident involving the Savannah up to a limit of U.S. $500 million. Agreement relating to the Use of United Kingdom Ports and Territorial Waters by the N.S. Savannah, June 19, 1964, 15 U.S.T. 1511; TIAS 5633. Similar agreements were concluded with other states whose waters the Savannah entered. For a list of thse agreements, see Marjorie M. Whiteman, *Digest of International Law*, Vol. 9, Washington, D.C.: U.S. Government Printing Office, 1968, p. 305. The Federal Republic of Germany also concluded a Treaty with The Netherlands concerning the Use of Netherlands Territorial Waters and Ports by [Nuclear-powered Ship] N.S. Otto Hahn, October 28, 1968, 781 UNTS 221. For a list of similar agreements, see Robin Churchill, Myron Nordquist and S. Houston Lay, eds., *New*

of similar agreements, see Robin Churchill, Myron Nordquist and S. Houston Lay, eds., *New Directions in the Law of the Sea*, Vol. VI, Dobbs Ferry, New York: Oceana, 1977, p. 772.

On May 25, 1962, a Convention on the Liability of Operators of Nuclear Ships was signed at Brussels, text in *American Journal of International Law*, Vol. 57 (1963), pp. 268-287, which provides that the operator of a nuclear ship is to be strictly liable for damage caused by a nuclear accident up to a maximum of 1.5 billion gold francs. However, this Convention has not yet entered into force.

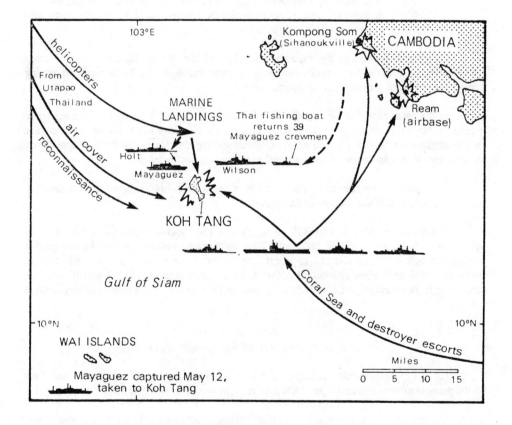

"Mayaguez Incident"
Figure 6-1

Source: *Time*, May 26, 1975. Copyright 1975 Time Inc. Reprinted by permission.

d. Civil and Criminal Jurisdiction

1982 UNITED NATIONS CONVENTION ON THE LAW OF THE SEA

Article 27
Criminal jurisdiction on board a foreign ship

1. The criminal jurisdiction of the coastal State should not be exercised on board a foreign ship passing through the territorial sea to arrest any person or to conduct any investigation in connection with any crime committed on board the ship during its passage, save only in the following cases:

   (a)   if the consequences of the crime extend to the coastal State;
   (b)   if the crime is of a kind to disturb the peace of the country or the good order of the territorial sea;
   (c)   if the assistance of the local authorities has been requested by the master of the ship or by a diplomatic agent or consular officer of the flag State; or
   (d)   if such measures are necessary for the suppression of illicit traffic in narcotic drugs or psychotropic substances.

2. The above provisions do not affect the right of the coastal State to take any steps authorized by its laws for the purpose of an arrest or investigation on board a foreign ship passing through the territorial sea after leaving internal waters.

3. In the cases provided for in paragraphs 1 and 2, the coastal State shall, if the master so requests, notify a diplomatic agent or consular officer of the flag State before taking any steps, and shall facilitate contact between such agent or officer and the ship's crew. In cases of emergency this notification may be communicated while the measures are being taken.

4. In considering whether or in what manner an arrest should be made, the local authorities shall have due regard to the interests of navigation.

5. Except as provided in Part XIII or with respect to violations of laws and regulations adopted in accordance with Part V, the coastal State may not take any steps on board a foreign ship passing through the territorial sea to arrest any person or to conduct any investigation in connection with any crime committed before the ship entered the territorial sea, if the ship, proceeding from a foreign port, is only passing through the territorial sea without entering internal waters.

Article 48
Civil jurisdiction in relation to foreign affairs

1. The coastal State should not stop or divert a foreign ship passing through the territorial sea for the purpose of exercising civil jurisdiction in relation to a person on board the ship.

2. The coastal State may not levy execution against or arrest the ship for the purpose of any civil proceedings, save only in respect of obligations or liabilities assumed or incurred by the ship itself in the course or for the purpose of its voyage through the waters of the coastal State.

3. Paragraph 2 is without prejudice to the right of the coastal State, in accordance with its laws, to levy execution against or to arrest, for the purpose of any civil proceedings, a foreign ship

laws, to levy execution against or to arrest, for the purpose of any civil proceedings, a foreign ship lying in the territorial sea, or passing through the territorial sea after leaving internal waters.

NOTE

Articles 19 and 20 of the 1958 Convention on the Territorial Sea and Contiguous Zone are identical to the above articles.

e.   Warships and Government Ships Operated for Non-Commercial Purposes

1982 UNITED NATIONS CONVENTION ON THE LAW OF THE SEA

Article 29
Definition of warships

For the purposes of this Convention, "warship" means a ship belonging to the armed forces of a State bearing the external marks distinguishing such ships of its nationality, under the command of an officer duly commissioned by the goverment of the State and whose name appears in the appropriate service list or its equivalent, and manned by a crew which is under regular armed forces discipline.

Article 30
Non-compliance by warships with the laws and regulations of the coastal State

If any warship does not comply with the laws and regulations of the coastal State concerning passage through the territorial sea and disregards any request for compliance therewith which is made to it, the coastal State may require it to leave the territorial sea immediately.

Article 31
Responsibility of the flag State for damage caused by a warship or
other government ship operated for non-commercial purposes

The flag State shall bear international responsibility for any loss or damage to the coastal State resulting from the non-compliance by a warship or other government ship operated for non-commercial purposes with the laws and regulations of the coastal State concerning passage through the territorial sea or with the provisions of this Convention or other rules of international law.

Article 32
Immunities of warships and other government ships operated for non-commercial purposes

With such exceptions as are contained in subsection A and in articles 30 and 31, nothing in this Convention affects the immunities of warships and other government ships operated for non-commercial purposes.

Louis Henkin, Richard C. Pugh, Oscar Schachter and Hans Smit, *International Law, Cases and Materials*, 2nd ed., St. Paul, Minn.: West Publishing Co., 1987, pp. 1259-1260. Reprinted by permission.

The 1958 Convention on the Territorial Sea and the Contiguous Zone provides:

> Article 23. If any warship does not comply with the regulations of the coastal State concerning passage through the territorial sea and disregards any request for compliance which is made to it, the coastal State may require the warship to leave the territorial sea.

The 1982 Convention, Article 30, adds the word "immediately."

Did the inclusion of Article 23 in the 1958 Convention imply that warships have a right of innocent passage through a foreign state's territorial sea? The International Law Commission had adopted an additional article, which was to have preceded the present Article 23, providing that a coastal state might make the passage of warships through its territorial sea "subject to previous authorization or notification." [1956] 2 Yb.I.L.C. 276. After lengthy discussion and the rejection of several amendments, the Commission's text was approved by the First Committee (3 U.N. Conf. on the Law of the Sea, Off. Rec. 127-31), but, after a majority of the Plenary Meeting had voted to delete the words "authorization or," vigorous opposition from the Afro-Asian-Soviet bloc prevented the article as a whole from obtaining the necessary two-thirds approval. 2 id. at 66-68. Many of these states have, on ratifying the Convention, made reservations asserting the coastal state's right to require warships to seek previous authorization before passing through the territorial sea. See Slonim, The Right of Innocent Passage and the 1958 Geneva Conference on the Law of the Sea, 5 Colum. J. Transnat'l L. 96 (1966).

A warship's right of innocent passage under customary law is unclear. Jessup concluded in 1927 that "the sound rule seems to be that they [warships] should not enjoy an absolute legal right to pass through a state's territorial waters any more than an army may cross the land territory." The Law of Territorial Waters and Maritime Jurisdiction 120 (1927). The Hague Codification Conference confined itself to observing that states ordinarily "will not forbid the passage of foreign warships" and "will not require a previous authorization or notification." 24 A.J.I.L. Supp. 246 (1930). For a collection of views, see 4 Whiteman at 404-17.

Is it persuasive, with respect to the innocent passage of warships, that Article 14(6) provides that "submarines are required to navigate on the surface and to show their flag"? See [1956] 2 Yb.I.L.C. 273; 3 U.N.Conf. on the Law of the Sea, Off. Rec. 111-12 (1958).

The 1958 Convention, while putting warships in a separate subsection, included it in the section entitled "Right of Innocent Passage" and the article providing that ships of all states shall enjoy the right of innocent passage was in a subsection entitled "Rules applicable to all ships." On the other hand, a subsection applicable to Government ships other than warships expressly provided that the rules applicable to all ships shall apply, while no such provision appears in the subsection applicable to warships. The 1982 Convention places warships and other government ships operated for non-commercial purposes in the same subsection of a section entitled "Innocent Passage in the Territorial Sea." The right of innocent passage is set forth in a subsection applicable to all ships. And see Delupis, Foreign Warships and Immunity for Espionage, 78 A.J.I.L. 53 (1984).

NOTE

Before the adoption of the 1982 United Nations Convention on the Law of the Sea on April 30, 1982, the President of the Third United Nations Conference on the Law of the Sea announced on April 26 that an amendment to Article 21, which would have allowed the coastal state to adopt laws and regulations for prevention of infringement of its security, was withdrawn "without prejudice to the rights of coastal states to adopt measures to safeguard their security interests, in accordance with articles 19 and 25" of the Convention. U.N. Doc. CONF. 62/L.117, *Third United Nations Conference on the Law of the Sea, Official Records*, Vol. 16, p. 132. Different interpretations were later given to that statement, some interpreting it as permitting adoption of regulations requiring prior notification or authorization for the passage of warships, and others read it as prohibiting such regulations. *See* Iranian statement of December 9, 1982 at the closing session of the Conference, *ibid.*, Vol. 17, p. 106 (for requiring prior notification) and United States statement of March 8, 1983, *ibid.*, pp. 243-244 (against requiring prior notification.)

THE SUDAN TERRITORIAL WATERS
AND CONTINENTAL SHELF ACT, 1970
(1970 Act No. 106)

Chapter II, Art. 8 (3)

The passage of military vessels in the territorial waters shall be subject to previous permission, and the Government may take all necessary action against ships committing any breach, and submarines shall navigate on the surface and shall show the flag of the nation to which they belong.

MEASURES GOVERNING THE CONTROL OF ENTRY OF FOREIGN WARSHIPS
INTO THE TERRITORIAL SEA OR PORTS OF THE REPUBLIC OF CHINA
December 9, 1980,
Chinese Yearbook of International Law and Affairs, Vol. 3 (1983), p. 213

Article 1.   The request by a foreign warship to seek consent to enter into our country's territorial sea or port should be forwarded to the Ministry of Foreign Affairs at least 10 days before its porposed arrival date by the government, embassy, consulate or representative organs to which the warship belongs. The request should include information on the specific role, name, class, identification number, tonnage, [radio] call signal, frequency, communication method, name of captain and crew members of the warship, whether it is equipped with airplanes, destination for mooring, arrival date and duration of stay. However, the above stated [advanced notice] restriction shall not be applied if an emergency request for entry is made on the ground of natural calamity, damage or accident.

REFERENCES

B. Chauhan, "Right of Innocent Passage for Warships Through the Territorial Sea," *Thesaurus Acrosium: The Law of the Sea*, Vol. VII, 1977, pp. 511-524; L.W. Kaye, "The Innocent Passage of Warships in Foreign Territorial Seas: A Threatened Freedom," *San Diego Law Review*, Vol. 15 (1978), pp. 573-602; D.P. O'Connell, "Innocent Passage of Warships," Thesaurus Acrosium: The Law of the Sea, Vol. VII, 1977, pp. 405-452; Robert J. Grammig, "The Yoron Jima Submarine Incident of August 1980: A Soviet Violation of the Law of the Sea," *Harvard International Law Journal*, Vol. 22 (1981), pp. 331-354; Ko Nakamura, "The Passage Through the Territorial Sea of

Foreign Warships Carrying Nuclear Weapons: An Interpretation of the Convention on the Territorial Sea and the Contiguous Zone and Its Application to the Broken Soviet Nuclear-Powered Submarine," *Japanese Annual of International Law*, Vol. 25 (1982), pp. 1-10; F. David Froman, "Uncharted Waters: Non-Innocent Passage of Warships in the Territorial Sea," *San Diego Law Review*, Vol. 21 (1984), pp. 625-689; Roma Sadurska, "Foreign Submarines in Swedish Waters: The Erosion of An International Norm," *Yale Journal of International Law*, Vol. 10 (1984), pp. 34-58; Erik Franck, "The U.S.S.R. Position on the Innocent Passage of Warship Through Foreign Territorial Waters," *Journal of Maritime Law & Commerce*," Vol. 18 (1987), pp. 33-65; Shao Jin, "The Question of Innocent Passage of Warships: After the UNCLOS III," *Marine Policy*, Vol. 13, No. 1 (1989), pp. 56-67; Lawrence Juda, "Innocent Passage by Warships in the Territorial Seas of the Soviet Union: Changing Doctrine," *Ocean Development and International Law*, Vol. 21 (1980), pp. 111-116.

UNITED STATES v. CONROY
589 F.2d 1258 (5th Cir. 1979)
rehearing denied, 594 F.2d 241 (1979);
certiorari denied, 100 S.Ct. 60 (1979)
Some notes omitted or renumbered.

ALVIN B. RUBIN, Circuit Judge:

If the Coast Guard cutter DAUNTLESS is not otherwise recorded in history, her forays to protect coasts of the United States from illicit imports will be commemorated in decisions of the Fifth Circuit. The defendants, convicted of either conspiracy or both conspiracy and attempting to import marijuana, charge that the zeal of her commanding officer exceeded his statutory authority and led him to violate their constitutional rights by boarding their American vessel in Haitian waters. Having recently attempted to chart the rules concerning coast guard authority with respect to domestic vessels in coastal waters as well as on the high seas, we now explore the same questions in the uncharted foreign domain.

I.

Once upon a time there was an informer, most of these tales begin. In this instance he was Flemming Larson Budal, a Danish citizen who was residing in the United States, had been an informer for several months, had worked on a number of other cases, and had been paid $200 a week by the Drug Enforcement Administration.

In December, 1975, Budal began a series of conversations with two of the defendants, Schubert and Conroy, in New England, and together they formulated a plan to smuggle a boatload of marijuana from Jamaica. During this time Budal was in constant communication with a special agent of the DEA.

Schubert obtained a 53-foot Gulfstar sailboard in Ft. Lauderdale. Soon afterwards Budal flew to Ft. Lauderdale where he was met by Dahl and Schubert, and another indictee who was separately tried. They were later joined by a fourth defendant, Jacobs, and together lived on the vessel, the NAHOA, until September 3, 1976, when they weighed anchor for Jamaica. Conroy remained in New England, allegedly to await the return of the other defendants with their cargo.

The DEA agent had furnished Budal two electronic devices of the kind known as beepers, one of which was to be turned on when the vessel was loaded. This device emits a signal by means of which its location can be determined by other electronic equipment. Rather than keep either on his person, Budal concealed one in the engine room and the other in an air vent on the NAHOA.

When the NAHOA was about 40 miles from Jamaica, the crew met the fifth defendant, Walker, who came out from the island on a small motorboat. Walker made four trips to the NAHOA ferrying marijuana.

The DAUNTLESS, under the command of Lieutenant Robert Council, was on border patrol in the Windward Passage between Haiti and Cuba, on guard for the NAHOA. When a DEA plane flying over nearby waters received an electronic signal from one of Budal's beepers, the DAUNTLESS attempted to establish a barrier patrol in the Windward Passage.

A day later the commanding officer of the DAUNTLESS recognized a radar beep on his scope as a vessel located about nine miles southwest of Haiti. He set his course for the vessel, and soon sighted her; it was, as anticipated, the NAHOA. He attempted to communicate with the vessel by radio, flag and flashing lights, all signaling her to heave to. Nevertheless, those aboard the vessel set course straight for Haiti, and entered that nation's territorial waters.

Oral approval, later confirmed in writing, to enter Haitian waters and search the NAHOA was obtained from the Haitian Chief-of-Staff, and the DAUNTLESS continued in pursuit. When on further signals, the NAHOA did not halt, the flag Sierra Quebec III was raised: this signifies, "stop or we'll shoot." The NAHOA then hove to, and Lieutenant Council pulled alongside her in a small boat. He smelled marijuana, and asked permission to board. Schubert denied his request, but Lieutenant Council went on the vessel and requested the ship's papers. Schubert prevented him from entering the ship's cabin; the lieutenant ordered a search, and found 7,000 pounds of marijuana.

Defendants Conroy, Schubert, Dahl and Jacobs contend that in this dramatic encounter the Coast Guard were little better, legally, than pirates. The installation of the beeper was an illegal search; the boarding of the vessel in Haitian waters exceeded the statutory authority of the Coast Guard and violated their constitutional rights because it was unreasonable and warrantless. In addition, defendant Walker, who was separately tried, alleges that there was insufficient evidence to convict him of conspiracy, and that procedural errors denied him a fair trial.

II.

. . . .

B. International Law

Our statutory interpretation of Coast Guard authority, premised on the concurring opinion of Mr. Justice Brandeis in *Maul*, is implicitly supported by principles of international law that justify law enforcement activities by the Coast Guard in foreign waters. International law is part of our domestic law. . . . The possible application of the law of nations to supplement the statute is consistent with the statement in the House of Representatives report, "The powers conferred by this act are not to be construed to affect any other powers conferred by existing law." H.R. Rep. No. 2452, at 4.

The law of nations classifies Coast Guard vessels as warships. Such vessels belong to the State, are under the direction of a military commander and manned by a military crew, and legally bear the ensign of the national navy. . . .

Early interpretations of the law of nations denied the right of innocent passage to warships; it was thought that armed vessels did not "enjoy an absolute legal right to pass through a state's territorial waters any more than an army may cross the land territory," P. Jessup, The Law of Territorial Waters and Maritime Jurisdiction 120 (1927), and prior permission had to be obtained. Until 1959, a regulation issued by the United States Office of the Chief of Naval Operations provided, "naval vessels should not be navigated in or near such claimed territorial waters without having obtained prior authorization from higher authority." 4 Whiteman Digest of International Law 417 (1965).[1]

The United-Nations-sponsored Convention on the Territorial Sea and the Contiguous Zone entered into force in 1964; the United States Senate had previously ratified the Convention in 1960, and the President had signed it in 1961. 15 U.S.T. 1606, T.I.A.S. No. 5639 (1958). Haiti is also a party to the Convention. Thus, the Convention represents existing U.S. policy, at least with respect to other party nations.

After much debate, the draftsmen of the multilateral treaty rejected any requirement of previous authorization by a coastal state for the entry of a foreign warship into its territorial waters. See 4 Whiteman, *supra*, at 415-16. Article 14(1) of the Convention on the Territorial Sea and the Contiguous Zone states simply, "Subject to the provisions of these articles, ships of all States, whether coastal or not, shall enjoy the right of innocent passage through the territorial sea." 15 U.S.T. at 1610. Article 16(1) provides that the coastal state may take "the necessary steps in its territorial sea to prevent passage which is not innocent." No distinction is made between warships and other vessels.

At least between parties to the Convention, such as the United States and Haiti, a warship of one nation may enter the territorial waters of the other without first giving notification and receiving authorization.[2] Ratification of the Convention by the United States manifests implicit authorization for its warships to do what the warships of other nations might do. The DAUNTLESS was not, of course, on a hostile mission. Indeed, it bears emphasis again that, despite the fact that presumably no consent by Haitian authority was required under the terms of the treaty, permission was in fact obtained. Therefore, in the ensuing search, there was a conjunction of implicit recognition by the United States Government of the power of its warship to make the search, and explicit approval of the search by the Haitian government.

Even had we been provided no guidance by the implicit authorization granted warships under the treaty, we would still be compelled to conclude that the defendants cannot assail the legality of the seizure of their vessel in Haitain waters. Since 1815 it has been established that redress for improper seizure in foreign waters is not due to the owner or crew of the vessel involved, but to the foreign government whose territoriality has been infringed by the action. In *The Richmond*, 1815, 13 U.S. (9 Cranch) 102, 3 L.Ed. 670, the Court rejected a challenge similar to the one we face here to the seizure of an American registered vessel in the territorial waters of Spain. Chief

---

[1]Indeed, on one occasion in 1957, the commanding officer of an American vessel was reprimanded for entering Mexican territorial waters without prior permission from the Mexican government. The purpose of the entry was to investigate a fishing vessel in Mexican waters believed to be of American registry. The reprimand followed a protest of the entry by the Mexican government. . . .

[2]Some nations, all from the communist bloc, adopted the Convention with a reservation declaring that they believed that a coastal state had the right to establish procedures for the authorization of passage of foreign warships through territorial waters. 4 Whiteman, supra, at 416. Haiti is a party to the Convention without such a reservation. Treaties in Force, January 1, 1978, p. 327.

Justice Marshall explained, "The seizure of an American vessel, within the territorial jurisdiction of a foreign power, is certainly an offense against that power, which must be adjusted between the two governments. This court can take no cognizance of it." 13 U.S. at 103, 3 L.Ed. at 671. Here, where not even the foreign government complains of the American assertion of sovereignty over its own vessel, defendants have no basis for complaint unless the seizure was improper on some other grounds.

. . . .

5. Entry in Distress

UNITED STATES v. MEXICO
("Kate A. Hoff Claim")
CLAIMS COMMISSION, UNITED STATES AND MEXICO
April 2, 1929
American Journal of International Law, Vol. 23 (1929), p. 860, at pp. 862-863.
Reprinted by permission of The American Society of International Law.

[The American schooner Rebecca bound for Tampico, Mexico, from Morgan City, Louisiana, had on board goods destined for Brazos Santiago, Texas, but before being able to deliver them was forced by high winds and rough seas to a point off the port of Tampico where she was disabled and in an unsafe condition. The Rebecca thereupon put into Tampico because of the dangeorus condition of the vessel. Mexican customs officials seized the merchandise originally destined for Brazos Santiago and charged the master of the Rebecca with smuggling (the merchandise for Brazos Santiago met the requirements of the law of the United States.) After a somewhat delayed trial, the Rebecca and its cargo were sold by court order. In the claim, it was asserted that the vessel, having entered Tampico in distress, should have been immune from local jurisdiction as regards the administration of the local customs laws. The relevant portions of the opinion of the Commission on the point are set forth below.]

It is of course well established that, when a merchant vessel belonging to one nation enters the territorial waters of another nation, it becomes amenable to the jurisdiction of the latter and is subject to its laws, except insofar as treaty stipulations may relieve the vessel from the operation of local laws. On the other hand, there appears to be general recognition among the nations of the world of what may doubtless be considered to be an exception, or perhaps it may be said two exceptions, to this general, fundamental rule of subjection to local jurisdiction over vessels in foreign ports.

Recognition has been given to the so-called right of "innocent passage" for vessels through the maritime belt insofar as it forms a part of the high seas for international traffic. Similarly, recognition has also been given--perhaps it may be said in a more concrete and emphatic manner-- to the immunity of a ship whose presence in territorial waters is due to a superior force. The principles with respect to the status of a vessel in "distress" find recognition both in domestic laws and in international law. For numerous, interesting precedents of both domestic courts and international courts, see Moore, *Digest*, Vol. II, p. 339 *et seq.*; Jessup, *The Law of Territorial Waters and Maritime Jurisdiction*, p. 194, *et seq.*

Domestic courts have frequently considered pleas of distress in connection with charges of infringement of customs laws. Interesting cases in which pleas of distress were raised came before American courts in the cases of vessels charged with violation of the interesting American so-called "non-intercourse" acts forbidding trade with French and British possession. 1 Stat. 565; 2

Stat. 308. In these cases it was endeavored on behalf of the vessels to seek immunity from prosecution under these laws by alleging that the vessels had entered forbidden ports as a result of *vis major*. A Mexican law of 1880 which was cited in the instant case appears to recognize in very comprehensive terms the principles of immunity from local jurisdiction which have so frequently been invoked. *Legislacion Mexicana*, Dublan & Lozano, vol. 14, p. 619, *et seq.*

The enlightened principle of comity which exempts a merchant vessel, at least to a certain extent, from the operation of local laws has been generally stated to apply to vessels forced into port by storm, or compelled to seek refuge for vital repairs or for provisioning, or carried into port by mutineers. It has also been asserted in defense of a charge of attempted breach of blockade. It was asserted by as early a writer as Vattel. *The Law of Nations*, p. 128. In the instant case we are concerned simply with distress said to have been occasioned by violent weather.

While recognizing the general principle of immunity of vessels in distress, domestic courts and international courts have frequently given consideration to the question as to the degree of necessity prompting vessels to seek refuge. It has been said that the necessity must be urgent. It seems possible to formulate certain reasonably concrete criteria applicable and controlling in the instant case. Assuredly a ship floundering in distress, resulting either from the weather or from other causes affecting management of the vessel, need not be in such a condition that it is dashed helplessly onthe shore or against rocks before a claim of distress can properly be invoked in its behalf. The fact that it may be able to come into port under its own power can obviously not be cited as conclusive evidence that the plea is unjustifiable. If a captain delayed seeking refuge until his ship was wrecked, obviously he would not be using his best judgment with a view to the preservation of the ship, the cargo and the lives of people on board. Clearly an important consideration may be the determination of the question whether there is any evidence in a given case of a fraudulent attempt to circumvent local laws. And even in the absence of any such attempt, it can probably be correctly said that a mere matter of convenience in making repairs or in avoiding a measure of difficulty in navigation cannot justify a disregard of local laws. . . .

THE PEOPLE OF THE STATE OF NEW YORK
v. PAUL NISSEN AND ALAN VAN HORN
Supreme Court, Criminal Term,
Suffolk County, Part II.
412 N.Y.S.2d 999
(Jan. 31, 1979)

. . .

JOSEPH JASPAN, Judge.

The defendants are charged with criminal possession of approximately 14,000 pounds of marijuana (P.L. 221.30) which was found on board a large sailboat of foreign registry manned by them and was at the time moving in a westerly direction just north of Gardiners Island within the territorial waters of the United States.

They seek to dismiss the one count indictment on the grounds that their vessel was in distress and only seeking a safe harbor at the time it was boarded and seized and was therefore immune from such action and consequential prosecution.

In the alternative, the defendants urge that, in any event, the boarding and search without a warrant constituted a violation of their Fourth Amendment rights and that 14 U.S.C. §89(a) under which the Coast Guard presumed to act is unconstitutional.

Facts

The following is a summary of the events surrounding the search and seizure of the *Scott Bader* on October 2, 1978 based upon the testimony given before the Grand Jury by a number of witnesses including the defendant Nissen and upon the moving papers of the defendants.

At approximately 6:00 p.m. on October 2, 1978 the Coast Guard cutter *Point Wells* left on a law enforcement patrol from Montauk, Point, Long Island. At approximately 7:25 p.m. Executive Petty Officer Keller saw the silhouette and red (port, leftside) running light of a large sailboat heading in a westerly direction. There-after, the cutter moved closer and by observation, determined that it was the *"Scott Bader"* from Cayman Islands, British Bahamas. At this time it was also noted that the vessel was riding heavy in the water although a blue water line was spotted periodically through the waves. The *Point Wells* then moved off to the *Scott Bader's* starboard quarter from which point it appeared that neither the green starboard or the masthead lights were visible and that the stern light was extremely dim.

Keller testified that these running lights are important to navigation so that approaching vessels may determine which side they are looking at and what action to take or direction to travel. Keller also testified that without lights emanating from starboard you cannot, without artificial light, determine the identity of the boat.

A determination was then made to board the *Scott Bader,* which was under both power and small sail. The *Point Wells* identified itself and told the occupants to prepare to be boarded.

At that time, the *Scott Bader* was .6 miles from the Gardiners Island ruins and approximately 1.8 miles north of Gardiners Island Point itself.

Gardiners Island is located within Suffolk County in the waters between Montauk and Orient Point astride the entrance to Gardiners Bay and Peconic Bay.

After hailing the *Scott Bader,* the cutter throttled back and got into position for the boarding. Nissen was on deck at this time. Keller identified himself and said that he was coming aboard to see if he complied with the federal law. Nissen asked, "Is this a safety inspection?" and Keller answered, "Well, I want to see if you have complied with all of the federal laws pertaining to equipment and paper."

At the time of the boarding, the *Scott Bader* was 1.1 miles southwest of the ruins and 1.6 miles northwest of Gardiners Island Point. The testimony indicates that it was headed to Cherry Harbor (apparently Cherry Hill Point) located on the west side of Gardiners Island.

Upon boarding, Nissen identified himself as the skipper and was asked for his documents. Nissen went forward to the cabin and Keller remained at the cabin entrance. While standing near the cabin entrance, Keller noticed the strong aroma of what he believed to be marijuana. (Keller also testified to his expertise in the field of narcotics.) Nissen got the documentation, and as it was dark outside suggested that Keller come below and use the light on the chart table. Thereafter, as Nissen went to get identification papers, Keller observed 12 to 15 rectangular burlap bales. When Nissen returned he was given his *Miranda* warnings by Keller who then cut open a burlap sack and the underlying plastic and found marijuana. Nissen was arrested. Subsequently, Van Horn, who was also aboard, was arrested and given his *Miranda* warnings. The Scott Bader was taken to Mantauk Station where 304 bales of marijuana were unloaded and delivered to the Drug Enforcement Agency who subsequently turned them over to the Suffolk police.

Defendants contend, however, that this safety stop was nothing more than a pretext and that the evidence in this case was obtained by law enforcement officials whose only purpose in boarding defendants' vessel was to look for narcotics violations. Defendants' position is that the Coast Guard did not immediately board but kept defendants' vessel under continuous surveillance for a period of approximately twenty-five minutes until they communicated with the Drug Enforcement Agency and learned that at some time in the past defendants' vessel had appeared on a "Hot" list of vessels suspected of being used to transport contraband. It is alleged that upon boarding defendants' vessel, these officers began an extensive and highly intrusive search of the vessel and that the search and the inquiries directed to the defendants were in no way connected with a safety and document inspection.

The Safe Harbor Theory

A foreign vessel has the right to enter the territory of a state when such entry is necessary for the safety of the vessel or persons aboard and to leave the territory once the conditions that made the entry necessary have ceased to exist (Restatement of the Law 2d--Foreign Relations Law of the United States, Section 48).

This right of entry for reasons of *force majeure* entitles the foreign vessel to claim, as of right, an entire immunity from the local jurisdiction (The Law of Territorial Waters and Maritime Law as published by Jennings Co., Inc., New York, 1927; republished by Kraus Reprint Co., New York, 1970).

No importation occurs within the meaning of the duty statutes "where goods are brought by superior force or by inevitable necessity into the United States." *The Brig Concord*, 9 Cr. 387, 388, (13 U.S.) 3 L.Ed. 768 (1815).

The necessity must be urgent and not merely a matter of convenience and the entry must be bona fide and made without intent to evade the laws of the host state (The *New York*, 3 Wheat. 59 (16 U.S. 59) 4 L.Ed. 333 (1818); *Latham v. United States*, 2 F.2d 208 (4th Cir., 1924).

A factual issue is presented by the claim of the defendants that they required a safe harbor. The parties agree that this threshold question of jurisdiction should be presented to the trial jury for resolution within the framework of the rules set forth above.

[Both defendants were found guilty and on appeal, the conviction was confirmed. The People, etc. v. Alan Van Horn and Paul Nissen, Supreme Court, Appellate Division, 2nd Dept., 430 N.Y.S. 2d 646 (July 28, 1980).]

1958 CONVENTION ON THE TERRITORIAL
SEA AND THE CONTIGUOUS ZONE

Article 14

. . . .

3. [Innocent] [p]assage includes stopping and anchoring, but only insofar as the same are incidental to ordinary navigation or are rendered necessary by *force majeure* or by distress.

NOTE

The 1982 Convention, in Article 18, paragraph 2 adds, "or for the purpose of rendering assistance to persons, ships or aircraft in danger or distress."

> *Restatement of the Foreign Relations Law of the United States*, 2nd ed., St. Paul, Minn.: American Law Institute Publishers, 1965, pp. 161-162. Copyright by The American Law Institute. Reprinted with the permission of The American Law Institute.

[The Third Revision of the Restatement removed the following section.]

§ 48

Entry in Distress

(1) A foreign vessel or aircraft has the right to enter the territory of a state when such entry is necessary for the safety of the vessel, aircraft or persons aboard, and to leave the territory once the conditions that made the entry necessary have ceased to exist.

(2) The territorial state may not exercise its jurisdiction under the rule stated in §20 to enforce rules prescribed by it with respect to:

(a) acts aboard a foreign vessel or aircraft necessary to effectuate entry in distress,

(b) the possession or carriage of property aboard a foreign vessel or aircraft entering in distress, bona fide and without intent to evade the customs and anti-smuggling laws of the coastal state, except insofar as such regulation may reasonably be necessary for reasons of health or safety of the coastal state.

REFERENCES

L.H. Liang, "American Fishing Vessels in Canadian Waters of the Pacific," *American Journal of International Law*, Vol. 26 (1932), pp. 374-379; M.S. McDougal & W.T. Burke, *The Public Order of the Oceans: A Contemporary International Law of the Sea*, New Haven and London: Yale University Press, 1962, p. 110; *1The May v. The King*, Canada, Supreme Court, April 28, 1931, *Annual Digest of Public International Law Cases 1931-1932*, pp. 154-156 (Case No. 81); *Rex v. Flahaut*, Canada, Supreme Court of New Brunswick (Appeal Division), October 9, 1934, *ibid.*, 1938-40, pp. 164-166 (Case No. 61); *The Diana*, 7 Wall. (74 U.S.) 354 (1868).

6.   Access to Ports

Restatement on the Foreign Relations Law of the United States, Third
Revision, Vol. 2, St. Paul, Minn.: American Law Institute, 1987, pp.
38-40. Copyright by The American Law Institute. Reprinted with the
permission of The American Law Institute.

Section 512, Editors' Notes:

3. *Access to ports.* It has been said that, as no civilized state has "the right to isolate itself wholly from the outside world," there is "a corresponding obligation imposed upon each maritime power not to deprive foreign vessels of commerce of access to all of its ports." 1 Hyde, International Law Chiefly as Intepreted and Applied by the United States 581 (2d ed. 1945). The LOS Convention does not mention a right of access of ships to foreign ports, but the customary law on the subject, as reflected in a number of international agreements, has been confirmed by at least one international decision. Thus, the Statute on the International Regime of Maritime Ports of 1923, confirmed the freedom of access to maritime ports by foreign vessels on condition of reciprocity; but it allows the coastal state "in exceptional cases, and for as short a period as possible," to deviate from this provision by measures which that state "is obliged to take in case of an emergency affecting the safety of the state or the vital interest of the country." 58 L.N.T.S. 285, 301, 305; 2 Hudson, International Legislation 1162 (1931). Although this Statute has been ratified by less than 30 states and the United States is not a party to it, the Statute has been accepted as reflecting a customary rule of international law. An arbitral tribunal, relying on this Statute, stated that "[a]ccording to a great principle of international law, ports of every State must be open to foreign merchant vessels and can only be closed when the vital interests of a State so require." Saudi Arabia v. Arabian American Oil Company (ARAMCO), Award of August 23, 1958, 27 Int'l L. Rep. 117, 212 (1963).

The Institute of International Law has considered this issue in 1898, 1928, and 1957, and each time, after a heated discussion, it affirmed the right of access to ports, subject to various conditions. In 1898, the Institute agreed that, as a general rule, access to ports "is presumed to be free to foreign ships," except when a state, "for reasons of which it is sole judge," declares its ports, or some of them, closed "when the safety of the State or the interest of the public health justifies the order," or when it refuses entrance to ships of a particular nation "as an act of just reprisal." Resolutions of the Institute of International Law 144 (J. Scott ed. 1916). In 1928, the Institute stated that, as a general rule, access to ports, "is open to foreign vessels," but, as an exception and for a term as limited as possible, "a state may suspend this access by particular or general measures which it is obliged to take in case of serious events touching the safety of the state or the public health"; it also confirmed the exception in case of reprisals. Institut de Droit International, Tableau Général des Résolutions, 1873-1956, at 102 (Wehberg ed., 1957); 22 Am. J. Int'l. L. 844; 847 (1928). In 1957, the Institute distinguished between internal waters and ports, and pointed out that a coastal state may deny access to internal waters, "[s]ubject to the rights of passage sanctioned either by usage or by treaty," but should abstain from denying such access to foreign commercial vessels "save where in exceptional cases this denial of access is imposed by imperative reasons." On the other hand, the Institute declared that "it is consistent with general practice of States to permit free access to ports and harbors by such vessels." [1957] 2 Annuaire de l'Institut de Droit International 485-86. For discussion, see *id.* 171, 180, 194-98, 202-09, 212-22, 253-67; for the text of the 1957 resolution, see also 52 Am. J. Int'l L. 103 (1958).

It seems, therefore, that it is now generally accepted that "in time of peace, commercial ports must be left open to international traffic," and that the "liberty of access to ports granted to foreign vessels implies their right to load and unload their cargoes; embark and disembark their passengers." Colombos, The International Law of the Sea 176 (6th ed. 1967). But see Khedivial Line, S.A.E. v. Seafarers' International Union, 278 F.2d 49, 52 (2d Cir. 1960) (plaintiff presented no precedents showing that "the law of nations accords an unrestricted right of access to harbors by vessels of all nations"); Lowe, "The Right of Entry into Maritime Ports in International Law," 14 San Diego L. Rev. 597, 622 (1977) ("the ports of a State which are designated for international trade are, in the absence of express provisions to the contrary made by a port State, presumed to be open to the merchant ships of all States," and they "should not be closed to foreign merchant ships except when the peace, good order, or security of the coastal State necessitates closure").

The general principle of open ports is confirmed by many bilateral agreements. For instance, the Treaty of Friendship, Establishment and Navigation between the United States and Belgium, Brussels, 1961 provides that "[v]essels of either Contracting Party shall have liberty, on equal terms with vessels of the other Party and on equal terms with vessels of any third country, to come with their cargoes to all ports, places and waters of such other Party open to foreign commerce and navigation. Such vessels and cargoes shall in the ports, places and waters of such other Party be accorded in all respects national treatment and most-favored-nation treatment." Art. 13, 14 U.S.T. 1284, T.I.A.S. No. 5432, 480 U.N. T.S. 149. See also [1957] 2 Annuaire de l'Institut de Droit International 209, 216 (according to Paul de La Pradelle, "the many conventions on commerce and navigation which provide for [access to ports] have established a rule of customary law," but others contended that all these treaty provisions would have been superfluous if this right of access were based on customary law). . . .

States may impose, however, special restrictions on certain categories of ships. For instance, the Convention on the Liability of Operators of Nuclear-Powered Ships, Brussels, 1962, provides that nothing in that Convention "shall affect any right which a Contracting State may have under international law to deny access to its waters, and harbours to nuclear ships licensed by another Contracting State, even when it has formally complied with all the provisions" of that Convention. Art. XVII, 57 Am. J. Int'l. L. 268 (1963). . . .

A coastal state can condition the entry of foreign ships into its ports on compliance with specified laws and regulations. This jurisdiction to prescribe may extend even to some matters relating to the internal affairs of the ship. See Patterson v. Bark Eudora, 190 U.S. 169, 178, 23 S.Ct. 821, 824, 47 L.Ed. 1002 (1903) (prohibiting prepayment of seamen's wages by certain foreign vessels.)

D. STRAITS USED FOR INTERNATIONAL NAVIGATION

1. Introduction

A strait is defined as a narrow passage of water joining two larger bodies of water. Before proceeding with the material in this subsection look at a world map and locate several straits of considerable economic and strategic importance -- Gibraltar, Hormuz, Bab el Mandeb, Malacca, Dover, and Bering.[1]

---

[1]See also R.H. Kennedy, "A Brief Geographical and Hydrographical Study of Straits Which Constitute Routes for International Traffic," U.N. Doc. A/CONF.13/6 and Add.1 (23 October 1957) in [First] United Nations Conference on the Law of the Sea, *Official Records*, Vol. I *Preparatory Documents*, pp. 115-116, 125-126, 129-130, 134-135, 142-143.

Which of these possess corridors of high seas under a three mile territorial sea breadth regime? Under a twelve mile breadth? Obviously, straits passage problems arise only when the straits consist entirely of territorial waters at some point, thus bringing into play the rules of innocent passage discussed in the last subsection. Where there is a corridor of high seas throughout the length of the strait, high seas freedom of navigation permits unregulated navigation.

The problem of straits passage is one of the most controversial issues involved in the law of the sea. At issue, essentially, is the conflict between littoral states and maritime powers. Littoral states have valid concerns about the nature and activities of vessels passing through their territorial waters, especially in narrow channels such as are usually found in straits. These concerns include military security and pollution. Maritime powers are interested in maintaining a free flow of commerce on the sea, without burdensome costs, and in ensuring naval mobility for their armed forces. As might be expected, all nations (maritime, littoral, even landlocked) have a common interest in the unimpeded shipment of goods on the sea. Accordingly, philosophical arguments are minimal on the question of merchant vessel passage through straits, most of the debate centering on technical rules concerning procedures for determining proper conduct and activities while in passage.

Transit of warships is another matter. Here there exists a wide philosophical gap between littoral nations and military powers. In reviewing the material in this subsection, then, be careful to distinguish the issues involved in merchant and military passage, and to note how the two are sought to be divided or interlocked in the positions taken by various nations in the Third U.N. Conference on the Law of the Sea.

Straits of Bab el Mandeb
Figure 6-2

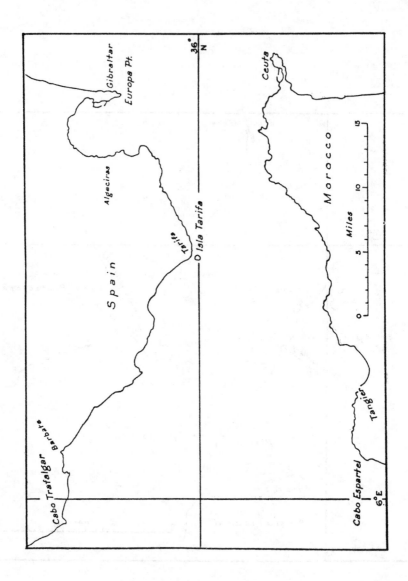

Strait of Gibraltar
Figure 6-3

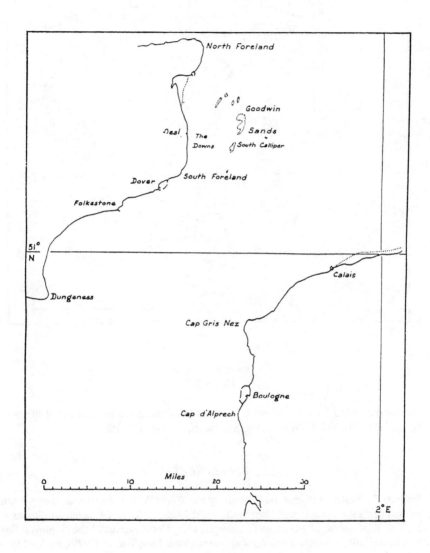

Dover Strait
Figure 6-4

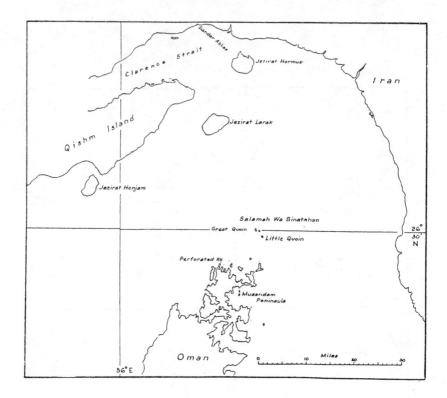

Strait of Hormuz
Figure 6-5

Figures 6-2 to 6-5 *Source*: [First] United Nations Conference on the Law of the Sea, *Official Records*, Vol. I, *Preparatory Documents*, pp. 145, 155, 159.

REFERENCES

William E. Butler, *International Straits of the World*, Vol. 1, *Northeast Arctic Passage*, Alphen aan den Rijn: Sijthoff and Noordhoff, 1978; Michael Leifer, *International Straits of the World*, Vol. 2, *Malacca, Singapore and Indonesia*, 1978; Donat Pharand, "The Northwest Passage in International Law," *Canadian Yearbook of International Law*, Vol. 17 (1979), pp. 99-133; R.K. Ramazani, *International Straits of the World*, Vol. 3, *The Persian Gulf and the Strait of Hormuz*, Alphen aan de Rijn: Sijthoff and Noordhoff, 1979; S.H. Amin, "The Regime of International Straits: Legal Implications for the Strait of Hormuz," *Journal of Maritime Law and Commerce*, Vol. 12 (1981), pp. 387-405; K.W. Ryan, "The Torres Strait Treaty," *Australian Yearbook of International Law*, Vol. 7 (1981), pp. 87-113; Gunnar Alexandersson, *International Straits of the World*, Vol. 6, *The Baltic Straits*, Alphen aan den Rijn: Sijthoff and Noordhoff, 1982; Ruth Lapidoth-Eschelbacher, *International Straits of the World*, Vol. 5, *The Red Sea and The Gulf of*

Aden, Alphen aan den Rijn: Sijthoff and Noordhoff, 1982; Yaacov Vertzberger, "The Malacca/Singapore Straits," *Asian Survey,* Vol. 22 (1982), pp. 609-629; Yaacov Vertzberger, "The Malacca/ Singapore Straits: The Suez of South-East Asia," *Conflict Studies* (London), No. 140 (1982), 28 pp.; Ruth Lapidoth-Eschelbacher, "The Straits of Tiran, The Gulf of Aqaba, and the 1979 Treaty of Peace between Egypt and Israel," *American Journal of International Law,* Vol. 77 (1983), pp. 84-108; A.L.C. De Mestral, "Reference re Ownership of the Bed of the Strait of Georgia and Related Areas and Reference Re Newfoundland Continental Shelf," *McGill Law Journal,* Vol. 30 (1985), pp. 293-301; Geoffrey Marston, "The Strait of Georgia Reference," *Canadian Yearbook of International Law,* Vol. 23 (1985),pp. 34-79; Mark J. Valencia and Abu Bakar, "Environmental Management of the Malacca/Singapore Straits: Legal and Institutional Issues," *Natural Resources Journal,* Vol. 25 (1985), pp. 195-232; Mark J. Valencia and James Barney Marsh, "Access to Straits and Sealanes in Southeast Asian Seas: Legal, Economic, and Strategic Considerations," *Journal of Maritime Law and Commerce,* Vol. 16 (1985), pp. 513-551; Ronnie Ann Wainwright, "Navigation Through Three Straits in the Middle East: Effects on the United States of Being a Nonparty to the 1982 Convention on the Law of the Sea," *Case Western Reserve Journal of International Law,* Vol. 18 (1986), pp. 361-414; Michael A. Morris, "The Politics of Caribbean Straits," *Ocean Development and International Law,* Vol. 18 (1987), pp. 459-477.

2. Customary International Law

CORFU CHANNEL CASE (MERITS)
(UNITED KINGDOM v. ALBANIA)
Judgment of April 9, 1949
I.C.J. Reports 1949, p. 4, at pp. 28-31.

[The *Corfu Channel Case* dealt *inter alia* with the question of the right of passage of warships in time of peace through straits connecting two parts of the high seas. The issue arose out of an incident in which British warships, navigating in the Corfu Channel off the Albanian coast, were damaged by mines placed in Albanian territorial waters. The Court dealt with the Albanian contention that Britain violated Albanian sovereignty by sending the warships through the Corfu Channel without prior authorization.]

It is, in the opinion of the Court, generally recognized and in accordance with international custom that States in time of peace have a right to send their warships through straits used for international navigation between two parts of the high seas without the previous authorization of a coastal State, provided that the passage is *innocent.* Unless otherwise prescribed in an international convention, there is no right for a coastal State to prohibit such passage through straits in time of peace.

The Albanian Government does not dispute that the North Corfu Channel is a strait in the geographical sense; but it denies that this Channel belongs to the class of international highways through which a right of passage exists, on the grounds that it is only of secondary importance and not even a necessary route between two parts of the high seas, and that it is used almost exclusively for local traffic to and from the ports of Corfu and Saranda.

It may be asked whether the test is to be found in the volume of traffic passing through the Strait or in its greater or lesser importance for international navigation. But in the opinion of the Court the decisive criterion is rather its geographical situation as connecting two parts of the high seas and the fact of its being used for international navigation. Nor can it be decisive that this

Strait is not a necessary route between two parts of the high seas, but only an alternative passage between the Aegean and the Adriatic Seas. It has nevertheless been a useful route for international maritime traffic. In this respect, the Agent of the United Kingdom Government gave the court the following information relating to the period from April 1st, 1936, to December 31st, 1937: "The following is the total number of ships putting in at the Port of Corfu after passing through or just before passing through the Channel. During the period of one year nine months, the total number of ships was 2,884. The flags of the ships are Greek, Italian, Romanian, Yugoslav, French, Albanian and British. Clearly, very small vessels are included, as the entries for Albanian vessels are high, and of course one vessel may make several journeys, but 2,884 ships for a period of one year nine months is quite a large figure. These figures relate to vessels visited by the Customs at Corfu and so do not include the large number of vessels which went through the Strait without calling at Corfu at all." There were also regular sailings through the Strait by Greek vessels three times weekly, by a British ship fortnightly, and by two Yugoslav vessels weekly and by two others fortnightly. The Court is further informed that the British Navy has regularly used this Channel for eighty years or more, and that it has also been used by the navies of other States.

One fact of particular importance is that the North Corfu Channel constitutes a frontier between Albania and Greece, that a part of it is wholly within the territorial waters of these States, and that the Strait is of special importance to Greece by reason of the traffic to and from the port of Corfu.

Having regard to these various considerations, the Court has arrived at the conclusion that the North Corfu Channel should be considered as belonging to the class of international highways through which passage cannot be prohibited by a coastal State in time of peace.

On the other hand, it is a fact that the two coastal States did not maintain normal relations, that Greece had made territorial claims precisely with regard to a part of Albanian territory bordering on the Channel, that Greece had declared that she considered herself technically in a state of war with Albania, and that Albania, invoking the danger of Greek incursions, had considered it necessary to take certain measures of vigilance in this region. The Court is of opinion that Albania, in view of these exceptional circumstances, would have been justified in issuing regulations in respect of the passage of warships through the Strait, but not in prohibiting such passage or in subjecting it to the requirement of special authorization.

For these reasons the Court is unable to accept the Albanian contention that the Government of the United Kingdom has violated Albanian sovereignty by sending the warships through the Strait without having obtained the previous authorization of the Albanian Government. . . .

The Albanian Government has further contended that the sovereignty of Albania was violated because the passage of the British warships on October 22nd, 1946, was not an *innocent passage*. The reasons advanced in support of this contention may be summed up as follows: The passage was not an ordinary passage, but a political mission; the ships were maneuvering and sailing in diamond combat formation with soldiers on board; the position of the guns was not consistent with innocent passage; the vessels passed with crews at action stations; the number of the ships and their armament surpassed what was necessary in order to attain their object and showed an intention to intimidate and not merely to pass; the ships had received orders to observe and report upon the coastal defenses and this order was carried out.

It is shown by the Admiralty telegram of September 21st, cited above, and admitted by the United Kingdom Agent, that the object of sending the warships through the Strait was not only to carry out a passage for purposes of navigation, but also to test Albania's attitude. As mentioned above, the Albanian Government, on May 15th, 1946, tried to impose by means of gunfire its view with regard to the passage. As the exchange of diplomatic notes did not lead to any clarification, the Government of the United Kingdom wanted to ascertain by other means whether the Albanian Government would maintain its illegal attitude and again impose its view by firing at passing ships. The legality of this measure taken by the Government of the United Kingdom cannot be disputed, provided that it was carried out in a manner consistent with the requirements of international law. The "mission" was designed to affirm a right which had been unjustly denied. The Government of the United Kingdom was not bound to abstain from exercising its right of passage, which the Albanian Government had illegally denied.

It remains, therefore, to consider whether the *manner* in which the passage was carried out was consistent with the principle of innocent passage and to examine the various contentions of the Albanian Government in so far as they appear to be relevant.

When the Albanian coast guards at St. George's Monastery reported that the British warships were sailing in combat formation and were maneuvering, they must have been under a misapprehension. It is shown by the evidence that the ships were not proceeding in combat formation, but in line, one after the other, and that they were not maneuvering until after the first explosion. Their movements thereafter were due to the explosions and were made necessary in order to save human life and the mined ships. It is shown by the evidence of witnesses that the contention that soldiers were on board must be due to a misunderstanding probably arising from the fact that the two cruisers carried their usual detachment of marines.

It is known from the above-mentioned order issued by the British Admiralty on August 10th, 1946, that ships, when using the North Corfu Strait, must pass with armament in fore and aft position. That this order was carried out during the passage on October 22nd is stated by the Commander-in-Chief, Mediterranean, in a telegram of October 26th to the Admiralty. The guns were, he reported, "trained fore and aft, which is their normal position at sea in peace time, and were not loaded." It is confirmed by the commanders of *Saumarez* and *Volage* that the guns were in this position before the explosions. The navigating officer on board *Mauritius* explained that all guns on that cruiser were in their normal stowage position. The main guns were in the line of the ship, and the anti-aircraft guns were pointing outward and up into the air, which is the normal position of these guns on a cruiser both in harbour and at sea. In the light of this evidence, the Court cannot accept the Albanian contention that the position of the guns was inconsistent with the rules of innocent passage.

In the above-mentioned telegram of October 26th, the Commander-in-Chief reported that the passage "was made with ships at action stations in order that they might be able to retaliate quickly if fired upon again." In view of the firing from the Albanian battery on May 15th, this measure of precaution cannot, in itself, be regarded as unreasonable. But four warships--two cruisers and two destroyers--passed in this manner, with crews at action stations, ready to retaliate quickly if fired upon. They passed one after another through this narrow channel, close to the Albanian coast, at a time of political tension in this region. The intention must have been, not only to test Albania's attitude, but at the same time to demonstrate such force that she would abstain from firing again on passing ships. Having regard, however, to all the circumstances of the case, as described above, the Court is unable to characterize these measures taken by the United Kingdom authorities as a violation of Albania's sovereignty.

Corfu Channel
Figure 6-6

Source: A.L. Shalowitz, *Shore and Sea Boundaries*, Vol. 1, Washington, D.C:: U.S.
Government Printing Office, 1962, p. 76.

REFERENCES

J.M. Jones, "The Corfu Channel Case: Merits," *British Yearbook of International Law*, Vol.
26 (1949), pp. 447-453; Q. Wright, "The Corfu Channel Case," *American Journal of International
Law*, Vol. 43 (1949), pp. 491-494; I.Y.O. Chung, *Legal Problems Involved in the Corfu Channel
Incident*, Geneva: Librairie E. Droz, 1959; M.S. McDougal & W.T. Burke, *The Public Order of
the Oceans: A Contemporary International Law of the Sea*, New Haven and London: Yale
University Press, 1962, pp. 196-214.

3.   **The 1958 Convention on the Territorial Sea and Contiguous Zone and Other International Regimes**

1958 CONVENTION ON THE TERRITORIAL SEA
AND THE CONTIGUOUS ZONE

Article 16

. . . .

3. Subject to the provisions of paragraph 4, the coastal State may, without discrimination amongst foreign ships, suspend temporarily in specified areas of its territorial sea the innocent passage of foreign ships if such suspension is essential for the protection of its security. Such suspension shall take effect only after having been duly published.

4. There shall be no suspension of the innocent passage of foreign ships through straits which are used for international navigation between one part of the high seas and another part of the high seas or the territorial sea of a foreign State.

THE CASE OF EDISTO AND EASTWIND
"Soviet Union Bars Completion of U.S.
Scientific Voyage," *Department
of State Bulletin*, Vol. 57, No. 1473
(September 18, 1967), p. 362.

On August 16 the United States Coast Guard announced that the 269-foot Coast Guard icebreakers *Edisto* and *Eastwind* planned an 8,000-mile circumnavigation of the Arctic Ocean, conducting scientific research enroute. Their itinerary called for them to travel north of the Soviet islands of Novaya Zemlya, Severnaya Zemlya, and the New Siberian Islands.

The planned course was entirely on the high seas and, therefore, the voyage did not require any previous clearance with Soviet authorities. Nevertheless, the Soviet Government was officially informed of these plans just prior to the public announcement.

However, heavy ice conditions made it impossible for the vessels to proceed north of Severnaya Zemlya. On August 24 our Embassy in Moscow notified the Soviet Ministry of Foreign Affairs of this situation and stated it would be necessary for the two vessels to pass through Vilkitsky Straits south of Severnaya Zemlya in order to complete their journey.

In response the Soviet Ministry of Foreign Affairs made a statement to our Embassy that the straits constituted Soviet territorial waters.

On August 28, as a result of a routine message from the icebreakers to the Soviet Ministry of the Maritime Fleet, the Soviet Ministry of Foreign Affairs reaffirmed its declaration of August 24 and made it clear that the Soviet Government would claim that passage of the ships through the Vilkitsky Straits would be a violation of Soviet frontiers.

Under these circumstances, the United States considered it advisable to cancel the proposed circumnavigation. The *Edisto* has now been ordered to proceed directly to Baffin Bay, and the *Eastwind* was ordered to remain in the area of the Kara and Barents Seas for about a month to

circumnavigation. The *Edisto* has now been ordered to proceed directly to Baffin Bay, and the *Eastwind* was ordered to remain in the area of the Kara and Barents Seas for about a month to conduct further oceanographic research.

On August 30 our Embassy in Moscow sent a note strongly protesting the Soviet position. The note pointed out that Soviet law cannot have the effect of changing the status of international waters and the rights of foreign ships with respect to them. These rights are set forth clearly in the Convention on the Territorial Sea and the Contiguous Zone of April 29, 1958, to which the Soviet Union is a party.

There is right of innocent passage for all ships through straits used for international navigation between two parts of the high seas, whether or not, as in the case of Vilkitsky Straits, they are described by the Soviet Union as being overlapped by territorial waters, and there is an unlimited right of navigation on the high seas of straits comprising both high seas and territorial waters. Clearly, the Soviet Government, by denying to U.S. vessels their rights under international law, has acted to frustrate a useful scientific endeavor and thus to deprive the international scientific community of research data of considerable significance.

QUESTIONS

Which nation has the better legal argument under the *Corfu Channel Case* and the Convention on the Territorial Sea and the Contiguous Zone? As in the last sub-section, would you expect the position of the Soviet Union to be the same today in view of its recent emergence as a major global naval power? For recent Soviet attitude on strait passages, see I.P. Blishchenko, general editor, *The International Law of the Sea*, Moscow: Progress Publishers, 1988, pp. 111-117.

REFERENCES

W.E. Butler, "Soviet Concepts of Innocent Passage," *Harvard International Law Club Journal*, Vol. 7 (1965), pp. 113-130; W.E. Butler, *The Law of Soviet Territorial Waters: A Case Study of Maritime Legislation and Practice*, New York: Praeger, 1967, Ch. 5; W.E. Butler, "The Legal Regime of Russian Territorial Waters," *American Journal of International Law*, Vol. 62 (1968), pp. 51-77; A.D. Pharand, "Soviet Union Warns United States Against Use of North East Passage," *American Journal of International Law*, Vol. 62 (1968), pp. 927-935, [in this excellent analysis, the author concludes that (1) the Vilkitsky Straits probably do not fit the "used for international navigation" definition of Art. 16(4); (2) Art. 16(3) would not apply because of the lack of prior publication; and (3) even if the vessels could be classified as "warships" under Art. 8(2) of the Convention on the High Seas, the Soviet Union's reservation to Art. 23 is contrary to the object and purpose of the treaty and thus is not a permitted (valid) reservation]; Wells, "The Icy 'Nyet!,' *U.S. Naval Institute Proceedings*, Vol. 94 (No. 4) (1968), p. 73; M.R. Deddish, "Right of Passage by Warships Through International Straits," *JAG Journal*, Vol. 24 (1969-70), pp. 79-86; Walker, "What is Innocent Passage?," *U.S. Naval War College Review*, Vol. 21 (No. 5) (1969), p. 53, 69-71.

NOTE

One approach to the straits problem is for the concerned nations to reach agreement on a passage regime for a particular strait. For examples of international agreements and other documents dealing with the Straits of the Dardanelles, the Sea of Marmora, and the Bosphorus; the Straits of Gibraltar; Fuca's Straits; the Straits of Magellan; and the Danish Straits, see "Guide to Instruments Affecting the Legal Status of Straits," U.N. Doc. A/CONF.13/14 (12 November

Instruments Affecting the Legal Status of Straits," U.N. Doc. A/CONF.13/14 (12 November 1957). Excerpts from one such arrangement follow.

CONVENTION CONCERNING THE REGIME
OF STRAITS -- DARDANELLES AND BOSPHORUS
Montreux, July 20, 1936; entered in force
November 9, 1936
League of Nations Treaty Series
Vol. 173, p. 213 *et seq.*

Article 1. The High Contracting Parties recognize and affirm the principle of freedom of transit and navigation by sea in the Straits.

The exercise of this freedom shall henceforth be regulated by the provisions of the present Convention.

Article 2. In time of peace, merchant vessels shall enjoy complete freedom of transit and navigation in the Straits, by day and by night, under any flag and with any kind of cargo, without any formalities, except as provided in article 3, below. No taxes or charges other than those authorized by Annex I to the present Convention shall be levied by the Turkish authorities on these vessels when passing in transit without calling at a port in the Straits.

In order to facilitate the collection of these taxes or charges merchant vessels passing through the Straits shall communicate to the officials at the stations referred to in article 3 their name, nationality, tonnage, destination and last port of call (provenance). . . .

Art. 4. In time of war, Turkey not being belligerent, merchant vessels, under any flag or with any kind of cargo, shall enjoy freedom of transit and navigation in the Straits subject to the provisions of articles 2 and 3. . . .

Art. 5. In time of war, Turkey being belligerent, merchant vessels not belonging to a country at war with Turkey shall enjoy freedom of transit and navigation in the Straits on condition that they do not in any way assist the enemy. . . .

[The Convention contains detailed provisions concerning passage in wartime. Parties are Bulgaria, France, the United Kingdom, India, Greece, Japan, Romania, Turkey, the Soviet Union, and Yugoslavia.]

REFERENCES

H.P. Kirkpatrick, *The Montreux Straits Convention*, Geneva: Geneva Research Center, 1936; D.A. Routh, "The Montreux Convention Regarding the Regime of the Black Sea Straits," *Survey of International Affairs*, London, 1936, p. 584; Gerald Fitzmaurice, "The Straits Convention of Montreux, 1936," *British Yearbook of International Law*, Vol. 18 (1937), pp. 186-191; J.T. Shotwell and F. Deak, *Turkey at the Straits: A Short History*, New York: Macmillan, 1940; F.A. Vali, *The Turkish Straits and NATO*, Stanford, California: Hoover Institution Press, 1972; F.D. Froman, "*Kiev* and the Montreux Convention: The Aircraft Carrier that Became a Cruiser to Squeeze through the Turkish Straits," *San Diego Law Review*, Vol. 14 (1977), pp. 681-717; H.G. Knight, "The *Kiev* and the Turkish Straits," *American Journal of International Law*, Vol. 71 (1977), pp. 125-129.

Sea of Marmara

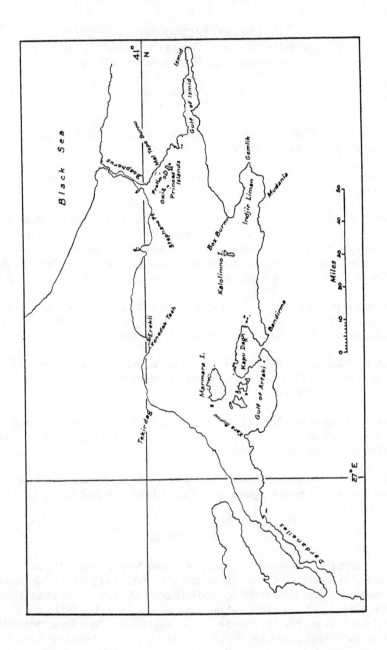

The Dardanelles and Bosphorus

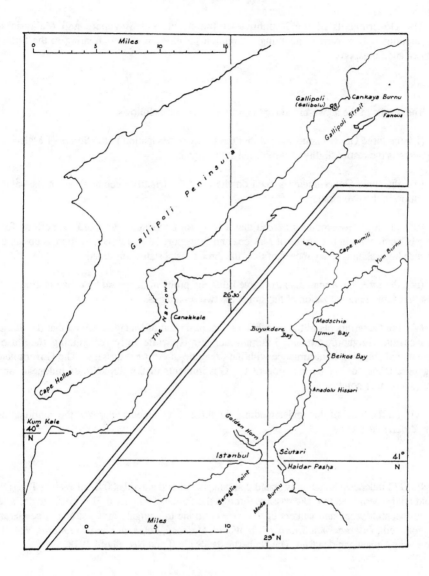

Turkish Straits
Figure 6-7

Source: [First] United Nations Conference on the Law of the Sea, *Official Records*, Vol.
I, *Preparatory Documents*, p. 161.

JOINT STATEMENT OF THE GOVERNMENTS OF
INDONESIA, MALAYSIA, AND SINGAPORE
November 16, 1971

The Governments of the Republics of Indonesia, and Singapore and Malaysia held consultations with a view to adopting a common position on matters relating to the Straits of Malacca and Singapore.

. . . .

The results of the above-mentioned consultations were as follows:

(i)   the three Governments agreed that the safety of navigation in the Straits of Malacca and Singapore is the responsibility of the coastal states concerned;

(ii)   the three Governments agreed on the need for tripartite cooperation on the safety of navigation in the two straits;

(iii)   the three Governments agreed that a body for cooperation to coordinate efforts for the safety of navigation in the Straits of Malacca and Singapore be established as soon as possible and that such body should be composed of only the three coastal states concerned;

(iv)   the three Governments also agreed that the problem of the safety of navigation and the question of internationalization of the straits are two separate issues;

(v)   the Governments of the Republic of Indonesia and of Malaysia agreed that the Straits of Malacca and Singapore are not international straits, while fully recognizing their use for international shipping in accordance with the principle of innocent passage. The Government of Singapore takes note of the position of the Governments of the Republic of Indonesia and of Malaysia on this point;

(vi)   on the basis of this understanding, the three Governments approved the continuation of the hydrographic survey.

NOTE

In 1972 Indonesia unilaterally stated that tankers larger than 200,000 Dead Weight Ton (DWT) would not be permitted to make passage through the Straits of Malacca. However, the declaration has not been enforced and tankers of that size continue to navigate in the straits. See Gerard J. Mangone, ed., *International Straits of the World, Malacca, Singapore, and Indonesia*, Vol. II, M. Leifer, ed., Alphen aan den Rün, The Netherlands: Sijthoff and Noordhoff, 1978.

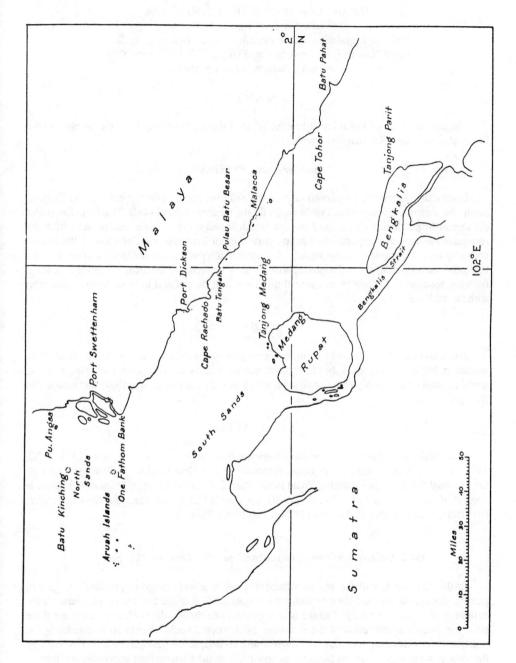

Strait of Malacca
Figure 6-8

Source: [First] United Nations Conference on the Law of the Sea, *Official Records*, Vol.
I, *Preparatory Documents*, p. 153.

JAPAN: LAW ON THE TERRITORIAL SEA
Law No. 30 of May 2, 1977
National Legislation and Treaties Relating to the Law of the Sea,
United Nations Legislative Series, ST/LEG/SER.B/19, New York:
The United Nations, 1980, pp. 56-57.

Article 1

The territorial sea of Japan comprises the areas of the sea extending from the baseline to the line twelve nautical miles seaward thereof. . . .

Supplementary Provisions

For the time being, the provisions of Article 1 shall not apply to the Soya Strait, the Tsugaru Strait, the eastern channel of the Tsushima Strait, the western channel of the Tsushima Strait and the Osumi Strait (including areas of the sea which are adjacent to these waters and which are recognized as forming respectively integral parts thereof from the point of view of the course normally used for navigation by vessels; hereinafter referred to as "designated areas"). The territorial sea pertaining to the designated areas shall be respectively the areas of the sea extending from the baseline to the line three nautical miles seaward thereof and to lines drawn connecting with the said line.

NOTE

Japan solved the straits problem in the same procedural manner (i.e., unilateral decree) as Indonesia-Malaysia-Singapore, but to achieve a diametrically opposed objective, *viz.*, keeping specified straits *open* for high seas navigation which includes, of course, overflight and submerged passage.

REFERENCES

A.H. Malcolm, "Japanese Extending National Sea Limits," *New York Times*, March 30, 1977, p. 5; T. Kuribayashi, "The Basic Structure of the New Regime of Passage Through International Straits -- An Emerging Trend in the Third UNCLOS and Japan's Situation," *Japanese Annual of International Law*, Vol. 21 (1977), pp. 29-41; Chi Young Pak, *The Korean Straits*, Dordrecht, Boston, London: Martinus Nijhoff Publishers, 1988.

4.   1982 United Nations Convention on the Law of the Sea

In the 1973-82 law of the sea negotiations, there is a wide range of proposals to govern passage through straits used for international navigation. One of the key issues, of course, is the definition of straits to be subject to the new regime. Once that hurdle is cleared, there are three basic approaches to resolution of the problem. First, vessels could be granted a completely (or nearly so) unregulated right of transit through straits; second, straits passage could be governed by the same principles of "innocent passage" as now apply to the territorial sea generally; and third, a new formulation, balancing the interests of littoral states and maritime nations, in the form of expanded articles on the innocent passage concept, could be adopted.

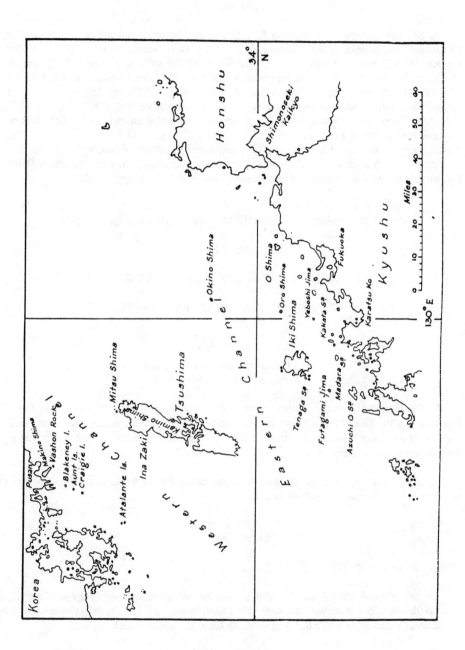

Chosen Strait
Figure 6-9

Source: [First] United Nations Conference on the Law of the Sea, *Official Records*, Vol.
I, *Preparatory Documents*, p. 151.

REFERENCES

"U.S. Draft Articles on Territorial Sea, Straits, and Fisheries Submitted to U.N. Seabeds Committee," *Department of State Bulletin*, Vol. 65, No. 1680 (September 6, 1971), pp. 261-268; Garwin, "Antisubmarine Warfare and National Security," *Scientific American*, Vol. 227 (No. 1), (1972), p. 14; H.G. Knight, "1971 Proposals on the Breadth of the Territorial Sea and Passage Through International Straits," *Oregon Law Review*, Vol. 51 (1972), pp. 759-785; H. Scoville, "Missile Submarines and National Security," *Scientific American*, Vol. 226 (1972), pp. 15-27; W.R. Slomanson, "Free Transit in Territorial Straits: Jurisdiction on an Even Keel?," *California Western International Law Journal*, Vol. 3 (1972-1973), pp. 375-396; R.E. Osgood, "U.S. Security Interests in Ocean Law," *Ocean Development and International Law*, Vol. 2 (1974), pp. 1-36; Pirtle, "Transit Rights and U.S. Security Interests in International Straits: the 'Straits Debate' Revisited," *Ocean Development and International Law*, Vol. 5 (1978), pp. 477-497.

1982 UNITED NATIONS CONVENTION ON THE LAW OF THE SEA

PART III

STRAITS USED FOR INTERNATIONAL NAVIGATION

SECTION 1.   GENERAL PROVISIONS

Article 34
Legal status of water forming straits
used for international navigation

1. The regime of passage through straits used for international navigation established in this Part shall not in other respects affect the legal status of the waters forming such straits or the exercise by the States bordering the straits of their sovereignty of jurisdiction over such waters and their air space, bed and subsoil.

2. The sovereignty or jurisdiction of the States bordering the straits is exercised subject to this Part and to other rules of international law.

Article 35
Scope of this Part

Nothing in this Part affects:

(a) any areas of internal waters within a strait, except where the establishment of a straight baseline in accordance with the method set forth in article 7 has the effect of enclosing as internal waters areas which had not previously been considered as such;

(b) the legal status of the waters beyond the territorial seas of States bordering straits as exclusive economic zones or high seas; or

(c) the legal regime in straits in which passage is regulated in whole or in part by long-standing international conventions in force specifically relating to such straits.

Article 36
High seas routes or routes through exclusive economic zones
through straits used for international navigation

This Part does not apply to a strait used for international navigation if there exists through the strait a route through the high seas or through an exclusive economic zone of similar convenience with respect to navigational and hydrographical characteristics; in such routes, the other relevant Parts of this Convention, including the provisions regarding the freedoms of navigation and overflight, apply.

SECTION 2.   TRANSIT PASSAGE

Article 37
Scope of this section

This section applies to straits which are used for international navigation between one part of the high seas or an exclusive economic zone and another part of the high seas or an exclusive economic zone.

Article 38
Right of transit passage

1. In straits referred to in article 37, all ships and aircraft enjoy the right of transit passage, which shall not be impeded; except that, if the strait is formed by an island of a State bordering the strait and its mainland, transit passage shall not apply if there exists seaward of the island a route through the high seas or through an exclusive economic zone of similar convenience with respect to navigational and hydrographical characteristics.

2. Transit passage means the exercise in accordance with this Part of the freedom of navigation and overflight solely for the purpose of continuous and expeditious transit of the strait between one part of the high seas or an exclusive economic zone and another part of the high seas or an exclusive economic zone. However, the requirement of continuous and expeditious transit does not preclude passage through the strait for the purpose of entering, leaving or returning from a State bordering the strait, subject to the conditions of entry to that State.

3. Any activity which is not an exercise of the right of transit passage through a strait remains subject to the other applicable provisions of this Convention.

Article 39
Duties of ships and aircraft during transit passage

1. Ships and aircraft, while exercising the right of transit passage, shall:

(a) proceed without delay through or over the strait;

(b) refrain from any threat or use of force against the sovereignty; territorial integrity or political independence of States bordering the strait, or in any other manner in violation of the principles of international law embodied in the Charter of the United Nations.

(c) refrain from any activities other than those incident to their normal modes of continuous and expeditious transit unless rendered necessary by *force majeure* or by distress;

(d) comply with other relevant provisions of this Part.

2. Ships in transit passage shall:

(a) comply with generally accepted international regulations, procedures and practices for safety at sea, including the International Regulations for Preventing Collisions at Sea;

(b) comply with generally accepted international regulations, procedures and practices for the prevention, reduction and control of pollution from ships.

3. Aircraft in transit passage shall:

(a) observe the Rules of the Air established by the International Civil Aviation Organization as they apply to civil aircraft; state aircraft will normally comply with such safety measures and will at all times operate with due regard for the safety of navigation;

(b) at all times monitor the radio frequency assigned by the competent internationally designated air traffic control authority or the appropriate international distress radio frequency.

Article 40
Research and survey activities

During transit passage, foreign ships, including marine scientific research and hydrographic survey ships, may not carry out any research or survey activities without the prior authorization of the States bordering straits.

Article 41
Sea lanes and traffic separation schemes in straits used for international navigation

1. In conformity with this Part, States bordering straits may designate sea lanes and prescribe traffic separation schemes for navigation in straits where necessary to promote the safe passage of ships.

2. Such States may, when circumstances require, and after giving due publicity thereto, substitute other sea lanes or traffic separation schemes for any sea lanes or traffic separation schemes previously designated or prescribed by them.

3. Such sea lanes and traffic separation schemes shall conform to generally accepted international regulations.

4. Before designating or substituting sea lanes or prescribing or substituting traffic separation schemes, States bordering straits shall refer proposals to the competent international organization with a view to their adoption. The organization may adopt only such sea lanes and traffic separation schemes as may be agreed with the States bordering the straits, after which the States may designate, prescribe or substitute them.

5. In respect of a strait where sea lanes or traffic separation schemes through the waters of two or more States bordering the strait are being proposed, the States concerned shall cooperate in formulating proposals in consultation with the competent international organization.

6. States bordering straits shall clearly indicate all sea lanes and traffic separation schemes designated or prescribed by them on charts to which due publicity shall be given.

7. Ships in transit passage shall respect applicable sea lanes and traffic separation schemes established in accordance with this article.

Article 42
Laws and regulations of States bordering straits relating to transit passage

1. Subject to the provisions of this section, States bordering straits may adopt laws and regulations relating to transit passage through straits, in respect of all or any of the following:

(a) the safety of navigation and the regulation of maritime traffic, as provided in article 41;

(b) the prevention, reduction and control of pollution, by giving effect to applicable international regulations regarding the discharge of oil, oily wastes and other noxious substances in the strait;

(c) with respect to fishing vessels, the prevention of fishing, including the stowage of fishing gear;

(d) the loading or unloading of any commodity, currency or person in contravention of the customs, fiscal, immigration or sanitary laws and regulations of States bordering straits.

2. Such laws and regulations shall not discriminate in form or in fact among foreign ships or in their application have the practical effect of denying, hampering or impairing the right of transit passage as defined in this section.

3. States bordering straits shall give due publicity to all such laws and regulations.

4. Foreign ships exercising the right of transit passage shall comply with such laws and regulations.

5. The flag State of a ship or the State of registry of an aircraft entitled to sovereign immunity which acts in a manner contrary to such laws and regulations or other provisions of this Part shall bear international responsibility for any loss or damage which results to States bordering straits.

Article 43
Navigational and safety aids and other improvements and
the prevention, reduction and control of pollution

User States and States bordering a strait should by agreement cooperate:

(a) in the establishment and maintenance in a strait of necessary navigational and safety aids or other improvements in aid of international navigation; and

(b) for the prevention, reduction and control of pollution from ships.

Article 44
Duties of States bordering straits

States bordering straits shall not hamper transit passage and shall give appropriate publicity to any danger to navigation or overflight within or over the strait of which they have knowledge. There shall be no suspension of transit passage.

SECTION 3.   INNOCENT PASSAGE

Article 45
Innocent passage

1. The regime of innocent passage, in accordance with Part II, section 3, shall apply in straits used for international navigation:

(a) excluded from the application of the regime of transit passage under article 38, paragraph 1; or

(b) between a part of the high seas or an exclusive economic zone and the territorial sea of a foreign State.

2. There shall be no suspension of innocent passage through such straits.

REFERENCES

Tadao Kuribayashi, "The Basic Structure of the New Regime of Passage through International Straits: An Emerging Trend in the Third UNCLOS and Japan's Situation," *Japanese Annual of International Law*, Vol. 21 (1977), pp. 29-47; Charles E. Pirtle, "Transit Rights and U.S. Security Interests in International Straits: The 'Straits Debate' Revisited," *Ocean Development and International Law*, Vol. 5 (1978), pp. 477-497; Kheng-lian Koh, *Contemporary Issues Relating to Straits Used for International Navigation*, Geneva: Institut Universitaire de Hautes Etudes Internationales, 1980; Morris F. Maduro, "Passage through International Straits: The Prospects Emerging from the Third United Nations Conference on the Law of the Sea," *Journal of Maritime Law and Commerce*, Vol. 12 (1980), pp. 65-95; Roger Mesznik, "Transit Fees for Ocean Straits and Their Impact on Global Economic Welfare," *Ocean Development and International Law*, Vol. 8 (1980), pp. 337-354; John Norton Moore, "The Regime of Straits and the Third United Nations Conference on the Law of the Sea," *American Journal of International Law*, Vol. 74 (1980), pp. 77-121; Michael Reisman, "The Regime of Straits and National Security: An Appraisal of International Lawmaking," *American Journal of International Law*, Vol. 74 (1980), pp. 48-74; Horace B. Robertson, "Passage through International Straits: A Right Preserved in the Third United Nations Conference on the Law of the Sea," *Virginia Journal of International Law*, Vol. 20 (1980), pp. 801-857; Awad El Mor, "The Regime of Passage in Straits Used for International Navigation in the Light of the 3rd UN Conference on the Law of the Sea," *Revue Egyptienne de Droit International*, Vol. 37 (1981), pp. 13-83; Edward J. Frank, "UNCLOS III and the Straits Passage Issue: The Maritime Powers' Perspective on Transit Passage," *Journal of International and Comparative Law*, Vol. 3 (1982), pp. 243-270; Kheng-lian Koh, *Straits in International Navigation*, Dobbs Ferry, New York: Oceana Publications, 1982; P. De Vries Lentsch, "The Right of Overflight Over Strait States and Archipelagic States: Developments and Prospects," *Netherlands Yearbook of International Law*, Vol. 14 (1983), pp. 165-225; Bruce A. Harlow, "UNCLOS III and Conflict Management in Straits," *Ocean Development and International Law*, Vol. 15 (1985), pp. 197-208; Lewis M. Alexander, "Exceptions to the Transit Passage Regime:

Straits with Routes of Similar Convenience," *Ocean Development and International Law*, Vol. 18 (1987), pp. 479-491; Hugo Caminos, "The Legal Regime of Straits in the 1982 United Nations Convention on the Law of the Sea," *Recueil des Cours* (Hague Academy of International Law), Vol. 205 (1987), pp. 9-245; Gerald J. Mangone, "Straits Used for International Navigation," *Ocean Development and International Law*, Vol. 17 (1987), pp. 391-409; Kazimierz Rowny, "The Right of Passage Through Straits Used for International Navigation and the United Nations Convention on the Law of the Sea," *Polish Yearbook of International Law*, Vol. 16 (1987), pp. 57-84; Said Mahmoudi, "Customary International Law and Transit Passage," *Ocean Development and International Law*, Vol. 20 (1989), pp. 157-174; J.B.R.L. Langdon, "The Extent of Transit Passage: Some Practical Anomalies," *Marine Policy*, Vol. 14 (1990), pp. 130-136.

> John Norton Moore, "The Regime of Straits and the Third United Nations Conference on the Law of the Sea," *American Journal of International Law*, Vol. 74 (1980), pp. 95-97. Reprinted by permission of The American Society of International Law and the author.

Submerged Transit

Text. An analysis of the full text makes clear that transit passage includes rights of submerged transit through straits for those straits covered by the transit passage regime. The innocent passage section includes a specific article requiring submarines "to navigate on the surface and to show their flag"; by contrast, there is no such requirement in either the transit passage section or the archipelagic states chapter dealing with the analogous archipelagic sea lanes passage, even though the transit passage section expressly enumerates the duties of ships during passage. That list of duties is clearly exhaustive since it ends with a catch-all obligation to "comply with the other relevant provisions *of this Part.*" Moreover, both the Territorial Sea Convention and the innocent passage section of UNCLOS establish a pattern that if submerged transit is to be prohibited, it will explicitly be so stated. In contrast, there is nowhere in the straits and archipelago chapters a duty to navigate on the surface through straits or "archipelagic sea lanes." In my judgment, these textual provisions, taken together, undeniably establish the right of submerged transit in straits, and nothing else, text or *travaux*, is needed. Nevertheless, the existence of the right of submerged passage is further attested to by a wide variety of other textual indications . . . .

The provision in Article 39(1)(c) that ships shall "[r]efrain from any activities other than those incident to their normal modes of continuous and expeditious transit" establishes, since it appears in a list of duties, that transit passage includes a right of transit in the "normal mode of continuous and expeditious transit." Because the "normal mode of continuous and expeditious transit" of modern submarines is submerged, a right of submerged transit is comprehended. It should be noted that normal mode in this regard is modified only by "of continuous and expeditious transit," not some other standard . . . .

The existence of Article 45 makes it clear that when a cross-reference is intended to the innocent passage section from the transit passage section, it is made explicitly. Similarly, Articles 29, 31, and 32 in the innocent passage chapter make it clear that when a provision of that part is intended to have effect beyond that part or to be affected by another part, it is so stated. This specific cross-reference practice is also followed in the environmental chapter on issues concerning navigational rights as spelled out in Articles 211(4), 220(2), and most importantly 233 and 236, which also apply in straits. Articles 233 and 236 particularly show that whenever an article outside of the straits part is intended to have an effect on the straits part, it is specifically stated to so apply or to apply to the entire convention. In short, the overall textual scheme of the convention is that in the absence of a specific cross-reference in at least one of the parts to be affected, nothing in the convention outside the straits chapter affects transit rights through straits used for international navigation.

E.   CONTIGUOUS ZONE

1.   The Origin and Development of the Regime of Contiguous Zone

CHURCH v. HUBBART
6 U.S. (2 Cranch.) 187 (1804)

[This case involved the seizure of a vessel on the basis that it was involved in illicit trade with the Portuguese colony of Brazil. On the question of the legality of the seizure and the interests which might thereby be legitimately protected, the Court noted as follows.]

The authority of a nation within its own territory is absolute and exclusive. The seizure of a vessel within the range of its cannon by a foreign force is an invasion of that territory, and is a hostile act which it is its duty to repel. But its power to secure itself from injury may certainly be exercised beyond the limits of its territory. Upon this principle the right of a belligerent to search a neutral vessel on the high seas for contraband of war is universally admitted, because the belligerent has a right to prevent the injury done to himself by the assistance intended for his enemy: so too a nation has a right to prohibit any commerce with its colonies. Any attempt to violate the laws made to protect this right, is an injury to itself which it may prevent, and it has a right to use the means necessary for its prevention. These means do not appear to be limited within any certain marked boundaries, which remain the same at all times and in all situations. If they are such as unnecessarily to vex and harass foreign lawful commerce, foreign nations will resist their exercise. If they are such as are reasonable and necessary to secure their laws from violation, they will be submitted to.

In different seas, and on different coasts, a wider or more contracted range, in which to exercise the vigilance of the government, will be assented to. Thus, in the channel, where a very great part of the commerce to and from all the north of Europe, passes through a very narrow sea, the seizure of vessels on suspicion of attempting an illicit trade, must necessarily be restricted to very narrow limits, but on the coast of South America, seldom frequented by vessels but for the purpose of illicit trade, the vigilance of the government may be extended somewhat further; and foreign nations submit to such regulations as are reasonable in themselves, and are really necessary to secure that monopoly of colonial commerce, which is claimed by all nations holding distant possessions.

If this right be extended too far, the exercise of it will be resisted. . . .

Nothing, then, is to be drawn from the laws or usages of nations, which gives to this part of the contract before the court the very limited construction which the plaintiff insists on, or which proves that the seizure of the *Aurora*, by the Portuguese governor, was an act of lawless violence.

CROFT v. DUNPHY

British Empire, Judicial Committee of the Privy Council, on appeal
from the Supreme Court of Canada, July 28, 1932 *Annual Digest of
Public International Law Cases 1931-1932*, pp. 157-160 (Case No. 82),
p. 158. Reproduced with permission from the *International Law
Reports*.

[This case concerned the validity of sections of the Customs Act of Canada (R.S. Can. 1927,
c. 42; amended by 18 & 19 Geo. 5, c. 16, 1928) authorizing the seizure of vessels registered in
Canada under certain circumstances within twelve marine miles from the coast. In affirming the
validity of the legislation, the Council noted, in part, as follows.]

It may be accepted as a general principle that States can legislate effectively only for their own
territories. To what distance seaward the territory of a State is to be taken as extending is a
question of international law upon which their Lordships do not deem it necessary or proper to
pronounce. But whatever be the limits of territorial waters in the international sense, it has long
been recognized that for certain purposes, notably those of police, revenue, public health, and
fisheries, a State may enact laws affecting the seas surrounding its coasts to a distance seaward
which exceeds the ordinary limits of its territory.

F.V. Garcia-Amador, *The Exploration and Conservation of the
Resources of the Sea*, Leiden, the Netherlands: A.W. Sijthoff, 1959,
pp. 59-65. Reprinted with the permission of the Kluwer Academic
Publishers Group.

Nature and function of the "contiguous zones."

The necessarily limited breadth of the territorial sea has not always enabled the coastal State to
ensure effective protection of all its interests and this inadequacy of the territorial sea was the
determining factor in the development, particularly in this century, of the area known as the
"contiguous zone." . . .

Origin and development of the institution; The Conference of The Hague.

The British *Hovering Acts* of the beginning of the eighteenth century seem to provide the
earliest proper examples of the "contiguous zone." A series of legislative measures was adopted in
Great Britain at different times during the century to check smuggling of various articles and to
prevent infringement of customs and excise regulations. These extended the jurisdictions of the
maritime policing of the State to two or more marine leagues, according to what was referred for
the effective application of the particular local regulations. In the earliest days of its independence,
United States Congress also began to enact laws fixing limits of its jurisdiction for the purpose of
suppressing smuggling and the slave trade. Once the concept of the territorial sea was defined and
a general consensus prevailed on the marine league rule, Great Britain repealed the *Hovering Acts*
and other measures it had adopted but the United States did not do the same, regarding these
extensions of competence as compatible with its acceptance of the marine league rule.

During the nineteenth century various European countries followed the Anglo-American
example. By the time the Conference of the Hague met in 1930 various Latin American States
had established zones contiguous to their territorial seas. Just prior to the Conference, States

passed from unilateral to collective action. The United States concluded sixteen treaties with other countries during the Prohibition period to establish the distance from the coast within which its authorities could exercise the right of search and detention over foreign ships suspected of smuggling alcoholic beverages. In 1925 eleven States signed a Convention for the same purpose. Thus, when the Codification Conference met there was no doubt at all that a general consensus already reigned with respect to the extensions of State competence in zones of the high seas contiguous to the territorial sea, within certain limits and for specific purposes.

[T]he concept of the "contiguous zone" during the discussions at The Hague had an indirect influence on the question of the breadth of the territorial sea and, to a certain extent, conditioned the agreements at the Conference on that point. One of the Bases of Discussion drawn up by the Preparatory Committee of the Conference, envisaged the recognition of this maritime area:

> On the high seas adjacent to its territorial waters, the coastal State may exercise the control necessary sufficient to ensure complete agreement, as the majority was divided within itself regarding both the nature of the interests to protect for which the State could extend its maritime jurisdiction and the distance within which it could be permitted to exercise such State competence. The main difficulties really arose in connection with the former, some delegations being in favor of recognizing the institution for fiscal and customs purposes only, while others wished to do so for purposes of state security, and others again to protect fishing interests. As a result of these differences of opinion the Conference was unable to reach a definition of the "contiguous zone.

Acceptance and subsequent development of the institution.

The Conference of The Hague did not succeed in defining the "contiguous zone". It seemed clear that in the view of the majority the fundamental idea behind these extensions of specialized competence was perfectly consistent with the principle of the freedom of the seas. To that extent, there seems no reason to doubt that, despite the opposition of certain States based on strict interpretations of the principle, the concept of this other area of sea had been accepted in international law.

Practice since 1930 abundantly confirms this impression. A vast number of legal measures has been adopted by States, both unilaterally and collectively, and particularly on fiscal and customs questions, to ensure the protection of such interests outside their territorial seas. One example is the Anti-Smuggling Act of 1935, empowering the President of the United States to delimit, on certain conditions, zones of the high seas beyond the 12-mile limit from the coast and to allow smuggling to be suppressed therein. The width of the *Customs Enforcement Area* provided for under the Act varies according to occasion and in direction; seawards, it can extend to 50 miles beyond the 12-mile line from the coast and laterally for a distance of 100 miles on each side, *i.e.*, to a total of 200 miles from the place in which the offense is committed. Similar enforcement areas for the same purpose, though within more modest limits, have been established by other countries: Argentina, Canada, Chile, Cuba, etc. (12 miles); Norway and Yugoslavia (10 miles); Ceylon, Finland and Poland (6 miles). The practice has also grown up of establishing such zones by international treaty; bilateral agreements on the subject are very common. Maritime jurisdiction has also been extended for considerations of neutrality and security, and especially in the latter case, the extension of competence has at times covered a considerable area. Some States have claimed 10 miles, others 12, and in some cases, such as that of Chile, 100 kilometers. Of the extensions of competence for this purpose, the most outstanding area those adopted collectively by the American Republics at the beginning of the second World War and shortly after it had ended, *e.g.*, the security zone established by the First Meeting of Foreign Ministers (Panama, October 1939), which at some points reached a breadth of 300 miles, and the zone established by the Inter-American Treaty of Mutual Assistance (Rio de Janeiro, 1947), which includes vast polar, Arctic and Antarctic regions.

REFERENCES

E.D. Dickinson, "Jurisdiction at the Maritime Frontier," *Harvard Law Review*, Vol. 40 (1926), pp. 1-29; W. Bishop, "The Exercise of Jurisdiction for Special Purposes in High Seas Areas Beyond the Outer Limit of Territorial Waters," *Congressional Record*, Vol. 99 (Pt. 2) (March 30, 1953), p. 2493; Gerald Fitzmaurice, "The Law and Procedure of the International Court of Justice, 1951-1954: Substantial Law, Part I," *British Yearbook of International Law*, Vol. 31 (1954), pp. 371, 376-381; Shigeru Oda, "The Territorial Sea and Natural Resources," *International and Comparative Law Quarterly*, Vol. 4 (1955), pp. 415-425; Shigeru Oda, "The Concept of the Contiguous Zone," *International and Comparative Law Quarterly*, Vol. 11 (1962), pp. 131-153; L.C. Fell, "Maritime Contiguous Zones," *Michigan Law Review*, Vol. 62 (1964), pp. 848-864; Janusz Symonides, "Origin and Legal Essence of the Contiguous Zone," *Ocean Development and International Law*, Vol. 20 (1989), pp. 203-211.

2.   **Article 24 of the 1958 Convention on the Territorial Sea and Contiguous Zone**

1958 CONVENTION ON THE TERRITORIAL SEA
AND THE CONTIGUOUS ZONE

Article 24

1. In a zone of the high seas contiguous to its territorial sea, the coastal State may exercise the control necessary to:

(a) Prevent infringement of its customs, fiscal, immigration or sanitary regulations within its territory or territorial sea;

(b) Punish infringement of the above regulations committed within its territory or territorial sea.

2. The contiguous zone may not extend beyond twelve miles from the baseline from which the breadth of the territorial sea is measured.

3. Where the coasts of two States are opposite or adjacent to each other, neither of the two States is entitled, failing agreement between them to the contrary, to extend its contiguous zone beyond the median line every point of which is equidistant from the nearest points on the baselines from which the breadth of the territorial seas of the two States is measured.

[The matter of apportionment of jurisdictional areas among opposite and adjacent states is dealt with in detail in Chapter 5, Section B, and thus need not be considered here.]

INTERNATIONAL LAW COMMISSION
1956 Commentary, Draft Article 66
Yearbook of the International Law Commission 1956,
Vol. II, pp. 294-295.

(1) International law accords States the right to exercise preventive or protective control for certain purposes over a belt of the high seas contiguous to their territorial sea. It is, of course, understood that this power of control does not change the legal status of the waters over which it is exercised. These waters are and remain a part of the high seas and are not subject to the sovereignty of the coastal State, which can exercise over them only such rights as are conferred on it by the present draft or are derived from international treaties.

(2) Many States have adopted the principle that in the contiguous zone the coastal State may exercise customs control in order to prevent attempted infringements of its customs and fiscal regulations within its territory or territorial sea, and to punish infringements of those regulations committed within its territory or territorial sea. The Commission considered that it would be impossible to deny to States the exercise of such rights.

(3) Although the number of States which claim rights over the contiguous zone for the purpose of applying sanitary regulations is fairly small, the Commission considers that, in view of the connection between customs and sanitary regulations, such rights should also be recognized for sanitary regulations.

(4) The Commission did not recognize special security rights in the contiguous zone. It considered that the extreme vagueness of the term "security" would open the way for abuses and that the granting of such rights was not necessary. The enforcement of customs and sanitary regulations will be sufficient in most cases to safeguard the security of the State. In so far as measures of self-defense against an imminent and direct threat to the security of the State are concerned, the Commission refers to the general principles of international law and the Charter of the United Nations.

(5) Nor was the Commission willing to recognize any exclusive right of the coastal State to engage in fishing in the contiguous zone. The Preparatory Committee of The Hague Codification Conference found, in 1930, that the replies from Governments offered no prospect of an agreement to extend the exclusive fishing rights of the coastal State beyond the territorial sea. The Commission considered that in that respect the position has not changed.

(6) The Commission examined the question whether the same attitude should be adopted with regard to proposals to grant the coastal State the right to take whatever measures it considered necessary for the conservation of the living resources of the sea in the contiguous zone. The majority of the Commission were unwilling to accept such a claim. They argued, first, that measures of this kind applying only to the relatively small area of the contiguous zone would be little practical value and, secondly, that having provided for the regulation of the conservation of living resources in a special part of the present draft, it would be inadvisable to open the way for a duplication of these rules by different provisions designed to regulate the same matters in the contiguous zone only. Since the contiguous zone is a part of the high seas, the rules concerning conservation of the living resources of the sea apply to it.

(7) The Commission did not maintain its previous decision to grant the coastal State, within the contiguous zone, a right of control in respect of immigration. In its report on the work of its fifth session the Commission commented on this provision as follows:

It is understood that the term 'customs regulations' as used in the article refers not only to regulations concerning import and export duties but also to other regulations concerning the exportation and importation of goods. In addition, the Commission thought it necessary to amplify the formulation previously adopted by referring expressly to immigration, a term which is also intended to include emigration.

Reconsidering this decision, the majority of the Commission took the view that the interests of the coastal State do not require an extension of the right of control to immigration and emigration. It considered that such control could and should be exercised in the territory of the coastal State and that there was no need to grant it special rights for this purpose in the contiguous zone.

(8) The commission considered the case of areas of the sea situated off the junction of two or more adjacent States, where the exercise of rights in the contiguous zone by one State would not leave any free access to the ports of another State except through that zone. The Commission, recognizing that in such cases the exercise of rights in the contiguous zone by one State may unjustifiably obstruct traffic to or from a port of another State, considered that in the case referred to it would be necessary for the two States to include a prior agreement on the exercise of rights in the contiguous zone. In view of the exceptional nature of the case, however, the Commission did not consider it necessary to include a formal rule to this effect.

(9) The Commission considers that the breadth of the contiguous zone cannot exceed twelve miles from the coast, the figure adopted by the Preparatory Committee of The Hague Codification Conference (1930). Until such time as there is unanimity in regard to the breadth of the territorial sea, the zone should be measured from the coast and not from the outer limit of the territorial sea. States which have claimed extensive territorial waters have in fact less need for a contiguous zone than those which have been more modest in their delimitation.

(10) The Commission thought it advisable to clarify the expression "from the coast" by stating that the zone is measured from the baseline from which the breadth of the territorial sea is measured.

(11) The exercise by the coastal State of the rights enunciated in this article does not affect the legal status of the air space above the contiguous zone. The question whether the establishment of such an air control zone could be contemplated is outside the scope of these rules of the law of the sea.

DEPARTMENT OF STATE
[Public Notice 358]
U.S. TERRITORIAL SEA AND CONTIGUOUS ZONE
Implementation and Enforcement of Laws
Federal Register, Vol. 37, No. 116
(June 15, 1972), p. 11906.

This notice is for the purposes of the implementation and enforcement of the laws and treaties of the United States applicable to its territorial sea and contiguous zone. It is the position of the United States in the conduct of its affairs that there exists off its coast a 3-mile territorial sea and a 9-mile contiguous zone of high seas seaward of the territorial sea for the purposes of the customs, fiscal, immigration, and sanitary controls described in Article 24 of the Convention on the Territorial Sea and the Contiguous Zone, and for the purposes of exclusive fisheries rights under

310   THE INTERNAL WATERS

Territorial Sea and the Contiguous Zone, and for the purposes of exclusive fisheries rights under Public Law 89-658 of October 14, 1966.

Date: June 1, 1972
John R. Stevenson,
The Legal Adviser.

QUESTION

Why did the United States not implement its rights under Article 24 of the Convention on the Territorial Sea and the Contiguous Zone until 1972?

REFERENCES

Gerald Fitzmaurice, "The Law and Procedure of the International Court of Justice, 1951-54. Substantive Law, Part I. Maritime Law," *British Yearbook of International Law*, Vol. 31 (1954), pp. 371, 378-381; Shigeru Oda, "The Territorial Sea and Natural Resources," *International and Comparative Law Quarterly*, Vol. 4 (1955), pp. 415-425; Gerald Fitzmaurice, "Some Results of the Geneva Conference on the Law of the Sea," *International and Comparative Law Quarterly*, Vol. 8 (1959), pp. 73, 108-121; Shigeru Oda, "The Concept of a Contiguous Zone," *International and Comparative Law Quarterly*, Vol. 11 (1962), pp. 131, 148-153; L.C. Fell, "Maritime Contiguous Zones," *Michigan Law Review*, Vol. 62 (1964), pp. 848-864; Shigeru Oda, "The Geneva Conventions on the Law of the Sea: Some Suggestions for Their Revision," *Natural Resources Lawyer*, Vol. 1 (No. 2) (1968), pp. 103, 107-110; A.V. Lowe, "The Development of the Concept of the Contiguous Zone," *British Yearbook of International Law*, Vol. 52 (1981), pp. 109-169; Alan M. Frommer, "The British Hovering Acts: A Contribution to the Study of the Contiguous Zone," *Revue Belge de Droit International*, Vol. 16 (1981-1982), pp. 434-458.

RE MARTINEZ AND OTHERS
Italy, Court of Cassation, November 25, 1959, *International Law Reports*,
Vol. 28, pp. 170-175. Reproduced with permission from the *International Law Reports*.

The Facts. -- Article 2 of the Italian Maritime Code fixes the limit of territorial waters at six miles from the coast. Article 33 of the Customs Law of September 25, 1940, on the other hand, provides that Italy shall be entitled to exercise jurisdiction over a further six-mile zone for the purpose of preventing and punishing smuggling along the Italian coast. This latter zone is referred to as the "zone of vigilance" (contiguous zone). The appellants, who were foreign nationals, were convicted of smuggling in the following circumstances: while their vessel was at a distance of nine miles from the coast, warning shots were fired, and upon these shots being ignored the vessel was pursued and ultimately captured at a distance of 54 miles from the coast. The appellants appealed against their conviction and contended that Article 24 of the Geneva Convention of 1958 on the Territorial Sea and the Contiguous Zone was declaratory of existing customary international law and accordingly a coastal State, while entitled to prevent customs offenses from being committed in the contiguous zone, was not entitled to exercise jurisdiction and inflict punishment in respect of such offenses; that jurisdiction could only be exercised if an offense had actually been committed within the territorial sea, and therefore Article 33 of the Customs Law was contrary to Article 10 of the Italian Constitution, which provided that Italian law must be consistent with international law. They therefore contended that their conviction should be quashed.

Held: that the appeal must be dismissed. (i) Article 24 of the Convention was not declaratory of existing customary international law, and there was no rule of international law which precluded a coastal State from exercising jurisdiction over offenses by foreign nationals which were committed in the contiguous zone of between six and twelve miles from the coast. (ii) Accordingly, Article 33 of the Customs Law was not contrary to Article 10 of the Constitution (or international law), and as the offense had been committed at a distance of nine miles from the coast when the pursuit of the vessel began, the Italian courts were entitled to exercise jurisdiction.

The Court said: "It is contended that Article 33 of the Customs Law, which extends the territorial sea beyond the limit of six nautical miles laid down in Article 2 of the Maritime Code, and confers on the coastal State sovereignty and jurisdiction over a stretch of sea between six and twelve miles, is contrary to Article 10 of the Italian Constitution which provides that Italian law shall be in conformity with the generally recognized rules of international law. By a rule of customary international law recognized and laid down in Article 24 of the 'Convention on the Territorial Sea and the Contiguous Zone', which was adopted at the Geneva Conference on February 24 and April 27, 1958, the sovereignty and jurisdiction of the coastal State--it is said--cannot extend beyond six miles, and sovereignty and jurisdiction over a belt being defined as the contiguous zone, are not recognized except in specially defined cases. According to the argument put forward on behalf of the appellants, the coastal State can exercise the requisite control for the purpose of preventing and punishing offenses against its customs, tax and sanitary laws over a portion of the high seas contiguous to the territorial sea, on condition only that the offenses have been committed in the territorial sea within six miles from the coast. It follows--so it is said--that the coastal State can exercise its jurisdiction over the contiguous zone only in respect of offenses committed in its territorial sea, the contiguous zone being the intermediate zone between the territorial sea and the high seas. This, it is said, would be contrary to Article 33 of the Customs Law, which, in delimiting the zone of customs vigilance as being twelve miles from the coast, includes in the latter the territorial sea as laid down in Article 2 of the Maritime Code and the zone of vigilance, which latter it makes coincide with the territorial sea.

"The contention that Article 33 of the Customs Law is contrary to the Constitution is misconceived and has been rejected by the judgment under appeal. It is undoubtedly true that the rule laid down in Article 10 of the Constitution, according to which Italian law must comply with generally recognized rules of international law, ensures the compatibility of Italian municipal law with international law, *viz.*, with the duties imposed upon the State by international law, so that rules of municipal law which are contrary to international law must be eliminated. However, in order for this to be so, it is necessary for the rules of international law to be generally recognized, and it is admitted on behalf of the defendants that the Geneva Convention, which has been signed by Italy, is not yet in force.

"It is not true that Article 24 of the Convention constitutes a customary rule of international law governing the delimitation of the territorial sea in the sense that the sovereignty of the coastal State is limited to the territorial sea itself, without being capable of being extended over the contiguous zone when smuggling has occurred in the latter and not in the territorial sea. No such rule can be said to have been generally accepted in international law. . . .

. . . .

". . . .Italy has not accepted the limit of the contiguous zone in the form in which it is expressed in Article 24. The rules of municipal law of coastal States have therefore remained in force. In Italy it is the rule laid down in Article 33 of the Customs Law, which cannot be said to be contrary to Article 10 of the Constitution. It follows that the offense of smuggling committed in the zone of vigilance, the so-called contiguous zone, is punishable in Italy, and that the arrest of a foreign national is lawful by Article 137 of the Customs Law. Equally lawful is the pursuit of a foreign vessel, which is recognized by customary international law except with regard to the limit of the territorial sea and the contiguous zone.

"We now come to the second and third grounds of appeal. The rule laid down in Article 33 of the Customs Law, which, as we have said, puts the zone of vigilance--the contiguous zone--on the same legal basis as the territorial sea for the purpose of customs offenses, is well established so far as concerns the right of pursuit. By virtue of this right a foreign vessel can be pursued if the competent authorities of a coastal State have good reason to suspect that the vessel has violated the law of that State, provided that the pursuit begins while the foreign vessel or one of its auxiliary craft is in internal waters, in the territorial sea or in the contiguous zone of the pursuing State; the pursuit can be extended beyond the limits of the territorial sea if it has not been interrupted. It follows that it is lawful to capture the crew and seize the vessel with its cargo of contraband.

"The appellants contend that as Article 2 of the Maritime Code fixes the limit of the territorial sea at six miles from the coast and provides that this is without prejudice to various legal provisions which are to apply in specific cases, the only purpose of the Code was to lay down a six-mile limit for the territorial sea, reserving the right to extend the limit for specific purposes other than sovereignty, and less extensive than the latter. Accordingly, the zone of vigilance provided for by Article 33 of the Customs Law as being between six and twelve miles is not the territorial sea but merely an area of the sea which is subject to control for the purpose of prevention only and not punishment. Although in theory it may seem as if in the contiguous zone only police and preventive measures may be taken, because this zone forms part of the open sea rather than the territorial sea, a different view must be taken when one considers that the draft code of the Institute of International Law on the contiguous zone clearly recognizes the right to exercise jurisdiction. The International Law Commission, in its report on the session held in 1953, was decidedly in favor of acknowledging the right to exercise jurisdiction, while in its 1951 draft it merely referred to preventive measures."

(Court then pointed out that Article 33 of the Customs Law was designed to give the widest possible powers to the Italian courts and not merely to enable the police to prevent smuggling in the vicinity of the Italian coast. It then considered the facts and found that warning shots had been fired at the foreign vessel concerned when the latter was at a distance of nine miles from the coast, and that upon the shots being ignored the vessel was pursued until it was captured at a distance of 54 miles from the coast. The appeal was accordingly dismissed.)

3.   **Article 33 of the 1982 United Nations Convention on the Law of the Sea**

THIRD UNITED NATIONS CONFERENCE ON THE LAW OF THE SEA
SECOND COMMITTEE, 31st MEETING
August 7, 1974
Third United Nations Conference on the Law of the Sea, 1973-1982,
Official Records, Vol. II (Second Session), pp. 234-235.

34.   *Mr. GOERNER* (German Democratic Republic) . . . The basic idea of the concept of the contiguous zone was to provide protection for the legitimate interests of coastal States which did not wish to extend their territorial sea to a breadth of 12 nautical miles. It was thus clear that the establishment and recognition of contiguous zones was closely connected with the breadth of

the territorial sea. Since every coastal State was entitled, under generally recognized international law, to establish a 12-mile territorial sea in which it exercised full sovereignty, it would seem logical that coastal States which claimed a territorial sea of less than 12 miles should have the right to exercise individual sovereign rights for the protection of their legitimate interests in a zone stretching for 12 miles measured from the baseline. The concept of the contiguous zone was thus based on the voluntary renunciation by some States of the exercise of their sovereign rights and was not directed against the interests of any other State. . . .

36. He could not accept the proposal that coastal States claiming a territorial sea of 12 miles should establish a contiguous zone adjacent to that territorial sea. The exercise of rights such as control of customs, immigration, fiscal and sanitary regulations should be restricted to an area of 12 nautical miles, in the form of the territorial sea or the territorial sea and contiguous zone. Any additional exercise of those rights could seriously interfere with international communication and the freedom of navigation. It was also important that the internationally recognized rights of other States should not be prejudiced by the application by the coastal State of the legal regime of the contiguous zone. . . .

42. *Mr. NIMER* (Bahrain) said that . . . the establishment of a contiguous zone for particular purposes beyond the territorial waters of a coastal State was not inconsistent with the concept of an exclusive economic zone since the latter, as its name implied, would be an area in which the utilization of resources and other economic matters were the sole concern.

43. A coastal State's rights in the contiguous zone were of a functional and protective nature. As indicated in article 24 of the 1958 Convention on the Territorial Sea and the Contiguous Zone, the coastal State's powers were confined to the control necessary to prevent infringement of its customs, fiscal, immigration and sanitary regulations and the punishment of infringements of such regulations, which were often committed under cover of the commendable principle of freedom of the high seas.

44. The contiguous zone was not a new concept in international sea law. As far back as the seventeenth century, States had had to resort to it in order to enforce their customs and fiscal regulations. Objections to the concept, over the years, had been motivated by fears lest its misuse should interfere with the traditional freedom of navigation on the high seas. But there were no grounds for such fears as long as the freedom of navigation was regulated by an acceptable and universal convention on the law of the sea.

45. The contiguous zone was very important to coastal States, particularly in areas where there were wide divergences in the prices of commodities and precious materials or where foreign labor was attracted away by better pay or working conditions. Many developing States did not possess the modern technical equipment or the large coastal fleets to protect the whole of their territorial belt from smugglers and infiltrators and to intercept suspicious vessels before they broke through into the territorial zone.

46. His delegation considered that the regime of the contiguous zone, in accordance with article 24 of the 1958 Geneva Convention, should be maintained; and that its limit should be extended to a distance of 12 miles beyond the territorial waters of the coastal State, in view of the current trend to extend the breadth of the territorial sea and the great advances in the speed and construction of modern ships. The ratio between the contiguous zone and the territorial sea would then be almost the same as the ratio formerly adopted and recognized by international law.

1982 UNITED NATIONS CONVENTION ON THE LAW OF THE SEA

Article 33
Contiguous Zone

1. In a zone contiguous to its territorial sea, described as the contiguous zone, the coastal State may exercise the control necessary to:

(a) prevent infringement of its customs, fiscal, immigration or sanitary laws and regulations within its territory or territorial sea;

(b) punish infringement of the above laws and regulations committed within its territory or territorial sea.

2. The contiguous zone may not extend beyond 24 nautical miles from the baselines from which the breadth of the territorial sea is measured.

NOTE

On December 27, 1989, the United States extends its territor-ial sea to 12 miles, see Section C, Subsection 3, e, but it has not extended its contiguous zone to 24 miles from its baseline of territorial sea.

REFERENCES

Constantine Economides, "The Contiguous Zone, Today and Tomorrow," in Christos L. Rozakis and Constantin A. Stephanou, eds., *The New Law of the Sea: Selected and Edited Papers of Athens Colloquium on the Law of the Sea*, Amsterdam: North-Holland, 1983, pp. 69-81; Frederick C. Leiner, "Maritime Security Zones: Prohibited yet Perpetuated," *Virginia Journal of International Law*, Vol. 24 (1984), pp. 967-992; Rose Varghese, "Territorial Sea and Contiguous Zone: Concept and Development," *Cochin University Law Review*, Vol. 9 (1985), pp. 436-459.

4. Pirate Broadcasting

D.W. Bowett, *The Law of the Sea*, Manchester: Manchester University
Press, 1967, pp. 52-55. Reprinted by permission.

Within recent years there has developed what many people would regard as an "abuse" of the freedom of the High Seas in the practice of broadcasting to a State's territory from a vessel or installation outside the territorial waters of that State. The way in which, within Europe, States have reacted to this practice affords an interesting example of one technique of dealing with such an "abuse of rights."

By and large, States tend to apply a closely-regulated system of licensing to all broadcasts within their territory and even in some cases, such as the United Kingdom, to impose a State monopoly on broadcasting. The case for regulation is clear: uncontrolled broadcasting can lead to breach of copyright and to interference with radio frequencies used by ships or aircraft (which may be in distress), with space research (which depends very much on radio techniques), or with the regular broadcasts of radio and television licensed within the State. Moreover, the whole arrangement for the allocation of frequencies within the International Telecommunications Union

arrangement for the allocation of frequencies within the International Telecommunications Union is jeopardized if States lose their capacity to regulate radio and television transmissions.

There are therefore two ways of dealing with this problem. One is for States to abandon their general tendency to limit their legislation on broadcasting to their own territory. Hence it might be possible to amend the U.K. Wireless Telegraphy Act of 1949 so as to make it applicable beyond the limit of territorial waters. This has already been done to a limited extent by the Continental Shelf Act, 1964, section 6 of which enables the 1949 Act to be extended to installations within the designated areas of the shelf. A number of other States seem to have taken this course, and it is at least arguable that such a limited extension of jurisdiction is necessary and justifiable. But there are hazards to this, for such action may well be contested by the flag State (normally a "flag of convenience" is used) and it is by no means clear that the concept of the Contiguous Zone allows for this kind of jurisdiction.

The other way is to proceed by way of international agreement so that a number of States take concerted action which will be tantamount to reciprocal protection, simply by utilizing their existing jurisdiction. This is, essentially, the way in which the European States have reacted. Under the auspices of the Council of Europe, a European Agreement for the Prevention of Broadcasts Transmitted from Stations outside National Territories was opened for signature.

The essence of the Agreement lies in the undertaking by each Party to make punishable under its own laws such broadcasting by its own nationals or even by aliens on its "territory, ships or aircraft, or on board any floating or airborne object under its jurisdiction." Moreover, (and here lies probably the most effective sanction), the prohibition shall extend to any acts of collaboration, which are defined in Article 2(2) as follows:

(a) the provision, maintenance or repairing of equipment;

(b) the provision of supplies;

(c) the provision of transport for, or the transporting of, persons, equipment or supplies;

(d) the ordering or production of material of any kind, including advertisements, to be broadcast;

(e) the provision of services concerning advertising for the benefit of the stations.

It may be noted, also, that Article 4 of the Agreement says that nothing in the Agreement shall prevent any Party from applying the provisions of this Agreement to "broadcasting stations installed or maintained on objects affixed to or supported by the bed of the sea." This clearly has in mind the several "pirate" stations established on the artificial Towers, constructed in the Thames Estuary and elsewhere off the English coasts as part of our coastal defenses during the Second World War.

The interesting aspect of this Agreement is that it does not contemplate any unusual jurisdiction: that is to say, the jurisdiction of each State is confined to its own territory, its own ships, aircraft or nationals--and this is perfectly consistent with the rules of international law. The "abuse" is thus met by a concerted action by several States on the basis of a recognition of their "common interest," and without importing any novel principles. Of course, there are possibilities of evasion; the Convention would not cover a vessel which was registered in and manned by nationals of a non-contracting Party. But even here, if deprived of all assistance or even business --

for this is what is covered by the definition of "acts of collaboration" -- from the coastal State, the risks of this are minimal: broadcasting would presumably cease to be an economic proposition.

NOTE

On the Strasbourg Convention and the case of *Regina v. Kent Justices*, [1967] 2 Q.B. 153, see note by J.R. Watts in *Harvard International Law Journal*, Vol. 9 (1968), pp. 317-324.

REFERENCES

N.M. Hummings, "Pirate Broadcasting in European Waters," *International and Comparative Law Quarterly*, Vol. 14 (1965), pp. 410-436; J.C. Woodliffe, "Some Legal Aspects of Pirate Broadcasting in the North Sea," *Netherlands International Law Review*, Vol. 12 (1965), pp. 365-384; H.F. van Panhuys and M.J. van Emde Boas, "Legal Aspects of Pirate Broadcasting: A Dutch Approach," *American Journal of International Law*, Vol. 60 (1966), pp. 303-341; D.E. Smith, "Pirate Broadcasting," *Southern California Law Review*, Vol. 41 (1968), pp. 769-815; M.J. Hanna, "Controlling 'Pirate' Broadcasting," *San Diego Law Review*, Vol. 15 (1978), pp. 547-571; H. Meijers and R.C.R. Siekmann, "The 'Magda Maria' and Customary Law of the Sea: A Casenote, "*Netherlands Yearbook of International Law*, Vol. 13 (1982), pp. 143-156; Horace B. Robertson, Jr., "The Suppression of Pirate Radio Broadcasting: A Test Case of the International System for Control of Activities Outside National Territory," *Law and Contemporary Problems*, Vol. 45 (1982), roblems, Vol. 45 (1982), pp. 71-101.

NOTE AND QUESTION

In the United States the Reverend Carl McIntire, a fundamentalist preacher claiming persecution by the U.S. Government for his conservative political views, attempted to continue radio broad-casts from an unlicensed transmitter on board a ship anchored more than three miles from the coast. The Federal Communications Commission referred to McIntire's vessel as a "pirate ship" and sought to terminate the broadcasts. On what jurisdictional bases could they proceed? Would reliance on any international agreement be necessary? See "F.C.C. Challenged by a 'Pirate' Ship," *New York Times*, September 20, 1973, p. 47.

1982 UNITED NATIONS CONVENTION ON THE LAW OF THE SEA

Article 109
Unauthorized broadcasting from the high seas

1. All States shall cooperate in the suppression of unauthorized broadcasting from the high seas.

2. For the purposes of this Convention, "unauthorized broadcasting" means the transmission of sound radio or television broadcasts from a ship or installation on the high seas intended for reception by the general public contrary to international regulations, but excluding the transmission of distress calls.

3. Any person engaged in unauthorized broadcasting may be prosecuted before the court of:

(a) the flag State of the ship;

(b) the State of registry of the installation;

(c) the State of which the person is a national;

(d) any State where the transmissions can be received; or

(e) any State where authorized radio communication is suffering interference.

4. On the high seas, a State having jurisdiction in accordance with paragraph 3 may, in conformity with article 110, arrest any person or ship engaged in unauthorized broadcasting and seize the broadcasting apparatus.

CHAPTER VII

THE HIGH SEAS

A.   INTRODUCTION

Readers should begin here to compare the historical pattern of treating the high seas as exempt from appropriation by any state with the emerging doctrine of shared use and regulation of activities. The Grotian concept of freedom of the high seas was codified in the 1958 Convention on the High Seas (Article 1) and the 1982 United Nations Convention on the Law of the Sea, Part VII (Articles 86-120) but also included was language recognizing the increased diversity and concentration of use of ocean space on a principle of shared utilization. Observe how the trend has shifted from a basically negative approach (non-appropriation) to a positive approach (recognition of "exercise" or "use" rights on an equitable basis). Clearly, the classical doctrine of freedom of the high seas has been eroded in the past half-century. This does not mean, however, that states have appropriated bodies of water in the same sense that European states did so during the Middle Ages. With few exceptions (e.g., limitations on passage through international straits as a result of extended territorial sea claims, and hazards to navigation posed by concentrations of offshore oil and gas drilling platforms) no significant interference with rights of navigation and access to the sea has occurred. The fact is simply that *other* uses of the ocean have developed--offshore mining, principally for oil and gas; laying of submarine cables; intensified fishing activity; waste disposal; recreation; and the like--and it has been necessary to *accommodate* these uses within the framework of the existing regime of the high seas. See Lewis M. Alexander, "National Jurisdiction and the Use of the Sea," *Natural Resource Journal*, Vol. 8 (1968), pp. 373-400, and Francis J. Christy, "Marine Resources and the Freedom of the Seas," *Natural Resource Journal*, Vol. 8 (1968), pp. 424-433.

Traditionally, the high seas include all parts of the sea not included in the territorial sea or internal waters. However, with the emergence of the regimes of exclusive economic zones, archipelagic waters and international control of the seabed beyond national jurisdiction, the scope of high seas has been reduced. Accordingly, this chapter deals with high seas in their present scope. The question of unauthorized broadcast from the high seas has been dealt with in Chapter VI, Section E, sub-section 4 and will not be discussed here.

B.   RECOGNIZED FREEDOMS OF THE HIGH SEAS

1958 CONVENTION ON THE HIGH SEAS

Article 1

The term "high seas" means all parts of the sea that are not included in the territorial sea or in the internal waters of a State.

Article 2

The high seas being open to all nations, no State may validly purport to subject any part of them to its sovereignty. Freedom of the high seas is exercised under the conditions laid down by these articles and by the other rules of international law. It comprises, *inter alia*, both for coastal and non-coastal States:

(1) Freedom of navigation;

(2) Freedom of fishing;

(3) Freedom to lay submarine cables and pipelines;

(4) Freedom to fly over the high seas.

These freedoms, and others which are recognized by the general principles of international law, shall be exercised by all States with reasonable regard to the interests of other States in their exercise of the freedom of the high seas.

INTERNATIONAL LAW COMMISSION
1956 Commentary, Draft Articles 26 and 27
Yearbook of the International Law Commission 1956,
Vol. II, pp. 277-278.

Commentary to Article 26

Some large stretches of water, entirely surrounded by dry land, are known as "lakes", others as "seas". The latter constitute internal seas, to which the regime of the high seas is not applicable. Where such stretches of water communicate with the high seas by a strait or arm of the sea, they are considered as "internal seas" if the coasts, including those of the waterway giving access to the high seas, belong to a single State. If that is not the case, they are considered as high seas. These rules may, however, be modified for historical reasons or by international arrangement.

Commentary to Article 27

The principle generally accepted in international law that the high seas are open to all nations governs the whole regulation of the subject. No State may subject any part of the high seas to its sovereignty; hence no State may exercise jurisdiction over any such stretch of water. States are bound to refrain from any acts which might adversely affect the use of the high seas by nationals of other States. Freedom to fly over the high seas is expressly mentioned in this article because the Commission considers that it follows directly from the principle of the freedom of the sea; . . .

.

The list of freedoms of the high seas . . . is not restrictive. The Commission has merely specified four of the main freedoms, but it is aware that there are other freedoms, such as freedom to undertake scientific research on the high seas--a freedom limited only by the general principle stated in the third sentence of [the preceding] paragraph . . . .

[T]he Commission [did not] make any express pronouncement on the freedom to undertake nuclear weapon tests on the high seas. In this connexion the general principle enunciated in the third sentence [referred to above] . . . is applicable . . . .

The term "submarine cables" applies not only to telegraph and telephone cables, but also to high-voltage power cables.

Any freedom that is to be exercised in the interests of all entitled to enjoy it, must be regulated. Hence, the law of the high seas contains certain rules, most of them already recognized in positive international law, which are designed, not to limit or restrict the freedom of the high seas, but to safeguard its exercise in the interests of the entire international community. These rules concern particularly:

(i) The right of States to exercise their sovereignty on board ships flying their flag;

(ii) The exercise of certain policing rights;

(iii) The rights of States relative to the conservation of the living resources of the high seas;

(iv) The institution by a coastal State of a zone contiguous to its coast for the purpose of exercising certain well-defined rights;

(v) The rights of coastal States with regard to the continental shelf.

These matters form the subject of the present articles.

REFERENCE

R. Lapidoth, "Freedom of Navigation and the New Law of the Sea," *Israel Law Review*, Vol. 10 (1976), pp. 456-502.

NOTE

The question of nuclear weapons testing on the high seas gave rise to substantial debate concerning the legality of such tests under principles of international law. Among the contributions to this analysis were: M.S. McDougal, "The Hydrogen Bomb Tests and the International Law of the Sea," *American Journal of International Law*, Vol. 49 (1955), pp. 356-361; M. S. McDougal and N. A. Schlei, "The Hydrogen Bomb Tests in Perspective," *Yale Law Journal*, Vol. 64 (1955), pp. 648-710; "U. S. Replies to Japan on Atom and Hydrogen Bomb Tests," *Department of State Bulletin*, Vol. 36, No. 956 (June 3, 1957), pp. 901-904; E. Margolis, "Hydrogen Bomb Experiments and International Law," *Yale Law Journal*, Vol. 64 (1955), pp. 629-647; G. Schwarzenberger, "The Legality of Nuclear Weapons," *Current Legal Problems*, Vol. 11 (1958), pp. 258, 287-289; M. M. Whiteman, *Digest of International Law*, Vol. IV, Washington, D.C.: United States Government Printing Office, 1965, pp. 544-607.

For the United States, the Soviet Union, and the United Kingdom the issue became moot on October 10, 1963, the effective date of the Treaty Banning Nuclear Weapon Tests in the Atmosphere, In Outer Space and Under Water [1963] 14 U.S.T. 1313, T.I.A.S. No. 5433. That treaty specifically forbids nuclear weapons testing on the high seas [Art I, para. 1(a)]. As of January 1, 1988, 115 nations were parties to the treaty, lending support to the argument that it expressed a rule of customary international law. However, two nuclear powers are not parties, *viz.*, France and the People's Republic of China. As a result, the high seas are not free from nuclear weapons testing by these two nations. See J. E. Mann, "French Nuclear Testing and International Law," *Rutgers Law Review*, Vol. 24 (1969), pp. 144-170; W. K. Ris, Jr., "French Nuclear Testing: A Crisis for International Law," *Denver Journal of International Law and Policy*, Vol. 4 (1974), pp. 111-132; S. A. Tiewul, "International Law and Nuclear Test Explosions on the High Seas," *Cornell International Law Journal*, Vol. 8 (1974), pp. 45-70.

The validity of high seas nuclear testing was brought before the International Court of Justice in 1974 as a result of a series of French nuclear tests in the South Pacific. However, France suspended its tests before the Court rendered an opinion on the merits and the case was thus dismissed as being moot. *Nuclear Tests (Australia v. France), Judgment of 20 December 1974, I. C. J. Reports 1974*, p. 253. See J. B. Elkind, "French Nuclear Testing and Article 41 -- Another

Blow to the Authority of the Court?," *Vanderbilt Journal of Transnational Law*, Vol. 8 (1974), pp. 39-84; SIPRI, *French Nuclear Tests in the Atmosphere: The Question of Legality*, Stockholm: Stockholm International Peace Research Institute, 1974; J. Dugard, "The Nuclear Test Cases and the South West Africa Cases: Some Realism About the International Judicial Decision," *Virginia Journal of International Law*, Vol. 16 (1976), pp. 463-504; J. B. Elkind, "Footnote to the Nuclear Test Cases: Abuse of Right - A Blind Alley for Environmentalists," *Vanderbilt Journal of Transnational Law*, Vol. 9 (1976), pp. 57-98; L. L. Herman, "Nuclear Test Case: Australia v. France; New Zealand v. France," *Dalhousie Law Journal*, Vol. 3 (1976), pp. 288-294.

It should be noted that Article 88 of the 1982 United Nations Convention on the Law of the Sea reserves high seas "for peaceful purposes" only. Whether this prohibits nuclear tests on the high seas is not clear.

1982 UNITED NATIONS CONVENTION ON THE LAW OF THE SEA

PART VII. HIGH SEAS

SECTION 1. GENERAL

Article 86
Application of the provisions of this Part

The provisions of this Part apply to all parts of the sea that are not included in the exclusive economic zone, in the territorial sea or in the internal waters of a State, or in the archipelagic waters of an archipelagic State. This article does not entail any abridgement of the freedoms enjoyed by all States in the exclusive economic zone in accordance with article 58.

Article 58
Rights and duties of other States in the exclusive economic zone

1. In the exclusive economic zone, all States, whether coastal or land-locked, enjoy, subject to the relevant provisions of this Convention, the freedoms referred to in article 87 of navigation and overflight and of the laying of submarine cables and pipelines, and other internationally lawful uses of the sea related to these freedoms such as those associated with the operation of ships, aircraft and submarine cables and pipelines, and compatible with the other provisions of this Convention.

2. Articles 88 and 115 and other pertinent rules of international law apply to the exclusive economic zone in so far as they are not incompatible with this Part.

3. In exercising their rights and performing their duties under this Convention in the exclusive economic zone, States shall have due regard to the rights and duties of the coastal State and shall comply with the laws and regulations adopted by the coastal State in accordance with the provisions of this Convention and other rules of international law in so far as they are not incompatible with this Part.

Article 87
Freedom of the High Seas

1. The high seas are open to all States, whether coastal or land-locked. Freedom of the high seas is exercised under the conditions laid down by this Convention and by other rules of international law. It comprises, *inter alia*, both for coastal and land-locked States:

(a) Freedom of navigation;

(b) Freedom of overflight;

(c) Freedom to lay submarine cables and pipelines, subject to Part VI;

(d) Freedom to construct artificial islands and other installations permitted under international law, subject to Part VI;

(e) Freedom of fishing, subject to the conditions laid down in section 2;

(f) Freedom of scientific research, subject to Parts VI and XIII.

2. These freedoms shall be exercised by all States, with due consideration for the interests of other States in their exercise of the freedom of the high seas, and also with due consideration for the rights under this Convention with respect to activities in the Area.

Article 88
Reservation of the high seas for peaceful purposes

The high seas shall be reserved for peaceful purposes.

Article 89
Invalidity of claims of sovereignty over the high seas

No state may validly purport to subject any part of the high seas to its sovereignty.

REFERENCES

(Freedom of the Sea) George Patrick Smith, III, *Restricting the Concept of Free Seas: Modern Maritime Law Re-evaluated*, Huntington, New York: Robert E. Krieger Publication, 1980; Gordon H. Warren, *Fountain of Discontent: The Trent Affairs and Freedom of the Seas*, Boston: Northeastern University Press, 1981; Ram Prakash Anand, "Freedom of the Sea: Past, Present and Future," in Rafael Gutierrez Girardot and others, eds., *New Directions in International Law: Essays in Honour of Wolfgang Abendroth*, Frankfurt/Main, 1982, pp. 215-233; Malte Diesselhorst, "Hugo Grotius and the Freedom of the Seas," *Grotiana*, Vol. 3 (1982), pp. 11-26; Jon M. Van Dyke and Christopher Yuen, "'Common Heritage' v. 'Freedom of the High Seas': Which Governs the Seabed?" *San Diego Law Review*, Vol. 19 (1982), pp. 493-551; E. D. Brown, "Freedom of the High Seas versus the Common Heritage of Mankind: Fundamental Principles in Conflict," *San Diego Law Review*, Vol. 20 (1983), pp. 521-560; Kay Hailbronner, "Freedom of the Air and the Convention on the Law of the Sea," *American Journal of International Law*, Vol. 77 (1983), pp. 490-520; L. J. Bouchez, "The New Law of the Sea and Right of Overflight," in E. Hey and A. W. Koers, eds., *The International Law of the Sea: Issues of Implementation in*

Indonesia, Rijswijk, The Netherlands: Netherlands Institute of Transport, 1984, pp. 52-58; Louis B. Sohn, "Interdiction of Vessels on the High Seas," *International Lawyer*, Vol. 18 (1984), pp. 411-420; Janusz Symonides, "The Freedoms of the High Seas in the Montego Bay Convention of 1982," *Polish Political Science Yearbook*, Vol. 15 (1985), pp. 171-190.

(Navigation) Edward H. Lueckenhoff, "Free Navigation: Examination of Recent Actions of the United States Coast Guard," *Vanderbilt Journal of Transnational Law*, Vol. 13 (1980), pp. 141-172; P. B. Beazley, "Navigational Implications of the Law of the Sea Conference," *Journal of Navigation*, Vol. 35 (1982), pp. 293-304; Elliot L. Richardson, "Law of the Sea: Navigation and Other Traditional National Security Considerations," *San Diego Law Review*, Vol. 19 (1982), pp. 553-576; Thomas A. Clingan, Jr., "Freedom of Navigation in the Post UNCLOS III Environment," *Law and Contemporary Problems*, Vol. 46 (1983), pp. 107-146; D. Uzunov, "Regime of Navigation in the Light of the 1982 UN Convention on the Law of the Sea," *Soviet Yearbook of Maritime Law*, 1984, pp. 95-97; Pyotr D. Barabolya, "Changes in the Legal Regime of the Sea and Their Influence on Navigation," in Budislav Vukas, ed., *Essays on the New Law of the Sea*, Zagreb, Yugoslavia: Faculty of Law, University of Zagreb, 1985, pp. 189-201; P. J. Slot, "The International Legal Regime for Navigation," *Ocean Development and International Law*, Vol. 15 (1985), pp. 89-98.

NOTE

In June 1977, the *Washington Post* reported French newspapers as saying that the Soviet Union was using an iceberg off northern Canada as a floating "spy base," conceivably for use in providing navigational assistance to Soviet submarines. The iceberg housed some 160 Soviets and was located north of Canada's Queen Elizabeth Islands and west of Greenland. The article also noted that the United States made similar use of icebergs for "surveillance purposes." See "Soviet Spies Said to Use Iceberg Base," *Washington Post*, June 26, 1977, p. 18.

Is this a recognized freedom of the high seas? Do such icebergs, when occupied, become territory of the occupying nation? Do such icebergs generate territorial waters? Does freedom of overflight (for counter-surveillance) apply to such floating ice masses? Who would have jurisdiction over criminal acts committed on such an ice island?

Article 88 of the 1982 United Nations Convention on the Law of the Sea provides that the high seas "shall be reserved for peaceful purposes." However, it is widely regarded as prohibiting only acts of aggression on the high seas, and will certainly be interpreted in that way by naval powers. See R. R. Churchill and A. V. Lowe, *The Law of the Sea*, 2nd ed., Manchester: Manchester University Press, 1988, p. 176.

For further references, see Oliver J. Lissitzyn, "Electronic Reconnaissance from the High Seas and International Law," in Richard B. Lillich and John Norton Moore, *Readings in International Law from the Naval War College Review 1947-1977*, Vol. I, *Role of International Law and Evolving Ocean Law*, Newport, Rhode Island: Naval War College, 1980, pp. 563-571; Myers S. McDougal, "Authority to Use Force on the High Seas," in ibid., pp. 551-562; "Exclusion of Ships from Nonterritorial Weapons Testing Zone," *Harvard Law Review*, Vol. 99 (1986), pp. 1040-1058; Boleslaw A. Boczek, "Peaceful Purposes Provisions of the United Nations Convention on the Law of the Sea," *Ocean Development and International Law*, Vol. 20 (1989), pp. 359-390; Owen Pawson, "Implications of Floating Communities for International Law," *Marine Policy Report*, Vol. 1, No. 2 (1989), pp. 101-118.

Restatement on the Foreign Relations Law of the United States, Third Revision, Vol. 2, St. Paul, Minn.: American Law Institute, 1987, p. 81. Reprinted by permission.

Section 521, Editors' Notes:

2. *Overflight and air defense.* The United States has established air defense areas, air defense identification zones (ADIZ), and, for Alaska, a distant early warning identification zone (DEWIZ). Some of these zones extend several hundred miles into the sea. Pilots entering these zones are obliged to report promptly and to provide specific data to United States authorities; a foreign aircraft not complying with this requirement is not permitted to enter the air space of the United States. See 14 C.F.R. § 99.23.

Similar zones have been established by other states. These zones have been generally accepted. It is uncertain, however, whether a coastal state can apply such regulations to aircraft passing through its declared air defense zone but not planning to enter its airspace. See Note, "Air Defense Identification Zones: Creeping Jurisdiction in the Airspace," 18 Va. J. Int'l L. 485 (1978); 4 Whiteman, Digest of International Law 496-97 (1965). See also § 511, Comment *k*.

C.   ENCLOSED AND SEMI-ENCLOSED SEAS

At the 1958 U.N. Conference on the Law of the Sea, Romania and the Ukrainian Soviet Socialist Republic proposed additional language for Article 1 of the Convention on the High Seas providing that "[f]or certain seas a special regime of navigation may be established for historical reasons or by virtue of international agreements" (U.N. Doc. A/CONF.13/C.2/L.26, [First] United Nations Conference on the Law of the Sea, *Official Records*, Vol. IV, p. 123). The United States, the United Kingdom, and others argued against the proposal on the ground that it was an opening wedge for "closed seas." According to the United States delegate the Soviet Union's concept of "closed seas" included: (1) seas communicating with other seas through one or several narrow straits and surrounded by the territory of a limited number of states, the regime of the straits being regulated by international agreement, and (2) seas surrounded by the territory of a limited number of states where the straits were not regulated by international agreement. *Official Records*, Vol. IV, p. 37. Obvious targets of the Soviet proposal were the Black Sea, the Baltic Sea, the Sea of Okhotsk, and the Sea of Japan. The Soviet Union argued that the proposal:

> [d]ealt with the special regimes of navigation which might be required for seas bounded by a limited number of states and communicating with the high seas only by a channel skirting the shores of the coastal states. . . .
> The importance of a special regime of navigation for those seas was due to the security requirements of the coastal states which had to be borne in mind in consequence of numerous historical circumstances or the conclusion of international agreements.

Official Records, Vol. IV, p. 40.

The Romanian representative argued that the proposal had its genesis in the commentary of the I.L.C. to Draft Article 26 which noted that "[t]hese rules may, however, be modified for historical reasons or by international agreement." *Official Records*, Vol. IV, p. 38. However, the Turkish representative pointed out that the I.L.C. Language arose over the question of internal waters only, and that the Soviet representative to the I.L. C. had so understood the language. *Official Records*, Vol. IV, p. 39. The representative of the United Kingdom noted that the I.L.C. had intended to refer to the "familiar cases of seas entirely surrounded by one coastal state, the access to which was bordered in both sides by that same state," *Official Records*, Vol. IV, p. 38. In the face of substantial opposition, the proposal was ultimately withdrawn and never voted upon. *Official Records*, Vol. IV, p. 53.

REFERENCES

(1) On the status of the Black Sea, see I. Brownlie, *Principles of Public International Law*, London and New York: Oxford University Press, 1966, pp. 207-208; C. J. Colombos, *The International Law of the Sea*, 6th ed., London: Longmans, 1967, pp. 192-193, 216-220.

(2) On the status of the Baltic Sea, see Brownlie, pp. 207-208; Colombos, pp. 193-194; B. Johnson "The Baltic Conventions," *International and Comparative Law Quarterly*, Vol. 25 (1976), pp. 1-14.

(3) On the status of the Sea of Okhotsk, see Dean W. Given, "The Sea of Okhotsk: USSR's Great Lake?" *U.S. Naval Institute Proceedings*, Vol. 96, No. 9 (1970), pp. 46-51.

(4) On the Soviet Union's view generally concerning semi-enclosed seas, see W. N. Harben, "Soviet Attitudes and Practices Concerning Maritime Waters; A Recent Historical Survey," *JAG Journal*, Vol. 15 Oct. - Nov. (1961), pp. 149-154; W. E. Butler, *The Law of Soviet Territorial Waters: A Case Study of Maritime Legislation and Practice*, New York: Praeger, 1967, Chs. 2-3; W. E. Bulter, "The Legal Regime of Russian Territorial Waters," *American Journal of International Law*, Vol. 62 (1968), pp. 51, 56-59; W. E. Butler, "Some Recent Developments in Soviet Maritime Law," *The International Lawyer*, Vol. 4 (1970), pp. 695, 700-702.

(5) On the status of Hudson Bay, see Thomas W. Balch, "Is Hudson Bay a Closed or an Open Sea?" *American Journal of International Law*, Vol. 6 (1912), pp. 409-459; Thomas W. Balch, "The Hudsonian Sea is a Great Open Sea," *American Journal of International Law*, Vol. 7 (1913), pp. 546-565; V. K. Johnston, "Canada's Title to Hudson Bay and Hudson Strait," *British Yearbook of International Law*, Vol. 15 (1934), pp. 10-20; C.J. Colombos, p. 186.

(6) On the status of the Great Lakes (U.S.-Canada), see Nicholas V. Olds, "The Law of the Lakes," *Michigan State Bar Journal*, Vol. 44, No. 2 (1965), pp. 14-20; D. C. Piper, *The International Law of the Great Lakes: A Study of Canadian-United States Co-operation*, Durham, North Carolina: Duke University Press, 1967.

1982 UNITED NATIONS CONVENTION OF THE LAW OF THE SEA

PART IX

ENCLOSED OR SEMI-ENCLOSED SEAS

Article 122
Definition

For the purpose of this Convention, "enclosed or semi-enclosed sea" means a gulf, basin or sea surrounded by two or more States and connected to another sea or the ocean by a narrow outlet or consisting entirely or primarily of the territorial seas and exclusive economic zones of two or more coastal States.

Article 123
Co-operation of States bordering enclosed or semi-enclosed seas

States bordering an enclosed or semi-enclosed sea should co-operate with each other in the exercise of their rights and in the performance of their duties under this Convention. To this end they shall endeavour, directly or through an appropriate regional organization:

(a) to co-ordinate the management, conservation, exploration and exploitation of the living resources of the sea;

(b) to co-ordinate the implementation of their rights and duties with respect to the protection and preservation of the marine environment;

(c) to co-ordinate their scientific research policies and undertake where appropriate joint programmes of scientific research in the area;

(d) to invite, as appropriate, other interested States or international organizations to co-operate with them in furtherance of the provisions of this article.

THIRD UNITED NATIONS CONFERENCE ON THE LAW OF THE SEA
SECOND COMMITTEE, 38TH MEETING
August 13, 1974
Third United Nations Conference on the Law of
the Sea, 1973 - 1982, *Official Records*, Vol. II
(Second Session), pp. 273, 276, 277.

1. *Mr. KAZEMI* (Iran) said that the particular cases of enclosed and semi-enclosed seas raised difficult problems which could not be solved within the framework of regional or bilateral agreements. Semi-enclosed seas were distributed all along the margin of the continents at varying distances from the major oceanic basin, which was why they were often called marginal seas. There were between 40 and 50 such seas in different regions of the world. Semi-enclosed seas like the Baltic, the Black Sea and the Persian Gulf fell into a special category because of the small volume of their waters and their single outlet to the ocean.

2. The problems raised by the semi-enclosed seas with regard to the management of their resources, international navigation and the preservation of the marine environment justified granting them a particular status constituting an exception to the general rule. When worked out on a regional basis, that status would obviously have to take into account the needs and interests of all the coastal States in the region.

3. As to the management of resources, the fact that the total area of the semi-enclosed seas lay above the continental shelf of the coastal States justified the working out of a special regime. In the connexion, the delimitation of the various areas of jurisdiction would present problems which were peculiar to semi-enclosed seas and which would have to be solved on the basis of the principles of justice, equity and equidistance. . . .

4. Apart from problems of delimitation, the exploitation of exclusive fishery zones in semi-enclosed seas raised a number of questions with regard to the preservation of species, and solutions would have to be tailored to fit the particular situation of those seas.

5. With regard to the international navigation in semi-enclosed seas, there was of course a marked difference between the coastal States of those seas, on the one hand, for which freedom of passage through straits connecting those seas to the oceans was vital to their trade and communications, and on the other hand all other States. Such freedom of passage must be fully guaranteed for the former category of States. However, a different regime should apply to the navigation of other States whose ships could pass through straits connecting the oceans with semi-enclosed seas only for the purpose of calling at one of the ports of the semi-enclosed sea.

6. The semi-enclosed seas were highly vulnerable to pollution owing to the small volume of their waters, which lowered their capacity for absorption, and the absence of currents to change the waters. A number of semi-enclosed seas like the Persian Gulf were the scene of intensive petroleum production and of heavy tanker traffic, which increased the threat of pollution . . . .

8. With regard to scientific research, semi-enclosed seas were not of great interest since the geomorphological structure of their basins was quite uncomplicated and had already been studied by numerous scientific expeditions. . . .

34. *Mr. QUENEUDEC* (France) said that the expression "enclosed or semi-enclosed seas" was not a traditional concept of international law. The notion of "enclosed seas" seemed rather to be a purely geographical one; the legal rules applicable to them were not part of international public maritime law and the Conference should not concern itself with them. The idea of "semi-enclosed seas" was extremely vague. The inclusion of the item in the agenda tended to give an ambiguous formula legal status.

35. Undoubtedly, the geographical situation of the coastal States of a semi-enclosed sea obliged them, in certain circumstances, to become aware of the links that bound them or to consider themselves coastal States in relation to a sort of interior sea. However, to make those maritime spaces subject to special rules would be to resuscitate the Roman formula of *mare nostrum*, with the consequent risk of establishing a *mare clausum*. What, in any case, was the purpose of the exercise?

36. It was inconceivable that the idea was to restrict the freedom of navigation and overflight in areas considered to be semi-enclosed seas. The institution of 200-mile economic zones would place all the renewable and non-renewable resources of the maritime areas concerned under the jurisdiction of the coastal States and there was thus no need for those coastal States to demand special provisions for semi-enclosed seas in the Convention; regional agreements should suffice. As far as preservation of the marine environment was concerned, the maritime areas in question were, like necessary in certain special circumstances, such as those recognized in a number of international conventions. There too, there was no need to establish a new legal category to solve the problems that might arise.

37. For the reasons stated, his delegation felt that there would be more disadvantages than advantages in introducing into the law of the sea a concept that was ambiguous and was not in conformity with the interests of the international community. . . .

49. *Mr. BARABOLYA* (Union of Soviet Socialist Republics) said he wished to draw attention to certain peculiarities of the problem under discussion. Firstly, a clear distinction must

be made between enclosed and semi-enclosed seas. From a juridical point of view, enclosed seas were comparatively small, had no outlet to the ocean, and did not serve as international shipping routes in the broadest sense. Such seas should be subject to specific regimes established by existing international agreements and international custom. Semi-enclosed seas, on the other hand, were large bodies of water with several outlets through which passed international waterways. They had never been subject to any special regime. Almost any sea could be called semi-enclosed, and it would be quite unjustified to compare such seas with enclosed seas. His country could not accept the establishment of a special regime benefiting any given country in waters that had traditionally been used by all countries for international shipping on a basis of equality. The question of enclosed seas had both a geographical and a juridical aspect. Was the Mediterranean, for example, an enclosed or semi-enclosed sea? He would say it was neither. It contained many other seas and could be compared to an ocean. It was an immense body of water used as a high sea by all countries for international shipping.

50. Another peculiarity of the issue was that the Geneva Conference had not laid down principles for enclosed seas, although the International Law Commission had confirmed the usefulness of extending a special regime to some seas. No specific proposals had been put forward in the Sea-Bed Committee, with the exception of a proposal submitted by Turkey; so there was only one chapter heading for the issue in the Committee's report. Nevertheless the question had been raised, mainly in connexion with the problem of the delimitation of marine areas. That question had recently become of some current interest as a result of the prospect of establishing economic zones of a breadth of up to 200 miles. Although the question of economic zones would cause no problems where the coastlines faced the open sea, it would create a number of problems in enclosed or semi-enclosed seas, as the representative of Turkey had pointed out, particularly in connexion with the delimitation of sea areas between States.

51. The point at issue was not a regime for enclosed seas, but the possibility of taking a regional approach to certain questions in specific marine areas where the application of certain provisions of international marine law by one coastal State might affect the rights and interests of other States. His country's position was that in those specific regions regional decisions on questions of sea law could be taken only within the framework of the international convention to be adopted by the Conference. Solutions to problems must be arrived at by agreement between the coastal States concerned, without prejudice to the legitimate interests of other countries of the world.

REFERENCES

A. B. Miller, "Ecological Balance in Semi-Enclosed Seas," *Environmental Affairs*, Vol. 2 (No. 1)(1972), pp. 191-203; L. M. Alexander, "Special Circumstances: Semi-Enclosed Seas," in J. K. Gamble and G. Pontecorvo, eds., *The Law of the Sea: The Emerging Regime of the Oceans*, Cambridge, Mass: Ballinger, 1974, pp. 201-215; L. M. Alexander, "Regionalism and the Law of the Sea: The Case of Semi-Enclosed Seas," *Ocean Development and International Law Journal*, Vol. 2 (1974), pp. 151-186; M. Hardy, "Regional Approaches to Law of the Sea Problems: The European Community," *International and Comparative Law Quarterly*, Vol. 24 (1975), pp. 336-348; M. W. Janis, "The Roles of Regional Law of the Sea," *San Diego Law Review*, Vol. 12 (1975), pp. 553-568; R. K. Walker and J. L. McNish, "Toward a Model Regional Fisheries Management Regime: An Immodest Proposal," *Kansas Law Review*, Vol. 23 (1975), pp. 461-497; L. M. Alexander, *Regional Arrangements in Ocean Affairs*, Washington D.C.: Fleet Analysis and Support Division, Office of Naval Research, 1977; C. O. Okidi, "Toward Regional Arrangements for Regulation of Marine Pollution: An Appraisal of Options," *Ocean Development and International Law*, Vol. 4 (1977), pp. 1-25; D. M. Johnson, ed., *Regionalisation of the Law of the Sea*, Cambridge, Mass.: Ballinger 1978; M. J. Valencia, "Southeast Asia: National Marine Interests and Marine Regionalism," *Ocean Development and International Law.*, Vol. 5 (1978), pp. 421-476; B. Buzan, "Maritime Issues in Northeast Asia: Their Impact on Regional Politics," *Marine Policy*, Vol. 3(3) (1979), pp. 190-200; M. E. Goncalves, "Concepts of Marine Region and the New Law of the Sea," *Marine Policy*, Vol. 3(4) (1979), pp. 255-263.

D. PROBLEM OF LAND-LOCKED STATES

1958 CONVENTION ON THE TERRITORIAL SEA AND THE CONTIGUOUS ZONE

Article 14

1. Subject to the provisions of these articles, ships of all States, whether coastal or not, shall enjoy the right of innocent passage through the territorial sea.

1958 CONVENTION ON THE HIGH SEAS

Article 2

. . . Freedom of the high seas . . . comprises, *inter alia*, both for coastal and non-coastal States:

(1) Freedom of navigation;

Article 3

1. In order to enjoy the freedom of the seas on equal terms with coastal States, States having no sea-coast should have free access to the sea. To this end States situated between the sea and a State having no sea-coast shall by common agreement with the latter and in conformity with existing international conventions accord:

(a) To the State having no sea-coast, on a basis of reciprocity, free transit through their territory; and

(b) To ships flying the flag of that State treatment equal to that accorded to their own ships, or to the ships of any other State, as regards access to seaports and the use of such ports.

2. States situated between the sea and a State having no sea-coast shall settle, by mutual agreement with the latter, and taking into account the rights of the coastal State or State of transit and the special conditions of the State having no sea-coast, all matters relating to freedom of transit and equal treatment in ports, in case such States are not already parties to existing international conventions.

Article 4

Every State, whether coastal or not, has the right to sail ships under its flag on the high seas.

NOTE

Article 17 of the 1982 United Nations Convention on the Law of the Sea is identical with Article 14 of the 1958 Territorial Sea Convention, except the phrase "this Convention" is used to replace "the provisions of these articles" in the 1958 Convention. Article 3 of the 1958 High Seas Convention is replaced by Articles 124 to 132 of the 1982 Convention (*see infra*). Article 90 of the 1982 Convention is identical with Article 4 of the 1958 Convention.

CONVENTION ON TRANSIT TRADE OF LAND-LOCKED STATES
Done at New York July 8, 1965
19 UST 7383; TIAS 6592; 597 UNTS 42.

Article 1
Definitions

For the purpose of this Convention,

(a) the term "land-locked State" means any Contracting State which has no sea-coast;

(b) the term "traffic in transit" means the passage of goods including unaccompanied baggage across the territory of a Contracting State between a land-locked State and the sea when the passage is a portion of a complete journey which begins or terminates within the territory of that land-locked State and which includes sea transport directly preceding or following such passage. The trans-shipment, warehousing, breaking bulk, and change in the mode of transport of such goods as well as the assembly, disassembly or reassembly of machinery and bulky goods shall not render the passage of goods outside the definition of "traffic in transit" provided that any such operation is undertaken solely for the convenience of transportation. Nothing in this paragraph shall be construed as imposing an obligation on any Contracting State to establish or permit the establishment of permanent facilities on its territory for such assembly, disassembly or reassembly;

(c) the term "transit State" means any Contracting State with or without a sea-coast, situated between a land-locked State and the sea, through whose territory "traffic in transit" passes;

Article 2
Freedom of transit

1. Freedom of transit shall be granted under the terms of this Convention for traffic in transit and means of transport. Subject to the other provisions of this Convention, the measures taken by Contracting States for regulating and forwarding traffic across their territory shall facilitate traffic in transit on routes in use mutually acceptable for transit to the Contracting States concerned. Consistent with the terms of this Convention, no discrimination shall be exercised which is based on the place of origin, departure, entry, exit or destination or on any circumstances relating to the ownership of the goods or the ownership, place of registration or flag of vessels, land vehicles or other means of transport used.

2. The rules governing the use of means of transport, when they pass across part or the whole of the territory of another Contracting State, shall be established by common agreement among the Contracting States concerned, with due regard to the multilateral international conventions to which these States are parties.

3. Each Contracting State shall authorize, in accordance with its laws, rules and regulations, the passage across or access to its territory of persons whose movement is necessary for traffic in transit.

4. The Contracting States shall permit the passage of traffic in transit across their territorial waters in accordance with the principles of customary international law or applicable international conventions and with their internal regulations.

. . . .

Article 11
Exceptions to Convention on grounds of public health, security, and protection of intellectual property

1. No Contracting State shall be bound by this Convention to afford transit to persons whose admission into its territory is forbidden, or for goods of a kind of which the importation is prohibited, either on grounds of public morals, public health or security, or as a precaution against diseases of animals or plants or against pests.

2. Each Contracting State shall be entitled to take reasonable precautions and measures to ensure that persons and goods, particularly goods which are the subject of a monopoly, are really in transit, and that the means of transport are really used for the passage of such goods, as well as to protect the safety of the routes and means of communication.

3. Nothing in this Convention shall affect the measures which a Contracting State may be called upon to take in pursuance of provisions in a general international convention, whether of a world-wide or regional character, to which it is a party, whether such convention was already concluded on the date of this Convention or is concluded later, when such provisions relate:

(a) to export or import or transit of particular kinds of articles such as narcotics, or other dangerous drugs, or arms; or

(b) to protection of industrial, literary or artistic property, or protection of trade names, and indications of source or appellations of origin, and the suppression of unfair competition.

4. Nothing in this Convention shall prevent any Contracting State from taking any action necessary for the protection of its essential security interests.

Article 12
Exceptions in case of emergency

The measures of a general or particular character which a Contracting State is obliged to take in case of an emergency endangering its political existence or its safety may, in exceptional cases and for as short a period as possible, involve a deviation from the provisions of this Convention on the understanding that the principle of freedom of transit shall be observed to the utmost possible extent during such a period.

NOTE

As of December 31, 1988, the following states were parties to the Transit Trade Convention [Note: (1) indicates a landlocked state; (2) indicates a coastal state with at least one landlocked bordering state]:

Australia	Nepal (1)
Belgium (2)	Netherlands
Burkina Faso (1) (formerly Upper Volta)	Niger (1)
Burundi (1)	Nigeria (2)
Byelorussian S.S.R. (1)	Norway
Chad (1)	Rwanda (1)
Chile (2)	San Marino (1)
Czechoslovakia (1)	Senegal (2)
Denmark	Swaziland (1)
Finland	Sweden
Hungary (1)	Turkey
Laos (1)	Ukranian S.S.R.
Lesotho (1)	U.S.S.R. (2)
Malawi (1)	United States
Mali (1)	Yugoslavia (2)
Mongolia (1)	Zambia (1)

See *Multilateral Treaties Deposited with the Secretary-General, Status as at 31 December 1988*, New York: The United Nations, 1989, p. 338. For a study of this Convention, see J. H. E. Fried, "The New Convention on Transit Trade of Land-Locked States and the Development of Law Under United Nations Auspices," *Journal of the Tribhuban University* (Department of Political Science, Kathmandu), 1966, pp. 16-29; J. H. E. Fried, "The 1965 Convention on Transit Trade of Land-Locked States," *Indian Journal of International Law*, Vol. 6 (1966), pp. 9-30; R. Makil, "Transit Rights of Land-Locked Countries; An Appraisal of International Conventions," *Journal of World Trade Law*, Vol. 4 (1970), pp. 35-51.

It should be noted that only six coastal states with land-locked neighboring states have seen fit to ratify the Convention, providing benefits only for Afghanistan, Austria, Bolivia, Chad, Czechoslovakia, Hungary, Luxembourg, Mali, Mongolia and Niger.

A relatively current but classic case of a land-locked nation seeking a corridor to the sea involves Bolivia, Chile, and Peru. In the 1879 "War of the Pacific" Bolivia lost a narrow strip of coastline to Chile. Now, although Chile appears willing to negotiate some sort of settlement with Bolivia, the 1929 Treaty of Santiago obligates Chile not to make any such agreement without the consent of Peru since the area was once subject to Peruvian sovereignty. For further study of this question, see J. H. Merryman and E. D. Ackerman, *International Legal Development and the Transit Trade of Land-locked States: The Case of Bolivia*, Hamburg: n.p., 1969;

"Venezuela Backs Bolivian Sea Outlet," *Washington Post*, August 7, 1975, p. A20; "Bolivia Pressing for Route to Sea," *New York Times*, October 19, 1975, p. 5; "Bolivia Still Seeks the Sea," *Washington Post*, May 6, 1976, p. A-21; "Bolivia Gets Free Zone in Key Argentine Port," *New York Times*, July 7, 1976, p. 5; "Peru proposes Bolivia passage," *The Sun* (Baltimore), November 21, 1976, p. A6; Juan de Onis, "Bolivia Seeks Corridor to Sea But Fears War," *New York Times*, December 9, 1976, p. 13; Enrique Zileri Gibson, "Seaward Bolivia," *New York Times*, October 28, 1979, p. E19; M. I. Glassner, "The Transit Problem of Land-locked States: The Cases of Bolivia and Paraguay," *Ocean Yearbook*, Vol. 4 (1983), pp. 366-389.

For other land-locked states, see Z. Cervenka, ed., *Land-Locked Countries of Africa*, Uppsala: Scandinavian Institute of African Studies, 1973; A. Sarup, "TransitTrade of Land-Locked Nepal, "*International and Comparative Law Quarterly*, Vol. 21 (1972), pp. 287-306; T. K. Jayaraman and O. L. Shrestha, "Some Trade Problems of Land-locked Nepal," *Asian Survey*, Vol. 16 (1976), pp. 1113-1123; M. I. Glassner, *Transit Problems of Three Asian Land-Locked Countries: Afghanistan, Nepal and Laos*, Baltimore: University of Maryland School of Law Occasional Papers/Reprints Series in Contemporary Asian Studies, No. 4-1983 (57).

LIST OF LANDLOCKED STATES

Name	Area (mi^2)	Population (1989)	Neighboring Coastal States
AFRICA			
Botswana	224,607	1,250,000	Namibia, South Africa
Bukina Faso (formerly Upper Volta)	105,869	8,714,000	Benin (formerly Dahomey), Ghana, Ivory Coast, Togo
Burundi	10,747	5,287,000	Tanzania, Zaire
Cen. African Rep.	240,324	2,813,000	Cameroon, Congo Rep., Sudan, Zaire
Chad	495,755	5,538,000	Cameroon, Libya, Sudan
Lesotho	11,720	1,715,000	South Africa
Malawi	45,747	8,515,000	Mozambique, Tanzania
Mali	478,841	7,911,000	Algeria, Guinea, Ivory Coast, Senegal

LIST OF LANDLOCKED STATES

Name	Area (mi²)	Population (1989)	Neighboring Coastal States
Niger	458,075	7,523,000	Algeria, Benin, Libya, Nigeria
Rwanda	10,169	6,989,000	Tanzania, Zaire
Swaziland	6,704	746,000	Mozambique, South Africa
Uganda	93,070	16,452,000	Kenya, Sudan, Tanzania, Zaire
Zambia	290,586	8,148,000	Angola, Mozambique, Tanzania, Zaire
Zimbabwe	150,873	9,122,000	Mozambique, South Africa
ASIA			
Afghanistan	251,825	14,825,000	Iran, Pakistan, USSR
Bhutan	18,150	1,408,000	China, India
Laos	91,400	3,936,000	Cambodia [Democratic Kampuchea], Thailand, Viet Nam
Mongolia	604,800	2,096,000	China, USSR
Nepal	56,827	18,452,000	China, India
EUROPE			
Andorra	181	50,000	France, Spain
Austria	32,377	7,603,000	Germany, Italy, Yugoslavia
Czechoslovakia	49,382	15,636,000	Germany, Poland, USSR

LIST OF LANDLOCKED STATES

Name	Area (mi²)	Population (1989)	Neighboring Coastal States
Hungary	35,920	10,580,000	Rumania, USSR, Yugoslavia
Liechtenstein	61.8	28,300	None (borders Switzerland and Austria
Luxembourg	999	377,000	Belgium, France, Germany
San Marino	23.63	22,860	Italy
Switzerland	15,943	6,689,000	France, Germany, Italy
Vatican	0.2	1,000	Italy
SOUTH AMERICA			
Bolivia	424,164	7,193,000	Argentina, Brazil, Chile, Peru
Paraguay	157,048	4,157,000	Argentina, Brazil

List of Land-Locked States
Figure 7-1

Source: 1990 Britannica Book of the Year, Chicago: Encyclopaedia Britannica, Inc., 1990. Vatican's information is from *Information Please Almanac, Atlas and Yearbook 1986*, 39th ed., Boston: Houghton Mifflin Co., 1986, p. 291. Land-locked countries constitute about 8.5% of the land of the world and 4% of the population of the world.

1982 UNITED NATIONS CONVENTION ON THE LAW OF THE SEA

PART X

RIGHT OF ACCESS OF LAND-LOCKED STATES TO AND FROM THE SEA AND FREEDOM OF TRANSIT

Article 124
Use of Terms

1. For the purposes of this Convention:

(a) "land-locked State" means a State which has no sea-coast;

(b) "transit State" means a State, with or without a sea-coast, situated between a land-locked State and the sea, through whose territory traffic in transit passes;

(c) "traffic in transit" means transit of persons, baggage, goods and means of transport across the territory of one or more transit States, when the passage across such territory, with or without trans-shipment, warehousing, breaking bulk or change in the mode of transport, is only a portion of a complete journey which begins or terminates within the territory of the land-locked State;

(d) "means of transport" means:
      (i) railway rolling stock, sea, lake and river craft and road vehicles;
      (ii) where local conditions so require, porters and pack animals.

2. Land-locked States and transit States may, by agreement between them, include as means of transport pipelines and gas lines and means of transport other than those included in paragraph 1.

Article 125
Right of access to and from the sea and freedom of transit

1. Land-locked States shall have the right of access to and from the sea for the purpose of exercising the rights provided for in this Convention including those relating to the freedom of the high seas and the common heritage of mankind. To this end, land-locked States shall enjoy freedom of transit through the territory of transit States by all means of transport.

2. The terms and modalities for exercising freedom of transit shall be agreed between the land-locked States and transit States concerned through bilateral, subregional or regional agreements.

3. Transit States, in the exercise of their full sovereignty over their territory, shall have the right to take all measures necessary to ensure that the rights and facilities provided for in this Part for land-locked States shall in no way infringe their legitimate interests.

Article 126
Exclusion of application of the most-favored-nation clause

The provisions of this Convention, as well as special agreements relating to the exercise of the right of access to and from the sea, establishing rights and facilities on account of the special geographical position of land-locked States, are excluded from the application of the most-favored-nation clause.

Article 127
Customs duties, taxes and other charges

1. Traffic in transit shall not be subject to any customs duties, taxes or other charges except charges levied for specific services rendered in connection with such traffic.

2. Means of transport in transit and other facilities provided for and used by land-locked States shall not be subject to taxes or charges higher than those levied for the use of means of transport of the transit State.

Article 128
Free zones and other customs facilities

For the convenience of traffic in transit, free zones or other customs facilities may be provided at the ports of entry and exit in the transit States, by agreement between those States and the land-locked States.

Article 129
Co-operation in the construction and improvement of means of transport

Where there are no means of transport in transit States to give effect to the freedom of transit or where the existing means, including the port installations and equipment, are inadequate in any respect, the transit States and land-locked States concerned may co-operate in constructing or improving them.

Article 130
Measures to avoid or eliminate delays or other difficulties of a technical nature in traffic in transit

1. Transit States shall take all appropriate measures to avoid delays or other difficulties of a technical nature in traffic in transit.

2. Should such delays or difficulties occur, the competent authorities of the transit States and land-locked States concerned shall co-operate towards their expeditious elimination.

Article 131
Equal treatment in maritime ports

Ships flying the flag of land-locked States shall enjoy treatment equal to that accorded to other foreign ships in maritime ports.

Article 132
Grant of greater transit facilities

This Convention does not entail in any way the withdrawal of transit facilities which are greater than those provided for in this Convention and which are agreed between States Parties to this Convention or granted by a State Party. This Convention also does not preclude such grant of greater facilities in the future.

REFERENCES

E. Lauterpacht, "Freedom of Transit in International Law," *Transactions of the Grotius Society*, Vol. 44 (1958-1959), pp. 313-356; N. J. G. Pounds, "A Free and Secure Access to the Sea," *Annals of the Association of American Geographers*, Vol. 49 (September 1959), pp., 256-268; M. I. Glassner, *Access to the Sea for Developing Land-Locked States*, The Hague: Martinus Nijhoff, 1970; V. C. Govindaraj, "Land-Locked States and Their Right of Access to the Sea," *Indian Journal of International Law*, Vol. 14 (1974), pp. 190-216; L. C. Caflisch, "The Access of Land-locked States to the Sea," *Revue Iranienne des Relations Internationales*, Vols. 5-6 (1975-76), pp. 53-76; A. Mpazi Sinjela, *Land-Locked States and the UNCLOS Regime*, New York: Oceana Publications, 1983, Chapter 3; Uys VanZyl, "Access to the Sea for Land-Locked States," *Sea Changes*, Vol. 6 (1987), pp. 112-133. For further references, see M. I. Glassner, ed., *Bibliography on Land-Locked States*, 2nd ed., Dordrecht, The Netherlands: Nijhoff, 1986; Kishor Uprety, *Land-locked States and Access to the Sea* (Toward a Universal Law), Katmandu: Nepal Law Society, 1989.

E. THE NATIONALITY OF SHIPS AND THE QUESTION OF THE FLAG OF CONVENIENCE

1. The Question of Stateless Ships

> Andrew W. Anderson, "Jurisdiction Over Stateless Vessels on the High Seas: An Appraisal Under Domestic and International Law," *Journal of Maritime Law and Commerce*, Vol. 13 (1982), pp. 327-328, 329-330, 334-337. Some notes omitted. Reprinted by permission of the Anderson Publishing Co. and the author.

[The Biaggi Act, P.L. 96-350, 94 Stat. 1159 (1980) amends the provisions of the 1970 Comprehensive] Drug Abuse Prevention and Control Act by adding a new section, 21 U.S.C. §955a, which explicitly prohibits any person on board a United States vessel, or *on board a vessel subject to the jurisdiction of the United States on the high seas* to knowingly or intentionally manufacture or distribute, or possess with intent to manufacture or distribute, a controlled substance. There need not be any proof that the United States is the destination of the controlled substance: possession alone is sufficient. The law further prohibits similar acts by American citizens on board any vessel, or by any persons on board any vessel within the customs waters of the United States. A broad prohibition was also included against any person, wherever located, who possesses, distributes or manufactures a controlled substance intending or knowing that it will be unlawfully imported into the United States. There have been few challenges to most of these provisions, as they fit well within most common principles of criminal legislation.

The provision extending United States jurisdiction to "any person . . . on board a vessel subject to the jurisdiction of the United States on the high seas. . ." has been the subject of intense debate.

The term "vessel subject to the jurisdiction of the United States" is further defined by the Act as including ". . . a vessel without nationality or a vessel assimilated to a vessel without nationality, in accordance with paragraph (2) of article 6 of the Convention on the High Seas, 1958."

Prosecutions under 21 U.S.C. §955a have repeatedly been attacked, albeit with limited success thus far, on the grounds that there is no jurisdiction over a stateless vessel. The court, it is argued by defense attorneys, lacks subject matter jurisdiction because under international law Congress lacked authority to extend United States law to a non-United States vessel on the high seas. It is argued, alternatively that even if Congress has such authority, §955a is invalid as applied to non-United States citizens on non-United States vessels because that such application would be a violation of international law, and the legislative history shows Congress intended to comply with international law, and not to violate it. . . .

The examination of whether United States courts should give effect to the authority claimed by Congress over vessels without nationality necessitates venturing into some fundamental areas of constitutional and international law. First, the question must be raised as to whether the defendants have the standing under international law to raise it as a bar to their prosecution. Normally, the rights and immunities granted under international law are given to nations and through them, to their citizens.[1] Violations of international law must be raised by nations on behalf of citizens. Although, for example, it is an acknowledged violation of international law for one nation to enforce its law within the sovereign territory of another nation without permission, the wrong is one under international and not domestic law. The person so arrested cannot raise it when he is brought before United States courts. The wrong, if any, is against the sovereignty and jurisdiction of the foreign nation and is for it to raise it as a defense. If the defendants were apprehended on a vessel without a nationality and their prosecution is not a violation of international law, then the absence of any international protest by the country of vessel registration or the country of the defendants' citizenship is evidence of its propriety under international law. In some cases, not even nations have standing under international law to raise treaty violations as a defense. In *United States v. Monroy*[2], the Fifth Circuit held that where a vessel was determined to be registered in a country which had not signed the Convention on the High Seas (Panama), neither the defendants boarded and arrested by the Coast Guard nor the Republic of Panama could raise restrictions of the treaty on the exercise of jurisdiction over foreign vessels on the high seas as a bar to prosecution. The court also held that the treaty protections were not available to defendants on a stateless vessel. . . .

The international law of the sea is conspicuously silent on the issue of stateless vessels, because the entire legal regime of the high seas is predicated on the assumption that every vessel has a nationality. The possession of a nationality is so essential to a vessel engaged in legitimate trade that many commentators simply could not envision a vessel not being properly registered in some country. This is not surprising when one considers the importance that nationality has for a vessel. The nationality of a vessel determines what nations it may trade with and what nations it may not, whether it may engage in the coastwise trade or fisheries of any nation, what law will be applied by the courts in case of disputes, the qualifications of its officers, the working conditions and wages of its crew, and the safety standards of the vessel and its equipment. Without a properly documented nationality, a vessel cannot enter through customs, load or discharge cargo, or leave a port with proper customs clearance. In short, without a proper nationality, a vessel cannot engage in legitimate trade or fisheries. It follows, therefore, that a vessel without a nationality is engaged, not in legitimate but in illegitimate trade.

---

[1]See, e.g., Mavrommatis Palestine Concessions (Greece v. United Kingdom) 1924 P.C.I.J., Ser. A, No. 2 at 11-12.

[2]614 F.2d 61 (5th Cir. 1980).

Nationality is also essential to a vessel on the high seas because the protections afforded a vessel on the high seas under international law are derived from its having been registered in a flag state in accordance with international law. A ship has the nationality of the state whose flag it is entitled to fly. Therefore, a ship that has not been granted the right by any state to fly its flag is without nationality. That this must be so becomes obvious after examining the international regime established for the regulation of vessels on the high seas. The exercise of jurisdiction with regard to administrative, technical and social matters, the use of signals and communications, the prevention of collisions, rendering aid to those in distress, the protection of submarine cables and pipelines, proper manning, labor conditions, proper construction, equipment and seaworthiness are all predicated on the effective control of the flag state. A vessel which is so registered and controlled enjoys a large degree of immunity on the high seas from interference by the vessels of other states.

The introduction of stateless vessels causes the international regime, predicated as it is on nationality, to break down and with this breakdown there is an attendant loss of the protections afforded by the system. It has been said by a noted commentator that registration of vessels is so important to prevent chaos on the high seas that a vessel that is not registered may be confiscated under the *jus gentium* by any State meeting with it. Another author has suggested that stateless vessels be equated to pirate or slave vessels, which are subject to universal jurisdiction. The noted international legal scholar, Professor Myres S. McDougal, stated:

> Every ship is required to have a nationality and scant protection is afforded to ships which have no nationality. . . . So great a premium is placed upon the certain identification of vessels for purposes of maintaining minimal order upon the high seas. . .that extraordinary deprivational measures are permitted with respect to stateless ships. Thus, it is commonly considered that ships either having no nationality or falsely assuming a nationality, are almost completely without protection.

These statements reflect the true nature of jurisdiction on the high seas. The high seas are not *res nullius* subject to the jurisdiction of no nation, but *res communis*, subject to the common jurisdiction of all nations. The protection that a registered vessel enjoys on the high seas is in the nature of an immunity. Not unlike a diplomat who would be subject to the jurisdiction of the country to which he is accredited but for his diplomatic passport, the registration papers of a vessel immunize it against interference from other states. The flag state does not gain its exclusive jurisdiction through the registration of a vessel. Rather, *but for* the registration, other states would have jurisdiction as well. Any other result would end in chaos and anarchy on the high seas. If only a country of registration could exercise jurisdiction at all, under any circumstances, then an unregistered vessel would be immune from interference by anyone. This result cannot be and has never been tolerated by the nations of the world. In the 1948 case of *Molvan v. Attorney General for Palestine*,[3] the Privy Council, citing with approval the writings of Oppenheim,[4] wrote:

> . . . [F]reedom of the open sea, whatever those words may connote, is a freedom of ships which fly, and are entitled to fly, the flag of a State which is within the comity of nations. No question of comity nor of

---

[3](1948) A.C. 351, 369.

[4]Lauterpacht, *Oppenheim's International Law*, Vol. 1, 646 (1934).

> any breach of international law can arise if there is no state under whose flag the vessel sails. Their Lordships would accept as a valid statement of international law, the following passage. . . . "In the interest of order on the open sea, a vessel not sailing under the maritime flag of a State enjoys no protection whatsoever, for the freedom of navigation on the open sea is the freedom for such vessels only as sail under the flag of a State."

As previously stated, a vessel has only the nationality of its country of registration and without registration it is without nationality. A vessel properly registered in a particular state is also said to be without nationality if it falsely claims another nationality. Since the only prohibition against interference with a vessel on the high seas by a warship is with regard to a "foreign" vessel, how can a vessel without nationality be "foreign" as to the warship?

Viewed in this light, the extension of United States jurisdiction over stateless vessels seems not only to be a reasonable claim but completely consistent with both customary and treaty international law. In fact, the United States Supreme Court held as long ago as 1820, in *United States v. Klintock*[5] and *United States v. Holmes*[6] that the United States could exercise criminal jurisdiction over the acts of non-United States citizens on board stateless vessels on the high seas.

2.   The Question of the Flag of Convenience

1958 CONVENTION ON THE HIGH SEAS

Article 4

Every State, whether coastal or not, has the right to sail ships under its flag on the high seas.

Article 5

1. Each State shall fix the conditions for the grant of its nationality to ships, for the registration of ships in its territory, and for the right to fly its flag. Ships have the nationality of the State whose flag they are entitled to fly. There must exist a genuine link between the State and the ship; in particular, the State must effectively exercise its jurisdiction and control in administrative, technical and social matters over ships flying its flag.

2. Each State shall issue to ships to which it has granted the right to fly its flag documents to that effect.

Article 6

1. Ships shall sail under the flag of one State only and, save in exceptional cases expressly provided for in international treaties or in these articles, shall be subject to its exclusive jurisdiction on the high seas. A ship may not change its flag during a voyage or while in a port of call, save in the case of a real transfer of ownership or change of registry.

---

[5] 18 U.S. 144 (1820).

[6] 18 U.S. 412 (1820): see also Clark, *Criminal Jurisdiction over Merchant Vessels Engaged in International Trade*, 11 J. Maritime Law & Com. 219, 230 (1980).

2. A ship which sails under the flags of two or more States, using them according to convenience, may not claim any of the nationalities in question with respect to any other State, and may be assimilated to a ship without nationality.

Article 7

The provisions of the preceding articles do not prejudice the question of ships employed on the official service of an inter-governmental organization flying the flag of the organization.

INTERNATIONAL LAW COMMISSION
1956 Commentary, Draft Article 29
Yearbook of the International Law Commission 1956,
Vol. II, pp. 278-279.

Each State lays down the conditions on which ships may fly its flag. Obviously the State enjoys complete liberty in the case of ships owned by it or ships which are the property of a nationalized company. With regard to other ships, the State must accept certain restrictions. As in the case of the grant of nationality to persons, national legislation on the subject must not depart too far from the principles adopted by the majority of States, which may be regarded as forming part of international law. Only on that condition will the freedom granted to States not give rise to abuse and to friction with other States. With regard to the national element required for permission to fly the flag, a great many systems are possible, but there must be a minimum national element.

On this principle, the Institute of International Law, as long ago as 1896, adopted certain rules governing permission to fly the flag. At its seventh session the Commission deemed these rules acceptable in slightly amended form, while realizing that, if the practical ends in view were to be achieved, States would have to work out more detailed provisions when incorporating these rules in their legislation.

At its eighth session, the Commission, after examining the comments of Governments, felt obliged to abandon this viewpoint. It came to the conclusion that the criteria it had formulated could not fulfill the aim it had set itself. Existing practice in the various States is too divergent to be governed by the few criteria adopted by the Commission. Regulations of this kind would be bound to leave a large number of problems unsolved and could not prevent abuse. The Commission accordingly thought it best to confine itself to enunciating the guiding principle that, before the grant of nationality is generally recognized, there must be a genuine link between the ship and the State granting permission to fly its flag. The Commission does not consider it possible to state in any greater detail what form this link should take. This lack of precision made some members of the Commission question the advisability of inserting such a stipulation. But the majority of the Commission preferred a vague criterion to no criterion at all. While leaving States a wide latitude in this respect, the Commission wished to make it clear that the grant of its flag to a ship cannot be a mere administrative formality, with no accompanying guarantee that the ship possess a real link with its new State. The jurisdiction of the State over ships, and the control it should exercise in conformity with article 34 of these articles, can only be effective where there exists in fact a relationship between the State and the ship other than mere registration or the mere grant of a certificate of registry.

Max Sorensen, "Law of the Sea," *International Conciliation*, No. 520, November, 1958, pp. 201-206. Reprinted by permission of Carnegie Endowment for International Peace.

Freedom of the high seas implies, as a general rule, that no ship is subject to the jurisdiction of a foreign state. As a counterpart and to avoid anarchy, there must be some certainty that the state to which the ship belongs effectively exercises certain minimum standards for safety of navigation and maintenance of good order. This condition, however, is far from being fulfilled, and thus it is a matter of international concern what state can legitimately claim to be considered as the home state of a ship.

International law has traditionally left each state free to determine under what conditions it will register and thereby confer its nationality upon a ship. This liberty is confirmed by Article 5 of the Convention on the High Seas: "Each State shall fix the conditions for the grant of its nationality to ships, for the registration of ships in its territory, and for the right to fly its flag. . . ."

This liberty has, however, been used by certain states, in particular Liberia and Panama and to a certain extent Honduras and Costa Rica as well, to enact "liberal" registration laws allowing for the registration even of ships owned and operated by foreigners. Tonnage sailing under the flags of these states for the convenience of the owners--hence the term, "flags of convenience"--has increased rapidly in recent years. Out of the total increase since 1939, 43 per cent has gone to these countries, which, at the end of 1957, had about 15.5 per cent of world tonnage under their flags. Liberia, which now holds fourth place among the maritime nations (surpassed only by the United States, United Kingdom, and Norway in that order), has more than seven million gross register tons corresponding to 6.77 per cent of world tonnage. The figures for Panama, which is number eight on the list, are more than four million tons and 3.75 percent of world tonnage. It is estimated that over 80 per cent of the tonnage under flags of convenience is owned either by United States interests, in particular the large oil companies, or by persons of Greek origin supported to a certain extent by United States capital.

Owners register their ships in such countries for various reasons. Taxation is very low, or practically nonexistent. Operating costs are lower because the legislation and collective agreements on wages, labor conditions, and social security of the traditionally maritime countries do not apply. Lack of adequate administrative machinery, especially inspection services, means that the countries concerned are unable to enforce effectively such laws and regulations as they may have enacted with respect to safety standards, accommodation and protection of crews, and so forth.

The problem of registration under flags of convenience was first raised by the International Transport Workers' Federation shortly after the Second World War as a problem affecting the economic and social security of seafarers. Because of improved conditions in the many modern ships registered under flags of convenience, the emphasis has shifted since then. The problem is now also viewed as one of economic competition between the merchant fleets of traditionally maritime countries and the new and efficient vessels operating with lower costs under the flags of countries to which they are attached only by the administrative formality of registration. The problem has therefore become one of mutual concern to governments, shipowners, and seafarers in the old maritime countries, and countermeasures are being sought on both national and international levels.

ILC [The International Law Commission], in recognizing the freedom of each state to fix the conditions of registration, formulated a rule limiting the scope of this freedom. The third sentence of its draft Article 29, corresponding to what is now Article 5 of the Convention on the High Seas, added the following provision: "Nevertheless, for purposes of recognition of the national character of the ship by other States, there must exist a genuine link between the State and the ship." In other words, if a "genuine link" did not exist between the state and the ship, a foreign state should be free not to recognize the purported nationality of the ship and to treat it as a stateless ship, having no right of access to its ports.

The Commission made no attempt, however, to define a "genuine link." It felt--as did the Geneva Conference--that the legislation of traditionally maritime states was too divergent to permit of any internationally binding definition. Among the criteria that may be used are nationality or domicile of the owner, his principal place of business, nationality of officers and crew. In the case of ships owned by joint-stock companies, the criteria may include nationality or domicile of the shareholders or of a certain proportion of them.

The very condition that there should be a "genuine link" between the state and the ship, whatever the precise implications of the term, was opposed at the Geneva Conference by Panama and Liberia, with the support of the United States. The Conference decided, however, to retain this condition. As an alternative, the same countries sought to deny foreign states the right to refuse recognition of a registration because of the absence of a "genuine link" between the ship and the state of registration. The argument was advanced that it would be contradictory to allow a state to fix the conditions of registration, but at the same time allow others not to consider themselves bound by an act of registration in conformity with those conditions. Against this argument, it was observed that there would be nothing extraordinary in such a legal situation. It is well established that each state has the right to determine the conditions under which it will grant its nationality to an individual, but a state is not in all circumstances bound to respect a naturalization effected by another state. Only if the grant of nationality is based upon a genuine connection between the state and the individuals, and is thus the legal expression of a real and effective nationality, can it be invoked against foreign states as a valid legal act.

In committee, the words "for purposes of recognition. . . by other States," on which a separate vote was taken, were retained by a large majority (39 to 13, with 6 abstentions). When the matter reached the plenary, however, a number of delegations had changed their minds, presumably as a result of extensive lobbying. This part of the sentence was then rejected by 30 negative votes to 15 affirmative and 17 abstentions.

Nevertheless, the final text requires, as a matter of principle, that there be a "genuine link" between the state and the ship. "In particular," it adds, "the state must effectively exercise its jurisdiction and control in administrative, technical, and social matters over ships flying its flag." This sentence, proposed originally by the Netherlands and French delegations, in effect relates the "genuine link" not only to the qualities of the ship and its owner, but also to the legal possibilities of the state to control the ship. If such possibilities are absent, the state is not entitled to enter or to maintain the ship on its register.

It is generally admitted that the problem of flags of convenience has not been solved by the Geneva Conference. Unless countries with liberal registration laws agree to modify their legislation and practice, the United States and other countries whose capital and shipping interests are seeking the advantages of a flag of convenience may have to discourage their own nationals from resorting to this means of competition in international shipping. But this is a problem of the regulation of international competition in an important industry rather than a problem of the law of the sea.

Apart from the question of flags of convenience, the nationality of ships has not given rise to serious problems. Article 6 of the Convention on the High Seas provides that ships shall sail under the flag of one state only and shall be subject to the exclusive jurisdiction of that state on the high seas. A change of flag may take place only in the case of a real transfer of ownership or change of registry. A ship may not sail under more than one flag, using them according to convenience.

ILC considered whether or not the United Nations or other international organizations should be recognized as having the right to sail ships exclusively under their own flags. The principal objection to recognizing such a right is that the United Nations has no legal system covering such matters as safety, manning, social conditions, civil and criminal jurisdiction, and so forth that would be applicable to ships sailing under its flag. The special rapporteur of the ILC, Professor J. P. A. Francois, submitted a report in which he proposed that special arrangements might be made between the Secretary-General and member states under which vessels owned by, or otherwise in the service of, the United Nations would be allowed to fly a national flag in combination with the United Nations flag. But no effect was given to this proposal and the question was left open. The Conference merely inserted as Article 7 a provision that the question should not be considered prejudiced by the other articles of the Convention concerning the nationality of ships.

D. W. Bowett, *The Law of the Sea*, Manchester: Manchester University Press, (1967), pp. 56-58. Reprinted by permission.

The adoption of the "genuine link" test of nationality has been severely criticized, and not least for its ambiguity. . . .

The real explanation for the opposition to "flags of convenience" lies almost entirely in the economic field. Even the opposition of the Trade Unions, although certainly quite genuinely based on a concern with safety and labor conditions, is more directly based upon the desire to see national ship-owners pay national, trade union rates and not avoid these by resorting to a foreign flag of convenience with foreign rates of pay and foreign labour for a crew. Even more important, the opposition of the European ship-owning interests is directly based upon the economic advantages which companies operating under such flags of convenience possess by reason of lower taxation of earnings and, somewhat less important, lower costs of operating the vessels (mainly due to lower crew salaries). . . .

The position of the United States is of particular interest, since it is generally opposed to that of the European States: the U.S.A. is, in other words, "sympathetic" to the use of flags of convenience. The reason, frankly admitted although not entirely popular with the U. S. trade unions, is simply this: that in time of war the U.S.A. would need to call on a vast mercantile marine fleet, that U.S. shipowners cannot in time of peace build, maintain and operate a fleet of this size under the U.S. flag, given the high costs of so doing, and that it is therefore necessary for these fleets to be operated under flags of convenience until such time as the U.S.A. would "requisition" them in time of war. We thus have again, as so often in the law of the sea, a conflict of interests which is primarily economic, but which involves considerable security aspects.

Restatement on the Foreign Relations Law of the United States, Third Revision, Vol. 2, St. Paul, Minn.: American Law Institute, 1987, pp. 10-11, 16-17. Copyright by The American Law Institute. Reprinted with the permission of The American Law Institute.

§ 501. Nationality of Ships

A ship has the nationality of the state that registered it and authorized it to fly the state's flag, but a state may properly register a ship and authorize it to fly the state's flag only if there is a genuine link between the state and the ship.

Comment:

b. *"Genuine link."* In general, a state has a "genuine link" entitling it to register a ship and to authorize the ship to use its flag if the ship is owned by nationals of the state, whether natural or juridical persons, and the state exercises effective control over the ship. In most cases a ship is owned by a corporation created by the state of registry. However, in determining whether a "genuine link" with the state of registry exists, the following additional factors are to be taken into account: whether the company owning the ship is owned by nationals of the state; whether the officers and crew of the ship are nationals of the state; how often the ship stops in the ports of the state; and how extensive and effective is the control that the state exercises over the ship.

Although international law requires a genuine link between the ship and the registering state, the lack of a genuine link does not justify another state in refusing to recognize the flag or in interfering with the ship. A state may, however, reject diplomatic protection by the flag state when the flag state has no genuine link with the ship. If another state doubts the existence of a genuine link, for instance, because there is evidence that the flag state has not been exercising its duties to control and regulate the ship (see § 502), it may require that the flag state "investigate the matter and, if appropriate, take any action necessary to remedy the situation." LOS Convention, Article 94 (6); § 502, Comment *f.*

Editor's Note:

. . . .

7. *Genuine link and flag of convenience.*

Complaints about the lack of genuine link are directed primarily against "flags of convenience." Such flags benefit both the states granting them and the owners and users of the ships sailing under these flags. The United Kingdom Committee of Inquiry into Shipping (the "Rochdale Committee") listed six major features of flags of convenience:

(i)   The country of registry allows ownership and/or control of its merchant vessels by noncitizens;

(ii)   Access to the registry is easy. A ship may usually be registered at a consul's office abroad. Equally important, transfer from the registry at the owner's option is not restricted;

(iii)   Taxes on the income from the ships are not levied by the flag state or are low. A registry fee and an annual fee, based on tonnage, are normally the only charges made. A guarantee or acceptable understanding regarding future freedom from taxation may also be

registry fee and an annual fee, based on tonnage, are normally the only charges made. A guarantee or acceptable understanding regarding future freedom from taxation may also be given;

(iv)   The country of registry is a small power with no national requirement under any foreseeable circumstances for all the shipping registered, but receipts from very small charges on a large tonnage may produce a substantial effect on its national income and balance of payments;

(v)   Manning of ships by non-nationals is freely permitted; and

(vi)   The country of registry has neither the power nor the administrative machinery effectively to impose any government or international regulations; nor has the country the wish or the power to control the companies themselves.

Cmnd. 4337, at 51 (1970); see also Osieke, "Flags of Convenience Vessels: Recent Developments," 73 Am.J.Int'l L. 604 (1979). . . .

8. *Effects of lack of genuine link.* Another state is not entitled to decide unilaterally that there is no genuine link between a ship and the flag state or to refuse on that basis to recognize the flag.

The existence of a "genuine link" between the state and the ship is not a condition of recognition of the nationality of a ship; that is, no state can claim the right to determine unilaterally that no genuine link exists between a ship and the flag state. Nevertheless there is a possibility that a state, with respect to a particular ship, may assert before an agreed tribunal, such an the International Court of Justice, that no genuine link exists. In such event, it would be for the Court to decide whether or not a "genuine link" existed.

S.Exec. Rep. No. 5 (Law of the Sea Conventions), 106 Cong.Rec. 1189, 1190 (86th Cong.2d sess., 1960), 9 Whiteman, Digest of International Law 14-15 (1968).

Moreover, as the court of appeals for the Second Circuit pointed out, "it would be unreasonable to conclude that . . . other states do not owe some obligations of respect" so long as the flag state effectively exercises its "jurisdiction and control in administrative, technical and social matters over ships flying its flag." *Empresa Hondurena de Vapores, S.A. v. McLeod,* 300 F.2d 222, 235-36 (2d Cir.1962), *reversed on other grounds, sub nom. McCulloch v. Sociedad Nacional de Marineros de Honduras,* 372 U.S. 10, 83 S.Ct. 671, 9 L.Ed.2d 547 (1962), citing the 1958 Convention on the High Seas, Art. 5(1) (followed with minor changes in LOS Convention, Art. 94(1)). The court of appeals had held in that case that the National Labor Relations Act should be interpreted as not intended to apply to maritime operations of foreign-flag ships employing alien seamen. 300 F.2d 222 at 231. In vacating the court of appeals judgment, and upholding a district court judgment in a related case, the Supreme Court referred to the "well-established rule of international law that the law of the flag state ordinarily governs the internal affairs of a ship." *McCulloch v. Sociedad Nacional de Marineros de Honduras,* 372 U.S. at 21, 83 S.Ct. at 677. For United Kingdom decisions relating to attempts by an international labor union to induce port workers to withdraw services from a ship navigating under a flag of convenience in order to compel owners to pay standard union wages to the crew, see *N.W.L. Ltd. v. Woods,* [1979] 3 All E.R. 614 (H.L.) (injunction against labor union rejected); *Merkur Island Shipping Co. v. Laughton,* [1983] 2 All E.R. 189 (H.L.) (injunction against labor union upheld).

International law probably does not permit a state to assert authority with respect to a vessel owned by its nationals but registered in another state merely on the ground that there is no genuine link between the vessel and the flag state.

9. *Imposition of nationality on ships owned by nationals.* A state cannot impose its nationality on a ship owned by its nationals if the ship is already registered elsewhere and is flying the flag of the state of registration.

CONSTITUTION OF THE MARITIME SAFETY COMMITTEE OF THE INTER-GOVERNMENTAL MARITIME CONSULTATIVE ORGANIZATION
Advisory Opinion of 8 June 1960
I.C.J. Reports 1960, p. 150, at pp. 166-167, 168-169.

[The 1968 Convention for the Establishment of the Inter-Governmental Maritime Consultative Organization provides in Article 28(a):

The Maritime Safety Committee shall consist of fourteen Members elected by the Assembly from the Members, governments of those nations having an important interest in maritime safety, of which not less than eight shall be the largest ship-owning nations, and the remainder shall be elected so as to ensure adequate representation of Members, governments of other nations with an important interest in maritime safety, such as nations interested in the supply of large numbers of crews or in the carriage of large numbers of berthed and unberthed passengers, and of major geographical areas.

Liberia and Panama were not elected to the Maritime Safety Committee in 1959 by the Assembly of the Inter-Governmental Maritime Consultative Organization (IMCO), despite the fact that their merchant fleets were respectively the third and the eighth largest of the IMCO members, according to Lloyd's Register of Shipping for 1958. They challenged the legality of the result of the election. The Assembly then requested the International Court of Justice to give an advisory opinion. Excerpts of the opinion are reproduced below.]

In order to determine which nations are the largest ship-owning nations, it is apparent that some basis of measurement must be applied. The rationale of the situation is that when Article 28 (a) speaks of "the largest ship-owning nations", it can only have in mind a comparative size vis-a-vis other nations owners of tonnage. There is no other practical means by which the size of ship-owning nations may be measured. The largest ship-owning nations are to be elected on the strength of their tonnage, the tonnage which is owned by or belongs to them. The only question is in what sense Article 28(a) contemplates it should be owned by or belong to them.

A general opinion, shared by the Court, is that it is not possible to contend that the words "ship-owning nations" in Article 28(a) mean that the ships have to be owned by the State itself.

There appear to be but two meanings which could demand serious consideration: either the words refer to the tonnage beneficially owned by the nationals of a State or they refer to the registered tonnage of a flag State regardless of its private or State ownership.

Liberia and Panama, supported by other States, have contended that the sole test is registered tonnage. On the other hand, it has been submitted by certain States that the proper interpretation of the Article requires that ships should belong to nationals of the State whose flag they fly. This submission was rather concretely expressed by the Government of Norway which suggested using the flag-tonnage as a point of departure, reducing this amount by the amount of tonnage not owned by nationals of the flag State and adding the tonnage which does belong to such nationals but is registered under a different flag.

The practice followed by the Assembly in relation to other Articles reveals the reliance placed upon registered tonnage.

Thus in implementing Article 17(c) of the Convention, which provides that two members of the Council "shall be elected by the Assembly from among the governments of nations having a substantial interest in providing international shipping services", the Assembly elected Japan and Italy. This was done after it had been reported to the Assembly that the representatives of the Members of the Council who were required under the terms of Article 18 to make their recommendation to the Assembly had

> therefore examined the claims of countries having a substantial interest in providing international shipping services. They did not feel that they should propose to the Assembly a long list of candidates, as two countries clearly surpassed the others in size of their tonnage; they recommended the election of Japan (with tonnage of about 5,500,000 tons) and of Italy (with tonnage of nearly 5,000,000).

The tonnages mentioned are those recorded in the list of the Secretary-General of the Organization, which was before the Assembly in the election under Article 28(a) and which is none other than a copy of *Lloyd's Register of Shipping for 1958*. The registered tonnages of the two countries were taken as the appropriate criterion, there was not suggestion of any other. There were only two Members to be elected under Article 17(c) and there were only two recommendations to the Assembly.

The apportionment of the expenses of the Organization among its Members under the provisions of Article 41 of the Convention is also significant. Under Resolution A.20(I) adopted by the Assembly of the Organization on 19 January 1959, the assessment on each Member State was principally "determined by its respective gross registered tonnage as shown in the latest edition of *Lloyd's Register of Shipping*". Those States whose registered tonnages were the largest paid the largest assessments.

Furthermore, the Assembly, when proceeding to elect the eight largest ship-owning nations under Article 28(a), took note of the Working Paper prepared by the Secretary-General of the Organization which embodies a list of the ship-owning nations with their respective registered tonnages formulated on the basis of *Lloyd's Register*. Liberia and Panama, countries which were among the eight largest on the list, were not elected by the Assembly but countries which ranked ninth and tenth were elected.

This reliance upon registered tonnage in giving effect to different provisions of the Convention and the comparison which has been made of the text of Articles 60 and 28(a), persuade the Court to the view that it is unlikely that when the latter Article was drafted and incorporated into the Convention it was contemplated that any criterion other than registered tonnage should determine which were the largest ship-owning nations. In particular it is unlikely that it was contemplated that the test should be the nationality of stock-holders and of others having beneficial interests in every merchant ship; facts which would be difficult to catalogue, to ascertain and to measure. To take into account the names and nationalities of the owners or shareholders of shipping companies would, to adopt the words of the representative of the United Kingdom during the debate which preceded the election, "introduce an unnecessarily complicated criterion." Such a method of evaluating the ship-owning rank of a country is neither practical not certain. Moreover, it finds no basis in international practice, the language of international jurisprudence, in maritime terminology, in international conventions dealing with safety at sea or in the practice followed by the Organization itself in carrying out the Convention. On the other hand, the criterion of registered tonnage is practical, certain and capable of easy application.

NOTE

One major reason for using the flag of convenience is the high cost of American maritime union laborers. As observed in the following:

> For a 50,000-ton tanker . . . a 32-man crew would cost [U.S.] $1.7 million a year at American wages. . . . by using the Liberian flag, a ship-owner can hire crews of other nationalities at the following rates: all-Italian, $600,000 a year; British, $500,000; Spanish, $450,000; Greek, $325,000; Chinese, $250,000; and Filipino, $250,000. . . . a "motley crew," one made up of various nationalities, would cost about $200,000.

John Kifner, "Liberia: A Phantom Maritime Power Whose Fleet is Steered by Big Business," *New York Times*, February 14, 1977, p. 14 c.

Another reporter observed:

> The classic way to cut operating costs in the tanker industry is to register the ship in an offshore nation with few regulatory controls, like Liberia or Panama. These "flags of convenience" allow shipowners to sidestep national rules that mandate the use of domestic crews, with obvious benefits.
>
> The basic monthly wage for seamen affiliated with the International Transport Workers' Federation, which includes unions mainly in developing nations, is $821 a month. By contrast, the going rate for Filipino seamen is $276 a month, for Bangladesh seamen $140 a month, and for Chinese seamen $50 a month, according to Lloyd's Shipping Economist, a monthly magazine.

Steve Lohr, "Tanker in Big Spill Typifies Freewheeling Industry," *New York Times*, July 3, 1989, p. 30.

The loose safety standards for merchant ships registered in major flag of convenience countries prompted the 62nd International Labor Conference to adopt the Convention concerning Minimum Standards in Merchant Ships on October 29, 1976, *International Legal Materials*, Vol. 15 (1976), pp. 1288-1292. Article 2 of the Convention provides:

Each member which ratifies this Convention undertakes--

(a) to have laws or regulations laying down, for ships registered in its territory--

(i) safety standards, including standards of competency, hours of work and manning, so as to ensure the safety of life onboard ship;

(ii) appropriate social security measures; and

(iii) shipboard conditions of employment and shipboard living arrangements, in so far as these, in the opinion of the Member, are not covered by collective agreements or laid down by competent courts in a manner equally binding on the shipowners and seafarers concerned; . . . .

(b) to exercise effective jurisdiction or control over ships which are registered in its territory in respect of--

(i) safety standards, including standards of competency, hours of work and manning, prescribed by national laws or regulations;

(ii) social security measures prescribed by national laws or regulations;

(iii) shipboard conditions of employment and shipboard living arrangements prescribed by national laws or regulations, or laid down by competent courts in a manner equally binding on the shipowners and seafarers concerned. . . .

For a study of this question, see Ebere Osieke, "The International Labour Organization and the Control of Substandard Merchant Vessels," *International and Comparative Law Quarterly*, Vol. 30 (1981), pp. 497-512. *See also* Irwin M. Heine, *The U.S. Maritime Industry in the National Interest*, Washington, D.C.: National Maritime Council, distributed by Acropolis Book Ltd., 1980.

On July 7, 1978, at the IMCO (now IMO) Conference, the International Convention on Standards of Training, Certification and Watchkeeping for Seafarers was adopted at London, United Kingdom Command Papers, Miscellaneous Series 6 (1979), 7543. The Convention contains, in the Annex, detailed Regulations establishing common standards for the training and others of seafarers. Parties undertake to apply these to seafarers on board most sea-going ships entitled to fly their flag.

1982 UNITED NATIONS CONVENTION ON THE LAW OF THE SEA

Article 90
Right of Navigation

Every State, whether coastal or land-locked, has the right to sail ships flying its flag on the high seas.

Article 91
Nationality of ships

1. Every State shall fix the conditions for the grant of its nationality to ships, for the registration of ships in its territory, and for the right to fly its flag. Ships have the nationality of the State whose flag they are entitled to fly. There must exist a genuine link between the State and the ship.

2. Every State shall issue to ships to which it has granted the right to fly its flag documents to that effect.

Article 92
Status of ships

1. Ships shall sail under the flag of one State only and, save in exceptional cases expressly provided for in international treaties or in this Convention, shall be subject to its exclusive jurisdiction on the high seas. A ship may not change its flag during a voyage or while in a port of call, save in the case of a real transfer of ownership or change of registry.

2. A ship which sails under the flags of two or more States, using them according to convenience, may not claim any of the nationalities in question with respect of any other State, and may be assimilated to a ship without nationality.

Article 93
Ships flying the flag of the United Nations, its specialized
agencies and the International Atomic Energy Agency

The preceding articles do not prejudice the question of ships employed on the official service of the United Nations, its specialized agencies or the International Atomic Energy Agency, flying the flag of the organization.

Article 94
Duties of the flag State

1. Every State shall effectively exercise its jurisdiction and control in administrative, technical and social matters over ships flying its flag.

2. In particular every State shall:

> (a) maintain a register of ships containing the names and particulars of ships flying its flag, except those which are excluded from generally accepted international regulations on account of their small size; and

> (b) assume jurisdiction under its internal law over each ship flying its flag and its master, officers and crew in respect of administrative, technical and social matters concerning the ship.

3. Every State shall take such measures for ships flying its flag as are necessary to ensure safety at sea with regard, *inter alia*, to:

> (a) the construction, equipment and seaworthiness of ships;

> (b) the manning of ships, labour conditions and the training of crews, taking into account the applicable international instruments;

> (c) the use of signals, the maintenance of communications and the prevention of collisions.

4. Such measures shall include those necessary to ensure:

   (a) that each ship, before registration and thereafter at appropriate intervals, is surveyed by a qualified surveyor of ships, and has on board such charts, nautical publications and navigational equipment and instruments as are appropriate for the safe navigation of the ship;

   (b) that each ship is in the charge of a master and officers who possess appropriate qualifications, in particular in seamanship, navigation, communications and marine engineering, and that the crew is appropriate in qualification and numbers for the type, size, machinery and equipment of the ship;

   (c) that the master, officers and, to the extent appropriate, the crew are fully conversant with and required to observe the applicable international regulations concerning the safety of life at sea, the prevention of collisions, the prevention, reduction and control of marine pollution, and the maintenance of communications by radio.

5. In taking the measures called for in paragraphs 3 and 4 each State is required to conform to generally accepted international regulations, procedures and practices and to take any steps which may be necessary to secure their observance.

6. A State which has clear grounds to believe that proper jurisdiction and control with respect to a ship have not been exercised may report the facts to the flag State. Upon receiving such a report, the flag State shall investigate the matter and, if appropriate, take any action necessary to remedy the situation.

7. Each State shall cause an inquiry to be held by or before a suitably qualified person or persons into every marine casualty or incident of navigation on the high seas involving a ship flying its flag and causing loss of life or serious injury to nationals of another State or serious damage to ships or installations of another State or to the marine environment. The flag State and the other State shall co-operate in the conduct of any inquiry held by that other State into any such marine casualty or incident of navigation.

NOTE

Articles 90 to 93 of the 1982 United Nations Convention on the Law of the Sea are essentially identical to Articles 4 to 7 of the 1958 Convention on the High Seas, but Article 91 omits the following language of Article 5:

". . .in particular, the State must effectively exercise its jurisdiction and control in administrative, technical and social matters over ships flying its flag."

The omitted part is replaced by more elaborate rules provided in Article 94 of the 1982 Convention.

REFERENCES

(Nationality of Ships in General) Herman Meyers, *The Nationality of Ships*, The Hague: Martinus Nijhoff, 1967; Nagendra Singh, *Maritime Flag and International Law*, Leyden: Sijthoff, 1978; Philip P. Jones, "British Flag--A Privilege or an Encumbrance--Or Just an Anachronism?,"

Lloyd's Maritime and Commercial Law Quarterly, 1981, pp. 241-249; Nagendra Singh, "Maritime Flag and State Responsibility," in Jerzy Makarczyk, ed., *Essays in International Law in Honour of Judge Manfred Lachs*, The Hague: Martinus Nijhoff, 1984, pp. 657-669.

(Registration and Documentation) Jane Marc Wells, "Vessel Registration in Selected Open Registries," *Maritime Lawyer*, Vol. 6 (1981), pp. 221-245; Michael P. Drzal and Phyllis D. Carnilla, "Documentation of Vessels: The Fog Lifts," *Journal of Maritime Law and Commerce*, Vol. 13 (1981-82), pp. 261-279; Vincent K. Hubbard, "Registration of a Vessel under Vanuatu Law," *Journal of Maritime Law and Commerce*, Vol. 13 (1981-82), pp. 235-244; "Conditions for Registration of Ships," [Report by the United Nations Conference on Trade and Development Secretariat, TD/B/AC.34/2 (January 22, 1982)], *Ocean Yearbook*, Vol. 4 (1983), pp. 492-514; Meredith L. Hathorn, "The Vessel Documentation Act of 1980," *Maritime Lawyer*, Vol. 7 (1982), pp. 303-317.

(Flag of Convenience) Myers S. McDougal, "Maintenance of Public Order at Sea and the Nationality of Ships," *American Journal of International Law*, Vol. 54 (1960), pp. 25-116; Boleslaw Boczek, *Flags of Convenience*, Cambridge, Massachusetts: Harvard University Press, 1962; Myers S. McDougal and William T. Burke, *The Public Order of the Oceans*, New Haven, Connecticut: Yale University Press, 1962, pp. 1008-1141; Thomas J. Romans, "The American Merchant Marine--Flags of Convenience and International Law," *Virginia Journal of International Law*. Vol. 3 (1963), pp. 121-152; Nagendra Singh, "Maritime Flag as an Attribute of Sovereignty," *Indian Journal of International Law*, Vol. 4 (1964), pp. 75-84; Marjorie M. Whiteman, *Digest of International Law*, Vol. 4, Washington, D.C.: U.S. Government Printing Office, 1965, pp. 633-645; John J. Clark, "Flags of Whose Convenience?," *U.S. Naval Institute Proceedings*, Vol. 94 No. 10 (1968), pp. 50-59; Michael D. Wellington, "The Better Part of Valour--Applicability of the Jones Act to the Flags of Convenience Fleet," *San Diego Law Review*, Vol. 7 (1970), pp. 674-683; "OECD Study on Flags of Convenience," *Journal of Maritime Law and Commerce*, Vol. 4 (1972-73), pp. 231-254; Enrico Argiroffo, "Flags of Convenience and Standard Vessels: A Review of the ILO's Approach to the Problem," *International Labour Review*, Vol. 110 (1974); pp. 437-453; James K. Pedley, "Under Foreign Flags: The Inequitable Avoidance of U.S. Taxation by American-Owned Ships," *Case Western Reserve Journal of International Law*, Vol. 8 (1976), pp. 188-203; John G. Kilgour, "Effective United States Control?", *Journal of Maritime Law and Commerce*, Vol. 8 (1976-77), pp. 337-348; Clarence R. Hallberg, "Shipping Under Flags of Convenience: Maritime Safety Aspects," *Fordham Corporate Law Institute Proceedings*, Vol. 4 (1977), pp. 231-240; Roy Albert Povell, "New Developments in Taxation of Shipping Under Flags of Convenience," *ibid.*, pp. 211-229; L.L. Herman, "Flags of Convenience--New Dimensions to an Old Problem," *McGill Law Journal*, Vol. 24 (1978), pp. 1-28; Comment [Edith A. Wittig], "Tanker Fleets and Flags of Convenience: Advantages, Problems, and Dangers," *Texas International Law Journal*, Vol. 14 (1979), p. 115-138; European Communities, Economic and Social Council, *EEC Shipping Policy: Flags of Convenience: Own-Initiative Opinion, Problems Currently Facing Shipping Policy, Particularly Maritime Safety, the Growing Importance of the New Shipping Nations, the Development of Flags of Convenience, and the Discrimination Against Certain Flags*, Brussels, 1979; Ebere Osieke, "Flags of Convenience Vessels: Recent Developments," *American Journal of International Law*, Vol. 73 (1979), pp. 604-627; Keith D. Ewing, "Union Action Against Flags of Convenience--The Legal Position in Great Britain," *Journal of Maritime Law and Commerce*, Vol. 11 (1979-80), pp. 503-508; Rodney P. Carlisle, "The American Century Implemented: Stettinius and the Liberian Flag of Convenience," *Business History Review*, Vol. 54 (1980), pp. 175-191; Albert T. Church, Jr., "Flags of Convenience or Flags of Necessity? An Interview with Bert Steeple," *U.S. Naval Institute Proceedings*, Vol. 106 (June 1980), pp. 52-57; Rodney P. Carlisle, "Liberia's Flag of Convenience: Rough Water Ahead," *ORBIS* Vol. 24 (1980-81), pp. 881-891;

Paul Stephen Dempsey and Lisa L. Helling, "Oil Pollution by Ocean Vessels,: An Environmental Tragedy: The Legal Regime of Flags of Convenience, Multilateral Conventions and Coastal States," *Denver Journal of International Law and Policy*, Vol. 10 (1980-81), pp. 37-87; Richard J. Payne, "Flags of Convenience and Oil Pollution: A Threat to National Security?," *Houston Journal of International Law*, Vol. 3 (1980-81), pp. 67-99; Rodney P. Carlisle, *Sovereignty for Sale: The Origin and Evolution of the Panamanian and Liberian Flags of Convenience*, Annapolis, Maryland: Naval Institute Press, 1981; Basil N. Metaxas, "Flags of Convenience," *Marine Policy*, Vol. 5 (1981), pp. 52-66; UNCTAD Shipping Committee Calls for Phasing Out Flags of Convenience," *UN Chronicle*, Vol. 18, No. 8 (1981), pp. 39-41; S. J. Bergstrand, *Buy the Flag: Developments in the Open Registry Debate*, London: Polytechnic of Central London, 1983; Herbert Roof Northrup and Richard L. Rowan, *The International Transport Workers' Federation and Flag of Convenience Shipping*, Philadelphia: Industrial Research Unit, Wharton School, University of Pennsylvania, 1983; Sheila Farrel, "The Use of Flags of Convenience by Latin American Shipping," *Maritime Policy and Management*, Vol. 11 (1984), pp. 15-20; J. Hannigan, "Flags of Convenience and Maritime Labour," *Industrial Relations Journal*, Vol. 15 (1984), pp. 35-40; Jacelyn Kelley and Valerie Paul, *Flags of Convenience: The Emerging Regime and the Canadian Experience*, Halifax, Nova Scotia: Canadian Marine Transportation Centre, Dalhousie University, 1984; I. M. Sinan, "UNCTAD and the Flag of Convenience," *Journal of World Trade Law*, Vol. 18 (1984), pp. 95-109; S. J. Bergstrand and R. Doganis, "The Impact of Flags of Convenience (Open Registries)," in William E. Butler, ed., *The Law of the Sea and International Shipping: Anglo-Soviet Post UNCLOS Perspectives*, Dobbs Ferry, New York: Oceana, 1985, pp. 413-432; Moira L. McConnell, "Darkening Confusion Mounted Upon Darkening Confusion: The Search for the Elusive Genuine Link," *Journal of Maritime Law and Commerce*, Vol. 16 (1985), pp. 365-396; Mervyn Rowlinson, "Flags of Convenience: The UNCTAD Case," *Maritime Policy and Management*, Vol. 12 (1985), pp. 241-244; G.S. Egiyan, "'Flag of Convenience' or 'Open Registration' of Ships," *Marine Policy*, Vol. 14 (1990), pp. 106-111.

1986 UNITED NATIONS CONVENTION ON CONDITIONS FOR
REGISTRATION OF SHIPS
Done at Geneva on February 7, 1986
UNCTAD Doc. TD/RS/CONF/23 (March 13, 1986),
in *Law of the Sea Bulletin*, No. 7 (April 1986), pp. 90-102.

Article 5
National Maritime Administration

1. The flag State shall have a competent and adequate national maritime administration, which shall be subject to its jurisdiction and control.

2. The flag State shall implement applicable international rules and standards concerning, in particular, the safety of ships and persons on board and the prevention of pollution of the marine environment.

3. The maritime administration of the flag State shall ensure:

(a) That ships flying the flag of such State comply with its laws and regulations concerning registration of ships and with applicable international rules and standards concerning, in particular, the safety of ships and persons on board and the prevention of pollution of the marine environment;

(b) That ships flying the flag of such State are periodically surveyed by its authorized surveyors in order to ensure compliance with applicable international rules and standards;

(c) That ships flying the flag of such State carry on board documents, in particular, those evidencing the right to fly its flag and other valid relevant documents, including those required by international conventions to which the State of registration is a Party;

(d) That the owners of ships flying the flag of such State comply with the principles of registration of ships in accordance with the laws and regulations of such State and the provisions of this Convention.

4. The State of registration shall require all the appropriate information necessary for full identification and accountability concerning ships flying its flag.

Article 6
Identification and Accountability

1. The State of registration shall enter in its register of ships, *inter alia*, information concerning the ship and its owner. Information concerning the operator, when the operator is not the owner, should be included in the register of ships or in the official record of operators to be maintained in the Office of the Registrar or be readily accessible to him, in accordance with the laws and regulations of the State of registration. The State of registration shall issue documentation as evidence of the registration of the ship.

2. The State of registration shall take such measures as are necessary to ensure that the owner or owners, the operator or operators, or any other person or persons who can be held accountable for the management and operation of ships flying its flag can be easily identified by persons having a legitimate interest in obtaining such information.

3. Registers of ships should be available to those with a legitimate interest in obtaining information contained therein, in accordance with the laws and regulations of the flag State.

4. A State should ensure that ships flying its flag carry documentation including information about the identity of the owner or owners, the operator or operators or the person or persons accountable for the operation of such ships, and make available such information to port State authorities.

5. Log-books should be kept on all ships and retained for a reasonable period after the date of the last entry, notwithstanding any change in a ship's name, and should be available for inspection and copying by persons having a legitimate interest in obtaining such information, in accordance with the laws and regulations of the flag State. In the event of a ship being sold and its registration being changed to another State, log-books relating to the period before such sale should be retained and should be available for inspection and copying by persons having a legitimate interest in obtaining such information, in accordance with the laws and regulations of the former flag State.

6. A State shall take necessary measures to ensure that ships it enters in its register of ships have owners or operators who are adequately identifiable for the purpose of ensuring their full accountability.

7. A State should ensure that direct contact between owners of ships flying its flag and its government authorities is not restricted.

Article 10
Role of Flag States in Respect of the Management of
Shipowning Companies and Ships

1. The State of registration, before entering a ship in its register of ships, shall ensure that the shipowning company or a subsidiary shipowning company is established and/or has its principal place of business within its territory in accordance with its laws and regulations.

2. Where the shipowning company or a subsidiary shipowning company or the principal place of business of the shipowning company is not established in the flag State, before entering a ship in its register of ships, that there is a representative or management person who shall be a national of the flag State, or be domiciled therein. Such a representative or management person may be a natural or juridical person who is duly established or incorporated in the flag State, as the case may be, in accordance with its laws and regulations, and duly empowered to act on the shipowner's behalf and account. In particular, this representative or management person should be available for any legal process and to meet the shipowner's responsibilities in accordance with the laws and regulations of the State of registration.

3. The State of registration should ensure that the person or persons accountable for the management and operation of a ship flying its flag are in a position to meet the financial obligations that may arise from the operation of such a ship to cover risks which are normally insured in international maritime transportation in respect of damage to third parties. To this end the State of registration should ensure that ships flying its flag are in a position to provide at all times documents evidencing that an adequate guarantee, such as appropriate insurance or any other equilavent means, has been arranged. Furthermore, the State of registration should ensure that an appropriate mechanism, such as a maritime lien, mutual fund, wage insurance, social security scheme, or any governmental guarantee provided by an appropriate agency of the State of the accountable person, whether that person is an owner or operator, exists to cover wages and related monies owed to seafarers employed on ships flying its flag in the event of default of payment by their employers. The State of registration may also provide for any other appropriate mechanism to that effect in its laws and regulations.

Article 11
Register of ships

1. The State of registration shall establish a register of ships flying its flag, which register shall be maintained in a manner determined by the State and in conformity with the relevant provisions of this Convention. Ships entitled by the laws and regulations of a State to fly its flag shall be entered in this register in the name of the owner or owners or, where national laws and regulations so provide, the bareboat charterer.

2. Such register shall, *inter alia*, record the following;

(a) The name of the ship and the previous name and registry if any;

(b) The place of port of registration or home port and the official number or mark of identification of the ship;

(c) The international call sign of the ship, if assigned;

(d) The name of the builders, place of build and year of building of the ship;

(e) The description of the main technical characteristics of the ship;

(f) The name, address and, as appropriate, the nationality of the owner or of each of the owners;

and, unless recorded in another public document readily accessible to the Registrar in the flag State:

(g) The date of deletion or suspension of the previous registration of the ship;

(h) The name, address and, as appropriate, the nationality of the bareboat charterer, where national laws and regulations provide for the registration of ships bareboat chartered-in;

(i) The particulars of any mortgages or other similar charges upon the ship as stipulated by national laws and regulations.

3. Furthermore, such register should also record:

(a) If there is more than one owner, the proportion of the ship owned by each;

(b) The name, address and, as appropriate, the nationality of the operator, when the operator is not the owner or the bareboat charterer.

4. Before entering a ship in its register of ships a State should assure itself that the previous registration, if any, is deleted.

5. In the case of a ship bareboat chartered-in a State should assure itself that right to fly the flag of the former flag State is suspended. Such registration shall be effected on production of evidence, indicating suspension of previous registration as regards the nationality of the ship under the former flag State and indicating particulars of any registered encumbrances.

Article 14
Measures to Protect the Interests of Labour-Supplying Countries

1. For the purpose of safeguarding the interests of labour-supplying countries and of minimizing labour displacement and consequent economic dislocation, if any, within these countries, particularly developing countries, as a result of the adoption of this Convention, urgency should be given to the implementation, *inter alia*, of the measures as contained in resolution 1 annexed to this Convention.

2. In order to create favorable conditions for any contract or arrangement that may be entered into by shipowners or operators and the trade unions of seamen or other representative seamen bodies, bilateral agreements may be concluded between flag States and labour-supplying countries concerning the employment of seafarers of those labour-supplying countries.

Annex 1

Resolution 1
Measures to protect the interests of labour-supplying countries

The United Nations Conference on Conditions for Registration of Ships

Having adopted the United Nations Convention on Conditions for Registration of Ships,

Recommends as follows:

1. Labour-supplying countries should regulate the activities of the agencies within their jurisdiction that supply seafarers for ships flying the flag of another country in order to ensure that the contractual terms offered by those agencies will prevent abuses and contribute to the welfare of seafarers. For the protection of their seafarers, labor-supplying countries may require, *inter alia*, suitable security of the type mentioned in article 10 from the owners or operators of ships employing such seafarers or from other appropriate bodies; . . . .

REFERENCES

G. Marston, "The UN Convention on Registration of Ships," *Journal of World Trade Law*, Vol. 20 (1986), pp. 575-580; H. W. Wefers Bettink, "Open Registry, the Genuine Link and the 1986 Convention of Registration Conditions for Ships," *Netherlands Yearbook of International Law*, Vol. 18 (1987), pp. 69-119; M. L. McConnell, "'Business as Usual': An Evaluation of the 1986 United Nations Convention on Conditions for Registration of Ships," *Journal of Maritime Law and Commerce*, Vol. 18 (1987), pp. 435-449; S. G. Sturmey, "The United Nations Convention on Conditions for Registration of Ships," *Lloyd's Maritime and Commerce Law Quarterly*, 1987, pp. 97-117; George C. Kasoulides, "The 1986 United Nations Convention on the Conditions for Registration of Vessels and the Question of Open Registry," *Ocean Development and International Law*, Vol. 20 (1989), pp. 543-576.

Liberia	57,985,747
Panama	39,366,187
Japan	37,189,376
Greece	30,751,092
Soviet Union	16,767,526
Norway	14,567,326
U.S.A.	13,922,244
United Kingdom	13,260,290
China, People's Republic	10,167,450
Italy	8,530,108
Cyprus	8,134,083
France	7,864,931
Korea, Republic of	6,621,898
Singapore	6,385,919
India	6,324,145

15 Largest "Ship-Owning" States (In Registered Tonnage)
of the World as of July 1, 1985
Figure 7-2

Source: *Law of the Sea Bulletin*, No. 7 (April 1986), pp. 103-106. At the end of 1988, the total merchant shipping tonnage registered in some of the above countries increased substantially (in millions of tons): Liberia 89.6, Panama 69.7, Japan 38.5, Greece 37.6 and Cyprus 32.2. "The Biggest Merchant Fleets," *New York Times*, July 3, 1989, p. 30.

Margaret G. Wachenfeld, "Reflagging Kuwaiti Tankers: A U.S. Response in the Persian Gulf," *Duke Law Journal*, Vol. 1988, pp. 181, 183, 184, 185-187. Notes omitted. Copyright 1988, Duke University School of Law. Reprinted by permission of the copyright holder and the author.

Since September 1986, Iranian air attacks on Persian Gulf shipping have focused on Kuwaiti vessels and vessels bound for Kuwaiti ports. Iran singled out Kuwait partially in retaliation for the aid Kuwait has given to Iraq during the course of the eight-year war between Iran and Iraq. In response to escalating attacks on its shipping, Kuwait sought assistance from the United States and the Soviet Union in protecting its vessels and maritime commerce. In March 1987, the United States responded by reflagging eleven Kuwaiti oil tankers as United States vessels. . . .

Title 46, chapter 121 of the United States Code, governing the documentation of vessels, codifies the domestic implementation of the 1958 Convention [on the High Seas]. The Code requires that the tankers be: (1) properly constructed and inspected by the United States Coast Guard, (2) manned by the appropriate number of United States crew and officers, and (3) documented as belonging to a United States citizen . . . .

Although the United States is not a party to the 1986 Convention [on Conditions for Registration of Ships] current United States vessel documentation requirements would qualify under 1986 standards because the critical provisions permit each State to implement the 1986 Convention according to its own law. The reflagging meets the ownership [Article 8, paragraph 2] and management provisions [Article 10], but does not meet the national crew requirement [Article 9]. Under the terms of the 1986 Convention, however, it need only meet the ownership *or* manning requirements, not both [Article 7].

The United States reflagging also meets the 1958 Convention criteria because the United States has established the conditions necessary for the registration of vessels under its domestic law. The United States has the authority to regulate the administrative, technical and social matters of the vessels, and it exercises effective jurisdiction and control over the vessels. . . .

2. Meeting the Domestic Standards. The domestic procedures applied to reflag the Kuwaiti tankers were based on preexisting policy and practice. No new laws were written specifically for the occasion; none were waived except by statutory authority; no extraordinary procedures were used. Because the Kuwaiti tankers met all necessary statutory requirements or conditions for waivers, the reflagging, under domestic law, was technically proper.

The Coast Guard conducted the inspection in Kuwait. As part of the permissible inspection procedures, the Department of Defense requested a one-year waiver from compliance with those United States requirements that exceed requirements set by certain international safety conventions. The Department of Defense request was premised on pre-existing national security waivers provided in the Code.

United States-flagged vessels normally must carry a full complement of United States officers and at least 75% United States crew upon leaving a United States port. If, however, a vessel is in a foreign port and is deprived of her crew, alien replacements are sufficient until the vessel returns to a United States port and can secure United States replacements. This exemption does not apply to the master; the master commanding a United States vessel must always be a United States citizen. The United States Coast Guard, over the objection of several seamen's groups, considered the Kuwaiti tankers as falling within the ambit of the exemption. Because the Kuwaiti tankers are not departing from or calling at a United States port, the 75% United States crew and 100% United States officer requirements were deemed inapplicable. The tankers are manned by non-U.S. citizens and U.S. masters; the Kuwaitis agreed to replace the Soviet-bloc sailors on four of its tankers with Filipino crew and European or Arab officers.

United States ownership requirements are satisfied if a vessel is owned by a United States citizen or corporation. Corporate citizenship requirements are satisfied if: (1) the corporation is incorporated under the laws of the United States or any state thereof; (2) the president or other chief executive officer and the chairman of the board of directors are United States citizens; and (3) the number of foreign directors is less than the number necessary to constitute a quorum. The reflagged tankers are owned by a Delaware corporation, Chesapeake Shipping, Inc., which was formed under Delaware law on May 15, 1987. The corporation assumed ownership and operation of the eleven reflagged tankers, previously owned by the Kuwait Oil Tanker Company; the corporation then chartered the tankers back to the Kuwait company. Because neither United States nor international law requires equity ownership, Chesapeake Shipping, Inc., with its Delaware registration, American president and chief executive officer, and a majority of United States citizens on its board of directors, meets the domestic statutory requirements for United States corporate ownership even though the corporation and tankers are still essentially owned by the Kuwaiti government.

NOTE

On September 16, 1988, the U. S. Defense Department had recommended that the Navy halt its full time escort operation for reflagged Kuwaiti tankers and other U.S.-registered vessels in the Persian Gulf, because there had been no significant shipping attacks in two months. *Facts on File*, Vol. 48, No. 2496 (September 23, 1988), p. 587. In late 1988, it was reported that the U. S. Navy shifted to a kind of "zone defense" in which vessels were accompanied at a distance. The number of U. S. warships in the Persian Gulf was also reduced. *Facts on File*, Vol. 48, No. 2510 (December 31, 1988), p. 966. In January 1989, it was reported that six of the eleven Kuwaiti tankers were removed from U S. protection. "U.S. to End Protection of 6 Kuwaiti Tankers," *New York Times*, January 18, 1989, p. 10.

REFERENCES

Oversight on the Reflagging of Kuwaiti Tankers: Hearings Before the House Committee on Merchant Marine and Fisheries, 100th Congress, 1st Session, Washington, D.C.: U. S. Government Printing Office, 1987; Jordan J. Paust, "Under International Law, Reflagging Doesn't Fly," *New York Times*, July 26, 1987, p. E26; Abraham D. Safaer [Legal Advisor of the Department of State], "Complied with U.S. Law," *New York Times*, August 16, 1987, p. E24; Scott Davidson, "United States Protection of Reflagged Kuwaiti Vessels in the Gulf War: The Legal Implication," *International Journal of Estuarine and Coastal Law*, Vol. 4, No. 3 (August 1989), pp. 173-191; Rudiger Wolfrum, "Reflagging and Escort Operation in the Persian Gulf: An International Law Perspective," *Virginia Journal of International Law*, Vol. 29 (1989), pp. 387-399.

F. DUTY TO RENDER ASSISTANCE AT SEA

1958 CONVENTION ON THE HIGH SEAS

Article 12

1. Every State shall require the master of a ship sailing under its flag, in so far as he can do so without serious danger to the ship, the crew or the passengers,

(a) To render assistance to any person found at sea in danger of being lost;

(b) To proceed with all possible speed to the rescue of persons in distress if informed of their need of assistance, in so far as such action may reasonably be expected of him;

(c) After a collision, to render assistance to the other ship, her crew and her passengers and, where possible, to inform the other ship of the name of his own ship, her port of registry and the nearest port at which she will call.

2. Every coastal State shall promote the establishment and maintenance of an adequate and effective search and rescue service regarding safety on and over the sea and - where circumstances so require - by way of mutual regional arrangements co-operate with neighboring States for this purpose.

[Article 98 of the 1982 United Nations Convention on the Law of the Sea is identical.]

INTERNATIONAL LAW COMMISSION
Commentary, Draft Article 36
Yearbook of the International Law Commission 1956,
Vol. II, p. 281.

The Commission deemed it advisable to include a provision to the effect that ships must render assistance to all persons in danger on the high seas. The Commission has borrowed the terms of article XI of the Brussels Convention of 23 September 1910 for the Unification of Certain Rules of Law respecting Assistance and Salvage at Sea, article 8 of the Convention of the same date for the Unification of Certain Rules of Law with respect to Collisions between Vessels, and Regulation 10 of Chapter V of the Regulations annexed to the International Convention on the Safety of Life at Sea, of June 10, 1948. In the opinion of the Commission, the article as worded above states the existing international law.

NOTE

Article 98 of the 1982 United Nations Convention on the Law of the Sea is essentially the same as that of Article 12 of the 1958 Convention, except in paragraph 2, the word "operation" is added after "the establishment." Despite the above stated duty to render assistance at sea, some ships on the high seas failed to carry out this obligation. E.g., see David E. Sanger, "Japanese Say 3 Ships Refused to Aid Boat People," *New York Times*, March 24, 1989, p. A6. On February 24, 1989, a United States Navy captain was reprimanded by a court-martial for dereliction of duty in failing to adequately assist Vietnamese refugees lost in the South China Sea in June 1988. Captain Alexander G. Balian, who was in charge of the Dubuque and the latter was en route to the

Persian Gulf to assist United States minesweepers, left the refugee boat after providing refugees there with food, water and navigational charts. The refugees were rescued by Filipino fisherman after 37 days at sea. Only 52 of the 110 refugees who left Vietnam survived. The court found Captain Balian guilty of failure to make a detailed inspection of the boat, make a proper medical evaluation of the refugees and provide navigational equipment to help them reach land. Therefore, he failed to comply with "the international tradition and custom of the seagoing mariner and long-established custom of the U.S. Navy to extend humanitarian assistance to people in peril at sea." See "Officer Convicted in Refugees Case," *New York Times*, February 25, 1989, p. 7.

A new convention on salvage was adopted recently--International Convention on Salvage, April 28, 1989. IMO Doc. LEG/CONF.7/26. For a study of this Convention, see N.J.J. Gaskell, "The International Convention on Salvage 1989," *International Journal of Esutarine and Coastal Law*, Vol. 4, No. 4 (1989), pp. 268-287; Donald A. Kerr, "The 1989 Salvage Convention: Expediency or Equity," *Journal of Maritime Law and Commerce*, Vol. 20 (1989), pp. 505-550.

G. IMMUNITIES

1958 CONVENTION ON THE HIGH SEAS

Article 8

1. Warships on the high seas have complete immunity from the jurisdiction of any State other than the flag State.

2. For the purposes of these articles, the term "warship" means a ship belonging to the naval forces of a State and bearing the external marks distinguishing warships of its nationality, under the command of an officer duly commissioned by the government and whose name appears in the Navy list, and manned by a crew who are under regular naval discipline.

Article 9

Ships owned or operated by a State and used only on government non-commercial service shall, on the high seas, have complete immunity from the jurisdiction of any State other than the flag State.

[Articles 95 and 96 of the 1982 United Nations Convention on the Law of the Sea are identical to the above provisions.]

NOTE

The principal issue raised by Article 9 concerns the status of government owned (both commercial and non-commercial) vessels. The International Law Commission (ILC) draft article 33 which was precedent for Article 9 of the Convention reads as follows:

> For all purposes connected with the exercise of powers on the high seas
> by States other than the flag State, ships owned or operated by a State

and used only on government service, *whether commercial* or non-commercial, shall be assimilated to and shall have the same immunity as warships. (Emphasis added). (*Yearbook of the International Law Commission 1956*, Vol. II, p. 280.)

In its commentary to this draft article, the ILC noted that:

> The Commission discussed the question whether ships used on commercial government service on the high seas could claim the same immunity as warships with respect to the exercise of powers by other States, and answered this question in the affirmative. Although aware of the objections to the granting of immunity to merchant ships used on government service, which led to the denial of this right in the International Convention for the Unification of Certain Rules relating to the Immunity of State-owned Vessels, signed at Brussels on 10 April 1926, the Commission held that, as regards navigation on the high sea, there were no sufficient grounds for not granting to State ships used on commercial government service the same immunity as other State ships. The Commission thinks it worth pointing out that the assimilation referred to in article 33 concerns only the immunity of ships for the purpose of the exercise of powers by other States, so that there is no question of granting to ships that are not warships policing rights over other ships, exercisable under international law by warships. (*Yearbook of the International Law Commission 1956*, Vol. II, p. 280.)

The United States proposed an amendment to the draft article submitted by the ILC (A/CONF.13/C.2/L.76, [First] United Nations Conference on the Law of the Sea, *Official Records*, Vol. IV, p. 135) which provided that "[s]hips owned or operated by a State and used only on government non-commercial service shall, when on the high seas, have complete immunity from jurisdiction of any State other than the flag State." The United States added a comment to its proposal which provided in part that:

> . . . .the International Law Commission's commentary indicates that it was not intended that government-owned ships other than warships should have policing rights on the high seas. As drafted, the article might be interpreted as meaning that other government-owned ships have such rights. The proposal clarifies the article to conform with the intent of the International Law Commission.

> "The United States delegation believes that the immunity of a vessel owned or operated by a State should be based on the purpose of its service."

In supporting the position of the Soviet Union in favor of extending immunity to governmental commercial ships, Mr. Keilin (U.S.S.R.) made the following observations, taken from the synopsis in the *Official Records* of the Conference:

> the immunity of government ships, including those operated for commercial purposes, was one of the oldest-established principles of international law. It was based on the generally accepted respect for the sovereignty of foreign States, in virtue of which no State was entitled

to exercise jurisdiction over another State; the time-honoured principle was expressed in the maxim: *par in parem non habet imperium* [an equal has no dominion over an equal].

The immunity of government ships, including those operated for commercial purposes was admitted in the legal practice of many States, among them States whose representatives in the Committee were opposed to that principle. There was an obvious contradiction between the statement of their representatives and the position adopted by certain States, which, when their own interests were directly affected, pleaded the immunity in question. . . .

In recent years, the United States of America had been trying to introduce a restrictive interpretation of immunity by differentiating between the functions exercised by a State in public and in private international law. But the protagonist of such an interpretation could not show any grounds for it. Indeed, it would be an inadmissable interference in the domestic affairs of a foreign State for any judicial organ to lay down which functions of the foreign State were exercised in public law and which in private law. It would surely be a violation of international law if national courts were to try to distinguish between the sovereign and non-sovereign acts of a foreign State, particularly since in some countries commercial vessels were state-owned and the operation of commercial navigation constituted a function of the State. . . .

The reasons for that attempt to restrict the immunity of government ships operated for commercial purposes were not difficult to surmise. On the one hand, there was a completely unfounded fear that to concede such immunity might place privately owned ships at a disadvantage in international trade by comparison with government ships. On the other hand, the question was being confused, possibly deliberately. The conception of immunity was being replaced by one of irresponsibility, although the immunity of government commercial ships in no way implied any irresponsibility. There had never been a case in which any valid claims in respect of Soviet Union ships had not been settled. Certain questions concerning suits brought against U.S.S.R. government commercial ships, and suits brought by such ships against foreign ships, had been and were being considered, to the satisfaction of the parties in dispute, by the Maritime Arbitration Commission of the Soviet Union, established some thirty years previously.

Established institutions of international law, such as the immunity of government ships, including those operated for commercial purposes, should be respected. The observance of that immunity did not encroach upon the interests of privately owned ships. For those reasons, the Soviet Union delegation objected to any restriction of the immunity of government ships, a restriction which ran counter to international law, and would vote for the adoption of article 33 of the International Law Commission's draft. *Official Record*, Vol. IV, pp. 69-70.

In rebuttal, the United States representative, Mr. Colclough, had the following observations, also taken from the synopsis in the *Official Records* of the Conference:

> he could not agree with the U.S.S.R. representative's statement made at the previous meeting that delegations which opposed the International Law Commission's draft of article 33 had assumed an inconsistent position and that their States recognized the principle of complete immunity of all state-owned vessels. In support of his contention, the U.S.S.R. representative had cited decisions of the United States Supreme Court, but had ignored the issue before the Committee, which was whether the Conference should adopt as a principle of international law the granting of complete immunity to state-owned vessels used for commercial purposes.
>
> There was no more complete immunity in the law of nations than that possessed by warships, to which it was proposed to assimilate all other state-owned vessels. But it was not that type of immunity to which the U.S.S.R. representative had referred. The cases he had cited reflected the state of domestic law as it had existed at the time of the judicial decisions in question. The development of international law should, however, be taken into account.
>
> A study of the law of sovereign immunity revealed the development of two conflicting concepts, that of the classical theory of absolute immunity and the modern or restricted theory, under which immunity was recognized with regard to sovereign or public acts of the State (*jus imperii*), but not with regard to private acts (*jus gestionis*). Before the twentieth century, it would have been virtually impossible to find any act of a sovereign State which was not the exercise of *jus imperii*, and hence immune from the jurisdiction of any other State. The advent of new political philosophies, however, had resulted in increasing inroads by the State into the private and commercial field; those inroads had been most marked in the case of the Soviet Union and other countries. International law had recognized the challenge of such new situations, and the creation of new States was contributing to that trend in international law. . . .
>
> Since the present attitude of the United States Government was completely different from the classical and absolute theory of sovereign immunity, it could not be seriously contended that the United States proposal (A/CONF.13/C.2/L.76) was inconsistent with its law and policy. If the law of nations was to remain responsive to the requirements of international relations, definite principles should be agreed upon and should be designed to safeguard and promote private commercial transactions, rather than to jeopardize and retard them by providing an unlimited advantage for state ownership. *Official Records1*, Vol. IV, pp. 71-72.

The United States proposal was adopted by 46 votes to nine, with two abstentions (*Official Records*, Vol. VI, p. 76). A United Kingdom proposal (A/CONF.13/C.2/L.113, *Official Records*, Vol. IV, p. 147) to define non-commercial purposes was also adopted by 24 votes to 14, with 21 abstentions (*Official Records*, Vol. IV., p. 76) but because of procedural irregularities was subsequently reconsidered and withdrawn (*Official Records*, Vol. IV, pp. 97-100). The proposal suggested a new article to read as follows:

> For the purposes of the present convention ships owned or operated by a State and used only on government non-commercial service are ships which, being owned or operated by a government, fall into one or other of the following categories:

> (i) Yachts, patrol vessels, hospital ships, fleet auxiliaries, military supply ships, troopships;

> (ii) Cable ships, ocean weather ships, vessels carrying out scientific investigation, fishery protection vessels;

> (iii) Vessels employed in services of a similar character to (i) and (ii).

As a result of the adoption of the United States amendment the following countries (all parties to the Convention) filed reservations concerning Article 9:   Albania, Bulgaria, Byelorussian S.S.R., Czechoslovakia, Hungary, Mexico, Poland, Romania, Ukrainian S.S.R. and the Soviet Union. Typical of the language used was that of the Soviet Union:

> The Government of the Union of Soviet Socialist Republics considers that the principle of international law according to which a ship on the high seas is not subject to any jurisdiction except that of the flag State applies without restriction to all government ships.

All of the reservations and declarations were objected to by the Netherlands, the United Kingdom and the United States; Australia objected to all except that made by Mexico which was not published at the time of Australia's objections. Portugal has objected to the Mexican reservation.

NOTE

Article 95, paragraph 1 and Article 96 of the 1982 United Nations Convention on the Law of the Sea contains provisions identical to Article 8, paragraph 1 and Article 9 of the 1958 Convention on the High Seas. Article 29 of the 1982 Convention on definition of warships is identical to Article 8, paragraph 2 of the 1958 Convention.

Sovereign immunity issues in the courts for the United States are now governed by the Foreign Sovereign Immunities Act of 1976, P.L. 94-583 (94th Cong., 2d Sess., October 21, 1976). The law exempts from sovereign immunity a wide range of activities, including actions based on commercial activities carried on in the United States by the foreign state and actions based on rights in property taken in violation of international law. Similar laws were also enacted in many Western countries. See *Materials on Jurisdictional Immunities of States and Their Property*, United Nations Legislative Series ST/LEG/SER. B/20, New York: The United Nations, 1982.

REFERENCES

W. L. McNair, "Legal Aspects of State Shipping," *Transactions of the Grotius Society*, Vol. 34 (1948), pp. 310-61; M. Brandon, "Sovereign Immunity of Government-Owned Corporations and Ships," *Cornell Law Quarterly*, Vol. 39 (1954), pp. 425-462; R. B. Lillich, "The Geneva

Conference on the Law of the Sea and the Immunity of Foreign State-Owned Commercial Vessels," *George Washington Law Review*, Vol. 28 (1960), pp. 408-420; L. T. Lee, "Jurisdiction over Foreign Merchant Ships in the Territorial Sea: An Analysis of the Geneva Convention of the Law of the Sea," *American Journal of International Law*, Vol. 55 (1961), pp. 77-96; T. K. Thommen, *Legal Status of Government Merchant Ships in International Law*, The Hague: Martinus Nijhoff, 1962; P. D. Clark, "Criminal Jurisdiction over Merchant Vessels Engaged in International Trade," *Journal of Maritime Law and Commerce*, Vol. 11 (1980), pp. 219-237.

H.   COLLISION JURISDICTION

1958 CONVENTION ON THE HIGH SEAS

Article 10

1. Every State shall take such measures for ships under its flag as are necessary to ensure safety at sea with regard *inter alia* to:

(a) The use of signals, the maintenance of communications and the prevention of collisions;

(b) The manning of ships and labour conditions for crews taking into account the applicable international labour instruments;

(c) The construction, equipment and seaworthiness of ships.

2. In taking such measures each State is required to conform to generally accepted international standards and to take any step which may be necessary to ensure their observance.

Article 11

1. In the event of a collision or of any other incident of navigation concerning a ship on the high seas, involving the penal or disciplinary responsibility of the master or of any other person in the service of the ship, no penal or disciplinary proceedings may be instituted against such persons except before the judicial or administrative authorities either of the flag State or of the State of which such person is a national.

2. In disciplinary measures, the State which had issued a master's certificate or a certificate of competence or license shall alone be competent, after due legal process, to pronounce the withdrawal of such certificates, even if the holder is not a national of the State which issued them.

3. No arrest or detention of the ship, even as a measure of investigation, shall be ordered by any authorities other than those of the flag State.

[Article 97 of the 1982 United Nations Convention on the Law of the Sea is identical with Article 11 of the 1958 Convention.]

INTERNATIONAL LAW COMMISSION
1956 Commentary, Draft Article 35
Yearbook of the International Law Commission 1956,
Vol. II, p. 281.

(1) The Commission thought that no account should be taken for the moment of private international law problems arising out of the question of collision, but considered it essential to determine what tribunal was competent to deal with any penal proceedings arising out of a collision. In view of the judgment rendered by the Permanent Court of International Justice on 7 September 1927 in the "Lotus" case, [P.C.I.J, Ser A., No. 10 (1927)], the Court held that "there is no rule of international law in regard to collision cases to the effect that criminal proceedings are exclusively within the jurisdiction of the state whose flag is flown"] the Commission felt obliged to take a decision on the subject. This judgment, which was carried by the President's casting vote after an equal vote of six to six, was very strongly criticized and caused serious disquiet in international maritime circles. A diplomatic conference held at Brussels in 1952 disagreed with the conclusions of the judgment. The Commission concurred with the decisions of the conference, which were embodied in the International Convention for the Unification of Certain Rules relating to the Penal Jurisdiction in matters of Collisions and Other Incidents of Navigation, signed at Brussels on 10 May 1952. It did so with the object of protecting ships and their crews from the risk of penal proceedings before foreign courts in the event of collision on the high seas, since such proceedings may constitute an intolerable interference with international navigation. In such a case, proceedings may take place only before the judicial or administrative authorities of the State whose flag was flown by the ship on which the persons in question were serving or of the State of which they are nationals. In making this latter addition, the Commission adopted the findings of the Brussels Conference in order to enable States to take penal or disciplinary measures against their nationals serving on board foreign vessels who are accused of causing collisions, since in such cases some States wish to be able to prosecute their nationals with a view to withdrawing the certificates issued to them. The power to withdraw or suspend certificates rests solely with the State which has issued them.

[For duty to render assistance after collision, see Article 12 of the 1958 Convention, mentioned in Section F.]

I. SLAVERY

1958 CONVENTION ON THE HIGH SEAS

Article 13

Every State shall adopt effective measures to prevent and punish the transport of slaves in ships authorized to fly its flag, and to prevent the unlawful use of its flag for that purpose. Any slave taking refuge on board any ship, whatever its flag, shall, *ipso facto*, be free.

[Article 99 of the 1982 United Nations Convention on the Law of the Sea is identical.]

NOTE

Unless authorized by special agreement, a ship suspected of slave trade may be visited and inspected by foreign law enforcement ships on the high seas for the purpose of verifying the ship's right to fly its flag, but the ship cannot be seized, unless authorized by the flag state. *See* Article

22(1)(b) of the 1958 Convention on the High Seas and Article 110 (1)(b) of the 1982 Convention on the Law of the Sea. Jurisdiction over slave trade of a ship remains with the flag state.

REFERENCES

H. H. Wilson, "Some Principal Aspects of British Efforts to Crush the African Slave Trade, 1807-1929," *American Journal of International Law*, Vol. 44 (1950), pp. 505-526; J. A. C. Gutteridge, "Supplementary Slavery Convention, 1956," *International and Comparative Law Quarterly*, Vol. 6 (1957), pp. 449-471; M. S. McDougal and W. T. Burke, *The Public Order of the Oceans: A Contemporary Law of the Sea*, New Haven and London: Yale University Press, 1962, pp. 879-885; M. M. Whiteman, *Digest of International Law*, Vol. 4, Washington, D.C., U.S. Government Printing Office, 1965, pp. 645-648.

J. PIRACY, ILLICIT TRAFFIC IN NARCOTIC DRUGS, UNLAWFUL ACTS AGAINST THE SAFETY OF NAVIGATION, WARSHIPS' RIGHT OF VISIT AND ENFORCEMENT JURISDICTION OVER FOREIGN SHIPS ON HIGH SEAS

1958 CONVENTION ON THE HIGH SEAS

Article 14

All States shall co-operate to the fullest possible extent in the repression of piracy on the high seas or in any other place outside the jurisdiction of any State.

Article 15

Piracy consists of any of the following acts:

(1) Any illegal acts of violence, detention or any act of depredation, committed for private ends by the crew or the passengers of a private ship or a private aircraft, and directed:

(a) On the high seas, against another ship or aircraft, or against persons or property on board such ship or aircraft;

(b) Against a ship, aircraft, persons or property in a place outside the jurisdiction of any State;

(2) Any act of voluntary participation in the operation of a ship or of an aircraft with knowledge of facts making it a pirate ship or aircraft;

(3) Any act of inciting or of intentionally facilitating an act described in sub-paragraph 1 or sub-paragraph 2 of this article.

Article 16

The acts of piracy, as defined in article 15, committed by a warship, government ship or government aircraft whose crew has mutinied or taken control of the ship or aircraft are assimilated to acts committed by a private ship.

Article 17

A ship or aircraft is considered a pirate ship or aircraft if it is intended by the persons in dominant control to be used for the purpose of committing one of the acts referred to in article 15. The same applies if the ship or aircraft has been used to commit any such act, so long as it remains under the control of the person guilty of that act.

Article 18

A ship or aircraft may retain its nationality although it has become a pirate ship or aircraft. The retention or loss of nationality is determined by the law of the State from which such nationality was derived.

Article 19

On the high seas, or in any other place outside the jurisdiction of any State, every State may seize a pirate ship or aircraft, or a ship taken by piracy and under the control of pirates, and arrest the persons and seize the property on board. The courts of the State which carried out the seizure may decide upon the penalties to be imposed, and may also determine the action to be taken with regard to the ships, aircraft or property, subject to the rights of third parties acting in good faith.

Article 20

Where the seizure of a ship or aircraft on suspicion of piracy has been effected without adequate grounds, the State making the seizure shall be liable to the State the nationality of which is possessed by the ship or aircraft, for any loss or damage caused by the seizure.

Article 21

A seizure on account of piracy may only be carried out by warships or military aircraft, or other ship or aircraft on government service authorized to that effect.

Article 22

1. Except where acts of interference derive from powers conferred by treaty, a warship which encounters a foreign merchant ship on the high seas is not justified in boarding her unless there is reasonable ground for suspecting:

(a) That the ship is engaged in piracy; or

(b) That the ship in engaged in slave trade; or

(c) That, though flying a foreign flag or refusing to show its flag, the ship is, in reality, of the same nationality as the warship.

2. In the case provided for in sub-paragraphs (a), (b) and (c) above, the warship may proceed to verify the ship's right to fly its flag. To this end, it may send a boat under the command of an officer to the suspected ship. If suspicion remains after the documents have been checked, it may proceed to a further examination on board the ship, which must be carried out with all possible consideration.

3. If the suspicions prove to be unfounded, and provided that the ship boarded has not committed any act justifying them, it shall be compensated for any loss or damage that may have been sustained.

UNITED STATES CONSTITUTION
Art. 1, §8, cl. 10

The Congress shall have power . . . . to define and punish piracies and felonies committed on the high seas, and offenses against the law of nations.

> *Restatement of the Foreign Relations Law of the United States*, Third Revision, Vol. 2., St. Paul, Minn,: American Law Institute, 1987, pp. 83-87, 89. Copyright by The American Law Institute. Reprinted with the permission of The American Law Institute.

§522. Enforcement Jurisdiction over Foreign Ships on High Seas

. . . . a warship or clearly-marked law enforcement ship of any state, may board such a ship if authorized by the flag state, or if there is reason to suspect that the ship

(a) is engaged in piracy, slave trade, or unauthorized broadcasting;

(b) is without nationality; or

(c) though flying a foreign flag or refusing to show its flag, is in fact of the same nationality as the warship or law enforcement ship.

Comment:

c. *Piracy.*

Not every act of violence committed on the high seas is piracy under international law. Only the following acts are considered piratical:

(i) Any illegal acts of violence, detention or depredation committed for private ends by the crew or the passengers of a private ship or a private aircraft, and directed against another ship or aircraft on the high seas, or against persons or property on board such other ship or aircraft; or against a ship, aircraft, persons, or property in a place outside the jurisdiction of any state;

(ii) any act of voluntary participation in the operation of a ship or of an aircraft with knowledge of facts making it a pirate ship or aircraft;

(iii) any act of inciting or of intentionally facilitating an act described in subparagraphs (1) or (2).

In addition, acts committed by a mutinous crew of a warship or other government ship or aircraft against another ship or aircraft, may also constitute piracy. 1958 Convention on the High Seas, Articles 15-16; LOS Convention, Articles 101-102.

REPORTER'S NOTES

2. *Piracy and hijacking* . . . .

The definition of piracy, Comment c, includes acts by a pirate ship or aircraft against "another ship or aircraft on the high seas" (para. (1)(a)). That clause was designed to cover acts against a ship or a sea plane floating on the sea; acts committed in the air by one aircraft against another were not included in the definition of piracy but left for regulation outside the framework of the law of the sea. The definition includes also acts committed in "a place outside the jurisdiction of any state" (para (1)(b)). That reference is to "acts committed by a ship or aircraft on an island constituting *terra nullius* or on the shores of an unoccupied territory," so as to ensure that such acts would not escape all penal jurisdiction. Report of the International Law Commission, [1956] 2 Y.B. Int'l L. Comm'n 282, 11 U.N. GAOR Supp. No. 9 at 28 . . . .

4. *Illicit traffic in narcotic drugs or psychotropic substances.*

A ship suspected of traffic in illicit drugs may be visited and inspected by a foreign law enforcement ship with the consent of the ship's master. Absent such consent, it may be visited and searched only pursuant to formal or informal agreement with the flag state, and such agreement is always required for the seizure of the ship. . . .

No such agreement is necessary, however, when the suspected ship is without nationality or is assimilated to one without nationality. . . .

6. *Other situations justifying inspection or seizure.*

It may be suggested that the right to inspect and to seize foreign ships be extended to ships carrying stolen nuclear materials or escaping terrorists, but the present international law on the subject in unclear . . . .

8. *Consent of flag state to seizure of ships.*

Except in cases of piracy, slave trade, or unauthorized broadcasting, . . . a state may interfere with the ships of another state on the high seas only when expressly authorized by international agreement. 1958 Convention on the High Seas, Art. 22; [1982 Law of the Sea] Convention, Art. 110. States have been reluctant to accord such authority, but a few states have done so in special circumstances.

For instance, by agreement in 1981, the United Kingdom gave permission to United States authorities to board, search and seize ships under the British flag in an area comprising the Gulf of Mexico, the Caribbean Sea, and a portion of the Atlantic Ocean, in any case in which United States authorities reasonably believe that a ship "has on board a cargo of drugs for importation into the United States in violation of the laws of the United States"; but the United States agreed to release the ship or any United Kingdom national found on board the ship, if the United Kingdom should, within a specified period, "object to the continued exercise of United States jurisdiction" over the ship or person. 1981 Agreement to Facilitate the Interdiction by the United States of Vessels of the United Kingdom Suspected of Trafficking in Drugs, T.I.A.S. No. 10296. . . .

In 1981, Haiti authorized United States authorities to board Haitian flag vessels on the high seas for the purpose of ascertaining whether there were any Haitians on board intending to commit an offense against United States immigration laws. The agreement authorized United States authorities to detain any vessel with such migrants aboard, and to return the vessel and persons aboard the vessel to a Haitian port or to release them on the high seas to a representative of Haiti. T.I.A.S. No. 10241. . . .

9. *United States jurisdiction over gambling ships.*

The Gambling Act of 1948 applies to "any citizen or resident of the United States or any other person who is on an American vessel or is otherwise under or within the jurisdiction of the United States," who commits certain acts on a gambling ship, "if such gambling ship is on the high seas, or is an American vessel or otherwise under or within the jurisdiction of the United States, and is not within the jurisdiction of any State." The Act defines an "American vessel" as either "any vessel documented or numbered under the laws of the United States" or "any vessel which is neither documented or numbered under the laws of the United States nor documented under the laws of any foreign country, if such vessel is owned by, chartered to, or otherwise controlled by one or more citizens or residents of the United States or corporations organized under the laws of the United States or of any State." 18 U.S.C. §§ 1081-1083. This law was applied to defendants engaged in gambling activity on the high seas on a Greek Line ship on a weekend voyage "to nowhere" from New York harbor, on the grounds that they were United States citizens and residents and that "citizenship alone, apart from locus, suffices to confer upon the United States jurisdiction over extraterritorial acts." United States v. Black, 291 F.Supp. 262, 265-66 (S.D.N.Y.1968).

1982 UNITED NATIONS CONVENTION ON THE LAW OF THE SEA

Article 100
Duty to co-operate in the repression of piracy

All States shall co-operate to the fullest possible extent in the repression of piracy on the high seas or in any other place outside the jurisdiction of any State.

Article 101
Definition of piracy

Piracy consists of any of the following acts:

(a) any illegal acts of violence or detention, or any act of depredation, committed for private ends by the crew or the passengers of a private ship or a private aircraft,and directed:

   (i) on the high seas, against another ship or aircraft, or against persons or property on board such ship or aircraft;

   (ii) against a ship, aircraft, persons or property in a place outside the jurisdiction of any State;

(b) any act of voluntary participation in the operation of a ship or of an aircraft with knowledge of facts making it a pirate ship or aircraft;

(c) any act of inciting or of intentionally facilitating an act described in sub-paragraphs (a) or (b).

Article 102
Piracy by a warship, government ship or government aircraft whose crew has mutinied

The acts of piracy, as defined in article 101, committed by a warship, government ship or government aircraft whose crew has mutinied and taken control of the ship or aircraft are assimilated to acts committed by a private ship or aircraft.

Article 103
Definition of a pirate ship or aircraft

A ship or aircraft is considered a pirate ship or aircraft if it is intended by the persons in dominant control to be used for the purpose of committing one of the acts referred to in article 101. The same applies if the ship or aircraft has been used to commit any such act, so long as it remains under the control of the persons guilty of that act.

Article 104
Retention or loss of the nationality of a pirate ship or aircraft

A ship or aircraft may retain its nationality although it has become a pirate ship or aircraft. The retention or loss of nationality is determined by the law of the State from which such nationality was derived.

Article 105
Seizure of a pirate ship or aircraft

On the high seas, or in any other place outside the jurisdiction of any State, every State may seize a pirate ship or aircraft, or a ship or aircraft taken by piracy and under the control of pirates, and arrest the persons and seize the property on board. The courts of the State which carried out the seizure may decide upon the penalties to be imposed, and may also determine the action to be taken with regard to the ships, aircraft or property, subject to the rights of third parties acting in good faith.

Article 106
Liability for seizure without adequate grounds

Where the seizure of a ship or aircraft on suspicion of piracy has been effected without adequate grounds, the State making the seizure shall be liable to the State the nationality of which is possessed by the ship or aircraft for any loss or damage caused by the seizure.

Article 107
Ships and aircraft which are entitled to seize on account of piracy

A seizure on account of piracy may be carried out only by warship or military aircraft, or other ships or aircraft clearly marked and identifiable as being on government service and authorized to that effect.

Article 108
Illicit traffic in narcotic drugs or psychotropic substances

1. All States shall co-operate in the suppression of illicit traffic in narcotic drugs and psychotropic substances engaged in by ships on the high seas contrary to international conventions.

2. Any State which has reasonable grounds for believing that a ship flying its flag is engaged in illicit traffic in narcotic drugs or psychotropic substances may request the co-operation of other States to suppress such traffic.

Article 109
Unauthorized broadcasting from the high seas

1. All States shall co-operate in the suppression of unauthorized broadcasting from the high seas.

2. For the purposes of the Convention, "unauthorized broadcasting" means the transmission of sound radio or television broadcasts from a ship or installation on the high seas intended for reception by the general public contrary to international regulations, but excluding the transmission of distress calls.

3. Any person engaged in unauthorized broadcasting may be prosecuted before the court of:

(a) the flag State of the ship;

(b) the State of registry of the installation;

(c) the State of which the person is a national;

(d) any State where the transmission can be received; or

(e) any State where authorized radio communication is suffering interference.

4. On the high seas, a State having jurisdiction in accordance with paragraph 3 may, in conformity with article 110, arrest any person or ship engaged in unauthorized broadcasting and seize the broadcasting apparatus.

Article 110
Rights of visit

1. Except where acts of interference derive from powers conferred by treaty, a warship which encounters on the high seas a foreign ship, other than a ship entitled to complete immunity in accordance with articles 95 and 96, is not justified in boarding it unless there is reasonable ground for suspecting that:

(a) the ship is engaged in piracy;

(b) the ship is engaged in the slave trade;

(c) the ship is engaged in unauthorized broadcasting and the flag State of the warship has jurisdiction under article 109;

(d) the ship is without nationality; or

(e) though flying a foreign flag or refusing to show its flag, the ship is, in reality, of the same nationality as the warship.

2. In the case provided for in paragraph 1, the warship may proceed to verify the ship's right to fly its flag. To this end, it may send a boat under the command of an officer to the suspected ship. If suspicion remains after the documents have been checked, it may proceed to a further examination on board the ship, which must be carried out with all possible consideration.

3. If the suspicions prove to be unfounded, and provided that the ship boarded has not committed any act justifying them, it shall be compensated for any loss or damage that may have been sustained.

4. These provisions apply *mutatis mutandis* to military aircraft.

5. These provisions also apply to any other authorized ships or aircraft clearly marked and identifiable as being on government service.

REFERENCES

E. D. Dickinson, "Is the Crime of Piracy Obsolete?" *Harvard Law Review*, Vol. 38 (1925), pp. 334-360; *In re Piracy Jure Gentium*, July 26, 1934, L. R. [1934] A.C. 586, reprinted in "Judicial Committee of the Privy Council," *American Journal of International Law*, Vol. 29 (1935), pp. 140-150; C. Fairman, "A Note on Re Piracy *Jure Gentium*," *American Journal of International Law*, Vol. 29 (1935), pp. 508-512; *Irish Law Times*, Vol. 68 (1934), pp. 287, 293; D. H. N. Johnson, "Piracy in Modern International Law," *Transactions of the Grotius Society*, Vol. 43 (1959), pp. 63-85; C. G. Fenwick, "'Piracy' in the Caribbean," *American Journal of International Law*, Vol. 56 (1961), pp. 426-428; B. Forman, "International Law of Piracy and the Santa Maria Incident," *JAG Journal*, Vol. 15 (1961), pp. 143-148, 166, 168; L. C. Green, "The Santa Maria: Rebels or Pirates?" *British Yearbook of International Law*, Vol. 37 (1961), pp. 496-505; M. S. McDougal and W. T. Burke, *The Public Order of the Oceans: A Contemporary International Law of the Sea*, New Haven and London, Yale University Press, 1962, pp. 875-879; B. H. Brittin, "Piracy: A Modern Conspectus," *British Yearbook of International Law*, Vol. 19 (1938), pp. 198-208; M. M. Whiteman, *Digest of International Law*, Vol. 4, Washington, D.C., U.S. Government Printing Office, 1965, pp. 648-667; R. W. Gehring, "Defense Against Insurgents on the High Seas: The Lyla Express and Johnny Express," *JAG Journal*, Vol. 27 (1973), pp. 317-348; Alfred P. Rubin, "Is Piracy Illegal?" *American Journal of International Law*, Vol. 70 (1976), pp. 92-95; Barry Hart Dubner, "The Law of International Sea Piracy," *1New York University Journal of International Law and Politics*, Vol. 11 (1978-79), pp. 471-517; Evelyn Berckman, *Victims of Piracy: The Admiralty Court, 1575-1678*, London: H. Hamilton, 1979; Lawrence C. Delay, "Yacht Theft: Loss by Pirates or Assailing Thieves?" *Maritime Lawyer*, Vol. 4 (1979), pp. 277-303; Alan D. Wiener, "Piracy: The Current Crime," *Lloyd's Maritime and Commercial Law Quarterly*, 1979, pp. 469-484; J. W. Boulton, "The Law of Piracy," *Indian Yearbook of International Affairs*, Vol. 18 (1980), pp. 97-127; Barry Hart Dubner, *The Law of International Sea Piracy*, The Hague: Maritnus Nijhoff, 1980; E. D. Brown, "Maritime Commercial Malpractice and Piracy Under International Law," *Maritime Policy and Management*, Vol. 8 (1981), pp. 99-107; J. W. Boulton, "Maritime Order and the Development of the

International Law of Piracy," *International Relations*, Vol. 7 (1981-83), pp. 2335-2350; J. W. Boulton, "The Modern International Law of Piracy: Content and Contemporary Relevance," *International Relations*, Vol. 7 (1981-83), pp. 2493-2511; Brian A.H. Parritt, ed., *Violence at Sea; A Review of Terrorism, Acts of War and Piracy, and Countermeasures to Prevent Terrorism*, Paris: ICC Publishing S.A., 1986.

NOTE

During recent years a number of cases of piracy have occurred. See, e.g., "Two Americans' Deaths Reported Off Colombia," *Washington Post*, July 20, 1976, p. A15, (the Caribbean Sea); "Pirates Plying Nigerian Seas," *New York Times*, January 9, 1977, p. 1 (African coast); "The Jolly Roger Still Flies," *Time Magazine*, July 31, 1978, p. 35 (Gulf of Thailand, Sulu Sea, Celebes Sea); "Pirates Attacks vs. 'Boat People,'" *Facts on File*, Vol. 44, No. 2280 (July 27, 1984), p. 551; A. P. Rubin, *The Law of Piracy*, Newport, Rhode Island: Naval War College Press, 1988, pp. 337-345; Daniel J. Dzurek, "Piracy in Southeast Asia," *Oceanus* (Boston), Vol. 32, No. 4 (Winter 1989/90), pp. 65-70.

UNITED NATIONS CONVENTION AGAINST ILLICIT TRAFFIC IN NARCOTIC DRUGS AND PSYCHOTROPIC SUBSTANCES
Adopted at Vienna on December 19, 1988, U.N. Doc. E/CONF.82/15

Article 17
Illicit Traffic by Sea

1. The Parties shall cooperate to the fullest extent possible to suppress illicit traffic by sea, in conformity with the international law of the sea.

2. A Party which has reasonable grounds to suspect that a vessel flying its flag or not displaying a flag or marks of registry is engaged in illicit traffic may request the assistance of other Parties in suppressing its use for that purpose. The Parties so requested shall render such assistance within the means available to them.

3. A Party which has reasonable grounds to suspect that a vessel exercising freedom of navigation in accordance with international law and flying the flag or displaying marks of registry of another Party is engaged in illicit traffic may so notify the flag State, request confirmation of registry and, if confirmed, request authorization from the flag State to take appropriate measures in regard to that vessel.

4. In accordance with paragraph 3 or in accordance with treaties in force between them or in accordance with any agreement or arrangement otherwise reached between those Parties, the flag State may authorize the requesting State to, *inter alia:*

(a) Board the vessel;

(b) Search the vessel;

(c) If evidence of involvement in illicit traffic is found, take appropriate action with respect to the vessel, persons and cargo on board.

5. Where action is taken pursuant to this article, the Parties concerned shall take due account of the need not to endanger the safety of life at sea, the security of the vessel and the cargo or to prejudice the commercial and legal interests of the flag State or any other interested State.

6. The flag State may, consistent with its obligations in paragraph 1 of this article, subject its authorization to conditions to be mutually agreed between it and the requesting Party, including conditions relating to responsibility.

7. For the purposes of paragraphs 3 and 4 of this article, a Party shall respond expeditiously to a request from another Party to determine whether a vessel that is flying its flag is entitled to do so, and to requests for authorization made pursuant to paragraph 3. At the time of becoming a Party to this Convention, each Party shall designate an authority or, when necessary, authorities to receive and respond to such requests. Such designation shall be notified through the Secretary-General to all other Parties within one month of the designation.

8. A Party which has taken any action in accordance with this article shall promptly inform the flag State concerned of the results of that action.

9. The Parties shall consider entering into bilateral or regional agreements or arrangements to carry out, or to enhance the effectiveness of, the provisions of this article.

10. Action pursuant to paragraph 4 of this article shall be carried out only by warships or military aircraft, or other ships or aircraft clearly marked and identifiable as being on government service and authorized to that effect.

11. Any action taken in accordance with this article shall take due account of the need not to interfere with or affect the rights and obligations and the exercise of jurisdiction of coastal States in accordance with the international law of the sea.

CONVENTION FOR THE SUPPRESSION OF UNLAWFUL
ACTS AGAINST THE SAFETY OF MARITIME NAVIGATION
Adopted at Rome on March 10, 1988. IMO Doc. SUA/CONF/15/Rev. 1,
reprinted in *Law of the Sea Bulletin*, No. 11 (July 1988), pp. 14-23.

Article 3

1. Any person commits an offense if that person unlawfully and intentionally:

(a) Seizes or exercises control over a ship by force or threat thereof or any other form of intimidation; or

(b) Performs an act of violence against a person on board a ship if that act is likely to endanger the safe navigation of that ship; or

(c) Destroys a ship or causes damage to a ship or to its cargo which is likely to endanger the safe navigation of that ship; or

(d) Places or causes to be placed on a ship, by any means whatsoever, a device or substance which is likely to destroy that ship, or cause damage to that ship or its cargo which endangers or is likely to endanger the safe navigation of that ship; or

(e) Destroys or seriously damages maritime navigational facilities or seriously interferes with their operation, if any such act is likely to endanger the safe navigation of a ship; or

(f) Communicates information which he knows to be false, thereby endangering the safe navigation of a ship; or

(g) Injures or kills any person, in connection with the commission or the attempted commission of any of the offenses set forth in subparagraphs (a) to (f).

2. Any person also commits an offense if that person:

(a) Attempts to commit any of the offenses set forth in paragraph 1; or

(b) Abets the commission of any of the offenses set forth in paragraph 1 perpetrated by any person or is otherwise an accomplice of a person who commits such an offense; or

(c) Threatens, with or without a condition, as is provided for under national law, aimed at compelling a physical or juridical person to do or refrain from doing any act, to commit any of the offenses set forth in paragraph 1, subparagraphs (b), (c) and (e), if that threat is likely to endanger the safe navigation of the ship in question.

Article 4

1. This Convention applies if the ship is navigating or is scheduled to navigate into, through or from waters beyond the outer limit of the territorial sea of a single State, or the lateral limits of its territorial sea with adjacent States.

2. In cases where the Convention does not apply pursuant to paragraph 1, it nevertheless applies when the offender or the alleged offender is found in the territory of a State Party other than the State referred to in paragraph 1.

[This article is to be understood in conjunction with paragraph 23 of the Final Act of the International Conference on the Suppression of Unlawful Acts Against the Safety of Maritime Navigation, which reads as follows:

23. In relation to article 4 of the Convention for the Suppression of Unlawful Acts against the Safety of Maritime Navigation, some delegations were in favor of the inclusion in article 4, paragraph 1, of straits used for international navigation. Other delegations pointed out that it was unnecessary to include them since navigation in such straits was one of the situations envisaged in article 4, paragraph 1. Therefore, the Convention will apply in straits used for international navigation, without prejudice to the legal status of the waters forming such straits in accordance with relevant conventions and other rules of international law.]

Article 5

Each State Party shall make the offenses set forth in article 3 punishable by appropriate penalties which take into account the grave nature of those offenses.

Article 6

1. Each State Party shall take such measures as may be necessary to establish its jurisdiction over the offenses set forth in article 3 when the offense is committed:

(a) Against or on board a ship flying the flag of the State at the time the offense is committed; or

(b) In the territory of that State, including its territorial sea; or

(c) By a national of that State.

2. A State Party may also establish its jurisdiction over any such offense when:

(a) It is committed by a stateless person whose habitual residence is in that State; or

(b) During its commission a national of that State is seized, threatened, injured or killed; or

(c) It is committed in an attempt to compel that State to do or abstain from doing any act.

3. Any State Party which has established jurisdiction mentioned in paragraph 2 shall notify the Secretary-General of the International Maritime Organization (hereinafter referred to as "the Secretary-General"). If such State Party subsequently rescinds that jurisdiction, it shall notify the Secretary-General.

4. Each State Party shall take such measures as may be necessary to establish its jurisdiction over the offenses set forth in article 3 in cases where the alleged offender is present in its territory and it does not extradite him to any of the States Parties which have established their jurisdiction in accordance with paragraphs 1 and 2 of this article.

5. This Convention does not exclude any criminal jurisdiction exercised in accordance with national law.

Article 7

1. Upon being satisfied that the circumstances so warrant, any State Party in the territory of which the offender or the alleged offender is present shall, in accordance with its law, take him into custody or take other measures to ensure his presence for such time as is necessary to enable any criminal or extradition proceedings to be instituted.

2. Such State shall immediately make a preliminary inquiry into the facts, in accordance with its own legislation.

3. Any person regarding whom the measures referred to in paragraph 1 are being taken shall be entitled to:

(a) Communicate without delay with the nearest appropriate representative of the State of which he is a national or which is otherwise entitled to establish such communication or, if he is a stateless person, the State in the territory of which he has his habitual residence;

(b) Be visited by a representative of that State.

4. The rights referred to in paragraph 3 shall be exercised in conformity with the laws and regulations of the State in the territory of which the offender or the alleged offender is present, subject to the proviso that the said laws and regulations must enable full effect to be given to the purposes for which the rights accorded under paragraph 3 are intended.

5. When a State Party, pursuant to this article, has taken a person into custody, it shall immediately notify the States which have established jurisdiction in accordance with article 6, paragraph 1, and if it considers it advisable, any other interested States, of the fact that such person is in custody and of the circumstances which warrant his detention. The State which makes the preliminary inquiry contemplated in paragraph 2 of this article shall promptly report its findings to the said States and shall indicate whether it intends to exercise jurisdiction.

Article 8

1. The master of a ship of a State Party (the "flag State") may deliver to the authorities of any other State Party (the "receiving State") any person who he has reasonable grounds to believe has committed one of the offenses set forth in article 3.

2. The flag State shall ensure that the master of its ship is obliged, whenever practicable, and if possible before entering the territorial sea of the receiving state carrying on board any person whom the master intends to deliver in accordance with paragraph 1, to give notification to the authorities of the receiving State of his intention to deliver such person and the reasons therefor.

3. The receiving State shall accept the delivery, except where it has grounds to consider that the Convention is not applicable to the acts giving rise to the delivery, and shall proceed in accordance with the provisions of article 7. Any refusal to accept a delivery shall be accompanied by a statement of the reasons for refusal.

4. The flag State shall ensure that the master of its ship is obliged to furnish the authorities of the receiving State with the evidence in the master's possession which pertains to the alleged offense.

5. A receiving State which has accepted the delivery of a person in accordance with paragraph 3 may, in turn, request the flag State to accept delivery of that person. The flag State shall consider any such request, and if it accedes to the request it shall proceed in accordance with article 7. If the flag State declines a request, it shall furnish the receiving State with a statement of the reasons therefor.

. . . .

NOTE

For the interesting problem of the jurisdiction over mutiny on the high seas, see George P. Smith II, "From Cutlass to Cat-O'-Nine Tails: The Case for International Jurisdiction of Mutiny on the High Seas," *Michigan Journal of International Law*, Vol. 10 (1989), pp. 277-303.

K. HOT PURSUIT

1958 CONVENTION ON THE HIGH SEAS

Article 23

1. The hot pursuit of a foreign ship may be undertaken when the competent authorities of the coastal State have good reason to believe that the ship has violated the laws and regulations of that State. Such pursuit must be commenced when the foreign ship or one of its own boats is within the internal waters or the territorial sea or the contiguous zone of the pursuing State, and may only be continued outside the territorial sea or the contiguous zone if the pursuit has not been interrupted. It is not necessary that, at the time when the foreign ship within the territorial sea or the contiguous zone receives the order to stop, the ship giving the order should likewise be within the territorial sea or the contiguous zone. If the foreign ship is within a contiguous zone, as defined in articles 24 of the Convention on the Territorial Sea and the Contiguous Zone, the pursuit may only be undertaken if there has been a violation of the rights for the protection of which the zone was established.

2. The right of hot pursuit ceases as soon as the ship pursued enters the territorial sea of its own country or of a third State.

3. Hot pursuit is not deemed to have begun unless the pursuing ship has satisfied itself by such practicable means as may be available that the ship pursued or one of its boats or other craft working as a team and using the ship pursued as a mother ship are within the limits of the territorial sea, or as the case may be within the contiguous zone. The pursuit may only be commenced after a visual or auditory signal to stop has been given at a distance which enables it to be seen or heard by the foreign ship.

4. The right of hot pursuit may be exercised only by warships or military aircraft, or other ships or aircraft on government service specially authorized to that effect.

5. Where hot pursuit is effected by an aircraft:

(a) The provision of paragraphs 1 to 3 of this article shall apply *mutatis mutandis*;

(b) The aircraft giving the order to stop must itself actively pursue the ship until a ship or aircraft of the coastal State, summoned by the aircraft, arrives to take over the pursuit, unless the aircraft is itself able to arrest the ship. It does not suffice to justify an arrest on the high seas that the ship was merely sighted by the aircraft as an offender or suspected offender, if it was not both ordered to stop and pursued by the aircraft itself or other aircraft or ships which continue the pursuit without interruption.

6. The release of a ship arrested within the jurisdiction of a State and escorted to a port of that State for the purposes of an inquiry before the competent authorities may not be claimed solely on the grounds that the ship, in the course of its voyage, was escorted across a portion of the high seas, if the circumstances rendered this necessary.

7. Where a ship has been stopped or arrested on the high seas in circumstances which do not justify the exercise of the rights of hot pursuit, it shall be compensated for any loss or damage that may have been thereby sustained.

INTERNATIONAL LAW COMMISSION
1956 Commentary Draft Article 47
Yearbook of the International Law Commission 1956,
Vol. II, p. 285.

(1) In the main, this article is taken from article 11 of the regulations adopted by the Second Committee of The Hague Codification Conference in 1930. The right concerned is not contested in international law. Only certain details as to the exercise of the right call for comment:

(i) It is not necessary that, at the time when the foreign ship within the territorial sea receives the order to stop, the ship giving the order would likewise be within the territorial sea. This rule applies in practice in the case of patrol vessels cruising for police purposes just outside the territorial sea. The essential point is that the ship committing the infringement must be in the territorial sea when the pursuit begins.

(ii) Hot pursuit must be continuous. Once it is broken off it cannot be resumed. The right of hot pursuit in any case ceases as soon as the ship pursued enters the territorial sea of its own country or of a third State.

(iii) Hot pursuit cannot be considered to have begun until the pursuing vessel has spotted the foreign ship in the territorial sea and has ordered it to stop by giving the prescribed signal. To prevent abuse, the Commission declined to admit orders given by wireless, as these could be given at any distance; the words "visual or auditory signals" exclude signals given at a great distance and transmitted by wireless.

(iv) The article also applies to ships which lie outside the territorial sea and cause their boats to commit unlawful acts in that sea. The Commission, however, refused to assimilate to such cases that of a ship staying outside the territorial sea and using, not its own boats, but other craft.

(2) The rules laid down above are all in conformity with those adopted by The Hague Conference. The article adopted by the Commission differs from that of 1930 on two points only:

(a) The majority of the Commission was of the opinion that the right of hot pursuit should also be recognized when the ship is in a zone contiguous to the territorial sea, provided such pursuit is undertaken on the ground of violation of rights for the protection of which the zone was established. Thus, a State which established a contiguous zone for the purposes of customs control cannot commence hot pursuit of a fishing boat accused of unlawful fishing in the territorial sea if the fishing boat is already in the contiguous zone. Some members of the Commission were of the opinion that since the coastal State does not exercise sovereignty in the contiguous zone, no pursuit commenced when the ship is already in the contiguous zone can be recognized. The majority of the Commission did not share that opinion. It admitted, however, that the offences giving rise to hot pursuit must always have been committed in internal waters or in the territorial sea; acts committed in the contiguous zone cannot confer upon the coastal State a right of hot pursuit.

(b) The Commission wished to make it clear that the right of hot pursuit may be exercised only by warships and ships on government service specially authorized by the flag State to that effect. It is quite natural that customs and police vessels should be able to exercise the right of hot pursuit, but there can be no question of government ships on commercial service, for example, claiming that right.

(c) The ship finally arresting the ship pursued need not necessarily be the same as the one which began the pursuit, provided that it has joined in the pursuit and has not merely effected an interception.

(d) The Commission also dealt with the right of hot pursuit of a ship by aircraft. In spite of the dissenting opinions of some of its members, it felt able to recognize the lawfulness of such a practice, provided it is exercised in accordance with the principles governing its exercise by ships. It accordingly made the exercise of an aircraft's right to pursue a ship on the high seas and to arrest it--if necessary in co-operation with a ship--subject to the conditions laid down in paragraph 5. It is essential for the purposes of the proper exercise of the right of hot pursuit that the ship pursued should have been ordered to stop while it was still in the territorial sea or the contiguous zone. The aircraft must be in a position to give a visible and comprehensible signal to that effect; signals by wireless are barred in the case of aircraft also.

(e) It is recommended that the ship or aircraft should establish the position of the ship pursued at the moment when hot pursuit commences; it must wherever possible mark this position by physical means, for example, by dropping a buoy.

(f) The Commission included in this article a case which presents some analogy with the right of hot pursuit which gave rise to differences of opinion, since it arose after the 1930 Conference. The question was whether a ship pursued and stopped in the territorial sea can be escorted to a port of the State of the pursuing vessel across the high seas, where there is no choice but to pass through the high seas. The Commission considered that it would be illogical to recognize the right of the pursuing vessel to seize a ship on the high seas and escort it to port across the high seas, while at the same time refusing to the government ship, in respect of a ship already apprehended in the territorial sea, the right to escort it to port across the high seas in cases where special circumstances forced it to leave the territorial sea in order to reach the port.

Restatement of the Foreign Relations Law of the United States, Third Revision, Vol. 2, St. Paul, Minn.: American Law Institute, 1987, p. 49. Copyright by The American Law Institute. Reprinted with the permission of The American Law Institute.

Section 513, Comment g.

g. Hot pursuit. International law permits a coastal state to engage in hot pursuit of a foreign ship beyond the state's territorial sea if the state has good reason to believe that the ship had violated the state's laws or regulations within its internal waters or its territorial sea. Hot pursuit may begin in the contiguous zone for violation of those regulations for which that zone was designed; it may begin in the exclusive economic zone or over the continental shelf for violations of economic rights of the coastal State committed in that zone or on that shelf. Hot pursuit may be exercised only by a warship, a military aircraft, or a duly authorized ship or aircraft clearly identifiable as being on government service. The right of hot pursuit may be continued only if it has not been interrupted, and ceases as soon as the ship pursued enters the territorial sea of its own state or of a third state. 1958 Convention on the High Seas, Article 23; LOC Convention, Article 111.

THE I'M ALONE
G. H. Hackworth, *Digest of International Law*, Vol. II,
Washington, D.C.: U.S. Government Printing Office, 1941, pp. 703-708.

On March 22, 1929, the *I'm Alone*, a rum-runner of Canadian registry, was sunk on the high seas about 200 miles south of the Louisiana coast in the Gulf of Mexico by the United States revenue cutter *Dexter*. Inquiry as to the facts having been made by the Canadian Minister in Washington, the Department of State, on March 28 following, transmitted a note to him in which the facts were stated as follows:

On March 20, 1929, the *I'm Alone* was sighted by the United States Coast Guard vessel *Wolcott* northwest of Trinity Shoal, within approximately ten and one half miles of the Coast of the United States. The *Wolcott* ordered the *I'm Alone* to heave to for boarding and examination, but this order was ignored; whereupon the *Wolcott* fired a warning shot across the bow of the *I'm Alone* and repeated its command for the vessel to heave to. When the second command was not complied with, the *Wolcott* fired through the sails and rigging of the vessel. The *I'm Alone* was proceeding seaward and the *Wolcott* took up the chase. The *Wolcott's* gun jammed and it could not therefore stop the *I'm Alone* but it kept in close chase and reported the incident to the Commanding Officer of the Coast Guard Base at Pascagoula, Mississippi, who dispatched the vessels *Dexter* and *Dallas* to assist the *Wolcott*.

The *Wolcott* continued the pursuit of the *I'm Alone* and, according to statements of the appropriate authorities, was at all times within sight of it. The Coast Guard vessel *Dexter* overhauled the *Wolcott* close up with the *I'm Alone* about eight a.m. on March 22 with the latter vessel heading toward Yucatan. The Commander of the *Dexter* ordered the *I'm Alone* to heave to but the master of the latter vessel refused saying that he would be sunk rather than stop. The commanding officer of the *Dexter* then spoke to the master of the *I'm Alone* through a megaphone and informed him that the *I'm Alone* would be sunk unless it obeyed the command to stop. Warning shots were fired ahead, and, when the vessel did not stop, the *Dexter* fired through the rigging and later put about a dozen shots into the hull of the *I'm Alone*. It is stated that the sea was too rough to permit the *I'm Alone* to be boarded and seized by force and that furthermore the master of the *I'm Alone* waved the revolver in a threatening manner indicating that he would resist forcibly any attempt to board his vessel.

The *I'm Alone* sank about 9:05 a.m. on March 22, in latitude 25°41' and longitude 90°45'. The Coast Guard vessels picked up the members of the crew of the *I'm Alone* with the exception of one person who was drowned. . . .

In its reply, the Canadian Legation stated that, according to the master of the vessel, the *I'm Alone* was anchored at a point not less that fourteen and a half miles off the coast of the United States; that even if the vessel was within approximately ten and a half miles, as contended by the Government of the United States, "she was then beyond an hour's sailing distance from the shore"; that the convention between the United States and Great Britain concluded on January 23, 1924, regarding the smuggling of intoxicating liquors (43 Stat. 1761), conferring rights of search and seizure, to be exercised at a distance not greater, from the United States coast, than could be transversed in one hour by the suspected vessel, or by any other vessel in which the liquor was to be conveyed to shore; that on the evidence available, the pursuit and sinking of the vessel appeared not to have been authorized by the terms of the convention of 1924 or by international law; and that:

. . . .It has been intimated that pursuit and seizure on the high seas might be justified on the ground of hot pursuit and continuous pursuit. It is agreed that international law recognizes that pursuit begun within territorial waters may be continued on the high seas, if immediate and continuous. The validity of this doctrine has been fully recognized by Canadian courts. It does not, however, appear to apply to the present case. The pursuit did not begin within the territorial 3-mile limit, which is an essential factor. . . .

It is further to be noted that the cutter which sank the schooner had not participated in the original pursuit, but had come up from an entirely different direction two days later. Under these circumstances, the most essential elements of justification under the doctrine of hot pursuit appear to be lacking.

To this the Department of State replied, on April 17, 1929, *inter alia*:

It is the contention of this Government that the *I'm Alone* was sighted and commanded to heave to at a point not more than 10.8 miles from the coast of the United States; that this distance is less that the distance which could be traversed by the vessel in one hour; . . . .and that under the doctrine of "hot pursuit," the Coast Guard vessels possessed authority to follow the *I'm Alone* beyond the distance of one hour's sailing stipulated in the treaty between the United States and Great Britain of January 23, 1924, and to compel it to comply with the orders of the Coast Guard officers to stop . . . .

In the estimation of this Government, the correct principle underlying the doctrine of hot pursuit is that if the arrest would have been valid when the vessel was first hailed, but was made impossible through the illegal action of the pursued vessel in failing to stop when ordered to do so, then hot pursuit is justified and the *locus* of the arrest and the distance of the pursuit are immaterial provided:

> (1) that it is without the territorial waters of any other state;

> (2) that the pursuit has been hot and continuous.

With regard to the duration of pursuit I may state that it is the view of this Government that this is unimportant, provided the other elements of hot pursuit are always present . . . .

With regard to the fact that the arrest of the *I'm Alone* was performed not by the original pursuing vessel but by another which had been called for assistance, I desire to present the following considerations.

It is submitted that so long as the *Wolcott* was present at all times and was actually cooperating with the *Dexter* in a joint endeavor to make the *I'm Alone* stop, the requirements of the doctrine "hot pursuit" were met and the additional factor that the *Dexter* joined in the chase does not invalidate the legality of the action of the American authorities . . . .

The dispute was submitted to two commissioners, the Right Honorable Lyman Poore Duff, appointed by Canada, and the Honorable Willis Van Devanter, appointed by the United States.

In a joint interim report, dated June 30, 1933, the commissioners stated that they were "not in agreement. . . .nor have they reached a final disagreement" as to whether the United States, under the convention of 1924, had the right of hot pursuit where the offending vessel was within an hour's sailing distance of the shore at the commencement of the pursuit and beyond that distance at its termination. The commissioners further stated that "based upon the *assumption* [italics added] that the United States Government had the right of hot pursuit in the circumstances and was entitled to exercise the rights under article 2 of the Convention at the time when the *Dexter* joined the *Wolcott* in the pursuit of the *I'm Alone*" and upon the assumption that the averments set forth in paragraph 8 on the answer of the United States are true (these related particularly to the manner and extent of the use of force), "the admittedly intentional sinking of the suspected vessel was not justified by anything in the Convention."   In a joint final report of January 5, 1935 the commissioners stated that "By their interim report the Commissioners found that the sinking of the vessel was not justified by anything in the Convention. The commissioners now add that it could not be justified by any principle of international law." In view of the fact that the *I'm Alone*, although of Canadian registry, was *de facto* owned, controlled, and at the critical times, managed, and her movements directed and her cargo dealt with and disposed of by a group of persons acting in concert who were entirely, or nearly so, citizens of the United States," the commissioners considered that no compensation ought to be paid for the loss of the ship or cargo. In view of the fact, however, that the "act of sinking the ship, . . .by officers of the United States Coast Guard, was. . . an unlawful act," the commissioners considered that the United States ought formally to acknowledge its illegality and apologize to His Majesty's Canadian Government, and to pay $25,000 to that Government "in respect of the wrong." The commissioners recommended that $25,666.50 should be paid to the captain and members of the crew, "none of whom was a party to the illegal conspiracy to smuggle liquor into the United States and sell the same there." On January 19, 1935 the United States, after pointing out that although the commissioners found that "the mission and use of the vessel at the time of its sinking were unlawful" and that nevertheless they also found that "its sinking by the United States was unlawful," tendered to His Majesty's Canadian Government an apology for the sinking of the vessel. On November 7, 1935 a check in the amount of $50,666.50 in full settlement of all claims for damages resulting from the sinking of the vessel was transmitted to the Charge d'Affaires ad interim of Canada by the Department of State.

GILLAM v. UNITED STATES
27 F.2d 296 (4th Cir. 1928)

[This case involved the seizure of a vessel sighted 7 1/2 miles from the United States coast but apprehended, after chase, at a distance of 12 3/4 miles from the coast. The vessel was carrying a cargo of liquor and the Court found that she was bound, illegally, for a U.S. port. On the validity of the seizure, the Court noted:]

On this question, the contention in behalf of the vessel is (1) that, as she was admittedly beyond the 3-mile limit at all times, she had not committed a crime within the territorial limits of the United States, and was therefore not subject to seizure; and (2) that under the Treaty with Great Britain on May 22, 1924, 43 Stat. 1761, seizure is authorized only when it appears that the vessel is within one hour's sailing distance of shore and has committed or is attempting to commit an offense against the laws of the United States, which prohibit the importation of alcoholic beverages. No point is made that the vessel was actually overhauled and the seizure actually made beyond the hour's sailing distance and beyond the 12-mile limit, if she were within these limits when signaled; and we think it is clear, under the "hot pursuit" doctrine, that if the right of seizure existed at the time the vessel was signaled, the right was not lost because she had succeeded in getting farther from shore in her attempt to run away. . . .

While it is true, as contended, that the vessel never came within the 3-mile limit of the territorial waters of the United States, we think that, as she was bound for the United States with an unmanifested cargo and came within 12 miles, or 4 marine leagues, of the coast, her seizure was justified under the revenue statutes of the United States, and these statutes constitute a valid exercise of the sovereign power of the government.

> J. R. Brock, "Hot Pursuit and the Right of Pursuit," *JAG Journal*, March-April, 1960, pp. 19-20. Reprinted by permission of the *Naval Law Review*, Naval Justice School, Newport, R.I. 02841. Views expressed in this article are the authors and do not purport to represent the views or policies of the Department of the Navy.

The doctrine of *Hot Pursuit* is internationally recognized as the right of a coastal State to pursue commercial vessels of a foreign State suspected of violating the laws or regulations of the coastal State applicable to its territorial sea or contiguous zone. *Hot Pursuit* is generally considered as a peacetime concept not connected with hostilities or the threat of hostilities by the military forces of a State. Pursuit under this doctrine does not include the right to pursue warships or military aircraft.

. . . .

It is obvious that the doctrine of *hot pursuit* is a doctrine of limited scope. It is not a right which gives a blank check to seapower. *Hot Pursuit* has no application to self-preservation. But this is only half the story. International law does recognize the right of a state or of men of war to take whatever measures are necessary in self-defense. Our fleets and task forces and our submarines, ships and aircraft on independent duty, may repel or resist a hostile act committed or threatened by foreign vessels, aircraft or missiles. This right includes the *right of pursuit* if pursuit is considered necessary to insure the safety of the threatened forces or territory.

The *right of pursuit* is a part of the right of self-preservation recognized by the Charter of the United Nations in Article 51 and in the numerous defense organization agreements which the United States had concluded with other nations of the world. The application of this right of self-preservation will depend, of course, upon the particular facts of each situation.

International law does not require a naval force at sea in time of peace to await the first blow before it can resort to its weapons at hand. Action occasioned by attack or fear of attack can be taken at anytime an opposing ship, aircraft or submarine is in a position to inflict great harm and is *manifestly* of hostile intent. As is apparent, this concept of self-preservation encompasses an area of broad authority for the naval commander. Even however during times of stress or threatened hostilities he is required by international law to exercise sound judgment and not extend the concept of right of pursuit beyond the bound of reasonableness. Of course, reasonableness is an elastic term; what is reasonable will be judged in the context of the stresses of the times and the peculiar situations at hand.

REFERENCES

The Ship North v. The King, 37 Can. Sup. 385 (1906); C. Eagleton, "The I'm Alone," *New York University Law Quarterly Review*, Vol. 7 (1929), pp. 159-166; K. C. Frazer, "The 'I'm Alone' Case and the Doctrine of 'Hot Pursuit'", *North Carolina Law Review*, Vol. 7 (1929), pp. 413-422; N. A. M. MacKenzie, "International Law -- Hot Pursuit -- The Freedom of the Seas,"

Canadian Bar Review, Vol. 7 (1929), pp. 407-410; J. S. H. Beck, "The Doctrine of Hot Pursuit," *Canadian Bar Review*, Vol. 9 (1931). pp. 85-114, 176-202, 249-270, 341-365; Sir Gerald Fitzmaurice, "The Case of the 'I'm Alone,'" *British Yearbook of International Law*, Vol. 17 (1936), pp. 82-111; G. L. Williams, "The Juridical Basis of Hot Pursuit," *British Yearbook of International Law*, Vol. 16 (1939), pp. 83-97; N. M. Poulantzas, "The Right of Hot Pursuit especially under the Geneva Convention of the High Seas," *Revue Hellenique de Droit International*, Vol. 14 (1961), pp. 198-224; M. S. McDougal and W. T. Burke, *The Public Order of the Oceans: A Contemporary International Law of the Sea*, New Haven and London: Yale University Press, 1962, pp. 893-923; M. M. Whiteman, *Digest of International Law*, Vol. 4, Washington, D.C.: U.S. Government Printing office, 1965, pp. 677-687; N. M. Poulantzas, *The Right of Hot Pursuit In International Law* Leyden: A. W. Sijthoff, 1969; S. Maidment, "Historical Aspects of the Doctrine of Hot Pursuit," *British Yearbook of International Law*, Vol. 46 (1972-73), pp. 365-381; Craig H. Allen, "Doctrine of Hot Pursuit: A Functional Interpretation Adaptable to Emerging Maritime Law Enforcement Technology and Practiices," *Ocean Development and International Law*, Vol. 20 (1989), pp. 309-341.

UNITED STATES v. F/V TAIYO MARU No. 28

395 F. Supp 413 (1975)

These two proceedings arise from the seizure of a Japanese fishing vessel, the F/V TAIYO MARU No. 28, by the United States Coast Guard for violation of United States fisheries law. On September 5, 1974, the Coast Guard sighted the TAIYO MARU 28 fishing at Latitude 43-35.9 North, Longitude 69-20 West. That point is approximately 16.25 miles off the coast of the State of Maine and approximately 10.5 miles seaward from Monhegan Island. It is conceded to be within the contiguous fisheries zone of the United States. 16 U.S.C. §1092. The Coast Guard signaled the TAIYO MARU 28 to stop, but the vessel attempted to escape by accelerating toward the high seas. The Coast Guard immediately pursued and seized the vessel on the high seas at Latitude 45-28 North, Longitude 68-24 West, a point approximately 67.9 miles at sea from the mainland of the continental United States. . . .

Defendant's sole contention is that the United States had no right to conduct hot pursuit from the contiguous zone and to effect seizure of the TAIYO MARU 28, because the vessel was seized on the high seas in violation of Article 23 of the 1958 Convention on the High Seas.

. . . .

Defendant asserts that Article 23 of the Convention on the High Seas must be read in conjunction with Article 24 of the Convention on the Territorial Sea and the Contiguous Zone. The argument is that since Article 24 only authorizes the establishment of a contiguous zone for the purposes of enforcing the coastal State's customs, fiscal, immigration or sanitary regulations, and since Article 23 permits hot pursuit of a foreign ship from such a contiguous zone only for the four purposes listed in Article 24, the United States was without authority to commence hot pursuit of the TAIYO MARU 28 from within the contiguous fisheries zone for the purpose of enforcing its fisheries regulations.

Both parties recognize that the general rule of law is that the power of the government to enforce a forfeiture or to prosecute a defendant is not impaired by the illegality of the method by which it has acquired control over the property or the defendant. . . . Defendant relies upon the exception to this general rule established in Cook v. United States, 288 U.S. 102, 53 S.Ct. 305, 77 L.Ed 641 (1933). In *Cook*, the United States Coast Guard seized a British vessel, the *Mazel Tov*, caught in rum-running, on the high seas outside the American jurisdictional limits set by a

British-American treaty covering the apprehension of prohibition law violators. The Supreme Court held that the United States "lacking power to seize, lacked power, because of the Treaty, to subject the vessel to our laws. To hold that adjudication may follow a wrongful seizure would go far to nullify the purpose and effect of the Treaty."....

Mr. Justice Brandeis made clear, however, that the exception to the general rule recognized in *Cook* covers the particular situation where the United States has by treaty "imposed a territorial limitation upon its own authority." ... As stated in Autry v. Wiley, the *Cook* doctrine is a "narrow" exception to the general rule; it "applies only to violations of a specific territorial jurisdictional circumscription set by treaty."

Defendant strenuously argues that the *Cook* exception destroys the jurisdiction of the Court in these proceedings because by Article 23 of the Convention on the High Seas, read together with Article 24 of the Convention of the Territorial Sea and the Contiguous Zone, the United States has undertaken a specific obligation not to institute hot pursuit of a foreign ship from the contiguous fisheries zone for violation of its fisheries law. Defendant's position is that Article 23 limits the government's right of hot pursuit from a contiguous zone to the four purposes for which Article 24 authorizes the establishment of such a zone, and the enforcement of domestic fisheries law is not one of the purposes recognized by Article 24. The Court is persuaded, however, that neither the language nor the history of the Conventions shows that the signatory parties intended to limit the right of a coastal State to exercise exclusive fishery jurisdiction within 12 miles of its coast, to establish a contiguous zone for such a purpose, or to conduct hot pursuit from such a zone.

Analysis of the text of Article 23 of the Convention on the High Seas shows that the Article provides general authority to undertake hot pursuit from a contiguous zone when the authorities of the coastal State have good reason to believe that a foreign vessel has violated the coastal State's laws and regulations. It is true that Article 23 permits hot pursuit from a contiguous zone, created for one of the four purposes enumerated in Article 24 of the Convention on the Territorial Sea and the Contiguous Zone, only if there has been a violation of the rights for the protection of which the zone was established. But Article 23 does not in terms deny a coastal State the right to commence hot pursuit from a contiguous zone established for a purpose other than one of the purposes listed in Article 24. Nor does Article 24 in terms prohibit the establishment of a contiguous zone for a purpose other than one of those specified in the Article. The language of Article 24, relating to the purposes for which a contiguous zone may be established, is permissive, rather than restrictive. It provides that a coastal State "may" establish a contiguous zone for the purposes of enforcing its customs, fiscal, immigration or sanitary regulations. Although Article 24 only affirmatively recognizes the right of a coastal State to create a contiguous zone for one of the four enumerated purposes, nothing in the Article precludes the establishment of such a zone for other purposes, including the enforcement of domestic fisheries law. In short, unlike the British-American treaty in *Cook*, the Conventions in the case at bar contain no specific undertaking by the United States not to conduct hot pursuit from a contiguous fisheries zone extending 12 miles from its coast. The *Cook* exception, therefore is not applicable, because the United States has not by treaty "imposed a territorial limitation upon its own authority."

The history of the 1958 Conventions confirms the conclusion that the United States did not specifically undertake to limit its authority to exercise exclusive fisheries jurisdiction within 12 miles of its coast, to establish a contiguous zone for such a purpose, or to conduct hot pursuit from such a zone. The Convention on the High Seas and the Convention on the Territorial Sea and the Contiguous Zone were the product of the Conference on the Law of the Sea, convened at Geneva in 1958 pursuant to Resolution 1105 of the General Assembly of the United Nations. ... Although the Conference was convened to resolve a variety of matters pertaining to the codification of the Law of the Sea, most commentators agree that the two principal issues presented for the Conference's consideration were the question of the breadth of the territorial sea, and the closely-related question of whether there should be an additional contiguous zone in which the coastal States could exercise exclusive jurisdiction over fishing. . . . The 1958 Geneva Conference was unable to achieve agreement on either issue, primarily because of the volatile political ramifications involved in setting a limit to the territorial sea. In recommending that the Senate give its advice and consent to ratification of the Conventions, the Senate Report from the Committee on Foreign Relations made clear that the Convention on the Territorial Sea and the Contiguous Zone did not define the width of the territorial sea, or circumscribe the right of a coastal State to assert exclusive fisheries jurisdiction:

> This convention does not fix the breadth of the territorial sea. This subject and the closely related one of the extent to which the coastal state should have exclusive fishing rights in the sea off its coast were hotly debated without any conclusion being reached.

It is clear from the foregoing history that, in becoming a signatory to the 1958 Conventions, the United States could not have intended to accept any limitation on its right to conduct hot pursuit for violations of exclusive fishery rights occurring within 12 miles of its coast, since the Geneva Conference could not agree as to whether a contiguous zone could be established for the purpose of enforcing domestic fisheries law.

It is apparent that Congress was well aware of its obligations under the 1958 Conventions when the 1966 Contiguous Fisheries Zone Act was enacted, and that Congress perceived no conflict between the Act and the treaty provisions. This is evident from the House Report, which discusses the Conventions and their relationship to the proposed legislation:

> In 1958, and again in 1960, the Law of the Sea Conferences held in Geneva, Switzerland, left unresolved the twin questions of the width of the territorial sea and the extent to which a coastal state could claim exclusive fishing rights in the high seas off its coast. At the second conference in 1960, the United States and Canada put forward a compromise proposal for a 6-mile territorial sea, plus a 6-mile exclusive fisheries zone (12 miles of exclusive jurisdiction in all) subject to the continuation for 10 years of traditional fishing by other states in the outer 6 miles. This compromise proposal failed by one vote to obtain the two-thirds vote necessary for adoption.

> Since the 1958 Law of the Sea Conference, there has been a trend toward the establishment of a 12-mile fisheries rule in international practice. Thirty-nine countries acting individually or in concert with other countries have extended their fisheries limits to 12 miles since 1958.

The Report also notes that, as of July 1, 1966, of the 99 United Nations coastal nations, slightly more than 60 countries asserted a 12-mile exclusive fishery zone, either as territorial sea or as territorial sea plus a contiguous zone.

Since the seizure of the TAIYO MARU 28 on the high seas following hot pursuit from the contiguous zone was not in violation of Article 23 of the 1958 Convention of the High Seas, and, moreover, was sanctioned by domestic law and in conformity with the prevailing consensus of international law and practice, this Court has jurisdiction to decide the present proceedings on their merits. Defendant's motions to dismiss for lack of jurisdiction are therefore denied.

REFERENCES

D. Ciobanu, "Hot Pursuit from a Fisheries Zone: A Further Comment on *United States v. Taiyo Maru No. 28; United States v. Kawaguchi*," *American Journal of International Law*, Vol. 70 (1976), pp. 546-553; D. E. Singer, "The Right of Hot Pursuit from Exclusive Fishery Zones: United States v. F/V Taiyo Maru No. 28," *Columbia Journal of Transnational Law*, Vol. 15 (1976), pp. 336-366; Eric Allan Sisro, "Hot Pursuit from a Contiguous Fisheries Zone--An Assault on the Freedom of the High Seas," *San Diego Law Review*, Vol. 14 (1979), pp. 656-680; Craig H. Allen, "Doctrine of Hot Pursuit: A Functional Interpretation Adaptable to Emerging Maritime Law Enforcement Technologies and Practices," *Ocean Development and International Law*, Vol. 20 (1989), pp. 309-342; N.D. Korolera, "The Right of Pursuit from the Exclusive Economic Zone," Marine Policy, Vol. 14 (1990), pp. 137-141.

1982 UNITED NATIONS CONVENTION OF THE LAW OF THE SEA

Article 111
Right of hot pursuit

1. The hot pursuit of a foreign ship may be undertaken when the competent authorities of a coastal State have good reason to believe that the ship has violated the laws and regulation of that State. Such pursuit must be commenced when the foreign ship or one of its boats is within the internal waters, the archipelagic waters, the territorial sea or the contiguous zone of the pursuing State, and may only be continued outside the territorial sea or the contiguous zone if the pursuit has not been interrupted. It is not necessary that, at the time when the foreign ship within the territorial sea or the contiguous zone receives the order to stop, the ship giving the order should likewise be within the territorial sea or the contiguous zone. If the foreign ship is within a contiguous zone, as defined in Article 33, the pursuit may only be undertaken if there has been a violation of the rights for the protection of which the zone was established.

2. The right of hot pursuit shall apply *mutatis mutandis* to violations in the exclusive economic zone or on the continental shelf, including safety zones around continental shelf installations, of the laws and regulations of the coastal State applicable in accordance with this Convention to the exclusive economic zone or the continental shelf, including such safety zones.

3. The right of hot pursuit ceases as soon as the ship pursued enters the territorial sea of its own State or of a third State.

4. Hot pursuit is not deemed to have begun unless the pursuing ship has satisfied itself by such practicable means as may be available that the ship pursued or one of its boats or other craft working as a team and using the ship pursued as a mother ship is within the limits of the territorial sea, or, as the case may be, within the contiguous zone or the exclusive economic zone or above the continental shelf. The pursuit may only be commenced after a visual or auditory signal to stop has been given at a distance which enables it to be seen or heard by the foreign ship.

5. The right of hot pursuit may be exercised only by warships or military aircraft, or other ships or aircraft clearly marked and identifiable as being on government service and authorized to that effect.

6. Where hot pursuit is effected by an aircraft:

(a) the provisions of paragraphs 1 to 4 shall apply *mutatis mutandis,*

(b) the aircraft giving the order to stop must itself actively pursue the ship until a ship or another aircraft of the coastal State, summoned by the aircraft, arrives to take over the pursuit, unless the aircraft is itself able to arrest the ship. It does not suffice to justify an arrest outside the territorial sea that the ship was merely sighted by the aircraft as an offender or suspected offender, if it was not both ordered to stop and pursued by the aircraft itself or other aircraft or ships which continue the pursuit without interruption.

7. The release of a ship arrested within the jurisdiction of a State and escorted to a port of that State for the purposes of an inquiry before the competent authorities may not be claimed solely on the ground that the ship, in the course of its voyage, was escorted across a portion of the exclusive economic zone or the high seas, if the circumstances rendered this necessary.

8. Where a ship has been stopped or arrested outside the territorial sea in circumstances which do not justify the exercise of the right of hot pursuit, it shall be compensated for any loss or damage that may have been thereby sustained.

NOTE

Except paragraph 2, the above Article is essentially identical to Article 23 of the 1958 Convention on the High Seas.

L. USE OF THE BED OF THE HIGH SEAS FOR SUBMARINE CABLES AND PIPELINES

1958 CONVENTION ON THE HIGH SEAS

Article 2

. . . . Freedom of the high seas. . . comprises, *inter alia,* . . . :

. . . .

(3) Freedom to lay submarine cables and pipelines;

. . . .

Article 26

1. All States shall be entitled to lay submarine cables and pipelines on the bed of the high seas.

2. Subject to its right to take reasonable measures for the exploration of the continental shelf and the exploitation of its natural resources, the coastal State may not impede the laying or maintenance of such cables or pipelines.

3. When laying such cables or pipelines the State in question shall pay due regard to cables and pipelines already in position on the seabed. In particular, possibilities of repairing existing cables or pipelines shall not be prejudiced.

Article 27

Every State shall take the necessary legislative measures to provide that the breaking or injury by a ship flying its flag or by a person subject to its jurisdiction of a submarine cable beneath the high seas done wilfully or through culpable negligence, in such a manner as to be liable to interrupt or obstruct telegraphic or telephonic communications, and similarly the breaking or injury of a submarine pipeline or high-voltage power cable shall be a punishable offence. This provision shall not apply to any break or injury caused by persons who acted merely with the legitimate object of saving their lives or their ships, after having taken all necessary precautions to avoid such break or injury.

Article 28

Every State shall take the necessary legislative measures to provide that, if persons subject to its jurisdiction who are the owners of a cable or pipeline beneath the high seas, in laying or repairing that cable or pipeline, cause a break in or injury to another cable or pipeline, they shall bear the cost of the repairs.

Article 29

Every State shall take the necessary legislative measures to ensure that the owners of ships who can prove that they have sacrificed an anchor, a net or any other fishing gear, in order to avoid injuring a submarine cable or pipeline, shall be indemnified by the owner of the cable or pipeline, provided that the owner of the ship has taken all reasonable precautionary measures beforehand.

1958 CONVENTION ON THE CONTINENTAL SHELF

Article 4

Subject to its right to take reasonable measures for the exploration of the continental shelf and the exploitation of its natural resources, the coastal State may not impede the laying or maintenance of submarine cables or pipelines on the continental shelf.

INTERNATIONAL LAW COMMISSION
1956 Commentary, Draft Article 70
Yearbook of the International Law Commission 1956,
Vol. II, p. 299.

(1) The coastal State is required to permit the laying of submarine cables on the seabed of its continental shelf, but in order to avoid unjustified interference with the exploitation of the natural resources of the seabed and subsoil, it may impose conditions concerning the route to be followed.

(2) The Commission considered whether this provision should not be extended to pipelines. In principle, the answer must be in the affirmative. The question is, however, complicated by the fact that it would often be necessary to install pumping stations at certain points which might hinder the exploitation of the soil more than cables. It follows that the coastal State might be less

liberal in this matter than in the case of cables. As the question does not yet seem to be of practical importance, the Commission has not expressly referred to pipelines in the present article.

REFERENCES

M. S. McDougal and W. T. Burke, *The Public Order of the Oceans: A Contemporary International Law of the Sea*, New Haven and London: Yale University Press, 1962, pp. 778-782, 842-848; M. M. Whiteman, *Digest of International Law*, Vol. 4, 1965, pp. 727-739.

1982 UNITED NATIONS CONVENTION ON THE LAW OF THE SEA

Article 112
Right to lay submarine cables and pipelines

1. All states are entitled to lay submarine cables and pipelines on the bed of the high seas beyond the continental shelf.

2. Article 79, paragraph 5, applies to such cables and pipelines.

Article 113
Breaking or injury of a submarine cable or pipeline

Every State shall adopt the laws and regulations necessary to provide that the breaking or injury by a ship flying its flag or a person subject to its jurisdiction of a submarine cable beneath the high seas done willfully or through culpable negligence, in such a manner as to be liable to interrupt or obstruct telegraphic or telephonic communications, and similarly the breaking or injury of a submarine pipeline or high-voltage power cable, shall be a punishable offense. This provision shall apply also to conduct calculated or likely to result in such breaking or injury. However, it shall not apply to any break or injury caused by persons who acted merely with the legitimate object of saving their lives or their ships, after having taken all necessary precautions to avoid such break or injury.

Article 114
Breaking or injury by owners of a submarine cable or pipeline of another submarine cable or pipeline

Every State shall adopt the laws and regulations necessary to provide that, if persons subject to its jurisdiction who are the owners of a submarine cable or pipeline beneath the high seas, in laying or repairing that cable or pipeline, cause a break in or injury to another cable or pipeline, they shall bear the cost of the repairs.

Article 115
Indemnity for loss incurred in avoiding injury to a submarine cable or pipeline

Every State shall adopt the laws and regulation necessary to ensure that the owners of ships who can prove that they have sacrificed an anchor, a net or any other fishing gear, in order to avoid injuring a submarine cable or pipeline, shall be indemnified by the owner of the cable or pipeline, provided that the owner of the ship has taken all reasonable precautionary measures beforehand.

CHAPTER VIII

CONTINENTAL SHELF

A. INTRODUCTION

The emergence of the continental shelf doctrine is a classic example of the development of a rule of customary international law, initiated by a unilateral act, through state practice. The basic principles of the doctrine were codified at the First U.N. Conference on the Law of the Sea in 1958.

At the 1973-82 Third U.N. Conference on the Law of the Sea, the following controversial problems were generally settled: (1) the seaward limit of continental shelf of a coastal state, (2) the principles for apportioning continental shelf areas between adjacent and opposite states (see Chapter 5, Section C), and (3) the rights and duties of the coastal state in the continental shelf. However, the Conference did not resolve the issue of the relationship between the continental shelf and the exclusive economic zone (see Chapter 9, Section D).

This chapter begins with some material on the physical nature of the continental shelf and methods for extracting its resources. Excellent supplemental reading would include several articles in *The Ocean: A Scientific American Book*, Red Bluff, California: H.P. Freeman, 1969.

B. THE GEOLOGY OF THE CONTINENTAL SHELF AND THE TECHNOLOGY OF EXPLORING OFFSHORE OIL AND GAS

> H.G. Knight, "The Draft United Nations Convention on the International Seabed Area: Background Description and Some Preliminary Thoughts," *San Diego Law Review*, Vol. 8 (1971), pp. 463-470. Copyright 1971 San Diego Law Review Association. Reprinted with the permission of the *San Diego Law Review*.

a. *The Continental Shelf*. The continental shelf is the seaward portion of the extension of the continental land mass which begins with the upland coastal plain and extends seaward until a marked increase in slope occurs. Although the continental shelf actually consists of the entire continental structure beginning at approximately the 600 foot contour above sea level, only the submerged portion is of interest to those concerned with marine resources, and the term has come generally to refer only to that submerged portion. The average water depth at the break in slope was traditionally considered to be 200 meters although in fact this average depth is approximately 72 fathoms or 130-140 meters. This average figure may be somewhat misleading, however, since there are few places in the world where the 72 fathom or 130-140 meter isobath actually coincides with the shelf edge. Rther, the shelf edge varies from water depths of 20 to 550 meters. The average slope of the shelf is given as 0° 07', or about ten feet per mile, and the average water depth over continental shelves as 30 fathoms. The width of the continental shelf also varies substantially, ranging from virtually zero breadth off the western coast of South America to 800 miles or more beneath the Bering Sea, averaging approximately 40 miles in width world-wide. In the United States, shelf width varies from as little as one mile off portions of California, to 100-150 miles off the Gulf coast, to over 200 miles off New England. The area of world continental shelves, based on a 200 meter isobath shelf edge, is generally given as 7.5-7.6 percent of the ocean floor area. Classification of continental shelf types and descriptions of their origins are beyond the scope of this review, but may be found elsewhere. The surface of the shelf shows some degree of topographical relief, including canyons (extending from the coast seaward) and parallel trenches. Most shelf areas are covered by a relatively thick layer of various types of unconsolidated sediment reaching depths of five kilometers, although areas exist without sediment. According to K.O. Emery, "[c]ontinental shelves are characterized by structure and stratigraphy that are similar to, or are natural continuations of, the structure and stratigraphy of the adjacent land." It is therefore not surprising that some mineral deposits found in upland locations are also found on and beneath the continental shelves. Some of the resources, such as fish and manganese nodules are, of course, unique to the shelf environment (vis-a-vis the upland), but large deposits of petroleum and natural gas are also present beneath shelves underlain by consolidated sedimentary strata. This area also is exploited to a lesser extent for sand and gravel, ilmenite, rutile, zircon, tin, monazite, iron, gold, and diamonds.

   b. *The Continental Slope*. The continental slope lies seaward of the continental shelf. . . . The term "continental margin" refers generally to the area of seabed including a seaward portion of the shelf, all of the slope, and a landward portion of the continental rise, excluding the ocean basin. The continental slope may be defined as the area of seabed extending from the outer margin of the continental shelf to, in the absence of a continental rise, the oceanic abyss. . . . The seaward limit of the slope is ill-defined, but is conventionally taken as the point where the change in gradient from the steep banked slope to the ocean floor reaches less than 1:40. The water depth at the seaward extent averages 2500 meters, the range running from less than 1000 meters to more than 4000 meters. As a result of an average declivity of 4° 07', the width of the continental slope extends from 15 to 50 kilometers. The area of the slope has been placed at 8.5 percent of the area beneath the oceans. Slopes, like shelves, are overlain by unconsolidated sedimentary deposits composed principally of mud, sand, and gravel, with the mud/sand ratio being higher than on shelves. . . . [A]lthough slopes, like shelves, contain irregularities, slopes are continuous between the shelf and the deep ocean floor with the exception of intermediate terraces or series of basins and ridges. These intermediate terraces are commonly referred to as continental borderlands or plateaus, the most notable off the United States coast being the Blake Plateau from which manganese nodules have recently been recovered, which lies at depths of 500-1100 meters, and which has an area of approximately 200,000 square kilometers. There is growing evidence that many natural resources, including hydrocarbons and surficial hard mineral deposits, occur on portions of the slope in quantities comparable to those occurring on the shelf. . . .

   c. *The Continental Rise*. The continental rise exists in situations where the steep portion of the continental slope is terminated on its seaward edge by a gentle slope which may extend for substantial distances into the deep-ocean basins. This sedimental structure creates a significant problem in some instances in locating the actual edge of the continental formation since it may overlie deep ocean structures at its seaward edge. . . . The rise occurs on the landward side in water depths ranging from 1200 meters to 3500 meters and on the seaward side from 3500 meters to 5500 meters. The area of the continental rise is about 5 percent of the total ocean bottom, has an average slope of approximately one-half degree, and may extend to a width of 1000 kilometers. . . .

>   C.M. Franklin, *The Law of the Sea: Some Recent Developments*,
>   Vol. 52 of *Naval War College, International Law Studies, 1959-1960*,
>   Washington, D.C.: U.S. Government Printing Office, 1961, pp. 12-
>   17.

   When geologists, geographers and other scientists use the term "continental shelf" in a broad sense they mean the submarine extension of the "continent" outward into the sea; a kind of pedestal on which the continents seem to rest in the ocean, lying "between the shore and the first substantial fall-off, on the seaward side, whatever its depth. . . ."

Perhaps we can best understand what the continental shelves are from a geological point of view if we visualize for a moment what the earth would look like if we removed all of the water (hydrosphere) from its surface. We would then see the earth's crust (lithosphere) has two predominant features: (1) the continents together with their gradually sloping continental shelves, and (2) the deep ocean basins whose steep-sloping sides are referred to as continental slopes. There are six such continents: North America, South America, Europe-Asia, Africa, Australia and Antarctica. The first five of these continents are surrounded by a more or less continuous continental shelf of varying widths. Indeed, if the continent of Antarctica did not exist we might speak of the continental shelves of the earth in the singular because "all the other continents lie within the confines of a single encircling belt of shallow water which is essentially continuous-- the continental shelf."

The configurations of the submarine areas of the three oceans (Pacific, Atlantic and Indian) vary greatly. Longitudinal ridges divide the oceans into elongated troughs which in turn are often cut by transverse ridges, thus creating a number of deep ocean basins. Mountain peaks on some of the ridges rise almost abruptly out of the ocean depths to form islands, some of which have little or no insular shelves.

Now, if we poured back from our mammoth container enough of the water to fill the deep ocean basins up to the outer edge of the continental shelf we would cover about 128,000,000 square miles, or approximately two-thirds of the earth's total surface. We would then have left, high and dry, the six continents including their continental shelves, whose total area would cover approximately 68,500,000 square miles. Of this total, the continental shelves of the world (including insular shelves) are estimated at approximately 10,500,000 square miles, roughly 18 percent of the 58,000,000 square miles of present dry land areas, and about 7.6 percent of the total ocean areas of the world. . . .

Then if we poured back the rest of the water remaining in our container after filling the deep ocean basins, it would spill over those basins on to the continental shelves up to the shore line of the dry land areas of the earth.

From a geological point of view, the present dry land areas of the world, which are traditionally referred to as *continents*, are only the major parts of the continents. More accurately, the continents include the present "dry land" areas totaling some 58,000,000 square miles *plus* their continental shelves of approximately 10,500,000 square miles.

Hence, when the continental shelves are defined it is important to stress this oneness of relationship of the shelves to their continents by referring to the shelves as the *outward extensions* of the continents covered by comparatively shallow waters which, at approximately 200 meters depth at the outer edges, drop off rather sharply down the continental slopes into the deep ocean basins.

It should be emphasized that the continental shelves do not project out from the continents of which they are an integral part like huge awnings hanging from the sides of a building. On the contrary, the continental shelves are generally the outward parts of a shelving plain extending *inland* from the shoreline to the foothills of the continental heights and extending *outward* from the shoreline under the ocean waters to the edge of the deep ocean basins. In some parts of the world, notably off the west coast of South America (in particular, off the coasts of Peru and Chile), and off the east coast of Africa, there is practically no continental shelf, the edge of the steep-sided ocean basin coming almost to the shoreline. This geological fact has given rise to some legal problems in connection with the extensive claims to sovereignty over the high seas by certain South American countries, notably Chile, Ecuador, and Peru.

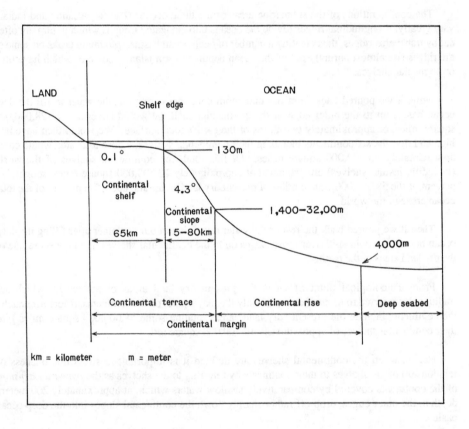

LAND   OCEAN

Shelf edge

0.1°   130m

Continental
shelf   4.3°

                   Continental   1,400-32,00m
                   slope

                                                      4000m

      65km   15-80km

      Continental terrace   Continental rise   Deep seabed

              Continental margin

km = kilometer   m = meter

Analysis of Continental Margin

Figure 8-1

Source: Henry Lee Berryhill, "The Worldwide Search for Petroleum Offshore--A Status Report for the Quarter Century, 1947-1972," U.S. Dept. of the Interior, 1974.

All maps tend to give an incorrect perspective of the true continental shelves because they show the shelves as beginning at the shore lines of the continents, whereas in fact that part of each shelf which begins at the water's edge and runs out to the start of the ocean basins at the 200 meter depth is merely the seaward or underwater part of the total continental shelf plain. . . .

. . . It is essential . . . to any intelligent discussion of the merits of various legal theories which have been advanced to justify the claims by states to the resources of their shelves to remember that geologically the continental shelves are as much a part of their respective continents as are the dry land areas. Therefore, from a geological standpoint, it is not a question of whether the continental shelves are contiguous (i.e., near to the continents), as has been suggested, but rather that they are in fact an integral part of the continents. Geologically, the question is not one of *contiguity* but of *continuity*.

REFERENCES

"Scientific Considerations Relating to the Continental Shelf," U.N. Doc. A/CONF. 13/2 and Add. 1, 20 September 1957 in [First] United Nations Conference on the Law of the Sea, 24 February - 27 April 1958, Geneva, *Official Records*, Vol. I. Preparatory Documents, pp. 39-46; C.A.M. King, *An Introduction to Oceanography*, New York: McGraw Hill, 1963, pp. 54-63; F.P. Shepard, *The Earth Beneath the Sea*, (rev. ed.), Baltimore: Johns Hopkins Press, 1967; K.O. Emery, "An Oceanographer's View of the Law of the Sea," in J. Sztucki, ed., *Proceedings of the Symposium on the International Regime of the Sea-Bed*, Rome: Academia Nazionale dei Lincei, 1970, pp. 47-63; A.J. Guilcher, "The Configuration of the Ocean Floor and its Subsoil: Geopolitical Implications," in J. Sztucki, ed., *Proceedings of the Symposium on the International Regime of the Seabed*, Rome: Academica Nazionale dei Lincei, 1970, pp. 3-27; H.D. Hedberg, "Continental Margins from the Viewpoint of the Petroleum Geologist," *American Association of Petroleum Geologists Bulletin*, Vol. 54 (1970), pp. 3-43; K.O. Emery, "Geological Limits of the 'Continental Shelf,'" *Ocean Development and International Law*, Vol. 10 (1981-82), pp. 1-11; C. Morales Siddayao, "Oil and Gas on the Continental Shelf: Potentials and Constraints in the Asia-Pacific Region," *Ocean Management*, Vol. 9 (1984), pp. 73-100.

Commission on Marine Science, Engineering and Resources, *Report of the Panel on Marine Engineering and Technology*, 1969, pp. VI-1, VI-164 - VI-169.

III. *Offshore Oil and Gas*

. . . .

C. *Exploration*

1. *Geophysical Surveys and Geological Analysis*

Exploration encompasses the broad reconnaissance surveys followed by more detailed surveys that actually delineate (i.e., exploration activities involve locating promising areas for drilling activities). Exploration begins with geologists making a general study of the structure of the earth to select an area with characteristics possibly favorable for oil or gas recovery.

After selecting a promising area, tests pinpoint the site to probe further for possible reserves. These can be simple magnetometer readings taken from an airplane or ship. By showing a variation in the earth's magnetic field, the tests indicate geologic structures below the ocean floor. In addition, towed marine gravimeters can determine very small variations in the earth's gravity field. Both types of geophysical surveys can be made in any depth of water and at any distance from land. However, in themselves, they usually do not provide information of sufficient accuracy to permit siting an exploratory well.

The most successful technique to locate test drilling sites is seismic profiling. Such surveys require much more expensive equipment but because of the high speed at which the surveys can be conducted, the actual cost per mile is about one third as much as on land. A sound pulse is generated, a portion of which is reflected from the layers of sediment and rock under the ocean floor. The reflections, when received at the surface, are recorded on a graph showing an approximation of the depth and characteristics of underlying geological structures. In earlier surveys black powder or dynamite was used to generate the sound pulse. Today, electrical sparking systems, air guns, contained-gas explosions, mechanical boomers, and other nonexplosive energy sources are used. Seismic data are recorded routinely on magnetic tape and processed by digital computers, enhancing quality and reliability.

The above-mentioned geophysical techniques are indirect methods for examining structures under our continental margins. The most satisfactory method to date for obtaining geologic samples of rocks on or at shallow depths under the sea floor has been with small coring devices operated from a surface ship. These devices drill a hole several hundred feet into the sea floor and recover samples of rock for further study. Similar holes have been drilled in the U.S. continental margin beyond the shelves to 1,000 feet beneath the sea floor in waters from 600 feet to 5,000 feet deep. Coring in such depths has been accomplished from floating, dynamically positioned vessels. As long ago as 1961, several experimental core holes were drilled in 11,700 feet of water as part of the early phase of Project Mohole.

Exploration technology has made rapid strides in new seismic energy sources and receiving systems. Computers permit analysis of the data while underway at sea. The Navy Navigation Satellite System will permit seismic teams to determine more accurately survey locations in remote areas.

2. *Exploratory Drilling.*

Determining the presence of oil or gas requires full scale drilling operations at the site, a much more difficult and expensive task than drilling shallow core holes. . . .

While the types of platforms used to support the drilling rigs vary greatly, the rigs are fairly standardized. They consist of: (1) a tall steel tower to hoist the bit, pipe, and other equipment in and out of the hole, (2) a system to rotate the pipe and bit, and (3) a system to circulate fluid to the bottom of the hole.

Fixed platforms supported by pilings were constructed in shallow offshore waters as the drillers followed the seaward extension of oil fields. As the industry moved into deeper waters, it continued using this type of foundation for exploitation drilling. However, for exploratory drilling, where the incidence of dry holes is inherently higher, fixed platforms soon became too costly.

The industry then began to develop mobile drilling platforms. This minimized the capital investment chargeable to each well site. The first mobile platforms were submersible barges for operation in 20 to 40 feet of water and evolved from the barge-mounted drilling rigs used in southern Louisiana marshlands. Later, jack-up mobile platforms were developed for greater water depths.

. . .There are three general types of mobile platforms -- submersible, jack-up, and floating.

The jack-up rig is mounted on a buoyant hull to which extendable legs are attached. The legs are raised for moving the rig and lowered to the ocean floor to lift the platform above the ocean waves during drilling operations. . . .

The submersible rig is mounted on a submersible hull that is ballasted with water and sunk to the ocean floor for support during drilling operations. . . .

The advantage of the jack-up and submersible rig is that they rest on the bottom while the platform stands clear of the highest waves, enabling them to operate in rough seas. The jack-up rig has more depth flexibility and capability while the submersible rig, a monolithic structure, can be towed more readily from one location to another.

While floating platforms lack the stability of the bottom support type, they are not as restricted to a given depth of water and are cost-competitive at 200 feet or more. The floating platform includes two major categories: semi-submersibles and the ship-shaped typed.

The semi-submersibles are floating platforms supported on tall columns which rise from buoyant barge-like hulls or cylindrical torpedo-shaped tubes . . . . Upon arrival on location they are ballasted so that approximately one-half the unit is below water. Their advantage over drilling ships or barges is that the major structure is located above or below the region of most severe wave action. This configuration provides improved stability by its large inertia, and by having a vertical natural frequency of movement which is affected little by wave forces.

The semi-submersibles can be raised by pumping ballast water from the tubes and columns. Finally, they can be used to drill while resting on the sea floor if in sufficiently shallow water.

Ship-shaped platforms consist of a drilling rig supported on a barge or self-propelled ship. A barge, because it is not self-propelled, must be moved by tugs to new assignments, but it has the advantage of low initial cost. The ship-shaped platform can transit at higher speeds and at less expense. A disadvantage of the ship-shaped vessel platforms is that much drilling time can be lost in bad weather due to vessel motion; however, this may not be an important consideration in protected drilling locations. . . .

REFERENCES

E. Keiffer, ed., *Mineral Resources of the World Ocean*, Kingston: University of Rhode Island, Graduate School of Oceanography (Occasional Publication No. 4), 1968; "Mineral Resources of the Sea," U.N. Secretariat, U.N. Doc. E/4680 (2 June 1969); M.B. Spangler, *New Technology and Marine Resource Development; A Study in Government-Business Cooperation*, New York: Praeger, in cooperation with the National Planning Association, 1970; "The Sea: Mineral Resources of the Sea," U.N. Secretariat, U.N. Doc. E/4973 (1971); M.O. Carmichael, *Offshore Drilling Technology*, Park Ridge, N.J.: Noyes Data Corp., Publ. Dept., 1975; H.R. Gould, "Offshore Petroleum Development and Potential," *Maritime Studies and Management*, Vol. 2 (1975), pp. 181-189; V. Asthana, "Mineral Resources of the Continental Margins: An Introduction," in Ram Prakash Anand, ed., *Law of the Sea: Caracas and Beyond*, The Hague:

Martinus Nijhoff, 1980, pp. 71-81; Lewis M. Alexander, ed., *New Developments in Marine Science Technology: Economic, Legal, & Political Aspects of Change*, Honolulu: University of Hawaii Law of the Sea Institute, 1989.

C. THE ORIGIN AND DEVELOPMENT OF THE REGIME OF CONTINENTAL SHELF

By "concept of the continental shelf" is meant its recognition as a *legal* entity rather than as a geological phenomenon. As a geological concept, the continental shelf has been known from the earliest days of ocean exploration. Legal consequences, however, did not arise until relatively recent times when technology permitted the extraction of hydrocarbons and other minerals from shelf areas *outside* the territorial sea. Nonetheless, some early uses had been made of the shelf outside the territorial sea, notable examples being the pearl fisheries of Australia, Ceylon, Mexico, Colombia and other states; coral exploitation off the coasts of Algeria, Sardinia and Sicily; and sponge bed harvesting off the coast of Tunisia. See T.W. Fulton, *The Sovereignty of the Sea, A Historical Account of the Claims of England to the Dominion of the British Seas*, Edinburgh and London: W. Black and Sons, 1911, pp. 697-698; and F.V. Garcia-Amador, *The Exploitation and Conservation of the Resources of the Sea*, Leyden: A.W. Sijthoff, 1959, p. 96. Although exclusive claims to such areas for the purpose of exploiting the particular resource were made and enforced, the magnitude of the enterprise was not sufficient to foster a general legal theory of the continental shelf.

E.J. Cosford, "Continental Shelf 1910-1945," *McGill Law Journal*, Vol. 4 (1958), pp. 245, 246-253.

Portugal in 1910 prohibited trawling by steam vessels within the limit of the shelf as defined by the 100 fathom isobath, or within a minimum of three miles from the coast. It was concerned with the depletion of fisheries resources above the narrow Portuguese shelf. The act marked the official introduction of the shelf into state practice. It was apparently used as both measure and basis of a claim of jurisdiction over trawl fishing. The shelf was said to be the birthplace and nursery of the young fish from which came the supply of fully developed fish found in waters deeper than 100 fathoms. The destructive effect of the trawl on the bottom environment near and on the bed of the shelf was implied the cause of concern.

Steam trawlers would be permitted to operate freely beyond the 100 fathom isobath. Restrictions applied within it. The decree would appear to imply its limited application to Portuguese trawlers only, although it would doubtless have been desired to apply it to foreign vessels. No record is available of any attempt to make it effective internationally.

The act was significant as providing for (1) a type of coastal fisheries jurisdiction beyond the territorial sea based on the presence of a subjacent shelf, and (2) delimitation of this zone by the 100 fathom isobath, evidently intended as the definition of the shelf. The shelf had, however, not apparently then been thought to provide sufficient justification for a claim of right valid against foreign states. Thus in its first appearance the shelf had a limited municipal role only . . . .

The chronologically second employ of the shelf in state practice came in an Imperial Russian pronouncement of 29th September, 1916. Allied and friendly powers were notified that certain specific islands and "others situated near the Asiatic coast of the Empire (are considered) an extension towards the north of the Siberian continental platform." Soviet Russia reaffirmed this claim on 4th November, 1924, holding the islands formed "the northern continuation of the Siberian continental plateau." Later Soviet claims, however, relied on the "sector theory" instead. The words *continental plateau or platform* were used in 1916 and 1924 by the Russians in a different sense and for a different purpose than in earlier fisheries jurisdiction and territorial sea contexts. This usage of the shelf must be examined in relation to grounds allegedly creative of title to territory, particularly, to the *hinterland, watershed, sector*, and other similar notions based on geographic contiguity. Original acquisition of territory is essentially founded on discovery and effective occupation.

Special propositions have been used at times to support claims of right to territory over which there was only minimal, if any, effective occupation, but which was geographically contiguous to a zone which had been effectively subjected to territorial sovereignty. Oppenheim rejected these "fanciful assertions" as having no legal basis. In the above Russian acts the mere fact of the islands being on the Siberian platform was apparently intended to result *ipso jure* in a vesting of sovereignty, without the necessity of "discovery" completed by "effective occupation"....

The Russian employ was a *sui generis* notion, the second in state practice, chronologically speaking, concerning the shelf. It would appear clearly contrary to existing law. This use appeared next incidentally in state practice in negative form in confirmation of the existing law in the 1942 acts concerning the submarine areas of the Gulf of Paria examined later....

A special implied application of the shelf was made by Ceylon in 1925. The *Pearl Fisheries Ordinance* of 1925 provided for the exclusive control by Ceylon of the adjacent pearl fisheries within a defined area based in large part on the 100 fathoms isobath. The boundary followed the 100-fathom line for a distance of some 45 to 50 nautical miles. The ordinance is still in effect. It clearly constituted a claim to at least part of the natural resources of the sea-bed, if not to the sea-bed itself, of that part of the adjacent shelf defined. Certain of the sedentary fisheries have recently been included within the general scope of the natural resources of the shelf by a number of authorities, chiefly including the International Law Commission of the UN, in 1953. This policy has been disputed, particularly by Japan, and is one of the important controversial points in the legal concept of the shelf involving direct interests in its sea-bed and subsoil.

The 1925 ordinance marked a partial shift of interest from the free-swimming fisheries of the sea above to resources more closely identified with the shelf itself. It should not, however, be regarded as a precedent for claims based on direct interest in the shelf or its mineral resources. The 100 fathom isobath was probably adopted by Ceylon for reasons of convenience as a definition of the outer limit of a pre-existing claim based on entirely different considerations than those inherent in the new shelf concept. Nevertheless, the ordinance was disinterested testimony of the utility of a chief feature of the continental shelf, a geographic isobath assigned as its more or less well-defined natural outer limit....

The chronological order of the three concepts' importance as effective legal concepts has been reversed. The earliest employ, the indirect fisheries interest, in 1958 ranks second in intensity of interests, and is clearly contrary to existing law, and the second employ chronologically, the territoriality of emergent islands situated on the adjacent shelf, receives virtually no support, and is also contrary to existing law. The third notion chronologically, that of direct interest in the shelf itself for the sake of its resources, and of the consequent need for appropriation of some form of jurisdiction, slowly gained ground as the economic possibilities became known and technology developed. It is today the most important of the three and the only one given general recognition.

During the preliminary period prior to 1945, however, there was no thought out differentiation of the three interests and the legal notions based on them, and no analysis of consequent legal problems. With the emergence by 1930 of the three notions of the utility of the shelf, however, all of the principal ingredients of the post 1945 controversy over the development of a determinate legal doctrine of the shelf had come into being. Events, legislation, and writings after 1930 amplified and made firm the questions at issue and prepared the way for the heavy spate of post Second World War state practice. The nature of some of the problems which would arise was early evident.

REFERENCES

Sir Cecil Hurst, "Whose is the Bed of the Sea?" *British Yearbook of International Law*, Vol. 4 (1923-24), pp. 34-43; C.H.M. Waldock, "The Legal Basis of Claims to the Continental Shelf," *Transactions of the Grotius Society*, Vol. 36 (1951), pp. 115-148; M.S. McDougal and W.T. Burke, *The Public Order of the Oceans: A Contemporary International Law of the Sea*, New Haven and London: Yale University Press, 1962, pp. 631-642.

The development of the concept of continental shelf is also discussed in *Petroleum Development Ltd. v. Sheikh of Abu Dhabi*, September 1951, [the award bears no exact date], in *International Law Reports*, Vol. 18 (1951), pp. 144-161. See also, *Petroleum Development (Qatar) Ltd. v. Ruler of Qatar*, April 1950 [the award bears no exact date], *International Law Reports*, Vol. 18 (1951), pp. 161-163; R. Young, "Lord Asquith and the Continental Shelf," *American Journal of International Law*, Vol. 46 (1952), pp. 512-515; *1* E.J. Cosford, "The Continental Shelf and the Abu Dhabi Award," *McGill Law Journal*, Vol. 1 (1953), pp. 109-127; Zaslawski, *Oil Under the High Seas*, 1960.

LETTER FROM SECOND ASSISTANT SECRETARY OF STATE (ADEE) TO
MR. FRANK R. NEWTON, September 10, 1918 MS. Department of State, file 312.11/8645
G.H. Hackworth, *Digest of International Law*, Vol. 2 Washington, D.C.:
U.S. Government Printing Office, 1940, pp. 679-680.

The Department is in receipt of your letter of August 20, 1918, concerning the alleged discovery of a large oil pool in the Gulf of Mexico about 40 miles from land on a reef where the water is less than 100 feet deep. With regard to this matter, you ask on behalf of yourself and other interested parties whether it would be possible to acquire property or leasehold rights to this tract of ocean bottom so as to be protected in an effort to obtain oil from this pool. You suggest that an artificial island might be erected and inquire whether such islands could be brought under the jurisdiction of the United States and whether it could protect your rights by giving you a lease to the property. You further suggest that, if protective rights could not be acquired by individuals, you would be willing to turn your discovery over to the Government for a consideration and allow the United States to operate the oil well.

In reply the Department informs you that the United States has no jurisdiction over the ocean bottom of the Gulf of Mexico beyond the territorial waters adjacent to the coast. Therefore, it does not appear possible for the United States to grant to you the leasehold or other property rights in the ocean bottom which you desire.

The Department further informs you that, unless the erection of an artificial island interfered with rights of the United States or of its citizens, or formed the subject of a complaint made upon apparently good grounds, by a foreign government, it is not likely that this Government would object to the erection by American citizens of such an island as you suggest. The Department is not in a position to procure information from other nations as to their attitude toward such a project, but it would seem that no foreign government would interfere with the erection of an artificial island in the Gulf of Mexico unless its interests or the rights of its citizens were injuriously affected thereby.

It may also be observed, although the Department can give no assurances on the subject, that it would seem possible that, if an island were constructed 40 miles from the coast of the United States by the efforts of American citizens and inhabited and controlled by them in the name of the United States, this Government would assume some sort of control over the island. However, it would seem that some special action by the President and Congress would be necessary to this end. If the island were erected, and if the United States assumed control over it, it would then be possible to take such steps as were necessary to protect the rights of the occupants.

NOTE

On February 26, 1942, the United Kingdom and Venezuela concluded the Treaty relating to the Submarine Areas of the Gulf of Paria, *League of Nations Treaty Series*, Vol. 205, pp. 121-127, which provided for the division of such areas between the United Kingdom and Venezuela (Trinidad, which is situated between the Gulf and the open sea, was then a British possession). "Submarine areas" was defined to mean the seabed and subsoil outside of the territorial waters of the parties. Subsequently, an Order in Council of the United Kingdom was passed which provided in part that:

As from the date of this Order all of the submarine areas of the Gulf of Paria [defined as the seabed and subsoil situated beneath the waters, excluding territorial waters, described in the Order] . . . shall be annexed to and form a part of His Majesty's dominion . . . . United Kingdom, *Statutory Rules and Order*, August 6, 1942, Vol. I, p. 919.

The order was not a general claim to continental shelf lands, but related exclusively to the Gulf of Paria continental shelf. Although not the first general claim, the most significant general claim was the proclamation of President Truman made on September 28, 1945.

POLICY OF THE UNITED STATES WITH RESPECT TO THE NATURAL
RESOURCES OF THE SUBSOIL AND SEA BED OF THE CONTINENTAL SHELF
Presidential Proclamation No. 2667, September 28, 1945
United States Statutes at Large, Vol. 59, (1945) pp. 884-885.

WHEREAS the Government of the United States of America, aware of the long range world-wide need for new sources of petroleum and other minerals, holds the view that efforts to discover and make available new supplies of these resources should be encouraged; and

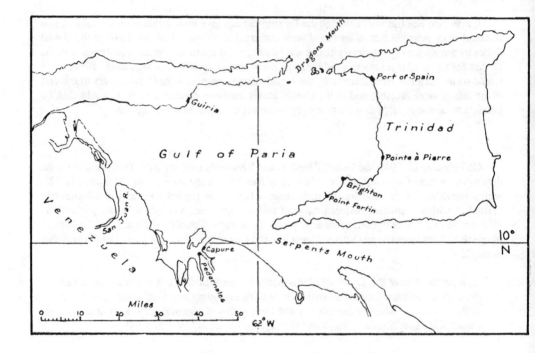

Gulf of Paria
Figure 8-2

Source: [First] United Nations Conference on the Law of the Sea, *Official Records*, Vol.
I, *Preparatory Documents*, p. 228.

WHEREAS its competent experts are of the opinion that such resources underlie many parts
of the continental shelf off the coasts of the United States of America, and that with modern
technological progress their utilization is already practicable or will become so at an early date; and

WHEREAS recognized jurisdiction over these resources is required in the interest of their
conservation and prudent utilization when and as development is undertaken; and

WHEREAS it is the view of the Government of the United States that the exercise of
jurisdiction over the natural resources of the subsoil and sea bed of the continental shelf by the
contiguous nation is reasonable and just, since the effectiveness of measures to utilize or conserve

these resources would be contingent upon cooperation and protection from the shore, since the continental shelf may be regarded as an extension of the landmass of the coastal nation and thus naturally appurtenant to it, since these resources frequently form a seaward extension of a pool or deposit lying within the territory, and since self-protection compels the coastal nation to keep close watch over activities off its shores which are of the nature necessary for utilization of these resources;

NOW, THEREFORE I, HARRY S. TRUMAN, President of the United States of America, do hereby proclaim the following policy of the United States of America with respect to the natural resources of the subsoil and sea bed of the continental shelf.

Having concern for the urgency of conserving and prudently utilizing its natural resources, the Government of the United States regards the natural resources of the subsoil and sea bed of the continental shelf beneath the high seas but contiguous to the coasts of the United States as appertaining to the United States, subject to its jurisdiction and control. In cases where the continental shelf extends to the shores of another State, or is shared with an adjacent State, the boundary shall be determined by the United States and the State concerned in accordance with equitable principles. The character as high seas of the waters above the continental shelf and the right to their free and unimpeded navigation are in no way thus affected.

PROCLAMATIONS CONCERNING UNITED STATES JURISDICTION
OVER NATURAL RESOURCES IN COASTAL AREAS AND THE HIGH SEAS
White House Press Release, September 28, 1945
Department of State Bulletin, Vol. 13 No. 327 (September 30, 1945), pp. 484-485.

. . . The Policy proclaimed by the President in regard to jurisdiction over the continental shelf does not touch upon the question of Federal versus State control. It is concerned solely with establishing the jurisdiction of the United States from an international standpoint. It will, however, make possible the orderly development of an underwater area 750,000 square miles in extent. Generally, submerged land which is contiguous to the continent and which is covered by no more than 100 fathoms (600 feet) of water is considered as the continental shelf.

Petroleum geologists believe that portions of the continental shelf beyond the three-mile limit contain valuable oil deposits. The study of sub-surface structures associated with oil deposits which have been discovered along the Gulf coast of Texas, for instance, indicates that corresponding deposits may underlie the offshore, or submerged land. The trend of oil-productive salt domes extends directly into the Gulf of Mexico off the Texas coast. Oil is also being taken at present from wells within the three mile limit off the coast of California. It is quite possible, geologists say, that the oil deposits extend beyond this traditional limit of national jurisdiction.

Valuable deposits of minerals other than oil may also be expected to be found in these submerged areas. Ore mines now extend under the sea from the coasts of England, Chile, and other countries.

While asserting jurisdiction and control of the United States over the mineral resources of the continental shelf, the proclamation in no way abridges the right of free and unimpeded navigation of waters of the character of high seas above the shelf, nor does it extend the present limits of the territorial waters of the United States.

The advance of technology prior to the present war had already made possible the exploitation of a limited amount of minerals from submerged lands within the three-mile limit. The rapid development of technical knowledge and equipment occasioned by the war now makes possible the determination of the resources of the submerged lands outside of the three-mile limit. With the need for the discovery of additional resources of petroleum and other minerals, it became advisable for the United States to make possible orderly development of these resources. The proclamation of the President is designed to serve this purpose.

REFERENCES

J.W. Bingham, "The Continental Shelf and the Marginal Belt," *American Journal of International Law*, Vol. 40 (1946), pp. 173-178; E. Borchard, "Resources of the Continental Shelf," *American Journal of International Law*, Vol. 40 (1946), pp. 53-70; F.A. Vallat, "The Continental Shelf," *British Yearbook of International Law*, Vol. 23 (1946), pp. 333-338; H. Lauterpacht, "Sovereignty over Submarine Areas," *British Yearbook of International Law*, Vol. 27 (1950), pp. 376-433; J.W. Bingham, "Juridical Status of the Continental Shelf," *Southern California Law Review*, Vol. 26 (1952), pp. 4-20; M.M. Whiteman, *Digest of International Law*, Vol. IV, Washington, D.C.: United States Government Printing Office, 1965, pp. 752-764; L. Juda and O.J. Lissitzyn, *Ocean Space Rights: Developing U.S. Policy*, New York: Praeger Publishers, 1975, chs. 2-3; A.L. Hollick, "U.S. Oceans Policy: The Truman Proclamations," *Virginia Journal of International Law*, Vol. 17 (1976), pp. 23-55; Donald Cameron Watt, "First Steps in the Enclosure of the Oceans--The Origins of Truman's Proclamation on the Resources of the Continental Shelf, 28 September 1945," *Marine Policy*, Vol. 3 (1979), pp. 211-224.

NOTE

Between the Gulf of Paria Order in Council and the Truman Proclamation, the Republic of Argentina issued Decree No. 1, 386 designating as "temporary zones of mineral reserves" the area, *inter alia*, of the epicontinental sea of Argentina. Thereafter virtually every coastal nation in the world issued decrees, proclamations or claims relating to the continental shelf or the mineral resources thereof, or ratified the 1958 Convention on the Continental Shelf. Table 8-3 indicates typical claims of this period [note the diversity of the extent of territory claimed (200 miles, 200 meter isobath, 100 fathom contour, geological shelf, to the depth of exploitability, indefinite) as well as the diversity of the type of legal regime asserted (jurisdiction, national sovereignty, control, national territory, sovereign rights, unspecified)]. The states selected for inclusion in the table were chosen only to illustrate the range of claims asserted. These widespread assertions gave rise to the claim that even though no international agreement had been reached on the subject, there had been created a customary rule of international law recognizing the existence of some degree of jurisdiction by coastal states over their respective continental shelves.

Typical Claims to Continental
Shelf Areas, 1948-1955

1. Brazil   –   By Decree No. 28840 of November 8, 1950, Brazil claimed that part of the seabed corresponding to its continental and insular territory as territory under the exclusive jurisdiction and dominion of the State.

2. Chile   –   By Presidential Proclamation of June 23, 1947, Chile claimed sovereignty over its continental shelf, to a distance of 200 miles from the coastline, and proclaimed and confirmed national sovereignty over the adjacent seas within the limits necessary in order to reserve, protect, preserve and exploit the natural resources found on, within and below that area.

3. Costa Rica   –   By Declaration of July 27, 1948, Decree Law No. 803 of November 2, 1949, and the Constitution of November 9, 1949, Costa Rica claimed sovereignty over the continental shelf to a distance of 200 miles from the coastline, including sovereignty over superjacent waters for purposes of exploring for and exploiting natural resources.

4. Ecuador   –   By Decree of November 6, 1950, and Congres-sional Decree of February 21, 1951, Ecuador claimed the continental shelf to a depth of 200 meters as belonging to the state.

5. India   –   By Proclamation of August 30, 1955, India claimed sovereign rights to the seabed and subsoil of the continental shelf.

6. Israel   –   By Proclamation of August 3, 1952, Israel claimed the seabed and subsoil of submarine areas to the extent that the depth of superjacent waters admitted of exploitation.

7. Mexico   –   By Presidential Proclamation of October 29, 1945, Mexico claimed the continental shelf, to the 200 meter isobath, and its natural resources.

8. Pakistan   –   By Declaration of the Governor-General on March 9, 1950, Pakistan claimed the seabed to the 100 fathom contour as national territory.

9. Saudi Arabia   –   By Royal Pronouncement of May 28, 1949, Saudi Arabia claimed jurisdiction and control over the seabed and subsoil of areas in the Persian Gulf contiguous to its coasts.

Figure 8-3

REFERENCES

R. Young, "Recent Developments with Respect to the Continental Shelf," *American Journal of International Law*, Vol. 42 (1948), pp. 849-857; H.W. Briggs, "Jurisdiction Over the Sea-Bed and Subsoil Beyond Territorial Waters, *American Journal of International Law*, Vol. 45 (1951), pp. 338-342; L.C. Green, "The Continental Shelf," *Current Legal Problems*, Vol. 4 (1951), pp. 54-80; E.C. Smith, "Expanded Maritime Jurisdiction," *George Washington Law Review*, Vol. 19 (1951), pp. 469-489; R. Young, "The Legal Status of Submarine Areas Beneath the High Seas," *American Journal of International Law*, Vol. 45 (1951), pp. 225-240; H. Holland, "The Juridical Status of the Continental Shelf," *Texas Law Review*, Vol. 30 (1952), pp. 586-598; M.W. Mouton, *The Continental Shelf*, The Hague: Martinus Nijhoff, 1952, pp. 32-39; A.A. Aramburu Y. Menchaca, "Character and Scope of the Rights Declared and Practiced Over the Continental Sea and Shelf," *American Journal of International Law*, Vol. 47 (1953), pp. 120-123; R. Young, "The Over-Extension of the Continental Shelf," *American Journal of International Law*, Vol. 47 (1953), pp. 454-456; T.A. Garaioca, "The Continental Shelf and the Extension of the Territorial Sea," *Miami Law Quarterly*, Vol. 10 (1956), pp. 490-498; C.M. Franklin, *The Law of the Sea: Some Recent Developments*, Vol. 52 of *U.S. Naval War College-International Law Studies 1959-1960*, Washington, D.C.: U.S. Government Printing Office, 1961, pp. 30-63; M.M. Whiteman, *Digest of International Law*, Vol. IV, Washington, D.C.: U.S. Government Printing Office, 1965, pp. 740-764.

NORTH SEA CONTINENTAL SHELF CASES
(Federal Republic of Germany/Denmark;
Federal Republic of Germany/Netherlands)
Judgment of February 20, 1969
I.C.J. Reports 1969, p. 3, at pp. 22, 38-39

19.   [T]he Court entertains no doubt [that] the most fundamental of all the rules of law relating to the continental shelf, enshrined in Article 2 of the 1958 Geneva Convention, though quite independent of it, [is] that the rights of the coastal State in respect of the area of continental shelf that constitutes a natural prolongation of its land territory into and under the sea exist *ipso facto* and *ab initio*, by virtue of its sovereignty over the land, and as an extension of it in an exercise of sovereign rights for the purpose of exploring the seabed and exploiting its natural resources. In short, there is here an inherent right. In order to exercise it, no special legal process has to be gone through, nor have any special legal acts to be performed. Its existence can be declared (and many States have done this) but does not depend on its being exercised. To echo the language of the Geneva Convention, it is "exclusive" in the sense that if the coastal State does not choose to explore or exploit the areas of shelf appertaining to it, that is its own affair, but no one else may do so without its express consent.

    . . . .

63.   [Articles 1 to 3 of the Continental Shelf Convention], it is clear, were then [1958] regarded as reflecting, or as crystallizing, received or at least emergent rules of customary international law relative to the continental shelf, amongst them the question of the seaward extent of the shelf; the juridical character of the coastal State's entitlement; the nature of the rights exercisable; the kind of natural resources to which these relate; and the preservation intact of the legal status as high seas of the waters over the shelf, and of the superjacent air-space.

REFERENCES

H.W. Roberts, "International Law--The High Seas, the Continental Shelf, and Free Navigation," *North Carolina Law Review*, Vol. 35 (1957), pp. 524-535; M.M. Whiteman, "Conference on the Law of the Sea: Convention on the Continental Shelf," *American Journal of International Law*, Vol. 52 (1958), pp. 640-648; J.A.C. Gutteridge, "The 1958 Convention on the

Continental Shelf," *British Yearbook of International Law*, Vol. 35 (1959), pp. 102, 120-122; M.M. Whiteman, *Digest of International Law*, Vol. IV, Washington, D.C.: U.S. Government Printing Office, 1965, pp. 871-882, 888-903; K.L. Koh, *The Continental Shelf: An Analytical Study of the Draft Articles on the Continental Shelf Adopted by the International Law Commission*, Seoul: Il Cho Kak, 1980; M.L. Jewett, "The Evolution of the Legal Regime of the Continental Shelf," *Canadian Yearbook of International Law*, Vol. 22 (1984), pp. 153-193 and Vol. 23 (1985), pp. 201-225.

D.   THE SEAWARD LIMIT OF THE CONTINENTAL SHELF

1.   The 1958 Convention on the Continental Shelf

a.   Adjacency, the 200 Meter Isobath, and the "Exploitability" Test

1958 CONVENTION ON THE CONTINENTAL SHELF

Article 1

For the purpose of these articles, the term "continental shelf" is used as referring (a) to the seabed and subsoil of the submarine areas adjacent to the coast but outside the area of the territorial sea, to a depth of 200 meters or, beyond that limit, to where the depth of the superjacent waters admits of the exploitation of the natural resources of the said areas; (b) to the seabed and subsoil of similar submarine areas adjacent to the coasts of islands.

. . . .

Article 7

The provisions of these articles shall not prejudice the right of the coastal State to exploit the subsoil by means of tunnelling irrespective of the depth of water above the subsoil.

NOTE

With respect to tunnelling, see M.M. Whiteman, *Digest of International Law*, Vol. IV, Washington, D.C.: U.S. Government Printing Office, 1965, pp. 918-920.

INTERNATIONAL LAW COMMISSION
1956 Commentary, Draft Article 67
Yearbook of the International Law Commission 1956
Vol. II, p. 297.

(5) The sense in which the term "continental shelf" is used departs to some extent from the geological concept of the term. The varied use of the term by scientists is in itself an obstacle to the adoption of the geological concept as a basis for legal regulation of this problem.

(6) There was yet another reason why the Commission decided not to adhere strictly to the geological concept of the continental shelf. The mere fact that the existence of a continental shelf in the geological sense might be questioned in regard to submarine areas where the depth of the sea would nevertheless permit of exploitation of the subsoil in the same way as if there were a continental shelf, could not justify the application of a discriminatory legal regime to these regions.

(7) While adopting, to a certain extent, the geographical test for the "continental shelf" as the basis of the juridical definition of the term, the Commission therefore in no way holds that the existence of a continental shelf, in the geographical sense as generally understood, is essential for the exercise of the rights of the coastal State as defined in these articles. Thus, if, as is the case in the Persian Gulf, the submarine areas never reach the depth of 200 meters, that fact is irrelevant for the purposes of the present article. Again, exploitation of a submarine area at a depth exceeding 200 meters is not contrary to the present rules, merely because the area is not a continental shelf in the geological sense. . . .

(9) Noting that it was departing from the strictly geological concept of the term, *inter alia*, in view of the inclusion of exploitable areas beyond the depth of 200 meters, the Commission considered the possibility of adopting a term other than "continental shelf." It considered whether it would not be better, in conformity with the usage employed in certain scientific works and also in some national laws and international instruments, to call these regions "submarine areas." The majority of the Commission decided to retain the term "continental shelf" because it is in current use and because the term "submarine areas" used without further explanation would not give a sufficient indication of the nature of the areas in question. The Commission considered that some departure from the geological meaning of the term "continental shelf" was justified, provided that the meaning of the term for the purpose of these articles was clearly defined. It has stated this meaning of the term in the present article.

(10) The term "continental shelf" does not imply that it refers exclusively to continents in the current connotation of that word. It also covers the submarine areas contiguous to islands.

(11) Lastly, the Commission points out that it does not intend limiting the exploitation of the subsoil of the high seas by means of tunnels, cuttings or wells dug from *terra firma*. Such exploitation of the subsoil of the high seas by a coastal State is not subject to any legal limitation by reference to the depth of the superjacent waters.

STUDY PREPARED BY THE SECRETARIAT OF THE UNITED NATIONS FOR
THE AD HOC COMMITTEE TO STUDY THE PEACEFUL USES OF THE SEA-BED
AND THE OCEAN FLOOR BEYOND THE LIMITS OF NATIONAL JURISDICTION
U.N. Doc. A/AC.135/19, Paragraphs 24-26, 28-34 June 21, 1968

(a)   *Question whether the whole submarine areas of the high seas can become part of the continental shelf.*

It has been contended that article 1 of the Convention could be interpreted as causing all the submerged areas in the oceans and seas to become part of the continental shelf, if technology should advance to the point where all such areas are exploitable. The ground advanced for this interpretation is the language of the definition which, referring to "the seabed and subsoil of the submarine areas adjacent to the coast," extends the continental shelf "to where the depth of the superjacent waters admits of the exploitation of the resources of the said areas." From this language, it is inferred that as technical capability develops, a coastal State may extend its jurisdiction across the deep sea floor until it encounters the limit of the similarly extended jurisdiction of the coastal State opposite, in accordance with rules for the delimitation of the boundaries of the continental shelf contained in article 6 of the Convention.

Opponents of this interpretation have argued that it ignores that element in the definition of the continental shelf requiring that such areas be "adjacent to the coast." On the basis of the language of article 1 of the Continental Shelf Convention, this requirement applies whether the sea-bed is less than 200 meters deep or whether it is deeper, but admits of exploitation. Although the concept of adjacency may be not very precise, it would, it is argued, prevent extending the continental shelf to the middle of the ocean. It has also been argued against that interpretation that the term "continental shelf" was deliberately retained by both the International Law Commission and the Geneva Conferences. The International Law Commission said in its report on its eighth session (1956) that it decided to retain the term "because the term 'submarine areas' used without further explanation would not give sufficient indication of the nature of the areas in question." The Commission also said in the same report that it was not possible "to disregard the geographical phenomenon whatever the term - propinquity, contiguity, geographical continuity, appurtenance or identity - used to define the relationship between the submarine areas in question and the adjacent non-submerged land." Likewise, several of the representatives in the Fourth Committee of the 1958 Geneva Conference referred to the fact that the continental shelf was a prolongation of the mainland as the basis for extending the rights of the coastal States over it. Moreover, it is pointed out that the Commission, in the commentary on article 27 of its final draft (later article 2 of the Convention on the High Seas) said:

> The Commission has not made specific mention of the freedom to explore or exploit the subsoil of the high seas. It considered that apart from the case of the exploitation or exploration of the soil or subsoil of a continental shelf . . . such exploitation had not yet assumed sufficient practical importance to justify special regulation.

It thus appears that the Commission's intention was not to deal with the "freedom to explore or exploit the subsoil of the high seas" (an expression which in itself differentiates such areas from the continental shelf), and that the Commission did not consider that the question of the regime of such areas would be automatically settled by the gradual extension of the continental shelf as the result of developing technology of exploitation. Finally, it is argued that if the International Law Commission and the Geneva Conference had had in mind the possibility of such a radical extension of national jurisdiction they would have undoubtedly made this clear.

The Government of France has formally adhered to the restrictive interpretation of the concept of adjacency by declaring in its instrument of accession to the Convention that with respect to article 1 "in the view of the Government of the French Republic, the expression 'adjacent' areas implies a notion of geophysical, geological and geographical dependence which *ipso facto* rules out an unlimited extension of the continental shelf." Two of the parties to the Convention [United Kingdom and the United States] have reserved their position as regards the declaration of the French Government concerning article 1. No party has specifically objected to it.

. . . .

(b)   *The question of the relation between the criterion of depth and the criterion of exploitability.*

According to the definition in article 1 of the Convention on the Continental Shelf, the continental shelf means "the seabed and subsoil of the submarine areas adjacent to the coast but outside the area of the territorial sea, to a depth of 200 meters, or beyond that limit, to where the depth of the superjacent waters admits of the exploitation of the natural resources of the said areas." There has been considerable discussion of the mutual relationship between the two criteria of depth and of exploitability set forth in the foregoing definition.

Some have considered that the two criteria were completely independent of each other, and have even stated that they were mutually incompatible. On this view, the result would tend to be that only the criterion of exploitability would have a real effect. Others find no incompatibility between the two criteria, but consider that they are complementary, so that all coastal States, regardless of their technical capability, would automatically acquire rights up to a depth of 200 meters, but beyond that point they would do so only through actual increase of exploitability.

Another view is that the criterion of exploitability has a supplementary and subordinate function, and was intended to permit a coastal State to exercise rights over activities carried out on the continental slopes and in the continental border land in continuation of activities begun, or in connection with those carried out, in zones with a depth of less than 200 meters. This view, however, recognizes that the development of technology might bring about the unexpected result that the criterion of exploitability, though originally intended to be ancillary, might come in practice to supplant the criterion of 200-meter depth.

Finally, the view has also been advanced that each criterion applies to a separate category of States; the criterion of 200 meters depth would apply to States bounded by a continental shelf, while the criterion of exploitability would apply to States having no true continental shelf.

(c)   *The question of the meaning of the criterion of exploitability.*

The part of the definition in article 1 of the Convention on the Continental Shelf which reads ". . . or beyond that limit, to where the depth of the superjacent waters admits of the exploitation of the natural resources of the said areas" has given rise to a number of questions. In the first place, there is a question whether, in order for a State to exercise rights in the continental shelf beyond a depth of 200 meters, there must be actual recovery of a natural resource, or whether it is sufficient simply that a possibility of such exploitation exists. The language of article 1, "admits of the exploitation," would seem to favor the latter interpretation. It may also be recalled that paragraph 2 of article 2 of the Convention makes it clear that the coastal State has exclusive rights even if it does not explore the continental shelf or exploit its natural resources. Paragraph 3 of article 2 of the Convention provides that "The rights of the coastal State over the continental shelf do not depend on occupation, effective or notional. . . ." At the 1958 Conference some delegations spoke in favor of the view that a State would have rights in the continental shelf whether or not it was itself actually able to exploit the natural resources contained therein.

In the second place, questions have been raised as to the meaning of exploitability. Is the phrase "admits of exploitation" to be understood as requiring that there be a possibility of real economic benefit, or does a mere scientific and technical possibility of carrying on activities on the sea-bed and in the subsoil suffice? If one State, without motives of profit, carries on purely scientific activities involving, for instance, drilling in an area of sea-bed which is more than 200 meters deep, does it thereby extend its rights and those of other States in the continental shelf? If a

State's activity consists simply of picking up from the sea-bed some relatively easily available natural resource such as manganese nodules, does this activity give the State rights over the resources of the subsoil, which are not exploitable by present technology? Does simple exploration constitute exploitation? If not, will not exploration of the bed of the deep sea be discouraged by lack of security of rights and of sanctions before the time when exploitation has been clearly proved possible?

Moreover, it has been pointed out that although article 1 of the Convention says ". . . to where the depth of the superjacent waters admits of . . . exploitation," there may be difficulties of exploitation from other causes than simple depth, so that even if the depth offers no obstacle, exploitation may still be impossible. In any event, it is claimed, it may be very difficult to prove that the depth permits exploitation by any other means than actual exploitation.

QUESTIONS

(1) Would exploitation by one nation at a depth in excess of 200 meters automatically extend continental shelf jurisdiction for all coastal nations? See M.W. Mouton, *The Continental Shelf*, The Hague: Martinus Nijhoff, 1952, p. 42; R. Young, "The Geneva Convention on the Continental Shelf: A First Impression," *American Journal of International Law*, Vol. 52 (1958), pp. 733, 735; C.M. Franklin, *The Law of the Sea: Some Recent Developments*, Vol. 52 of *U.S. Naval War College-International Law Studies 1959-1960*, Washington, D.C.: U.S. Government Printing Office, 1961, p. 23. Cf. Senate Report No. 528, 89th Congress, 1st Session, 1965, pp. 11, 14; N. Ely, "American Policy Options in the Development of Undersea Mineral Resources," *International Lawyer*, Vol. 2 (1968), pp. 215, 219; See also R. Young, "The Legal Regime of the Deep-Sea Floor," *American Journal of International Law*, Vol. 62 (1968), pp. 641, 645 (n. 16 and accompanying text).

(2) Would exploitation of sedentary species of living resources at 330 meters water depth automatically extend continental shelf jurisdiction for petroleum and natural gas to the same depth?

(3) Is the achievement of commercial production of petroleum or natural gas in 500 meters of relatively calm Gulf of Mexico waters indicative of technological capability to produce those resources from 500 meters water depth off the coast of Alaska with its severe weather and great tide ranges?

REFERENCES

E.D. Brown, "The Outer Limit of the Continental Shelf," *Juridical Review*, Vol. 13 (1968), pp. 111-146; L.F.E. Goldie, "The Exploitability Test--Interpretation of Potentialities," *Natural Resources Journal*, Vol. 8 (1968), pp. 434-477; Shigeru Oda, "Boundary of the Continental Shelf," *Japanese Annual of International Law*, Vol. 12 (1968), pp. 264-284; Shigeru Oda, "Proposals for Revising the Convention on the Continental Shelf," *Columbia Journal of Transnational Law*, Vol. 7 (1968), pp. 1-31; N. Ely, "Deep Sea Minerals and American National Interests," in L.M. Alexander, ed., *The Law of the Sea: International Rules and Organization for the Sea*, Kingston: University of Rhode Island, 1969, p. 423; R. Denorme, "The Seaward Limit of the Continental Shelf," in L.M. Alexander, ed., *The Law of the Sea: National Policy Recommendations*, Kingston, University of Rhode Island, 1970, pp. 263-274; L.F.E. Goldie, "Where is the Continental Shelf's Outer Boundary," *Journal of Maritime Law and Commerce*, Vol. 1 (1970), pp. 461-472; O.L. Stone, "Some Aspects of Jurisdiction Over Natural Resources Under the Ocean Floor," *Natural Resources Lawyer*, Vol. 3 (1970), pp. 155-194; L.F.E. Goldie, "The Continental Shelf's Outer Boundary--A Postscript," *Journal of Maritime Law and Commerce*, Vol.

2 (1971), pp. 173-177; Pacem in Maribus, *Legal Foundations of the Ocean Regime*, Vol. 2, Royal University of Malta Press, 1971, Part I ("The Limits of National Jurisdiction"); L.F.E. Goldie, "A Lexicographical Controversy--The Word 'Adjacent' in Article 1 of the Continental Shelf Convention," *American Journal of International Law*, Vol. 66 (1972), pp. 829-835; B.H. Oxman, "The Preparation of Article 1 of the Convention on the Continental Shelf," *Journal of Maritime Law and Commerce*, Vol. 3 (1972), pp. 245-305, 445-472, 683-723 (3 Parts); R.P. Anand, "Limits of National Jurisdiction in the Sea-Bed," *India Quarterly*, Vol. 29 (1973), pp. 79-103; J.M. Ruda, "The Outer Limit of the Continental Shelf," in N.S. Rodley and C.N. Ronning, eds., *International Law in the Western Hemisphere*, The Hague: Martinus Nijhoff, 1974, pp. 38-69; N. Ely and R.F. Pietrowski, "Boundaries of Seabed Jurisdiction Off the Pacific Coast of Asia," *Natural Resources Lawyer*, Vol. 8 (1975), pp. 611-629; H.D. Hedberg, "Relation of Political Boundaries on the Ocean Floor to the Continental Margin," *Virginia Journal of International Law*, Vol. 17 (1976), pp. 57-75; F.A. Eustis, IV, "Method and Basis of Seaward Delimitation of Continental Shelf Jurisdiction," *Virginia Journal of International Law*, Vol. 17 (1976), pp. 107-130.

NOTE

Obviously, the most important criterion in delimiting this boundary concerned wealth acquisition. If the national area were broad, virtually all of the presently accessible wealth of the ocean would be accorded to coastal states; if, on the other hand, the national area were to be narrow, real wealth would be available for administration by an international agency, presumably for the benefit of developing nations. It should be understood, however, that some of the early arguments for narrow or wide national jurisdiction over seabed minerals were based on interpretation of Article 1 of the 1958 Convention on the Continental Shelf, while later positions tended to be based on perceived national economic or security interests, entirely without regard to Article 1.

Leaving aside the positions taken on a self-interest basis with respect to broad or narrow national seabed jurisdiction, there are two further issues which should be considered in the context of materials on the seaward limit of the continental shelf. First, what options are available in determining the seaward limit of national seabed mineral jurisdiction, and, second, what specific boundary can or ought to be adopted to demarcate the national-international boundary.

NORTH SEA CONTINENTAL SHELF CASES
(Federal Republic of Germany/Denmark
Federal Republic of Germany/Netherlands)
I.C.J. Reports *1969*, p. 3.

43. More fundamental than the notion of proximity appears to be the principle--constantly relied upon by all the Parties--of the natural prolongation or continuation of the land territory or domain, or land sovereignty of the coastal State into and under the high seas via the bed of its territorial sea which is under the full sovereignty of that State. There are various ways of formulating this principle, but the underlying idea, namely of an extension of something already possessed, is the same, and it is this idea of extension which is, in the Court's opinion, determinant. Submarine areas do not really appertain to the coastal State because--or not only because--they are near it. They are near it of course; but this would not suffice to confer title, any more than, according to a well-established principle of law recognized by both sides in the present case, mere proximity confers *per se* title to land territory. What confers the *ipso jure* title which international law attributes to the coastal State in respect of its continental shelf, is the fact that

the submarine areas concerned may be deemed to be actually part of the territory over which the coastal State already has dominion--in the sense that, although covered with water, they are a prolongation or continuation of that territory, an extension of it under the sea.

REFERENCES

H.D. Hedberg, "National-International Jurisdictional Boundary on the Ocean Floor," Occasional Paper No. 16, Law of the Sea Institute, University of Rhode Island, Kingston, 1972; L.F.E. Goldie, "The International Court of Justice's 'Natural Prolongation' and the Continental Shelf Problem of Islands," *Netherlands Yearbook of International Law*, Vol. 4 (1973), pp. 237-261; G.T. Yates and J.H. Young, eds., *Limits to National Jurisdiction Over the Sea*, Charlottesville: University Press of Virginia, 1974; H. Orlin, "Offshore Boundaries: Engineering and Economic Aspects," *Ocean Development and International Law Journal*, Vol. 3 (1975), pp. 87-96.

b. Irregularities in Continental Shelf Structure

INTERNATIONAL LAW COMMISSION
1956 Commentary, Draft Article 67
[Article 1 of the 1958 Convention]
Yearbook of the International Law Commission 1956
Vol. II, p. 297

(8) In the special cases in which submerged areas of a depth less than 200 meters, situated fairly close to the coast, are separated from the part of the continental shelf adjacent to the coast by a narrow channel deeper than 200 meters, such shallow areas could be considered as adjacent to that part of the shelf. It would be for the State relying on this exception to the general rule to establish its claim to an equitable modification of the rule. In case of dispute it must be a matter for arbitral determination whether a shallow submarine area falls within the rule as here formulated.

SCIENTIFIC CONSIDERATIONS RELATING TO THE CONTINENTAL
SHELF MEMORANDUM BY THE SECRETARIAT OF U.N.E.S.C.O.
U.N. Doc. A/CONF.13/2 and Add. (September 20, 1957)
[First] United Nations Conference on the Law of the Sea,
Official Records, Vol. I, *Preparatory Documents*, pp. 43-44.

III. The Problem of Irregularities in the Shelf

29. The term shelf or platform does not necessarily imply an absolutely flat relief, but only a configuration where, except in glaciated areas, the unevenness is not very considerable: 100 meters at most, and usually of lesser order. If we were to insist on absolutely flat areas between the coast and the outer limits suggested above, we would not find very many continental shelves in the worlds. Besides, isolated rises and depressions of a much greater scale can be found on the shelves; but in continental terminology, it is admitted that such heights and depressions do not form part of the platform.

30. Shallowly embedded submarine valleys (some 40 or 50 meters deep) that are found on the shelves in different parts of the world should certainly be considered as integral parts of the shelves. Examples are found on the shelf off the mouth of the Hudson River, in the Java Sea between Java, Sumatra and Borneo, in the Arafura Sea, north of Australia, and in front of Guinea. These valleys (so-called shelf channels), cut by subaerial rivers during the Pleistocene period at a time when glaciation caused a lowering of the sea level, are but a witness of the fact that the shelf is a borderline area alternately submerged and exposed, a true extension of the neighboring continents. Another evidence of the mixed origin of the shelves is the existence on various shelves of hills of glacial origin and of Quaternary Age (north-east coast of North America, North Sea, Baltic Sea). There are also channels of fluviatile or origin, which have been excavated to greater or lesser extent by tidal current scour.

31. The case of isolated and narrow but deeper depressions is more controversial. . . . It will no doubt be unanimously agreed that these isolated deeps form part of the shelf in which they are embedded, so long as they do not occupy more than a very small part of the sea bottom and are encircled by much shallower depths.

32. However, certain continental shelves are marked by much deeper and bigger depressions . . . . Three categories can be distinguished: a) the depressions that communicate with the deep sea beyond the outer edge of the shelf only over a sill at the level, or nearly at the level of the shelf floor; b) wide flat-floored troughs lacking a sill in the outer part; c) the narrow canyon-like valleys which slope out to the deep-sea floor.

a) The depressions of the first kind are frequent on continental shelves in higher latitudes that have been glaciated. They are sometimes longitudinal and thus form a kind of large trough parallel to the general direction of the coast, for example around Norway . . . , sometimes transversal, and thus correspond to the openings of fjords, for example, the coast of British Columbia. . . . The glaciers of the Ice Age are evidently responsible for the modelling.

b) The depression of the second type so far as known are all off glaciated coasts, for example the Cabot Strait Trough, south of Newfoundland. . . .

c) Depressions of the third type, much more numerous but narrower, are the submarine canyons, concerning which a considerable literature is in existence . . . ; they are valleys with a V-shaped cross-section, often ramified, deeply embedded in the shelf, with relative depths of several hundred meters, sometimes even exceeding 1,000 meters. They are thus distinguished from the "shelf channels" described [above]. Furthermore, they have a very steep and irregular longitudinal profile, but, generally, without very marked counter-slopes. Many submarine canyons only cut into the fringe of the continental shelf without penetrating deeply into it; but others traverse it almost completely and nearly reach the coast or even enter the mouths of certain rivers, as is the case of the Congo Canyon on the west coast of Africa, the Gouf de Cap Breton, off the south-western coast of France; and the canyons off California.

33. The problem whether these various depressions do or do not form part of the continental shelf is one which will arise in many areas since submarine canyons exist in a considerable number of regions; they are known to be found on the coasts of both Americas, many Mediterranean coasts, coasts of east and west Africa, off the entrance of the English Channel, in the Beaufort Sea, around the Philippines, Japan, etc. . . . Though the exploitation by man of their bottom and sides are not as yet begun nor envisaged, it is foreseen that jurists will one day be faced with this problem.

34. From the morphological point of view, when a depression of the first type mentioned above is concerned, that is, one communicating with the ocean over a sill nearly level with the shelf, it would seem reasonable to consider this depression as constituting a part of the shelf, even if the depression is very deep. In this case the depression is perhaps anomalous to the shelf, it is true, but totally enclosed therein. It is suggested that the depressions in the Norwegian shelf should not be dissociated therefrom because they form an integral part of the shelf from the morphogenetic point of view and many continue far inside the coastline as fjords. It is also suggested that the Norwegian Trough forms part of the North Sea Shelf because of its sill.

35. A more difficult problem arises concerning depressions of the second type, that is, extending across to the break in slope without a sill. A type example is provided by the trough coming out of the Gulf of St. Lawrence through Cabot Strait. The depths along the entire length of this trough are in excess of those of the shelf on either side, and the trough has a width of about 100 kilometers. On the other hand, the trough is morphologically related to the shelf. Furthermore, the depths are not in excess of many of the basins on other glaciated shelves and it would be difficult to draw a line between this trough and the numerous other troughs of the glaciated shelves. However, the problem of the inclusion of this kind of trough in the continental shelves is more controversial than the preceding case.

36. The situation is very different from that of submarine canyons which tend to slope continuously out from their head to the deep-sea floor, thus forming part of the continental slope. The narrow upper part of submarine canyons, although belonging technically more to the slope than to the surface of the terrace, could nevertheless be considered part of the surrounding shelf from the point of view of convenience for international legislation.

37. In this regard, the notion of the straight baseline might be taken into consideration. This is the baseline from which the width of territorial waters are calculated in the case of deep coastal indentations. The question would then be to know what would be the width of the indentation in the shelf beyond which a straight line should be drawn from one side to the other, to define the limits of the shelf at this point. The critical width to be adopted should be discussed by jurists.

NORTH SEA CONTINENTAL SHELF CASES
(Federal Republic of Germany/Denmark;
Federal Republic of Germany/Netherlands)
Judgment of February 20, 1969
I.C.J. Reports 1969, p. 3.

45. The fluidity of all these notions is well illustrated by the case of the Norwegian Trough. . . . Without attempting to pronounce on the status of that feature, the Court notes that the shelf areas in the North Sea separated from the Norwegian coast by the 80-100 kilometers of the Trough cannot in any physical sense be said to be adjacent to it, nor to be its natural prolongation. They are nevertheless considered by the States parties to the relevant delimitations . . . to appertain to Norway up to the median lines. . . . True these median lines are themselves drawn on equidistance principles; but it was only by first ignoring the existence of the Trough that these median lines fell to be drawn at all.

R. Young, "Offshore Claims and Problems in the North Sea," *American Journal of International Law*, Vol. 59 (1965), pp. 505, 506, 511.

[I]n geological terms the rim of the Norwegian Trough is not a true shelf edge, but . . . the Trough is rather a deep gouge in the wide North Sea shelf caused largely by glacial action of the kind so conspicuous on the Norwegian mainland. . . .

. . . .

[I]t appears to be still the official view that Norway should not join in the [Convention on the Continental Shelf]. The reason seems to be primarily geographical: because of the Norwegian Trough, Norway is apparently reluctant to accept a shelf definition which refers to the 200-meter depth line, even though the alternative criterion of exploitability is also recognized in the Convention text. Norway's position is that the Trough is only a depression in the shelf properly appertaining to Norway, and that Norway is entitled to this full expanse of shelf, under generally accepted principles of international law irrespective of the Convention, as far out as median lines between Norway and the opposite states. [T]here is scientific support for this view, and it was also affirmed by Norway at the 1958 Conference without exception being taken by other states.

REFERENCES

C.A.M. King, *An Introduction to Oceanography*, New York: McGraw Hill, 1963, p. 64 *et seq.*; F.P. Shepard, *The Earth Beneath the Sea*, rev. ed., Baltimore: Johns Hopkins Press, 1967, pp. 115-138; J.H. Whitaker, ed., *Submarine Canyons & Deep-Sea Fans*, San Diego, California: Academie Press, 1976; Asnani Usman, "The Timor Gap in the Delimitation of the Continental Shelf Boundary Between Indonesia and Australia," *Indonesian Quarterly*, Vol. 14 (1986), pp. 375-392.

NOTE

A modern version of the "trough" problem occurs in the East China Sea dispute over continental shelf resources where Japan's shelf is cut laterally by the Okinawa Trough. Japan naturally favors an equidistance apportionment formula which ignores the anomaly in the same manner that the North Sea allocation ignored the Norwegian Trough. China, on the other hand, is urging acceptance of the "natural prolongation" concept enunciated by the International Court of Justice in the *North Sea Continental Shelf Cases* so that it would receive rights in the shelf up to the Okinawa Trough, well beyond any proposed median line. See Choon-ho Park, "The Sino-Japanese-Korean Sea Resources Controversy and the Hypothesis of a 200-Mile Economic Zone," *Harvard International Law Journal*, Vol. 16 (1975), pp. 41-42 and Hungdah Chiu, "The 1982 United Nations Convention on the Law of the Sea and the Settlement of China's Maritime Boundary Dispute," in Thomas Buergenthal, ed., *Contemporary Issues in International Law, Essays in Honor of Louis B. Sohn*, Kehl/Strasbourg/Arlington: N.P. Engel, 1984, pp. 200-201. See also K.T. Chao, "East China Sea: Boundary Problems Relating to the Tiao-yu-t'ai Islands," *Chinese Yearbook of International Law and Affairs*, Vol. 2 (1982), pp. 45-97; Ying-jeou Ma, "The East Asian Seabed Controversy Revisited: Relevance (or Irrelevance) of the Tiao-yu-t'ai (Senkaku) Islands Territorial Dispute," *Chinese Yearbook of International Law and Affairs*, Vol. 2 (1982), pp. 1-44; H. Schulte Nordholte, "Delimitation of the Continental Shelf in the East China Sea," *Netherlands International Law Review*, Vol. 32 (1985), pp. 123-159.

2.   1982 United Nations Convention on the Law of the Law

a.   Definition, Scope and Revenue Sharing

1982 UNITED NATIONS CONVENTION ON THE LAW OF THE SEA

Article 76
Definition of the continental shelf

1. The continental shelf of a coastal State comprises the sea-bed and subsoil of the submarine areas that extend beyond its territorial sea throughout the natural prolongation of its land territory to the outer edge of the continental margin, or to a distance of 200 nautical miles from the baselines from which the breadth of the territorial sea is measured where the outer edge of the continental margin does not extend up to that distance.

2. The continental shelf of a coastal State shall not extend beyond the limits provided for in paragraphs 4 to 6.

3. The continental margin comprises the submerged prolongation of the land mass of the coastal state, and consists of the sea-bed and subsoil of the shelf, the slope and the rise. It does not include the deep ocean floor with its oceanic ridges or the subsoil thereof.

4. (a) For the purposes of this Convention, the coastal State shall establish the outer edge of the continental margin wherever the margin extends beyond 200 nautical miles from the baselines from which the breadth of the territorial sea is measured, by either:

> (i) a line delineated in accordance with paragraph 7 by reference to the outermost fixed points at each of which the thickness of sedimentary rocks is at least 1 percent of the shortest distance from such point to the foot of the continental slope; or

> (ii) a line delineated in accordance with paragraph 7 by reference to fixed points not more than 60 nautical miles from the foot of the continental slope.

(b) In the absence of evidence to the contrary, the foot of the continental slope shall be determined as the point of maximum change in the gradient at its base.

5. The fixed points comprising the line of the outer limits of the continental shelf on the sea-bed, drawn in accordance with paragraph 4(a)(i) and (ii), either shall not exceed 350 nautical miles from the baselines from which the breadth of the territorial sea is measured or shall not exceed 100 nautical miles from the 2,500 meter isobath, which is a line connecting the depth of 2,500 meters.

6. Notwithstanding the provisions of paragraph 5, on submarine ridges, the outer limit of the continental shelf shall not exceed 350 nautical miles from the baselines from which the breadth of the territorial sea is measured. This paragraph does not apply to submarine elevations that are natural components of the continental margin, such as its plateaux, rises, caps, banks and spurs.

7. The coastal State shall delineate the outer limits of its continental shelf, where that shelf extends beyond 200 nautical miles from the baselines from which the breadth of the territorial sea is measured, by straight lines not exceeding 60 nautical miles in length, connecting fixed points, defined by coordinates of latitude and longitude.

8. Information on the limits of the continental shelf beyond 200 nautical miles from the baselines from which the breadth of the territorial sea is measured shall be submitted by the coastal State to the Commission on the Limits of the Continental Shelf set up under Annex II on the basis of equitable geographical representation. The commission shall make recommendations to coastal States on matters related to the establishment of the outer limits of their continental shelf. The limits of the shelf established by a coastal State on the basis of these recommendations shall be final and binding.

9. The coastal State shall deposit with the Secretary-General of the United Nations charts and relevant information, including geodetic data, permanently describing the outer limits of its continental shelf. The Secretary-General shall give due publicity thereto.

10. The provisions of this article are without prejudice to the question of delimitation of the continental shelf between States with opposite or adjacent coasts.

. . . .

Article 82
Payments and contributions with respect to the exploitation
of the continental shelf beyond 200 nautical miles

1. The coastal State shall make payments or contributions in kind in respect of the exploitation of the non-living resources of the continental shelf beyond 200 nautical miles from the baselines from which the breadth of the territorial sea is measured.

2. The payments and contributions shall be made annually with respect to all production at a site after the first five years of production at that site. For the sixth year, the rate of payment or contribution shall be 1 percent of the value or volume of production at the site. The rate shall increase by 1 percent for each subsequent year until the twelfth year and shall remain at 7 percent thereafter. Production does not include resources used in connection with exploitation.

3. A developing State which is a net importer of a mineral resource produced from its continental shelf is exempt from making such payments or contributions in respect of that mineral resource.

4. The payments or contributions shall be made through the Authority, which shall distribute them to States Parties to this Convention, on the basis of equitable sharing criteria, taking into account the interests and needs of developing States, particularly the least developed and the land-locked among them.

Article 84
Charts and lists of geographical coordinates

1. Subject to this Part, the outer limit lines of the continental shelf and the lines of delimitation drawn in accordance with article 83 shall be shown on charts of a scale or scales adequate for ascertaining their position. Where appropriate, lists of geographical coordinates of points, specifying the geodetic datum, may be substituted for such outer limit lines or lines of delimitation.

2.   The coastal State shall give due publicity to such charts or lists of geographical coordinates and shall deposit a copy of each such chart or list with the Secretary-General of the United Nations and, in the case of those showing the outer limit lines of the continental shelf, with the Secretary-General of the Authority.

REFERENCES

Vincent J. Nigrelli, "Ocean Mineral Revenue Sharing," *Ocean Development and International Law*, Vol. 5 (1978), pp. 153-180; Ram Prakash Anand, "Legal Continental Shelf," in Ram Prakash Anand, ed., *Law of the Sea: Caracas and Beyond*, The Hague: Martinus Nijhoff, 1980, pp. 145-179; Maurice Hope-Thompson, "The Third World and the Law of the Sea. The Attitude of the Group of 77 Toward the Continental Shelf," *Boston College Third World Law Journal*, Vol. 1 (1980), pp. 37-70; Takeshi Minagawa, "The Nature of the Continental Shelf Rights in International Law," *Hitotsubashi Journal of Law & Politics*, Vol. 10 (1981), pp. 1-14; Vincent E. McKelvey, "Interpretation of the UNCLOS III Definition of the Continental Shelf," in Douglas M. Johnston and Norman G. Letalik, eds., *The Law of the Sea and Ocean Industry: New Opportunities and Restraints*, Honolulu: The Law of the Sea Institute, University of Hawaii, 1984, pp. 465-472; Adam J. Kerr and Michael J. Keen, "Hydrographic and Geologic Concerns of Implementing Article 76," *International Hydrographic Review*, Vol. 52 (1985), pp. 139-148; Makhdoom Ali Khan, "The Juridical Concept of the Continental Shelf," *Pakistan Horizon*, Vol. 38, No. 2 (1985), pp. 19-40.

b.   Settlement of Dispute on Seaward Limit Beyond 200 Miles

1982 UNITED NATIONS CONVENTION ON THE LAW OF THE SEA

ANNEX II. COMMISSION ON THE LIMITS
OF THE CONTINENTAL SHELF

Article 1

In accordance with the provisions of Article 76, a Commission on the Limits of the Continental Shelf beyond 200 nautical miles shall be established in conformity with the following articles.

Article 2

1.   The Commission shall consist of 21 members who shall be experts in the field of geology, geophysics or hydrography, elected by States Parties to this Convention from among their nationals, having due regard to the need to ensure equitable geographical representation, who shall serve in their personal capacities.

2.   The initial election shall be held as soon as possible but in any case within 18 months after the date of entry into force of this Convention. At least three months before the date of each election, the Secretary-General of the United Nations shall address a letter to the States Parties, inviting the submission of nominations, after appropriate regional consultations, within three months. The Secretary-General shall prepare a list in alphabetical order of all persons thus nominated and shall submit it to all the States Parties.

3. Elections of the members of the Commission shall be held at a meeting of States Parties convened by the Secretary-General at United Nations Headquarters. At that meeting, for which two-thirds of the States Parties shall constitute a quorum, the persons elected to the Commission shall be those nominees who obtain a two-thirds majority of the votes of the representatives of States Parties present and voting. Not less than three members shall be elected from each geographical region.

4. The members of the Commission shall be elected for a term of five years. They shall be eligible for re-election.

5. The State Party which submitted the nomination of a member of the Commission shall defray the expense of that member while in performance of Commission duties. The coastal State concerned shall defray the expenses incurred in respect of the advice referred to in article 3, paragraph 1(b), of this Annex. The secretariat of the Commission shall be provided by the Secretary-General of the United Nations.

Article 3

1. The functions of the Commission shall be:

(a) to consider the data and other material submitted by coastal States concerning the outer limits of the continental shelf in areas where those limits extend beyond 200 nautical miles, and to make recommendations in accordance with article 76 and the Statement of Understanding adopted on 29 August 1980 by the Third United Nations Conference on the Law of the Sea;

(b) to provide scientific and technical advice, if requested by the coastal State concerned during the preparation of the data referred to in subparagraph (a).

2. The Commission may cooperate, to the extent considered necessary and useful, with the Intergovernmental Oceanographic Commission of UNESCO, the International Hydrographic Organization and other competent international organizations with a view to exchanging scientific and technical information which might be of assistance in discharging the Commission's responsibilities.

Article 4

Where a coastal State intends to establish, in accordance with article 76, the outer limits of its continental shelf beyond 200 nautical miles, it shall submit particulars of such limits to the Commission along with supporting scientific and technical data as soon as possible but in any case within 10 years of the entry into force of this Convention for that State. The coastal State shall at the same time give the names of any Commission members who have provided it with scientific and technical advice.

Article 5

Unless the Commission decides otherwise, the Commission shall function by way of sub-commissions composed of seven members, appointed in a balanced manner taking into account the specific elements of each submission by a coastal State. Nationals of the coastal State making the submission who are members of the Commission and any Commission member who has assisted a coastal State by providing scientific and technical advice with respect to the delineation shall not be a member of the sub-commission dealing with that submission but has the right to participate as a member in the proceedings of the Commission concerning the said submission. The coastal State which has made a submission to the Commission may send its representatives to participate in the relevant proceedings without the right to vote.

Article 6

1. The sub-commission shall submit its recommendations to the Commission.

2. Approval by the Commission of the recommendations of the sub-commission shall be by a majority of two-thirds of Commission members present and voting.

3. The recommendations of the Commission shall be submitted in writing to the coastal State which made the submission and to the Secretary-General of the United Nations.

Article 7

Coastal States shall establish the outer limits of the continental shelf in conformity with the provisions of article 76, paragraph 8, and in accordance with the appropriate national procedures.

Article 8

In the case of disagreement by the coastal State with the recommendations of the Commission, the coastal State shall, within a reasonable time, make a revised or new submission to the Commission.

Article 9

The actions of the Commission shall not prejudice matters relating to delimitation of boundaries between States with opposite or adjacent coasts.

REFERENCES

K.O. Emery, "Geological Limits of the Continental Shelf," *Ocean Development and International Law*, Vol. 10 (1981), pp. 1-11; Emmanuel Gounaris, "The Continental Shelf Doctrine and Its Implications in the Greek and German Foreign Policy," *Hellenic Review of International Relations*, Vol. 2 (1981/82), No. 2, pp. 660-666; P.R. Gardiner, "Reasons and Methods for Fixing the Outer Limit of the Legal Continental Shelf Beyond 200 Nautical Miles," *Revue Iranienne Des Relations Internationales*, Vols. 11/12 (Spring 1978), pp. 145-170; Ted L. McDorman, "The Definition of 'Canada Lands' and the Determination of the Outer Limit of the Continental Shelf," *Journal of Maritime Law and Commerce*, Vol. 14 (1983), pp. 195-223; D.N. Hutchinson, "The Seaward Limit to Continental Shelf Jurisdiction in Customary International Law," *British Yearbook of International Law*, Vol. 56 (1985), pp. 111-188; Duncan J. McMillan, "The Extent of the Continental Shelf: Factors Affecting the Accuracy of a Continental Margin Boundary," *Baden-Württembergische Verwaltungspraxis* (Stuttfurt, Germany), Vol. 9 (1985), No. 2, pp. 148-156; Kilaparti Ramakrishna, Robert E. Bowen and Jack H. Archer, "Outer Limits of Continental Shelf. A Legal Analysis of Chilean and Ecuadorian Island Claims and U.S. Response," *Marine Policy*, Vol. 11 (1987), No. 1, pp. 58-68; Stephen Vasciannie, "Land-locked and Geographically Disadvantaged States and the Question of the Outer Limit of the Continental Shelf," *British Yearbook of International Law*, Vol. 58 (1987), pp. 271-302.

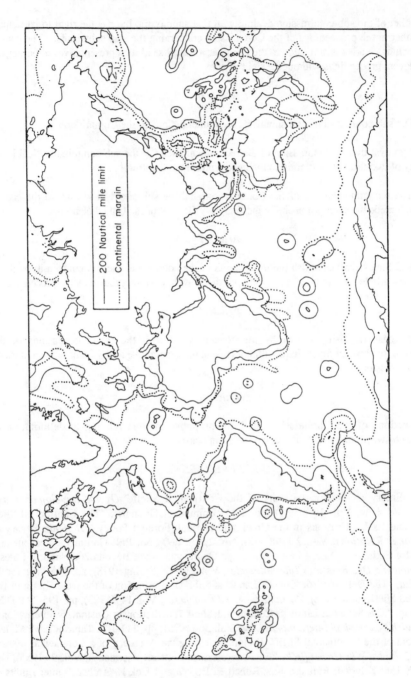

The 200 mile limit and continental shelf margin
Figure 8-4

Source: R.R. Churchill and A.V. Lowe, *The Law of the Sea*, 2nd ed., Manchester: Manchester University Press, 1988, p. 132. Reprinted by permission.

E. THE RIGHTS AND DUTIES OF THE COASTAL STATE OVER THE CONTINENTAL SHELF

1958 CONVENTION ON THE CONTINENTAL SHELF

Article 2

1. The coastal State exercises over the continental shelf sovereign rights for the purpose of exploring it and exploiting its natural resources.

2. The rights referred to in paragraph 1 of this article are exclusive in the sense that if the coastal State does not explore the continental shelf or exploit its natural resources, no one may undertake these activities, or make a claim to the continental shelf, without the express consent of the coastal State.

3. The rights of the coastal State over the continental shelf do not depend on occupation, effective or notional, or on any express proclamation.

4. The natural resources referred to in these articles consist of the mineral and other non-living resources of the seabed and subsoil together with living organisms belonging to sedentary species, that is to say, organisms which, at the harvestable stage, either are immobile on or under the seabed or are unable to move except in constant physical contract with the seabed or the subsoil.

INTERNATIONAL LAW COMMISSION
1956 Commentary, Draft Article 68
Yearbook of the International Law Commission, 1956,
Vol. II, p. 298.

(5) It is clearly understood that the rights in question do not cover objects such as wrecked ships and their cargoes (including bullion) lying on the seabed or covered by the sand of the subsoil.

(6) In the view of the Commission, the coastal State, when exercising its exclusive rights, must also respect the existing rights of nationals of other States. Any interference with such rights, when unavoidably necessitated by the requirements of exploration and exploitation of natural resources, is subject to the rules of international law concerning respect for the rights of aliens. However, apart from the case of acquired rights, the sovereign rights of the coastal State over its continental shelf also cover "sedentary" fisheries in the sense indicated above. As regards fisheries which are also sometimes described as "sedentary" because they are conducted by means of equipment fixed in the sea, but which are not concerned with natural resources attached to the seabed, the Commission refers to article 60 of these rules.

(7) The rights of the coastal State over the continental shelf do not depend on occupation, effective or notional, or on any express proclamation.

(8) The Commission does not deem it necessary to expatiate on the question of the nature and legal basis of the sovereign rights attributed to the coastal State. The considerations relevant to this matter cannot be reduced to a single factor. In particular, it is not possible to base the sovereign rights of the coastal State exclusively on recent practice, for there is no question in the

present case of giving the authority of a legal rule to a unilateral practice resting solely upon the will of the States concerned. However, that practice itself is considered by the Commission to be supported by considerations of law and of fact. In particular, once the seabed and the subsoil have become an object of active interest to coastal States with a view to the exploration and exploitation of their resources, they cannot be considered as *res nullius*, i.e., capable of being appropriated by the first occupier. It is natural that coastal States should resist any such solution. Moreover, in most cases, the effective exploitation of natural resources must presuppose the existence of installations on the territory of the coastal State. Neither is it possible to disregard the geographical phenomenon whatever the term--propinquity, contiguity, geographical continuity, appurtenance or identity--used to define the relationship between the submarine areas in question and the adjacent non-submerged land. All these considerations of general utility provide a sufficient basis for the principle of the sovereign rights of the coastal State as now formulated by the Commission. As already stated, that principle, which is based on general principles corresponding to the present needs of the international community, is in no way incompatible with the principle of the freedom of the seas.

REFERENCES

M.M. Whiteman, "Conference on the Law of the Sea: Convention on the Continental Shelf," *American Journal of International Law*, Vol. 52 (1958), pp. 629, 636-640; M.M. Whiteman, *Digest of International Law*, Vol. IV, Washington, D.C.: U.S. Government Printing Office, 1965, pp. 842-871; F.V.W. Penick, "The Legal Character of the Right to Explore and Exploit the Natural Resources of the Continental Shelf," *San Diego Law Review*, Vol. 22 (1985), pp. 765-778.

TREASURE SALVORS v. UNIDENTIFIED WRECKED, ETC.
569 F.2d 330 (Fifth Circuit 1978)

Treasure Salvors, Inc., and Armada Research Corp., Florida corporations, sued for possession of and confirmation of title to an unidentified wrecked and abandoned vessel thought to be the *Nuestra Senora de Atocha*. The *Atocha* sank in the sea off the Marquesas Keys in 1622 while en route to Spain. The United States intervened, answered, and counterclaimed, asserting title to the vessel. Summary judgment was entered for the plaintiffs, 408 F. Supp. 907 (S.D. Fla. 1976), and the government appealed. . . .

The Antiquities Act

The Antiquities Act authorizes executive designation of historic landmarks, historic and prehistoric structures, and objects of historic or scientific interests situated upon lands owned or controlled by the United States as national monuments. Permission to examine ruins, excavate archaeological sites, and gather objects of antiquity must be sought from the secretary of the department exercising jurisdiction over such lands. As the district court noted, the Antiquities Act applies by its terms only to *lands owned or controlled by the Government of the United States*. The wreck of the *Atocha* rests on the continental shelf, outside the territorial waters of the United States.

The government asserts that the Outer Continental Shelf Lands Act (OCSLA), 43 U.S.C. §1331 *et seq.*, demonstrates Congressional intent to extend the jurisdiction and control of the United States to the outer continental shelf. OCSLA was passed, along with the Submerged Lands Act, 43 U.S.C. §1301 *et seq.*, to clarify the respective interests of coastal states and the United

States in the natural resources of the subsoil and seabed of the continental shelf. A look at the background and interpretation of OCSLA is necessary to determine its scope.

The Truman proclamation of September 28, 1945, spurred national and international interest in exploitation of the mineral wealth of the oceans. The proclamation asserted the jurisdiction and control of the United States over the mineral resources of the continental shelf, but was not intended to abridge the right of free and unimpeded navigation of waters above the shelf, nor to extend the limits of American territorial waters. See 13 Dep't State Bull. 485 (Sept. 30, 1945). The Convention on the Continental Shelf, written thirteen years later, assured to each coastal nation the exclusive right to explore and exploit the resources of the seabed and subsoil, not only of its territorial sea, but also of the adjacent continental shelf beyond the territorial sea. See Master's Report, *supra* n.14, at 69.

During the years following the Truman proclamation, intense interest in exploiting ocean resources resulted in disputes between the United States and coastal states asserting jurisdiction over territorial waters. In *United States v. California*, 332 U.S. 19, 67 S.Ct. 1658, 91 L.Ed 1889 (1947), and its progeny, the United States was held to have rights in the offshore seabed superior to and exclusive of the states. The political reaction to these decisions led to passage of the Submerged Lands Act in May 1953 and the Outer Continental Shelf Lands Act a few months later. See 15 Va. J. Int'l L. 1009, 1011 (1975). By enactment of the Submerged Lands Act, Congress recognized the coastal states' title to and ownership of the lands and natural resources beneath navigable waters within the territorial sea. See *United States v. Maine*, 420 U.S. 515, 525, 95 S.Ct. 1155, 1160, 43 L.Ed. 2d 363, 370-71 (1975). In the Outer Continental Shelf Lands Act, "Congress emphatically implemented its view that the United States has paramount rights to the seabed beyond the three-mile limit." *Id.* at 526, 95 S.Ct. at 1161, 43 L.Ed.2d at 371.

The superiority of the federal claim to resources on the outer continental shelf to the claims of the states was clearly established in 1975 in *United States v. Maine, supra.* The United States asserted in its complaint in *Maine* only ". . . sovereign rights over the seabed and subsoil underlying the Atlantic Ocean, lying more than three geographic miles seaward from the coastline to the outer edge of the continental shelf for the purpose of exploring the area and exploiting its natural resources. . . ." Master's Report, *supra* n.14 at 3. The special master found the "basic question involved" in the litigation to be "whether the right to explore and exploit the natural resources of the seabed and subsoil of that portion of the continental shelf . . . belongs to the United States or to the defendant States or any of them." *Id.* at 1. After *Maine,* the primacy of federal over state interests in the natural resources of the outer continental shelf cannot be doubted. But the decision in *Maine* did not address the extent of control by the United States of the shelf in all circumstances.

43 U.S.C. §1332(a) declares the policy of the United States to be "that the subsoil and seabed of the outer Continental Shelf appertain to the United States and are subject to its jurisdiction, control, and power of disposition as provided in this subchapter." Certain language in the Conference Committee report on the bill supports the view that Congress intended to extend the jurisdiction and control of the United States to both the seabed and subsoil. However, this language must be taken in the context of the bill's stated purpose ". . . to amend the Submerged Lands Act in order that the area in the outer Continental Shelf beyond boundaries of the States may be leased and developed by the Federal Government. . . ."

This court held in *Guess v. Read,* 290 F.2d 622, 625 (1961), *cert. denied,* 386 U.S. 957, 82 S.Ct. 394, 7 L.Ed.2d 388 (1962), that "[t]he Continental Shelf Act was enacted for the purpose, primarily, of asserting ownership of and jurisdiction over the minerals in and under the Continental

Shelf." The structure of the Act itself, which is basically a guide to the administration and leasing of offshore mineral-producing properties, reinforces this conclusion. The Act consists almost exclusively of specific measures to facilitate exploitation of natural resources on the continental shelf. In addition, 43 U.S.C. §1332(b) provides that the Act "shall be construed in such manner that the character as high seas of the waters above the outer Continental Shelf and the right to navigation and fishing therein shall not be affected." As the court below noted, an extension of jurisdiction for purposes of controlling the exploitation of the natural resources of the continental shelf is not necessarily an extension of sovereignty.

We believe that a limited construction of the Act comports with the primary purpose of resolving competing claims to ownership of the natural resources of the offshore seabed and subsoil. So read, the Act is consistent with Article 2 of the Convention on the Continental Shelf:

1.   The coastal state [nation] exercises over the continental shelf sovereign rights for the purpose of exploring it and exploiting its natural resources.

The Convention on the Continental Shelf was a product of the United Nations Conference on the Law of the Sea convened at Geneva in 1958. It was the result of eight years' work by the International Law Commission. See generally Neblett, *The 1958 Conference on the Law of the Sea: What Was Accomplished,* in the Law of the Sea (L. Alexander ed. 1967). The Convention on the Continental Shelf became effective as law in the United States eleven years after passage of the Outer Continental Shelf Lands Act and superseded any incompatible terminology in the domestic statute. *United States v. Ray,* 423 F.2d 16, 21 (5th Cir. 1970). See *Cook v. United States,* 288 U.S. 102, 118-19, 53 S.Ct. 305, 311, 77 L.Ed. 641, 649-50 (1932).

Interpretations of the Convention and the Act by legal scholars have, with remarkable accord, reached the same conclusion regarding the nature of control of the United States over the continental shelf. The most compelling explication of the Convention regarding national control over non-resource-related material in the shelf area is contained in the comments of the International Law Commission:

It is clearly understood that the rights in question do not cover objects such as wrecked ships and their cargoes (including bullion) lying on the seabed or covered by the sand of the subsoil.

This comment is consistent with the Commission's general perception of national jurisdiction over the continental shelf:

[The Commission] was unwilling to accept the sovereignty of the coastal State over the seabed and subsoil of the continental shelf . . . . the text as now adopted leaves no doubt that the rights conferred upon the coastal state cover all rights necessary for and connected with the exploration and exploitation of the natural resources of the continental shelf.

We have demonstrated the limited scope of American control over the wreck site. We conclude that the remains of the *Atocha* are not situated on lands owned or controlled by the United States under the provisions of the Antiquities Act.

. . . .

The judgement is modified and as modified as AFFIRMED.

REFERENCE

David A. Balinsky, "Treasure Salvors, Inc. v. The Unidentified Wrecked and Abandoned Sailing Vessels, Etc., Atocha," *Brooklyn Journal of International Law*, Vol. 5 (1979), pp. 178-190.

NOTE

On March 15, 1960 President Eisenhower issued Presidential Proclamation No. 3339 [*United States Statutes at Large*, Vol. 74 (1960), pp. C48-C50] which designated certain submerged lands off the coast of Florida as the Key Largo Coral Reef Preserve. Regulations were subsequently issued protecting that natural resource. See also Order No. 2978 of the Secretary of the Interior [40 Fed. Reg. 42039 (September 10, 1975)] which effectuates a program designed to conserve and prevent the waste of the coral reefs located on the outer continental shelf of the United States.

Were these two actions compatible with United States international obligations concerning the continental shelf? How do they differ from the *Treasure Salvors* case? What would have happened if, prior to Order No. 2978, an entrepreneur wished to construct an offshore resort hotel on a coral reef?

PLAISANCE v. UNITED STATES
433 F. Supp 936 (E.D. La. 1977)

This tax refund case raises the question: Is an American citizen within a foreign country during the time when he is the captain of a tug boat navigating in waters off the coast of England, beyond the three mile limit? For reasons set forth below, he is not. Hence, his claim for a tax refund, based on 26 U.S.C. §911(a)(2), is denied.

I.

The plaintiff, Lester A. Plaisance, is a United States citizen whose domicile is in Louisiana. During the years 1967 and 1968, he worked for Nolty Theriot, Inc. as a tug boat captain. His employer assigned him to work on tugs in the North Sea prior to July 1, 1967, and, thereafter, he worked either in the North Sea, or in England or another country contiguous to the North Sea, except for a brief trip to the United States. During at last 510 full days of a consecutive eighteen month period during 1967 and 1968, Mr. Plaisance was either on the tug in the North Sea or in a contiguous country.

In his income tax returns, Mr. Plaisance claimed the benefit of the exclusion provided for in Section 911(a)(2) of the Internal Revenue Code of 1954. . . .

Plaintiff contends that he was present in a foreign country within the meaning of U.S.C. §911(a)(2) for 510 full days during an 18 month consecutive period in 1967 and 1968, by virtue of his presence in the North Sea or a contiguous country. Treasury Regulation §1.911-2(f) states that the term foreign country, as used in the statute, means "territory under the sovereignty of a government other than that of the United States and includes the air space over such territory." The government takes the position that, during the time Mr. Plaisance was on a boat in the North

Sea, he was not "within a foreign country" as that term is used in the statute and defined in the regulation.

II.

At a meeting of the United Nations Conference of the Law of the Sea, in Geneva, in 1958, the Convention on the Continental Shelf was adopted. The United States ratified this Convention on April 12, 1961. In 1964, the English Parliament adopted the Outer Continental Shelf Act of 1964, which vested in Her Majesty all rights exercisable by the United Kingdom outside its territorial waters with respect to the continental shelf.

Article 1 of the Convention defines the continental shelf as the sea bed and subsoil of the submarine area adjacent to the coast but outside the area of the territorial sea, to a depth of 200 meters or, beyond that limit, to where the depth of the superjacent waters admits of the exploitation of the natural resources of the area. Article 2 states, "The coastal State exercises over the continental shelf sovereign rights for the purpose of exploring it and exploiting its natural resources." The Convention does not, therefore, recognize that the coastal State has full sovereignty over the continental shelf, but only that it has "sovereign rights" for the purpose of natural resource development.

What is implicit in the limited grant contained in Article 2 is made explicit by restrictions contained in Article 3 of the Convention, which states:

> The rights of the coastal State over the continental shelf do not affect
> the legal status of the superjacent waters as high seas, or that of the
> airspace above those waters.

This makes it clear that the waters above the continental shelf and the airspace above those waters retain their prior legal status and are not under the dominion of the coastal states.

Article 5 of the Convention expresses other limitations on the powers of the coastal states, and clarifies the continued international status of the continental shelf waters:

> The exploration of the continental shelf and the exploitation of its
> natural resources must not result in any unjustifiable interference with
> navigation, fishing or the conservation of the living resources of the
> sea, nor result in any interference with fundamental oceanographic or
> other scientific research carried out with the intention of open . . . .

Similarly, Restatement 2d, Foreign Relations Law §23 (1965), recognizes sovereignty to "prescribe and to enforce rules of law concerning the exploration and exploitation of the continental shelf off its coast and beyond the outer limit of its territorial sea." But this rule "gives jurisdiction in the continental shelf . . . only for the purpose of exploring and exploiting its natural resources." *Id.*, Comment a.

Counsel for the taxpayer points to actions of Great Britain with respect to the continental shelf waters as amounting to the exercise of sovereignty in the area. Even if such acts could be shown, they would not necessarily make the waters a foreign country for purposes of a United States tax statute. But, in fact, the legislation of Great Britain has been limited, and that nation has not undertaken to exercise sovereign rights over the waters beyond its three-mile limit.

Thus, Great Britain has vested its government with the exclusive right to search for and develop petroleum resources by the Petroleum (Production) Act 1934, 24 & 25 Geo. 5, ch. 36. Great Britain's Continental Shelf Act 1964, ch. 29, (the "Shelf Act") vested in the government of Great Britain any rights exercisable by the United Kingdom with respect to the sea bed and subsoil and their natural resources. Section 1(3) of that Act makes sections 2, 3, and 6 of the Petroleum Act applicable with respect to the United Kingdom's Continental Shelf. By a combination of the two Acts, the United Kingdom grants licenses to those people who desire to explore and exploit the natural resources of the North Sea within the United Kingdom's continental shelf area. Only English residents held such licenses, and only they are permitted to explore and exploit its continental shelf area. See Notes following Finance Act 1973, ch. 51, §38. In addition, those license holders acquire ancillary rights in the North Sea in order to exercise their rights. Mines Act, ch. 4, §2.

The Shelf Act goes beyond the Petroleum Act in its exercise of jurisdiction over the continental shelf and superjacent waters. The regulations which the Board of Trade is to promulgate pursuant to the Petroleum Act are broadened by Section 1(4) of the Shelf Act, which requires the inclusion of provisions for the safety, health and welfare of persons employed on operations undertaken under authority of any license granted pursuant to the Petroleum Act.

But these Acts extend British power only to natural resource development. Thus, the Minister of Power may prohibit ships from entering designated areas, but only in order to protect installations in those areas. Shelf Act, §2(1). The Act extends the civil and criminal law of the United Kingdom only to zones around installations within designated areas, *Id.*, §3(1), not generally to the waters above the coastal zone. Similarly, when, in the Finance Act of 1973, the United Kingdom exercised its taxing power and taxed all the continental shelf, it did not tax all persons aboard vessels in the North Sea.

The sovereign rights exercisable by a coastal state with respect to its continental shelf area, and the rights asserted in particular by Great Britain, do not, as the plaintiff concedes, constitute total or absolute sovereignty, for the rights of coastal states are limited by the Convention to those necessary for natural resource development.

The United States alone can determine, for purposes of its tax laws, as applied to its own nationals, whether a territory shall be recognized as being under the sovereignty of a foreign state. This is a political decision made by the political branches of the government, that is, the legislative and executive, not by the judiciary. . . . as stated by the Supreme Court in *Jones v. United States*, 1890, 137 U.S. 202, 212, 11 S. Ct. 80, 83, 34 L. Ed. 691. . . .

All countries recognize that a coastal state possesses sovereignty or territorial jurisdiction within three miles of its coasts. The Digest of International Law, Vol. 4, which was prepared by Marjorie M. Whiteman, Assistant Legal Advisor, the Department of State. However, such sovereignty does not extend past this three-mile limit. *Id.* at pp. 1-195. Restatement 2d, *supra*, §15(2), Reporters' Note 1.

In *United States v. Louisiana*, 1960, 363 U.S. 1, 34, 80 S. Ct. 961, 981, 4 L. Ed. 2d 1025, the Supreme Court indicated that the State Department did not recognize national boundaries to extend in excess of three miles off shore. The high seas, as distinguished from inland waters, it said, are conceded by modern nations to be subject to the "exclusive sovereignty of no single nation. . . . The extent to which a nation can extend its power into the sea for any purpose is subject to the consent of other nations, and assertions of jurisdiction to different distances may be recognized for different purposes."

The failure of the Department of State to recognize that a foreign country had jurisdiction over the territory in question in 1968 further supports the conclusion that the plaintiff was not in a foreign country, within the meaning of Treasury Regulation §1.911-2(f), when he was on a tug boat in the North Sea. Of course, the United States may have a different understanding of a foreign nation's sovereign limits for tax purposes than for political purposes. But there is no support either in the record or in materials of which the court might take judicial notice that such a different understanding exists or was intended to exist. Accordingly, the taxpayer was not in a foreign country within the meaning of 26 U.S.C. §911(a)(2), and his claim for a tax refund is denied.

REFERENCES

"Tax Status of Off-Shore Petroleum Operations," *International Business Lawyer* (London), Vol. 9, Nos. 7/8 (July/August 1981), pp. 267-292.

UNITED STATES v. RAY
423 F.2d 16 (Fifth Circuit, January 22, 1970)

The United States brought this action for injunctive relief against Louis M. Ray and Acme General Contractors, Inc. alleging interference with the rights of the United States on coral reefs located on its Continental Shelf on two grounds. In the first count the Government alleged that the activities of these defendants in building caissons on the reefs, dredging material from the seabed and depositing that material within the caissons was causing irreparable injury to the reefs which are subject to the control of the United States, and that these activities constituted trespass. The second count alleged that these activities were being unlawfully conducted without the required authorization of the Secretary of the Army. See 33 U.S.C. §403; 43 U.S.C. §1333(f). A preliminary injunction was granted against defendants. Thereafter Atlantis Development Corporation, Ltd., which was also contemplating commercial development of the reefs, was allowed by this Court to intervene in the proceedings. Intervenor filed a cross claim, alleging its superior title to the property by virtue of discovery of the reefs by its predecessor. After an extensive nonjury trial, at which numerous witnesses, lay and expert, testified and at which voluminous exhibits were introduced, the District Court adopted all of the facts stipulated by the parties and further found:

"1.   Triumph and Long Reefs are a part of the Continental Shelf extending seaward from the East Coast of Florida, and all waters overlying the reefs do not exceed one hundred fathoms in depth.

"2.   Triumph and Long Reefs are completely submerged at all times, except when their highest projections are fleetingly visible while awash at mean low water. Accordingly, Triumph and Long Reefs are part of the 'seabed' and 'subsoil' of the Outer Continental Shelf within the Outer Continental Shelf Lands Act of 1953 .
        . . .

"3.   These reefs, together with the organisms attached thereto, are 'natural resources' within the Outer Continental Shelf Lands Act, and the Geneva Convention on the Continental Shelf.

"4.   The caissons positioned by Ray and the jack platform construction or 'boathouses' built on pilings proposed by Atlantis constitute 'artificial islands and fixed structures . . . erected . . . for the purpose of . . . developing' the reefs, within the Outer Continental Shelf Lands Act."

The District Court denied all claims of defendants and intervenor, granted the claim of the Government under its second count, but denied the Government's claim of trespass under the first count. In so doing, the District Court recognized the sovereign rights of the United States, but concluded that those rights are limited as the claimed interest of the United States is something less than a property right, consisting of neither ownership nor possession, and consequently not supporting a common law action for trespass *quare clausum fregit.*

All parties have appealed. The Government's appeal is limited to the Court's denial of an injunction on count one of the amended complaint. We affirm the District Court's factual findings and its grant of injunctive relief under the Government's second count. However, we reverse the Court's denial of injunctive relief on the first count of the Government's amended complaint.

. . . .

It is clear that the reefs in question are within the area designated as the Continental Shelf by both national (Outer Continental Shelf Lands Act) . . . and international (Geneva Convention on the Continental Shelf . . .) law.

The Outer Continental Shelf Lands Act, 43 U.S.C. § 1331(a), in pertinent part provides:

"The term 'outer Continental Shelf' means all submerged lands lying seaward and outside of the area of lands beneath navigable waters as defined in section 1301 of this title, and of which the subsoil and seabed appertain to the United States and are subject to its jurisdiction and control."

Article 1 of the international Convention on the Continental Shelf similarly reads:

"For the purpose of these articles, the term 'continental shelf' is used as referring (a) to the seabed and subsoil of the submarine areas adjacent to the coast but outside the area of the territorial sea, to a depth of 200 meters or, beyond that limit, to where the depth of the superjacent waters admits of the exploitation of the natural resources of the said areas; . . ." 15 U.S.T. 473.

The evidence shows that the reefs are completely submerged at mean high water, and as the Court specifically found, "at all times, except when their highest projections are fleetingly visible while awash at mean low water." Thus, the reefs are contemplated within the definition of the Outer Continental Shelf Lands Act and the Geneva Convention on the Continental Shelf, if they meet the definition of "seabed" or "subsoil" contained therein. Webster defines "seabed" as "lands underlying the sea." The evidence establishes that the term "seabed" is commonly understood to be any terrain below the high water line. The federal and common law comports with this understanding in defining the "bed" of a body of water as lands below the ordinary high water mark. . . . The record shows that on the death of the coral, which has a natural predilection for cementing itself onto preexisting rocky structures, its skeletal remains become part of the seabed of the Continental Shelf. The District Court's finding that the reefs are part of the "seabed" of the Shelf is fully supported by substantial evidence of record.

The same national and international laws (The Outer Continental Shelf Lands Act and the Geneva Convention on the Continental Shelf) explicitly recognize the sovereign rights of the

United States and the exclusiveness of those rights to explore the Shelf and exploit its natural resources.

The Outer Continental Shelf Lands Act (43 U.S.C. § 1332(a)) states:

"It is declared to be the policy of the United States that the subsoil and seabed of the outer Continental Shelf appertain to the United States and are subject to its jurisdiction, control, and power of disposition as provided in this subchapter."

To the extent that any of the terms of the Act are inconsistent with the later adopted Geneva Convention on the Continental Shelf, they should be considered superseded. . . . But there is nothing in the pertinent language of the Geneva Convention on the Continental Shelf which detracts from or is inconsistent with the Outer Continental Shelf Lands Act. To the contrary, the Geneva Convention confirms and crystallizes the exclusiveness of those rights, particularly with reference to the natural resources of the Shelf.

. . . .

It is unnecessary for us to decide whether the Outer Continental Shelf Lands Act, Section 1332(a). . . (which does not limit the nation's "jurisdiction, control, and power of disposition" to the natural resources of the Shelf), alone confers rights sufficient to authorize the injunctive relief sought. The right of the United States to control those resources is implicit in Article 2, paragraphs 1, 2 and 3, . . . of the Geneva Convention on the Continental Shelf, and explicitly recognized in the Submerged Lands Act, 43 U.S.C. § 1301 et seq. This Act further provides (43 U.S.C. § 1302) the definition of "natural resources" of the Continental Shelf:

"Nothing in this chapter shall be deemed to affect in any way the rights of the United States to the natural resources of that portion of the subsoil and seabed of the Continental Shelf lying seaward and outside of the area of lands beneath navigable waters, as defined in Section 1301 of this title, all of which natural resources appertain to the United States, and the jurisdiction and control of which by the United States is confirmed."

Section 1301, referred to within the above-quoted section, defines "natural resources" as including, "*without limiting the generality thereof*, oil, gas, and all other minerals, and *fish*, shrimp, oysters, clams, crabs, lobsters, sponges, kelp, *and other marine animal* and plant *life* . . ." (Emphasis supplied.) 43 U.S.C. § 1301(e).

Article 2, paragraph 4, of the Geneva Convention on the Continental Shelf includes in its definition of "natural resources" both living and non-living resources, for it defines the term as consisting of ". . . mineral and other non-living resources of the seabed and subsoil together with living organisms belonging to sedentary species. . . ."

Having thus concluded that the United States has the exclusive right for purposes of exploration and exploitation of the reefs, there remains only the question of whether injunctive relief was improperly denied to the Government on its first count which alleged trespass.

Although the complaint is inaccurately framed in terms of trespass in count one, the Government repeatedly stresses that it is not claiming ownership of the reefs. We do not question the District Court's conclusion that the Government's interest, being something less than fee simple, cannot support a common law action for trespass *quare clausum fregit*. But we do not understand that claim to seek such a remedy, despite the language in which the petition is couched.

Damages, an inseparable element in the common law action for trespass, are not sought here, and the only relief requested is restraint from interference with rights to an area which appertains to the United States and which under national and international law is subject not only to its jurisdiction but its control as well. It is in this light that we consider the allegations of amended count one.

Neither ownership nor possession is, however, a necessary requisite for the granting of injunctive relief. This principle is implicit in the companion decisions of the Supreme Court, United States v. State of Louisiana, 339 U.S. 699, 70 S.Ct. 914, 94 L.Ed. 1216 (1950); United States v. State of Texas, 339 U.S. 707, 70 S.Ct. 918, 94 L.Ed. 1221 (1950), in which injunctive relief was granted to protect "paramount rights" of the United States beyond the territorial limits of Louisiana and Texas, to distances farther out in international waters than that involved here and at a time when those rights had not yet been statutorily established.

In United States v. Republic Steel Corp., 362 U.S. 482, 80 S.Ct. 884, 4 L.Ed. 2d 903 (1960), the Supreme Court did not consider lack of specific statutory authority a bar to injunctive relief for the United States in an action alleging activities which resulted in obstruction to commerce in a navigable inland river. The test for such relief, the Court said, citing United States v. San Jacinto Tin Co., 125 U.S. 273, 8 S.Ct. 850, 31 L.Ed. 747, was "whether the United States had an interest to protect or defend." 362 U.S. at 492, 80 S.Ct. at 890. . . .

The evidence overwhelmingly shows that the Government has a vital interest, from a practical as well as an aesthetic viewpoint, in preserving the reefs for public use and enjoyment.

The protective underwater crannies of the reefs serve as a haven and spawning ground for myriad species of tropical and game fish. The unique and spectacular formations of the submerged coral deposits attract scores of water sports enthusiasts, skin divers, nature students, and marine researchers. Certain organisms living on the reefs contain substances useful in pharmacology. The reefs protect the inland waters from the heavy wave action of the open sea, thus making the area conducive to boating and other water sports. Congress, intent on conserving the value and natural beauty of the area, recently enacted the Biscayne National Monument Bill establishing the area, which includes both Triumph and Long Reefs, as a national monument. The reefs are a part of the series of coral reefs which dot the coastal and international waters extending out from southeastern Florida. Slightly to the south and west of the Triumph and Long Reefs, and straddling the three-mile dividing line between federal and state waters, is the huge federal-approved John Pennekamp Coral Reef State Park, also known as Key Largo Coral Reef Preserve. The fact that the area is worthy of preservation is abundantly demonstrated by the evidence. But more importantly, the evidence shows that protective action by the Government to prevent despoliation of these unique natural resources is of tantamount importance. There was convincing evidence that the activities of defendants in dredging and filling the reefs has and would continue to kill the sensitive corals by smothering them; that the construction would constitute a navigational hazard to pleasure craft, and would destroy a very productive marine area and other natural resources. Obviously the United States has an important interest to protect in preventing the establishment of a new sovereign nation within four and one-half miles of the Florida Coast, whether it be Grand Capri Republic or Atlantis, Isle of Gold.

The rights of the United States in and to the reefs and the vital interest which the Government has in preserving the area require full and permanent injunctive relief against any interference with those rights by defendants and intervenor.

We find without merit the additional errors alleged, particularly the challenge to the District Court's jurisdiction. The District Court held, and we agree, that jurisdiction lies under 28 U.S.C.

§ 1345 (an action by the United States); under 28 U.S.C. § 1331 (a case or controversy arising under the Constitution, laws or treaties of the United States involving more than $10,000); under the Court's general equity and ancillary jurisdiction; and under 43 U.S.C. § 1333(b) (the Outer Continental Shelf Lands Act). . . .

REFERENCES

Atlantis Development Corporation v. United States, 379 F.2d 818 (1967); J.T. Drew, "Continental Shelf Law: Outdistanced by Science and Technology," *Louisiana Law Review*, Vol. 31 (1970), pp. 108-120.

1982 UNITED NATIONS CONVENTION ON THE LAW OF THE SEA

Article 77
Rights of the coastal State over the continental shelf

1. The coastal State exercises over the continental shelf sovereign rights for the purpose of exploring it and exploiting its natural resources.

2. The rights referred to in paragraph 1 are exclusive in the sense that if the coastal State does not explore the continental shelf or exploit its natural resources, no one may undertake these activities without the express consent of the coastal State.

3. The rights of the coastal State over the continental shelf do not depend on occupation, effective or notional, or on any express proclamation.

4. The natural resources referred to in this Part consist of the mineral and other non-living resources of the seabed and subsoil together with living organisms belonging to sedentary species, that is to say, organisms which, at the harvestable stage, either are immobile on or under the seabed or are unable to move except in constant physical contact with the seabed or the subsoil.

Article 78
*Legal status of the superjacent waters and air space
and the rights and freedoms of other States*

1. The rights of the coastal State over the continental shelf do not affect the legal status of the superjacent waters or of the air space above those waters.

2. The exercise of the rights of the coastal State over the continental shelf must not infringe or result in any unjustifiable interference with navigation and other rights and freedoms of other States as provided for in this Convention.

Article 81
Drilling on the continental shelf

The coastal State shall have the exclusive right to authorize and regulate drilling on the continental shelf for all purposes.

Article 85
Tunnelling

This Part does not prejudice the right of the coastal State to exploit the subsoil by means of tunnelling, irrespective of the depth of water above the subsoil.

REFERENCES

John Briscoe and Jo Lynn Lambert, "Seabed Mineral Discoveries with National Jurisdiction and the Future of the Law of the Sea," *University of San Francisco Law Review*, Vol. 18 (1984), pp. 433-487; John Warren Kindt, "Claims to Jurisdiction Over the Environment of the Continental Shelf," *California Western Law Review*, Vol. 21 (1984), pp. 1-46; F.V.W. Penick, "The Legal Character of the Right to Explore and Exploit the Natural Resources of the Continental Shelf," *San Diego Law Review*, Vol. 22 (1985), pp. 765-778.

F. STRUCTURE PERMITTED ON THE CONTINENTAL SHELF

1958 CONVENTION ON THE CONTINENTAL SHELF

Article 3

The rights of the coastal State over the continental shelf do not affect the legal status of the superjacent waters as high seas, or that of the air space above those waters.

Article 4

Subject to its right to take reasonable measures for the exploration of the continental shelf and the exploitation of its natural resources, the coastal State may not impede the laying or maintenance of submarine cables or pipelines on the continental shelf.

Article 5

1. The exploration of the continental shelf and the exploitation of its natural resources must not result in any unjustifiable interference with navigation, fishing or the conservation of the living resources of the sea, nor result in any interference with fundamental oceanographic or other scientific research carried out with the intention of open publication.

2. Subject to the provisions of paragraphs 1 and 6 of this article, the coastal State is entitled to construct and maintain or operate on the continental shelf installations and other devices necessary for its exploration and the exploitation of its natural resources, and to establish safety zones around such installations and devices and to take in those zones measures necessary for their protection.

3. The safety zones referred to in paragraph 2 of this article may extend to a distance of 500 meters around the installations and other devices which have been erected, measured from each point of their outer edge. Ships of all nationalities must respect these safety zones.

4. Such installations and devices, though under the jurisdiction of the coastal State, do not possess the status of islands. They have no territorial sea of their own, and their presence does not affect the delimitation of the territorial sea of the coastal State.

5. Due notice must be given of the construction of any such installations, and permanent means for giving warning of their presence must be maintained. Any installations which are abandoned or disused must be entirely removed.

6. Neither the installations or devices, nor the safety zones around them, may be established where interference may be caused to the use of recognized sea lanes essential to international navigation.

7. The coastal State is obliged to undertake, in the safety zones, all appropriate measures for the protection of the living resources of the sea from harmful agents.

. . . .

INTERNATIONAL LAW COMMISSION
1956 Commentary, Draft Articles 69, 70 and 71
Yearbook of International Law Commission 1956,
Vol. II, pp. 298-300.

Commentary on Draft Article 69

Article 69 is intended to ensure respect for the freedom of the seas in face of the sovereign rights of the coastal State over the continental shelf. It provides that the rights of the coastal State over the continental shelf do not affect the legal status of the superjacent waters as high seas or of the airspace above the superjacent waters. A claim to sovereign rights in the continental shelf can only extend to the seabed and subsoil and not to the superjacent waters; such a claim cannot confer any jurisdiction or exclusive right over the superjacent waters, which are and remain a part of the high seas. The articles on the continental shelf are intended as laying down the regime of the continental shelf, only as subject to and within the orbit or the paramount principle of the freedom of the seas and of the airspace above them. No modification of or exceptions to that principle are admissible unless expressly provided for in the various articles.

Commentary on Draft Article 70

(1) The coastal State is required to permit the laying of submarine cables on the seabed of its continental shelf, but in order to avoid unjustified interference with the exploitation of the natural resources of the seabed and subsoil, it may impose conditions concerning the route to be followed.

(2) The Commission considered whether this provision should not be extended to pipelines. In principle, the answer must be in the affirmative. The question is, however, complicated by the fact that it would often be necessary to install pumping stations at certain points, which might hinder the exploitation of the soil more than cables. It follows that the coastal State might be less liberal in this matter than in the case of cables. As the question does not yet seem to be of practical importance, the Commission has not expressly referred to pipelines in the present article.

Commentary on Draft Article 71

(1) While article 69 lays down in general terms the basic principle of the unaltered legal status of the superjacent sea and the air above it, article 71 applies that basic principle to the main manifestations of the freedom of the seas, namely, freedom of navigation and of fishing. Paragraph 1 of this article lays down that the exploration of the continental shelf must not result in any unjustifiable interference with navigation, fishing or the conservation of the living resources of the sea. It will be noted, however, that what the article prohibits is not any kind of interference, but only unjustifiable interference. The manner and the significance of that qualification were the subject of prolonged discussion in the Commission. The progressive development of international law, which takes place against the background of established rules, must often result in the modification of those rules by reference to new interests or needs. The extent of that modification must be determined by the relative importance of the needs and interests involved. To lay down, therefore, that the exploration and exploitation of the continental shelf must never result in any interference whatsoever with navigation and fishing might result in many cases rendering somewhat nominal both the sovereign rights of exploration and exploitation and the very purpose of the articles as adopted. The case is clearly one of assessment of the relative importance of the interests involved. Interference, even if substantial, with navigation and fishing might, in some cases, be justified. On the other hand, interference even on an insignificant scale would be unjustified if unrelated to reasonably conceived requirements of exploration and exploitation of the continental shelf. . . .

(2) With regard to the conservation of the living resources of the sea, everything possible should be done to prevent damage by exploitation of the subsoil, seismic exploration in connection with oil prospecting, and leaks from pipelines.

(3) Paragraphs 2 to 5 relate to the installations necessary for the exploration and exploitation of the continental shelf, as well as to safety zones around such installations and the measures necessary to protect them. These provisions, too, are subject to the overriding prohibition of unjustified interference. Although the Commission did not consider it essential to specify the size of the safety zones, it believes that generally speaking a maximum radius of 500 meters is sufficient for the purpose.

(4) Interested parties, i.e., not only Governments but also groups interested in navigation and fishing, should be duly notified of the construction of installations, so that these may be marked on charts. In any case, the installations should be equipped with warning devices (lights, audible signals, radar, buoys, etc.).

(5) There is, in principle, no duty to disclose in advance plans relating to contemplated construction of installations. However, in cases where the actual construction of provisional installations is likely to interfere with navigation, due means of warning must be maintained, in the same way as in the case of installations already completed, and as far as possible due notice must be given. If installations are abandoned or disused they must be entirely removed.

(6) With regard to the general status of installations, it has been thought useful to lay down expressly in paragraph 3 of this article, that they do not possess the status of islands and that the coastal State is not entitled to claim for installations any territorial waters of their own or treat them as relevant for the delimitation of territorial waters. In particular, they cannot be taken into consideration for the purpose of determining the baseline. On the other hand, the installations are under the jurisdiction of the coastal State for the purpose of maintaining order and of the civil and criminal competence of its courts.

(7) While, generally, the Commission, by formulating the test of unjustifiable interference, thought it advisable to eliminate any semblance of rigidity in adapting the existing principle of the freedom of the sea to what is essentially a novel situation, it thought it desirable to rule out expressly any right of interference with navigation in certain areas of the sea. These areas are defined in paragraph 5 of this article as narrow channels or recognized sea lanes essential to international navigation. They are understood to include straits in the ordinary sense of the word. The importance of these areas for the purpose of international navigation is such as to preclude, in conformity with the tests of equivalence and relative importance of the interests involved, the construction of installations or the maintenance of safety zones therein, even if such installations or zones are necessary for the exploration or exploitation of the continental shelf.

1982 UNITED NATIONS CONVENTION ON THE LAW OF THE SEA

Article 79
Submarine cables and pipelines on the continental shelf

1. All States are entitled to lay submarine cables and pipelines on the continental shelf, in accordance with the provisions of this article.

2. Subject to its right to take reasonable measures for the exploration of the continental shelf, the exploitation of its natural resources and the prevention, reduction and control of pollution from pipelines, the coastal State may not impede the laying or maintenance of such cables or pipelines.

3. The delineation of the course for the laying of such pipelines on the continental shelf is subject to the consent of the coastal State.

4. Nothing in this Part affects the right of the coastal State to establish conditions for cables or pipelines entering its territory or territorial sea, or its jurisdiction over cables and pipelines constructed or used in connection with the exploration of its continental shelf or exploitation of its resources or the operations of artificial islands, installations and structures under its jurisdiction.

5. When laying submarine cables or pipelines, States shall have due regard to cables or pipelines already in position. In particular, possibilities of repairing existing cables or pipelines shall not be prejudiced.

Article 80
Artificial islands, installations and structures on the continental shelf

Article 60 applies *mutatis mutandis* to artificial islands, installations and structures on the continental shelf. [Article 60 is reproduced in Chapter IX, Section C, Sub-section 3.]

REFERENCES

Rex J. Zedalis, "Military Installations, Structures and Devices on the Continental Shelf: A Response," *American Journal of International Law*, Vol. 75 (1981), pp. 926-933; R. Jaganmohan Rao, "The International Legal Regime of ODAS and Other Off Shore Research Installations," *Indian Journal of International Law*, Vol. 22 (1982), Nos. 3/4, pp. 375-395.

NOTE

On March 10, 1988, a Protocol for the Suppression of Unlawful Acts Against the Safety of Fixed Platforms Located on the Continental Shelf, IMO Doc. SUA/CONF/16/Rev. 2 dated 10 March 1988, reprinted in *Law of the Sea Bulletin*, No. 11 (July 1988), pp. 24-27, was adopted which in Article 3 obligated a contracting party to "take such measures as may be necessary to establish its jurisdiction over the offenses" relating to certain acts against safety of fixed platforms as provided in Article 2 as follows:

1. Any person commits an offence if that person unlawfully and intentionally:

(a) Seizes or exercises control over a fixed platform by force or threat thereof or any other form of intimidation; or

(b) Performs an act of violence against a person on board a fixed platform if that act is likely to endanger its safety; or

(c) Destroys a fixed platform or causes damage to it which is likely to endanger its safety; or

(d) Places or causes to be placed on a fixed platform, by any means whatsoever, a device or substance which is likely to destroy that fixed platform or likely to endanger its safety; or

(e) Injures or kills any person in connection with the commission or the attempted commission of any of the offences set forth in subparagraphs (a) to (d).

2. Any person also commits an offence if that person:

(a) Attempts to commit any of the offences set forth in paragraph 1; or

(b) Abets the commission of any such offences perpetrated by any person or is otherwise an accomplice of a person who commits such an offence; or

(c) Threatens, with or without a condition, as is provided for under national law, aimed at compelling a physical or juridical person to do or refrain from doing any act, to commit any of the offences set forth in paragraph 1, subparagraphs (b) and (c), if that threat is likely to endanger the safety of the fixed platforms.

OUTER CONTINENTAL SHELF LANDS ACT OF THE UNITED STATES
67 Stat. 462; 43 U.S.C. § 1333(f)

. . . .

(f) The authority of the Secretary of the Army to prevent obstruction to navigation in the navigable waters of the United States is extended to artificial islands and fixed structures located on the outer Continental Shelf.

NOTE

The Secretary's authority, referred to in § 1333(f), is contained in the Rivers and Harbors Act of 1899. That Act specifies that no structure posing a potential interference with navigation may be constructed in navigable waters of the United States except upon the permission of the Secretary. Section 1333(f) does not declare that the ocean above the outer continental shelf is "navigable water of the United States," but simply extends the Secretary's authority to prevent obstructions to navigation to continental shelf structures. Thus, petroleum companies wishing to emplace a rig on the continental shelf for exploratory or production work must first secure a permit from the U.S. Army Corps of Engineers. Of course, such structures must also comply with regulations promulgated by the Coast Guard (for safety purposes) and other affected Federal agencies.

REFERENCES

R.H. Kierr, "Beyond the Blue Horizon," *Louisiana Bar Journal*, Vol. 15 (1967), pp. 105-116; W.L. Griffin, "Accommodation of Conflicting Uses of Ocean Space with Special Reference to Navigation Safety Lanes," in L.M. Alexander, ed., *The Law of the Sea: The Future of the Sea's Resources*, Kingston: University of Rhode Island, 1968, pp. 73-83; T.A. Clingan, "Transportation Industry and the Continental Shelf," in L.M. Alexander, ed., *The Law of the Sea: International Rules and Organization for the Sea*, Kingston: University of Rhode Island, 1969, pp. 207-224; H.G. Knight, "Shipping Safety Fairways: Conflict Amelioration in the Gulf of Mexico," *Journal of Maritime Law and Commerce*, Vol. 1 (1969), pp. 1-20; C.W. Walker, "Jurisdictional Problems Created by Artificial Islands," *San Diego Law Review*, Vol. 10 (1973), pp. 638-663.

G. UNITED STATES PRACTICE AND LEGISLATION RELATING TO CONTINENTAL SHELF

Louis B. Sohn and Kristen Gustafson, *The Law of the Sea*, St. Paul, Minn.: West Publishing Co., 1984, pp. 165-171. Reprinted with the permission of West Publishing Co.

After issuance of the Truman Proclamation, disputes arose among the states and the federal government over the rights of each in the natural resources of the continental shelf. Many states enacted legislation establishing a regulatory system for the leasing, exploration and exploitation of the natural resources of the continental shelf in the territorial sea adjacent to their coasts. The United States instituted several actions to enjoin the states from implementing these regulatory schemes, and to claim ownership of the natural resources of the continental shelf in these areas. In 1947, the United States Supreme Court held that the United States was "possessed of paramount rights in, and full dominion and power over, the lands, minerals and other things" underlying the waters seaward of the low-water mark and outside of the inland waters of the coastal states, and that the coastal states had "no title thereto or property interest therein." United States v. California, 332 U.S. 19 (1947), and Decree, 332 U.S. 804, 805 (1947). The principle of federal sovereignty over the natural resources of the continental shelf was applied again in United States v. Louisiana, 339 U.S. 699 (1950) and Decree, 340 U.S. 899 (1950), and in United States v. Texas, 339 U.S. 707 (1950) and Decree, 340 U.S. 900 (1950).

In 1953, Congress enacted the Outer Continental Shelf Lands Act (OCSLA) which established a regulatory system for the leasing, exploration and exploitation of the non-living resources of the continental shelf beyond three miles (or nine miles in certain historic cases) from the baseline from which the territorial sea is measured. 43 U.S.C. §§ 1331 et seq. The simultaneously enacted Submerged Lands Act relinquished all rights, title and interest of the United States in the continental shelf and its resources within three miles of the baseline (or within nine miles in certain historic cases) to the adjacent states. 43 U.S.C. §§ 1301 et seq. The United States reserved its powers of regulation and control in those areas for purposes of commerce, navigation, national defense, and international affairs, and specifically reserved its rights in and title to the continental shelf seaward of the conceded areas. 43 U.S.C. § 1314.

In United States v. States of Louisiana, Texas, Mississippi, Alabama, and Florida, 363 U.S. 1 (1959), and United States v. Florida, id. at 121, the Supreme Court found that, based upon historic circumstances, the relevant boundary for Texas and the Gulf side of Florida for purposes of the Submerged Lands Act extended to a distance of three marine leagues (nine miles) beyond the baseline. The other states were entitled only to those lands, minerals and other natural resources underlying the Gulf to a distance of three geographical miles of the baseline.

The OCSLA established very general guidelines and directives for the Secretary of the Interior in managing the resources of the "outer continental shelf" (the continental shelf beyond the areas conceded to the states) and in leasing tracts for oil, gas and other mineral exploration and development. The Secretary was authorized to grant oil and gas leases on tracts not exceeding 5,760 acres (3 miles by 3 miles) for a period of five years and for as long thereafter as approved by the Secretary. Leases were to be granted by competitive bidding on the basis of a cash bonus with a fixed royalty. Under this system, whoever offered the most "front end" money was awarded the lease. 43 U.S.C. § 1337 (1964). Other than providing this skeletal framework, the OCSLA granted the Secretary broad discretion in structuring and implementing the Act.

The increased need for exploration and exploitation of continental shelf resources resulting from the oil shortage of the 1970's produced dissatisfaction, primarily from the states and environmental groups, with the over-general directives of the OCSLA. The OCSLA was amended in 1978 to establish a comprehensive national policy for continental shelf exploration and exploitation, to revise the federal leasing system significantly, to provide coastal states with an increased role in federal exploration and exploitation decisions on the continental shelf beyond state boundaries, to provide for safety standards on off-shore installations and other exploration and exploitation operations, to enhance environmental protection, and to establish an oil spill liability fund. 43 U.S.C. §§ 1331-1356.

Under the 1978 amendments, alternative bidding systems other than cash bonus bidding "shall be applied to not less than 20 per centum and not more than 60 per centum of the total area offered" for a five-year period following enactment of the amendments. 43 U.S.C. § 1337(a)(5)(B). Six alternative methods are set forth in the amendments, and the Secretary of the Interior is authorized to use others. 43 U.S.C. § 1337(a)(1)(A)-(H).

The Secretary must prepare and periodically revise a five-year schedule of proposed oil and gas lease sales, taking into account a list of designated factors intended to ensure a proper balance among the disparate concerns involved. 43 U.S.C. § 1334(a). To ensure that the Secretary takes into account all relevant policy considerations, the 1978 amendments provide for participation by affected state and local governments, relevant federal agencies and the public. 43 U.S.C. § 1344. When the states of Alaska and California challenged the 1980-85 oil and gas lease plan prepared by the Secretary of the Interior, the court found much of the Secretary's program free from fault, but held that he erred in several regards, including a failure "to strike a proper balance incorporating environmental and coastal zone factors and not simply administrative need and economic factors such as potential oil and gas recovery." California v. Watt, 668 F.2d 1290, 1325 (D.C. Cir. 1981). The plan was remanded to the Secretary for revision. The revised plan for 1982-87 set forth a leasing program which would offer, in 41 oil and gas lease sales, almost all of the one billion acres comprising the United States OCS. The revised plan has been upheld. California v. Watt, 712 F.2d 584 (D.C. Cir. 1983).

In 1981, the Secretary of the Interior announced an OCS lease sale of the entire Santa Maria basin offshore a scenic stretch of coastline extending from Big Sur to Santa Barbara. The lease sale was enjoined in an action brought by California, which demanded a showing that the lease sales would be consistent with its coastal zone management program pursuant to Section 307 of the Coastal Zone Management Act, 16 U.S.C. § 1456(c)(1). The United States Supreme Court held that lease sales on the OCS are not activities "directly affecting" the coastal zone and therefore need not be shown to be consistent with a state's management plan. Secretary of the Interior v. California, 104 S.Ct. 656 (1984).

Environmental impact studies must be prepared for each area included in any oil and gas lease sale and must be submitted for public review. 43 U.S.C. § 1346. Inadequate environmental impact statements have been the basis for several suits challenging oil and gas lease sale programs. See, e.g., Natural Resources Defense Council, Inc. v. Morton, 458 F.2d 827 (D.C. Cir. 1972) (environmental impact statement relating to oil and gas lease sale off the coast of Louisiana was inadequate due to failure to discuss the environmental risks incident to alternative energy sources).

Where a proposed lease area underlies both the outer continental shelf and the continental shelf seaward of the territorial sea, the adjacent state is entitled to enter an agreement to permit an equitable division of any resulting revenues. 43 U.S.C. § 1337(g).

REFERENCES

Geoffrey D.C. Best, "Oil and Gas Operations in the Atlantic Outer Continental Shelf: An Overview of the Regulatory and Litigation-Related Constraints to Development," Connecticut Law Review, Vol. 11 (1979), pp. 459-481; Stanhope B. Denegre, "A Broad Overview of the Outer Continental Shelf Lands Act Amendments of 1978," Maritime Lawyer, Vol. 4 (1979), pp. 108-131; Russell O. Jones, Walter J. Mead and Philip E. Sorensen, "The Outer Continental Shelf Lands Act Amendments of 1978," Natural Resources Journal, Vol. 19 (1979), pp. 885-908; Robert B. Krueger and Louis H. Singer, "An Analysis of the Outer Continental Shelf Lands Act Amendments of 1978," Natural Resources Journal, Vol. 19 (1979), pp. 909-927; Gordon L. James, "The Outer Continental Lands Act Amendments of 1978: Balancing Energy Needs with Environmental Concerns?," Louisiana Law Review, Vol. 40 (1979-80), pp. 177-206; Dennis M. Hughes, "California v. Kleppe: Who Regulates Air Quality Over the Outer Continental Shelf?," Catholic University Law Review, Vol. 29 (1980), pp. 461-483; Bruce F. Vild, "State Government and OCS Policy: An Analysis of the Outer Continental Shelf Lands Act and the 1978 Amendments," Marine Affairs Journal, Vol. 6 (1980), pp. 39-59; Janet L. Dolgin, "A Jurisprudential Problem in the Submerged Lands Cases: International Law in Domestic Dispute," Yale Law Journal, Vol. 90 (1980-81), pp. 1651-1669; G. Kevin Jones, "The Legal Framework for Energy Development on the Outer Continental Shelf," UCLA-Alaska Law Review, Vol. 10 (1980-81), pp. 143-173; Donald B. Craven and Robert E. Montgomery, New Directions at the Department of Interior: Opportunities for the Energy Industry on Federal Lands, New York: Law & Business, 1981; Mary Ann Louise Garcia, "USDI's Outer Continental Shelf Lease Sale in the Beaufort Sea Contested," Natural Resources Journal, Vol. 21 (1981), pp. 943-959; Chrystal R. Brand, "The Seaweed Rebellion: Federal-State Conflicts Over Offshore Oil and Gas

Development," *Willamette Law Review*, Vol. 18 (1982), pp. 535-561; Thomas M. Richard, "State Court Jurisdiction Under the Outer Continental Shelf Lands Act (Gulf Offshore Co. v. Mobil Oil Corp.)," *Loyola Law Review*, Vol. 28 (1982), pp. 343-359; Theodore I. Yi, "Application of the Coastal Zone Management Act to Outer Continental Shelf Lease Sales," *Harvard Environmental Law Review*, Vol. 6 (1982), pp. 159-183; Jonathan I. Charney, "The Offshore Jurisdiction of the States of the United States and the Provinces of Canada: A Comparison," *Ocean Development and International Law*, Vol. 12 (1982-83), pp. 301-335; Michele Mitchell, "Cooperative Federalism for the Coastal Zone and the Outer Continental Shelf: A Legislative Proposal," 1983 *Brigham Young University Law Review*, pp. 123-146. Theodora Berger and John A. Saurenman, "The Role of Coastal States in Outer Continental Shelf Oil and Gas Leasing: A Litigation Perspective," *Virginia Journal of Natural Resources Law*, Vol. 3 (1983), pp. 35-67; Ian Townsend Gault, "Recent Developments in the Federal-Provincial Dispute Concerning Jurisdiction Over Offshore Petroleum Resources," *Alberta Law Review*, Vol. 21 (1983), pp. 97-113; Leslie E. Grayson, Henry Canaday, R. Dan Brumbaugh, Roger Sherman and Timothy F. Sutherland, "Issues of Competition on the Outer Continental Shelf," *Virginia Journal of Natural Resources Law*, Vol. 3 (1983), pp. 69-103; Edward Corwin, "Prospects for Increased State and Public Control Over OCS Leasing: The Timing of the Environmental Impact Statement," *San Diego Law Review*, Vol. 21 (1984), pp. 703-731; William C. Gilmore, "The Newfoundland Continental Shelf Dispute in the Supreme Court of Canada," *Marine Policy*, Vol. 8 (1984), No. 4, pp. 323-329; Susan Harvey, "Federal Consistency and OCS Oil and Gas Development: A Review and Assessment of the 'Directly Affecting' Controversy," *Ocean Development and International Law*, Vol. 13 (1984), pp. 481-533; Daniel S. Miller, "Offshore Federalism: Evolving Federal-State Relations in Offshore Oil and Gas Development," *Ecology Law Quarterly*, Vol. 11 (1984), pp. 401-450; Michael E. Shapiro, "Sagebrush and Seaweed Robbery: State Revenue Losses from Onshore and Offshore Federal Lands," *Ecology Law Quarterly*, Vol. 12 (1984-85), pp. 481-509; Donna Darm, "The Outward Limit of the Department of Interior's Authority Over Submerged Lands--The Effect of Customary International Law on the Outer Continental Shelf Lands Act," *Washington Law Review*, Vol. 60 (1985), pp. 673-696.

CHAPTER IX

EXCLUSIVE ECONOMIC ZONE

A. HISTORICAL BACKGROUND

David Joseph Attard, *The Exclusive Economic Zone in International Law*, New York and London: Oxford University Press, 1987, pp. 3, 4-7, 9, 14-15, 17-27, 29, 31. Notes omitted. Reprinted by permission of Oxford University Press. [The following abbreviations are used in the following excerpts: AALCC=Asian-African Legal Consultative Committee; CEP=Chile, Ecuador, Peru; EFZ=Exclusive Fishery Zone; EEZ=Exclusive Economic Zone; GDS=Geographically Disadvantaged States; LLS=Land-locked States; OAU=Organization of African Unity; UNCLOS=United Nations Conference on the Law of the Sea.]

2.   THE TRUMAN PROCLAMATIONS

. . . Prior to 1945, the division of the sea into the territorial sea and the high seas, with an overlapping contiguous zone, had been accepted. Ironically, it was the United States, one of the staunchest supporters of the 3-n.m. territorial sea doctrine, that opened an era of extensive maritime claims. President Truman issued two proclamations [in 1945], the catalytic effect of which was not due solely to the United States' political weight but also to the rapid developments in the exploitation techniques of the sea-bed and fisheries. Through the Proclamation with Respect to the Natural Resources of the Subsoil and Sea-bed of the Continental Shelf, the United States claimed the natural resources of the subsoil and the sea-bed of the shelf "beneath the high seas but contiguous to" its coasts, to be "subject to its jurisdiction and control." While no outer shelf boundary was specified, an accompanying White House release indicated a 100-fathom isobath (200 metres) as determinative of the limit, a move clearly intended to prevent other States from approaching closer to the coasts of the United States for the purpose of exploiting submarine mineral resources.

Through the Proclamation with Respect to Coastal Fisheries in Certain Areas of the High Seas, the United States proposed the establishment of fishery-conservation zones in waters contiguous to its coast but beyond the 3-n.m. territorial sea. These zones were to be regulated and controlled by the United States where fishing was carried out by nationals, and by joint State management where nationals of other countries were also engaged in fishing activities. The Proclamations emphasized that the character as high seas of the waters above the shelf or the area in which conservation zones are established "and the right to their free and unimpeded navigation are in no way thus affected . . . ."

It is noteworthy that the second Proclamation was never applied. Nevertheless, the introduction of these Proclamations marked a turning-point in the law of the sea by encouraging other States to establish extensive maritime claims. They afforded the plausible grounds for enlarging States' offshore control. However, whilst the Proclamations were carefully drafted to balance the rights of concerned states within the high-seas regime, the same cannot be said for most of the bolder initiatives they provoked . . . .

3. EARLY LATIN AMERICAN CLAIMS

(A) UNILATERAL CLAIMS

. . . The Mexican Executive, in its proposed 1945 amendment to the Constitution, Article 27, held that: "direct dominion over the continental shelf and the submarine terraces belongs to the nation . . . the waters of the seas over the continental shelf and submarine terraces are also the property of the nation . . . ." In 1946, Argentina issued Decree No. 14,708 Concerning National Sovereignty over the Epicontinental Sea and the Continental Shelf, which described the waters over the shelf --the epicontinental sea-- as: "transitory zones of mineral reserves . . . characterized by extraordinary biological activity, owing to the influence of the sunlight, which stimulates plant life (as exemplified in algae, mosses etc.) and the life of innumerable species of animals, both susceptible of industrial utilization." Then, in an obvious misconstruction of the Truman Proclamations, Argentina declared that:

> whereas...the governments of the United States and of Mexico have issued declarations asserting the sovereignty of each of the two countries over the respective peripheral epicontinental seas and continental shelves...it is hereby declared that the Argentina Epicontinental Sea and Continental Shelf are subject to the sovereign power of the Nation...

The Declaration did, however, specify that the "character" of the waters in question would remain unaffected for the purpose of 'free navigation'.

Panama in its 1946 Constitution proclaimed State ownership over both the territorial sea and the shelf. However, Decree 449 (1946) proclaimed "national jurisdiction for the purpose of fishing in general" over its territorial sea and the superjacent waters of the shelf. All fisheries, which it considered a "national product" within these limits, were subjected to the provisions of national legislation. The Congress of Nicaragua on 1 May 1947 adopted a declaration extending its national sovereignty over the adjacent shelf, which on the Atlantic side is the most extensive in Central America.

Chile was the first State to establish a 200-n.m. maritime zone. Through the Presidential Declaration of 23 June 1947, it proclaimed "national sovereignty" (a) over its shelf and the resources therein; and (b) over

> the seas adjacent to its coasts whatever may be their depths, and within those limits necessary in order to reserve, protect, preserve, and exploit the natural resources of whatever nature found on, within, and below the said seas, placing within the control of the government especially all fisheries and whaling activities with the object of preventing the exploitation of natural riches of this kind to the detriment of the inhabitants of Chile and to prevent the spoiling or destruction of the said riches to the detriment of the country and the American continent.

Chile stated that its Declaration did not "disregard the similar legitimate rights of other States on a basis of reciprocity, [nor did it] affect the rights of free navigation on the high seas." The zone's breadth was fixed at 200 n.m. without prejudice to future enlargements or modifications. This limit, it claimed, was consistent with the security zone adopted in the 1939 Declaration of Panama.

Under Presidential Decree No. 781, Peru extended national sovereignty and jurisdiction to the submarine areas regardless of the depth of the superjacent waters, and to the adjacent sea to the extent necessary for the preservation, protection, conservation, and exploitation of the natural wealth and resources therein. The zone's width was 200 n.m., within which the right of free navigation of all States would not suffer "any prejudice" in accordance with international law . . . .

By Decree 116 (1948) Costa Rica proclaimed its "national sovereignty over the seas adjacent to the continental and insular coasts of the national territory, whatever their depth, and to the extent necessary to protect, conserve, and utilize the natural resources and wealth." This Decree also claimed: "the protection and control of the State . . . over all the sea included within the perimeter formed by the coasts and by a mathematical parallel, projected out to sea at a distance of 200 maritime miles." The Decree was revised by Legislative Decree 803 (1949), which changed the expression "national sovereignty" to "rights and interests of Costa Rica" and the word "control" applicable to the 200-mile zone was deleted.

The 1950 Constitution of El Salvador established a 200-n.m. claim: "The territory of the Republic within its present boundaries is irreducible. It includes the adjacent seas to a distance of 200 sea miles from the low-water line and the corresponding air space, subsoil and continental shelf." However, within this zone freedom of navigation was not affected. The inclusion of the "corresponding air space" was a new variation not found in the previous claims. This constitutional provision with regard to fishing and marine hunting was implemented by means of Law No. 1961 (1955).

Similarly, Honduras passed Legislative Decree No. 25 (1951) which extended national sovereignty over the shelf and "the waters covering it," at whatever depth it might be found and whatever its extent might be; it claimed full, inalienable, and imprescriptible dominion over all the resources which were found in the area . . . .

Most of the above claims went beyond the Truman Proclamations in at least two respects: they undertook to effect a categorical extension of sovereignty over the continental shelf and sea-bed, and over the superjacent waters. These differences reflect the divergent approaches to the problems of maritime jurisdiction. The Truman Proclamation on the shelf only referred to the natural resources of its shelf as appertaining to the United States. The Truman Proclamation, in attempting to establish fishing conservation zones in areas of the high seas contiguous to its coasts, made no reference to the shelf, but proceeded on a general theory of the right of a coastal State to protect its contiguous fisheries. The Latin American States, however, sought to achieve their objectives through a single comprehensive claim over the shelf and its superjacent waters, an assertion of sovereignty which went beyond anything put forward in either of the Truman Proclamations and revived the early formulations of the shelf theory.

(B) REGIONAL CLAIMS

The above-mentioned Latin American claims were challenged generally on the grounds that they violated the freedoms of the high seas. In the light of the status of the law of the sea during this period, the legal validity of these claims must be considered questionable. The United States held that these claims appeared to be "at variance with the generally accepted principles of international law" and "reserved the rights and interests of the United States so far as concerned any effects" of these decrees or of any measures designed to put them into operation. In its view, the Argentine declaration, for example, asserted sovereignty over the shelf and the seas adjacent to the coasts beyond the generally accepted limits of the territorial sea and, with respect to fishing, it failed to accord recognition to the United States' rights and interests in the high seas off the

failed to accord recognition to the United States' rights and interests in the high seas off the Argentine coast.

As the controversy developed further, there evolved total confusion over the legal nature of the said claims. What was certain was that these States were determined exclusively to control and exploit the offshore marine resources. Unable to do this under the traditional concepts of the law of the sea, they claimed sovereignty over areas of the high seas with the purpose of exercising only certain functions of this sovereignty, primarily the exclusive control over fishing. Chile, fearing the offshore whaling operations of European fishing fleets, began consultations with its neighbours in order to muster support of its position. Both Ecuador and Peru offered support, albeit for different reasons, as their whaling rarely took place beyond 25 n.m. from the shore. Nonetheless, they were keen to protect their fishing fleets, as the prospect of United States tuna fishing in their waters was growing . . . .

The three States met in 1952 and signed the Santiago Declaration on the Maritime Zone which they subsequently ratified and which was acceded to by Costa Rica in 1955. The introduction of the operative part of the Declaration reflected the above-mentioned fears:

> 1. Governments are bound to ensure for their peoples access to the necessary food supplies. 2. It is therefore the duty of each Government to ensure the conservation and protection of its natural resources and to regulate the use thereof to the greatest possible advantage of its country. 3. Hence it is likewise the duty of each Government to prevent the said resources from being used outside the area of its jurisdiction so as to endanger their existence, integrity, and conservation to the prejudice of peoples so situated geographically that their seas are irreplaceable sources of essential food and economic materials....

The CEP States went on to proclaim: "as a principle of their international policy that each of them possesses sole sovereignty and jurisdiction over the area of sea adjacent to the coasts of their respective countries, to a minimum distance of 200 n.m. from the said coasts." With regard to navigation, the Declaration was not to "be construed as disregarding the necessary restrictions on the exercise of sovereignty and jurisdiction imposed by international law to permit the innocent and inoffensive passage of vessels of all nations through the zone aforesaid" . . . .

7. THE POST-GENEVA PERIOD

. . . .

(B) LATIN AMERICA

In 1965 Nicaragua claimed a 200-mile national fishing zone "for the better conservation and national exploitation of our fish and other resources" and submitted any fishing therein to its domestic legislation. Article I of the General Law on the Exploitation of Natural Resources (1958), which was made applicable to the zone, stated that the General Law: "has the purpose of establishing the basic conditions that shall govern the exploration and exploitation of the natural resources belonging to the State." Ecuador, through Decree No. 1542 (1966), extended to 200 n.m. the breadth of its territorial sea. It also declared the airspace over the territorial sea to be "national domain."

Next came the Argentine claim which, owing to the terms in which the basic law was concluded, caused considerable debate as to its scope and nature. The matter was further complicated by the fact that other instruments, not intended to be supplementary to that law but having a bearing on it, also contained terms the full meaning of which was unclear. The basic law referred to is Law No. 17094 (1966) which, whilst providing that: "the sovereignty of the Argentine nation shall extend over the sea adjacent to its territory for a distance of 200 nautical miles measured from the line of the lowest tide," expressly declared that neither this nor any other provision of the law were to affect freedom of navigation and overflight, thereby creating confusion as to the legislator's actual intention. The situation was further complicated when Law No. 17500 (1967) referred to the "Argentine territorial sea" and apparently identified it with the 200-n.m. adjacent sea, without referring to freedom of navigation and overflight.

Panama entered a true claim to a 200-n.m. territorial sea in its Law 31 (1967). Article I held that: "sovereignty of the Republic of Panama extends beyond its continental and insular territory and its inland waters to a zone of territorial sea 200 nautical miles wide, to the sea-bed and the subsoil of that zone, and to the airspace above it . . . ."

(D) REGIONAL LATIN AMERICAN APPROACHES

In accordance with the semantic confusion found in other Latin American legislation, Uruguay promulgated Law No. 13833 (1969) which stated in Article 2:

> The sovereignty of the Eastern Republic of Uruguay extends beyond its continental and insular territory and internal waters to a zone of territorial sea 200 nautical miles wide measured from the baseline...the sovereignty of the Republic also extends to the airspace situated above the territorial sea, as well as to the sea-bed and the subsoil beneath that sea.

A subsequent article recognized the right of innocent passage up to 12 n.m., and beyond this limit the "provisions of this law did not affect free navigation and overflight." Fishing was reserved in the 12-n.m. zone for vessels flying the Uruguayan flag and foreign vessels were required to obtain authorization in order to fish beyond 12 n.m.

Brazil put forward her claim in unequivocal terms and proclaimed a 200-n.m. territorial sea in its Decree Law No. 1098 (1970). It claimed control over the water column, sea-bed, subsoil, and airspace throughout the zone, allowing only the right of innocent passage. Through Decree Law No. 68.459 (1971), two "fishing zones," each of 100-n.m. width, were established. However, this let the status of the territorial waters unaffected. Whilst the first 100-n.m. zone was reserved for nationals, foreigners were allowed to fish in the outer 100-n.m. zone under license.

The Latin American States also felt the need to consolidate their position on the 200-n.m. zone. In 1970, Uruguay invited Latin American 200-n.m. claimants to a meeting with the purpose of "exchanging points of view and co-ordinating their position." Only nine States attended and on 8 May 1970 they unanimously adopted the Montevideo Declaration on the Law of the Sea. In the preamble, mention was made of the ties of a geographic, economic, and social nature binding the sea, the land, and man who inhabits it, which give the coastal State a "legitimate priority" to benefit from the resources found in the marine environment. Under these circumstances, the Declaration recognized the coastal States' right to exercise control over the marine resources adjacent to their coasts and of the sea-bed and subsoil thereof: "in order to achieve the maximum development of their economy and to raise the living standards of their peoples."

The limit of this control was to be: "in accordance with their geographical and geological characteristics and with factors governing the existence of marine resources and the need for their national utilization."

The Declaration also stipulated that the right to adopt measures in areas under maritime sovereignty and jurisdiction should be exercised "without prejudice to freedom of navigation by ships and overflight by aircraft of any flag." While this preserved *expressis verbis* the freedom of navigation and overflight, statements of five States attached to the Declaration gave a restrictive interpretation. For example, Brazil equated the freedom of navigation to "innocent passage, as Brazilian legislation defines it"; similarly, it declared: "that the reference to overflight does not mean that the rules normally applied to the airspace above the territorial sea should be abolished." Peru's observation also limited freedom of navigation in the zone to that of "innocent passage," as established in the Santiago Declaration (1952) . . . [However,] by 1970 only ten out of some twenty-two Latin American States had established a 200-n.m. limit . . . .

The Conference also decided to call another meeting at Lima in August 1970.

The Lima meeting was for all Latin American States. In all, twenty States attended, but only fourteen adopted the Declaration of Latin American States on the Law of the Sea. In the hope of securing broad recognition, observers were invited from Canada, India, Iceland, Egypt, Senegal, Korea (R), Yugoslavia, the UN, the OAU, and the Standing Commission of the South Pacific. The Declaration did not differ in essence from the Montevideo Declaration, however, no mention was made of the 200-n.m. limit which was left to be decided by each State in accordance with reasonable criteria, having regard to its geographical, geological, and biological characteristics, and the need to make rational use of its resources. As was the case with the Montevideo Declaration, most States made reservations to the effect that [the] paragraph . . . prescribing freedom of navigation and overflight, did not apply to them. The States which did not sign the Lima Declaration can be divided into two groups: (a) the LLS, which held that the Declaration gave coastal States expansive powers and neglected their rights; and (b) the Caribbean States.

In June 1972, the Caribbean States produced the Declaration of Santo Domingo, which explicitly proposed a 12-n.m. territorial sea and a 200-n.m. patrimonial sea wherein the coastal State had "sovereign rights over the renewable and non-renewable resources" and jurisdiction over measures to prevent marine pollution and the regulation of scientific research. The freedoms of movement and communication were recognized, subject to the limitation "resulting from the exercise by the coastal State of its rights within the area."

Finally, reference must be made to the Resolution of the Inter-American Juridical Committee dated 9 February 1973 . . . . The Resolution declared that the "sovereignty or jurisdiction of a coastal state extends . . . up to a maximum distance of 200 nautical miles as well as to the airspace above and the bed and subsoil of that sea." Within this zone, the coastal State had *inter alia* and the "power" to regulate the exploration and exploitation of the living and non-living resources therein; to promulgate environmental measures; and to promote scientific research activities.

Provision was also made to safeguard the freedoms of movement, overflight, and communication subject to the coastal powers mentioned above. Of particular interest is the Resolution's proposal that enabled LLS to exploit the zone's living resources by granting them "preferential rights in relation to third states . . . . " Previous Latin American declarations had failed to refer to the rights of LLS . . . .

(E) AFRICA

Two important developments occurred which favoured the Latin American position: the emergence of new independent States in Africa and Asia, and the spectacular explosion of fishing activities in international waters. The West African States, in particular, were facing a serious threat due to the over-exploitation of their offshore fisheries by foreigners. The situation was made worse by the fact that these fleets were self-sufficient and did not even need to utilize the facilities offered by coastal States . . . .

The OAU also played a crucial role. In December 1971, it passed a resolution which endorsed a recommendation of the Scientific Council for Africa that African States should extend their territorial waters to 200 n.m., establish a 212-n.m. non-pollution zone, and create a restricted national fishery zone in the 12-n.m. belt adjacent to the territorial-sea baselines. It was held that "the 212-n.m. limit would thus constitute the national economic limit in the oceans and seas surrounding Africa."

The question relating to coastal State jurisdiction over offshore resources was also considered by the AALCC . . . .

At the 1971 Colombo Session of the [AALCC] --which was also attended by observers from Argentina, Brazil, Ecuador, Peru, and the United States--the idea of an "exclusive economic juris-diction" zone was vented by some States. No effort seems to have been made to define the coastal State's rights within this zone. However, the session also set up a Working Group to consider law-of-the-sea questions. This Group only formulated a general description of the said zone's purpose, and did not provide any detailed provisions relating to the regime which would regulate the zone.

At the 1972 Lagos session, Kenya took the initiative and presented a working paper on the "Exclusive Economic Zone concept." It described the zone's purpose as the safeguard of the coastal State's economic interests without interfering unduly with other States' legitimate interests, particularly in movement and communication. It proposed a 200-n.m. limit for the zone, motivated by "the economic need not only for the present but over the foreseeable future." Fishery and pollution control within the zone would fall under the coastal State's exclusive jurisdiction. Although the 1972 session did not adopt any resolution on the matter, the Kenyan proposal received widespread support within the AALCC.

The Kenyan working paper represents only the start of the EEZ concept as it dealt solely with fishery and pollution control, omitting such matters as the exploitation of non-living resources and scientific research. Nevertheless, the Kenyan initiative had a catalytic effect as it encouraged other States to consider the question further. Indeed, in June 1972, the matter was raised again at the African States Regional seminar on the Law of the Sea held at Yaounde, Cameroon.

The seventeen participating African States demonstrated their unified position on this issue at the regional level by adopting an aggressive stance on coastal jurisdiction. The report which emerged, which was adopted unanimously with no reservations, reflected the firm support for the establishment of an "economic zone." It recommended that, whilst the territorial sea should not extend beyond 12 n.m., an economic zone should be established wherein the coastal State would have exclusive jurisdiction for the purpose of control, regulation, and exploitation of living resources and their reservation for the primary benefit of their peoples and their respective economies; and for the prevention and control of pollution. Freedom of navigation, overflight, and laying of submarine cables and pipelines was recognized.

Although no specific breadth for the zone was mentioned, the report recommended that in fixing the limit of the zone due account should be taken of the resources of the region and the rights of land-locked and quasi-land-locked States. It also recommended that the zone should include "at least the continental shelf;" thereby embodying "all economic resources and comprising both living and non-living resources such as oil, natural gas, and other mineral resources . . . ."

The first attempt to articulate the EEZ concept came again from Kenya which, no doubt encouraged by the positive reception its paper received in the AALCC forum, presented draft articles to the Sea-bed Committee in 1972. It proposed a 200-n.m. EEZ, wherein the coastal State was to: "have exclusive jurisdiction for the purpose of control, regulation and exploitation of both living and non-living resources of the Zone and their preservation, and for the purpose of prevention and control of pollution." Kenya's proposal, whilst guaranteeing the freedoms of navigation, overflight, and communication within the zone, envisaged the exercise of jurisdiction therein to: "encompass all the resources of the area, living and non-living, either on the water surface or within the water column, or on the soil or subsoil of the sea-bed and ocean floor below."

The EEZ concept found further support at the OAU. In May 1973, its Council of Ministers issued the Declaration on the Issues of the Law of the Sea. This Declaration recognized the right of each State to establish an EEZ beyond its territorial sea up to a limit of 200 n.m. Within the zone the coastal State was to exercise "permanent sovereignty" over living and non-living resources: "without undue interference with the other legitimate uses of the sea, namely, freedom of navigation, overflight, and laying of cables and pipelines," marine scientific research and pollution too were to be subject to the State's jurisdiction. The Declaration was incorporated into a proposal by fourteen African States and presented to the Sea-bed Committee in 1973.

In their proposal entitled Draft Articles on Exclusive Economic Zone the fourteen sponsors further elaborated the 1972 Kenyan Draft Articles. Coastal States were recognized as having the right to establish an "Economic Zone" wherein:

> they shall have sovereignty over the renewable and non-renewable
> natural resources for the purpose of exploration and exploitation.
> Within the zone they shall have exclusive jurisdiction for the purpose
> of control, regulation and exploitation of both living and non-living
> resources of the Zone and their preservation, and for the purpose of
> prevention and control of pollution.

The rights exercised over the Economic Zone shall be exclusive . . . .

The proposal also dealt with, *inter alia*, the freedoms of navigation, overflight, and communication, LLS and GDS, delimitation, and scientific research.

In conjunction with the fourteen-State proposal, Kenya together with three other States presented Draft Articles on Fisheries which were intended to be part of and complementary to the EEZ concept. The articles contained elaborate provisions which allowed the coastal State to exercise within an EEZ "sovereign rights for the purpose of exploration, exploitation, conservation, and management, over the living resources, including fisheries, and shall adopt from time to time such measures as it may deem necessary and appropriate."

The proposal imposed on the coastal State responsibilities for conservation and management of the living resources in the zone. Furthermore, the articles also dealt with, *inter alia*, participation by other States such as LLS, highly migratory fisheries, and settlement of disputes. A large number of other drafts dealing with specific aspects of the concept were also introduced to the Sea-bed Committee.

There can be little doubt that 1973 was the year when the EEZ concept took off. The above-mentioned 1973 proposals represent a concrete attempt by States, principally African, to elaborate and articulate comprehensively the concept's constituent elements. Indeed, these proposals foreshadowed the concept as found in UNCLOS III's texts and the 1982 Convention. Parallel to these proposals, Latin American States that year continued to sponsor articles aimed at promoting the patrimonial- or epicontinental-sea concepts. Eventually, however, through the course of the Sea-bed Committee and the 1974 UNCLOS III sessions, these concepts gradually fused into or were displaced by the EEZ concept . . . .

(F) NORTH AMERICA

. . . .

The United States' policy against extended coastal jurisdiction was the main reason behind its refusal to accept the demands of the developing States to hold a conference to deal with all law-of-the-sea issues. However, as it became clear that American interests were not decisively opposed to the EEZ concept, it changed its policy. Adopting the principle of the "common heritage of mankind," it submitted a working paper to the Sea-bed Committee in August 1970 which proposed the establishment of two zones: (1) an area of national jurisdiction to the 200-metre isobath and (2) an International Sea-bed Area seaward of this limit. International reaction, particularly that of developing States, was not favourable.

The American proposals also found internal opposition. The fishing industry wanted a 200-n.m. zone to protect itself from the Soviet and Japanese distant fishing fleets. The petroleum industry was against any proposals that involved the sharing of profits derived from the shelf resources. This growing domestic pressure caused the United States to modify its position and to focus more on resource exploitation. The shift was also the result of geographical factors: long coastlines on two oceans and the Gulf of Mexico as well as archipelagic conditions off Hawaii and parts of Alaska, assure the United States the world's largest EEZ. Moreover, during the work of the Sea-bed Committee it soon became clear that an agreement on almost any issue was possible only as part of a comprehensive "package deal" which would have to incorporate a 200-n.m. EEZ. Thus, a highly developed State with an extensive merchant and military fleet came significantly closer to the position of the developing States. Indeed, by August 1974, it presented its own draft articles on the economic zone and the continental shelf. It proposed a maximum limit of 200 n.m. for the zone, wherein the coastal State would have the jurisdiction and the sovereign and exclusive rights for the purposes of exploiting the living and non-living resources . . . .

8. THE SEA-BED COMMITTEE AND UNCLOS III

At Caracas, the agreement on a 12-n.m. territorial sea was so widespread that there was virtually no reference to any other limit in the public debate. Its acceptance for many States was, however, subject to agreement on unimpeded transit of straits and the 200-n.m. EEZ. In fact some hundred States spoke in favour of the EEZ as a part of an overall treaty settlement, although there was considerable disagreement over the quality of coastal States' rights therein. Even the United States and the Soviet Union gave their conditional support to the concept. By agreeing to the inevitable, they hoped to induce the other participants to act favourably with regard to their main interest, freedom of navigation. This general support for the concept is understandable, as

118 Conference participants were coastal States. The United States, for example, has a potential EEZ covering some 2,831,400-sq.n.m. . . .

At the beginning of UNCLOS III, in an effort to gain further support, the patrimonial-sea proposals were gradually merged into or were supplanted by the EEZ concept. In fact, by August 1974 the Chairman of Committee II was able to state that the idea of a 12-n.m. territorial sea and a 200-n.m. EEZ was the "keystone" of the compromise solution to offshore coastal jurisdiction favoured by the participants . . . .

REFERENCES

J. Castaneda, "The Concept of Patrimonial Sea in International Law," *Indian Journal of International Law*, Vol. 12 (1972), pp. 535-542; P.S. Rao, "Offshore Natural Resources: An Evaluation of African Interests," *Indian Journal of International Law*, Vol. 12 (1972), pp. 345-367; A.M. Aguilar, "The Patrimonial Sea," in L.M. Alexander, ed., *The Law of the Sea: The Needs and Interests of the Developing Countries*, Kingston, Rhode Island: University of Rhode Island, 1973, pp. 161-165; D.M. Johnston and E. Gold, *The Economic Zone in the Law of the Sea: Survey, Analysis and Appraisal of Current Trends, Occasional Paper No. 17*, Kingston, Rhode Island: Law of the Sea Institute, University of Rhode Island, (June, 1973); L.D.M. Nelson, "The Patrimonial Sea," *International and Comparative Law Quarterly*, Vol. 22 (1973), pp. 668-686; K.G. Nweihed, "Venezuela's Contribution to the Contemporary Law of the Sea," *San Diego Law Review*, Vol. 11 (1974), pp. 603-632; Shigeru Oda, "New Directions in the International Law of Fisheries," *Japanese Annual of International Law*, Vol. 17 (1973), pp. 84-90; A.M. Aguilar, "The Patrimonial Sea or Economic Zone Concept," *San Diego Law Review*, Vol. 11 (1974), pp. 575-602; F.V. Garcia-Amador, "The Latin American Contribution to the Development of the Law of the Sea," *American Journal of International Law*, Vol. 68 (1974), pp. 33-50; L.M. Alexander and R.D. Hodgson, "The Impact of the 200-Mile Economic Zone on the Law of the Sea," *San Diego Law Review*, Vol. 12 (1975), pp. 569-599; W.R. Edeson, "The Impact on Fisheries of Two-Hundred-Mile Zones," *Maritime Studies and Management*, Vol. 2 (1975), pp. 138-143; R.D. Hodgson, "National Maritime Limits: The Economic Zone and the Seabed," in F.T. Christy, et al., eds., *Law of the Sea: Caracas and Beyond*, Cambridge, Mass.: Ballinger, 1975, pp. 183-192; D.M. Johnston, "The Economic Zone in North America: Scenarios and Options," *Ocean Development and International Law Journal*, Vol. 3 (1975), pp. 53-68; Stephen R. Katz, "Consequences of the Economic Zone for Catch Opportunities of Fishing Nations," *Maritime Studies and Management*, Vol. 2, No. 2 (1975), pp. 144-153; E. Osieke, "The Contribution of States from the Third World to the Development of the Law on the Continental Shelf and the Concept of the Economic Zone," *Indian Journal of International Law*, Vol. 15 (1975), pp. 313-332; D.E. Pollard, "The Exclusive Economic Zone--The Elusive Consensus," *San Diego Law Review*, Vol. 12 (1975), pp. 600-623; R. Khan, "The Fisheries Regime of the Exclusive Economic Zone: A Comment on the Single Negotiating Text Adopted by UNCLOS III at Geneva, 1975," *Indian Journal of International Law*, Vol. 16 (1976), pp. 169-186; M.K. Nawaz, "The Emergence of Exclusive Economic Zones: Implications for a New Law of the Sea," *Indian Journal of International Law*, Vol. 16 (1976), pp. 471-488; M. Shyam, "Rights of the Coastal States to Fisheries Resources in the Economic Zone, An Empirical Analysis of State Preferences," *Ocean Management*, Vol. 3(1) (1976), pp. 1-30; F.T. Christy, "Transitions in the Management and Distribution of International Fisheries," *International Organization*, Vol. 31(2) (1977), pp. 235-266; T.A. Clingan, "Emerging Law of the Sea: The Economic Zone Dilemma," *San Diego Law Review*, Vol. 14 (1977), pp. 530-547; C.A. Fleischer, "Right to a 200-Mile Exclusive Economic Zone or a Special Fishery Zone," *San Diego Law Review*, Vol. 14 (1977), pp. 548-583; A.L. Hollick, "Origins of the 200-Mile Offshore Zones," *American Journal of International Law*, Vol. 71 (1977), pp. 494-500; D.C. Kapoor, "The Delimitation of Exclusive Economic Zones,"

Maritime Policy and Management, Vol. 4 (1977), pp. 255-263; A. Szekely, "Mexico's Unilateral Claim to a 200-Mile Exclusive Economic Zone: Its International Significance," *Ocean Development and International Law Journal*, Vol. 4 (1977), pp. 195-211; "Symposium on the Exclusive Economic Zone," *Maritime Policy and Management*, Vol. 4 (No. 6) (1977), pp. 313-451; W.C. Extavour, *The Exclusive Economic Zone -- A Study of the Evolution and Progressive Development of the International Law of the Sea*, Geneva: Institut Universitaire de Hautes Etudes Internationales, Collection de Droit International, 1978; F. Mirvahabi, "Conservation and Management of Fisheries in the Exclusive Economic Zone," *Journal of Maritime Law and Commerce*, Vol. 9 (1978), pp. 225-250; F. Mirvahabi, "Significant Fishery Management Issues in the Law of the Sea Conference: Illusions and Realities," *San Diego Law Review*, Vol. 15 (1978), pp. 493-524; K. Ouchi, "A Perspective on Japan's Struggle for its Traditional Rights on the Oceans," *Ocean Development and International Law Journal*, Vol. 5 (1978), pp. 107-134; Winston Conrad Extavour, *The Exclusive Economic Zone: A Study of the Evolution and Progressive Development of the International Law of the Sea*, Geneve: Institute Universitaire de Hautes Etudes Internationales, 1979; R.B. Krueger and M.H. Nordquist, "The Evolution of the 200-Mile Exclusive Economic Zone: State Practice in the Pacific Basin," *Virginia Journal of International Law*, Vol. 19 (1979), pp. 321-400; Jorge A. Vargas, "The Legal Nature of Patrimonial Sea - A First Step Towards the Definition of the EEZ," *German Yearbook of International Law*, Vol. 22 (1979), pp. 142-177; Alan T. Leonhard, "Ixtoc I: A Test for the Emerging Concept of the Patrimonial Sea," *San Diego Law Review*, Vol. 17 (1980), pp. 617-627; J.C. Phillips, "The Economic Resources Zone: Progress for the Developing Coastal States," *Journal of Maritime Law and Commerce*, Vol. 11 (1980), pp. 349-365; Paolo Mengozzi, "Common Heritage of Mankind and Exclusive Economic Zone," *Italian Yearbook of International Law*, Vol. 5 (1980-1981), pp. 65-84; Winston Conrad Extravour, *The Exclusive Economic Zone, A Study of the Evolution and Progressive Development of the International Law of the Sea*, 2nd ed., Geneva: Institut universitaire de hautes études internationales, 1981; Wil D. Verwey, "The New Law of the Sea and the Establishment of A New International Economic Order: The Role of the Exclusive Economic Zone," *Indian Journal of International Law*, Vol. 21 (1981), pp. 387-423; Jorge Casteneda, "Negotiations on the Exclusive Economic Zone at the Third United Nations Conference on the Law of the Sea," in Jerzy Makarczyk, ed., *Essays in International Law in Honour of Judge Manfred Lachs*, The Hague: Martinus Nijhoff, 1984, pp. 605-623; James E. Bailey III, "The Exclusive Economic Zone: Its Development and Future in International and Domestic Law," *Louisiana Law Review*, Vol. 45 (1985), pp. 1269-1297; Jonathan I. Charney, "The Exclusive Economic Zone and Public International Law," *Ocean Development and International Law*, Vol. 15 (1985), pp. 233-288; Sokrat Plaka, "The Exclusive zone: An Important Institution in the Hands of the Sovereign States to Protect Their Maritime Assets," *Albania Today* (Tirana), Vol. 5, No. 96 (1987), pp. 34-42; Tommy T.B. Koh, "The Exclusive Economic Zone," *Malaya Law Review*, Vol. 30 (1988), pp. 1-13; Barbara Kwiatkowska, *The 200 Miles Exclusive Economic Zone in the New Law of the Sea*, Dordrecht, Boston and London: Martinus Nijhoff Publishers, 1989; Francisco Orrego Vicuna, *The Exclusive Economic Zone, Regime and Legal Nature Under International Law*, Cambridge, England: Cambridge University Press, 1989.

B. THE REGIME OF THE EXCLUSIVE ECONOMIC ZONE UNDER THE 1982 UNITED NATIONS CONVENTION ON THE LAW OF THE SEA

1. The Legal Status

> R.R. Churchill and A.V. Lowe, *The Law of the Sea*, 2nd ed., Manchester: Manchester University Press, 1988, pp. 136-137. Reprinted by permission.

During the earlier stages of UNCLOS there was considerable discussion as to the exact legal nature of the EEZ. Many maritime States argued, because of a fear of "creeping jurisdiction," that the EEZ should have a residual high seas character, i.e., any activity not falling within the clearly defined rights of the coastal State would be subject to the regime of the high seas. This approach did not find favour with the majority of UNCLOS participants, and articles 55 and 86 of the Law of the Sea Convention make it clear that the EEZ does not have a residual high seas character. Equally it is clear that the EEZ does not have a residual territorial sea character, which would have created a presumption that any activity not falling within the clearly defined rights of non-coastal States would come under the jurisdiction of the coastal State - as was desired by some UNCLOS participants (notably those Latin American States claiming a 200 mile territorial sea). Instead, the EEZ must be regarded as a separate functional zone of a *sui generis* character, situated between the territorial sea and the high seas. The *sui generis* legal character of the EEZ has three principal elements: (1) the rights and duties which the Law of the Sea Convention accords to the coastal State; (2) the rights and duties which the Convention accords to other States; and (3) the formula provided by the Convention for regulating activities which do not fall within either of the two previous categories.

> *Restatement of the Foreign Relations Law of the United States*, Third Revision, Vol. 2, St. Paul, Minn.: American Law Institute, 1987, pp. 56, 57, 62-63. Reprinted by permission.

§ 514. Exclusive Economic Zone

In the exclusive economic zone:

(2) .... All states enjoy, as on the high seas, the freedoms of navigation and overflight, freedom to lay submarine cables and pipelines, and the right to engage in other internationally lawful uses of the sea related to these freedoms, such as those associated with the operation of ships or aircraft.

Comment:

b. Relation of exclusive economic zone to high seas. The LOS Convention does not explicitly designate the exclusive economic zone as part of the high seas. . . . According to the United States and other maritime states, however, the Convention reflects the general understanding that, as a matter of customary law as well as under the Convention, the rights and freedoms of other states in the zone, set forth in Subsection (2), are the same as on the high seas. . . . As to matters not expressly covered by this section, any conflict that might arise between the interests of a coastal state and those of any other state concerning their respective rights and duties in the exclusive economic zone should be resolved "on the basis of equity and in the light of all the relevant circumstances, taking into account the respective importance of the interests involved to the parties as well as to the international community." LOS Convention, Article 59. Special procedures for settling such disputes are provided in the Convention, but will not apply to states not parties. Id. Article 297(1).

REPORTER'S NOTES

2. Exclusive economic zone and high seas. At the Third United Nations Conference on the Law of the Sea, maritime states pressed for having the waters of the exclusive economic zone designated as "high seas" subject to special rights for coastal states in the resources of the area. Coastal states generally insisted that the exclusive economic zone be designated not as high seas but as a special zone of the coastal state subject to rights of navigation and overflight for other states. In the end, the maritime states did not insist on expressly designating the zone as high seas, but the history of the negotiations indicates that they consider that the zone remains high seas, although it will be subject to exceptional rights in favor of the adjacent coastal state. Conflicts may arise over assertions of rights in the zone, under the principle of freedom of the sea, with respect to matters not explicitly covered in the LOS Convention....

1982 UNITED NATIONS CONVENTION ON THE LAW OF THE SEA

Article 55
Specific legal regime of the exclusive economic zone

The exclusive economic zone is an area beyond and adjacent to the territorial sea, subject to the specific legal regime established in this Part, under which the rights and jurisdiction of the coastal State and the rights and freedoms of other States are governed by the relevant provisions of this Convention.

REFERENCES

Awadh Mohamed Al-Mour, "The Legal Status of the Exclusive Economic Zone," *Revue Egyptienne de Droit International*, Vol. 33 (1977), pp. 35-69; F. Kovalyov, "The Economic Zone and its Legal Status," *International Affairs* (Moscow), 1979, No. 2, pp. 58-64; Carolyn Hudson, "Fishery and Economic Zones as Customary International Law," *San Diego Law Review*, Vol. 17 (1980), pp. 661-689; A. Benniou, "The Status of the Exclusive Economic Zone," *Revue Egyptienne deDroit International*, Vol. 42 (1986), pp. 189-227; Francisco Orrego Vicuna, *The Exclusive Economic Zone: Regime and Legal Nature Under International Law*, Cambridge, United Kingdom: Cambridge University Press, 1989.

2. Rights and Jurisdiction

1982 UNITED NATIONS CONVENTION ON THE LAW OF THE SEA

Article 56
Rights, jurisdiction and duties of the coastal State in the exclusive economic zone

1. In the exclusive economic zone, the coastal State has:

(a) sovereign rights for the purpose of exploring and exploiting, conserving and managing the natural resources, whether living or non-living, of the waters superjacent to the sea-bed and of the sea-bed and its subsoil, and with regard to other activities for the economic exploitation and exploration of the zone, such as the production of energy from the water, currents and

and exploration of the zone, such as the production of energy from the water, currents and winds;

(b) jurisdiction as provided for in the relevant provisions of this Convention with regard to:

    (i) the establishment and use of artificial islands, installations and structures;

    (ii) marine scientific research;

    (iii) the protection and preservation of the marine environment;

(c) other rights and duties provided for in this Convention.

2. In exercising its rights and performing its duties under this Convention in the exclusive economic zone, the coastal State shall have due regard to the rights and duties of other States and shall act in a manner compatible with the provisions of this Convention.

3. The rights set out in this article with respect to the sea-bed and subsoil shall be exercised in accordance with Part VI.

Article 57
Breadth of the exclusive economic zone

The exclusive economic zone shall not extend beyond 200 nautical miles from the baselines from which the breadth of the territorial sea is measured.

Article 58
Rights and duties of other States in the exclusive economic zone

1. In the exclusive economic zone, all States, whether coastal or land-locked, enjoy, subject to the relevant provisions of this Convention, the freedoms referred to in article 87 of navigation and overflight and of the laying of submarine cables and pipelines, and other internationally lawful uses of the sea related to these freedoms, such as those associated with the operation of ships, aircraft and submarine cables and pipelines, and compatible with the other provisions of this Convention.

2. Articles 88 to 115 and other pertinent rules of international law apply to the exclusive economic zone in so far as they are not incompatible with this Part.

3. In exercising their rights and performing their duties under this Convention in the exclusive economic zone, States shall have due regard to the rights and duties of the coastal state and shall comply with the laws and regulations adopted by the coastal state in accordance with laws and regulations adopted by the coastal state in accordance with the the provisions of this Convention and other rules of international law insofar as they are not incompatible with this Part.

Article 59
Basis for the resolution of conflicts regarding the attribution

of rights and jurisdiction in the exclusive economic zone

In cases where this Convention does not attribute rights or jurisdiction to the coastal State or to other States within the exclusive economic zone, and a conflict arises between the interests of the coastal State and any other State or States, the conflict should be resolved on the basis of equity and in the light of all the relevant circumstances, taking into account the respective importance of the interests involved to the parties as well as to the international community as a whole.

REFERENCES

G.L. Becker, "Rights, Obligations and Liabilities of Commercial Shipping in the EEZ," *Marine Technology Society Journal*, Vol. 13 (1979), pp. 10-14; Benedetto Conforti, "The Exclusive Economic Zone: Some Transitional Law Problems," *Italian Yearbook of International Law*, Vol. 5 (1980-1981), pp. 14-21; Christopher C. Joyner, "The Exclusive Zone and Antarctica," *Virginia Journal of International Law*, Vol. 21 (1981), pp. 691-725; J.C. Phillips, "The Economic Resources Zone and the Southwest Pacific," *International Lawyer*, Vol. 16 (1982), pp. 265-278; William T. Burke, "Exclusive Fisheries Zones and the Freedom of Navigation," *San Diego Law Review*, Vol. 20 (1983), pp. 595-623; Horace B. Robertson, Jr., "Navigation in the Exclusive Economic Zone," *Virginia Journal of International Law*, Vol. 24 (1984), pp. 865-915; Maynard Silva and William Westermeyer, "The Law of the Sea and the U.S. Exclusive Economic Zone: Perspectives on Marine Transportation and Fisheries," *Ocean Development and International Law*, Vol. 15 (1985), pp. 321-353; Janusz Symonides, "The Exclusive Economic Zone," *Polish Yearbook of International Law*, Vol. 14 (1985), pp. 43-63; Casey Jarman, "The Public Trust Doctrine in the Exclusive Economic Zone," *Oregon Law Review*, Vol. 65 (1986), pp. 1-33; Lawrence Juda, "The Exclusive Economic Zone and Ocean Management," *Ocean Development and International Law*, Vol. 18 (1987), pp. 305-331; Christopher C. Joyner, "The Exclusive Economic Zone and Antarctica: The Dilemmas of Non-Sovereign Jurisdiction," *Ocean Development and International Law*, Vol. 19 (1988), pp. 469-492.

3.   Artificial Islands, Installations, Structures and Deepwater (Super) Ports

1982 UNITED NATIONS CONVENTION ON THE LAW OF THE SEA

Article 60
Artificial islands, installations and structures in the exclusive economic zone

1.   In the exclusive economic zone, the coastal State shall have the exclusive right to construct and to authorize and regulate the construction, operation and use of:

(a) artificial islands;

(b) installations and structures for the purposes provided for in article 56 and other economic purposes;

(c) installations and structures which may interfere with the exercise of the rights of the coastal State in the zone.

2. The coastal State shall have exclusive jurisdiction over such artificial islands, installations and structures, including jurisdiction with regard to customs, fiscal, health, safety and immigration laws and regulations.

3. Due notice must be given of the construction of such artificial islands, installations or structures, and permanent means for giving warning of their presence must be maintained. Any installations or structures which are abandoned or disused shall be removed to ensure safety of navigation, taking into account any generally accepted international standards established in this regard by the competent international organization. Such removal shall also have due regard to fishing, the protection of the marine environment and the rights and duties of other States. Appropriate publicity shall be given to the depth, position and dimensions of any installations or structures not entirely removed.

4. The coastal State may, where necessary, establish reasonable safety zones around such artificial islands, installations and structures in which it may take appropriate measures to ensure the safety both of navigation and of the artificial islands, installations and structures.

5. The breadth of the safety zones shall be determined by the coastal State, taking into account applicable international standards. Such zones shall be designed to ensure that they are reasonably related to the nature and function of the artificial islands, installations or structures, and shall not exceed a distance of 500 metres around them, measured from each point of their outer edge, except as authorized by generally accepted international standards or as recommended by the competent international organization. Due notice shall be given of the extent of safety zones.

6. All ships must respect these safety zones and shall comply with generally accepted international standards regarding navigation in the vicinity of artificial islands, installations, structures and safety zones.

7. Artificial islands, installations and structures and the safety zones around them may not be established where interference may be caused to the use of recognized sea lanes essential to international navigation.

8. Artificial islands, installations and structures do not possess the status of islands. They have no territorial sea of their own, and their presence does not affect the delimitation of the territorial sea, the exclusive economic zone or the continental shelf.

DEEPWATER PORT ACT OF 1974
As Amended of 1984, 33 U.S.C. §1501 et seq.

§ 1502. Definitions

As used in this chapter unless the context otherwise requires, the term . . . .

(10) "deepwater port" means any fixed or floating manmade structures other than a vessel, or any group of such structures, located beyond the territorial sea and off the coast of the United States and which are used or intended for use as a port or terminal for the loading or unloading and further handling of oil for transportation to any State . . . .

§ 1509. Marine environmental protection and navigational safety

(d) Safety zones; designation; construction period;
permitted activities

(1) Subject to recognized principles of international law and after consultation with the Secretary of the Interior, the Secretary of Commerce, the Secretary of State, and the Secretary of Defense, the Secretary shall designate a zone of appropriate size around and including any deepwater port for the purpose of navigational safety. In such zone, no installations, structures, or uses will be permitted that are incompatible with the operation of the deepwater port. The Secretary shall by regulation define permitted activities within such zone . . . .

§ 1517. Liability

(a)   Oil discharge; prohibition; penalty; notice and hearing; separate
offense; vessel clearance: withholding, bond or surety

(1) The discharge of oil into the marine environment from a vessel within any safety zone, from a vessel which has received oil from another vessel at a deepwater port, or from a deepwater port is prohibited.

(2) The owner or operator of a vessel or the licensee of a deepwater port from which oil is discharged in violation of this subsection shall be assessed a civil penalty of not more than $10,000 for each violation. No penalty shall be assessed unless the owner or operator or the licensee has been given notice and opportunity for a hearing on such charge. Each violation is a separate offense. The Secretary of the Treasury shall withhold, at the request of the Secretary, the clearance required by section 91 of Title 46, of any vessel the owner or operator of which is subject to the foregoing penalty. Clearance may be granted in such cases upon the filing of a bond or other surety satisfactory to the Secretary.

(b)   Oil discharge; notification; penalty; use of notification in
criminal cases limited

Any individual in charge of a vessel or a deepwater port shall notify the Secretary as soon as he has knowledge of a discharge of oil. Any such individual who fails to notify the Secretary immediately of such discharge shall, upon conviction, be fined not more than $10,000 or imprisoned for not more than 1 year, or both. Notification received pursuant to this subsection, or information obtained by the use of such notification, shall not be used against any such individual in any criminal case, except a prosecution for perjury or for giving a false statement.

(c)   Oil removal; drawing upon Fund money for cleanup costs

(1) Whenever any oil is discharged from a vessel within any safety zone, from a vessel which has received oil from another vessel at a deepwater port, or from a deepwater port, the Secretary shall remove or arrange for the removal of such oil as soon as possible, unless he determines such removal will be done properly and expeditiously by the licensee of the deepwater port or the owner or operator of the vessel from which the discharge occurs.

§ 1518. Relationship to other laws

(a) Federal Constitution, laws, and treaties applicable; other Federal requirements applicable; status of deepwater port; Federal or State authorities and responsibilities within territorial seas unaffected; notification by Secretary of State of intent to exercise jurisdiction; objections by foreign governments

(1) The Constitution, laws, and treaties of the United States shall apply to a deepwater port licensed under this chapter and to activities connected, associated, or potentially interfering with the use or operation of any such port, in the same manner as if such port were an area of exclusive Federal jurisdiction located within a State. Nothing in this chapter shall be construed to relieve, exempt, or immunize any person from any other requirement imposed by Federal law, regulation, or treaty. Deepwater ports licensed under this chapter do not possess the status of islands and have no territorial seas of their own.

(2) Except as otherwise provided by this chapter, nothing in this chapter shall in any way alter the responsibilities and authorities of a State or the United States within the territorial seas of the United States.

(3) The Secretary of State shall notify the government of each foreign state having vessels registered under its authority or flying its flag which may call at or otherwise utilize a deepwater port but which do not currently have an agreement in effect as provided in subsection (c)(2)(A)(i) of this section that the United States intends to exercise jurisdiction over vessels calling at or otherwise utilizing a deepwater port and the persons on board such vessels. The Secretary of State shall notify the government of each such state that, absent its objection, its vessels will be subject to the jurisdiction of the United States whenever they --

(A) are calling at or otherwise utilizing a deepwater port; and

(B) are within the safety zone of such a deepwater port and are engaged in activities connected, associated, or potentially interfering with the use and operation of the deepwater port.

The Secretary of State shall promptly inform licensees of deepwater ports of all objections received from governments of foreign states in response to notifications made under this paragraph.

(b)   Law of nearest adjacent coastal State as applicable Federal law; Federal administration and enforcement of such law; nearest adjacent coastal State defined

The law of the nearest adjacent coastal State, now in effect or hereafter adopted, amended, or repealed, is declared to be the law of the United States, and shall apply to any deepwater port licensed pursuant to this chapter, to the extent applicable and not inconsistent with any provision or regulation under this chapter or other Federal laws and regulations now in effect or hereafter adopted, amended, or repealed. All such applicable laws shall be administered and enforced by the appropriate officers and courts of the United States. For purposes of this subsection, the nearest adjacent coastal State shall be that State whose seaward boundaries, if extended beyond 3 miles, would encompass the site of the deepwater port.

(c)   Vessels of United States and foreign states subject to Federal jurisdiction; objections to jurisdiction; designation of agent for

jurisdiction; objections to jurisdiction; designation of agent for
service of process; duty of licensee

(1) The jurisdiction of the United States shall apply to vessels of the United States
and persons on board such vessels. The jurisdiction of the United States shall also apply to
vessels, and persons on board such vessels, registered in or flying the flags of foreign states,
whenever such vessels are--

(A) calling at or otherwise utilizing a deepwater port; and

(B) are within the safety zone of such a deepwater port, and are
engaged in activities connected, associated, or potentially interfering
with the use and operation of the deepwater port.

The jurisdiction of the United States under this paragraph shall not, however, apply to vessels
registered in or flying the flag of any foreign state that has objected to the application of such
jurisdiction.

AGREEMENT RELATING TO JURISDICTION OVER
VESSELS UTILIZING THE LOUISIANA OFFSHORE OIL PORT
Exchange of Notes at Washington on May 14 and 25, 1979
30 UST 5926; TIAS 9525

The Secretary of State to the British Ambassador

May 14, 1979

Excellency:

I have the honor to refer to the discussions which have taken place between
representatives of our two Governments in connection with the establishment of deepwater
ports off the coast of the United States and the jurisdictional requirements of the United States
Deepwater Port Act of 1974, and to confirm that the two Governments are in agreement that
vessels registered in the United Kingdom, the West Indies Associated States or its other
territories or flying the flag of the United Kingdom and the personnel on board such vessels
utilizing the Louisiana Offshore Oil Port (LOOP, Inc.), a deepwater port facility established
under the Deepwater Port Act of 1974, for the purposes stated therein shall, whenever they
may be present within the safety zone of such deepwater port, be subject to the jurisdiction of
the United States and the United Kingdom on the same basis as when in coastal ports of the
United States.

It is the understanding of the Government of the United States and of the Government
of the United Kingdom that this agreement shall not apply to vessels registered in the United
Kingdom, the West Indies Associated States or its other territories or flying the flag of the
United Kingdom merely passing through the safety zone of the Louisiana Offshore Oil Port
without calling at or otherwise utilizing the port.

If the foregoing is acceptable to the Government of the United Kingdom, I have the
honor to propose that this note, together with your reply thereto, shall constitute an
Agreement between our two Governments, to enter into force upon the date of your reply to
that effect, and to remain in force until terminated by six months' written notice by either
party to the other.

Accept, Excellency, the renewed assurances of my highest consideration.

For the Secretary of State:

James R. Atwood

The British Ambassador to the Secretary of State

25 May 1979

Sir,

I have the honour to acknowledge receipt of your Note of 14 May 1979, the terms of which are as follows:

[Quoting U.S. Note.]

I have the honour to inform you that the foregoing proposals are acceptable to the Government of the United Kingdom, who therefore agree that your Note, together with the present reply, shall constitute an Agreement between the two Governments in this matter, which shall enter into force from today and remain in force until terminated by six months' written notice by either party to the other.

Accept, Sir, the assurance of my highest consideration.

Peter Jay

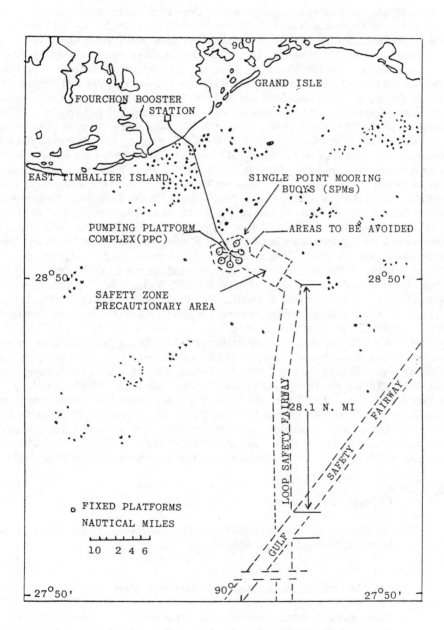

Deepwater Port Routing Measures in Louisiana
Figure 9-1

Source: Based on *Federal Register*, Vol. 45, No. 32 (February 14, 1980), p. 10175.

REFERENCES

Gary Knight, "International Legal Aspects of Deep Draft Harbor Facilities," *Journal of Maritime Law & Commerce*, Vol. 4 (1973), pp. 367-395; Gary Knight, "International Legal Problems in the Construction and Operation of Offshore Deep Draft Port Facilities," in Thomas A. Clingan and Lewis M. Alexander, eds., *Hazards of Maritime Transit*, Cambridge, Mass.: Ballinger, 1973, pp. 91-135; William H. Lawrence, "Superports, Airports & Other Fixed Installations on the High Seas," *Journal of Maritime Law & Commerce*, Vol. 6 (1975), pp. 575-591; J.H. Gnann, Jr., "Deepwater Port Act of 1974: Some International and Environmental Implications," *Georgia Journal of International & Comparative Law*, Vol. 6 (1976), pp. 535-563; Steven C. Barkley, "The Deepwater Port Act of 1974: The Definition of Adjacent Coast States," *Baylor Law Review*, Vol. 29 (1977), pp. 1051-1063; R.B. Krueger, M.H. Nordquist and R.P. Wessely, "New Technology and International Law: The Case of Deepwater Ports," *Virginia Journal of International Law*, Vol. 17 (1977), pp. 597-643; Tobey L. Winters, *Deepwater Ports in the United States: An Economic & Environmental Impact Study*, New York: Praeger, 1977; Ved Nanda, "The Legal Status of Surface Devices Functioning at Sea Other than Ships (Drilling Rigs, Offshore Platforms, etc.)," *American Journal of Comparative Law, Supplement*, Vol. 26 (1978), pp. 233-243; Max K. Morris and John W. Kindt, "The Law of the Sea: Domestic and International Considerations Arising from the Classification of Floating Nuclear Power Plants and Their Breakwaters as Artificial Islands," *Virginia Journal of International Law*, Vol. 19 (1979), pp. 299-319; Tullio Treves, "Military Installations, Structures and Devices on the Seabed," *American Journal of International Law*, Vol. 74 (1980), pp. 808-857; Warren Rose, "Facilitating U.S. Oil Import: Deepwater Ports in the Gulf of Mexico," *Transportation Journal*, Vol. 20 (No. 2, 1980-81), pp. 41-49; Rex J. Zedalis, "Military Installations, Structures and Devices on the Continental Shelf: A Response," *American Journal of International Law*, Vol. 75 (1981), pp. 926-933; R. Jaganmohan Rao, "The International Legal Regime of ODAS [Ocean Data Acquisition System] and other Offshore Research Installations," *Indian Journal of International Law*, Vol. 22, Nos. 3/4 (July/December 1982), pp. 375-395; Jean Dominique Wahiche, "Artificial Structures and Traditional Uses of the Sea: The Field of Conflict," *Marine Policy*, Vol. 7 (1983), No. 1, pp. 37-52; Paul Peters, Alfred H.A. Soons and Lucie A. Zima, "Removal of Installations in the Exclusive Economic Zone," *Netherlands Yearbook of International Law*, Vol. 15 (1984), pp. 167-207; U.S. Congress, House, Committee on Pubic Works and Transportation, Subcommittee on Water Resources, *Deepwater Port Act Amendments of 1984: Hearing, 98th Congress, 2nd Session on H.R. 2353, February 22, 1984*, Washington, D.C.: U.S. Government Printing Office, 1984.

4.   Fishery Management

See Chapter XI International Fishery Management and Protection of Marine Mammals, Section E, 1 [pp. 626-643].

5.   Land-locked/Geographically Disadvantaged States

[Here deals with general problems of access of these states to the resources of the Exclusive Economic Zone at the Third United Nations Conference on the Law of the Sea. For specific fishery problem, see Chapter XI, Section E, 1, h.]

DISCUSSIONS AT THE 32ND MEETING OF THE SECOND COMMITTEE OF
THE THIRD UNITED NATIONS CONFERENCE ON THE LAW OF THE SEA,
AUGUST 8, 1974.
Third United Nations Conference on the Law of the Sea, *Official Records*,
Vol. II, pp. 239-244.

Mr. KAFANDO (Upper Volta) said that his delegation was guided by the principle that the sea
was a factor in the development of peoples, an element of solidarity between the nations and a zone
of peace and security. The three priorities with respect to the land-locked countries' rights were the
right of access to the sea, the right of transit and the right of participation by developing land-
locked countries in the exploration and exploitation of the resources of the exclusive economic
zone . . . .

The old legal order governing the use of the oceans which had been based on political concerns
and the desire for hegemony by the great maritime Powers, had undergone a radical change. The
res communis which was now the basis for that law was primarily economic considerations. A
new concept of equality of rights had been introduced, placing all States, coastal or non-coastal, on
an equal footing. However, that *de jure* equality had to be made *de facto* since the coastal States at
present enjoyed certain priorities . . . .

The fact remained, however, that the land-locked countries were far more deprived than their
coastal neighbours, as reflected in their classification by UNCTAL among the least developed
countries. The Conference should therefore find a definitive solution in order to ease the economic
plight of the land-locked countries resulting from heavy transport costs, lack of industry and high
cost of imports, all of which reduced their foreign exchange earnings. It was for that reason that
the land-locked countries were attempting to ensure that transit traffic should not be subjected to
any customs duties or taxes other than for services rendered. If free transit was recognized as a
right, then the principle of reciprocity did not exist.

The land-locked countries should have the right to participate in the exploration and
exploitation of the resources of the exclusive economic zone. As the representative of Senegal had
pointed out, that was one of the basic tenets of the West African Economic Community. While
his country maintained excellent bilateral co-operation with Ghana and the Ivory Coast [Cote
d'Ivoire], the experience of regional integration showed that political considerations did enter into
the picture. The rights of the land-locked countries, in order to be safeguarded, should therefore be
laid down in a multilateral convention. Bilateral and regional arrangements should exist, but only
in order to regulate the modalities and details of transit in the context of the laws of the coastal
States. That was a flexible formula that would permit a reconciliation between respect for the
sovereignty of the coastal States and the rights of the land-locked countries. He urged the States
represented at the Conference to transcend national self-interest and negotiate a new, enlightened
law of the sea by accepting compromise solutions . . . .

Mr. KUMI (Ghana) said that the problems of special interest groups involved rather delicate
issues; the need for tact and care in assessing and evaluating them had been underscored on several
occasions. The Conference should not threaten the unity of cohesive groups or see them
dismembered. Any solution to the problem involved must accommodate conflicting interests.

There were two elements involved: the incontestable right of all States to the resources of the
sea-bed and ocean floor beyond the limits of national jurisdiction as the common heritage of
mankind, and agreement on appropriate measures to ensure that geographically disadvantaged
countries had access to resources under the sovereign jurisdiction of coastal States. It was the

countries had access to resources under the sovereign jurisdiction of coastal States. It was the second element that had led to controversy and disagreement.

It would be virtually impossible for the Conference to try to spell out the details of regional or bilateral agreements conferring the right of transit through coastal States to the sea, but the Convention should contain provisions that would make the conclusion of such agreements mandatory. There was no doubt that regional integration was fast becoming a fact of life: paragraph 9 (part C) of the OAU Declaration on the Issues of the Law of the Sea (A/CONF.62/33) adequately reflected a spirit of accommodation and the trend towards integration.

His delegation sympathized with and shared the concerns of those who wished to see regional or subregional economic zones established as a solution to the problems of the land-locked and other geographically disadvantaged countries. There was considerable merit in the idea of establishing regional fishery zones, and to do so would be a welcome move towards regional economic integration. But the issue should be taken up by the appropriate continental or regional organizations. Even if the concept of a regional economic zone was accepted, there would still remain the crucial issue of the access of land-locked and other geographically disadvantaged countries to the zone. Such access should not compromise the security of coastal States, and it must reflect the underlying principle of bilateral or multilateral agreements.

His delegation supported the legitimate demands of land-locked States for access to and the right to benefit from the living resources of the economic zone of neighbouring countries. The OAU Declaration had endorsed that provision as a right and not merely as a principle. It followed that his delegation could not fully support all the articles submitted in document A/CONF.62/C.2/L.39, but it could accept the articles referring to the sharing of the living resources in the economic zone. His delegation interpreted the word "neighbouring" in terms of adjacency . . . .

Mr. ANDRES (Switzerland) [said that] it went without saying that the institution of a broad zone in which the coastal State would have rights over all the resources would further aggravate [the] inequitable situation. that was why his delegation had decided to sponsor document A/CONF.62/C.2/L.39. The circumstances in which the land-locked countries now found themselves justified their demand to participate in the exploitation of the resources of the economic zone or, failing that, to receive adequate compensation. It must be remembered that the land-locked countries were all small States, of which most were developing and some were among the least developed. On the other hand, the majority of the States that would benefit from the creation of the economic zone were not poor.

There was nothing in law or in equity to justify a distinction between living and non-living resources. Furthermore, the advocates of the economic zone concept did not draw any such distinction. Consequently any attempt to exclude the land-locked countries from the exploitation of either category of resources or the resultant benefits would be misguided, particularly where regional agreements implying solidarity between the signatory States had been concluded.

Many land-locked and geographically disadvantaged countries were sorely lacking in mineral resources; Switzerland, for example, had none at all. Their interest in living resources to feed their population was self-evident.

Some delegations maintained that only the developing land-locked and geographically disadvantaged countries should be allowed to exploit the living resources of the economic zone. That view was, moreover, reflected in article 19 of document A/CONF.62/ L.4. His delegation had already pointed out that such a discriminatory attitude was completely unjustifiable. The representative of Austria had rightly stated, moreover, that the sponsors of document A/CONF.62/L.4 drew no distinction between developed and developing coastal States when advocating the creation of an exclusive economic zone and that they were therefore unjustified in making a distinction when it came to the interests of the land-locked or geographically disadvantaged States within that zone. There seemed to be a confusion between the concept of the economic zone and that of the international sea-bed area; each would serve a completely different purpose. The proposed economic zone was designed to protect the economic interests of all coastal States without distinction. The inequalities that would result from its creation as far as the land-locked and geographically disadvantaged countries were concerned should be offset by granting such countries the right to benefit directly or indirectly from the resources of the economic zones of the region. The international sea-bed area, on the other hand, would belong to and should benefit everyone, particularly the developing countries. Thus a distinction was drawn between developed and developing States with regard to that area, whereas in the case of the economic zone it was not.

The regime for the international sea-bed area should explicitly grant to the land-locked countries the right of free access to and from the area and the right to preferential benefits from the resources of the area. Furthermore, the land-locked countries should be represented in the body of the authority which would be responsible for administering those resources.   Measures along those lines were not a charitable gesture but a meaningful application of the common heritage of mankind principle . . . .

Mr. KAZEMI (Iran) said that . . . [t]he land-locked States should have the right to participate in the exploration and exploitation of the sea-bed area beyond the limits of national jurisdiction and to be represented in the organs of the sea-bed authority on an equal footing with coastal States. However, his delegation maintained its view that the coastal State held exclusive and inalienable rights over its continental shelf and that they could not be fundamentally modified. Therefore it could not agree with any proposal that would involve the sharing of revenues derived from the exploitation of the resources of the continental shelf. It would like that view, which was shared by a number of other delegations, to be reflected in the revised text of informal working paper number 3 as an alternative to provision XII of that paper.

His delegation wished to make some suggestions with regard to the legitimate aspirations of the land-locked countries to participate in the exploitation of the living resources in the seas adjacent to that neighbouring State. Firstly, coastal States, whether transit or non-transit States, should, under bilateral or regional agreements, accord to the nationals of the land-locked States of their region or subregion preferential rights to fish in certain areas of their exclusive economic zones.   Secondly, in view of the fact that the adoption of the 200-mile limit as the maximum breadth of the exclusive economic zone would place some oceanic States in an extreme enviable position in terms of the living resources of the sea, it seemed only right to provide that any State whose total gain in terms of actual economic zone would exceed 50 per cent or the outer limits of whose economic zone would exceed 100 miles should have the obligation to contribute a reasonable portion of the revenue from the exploitation of its living resources to the sea-bed authority, for distribution among all land-locked countries, with special consideration given to the least developed land-locked States.

REFERENCES

"Memorandum Concerning the Question of Free Access to the Sea of Land-Locked Countries," U.N. Doc. A/CONF. 13/29 and Add. 1 (14 January 1958); E. Lauterpacht, "Freedom of Transit in International Law," *Transactions of the Grotius Society*, Vol. 44 (1958-1959), pp.

313-356; F. Boas, "Landlocked Countries and the Law of the Sea," *American Bar Association Section on International and Comparative Law Bulletin*, No. 22, Dec., 1959, p. 22; N.J.G. Pounds, "A Free and Secure Access to the Sea," *Annals of the Association of American Geographers*, Vol. 49 (September, 1959), pp. 256-268; M.I. Glassner, *Access to the Sea for Developing Land-Locked States*, The Hague: Martinus Nijhoff, 1970; R. Makil, "Transit Rights of Land-Locked Countries, *Journal of World Trade Law*, Vol. 4 (1970), pp. 35-51; "Study of the Question of Free Access to the Sea of Land-Locked Countries and of Special Problems of Land-Locked Countries Relating to the Exploration and Exploitation of the Resources of the Sea-Bed and the Ocean Floor Beyond the Limits of National Jurisdiction," U.N. Doc A/AC.138/37 and Corr. 1 and 2, 11 June 1971; P. Childs, "The Interests of Land-Locked States in Law of the Sea," *San Diego Law Review*, Vol. 9 (1972), pp. 701-732; V.C. Govindaraj, "The 1971 Treaty of Trade and Transit Between Nepal and India," *Indian Journal of International Law*, Vol. 12 (1972), pp. 247-251; A. Sarup, "Transit-Trade of Land-Locked Nepal," *International and Comparative Law Quarterly*, Vol. 21 (1972), pp. 287-306; M.I. Glassner, "The Status of Developing Land-Locked States Since 1965," *Lawyer of the Americas*, Vol. 5(3) (October, 1973), pp. 480-498; V. Ibler, "The Land and Shelf-Locked States and the Development of the Law of the Sea," *Annales d'Etudes Internationales*, Vol. 4 (1973), pp. 55-65; T.M. Franck, et al., "The New Poor; Land-Locked, Shelf-Locked and Other Geographically Disadvantaged States," *New York University Law Review*, Vol. 7 (1974), pp. 33-57; M.I. Glassner, "Developing Land-Locked States and the Resources of the Seabed," *San Diego Law Review*, Vol. 11 (1974), pp. 633-655; I. Delupis, "Landlocked States and the Law of the Sea," *Scandinavian Studies in Law*, Vol. 19 (1975), pp. 101-120; S. Ferguson, "UNCLOS III: Last Chance for Landlocked States?," *San Diego Law Review*, Vol. 14 (1977), pp. 637-655; L.C. Caflisch, "Land-Locked States and Their Access To and From the Sea," *British Yearbook of International Law*, Vol. 49 (1978), pp. 71-100; Povolny, "Landlocked States and the Law of the Sea," *Marine Policy Reports* (University of Delaware), Vol. 2, No. 4 (March, 1980); Shafqat Hussain Naghmi, "Exclusive Economic Zone and the Land-Locked States," *Pakistan Horizon*, Vol. 33 (1980), pp. 37-48; International Law Association, *59th Conference (Belgrade 1980) Report*, London: The Association, 1982, pp. 310-336; A.M. Sinjela, *Land-Locked States and the UNCLOS Regime*, Dobbs Ferry, New York: Oceana, 1983; Ijaz Hussain, "A Study of Pakistan's Attitude Towards the Question of Free Access to the Sea of Land-Locked States," *Indian Journal of International Law*, Vol. 24 (1984), pp. 319-345; A. Mpazi, "Land-locked States' Rights in the Exclusive Economic Zone from the Perspective of the UN Convention on the Law of the Sea: An Historical Evaluation," *Ocean Development and International Law*, kVol. 20 (1989), pp. 63-82.

NOTE ON THE GEOGRAPHICALLY DISADVANTAGED STATES

Some states, though technically not landlocked, nonetheless fare poorly in terms of geographical advantages. Some have virtually no continental shelves while others are in such close proximity to their neighboring states that median line boundaries leave them little of value in ocean resources. Commonly known as "geographically disadvantaged states," these nations have much in common with landlocked nations in their quest for a larger share of ocean wealth than would be dictated by geographical factors alone. For further references, see L.M. Alexander and R.D. Hodgson, "The Role of the Geographically-Disadvantaged States in the Law of the Sea," *San Diego Law Review*, Vol. 13 (1976), pp. 558-582; J. Symonides, "Geographically Disadvantaged States and the New Law of the Sea," *Polish Yearbook of International Law*, Vol. 8 (1976), pp. 55-74; S. Jayakumar, "The Issue of the Rights of Landlocked and Geographically Disadvantaged States and the New Law of the Sea," *Thesaurus Acroasium: The Law of the Sea*, Vol. 7 (1977), p. 341; F. Mirvahabi, "The Rights of the Landlocked and Geographically Disadvantaged States in Exploitation of Marine Fisheries," *Netherlands International Law Review*, Vol. 26(2), (1979), pp. 130-162; J.C. Phillips, "The Economic Resources Zone -- Progress for the

Developing Coastal States," *Journal of Maritime Law and Commerce*, Vol. 11 (1980), pp. 349-365; Robert E. Bowen, "The Land-Locked and Geographically Disadvantaged States and the Law of the Sea," *Political Geography Quarterly*, Vol. 5 (1986), pp. 63-69; Janusz Symonides, "Geographically Disadvantaged States Under the 1982 Convention on the Law of the Sea," *Recueil des Cours* (Hague Academy of International Law), Vol. 208(1) (1988), pp. 283-406.

C. NATIONAL EXCLUSIVE ECONOMIC ZONE CLAIMS AND LEGISLATION

1. Countries Proclaimed Exclusive Economic Zone

Up to mid-1990, there are 80 countries proclaimed Exclusive Economic Zones: Antiqua and Barbuda, Argentina, Bangladesh, Barbados, Bulgaria, Burma (now Myanmar), Cape Verde, Chile, Republic of China (Taiwan),[1] Columbia, Comoros, Cook Islands, Costa Rica, Cote d'Ivoire (Ivory Coast), Cuba, Democratic Kampuchea (Cambodia), Democratic People's Republic of Korea, Democratic Yemen, Djibouti, Dominica, Dominican Republic, Egypt, Equatorial Guinea, Fiji, France, Gabon, Ghana, Grenada, Guatemala, Guinea, Guinea-Bissau, Haiti, Honduras, Iceland, India, Indonesia, Kenya, Kiribati, Madagascar, Malaysia, Marshall Islands, Mauritania, Mauritius, Mexico, Micronesia, Morocco, Mozambique, New Zealand, Nigeria, Niue, Norway, Oman, Pakistan, Philippines, Portugal, Romania, St. Kitts and Nevis, Saint Lucia, St. Vincent and the Grenadines, Samoa, Sao Tome and Principe, Senegal, Seychelles, Solomon Islands, Spain, Sri Lanka, Suriname, Thailand, Togo, Tonga, Trinidad and Tobago, Tuvalu, Ukarainian SSR, Union of Soviet Socialist Republics, United States, Tanzania, Vanuatu, Venezuela, Vietnam, Zaire. [2]

REFERENCES

Robert W. Smith, *Exclusive Economic Zone Claims, An Analysis and Primary Documents*, Dordrecht/Boston/Lancaster: Martinus Nijhoff Publishers, 1986; Office of the Special Representative of the Secretary-General for the Law of the Sea, *The Law of the Sea, National Legislation on the Exclusive Economic Zone, the Economic Zone and the Exclusive Fishery Zone*, New York: The United Nations, 1986.

2. Selected National Legislation

a. Proclamation

PROCLAMATION 5030 OF THE
PRESIDENT OF THE UNITED STATES OF AMERICA
March 10, 1983
International Legal Materials, Vol. 22 (1983), p. 465.

Now, Therefore, I, Ronald Reagan, by the authority vested in me as President by the Constitution and laws of the United States of America, do hereby proclaim the sovereign rights and jurisdiction of the United States of America and confirm also the rights and freedoms of all States within an Exclusive Economic Zone, as described herein.

---

[1]*Chinese Yearbook of International Law and Affairs*, Vol. 1 (1981), pp. 151-152.

[2]*Law of the Sea Bulletin*, No. 15 (May 1990), pp. 29-38.

The Exclusive Economic Zone of the United States is a zone contiguous to the territorial sea, including zones contiguous to the territorial sea of the United States, the Commonwealth of Puerto Rico, the Commonwealth of the Northern Mariana Islands (to the extent consistent with the covenant and the United Nations Trusteeship Agreement), and United States overseas territories and possessions. The Exclusive Economic Zone extends to a distance 200 nautical miles from the baseline from which the breadth of the territorial sea is measured. In cases where the maritime boundary with a neighbouring State remains to be determined, the boundary of the Exclusive Economic Zone shall be determined by the United States and other State concerned in accordance with equitable principles.

Within the Exclusive Economic Zone, the United States has, to the extent permitted by international law, (a) sovereign rights for the purpose of exploring, exploiting, conserving and managing natural resources, both living and non-living, of the sea-bed and subsoil and the superjacent waters and with regard to other activities for the economic exploitation and exploration of the zone, such as the production of energy from the water, currents and winds; and (b) jurisdiction with regard to the establishment and use of artificial islands, and installations and structures having economic purposes, and the protection and preservation of the marine environment.

This Proclamation does not change existing United States policies concerning the continental shelf, marine mammals and fisheries, including highly migratory species of tuna which are not subject to United States jurisdiction and require international agreements for effective management.

The United States will exercise these sovereign rights and jurisdiction in accordance with the rules of international law.

Without prejudice to the sovereign rights and jurisdiction of the United States, the Exclusive Economic Zone remains an area beyond the territory and territorial sea of the United States in which all States enjoy the high seas freedoms of navigation, overflight, the laying of submarine cables and pipelines, and other internationally lawful uses of the sea.

REFERENCES

National Advisory Committee on Oceans and Atmosphere, *The Exclusive Economic Zone of the United States: Some Immediate Policy Issues -- A Special Report to the President and the Congress*, Washington, D.C.: The Committee, 1984; Bibiana Cicin-Sain and Robert W. Knecht, "The Problem of Governance of U.S. Ocean Resources and the New Exclusive Economic Zone," *Ocean Development and International Law*, Vol. 15 (1985), pp. 289-320; Maynard Silva and William Westermeyer, "The Law of the Sea and U.S. Exclusive Economic Zone: Perspectives on Marine Transportation and Fisheries," *Ocean Development and International Law*, Vol. 15 (1985), pp. 321-354; Alexander Holser, "Offshore Lands of the U.S.A.: The U.S. Exclusive Economic Zone, Continental Shelf and Outer Continental Shelf," *Marine Policy*, Vol. 12 (1988), pp. 2-8; Jon M. Van Dyke, Joseph Morgan and Jonathan Gurish, "The Exclusive Economic Zone of the Northwestern Hawaiian Islands: When Do Uninhabited Islands Generate an EEZ?" *San Diego Law Review*, Vol. 25 (1988), pp. 425-494.

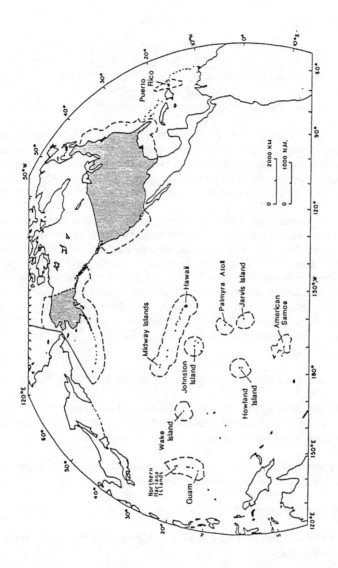

Sketch Map Showing Approximate Outlines of Exclusive Economic Zone of
the United States, Commonwealth of Puerto Rico, Commonwealth of the
Northern Mariana Islands and United States Overseas Possessions.
Figure 9-2

Source: *International Legal Materials*, Vol. 22 (1983), p. 463. (Based on map published
by U.S. Geological Survey, Department of the Interior, to show compilation of
subsea energy and mineral resource (MF-1360) but not drawn to determine legal
boundaries.) Reprinted by permission of the American Society of International
Law.

b.   Specific Legislation

ROMANIA

DECREE OF THE COUNCIL OF STATE CONCERNING THE
ESTABLISHMENT OF THE EXCLUSIVE ECONOMIC ZONE OF
THE SOCIALIST REPUBLIC OF ROMANIA IN THE BLACK SEA
(No. 142, 25 April 1986)
Law of the Sea Bulletin, No. 8 (November 1986), pp. 17-22.

Article 1. - In the ocean space off the Romanian coast in the Black Sea, beyond and adjacent to the limits of the territorial waters, there shall be established the exclusive economic zone of the Socialist Republic of Romania, in which it shall exercise sovereign rights and jurisdiction over the natural resources of the sea-bed, its subsoil and the superjacent water column and with regard to the different activities related to their exploration, exploitation, conservation and management.

Article 2. - The outer part of the exclusive economic zone shall extend to a distance of 200 nautical miles from the baselines from which the breadth of the territorial sea is measured; owing to the narrow dimensions of the Black Sea, the effective extent of the exclusive economic zone of the Socialist Republic of Romania shall be determined by delimiting it within the framework of negotiations with the neighbouring States with coasts opposite or adjacent to the Romanian Black Sea coast. The delimitation shall be carried out with due regard for the legislation of the Socialist Republic of Romania, by means of agreements with those States, through the application, according to the specific circumstances of each area to be delimited, of the delimitation principles and criteria generally recognized in international law and in the practice of States, in order to arrive at equitable solutions.

Article 3. - In its exclusive economic zone, the Socialist Republic of Romania shall exercise:

(a) Sovereign rights for the purpose of exploring and exploiting, conserving and managing the living and non-living natural resources and other resources on the sea-bed, in its subsoil and in the superjacent water column;

(b) Sovereign rights with regard to other activities related to the economic exploitation and exploration of the zone, such as the production of energy from the water, currents and winds;

(c) Jurisdiction with regard to:

The establishment and use of artificial islands, installations and structures;
Marine scientific research;

The protection and conservation of the marine environment;

(d) Other rights provided for in this Decree or in other legislation of the Socialist Republic of Romania and in the generally recognized norms of international law.

The sovereign rights and the jurisdiction provided for in this article shall be exercised in accordance with the legislation of the Socialist Republic of Romania.

Article 4. - The Socialist Republic of Romania may co-operate in its exclusive economic zone with the other coastal States of the Black Sea so as to ensure the conservation and rational exploration of the living resources and the protection and preservation of the marine environment, particularly in the areas adjacent to that zone, taking account of the specific characteristics of the Black Sea as a semi-enclosed sea with limited biological potential.

Article 5. - In the exclusive economic zone of the Socialist Republic of Romania, all States, whether coastal or land-locked, shall enjoy the freedoms of navigation and overflight, the freedom to lay submarine cables and pipelines and other internationally lawful ways of using the sea related to these freedoms, provided that respect is shown for the provisions of this Decree and other legislation of the Socialist Republic of Romania and for the generally recognized norms of international law.

Article 6. - The Socialist Republic of Romania has priority interests with regard to the anadromous stocks which originate in its waters and shall therefore exercise its rights in respect of them.

The competent Romanian organs shall take measures to ensure the conservation of these anadromous stocks, by means of appropriate actions, and to establish rules to regulate fishing for them, including the determination of the total authorized catch, and shall co-operate to this end with the organs of the other interested States, when such stocks migrate landward of the limits of the exclusive economic zone of the Socialist Republic of Romania.

Article 7. - The Socialist Republic of Romania shall ensure the optimum utilization of the fish and other living resources in its exclusive economic zone, by taking the measures required for the conservation and management of such resources, taking into account the best scientific evidence and, when it deems it necessary, in co-operation with the international organizations which are competent in this field.

To this end, the competent Romanian organs shall annually determine the total authorized catch for each species of fish and other living resources and shall also prescribe measures to ensure the rational conduct of fishing operations, the conservation and reproduction of the living resources and their protection, including the inspection, boarding and arrest of vessels.

The fishing vessels of other States may have access to the exclusive economic zone of the Socialist Republic of Romania through agreements, under conditions of reciprocity.

Article 8. - The Socialist Republic of Romania shall have the exclusive right to construct and to authorize and regulate the construction, operation and use in its economic zone of all types of artificial islands and all types of installations and structures intended for the conduct of scientific research in its economic zone and for the exploration and exploitation of its natural resources.

Article 9. - In its economic zone, the Socialist Republic of Romania shall have exclusive jurisdiction over artificial islands, installations and structures, including the right to exercise control in order to prevent infractions and other violations of customs, fiscal, health and immigration regulations and of safety laws and regulations.

Safety zones shall be established around the artificial islands, installations and structures in the exclusive economic zone of the Socialist Republic of Romania and shall extend a maximum distance of 500 metres measured from each point of their outer edge, except where generally recognized international norms provide otherwise. The competent Romanian organs shall specify the measures which are necessary in these zones in order to ensure the safety of both navigation and the artificial islands, installations and structures.

Romanian organizations and foreign individuals and legal entities that have the right to construct, maintain and operate the aforementioned artificial islands, installations and structures shall be obliged to ensure that the permanent means for giving warning of their presence are maintained in working order.

Notification of the construction of artificial islands, installations and structures, the establishment of safety zones around them and the total or partial dismantling of these installations and structures shall be provided through "Warnings for Navigators."

Article 10. - Marine scientific research in the exclusive economic zone of the Socialist Republic of Romania shall be conducted in compliance with the legislation of the Socialist Republic of Romania; account shall also be taken of the treaties to which the Socialist Republic of Romania is a party.

Scientific research in the exclusive economic zone of the Socialist Republic of Romania, conducted exclusively for peaceful purposes and to increase scientific knowledge of the marine environment, for the benefit of all mankind, may also be carried out by foreign States or by international organizations, but only with the prior agreement of the competent Romanian organs.

When conducting marine scientific research in the exclusive economic zone of the Republic of Romania, foreign States and international organizations which are competent in this field and have obtained the agreement of the Romanian organs to this end shall be obliged:

(a) To ensure the participation of Romanian representatives in the marine scientific research work, including work on board research vessels or marine scientific research installations;

(b) To present to the competent Romanian organs, at their request, preliminary reports and the final results and conclusions after the completion of the research;

(c) To grant access for the competent Romanian organs, at their request, to all data derived from the marine scientific research;

(d) Not to prejudice, in any manner whatsoever, by their activities, the sovereign rights and jurisdiction of the Socialist Republic of Romania over its exclusive economic zone, as provided for by this Decree.

Article 11. - The prevention, reduction and control of pollution of the marine environment caused by or related to activities in the exclusive economic zone of the Socialist Republic of Romania shall be effected in compliance with Romanian legislation and the treaties to which the Socialist Republic of Romania is party.

The competent Romanian organs shall establish rules relating to the prevention, reduction and control of pollution of the marine environment and the safety of navigation specifically for the exclusive economic zone of the Socialist Republic of Romania; notification of these rules shall be provided through "Warnings of Navigators."

Where there are clear grounds for believing that a vessel which has passed through the exclusive economic zone of the Socialist Republic of Romania has violated the provisions of Romanian legislation or applicable international rules regarding the prevention, reduction and control of pollution of the marine environment, the competent Romanian organs shall have the right to require the vessel concerned to provide explanations concerning such violation and to inspect that vessel if it has refused to provide such explanations or where the explanations received did not correspond to the facts.

Where there is clear objective evidence that a vessel navigating in the exclusive economic zone of the Socialist Republic of Romania has, in that zone, violated the rules contained in the first and second paragraphs and has disposed of wastes causing major damage or threat of major damage to the Romanian coastline or to the resources of the territorial waters or to the Romanian exclusive economic zone, proceedings, including detention of the vessel, may be instituted in respect of such a violation, in accordance with the legislation of the Socialist Republic of Romania.

If the foreign vessel is within a Romanian port, the competent organs of the Socialist Republic of Romania may institute legal proceedings in respect of any violation committed by that vessel in the exclusive economic zone of the Socialist Republic of Romania.

Article 12. - Where vessels collide, run aground or suffer any other maritime damage in the exclusive economic zone of the Socialist Republic of Romania, and if the actions related to such damage can have particularly harmful consequences for the exclusive economic zone or for the Romanian coastline, the competent Romanian organs shall have the right to prescribe, in accordance with international law, the necessary measures corresponding to the actual harm or to the threat posed by such damage, in order to protect against pollution or the threat of pollution.

Article 13. - The following acts, if they are committed in such circumstances as to be considered offences under criminal law, shall constitute contraventions and shall be punishable by a fine of from 100,000 to 1,200,000 lei, which shall be imposed at the place where the contravention is recorded:

(a) The unlawful exploration and exploitation of the natural resources of the exclusive economic zone of the Socialist Republic of Romania;

(b) Pollution and the act of unlawfully introducing, for purposes of disposal within the exclusive economic zone of the Socialist Republic of Romania, by vessels or aircraft or from artificial islands, installations or structures constructed in the sea, substances which are harmful to human health or to the living resources of the sea or other waste and materials which could cause damage or create obstacles to the lawful use of the sea;

(c) The undertaking of activities in the exclusive economic zone of the Socialist Republic of Romania without the consent of the competent Romanian organs;

(d) Failure to comply with the "Warnings of Navigators" and with signals relating to the construction of artificial islands, installations and structures;

(e) The construction of artificial islands, installations and structures in the exclusive economic zone of the Socialist Republic of Romania, without the necessary approval;

(f) Failure to protect the installations and other equipment in the exclusive economic zone of the Socialist Republic of Romania with permanent means for giving warning of their presence and failure to comply with the standards relating to the maintenance of these means in good working order and with the standards relating to the dismantling of installations and equipment the use of which has been permanently prohibited.

Where the aforementioned acts have caused major damage, had other serious consequences or have been committed repeatedly, the fine shall be from 1 million to 2 million lei.

In particularly serious situations, the competent Romanian organs may take the additional steps of confiscating the vessel, installations, fishing gear, equipment and other objects belonging to the offender, as well as the goods acquired unlawfully.

The penalties may also be imposed on legal entities.

The acts referred to in the first paragraph shall not constitute contraventions if they have been committed in order to guarantee the safety of navigation, to save human lives or to avoid damage to a vessel or its cargo.

Article 14. - The contravention shall be recorded and the penalty imposed by navigation monitoring and control organs specially empowered to do so by the Ministry of Transport and Telecommunication, by organs of the Ministry for the Food Industry and the Acquisition of Agricultural Products and by other legally authorized organs.

Objections to the contravention report may be filed with the Sea and River Section of the Civil Court of the town of Constanta, no later than 15 days following the date of the communication.

. . . .

Article 16. - The fines levied on foreign individuals or legal entities shall be paid in convertible currency, by converting the fines in lei at the exchange rate for non-commercial transactions.

Article 17. - The imposition of fines for contraventions shall not exempt the offender from the obligation of making reparation for the damage caused in the exclusive economic zone of the Socialist Republic of Romania, in compliance with Romanian legislation.

Article 18. - Where acts have been committed which, under Romanian law, result in the arrest of the commander or the detention of the foreign vessel, the competent Romanian organs shall immediately inform the flag State of the measures taken. The detained vessel and its crew shall be released immediately upon the payment of adequate security.

REFERENCES

Ioan Condor, "The Legal Regime of Romania's Exclusive Economic Zone in the Black Sea," *Review of Socialist Law*, Vol. 13 (1987), pp. 199-204; Erik Franckx, "Romania's Proclamation of a 200-mile Exclusive Economic Zone," *International Journal of Estuarine and Coastal Law*, Vol. 2 (1987), pp. 144-153; Olimpiu Craucinc, "The Exclusive Economic Zone of the Socialist Republic of Romania," *Revue Roumaine D'Etudes Internationales*, Vol. 24, No. 4 (July-August 1988), pp. 325-334.

c.   Mixed Legislation

SEYCHELLES
THE MARITIME ZONES ACT, 1977
National Legislation and Treaties Relating to the Law of the Sea
United Nations Legislative Series, ST/LEG/SER.B/19
New York: The United Nations, 1980, pp. 102-106.
[Section 1 of the Act is from Supplement to *Official Gazette*, May 23, 1977, p. 143.]

An Act to provide for certain matters relating to the territorial waters, the continental shelf, the exclusive economic zone and the historic waters of Seychelles.

ENACTED by the Parliament of Seychelles.

1.   *Citation and commencement.*

This Act may be cited as the Maritime Zones Act, 1977 and shall come into operation on such date as the President may, by order, appoint.

2.   *Interpretation.*

In this Act --

. . . .

"resources" includes living and non-living resources as well as resources for the production of energy from tides, winds and currents.

3. *Sovereignty over and limits of territorial waters.*

. . . .

4. *Use of territorial waters by foreign ships.*

(1) Without prejudice to any other enactment in force but subject to subsection (2), (3) and (4), all foreign ships (other than warships, including submarines) shall enjoy the right of innocent passage through the territorial waters,

(2) Foreign warships, including submarines, may enter or pass through the territorial waters after giving notice to the President's Office.

(3) Submarines shall, while passing through the territorial waters, navigate on the surface and show their flag.

(4) Where the President is satisfied that it is necessary to do so --

(a) in the interest of public safety, public order, defence or security of Seychelles or any part thereof; or

(b) in pursuance of any treaty to which Seychelles is a party, he may, by Order published in the *Gazette*, suspend, whether absolutely or subject to such exceptions and qualifications as may be specified in the Order, the entry of any class of foreign ships into such area of the territorial waters as may be specified in the Order.

5. *Continental Shelf.*

(1) The continental shelf comprises the seabed and subsoil of the submarine areas that extend beyond the limit of the territorial waters throughout the natural prolongation of the land territory of the Seychelles --

(a) to the outer edge of the continental margin; or

(b) to a distance of two hundred nautical miles from the baseline where the outer edge of the continental shelf does not extend up to that distance.

(2) Seychelles has, and always had, full and exclusive sovereign rights in respect of the continental shelf.

6. *Exclusive economic zone.*

(1) The exclusive economic zone is the area beyond and adjacent to the territorial waters and which extends to a distance of two hundred nautical miles from the baseline.

(2) Notwithstanding anything contained in subsection (1), where the President considers it necessary so to do having regard to International Law and State practice, he may, subject to subsection (3), by Order published in the *Gazette*, amend the limit of the exclusive economic zone as specified in subsection (1).

7. *Rights over continental shelf and exclusive economic zones.*

(1) Without prejudice to sections 3, 5 and 6, but subject to subsection (3) and (6), Seychelles has, in the continental shelf and the exclusive economic zone --

(a) sovereign rights for the purposes of exploration, exploitation, conservation and management of all resources;

(b) exclusive rights and jurisdiction for the constructions, maintenance or operation of artificial islands, off-shore terminals, installations and other structures and devices necessary for the exploration and exploitation of resources or for the convenience of shipping or for any other purpose;

(c) exclusive jurisdiction to authorize, regulate and conduct scientific research;

(d) exclusive jurisdiction to preserve and protect the marine environment and to prevent and control marine pollution; and

(e) such other rights as are recognized by International Law or State practice.

(2) Except in accordance with the terms of any agreement entered into with Seychelles or of license granted by or under the authority of the President, no person shall, in

Seychelles or of license granted by or under the authority of the President, no person shall, in relation to the continental shelf or the exclusive economic zone --

        (a) explore or exploit any resources;

        (b) carry out any search, excavation or drilling operations;

        (c) conduct any research;

        (d) construct, maintain or operate any artificial island, off-shore terminal, installation or other structure or device.

        (3) Subject to subsection (d) and to any measures that may be necessary for protecting the interest of Seychelles, foreign States may lay or maintain cables or pipelines on the continental shelf and the seabed of the exclusive economic zone.

        (4) No cables or pipelines shall be laid on the continental shelf or on the seabed of the exclusive economic zone unless the authority of the President has been obtained for the delineation of the course of the cables or pipelines.

        (5) Nothing in subsection (2) shall apply in relation to fishing by a citizen of Seychelles or a body corporate registered in Seychelles and approved by the Minister of Fisheries.

        (6) Ships and aircraft of all States shall, subject to the exercise by Seychelles of its sovereign rights over its continental shelf or within the exclusive economic zone enjoy the following freedoms --

        (a) freedom of navigation; and

        (b) freedom of overflight.

    8. *Historic waters.*

        (1) The President may, by Order published in the *Gazette*, specify the limits of the historic waters.

        (2) The sovereign rights of Seychelles extends, and has always extended, to the historic waters and to the seabed and subsoil underlying, and the air space over, the historic waters.

    9. *Designated areas of the continental shelf and the exclusive economic zone.*

    The President may, by Order published in the *Gazette*-
        (a) declare any area of the continental shelf or the exclusive economic zone to be a designated area; and

        (b) make such provisions as he considers necessary with respect to --

        (i) the exploration, exploitation and protection of the resources within the designated area;

(ii) the safety and protection of artificial islands, off-shore terminals, installations and other structures and devices in the designated area;

(iii) the regulation and conduct of scientific research in the designated area;

(iv) the protection of the marine environment in the designated area;

(v) customs and other fiscal matters in relation to the designated area;

(vi) the regulation of entry into and passage of foreign ships through the designated area;

(vii) the establishment of fairways, sealanes, traffic separation schemes or any mode of ensuring freedom of navigation which is not prejudicial to the interest of Seychelles.

10. *Extension of enactments.*

The President may, by Order published in the *Gazette* --
(a) extend with such restrictions and modifications as he thinks fit, any enactment in force to the continental shelf or the exclusive economic zone, or any part thereof, including any designated area;

(b) make such provisions as he considers necessary for facilitating the enforcement of that enactment.

11. *Publication of charts.*

The President may cause the baseline, the limits of the territorial waters, the continental shelf, the exclusive economic zone and the historic waters to be published in charts.

12. *Offences.*

(1) Any person who contravenes any provisions of this Act or any regulation or Order made under this Act, shall commit an offence and shall, on conviction, be liable to a fine not exceeding two hundred thousand rupees or to imprisonment for a term not exceeding five years.

(2) Any person who commits an offence shall be tried in the Supreme Court.

13. *Offences by agent and body corporate.*

(1) Where an offence is committed by --

(a) an agent, the person for whom the agent is acting;

(b)   a body corporate, every person who, at the time of the commission of the offence, was concerned in the management of the body corporate or was purporting to act in a managerial capacity, shall also commit the like offence, unless he proves that the offence was committed without his knowledge or consent and that he took all reasonable steps to prevent the commission of the offence.

(2) Notwithstanding subsection (1), where an offence has been committed by a body corporate and it is proved that the offence has been committed with the consent, whether express or implied, or the connivance of, or is attributable to any neglect on the part of the director, manager, secretary, or other officer of the body corporate, such director, manager, secretary or other officer shall commit the like offence.

14. *Application of Act.*

Where any provision of this Act or of any regulation or Order made under this Act is in conflict with the provision of any other enactment in force, such provision of this Act or of such regulation or Order shall prevail.

15. *Regulations.*

(1) The President may make such regulations as he considers necessary for carrying out the purposes of this Act.

(2) In particular and without prejudice to the foregoing power, regulations made under subsection (1) may provide for all or any of the following matters --

(a) the regulation of the conduct of any person in the territorial waters, the continental shelf, the exclusive economic zone or the historical waters;

(b) the regulation of the exploration and exploitation, conservation and management of the resources of the continental shelf and the exclusive economic zone;

(c) the regulation of the construction, maintenance of artificial islands, off-shore terminals, installations and other structures and devices;

(d) the preservation and the protection of the marine environment and the prevention and control of marine pollution;

(e) the regulation and conduct of scientific research;

(f) the fees in relation to licenses; and

(g) any matter incidental to any of the matters specified in paragraphs (a) to (f).

NOTE

The reader should compare the basic provisions of the national legislation with each other and with the provisions dealing with the Exclusive Economic Zone in the 1982 United Nations Convention on the Law of the Sea. For a collection of national legislation, see *The Law of the Sea, National Legislation on the Exclusive Economic Zone, the Economic Zone and the Exclusive*

Sea, National Legislation on the Exclusive Economic Zone, the Economic Zone and the Exclusive Fishery Zone, New York: The United Nations, 1986.

REFERENCES

William T. Burke, "National Legislation on Ocean Authority Zones and the Contemporary Law of the Sea," *Ocean Development and International Law*, Vol. 9 (1981), pp. 289-322; B. Obinna Okere, "Nigeria's Exclusive Economic Zone and Freedom of Navigation," *Ocean Development and International Law*, Vol. 13 (1983-84), pp. 535-538; E.E.E. Mtango and Friedl Weiss, "The Exclusive Economic Zone and Tanzania: Considerations of a Developing Country," *Ocean Development and International Law*, Vol. 14 (1984), pp. 1-54; B. Obinna Okere, "Nigeria's Exclusive Economic Zone," *Nigerian Law Journal*, Vol. 12 (1984), pp. 65-78; F. Orrego Vicuna, ed., *The Exclusive Economic Zone: A Latin American Perspective*, 1984; Lawrence Juda, "The Exclusive Economic Zone: Compatibility of National Claims and the UN Convention on the Law of the Sea," *Ocean Development and International Law*, Vol. 16 (1986), pp. 1-58; Hamisi S. Kibola, "A Note on Africa and the Exclusive Economic Zone," *Ocean Development and International Law*, Vol. 16 (1986), pp. 369-380; Barbara Kwiakowska, "New Soviet Legislation on the 200 Mile Economic Zone and Certain Problems of Evolution of Customary Law," *Netherland International Law Review*, Vol. 33 (1986), pp. 24-64; Davorin Rudolf, "Yugoslav Economic Zone in the Adriatic Sea? *Jugoslovenska Revija Za Medunarodno Pravo*, Vol. 35, No. 1 (1988), pp. 52-61; Theodore C. Kariotis, "The Case for a Greek Exclusive Economic Zone in the Aegean Sea," *Marine Policy*, Vol. 14, No. 1 (January 1990), pp. 3-14.

D. THE EXCLUSIVE ECONOMIC ZONE AND THE CONTINENTAL SHELF

David Attard, *The Exclusive Economic Zone in International Law*, New York and London: Oxford University Press, 1987, pp. 137-145. Notes omitted. Reprinted by permission.

A review of State practice reveals that the fishery-zone and continental shelf concepts have managed to co-exist with a certain amount of success. It is submitted that this is due mainly to the fact that the institutions deal with different resources. There is a clear-cut distinction between the applicable regimes: the fishery zone concerns only living resources . . . .

In considering the relationship between the EEZ and the shelf . . . [it should be noted that] the EEZ grants the coastal State rights over the sea-bed and its subsoil up to 200 n.m., which are similar to those allowed under the shelf regime.

Before proceeding further, it may therefore be prudent to ask whether the EEZ has absorbed the shelf. In the course of the UNCLOS III negotiations, there were differences amongst the EEZ's proponents concerning the advisability of retaining the institution of the shelf. It is possible to identify three major trends on the matter. The first advocated the incorporation of both institutions into one regime which would regulate both the living and the non-living resources in the 200-n.m. zone. The second wanted to apply the EEZ regime within the 200-n.m. limit. Outside this limit the shelf regime would remain applicable. The final and prevailing trend envisaged the two institutions as autonomous. They would be complementary and not mutually exclusive. The shelf regime would be retained. It would comprise the sea-bed and subsoil up to the end of the continental margin or to a distance of 200 n.m. where the margin did not extend up to that distance . . . .

Articles 56(1) and 57 on the EEZ in the 1982 Convention cover the same sea-bed and subsoil up to 200 n.m. referred to in Article 76(1) on the shelf. Article 56(1) grants the coastal State sovereign rights for the purpose of exploring and exploiting, conserving, and managing the natural resources of the sea-bed and subsoil. Article 77(1) states that the coastal State exercises over the shelf sovereign rights for the purpose of exploring it and exploiting its natural resources. Furthermore, Article 56(3) states that the EEZ rights with respect to the sea-bed and the subsoil set out in Article 56 "shall be exercised in accordance with Part VI." It may therefore be argued that these provisions merge the shelf regime with that of the EEZ regime.

It is submitted that a more reasonable view would interpret Article 56(3) as recognizing the autonomy of both institutions by ensuring that with respect to the rights over the sea-bed and subsoil it is the shelf regime that remains applicable. This view is confirmed by the drafting of the Convention which deals with the EEZ and the shelf in two parts: Part V, entitled "Exclusive Economic Zone" and Part VI, entitled "Continental Shelf." In these parts, two related but separate and independent regimes are set up . . . .

If it were to be accepted that the EEZ and the shelf have merged, then serious problems would be encountered with respect to existing shelf boundaries. The fusing of the two institutions would suggest that there was little or no possibility of having separate boundaries for the EEZ and the shelf. A single EEZ boundary, covering the shelf and its superjacent waters, would have to be drawn. However, it would hardly seem realistic to expect this boundary automatically to follow existing shelf boundaries, particularly as they may have been based on considerations which bear no direct relevance to the superjacent waters.

The view which favours the autonomy of both institutions finds further support in the deliberations of UNCLOS III on the treatment of resources within the EEZ. At the Conference, there was a general understanding that the recognition of the right to access by foreign fisherman to certain living resources within the 200-n.m. zone was essential to the widespread acceptance of the EEZ. Whilst the legal novelty presented by the EEZ concept allowed States to negotiate for fishing rights, the retention of the established shelf regime ensured to a large extent that there was no justification for a right to participate in the zone's non-living resources. Even sedentary species, which fell under the shelf regime, were excluded from the EEZ, despite the fact that it covers all the living resources in the same area.

It has been seen above that even under customary law the coastal State is granted sea-bed rights and jurisdiction under both the EEZ and the shelf. However, as far as can be ascertained, the very large majority of EEZ claimants have not fused the two institutions. Indeed, a number of States explicitly declare that their EEZ claims do not affect the shelf regime. The United States' EEZ Proclamation, for example, clearly states that the Proclamation "does not change existing United States policies concerning the continental shelf . . . ." Other States which have retained the autonomy of the EEZ and the shelf regimes in their legislation are: Bangladesh, Burma, Colombia, Democratic Yemen, Dominican Republic, France, Guyana, Iceland, Indonesia, Ivory Coast, Pakistan, Portugal, Seychelles, Sri Lanka, Vanuatu, and Venezuela . . . .

Whilst both institutions are concerned with resource jurisdiction, their historical development and contents differ. Unlike the shelf regime, there is no reference to natural prolongation in the EEZ, for like the territorial sea and contiguous zone it is a zone measured from the coast. It is a zone which bears no relation, for example, to the geophysical features of the sea-bed. The EEZ regime concerns all natural resources, including living and non-living resources, and other activities relating to the economic exploitation of the zone. The shelf regime mainly concerns non-living resources with the exception of sedentary species.

Perhaps one of the most fundamental differences between the two institutions relates to the fact that the rights over the continental shelf do not depend on occupation, effective or notional, or on any express proclamation, as they exist *ipso facto* and *ab initio*. In short, they are inherent rights. On the other hand, . . . there is no compelling reason to indicate that under customary law, the EEZ exists *ipso facto*. The exercise of the EEZ rights depends on express proclamation. Consequently, whilst a State may have a shelf without an EEZ, the converse is not possible. Furthermore, it should be recalled that in the case of the EEZ, the 200-n.m. limit represents the maximum breadth. In the case of the shelf, it represents the minimum breadth. Thus, beyond the 200-n.m. EEZ a State may still have a shelf.

The differences referred to in the last paragraph are reflected in Article 78(1) of the 1982 Convention which states: "the rights of the coastal State over the continental shelf do not affect the legal status of the superjacent waters or of the airspace above those waters." This provision, unlike Article 3 of the 1958 Shelf Convention, omits any reference to the "superjacent waters being high seas." This omission was rendered necessary by the introduction of the EEZ. If a State has declared an EEZ, the shelf's superjacent waters are no longer part of the high seas but form a part of the EEZ. Beyond the EEZ's outer limit, the superjacent waters of any existing shelf retain their high-seas status. In this regard, it is difficult to understand why the 1982 Convention leaves out Article 13 found in the 1958 Fisheries Convention, which made provisions for fishing carried out from embedded installations in the high seas. It is clear, for example, that when a State does not claim an EEZ, the area adjacent to the territorial sea remains high seas.

Under customary law and the 1982 Convention, whilst there is no obligation to give foreign access to shelf resources, there exists an . . to give other States the right to participate in the surplus allowable catch of the EEZ's living resources. This differentiation leads to the conclusion that the concept of "sovereign rights" differs qualitively according to the regime in question. Thus, whilst living resources falling under the EEZ regime are subject to exploitation by other States, sedentary fisheries are not, as they fall under the shelf regime. Indeed, under Article 77(1), the 1982 Convention refers to the sovereign rights only rights only for the purpose of exploring the shelf and exploiting its resources. The reference to conservation and management found in Article 56(1) has been left out. This omission reflects the exclusive nature of shelf rights. It should, however, be noted that under Article 82 of the 1982 Convention, the coastal State is obliged to make payments or contributions in kind in respect of the exploitation of the non-living resources of the shelf beyond 200 n.m. There is no equivalent obligation under the EEZ regime.

There are other notable differences between the two institutions to be found in the 1982 Convention. Article 56(2) deals with the duties of the coastal State in the EEZ. Part VI on the shelf does not contain a similar provision. Article 77 refers only to the rights of the coastal State over the shelf. Under the shelf regime, all States are entitled to lay pipelines on the shelf, but their delineation is subject to the consent of the coastal States. Under the EEZ regime no such consent is explicitly mentioned.

Despite these differences, efforts to harmonize the shelf regime with that of the EEZ are evident both under customary law and the 1982 Convention. The coastal State enjoys similar sovereign rights for the purpose of exploring and exploiting the non-living resources of the sea-bed and the subsoil under both regimes. Perhaps the greatest manifestation of the need to harmonize both regimes is reflected by the incorporation of the distance principle in the shelf's definition, as a criterion for determining the legal status of the submerged lands. The introduction of the 200-n.m. limit measured from the same baselines used to measure the EEZ's breadth, abrogates the depth and exploitability tests found in the 1958 Shelf Convention and draws the shelf closer to the EEZ. In effect, this means that all the EEZ's sea-bed and the subsoil up to 200 n.m. will now be covered

effect, this means that all the EEZ's sea-bed and the subsoil up to 200 n.m. will now be covered by the shelf regime without the need to apply, for example, the exploitability test . . . .

The exclusive right to construct, authorize, and regulate the construction, operation and use of artificial islands, installations, and structures in the EEZ applies *mutatis mutandis* to the continental shelf. Article 246 of the 1982 Convention deals with the question of MSR [Marine Scientific Research] in the EEZ and on the shelf. Its provisions apply the same regime for the conduct of MSR in the zone and on the shelf. In fact, it was seen above that the introduction of the EEZ was one of the reasons for changes made in the 1982 Convention to the rules of the 1958 Shelf Convention regarding scientific research on the shelf.

Efforts to harmonize both regimes are also evident in State practice. In this respect, of particular interest is the Seychelles Maritime Zones Act (1977), which includes both institutions, but provides one regime for the exploitation of the EEZ and shelf resources. [See Section C, 2, c]. . . .

An important consequence of the autonomy of the two institutions relates to the accommodation of the exercise of shelf rights and the freedoms of movement . . . . [U]nder customary law and the 1958 Shelf Convention, the shelf's exploration or the exploitation of its natural resources must not result in any unjustifiable interference with navigation. The EEZ's introduction may be considered to have tilted this balance of interests further in favour of the coastal State. Because EEZ rights also cover shelf resources, a coastal State, in defending measures to exploit its shelf resources, can now also be expected to quote its EEZ rights as a further justification to interfere with the said freedoms.

In this regard, reference should be made to Article 78(2) of the 1982 Convention, which states: "the exercise of the rights of the coastal State over the continental shelf must not infringe or result in any unjustifiable interference with navigation and other rights and freedoms of other States as provided for in this Convention." This provision is similar to Article 5(1) of the 1958 Shelf Convention; however, it contains another limitation on the exercise of a State's shelf rights. Their exercise must neither cause unjustifiable interference nor must it "infringe" the said freedoms, the inference being that the concept of "unjustifiable interference" was not felt to be sufficient to safeguard the international community's interests in view of the new extensive EEZ powers allocated to the coastal State. It must also be pointed out that interference, even if substantial, may be justified, whilst certain forms of interference, even if insignificant, may be unjustifiable and may constitute an infringement of the freedom to navigate in the EEZ. In such case an assessment must be made of the interests involved. Thus, for example, the estimated value of the resource-deposit and the cost to shipping of alternative routes are just two elements which would have to be considered.

The autonomy of both institutions will also lead to serious problems in delimiting overlapping claims of the same kind . . . . The equitable considerations to be taken into account when delimiting both institutions may vary considerably. The historical development of the legal shelf relates it to geophysical factors. The geomorphological and the geological structures of the shelf which could be relevant to its delimitation bear no direct relevance to the superjacent waters. The EEZ is a zone which covers not only the sea-bed but also its superjacent waters. Hence, certain equitable considerations which are not applicable to shelf-delimitations, such as historic fishing rights, may be relevant to the delimitation of the EEZ. It is therefore possible that in delimiting overlapping claims of States, no common EEZ shelf boundary will necessarily emerge, even if the similar formulae for the delimitation of the EEZ and the shelf found in the 1982 Convention are used. This is particularly true in cases where the overlapping claims to the shelf

Convention are used. This is particularly true in cases where the overlapping claims to the shelf have already been delimited, and in cases where the shelf extends beyond the 200-n.m. EEZ limit.

The overlapping of an EEZ of one State with the shelf of another can lead to serious problems . . . . In view of the autonomy of the two institutions, such an occurrence is possible. The harmonization and alignment of the two institutions, particularly by giving preference to their common elements, would assist in ensuring that such occurrences are kept to a bare minimum.

REFERENCES

Surya P. Sharma, "The Single Maritime Boundary Regime and the Relationship Between the Continental Shelf and the Exclusive Economic Zone," *International Journal of Estuarine and Coastal Law*, Vol. 2 (1987), pp. 203-226.

CHAPTER X

EXPLOITATION AND USE OF THE SEABED
BEYOND NATIONAL JURISDICTION

A. INTRODUCTION

As most interpretations of the 1958 Convention on the Continental Shelf make clear, national (coastal state) jurisdiction over natural resources in the seabed and subsoil does not extend to mid-ocean but terminates at some point off the coast. This limit is now established by the 1982 United Nations Convention on the Law of the Sea at 200 miles or the edge of the continental margin, whichever is farther seaward. That leaves a large portion of the floor of the ocean beyond limits of national jurisdiction. Historically the resources of that area have been considered *res nullius*, subject to appropriation by individuals or nations much in the same manner as free swimming fish beyond the limit of territorial waters. With the initiation of the debate on the "seabed question" in the General Assembly in 1967, that status has been thrown into doubt, though some Western scholars still support *res nullius* for the manganese nodules situated on the deep ocean floor.

As the law of the sea negotiations progressed toward the Third U.N. Conference on the Law of the Sea, it became clear that some new legal regime and appropriate international organization would be developed to govern mining activities on the deep seabed. At issue were the precise nature and authority of such an organization, and the rules pursuant to which such exploitation would take place. Major philosophical differences plague the negotiating states, as will be evident from the documents in this chapter. Some nations have even supported the concept of granting power to the seabed agency with respect to other uses of the area besides deep seabed mining.

The materials in this chapter are organized, following an introductory section on seabed geology, in roughly chronological order, beginning with the introduction of the seabed question to the agenda of the 1967 U.N. General Assembly and concluding with the Montago session of the Conference, held in December 1982. The history of the Conference has been discussed in Chapter 3 and will not be repeated here. Subsequent sections (D to F) are concerned with, respectively, the deep seabed mining regime provided in the 1982 Convention, the United States attitude toward that regime and domestic legislation on deep seabed mining and mini-treaties among the industrialized countries.

REFERENCES

M. I. Lazarev, "Scientific-Technological Progress and the Search for Legal Regulation of Possible Seabed Uses," *Ocean Development & International Law*, Vol. 3 (1975), pp. 75-86; *Deep Seabed Minerals: Resources, Diplomacy, and Strategic Interest*, Library of Congress Report, 95th Cong., 2d Sess., March 1, 1978; J. N. Barkenbus, *Deep Seabed Resources: Politics and Technology*, New York: Free Press, 1979.

B. SOME MARINE GEOLOGY AND SEABED MINING TECHNOLOGY

V.E. McKelvey and Frank F.H. Wang, *World Subsea Mineral Resources*, Department of the Interior, U.S. Geological Survey, 1969.

The physiography of the large ocean basins beyond the continental margin and rise is also varied but is dominated by the following features . . . : (1) Oceanic ridges and rises, often called "midoceanic" although they do not everywhere occur in midocean. These form a nearly continuous but branching world-wide mountain chain with a total length of about 75,000 miles. A rift valley along the crest is a prominent feature of the ridges in many places, as are volcanoes and volcanic fields, many of which are islands. (2) Abyssal plains and hills, lying on both sides of the oceanic rises and underlain by a thin veneer of pelagic sediments. (3) Individual volcanoes and composite volcanic ridges formed by over-lapping volcanoes, and scattered over the ocean basins but often clustered to form groups of islands or seamounts and linear chains along oceanic margins. (4) Trenches, commonly present along volcanic island arcs or young mountain chains at the periphery of the large ocean basins.

In some places small ocean basins lie between two continents or between continents and offshore island arcs. Characteristically, they have an abyssal plain below a depth of 2000 meters, and a few also have trenches along the concave side of the bordering island arcs. Those that border land areas with large surface runoff have trapped erosional debris and hence contain thick accumulations of sediments analogous to those beneath the continental rises.

Many physiographic features of the ocean basins are related to volcanism, crustal subsidence, and possibly to a process of ocean-floor spreading that brings basaltic igneous rock to the surface along the oceanic ridges, and carries new crust away from the mid-oceanic ridge at the rate of a few to 10-15 cm a year. Much is still to be learned about this process, but many now believe that the continents have split apart, along what are now these oceanic ridges, and drifted away from each other, and that the continental mass is still in the process of separation in the Atlantic Ocean, Gulf of California, Red Sea, and African rift-valley system. . . .

In contrast to continental crust, oceanic crust is thin and relatively uniform in composition. Basaltic bedrock lies at or near the surface over much of the oceanic rise and ridge; and, although sediments increase in thickness toward the edge of the ocean basin (reflecting the longer time available for their accumulation on the older parts of the ocean floor), they probably do not attain a thickness of more than a few hundred meters in most places. The basalt originates by partial melting of rocks in the underlying mantle; and while other rocks and minerals are produced in this process, they are not as varied in composition as those that result from the action and interaction of the processes operating on and within the continental crust. Nevertheless, the ocean basins contain large concentrations of manganese, nickel, copper, cobalt, and other metals in manganese-oxide nodules, crusts, and pavements on the surface of the sea bottom; and the ocean basins probably also contain these and other metals, such as zinc, mercury, chromite, and platinum, in other kinds of deposits formed from the differentiation of the mantle material from which the basalt itself was derived. . . .

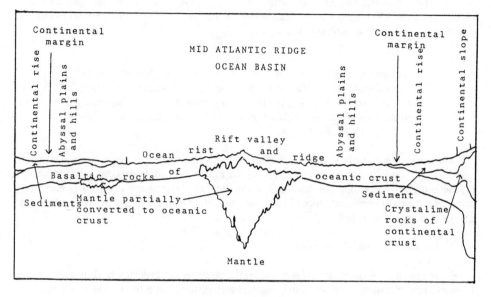

Mid-Atlantic Ridge
Figure 10-1

Manganese-Oxide Nodules

Surficial deposits of manganese-oxide nodules, crusts, and pavements, which are currently of more interest for their content of nickel, copper, and cobalt than for manganese, are largely confined to the deep ocean floor, generally at depths of 3500 to 4500 meters, and to the seamounts within it. In several areas, however, they occur near land--notably on the Blake Plateau off the eastern United States, off the west coast of Baja, California, in the Baltic Sea, and near some of the islands in large ocean basins. . . . In most of these near-shore areas, however, their metal content is much lower than that of the nodules far from land. Although bottom photographs and closely spaced samples show that nodules are extensive in many areas, the same kinds of data show that both their abundance and composition vary. Available information is not sufficient to infer their continuity between stations from which they have been reported or their absence in areas where they have not yet been found. Cores show that they are present in the sediments a few meters beneath the surface at some stations . . . where they are not present at the surface. Inspection of the results of available bottom photographs in the Pacific . . . however, suggests that nodules are absent from the surface of the bottom in some large areas and that they are particularly abundant in others. . . . Even if subsequent exploration shows that the nodules and related deposits are continuous over large areas, the minability may be adversely affected locally by irregularity of the bottom surface, presence of extensive crusts or pavements troublesome to break and lift, and deleterious impurities.

The composition of the nodules also varies greatly. Again there appear to be regional variations, but published attempts to define the pattern of variation have not been satisfactory. . . . Manganese is nearly 50 percent in some samples, which are generally low in the other metals. Copper and nickel tend to vary in rough proportion to each other and may be as much as 2 percent; cobalt also may be as much as 2 percent. Whether or not minable quantities contain such concentrations remains to be demonstrated.

The nodules constitute a huge resource. Mero . . . estimates that they aggregate 1.7 trillion tons and contain 400 billion tons of manganese, 16.4 billion tons of nickel, 8.8 billion tons of copper, and 918 billion tons of cobalt. . . .

> "Economic Implications of Sea-Bed Mineral Development in the International Area: Report of the Secretary-General," U.N. Doc. A/CONF.62/25 (May 22, 1974), in Third United Nations Conference on the Law of the Sea, *Official Records*, Vol. III (Documents of the Conference), pp. 8-14.

Deep sea-bed mining is a complex, multifaceted undertaking. Exploitation of nodules may be classified into three broad stages, namely: (1) the search for nodule deposits, (2) mining, and (3) metallurgical processing. A summary of the most important steps involved in each stage along with the most recent activities of companies and other institutions involved in research and development is presented below.

1. *The search for nodule deposits*

In the search for nodules, activities of a scientific character can generally be distinguished from the stages of exploration and evaluation because of their different objectives. Together they form a continuum in the accumulation of knowledge about sea-bed resources needed prior to commencement of commercial mining operations, and it is difficult to define where the scientific inquiry ends and the stage of exploration begins and where this stage ends and evaluation starts.

(a) *Procedures used*

Exploration is the broadly based survey using all available methods: the search generally begins over a large area and progressively narrows down to sites with mining potential. In industry circles this stage is generally referred to as "prospecting." It requires mapping, sampling of surficial and sub-bottom materials and making geophysical and geochemical measurements, and is best approached as a phased programme of increasingly more detailed surveys.

A large array of scientific instruments and devices are required to collect the necessary data. . . . Exploration vessels must carry sophisticated positioning equipment (satellite, celestial) and computers to correlate all sample data and other observations with precise coordinates. Acoustic and magnetic systems are used to obtain geophysical information about the nature of the sea bottom. The actual search for nodule deposits is made through optical systems such as closed-circuit T.V. and still and movie cameras.

The spacing at which samples are taken depends on results obtained, and generally range from 5 to 50 miles. The devices most commonly used for collecting samples are the free-fall sampler also called "boomerang," gravity-corer, piston-corer and dredge. The free-fall sample is extensively used by institutions and industry groups such as Kennecott, Centre national pour l'exploitation des océans (CNEXO), Preussag and Global Marine. These free-fall devices grab a small sample of nodules from an area of about 1 square foot. Corers are used to derive information on the sediments underlying the nodule deposit. Dredge sampling is used to collect a large volume of nodules for metallurgical testing from areas known to contain attractive nodule deposits.

A detailed appraisal follows the discovery and outlining of a potential mine site. The objective is to provide information upon which to base feasibility studies. Recoverable nodule grade and concentration estimates are the key parameters sought in evaluation surveys. The equipment required for evaluation is similar to that needed for the exploration stage. However, greater attention must be given to the precise correlation of sample data and other observations with their geographic location. . . .

2. *Nodule mining technology*

The mining systems under development comprise four major components: the mining/loading head; materials elevation/hoisting system; surface facility; and product transportation to shore plant. . . . [See Figure 10-2.]

(a) *Nodule collection*

Several forms of nodule gathering apparatus are under development. The dredge variety currently is thought to have the best potential for use in commercial production. Typically the dredge incorporates a sizing system to pick up nodules within a certain size range while excluding very large pieces as well as fine bottom silt. It is usually sufficient to drag the dredge head across the ocean floor to loosen the nodules from the substratum. The mining equipment must be kept as mechanically simple as possible to minimize maintenance. One problem encountered, however, is the construction and operation of the very wide dredge head needed to collect the desired volume of nodules per hour (200 to 400 tons). The large dredge size is required because of the relatively low nodule concentration at the sea floor (1.5 to 5 lb/sq. ft.) and the maximum practical speed for operation of the system (1 to 3 knots). . . .

(b) *Materials elevation*

Another critical factor in nodule mining is the materials elevation/hoisting system. Continuous systems can be based on: air lift, hydrolift (hydraulic hoisting), light-media lift and mechanical lift such as the CLB [Continuous Line Bucket] system. Batch systems include wireline dredging which, although useful for collecting tonnage samples, is not regarded as an economic large-scale production system due to its high cost when used at great depths. A buoyant hopper (submersible hopper) system has been proposed. Whether this system is being developed for materials elevation is not known, although the concept is somewhat akin to the Summa Corporation barge.

An air-lift is technically a three phase flow--air, nodules, and water. Compressed air is injected into the main pipe at various water depths to sustain the lifting action. Deepsea Ventures successfully tested an airlift device in 2,500 feet of water over the Blake Plateau in 1970. . . .

A hydrolift is technically a two-phase flow--nodules and water. The pump can be located close to the bottom or at an intermediate depth. . . . The technology for hydraulic and hydrolift pumping is well-developed and is used, for instance, in the coal industry. But working at such depths and lifting such volumes as required in nodule mining represent giant steps beyond current capability. . . .

The Hughes system is thought to operate on the hydro-lift principle. The major components of the system are the 36,000-ton Hughes Glomar Explorer and a sea floor mining vehicle which is connected to the ship by a string of 16-inch pipe and an umbilical cable that supplies electric power and control circuits. A large submersible barge plays a key role in the system. The mining vehicle is too large and heavy to be handled by the ship's gear in a conventional manner and must be installed from beneath the ship. The unit is loaded onto the submersible barge which meets the ship in calm waters of a specified depth. There, the barge submerges and the docking legs of the ship engage the mining vehicle which is then connected to pipestring lowered from the ship's rugged derrick. . . .

The CLB system uses a continuous polypropylene braided rope with dredge buckets attached. At the top, the loop is wound through traction motors while the bottom part of the loop drags along the ocean bottom. The CLB system was tested off Tahiti in August 1970. A later CLB test in August/September 1972 recovered seven tons of nodules off Hawaii. Several participants of the CLB consortium under the leadership of CNEXO of France are continuing work on a modification of the CLB, which would use two ships working in tandem; . . . the main components of this modified system are expected to be ready for tests in 1974. Sumitomo is developing continuous ship handling equipment for the dredge baskets and is also doing additional research in the operation of the CLB system.

(c) Surface vessel

The so-called first generation mining systems are likely to use the ship itself as the surface platform. Tug assistance may be used for directional movement in some systems. A pipe system for nodule lifting will require a derrick on board ship. Alternatives to a mine ship are a spar buoy or a semi-submersible platform. A spar buoy is a long cigar-shaped semi-submersible which when tilted on one end creates a small but highly stable working platform on its other end. Semi-submersible floating platforms are extensively used in the off-shore oil industry for work in deeper waters. . . . Both the spar buoy and the semi-submersibles, however, have a poor capability for lateral movement.

The first generation of mining ships will do minimal processing at sea--perhaps crushing and/or drying the nodules--and the nodules will be transported in bulk by the mining ship itself (particularly a CLB mining ship) or transferred at sea to a dry or bulk carrier.

3. Metallurgical processing

Nodules have a complex microscopic structure and are composed of fine-grained oxide material. They can vary widely in chemical and physical properties according to location, e.g., Blake Plateau nodules from the Atlantic are high in calcium, whereas those from the North Pacific are more siliceous. As a result, processing technology and costs for one type of nodule may not apply elsewhere. . . .

The two basic approaches to nodule processing can be classified as pyrometallurgical and hydrometallurgical, the latter based on chloride, ammonia or sulfur oxide reaction. Some of these processes are considered technically possible, but not necessarily economically feasible. Heavy emphasis is being placed on the development of hydrometallurgical nodule processing systems.

REFERENCES

(1) *On Geology.* Charles H. Cotter, *The Physical Geography of the Oceans*, New York: American Elsevier Publishing Co., 1966; F.P. Shepard, *The Earth Beneath the Sea*, rev. ed., Baltimore: Johns Hopkins Press, 1967; P.A. Rona and L.T. Neuman, "Energy and Mineral Resources of the Pacific Region in Light of Plate Tectonics," *Ocean Management*, Vol. 3(1) (1976), pp. 57-78; K.O. Emery and B.J. Skinner, "Mineral Deposits of the Deep-Ocean Floor," *Marine Mining*, Vol. 1 (1977), pp. 1-71.

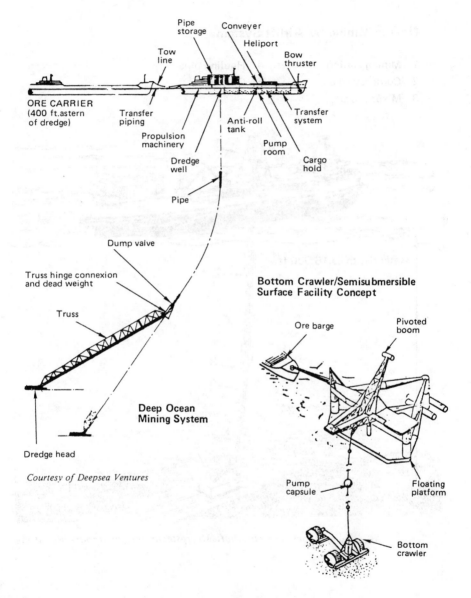

Deepsea Ventures Ocean Mining System
Figure 10-2

Source: Third United Nations Conference on the Law of the Sea, *Official Records*, Vol. III, *Documents of the Conference*, p. 11.

Nodule Mining by Airlift System

1 Mining station	4 Hauling pipe
2 Compressed air	5 Collector
3 Mixer nozzles	

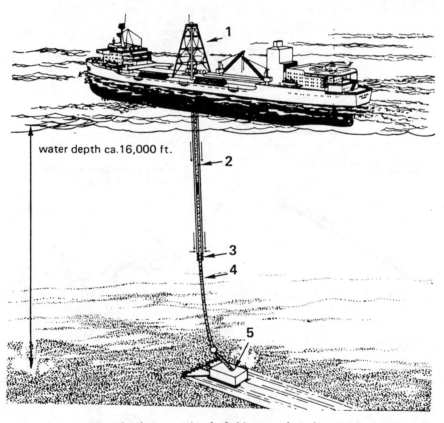

water depth ca.16,000 ft.

Courtesy of Arbeitsgemeinschaft Meerestechnischgewinnbare Rohstoffe

Nodule Mining by Airlift System
Figure 10-3

Source: Third United Nations Conference on the Law of the Sea, *Official Records*, Vol.
III, *Documents of the Conference*, p. 11.

(2) *On Nodules*. J.L. Mero, "Minerals on the Ocean Floor," *Scientific American*, Vol. 203 (No. 6) (1960), pp. 64-72; J.L. Mero, *The Mineral Resources of the Sea*, Amsterdam-London-New York: Elsevier Publishing Company, 1965; D.B. Brooks, "Deep Sea Manganese Nodules: From Scientific Phenomena to World Resources," *Natural Resources Journal*, Vol. 8(3) (1968), pp. 401-423; D.R. Horn, "Worldwide Distribution of Manganese Nodules," *Ocean Industry*, Vol. 7 (1972), pp. 26-29; F.M. Auburn, "Some Legal Problems of the Commercial Exploitation of Manganese Nodules in the Pacific Ocean," *Ocean Development and International Law*, Vol. 1 (1973), pp. 185-201; H.D. Drechsler, "Exploitation of the Sea: A Preliminary Cost-Benefit Analysis of Nodule Mining and Processing," *Maritime Studies and Management*, Vol. 1 (1973), pp. 53-66; O.C. Herfindahl, "Some Problems in the Exploitation of Manganese Nodules," in L.M. Alexander, ed., *The Law of the Sea: Needs and Interests of the Developing Countries*, Kingston: University of Rhode Island, 1973, pp. 28-40; "Ocean Manganese Nodules," Senate Committee on Interior and Insular Affairs (94th Congress, 1st Session, June 1975); "Ocean Manganese Nodules, Second Edition," Senate Committee on Interior and Insular Affairs (94th Congress, 2nd Session, February, 1976); E.N. Cameron, "Our Mineral Problems: The Context of Ocean Mining," *Marine Mining*, Vol. 1 (1977), pp. 73-84; J.Z. Frazer, "Manganese Nodule Reserves: An Updated Estimate," *Marine Mining*, Vol. 1 (1977), pp. 103-123; J. Greenslate, "Manganese Concentration Wet Density: A Marine Geochemistry Constant," *Marine Mining*, Vol. 1 (1977), pp. 125-148; K.M. Keith, "Manganese Nodule Processing in Hawaii--An Environmental Prospectus," *Hawaii Bar Journal*, Vol. 14 (1978), pp. 103-121; H.W. Menard and J.Z. Frazer, "Manganese Nodules on the Sea Floor: Inverse Correlation Between Grade and Abundance," *Science*, Vol. 199 (March 3, 1978), p. 969-971; J.E. Andrews and G.H.W. Friedrich, "Distribution Patterns of Manganese Nodule Deposits in the Northeast Equatorial Pacific," *Marine Mining*, Vol. 2 (1-2) (1979), pp. 1-43; K.N. Han, et al., "The Effect of Temperature on the Physio-Chemical Characteristics of Deep-Sea Manganese Nodules," *Marine Mining*, Vol. 2 (1979), pp. 131-149; Peter Halbach, "Deep-Sea Metallic Deposits," *Ocean Management*, Vol. 9 (1984), pp. 35-60; Ronald K. Sorem, "Manganese Nodules as Ore: Research Methods and Applications," *Marine Mining*, Vol. 8, No. 2 (1989), pp. 185-200.

(3) *On Marine Mining*. W. Bascom, "Mining in the Sea," in L.M. Alexander, ed., *The Law of the Sea: Offshore Boundaries and Zones*, Columbus, Ohio: Ohio State University Press, 1967, pp. 160-167; G. Pontecorvo, "Reflections on the Economics of the Common Heritage of Mankind: The Organisation of the Deep-Sea Mining Industry and the Expected Benefits from Resource Exploitation," *Ocean Development and International Law*, Vol. 2 (1974), pp. 203-216; J.E. Flipse, "Deep Ocean Mining Technology and its Impact on the Law of the Sea," in F.T. Christy, ed., *Law of the Sea: Caracas and Beyond*, Cambridge, Mass., Ballinger, 1975, pp. 325-333; C.C. Joyner, ed., *International Law of the Sea and the Future of Deep Seabed Mining*, Charlottesville, Virginia: Accent Printing Co., 1975; J.L. Mero, "The Great Nodule Controversy," in F.T. Christy, ed., *Law of the Sea: Caracas and Beyond*, Cambridge, Mass., Ballinger, 1975, pp. 343-350; J.E. Flipse, "The Science, Engineering, Economics, and Politics of Ocean Hard Mineral Development," Proceedings, 4th Annual Sea Grant Lecture, MIT Publishing No. MIT-W-75-001, 1976; A. Xavier, "The Exploitation of Deep-Sea Manganese Nodules: Progress and Prospects, *Maritime Policy and Management*, Vol. 4 (July, 1976), pp. 33-40; *The Deep Seabed and Its Mineral Resources, Proceedings of the Third International Ocean Symposium*, November 15-17, 1978, Japan Shipping Club, Tokyo: Ocean Association of Japan, 1979; J.C. Agarwal, et al., "Comparative Economics of Recovery of Metals from Ocean Nodules," *Marine Mining*, Vol. 2 (1-2) (1979), pp. 119-130; R. Young, "Inducement for Exploration by Companies," *Syracuse Journal of International Law & Commerce*, Vol. 6 (1979), pp. 199-205; E.M. Borgese and P.M.T. White, eds., *Seabed Mining: Scientific, Economic, Political Aspects: An Interdisciplinary Manual*, Msida, Malta: International Ocean Institute [1981]; H. Cameron, L.G. Georghiou, J.G. Perry and P. Wiley, "The Economic Feasibility of Deep-Sea Mining," *Engineering Costs and Production*

Economics, Vol. 5 (1981), pp. 279-287; T. Marjoram, H. Cameron, G. Ford, Angela Garner and M. Gibbons, "Manganese Nodules and Marine Technology," *Resources Policy*, Vol. 7 (1981), pp. 45-57; K.M. Shusterich, "Mining the Deep Seabed: A Complex and Innovative Study," *Marine Policy*, Vol. 6 (1982), pp. 175-192; M.A. Post, *Deepsea Mining and the Law of the Sea*, The Hague: Nijhoff, 1983; Jean-Pierre Lévy and N.A. Odunton, "Economic Impact of Sea-Bed Mineral Resources Development in Light of the Convention on the Law of the Sea," *Natural Resources Forum*, Vol. 8 (1984), pp. 147-161; William J. Broad, "Undersea Robots Open a New Age of Exploration," *New York Times*, November 13, 1990, pp. C1, C6.

C. THE SEABED QUESTION AT THE UNITED NATIONS AND THE THIRD UNITED NATIONS CONFERENCE ON THE LAW OF THE SEA

1.   Legal Status of the Seabed Beyond National Jurisdiction and the Question of the Freedom of the High Seas

> D.P. O'Connell, *The International Law of the Sea*, edited by I.A. Shearer, Vol. 1, New York: Oxford University Press, 1982, pp. 457-458. Footnotes omitted. Reprinted by permission of Oxford University Press.

The question whether the seabed is *res nullius* or *res communis* has been thought to be critical to any investigation of the law governing the recovery of minerals from the seabed and subsoil "beyond the limits of national jurisdiction" (i.e., beyond the limits of the continental shelf or the EEZ, whichever is the more extensive). If the seabed is *res nullius*, then individual States could acquire title to it and exercise sovereignty over it in the same way as on land, whereas if it is *res communis*, it is not susceptible of appropriation at all.

In fact, the issue between these two possible views of the status of the abyssal seafloor is not as sharp as it may appear, because, even if the seabed is to be characterized as *res nullius*, the requirement for the acquisition and consolidation of title would not be easily met. It would be insufficient to rely upon paper claims to sovereignty; these would need to be supported by a physical presence sufficiently permanent to guarantee the exclusion of others. And while the rules of international law for acquisition of title in remote and inhospitable places are loose and adaptable, they are at least sufficiently rigorous to deny that title could be based only upon spasmodic acts of recovery of minerals. The situation in this respect is likely to be what it was in the seventeenth century in seas over which sovereignty was claimed: the ephemeral presence of fleets was deemed insufficient to create exclusive rights, and their permanent presence proved impracticable.

Therefore, in practice it would seem that occupation of the seabed could only occur in the cases of seamounts or guyots where a physical presence would be possible. Exploration blocks of the seabed may be granted by governments, but it is difficult to conceive how entrepreneurs could establish themselves there so as to exclude others, or how limits could be drawn to the size of such blocks by acts of exploration.

The likely outcome of exploration and exploitation of the abyssal seabed would be, therefore, competition between nations on the basis of the freedom of the seas. In that sense, the case of deep-sea mining would be legally no different from that of high seas fishing: a recovery vessel would take what resources it could by suction or drilling or scooping, without these actions conferring upon its flag State any rights to the area; and other nations' vessels would be free to do the same in the same areas and at the same time, subject to observance of the rules of the road. The suggestion has been made that flag-State activity could confer flag-State "jurisdiction" over the area subject to the activity, but this is not plausible considering the evolutionary history of the freedom of the seas, and in any event would offer a very insecure title.

The real issue in the characterization of the seabed is whether there is any right at all to exploit the mineral resources of the seabed beyond the limits of national jurisdiction. If the seabed is *res nullius*, or if the doctrine of the freedom of the seas applies, there is that right. But because a *res communis* is said to be beyond appropriation, the inference is sometimes drawn that if the seabed is so characterized, there is no right to exploit at all without international sanction. To that extent, the characterization of the seabed as *res communis* is tendentious. But, like the concept of *res nullius*, the concept of *res communis* is also ambiguous; it can be regarded as endorsing common, or unrestricted, exploitation as much as outlawing exploitation altogether.

REFERENCES

Richard J. Grunawalt, "The Acquisition of the Resources of the Bottom of the Sea--A New Frontier of International Law," *Military Law Review*, Vol. 34 (1966), pp. 101-133; E.D. Brown, "Deep-Sea Mining: The Legal Regime of 'Inner Space,'" *Yearbook of World Affairs*, Vol. 22 (1968), pp. 165-190; David S. Browning, "Exploitation of Submarine Mineral Resources Beyond the Continental Shelf," *Texas International Forum*, Vol. 4 (1968), pp. 1-27; Francis T. Christy, Jr., "Alternative Regimes for Marine Resources Underlying the High Seas," *Natural Resources Lawyer*, Vol. 1 (1968), pp. 63-77; Francis T. Christy, Jr., "Communications: A Social Scientist Writes on Economic Criteria for Rules Governing Exploitation of Deep Sea Minerals," *The International Lawyer*, Vol. 2 (1968), pp. 224-242; Robert A. Creamer, "Title to the Deep Sea-Bed: Prospects for the Future," *Harvard International Law Journal*, Vol. 9 (1968), pp. 205-231; A. Pardo, "Who Will Control the Seabed?," *Foreign Affairs*, Vol. 47 (October, 1968), pp. 123-137; Steven J. Burton, "Freedom of the Seas: International Law Applicable to Deep Seabed Mining Claims," *Stanford Law Review*, Vol. 29 (1977), pp. 1135-1180; Bernard H. Oxman, "The High Seas and the International Seabed Area," *Michigan Journal of International Law*, Vol. 10 (1989), pp. 526-542.

2.   **At the United Nations and the Third Law of the Sea Conference**

D.P. O'Connell, *The International Law of the Sea*, edited by I.A. Shearer, Vol. 1, New York and London: Oxford University Press, 1982, pp. 459-464. Footnotes omitted. Reprinted by permission of Oxford University Press.

(1) The Moratorium

The idea of putting bounds to the search for minerals of the seabed was put forward in 1967 by the delegate of Malta to the United Nations. He pointed out that recent recoveries of manganese nodules from the floor of the ocean at great depths portended a race on the part of the technologically equipped nations to exploit this newly revealed resource, which would thus accrue to the benefit of the rich and developed countries when really it was a resource that could be said to belong to mankind. He gave some figures of exploitable quantities and values, and argued that if the resource was subject to international control and the benefit distributed to developing countries, the world economy would be transformed. The figures were uncritically accepted by many at the time, although they assumed, wrongly as it turned out, that the continental slope would lie beyond the limits of national jurisdiction, and they took little account of the extent of risk capital needed, the economics of marketing, or the effect of seabed recoveries upon the price of land-recovered minerals.

Malta introduced a resolution which aimed to exclude the ocean floor "beyond the limits of national jurisdiction" from national appropriation, and would permit the exploration of the ocean floor to be undertaken only in a manner consistent with the principles and purposes of the United Nations Charter; provided for the use of the ocean floor and its economic exploitation to be undertaken only with the aim of safeguarding the interests of mankind; designated the financial benefits derived from the use and exploitation of the ocean floor as primarily to promote the development of poorer countries; and proclaimed that the ocean floor should be reserved exclusively for peaceful purposes.

The resolution then proposed the establishment of an international agency to regulate, supervise, and control all ocean floor activities beyond the limits of national jurisdiction. This agency would assume jurisdiction as a trustee for all countries over the ocean floor, would regulate, supervise and control all activities thereon; and would ensure that the activities undertaken would conform to the principles of the provisions of an international seabed treaty established to embody the proposals.

These proposals were accepted in a mood of unbridled optimism and enthusiasm, and provoked a series of symposia, conferences and juristic papers. At the United Nations level, a first step towards its implementation was taken on 18 December 1967 when the General Assembly established an *ad hoc* committee of thirty-five members to study the matter. This committee met three times, but while there was universal lip-service paid to the moral objectives of the proposal, there was disagreement on the nature and functions of the seabed authority which would be set up to supervise exploration. The major industrial powers did not support the setting up of a permanent committee to study the establishment of such an authority. Nonetheless, the following year the General Assembly set up such a committee of forty-two members, called the Seabed Committee, with a mandate to study the legal principles and norms that would promote international cooperation in the exploration and use of the seabed and subsoil beyond the limits of national jurisdiction, and the means of encouraging the exploitation and use of the resources of this area in the light of foreseeable technological development and economic implications, bearing in mind the fact that such exploitation should benefit mankind as a whole.

The Seabed Committee submitted its report in 1969 to the First Committee of the General Assembly. This revealed that, while there was general agreement that part of the ocean floor lay outside the limits of national jurisdiction, there was little agreement as to what those limits were, and consequently how large the excluded area would be. The report stated that the concept that the resources of the seabed beyond these limits "are the common heritage of mankind" was "widely supported but not acceptable to all"; and that, while there was a general consensus on the establishment of a regime on the use of the resources of the ocean floor for the benefit of mankind, irrespective of the geographical location of States and taking into account the special interest and need of the developing countries, little progress was made on the functions, structure and geographical competence of such a regime.

The General Assembly, in accepting this report, raised the question of a Third Law of the Sea Conference. Because the Committee's debates had revealed that agreement on deep-sea mining was unlikely to be reached without some trading off, other aspects of the Law of the Sea had inevitably intruded; and so the General Assembly envisaged that the Conference would review the regimes of the high seas, the continental shelf, territorial sea, contiguous zone, fishing and conservation of the living resources of the high seas, although it would be convened "particularly in order to arrive at a clear, precise and internationally accepted definition of the area of the seabed and ocean floor which lies beyond the limits of national jurisdiction, the type of international regime to be established for that area."

Since it would take some time to convene the Conference, and in the meantime it was feared that there would develop a scramble for the recovery of manganese nodules, the General Assembly adopted what became known as the Moratorium Resolution on 15 December 1969. This declared that, pending the establishment of the proposed international regime, States and persons "are bound to refrain from all activities of exploitation of the resources of the area of the seabed and ocean floor, and the subsoil thereof, beyond the limits of national jurisdiction. . . ." It added that no claim to any part of that area or its resources should be recognized.

The legal status of the Moratorium Resolution has been the subject of debate. Certain major powers dissented; one or two took the position that the resolution was recommendatory in character only, and not binding. On the other hand, Governments did make efforts to curb attempts at exploiting the abyssal seabed, and it is a fact that such attempts have not been made on any scale, although this probably is due as much to economic as to legal and political considerations.

On 17 December 1970, the General Assembly adopted a resolution proclaiming the principles governing the seabed beyond the limits of national jurisdiction. It reiterated the doctrine of the common heritage of mankind, and stated that exploration should be carried out for the benefit of mankind. . . .

The motivation leading to a degree of consensus as to the desirability of regulating deep-sea mining has been that unregulated exploitation could become anarchic and lead to confrontations in the high seas, while want of security might lead to reluctance to put risk capital at work in exploitation from which others might then profit. Industry as well as governments would prefer a licensing system, but too much regulation or restrictive practices on the part of an international seabed authority could be an even greater deterrent to enterprise than total liberty. The problem that proved central in the work of the Enlarged Seabed Committee leading to the Third Law of the Sea Conference was how to provide some element of security of tenure for exploitation while at the same time minimizing the risk of discrimination on the basis of national wealth, political complexion or otherwise.

The structure of an international seabed authority was thus the central question. One proposal was that such an authority should itself engage, exclusively or in collaboration with private enterprise, in exploitation, this being the idea most consonant with the notion of "the heritage of mankind." Another was that the authority would merely license private enterprise on blocks of the seabed, although this might be done either directly by the authority itself or through the medium of governments. And a third was that the authority should be merely a supervisory and consultative body.

(2) The Third Law of the Sea Conference

The proposals made at the Conference, to develop the theories respecting the seabed which had been accumulated during the period of work of the Seabed Committee, took the form of designating the seabed and ocean floor and subsoil thereof everywhere beyond the limits of national jurisdiction (meaning beyond the limits of the EEZ or of the continental shelf, whichever is the greater) as the "Area"; and this, together with its "resources," which means minerals *in situ*, is proclaimed "the common heritage of mankind." No State may claim or exercise sovereignty or sovereign rights over any part of the Area or its resources, nor may any State or natural or juridical person appropriate any part thereof. No such claim or exercise of sovereignty or sovereign rights, nor any such appropriation, shall be recognized by other States.

REFERENCES

R.B. Bilder. "Emerging Legal Problems of the Deep Seas and Polar Regions," *Naval War College Review*, Vol. 20 (5) (1967), pp. 34-49; Northcutt Ely, "American Policy Options in the Development of Undersea Mineral Resources," *International Lawyer*, Vol. 2 (1968), pp. 215-223; Arthur J. Goldberg, "U.N. Establishes Ad Hoc Committee to Study Use of Ocean Floor," *Department of State Bulletin*, Vol. 58, No. 1491 (January 22, 1968), pp. 125-127; Herman Pollack, "National Interest, Foreign Affairs, and the Marine Sciences," *Department of State Bulletin*, Vol. 58, No. 1494 (February 12, 1968), pp. 211-215; David H. Popper, "U.S. Calls for Broad Inquiry on Peaceful Uses of the Seabed," *Department of State Bulletin*, Vol. 58, No. 1504 (April 22, 1968), pp. 543-545; "Reservation of the Sea-Bed and Ocean Floor for Peaceful Purposes," *U.N. Monthly Chronicle*, Vol. 5, No. 1 (January 1968), pp. 28-40; Joseph J. Sisco, "Recent International Developments Concerning the Ocean Floor," *Department of State Bulletin*, Vol. 58, No. 1488 (January 1, 1968), pp. 17-19; L.F. Ballah, "Activities of the United Nations General Assembly since 1966 Relating to the Seabed and Ocean Floor," in L.M. Alexander, ed., *The Law of the Sea: The United Nations and Ocean Management*, Kingston: University of Rhode Island, 1971, p. 29-33.

NOTE ON THE WORK OF THE AD HOC COMMITTEE

The *Ad Hoc* Committee held three sessions (United Nations Headquarters, March 18-27, 1968, and June 17-July 9, 1968; Rio de Janeiro, August 19-30, 1968). Two working groups were established, one concerned with economic and technical aspects of the item, the other concerned with the legal aspects. The Chairman of the *Ad Hoc* Committee was Mr. Hamilton Shirley Amerasinghe of Ceylon; the Chairman of the Economic and Technical Working Group was Mr. Roger Denorme of Belgium; and the chairman of the Legal Working Group was Mr. Leopoldo Benites of Ecuador. The "Report of the *Ad Hoc* Committee to Study the Peaceful Uses of the Sea-Bed and the Ocean Floor Beyond the Limits of National Jurisdiction," U.N. Doc. A/7230, was adopted by the Committee on August 30, 1968, and was subsequently delivered to the twenty-third session of the General Assembly.

The Report of the *Ad Hoc* Committee was included on the agenda of the twenty-third session of the General Assembly and was allocated to the First Committee (Political and Security) for consideration and report. The First Committee considered the item from October 28 to November 11, and from December 18 to December 20, 1968. At the conclusion of its deliberations, the First Committee recommended to the General Assembly the adoption of four draft resolutions. The General Assembly considered the recommendations of the First Committee at its 1752nd meeting held on December 21, 1968. All of the resolutions were adopted by the General Assembly without modification.

For the work of this Committee, see *Yearbook of the United Nations 1967*, pp. 41-49 and . . . *1968*, pp. 69-84; "Ad Hoc Committee on Peaceful Uses of Seabed: Holds First Session," *UN Monthly Chronicle*, Vol. 5, No. 4 (April 1968), pp. 50-51, ". . .: Begins Second Session," No. 7 (July-August 1968), pp. 46-49, ". . .: Adopts Report to Assembly," No. 2 (September 1968), pp. 97-100; David H. Popper, "The Deep Ocean Environment: US and International Policy,"

Department of State Bulletin, Vol. 59, No. 1520 (August 12, 1968), pp. 171-177; "Reservation of the Sea-Bed and Ocean Floor for Peaceful Purposes," *U.N. Monthly Chronicle*, Vol. 5, No. 11 (December 1968), pp. 53-61; Peter S. Thacher, "U.S. Reviews Word of 2nd Session of U.N. Ad Hoc Committee on Seabed," *Department of State Bulletin*, Vol 59, No. 1521 (August 5, 1968), pp. 150-153; James Russell Wiggins, "U.S. Suggests Possible Steps by U.N. to Promote Peaceful Uses of the Deep Ocean Floor," *Department of State Bulletin*, Vol. 59, No. 1535 (November 25, 1968), pp. 554-558; *Report of the First Committee--Examination of the Question of the Reservation Exclusively for Peaceful Purposes of the Sea-Bed and the Ocean Floor, and the Subsoil thereof, Underlying the High Seas Beyond the Limits of Present National Jurisdiction, and the Use of their Resources in the Interests of Mankind*, U.N. Doc. A/7477 (December 20, 1968); G. Winthrop Haight, "The Seabed and the Ocean Floor," *International Lawyer*, Vol. 3 (1969), pp. 642-681; K.K. Rao, "The Legal Regime of the Sea-Bed and Ocean Floor," *Indian Journal of International Law*, Vol. 9 (1969), pp. 1-18; "Reservation of the Sea-Bed and Ocean Floor for Peaceful Purposes," *U.N. Monthly Chronicle*, Vol. 6, No. 1 (January 1969), pp. 56-62.

NOTE ON THE WORK OF THE SEABED COMMITTEE

Beginning in 1969 and continuing through 1973 the U.N. Seabed Committee met twice annually. One meeting was held in the spring, the other in late summer. Following each meeting, resolutions were proposed and adopted by the U.N. General Assembly. The substantive machinations of the Committee are too detailed for inclusion in this book. However, the references contain citations to both the *United Nations Monthly Chronicle* and the *Department of State Bulletin* (U.S.) which provide a narrative account of the major issues discussed. Analytical references are also included.

The Seabed Committee established two working subcommittees at its meeting of February 6, 1969. These subcommittees were designated as the (1) Economic and Technical Subcommittee and (2) Legal Subcommittee. The full Committee held three sessions in 1969: February 6-7, March 10-28, and August 11-29. The Economic and Technical Subcommittee met from March 11-27 and August 12-28, 1969, and the Legal Subcommittee met from March 12-26 and August 11-28, 1969. The Economic and Technical Subcommittee presented its Report (U.N. Doc. A/AC.138/17) to the Committee, and on August 28, 1969, the Legal Subcommittee presented its Report (U.N. Doc. A/AC.138/18 and Add. 1). The full committee's report was subsequently published as U.N. Document No. A/7622. Further work by the Seabed Committee through December, 1969 included the preparation of a Study [as requested by General Assembly Resolution 2467 C (XXIII)] on the question of establishing in due time appropriate international machinery for the promotion of the exploration and exploitation of the resources of the deep ocean floor (U.N. Doc. A/AC.138/12, June 18, 1969).

For the work of this Committee, see *Yearbook of the United Nations 1969*, pp. 57-70, . . .*1970*, pp. 60-83, . . .*1971*, pp. 46-49, . . .*1972*, pp. 31-40 and . . .*1973*, pp. 38-46; U. Alexis Johnson, "Department Reviews History of International Efforts Governing Activities on the Seabed," *Department of State Bulletin*, Vol. 61 (1969), pp. 191-194; "Peaceful Uses of the Seabed," *U.N. Monthly Chronicle*, Vol. 6, No. 7 (July-August, 1969), pp. 126-128; Christopher H. Phillips and Vincent E. McKelvey, "August Session of UN Seabed Committee Held at New York," *Department of State Bulletin*, Vol. 61, No. 1579 (September 29, 1969), pp. 285-294; David H. Popper, "U.N. Seabed Committee Concludes Spring Session," *Department of State Bulletin*, Vol. 60, No. 1556 (April 21, 1969), pp. 342-345; "Reservation of the Sea-Bed and Ocean Floor for Peaceful Purposes: Standing Committee Holds First Session," *U.N. Monthly Chronicle*, Vol. 6, No. 3 (March 1969), pp. 9-10 and ". . .: Committee Holds Second Session," No. 4 (April 1969), pp. 53-56; David S. Browning. "The United Nations and Marine Resources,"

William & Mary Law Review, Vol. 10 (1969), pp. 690-740; Jared G. Carter, "The Seabed Beyond the Limits of National Jurisdiction," *Stanford Journal of International Studies*, Vol. 4 (1969), pp. 1-31; "Committee on Peaceful Uses of the Sea-Bed: Special Session Held," *U.N. Monthly Chronicle*, Vol. 6, No. 11 (December, 1969), pp. 78-80; "Peaceful Uses of the Sea-Bed: Committee Concludes General Debate," *U.N. Monthly Chronicle*, Vol. 6, No. 11 (December 1969), pp. 60-66; G. W. Haight, "Sea-Bed Discussions in the Twenty-Fourth General Assembly," *Natural Resources Lawyer*, Vol. 3 (1970), pp. 405-429; Avid Pardo, "Development of Ocean Space--An International Dilemma," *Louisiana Law Review*, Vol. 31 (1970), pp. 45-72; "Reservation of the Sea-Bed and Ocean Floor for Peaceful Purposes," *U.N. Monthly Chronicle*, Vol. 7, No. 1 (January 1970), pp. 72-80; William Rogers, "U.S. Gives Views on Convening Conference on Law of the Sea, *Department of State Bulletin*, Vol. 63, No. 1620 (July 13, 1970), pp. 38-39; John R. Stevenson, "International Law and the Oceans," *Department of State Bulletin*, Vol. 62, No. 1603 (March 6, 1970), pp. 339-343; J.L. Lovald, "In Search of an Ocean Regime: The Negotiations in the General Assembly's Seabed Committee 1968-1970," *International Organization*, Vol. 29, (1975), pp. 681-709; Paul Laurence Saffo, "The Common Heritage of Mankind: Has the General Assembly Created a Law to Govern Seabed Mining?" *Tulane Law Review*, Vol. 53 (1979), pp. 492-520; "Draft U.N. Convention on the International Seabed Area: U.S. Working Paper Submitted to U.N. Seabeds Committee," *Department of State Bulletin*, Vol. 63, No. 1626 (August 24, 1970), pp. 209-218; Richard M. Nixon, "United States Policy for the Seabed," *Department of State Bulletin*, Vol. 62, No. 1616 (June 15, 1970), pp. 737-741; "Peaceful Uses of the Sea-Bed: Committee Adopts Report," *U.N. Monthly Chronicle*, Vol. 7, No. 8 (July-August, 1970), pp. 40-43; "Reservation of the Sea-Bed and Ocean Floor for Peaceful Purposes: Committee Begins 1970 Work," *U.N. Monthly Chronicle*, Vol. 7, No. 4 (April 1970), pp. 40-43; "Peaceful Use of Seabed," *U.N. Monthly Chronicle*, Vol. 8, No. 1 (January 1971), pp. 37-42; ". . .: Committee Holds Session," No. 4 (April 1971), pp. 21-26; ". . .: Committee Adopts Report," No. 8 (August-September 1971), pp. 51-54; "Peaceful Uses of the Seabed: Committee Concludes Session," *U.N. Monthly Chronicle*, Vol. 9, No. 4 (April 1972), pp. 36-42. The reports and certain documents of the Seabed Committee are published in *Report of the Committee on the Peaceful Uses of the Sea-Bed and the Ocean Floor Beyond the Limits of National Jurisdiction*, United Nations General Assembly, *Official Records*: 28th Session, Supplement No. 21, U.N. Doc. A/9021 (1973), 6 vols.

3.   **The United Nations Resolutions on "Moratorium" and "Principles" of Seabed Exploitation**

a.   **"Moratorium"**

UNITED NATIONS GENERAL ASSEMBLY, RESOLUTION 2574-D
(XXIV), December 15, 1969 (Adopted by 62-28-28)

The General Assembly,

Recalling its resolution 2467 A (XXIII) of 21 December 1968 to the effect that the exploitation of the resources of the sea-bed and the ocean floor, and the subsoil thereof, beyond the limits of national jurisdiction, should be carried out for the benefit of mankind as a whole, irrespective of the geographical location of States, taking into account the special interests and needs of the developing countries,

Convinced that it is essential, for the achievement of this purpose, that such activities be carried out under an international regime, including appropriate international machinery,

Noting that this matter is under consideration by the Committee on the Peaceful Uses of the Sea-Bed and the Ocean Floor beyond the Limits of National Jurisdiction,

Recalling its resolution 2340 (XXII) of 18 December 1967 on the importance of preserving the sea-bed and the ocean floor, and the subsoil thereof, beyond the limits of national jurisdiction, from actions and uses which might be detrimental to the common interests of mankind,

Declares that, pending the establishment of the aforementioned international regime:

(a) States and persons, physical or juridical, are bound to refrain from all activities of exploitation of the resources of the area of the sea-bed and ocean floor, and the subsoil thereof, beyond the limits of national jurisdiction;

(b) No claim to any part of that area or its resources shall be recognized.

"U.S. Explains Its Votes on Seabed Resolutions," *State Department Bulletin*, Vol. 62, No. 1596 (January 26, 1970), pp. 92-93.

[Statement by Ambassador Phillips] Plenary Session, December 15, [1970].

The United States delegation is opposed to [Resolution 2574-D] and will vote against it. I should like to explain again the reasons for our position.

First of all, it proceeds on a premise which is unsound and self-defeating: that the development of deep seabed exploitation, and accordingly the development of the technological capacity for such exploitation, should be retarded. What has struck us as doubly surprising about this proposition is that it is put forward in connection with an item whose very existence is due in substantial measure to the conviction that all mankind stands to benefit by the promotion of the exploitation of deep seabed resources. The question is, therefore, whose interests--if anybody's-- would such retardation serve? This is the question to which we have as yet heard no adequate answer.

We are aware, of course, that a rather simplistic picture has sometimes been painted of developed maritime powers monopolizing seabed technology and rushing greedily to exhaust seabed resources before the international community can establish a regime to regulate their exploitation. To knowledgeable people, however, this picture is defective in at least two respects. First, to the extent that the technology of deep seabed exploitation exists at all, it exists only in embryonic form. If its development does not move forward to the point where commercially viable exploitation of deep seabed resources is possible on a significant scale, there will be no exploitation of deep seabed resources and no benefit to anyone--developed or developing, coastal or landlocked, east or west, north or south. Secondly, so far as my delegation is aware, there is simply no possibility of one country or group of countries having exclusive use of seabed exploitation technology, any more than one country or group of countries has exclusive use of the technology of exploiting resources on land.

If there are individual countries having special reasons for preferring a retardation of seabed exploitation, reasons not generally applicable and perhaps not generally understood, then it would be useful to have these considerations explained. Until convincing reasons are presented, however, we respectfully suggest that, in a time when the demands of economic development are being pressed insistently upon the entire international community, any proposal which posits the desirability of retarding development in a potentially important field requires looking at with a very skeptical eye indeed.

Secondly . . . the tendency of this resolution is to encourage national action which will make the issues now entrusted to the Seabed Committee for negotiation and solution progressively more difficult to solve. The resolution has been presented to us as a call for national self-restraint, intended to prevent unilateral action which would be prejudicial to the solution of issues currently pending before the committee. My delegation would not question the sincerity of these intentions; and in any case, motives are not the issue. What is the issue are practical consequences. In practical effect, this resolution is likely to encourage some states that may feel it useful or necessary to engage in exploration or exploitation of seabed resources to move toward unjustifiably expansive claims of national jurisdiction, just in order to remove these activities of exploitation from the scope of the prohibition contained in the resolution and thus render them in their view legitimate. It is not enough to say that the prohibition which the resolution contains is without binding legal effect; that is the case with almost any General Assembly resolution and certainly is the case for any General Assembly resolution purporting to prescribe standards of conduct for states in the oceans. The point is that such a resolution by the Assembly may be taken by some to raise a question of the legitimacy of exploitation undertaken in certain areas of the seabed which, in view of the very substantial investment of capital which such exploitation or even exploration may require, might well be sufficient to generate an unjustifiably expansive claim of national jurisdiction as a precautionary protective measure.

b.   The Principles

UNITED NATIONS GENERAL ASSEMBLY, RESOLUTION 2749
(XXV), December 17, 1970 (Adopted by 108-0-14)

The General Assembly,

Recalling its resolutions 2340 (XXII) of 18 December 1967, 2467 (XXIII) of 21 December 1968 and 2574 (XXIV) of 15 December, 1969, concerning the area to which the title of the item refers,

Affirming that there is an area of the sea-bed and the ocean floor, and the subsoil thereof, beyond the limits of national jurisdiction, the precise limits of which are yet to be determined,

Recognizing that the existing legal regime of the high seas does not provide substantive rules for regulating the exploration of the aforesaid area and the exploitation of its resources,

Convinced that the area shall be reserved exclusively for peaceful purposes and that the exploration of the area and the exploitation of its resources shall be carried out for the benefit of mankind as a whole,

Believing it essential that an international regime applying to the area and its resources and including appropriate international machinery should be established as soon as possible,

Bearing in mind that the development and use of the area and its resources shall be undertaken in such a manner as to foster healthy development of the world economy and balanced growth of international trade, and to minimize any adverse economic effects caused by fluctuation of prices of raw materials resulting from such activities,

Solemnly declares that:

1. The sea-bed and ocean floor, and the subsoil thereof, beyond the limits of national jurisdiction (hereinafter referred to as the area), as well as the resources of the area, are the common heritage of mankind.

2. The area shall not be subject to appropriation by any means by States or persons, natural or juridical, and no State shall claim or exercise sovereignty or sovereign rights over any part thereof.

3. No State or person, natural or juridical, shall claim, exercise or acquire rights with respect to the area or its resources incompatible with the international regime to be established and the principles of this Declaration.

4. All activities regarding the exploration and exploitation of the resources of the area and other related activities shall be governed by the international regime to be established.

5. The area shall be open to use exclusively for peaceful purposes by all States whether coastal or land-locked, without discrimination, in accordance with the international regime to be established.

6. States shall act in the area in accordance with the applicable principles and rules of international law including the Charter of the United Nations and the Declaration on Principles of International Law concerning Friendly Relations and Co-operation among States in accordance with the Charter of the United Nations, adopted by the General Assembly on 24 October 1970, in the interests of maintaining international peace and security and promoting international co-operation and mutual understanding.

7. The exploration of the area and the exploitation of its resources shall be carried out for the benefit of mankind as a whole, irrespective of the geographical location of States, whether land-locked or coastal, and taking into particular consideration the interests and needs of the developing countries.

8. The area shall be reserved exclusively for peaceful purposes, without prejudice to any measures which have been or may be agreed upon in the context of international negotiations undertaken in the field of disarmament and which may be applicable to a broader area. One or more international agreements shall be concluded as soon as possible in order to implement effectively this principle and to constitute a step towards the exclusion of the sea-bed, the ocean floor and the subsoil thereof from the arms race.

9. On the basis of the principles of this Declaration, an international regime applying to the area and its resources and including appropriate international machinery to give effect to its provisions shall be established by an international treaty of a universal character, generally agreed upon. The regime shall, *inter alia*, provide for the orderly and safe development and rational management of the area and its resources and for expanding opportunities in the use thereof and ensure the equitable sharing by States in the benefits derived therefrom, taking into particular consideration the interests and needs of the developing countries, whether land-locked or coastal.

10. States shall promote international co-operation in scientific research exclusively for peaceful purposes:

(a) By participation in international programs and by encouraging co-operation in scientific research by personnel of different countries;

(b) Through effective publication of research programs and dissemination of the results of research through international channels;

(c) By co-operation in measures to strengthen research capabilities of developing countries, including the participation of their nationals in research programs.

No such activity shall form the legal basis for any claims with respect to any part of the area or its resources.

11. With respect to activities in the area and acting in conformity with the international regime to be established, States shall take appropriate measures for and shall co-operate in the adoption and implementation of international rules, standards and procedures for, *inter alia*:

(a) Prevention of pollution and contamination, and other hazards to the marine environment, including the coastline, and of interference with the ecological balance of the marine environment;

(b) Protection and conservation of the natural resources of the area and prevention of damage to the flora and fauna of the marine environment.

12. In their activities in the area, including those relating to its resources, States shall pay due regard to the rights and legitimate interests of coastal States in the region of such activities, as well as of all other States which may be affected by such activities. Consultations shall be maintained with the coastal States concerned with respect to activities relating to the exploration of the area and the exploitation of its resources with a view to avoiding infringement of such rights and interests.

13. Nothing herein shall affect:

(a) The legal status of the waters superjacent to the area or that of the air space above those waters;

(b) The rights of coastal States with respect to measures to prevent, mitigate or eliminate grave and imminent danger to their coastline or related interests from pollution or threat thereof resulting from, or from other hazardous occurrences caused by, any activities in the area, subject to the international regime to be established.

14. Every State shall have the responsibility to ensure that activities in the area, including those relating to its resources, whether undertaken by governmental agencies, or non-governmental entities or persons under its jurisdiction, or acting on its behalf, shall be carried out in conformity with the international regime to be established. The same responsibility applies to international organizations and their members for activities shall entail liability.

15. The parties to any dispute relating to activities in the area and its resources shall resolve such dispute by the measures mentioned in Article 33 of the Charter of the United Nations and such procedures for settling disputes as may be agreed upon in the international regime to be established.

REFERENCES

Francis T. Christy, Jr., "Communications: A Social Scientist Writes on Economic Criteria for Rules Governing Exploitation of Deep Sea Minerals," *The International Lawyer*, Vol. 2 (1968), pp. 224-242; Robert A. Creamer, "Title to the Deep Sea-Bed: Prospects for the Future," *Harvard International Law Journal*, Vol. 9 (1968), pp. 205-231; A. Pardo, "Who Will Control the Seabed?," *Foreign Affairs*, Vol. 47 (October, 1968), pp. 123-137; John R. Stevenson, "The Search for Equity on the Seabeds," *Department of State Bulletin*, Vol. 64, No. 1660 (April 19, 1971), pp. 529-533; John R. Stevenson, "Legal Regulation of Mineral Exploitation in the Deep Seabed," *Department of State Bulletin*, Vol. 65, No. 1672 (July 12, 1971), pp. 48-55; "UN Adopts Principles Governing Seabed Exploitation and Decides to Convene Comprehensive Law-of-the-Sea Conference in 1973," *Department of State Bulletin*, Vol. 64, No. 1649 (February 1, 1971), pp. 150-159; A.C. Wolf, "The U.N. Declaration of Principles Governing the Deep Sea-Bed," in N.S. Rodley and C.N. Ronning, eds., *International Law in the Western Hemisphere*, The Hague: Martinus Nijhoff, 1974, pp. 70-87; Steven J. Burton, "Freedom of the Seas: International Law Applicable to Deep Seabed Mining Claims," *Stanford Law Review*, Vol. 29 (1977), pp. 1135-1180; Paul Laurence Saffo, "The Common Heritage of Mankind: Has the General Assembly Created a Law to Govern Seabed Mining?" *Tulane Law Review*, Vol. 53 (1979), pp. 492-520; Jorge Coquia, "The Common Heritage of Mankind: A New Hope of Developing States," *Foreign Relations Journal* (Manila), Vol. 3, No. 4 (December 1988), pp. 17-41.

D. THE DEEP SEABED MINING REGIME UNDER THE 1982 UNITED NATIONS CONVENTION ON THE LAW OF THE SEA

[Only the table of contents and the summary of the provisions of the deep sea-bed part of the Convention are reproduced here. The summary is taken from *Yearbook of the United Nations*, Vol. 36 (1982), New York: The United Nations, 1986, pp. 204-227.]

1. Overall Description

TABLE OF CONTENTS OF THE DEEP SEABED
PART OF THE 1982 UNITED NATIONS CONVENTION
ON THE LAW OF THE SEA

PART XI. THE AREA

Convention provisions. The legal regime governing the deep sea-bed area beyond national jurisdiction, including the constitutional provisions for the International Sea-Bed Authority, was set out in part XI of the Convention on the Law of the Sea and in two annexes: annex III, on basic conditions of prospecting, exploration and exploitation, and annex IV, containing the Statute of the Enterprise, the Authority's sea-bed mining organ. In addition, resolution I of the Conference on the Law of the Sea provided for the establishment of a Preparatory Commission to exercise certain interim authority until the Convention entered into force, and resolution II governed preparatory investment in pioneer activities relating to polymetallic nodules on the deep sea-bed. The resolutions were adopted by the Conference on 30 April 1982 as part of a package with the Convention.

The Convention and associated resolutions provided in detail for arrangements regarding sea-bed mining, the structure and functions of the Authority and special dispute settlement machinery. They also contained a number of general provisions and principles relating to what the Convention referred to as the Area--defined in part I as the sea-bed and ocean floor and subsoil thereof beyond the limits of national jurisdiction--and to activities in the Area, defined in part I as resource exploration and exploitation.

The Convention defined the resources it covered to include all solid, liquid or gaseous mineral resources in the Area at or beneath the sea-bed, including polymetallic nodules (mineral masses yielding mainly copper, nickel, cobalt and manganese) (article 133). Part XI of the Convention applied to the Area (article 134) and had no effect on the legal status of the waters or airspace above (article 135).

The section defining the principles governing the Area began with the statement that the Area and its resources were the common heritage of mankind (article 136). No State could claim or exercise sovereignty or sovereign rights over any part of the Area or its resources, nor could any State, person or entity appropriate any part thereof; all rights in the Area's resources were vested in mankind as a whole, on whose behalf the Authority was to act (article 137).

The general conduct of States in relation to the Area was to be in accordance with this part of the Convention, the principles of the Charter of the United Nations and other rules of international law, in the interests of maintaining peace and security and promoting international co-operation and mutual understanding (article 138). The Convention made States parties and international organizations responsible for ensuring that activities in the Area carried out by them or by persons under their control conformed to the Convention, and also made them liable for damage caused by failure to carry out that responsibility (article 139).

Activities in the Area were to be carried out for the benefit of mankind as a whole, taking into particular consideration the interests and needs of developing States and of peoples who had not attained full independence or self-government; the Authority was to provide for the equitable and non-discriminatory sharing of financial and other economic benefits derived from the Area (article 140). The Area was open for use exclusively for peaceful purposes by all States without discrimination (article 141). Activities in the Area with respect to resource deposits lying across limits of national jurisdiction must be conducted with due regard to the rights and legitimate interests of the coastal State concerned, including consultations with that State and a system of prior notification; the coastal State retained the right to protect its coastline from grave and imminent danger due to pollution or other hazards resulting from activities in the Area (article 142).

Marine scientific research in the Area must be carried out exclusively for peaceful purposes and for the benefit of mankind as a whole; both the Authority and States parties could conduct such research, and the latter were obliged to promote international co-operation by participating in international programs, ensuring that programs were developed to strengthen the research capabilities and train the personnel of developing States, and disseminating research results (article 143). Technology transfer was to be promoted (article 144).

Measures were to be taken to ensure effective protection of the marine environment from harmful effects arising from activities in the Area; these were to include the adoption by the Authority of rules, regulations and procedures (referred to below as rules) for the control of pollution and other environmental hazards resulting in particular from such activities as drilling, dredging, excavation, waste disposal, and construction and operation or maintenance of installations, pipelines and other devices (article 145). Measures to ensure protection of human life were to include the adoption by the Authority of rules to supplement existing international law (article 146). The Convention set out conditions for installations used to carry out activities in the Area, including due notice of emplacement and removal, non-interference with navigation and fishing, safety zones, and use exclusively for peaceful purposes; such installations would not have the status of islands (article 147).

The Convention called for promoting the participation of developing States in activities in the Area, with particular regard for the special need of land-locked and geographically disadvantaged States to overcome obstacles arising from their disadvantaged location and remoteness from the Area (article 148). It also provided that archaeological and historical objects found in the Area must be preserved or disposed of for the benefit of mankind as a whole, with particular regard to the preferential rights of the country of origin (article 149).

REFERENCES

Francisco Orrego Vicuña, "The Regime for the Exploitation of the Seabed Mineral Resources and the Quest for a New International Economic Order of the Oceans: a Latin-American View," *Lawyer of the Americas*, Vol. 10 (1978), pp. 774-798; Leigh S. Ratiner and Rebecca L. Wright, "The Billion Dollar Decision: Is Deepsea Mining a Prudent Investment?," *Lawyer of the Americas*, Vol. 10 (1978), pp. 713-773; George Aldrich, "A System of Exploitation," *Syracuse Journal of International Law and Commerce*, Vol. 6 (1978-1979), pp. 245-263; Ronald S. Katz, "Financial Arrangements for Seabed Mining Companies: an NIEO Case Study," *Journal of World Trade Law*, Vol. 13 (1979), pp. 209-222; Jean-Pierre Levy, "The Evolution of a Resource Policy for the Exploitation of Deep Sea-bed Minerals," *Ocean Management*, Vol. 5, No. 1 (1979), pp. 49-78; Vatsala Mani, "Exploitation of Deep Sea-bed Minerals: Some Economic Issues," *India Quarterly*, Vol. 31, No. 1 (1979), pp. 49-78; Tariq Rauf, "Arms Control on the Seabed," *Strategic Studies*, Vol. 3 (Summer 1980), pp. 14-26; James K. Sebenius and Mati L. Pal, "Evolving Financial Terms of Mineral Agreements: Risks, Rewards and Participation in Deep Sea-bed Mining. Symposium in the Uses of the Oceans," *Columbia Journal of World Business*, Vol. 15, No. 4 (Winter 1980), pp. 75-83; Tullio Treves, "Seabed Mining and the United Nations Law of the Sea Convention," *Italian Yearbook of International Law*, Vol. 5 (1980-1981), pp. 22-51; Dennis W. Arrow, "The 'Alternative' Seabed Mining Regime: 1981," *Fordham International Law Journal*, Vol. 5 (1981-1982), pp. 1-34; Dennis W. Arrow, "The Customary Norm Process and the Deep Seabed," *Ocean Development and International Law*, Vol. 9 (1981), pp. 1-59; Charles E. Pirtle, "Alternative Regimes for Harvesting the Seabed: A Review Article," *Ocean Development and International Law*, Vol. 9 (1981), pp. 77-99; D.C. Watt, "The Law of the Sea Conference and the Deep Sea Mining Issue: The Need for an Agreement, *International Affairs* (London), Vol. 58(1) (Winter 1981-1982), pp. 78-94; William C. Brewer, Jr., "Deep Seabed Mining: Can an Acceptable Regime Ever be Found?," *Ocean Development and International Law*, Vol. 11 (1981), pp. 25-67; Euripides L. Evriviades, "The Third World's Approach to the Deep Seabed," *Ocean Development and International Law*, Vol. 11 (1982), pp. 201-264; David Hegwood, "Deep Seabed Mining: Alternative Schemes for Protecting Developing Countries from Adverse Impacts," *Georgia Journal of International and Comparative Law*, Vol. 12 (1982), pp. 173-192; Alexandra M. Post, "United Nations Involvement in Ocean Mining," *Ocean Development and International Law*, Vol. 10 (1982), pp. 275-313; Jon Van Dyke and Christopher Yuen, "'Common Heritage' v.

'Freedom of the High Seas': Which Governs the Seabed?," *San Diego Law Review*, Vol. 19 (1982), pp. 493-551; Per Magnus Wijkman, "Managing the Global Commons, *International Organization*, Vol. 36 (1982), pp. 511-536; P.N. Kirthisingha, "International Policies on the Economic Resources of the Deep-Seabed," *Resources Policy* (June 1983), pp. 77-98; Brad Shingleton, "UNCLOS III and the Struggle for Law: The Elusive Customary Law of Seabed Mining," *Ocean Development and International Law*, Vol. 13 (1983), pp. 33-63; A. Mpazi Sinjela, "'Reaching for the Stars or What's a Heaven for': The Ideals of Deep Sea-bed for the Future of Developing Nations," *International Property Investment Journal*, Vol. 1, pp. 467-518; Tulio Treves, "The Adoption of the Law of the Sea Convention: Prospects for Seabed Mining," *Marine Policy*, Vol. 7 (1983), pp. 3-13; Dennis W. Arrow, "Seabeds, Sovereignty and Objective Regimes," *Fordham International Law Journal*, Vol. 7 (1983-84), pp. 169-243; William C. Brewer, Jr., "The Prospect for Deep Seabed Mining in a Divided World," *Ocean Development and International Law*, Vol. 14 (1985), pp. 363-381; Clifton E. Curtis, "Legality of Seabed Disposal of High-level Radioactive Wastes Under the London Dumping Convention," *Ocean Development and International Law*, Vol. 14 (1985), pp. 383-415.

2. Seabed Mining

Convention provisions. With respect to the development of resources of the sea-bed area beyond national jurisdiction, the Convention laid down several broad objectives for activities in the Area, including: the development and orderly, safe and rational management of resources; expansion and enhancement of opportunities for participation by all States parties, and prevention of monopolization; participation in revenues by the Authority and technology transfer to the Enterprise and developing States; increased availability of sea-bed minerals as needed in conjunction with minerals from other sources; promotion of just and stable prices remunerative to producers and fair to consumers, and promotion of long-term equilibrium between supply and demand; protection of developing countries from adverse economic effects on mineral prices or exports caused by sea-bed activities; development of the common heritage to benefit mankind as a whole; and conditions of access to mineral markets that were no more favorable to sea-bed minerals than to those from other sources (article 150).

A "parallel system" for exploring and exploiting the deep sea-bed was to be established (article 153). Under this system, activities in the Area would be organized, carried out and controlled by the Authority, which would be authorized to conduct its own mining operations through its Enterprise. At the same time, the Authority would contract with States or State enterprises or private ventures to give them mining rights, including security of tenure. The Authority was required to avoid discrimination in the exercise of its powers and functions, though special consideration was permitted for developing States, particularly the land-locked and geographically disadvantaged (article 152).

The whole range of sea-bed activities, as well as other aspects of the system's operation, were to be governed by rules to be established by the Authority in accordance with basic conditions of prospecting, exploration and exploitation set out in the 22 articles of annex III to the Convention.

Prospecting could be conducted only after the Authority received a satisfactory written undertaking that the proposed prospector would comply with the Convention and the Authority's rules; no further authorization would be required (annex III, article 2). Exploration and exploitation, however, would require approval by the Authority of a plan of work, in the form of a contract, conferring on the operator the exclusive right to explore for and exploit specified categories of resources in a specified geographical area (article 3). A contract applicant would have to meet certain financial and technical qualifications and would have to be sponsored by its

to meet certain financial and technical qualifications and would have to be sponsored by its Government, State party to the Convention (article 4).

Each application would have to cover an area large enough and of sufficient commercial value to allow two mining operations; the Authority would reserve one of them for its future use and assign the other to the applicant (article 8). The reserved area would then be available to the Enterprise, which could decide whether it intended to carry out activities there, either by itself or in a joint venture with another entity; an area where the Enterprise did not elect to work would be available to an applicant from a developing State (article 9).

Once an applicant was found qualified and a site was assigned, the mining contractor would need two more approvals before it could operate in the international area: a plan of work, authorizing it to develop the minesite (article 6), and a production authorization, permitting it to produce up to a specified quantity of minerals from that site (article 7). The Authority would be required by the Convention to approve plans of work and production authorizations which met the specified requirements--including anti-monopoly provisions designed to prevent any country from obtaining access to an excessive share of the Area--except that there would be a selection system for production authorizations to keep them within an overall production limitation. An operator which had an approved plan of work for exploration would be given preference over other applicants for a plan of work covering exploitation of the same area and resources (article 10).

With respect to the financial terms of contracts, the annex outlined a schedule of payments to the Authority, including a $500,000 fee for approval of a plan of work, a $1 million annual fee payable once the contract entered into force and, once production started, a production charge--actually a tax scheme--based on a percentage of the market value of the processed metals produced; if the operator chose, it could pay a combination of production charge and a share of net proceeds (article 13).

In addition to the aforementioned obligations, the operator would be required to transfer to the Authority whatever data it needed to exercise its powers and functions in the area covered by the plan of work (article 14), and to transfer technology to the Enterprise.

In return for these contractual obligations, the Authority would accord to the operator the exclusive right to explore and exploit the area covered by the plan of work, and ensure that no other entity operated in the same area for a different category of resources in a manner that might interfere with the contractor's operations (article 16). The operator's rights under the contract could be suspended or terminated, or monetary penalties imposed, only in cases in which its activities had resulted in serious, persistent and wilful violations of the contract's fundamental terms, the Convention or the Authority's rules (article 18). The contractor and the Authority would be responsible or liable for any damage arising out of wrongful acts in the conduct of their operations, liability being for the actual amount of damage (article 22).

Where either party believed that a contract had become inequitable or that its objectives could no longer be achieved because of changed circumstances, the parties would enter into negotiations on its revision (article 19). Rights and obligations under the contract could be transferred only with the Authority's consent (article 20). The applicable law for judging rights and obligations under the contract would be the terms of the contract itself, the Authority's rules, the sea-bed provisions of the Convention and other compatible rules of international law (article 21).

The Convention and annex III also provided for a system of production control, technology transfer from contractors to the Enterprise and developing countries, principles for the operation of the Enterprise and future reviews of the operation of the entire sea-bed mining system. For the period pending entry into force of the Convention, a Conference resolution established a scheme for regulating pioneer investors.

REFERENCES

L.F.E. Goldie, "A Selection of Books Reflecting Perspectives in the Seabed Mining Debate," *International Lawyer*, Vol. 15 (1981), pp. 293-337, 445-498; E.D. Brown, "Deep-sea Mining: The Consequences of Failure to Agree at UNCLOS III," *Natural Resources Forum*, Vol. 7 (1983), pp. 55-70; Robert L. Brooke, "The Current Status of Deep Seabed Mining," *Virginia Journal of International Law*, Vol. 24 (1983), pp. 361-417; Brad Shingleton, "UNCLOS III and the Struggle for Law: The Elusive Customary Law of Seabed Mining," *Ocean Development and International Law*, Vol. 13 (1983), pp. 33-63; Mina Mashayekhi, "The Present Legal Status of Deep Seabed Mining," *Journal of World Trade Law*, Vol. 19 (1985), pp. 229-250; Conrad G. Welling, "Mining of the Deep Seabed in the Year 2010," *Louisiana Law Review*, Vol. 45 (1985), pp. 1249-1267; Lee Kimball, "Turning Points in the Future of Deep Seabed Mining," *Ocean Development and International Law*, Vol. 17 (1986), pp. 367-398; David L. Larson, "Deep Seabed Mining: A Definition of the Problem," *Ocean Development and International Law*, Vol. 17 (1986), pp. 271-308; Sally A. Meese, "The Legal Regime Governing Seafloor Polymetallic Sulfide Deposits," *Ocean Development and International Law*, Vol. 17 (1986), pp. 131-162; Said Mahmoudi, *The Law of Deep Sea-bed Mining: A Study of the Progressive Development of International Law Concerning the Management of the Polymetallic Nodules of the Deep Sea-bed*, Stockholm: Almgrist & Wiksell International, 1987; Federico Foders, "International Organizations and Ocean use: The Case of Deep-Sea Mining," *Ocean Development and International Law*, Vol. 20 (1989), pp. 519-530; Francisco Orrego Vicuna, "The Deep Seabed Mining Regime: Terms and Conditions for Its Renegotiation," *Ocean Development and International Law*, Vol. 20 (1989), pp. 531-539.

3. Production Control

The Convention on the Law of the Sea set out a sea-bed production policy whose basic aim would be to encourage sea-bed production at prices remunerative to producers and fair to consumers, with the least possible harm to land-based producers of the same minerals (article 151). This policy would be enforced through the issuance by the Authority of production authorizations to approved sea-bed operators, specifying an annual production rate for each. An annual sea-bed production ceiling would be fixed, based on the trend of nickel consumption, calculated in such a way as to allow sea-bed producers a share of any increase in such consumption and leaving the rest to land-based producers. Under the pioneer investors' scheme provided for in Conference resolution II, such investors would have certain guarantees in regard to production authorizations.

To the extent that economic hardship for land-based producers could not be avoided, a compensation scheme would be set up for their benefit. Initial steps in respect of this scheme would be taken by the Preparatory Commission for the International Sea-Bed Authority and for the International Tribunal for the Law of the Sea, which would establish a special commission on the subject. Once the Authority became operational, its Assembly would be empowered to establish, on the recommendation of the Council based on advice from its Economic Planning Commission, a compensation system or other economic adjustment assistance measures (article 160).

The Authority would be obliged to issue production authorizations if all of those applied for could be approved without exceeding the overall production limitation or contravening the Authority's obligations under a commodity agreement (annex III, article 7). If a selection had to be made among applicants in order to remain within the overall limit, the Authority would apply objective and non-discriminatory standards to be specified in its rules, giving priority to applicants which provided better assurance of performance or earlier financial benefits, had already invested the most or had not been selected in earlier periods.

REFERENCES

Lawrence L. Herman, "The Niceties of Nickel--Canada and the Production Ceiling Issue at the Law of the Sea Conference," *Syracuse Journal of International Law and Commerce*, Vol. 6 (1978-79), pp. 265-294; Linda Filardi, "Canadian Perspectives on Seabed Mining: the Case of the Production Limitation Formula," *Ocean Development and International Law*, Vol. 13 (1984), pp. 457-480; David W. Pasho, "Canada and the Ocean Mining," *Marine Technology Society Journal*, Vol. 19, No. 4 (1985), pp. 26-30; United Nations Department of International Economic and Social Affairs, *Methodologies for Assessing the Impact of Deep Sea-Bed Minerals on the World Economy*, New York: The United Nations, 1986.

4.   Technology Transfer

The Convention on the Law of the Sea contained general rules empowering the Authority to acquire for the Enterprise technology and scientific knowledge relating to sea-bed activities and to promote and encourage their transfer to developing States (article 144). Specific provisions were laid down in annex III (article 5), obliging contractors to make available to the Enterprise, on commercial terms, the technology they employed in their sea-bed mining ventures. That obligation extended to technology owned by the contractor or which he was otherwise entitled to transfer to others, as well as to so-called "third-party" technology; in the latter instance, the contractor would be obliged to acquire from the owner the right to transfer the technology to the Enterprise if that could be done without substantial cost. Disputes over these undertakings would be subject to compulsory settlement. If the Enterprise was unable to obtain the technology it needed, a group of States parties with access to such technology would be convened to take measures to ensure that it was made available to the Enterprise on fair and reasonable terms and conditions.

In order to ensure that the Enterprise was able to operate in the Area before the Convention entered into force in such a manner as to keep pace with States and other entities, Conference resolution II established the same technology transfer obligations for every registered pioneer investor.

In addition, the part of the Convention concerned with marine technology development and transfer contained a set of objectives to be followed by the Authority in helping developing States to obtain such technology.

REFERENCES

M.C.W. Pinto, "Transfer of Technology Under the U.N. Convention on the Law of the Sea," *Ocean Yearbook*, Vol. 6, Chicago: University of Chicago Press, 1986, pp. 241-270; Chennat Gopalakrishnan, "Transnational Corporations and Ocean Technology Transfer: New Economic Zones Are Being Developed by Public/Private Partnerships But Deep Sea Miners Balk on

Royalties," *American Journal of Economics and Sociology*, Vol. 48, No. 3 (July 1989), pp. 373-383. For further references, see Chapter XIII, I.

5. Review Conference

The Convention on the Law of the Sea provided for a review of the operation of the sea-bed mining system every five years by the Assembly of the Authority (article 154) and 15 years after the start of commercial production by a Review Conference (article 155). The Review Conference would consider whether the system had achieved its aims, reserved areas had been effectively exploited, seabed development had fostered a healthy world economy and balanced growth of international trade, monopolization had been prevented, the production policies had been fulfilled and benefits had been equitably shared. It could, by a three-fourths majority vote, introduce amendments to the system that would take effect for all parties after ratification or accession by three fourths of them. Prior to the Review Conference, amendments not prejudicing the exploitation system could be made with the approval of both the Council and the Assembly, subject to the same ratification procedure.

6. Pioneer Investors

The scheme devised by the Conference on the Law of the Sea to protect investments made by States and private consortia before the Convention entered into force was set out in resolution II, adopted along with the Convention. In addition, under resolution I, the Preparatory Commission for the International Sea-Bed Authority and for the International Tribunal for the Law of the Sea was to exercise powers and functions in relation to those investments.

The scheme would enable States and private investors to qualify for registration by the Commission as pioneer investors. This would entitle them to explore--but not commercially exploit--a selected area of the sea-bed beyond national jurisdiction until the Convention entered into force. It would also guarantee them priority over all others--except for the Authority's Enterprise-- once the Authority permitted commercial production from the sea-bed.

Pioneer investors were defined by the resolution, which placed them in three groups: (1) France, India, Japan and the USSR, and their State enterprises and corporations; (2) four entities made up of firms having the nationality of or controlled by Belgium, Canada, the Federal Republic of Germany, Italy, Japan, the Netherlands, the United Kingdom or the United States, or any combination of those States; and (3) any developing State or group of such States, or any State enterprise or corporation from such State. To qualify for pioneer status, the State concerned must have signed the Convention and the applicant would have had to have spent at least $30 million on sea-bed activities by 1 January 1983 (1 January 1985 in the case of the developing States other than India), not less than 10 percent of which must have been spent on investigation of a specific portion of the sea-bed.

Pioneer investors would be confined during the pre-Convention period to exploration and prospecting for polymetallic nodules in an allocated area; commercial exploitation would be excluded before the Convention entered into force. Each applicant would receive only one site, not to exceed 150,000 square kilometers. The resolution specified that nothing in it derogated from the anti-monopoly provisions of the Convention.

In order to obtain pioneer investor status, the prospective pioneer, certified by a signatory State, would have to apply to the Preparatory Commission for registration. Certifying States would have to ensure, before applications were submitted, that claims for particular areas did not overlap.

Sites would be allocated in a manner similar to that provided for in the Convention: The applicant would have to present an area large enough for two commercial mining operations, whereupon the Commission would allocate one part to the pioneer investor and reserve a commercially equivalent part for development by the Enterprise. Within the area allocated to it, the pioneer investor would have exclusive exploration rights. However, it would have to relinquish progressively half of the pioneer area over an eight-year period, freeing those portions for future allocation.

Each pioneer investor would pay to the Commission a $250,000 registration fee, plus another $250,000 to the Authority--instead of the $500,000 provided for in the Convention--when it applied for a plan of work (mining contract). There would be an additional fee of $1 million a year from the time the pioneer area was allocated, payable to the Authority when the investor's plan of work was approved. Investors would have to spend a minimum amount on their site, as determined by the Commission in relation to the size of the area and the expenditures expected of an operator that intended to mine the site commercially within a reasonable time.

Pioneer investors would be guaranteed entry into sea-bed mining under the Convention once it entered into force. This would be accomplished by a provision requiring the Authority to approve their contract application as long as they met the requirements applicable to all, but only if their certifying State was a party to the Convention. In addition to a contract, they would be entitled to a production authorization permitting them to produce from at least one mine site each, while the Enterprise would be guaranteed production authorizations for two sites.

The resolution spelt out three commitments which pioneer investors would have to undertake in order to ensure that the Enterprise was able to carry out sea-bed activities in such a manner as to keep pace with States and other entities: at the Commission's request, to explore the area reserved for the Enterprise, for which their costs would be reimbursed; to provide training for personnel designated by the Commission; and to undertake to perform the technology transfer obligations prescribed in the Convention. To the same purpose, every certifying State would ensure that the necessary funds were available to the Enterprise once the Convention entered into force and would report to the Commission on its sea-bed activities and those carried out by entities under its jurisdiction.

NOTE

In 1982, the Preparatory Commission for the International Sea-Bed Authority and for the International Tribunal for the Law of the Sea was established, but up to mid-1989, it has not worked out rules for "pioneer investors." Registered as "pioneer investors" so far are France, India, Japan and the USSR. See "Sea Law Commission, 'pioneer investor' duties; rules for sea-bed institutions considered," *U.N. Chronicle*, Vol. XXVI, No. 2 (June 1989), pp. 38-39. The Preparatory Commission, at its resumed seventh session (New York, August 1 - September 1, 1989), approved a draft proposal for the training program, to be in cooperation with the registered pioneer investors, for the future Enterprise--the sea-bed mining arm of the International Sea-bed Authority. See "Sea Law Commission focuses on pioneer investor duties, training programme approved," *U.N. Chronicle*, Vol. XXVI, No. 4 (December 1989), pp. 34-35.

REFERENCES

"Commission Studies Sea-Bed Mining Rules: 'Pioneer Investor' Arrangements a Main Issue," *U.N. Chronicle*, Vol. 21, No. 4 (April 1984), pp. 44-50; "Preparing for Sea-Bed Regime: An Agreement on Claims Procedure," *U.N. Chronicle*, Vol. 21, No. 7 (July 1984), pp. 28-34; "Preparing Commission Agrees on Procedure for Registering Pioneer Investors in Deep Sea-Bed Mining," *U.N. Chronicle*, Vol. 23, No. 5 (November 1986), pp. 89-91; "Sea-Bed Commission postpones registration of pioneer investors," *U.N. Chronicle*, Vol. 24, No. 3 (August 1987), pp. 40-41; Moritaka Hayashi, "Registration of the First Group of Pioneer Investors by the Preparatory Commission for the International Sea-Bed Authority and for the International Tribunal for the Law of the Sea," *Ocean Development and International Law*, Vol. 20 (1989), pp. 1-34.

7. International Seabed Authority and the Enterprise

The Convention on the Law of the Sea provided for the establishment of the International Sea-Bed Authority, with all States parties to the Convention as members and with its seat in Jamaica (article 156). The Authority was described as the organization through which States parties would organize and control activities in the international sea-bed area in accordance with the Convention (article 157). Its principal organs would be an Assembly, a Council and a Secretariat; there would also be an Enterprise for mining operations. Advance arrangements for the Authority were to be made by the Preparatory Commission.

Assembly

The Assembly, composed of all members of the Authority, would [m]ake decisions on all matters of substance by a two-thirds majority of those present and voting (article 159). It was described by the Convention as the supreme organ of the Authority, with the power to establish general policies on any question within the Authority's competence, and specifically authorized to elect the members of the Council and the Governing Board of the Enterprise, assess budgetary contributions and approve the Authority's annual budget, approve rules for sea-bed mining and the Authority's financial management and administration, decide on the equitable sharing of benefits from sea-bed activities, examine reports from the Council and the Enterprise, initiate studies and make recommendations to promote international co-operation on sea-bed activities, establish a compensation system or other economic adjustment measures for affected land-based producers, and suspend the rights and privileges of members (article 160).

The Assembly would meet on the date the Convention entered into force, at which time it would elect the Council (article 308).

Council

Several aspects of the membership, voting procedures, functions and subsidiary bodies of the executive organ of the Authority--the Council--were spelt out in the Convention on the Law of the Sea.

Membership. The Convention provided for a Council of 36 members, each elected by the Assembly for a four-year term at elections to be held every second year (article 161). Half of them would come from one of four major interest groups, while the rest would be elected in such a way as to ensure equitable geographical representation in the Council as a whole. The four groups were: the major consumers or importers of the minerals found on the sea-bed (four States), major land-based exporters of the same minerals (four States), the largest investors in sea-bed mining (four States), and developing countries representing "special interests" (six States). The "special interests" category included developing States with large populations, the land-locked or geographically disadvantaged, major mineral importers, potential producers of the minerals in question and the least developed.

Voting procedures and functions. The Convention provided for an elaborate scheme of decision-making majorities in which the Council was to decide the most important questions by consensus rather than voting (article 161). Consensus--defined as the absence of a formal objection---would be required for adoption of the rules, regulations and procedures (referred to below as rules) for all sea-bed activities, pending approval by the Assembly, and rules for the Authority's administration and financial management, as well as measures to protect land-based producing countries from adverse economic effects of sea-bed mining, recommendations to the Assembly on economic adjustment assistance for such countries and adoption of amendments to the sea-bed provisions of the Convention. Other substantive matters would be resolved by voting majorities of three fourths or two thirds, depending on the nature of the issue. The Council was to have the power to establish, in conformity with the Convention and the general policies established by the Assembly, the specific policies to be pursued by the Authority (article 162).

Subsidiary bodies. The Convention established, as organs of the Council, an Economic Planning Commission and a Legal and Technical Commission, each to have 15 members elected by the Council with due regard for equitable geographical distribution, or more if the Council decided to expand their membership having due regard to economy and efficiency (article 163). The Economic Planning Commission--which would include at least two members from developing States whose exports of minerals also found on the sea-bed had a substantial bearing on their economies--was to review supply, demand and prices of sea-bed materials; make recommendations to the Council on likely adverse effects of sea-bed mining on land-based producing countries, and propose a compensation system or other economic adjustment measures for such countries (article 164). The Legal and Technical Commission was to make recommendations on plans of work for sea-bed activities, supervise activities in the international area, recommend environmental protection measures, formulate and submit to the Council the rules governing the sea-bed mining system, calculate the production ceiling and recommend production authorizations for individual contractors (article 165).

Enterprise

The Convention on the Law of the Sea provided that the Authority's Enterprise was to carry out sea-bed activities directly, as well as the transport, processing and marketing of recovered minerals (article 170). Specific provisions were set out in a 13-article Statute which constituted annex IV to the Convention.

As stated in this annex, the Enterprise was to operate in accordance with sound commercial principles (article 1). It was to enjoy autonomy in the conduct of its operations, while acting in accordance with the general policies of the Authority's Assembly and the directives of the Authority's Council (article 2). A Governing Board of 15 members elected by the Assembly was to decide all matters by simple majority vote (article 5). The Board was to direct the operations of the Enterprise, including preparation of plans of work and production authorizations for approval by the Council, authorization of negotiations for the acquisition of technology, approval of the results of negotiations with other entities for joint ventures and other joint arrangements, and borrowing of funds (article 6). A Director-General, nominated by the Board and elected by the Assembly on the Council's recommendation, was to be chief executive, responsible for the staff

Assembly on the Council's recommendation, was to be chief executive, responsible for the staff (article 7). The principal office of the Enterprise was to be at the seat of the Authority (article 8).

The Enterprise was to submit financial reports to the Council on a regular basis (article 9). It was to make the same payments to the Authority as any commercial producer, except during an initial grace period of not more than 10 years, intended to enable it to become self-supporting; aside from a share to be retained as reserves, it was to transfer its net income to the Authority (article 10). Its funds were to include amounts from the Authority, voluntary contributions by States parties to the Convention, borrowings and income from operations; half of the funds received from the Authority were to come from long-term interest-free loans which each State party must provide according to its share of the United Nations regular budget, and the other half from Enterprise borrowings guaranteed by those States (article 11).

The Enterprise was to sell its products on a non-discriminatory basis, and only commercial considerations were to be relevant to its decisions (article 12). Its property and assets were to be immune from seizure and discriminatory restrictions, and it was to negotiate tax exemptions in States where its offices were located (article 13).

The Enterprise's sea-bed activities were to be governed by the Authority's rules and decisions (annex III, article 12). A special commission for the Enterprise was to be established by the Preparatory Commission. As part of the scheme for pioneer investors, and to ensure that the Enterprise would be able to keep pace with States and other entities engaged in sea-bed activities, those investors, prior to the entry into force of the Convention, were to be required to explore areas reserved for the Enterprise on a cost-plus-interest basis, train personnel and undertake to transfer technology as provided in the Convention; in addition, the States certifying those investors were to ensure that funds were made available to the Enterprise for its first two mining operations.

The role of the Enterprise in the parallel system of sea-bed mining to be established under the Convention was spelt out in annex III, on basic conditions for prospecting, exploration and exploitation.

Financing

According to the Convention on the Law of the Sea (article 171), the International Sea-Bed Authority was to be financed from six sources: assessed contributions from its member States on a scale based on that used by the United Nations for its regular budget, receipts from the taxes (fees and charges) collected from sea-bed operators, part of the Enterprise's net income, possible borrowings, voluntary contributions, and payments to a compensation fund for affected land-based producing States. The Authority's annual budget would be subject to approval by the Assembly after consideration by the Council (article 172). Any funds not needed for administrative expenses could be shared with member States, transferred to the Enterprise or used to compensate developing States that suffered economic harm from sea-bed production (article 173).

The Authority would be empowered to borrow funds within limits imposed by the Assembly and with specifics to be decided by the Council (article 174). The financial statements and accounts would be audited annually by an independent auditor appointed by the Assembly (article 175).

Resolution I of the Conference on the Law of the Sea, on preparations for the Authority, provided that the budget for the Authority's first financial period was to be recommended by the Preparatory Commission.

The Convention made separate arrangements for the financing of the Enterprise, initially through loans and loan guarantees arranged through the Authority and eventually from the proceeds of its mining activities. Resolution II, on pioneer investors, provided that States certifying such investors (sea-bed mining States) were to ensure that funds were made available to the Enterprise for its initial mining operations.

Other Aspects

The Convention on the Law of the Sea provided for the establishment of a Secretariat of the Authority, headed by a Secretary-General elected by the Assembly for a four-year, renewable term from candidates proposed by the Council (article 166). As in the case of the United Nations Secretariat, the paramount consideration in staff recruitment would be efficiency, competence and integrity, with due regard to recruitment on as wide a geographical basis as possible (article 167). Staff members would be prohibited, even after the termination of their functions, from disclosing industrial secrets or other confidential information they had learned by reason of their employment with the Authority (article 168). The Secretary-General was empowered to make arrangements for consultation and cooperation with international and non-governmental organizations (article 169).

The Authority was to have the legal capacity needed for the exercise of its functions (article 176). This was to include certain privileges and immunities (article 177), including immunity from legal process (article 178) and from search and seizure of its property and assets (article 179), and exemption from restrictions, regulations, controls and moratoria (article 180). Its archives were to be inviolable and its official communications were to be accorded treatment no less favourable than that given to other international organizations (article 181).

Representatives of States parties attending meetings, as well as the Secretary-General and staff, were to be immune from legal process with respect to their official acts, and were to be accorded the same exemptions from immigration restrictions and alien registration requirements, and the same treatment with regard to currency exchange restrictions and travel facilities, as officials and employees of comparable rank of other States parties (article 182). The Authority was to be exempt from direct taxes and customs duties on its property and official transactions, and the staff were to be exempt from paying income tax to any State other than that of which they were nationals (article 183).

A state party that fell two years or more in arrears in respect of its financial contributions to the Authority would have its voting rights suspended, unless the Assembly decided that failure to pay was due to conditions beyond the member's control (article 184). Gross and persistent violations of the sea-bed provisions, as determined by the Sea-Bed Disputes Chamber, could lead to a decision by the Assembly, on the Council's recommendation, to suspend the rights and privileges of membership (article 185).

REFERENCES

L.F.E. Goldie, "The Contents of Davy Jones' Locker--A Proposed Regime for the Seabed and Subsoil," *Rutgers Law Review*, Vol. 22 (1967), pp. 1-66; E.D. Brown, "Deep-Sea Mining: The Legal Regime of 'Inner Space'," *Yearbook of World Affairs*, Vol. 22 (1968), pp. 165-190; Arvid Pardo, "An International Regime for the Deep Seabed: Developing Law or Developing Anarchy?," *Texas International Law Forum*, Vol. 5 (1969), pp. 204-217; W.M. Chapman, "The Ocean Regime in the Real World," in L.M. Alexander, ed., *The Law of the Sea: National Policy Recommendations*, Kingston: University of Rhode Island, 1970, pp. 446-469; Arvid Pardo, "Some General Considerations on the Need for and the Requirements of an International Regime for the Sea-bed and the Ocean Floor," in J. Sztucki, ed., *Symposium on the International Regime of the Sea-bed*, Rome: Academia Nazionales dei Lincei, 1970, pp. 363-368; L.B. Sohn, "Possible Future Regimes of the Sea-Bed Resources: International Regulatory Agency," in J. Sztucki, ed., *Symposium on the International Regime of the Sea-Bed*, Rome, Academia Nazionales dei Lincei, 1970, pp. 387-405; Northcutt Ely, "The Draft U.N. Convention on the International Seabed Area-- American Bar Association Position," *Natural Resources Lawyer*, Vol. 4 (1971), pp. 60-72; H.G. Knight, "The Draft United Nations Convention on the International Seabed Area: Background Description and Some Preliminary Thoughts," *San Diego Law Review*, Vol. 8 (1971), pp. 459- 550; J.R. Stevenson, "The United States Proposal for Legal Regulation of Seabed Mineral Exploitation Beyond National Jurisdiction," *Natural Resources Lawyer*, Vol. 4 (1971), pp. 571- 581; D. Paget, "Towards a Regime for the Sea-Bed: An Examination of Official Proposals," *Queens Law Journal*, Vol. 1 (1972), pp. 484-512; L.M. Alexander, "Future Regimes: A Survey of Proposals," in R. Churchill, et al., eds., *New Directions in the Law of the Sea: Collected Papers*, Vol. III, 1973, pp. 119-133; R.P. Anand, "International Machinery for Seabed: Issues and Prospects," *Indian Journal of International Law*, Vol. 13 (1973), pp. 351-366; A.L. Danzig, "Draft Treaty Proposals by the United States, the United Kingdom, and France on the Exploitation of the Seabed: An Analysis," *Ocean Management*, Vol. 1 (1973), pp. 55-82; M. Hayashi, "An International Machinery for the Management of the Seabed: Birth and Growth of the Idea," *Annals of International Studies*, Vol. 4 (1973), pp. 251-279; E. Wenk, "International Institutions for Rational Management of Ocean Space," *Ocean Management*, Vol. 1 (1973), pp. 171-200; K.W. Clarkson, "International Law, U.S. Seabeds Policy and Ocean Resource Management," *Journal of Law and Economics*, Vol. 17 (1974), pp. 117-142; R.J. Eckert, "Exploitation of Deep Ocean Minerals: Regulatory Mechanisms and United States Policy," *Journal of Law & Economics*, Vol. 17 (1974), pp. 143-177; R.J. Sweeney, *et al.*, "Market Failure, the Common-Pool Problem, and Ocean Resource Exploitation," *Journal of Law & Economics*, Vol. 17 (1974), pp. 179-192; C.F. Amerasinghe, "Basic Principles Relating to the International Regime of the Oceans at the Caracas Session of the U.N. Law of the Sea Conference," *Journal of Maritime Law & Commerce*, Vol. 6 (1975), pp. 213-248; Thomas N. Franck and Evan R. Chesler, "An International Regime for the Sea-Bed Beyond National Jurisdiction," *Osgoode Hall Law Journal*, Vol. 13 (1975), pp. 579-601; S.K. Kuba, "The Conditions of Exploration and Exploitation of the Sea Bed Activities in the Proposed 'Area'," *Indian Journal of International Law*, Vol. 15 (1975), pp. 216-232; Jonathan I. Charney, "The International Regime for the Deep Seabed: Past Conflicts and Proposals for Progress," *Harvard International Law Journal*, Vol. 17 (1976), pp. 1-50; M.I. Glassner, "The Illusory Treasure of Davy Jones' Locker," *San Diego Law Review*, Vol. 13 (1976), pp. 533-551; S. Kotz, "'The Common Heritage of Mankind': Resource Management of the International Seabed," *Ecology Law Quarterly*, Vol. 6 (1976), pp. 65-108; A.V. Lowe, "The International Seabed and the Single Negotiating Text," *San Diego Law Review*, Vol. 13 (1976), pp. 489-532; John W. Murphy, "Deep Ocean Mining: Beginning of a New Era," *Case Western Reserve Journal of International Law*, Vol. 8 (1976), pp. 46-68; James R. Silkenat, "Solving the Problem of the Deep Seabed: The Informal Composite Negotiating Text for the First Committee of UNCLOS III," *New York University Journal of International Law and Politics*, Vol. 9 (1976), pp. 177-201; Theodore M. Beuttler, "The Composite Text and Nodule Mining: Over-Regulation as a Threat to the 'Common Heritage of Mankind'," *Hastings International & Comparative Law Review*, Vol. 1 (1977), pp. 167-193; Christa G. Conant and Melvin A. Conant, "Resource Development and the Seabed Regime of UNCLOS III: A Suggestion for Compromise," *Virginia Journal of International Law*, Vol. 18 (1977), pp. 61-68; M. Hardy, "The Implications of Alternative Solutions for Regulating the Exploitation of Seabed Minerals," *International Organization*, Vol. 31 (1977), pp. 313-342; John Norton Moore, "In Search of Common Nodules at UNCLOS III," *Virginia Journal of International Law*, Vol. 18 (1977), pp. 1-29; Robert F. Pietrowski Jr., "Hard Minerals on the Deep Ocean Floor: Implications for American Law and Policy," *William & Mary Law Review*, Vol. 19 (1977), pp. 43-75; Katherine W. Schoonover, "The History of Negotiations

Concerning the System of Exploitation of International Seabed," *New York University Journal of International Law and Politics*, Vol. 9(3) (1977), pp. 483-514; John Thomas Smith, "Seabed Negotiation and the Law of the Sea Conference--Ready for a Divorce?," *Virginia Law of International Law*, Vol. 18 (1977), pp. 43-59; L.S. Ratiner and R.L. Wright, "The Billion Dollar Decision: Is Deepsea Mining a Prudent Investment?," *Lawyer of the Americas*, Vol. 10(3) (Winter 1978), pp. 713-773; F.O. Vicuna, "The Regime for the Exploitation of the Seabed Mineral Resources: A Latin American View," *Lawyer of the Americas*, Vol. 10 (1978), pp. 774-783; A.O. Adede, "The Group of 77 and the Establishment of the International Sea-Bed Authority," *Ocean Development and International Law*, Vol. 7 (1979), pp. 31-64; J.N. Barkenbus, *Deep Seabed Resources: Politics and Technology*, New York: The Free Press, 1979; L. Juda, "UNCLOS III and the New International Economic Order," *Ocean Development and International Law Journal*, Vol. 7 (1979), pp. 221-255; T.G. Kronmiller, *The Lawfulness of Deep Seabed Mining*, Dobbs Ferry, New York: Oceana Publications, 1979, 2 Vols.; J.J. Logue, "The Nepal Proposal for a Common Heritage Fund," *California Western International Law Journal*, Vol. 9 (1979), pp. 598-628; "Symposium--Mining the Deep Seabed: A Range of Perspectives," *Syracuse Journal of International Law and Commerce*, Vol. 6 (1979), pp. 167-309; Roy S. Lee, "The Enterprise: Operational Aspects and Implications," in Symposium on the Uses of the Oceans, *Columbia Journal of World Business*, Vol. 15 (1980), pp. 62-74; William C. Lynch, "The Nepal Proposal for a Common Heritage Fund: Panacea or Pipedream?," *California Western International Law Journal*, Vol. 10 (Winter 1980), pp. 25-52; Elisabeth Mann Borgese, "The Role of the International Seabed Authority in the 1980's," *San Diego Law Review*, Vol. 18 (1981), pp. 395-407; Hugh Cameron and Luke Georghiou, "Decision Making in the International Seabed Authority: Production Limits--Who Benefits?," *Marine Policy*, Vol. 5 (1981), No. 3, pp. 267-270; E.J. Langevad, "Decision Making in the International Seabed Authority: Production Policy for Deep Sea Mineral Resources," *Marine Policy*, Vol. 5 (1981), No. 3, pp. 264-267; Elliot L. Richardson, "Decision Making in the International Seabed Authority," *Marine Policy*, Vol. 5 (1981), No. 3, pp. 256-260; G.J.F. Van Hegelsom, "Decision Making in the International Sea-bed Authority: the Argument for an Interim Arrangement," *Marine Policy*, Vol. 5 (1981), No. 3, pp. 260-264; Augusto Caesar Espiritu, "The International Seabed Authority and the New International Order," *Philippine Yearbook of International Law*, Vol. 8 (1982), pp. 13-23; Rema Puri, "International Seabed Regime Versus Consortia," *Foreign Affairs Reports* (New Delhi), Vol. 31, No. 10 (October 1982), pp. 171-192; William B. Jones, "The International Sea-Bed Authority Without the U.S. Participation," *Ocean Developments and International Law*, Vol. 12 (1982-83), pp. 151-171; Lucius Caflisch, "A New Type of Intergovernmental Organisation: The International Seabed Authority," *Philippine Yearbook of International Law*, Vol. 9 (1983), pp. 1-46; Wojciech Goralczyk, "The International Sea-Bed Authority," *Polish Yearbook of International Law*, Vol. 12 (1983), pp. 77-93; William B. Jones, "The International Sea-Bed Authority Without the U.S. Participation," *Ocean Development and International Law*, Vol. 12 (1983), pp. 151-171; Kathryn E. Yost, "The International Sea-Bed Authority Decision-Making Process: Does it Give a Proportionate Voice to the Participant's Interests in Deep Sea Mining?," *San Diego Law Review*, Vol. 20 (1983), pp. 659-678; Felipe H. Paolillo, "The Institutional Arrangements for the International Sea-Bed and Their Impact on the Evolution of International Organizations," *Academie de Droit International, Recueil des Cours*, Vol. 188 (1984), pp. 135-338; "The Preparatory Commission for the International Sea-Bed Authority and for the International Tribunal for the Law of the Sea," *Ocean Yearbook*, Vol. 5 (1985), pp. 445-463; Bhimsen Rao, "Preparatory Commission for the International Seabed Authority and for the International Tribunal for the Law of the Sea," *Indian Journal of International Law*, Vol. 25 (1985), pp. 226-244; Bradley Larschan, "The International Legal Status of the Contractual Rights of Contractors Under the Deep Sea-bed Mining Provisions (part XI) of the Third United Nations Convention on the Law of the Sea," *Denver Journal of International Law & Policy*, Vol. 14(2/3) (1986), pp. 207-229.

8. Seabed Disputes

The establishment of a Sea-Bed Disputes Chamber as an organ of the International Tribunal for the Law of the Sea was provided for in the Convention on the Law of the Sea (article 186). This Chamber would handle disputes between States parties to the Convention on the interpretation or application of the sea-bed provisions, as well as disputes involving the Authority and contractors (article 187). States could also submit their disputes to a special chamber of the Tribunal or an *ad hoc* chamber of the Sea-Bed Disputes Chamber; contract disputes could be submitted to a commercial arbitral tribunal for binding arbitration (article 188). The Sea-Bed Disputes Chamber could not decide questions involving the discretionary powers of the Authority or the validity of its rules, regulations and procedures (referred to below as rules) (article 189). A State sponsoring a corporation involved in a dispute would be entitled to take part in the proceedings (article 190). The Assembly or the Council could obtain advisory opinions from the Chamber on legal questions (article 191).

Further details regarding this Chamber were set out in the Tribunal's Statute (annex VI to the Convention). The Chamber would be composed of 11 members of the Tribunal, selected by a majority of the Tribunals' members to serve a three-year term (article 35). The Chamber would form an *ad hoc* chamber to deal with a particular dispute, composed with the approval of the parties (article 36). The Chamber would be open to the States parties to the Convention, the Authority and other entities (article 37). It would apply the rules of the Authority and the terms of contracts governing sea-bed activities (article 38). Its decisions would be enforceable in the territories of States parties in the same manner as judgments of the State's highest court (article 39). The other provisions of the Tribunal's Statute not incompatible with those specifically relating to the Chamber applied to the Chamber (article 40).

REFERENCES

Frederick Arnold, "Toward a Principled Approach to the Distribution of Global Wealth: An Impartial Solution to the Dispute Over Seabed Manganese Nodules," *San Diego Law Review*, Vol. 17 (1980), pp. 557-589; James H. Breen, "The 1982 Dispute Resolving Agreement: The First Step Toward Unilateral Mining Outside the Law of the Sea Convention," *Ocean Development and International Law*, Vol. 14 (1984), pp. 201-233; Lee Kimball, "Status Report: Resolution of Overlapping Pioneer Mine Site Claims," *Ocean Yearbook*, Vol. 5, Chicago: University of Chicago Press, 1985, pp. 469-477. For further references, see Chapter XIV, C.

9. The Preparatory Commission

On April 30, 1982, the Third United Nations Conference on the Law of the Sea adopted, among others, Resolution I on Establishment of the Preparatory Commission for the International Seabed Authority and for the International Tribunal for the Law of the Sea. The Resolution was attached to Annex I of the Final Act of the Conference adopted on December 10, 1982. U.N. Doc. A/CONF.62/121, in Third United Nations Conference on the Law of the Sea, *Official Records*, Vol. XVII, pp. 145-146. The Commission began to function in 1983, but has not yet worked out a draft on the Seabed Authority and the Tribunal.

REFERENCES

Elisabeth Mann Borgese, "Implementing the Convention: Developments in the Preparatory Commission," in Elisabeth Mann Borgese, Norton Ginsburg, and Joseph R. Morgan, eds., *Ocean Yearbook*, Vol. 7, Chicago: University of Chicago Press, 1988, pp. 1-13; Renate Platzoder, ed.,

The Law of the Sea: Documents 1983-1989 (Preparatory Commission for the International Seabed Authority and for the International Tribunal for the Law of the Sea), 10 Vols., Dobbs Ferry, New York: 1990-.

The activities of the Preparatory Commission is summarized in *Law of the Sea Bulletin*, No. 12 (December 1988), pp. 37-74, No. 14 (December 1989), pp. 88-105 and No. 15 (May 1990), pp. 54-62.

E. THE UNITED STATES AND THE UNITED NATIONS DEEP SEABED MINING REGIME

STATEMENT BY AMBASSADOR JAMES L. MALONE,
SPECIAL REPRESENTATIVE OF THE PRESIDENT OF THE UNITED
STATES FOR THE THIRD UNITED NATIONS CONFERENCE ON THE
LAW OF THE SEA, BEFORE THE HOUSE MERCHANT MARINE
AND FISHERIES COMMITTEE, ON FEBRUARY 23, 1982.
Myron H. Nordquist and Choon-ho Park, eds., *Reports of the United States
Delegation to the Third United Nations Conference on the Law of the Sea*,
Honolulu: Law of the Sea Institute, University of Hawaii, 1983, pp. 557-562.

. . . . . The President stated that we will seek changes necessary to correct unacceptable elements of the draft treaty and to achieve our six objectives." [For text of President Reagan's statement, see Nordquist and Park, eds., *Reports of the United States Delegation. . . .*, pp. 554-555.]

First, the treaty must not deter development of any deep seabed mineral resources to meet national and world demand.

The United States believes that its interests, those of its allies, and, indeed, the interests of the vast majority of nations will best be served by developing the resources of the deep seabed as market conditions warrant. We have a consumer-oriented philosophy. The draft treaty, in our judgment, reflects a protectionist bias which would deter the development of deep seabed mineral resources, including manganese nodules and any other deep seabed minerals such as the polymetallic sulfide deposits which have received considerable publicity recently.

Many different provisions of the draft treaty discourage development of seabed resources. Chief among them are:

--The production policies of the Authority which place other priorities ahead of economically efficient resource development;

--The production ceiling which limits the availability of minerals for global consumption;

--The limit on the number of mining operations which could be conducted by any one country, thus potentially limiting our ability to supply U.S. consumption needs from the seabed; and

--Broad areas of administrative and regulatory discretion which, if implemented in accordance with the Authority's production policies, would deter seabed mineral development.

To meet the President's first objective, these and other related areas of Part XI would require change and improvement.

Second, the treaty must assure national access to those resources by current and future qualified entities to enhance U.S. security of supply, avoid monopolization of the resources by the operating arm of the international Authority, and promote the economic development of the resources.

The draft treaty provides no assurance that qualified private applicants sponsored by the U.S. Government will be awarded contracts. It is our strong view that all qualified applicants should be granted contracts and that the decision whether to grant a contract should be tied exclusively to the question of whether an applicant has satisfied objective qualification standards. We believe that when a sovereign State sponsors an applicant and certifies that the applicant meets the treaty's qualification standards, the Authority should accept such a certification unless a consensus of objective technical experts votes that the applicant's qualifications were falsely or improperly certified.

The Draft Convention also should make specific provision for the rights of private companies that have made pioneer investments in deep seabed mining. We are all aware that a few companies have devoted substantial resources to prospecting for deep seabed minerals and developing new technologies for their extraction. We recognize that there are different views as to the rights which pioneer investors have acquired, but practicality should guide us in this matter. Deep seabed mineral resources will not be made available for the benefit of mankind without the continuing efforts of pioneer miners. I am confident, therefore, that the conference can find ways and means to accommodate their special circumstances.

In addition, the draft treaty creates a system of privileges which discriminates against the private side of the parallel system. Rational private companies would, therefore, have little option but to enter joint ventures or other similar ventures either with the operating arm of the Authority, the Enterprise, or with developing countries. Not only would this deny the United States access to deep seabed minerals through its private companies because the private access system would be uncompetitive but, under some scenarios, the Enterprise could establish a monopoly over deep seabed mineral resources.

To meet the President's second objective, therefore, qualified applicants should be granted contracts, the legal and commercial position of pioneer operators should be accommodated, and the parallel system should be designed to permit private miners to operate independently.

Third, the treaty must provide a decision-making role in the deep seabed regime that fairly reflects and effectively protects the political and economic interests and financial contributions of participating States.

The United States has a strong interest in an effective and fair Law of the Sea treaty which includes a viable seabed mining regime. As the largest potential consumer of seabed minerals, as a country whose private firms could invest substantial amounts in seabed mining, and as potentially the largest contributor to the Seabed Authority and to the financing of the Enterprise, our political and economic interests in any new international organization are far-reaching. The decision-making system in the Seabed Authority must reflect these realities. For example, a treaty which makes American access to natural resources of the seabed dependent on the voting power either of its competition or of those countries which do not wish to see these resources produced would not meet the President's objectives.

Similarly, the President's objectives would not be satisfied if minerals other than manganese nodules could be developed only after a decision was taken to promulgate rules and regulations to allow the exploitation of such minerals. In our judgment, the development of other seabed resources should proceed without restraint pending the development of rules and regulations.

We must be candid--many countries do not wish to see new sources of minerals produced from the seabed, because they believe that such production will jeopardize their own competitive position in the world markets. We do not criticize them for holding this view but do expect them to understand that the U.S. national interest is not consistent with impediments to the production of seabed minerals. A seabed mining regime which deters production is antithetical to the interests of all nations in the economically efficient development of resources.

A way must be found to assure that any nation like the United States, having a vital stake in the Authority's decisions, has influence sufficient to protect its interests. The decision-making system should provide that, on issues of highest importance to a nation, that nation will have affirmative influence on the outcome. Conversely, nations with major economic interests should be secure in the knowledge that they can prevent decisions adverse to their interests. We will make detailed proposals to the conference on ways to achieve these objectives.

Fourth, the treaty must not allow for amendments to come into force without approval of the participating States, including in our case the advice and consent of the Senate.

The draft treaty now permits two-thirds of the States parties acting at the review conference to adopt amendments to Part XI of the treaty which would be binding on all States parties without regard to their concurrence. It has been argued that a State which objects to an amendment has the option to withdraw from the treaty if the amendment is imposed without his consent. This proposal is obviously not acceptable when dealing with major economic interests of countries which have invested significant capital in the development of deep seabed mining in an international treaty regime. We believe there are ways to solve this problem, and we will be exploring them during the negotiations.

Fifth, the treaty must not set other undesirable precedents for international organizations . . . . In solving problems in the draft treaty, we will be alert to the possibility that a particular solution may be viable in the context of the Law of the Sea treaty but inappropriate as a precedent for some future negotiation. As we proceed to seek solutions to problems in the Law of the Sea negotiations, we will be mindful of the broadest national interests and the relationship of these negotiations to U.S. participation in other global institutions.

Sixth, the treaty must be likely to receive the advice and consent of the Senate. In this regard, the Convention should not contain provisions for the mandatory transfer of private technology and participation by and funding for national liberation movements.

The comprehensive policy review process was initiated because this Administration recognized that the Senate could not and would not give its consent to the emerging draft treaty on the Law of the Sea. It is, however, our judgment that, if the President's objectives as outlined are satisfied, the Senate would approve the Law of the Sea treaty. It would be necessary, of course, to demonstrate concretely how any renegotiated treaty texts have solved the problems raised by Members of the Congress and the public which led to the review and how they have met the President's objectives.

In this regard, there are certain issues to which special attention must be called. The President highlighted these in his sixth objective. The mandatory transfer of private technology and participation by and funding for national liberation movements create commercial and political difficulty of such consequence that they must be singled out as issues requiring effective solutions. These solutions will have to be clearly defensible as total solutions to the problem.

There is a deeply held view in our Congress that one of America's greatest assets is its capacity for innovation and invention and its ability to produce advanced technology. It is understandable, therefore, that a treaty would be unacceptable to many Americans if it required the United States or, more particularly, private companies to transfer that asset in a forced sale. That is why the problem must be solved. . . .

STATEMENT MADE BY AMBASSADOR JAMES L. MALONE
AT THE 182ND PLENARY MEETING OF THE THIRD UNITED
NATIONS CONFERENCE ON THE LAW OF THE SEA
April 30, 1982.
Third United Nations Conference on the Law of the Sea
Official Records, Vol. XVI, pp. 155-156.

40. Three misconceptions had arisen about United States motivations. The first misconception had been that the United States was seeking essentially to nullify the basic bargain reflected in the draft convention. In fact, even if all the changes proposed by the United States had been accepted, there would still have been an international regulatory system for the deep sea-bed and an international mining entity. There had been no desire to destroy that system at all; rather the intention had been to structure it in a way that would best serve the interests of all nations by enhancing sea-bed resource development.

41. The second misconception had been that the primary interest of the United States in the deep sea-bed regime related to protecting a few United States business interests. That was a drastic misjudgment of the United States motivation and its commitment to certain principles. Finally, a widespread view which was also false was that the United States would in the end accept an unsatisfactory deep sea-bed regime because of the navigation provisions that served other national interests. On the contrary, the United States had consistently maintained that every part of the convention must be satisfactory.

42. His delegation had come to the current session determined to work with others to reach improvements that would accord with its objectives and ensure a viable sea-bed mining regime. Unfortunately, hopes that the task would be concluded successfully and an acceptable outcome reached had not been realized. . . .

43. It was important to make clear how far the Conference has fallen short of the objectives of the United States. First, the sea-bed mining provisions would deter the development of deep sea-bed mineral resources; such development was in the interest of all countries and especially of the developing countries. By denying the play of basic economic forces in the market-place, the Convention would create yet another barrier to rational economic development. Second, while there had been improvements to ensure access to deep sea-bed minerals for existing miners, the United States did not believe that the access necessary in the future to promote the economic development of those resources had been assured. At the same time, a system of privileges would be established for the Enterprise that would discriminate against private and national miners. Third, the decision-making process established in the deep sea-bed regime did not give a

proportionate voice to the countries most affected by the decisions and would thus not fairly reflect and effectively protect their interests. Fourth, the Convention would allow amendments to come into force for a State without its consent, which was clearly incompatible with United States processes for incurring treaty obligations. Moreover, after having made substantial investments in deep sea-bed mining, the choice of either accepting an amendment at some future time or being forced to withdraw from the Convention entirely was not acceptable. Lastly, the deep sea-bed régime continued to pose serious problems for the United States by creating precedents that were inappropriate; the provisions on mandatory transfer of technology, potential distribution of benefits to national liberation movements and production limitations posed key problems for the United States Congress.

44. Consequently, although other provisions of the Convention were generally acceptable, the inescapable conclusion was that the Convention in its existing form did not fully satisfy any of the objectives of the United States with regard to the deep sea-bed régime. His delegation had therefore been forced to vote against the convention and would have to report to his Government that its efforts to achieve an acceptable regime had not been successful. . . .

STATEMENT BY AMBASSADOR THOMAS CLINGAN,
HEAD OF THE DELEGATION OF THE UNITED STATES OF AMERICA
AT THE FINAL SESSION OF THE THIRD UNITED NATIONS
LAW OF THE SEA CONFERENCE, MONTEGO BAY, JAMAICA
December 9, 1982
Third United Nations Conference on the Law of the Sea
Official Records, Vol. XVII, pp. 116-117.

3. The United States recognizes that certain aspects of the Convention represent positive accomplishments. Indeed, those parts of the Convention dealing with navigation and overflight and most other provisions of the Convention serve the interests of the international community. These texts reflect prevailing international practice. They also demonstrate that the Conference believed that it was articulating rules in most areas that reflect the existing state of affairs--a state of affairs that we wished to preserve by enshrining these beneficial and desirable principles in treaty language.

4. Unfortunately, despite these accomplishments, the deep sea-bed mining regime that would be established by the Convention is unacceptable and would not serve the interests of the international community.

5. The Conference undertook, for the first time in history, to create novel institutional arrangements for the regulation of sea-bed mining beyond the limits of national jurisdiction. It attempted to construct new and complex institutions to regulate the exploitation of these resources in a field requiring high technology that has not yet been fully developed, and massive investments. We had all hoped that these institutions would encourage the development of sea-bed resources which, if left undeveloped, would benefit no one. A regime which would promote sea-bed mining to the advantage of all was the objective towards which we labored.

6. We regret that that objective was not achieved. Our major concerns with the sea-bed mining texts have been set forth in the records of this Conference and I shall not use this occasion to repeat them. Suffice it to say that along the road some lost sight of what it was the world community had charged us to do. They forgot that in the process of political interchange, the political and economic costs can become too high for some participants to bear. They forgot that

to achieve the global consensus we all sought, no nation should be asked to sacrifice fundamental national interests.

7. The result is that consensus eluded us on deep sea-bed mining. Each nation must now evaluate how it must act to protect its national interests in the years to come.

8. We need not fear the future. In particular, those elements which promote the general community interests with respect to navigation and the conservation and utilization of resources within national jurisdiction reflect long-standing practice. The expectations of the international community in these areas can and should be realized, because we recognize that certain practices are beneficial to the community as a whole. For example, the Convention has recognized the sovereign rights of the coastal State over the resources of the exclusive economic zone, jurisdiction over artificial islands, and jurisdiction over installations and structures used for economic purposes therein, while retaining the international status of the zone in which all States enjoy the freedoms of navigation, overflight, the laying of submarine cables and pipelines and other internationally lawful uses of the sea, including military operations, exercises and activities. In addition, the Conference record supports the traditional United States position concerning innocent passage in the territorial sea. The rules reflect the hopes of the international community: they are very wise and obviously meant to last.

9. Institutions, however, that do not command consensus and that are not beneficial to the community as a whole raise serious problems. In these circumstances, alternative ways of preserving national access to deep sea-bed resources are necessary, just and permitted by international law. . . .

NOTE

Recall President Reagan's statement in Chapter III, Sec. C [p. 47].

REFERENCES

Bernard H. Oxman, David D. Caron and Charles L.O. Buderi, eds., *Law of the Sea, U.S. Policy Dilemma*, San Francisco: Institute for Contemporary Studies, 1983; Susan M. Banks, "Protection of Investment in Deep Seabed Mining: Does the United States Have a Viable Alternative to Participation in UNCLOS?," *Boston University International Law Journal*, Vol. 2 (1983), pp. 267-297; Charles E. Biblowit, "Deep Seabed Mining: The United States and the United Nations Convention on the Law of the Sea," *St. John's Law Review*, Vol. 58 (1983-84), pp. 267-305; Jon M. Van Dyke and David L. Teichmann, "Transfer of Seabed Mining Technology: A Stumbling Block to U.S. Ratification on the Law of the Sea Convention?," 13 *Ocean Development and International Law*, Vol. 13 (1983-84), pp. 427-455; Bharat Dube, "The Deep Seabed and North-South Politics: Cooperation or Confrontation?," *Indian Journal of International Law*, Vol. 25 (1985), pp. 245-261; Mark W. Zacher and James G. McConnell, "Down to the Sea with Stakes: The Evolving Law of the Sea and the Future of the Deep Seabed Regime," *Ocean Development and International Law*, Vol. 12 (1990), pp. 71-104.

Restatement on the Foreign Relations Law of the United States, Third Revision, Vol. 2, St. Paul, Minn: American Law Institute, 1987, pp. 89-90. Copyright by the American Law Institute. Reprinted with the permission of the American Law Institute.

§ 523. Exploitation of Mineral Resources of Deep Sea-Bed

(1) Under international law,

    (a)   no state may claim or exercise sovereignty or sovereign or exclusive rights over any part of the sea-bed and subsoil beyond the limits of national jurisdiction, or over its mineral resources, and no state or person may appropriate any part of that area;

    (b)   unless prohibited by international agreement, a state may engage, or authorize any person to engage, in activities of exploration for and exploitation of the mineral resources of that area, provided that such activities are conducted

        (i)   without claiming or exercising sovereignty or sovereign or exclusive rights in any part of that area, and

        (ii)   with reasonable regard for the right of other states or persons to engage in similar activities and to exercise the freedoms of the high sea;

    (c)   minerals extracted in accordance with paragraph (b) become the property of the mining state or person.

(2) Under the law of the United States, a citizen of the United States may engage in activities of exploration for, or exploitation of, the mineral resources of the area of the sea-bed and subsoil beyond the limits of national jurisdiction only in accordance with a license issued by the Federal Government pursuant to law or international agreement.

F. NATIONAL LEGISLATION ON DEEP SEABED MINING AND MINI-TREATIES

1. The United States

UNITED STATES: DEEP SEABED HARD MINERAL RESOURCES ACT
June 28, 1980
94 Stat. 553; 30 U.S.C. §§ 1401-1473

§ 1401. Congressional findings and declaration of purpose

(a) Findings

The Congress finds that--

. . . .

(7) on December 17, 1970, the United States supported (by affirmative vote) the United Nations General Assembly Resolution 2749 (XXV) declaring inter alia the principle that the mineral resources of the deep seabed are the common heritage of mankind, with the expectation that this principle would be legally defined under the terms of a comprehensive international Law of the Sea Treaty yet to be agreed upon;

(8) it is in the national interest of the United States and other nations to encourage a widely acceptable Law of the Sea Treaty, which will provide a new legal order for the oceans covering a broad range of ocean interests, including exploration for and commercial recovery of hard mineral resources of the deep seabed;

(9) the negotiations to conclude such a Treaty and establish the international regime governing the exercise of rights over, and exploration of, the resources of the deep seabed, referred to in General Assembly Resolution 2749 (XXV) are in progress but may not be concluded in the near future;

(10) even if such negotiations are completed promptly, much time will elapse before such an international regime is established and in operation;

(11) development of technology required for the exploration and recovery of hard mineral resources of the deep seabed will require substantial investment for many years before commercial production can occur, and must proceed at this time if deep seabed minerals are to be available when needed;

(12) it is the legal opinion of the United States that exploration for and commercial recovery of hard mineral resources of the deep seabed are freedoms of the high seas subject to a duty of reasonable regard to the interests of other states in their exercise of those and other freedoms recognized by general principles of international law;

(13) pending a Law of the Sea Treaty, and in the absence of agreement among states on applicable principles of international law, the uncertainty among potential investors as to the future legal regime is likely to discourage or prevent the investments necessary to develop deep seabed mining technology;

(14) pending a Law of the Sea Treaty, the protection of the marine environment from damage caused by exploration or recovery of hard mineral resources of the deep seabed depends upon the enactment of suitable interim national legislation;

(15) a Law of the Sea Treaty is likely to establish financial arrangements which obligate the United States or United States citizens to make payments to an international organization with respect to exploration or recovery of the hard mineral resources of the deep seabed; and

(16) legislation is required to establish an interim legal regime under which technology can be developed and the exploration and recovery of the hard mineral resources of the deep seabed can take place until such time as a Law of the Sea Treaty enters into force with respect to the United States.

. . . .

§ 1402. International objectives

(a) Disclaimer of extraterritorial sovereignty

By the enactment of this chapter, the United States--

(1) exercises its jurisdiction over United States citizens and vessels, and foreign persons and vessels otherwise subject to its jurisdiction, in the exercise of the high seas freedom to engage in exploration for, and commercial recovery of, hard mineral resources of the deep seabed in accordance with generally accepted principles of international law recognized by the United States; but

(2) does not thereby assert sovereignty or sovereign or exclusive rights or jurisdiction over, or the ownership of, any areas or resources in the deep seabed.

. . . .

§ 1403. Definitions

For purposes of this chapter, the term--

. . . .

(2) "Continental Shelf" means--

(A) the seabed and subsoil of the submarine areas adjacent to the coast, but outside the area of the territorial sea, to a depth of 200 meters or, beyond that limit, to where the depth of the superjacent waters admits of the exploitation of the natural resources of such submarine area; and

(B) the seabed and subsoil of similar submarine areas adjacent to the coast of islands;

. . . .

(4) "deep seabed" means the seabed, and the subsoil thereof to a depth of ten meters, lying seaward of and outside--

(A) the Continental Shelf of any nation; and

(B) any area of national resource jurisdiction of any foreign nation, if such area extends beyond the Continental Shelf of such nation and such jurisdiction is recognized by the United States;

(5) "exploration" means--

(A) any at-sea observation and evaluation activity which has, as its objective, the establishment and documentation of--

(i) the nature, shape, concentration, location, and tenor of a hard mineral resource; and

(ii) the environmental, technical, and other appropriate factors which must be taken into account to achieve commercial recovery; and

(B) the taking from the deep seabed of such quantities of any hard mineral resource as are necessary for the design, fabrication, and testing of equipment which is intended to be used in the commercial recovery and processing of such resource;

(6) "hard mineral resource" means any deposit or accretion on, or just below, the surface of the deep seabed of nodules which include one or more minerals, at least one of which contains manganese, nickel, cobalt, or copper; . . . .

(14) "United States citizen" means--

(A) any individual who is a citizen of the United States;

(B) any corporation, partnership, joint venture, association, or other entity organized or existing under the laws of any of the United States; and

(C) any corporation, partnership, joint venture, association, or other entity (whether organized or existing under the laws of any of the United States or a foreign nation) if the controlling interest in such entity is held by an individual or entity described in subparagraph (A) or (B).

. . . .

SUBCHAPTER I--REGULATION OF EXPLORATION AND COMMERCIAL RECOVERY BY UNITED STATES CITIZENS

§ 1411. Prohibited activities by United States citizens

(a) Prohibited activities and exceptions

(1) No United States citizen may engage in any exploration or commercial recovery unless authorized to do so under--

(A) a license or a permit issued under this subchapter;

(B) a license, permit, or equivalent authorization issued by a reciprocating state; or

(C) an international agreement which is in force with respect to the United States.

(2) The prohibitions of this subsection shall not apply to any of the following activities:

(A) Scientific research, including that concerning hard mineral resources.

(B) Mapping, or the taking of any geophysical, geochemical, oceanographic, or atmospheric measurements or random bottom samplings of the deep seabed, if such taking does not significantly alter the surface or subsurface of the deep seabed or significantly affect the environment.

(C) The design, construction, or testing of equipment and facilities which will or may be used for exploration or commercial recovery, if such design, construction, or testing is conducted on shore, or does not involve the recovery of any but incidental hard mineral resources.

(D) The furnishing of machinery, products, supplies, services, or materials for any exploration or commercial recovery conducted under a license or permit issued under this subchapter, a license or permit or equivalent authorization issued by a reciprocating state, or under an international agreement.

(E) Activities, other than exploration or commercial recovery activities, of the Federal Government. . . .

(c) Interference

No United States citizen may interfere or participate in interference with any activity conducted by any licensee or permittee which is authorized to be undertaken under a license or permit issued by the United States to the licensee or permittee under this chapter or with any activity conducted by the holder of, and authorized to be undertaken under, a license or permit or equivalent authorization issued by a reciprocating state for the exploration or commercial recovery of hard mineral resources. United States citizens shall exercise their rights on the high seas with reasonable regard for the interests of other states in their exercise of the freedoms of the high seas.

. . . .

§ 1413. License and permit applications, review, and certification

(a) Applications

(1) Any United States citizen may apply to the Administrator for the issuance or transfer of a license for exploration or a permit for commercial recovery.

(2)(A) Applications for issuance or transfer of licenses for exploration and permits for commercial recovery shall be made in such form and manner as the Administrator shall prescribe in general and uniform regulations and shall contain such relevant financial, technical, and environmental information as the Administrator may by regulations require as being necessary and appropriate for carrying out the provisions of this subchapter. In accordance with such regulations, each applicant for the issuance of a license shall submit an exploration plan as described in subparagraph (B), and each applicant for a permit shall submit a recovery plan as described in subparagraph (C).

(B) The exploration plan for a license shall set forth the activities proposed to be carried out during the period of the license, describe the area to be explored, and include the intended exploration schedule and methods to be used, the development and testing of systems for commercial recovery to take place under the terms of the license, an estimated schedule of expenditures, measures to protect the environment and to monitor the effectiveness of environmental safeguards and monitoring systems for commercial recovery, and such other information as is necessary and appropriate to carry out the provisions of this subchapter. The area set forth in an exploration plan shall be of sufficient size to allow for intensive exploration.

(C) The recovery plan for a permit shall set forth the activities proposed to be carried out during the period of the permit, and shall include the intended schedule of commercial recovery, environmental safeguards and monitoring systems, details of the area or areas proposed for commercial recovery, a resource assessment thereof, the methods and technology to be used for commercial recovery and processing, the methods to be used for disposal of wastes from recovery and processing, and such other information as is necessary and appropriate to carry out the provisions of this subchapter.

(D) The applicant shall select the size and location of the area of the exploration plan or recovery plan, which area shall be approved unless the Administrator finds that--

(i) the area is not a logical mining unit; or

(ii) commercial recovery activities in the proposed location would result in a significant adverse impact on the quality of the environment which cannot be avoided by the imposition of reasonable restrictions.

(E) For purposes of subparagraph (D), "logical mining unit" means--

(i) in the case of a license for exploration, an area of the deep seabed which can be explored under the license in an efficient, economical, and orderly manner with due regard for conservation and protection of the environment, taking into consideration the resource data, other relevant physical and environmental characteristics, and the state of the technology of the applicant as set forth in the exploration plan; or

(ii) in the case of a permit, an area of the deep seabed--

(I) in which hard mineral resources can be recovered in sufficient quantities to satisfy the permittee's estimated production requirements over the initial 20-year term of the permit in an efficient, economical, and orderly manner with due regard for conservation and protection of the environment, taking into consideration the resource data, other relevant physical and environmental characteristics, and the state of the technology of the applicant set out in the recovery plan;

(II) which is not larger than is necessary to satisfy the permittee's estimated production requirements over the initial 20-year term of the permit; and

(III) in relation to which the permittee's estimated production requirements are not found by the Administrator to be unreasonable.

(b) Priority of right for issuance

Subject to section 1411(b) of this title, priority of right for the issuance of licenses to applicants shall be established on the basis of the chronological order in which license applications which are in substantial compliance with the requirements established under subsection (a)(2) of this section are filed with the Administrator. Priority of right shall not be lost in the case of any application filed which is in substantial but not full compliance with such requirements if the applicant thereafter brings the application into conformity with such requirements within such reasonable period of time as the Administrator shall prescribe in regulations. . . .

§ 1415.   License and permit terms, conditions, and restrictions; issuance and transfer of licenses and permits

(a) Eligibility for issuance or transfer of license or permit

Before issuing or transferring a license for exploration or permit for commercial recovery, the Administrator must find in writing, after consultation with interested departments and agencies pursuant to section 1413(e) of this title, and upon considering public comments received with respect to the license or permit, that the exploration or commercial recovery proposed in the application--

(1) will not unreasonably interfere with the exercise of the freedoms of the high seas by other states, as recognized under general principles of international law;

(2) will not conflict with any international obligation of the United States established by any treaty or international convention in force with respect to the United States;

(3) will not create a situation which may reasonably be expected to lead to a breach of international peace and security involving armed conflict;

(4) cannot reasonably be expected to result in a significant adverse effect on the quality of the environment, taking into account the analyses and information in any applicable environmental impact statement prepared pursuant to section 1419(c) or 1419(d) of this title; and

(5) will not pose an inordinate threat to the safety of life and property at sea. . . .

§ 1417. Duration of licenses and permits

(a) Duration of a license

Each license for exploration shall be issued for a period of 10 years. If the licensee has substantially complied with the license and the exploration plan associated therewith and has requested extensions of the license, the Administrator shall extend the license on terms, conditions, and restrictions consistent with this chapter and the regulations issued under this chapter for periods of not more than 5 years each.

(b) Duration of a permit

Each permit for commercial recovery shall be issued for a term of 20 years and for so long thereafter as hard mineral resources are recovered annually in commercial quantities from the area to which the recovery plan associated with the permit applies. The permit of any permittee who is not recovering hard mineral resources in commercial quantities at the end of 10 years shall be terminated; except that the Administrator shall for good cause shown, including force majeure, adverse economic conditions, unavoidable delays in construction, major unanticipated vessel repairs that prevent the permittee from conducting commercial recovery activities during an annual period, or other circumstances beyond the control of the permittee, extend the 10-year period, but not beyond the initial 20-year term of the permit. . . .

§ 1419. Protection of the environment

(a) Environmental assessment

(1) Deep ocean mining environmental study (DOMES)

The Administrator shall expand and accelerate the program assessing the effects on the environment from exploration and commercial recovery activities, including seabased processing and the disposal at sea of processing wastes, so as to provide an assessment, as accurate as practicable, of environmental impacts of such activities for the implementation of subsections (b), (c), and (d) of this section.

(2) Supporting ocean research

The Administrator also shall conduct a continuing program of ocean research to support environmental assessment activity through the period of exploration and commercial recovery authorized by this chapter. The program shall include the development, acceleration, and expansion, as appropriate, of studies of the ecological, geological, and physical aspects of the deep seabed in general areas of the ocean where exploration and commercial development under the authority of this chapter are likely to occur, including, but not limited to--

(A) natural diversity of the deep seabed biota;

(B) life histories of major benthic, midwater, and surface organisms most likely to be affected by commercial recovery activities;

(C) long- and short-term effects of commercial recovery on the deep seabed biota; and

(D) assessment of the effects of seabased processing activities.

Within 160 days after June 28, 1980, the Administrator shall prepare a plan to carry out the program described in this subsection, including necessary funding levels for the next five fiscal years, and shall submit the plan to the Congress.

(b) Term, conditions, and restrictions

Each license and permit issued under this subchapter shall contain such terms, conditions, and restrictions, established by the Administrator, which prescribe the actions the licensee or permittee shall take in the conduct of exploration and commercial recovery activities to assure protection of the environment. The Administrator shall require in all activities under new permits, and wherever practicable in activities under existing permits, the use of the best available technologies for the protection of safety, health, and the environment wherever such activities would have a significant effect on safety, health, or the environment, except where the Administrator determines that the incremental benefits are clearly insufficient to justify the incremental costs of using such technologies. Before establishing such terms, conditions, and restrictions, the Administrator shall consult with the Administrator of the Environmental Protection Agency, the Secretary of State, and the Secretary of the department in which the Coast Guard is operating, concerning such terms, conditions, and restrictions, and the Administrator shall take into account and give due consideration to the information contained in each final environmental impact statement prepared with respect to such license or permit pursuant to subsection (d) of this section.

(c) Programmatic environmental impact statement

(1) If the Administrator, in consultation with the Administrator of the Environmental Protection Agency and with the assistance of other appropriate Federal agencies, determines that a programmatic environmental impact statement is required, the Administrator shall, as soon as practicable after June 28, 1980, with respect to the areas of the oceans in which any United States citizen is expected to undertake exploration and commercial recovery under the authority of this chapter--

(A) prepare and publish draft programmatic environmental impact statements which assess the environmental impacts of exploration and commercial recovery in such areas;

(B) afford all interested parties a reasonable time after such dates of publication to submit comments to the Administrator on such draft statements; and

(C) thereafter prepare (giving full consideration to all comments submitted under subparagraph (B)) and publish final programmatic environmental impact statements regarding such areas.

(2) With respect to the area of the oceans in which exploration and commercial recovery by any United States citizen will likely first occur under the authority of this chapter, the Administrator shall prepare a draft and final programmatic environmental impact statement as required under paragraph (1), except that--

(A) the draft programmatic environmental impact statement shall be prepared and published as soon as practicable but not later than 270 days (or such longer period as the Administrator may establish for good cause shown) after June 28, 1980; and

(B) the final programmatic environmental impact statement shall be prepared and published within 180 days (or such longer period as the Administrator may establish for good cause shown) after the date on which the draft statement is published.

(d) Environmental impact statements on issuance of licenses and permits

The issuance of, but not the certification of an application for, any license or permit under this subchapter shall be deemed to be a major Federal action significantly affecting the quality of the human environment for purposes of section 4332 of Title 42. In preparing an environmental impact statement pursuant to this subsection, the Administrator shall consult with the agency heads referred to in subsection (b) of this section and shall take into account, and give due consideration to, the relevant information contained in any applicable studies and any other environmental impact statement prepared pursuant to this section. Each draft environmental impact statement prepared pursuant to this subsection shall be published, with the terms, conditions, and restrictions proposed pursuant to section 1415(b) of this title, within 180 days (or such longer period as the Administrator may establish for good cause shown in writing) following the date on which the application for the license or permit concerned is certified by the Administrator. Each final environmental impact statement shall be published 180 days (or such longer period as the Administrator may establish for good cause shown in writing) following the date on which the draft environmental impact statement is published. . . .

§ 1420. Conservation of natural resources

For the purpose of conservation of natural resources, each license and permit issued under this subchapter shall contain, as needed, terms, conditions, and restrictions which have due regard for the prevention of waste and the future opportunity for the commercial recovery of the unrecovered balance of the hard mineral resources in the area to which the license or permit applies. In establishing these terms, conditions, and restrictions, the Administrator shall consider the state of the technology, the processing system utilized and the value and potential use of any waste, the environmental effects of the exploration or commercial recovery activities, economic and resource data, and the national need for hard mineral resources. As used in this chapter, the term "conservation of natural resources" is not intended to grant, imply, or create any inference of production controls or price regulation, in particular those which would affect the volume of production, prices, profits, markets, or the decision of which minerals or metals are to be recovered, except as such effects may be incidental to actions taken pursuant to this section.

§ 1421.   Prevention of interference with other uses of the high seas

Each license and permit issued under this subchapter shall include such restrictions as may be necessary and appropriate to ensure that exploration or commercial recovery activities conducted by the licensee or permittee do not unreasonably interfere with the interests of other states in their exercise of the freedoms of the high seas, as recognized under general principles of international law.

. . . .

§ 1428. Reciprocating states

(a) Designation

The Administrator, in consultation with the Secretary of State and the heads of other appropriate departments and agencies, may designate any foreign nation as a reciprocating state if the Secretary of State finds that such foreign nation--

(1) regulates the conduct of its citizens and other persons subject to its jurisdiction engaged in exploration for, and commercial recovery of, hard mineral resources of the deep seabed in a manner compatible with that provided in this chapter and the regulations issued under this chapter, which includes adequate measures for the protection of the environment, the conservation of natural resources, and the safety of life and property at sea, and includes effective enforcement provisions;

(2) recognizes licenses and permits issued under this subchapter to the extent that such nation, under its laws, (A) prohibits any person from engaging in exploration or commercial recovery which conflicts with that authorized under any such license or permit and (B) complies with the date for issuance of licenses and the effective date for permits provided in section 1412(c)(1)(D) of this title;

(3) recognizes, under its procedures, priorities of right, consistent with those provided in this chapter and the regulations issued under this chapter, for applications for licenses for exploration or permits for commercial recovery, which applications are made either under its procedures or under this chapter; and

(4) provides an interim legal framework for exploration and commercial recovery which does not unreasonably interfere with the interests of other states in their exercise of the freedoms of the high seas, as recognized under general principles of international law.

(b) Effect of designation

No license or permit shall be issued under this subchapter permitting any exploration or commercial recovery which will conflict with any license, permit, or equivalent authorization issued by any foreign nation which is designated as a reciprocating state under subsection (a) of this section.

(c) Notification

Upon receipt of any application for a license or permit under this subchapter, the Administrator shall immediately notify all reciprocating states of such application. The notification shall include those portions of the exploration plan or recovery plan submitted with respect to the application, or a summary thereof, and any other appropriate information not required to be withheld from public disclosure by section 1423(c) of this title.

(d) Revocation of reciprocating state status

The Administrator, in consultation with the Secretary of State and the heads of other appropriate departments and agencies, shall revoke the designation of a foreign nation as a reciprocating state if the Secretary of State finds that such foreign nation no longer complies with the requirements of subsection (a) of this section. At the request of any holder of a license, permit, or equivalent authorization of such foreign nation, who obtained the license, permit, or equivalent authorization while such foreign nation was a reciprocating state, the Administrator, in consultation with the Secretary of State, may decide to recognize the license, permit, or equivalent authorization for purposes of subsection (b) of this section.

(e) Authorization

The President is authorized to negotiate agreements with foreign nations necessary to implement this section.

(f) International consultations

The Administrator, in consultation with the Secretary of State and the heads of other appropriate departments and agencies, shall consult with foreign nations which enact, or are preparing to enact, domestic legislation establishing an interim legal framework for exploration and commercial recovery of hard mineral resources. Such consultations shall be carried out with a view to facilitating the designation of such nations as reciprocating states and, as necessary, the negotiation of agreements with foreign nations authorized by subsection (e) of this section. In addition, the Administrator shall provide such foreign nations with information on environmental impacts of exploration and commercial recovery activities, and shall provide any technical assistance requested in designing regulatory measures to protect the environment.

. . . .

SUBCHAPTER II--TRANSITION TO INTERNATIONAL AGREEMENT

§ 1441. Declaration of Congressional intent

It is the intent of Congress--

(1) that any international agreement to which the United States becomes a party should, in addition to promoting other national oceans objectives--

(A) provide assured and nondiscriminatory access, under reasonable terms and conditions, to the hard mineral resources of the deep seabed for United States citizens, and

(B) provide security of tenure by recognizing the rights of United States citizens who have undertaken exploration or commercial recovery under subchapter I of this chapter before such agreement enters into force with respect to the United States to continue their operations under terms, conditions, and restrictions which do not impose significant new economic burdens upon such citizens with respect to such operations with the effect of preventing the continuation of such operations on a viable economic basis;

(2) that the extent to which any such international agreement conforms to the provisions of paragraph (1) should be determined by the totality of the provisions of such agreement, including, but not limited to, the practical implications for the security of investments of any discretionary powers granted to an international regulatory body, the structures and decision making procedures of such body, the availability of impartial and effective procedures for the settlement of disputes, and any features that tend to discriminate against exploration and commercial recovery activities undertaken by United States citizens; and

(3) that this chapter should be transitional pending--

(A) the adoption of an international agreement at the Third United Nations Conference on the Law of the Sea, and the entering into force of such agreement, or portions thereof, with respect to the United States, or

(B) if such adoption is not forthcoming, the negotiation of a multilateral or other treaty concerning the deep seabed, and the entering into force of such treaty with respect to the United States.

§ 1442. Effect of international agreement

If an international agreement enters into force with respect to the United States, any provision of subchapter I of this chapter, this subchapter, or subchapter III of this chapter, and any regulation issued under any such provision, which is not inconsistent with such international agreement shall continue in effect with respect to United States citizens. In the implementation of such international agreement the Administrator, in consultation with the Secretary of State, shall make every effort, to the maximum extent practicable consistent with the provisions of that agreement, to provide for the continued operation of exploration and commercial recovery activities undertaken by United States citizens prior to entry into force of the agreement. The Administrator shall submit to the Congress, within one year after the date of such entry into force, a report on the actions taken by the Administrator under this section, which report shall include, but not be limited to--

(1) a description of the status of deep seabed mining operations of United States citizens under the international agreement; and

(2) an assessment of whether United States citizens who were engaged in exploration or commercial recovery on the date such agreement entered into force have been permitted to continue their operations.

§ 1443. Protection of interim investments

In order to further the objectives set forth in section 1441 of this title, the Administrator, not more than one year after June 28, 1980--

(1) shall submit to the Congress proposed legislation necessary for the United States to implement a system for the protection of interim investments that has been adopted as part of an international agreement and any resolution relating to such international agreement; or

(2) if a system for the protection of interim investments has not been so adopted, shall report to the Congress on the status of negotiations relating to the establishment of such a system.

§ 1444. Disclaimer of obligation to pay compensation

Sections 1441 and 1442 of this title do not create or express any legal or moral obligation on the part of the United States Government to compensate any person for any impairment of the value of that person's investment in any operation for exploration or commercial recovery under subchapter I of this chapter which might occur in connection with the entering into force of an international agreement with respect to the United States.

SUBCHAPTER III--ENFORCEMENT AND MISCELLANEOUS PROVISIONS

§ 1472. Deep Seabed Revenue Sharing Trust Fund; establishment

(a) Creation of Trust Fund

There is established in the Treasury of the United States a trust fund to be known as the "Deep Seabed Revenue Sharing Trust Fund" (hereinafter in this section referred to as the "Trust Fund"), consisting of such amounts as may be appropriated or credited to the Trust Fund as provided in this section.

(b) Transfer to Trust Fund of amounts equivalent to certain taxes

(1) In general

There are hereby appropriated to the Trust Fund amounts determined by the Secretary of the Treasury to be equivalent to the amounts of the taxes received in the Treasury under section 4495 of Title 26.

(2) Method of transfer

The amounts appropriated by paragraph (1) shall be transferred at least quarterly from the general fund of the Treasury to the Trust Fund on the basis of estimates made by the Secretary of the Treasury of the amounts referred to in paragraph (1) received in the Treasury. Proper adjustments shall be made in the amounts subsequently transferred to the extent prior estimates were in excess of or less than the amount required to be transferred.

(c) Management of Trust Fund. . . .

(d) Expenditures from Trust Fund

If an international deep seabed treaty is ratified by and in effect with respect to the United States on or before the date ten years after June 28, 1980, amounts in the Trust Fund shall be available, as provided by appropriations Acts, for making contributions required under such treaty for purposes of the sharing among nations of the revenues from deep seabed mining. Nothing in this subsection shall be deemed to authorize any program or other activity not otherwise authorized by law.

(e) Use of funds

If an international deep seabed treaty is not in effect with respect to the United States on or before the date ten years after June 28, 1980, amounts in the Trust Fund shall be available for such purposes as Congress may hereafter provide by law. . . .

§ 1473.   Revenue and customs or tariff treatment of deep seabed mining unaffected

Except as otherwise provided in sections 4495 to 4498 of Title 26, nothing in this chapter shall affect the application of Title 26. Nothing in this chapter shall affect the application of the customs or tariff laws of the United States.

NOTE

For implementing regulations issued by U.S. Department of Commerce National Oceanographic and Atmospheric Administration (NOAA), see Deep Seabed Mining Regulations for Exploration Licenses, effective on October 15, 1981, *Federal Register*, Vol. 46, No. 178 (September 15, 1981), pp. 45890-920, reprinted in *International Legal Materials*, Vol. 20 (1981), pp. 1228-1258. A Correction to the above Regulations was later issued and became effective on February 9, 1982, *Federal Register*, Vol. 47, No. 27 (February 9, 1982), pp. 5966-71, reprinted in *International Legal Materials*, Vol. 21 (1982), pp. 867-871. In 1984, four licenses for deep seabed exploration were granted by the United States National Oceanic and Atmospheric Administration of the Commerce Department to Ocean Minerals Co., Kennecott Consortium, Ocean Management Inc. and Ocean Mining Associates. On January 13, 1986, the United States notified the Secretary General of the United Nations of the issuance of these licenses. See *Law of the Sea Bulletin*, No. 7 (April 1, 1986), pp. 74-86.

2.   Italy

ITALY: LAW ON THE EXPLORATION AND EXPLOITATION
OF THE MINERAL RESOURCES OF THE DEEP SEABED
February 20, 1985
International Legal Materials, Vol. 24 (1985), pp. 983-996.

Law No. 41 of February 20, 1985

Regulations on the Exploration and Exploitation of the Mineral Resources of the Deep
Seabed

. . . .

Article 1 - Purpose

This law regulates the exploration and exploitation of the mineral resources of the deep seabed
by Italian citizens or organizations, or by companies headquartered in Italy, hereinafter referred to as
"Italian nationals."

The provisions of this law are aimed at assuring the rational utilization of the mineral
resources of the deep seabed. It is a temporary measure pending the entry into force for Italy of an
international convention on the same subject concluded within the framework of the Third United
Nations Conference on the Law of the Sea.

Article 2 - Definitions

For the purposes of this law, the term

"deep seabed" means the seabed and the underlying subsoil beyond the areas which according to
international law are subject to the national jurisdiction of the coastal states;

"prospecting" means the general observation of large areas of the deep seabed for the purpose
of gathering, especially by means of samples, the necessary indications for locating mineral
deposits;

"exploration" means detailed observation, employing major technical and financial means, of a
specific area of the deep seabed in order to locate the economically exploitable mineral deposits and
to establish the technical modalities and conditions of exploitation. This operation also includes
the taking of samples and the extraction of sufficient mineral resources to allow for carrying out
tests prior to exploitation;

"exploitation" means the recovery of mineral resources for economic purposes.

*Article 3 - Obligation to Obtain Exploration and Exploitation Permits and Compliance with
International Rules*

Exploration and exploitation of the mineral resources of the deep seabed by Italian nationals
require a permit issued by the Italian Government in accordance with the present law, or a permit
issued by a State ensuring reciprocity under Article 16.

The permit gives the holder the exclusive right to carry out exploration or exploitation of a certain area of the deep seabed and does not entail claims to, or exercise of, rights of sovereignty over any part of the seabed itself.

The activities allowed under the permits mentioned in the first paragraph shall be governed by the principles of international law and conventions relating to:

a)   the use of the high seas, particularly as regards the freedoms of navigation, scientific research, and fishing;
b)   the protection and preservation of the marine environment;
c)   the safety and protection of human life at sea.

Italian nationals are prohibited from unduly interfering in activities carried out under a permit issued in compliance with the present law or by a State ensuring reciprocity.

Article 4 - Prospecting

No permits are required for prospecting. However, prospecting cannot be carried out in areas already included in exploration or exploitation permits if it is aimed at finding the very resources for which the exploration or exploitation permits have been issued.

Article 5 - Permits Issued by States Ensuring Reciprocity

Italian nationals applying for exploration or exploitation permits to States ensuring reciprocity under Art. 16 are required to simultaneously request the Ministry of Industry, Commerce and Crafts to register their applications.

For all practical purposes, the activities carried out are recognized from the date of the request for registration or from an earlier date if so recognized by the foreign State.

Article 6 - Participation of Italian Nationals in Foreign Organizations

The obligation to register mentioned in the above paragraph also applies to Italian nationals holding a substantial interest, either directly or indirectly, in companies, associations, or other foreign organizations.

Activities carried out in relation to the above interest are recognized for all practical purposes as dating from the request for registration or from an earlier date if so recognized by the foreign State with regard to the company, association, or organization.

Article 7 - Issuing of Permits

The exploration and exploitation permits are issued by the Ministry of Industry, Commerce, and Crafts in concert with the Ministry of Foreign Affairs and the Ministry of the Merchant Marine, subject to approval of work programs, and after consultation with the technical advisory committee for the deep seabed, as mentioned in Art. 17, on all technical and financial aspects relating to the programs themselves.

The permits may be denied if the Ministry of Foreign Affairs holds that granting them might seriously harm international relations.

In granting the permits, the following considerations are taken into account:

- that they do not exceed a reasonable area, taking the interest of the other States into account;

- the safeguarding of the country's interest in the supply of raw materials;

- the promotion of the development of the necessary technologies for the economic exploitation of the deep seabed.

Applicants for permits must have the technical and financial capacity required for exploration or exploitation in accordance with the principles and purposes of the present law.

Permits may be registered in the names of several Italian nationals meeting the requirements mentioned in the above paragraph, according to the quotas indicated in the permit application. Co-holders are jointly and severally responsible to the public administration for obligations connected with exploration or exploitation and are also jointly and severally answerable to third parties. One common representative must be chosen by the co-holders of the permit for their relations with public administration and third parties.

The holder of an exploration permit shall receive priority treatment for his application for an exploitation permit referring to the same area for which he holds the exploration permit, taking the results of the exploration into account.

In cases of competing applications for the same area, account is taken, *inter alia*, of the rationality and completeness of the work program, and the guarantees offered for carrying out the program, with particular consideration of the experience gained in that sector. Applications submitted within three months of the registration of the first application and referring to more than 30% of the same area are considered competing applications.

Article 8 - Duration of Exploration Permits and Extension of the Area

The initial duration of the exploration permit must allow for the implementation of the program and cannot exceed 10 years, but may be extended for successive three-year periods for justified reasons.

Extension of the area covered by the exploration permit is determined on the basis of the known characteristics of the site and the work program.

Article 9 - Duration of Exploitation Permits and Extension of the Area

The duration of the exploitation permit must be compatible with the general economy of the program and cannot exceed 25 years, but may be extended on justified grounds.

Extension of the area covered by the exploitation permit is granted for the purpose of allowing the rational exploitation of the mineral resources and taking the characteristics of the deposit and the available technology into account.

Article 10 - Modification and Revocation of Permits

The permit may be modified or revoked in the ways described in Article 7 if it appears necessary on the basis of the development of the technical or scientific state of the art or if it seems in the public interest or in order to bring them into compliance with obligations undertaken by the Italian Government on the international level. The permits may also be modified for valid reasons upon the holder's request.

The permits may also be modified and revoked by decree of the Minister of Industry, Commerce, and Crafts, in concert with the Minister of Foreign Affairs and the Minister of the Merchant Marine, if the Minister of Foreign Affairs finds that their continuation in the present form could seriously damage international relations.

Article 11 - Termination of Permits

The permit is declared terminated in accordance with Article 7, provided the reasons for the termination have been proven, and an adequate period of time has been granted to the holder to present his case, if the holder:

1) loses the required technical and financial means;
2) does not fulfill his obligations under the present law or provisions of the permit;
3) seriously violates his obligations concerning safety, health, working conditions, and the protection of the environment;
4) seriously falls behind in the observance of the time schedules and conditions set out in the work program;
5) cedes the permit without proper authorization;
6) delays payment of the amounts owed in connection with the exploitation in accordance with Article 15 for more than two years.

Article 12 - Transfer and Abandonment

The transfer of the permit or a part of it is subject to prior authorization by the Minister of Industry, Commerce, and Crafts, in concert with the Minister of Foreign Affairs and the Minister of the Merchant Marine after hearing the co-holders, if any, and after technical and financial evaluation of the transferee.

Any transfer without prior authorization is null and void, not only with regard to the parties involved, but also in relation to the public administration, without prejudice to the provisions of Article 11.

The abandonment of the permits must be requested by the holders and authorized by the Minister of Industry, Commerce, and Crafts, in concert with the Minister of Foreign Affairs and the Minister of the Merchants Marine after consultation with the technical advisory committee for the deep seabed.

Article 13 - Obligations of the Permit Holder

Without prejudice to the obligations deriving from membership in the European Economic Community, the holders of exploitation permits are obliged to use vessels, barges, installations, and aircraft flying the Italian flag or registered in Italy for the recovery and other activities connected with the processing of the minerals, as well as for the transport of the recovered resources.

They must also give priority to the national market with regard to the recovered products, if the processing of the recovered minerals is not performed in Italy.

Waivers for the provision of the first paragraph may be obtained from the Minister of the Merchant Marine is concert with the Minister of Foreign Affairs and the Minister of Industry, Commerce, and Crafts, and for the provisions of the second paragraph from the Minister of Industry, Commerce and Crafts in concert with the Minister of Foreign Affairs and the Minister of the Merchant Marine, in both cases after consultation with the technical advisory committee for the deep seabed.

Article 14 - Supervision and Control

The supervision and control of the activities governed by this law are exercised by the Ministry of Industry, Commerce, and Crafts and the Ministry of the Merchant Marine with regard to their respective competencies.

The costs for the exercise of supervision and control are borne by the permit holders.

The engineers of the Corps of Engineers as well as the functionaries of the Ministry of the Merchant Marine who are charged by ministerial decree with exercising the supervision and control in accordance with the first paragraph shall be considered officers of the criminal police for the purposes of this law.

Article 15 - Financial Burdens to be Borne by Permit Holders

The application for a permit in accordance with Article 7 must be accompanied by payment of a fee payable to the State, the amount of which and the manner of payment are established by the implementation regulations of Article 21.

For the purposes of the Italian Aid to the Developing Countries, the holder of an exploitation permit obtained under this law must pay 3.75% of the median market value of the minerals recovered from the deep seabed to the State. For minerals for which there is no market value, an equivalent value is determined by means of the implementation regulations of Article 21.

Article 16 - Reciprocating States

For the purposes of this law, to be recognized as a reciprocating state, a state must have a law which:

a)   regulates the exploration and exploitation of the mineral resources of the deep seabed in a manner equivalent to the purposes and results as provided by this law;

b)   recognizes the permits issued in accordance with this law;

c)   prevents the issuing of permits for areas which are, in total or in part, the subject of permits issued in accordance with this law.

The character of reciprocating state is accorded by the Minister of Foreign Affairs after consultation with the Minister of Industry, Commerce, and Crafts, and the Minister of the Merchant Marine after conclusion of the necessary agreements with the state in question, on the condition that that state also recognize Italy as a reciprocating state.

The agreements mentioned in the preceding paragraph shall serve the purpose of safeguarding the interests mentioned in Article 13, first and second paragraph, as well as the cases dealt with in Articles 5 and 6.

The exploration and exploitation permits issued by a reciprocating state are considered equally valid as those issued in accordance with this law.

[Articles 17 to 21 omitted.]

NOTE

The following countries also enacted national legislation on deep seabed mining: France: Law on the Exploration and Exploitation of Mineral Resources of the Deep Seabed, December 23, 1981, *International Legal Materials*, Vol. 21 (1982), pp. 808-814; Germany: Act of Interim Regulation on Deep Seabed Mining, August 22, 1980, *ibid.*, Vol. 20 (1981), pp. 393-398 and Amendment of February 12, 1982, *ibid.*, Vol. 21 (1982), pp. 832-833; Japan: Law on Interim Measures for Deep Seabed Mining, July 20, 1982, *ibid.*, Vol. 22 (1983), pp. 102-122 and United Kingdom: Deep Sea Mining (Temporary Provisions) Act 1981, July 28, 1981, **ibid**., Vol. 20 (1981), pp. 1218-1227.

3. Mini-Treaties

FRANCE-FEDERAL REPUBLIC OF GERMANY-UNITED KINGDOM-UNITED STATES: AGREEMENT CONCERNING INTERIM ARRANGEMENTS RELATING TO POLYMETALLIC NODULES OF THE DEEP SEA BED
Done at Washington and entered into force, September 2, 1982,
TIAS 10562; *International Legal Materials*, Vol. 21 (1982), pp. 950-962.

THE PARTIES TO THIS AGREEMENT:

− HAVING regard to investments made in exploration, research and other pioneer activities relating to the polymetallic nodules of the deep sea bed;

− NOTING the adoption by the Third United Nations Conference on the Law of the Sea of a Convention on the Law of the Sea and of a Resolution Governing Preparatory Investment in Pioneer Activities Relating to Polymetallic Nodules prior to the entry into force of the Convention on the Law of the Sea, and the provision of that Resolution concerning resolution of conflicts among pioneer operators;

− RECALLING the interim character of legislation with respect to deep sea bed operations enacted by certain parties;

− DESIRING to make appropriate provisions for avoiding overlaps in the areas claimed for future pioneer activities in the deep sea bed and to ensure that, during the interim period, such activities are carried out in an orderly and peaceful manner;

− EMPHASIZING that this Agreement is without prejudice to the decisions of the Parties with respect to the Convention on Law of the Sea adopted by the Third United Nations Conference on the Law of the Sea;

− DESIRING also to avoid any discrimination among Parties in the implementation of this Agreement;

– DESIRING further to insure that adequate areas containing polymetallic nodules remain available for operations by other states and entities in conformity with international law;

HAVE AGREED AS FOLLOWS:

1. The object of the present Agreement is to facilitate the identification and resolution of conflicts which may arise from the filing and processing of applications for authorizations made by Pre-Enactment Explorers (PEEs) on or before March 12, 1982 under legislation in respect of deep seabed operations enacted by any of the Parties.

2. In the case of a conflict between the areas claimed in such applications, the Parties shall afford the applicants adequate opportunity, and shall encourage them, to resolve such conflict in a timely manner by voluntary procedures.

3. The Parties with whom applications for authorizations have been made by PEEs on or before March 12, 1982 shall follow the procedures set out in Part I of the Schedule hereto in respect of such applications.

4. The Parties shall consult together:

  (a)   with a view to coordinating and reviewing implementation of this Agreement;
  (b)   before issuing any authorization under their respective laws relating to deep sea bed operations;
  (c)   in regard to consideration of any arrangement to facilitate mutual recognitions of such authorizations, it being understood that any such arrangement shall not enter into force before January 1, 1983;
  (d)   before entering into any other bilateral or any multilateral arrangement between themselves or any arrangement with other States, with respect to deep sea bed operations.

5. In the event that any of the Parties with whom applications for authorizations have been made by PEEs on or before March 12, 1982 enter into an agreement for the mutual recognition of authorizations granted under their respective laws in respect of deep sea bed operations, the Parties concerned shall apply the procedures and impose the requirements set out in Part II of the Schedule hereto.

6. To the extent permissible under national law, a Party shall maintain the confidentiality of the coordinates of application areas and other proprietary or confidential commercial information received in confidence from any other Party in pursuance of cooperation under this Agreement in accordance with the principles set out in Part III of the Schedule hereto.

7. The Parties shall settle any dispute arising from the interpretation or application of this Agreement by appropriate means. The Parties to the dispute shall consider the possibility of recourse to binding arbitration and, if they agree, shall have recourse to it.

8. The Schedule hereto is an integral part of this Agreement and Part IV thereof shall apply for the interpretation of this Agreement.

9. The Parties shall not enter into any supplementary international agreement inconsistent with this Agreement.

10. This Agreement may be amended by written agreement of all the Parties.

11. This Agreement shall enter into force upon signature.

12. After entry into force of this Agreement, additional States may be invited to accede to this Agreement at any time with the consent of all Parties.

13. Any Party may denounce this Agreement on 30 days notice to the Government of the United States of America, and in no case shall the denunciation have effect before January 3, 1983.

DONE at Washington this second day of September, 1982, in the English, German and French languages, all texts being equally authentic, in a single copy which be deposited in the archives of the Government of the United States of America, which will transmit a duly certified copy to each of the other signatory Governments.

. . . .

THE SCHEDULE

PART I

APPLICATION PROCEDURES FOR PRE-ENACTMENT EXPLORERS

1. Each Party as provided in paragraph 3 of the Agreement shall forthwith inform the other Parties of entities which have filed applications with it.

2. Any application filed on or before March 12, 1982 shall be deemed to be filed on that date.

3. Each Party shall with all dispatch determine whether:

    (a)   each application filed with it fulfills its domestic requirements;

    (b)   the applicant is a PEE with respect to the area applied for (an applicant filing on behalf of a PEE shall itself be deemed a PEE for that application);

    (c)   the area is bounded by a continuous boundary;

    (d)   the area is reasonably compact.

4. Each Party shall:

    (a)   notify the other Parties of the results of the initial processing under paragraph 3 above;

    (b)   with the other Parties establish the final list of applications to which this Agreement applies;

    (c)   inform the other Parties whether the applicant has applied for the same area, or substantially the same area, to one or more other Parties;

(d)   if the applicant agrees, inform the other Parties of the coordinates of the area specified in any application filed with it;

(e)   endeavor to determine the exact locations of any conflicts.

5. No Party shall issue any authorization before January 3, 1983.

6. Where it is informed of the relevant coordinates, each Party shall notify each of its applicants who is involved in a conflict that a conflict exists. Such notification shall include coordinates identifying the areas in conflict and the identity of each applicant with whom conflict has arisen.

7. Each Party shall ensure that domestic conflicts are resolved pursuant to its respective domestic requirements. Upon agreement of the applicants, domestic conflicts may be resolved in accordance with the international conflict resolution procedures specified in the Schedule. The Parties shall enter into consultations if it appears that the resolution of a domestic conflict might affect the international conflict resolution procedures, or *vice versa*.

8. (1)   Each Party shall accept amendments to applications to which this Agreement applies only if they:

     (a)   pertain to areas with respect to which the applicant is a PEE (the area applied for in an amendment need not be adjacent to the area applied for in the original application); and

     (b)   are made in order to resolve an existing conflict with respect to that application.

(2)   Each Party shall process any amendment filed pursuant to this paragraph in accordance with the procedures described in the foregoing provisions of this Part except that paragraphs 2, 3(c), 3(d), and 4(c) shall not apply to amendments.

(3)   Amendments filed under paragraph 8 of the Schedule shall be eligible for mutual recognition in accordance with the terms of an agreement entered into by any of the Parties pursuant to paragraph 5 of the Agreement.

PART II

CONFLICT RESOLUTION FOR PRE-ENACTMENT EXPLORERS

9. (1)   Where there is an international conflict, the Parties shall use their good offices to assist the applicants to resolve the conflict by voluntary procedures.

(2)   If, within six months from the entry into force of an agreement between the Parties referred to in paragraph 5 of the Agreement, notwithstanding the good offices of the Parties, all applicants involved in an international conflict have not resolved that conflict, or are not parties to a written agreement submitting the conflict to a specified binding conflict resolution procedure, the conflict shall be resolved by binding arbitration in accordance with Appendices 1 and 2 if a Party so elects.

(3)   The procedures provided in the Appendices shall commence ten days after a Party notifies the other Party or Parties of the decision to elect arbitration.

PART III

PRINCIPLES OF CONFIDENTIALITY

10. In implementing the provisions of paragraph 6 of the Agreement, Parties shall apply the following principles:

(a)   The confidentiality of the coordinates of application areas shall be maintained until any conflict involving such area is resolved and the relevant authorization is issued, except on the basis of a demonstrated need to know and adequate assurances that the confidentiality of the information shall be maintained by the recipient;

(b)   The confidentiality of other proprietary or confidential commercial information shall be maintained in accordance with domestic law as long as such information retains its character as such.

PART IV

DEFINITIONS

11. In this Agreement:

(a)   "activities" means the undertakings, commitments of resources, investigations, findings, research, engineering development, and other activities relevant to the identification, discovery, and systematic analysis and evaluation of polymetallic nodules and to the determination of the technical and economic feasibility of exploitation;

(b)   "authorization" means any license, permit, or other authorization issued under the national law of a Party which authorizes the holder to engage in deep sea bed operations in a specified area or areas;

(c)   "conflict" means the existence of more than one application or amendment covered by this Agreement submitted by different applicants:

(1)   whether filed with the same Party or with more than one Party; and
(2)   in which the deep sea bed areas applied for overlap in whole or part, to the extent of the overlap;

"international conflict" means a conflict arising from applications or amendments filed with more than one Party;

"domestic conflict" means any other conflict;

(d)   a "pre-enactment explorer" ("PEE") is an entity which was engaged, prior to the earliest date of enactment of domestic legislation by any Party, in deep sea bed polymetallic nodule exploration by substantial surveying activity with respect to the area applied for; and

(e)   "polymetallic nodules" means any deposit or accretion on or just below the surface of the deep sea bed consisting of nodules which contain manganese, nickel, cobalt, or copper.

[Appendix 1, Arbitration Procedure and Appendix 2, Principles for Resolution of Conflicts, omitted.]

BELGIUM-FRANCE-FEDERAL REPUBLIC OF GERMAN-ITALY-JAPAN-NETHERLANDS UNITED KINGDOM-UNITED STATES: PROVISIONAL UNDERSTANDING REGARDING DEEP SEABED MINING
Done at Geneva, August 3, 1984 entered into force, September 2, 1984
International Legal Materials, Vol. 23 (1984), pp. 1354-1365.

1.   (1) No Party shall issue an authorization in respect of an application, or seek registration, for an area included:

(a) within an area which is covered in another application filed in conformity with the agreements for voluntary conflict resolution reached on 18 May 1983 and 15 December 1983 and being still under consideration by another Party;

(b) within an area claimed in any other application which has been filed in conformity with national law and this Agreement.

(i) prior to the signature of this Agreement, or

(ii) earlier than the application or request for registration in question, and which is still under consideration by another Party; or

(c)   within an authorization granted by another Party in conformity with this Agreement.

(2) No party shall itself engage in deep seabed operations in an area for which, in accordance with this paragraph, it shall not issue an authorization or seek registration.

2. The Parties shall, as far as possible, process applications without delay. To this end, each Party shall, with reasonable dispatch, make an initial examination of each application to determine whether it complies with requirements for minimum content of applications under its national law, and thereafter determine the applicant's eligibility for the issuance of an authorization.

3. Each Party shall immediately notify the other Parties of each application for an authorization which it accepts, including applications already received, and of each amendment to such an application. Each Party shall also immediately notify the other Parties after it has taken action subsequently with respect to an application or any action with respect to an authorization.

4. No Party shall authorize, or itself engage in, exploitation of the hard mineral resources of the deep seabed before 1 January 1988.

5. (1) The Parties shall consult together:

(a)   prior to the issuance of any authorization or before themselves engaging in deep seabed operations or seeking registration for an area;

(b)   with regard to any arrangements between one or more Parties and another State or States for the avoidance of overlapping in deep seabed operations;

(c)   with regard to relevant legal provisions and any modification thereof; and

(d)   generally with a view to coordinating and reviewing the implementation of this Agreement.

(2) The relevant Parties shall consult together in the event that two or more applications are filed simultaneously.

6. (1) To the extent permissible under national law, a Party shall maintain the confidentiality of the coordinates of application areas and other proprietary or confidential commercial information received in confidence from any other Party in pursuance of cooperation in regard to deep seabed operations. In particular:

(a)   the confidentiality of the coordinates of application areas shall be maintained until any overlap involving such an area is resolved and the relevant authorization is issued; and

(b)   the confidentiality of other proprietary or confidential commercial information shall be maintained in accordance with national law as long as such information retains its character as such.

(2) Denunciation or other action by a Party pursuant to paragraph 14 of this Agreement shall not affect the Parties' obligations under this paragraph.

7. (1) The rights and interests of an applicant or of the grantee of an authorization may be transferred, in whole or in part, consistent with national law. Subject to national law, the rights, interests, and obligations of the transferee shall be as set forth in an agreement between the transferor and the transferee.

(2) For the purpose of this Agreement, the transferee is deemed to stand in the same position as that of the transferor for his rights and interests including the right of priority to the extent those rights and interests represent in whole or in part the original rights and interests of the transferor.

8. The Parties shall seek consistency in their application requirements and operating standards.

9. The Parties shall implement this Agreement in accordance with relevant national laws and regulations.

10. The Parties shall settle any dispute arising from the interpretation or application of this agreement by appropriate means. The Parties to the dispute shall consider the possibility of recourse to binding arbitration and, if they agree, shall have recourse to it.

11. This agreement, which includes Appendices I and II, may be amended only by written agreement of all Parties.

12. (1) This Agreement shall enter into force 30 days after signature.

(2) A Party which has not adopted the necessary legal provisions for the issue of authorizations may, by a declaration relating to its signature of this Agreement, limit the application of this Agreement to the parts thereof other than those relating to the issue of authorizations. Where such a Party adopts legal provisions which, in the view of the other Parties, are similar in aims and effects to their own legal provisions, the first mentioned Party shall notify all other Parties that it accepts fully the provisions of this Agreement. Such a Party may also declare, upon signature, that, for constitutional reasons, this Agreement shall become effective for it only after notification to all other Parties.

13. After entry into force of this Agreement, additional States may, with the consent of all Parties, be invited to accede to this Agreement.

14. (1) A Party may denounce this Agreement by written notice to all other Parties, subject to the provisions of paragraph 6. Such denunciation shall become effective 180 days from the date of the latest receipt of such notice.

(2) A Party may, for good cause related to the implementation of this Agreement, after consultation, serve written notice on another Party that, from a date not less than 90 days thereafter, it will cease to give effect to paragraph 1 of this Agreement in respect of such other Party. The rights and obligations of these two Parties towards the other Parties remain unaffected by such notice.

(3) Subsequent to such notice referred to in subparagraphs (1) and (2), the Parties concerned shall seek, to the extent possible, to mitigate adverse effects resulting therefrom.

15. This Agreement is without prejudice to, nor does it affect, the positions of the Parties, or any obligations assumed by any of the Parties, in respect of the United Nations Convention on the Law of the Sea.

Done at Geneva on 3 August 1984, in eight copies in the English, French, German, Italian, Japanese and Netherlands languages, each of which shall be equally authentic.

[Appendix 1, Definition and Appendix 2, Notification, in *International Legal Materials*, Vol 23 (1984), pp. 1357-1358; the memorandum of implementation, *ibid.*, pp. 1358-1360; the exchange of notes between the United States and the United Kingdom, the Federal Republic of Germany, France, and Japan, the four countries with national legislation on deep seabed mining, at ibid., pp. 1361-1362; the German declaration on Berlin, *ibid.*, p. 1363 and the declarations of Belgium, Italy (in 1984), and The Netherlands, the three countries without legislation on deep seabed mining at that time, *ibid.*, pp. 1364-1365, are omitted here.]

NOTE

On August 14, 1987, the United Kingdom and the Soviet Union concluded an Exchange of Notes Concerning Deep Seabed Mining Areas together with an Agreement between Canada, Belgium, Italy, The Netherlands and the Soviet Union on Resolution of Practical Problems with Respect to Deep Seabed Mining Areas, text in *Law of the Sea Bulletin*, No. 11 (July 1988), pp. 29-45.

REFERENCES

Benedetto Conforti, "Notes on the Unilateral Exploitation of the Deep Seabed," *Italian Yearbook of International Law*, Vol. 14 (1978-79), pp. 3-19; John M. Murphy, "The Politics of Manganese Nodules: International Considerations and Domestic Legislation," *San Diego Law Review*, Vol. 16 (1979), pp. 531-544; Ram Prakash Anand, "The Legality of Interim Seabed Mining Regime," *Foreign Affairs Reports* (New Delhi), Vol. 29, No. 2 (February 1980), pp. 29-48; Dennis W. Arrow, "The Proposed Regime for the Unilateral Exploitation of Deep Seabed Mineral Resources by the United States," *Harvard International Law Journal*, Vol. 21 (1980), pp. 334-417; Gonzalo Biggs, "Deep Seabed Mining and Unilateral Legislation," *Ocean Development and International Law*, Vol. 8 (1980), pp. 223-257; David D. Caron, "Municipal Legislation for Exploitation of the Deep Seabed," *Ocean Development and International Law*, Vol. 8 (1980), pp. 259-297; Theodore G. Kronmiller, *The Lawfulness of Deep Seabed Mining*, Dobbs Ferry, N.Y.: Oceana, 1980, 3 Vols.; Mark S. Bergman, "The Regulation of Seabed Mining Under the Reciprocating State Regime," *American University Law Review*, Vol. 30 (1981), pp. 477-518; David D. Caron, "Deep Seabed Mining: A Comparative Study of U.S. and West German Municipal Legislation," *Marine Policy*, Vol. 5 (1981), pp. 4-16; Harry M. Collins, "Deep Seabed Hard Mineral Resources Act: Matrix for United States Deep Seabed Mining," *Natural Resources Journal*, Vol. 13 (1981), pp. 571-580; Lilliana Torreh-Bayouth, "UNCLOS III: The Remaining Obstacles to Consensus on the Deep Sea Mining Regime," *Texas International Law Journal*, Vol. 16 (1981), pp. 79-115; F. Patterson Willsey, "The Deep Seabed Hard Mineral Resources Act and the Third United Nations Conference on the Law of the Sea: Can the Conference Meet the Mandate Embodied in the Act?," *San Diego Law Review*, Vol. 18 (1981), pp. 509-532; E. D. Brown, "The Impact of Unilateral Legislation on the Future Legal Regime of Deep-Sea Mining," *Archive des Völkrrechts*, Vol. 20 (1982), pp. 145-182; Roger A. Geddes, "The Future of United States Deep Seabed Mining: Still in the Hands of Congress," *San Diego Law Review*, Vol. 19 (1982), pp. 613-630; Michael R. Molitor, "The U.S. Deep Seabed Mining Regulations: The Legal Basis for an Alternative Regime," *San Diego Law Review*, Vol. 19 (1982), pp. 599-612; Virginia A. Pruitt, "Unilateral Deep Seabed Mining and Environmental Standards: A Risky Venture," *Brooklyn Journal of International Law* (Brooklyn, N.Y.), Vol. 8(2) (Summer 1982), pp. 345-363; Jeffrey D. Wilson, "Mining the Deep Seabed: Domestic Regulation, International Law and UNCLOS III," *Tulsa Law Journal*, Vol. 18 (1982-83), pp. 207-260; Richard Todd Luoma, "A Comparative Study of National Legislation Concerning the Deep Sea Mining of Manganese Nodules," *Journal of Maritime Law and Commerce*, Vol. 14 (1983), pp. 243-268; Ronald Scott Moss, "Insuring Unilaterally Licensed Deep Seabed Mining Operations Against Adverse Rulings by the International Court of Justice: An Assessment of the Risk," *Ocean Development and International Law*, Vol. 14 (1984), pp. 161-191; L.F.E. Goldie, "Special Problems Concerning Deep Seabed Mining in the Event of Non-participation in UNCLOS: Prospect for a Reciprocating States Regime, Site Certainty, Investment Assurance and Potential Litigation," *German Yearbook of International Law*, Vol. 28 (1985), pp. 268-296; Moritaka Hayashi, "Japan and Deep Seabed Mining," *Ocean Development and International Law*, Vol. 17 (1986), pp. 351-365; William B. Jones, "Risk Assessment: Corporate Ventures in Deep Seabed Mining Outside the Framework of the UN Convention on the Law of the Sea, *Ocean Development and International Law*, Vol. 16

(1986), pp. 341-351; Manjula R. Shyam, "Deep Seabed Mining: An Indian Perspective, *Ocean Development and International Law*, Vol. 17, (1986), pp. 325-349; Richard G. Hildreth, "Legal Regimes for Seabed Hard Mineral Mining: Evolution at the Federal and State Level," *Ocean Development and International Law*, Vol. 20 (1989), pp. 141-156.

CHAPTER XI

INTERNATIONAL FISHERY MANAGEMENT AND PROTECTION OF MARINE MAMMALS

A. GENERAL BACKGROUND ON THE BIOLOGY AND ECONOMICS OF INTERNATIONAL FISHERIES MANAGEMENT

Gary Knight, "International Law of Fisheries," Louisiana State University, *Marine Science Teaching Aid*, Issue No. 2, January, 1973, Baton Rouge, Louisiana: Center for Wetland Resources, Louisiana State University, sponsored by the Office of Sea Grant, NOAA, U.S. Department of Justice. Reprinted by permission.

Introduction

Man has always obtained food from the sea. In some societies seafood is the principal protein supply, as well as a major revenue source. At present, approximately 60 million metric tons of fish are harvested each year from the world's oceans, and some scientists estimate that an additional 200 million metric tons could be harvested annually on a continuing basis.

Fishery resources are not distributed evenly throughout the oceans. Ninety percent of the sea by area is relatively unproductive; another 9.9% has moderate production (concentrated mainly above continental shelves); and only 0.1% has very high productivity (principally in areas where the upwelling of deep water brings life-supporting nutrients to the surface). Further, human tastes tend toward certain types of seafood, thus causing fishermen to concentrate on a few favored species in a few select locations. This congestion of effort has created difficult problems for high-seas fishery management.

To understand the complexities of modern international law of the sea with respect to fisheries, it is necessary to examine the relevant aspects of ocean resources law, fisheries biology, and economics. . . .

The Idea of Maximum Sustainable Yield

Fisheries biologists have determined that the growth pattern indicated in Figure 11-1 is typical of an emerging fish stock. From t_0 to t_1 the population increases slowly because of the small numbers of fish available for reproduction, but from t_1 to t_2 there is a period of rapid growth occasioned by the presence of more fish of breeding age and lack of pressure on food supplies. After t_2 the growth rate slows because of pressure on food supplies. Plotting the rate of change of density (dP/dt) against the population (P) yields a curve like that shown in Figure 11-2. This curve indicates that a constant harvest at h_0 will produce the maximum sustainable yield. The harvest should occur at the point of maximum recruitment to the stock and should, to maximize catch, be equal to that recruitment.

Maximum sustainable yield for a given stock cannot be determined and forgotten, however. Natural mortality rates are altered in response to environmental changes in salinity, water temperature, and other factors. Thus, there is a necessity for continuous monitoring of stocks in order to adjust maximum sustainable yield figures to changes in stock density and rate of growth.

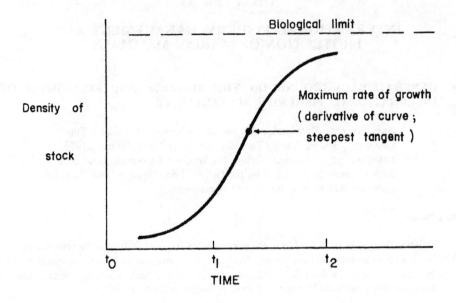

Growth Pattern of Emerging Fish Stock
Figure 11-1

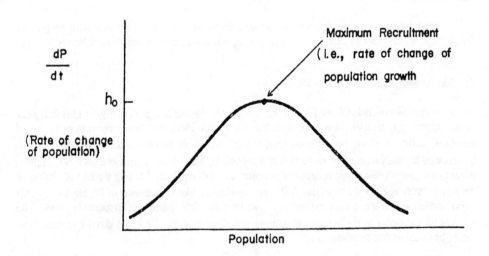

Maximum Sustainable Yield
Figure 11-2

Fisheries Economics

Beginning with an article written in 1954 by H. Scott Gordon, economists began examining the high seas fishery because it constituted a classic case of "common property resource." As noted above, this status was accorded the fishery because of the rule of "freedom of the high seas." Figure 11-3 is a simplified analysis of total costs and revenues for a particular fish stock. It has been established that the fishing effort required to produce maximum economic rent (profit), E_1, will always be less than required to produce maximum sustainable yield (msy), E_2. Unfortunately, most fishing takes place at the level of effort E_3 and even beyond, making the fishery one of the less profitable enterprises. Obviously, economists would like to see fishing effort at E_1, with the additional effort between E_1 and E_2 going into an activity where the effort would be more efficiently spent. Restricting entry into a fishery (or using other devices to reduce effort) is very difficult, however, for under the principle of freedom of the high seas, the only method for reducing effort is voluntary agreement among nations, a device not always easy to implement.

It should be obvious, however, that in order to achieve either msy or maximum rent, some restrictions or regulations must be imposed on the high-seas fisheries. In looking at attempts in this direction, it would be wise to analyze the critical issues involved in fisheries management and to determine exactly what it is one wants to achieve.

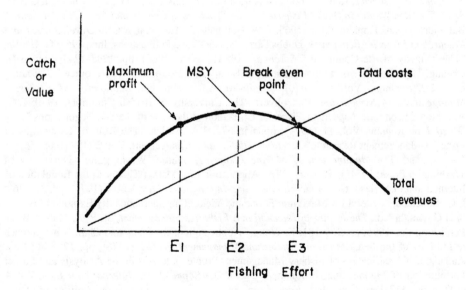

Total Costs and Revenues for A Particular Fish Stock
Figure 11-3

REFERENCES

(1) *On biology*

R.J.H. Beverton and S.J. Holt, "The Theory of Fishing," in M. Graham, ed., *Sea Fisheries: Their Investigation in the United Kingdom*, London: Edward Arnold, 1956, pp. 372-441; D.H. Cushing, *Fisheries Biology: A Study in Population Dynamics*, Madison, Wi.: University of Wisconsin Press, 1968; J.A. Gulland, *The Management of Marine Fisheries*, Seattle, Washington: University of Washington Press, 1974; D.L. Averson, "Opportunities to Increase Food Production from the World's Oceans," *Marine Technology Society Journal*, Vol. 9(5) (1975), pp. 33-40; D.H. Cushing, *Fisheries Resources of the Sea and Their Management*, London: Oxford University Press, 1975; P.M. Roedel, ed., "Optimum Sustainable Yield as a Concept in Fisheries Management," American Fisheries Society, *Special Publication 9*, Washington, D.C., 1975; J.A. Gulland, "World Fisheries and Fish Stocks," *Marine Policy*, Vol. 1 (July, 1977), pp. 179-189; P.A. Larkin, "An Epitaph for the Concept of Maximum Sustained Yield," *Transactions of the American Fisheries Society*, Vol. 106(1) (1977), pp. 1-11; M.A. Robinson, "World Fisheries to 2000: Supply, Demand and Management," *Marine Policy*, Vol. 4 (1980) No. 1, pp. 19-32; FAO Fisheries Department, *Atlas of the Living Resources of the Seas*, Rome: Food & Agriculture Organization of the UN, 1981; Edward J. Philips, "Biological Sources of Energy from the Sea, *Sea Frontiers* (Miami, Florida), Vol. 28 (Jan./Feb. 1982) No. 1, pp. 36-46.

(2) *On economics*

H.S. Gordon, "The Economic Theory of a Common-Property Resource: The Fishery," *Journal of Political Economy*, Vol. 62 (1954), pp. 124-142; R. Turvey and J. Wiseman, eds., *The Economics of Fisheries*, Rome: Food and Agriculture Organisation, 1957; F.T. Christy and A.D. Scott, *Common Wealth in Ocean Fisheries: Some Problems of Growth and Economic Allocation*, Baltimore: Johns Hopkins Press, 1965; F.W. Bell and J.E. Hazelton, *Recent Developments and Research in Fisheries Economics*, Dobbs Ferry, N.Y., Oceana Publications, Inc., 1967; G. Hardin, "The Tragedy of the Commons," *Science*, Vol. 162 (Dec. 1968), pp. 1243-1247; Steven N. Cheung, "The Structure of a Contract and the Theory of a Non-Exclusive Resource," *Journal of Law & Economics*, Vol. 13 (1970), pp. 49-70; A.D. Scott, ed., *Economics of Fisheries Management: A Symposium*, Vancouver: The University of British Columbia, 1970; L.G. Anderson, "Economic Aspects of Fisheries Utilization in the Law of the Sea Negotiations," *San Diego Law Review*, Vol. 11 (1974), pp. 656-679; J.A. Butlin, "The Role of Economics in Fisheries Management Research," *Maritime Studies and Management*, Vol. 2 (1974), pp. 56-65; J.A. Gulland, *The Management of Marine Fisheries*, Seattle, Washington: University of Washington Press, 1974; C.R. Kury, "The Application of a Market Theory to the Regulation of International Fisheries," *Ocean Development and International Law*, Vol. 1 (1974), pp. 355-369; L.G. Anderson, "Criteria for Maximum Economic Yield of an Internationally Exploited Fishery, in H.G. Knight, ed., *The Future of International Fisheries Management*, St. Paul, Minn.: West Publishing Co., 1975, pp. 159-181; E. Wong, "Application of the Economic Club: An Approach to the Law of the Sea," *Maritime Studies and Management*, Vol. 3 (1976), pp. 175-186; L.G. Anderson, "Classification of Fishery Management Problems to Aid in the Analysis and Proper Formulation of Management Problems," *Ocean Development and International Law*, Vol. 4 (1977), pp. 113-120; F.W. Bell, *Food from the Sea: The Economics and Politics of Ocean Fisheries*, Boulder: Co.: Westview, 1978; Sidney Holt, "Marine Fisheries," *Ocean Yearbook*, Vol. 1, Chicago: University of Chicago Press, 1978, pp. 38-83; Sidney Holt and C. Vanderbilt, "Marine Fisheries Ocean Yearbook, Vol. 2, Chicago: University of Chicago Press, 1980, pp. 9-56; Wilfred Prewo, "Ocean Fishing: Economic Efficiency and the Law of the Sea," *Texas International Law Journal*, Vol. 15 (1980), pp. 261-285; M.A. Robinson, "World Fisheries to

2000: Supply, Demand and Management," *Marine Policy*, Vol. 4 (1980) No. 1, pp. 19-32; Brian J. Rothschild, ed., *Global Fisheries: Perspectives for the 1990s*, New York: Springer-Verlag, 1983.

(3) On technology

F.T. Christy and A.D. Scott, *Common Wealth in Ocean Fisheries: Some Problems of Growth and Economic Allocation*, Baltimore: Johns Hopkins Press, 1965; J.L. Jacobson, "Future Fishing Technology and its Impact on the Law of the Sea," in F.T. Christy et al., eds., *Law of the Sea: Proceedings of the Ninth Annual Conference of the Law of the Sea Institute*, Cambridge, Mass: Ballinger, 1975, pp. 237-250; Shigeru Oda, "Impact of the Fishery Technology on International Law," *ibid.*, pp. 251-258; J. Scharfe, "Interrelations Between Fishing Technology and the Coming International Fishery Regime," *ibid.*, pp. 259-265; Vladimir M. Kaczynski, "Factory Motherships and Fish Carriers," *Journal of Contemporary Business*, Vol. 10 (1981), pp. 59-74; *Pelagic Drift Fisheries*, Hearings Before the National Ocean Policy, Study of the Senate Commerce, Science and Transportation Committee (98th Congress, 1st Session, 1985); Robert Eisenbud, "Problems and Prospects for the Pelagic Driftnet," *Boston College Environmental Affairs Law Review*, Vol. 12 (1985), pp. 473-490; David Whitmarsh, "Technological Change and Marine Fisheries Development," *Marine Policy*, Vol. 14 (1990), pp. 15-22.

B. OVERVIEW OF FISHERIES MANAGEMENT PROBLEMS

This textual section introduces the major issues involved in international fisheries management in terms of (1) the objectives of fishery management, (2) conservation of fishery resources, and (3) allocation of fishery resources. This overview is designed to permit acquisition of a broader perspective on the major problems before looking at documents and cases associated with specific problems.

> Gary Knight, "International Fisheries Management--A Background Paper," in Gary Knight, ed., *The Future of International Fisheries Management*, St. Paul, Minn.: West Publishing Co., 1975, pp. 16-37. Notes omitted. Some editorial changes have been made from the published version by Gary Knight. Reprinted with the permission of West Publishing Co.

1.   Objectives of Fisheries Management

. . . .

Some of the objectives identified are primary ones, which could form the primary basis of a management system. Others are clearly secondary, being sought only in conjunction with primary objectives. It should also be noted that even among a few selected objectives, it is likely not possible to maximize all because each will require some resource allocation useful in connection with others. Thus the most that could be achieved would be to optimize several selected objectives.

a. *Maximization of Food Production; Conservation*

A commonly asserted goal of international fisheries management is maximization or optimization of food production from the sea. This objective was expressly recognized in the

Convention on Fishing and Conservation of the Living Resources of the High Seas which provides in Article 2:

> As employed in this Convention, the expression "conservation of the living resources of the high seas" means the aggregate of the measures rendering possible the optimum sustainable yield from those resources so as to secure a maximum supply of food and other marine products. Conservation programs should be formulated with a view to securing in the first place a supply of food for human consumption.

Most international fisheries agreements also reflect this objective (see, e.g., the preamble to the International Convention for the Northwest Atlantic Fisheries). Within the scope of this general objective, one can advocate short term maximization of food production, in which a stock is fished to the point where the size of the catch does not warrant further expenditures of labor or capital, either with or without assurance that it will reconstitute itself over a period of years. This objective has never been formally asserted as the basis for management in any agreement, and although there is evidence that some states (principally those supporting sophisticated distant water fishing fleets) engage in this practice, it has never been asserted as a matter of national policy.

The usual expression for this objective is securing maximum sustainable yield, reflecting the goal of providing a recurring, long-term source of food from the ocean, based on the renewable resource characteristics of the fishery. Implementing the goal of maximum sustainable yield presents some practical problems, however. First, it is often difficult to define with accuracy the maximum sustainable yield of a given fish stock because of variations in environmental conditions and other factors. Second, two or more fishery stocks may be closely interrelated and it is sometimes difficult to predict the effect of a particular practice with respect to the catch of one stock on the sustainable yield of another. Third, the objective of producing maximum sustainable yield does not take into consideration the net economic return from the enterprise and, according to some economic theorists, automatically precludes maximizing economic return. These problems will be discussed in more detail in subsequent sections.

As with virtually all management objectives, the goal of maximizing sustained physical yield from the living resources of the ocean requires regulatory efforts which in turn demand some form of jurisdictional authority, whether supranational, international, or national.

b. *Maximization of Net Economic Return*

A newer suggested objective is securing the greatest economic value possible from the fishery, taking into consideration all costs of operation. This objective has not yet been implemented in any agreement or in practice, with the possible exception of arrangements concerning the fur seals, but is increasingly urged as the only valid objective for fisheries management. Generally stated as "maximizing the net economic revenues of the sea," this goal would transfer to other spheres the extra, uneconomic effort expended in maximizing sustained yield.

Among the costs often sought to be minimized in this approach are not only those of operations, but also those imposed by the competitive, open access characteristic of the high seas. To achieve this, as in maximizing sustainable yield, requires some jurisdictional authority with power to limit entry, regulate fishing activities, and the like. Among costs not generally discussed in this respect are costs of management, i.e., the costs of staffing and operating the requisite national or international management organizations.

One must also realize that maximization of economic return may not be the most desirable objective in particular situations. For example, it may be desired in certain countries to intensify the employment opportunities in fisheries in order to accomplish national employment objectives. In this case, the government may be willing to bear subsidy costs in terms of allowing the industry to operate at less than maximum efficiency in order to secure the objectives of higher employment.

c. *Avoidance of International Conflict*

The United Nations Charter contains a prohibition against the use or the threat of the use of force in the conduct of international relations. Resource management systems which are prone to produce conflict are clearly opposed to the spirit of international order which has evolved since World War II. Another objective of international fisheries management, then, would be to design a regime which will minimize the possibilities for international conflict.

Although relatively isolated, there are many examples of conflict escalated to violence in fishery situations. These have occurred in the Iceland-United Kingdom dispute over fishing rights in waters adjacent to the coast of Iceland; in the South Pacific between Chile, Ecuador, and Peru, on the one hand, and the United States, on the other; between France and Brazil over the lobster fishery off the coast of Brazil; and between Japan and the Soviet Union with respect to sedentary species of living resources on the Northwest Pacific Ocean seabed. Such conflicts often arise as a result of extensive claims of coastal state competence being challenged by fishermen from distant water fishing states. In other instances disputes have arisen over the question whether particular species fall within the legitimate competence of the coastal state under the sedentary resources provision of the Convention on the Continental Shelf.

The primary concern in this objective should not so much be the physical danger from the isolated instances of violence arising from such conflicts, but rather the poisoning effect which such continuing conflicts have on international relations among the states involved. For example, the personal injuries and property damage resulting from the entire history of the United States-CEP dispute in the South Pacific probably do not approach that from automobile accidents in a large United States city on a single day. Yet the conflict has affected United States-Latin American relations involving countries other than Chile, Ecuador, and Peru; has been a thorn in the side of negotiators on issues other than fisheries; and has created internal political difficulties far out of proportion to the values involved. Thus, in considering this objective, one must look beyond the immediate conflict manifestations, and determine the long range effects of a failure to come to grips with situations generative of conflict.

This objective of fisheries management also goes beyond the mere inclusion in any international or regional agreement of dispute settlement provisions, and relates to the substance of the regime agreed upon, for unless the substance deals with the past conflicts and develops a system to avoid their repetition, conflict settlement provisions will be relatively worthless.

d. *Maximum Utilization of the Fishery for Employment Purposes*

Some coastal states may perceive value in achieving increased employment, by utilizing the fishery as a labor intensive effort. This approach would generally contravene the objective of maximization of net economic return, and perhaps even of maximizing sustained yield, and would be the result of a political decision to effectuate a social rather than an economic or biologic policy.

e. *Equitable Allocation of Fishery Resources*

Another possible goal of international fisheries management is the distribution of fishery resources based on some criteria other than the open access principle or coastal state preferences. Such criteria might include protein deficiency or general economic underdevelopment, on a per capita basis.

Although this alternative seems to have little promise on an international scale because of the logistics involved, if considered in a narrow regional context or even in the context of a bilateral or low-party multilateral agreement, there might be some validity in it. Difficulties, of course, would be in securing agreement on the criteria determining allocation, and in making allocations pursuant to those criteria.

f. *Development of Knowledge and Technology*

Another objective of international fisheries management would be the development of knowledge and technology through the management system in order to (i) increase biologic output, (ii) increase economic efficiency, or (iii) develop new resources. As noted in a previous section, one of the functions of most fisheries commissions is to perform scientific research and make determinations about the stocks of fish with which it is concerned in order to maximize biologic output. However, few if any commissions to date have been concerned with increasing economic efficiency or developing new resources from the sea.

g. *Minimization of Interference with Other Uses of Ocean Space*

This objective differs from the objective of avoidance of international conflict in that the latter has as its goal the reduction of conflict between states or individuals involved in fishing activities while the objective now under discussion has as its goal the avoidance of conflict between fishing activities and other uses of the marine environment.

Such conflicts can be classified in two categories--conflicts over space and effects on the fishery resource itself. In the former would be such other activities as the emplacement of artificial structures on the continental shelf for petroleum and natural gas exploitation, naval maneuvers and other sea based military operations, general maritime navigation, and recreational activities. In the second category would be pollution or intentional modification of the marine environment.

In each of these cases, as well as others, it may be desirable to develop the concept of multiple or compatible use rather than limiting the use of a particular area of ocean space to a single endeavor. Thus another objective of an international fisheries management system might be to ensure that the activities carried on by the fishing industry are not inconsistent with other traditional uses of the areas involved, and vice versa.

h. *Political Acceptability*

This objective differs from the others in that it does not go to the substance of an international fisheries management regime as such but rather to perceptions about that substance held by members of the international community. Any international fisheries regime must, in order to be effectuated, be acceptable to a substantial majority of nations (perhaps a two-thirds majority if the route of international agreement in the context of the Third Conference is utilized). This acceptability will itself depend on the perceptions of coastal states about their national interests in international fisheries management. . . .

It should be noted, however, that acceptability can be as much a matter of education as of perception. In ensuring acceptability, then, an objective of fisheries management regimes might be the education of decision-makers in all nations concerning the scientifically determinable facts about fishery stocks, the technology for their harvest, and the economics of their consumption. What would be politically unacceptable today because of ignorance of the facts could become feasible tomorrow through logical explanations of the workings of the international fishery.

2.   Conservation

. . .[C]onservation refers to the objective of ensuring a renewable yield from a resource stock. . . .

a. *Determination of Maximum or Optimum Sustainable Yield*

Optimum sustainable yield was established as the international management criterion for fisheries in the Convention on Fishing and Conservation of the Living Resources of the High Seas. It has generally been accepted by scientists and political authorities alike as one of the most desirable goals of fisheries management. This is not to suggest that future regimes might not contain a blend of other goals or that other goals have not been sought in the past.

Determination of maximum sustainable yield involves the gathering of basic scientific data about fishery stocks--their migratory patterns, breeding habits, natural predation, and other factors. The object is to determine for a given time period the amount of fish which can be harvested from a particular stock while ensuring a similar return from the stock in future time periods. Two of the issues involved in this effort are of particular importance because they are at the frontier of the current move toward an international fisheries management.

First, there is in some situations a difficulty in determining sustainable yield figures because of the complex interrelationship among various species of fish in a given area. These inter-relationships are sometimes not well understood and present serious obstacles to data analysis. Suppose, for instance, that the maximum sustainable yield for two interrelated stocks of fish, A and B, were set up at 2000 and 5000 units, respectively, on the basis of research on the species in isolation. Assume further that stock A is a predator of stock B. If stock B is fished at the maximum sustainable yield of 5000 units, this will cause a reduction in food supply for stock A which could result in diminutions of its total mass. That being the case, the figure of 2000 units as maximum sustainable yield for stock A, although correct on an isolated analysis, would at that point probably be excessive. A further difficulty--related to the actual catch rather than the determination of an acceptable figure--is that of "incidental catch." Even if acceptable sustainable yield figures can be developed, ensuring adherence to the limit is difficult in practice because of the incidental harvest of stocks and the unreliability of data inputs on this practice.

Second, raw data is always subject to interpretation and, as with the interpretation of geophysical data concerning fossil fuel deposits in submerged lands, there can be as many interpretations of fisheries data as there are interpreters. In the fisheries situation the issue is further complicated by the fact that national interests are at stake, and one can at least question the impartiality of the interpreters of data when the positions of their respective nation states may depend upon the outcome of the analysis. Naturally, one is loathe to suggest any lack of impartiality on the part of scientists, but within the legitimate confines of given discipline there are always doctrinal disputes and much room for variation in interpretation, so that within the present system of fishery commissions there may be some problems associated with the nation-state approach to international order which might well be relieved through a new or more imaginative approach to fisheries management.

b. *Machinery*

The application of conservation systems with respect to high seas fisheries requires some national, regional, or international machinery which can conduct the research necessary for establishing standards, which can make recommendations based on that research, and which can exercise the requisite enforcement authority with respect to such recommendations. The principal issue is the locus in the world governmental hierarchy of this authority--national, regional, or international. . . .

Of course, some overall international machinery could be desirable from the standpoint of adopting rather general, fundamental standards for the conduct of fisheries regulation regarding such areas of avoidance of international conflict and minimization of interference with other uses of ocean space. These types of issues, if left at the regional or national level, might be unattainable due to national or regional conflicts.

Finally, one must also consider that there already exist some twenty international fishery management bodies, and it may be desirable to develop a "new order" utilizing these existing mechanisms rather than simply scrapping them.

c. *Enforcement Mechanisms*

. . . .a critical aspect of any conservation system is the development of a mechanism by which the standards adopted can be enforced in practice. This, of course, requires concessions on the part of nations concerning aspects of their sovereignty with respect to territorial water areas, economic resource zones, or their nationals. In given situations this may be more or less difficult to achieve. For instance, virtually all nations have refused to accept any enforcement mechanisms external to their own national interests.

d. *Costs of Management*

Little consideration has been given in the past in analyzing the effectiveness of fishery management systems in terms of the costs involved in the management system itself. These costs involve the salaries paid to staffs of fishery commissions, funds allocated for special studies, supplies and equipment necessary to carry out scientific investigations, and the economic outlay to generally administer and enforce such agreements. If in fact these costs result in a negative economic return from a particular stock, it is questionable whether the management effort itself is an acceptable goal. On the other hand, one must compare to that situation one in which there is no regulation and concomitant on overfishing and destruction of the fishery stock. The costs in the latter case may outweigh the ultimate costs even though there is a heavy burden from management.

3.   Allocation

[A]llocation concerns the issue of the distribution of the catch or revenue therefrom among participants or non-participants in the fishery. . . .

Virtually all of the issues concerned with allocation . . . arise from efforts to modify or restrict the effect of the open access system. . . .

a. *Distant Water Versus Coastal Fishing Nations*

At the core of the allocation dispute between coastal and distant water fishing nations is the open access character of the high seas fishery. In recent years several nations have subsidized their fishing fleets and have developed sophisticated, efficient gear with which to roam the world oceans in pursuit of fish stocks. Beyond the limits of a territorial sea or recognized exclusive fisheries zone, these fleets are free to exploit fishery resources even though coastal states may also have an interest in those stocks. The issue is not clear cut in favor of allocating the resource to either party. There are a number of factors involved, including:

(i) *Historic Rights*. One issue concerns historic fishing rights which may have been established by either coastal or distant water fishing nations through long usage of a particular area of the high seas for the purpose of taking fishery resources. For example, when the United States adopted a twelve mile exclusive fisheries zone in 1966, traditional fishing rights in the three to twelve mile belt by citizens of Mexico, *inter alia*, were recognized and were handled on a "phase out" basis. This in itself does not constitute any explicit recognition that Mexico had legal rights in the fisheries in this zone, but does reflect the fact of political and economic life that it would be generative of conflict to suddenly and unilaterally eliminate either the distant water state or the coastal state from an area in which it had traditionally derived resources and revenues.

(ii) *Bilateral Agreements*. One method of handling the conflict between distant water and coastal fishing nations with respect to allocation of the resource has been to enter into bilateral agreements by which one party trades off certain interests or rights for another. Some of these agreements concern reciprocal access, some relate to closing of open access areas in return for opening of closed access areas, while still others contain tradeoffs completely external to the fishery.

(iii) *Exclusive Fishing Zones*. The solution of allocation adopted (or preferred) by some nations is to establish zones of exclusive fishing rights extending to substantial distances in the sea, thus totally excluding the distant water state and allocating to the coastal state the entirety of the stock in question. Obviously, this is unsatisfactory to the distant water states which tend to base their arguments on either historic rights or on the conclusion of special bilateral and low party multilateral agreements involving tradeoffs for the maintenance of their fishing rights. [The issue is now generally moot as the 1982 United Nations Convention on the Law of the Sea establishes the regime of Exclusive Economic Zone up to 200 miles from the baseline of the territorial sea.]

b. *New Entrants*

One method of managing fishery stocks is for all the states concerned with the exploitation of that fishery to agree on maximum sustainable yield (or other objectives) and upon an allocation of the resultant catch among themselves. A problem is created, however, when a new state, not previously engaged in the fishery, also wishes to exploit that stock. Because of the open access character of the high seas and the resources thereof, there is no international law principle to prevent the new entrant from entering the fishery. However, this entry usually renders ineffective the conservation and allocation system agreed upon by the party to the agreement. There have been several proposals for handling the problem of new entrants, one of which is to allocate a certain percentage of the maximum sustainable yield for new entrants on an annual basis. Quotas would then be adjusted to reflect the new participant. Still another proposal is that new entrants be "bought off" by those states affected through revenues generated from the fishery.

With one non-relevant exception, neither of these systems has even been utilized in practice, and the problem of the new entrant is likely to become more severe in the next two decades as a result of developing countries' emphasis on fishery industries coupled with technical assistance from F.A.O. [Food and Agriculture Organization] and other organizations.

c. *Abstention*

An issue related to that of new entrants is the "doctrine of abstention." This doctrine would require a state not previously engaged in a fishery, which fishery was subject to a conservation and allocation system pursuant to international agreement, to abstain from entering into that fishery. It can also refer to the concept that a state will refrain from taking anadromous species on the high seas to ensure adequate stock return to spawning grounds subject to coastal state management systems.

In fact, the "doctrine" of abstention is not now nor has it ever been a rule of international law. It was proposed by the United States as a method of preserving the salmon and other fisheries in the Northwest Pacific Ocean. It has also been suggested as a means of handling the problem of new entrants, but, in fact, this is a non-solution because there is no benefit to the new entrant from simple abstention. If a simple *quid pro11 quo* were found for such a situation, the result would be properly described as a bilateral agreement which one state gives up the right of access in return for another payoff, and "abstention" as such would not enter into the picture as a legal doctrine.

d. *Open Access or Allocation of Rights*

The open access character of the high seas and the resources thereof means that allocation is determined by a first-come first-served basis. Opposing this system would be some mechanism for allocation of rights on the high seas much as mineral rights are allocated on an exclusive basis on the continental shelf or in upland areas. This requires some governmental entity possessing the requisite jurisdiction to enforce regulations concerning limitation of entry. If 200 mile economic resource zones were adopted, each individual coastal state would then possess the requisite authority to grant rights or licenses on a stock or area basis if it so chose although such a management system would suffer from the defects associated with migratory species which do not remain during their entire life cycle within the jurisdiction of a single state. Beyond the limits of national jurisdiction there would have to be established an international organization which would be given powers by its constituent nations to regulate access.

In view of the traditional character of the fishery, however, there is likely to be industry resistance to such a scheme and there will also probably be resistance from national governments (partly as a result of influence from their respective industries) to any international organization possessing the requisite jurisdiction to develop limitation of entry systems. Nonetheless, it is clear that with the continued congestion involved in productive fishing areas, some form of allocation of rights should be adopted because completely unregulated open access results in economic and biologic waste. Whether the existing systems of bilateral or low party multilateral conventions will suffice is problematical.

e. *Machinery*

. . . . The principal issue is whether the machinery for allocating the catch of a particular stock will be operative at a national, regional, or international level. Also critical is the method of allocation of rights and the decision-making process therefor within the national, regional, or international organization. However, questions of allocation are much more politically charged than questions of conservation. Thus it would seem likely that states would be more reluctant to give up aspects of sovereignty necessary to confer upon their regional or international organization the authority for allocating catch. Rather the mechanism that has evolved in the few instances where quotas are established is simply one of international negotiation--each nation negotiates within the context of its own national priorities for the maximum allocation of the stocks in which it has the greatest interest.

It may be more desirable at some time in the future (taking into consideration the issue of political acceptability) to move this process up the ladder to regional or international organizations which will allocate resources on the basis of specified criteria and data furnished by appropriate fishery commissions concerning conservation and catch figures.

f. *Anadromous Species*

.... The argument asserted by coastal states in whose fresh water anadromous species spawn is that such coastal states are, from both a biologic and economic viewpoint, the only logical repositories of management authority. For example, it has been suggested that the only rational location for the taking of an anadromous species is within the territorial waters of the state upon return of the species to its spawning ground. This would entirely preclude the taking of the species on the high seas, and thus would result in a complete allocation of resources to the coastal state. If such an approach is to be politically acceptable, it will likely have to be coupled with some form of "phase out" arrangement or an economic "payoff" for non-access.

It has also been argued that the economic investment which a coastal state makes in maintaining water quality in spawning areas, in constructing ladders providing greater access to spawning groups, and the like, justifies some preferential catch rights to the stock as a basis for ensuring a fair rate of return on the investment. . . .

g. *Wide Ranging Species*

Wide ranging species, predominantly tuna and whales, do not migrate exclusively in coastal waters or predominantly off the waters of any single state. Unlike anadromous species, they do not return to fresh waters of a single state. There is growing support for treating these species on an international basis apart from any coastal state-oriented economic zone since the contact therewith is minimal. . . .

h. *Sedentary Species*

Sedentary species of living resources, defined by international agreement as organisms which, at the harvestable stage either are immobile on or under the seabed or unable to move except in physical contract with the seabed or the subsoil, were placed under the exclusive jurisdiction of the coastal state in the Convention on the Continental Shelf [Art. 2(4)]. The principal conflict which has arisen concerning the treatment of sedentary species is the precise nature of such species included within the definition contained in Art. 2(4) of the Continental Shelf Convention. Disputes have arisen between France and Brazil, and among Japan, the Soviet Union, Australia and the United States on this issue. Various species of lobster have usually been at the core of such disputes. [The issue is now moot as the 1982 United Nations Convention on the Law of the Sea grants coastal states exclusive jurisdiction with respect to these resources within Exclusive Economic Zone whether they were sedentary or demersal.]

i. *Role of Landlocked States*

The traditional interest of landlocked states in the ocean has been in securing access through their neighboring coastal states to the sea for purposes of importing and exporting commodities. Although arguments have been made to the effect that such a right exists as a matter of principle, no international agreement afforded to landlocked states a right to access to the sea prior to the Convention on Transit Trade of Landlocked Countries. Few coastal states have become party to this convention, so that the plight of the landlocked state in terms of access is still essentially relegated to a question of negotiation with its coastal neighbor. The Convention on the High Seas does impose an obligation on the coastal state to negotiate in a reasonable manner, but does not impose any duty to admit the passage. . . .

Pursuant to Article 2 of the Convention on the High Seas, landlocked states have the right to fish the high seas on an open access basis for these resources. . . . [The 1982 United Nations Convention on the Law of the Sea now recognizes certain rights of land-locked states in securing access to neighboring coastal states' fishery resources.]

REFERENCES

D.E. Bevan, "Methods of Fishery Regulation," in J.A. Crutchfield, ed., *The Fisheries*, Seattle, University of Washington Press, 1965, pp. 25-41; W.M. Chapman, "Governmental Aspects of Harvesting the Living Resources of the Sea," *Natural Resources Lawyer*, Vol. 1(3) (1968), pp. 119-129; P.M. Dodyk, *Comments on International Law and Fishery Policy*, Washington, D.C.: The Clearinghouse for Federal Scientific and Technical Information, pp. 179-427, 1968; V.L. Arnold and D.W. Bromley, "Social Goals, Problem Perception, and Public Intervention: The Fishery," *San Diego Law Review*, Vol. 7 (1970), pp. 469-487; W.M. Chapman, "The Theory and Practice of International Fishery Development--Management," *San Diego Law Review*, Vol. 7 (1970), pp. 408-454; M.B. Schaefer, "Some Recent Developments Concerning Fishing and Conservation of the Living Resources of the High Seas," *San Diego Law Review*, Vol. 7 (1970), pp. 371-407; W.T. Burke, "Some Thoughts on Fisheries and a New Conference on the Law of the Sea," *Occasional Paper No. 9*, Law of the Sea Institute, University of Rhode Island, Kingston, 1971; R. Eisenbud, "Understanding the International Fisheries Debate," *Natural Resources Lawyer*, Vol. 4 (1971), pp. 19-46; W.E. Hale and D.F. Wittusen, *World Fisheries: A Tragedy of the Commons?*", Princeton, N.J., 1971; J.L. Jacobson, "Bridging the Gap to International Fisheries Agreement: A Guide for Unilateral Action," *San Diego Law Review*, Vol. 9 (1972); F.T. Christy, "Alternative Arrangements for Marine Fisheries: An Overview," *Resources for the Future, Paper 1*, Washington, D.C. Program of International Studies of Fishery Arrangements, 1973; H. Kasahara, "Problems of Allocation as Applied to the Exploitation of the Living Resources of the Sea," in L.M. Alexander, ed., *The Law of the Sea: The Needs and Interests of the Developing Countries*, Kingston: The University of Rhode Island, 1973, pp. 94-100; R. Khan, "On the Fairer and Equitable Sharing of the Fishery Resources of the Oceans," *Indian Journal of International Law*, Vol. 13 (1973), pp. 87-95; A.W. Koers, "The International Regulation of Marine Fisheries: Some Problems and Proposals," *Annals of International Studies*, Vol. 4 (1973), pp. 191-211; R. Lakshmanan, "International Regulation of Fisheries," *Indian Journal of International Law*, Vol. 13 (1973), pp. 367-388; Shigeru Oda, "New Directions in the International Law of Fisheries," *Japanese Annual of International Law*, Vol. 17 (1973), pp. 84-90; G.R. Ottenheimer, "Patterns of Development in International Fishery Law," *Canadian Yearbook of International Law*, Vol. 11 (1973), pp. 37-47; J.P. Rivers, "International Fisheries Regulation," *Georgia Journal of International and Comparative Law*, Vol. 3 (1973), pp. 387-407; Freeman, *The Abstention Doctrine*, University of North Carolina Sea Grant Pub. No.

UNC-SG-74-07 (1974); E. Miles, *Organizational Arrangements to Facilitate Global Management of Fisheries*, edited by J. Conny and J. Tron, Washington, D.C., 1974; T.A. Clingan, Jr., "Changing Global Pattern of Fisheries Management," *Lawyer of the Americas*, Vol. 10 (Winter 1978), pp. 658-685; Douglas M. Johnston, *The International Law of Fisheries: A Framework for Policy-Oriented Inquiries*, New Haven, Conn.: New Haven Press, 1987; Mahdi El-Baghdadi, "An Effort to Establish a Novel Organizational Structure for the Management of Resources on the Basis of Efficiency and Equity," *International Review of Administrative Sciences*, Vol. 54, No. 4 (December 1988), pp. 585-611; Carl August Fleischer, "The New Regime of Maritime Fisheries," *Recueil des Cours* (Hague Academy of International Law), Vol. 209(2) (1988), pp. 95-222; Warren S. Wooster, *Fishery Science and Management: Objectives and Limitations*, Heidelberg, Germany: Springer-Verlag, 1988; David D. Caron, "International Sanctions, Ocean Management, and the Law of the Sea: A Study of Denial of Access to Fisheries," *Ecology Law Quarterly*, Vol. 16 (1989), pp. 311-354; Svein Jentoft, "Fisheries Co-Management: Delegating Government Responsibility to Fishermen's Organizations," *Marine Policy*, Vol. 13, No. 2 (April 1989), pp. 137-154.

C. INTERNATIONAL FISHERIES MANAGEMENT BEFORE MID-1970'S

1. Overview

> R.R. Churchill and A.V. Lowe, *The Law of the Sea*, 2nd ed., Manchester: Manchester University Press, 1988, pp. 227-231. Reprinted by permission.

Access to Resources

The way in which international law regulated access to fishery resources during this period is best understood by considering, first, the various jurisdictional zones of coastal States and, secondly, the regime of the high seas.

Internal waters and territorial sea. . . .internal waters and the territorial sea form part of a State's territory and the only right which other States enjoy under general international law in these waters is a right of innocent passage in the territorial sea and, in very limited circumstances, in internal waters. It therefore follows that a State enjoys exclusive access to the fish stocks in its internal waters and territorial sea, unless a foreign State is accorded access by agreement (as under the EEC's Common Fisheries Policy); this, however, is most unusual in practice.

The exclusive fishery zone. The exclusive fishery zone (EFZ) is a concept of relatively recent origin in the international law of the sea. While there had been a few claims to EFZs before 1958, notably the claims made in the late 1940s and early 1950s by some of the Pacific coast Latin American States to 200 mile zones, the EFZ is essentially a product of the failure of UNCLOS I and II to agree on the breadth of the territorial sea or to accord coastal States any special rights of access to fish stocks beyond the territorial sea. This failure led to a wave of unilateral claims by coastal States to twelve-mile EFZs (and some zones of greater breadth), a number of bilateral agreements recognising these claims, and at a regional level in Western Europe the Fisheries Convention of 1964. The development of this practice was such that, in the 1974 *Fisheries Jurisdiction* cases, the International Court of Justice had no hesitation in pronouncing that the twelve-mile EFZ had become established as a rule of customary international law. Within the EFZ the coastal State had exclusive or priority access to the resources of the zone, although in most cases States whose vessels had traditionally fished in the waters embraced by the new zones were given a period of time in which to phase out their activities and in some cases indefinite, thouh limited, continued access.

The continental shelf. Articles 1-3 of the Convention on the Continental Shelf, which the International Court of Justice in the *North Sea Continental Shelf* cases (1969) said also represent customary international law, give the coastal State exclusive access to the natural resources of its continental shelf. These include "living organisms belonging to sedentary species, that is to say, organisms which, at the harvestable stage, either are immobile on or under the seabed or are unable to move except in constant physical contact with the seabed or the subsoil" [Shelf Convention, art. 2(4)). While these sedentary species clearly include such things as oysters, clams and mussels, there has been considerable controversy as to whether they include creatures such as crabs and lobsters. Reference was made in chapter eight to some of the disputes that have arisen in this area.

High seas. . . .the high seas are not susceptible to appropriation and are open to use by all States. Thus the vessels of all States have access to the fish stocks of the high seas. However, this freedom of access is clearly of most benefit to those States that have the capital and technology to take advantage of it, that is, in the main, developed distant-water fishing nations. While access to the fishery resources of the high seas is in principle free and unrestricted, in practice many States have agreed, through arrangements regulating high seas fisheries, to limit their access. These arrangements will be considered in the next section. A common consequence of freedom of fishing on the high seas, particularly where access is not limited through agreement, is that more vessels engage in fishing than is economically justifiable, i.e., fishing is often at a level considerably above the MEY.

In the *Fisheries Jurisdiction* cases, where the International Court of Justice was faced with determining the validity of Iceland's extension of its fishing limits in 1972 from twelve to fifty miles, the Court held that under customary international law a coastal State particularly dependent on fishing for its economic livelihood in certain circumstances enjoyed preferential rights of access to the high seas fishery resources in the waters adjacent to its coasts. This finding by the International Court has been criticised because of the lack of evidence for and the imprecision of the alleged rule, and in practice no coastal State, either before or since the Court's judgment, has sought to rely on it.

Conservation

As regards conservation (i.e. the prevention of overfishing), the concern of international law was originally largely limited to allocating the competence to adopt conservation measures, but later international law became directly and increasingly concerned with substantive rules of conservation through the establishment of international fishery commissions and a number of *ad hoc* agreements regulating fishing.

As far as the competence to adopt conservation measures was concerned, this was distributed between coastal States, flag States and international fishery commissions. By virtue of the fact that internal waters and the territorial sea form part of its territory, a State has the competence to prescribe regulations governing fishing in those waters by vessels of whatever nationality and the competence to enforce such regulations. The coastal State has a similar competence in its EFZ and in respect of the sedentary species of its continental shelf. A flag State has the competence to prescribe fishery regulations for vessels flying its flag, wherever they may be. The flag State may take action to enforce such regulations, however, only on the high seas or in its own internal waters, territorial sea or EFZ. It thus follows that the only way in which regulations may be prescribed and enforced in respect of vessels fishing on the high seas is through flag States.

This division of jurisdictional competence between coastal States and flag States did not provide an adequate framework for effective conservation. Since in most areas of the world territorial seas and EFZs formed a rather narrow band of waters, coastal States had in practice control only over a comparatively small area containing rather limited fish stocks: furthermore, in many cases fish stocks which were found within their areas of control migrated outside those areas at certain times of the year. As far as flag States were concerned, while they alone could regulate fishing on the high seas, there was in practice little incentive for them to take conservation measures. If a flag State took measures to conserve a particular fish stock, those measures would not have any beneficial effect unless other flag States fishing the same stock took similar measures; but there was no way in which other flag States could be compelled to do so. The fact that article 2 of the High Seas Convention provides that the freedom of fishing on the high seas "shall be exercised by all States with reasonable regard to interests of other States in their exercise of the freedom of the high seas" appears in practice not to have been a factor encouraging flag States to take conservation measures, either singly or in concert, or restraining them from excessive fishing.

In order to try to overcome some of the drawbacks of flag State jurisdiction and narrow coastal State jurisdiction--although it must be emphasized, without attempting to change the basic nature of the jurisdiction enjoyed by coastal and flag States or the distribution of jurisdiction betwen them--some twenty or more international fishery commissions were established, the vast majority since 1945. These commissions were either set up to regulate particular species (e.g., whales, seals, tuna) or to regulate fisheries in particular regions (e.g., the North Atlantic, the North Pacific, the Baltic, Mediterranean, etc.). The functions and powers of these commissions varied considerably, but they all tended to have the same shortcomings: the inability to agree on conservation measures recommended by scientists as essential; the possibility of opting out of any conservation measures adopted; and poor enforcement of such measures. The last two tend to be self-perpetuating in the sense that if one State sees another not accepting a recommendation, or not properly enforcing it, there is no incentive for it to adhere to its obligations, since this will put its fishermen at a disadvantage compared with the fishermen of the defaulting State. Finally, an international fishery commission cannot control the fishing activities of those States which are unwilling to become members of it.

Apart from international fishery commissions, there were a number of international agreements, largely of an *ad hoc* character, which attempted to conserve fisheries on the high seas. Most of these agreements were bilateral or regional, as well as often being short-term, in character, but there was one general multilateral agreement--the 1958 Convention on Fishing and Conservation of the Living Resources of the High Seas, adopted at UNCLOS I. This convention required States parties to it to agree upon measures to conserve the fishery resources of the high seas: in certain very limited circumstances it gave a coastal State the right unilaterally to adopt conservation measures for areas of the high seas adjacent to its territorial sea. However, the Convention largely proved to be a dead letter. Many major fishing nations did not ratify it, since it did not correspond to the interests of coastal States, and since in many regions international fishery commissions had already been set up to take conservation measures.

Avoidance of gear conflicts

The avoidance and resolution of conflicts arising out of fishing activities, particularly conflicts between different types of gear, such as the interference and damage trawling may cause to standing nets, have been the subject of a number of bilateral treaties and one regional agreement. The latter is the 1967 Convention on Conduct of Fishing Operations in the North Atlantic, which is aimed at preventing collisions between vessels while fishing and conflicts between trawling and the users of fixed gear, and at facilitating the resolution of disputes arising out of such collisions and conflicts. Of the bilateral agreements, one of the most important in practice and most sophisticated in the institutional machinery it provides for conflict resolution is the 1973 Agreement between the USSR and USA relating to the Consideration of Claims resulting from Damage to Fishing Vessels or Gear and Measures to Prevent Fishing Conflicts. These kinds of agreements are still important, although as the trend in the reduction of foreign fishing in the 200 mile zones of coastal States increases their practical application will decrease.

2. U.S.-Chile, Ecuador and Peru (CEP) Dispute

The conflict between the Latin American states' assertions of 200 mile exclusive fishing zones, on the one hand, and the claim of high seas freedom of fishing by United States nationals, on the other, gave rise following World War II to the so-called "tuna war" or "U.S.-CEP" dispute (the initials representing the three west coast South American nations--Chile, Ecuador and Peru). The materials which follow give some indication of the nature of the dispute, attempts at resolution, and U.S. domestic legislation aimed at preserving existing high seas rights.

> "Department Reviews Fisheries Disputes and Their Effect on Inter-American Relations," *Department of State Bulletin*, Vol. 66, No. 1706 (March 6, 1972), pp. 284-287. [This is the statement made by Charles A. Meyer, Assistant Secretary for Inter-American Affairs before the Subcommittee on Inter-American Affairs of the House Committee on Foreign Affairs on February 3, 1972.]

Fisheries disputes arise from differences we have with certain Latin American countries regarding the breadth of the territorial sea and coastal state rights over resources of the waters adjacent to their coasts. The United States recognizes a 3-mile territorial sea and, in addition, claims a 9-mile contiguous zone of exclusive jurisdiction over fisheries. Ecuador, Peru, and Brazil, the countries whose names are most closely associated with the fisheries problem, claim 200 miles of sovereignty or exclusive jurisdiction over the waters off their coasts. Thus, in some ways, fisheries disputes can be seen as the result of a contest between those who believe that the waters beyond 12 miles are high seas and those who claim 200 miles. . . .

The elements of the fisheries disputes date from the middle and late 1940's. In 1945, when the world was populated by countries claiming less than 12 miles of territorial seas, President Truman issued two proclamations dealing with ocean resources off our own coasts. One of these proclamations stated U.S. policy with respect to the resources of the continental shelf. In reserving for the coastal state the resources of the continental shelf, President Truman carefullly reaffirmed the United States view that existing international law provided for a 3-mile territorial sea. We also clearly stated that it was not our intention to affect the high seas character of the waters above the continental shelf and the right thereon to free and unimpeded navigation.

In spite of our intentions, in 1947, Peru and Chile, noting that the United States had acted unilaterally to protect resource interests in an area off its own coast, laid claim to sovereignty and national jurisdiction over the seas adjacent to their coasts extending to a distance of 200 nautical miles. They were joined in 1952 by Ecuador when all three countries signed the Santiago Declaration on the Maritime Zone. It was the thesis of the three nations that the region delineated by this zone cosititues a distinct ecological unit within which a dynamic balance of nature is maintained.

The Declaration of Santiago suggests that the claim of Chile, Ecuador, and Peru is essentially a claim to resources, although in the years since 1952, it has been treated both as a resource claim and as a territorial sea claim. With it, conflict over fisheries resources became inevitable. I say "inevitable" because differences with countries that make claims with which we disagree, and which we protest, cannot always wait on the slow process of writing new international law. Where the American distant-water fishing fleet must continue to operate pending agreement, the differences manifest themselves not only in the exchange of notes protesting juridical positions but, most seriously, in fisheries disputes.

There are, as I said, now 10 Latin American countries with similar claims. In addition to Chile, Ecuador, and Peru, these are El Salvador, Nicaragua, Argentina, Panama, Uruguay, and Brazil. Costa Rica has had a 200-mile conservation zone. Of all of these states, the disputes which concern us today involve only Ecuador, Peru, Chile (because of the tie of the Santiago Declaration), and Brazil.

Two international law-of-the-sea conferences, one in 1958 and one in 1960, have failed to resolve the basic issues on territorial seas and resource jurisdiction. We are now looking to a new conference in 1973 to do so. Our experience with fisheries disputes and the proliferation of 200-mile claims in the hemisphere in the decade of the sixties compel us to conclude that this conference must be successful if we are to insure the navigational rights on the world's oceans which are essential to our security and if we are to resolve existing conflicts or, more, to prevent new conflicts over rights to the oceans' resources. Unfortunately, the necessity for international agreement and the difficulty of waiting for it are being most clearly demonstrated in the hemisphere.

Over the years the elements for a full-scale demonstration of the implications for the United States of disagreements over issues of law of the sea have been gathering, with little obvious relation to each other. The American distant-water fishing fleet, particularly our tuna fleet, has been modernizing and improving its technology. It has sailed to more distant seas in search of tuna for a growing American market. Flying the American flag, vessel owners are not obligated, in our view, to buy licenses to fish waters beyond 12 miles, although we do not object when they decide for themselves that they want to. As a consequence of the seizures which began in 1953, when Ecuador and Peru began enforcing their 200-mile claims against unlicensed American fishing vessels, the Congress acted in 1954 to begin assisting the tunaboat owners to meet the costs to them as individuals of an unresolved dispute between governments. Amended in 1968, the Fishermen's Protective Act now permits reimbursement for fines paid and licenses purchased to obtain release after seizure. Other pieces of legislation have been passed by Congress as the vessel seizures have drawn increasing attention to the problem. This body of legislation calls upon the executive branch to act or consider acting against countries that seize American fishing vessels with respect to military sales, economic assistance, military assistance, and ship loan programs. Other drafts of legislation are periodically put forward which are either more stringent or are intended to add to the list of retaliations available for use against seizing countries. We have opposed punitive legislation consistently. Without exception, it does not address the problem of how we end seizures. Instead, it increases the scope of the problem, either by placing new obstacles in the way of returning to negotiations or by complicating the issue by adding others to it, or both.

Throughout 1967 and 1968, in a new effort to find a solution, we urged Chile, Ecuador, and Peru to join us at a conference table. Seizures in 1969, to which we responded by applying the laws then in force, threatened to lead us to bitter confrontation. At that time, however, perhaps because for a brief moment we all had a glimpse of what could happen in a spiral of escalating action and reaction, the United States, Chile, Ecuador, and Peru agreed at last to convene a Quadripartite Fisheries Conference. Taking note of the fact that by that time we were all engaged in the steps leading to the United Nations resolution of 1970 calling for a new law-of-the-sea conference, the Quadripartite Fisheries Conference was to consider practical solutions that set aside our differences on the broader issues of international law.

The Quadripartite Fisheries Conference met in its first session in Buenos Aires in 1969 and met again in that same city in 1970. It was to have reconvened in a third session no later than July 31, 1971.

As I indicated in the beginning of my statement, 1971 was the year for demonstrating the dimensions of the confrontation that can flow from unresolved fisheries disputes. Between January 11 and March 27 and again in November and December, the Ecuadorean Navy made 51 seizures of American fishing vessels. The vessel owners paid a total of $2.4 million for the forced purchase of licenses and fines to obtain their release. This amount will be reimbursed to them under the terms of the Fishermen's Protective Act. The executive branch, because of the legislation passed throughout the years of the dispute, announced on January 18, 1971, the suspension of military sales and credits to Ecuador under the terms of the Foreign Military Sales Act. All other programs which were the subject of discretionary legislation were placed under review. Given your own experience with the countries of the hemisphere, you will not be surprised when you recall that this step of January 18 was quickly followed by an Ecuadorean appeal to the OAS to consider charges of economic aggression and to the expulsion of the United States Military Group from Ecuador. . . .

REFERENCES

S.A. Bayitch, "International Fishery Problems in the Western Hemisphere," *Miami Law Quarterly*, Vol. 10 (1956), pp. 499-506; P.E. Kinsey, "The Tunaboat Dispute and the International Law of Fisheries," *California Western Law Review*, Vol. 6 (1969), pp. 114-133; J.S. Wiegand, "Seizures of U.S. Fishing Vessels--The Status of the Wet War," *San Diego Law Review*, Vol. 6 (1969), pp. 428-446; D.C. Lecuona, "The Ecuador Fisheries Dispute," *Journal of Maritime Law and Commerce*, Vol. 2 (1970), pp. 91-114; Smetherman, "The CEP Claims, U.S. Tuna Fishing and Inter-American Relations," *Orbis*, Vol. 14 (1970-71), p. 951; Thomas Wolff, "Peruvian-United States Relations Over Maritime Fishing: 1945-1969," *Occasional Paper No. 4, Law of the Sea Institute*, Kingston, Rhode Island: University of Rhode Island, 1970; Thomas Wolff, "The United States, Chile, Ecuador and Peru: Some Reflections on the 1969 Report of the Commission on Marine Science, Engineering and Resources," in L.M. Alexander, ed., *The Law of the Sea: National Policy Recommendations*, Kingston, Rhode Island: University of Rhode Island, 1970, pp. 492-494; David C. Loring, "United States-Peruvian Fisheries Dispute," *Stanford Law Review*, Vol. 23 (1971), pp. 391-453; D.C. Edmonds, "200 Mile Fishing Rights Controversy--Ecology or High Tariffs?," *Inter-American Economic Affairs*, Vol. 26 (Spring 1973), pp. 3-18; R.O. Freeman, "Possible Solutions to the 200-mile Territorial Limit," *International Lawyer*, Vol. 7 (1973), pp. 387-395; Warren S. Wooster, "Scientific Aspects of Maritime Sovereignty Claims," *Ocean Development and International Law Journal*, Vol. 1 (1973), pp. 13-20; B.B. Smetherman and R.M. Smetherman, *Territorial Seas and Inter-American Relations--With Case Studies of the Peruvian and U.S. Fishing Industries*, New York and London: Praeger Publishers, 1974; J.M. Fisher, S. Wood, and E.T. Burge, "Latin American Unilateral Declarations of 200-mile Offshore Exclusive Fisheries: Toward Resolving the Problems of Access Faced by the U.S. Tunafish Industry," *Southwestern University Law Review*, Vol. 9 (1977), pp. 643-670; J. Joseph and J.W. Greenough, *International Management of Tuna, Porpoise, and Billfish: Biological, Legal and Political Aspects*, Seattle: University of Washington Press, 1979.

NOTE

In 1970 Brazil extended its exclusive fishing jurisdiction to 200 miles, thus posing a problem for United States shrimp fishermen who traditionally fished for shrimp off the Brazilian coast. Rather than launching an Atlantic version of the acrimonious "tuna war," the two nations quickly reached accord on an access agreement on shrimp on March 14, 1973 and revised on March 14, 1975, TIAS 7862. With the general acceptance of the regime of 200 miles exclusive economic zone since mid-1970s, the issue became moot and the agreement expired. For similar reasons, the "tuna war" issue between the United States and the CEP countries became moot after the mid-1970s.

SOUZA v. COMMISSIONER OF INTERNAL REVENUE
33 T.C. 817, 822-823 (1960)

[The Tax Court disallowed petitioner's claim based on residence in Peru under section 911(a)(2), I.R.C. 1954, on the ground that he was not within the territorial waters of Peru while fishing in waters within 200 miles of the Peruvian coastline but not within 3 miles thereof.]

Petitioner's argument that because he was fishing in the waters within 200 miles of Peru over which that nation claimed sovereignty, he was present in the territory of Peruvian sovereignty, cannot prevail. It is stipulated by the parties "[[t]hat the Executive Department of the Government the United States does not recognize the claim of Peru to sovereignty over the seas to a minimum of 200 miles from its coastlines, but recognizes the sovereignty of Peru over its waters to a distance of three miles from its coastlines." Further, we take judicial notice of the facts that the executive branch in its conduct of foreign affairs has traditionally denied asserted extensions by foreign countries of territorial waters beyond 3 miles, and that the executive branch protested the extension claimed by Peru. Congress, also, denied such claims in enacting a bill, 22 U.S.C. sections 1971-1976 for the protection of American-flag vessels seized by foreign countries....

The determination of the boundaries of nations is a matter of foreign affairs which is the function of the political departments of government, not the judicial. . . . Petitioner was not physically present within the territorial limits of Peru, when fishing in waters beyond 3 miles from the Peruvian coastline.

NOTE

Beginning in 1954, the United States Congress enacted a series of measures designed to protect national interests and to apply pressure to Ecuador to change its position on the issue. See Fishermen's Protection Act, 22 United States Code, Sections 1971-1979, originally enacted on August 27, 1954, 68 Stat. 883, and the Bartlett Act, United States Code, Section 1081 et seq., originally enacted on May 20, 1964, 78 Stat. 194. The Bartlett Act is repealed as of March 1, 1977, by § 402(b) of the "Fishery Conservation and Management ACt of 1976," P.L. 94-265 (April 13, 1976) which incorporates the essential provisions of the Bartlett Act for the United States new 200-mile exclusive fishery management zone.

REFERENCES

Hearings on S. 1988 before the Subcommittee on Merchant Marine and Fisheries of the Senate Commitee on Commerce (88th Cong., 1st Sess., 1963); Hearings on S. 1988 before the House Committtee on Merchant Marine and Fisheries (88th Cong., 2d Sess., 1964); M.M.

Whiteman, *Digest of International Law*, Vol. 4, Washington, D.C.: U.S. Government Printing Office, 1965, pp. 936-938; Eugene R. Fidell, "10 Years Under the Bartlett Act: A Status Report on the Prohibition on Foreign Fishing," *Boston University Law Review*, Vol. 54 (1974), pp. 703-756.

DEPARTMENT OF STATE
SECRETARIAL DETERMINATION

SUBJECT: *Transfer of Foreign Assistance Funds under the Fishermen's Protective Act*

Pursuant to Section 5(b) of the Fishermen's Protective Act of 1967, as amended, and in accordance with Executive Order 11772, I hereby certify that it is in the national interest not to transfer to the Fishermen's Protective Fund established by Section 9 or to the account established in the Treasury pursuant to Section 7(c) of the Fishermen's Protective Act of 1967, as amended, funds from the Foreign Assistance Act of 1961 programmed for Ecuador in the amount of $395,404.50 which is equal to the amounts specified in the attached lists paid by the Secretary of Commerce and reimbursed by the Secretary of Treasury in accordance with Section 3 and Section 7 of the Fishermen's Protective Act of 1967, as amended, for fishing boat seizures as follows:

[Names of various vessels seized between January 25 and February 1, 1975 omitted.]

Date: July 30, 1976

Henry A. Kissinger

REFERENCES

Hearings on S.3594 before a Subcommittee of Senate Committee on Interstate & Foreign Commerce (83d Cong., 2d Sess., 1954); Theodor Meron, "The Fishermen's Protective Act: A Case Study in Contemporary Legal Strategy of the United States," *American Journal of International Law*, Vol. 69 (1975), pp. 290-309; Steven J. Burton, "The 1976 Amendments to the Fishermen's Protective Act," *American Journal of International Law*, Vol. 71 (1977), pp. 740-744.

FOREIGN ASSISTANCE ACT
22 U.S.C. § 2370(o)
(Originally enacted September 6, 1965; 79 Stat. 659)

In determining whether or not to furnish assistance under this chapter, consideration shall be given to excluding from such assistance any country which hereafter seizes, or imposes any penalty or sanction against, any United States fishing vessel on account of its fishing activities in international waters. The provisions of this subsection shall not be applicable in any case governed by international agreement to which the United States is a party.

FOREIGN MILITARY SALES ACT
22 U.S.C. § 2753(b)
(Originally enacted January 12, 1971; 84 Stat. 2053)

No sales, credits, or guarantees shall be made or extended under this chapter to any country during a period of one year after such country seizes, or takes into custody, or fines an American fishing vessel for engaging in fishing more than twelve miles from the coast of that country. The President may waive the provisions of this subsection when he determines it to be importnat to the security of the United States or he receives reasonable assurances from the country involved that future violations will not occur, and promptly so reports to the Speaker of the House of Representatives and the Committee on Foreign Relations of the Senate. The provisions of this subsection shall not be applicable in any case governed by an international agreement to which the United States is a party.

[On January 18, 1971, the United States suspended all military sales and credits to Ecuador, and other assistance programs subject to discretionary legislation (e.g., 22 U.S.C. § 2370(o) were placed under review.]

FOREIGN ASSISTANCE AND RELATED PROGRAM APPROPRIATION ACT, 1972
86 Stat. 48, at 52.

§ 113. No part of any appropriations contained in this Act may be used to provide assistance to Ecuador unless the President determines that the furnishing of such assistance is important to the national interest of the United States.

"Assistance to Ecuador Determined Important to U.S. National Interest," *Department of State Bulletin*, Vol. 66, No. 1711 (April 10, 1972), p. 546.

SECRETARIAL DETERMINATION

Subject: *Assistance to Ecuador*

. . . .

Executive Order 10973, as amended, delegates to me as Secretary of State authority to make the determination permitted by Section 113 with respect to assistance furnished pursuant to the Foreign Assistance Act 1961, as amended.

I have reached the conclusion that the continued furnishing of assistance to Ecuador is important to the national interest for the following reasons:

1. Termination of assistance to Ecuador, pursuant to Section 113, would not assist in resolving the several issues on which the GOE [Government of Ecuador] and USG are in disagreement. To the contrary, such action would seriously reduce the possibility of reaching a negotiated settlement of these issues.

2. Termination of assistance to Ecuador, pursuant to Section 113, would adversely affect other important U.S. interests in our relations with that country.

3. Termination of assistance to Ecuador, pursuant to Section 113, could prejudice a broad range of U.S. interests in other countries of the Western Hemisphere.

4. Because of the effects outside Ecuador, the prospects for the successful negotiation of an acceptable convention on Law of the Sea next year could be reduced.

On the basis of the considerations indicated above, and pursuant to Section 113 of the Foreign Assistance and Related Programs Appropriation Act, 1972, I hereby determine that the furnishing of assistnace to Ecuador pursuant to the Foreign Assistance Act of 1961, as amended, is important to the national interest of the United States.

William P. Rogers
Date: March 9, 1972

3.   The "Cod War" Between Iceland and the United Kingdom and the Federal Republic of Germany

FISHERIES JURISDICTION CASES (UNITED KINGDOM v. ICELAND;
FEDERAL REPUBLIC OF GERMANY v. ICELAND)
Judgment of July 25, 1974
I.C.J. Reports, 1974, p. 3.

[The following summary of the Court's judgment relating to the United Kingdom is taken from *UN Monthly Chronicle*, Vol. XI, No. 8 (August-September 1974), pp. 102-106. The Judgment relating to the Federal Republic of Germany is essentially the same.]

By 10 votes to 4 the Court has:

(1)   found that the Icelandic Regulations of 1972 constituting a unilateral extension of the exclusive fishing rights of Iceland to 50 nautical miles from the baselines are not opposable to the United Kingdom;

(2)   found that Iceland is not entitled unilaterally to exclude United Kingdom fishing vessels from areas between the 12-mile and 50-mile limits, or unilaterally to impose restrictions on their activities in such areas;

(3)   held that Iceland and the United Kingdom are under mutual obligations to undertake negotiations in good faith for an equitable solution of their differences;

(4)   indicated certain factors which are to be taken into account in these negotiations (preferential rights of Iceland, established rights of the United Kingdom, interests of other States, conservation of fishery resources, joint examination of measures required).

. . . .

History of the Dispute--Jurisdiction of the Court
(paras. 19-48 of the Judgment)

The Court recalled that in 1948 the Althing (the Parliament of Iceland) had passed a law concerning the Scientific Conservation of the Continental Shelf Fisheries which empowered the Government to establish conservation zones wherein all fisheries should be subject to Icelandic rules and control to the extent compatible with agreements with other countries. Subsequently, the 1901 Anglo-Danish Convention which had fixed a limit for Iceland's exclusive right of fishery round its coasts was denounced by Iceland as from 1951, new Icelandic Regulations of 1958 proclaimed a 12-mile limit and the Althing declared by a resolution in 1959 "that recognition should be obtained of Iceland's right to the entire continental shelf area in conformity with the policy adopted by the Law of 1948." Following a number of incidents and a series of negotiations, Iceland and the United Kingdom agreed on an Exchange of Notes which took place on 11 March 1961 and specified *inter alia* that the United Kingdom would no longer object to a 12-mile fishery zone, that Iceland would continue to work for the implementation of the 1959 resolution regarding the extension of fisheries jurisdiction but would give the United Kingdom six months' notice of such extension and that "in case of a dispute in relation to such extension, the matter shall, at the request of either Party, be referred to the International Court of Justice."

In 1971, the Icelandic Government announced that the agreement on fisheries jurisdiction with the United Kingdom would be terminated and that the limit of exclusive Icelandic fisheries jurisdiction would be extended to 50 miles. In an aide-mémoire of 24 February 1972, the United Kingdom was formally notified of this intention. In reply the latter emphasized that the Exchange of Notes was not open to unilateral denunciation and that in its view the measure contemplated "would have no basis in international law." On 14 July 1972 new Regualtions were introduced whereby Iceland's fishery limits would be extended to 50 miles as from 1 September 1972 and all fishing activities by foreign vessels inside those limits be prohibited. Their enforcement gave rise, while proceedings before the Court were continuing and Iceland was refusing to recognize the Court's decisions, to a series of incidents and negotiations which resulted on 13 November 1973 in an Exchange of Notes constituting an interim agreement between the United Kingdom and Iceland. This agreement, concluded for two years, provided for temporary arrangements "pending a settlement of the substantive dispute and without prejudice to the legal position or rights of either Governmenmt in relation thereto."

The Court considered that the existence of the interim agreement ought not to lead it to refrain from pronouncing judgment: it could not be said that the issues before the Court had become without object, since the dispute still continued; and, though it was beyond the powers of the Court to declare the law between the Parties as it might be at the date of expiration of the interim agreement, that could not relieve the Court from its obligation to render a judgment on the basis of the law as it now existed; furthermore, the Court ought not to discouarage the making of interim arrangements in future disputes with the object of reducing friction.

Reverting to the 1961 Exchange of Notes, which in the Court's Judgment of 1973 was held to be a treaty in force, the Court emphasized that it would be too narrow an interpretation of the compromissory clause [in Exchange of notes of March 11, 1961] to conclude that it limited the Court's jurisdiction to giving an affirmative or a negative answer to the question of whether the Icelandic Regulations of 1972 were in conformity with international law. It seemed evident that the dispute between the Parties included disagreements as to their respective rights in the fishery resources and the adequacy of measures to conserve them. It was within the power of the Court to take into consideration all relevant elements.

Applicable Rules of International Law
(paras. 49-78 of the Judgment)

The first United Nations Conference on the Law of the Sea (Geneva 1958) had adopted a Convention on the High Seas, Article 2 of which declared the principle of the freedom of the high seas, that is to say, freedom of navigation, freedom of fishing, etc., to "be exercised by all States with reasonable regard to the interests of other States in their exercise of the freedom of the high seas.

The question of the breadth of the territorial sea and that of the extent of the coastal State's fishery jurisdiction and been left unsettled at the 1958 Conference and were not settled at a second Conference held in Geneva in 1960. However, arising out of the general consensus at that second Conference, two concepts had since crystallized as customary law: that of a fishery zone, between the territorial sea and the high seas, within which the coastal State could claim exclusive fisheries jurisdiction--it now being generally accepted that that zone could extend to the 12-mile limit--and the concept, in respect of waters adjacent to the zone of exclusive fishing rights, of preferential fishing rights in favour of the coastal State in a situation of special dependence on its fisheries. The Court was aware that in recent years a number of States had asserted an extension of their exclusive fishery limits. The Court was likewise aware of present endeavours, pursued under the auspices of the United Nations, to achieve in a third Conference on the Law of the Sea the further codification and progressive development of that branch of the law, as it was also of various proposals and preparatory documents produced in that framework. But, as a court of law, it could not render judgment *sub specie legis ferendae* or anticipate the law before the legislator had laid it down. It must take into account the existing rules of international law and the Exchange of Notes of 1961.

The concept of preferential fishing rights had originated in proposals submitted by Iceland at the Geneva Conference of 1958, which had confined itself to recommending that: "... where, for the purpose of conservation, it becomes necessary to limit the total catch of a stock or stocks of fish in an area of the high seas adjacent to the territorial sea of a coastal State, any other States fishing in that area should collaborate with the coastal State to secure just treatment of such situation, by establishing agreed measures which shall recognize any preferential requirements of the coastal State resulting from its dependence upon the fishery concerned while having regard to the interests of the other States."

At the 1960 Conference the same concept had been embodied in an amendment incorporated by a substantial vote into one of the proposals concerning the fishing zone. The contemporary practice of States showed that that concept, in addition to its increasing and widespread acceptance, was being implemented by agreements, either bilateral or multilateral. In the present case, in which the exclusive fishery zone within the limit of 12 miles was not in dispute, the United Kingdom had expressly recognized the preferential rights of the other Party in the disputed waters situated beyond that limit. There could be no doubt of the exceptional dependence of Iceland on its fisheries and the situation appeared to have been reached when it was imperative to preserve fish stocks in the interests of rational and economic exploitation.

However, the very notion of preferential fishery rights for the coastal State in a situation of special dependence, though it implied a certain priority, could not imply the extinction of the concurrent rights of other States. The fact that Iceland was entitled to claim preferential rights did not suffice to justify its claim unilaterally to exclude British fishing vessels from all fishing beyond the limit of 12 miles agreed to in 1961.

The United Kingdom had pointed out that its vessels had been fishing in Icelandic waters for centuries, that they had done so in a manner comparable with their present activities for upwards of 50 years and that their exclusion would have very serious adverse consequences. There too the economic dependence and livelihood of whole communities were affected, and the United Kingdom shared the same interest in the conservation of fish stocks as Iceland, which had for its part admitted the existence of the Applicant's historic and special interests in fishing in the disputed waters. Iceland's 1972 Regulations were therefore not opposable to the United Kingdom, they disregarded the established rights of that State and also the Exchange Notes of 1961, and they constituted an infringement of the principle (1958 Convention on the High Seas, Art. 2) of

constituted an infringement of the principle (1958 Convention on the High Seas, Art. 2) of reasonable regard for the interests of other States, including the United Kingdom.

In order to reach an equitable solution of the present dispute it was necessary that the preferential fishing rights of Iceland should be reconciled with the traditional fishing rights of the United Kingdom through the appraisal at any given moment of the relative dependence of either State on the fisheries in question, while taking into account the rights of other States and the needs of conservation. Thus Iceland was not in law entitled unilaterally to exclude United Kingdom fishing vessels from areas to seaward of the limit of 12 miles agreed to in 1961 or unilaterally to impose restrictions on their activities. But that did not mean that the United Kingdom was under no obligation to Iceland with respect to fishing in the disputed waters in the 12-mile to 50-mile zone. Both Parties had the obligation to keep under review the fishery resources in those waters and to examine together, in the light of the information available, the measures required for the conservation and development, and equitable exploitation, of those resources, taking into account any international agreement that might at present be in force or might be reached after negotiation.

The most appropriate method for the solution of the dispute was clearly that of negotiation with a view to delimiting the rights and interests of the Parties and regulating equitably such questions as those of catch-limitation, share allocations and related restrictions. The obligation to negotiate flowed from the very nature of the respective rights of the Parties and corresponded to the provisions of the United Nations Charter concerning peaceful settlement of disputes. The Court could not accept the view that the common intention of the Parties was to be released from negotiating throughout the whole period covered by the 1973 interim agreement. The task before them would be to conduct their negotiations on the basis that each must in good faith pay reasonable regard to the legal rights of the other, to the facts of the particular situation and to the interests of other States with established fishing rights in the area.

REFERENCES

(Prior to the I.C.J. Decision)

R. Goy, "The Icelandic Fisheries Question," *Journal du Droit International*, Vol. 87 (1960), pp. 370-407; L.C. Green, "The Territorial Sea and the Anglo-Icelandic Dispute," *Journal of Public Law*, Vol. 9 (1960), pp. 53-73; Richard B. Bilder, "The Anglo-Icelandic Fisheries Dispute," *Wisconsin Law Review*, Vol. 37 (1973), pp. 37-132; S.R. Katz, "Issues Arising in the Icelandic Fisheries Case," *International and Comparative Law Quarterly*, Vol. 22 (1973), pp. 83-108; K. Reese, "The Making of a Case for the International Court of Justice--Icelandic Fishing Rights," *Comparative and International Law Journal of Southern Africa*, Vol. 6(3) (Nov. 1973), pp. 394-402; J. Thornodsson, "Some Legal Aspects of the Conservation of Fish Stocks in the North-East Atlantic Ocean," *Ulfjotur*, Vol. 26(2) (1973), Supplement; R.P. Barston and H.W. Hanneson, "The Anglo-Icelandic Fisheries Dispute," *International Relations*, Vol. 4(6) (1974), pp. 559-584; G.G. Schramm, "Iceland's 50-Mile Fisheries Zone," *Ocean Management*, Vol. 2 (1974), pp. 127-138; J.A. Hart, *The Anglo-Icelandic Cod War of 1972-1973: A Case Study of a Fishery Dispute*, Berkeley: University of California, Institute of International Studies, 1976.

(On the I.C.J. Decision)

Sylvanus A. Tiewul, "The Fisheries Jurisdiction Cases and the Ghost of Rebus Sic Stantibus," *New York University Journal of International Law and Politics*, Vol. 6, No. 3 (1973), pp. 455-472; Peter J. Goldsworthy, "Interim Measures of Protection in the International Court of Justice," *American Journal of International Law*, Vol. 68 (1974), pp. 258-277; R.A. Birney, "The

Icelandic Fisheries Dispute: A Decision is Finally Rendered," *Georgia Journal of International and Comparative Law*, Vol. 5 (1975), pp. 248-256; R.R. Churchill, "The Fisheries Jurisdiction Cases: The Contribution of the International Court of Justice to the Debate on Coastal States' Fisheries Rights," *International and Comparative Law Quarterly*, Vol. 24 (1975), pp. 82-105; Daniel J. Foucheaux, Jr., "International Law--International Court of Justice--Iceland's Regulations Establishing a Fishery Zone with a 50-Mile Limit Are Not Opposable to the United Kingdom and the Federal Republic of Germany," *Texas International Law Journal*, Vol. 10 (1975), pp. 150-171; R. Khan, "Fisheries Jurisdiction Case--A Critique," *Indian Journal of International Law*, Vol. 15 (1975), pp. 1-16; Jeffery G. Weil, "Law of the Sea--Exclusive Economic Zone," *Harvard International Law Journal*, Vol. 16 (1975), pp. 474-490; R.P. Anand, "Iceland's Fisheries Dispute," *Indian Journal of International Law*, Vol. 16 (1976), pp. 43-53; Donald A. Young, "Contributions to International Law and World Order by the World Court's Adjudication of the Icelandic Fisheries Controversy," *Boston College International and Comparative Law Journal*, Vol. 1(1) (1977), pp. 175-196.

NOTE

The decision of the International Court of Justice did not resolve the dispute. In October, 1975, Iceland extended her fishing limits from 50 to 200 miles, setting off another round in the war, this time involving naval units of both Britain and Iceland. Even the NATO alliance was threatened by Iceland's threat to withdraw from the organization. See "Iceland Closes Air to British Planes in Fishing Dispute," *New York Times*, November 27, 1975, p. 14; "Britain Launches Another Cod War," *Washington Post*, November 26, 1975, p. A-8; "Icelandic Gunboat Rammed, Fires on 2 British Vessels," *New York Times*, December 12, 1975, p. 12; "NATO Chief Offers to Help Avert Iceland-Britain Split," *New York Times*, January 1, 1976, p. 3; "British Order Halt, Then a Resumption, of Iceland Fishing," *New York Times*, January 27, 1976, p. 7; "Iceland Breaks Relations with Britain over Fishing," *New York Times*, February 20, 1976, p. 3; "British-Icelandic Fishing Dispute Involves Far More than Just Cod," *New York Times*, March 11, 1976, p. 2.

In November, 1975, Belgium and the Federal Republic of Germany signed agreements with Iceland concerning the conduct of their fishing activities within Iceland's 200-mile fishing zone. See Fisheries Agreement between Iceland and Belgium Relating to the Extension of the Icelandic Fishery Limits to 200 Nautical Miles, November 28, 1975, *International Legal Materials*, Vol. 15 (1976), pp. 1-4 and similar agreement with Federal Republic of Germany, November 28, 1975, *ibid.*, pp. 43-47. In June, 1976, Iceland and the United Kingdom finally reached an agreement on British fishing within the 200-mile limit, providing for a substantial reduction in British fishing effort. See "Iceland-United Kingdom: Agreement Concerning British Fishing in Icelandic Waters, June 1, 1976," *International Legal Materials*, Vol. 15 (1976), pp. 878-890. See also "Icelandic Dispute Eased by Britain," *New York Times*, May 31, 1976, p. 1; "Britain and Iceland Begin Fishery Negotiations," *New York Times*, June 1, 1976, p. 4; "Icelandic Accord Signed by Britain," *New York Times*, June 2, 1976, p. 15.

D. U.S. LEGISLATION ON FISHERIES MANAGEMENT AND INTERNATIONAL FISHERIES AGREEMENTS

1. Fishermen's Protective Act of 1967 (Pelly Amendment)

FISHERMEN'S PROTECTIVE ACT OF 1967
P.L. 90-482, August 12, 1968
22 U.S.C. § 1978

§ 1978.   Restriction on importation of fishery or wildlife products from countries which violate international fishery or endangered or threatened species programs

Certification to President

(a)(1) When the Secretary of Commerce determines that nationals of a foreign country, directly or indirectly, are conducting fishing operations in a manner or under circumstances which diminish the effectiveness of an international fishery conservation program, the Secretary of Commerce shall certify such fact to the President.

(2) When the Secretary of Commerce or the Secretary of the Interior finds that nationals of a foreign country, directly or indirectly, are engaging in trade or taking which diminishes the effectiveness of any international program for endangered or threatened species, the Secretary making such finding shall certify such fact to the President.

(3) Upon receipt of any certification made under paragraph (1) or (2), the President may direct the Secretary of the Treasury to prohibit the bringing or the importation into the United States of fish products (if the certification is made under paragraph (1)) or wildlife products (if the certification is made under paragraph (2)) from the offending country for such duration as the President determines appropriate and to the extent that such prohibition is sanctioned by the General Agreement on Tariffs and Trade.

Notification to Congress

(b) Within sixty days following certification by the Secretary of Commerce or the Secretary of the Interior, the President shall notify the Congress of any action taken by him pursuant to such certification. In the event the President fails to direct the Secretary of the Treasury to prohibit the importation of fish products or wildlife products of the offending country, or if such prohibition does not cover all fish products or wildlife products of the offending country, the President shall inform the Congress of the reasons therefore.

Importation of fish products from offending country prohibited

(c) It shall be unlawful for any person subject to the jurisdiction of the United States knowingly to bring or import into, or cause to be imported into, the United States any fish products or wildlife products prohibited by the Secretary of the Treasury pursuant to this section.

. . . .

2.   Fishery Conservation and Management (Magnuson) Act of 1976

THE FISHERY CONSERVATION AND MANAGEMENT (MAGNUSON) ACT OF 1976
P.L. 94-265, April 13, 1976
16 U.S.C. § 1801 to § 1861 (Amended in 1978, 1980, 1983, 1986)

§ 1802. *Definitions*

As used in this Act, unless the context otherwise requires--

. . . .

(10) The term "fishing" means--

   (A)   the catching, taking, or harvesting of fish;

   (B)   the attempted catching, taking, or harvesting of fish;

   (C)   any other activity which can reasonably be expected to result in the catching, taking, or harvesting of fish; or

   (D)   any operations at sea in support of, or in preparation for, any activity described in subparagraphs (A) through (C).

Such term does not include any scientific research activity which is conducted by a scientific research vessel.

. . . .

(18) The term "optimum," with respect to the yield from a fishery, means the amount of fish--

   (A)   which will provide the greatest overall benefit to the Nation, with particular reference to food production and recreational opportunities; and

   (B)   which is prescribed as such on the basis of the maximum sustainable yield from such fishery, as modified by any relevant economic, social, or ecological factor.

. . . .

(20) The term "Secretary" means the Secretary of Commerce or his designee.

. . . .

(23) The term "treaty" means any international fishery agreement which is a treaty within the meaning of section 2 of article II of the Constitution.

. . . .

TITLE I--FISHERY MANAGEMENT AUTHORITY OF THE UNITED STATES

§ 1811. *Fishery Conservation Zone*

There is established a zone contiguous to the territorial sea of the United States to be known as the fishery conservation zone. The inner boundary of the fishery conservation zone is a line coterminous with the seaward boundary of each of the coastal States, and the outer boundary of such zone is a line drawn in such a manner that each point on it is 200 nautical miles from the baseline from which the territorial sea is measured.

§ 1812. *Exclusive Fishery Management Authority*

The United States shall exercise exclusive fishery management authority, in the manner provided for in this Act, over the following:

(1) All fish within the fishery conservation zone.

(2) All anadromous species throughout the migratory range of each such species beyond the fishery conservation zone; except that such management authority shall not extend to such species during the time they are found within any foreign nation's territorial sea or fishery conservation zone (or the equivalent), to the extent that such sea or zone is recognized by the United States.

(3) All Continental Shelf fishery resources beyond the fishery conservation zone.

§ 1813. *Highly Migratory Species*

The exclusive fishery management authority of the United States shall not include, nor shall it be construed to extend to, highly migratory species of fish.

. . . .

§ 1821. *Foreign fishing*

(a) *In general*

After February 28, 1977, no foreign fishing is authorized within the fishery conservation zone, or for anadromous species or Continental Shelf fishery resources beyond the fishery conservation zone, unless such foreign fishing--

(1) is authorized under subsection (b) or (c) of this section;

(2) is not prohibited by subsection (g) of this section; and

(3) is conducted under, and in accordance with, a valid and applicable permit issued pursuant to section 1824 of this title.

(b) *Existing international fishery agreements*

Foreign fishing described in subsection (a) of this section may be conducted pursuant to an international fishery agreement (subject to the provisions of section 1822(b) or (c) of this title), if

international fishery agreement (subject to the provisions of section 1822(b) or (c) of this title), if such agreement--

(1) was in effect on April 13, 1976; and

(2) has not expired, been renegotiated, or otherwise ceased to be of force and effect with respect to the United States.

(c) *Governing international fishery agreements*

Foreign fishing described in subsection (a) of this section may be conducted pursuant to an international fishery agreement (other than a treaty) which meets the requirements of this subsection if such agreement becomes effective after application of section 1823 of this title. Any such international fishery agreement shall hereafter in this chapter be referred to as a "governing international fishery agreement." Each governing international fishery agreement shall acknowledge the exclusive fishery management authority of the United States, as set forth in this chapter. It is the sense of the Congress that each such agreement shall include a binding commitment, on the part of such foreign nation and its fishing vessels, to comply with the following terms and conditions:

(1) The foreign nation, and the owner or operator of any fishing vessel fishing pursuant to such agreement, will abide by all regulations promulgated by the Secretary pursuant to this chapter, including any regulations promulgated to implement any applicable fishery management plan or any preliminary fishery management plan.

(2) The foreign nation, and the owner or operator of any fishing vessel fishing pursuant to such agreement, will abide by the requirement that--

    (A)   any officer authorized to enforce the provisions of this chapter (as provided for in section 1861 of this title) be permitted--

    (i)   to board, and search or inspect, any such vessel at any time,

    (ii)   to make arrests and seizures provided for in section 1861(b) of this title whenever such officer has reasonable cause to believe, as a result of such a search or inspection, that any such vessel or any person has committed an act prohibited by section 1857 of this title, and

    (iii)   to examine and make notations on the permit issued pursuant to section 1824 of this title for such vessel;

    (B)   the permit issued for any such vessel pursuant to section 1824 of this title be predominantly displayed in the wheelhouse of such vessel;

    (C)   transponders, or such other appropriate position-fixing and identification equipment as the Secretary of the department in which the Coast Guard is operating determines to be appropriate, be installed and maintained in working order on each such vessel;

    (D)   United States observers required under subsection (i) of this section be permitted to be stationed aboard any such vessel and that all of the costs incurred incident to such stationing, including the costs of data editing and entry and observer monitoring, be paid for, in accordance with such subsection, by the owner or operator of the vessel;

(E)   any fees required under section 1824(b)(10) of this title be paid in advance;

(F)   agents be appointed and maintained within the United States who are authorized to receive and respond to any legal process issued in the United States with respect to such owner or operator; and

(G)   responsibility be assumed, in accordance with any requirements prescribed by the Secretary, for the reimbursement of United States citizens for any loss of, or damage to, their fishing vessels, fishing gear, or catch which is caused by any fishing vessel of that nation;

and will abide by any other monitoring, compliance, or enforcement requirement related to fishery conservation and management which is included in such agreement.

(3) The foreign nation and the owners or operators of all of the fishing vessels of such nation shall not, in any year, harvest an amount of fish which exceeds such nation's allocation of the total allowable level of foreign fishing, as determined under subsection (e) of this section.

(4) The foreign nation will--

(A)   apply, pursuant to section 1824 of this title, for any required permits;

(B)   deliver promptly to the owner or operator of the appropriate fishing vessel any permit which is issued under that section for such vessel;

(C)   abide by, and take appropriate steps under its own laws to assure that all such owners and operators comply with, section 1824(a) of this title and the applicable conditions and restrictions established under section 1824(b)(7) of this title; and

(D)   take, or refrain from taking, as appropriate, actions of the kind referred to in subsection (e)(1) of this section in order to receive favorable allocations under such subsection.

(d) *Total allowable level of foreign fishing*

. . . .

(e) *Allocation of Allowable Level*

. . . .

[Packwood-Magnuson Amendment]

(2)   (A) For the purposes of this paragraph--

    (i)   The term "certification" means a certification made by the Secretary that nationals of a foreign country, directly or indirectly, are conducting fishing operations or engaging in trade or taking which diminishes the effectiveness of the International Convention for the Regulation of Whaling. A certification under this section shall also be deemed a certification for the purposes of section 1978(a) of Title 22.

    (ii)   The term "remedial period" means the 365-day period beginning on the date on which a certification is issued with respect to a foreign country.

    (B)   If the Secretary issues a certification with respect to any foreign country, then each allocation under paragraph (1) that--

    (i)   is in effect for that foreign country on the date of issuance; or

    (ii)   is not in effect on such date but would, without regard to this paragraph, be made to the foreign country within the remedial period; shall be reduced by the Secretary of State, in consultation with the Secretary by not less than 50 percent.

(g) *Reciprocity*

Foreign fishing shall not be authorized for the fishing vessels of any foreign nation unless such nation satisfies the Secretary and the Secretary of State that such nation extends substantially the same fishing privileges to fishing vessels of the United States, if any, as the United States extends to foreign fishing vessels.

. . . .

§ 1822. International fishery agreements

(a) Negotiations

The Secretary of State--

(1) shall renegotiate treaties as provided for in subsection (b) of this section;

(2) shall negotiate governing international fishery agreements described in section 1821(c) of this title;

(3) may negotiate boundary agreements as provided for in subsection (d) of this section;

(4) shall, upon the request of and in cooperation with the Secretary, initiate and conduct negotiations for the purpose of entering into international fishery agreements--

    (A)   which allow fishing vessels of the United States equitable access to fish over which foreign nations assert exclusive fishery management authority, and

      (B)   which provide for the conservation and management of anadromous species and highly migratory species; and

    (5) may enter into such other negotiations, not prohibited by subsection (c) of this section, as may be necessary and appropriate to further the purposes, policy, and provisions of this chapter.

(b) Treaty renegotiation

    The Secretary of State, in cooperation with the Secretary, shall initiate, promptly after April 13, 1976, the renegotiation of any treaty which pertains to fishing within the fishery conservation zone (or within the area that will constitute such zone after February 28, 1977), or for anadromous species or Continental Shelf fishery resources beyond such zone or area, and which is in any manner inconsistent with the purposes, policy, or provisions of this chapter, in order to conform such treaty to such purposes, policy, and provisions. It is the sense of Congress that the United States shall withdraw from any such treaty, in accordance with its provisions, if such treaty is not so renegotiated within a reasonable period of time after April 13, 1976.

(c) International fishery agreements

    No international fishery agreement (other than a treaty) which pertains to foreign fishing within the fishery conservation zone (or within the area that will constitute such zone after February 28, 1977), or for anadromous species or Continental Shelf fishery resources beyond such zone or area--

    (1) which is in effect on June 1, 1976, may thereafter be renewed, extended, or amended; or

    (2) may be entered into after May 31, 1976;

by the United States unless it is in accordance with the provisions of section 1821(c) of this title.

(d) Boundary negotiations

    The Secretary of State, in cooperation with the Secretary, may initiate and conduct negotiations with any adjacent or opposite foreign nation to establish the boundaries of the fishery conservation zone of the United States in relation to any such nation.

(e) Nonrecognition

    It is the sense of the Congress that the United States Government shall not recognize the claim of any foreign nation to a fishery conservation zone (or the equivalent) beyond such nation's territorial sea, to the extent that such sea is recognized by the United States, if such nation--

    (1) fails to consider and take into account traditional fishing activity of fishing vessels of the United States;

    (2) fails to recognize and accept that highly migratory species are to be managed by applicable international fishery agreements, whether or not such nation is a party to any such agreement; or

(3) imposes on fishing vessels of the United States any conditions or restrictions which are unrelated to fishery conservation and management.

. . . .

§ 1824. Permits for foreign fishing

(a) In general

After February 28, 1977, no foreign fishing vessel shall engage in fishing within the fishery conservation zone, or for anadromous species or Continental Shelf fishery resources beyond such zone, unless such vessel has on board a valid permit issued under this section for such vessel.

(b) Applications and permits under governing
international fishery agreements

(1) Eligibility

Each foreign nation with which the United States has entered into a governing international fishery agreement shall submit an application to the Secretary of State each year for a permit for each of its fishing vessels that wishes to engage in fishing described in subsection (a) of this section.

. . . .

(9) Disapproval of applications

If the Secretary does not approve any application submitted by a foreign nation under this subsection, he shall promptly inform the Secretary of State of the disapproval and his reasons therefor. The Secretary of State shall notify such foreign nation of the disapproval and the reasons therefor. Such foreign nation, after taking into consideration the reasons for disapproval, may submit a revised application under this subsection.

. . . .

(12) Sanctions

If any foreign fishing vessel for which a permit has been issued pursuant to this subsection has been used in the commission of any act prohibited by section 1857 of this title the Secretary may, or if any civil penalty imposed under section 1858 of this title or any criminal fine imposed under section 1859 of this title has not been paid and is overdue the Secretary shall--

(A)   revoke such permit, with or without prejudice to the right of the foreign nation involved to obtain a permit for such vessel in any subsequent year;

(B)   suspend such permit for the period of time deemed appropriate; or

(C)   impose additional conditions and restrictions on the approved application of the foreign nation involved and on any permit issued under such application.

Any permit which is suspended under this paragraph for nonpayment of a civil penalty shall be reinstated by the Secretary upon the payment of such civil penalty together with interest thereon at the prevailing rate.

. . . .

§ 1825. Import prohibitions

(a) Determinations by Secretary of State

If the Secretary of State determines that--

(1) he has been unable, within a reasonable period of time, to conclude with any foreign nation an international fishery agreement allowing fishing vessels of the United States equitable access to fisheries over which that nation asserts exclusive fishery management authority, as recognized by the United States, in accordance with traditional fishing activities of such vessels, if any, and under terms not more restrictive than those established under sections 1821(c) and (d) and 1824(b)(7) and (10) of this title, because such nation has (A) refused to commence negotiations, or (B) failed to negotiate in good faith;

(2) any foreign nation is not allowing fishing vessels of the United States to engage in fishing for highly migratory species in accordance with an applicable international fishery agreement, whether or not such nation is a party thereto;

(3) any foreign nation is not complying with its obligations under any existing international fishery agreement concerning fishing by fishing vessels of the United States in any fishery over which that nation asserts exclusive fishery management authority; or

(4) any fishing vessel of the United States, while fishing in waters beyond any foreign nation's territorial sea, to the extent that such sea is recognized by the United States, is seized by any foreign nation--

(A)   in violation of an applicable international fishery agreement;

(B)   without authorization under an agreement between the United States and such nation; or

(C)   as a consequence of a claim of jurisdiction which is not recognized by the United States;

he shall certify such determination to the Secretary of the Treasury.

(b) Prohibitions

Upon receipt of any certification from the Secretary of State under subsection (a) of this section, the Secretary of the Treasury shall immediately take such action as may be necessary and appropriate to prohibit the importation into the United States--

(1) of all fish and fish products from the fishery involved, if any; and

(2) upon recommendation of the Secretary of State, such other fish or fish products, from any fishery of the foreign nation concerned, which the Secretary of State finds to be appropriate to carry out the purposes of this section.

(c) Removal of prohibition

If the Secretary of State finds that the reasons for the imposition of any import prohibition under this section no longer prevail, the Secretary of State shall notify the Secretary of the Treasury, who shall promptly remove such import prohibition.

. . . .

§ 1827. Observer program regarding certain foreign fishing

(a) Definitions

As used in this section--

(1) The term "Act of 1976" means the Magnuson Fishery Conservation and Management Act (16 U.S.C. 1801 et seq.).

(2) The term "billfish" means any species of marlin, spearfish, sailfish or swordfish.

(3) The term "Secretary" means the Secretary of Commerce.

(b) Observer program

The Secretary shall establish a program under which a United States observer will be stationed aboard each foreign fishing vessel while that vessel--

(1) is in waters that are within--

    (A)   the fishery conservation zone established under section 101 of the Act of 1976 [16 U.S.C.A. § 1811], and

    (B)   the Convention area as defined in Article I of the International Convention for the Conservation of Atlantic Tunas; and

(2) is taking or attempting to take any species of fish if such taking or attempting to take may result in the incidental taking of billfish.

The Secretary may acquire observers for such program through contract with qualified private persons.

(c) Functions of observers

United States observers, while aboard foreign fishing vessels as required under subsection (b) of this section, shall carry out such scientific and other functions as the Secretary deems necessary or appropriate to carry out this section.

(d) Fees

There is imposed for each year after 1980 on the owner or operator of each foreign fishing vessel that, in the judgment of the Secretary, will engage in fishing in waters described in subsection (b)(1) of this section during that year which may result in the incidental taking of billfish a fee in an amount sufficient to cover all of the costs of providing an observer aboard that vessel under the program established under subsection (a) of this section. The fees imposed under this subsection for any year shall be paid to the Secretary before the year begins. All fees collected by the Secretary under this subsection shall be deposited in the Fund established by subsection (e) of this section.

. . . .

REFERENCES

Eugene R. Fidell, "The Coast Guard and Fisheries Law Enforcement," *U.S. Naval Institute Proceedings*, Vol. 102 (No. 3) (1976), pp. 70-75; E.R. Fidell, "Fisheries Legislation: Naval Enforcement," *Journal of Maritime Law and Commerce*, Vol. 7(2) (January 1976), pp. 351-366; F.D. Froman, "The 200-Mile Exclusive Economic Zone: Death Knell for the American Tuna Industry," *San Diego Law Review*, Vol. 13 (1976), pp. 707-741; H. Gary Knight, "International Fisheries Management Without Global Agreement: United States Policies and Their Impact on the Soviet Union," *Georgia Journal of International and Comparative Law*, Vol. 6 (1976), pp. 119-142; "Symposium on the Fishery Conservation and Management Act of 1976," *Washington Law Review*, Vol. 52 (1977), pp. 425-745; Jorge Dopico, "Amendments to the Fishery Conservation and Management Act of 1976: The Path to Expanded Protection for American Fish Processors," *Law and Policy in International Business*, Vol. 10 (1978), pp. 1325-1337; Geoffrey S. Yarema, "Foreign Access to U.S. Fisheries in the Wake of the Fishery Conservation and Management Act," *Virginia Journal of International Law*, Vol. 18 (1978), pp. 513-567; United States National Marine Fisheries Service, *Calendar Year Report on the Implementation of the Fishery Conservation and Management Act of 1976*, Washington, D.C.: U.S. Department of Commerce, National Oceanic and Atmospheric Administration, National Marine Fisheries Service. 1978--; United States General Accounting Office, *The Fishery Conservation and Management Act's Impact on Selected Fisheries: Report by the Comptroller General of the United States*, Washington, D.C.: The Office, 1979; D.R. Christie, "Regulation of International Joint Ventures in the Fishery Conservation Zone," *Georgia Journal of International & Comparative Law*, Vol. 10 (1980), pp. 85-100; Robert L. Stokes, "Prospects for Foreign Fishing Vessels in U.S. Fisheries Development," *Marine Policy*, Vol. 4 (1980), No. 1, pp. 33-41; United States National Marine Fisheries Service, *Fishery Conservation and Management Act (FCMA): Operations Handbook*, Washington, D.C.: The Service, 1980, I Volume (looseleaf); Robert L. Stokes and Brian H. Offord, "Alaska Groundfish: A Financial Feasibility Analysis," *Ocean Development and International Law*, Vol. 9 (1981), pp. 61-76; G. Kevin Jones, "Freedom of Fishing in Decline: The Fishery Conservation and Management Act of 1976 and the Implication for Japan," *California Western International Law Journal*, Vol. 11 (1981), pp. 51-110; Langdon S. Warner, Barbara A. Finamore, and Michael J. Bean, "Practical Application of the Conservation Aspects of the Fishery Conservation and Management Act," *Harvard Environmental Law Review*, Vol. 5 (1981), pp. 30-70; Oran R. Young, "The Political Economy of Fish: The Fishery Conservation and Management Act of 1976," *Ocean Development and International Law*, Vol. 10 (1982), pp. 199-273; Gary M. Shinaver, "Fishery Conservation: Is the Categorical Exclusion of Foreign Fleets the Next Step?", *California Western International Law Journal*, Vol. 12 (1982), pp. 154-203; Scott C. Truver and David E. Little, "U.S.-Flag Fish Processing Plantships for the Alaskan Groundfish Fishery," *Ocean Development and International Law*, Vol. 13 (1983), pp. 87-102; Langdon S. Warner,

"Conservation Aspects of the Fishery Conservation and Management Act and the Protection of Critical Marine Habitat," *Natural Resources Journal*, Vol. 23 (1983), pp. 97-103; Roger W. Rosendahl, "The Development of Mexican Fisheries and Its Effect on United States--Mexican Relations," *UCLA Pacific Basin Law Journal*, Vol. 3 (1984), pp. 1-20; Biliana Cicin-Sain and Robert W. Knecht, "The Problem of Governance of U.S. Ocean Resources and the New Exclusive Economic Zone," *Ocean Development and International Law*, Vol. 15 (1985), pp. 289-320; Maynard Silva and William Westemeyer, "The Law of the Sea and the U.S. Exclusive Economic Zone: Perspectives on Marine Transportation and Fisheries," *Ocean Development and International Law*, Vol. 15 (1985), pp. 321-353; Cameron Crone Bilger, "U.S.-Soviet Fishing Agreement, Treaty Authorizing Soviet Fishing in U.S. Waters," *Marine Policy*, Vol. 10 (1986), No. 1, pp. 51-56; Stephen R. Crutchfield, "Extended Fisheries Jurisdiction in the U.S.A., An Economic Appraisal," *Marine Policy*, Vol. 10 (1986), No. 4, pp. 271-278; Susan O'Malley Wade, "A Proposal to Include Tunas in U.S. Fishery Jurisdiction," *Ocean Development and International Law*, Vol. 16 (1986), pp. 255-304.

NOTE

There are many congressional hearings on the FCMA, e.g., see *Implementation of the Fishery Conservation and Management Act*, Hearings before the Senate Committee on Commerce (95th Congress, 1st Session, January 24-25, 1977); *Need for Congressional Approval of Governing Fishery Agreements*, Hearing before the Senate Committee on Foreign Relations (95th Congress, 1st Session, February 3, 1977); *International Fishery Agreements*, Hearings before the Subcommittee on Fisheries and Wildlife Conservation and the Environment of the House Committee on Merchant Marine and Fisheries (95th Congress, 1st Session, February-March, 1977); *200-Mile Fishery Oversight--Joint Ventures*, Hearings before the Subcommittee on Fisheries and Wildlife Conservation and the Environment of the House Committee on Merchant Marine and Fisheries (95th Congress, 1st Session, April, July, 1977); *Fishery Conservation and Management Act*, Hearings before the Subcommittee on Fisheries and Wildlife Conservation and the Environment of the House Committee on Merchant Marine and Fisheries (96th Congress, 1st Session, June 22 - October 12, 1979); *West Coast Fishery Management*, Hearings before the Subcommittee on Fisheries and Wildlife Conservation and the Environment of the House Committee on Merchant Marine and Fisheries (98th Congress, 1st Session, August 27, 1983, Long Beach, Calif.; August 29, 1983, Monterey, Calif.; August 30, 1983, Eureka, Calif.).

In at least two cases, the FCMA was applied by courts. In *Maine v. Kreps*, 563 F.2d 1043 (1st Cir. 1977), it was held that the FCMA did not preclude the selection of an optimum yield figure large enough to allow some foreign fishing, even though a lower figure would have rebuilt depleted fishery stock more quickly. In *U.S. v. Kaiyo Maru No. 53*, 503 F. Supp. 1075 (D. Alaska 1980), the court upheld a warrantless search of a foreign fishing vessel under the FCMA and confirmed that under the FCMA all fishes illegally caught must be forfeited. However, the forfeiture of the foreign vessel was within the court's discretion and the court may permit any judgment to be recovered on the bond.

For a discussion of the compatibility of the FCMA and the 1982 United Nations Convention on the Law of the Sea, see William T. Burke, "United States Fishery Management and the New Law of the Sea," *American Journal of International Law*, Vol. 76 (1982), pp. 24-55.

In January 1988, U.S. Federal officials met at Anchorage, Alaska to investigate evidence that foreign trawlers might have been fishing illegally in rich waters off the Aleutian Islands in Alaska. American fishermen have alleged that illegal fishing by foreign vessels costs them up to U.S. $650 million each year. See Timothy Egan, "Foreign Trawlers Accused of Violating U.S. Zone,"

$650 million each year. See Timothy Egan, "Foreign Trawlers Accused of Violating U.S. Zone," *The New York Times*, January 21, 1988, pp. A1, B9.

3. United States International Fisheries Agreement

HIGH SEAS FISHERIES OF THE NORTH PACIFIC OCEAN. PROTOCOL AMENDING THE CONVENTION OF MAY 9, 1952 BETWEEN THE UNITED STATES, CANADA AND JAPAN, AS AMENDED
Signed at Tokyo on April 25, 1978 and Entered Into Force February 15, 1979.
United States T.I.A.S. 9242.

Article II

1. The Contracting Parties shall maintain the International North Pacific Fisheries Commission, hereinafter referred to as "the Commission."

2. The Commission shall be composed of three national sections, each consisting of not more than four members appointed by the Governments of the respective Contracting Parties.

3. Each national section shall have one vote. All proposals, recommendations and other decisions of the Commission shall be made only by a unanimous vote of the three national sections.

4. The Commission may decide upon and amend, as occasion may require, by-laws or rules for the conduct of its meetings.

5. The Commission shall meet at least once each year and at such other times as may be requested by a majority of the national sections. . . .

8. Each Contracting Party may establish an Advisory Committee for its national section, to be composed of persons who shall be well informed concerning North Pacific fishery problems of common concern. Each such Advisory Committee shall be invited to attend all sessions of the Commission except those which the Commission decides to be *in camera.*

9. The Commission may hold public hearings. Each national section may also hold public hearings within its own country. . . .

. . . .

Article V

. . . .

2. The Contracting Parties agree that in fishing for anadromous species in the Convention area, they shall respect the conservation measures specified in the Annex to this Convention and that any infringement of these measures shall be deemed to be in violation of the terms of this Convention.

3. The nationals and fishing vessels of the Contracting Parties shall abide by the conservation measures specified in the Annex to this Convention.

Article IX

1. The Contracting Parties agree that within the Convention area:

(a)   each Contracting Party shall enforce the provisions of this Convention within its 200 nautical mile fishery zone in accordance with its domestic law;

(b)   outside the 200 nautical mile fishery zone of any Contracting Party, any Contracting Party may enforce the provisions of this Convention in accordance with the following:

(i)   The duly authorized officials of any Contracting Party may board vessels fishing for anadromous species of the other Contracting Parties to inspect equipment, logs, documents, catch and other articles and question the persons on board for the purpose of carrying out the provisions of this Convention. Such inspections and questioning shall be made so that the vessels suffer the minimum interference and inconvenience. Such officials shall present credentials issued by their respective Governments if requested by the master of the vessel.

(ii)   When any such person or fishing vessel is actually engaged in operations in violation of the provisions of this Convention, or there is reasonable ground to believe was obviously so engaged prior to boarding of such vessel by any such official, the latter may arrest or seize such person or vessel and further investigate the circumstances if necessary. The Contracting Party to which the official belongs shall notify promptly the Contracting Party to which such person or vessel belongs of such arrest or seizure, and shall deliver such person or vessel as promptly as practicable to the authorized officials of the Contracting Party to which such person or vessel belongs at a place to be agreed upon by both Parties. Provided, however, that when the Contracting Party which receives such notification cannot immediately accept delivery, the Contracting Party which gives such notification may keep such person or vessel under surveillance within the waters of the Convention area or within its own territory under the conditions agreed upon by both the Contracting Parties.

(iii)   Only the authorities of the Contracting Party to which the above-mentioned person or fishing vessel belongs may try the offense and impose penalties therefor. The witnesses and evidence necessary for establishing the offense, so far as they are under the control of any of the Contracting Parties to this Convention, shall be furnished as promptly as possible to the Contracting Party having jurisdiction to try the offense and shall be taken into account, and utilized as appropriate, by the executive authority of that Contracting Party having jurisdiction to try the offense.

(c)   the Contracting Parties shall take appropriate measures to ensure that their fishing vessels allow and assist boardings and inspections carried out in accordance with this Convention of such vessels by the duly authorized officials of any Contracting Party, and cooperate in such enforcement action as may be undertaken.

2. Each Contracting Party agrees, for the purpose of rendering effective the provisions of this Convention, to enact and enforce necessary laws and regulations, with appropriate penalties against

violations thereof, and to transmit to the Commission a report on any action taken by it in regard thereto.

ANNEX

1. The following measures shall apply to salmon fishery operations conducted by Japanese nationals and fishing vessels in the waters of the Convention area:

(a)   North of 56° North Latitude, east of 175° East Longitude and outside the United States fishery conservation zone, beginning on June 26 (Japan Standard Time) (1500 June 25 GMT) of each year, the Japanese mothership fishery shall conduct no more than 22 mothership fleet days in the area between 175° East Longitude and 180° Longitude and no more than 31 mothership fleet days in the area between 180° Longitude and 175° West Longitude.

(b)   North of 46° North Latitude, between 175° East Longitude and 170° East Longitude, and outside the United States fishery conservation zone, salmon fishery operations shall not begin before June 1 (Japan Standard Time) (1501 May 31 GMT) of each year.

(c)   West of 175° East Longitude, and within the United States fishery conservation zone, salmon fishery operations shall not begin before June 10 (Japan Standard Time) (1500 June 9 GMT) of each year. Fishing vessels engaged in this fishery shall be required to have on board a registration permit which shall be issued by the Government of the United States. Such vessels may be required by the Government of the United States to accept on board scientific observers and to bear the expenses incurred in such boarding. The requirement of the Government of the United States that Japanese fishing vessels engaged in this fishery have on board a Certificate of Inclusion relating to the incidental taking of marine mammals shall be suspended for the period ending June 9, 1981 during which period the Governments of Japan and the United States shall conduct joint research, shall cooperate to determine the effect of the Japanese salmon fishery on marine mammal populations, and shall work to reduce or eliminate the incidental catch of marine mammals in the fishery.

(d)   Except for the areas specified in (a) above, there shall be no salmon fishery operations east of 175° East Longitude, unless such fishery operations are agreed to for a temporary period among the three Contracting Parties.

2. For the purposes of this Annex, a mothership fleet day is defined as one mothership with no more than forty-one catcher-boats present during a portion of any one calendar day in the areas specified in paragraph 1.(a) of this Annex. Any increase in the number of catcher-boats assigned to a mothership will be reflected in a proportional reduction in the number of authorized fleet days. Modifications to gear or fishing procedures which might affect current fishing efficiency shall be undertaken only after consultations among the three Contracting Parties. In such consultations the Contracting Parties shall examine the necessity of change in the number of authorized fleet days to take account of any increase in fishing efficiency.

. . . .

UNITED STATES-BULGARIA AGREEMENT ON FISHERIES
OFF THE UNITED STATES COASTS
Signed at Washington, September 22, 1983 and Entered Into Force on April 14, 1984.
United States T.I.A.S. 10816.

ARTICLE IV

In determining the portion of the surplus that may be made available to vessels of each country, including the People's Republic of Bulgaria, the Government of the United States of America will decide on the basis of the factors identified in United States law including:

1. whether, and to what extent, such nations impose tariff barriers or nontariff barriers on the importation, or otherwise restrict the market access, of United States fish or fishery products;

2. whether, and to what extent such nations are cooperating with the United States in the advancement of existing and new opportunities for fisheries trade, particularly through the purchase of fish or fishery products from United States processors or from United States fishermen;

3. whether, and to what extent, such nations and the fishing fleets of such nations have cooperated with the United States in the enforcement of United States fishing regulations;

4. whether, and to what extent, such nations require the fish harvested from the exclusive economic zone for their domestic consumption;

5. whether, and to what extent, such nations otherwise contribute to, or foster the growth of, a sound and economic United States fishing industry, including minimizing gear conflicts with fishing operations of United States fishermen, and transferring harvesting or processing technology which will benefit the United States fishing industry;

6. whether, and to what extent, the fishing vessels of such nations have traditionally engaged in fishing in such fishery;

7. whether, and to what extent, such nations are cooperating with the United States in, and making substantial contributions to, fishery research and the identification of fishery resources; and

8. such other matters as the United States deems appropriate.

ARTICLE V

The Government of the People's Republic of Bulgaria shall cooperate with and assist the United States in the development of the United States fishing industry and the increase of United States fishery exports by taking such measures as reducing or removing impediments to the importation and sale of United States fishery products, providing information concerning technical and administrative requirements for access of United States fishery products into the People's Republic of Bulgaria, providing economic data, sharing expertise, facilitating the transfer of harvesting or processing technology to the United States fishing industry, facilitating appropriate joint venture and other arrangements, informing its industry of trade and joint venture opportunities with the United Stats, and taking other actions as may be appropriate. . . .

ARTICLE VIII

The Government of the People's Republic of Bulgaria shall ensure that nationals and vessels of the People's Republic of Bulgaria refrain from harassing, hunting, capturing or killing, or attempting to harass, hunt, capture or kill, any marine mammal within the United States exclusive economic zone, except as may be otherwise provided by an international agreement respecting marine mammals to which the United States is a party, or in accordance with specific authorization for and controls on incidental taking of marine mammals established by the Government of the United States of America. . . .

ARTICLE X

The Government of the People's Republic of Bulgaria shall take all appropriate measures to assist the United States in the enforcement of its laws pertaining to fishing in the exclusive economic zone and to ensure that each vessel of the People's Republic of Bulgaria that engages in fishing for living resources over which the United States has sovereign rights to explore, exploit, conserve and manage shall allow and assist the boarding and inspection of such vessel by any duly authorized enforcement officer of the United States and shall cooperate in such enforcement action as may be undertaken pursuant to the laws of the United States.

ARTICLE XI

1. The Government of the United States of America will impose appropriate penalties, in accordance with the laws of the United States, on vessels of the People's Republic of Bulgaria or their owners, operators or crews, that violate the requirements of this Agreement or of any permit issued hereunder.

2. Arrested vessels and their crews shall be promptly released, subject to such reasonable bond or other security as may be determined by the court.

3. In any case arising out of fishing activities under this Agreement, the penalty for violation of fishery regulations shall not include imprisonment or any other form of corporal punishment except in the case of enforcement related offenses such as assault on an enforcement officer or refusal to permit boarding and inspection.

4. In cases of seizure and arrest of a vessel of the People's Republic of Bulgaria by the authorities of the Government of the United States of America, notification shall be given promptly through diplomatic channels informing the Government of the People's Republic of Bulgaria of the action taken and of any penalties subsequently imposed.

AGREEMENT BETWEEN THE UNITED STATES AND THE UNION OF SOVIET SOCIALIST REPUBLICS ON MUTUAL FISHERIES RELATIONS
May 31, 1988

ARTICLE III

1. Each Party agrees that its nationals and vessels shall be subject to the relevant laws and regulations of the other Party when engaged in fishing in the zone of the other Party. Each Party further agrees that its nationals and vessels shall be subject to the relevant laws and regulations of the other Party pertaining to fisheries resource management when engaged in fishing outside the

respective zones of either Party for living resources of the continental shelf appertaining to the other Party or for anadromous resources that originate in the waters of the other Party.

2. Each Party shall notify the other Party of the national laws and regulations referred to in paragraph 1 of this Article and any changes thereto.

ARTICLE IV

Each Party, consistent with its national law, shall take appropriate measures to ensure that its nationals and vessels:

(a)   conduct fishery operations within the zone of the other Party consistent with the national laws and regulations of the other Party;

(b)   refrain from fishing beyond its zone for fish resources over which the other Party, consistent with international law, has sovereign rights or management authority, except as authorized pursuant to this Agreement; and

(c)   comply with the provisions of permits issued pursuant to this Agreement and the applicable laws of the other Party.

. . . .

ARTICLE VIII

1. Each Party consents to and, to the extent allowable under its own law, will assist and facilitate boardings and inspections of its vessels by duly authorized officers of the other Party for compliance with laws and regulations referred to in Article III. If, upon boarding and inspection of a vessel by a Party's duly authorized officer, such law or regulation is found to have been violated, each Party agrees that it will not object to appropriate enforcement action undertaken pursuant to the laws of that other Party, including seizure and arrest of the vessel and the individuals on board.

2. Each Party shall impose appropriate penalties, in accordance with its laws, for violations of the laws or regulations referred to in Article III. In the case of arrest and seizure of a vessel of a Party by the authorities of the other Party, notification shall be given promptly through diplomatic channels informing the flag state party of the facts and actions taken.

3. Each Party shall release vessels of the other Party and their crews promptly, subject to the posting of reasonable bond or other security.

4. The penalty for violation of a limitation or restriction on the fishing operations of a Party shall be limited to appropriate fines, forfeitures or revocation or suspension of fishing privileges.

ARTICLE XI

1. The Parties shall cooperate and consult directly or through appropriate international organizations to ensure proper conservation and management of living marine resources in the areas beyond the zones of the Parties and beyond the zone of any third party. The Parties may consult on questions of mutual interest which may be considered by such organizations.

2. The Parties shall cooperate in the exercise of their rights and duties under international law in order to coordinate conservation, exploitation and management of the living marine resources of

the Bering Sea and the North Pacific Ocean. In particular, the Parties shall consult on actions to address the effects of unregulated fishing in the areas of the Bering Sea and North Pacific Ocean beyond the zones of the Parties.

. . . .

ARTICLE XVII

1. This Agreement shall enter into force on the date of the exchange of notes notifying the completion of internal procedures of both Parties, and remain in force for five years, unless extended by an exchange of notes between the Parties. Notwithstanding the foregoing, either Party may terminate this Agreement after giving written notice of such termination to the other Party twelve months in advance. . . .

4. Driftnet Impact Monitoring, Assessment, and Control Act of 1987 and Related International Agreements

DRIFTNET IMPACT MONITORING, ASSESSMENT, AND CONTROL ACT OF 1987
Title IV of Public Law 100-220 [§ 4001-4009]
100 Stat. 1458, approved December 29, 1987.

SEC. 4002. FINDINGS

The Congress finds that--
(1) the use of long plastic driftnets is a fishing technique that may result in the entanglement and death of enormous numbers of target and nontarget marine resources in the waters of the North Pacific Ocean, including the Bering Sea;

(2) there is a pressing need for detailed and reliable information on the number of marine resources that become entangled and die in actively fished driftnets and in driftnets that are lost, abandoned, or discarded; and

(3) increased efforts are necessary to monitor, assess, and reduce the adverse impacts of driftnets.

SEC. 4003. DEFINITIONS.

As used in this title--

(1) DRIFTNET--The term "driftnet" means a gillnet composed of a panel of plastic webbing one and one-half miles or more in length.

(2) DRIFTNET FISHING--The term "driftnet fishing" means a fish-harvesting method in which a driftnet is placed in water and allowed to drift with the currents and winds for the purpose of entangling fish in the webbing.

(3) EXCLUSIVE ECONOMIC ZONE OF THE UNITED STATES--The term "exclusive economic zone of the United States" means the zone defined in section 3(6) of the Magnuson Fishery Conservation and Management Act (16 U.S.C. 1802(b)).

(4) MARINE RESOURCES--The term "marine resources" includes fish, shellfish, marine mammals, seabirds, and other forms of marine life or waterfowl.

(5) MARINE RESOURCES OF THE UNITED STATES--The term "marine resources of the United States" means--

> (A)   marine resources found in, or which breed within, areas subject to the jurisdiction of the United States, including the exclusive economic zone of the United States; and

> (B)   species of fish, wherever found, that spawn in the fresh or estuarine waters of the United States.

(6) SECRETARY--The term "Secretary" means the Secretary of Commerce.

SEC. 4004. MONITORING AGREEMENTS.

(a) NEGOTIATIONS--The Secretary, through the Secretary of State and in consultation with the Secretary of the Interior, shall immediately initiate, negotiations with each foreign government that conducts, or authorizes its nationals to conduct, driftnet fishing that results in the taking of marine resources of the United States in waters of the North Pacific Ocean outside of the exclusive economic zone and territorial sea of any nation, for the purpose of entering into agreements for statistically reliable cooperative monitoring and assessment of the numbers of marine resources of the United States killed and retrieved, discarded, or lost by the foreign government's driftnet fishing vessels. Such agreements shall provide for--

> (1)   the use of a sufficient number of vessels from which scientists of the United States and the foreign governments may observe and gather reliable information; and

> (2)   appropriate methods of sharing equally the costs associated with such activities.

(b) REPORT--The Secretary, in consultation with the Secretary of State, shall provide to the Congress not later than 1 year after the date of enactment of this Act a full report on the results of negotiations under this section.

SEC. 4005. IMPACT REPORT.

(a) IN GENERAL--The Secretary shall provide to the Congress within 1 year after the date of the enactment of this Act, and at such other times thereafter as the Secretary considers appropriate, a report identifying the nature, extent, and effects of driftnet fishing in waters of the North Pacific Ocean on marine resources of the United States. The report shall include the best available information on--

> (1)   the number and flag state of vessels involved;
> (2)   the areas fished;
> (3)   the length, width, and mesh size of driftnets used;
> (4)   the number of marine resources of the United States killed by such fishing;
> (5)   the effect of seabird mortality, as determined by the Secretary of the Interior, on seabird populations; and

(6)   any other information the Secretary considers appropriate.

(b) INFORMATION FROM FOREIGN GOVERNMENTS--The Secretary, through the Secretary of State, shall--

(1)   request relevant foreign governments to provide the information described in subsection (a), and

(2)   include in a report under this section the information so provided and an evaluation of the adequacy and reliability of such information.

SEC. 4006. ENFORCEMENT AGREEMENTS.

(a) NEGOTIATIONS--The Secretary shall immediately initiate, through the Secretary of State and in consultation with the Secretary of the Department in which the Coast Guard is operating negotiations with each foreign government that conducts, or authorizes its nationals to conduct, driftnet fishing that results in the taking of marine resources of the United States in waters of the North Pacific Ocean outside of the exclusive economic zone and territorial sea of any nation, for the purpose of entering into agreements for effective enforcement of laws, regulations, and agreements applicable to the location, season, and other aspects of the operations of the foreign government's driftnet fishing vessels. Such agreements shall include measures for--

(1)   the effective monitoring and detection of violations;

(2)   the collection and presentation of such evidence of violations as may be necessary or the successful prosecution of such violations by the responsible authorities;

(3)   reporting to the United States of penalties imposed by the foreign governments for violations; and

(4)   appropriate methods for sharing equally the costs associated with such activities.

(b) CERTIFICATION FOR PURPOSES OF FISHERMEN'S PROTECTIVE ACT OF 1967--If the Secretary, in consultation with the Secretary of State, determines that a foreign government has failed, within 18 months after the date of the enactment of this Act, to enter into and implement an agreement under subsection (a) or section 4004(a) that is adequate, the Secretary shall certify such fact to the President, which certification shall be deemed to be a certification for the purposes of section 8(a) of the Fishermen's Protective Act of 1967 (22 U.S.C. 1978(a)).

SEC. 4007. EVALUATIONS AND RECOMMENDATIONS.

(a) MARKING, REGISTRY, AND IDENTIFICATION SYSTEM--The Secretary shall evaluate, in consultation with officials of other Federal agencies and such other persons as may be appropriate, the feasibility of and develop recommendations for the establishment of a driftnet marking, registry, and identification system to provide a reliable method for the determination of the origin by vessel, of lost, discarded, or abandoned driftnets and fragments of driftnets. In conducting such evaluation, the Secretary shall consider the adequacy of existing driftnet identification systems of foreign nations and the extent to which these systems achieve the objectives of this title.

(b) ALTERNATIVE DRIFTNET MATERIALS--The Secretary, in consultation with such other persons as may be appropriate, shall evaluate the feasibility of, and develop appropriate recommendations for, the use of alternative materials in driftnets for the purpose of increasing the

other persons as may be appropriate, shall evaluate the feasibility of, and develop appropriate recommendations for, the use of alternative materials in driftnets for the purpose of increasing the rate of decomposition of driftnets that are discarded or lost at sea.

(c) DRIFTNET BOUNTY SYSTEM--The Secretary, in consultation with such other persons as may be appropriate, shall evaluate the feasibility of and develop appropriate recommendations for the implementation of a driftnet bounty system to pay persons who retrieve from the exclusive economic zone and deposit with the Secretary lost, abandoned, and discarded driftnet and other plastic fishing material.

(d) DRIFTNET FISHING VESSEL TRACKING SYSTEM--The Secretary, in consultation with such other persons as may be appropriate, shall evaluate the feasibility of, and develop appropriate recommendations for, the establishment of a cooperative driftnet fishing vessel tracking system to facilitate efforts to monitor the location of driftnet fishing vessels.

(e) REPORT--The Secretary shall transmit to the Congress not later than 18 months after the date of the enactment of this Act a report setting forth--

(1)   the evaluations and recommendations developed under subsections (a), (b), (c), and (d);

(2)   the most effective and appropriate means of implementing such recommendations;

(3)   any need for further research and development efforts and the estimated cost and time required for completion of such efforts; and

(4)   any need for legislation to provide authority to carry out such recommendations.

SEC. 4008. CONSTRUCTION WITH OTHER LAWS.

This title shall not serve or be construed to expand or diminish the sovereign rights of the United States, as stated by Presidential Proclamation Numbered 5030, dated March 10, 1983, and reflected in existing law on the date of the enactment of this Act.

SEC. 4009. AUTHORIZATION OF APPROPRIATIONS.

There are authorized to be appropriated to the Department of Commerce and the Department of State, such sums as may be necessary to carry out the purposes of this title.

ANNEX TO EXCHANGE OF LETTERS BETWEEN THE COORDINATION COUNCIL
FOR NORTH AMERICAN AFFAIRS (CCNAA) [THE REPUBLIC OF CHINA (TAIWAN)]
AND THE AMERICAN INSTITUTE IN TAIWAN (AIT) [THE UNITED STATES]
REGARDING THE HIGH SEAS DRIFTNET FISHING IN THE NORTH PACIFIC OCEAN
July 13, 1989.
Chinese Yearbook of International Law and Affairs
Vol. 8 (1988-1989), pp. 512-518.

ARTICLE I.--FISHING GROUNDS

The party represented by CCNAA shall ensure that all driftnet vessels of the territory represented by CCNAA are to adhere to the following fishing grounds while operating in the North

Pacific Ocean beyond national 200 nautical mile Exclusive Economic Zones. Each driftnet vessel is required to confine fishing operations and all other vessel activities and movements to the area west of 145 degrees W longitude and south of the following monthly northernmost latitudinal lines of the fishery:

(a) For the area west of 170 degrees E longitude--

January through April	Latitude 36 degrees N
May	Latitude 38 degrees N
June	Latitude 40 degrees N
July	Latitude 42 degrees N
August	Latitude 44 degrees N
September	Latitude 46 degrees N
October	Latitude 44 degrees N
November	Latitude 42 degrees N
December	Latitude 40 degrees N

(b)   For the area between 170 degrees E to 145 degrees W longitude--

January through April	Latitude 20 degrees N
May	Latitude 34 degrees N for large mesh only
June	Latitude 40 degrees N
July	Latitude 42 degrees N
August	Latitude 44 degrees N
September	Latitude 46 degrees N
October	Latitude 44 degrees N
November	Latitude 42 degrees N
December	Latitude 40 degrees N

ARTICLE II.--TRANSMITTERS

(a) The party represented by CCNAA will install real-time automatic satellite position fixing devices identified here as transmitters, on ten percent of its North Pacific driftnet fishing vessels for an experimental test during the 1989 fishing season. Unless CCNAA and AIT agree after consultations that the transmitters are ineffective for monitoring vessel locations, after January 1, 1990, no driftnet fishing vessel will be permitted to fish in the North Pacific without a transmitter that will allow automatic, real time monitoring of the location and identity of the vessel by the parties represented by AIT and CCNAA. . . .

(c) Each driftnet vessel is required to validate the time and location of catch and fishing effort, including the use of location records from an automatic navigation system, and will report such data to the appropriate officials of the party represented by CCNAA.

(d) The party represented by AIT understands that such installation efforts made by the party represented by CCNAA need multi-agency coordination among the Ministry of National Defense, the Ministry of Communications, and the Council of Agriculture of the party represented by the CCNAA. The party represented by AIT will take into consideration practical or legal difficulties in implementing this provision.

ARTICLE III.--OPERATING PROCEDURES

(a) No driftnet vessel may harvest anadromous species of fish.

(b) Any anadromous species of fish incidentally taken in the driftnet fishery is to be immediately returned to the water and included in catch records outlined below in Article III (i).

(c) Each driftnet vessel seeking to operate in the North Pacific Ocean will have a license issued by the appropriate officials of the party represented by CCNAA.

(d) All marine resources harvested by driftnet vessels of the territory represented by CCNAA must be landed or, in the case of tuna shipments to Thailand, thoroughly inspected, in ports of the territory represented by CCNAA, with the exception of tuna shipped to American Samoa and Puerto Rico. For the sake of effective enforcement, the party represented by CCNAA will, upon signing of the agreement, promptly take the following measures:

(1)   All tuna and squid transport ships operating in the North Pacific shall be equipped with a transmitter that will allow automatic, real-time monitoring of the location and identity of the vessel by the parties represented by AIT and CCNAA;

(2)   The party represented by AIT will assist the party represented by CCNAA in procuring transmitters immediately. Once the transmitters are available, no transport vessel of the territory represented by CCNAA will be permitted to leave port for the North Pacific without an operating transmitter;

(3)   CCNAA will provide AIT with a list of transport vessels;

(4)   Squid transport ships shall only sail between North Pacific fishing grounds and ports in the territory represented by CCNAA;

(5)   All squid caught from the North Pacific fishing grounds may only be transshipped to transport vessels of the territory represented by CCNAA and must be landed at ports in the territory represented by CCNAA;

(6)   When a tuna or squid transport ship leaves port to carry on transshipment at sea, prior permission must be obtained from the competent agency of the party represented by CCNAA. CCNAA will forward this information promptly to designated AIT officials;

(7)   Detailed records shall be kept by all squid transport ships in connection with the transshipment they carry on, including the name of the fishing vessel from which the transshipped squid is received and the quantity of the squid. Upon return of the transport ship to the port in the territory represented by CCNAA it shall immediately report to the competent agency of the party represented by CCNAA for inspection.

The appropriate authorities of the party represented by CCNAA will establish a port inspection program to monitor landings of all driftnet vessels at all pertinent ports in the territory represented by CCNAA.

If the above measures should fail to bring about the desired result in six months, the authorities of the party represented by CCNAA will immediately introduce a bill to its Legislature for the prohibition of any and all transshipment of squid in the North Pacific.

(e) Authorities of the party represented by CCNAA shall take steps to introduce a bill as soon as possible to its Legislature to prohibit vessels from carrying both large-mesh gear (mesh size of 18 centimeters or greater) and small-mesh gear (less than 18 centimeters).

(f) Each driftnet vessel will be assigned an international radio call sign (IRCS) which is to be displayed amidships on both the port and starboard sides of the deckhouse or hull, and on a weather deck, in a color in contrast to the background and permanently affixed to the vessel in block roman alphabet letters and arabic numerals at least one meter in height.

(g) Each driftnet vessel is to use methods to identify the driftnet gear it deploys by permanently marking at every 50 meter interval of net with the name of the vessel and its corresponding IRCS. Each vessel is also required to refrain from discarding used or damaged driftnets and related gear while at sea. Such fishing equipment is to be stowed on the vessel and returned to port for proper disposal upon completion of the vessel's voyage. The location, date, and amount of lost fishing gear must be reported to the appropriate authorities of the party represented by CCNAA.

(h) CCNAA shall provide AIT with a list of licensed driftnet vessels, including name, corresponding IRCS numbers, the CT number and size by tonnage.

(i) CCNAA will provide AIT total catch and fishing effort of the driftnet fleet, stratified by month and delineated by five degree latitude by five degree longitude areas for the 1989 fishing season and one degree latitude by one degree longitude areas for the 1990 fishing season. Catch data is to include records of harvests of target species, incidental takes of anadromous species, marine mammals, seabirds, and other living marine resources. This information will be provided to AIT not later than June 30th of the following year.

ARTICLE IV.--ENFORCEMENT

(a) The authorities of the party represented by CCNAA shall ensure that enforcement boardings of driftnet fishing vessels are conducted by personnel of the party represented by CCNAA, both dockside and at sea within and beyond the fishing area authorized by the party represented by CCNAA.

(b) The parties represented by AIT and CCNAA may exchange enforcement observers to facilitate driftnet fishery enforcement activities. These exchanges may include:

(1)   participation by enforcement observers of the party represented by AIT on enforcement cruises conducted by the party represented by CCNAA;

(2)   participation by enforcement observers of the party represented by CCNAA on enforcement patrols conducted by the party represented by AIT.

(c) CCNAA Shall ensure that authorities of the party represented by CCNAA prosecuting administrative or judicial cases involving fishing violations shall treat the evidence supplied by or through AIT in the same manner as the evidence supplied by enforcement authorities of the party represented by CCNAA. The party represented by AIT understands that, under the judicial system of the party represented by CCNAA acceptance of evidence supplied by or through AIT, as well as evidence supplied by enforcement authorities of the party represented by CCNAA, would not necessarily have binding force should any alleged violations become a court case.

ARTICLE V.--VISIT AND VERIFICATION

Enforcement authorities of the party represented by AIT may visit flag vessels of the territory represented by CCNAA for the purpose of verifying fishing violations as follows:

(a) *Outside the Fishing Area Authorized by the Party Represented by CCNAA.* Personnel from the party represented by AIT may visit driftnet vessels of the territory represented by CCNAA wherever found if detected outside the authorized fishing area upon transmission of prior notification to CCNAA.

(b) *Inside the Fishing Area Authorized by the Party Represented by CCNAA.* Personnel from the party represented by AIT may visit driftnet vessels of the territory represented by CCNAA inside the authorized fishing area upon the occurrence of any of the following events and upon transmission of prior notification to CCNAA:

(1)   Prohibited species are observed on board;

(2)   Transfer of catch is observed in progress where there is reason to believe that catch being transferred is of anadromous species;

(3)   Identification of the vessel is obscured in any way;

(4)   Transmitter is not operating;

(5)   Vessel is not on the list provided by CCNAA of registered driftnet vessels; or

(6)   Vessel is evading detection or fleeing.

(c) Personnel from the party represented by AIT may visit transport vessels of the territory represented by CCNAA upon transmission of prior notification to CCNAA.

(d) Upon discovery of a fishing violation, AIT and CCNAA will consult regarding further steps in the handling of the vessel.

(e) Enforcement authorities of the party represented by AIT will take all reasonable measures to ensure a minimum interference to legitimate fishing operations of fishing vessels of the territory represented by CCNAA. Enforcement authorities of the party represented by AIT will conduct their operations in accordance with applicable rules of international law and practice and show the necessary courtesy to the master and crew of fishing vessels of the territory represented by CCNAA.

The foregoing is based upon the universally recognized principle of reciprocity.

ARTICLE VI.--DEPLOYMENT OF PATROL VESSELS.

(a) The party represented by AIT fully understands that the party represented by CCNAA currently has a rather limited number of vessels which can be deployed for patrolling the North Pacific. Nevertheless, the party represented by CCNAA will dispatch two dedicated patrol vessels for 200 vessel-days in the North Pacific during the balance of the 1989 fishing season to ensure a continuous enforcement presence throughout the season in the vicinity of the fishing grounds.

(b) For the 1990 fishing season, the number of dedicated patrol vessels will be increased to a minimum of three so that the total vessel-days will be 310 to ensure a continuous enforcement presence throughout the season in the vicinity of the fishing ground.

(c) CCNAA shall provide AIT with planned enforcement activities before the fishing season begins and annual reports on the patrols conducted, boardings made, violations detected, and penalties assessed by enforcement officials of the party represented by CCNAA at the conclusion of each fishing season.

ARTICLE VII.--MONITORING PROGRAM.

The party represented by CCNAA will implement with the party represented by AIT a cooperative monitoring program involving the deployment of scientific observers of the parties represented by AIT and CCNAA aboard driftnet vessels of the territory represented by CCNAA in the North Pacific Ocean. Each side will be responsible for bearing the personnel cost of its scientific observers. . . .

ARTICLE VIII.--MANAGEMENT OF THE DRIFTNET FISHING FLEET

The party represented by CCNAA will take steps to limit the size of its driftnet fleet during the term of this agreement and will consult further with the party represented by AIT on this matter. The authorities of the party represented by CCNAA will introduce at the earliest possible date the necessary laws and regulations for the management and control of driftnet fisheries. In doing so, they will take into account the relevant biological and socio-economic factors. CCNAA will inform AIT of the results of such efforts.

ARTICLE IX.--OPERATION OF THE AGREEMENT.

The parties to this Agreement shall consult periodically in order to review the operation and application of this agreement so as to assure that, with the passage of time and changes in circumstances, the objectives of this Agreement may be effectively maintained. The parties shall consult on enforcement and monitoring agreements for subsequent years.

Notwithstanding the undertakings by CCNAA under the agreement and the reply to AIT letter, the party represented by CCNAA reaffirms its rights and privileges under international law and practice.

NOTE

After the United States terminated its diplomatic relations with the Republic of China on Taiwan on January 1, 1979 and recognized the People's Republic of China (Communist government), its relations with Taiwan have been maintained through the CCNAA (representing Taiwan) and AIT (representing the United States). Pursuant to Section 12(a) of the United States Taiwan Relations Act (Public Law 96-8; 93 Stat. 14) agreements concluded between the AIT and the CCNAA are required to be transmitted to the Congress; and pursuant to sections 6 and 10(a) of the Act, such agreements have full force and effect under the law of the United States. See *Federal Register*, Vol. 51, No. 9 (January 14, 1986), p. 1558.

For a summary of the agreement with Taiwan and its background, see Clyde Farnsworth, "Taiwan to Let U.S. Monitor Drift-Net Fishing Practices," *New York Times*, August 26, 1989, pp. 29, 33.

Similar driftnet agreements were concluded by the United States with the Republic of Korea and Japan in September 1989. See "U.S. to Track S. Korean Fishing Boats, Agreement Reached on Pact to Curb Illegal Use of Drift Nets," Associated Press, *Washington Post*, September 9, 1989, p. A16; and David E. Sanger, "Japan to Limit Ships with Huge Nets," *New York Times*, September 20, 1989, p. A3. For international efforts to ban 'driftnet' fishing, see Section E, subsection 3 of this Chapter.

REFERENCES

Pelagic Driftnet Fisheries, Hearings before the National Ocean Policy Study of the Senate Commerce, Robert Eisenbud, "Problems and Prospects for the Pelagic Driftnet," *Boston College Environmental Affairs Law Review*, Vol. 12 (1985), pp. 473-490; *Driftnet Impact Monitoring, Assessment and Control Act of 1986*, Senate Report 99-529 on S. 2611 (99th Congress, 2nd Session, October 6, 1986); *Driftnet Impact Monitoring and Control Act of 1987*, Senate Report 100-261 on S. 62 (100th Congress, 1st Session, December 16, 1987); Science and Transportation Committee (99th Congress, 1st Session, October 9, 1985); Eric J. Fjelstad, The Ghosts of Fishing Net Past: A Proposal for Regulating Derelict Fishing Nets," *Washington Law Review*, Vol. 63 (1988), pp. 677-699; Marlise Simons, "Fishing Nets Trap Dolphins In the Mediterranean, Too," *New York Times*, September 6, 1989, pp. A1, A5; *1*Colin James, "Driftnet Methods Raise the Ire of Pacific States, A Catch-All Dilemma," *Far Eastern Economic Review*, Vol. 145, No. 39 (September 28, 1989), pp. 139-140; Secretary of Commerce, *Report to the Congress of the United States on the Nature, Extent and Effects of Driftnet Fishing in Waters of the North Pacific Pursuant to Section 4005 of Public Law 100-220, The Driftnet Impact Monitoring, Assessment and Control Act of 1987*, Washington, D.C.: U.S. Government Printing Office, 1989.

E. FISHERIES MANAGEMENT UNDER THE 1982 UNITED NATIONS CONVENTION ON THE LAW OF THE SEA

1. Within Exclusive Economic Zone

a. The Coastal State's Right to Manage Fisheries

1982 UNITED NATIONS CONVENTION ON THE LAW OF THE SEA

Article 56
Rights, jurisdiction and duties of the coastal State in the exclusive economic zone

1. In the exclusive economic zone, the coastal State has: (a) sovereign rights for the purpose of exploring and exploiting, conserving and managing the natural resources, whether living or non-living, of the waters superjacent to the seabed and of the sea-bed and its subsoil, and with regard to other activities for the economic exploitation and exploration of the zone. . . .

REFERENCES

Robin Rolf Churchill, *EEC Fisheries Law*, Dordrecht, Boston, London: Martinus Nijhoff Publishers, 1987; Vladimir M. Kaczynski, "Foreign Fishing Fleets in the Sub-Saharan West African EEZ: The Coastal State Perspective," *Marine Policy*, Vol. 13, No. 1 (January 1989), pp. 2-15; Ted L. McDorman, "French Fishing Rights in Canadian Waters: The 1986 La Bretagne Arbitration," *International Journal of Estuarine and Coastal Law*, Vol. 4, No. 1 (February 1989), pp. 52-64; Kitlemariam Melake, "Problems of Marine Fisheries in Developing Countries: The Ethiopian Case, "*Ocean and Shoreline Management*, Vol. 12, No. 4 (1989), pp. 347-361.

b.   Conservation and Utilization of Living Resources

1982 UNITED NATIONS CONVENTION ON THE LAW OF THE SEA

Article 61
Conservation of the living resources

1.   The coastal State shall determine the allowable catch of the living resources in its exclusive economic zone.

2.   The coastal State, taking into account the best scientific evidence available to it, shall ensure through proper conservation and management measures that the maintenance of the living resources in the exclusive economic zone is not endangered by over-exploitation. As appropriate, the coastal State and competent international organizations, whether subregional, regional or global, shall co-operate to this end.

3.   Such measures shall also be designed to maintain or restore populations of harvested species at levels which can produce the maximum sustainable yield, as qualified by relevant environmental and economic factors, including the economic needs of coastal fishing communities and the special requirements of developing States, and taking into account fishing patterns, the interdependence of stocks and any generally recommended international minimum standards, whether subregional, regional or global.

4.   In taking such measures the coastal State shall take into consideration the effects on species associated with or dependent upon harvested species with a view to maintaining or restoring populations of such associated or dependent species above levels at which their reproduction may become seriously threatened.

5.   Available scientific information, catch and fishing effort statistics, and other data relevant to the conservation of fish stocks shall be contributed and exchanged on a regular basis through competent international organizations, whether subregional, regional or global, where appropriate and with participation by all States concerned, including States whose nationals are allowed to fish in the exclusive economic zone.

Article 62
Utilization of the living resources

1.   The coastal State shall promote the objective of optimum utilization of the living resources in the exclusive economic zone without prejudice to article 61.

2.   The coastal State shall determine its capacity to harvest the living resources of the exclusive economic zone. Where the coastal State does not have the capacity to harvest the entire allowable catch, it shall, through agreements or other arrangements and pursuant to the terms, conditions, laws and regulations referred to in paragraph 4, give other States access to the surplus of the allowable catch, having particular regard to the provisions of articles 69 and 70, especially in relation to the developing States mentioned therein.

3.   In giving access to other States to its exclusive economic zone under this article, the coastal State shall take into account all relevant factors, including *inter alia*, the significance of the living resources of the area to the economy of the coastal State concerned and its other national interests, the provisions of articles 69 and 70, the requirements of developing States in the

subregion or region in harvesting part of the surplus and the need to minimize economic dislocation in States whose nationals have habitually fished in the zone or which have made substantial efforts in research and identification of stocks.

4. Nationals of other States fishing in the exclusive economic zone shall comply with the conservation measures and with the other terms and conditions established in the laws and regulations of the coastal State. These laws and regulations shall be consistent with this Convention and may relate, *inter alia,* to the following:

(a) licensing of fishermen, fishing vessels and equipment, including payment of fees and other forms of remuneration, which, in the case of developing coastal States, may consist of adequate compensation in the field of financing, equipment and technology relating to the fishing industry;

(b) determining the species which may be caught, and fixing quotas of catch, whether in relation to particular stocks or groups of stocks or catch per vessel over a period of time or to the catch by nationals of any State during a specified period;

(c) regulating seasons and areas of fishing, the types, sizes and amount of gear, and the types, sizes and number of fishing vessels that may be used;

(d) fixing the age and size of fish and other species that may be caught;

(e) specifying information required of fishing vessels, including catch and effort statistics and vessel position reports;

(f) requiring, under the authorization and control of the coastal State, the conduct of specified fisheries research programmes and regulating the conduct of such research, including the sampling of catches, disposition of samples and reporting of associated scientific data;

(g) the placing of observers or trainees on board such vessels by the coastal State;

(h) the landing of all or any part of the catch by such vessels in the ports of the coastal State;

(i) terms and conditions relating to joint ventures or other co-operative arrangements;

(j) requirements for the training of personnel and the transfer of fisheries technology, including enhancement of the coastal State's capability of undertaking fisheries research;

(k) enforcement procedures.

5. Coastal States shall give due notice of conservation and management laws and regulations.

William T. Burke, "The Law of the Sea Convention Provisions on Conditions of Access to Fisheries Subject to National Jurisdiction," *Oregon Law Review*, Vol. 63 (1984), pp. 78-79, 84-85, 87-89. Copyright by University of Oregon. Reprinted by permission also of the author.

(a) Allowable catch

Article 61 of the Convention provides that the coastal State "shall determine the allowable catch of the living resources in its exclusive economic zone." The allowable catch could normally embrace both those stocks harvested intentionally, for commercial, recreational or other purposes, and those taken incidentally while harvesting a target species. Since the incidental catch regulations may require that harvesting be terminated before the target catch level has been reached, in some actual management situations the level of permissible incidental catch may be more significant for fishermen than the target catch level. If the permissible incidental catch is taken first, some coastal State regulations require that fishing for target species be halted even though the catch of target species is far short of the permissible yield.

The use of the mandatory "shall" in article 61 indicates that the coastal State is obligated to decide upon an allowable catch; however, the article does not define the scope of that obligation. Common sense would suggest that the obligation does not require purely theoretical catch calculations for all living resources, but rather applies to stocks that are believed to be significantly affected by exploitation, whether as target or incidental catch. Accordingly, unless there is some actual or highly probable exploitation, a coastal State would not be in default of its obligation if it did not determine an allowable catch. Despite the literal language of article 61, the coastal State is not required to determine the allowable catch of all "living resources" within the State's EEZ. In any event, as noted below, the Convention provides no compulsory mechanism for resolving a dispute about the coastal State's obligation in this regard.

The Convention clearly provides that the determination of the amount of the allowable catch is at the coastal State's discretion. Article 61, paragraph 2, contains only the very general limitation that the coastal State is obliged to employ measure to "ensure" that "the maintenance of the living resources in the exclusive economic zone is not endangered by over-exploitation." This is a very generally worded obligation that imposes but slight restriction on coastal State authority. Furthermore, other obligations, which only the coastal State can undertake, appear to require discretion in setting the allowable catch. For example, under article 61, paragraph 4, coastal States are to consider the effects that fishing of target stocks will have upon associated or dependent species, and this could mean altering the allowable catch, but such a decision is solely within coastal State control. Apart from the single qualification concerning over-exploitation and the obligation towards other species, the coastal State may set the allowable catch as it may wish . . .

(d) Scientific Standards in Adoption of Conservation and Management Measures

In adopting conservation and management measures the coastal State is to take into account the "best scientific evidence available to it." This appears to mean that the coastal State may proceed to adopt measures even though the evidence gathered by the State is not complete or is recognized to be of low quality. More specifically, the coastal State may proceed to make conservation and management decisions even though there is a gap in the data available, or the interpretation of certain data is questionable because it is incomplete or not fully understood.

An important issue in this connection is how much effort a coastal State is required to exert to improve the quality and quantity of available evidence. If the coastal State is obliged to determine the allowable catch and to ensure against endangering a resource, is it required to invest resources in the effort to develop better data than previously available for its decisions? Nothing in the Convention expressly addresses this question. However, it might be inferred from the repetition of the term "available" in paragraphs 2 and 5 of article 61 that the coastal State's primary duty is to make use of the evidence accessible in normally expected sources, but that the Convention imposes no express duty to improve what might be available or go beyond these sources. The emphasis on "available" might reasonably be understood to signify that there is no absolute duty to pursue data and information, except data that might otherwise be secured in light of the coastal State's capacity to allocate resources and skills to the task.

In this context the term "available" should be understood to refer not only to data in the hands of the coastal State, but also to data or evidence from other sources, including foreign fleets, international organizations, and other States involved in the fisheries under management. Under article 61, paragraph 5, the various entities mentioned are expected to contribute and exchange "[a]vailable scientific information, catch and fishing effort statistics, and other data relevant to the conservation of fish stocks." The coastal State is authorized to condition access to its EEZ upon provision of information that it specifies, including catch and effort statistics, and upon the conduct of fisheries research and the reporting of scientific data. Any data and information that might reasonably be obtained from these sources should be considered "available" to the coastal State. Failure to seek or to use such data and information should not be permitted as a defense against a charge of failure to discharge a Convention obligation.

(f) The Obligation to Promote Optimum Utilization

Entitled "Utilization of the living resources," article 62 obligates the coastal State to "promote the objective of optimum utilization of the living resources in the exclusive economic zone without prejudice to Article 61." This language leaves no doubt that the Convention does not impose any obligation on the coastal State to provide for "full" or "maximum" utilization of fisheries in the EEZ. The reasons for this conclusion follow.

First, the term chosen is "optimum utilization," despite the United States proposal employing "maximum" and the Australia-New Zealand suggestion that allowable catch be tied to MSY [at the Third UN Conference on the Law of the Sea.] This choice emphasizes that the objective of management need not be classified or measured only in terms of the largest possible catch of fish. "Optimum" permits consideration of a variety of objectives in management. The selection of this term is the more significant because while the fishery provisions of CLOS generally follow the structure of the United States proposal, they differ from it in this specific instance, as well as in other operational concepts and details.

Second, article 61 requires the coastal State to "promote optimum utilization," which assumes that it is the coastal State which has the decision-making authority. No other State could implement the goal of optimum utilization, however defined, because no other State is competent to choose management goals, policies, principles, or tactics in the EEZ. States whose nationals fish for anadromous and highly migratory species do have a claim to be consulted or engaged in some cooperative activity regarding optimum utilization. In any event, the injunction to "promote" a particular objective seems neither onerous nor especially demanding, other than possibly forbidding extreme options such as prohibiting, without reason, any use of commonly exploited species.

Third, the obligations to "promote optimum utilization" is "without prejudice to Article 61." This qualification means that the coastal State's authority under article 61 is not affected by any obligation regarding "optimum utilization." Article 61 principally authorizes (1) determining the allowable catch, (2) establishing measures to ensure against endangering EEZ resources by overexploitation, and (3) establishing permissible yields. None of these determinations need be affected by any obligation to observe or to maintain a particular level of utilization above zero from a particular fishery. In light of article 62, paragraph 1, article 61 authority could be exercised to set an allowable catch or a permissible yield, at whatever level the coastal State determines to be in the interests of its harvesting effort or whatever other lawful interest it seeks to enhance. Apart from the obligation to avoid endangering target species and to avoid threatening the reproduction of associated/dependent species, the only legal qualification to the article 61 authority is the article 64 obligation to "cooperate" concerning specified highly migratory species. The obligation to "cooperate" should be interpreted as requiring negotiations that actively take into account and respond to the interests of other fishing and coastal States.

The conclusion that "optimum utilization" is to be decided solely by the coastal State is reinforced by the provisions on dispute settlement in CLOS Part XV. Article 297, paragraph 3(a), excepts from the compulsory and binding dispute settlement mechanisms of Part XV, section 2, any dispute arising from a coastal State's sovereign rights and discretionary powers that together determine how much of the coastal State's EEZ fish can be taken, by whom, when, and on what other conditions. Under CLOS the specific meaning of optimum utilization in any specific context is a matter exclusively for coastal State decision. It should be noted, however, that in the case of highly migratory species article 64 requires good faith negotiations with other States (both those which fish in the region and other coastal States) to seek to provide for utilization and conservation in the region.

c. Shared or Straddling Stock

1982 UNITED NATIONS CONVENTION ON THE LAW OF THE SEA

Article 63
Stocks occurring within the exclusive economic zones of two or more coastal States
or both within the exclusive economic zone and in an area beyond and adjacent to it

1. Where the same stock or stocks of associated species occur within the exclusive economic zones of two or more coastal States, these States shall seek, either directly or through appropriate subregional or regional organizations, to agree upon the measures necessary to co-ordinate and ensure the conservation and development of such stocks without prejudice to the other provisions of this Part.

2. Where the same stock or stocks of associated species occur both within the exclusive economic zone and in an area beyond and adjacent to the zone, the coastal State and the States fishing for such stocks in the adjacent area shall seek, either directly or through appropriate subregional or regional organizations, to agree upon the measures necessary for the conservation of these stocks in the adjacent area.

William L. Sullivan, Jr., "Special Problems Concerning Fishing," in
*United States Law of the Sea Policy: Options for the Future, Ocean
Policy Study Series*, No. 6, New York: 1985, pp. 255-258. Reprinted
with the permission of Oceana Publications, Inc.

Article 63 requires adjacent coastal states to seek agreement concerning transboundary stocks
in their zones. If they do not reach agreement, there is not much that can be done about it since
each of them has virtually total discretion in its zone, although the stock may be expected to suffer.
There is not much that can be done outside the treaty either, unless they agree to some form of
dispute settlement. The Article also requires a coastal state and a distant-water fishing state to seek
agreement on fishing a "straddling stock" in the area outside the coastal state's zone. If they fail to
do so, it might appear that there is no effective remedy, as the distant-water state is exercising its
high seas freedom of fishing. If it is conducting a significant fishery, and the dispute is protracted,
the coastal state might come to feel that it must protect its coastal fisheries through "creeping
jurisdiction," in spite of the 200 mile limitation in Article 56. A former Canadian Minister of
Fisheries has already called for jurisdiction over that portion of the Grand Banks which lies beyond
the Canadian 200 mile limit. However, Article 63 must be read in conjunction with Articles 87
and 116 concerning the right to fish on the high seas and other pertinent articles. Doing so reveals
that an effective remedy may exist which appears to strengthen the already strong coastal state
authority over coastal fisheries provided by the treaty.

The use of the term "sovereign rights" regarding fisheries (and other resources) in Article 56
means that the coastal state rights with regard to fisheries are the broadest of all the coastal State
rights mentioned in the EEZ part of the treaty. In contrast, Article 56 provides only for
"jurisdiction" over structures, marine scientific research, and the environment, and generally refers
to other "rights and duties." The terms "rights" and "jurisdiction" are used extensively throughout
the treaty, but the use of the term "sovereignty" or "sovereign rights" in addition to Article 56 is
limited to matters such as the territorial sea, archipelagoes, and the continental shelf, where, with
limited and specific exceptions, the coastal states have broad authority. The use of "sovereign
rights" in Article 56 with regard to fisheries must convey a similar meaning. Article 87 provides
that the high seas "freedom of fishing" beyond 200 miles is "subject to the conditions" set out in
later Articles. Article 116(b) specifically subjects high seas fishing rights to "the rights and duties
as well as the interests of coastal states provided for, inter alia, in Article 63, paragraph 2." Thus,
not only is the right to fish for straddling stocks on the high seas subject to the Article 63 mandate
to seek agreement, but because of the "inter alia", the "sovereign rights" under Article 56 and the
rights and duties of the coastal state for conservation and management under Articles 61 and 62 and
others become pertinent. Since the Articles referred to specifically in Article 116(b) pertain in part
to the high seas, the "inter alia" clarifies that the broad rights and duties of coastal States under
other Articles may be pertinent to high seas fisheries. Moreover, those "sovereign rights" are
nearly exempt from all forms of dispute settlement under Article 297.

With the interests of the coastal State firmly established in a straddling stock, as well as its
broad discretion, considered with the rights of the high seas fishing state constrained by Articles 87
and 116(b), it appears that the coastal state can insist that the high seas fishery on a straddling
stock cease in the absence of agreement, at least if the conservation of the stock or the coastal state
fishery in the EEZ is threatened. If the high seas fishery were to continue in such a circumstance,
the coastal state could invoke "binding compulsory dispute settlement" against the high seas
fishing state under Articles 286 to 296 (note that this is quite different from "compulsory
conciliation" under Article 297 discussed above). The high seas state would have difficulty
invoking the weak compulsory conciliation provision against the coastal state under Article 297,
because the coastal state's management actions are subject to its sole discretion, specifically

exempted from review by any conciliation commission. Unlike the severe limitations on invoking compulsory dispute settlement or compulsory conciliation against a coastal state in Article 297, there are no treaty limitations on invoking binding compulsory dispute settlement against a high seas fishing state.

A straddling stock may simultaneously be a transboundary stock, and thus the action of one of the coastal states concerned against a high seas fishing state may not be effective. While this may not be a big problem for the United States, it could be serious in some regions, such as West Africa. The circumstances in each case will have to determine how effective such a remedy would be. If the stock is mainly in the EEZ of the coastal state and the adjoining high seas area, it would still be effective. If the stock were only marginally in the EEZ and the immediately adjacent area, it would not be very effective, but the problem would not be very great either. There could be many gradations between. Certainly if all the coastal states concerned agreed, they would have a very strong position vis-à-vis the high seas fishing state, and an effective remedy.

The overwhelming priority of the fisheries provisions of the treaty is to serve coastal state interests. Not only has the traditional freedom of fishing been subjected to the virtually exclusive discretion of the coastal state within 200 miles of its coast, but the traditional freedom of fishing has been restricted even beyond 200 miles. Moreover, under Article 290 a court or tribunal would be able to impose "provisional measures" on any fishery beyond 200 miles in the event of a dispute, pending a binding settlement of the dispute outside 200 miles. In addition to straddling stocks, Article 116(b) also refers specifically to the Articles on highly migratory species, marine mammals, anadromous stocks, and catadromous species, as well as to whatever the "inter alia" clause encompasses. Hence, what "freedom" of fishing may exist on the high seas in the future pales compared to the authority of the coastal state.

The requirement to seek agreement concerning transboundary and straddling stocks may be considered to be customary international law, because most fisherfolk accept that agreement must be sought in fisheries disputes. It is less clear whether customary international law extends to cover the interests of the coastal state in a straddling stock beyond its zone. On the one hand, this may be considered to be new, and certainly the dispute settlement mechanism is new. On the other hand, it may be considered to be an aspect of the very strong coastal authority over fisheries which is found both in current state practice and in the provisions of the treaty. From the standpoint of the United States and our interest in preventing creeping jurisdiction, and from the world's interest in preventing protracted disputes in such fisheries, it might be to the world community's advantage to hold that these Articles constitute customary international law. Initially, non-parties to the treaty may have difficulties in invoking dispute settlement but I expect that this reading will become accepted as customary international law unless a significant number of distant-water states successfully defy coastal state interests. In view of the strong position of the coastal state both in the treaty and in evolving customary law, I doubt a successful defense is possible.

REFERENCE

Edward L. Miles and William T. Burke, "Pressures on the United Nations Convention on the Law of the Sea of 1982 Arising from New Fisheries Conflicts: The Problem of Straddling Stocks," *Ocean Development and International Law*, Vol. 20 (1989), pp. 343-359; Ellen Hey, *The Regime for the Exploitation of Transboundary Marine Fisheries Resources*, Dordrecht, Boston, London: Martinus Nijhoff Publishers, 1989; Karl M. Sullivan, "Conflict in the Management of A Northwest Atlantic Transboundary Cod Stock," *Marine Policy*, Vol. 13, No. 2 (April 1989), pp. 118-136.

d.   Highly Migratory Species

1982 UNITED NATIONS CONVENTION ON THE LAW OF THE SEA

Article 64
Highly migratory species

1. The coastal State and other States whose nationals fish in the region for the highly migratory species listed in Annex I shall co-operate directly or through appropriate international organizations with a view to ensuring conservation and promoting the objective of optimum utilization of such species throughout the region, both within and beyond the exclusive economic zone. In regions for which no appropriate international organization exists, the coastal State and other States whose nationals harvest these species in the region shall co-operate to establish such an organization and participate in its work.

2. The provisions of paragraph 1 apply in addition to the other provisions of this Part.

. . . .

ANNEX 1. HIGHLY MIGRATORY SPECIES

1. Albacore tuna: *Thunnus alalunga.*

2. Bluefin tuna: *Thunnus thynnus.*

3. Bigeye tuna: *Thunnus obesus.*

4. Skipjack tuna: *Katsuwonus pelamis.*

5. Yellowfin tuna: *Thunnus albacares.*

6. Blackfin tuna: *Thunnus atlanticus.*

7. Little tuna: *Euthynnus alletteratus; Euthynnus affinis.*

8. Southern bluefin tuna: *Thunnus maccoyii.*

9. Frigate mackerel: *Auxis thazard; Auxis rochei.*

10. Pomfrets: *Family Bramidae.*

11. Marlins: *Tetrapturus angustirostris; Tetrapturus belone; Tetrapturus pflugeri; Tetrapturus albidus; Tetrapturus audax; Tetrapturus georgei; Makaira mazara; Makaira indica; Makaira nigricans.*

12. Sail-fishes: *stiophorus platypterus; Istiophorus albicans.*

13. Swordfish: *ipias gladius.*

14. Sauries: *Scomberesox saurus; Cololabis saira; Cololabis adocetus; Scomberesox saurus scombroides.*

15. Dolphin: *oryphaena hippurus; Coryphaena equiselis.*

16. Oceanic sharks: *Hexanchus griseus; Cetorhinus maximus; Family Alopiidae; Rhincodon typus; Family Carcharhinidae; Family Sphyrnidae; Family Isurida.*

17. Cetaceans: *Family Phytseteridae, Family Balaenopteridae; Family Balaenidae; Family Eschrichtiidae; Family Monodontidae; Faily Ziphiidae; Family Delphinidae.*

NOTE

There are four major international organizations concerned with the scientific study and management of tuna:

(i)   The Inter-American Tropical Tuna Commission (IATTC).
(ii)   The International Commission for the Conservation of Atlantic Tunas (ICCAT).
(iii)   The Indian Ocean Fishery Commission (IOFC).
(iv)   The Indo-Pacific Fisheries Council (IPFC).

The first two organizations are concerned with tuna, tuna-like species and tuna baitfish. Moreover, the IATTC is also concerned with several species of porpoise that are captured in association with tuna. The last two organizations are responsible for all species within their geographical areas, including tuna.

REFERENCES

James Joseph and Joseph W. Greenough, *International Management of Tuna, Porpoise, and Billfish, Biological, Legal, and Political Aspects*, Seattle: University of Washington Press, 1979 and N. Peter Rasmussen, "The Tuna War: Fishery Jurisdiction in International Law," 1981 *University of Illinois Law Review*, pp. 755-774; Jon Van Dyke and Susan Heftel, "Tuna Management in the Pacific: An Analysis of the South Pacific Forum Fisheries Agency," *Hawaii Law Review*, Vol. 3 (1981), pp. 1-65; David C. Hoover, "A Case Against International Management of Highly Migratory Marine Fishery Resources: The Atlantic Blue Fin Tuna," *Boston College Environmental Affair Law Review*, Vol. 11 (1983), pp. 11-61; B. Martin Tsamenyi, "The South Pacific States, the USA and Sovereignty over Highly Migratory Species," *Marine Policy*, Vol. 10 (1986), No. 1, pp. 29-41; Christopher R. Kelly, "Law of the Sea: The Jurisdictional Dispute Over Highly Migratory Species of Tuna," *Columbia Journal of Transnational Law*, Vol. 26 (1988), pp. 475-513; James Kevin McElroy, "Indonesia's Tuna Fisheries: Past, Present and Future Prospects," *Marine Policy*, Vol. 13 No. 4 (October 1989), pp. 285-308; B. Martin Tsamenyi, "The Treaty on Fisheries between the Governments of Certain Pacific Island States and the Government of the United States: The Final Chapter in the United States Tuna Policy," *Brooklyn Journal of International Law*, Vol. 15 (1989), pp. 183-221; Christopher M. Weld, "Critical Evaluation of Existing Mechanisms for Managing Migratory Pelagic Species in the Atlantic Ocean," *Ocean Development and International Law*, Vol. 20 (1989), pp. 285-296.

e. **Anadromous Species**

CANADA: WORKING PAPER ON THE SPECIAL CASE OF SALMON--
THE MOST IMPORTANT ANADROMOUS SPECIES, U.N. DOC.
A/CONF. 62/C.2/L81 (August 23, 1974).
Third United Nations Conference on the Law of the Sea,
Official Records, Vol. III (Documents) p. 240.

This paper summarizes the unique position of the various species of salmon in the world of fisheries management. It is submitted to provide the basis in fact and in equity for the development of an appropriate regime for the best use of this valuable resource.

Salmon are unique in returning from the sea to the same fresh waters where they were born, to spawn and leave their fertilized eggs to develop in the same gravel beds. Following hatching, some salmon migrate directly to the sea as small fry; other species must live for one to several years in fresh water lakes or streams.

While salmon grow and mature in the open sea, they occupy the upper layers of cold northern waters where they are not serious competitors for the food supply of other valuable species. In the open sea they are found mainly in areas within the proposed 200-mile economic zones, but also, to a considerable degree, in areas beyond national jurisdiction.

Salmon are the only fish occurring in the open sea which man can and does increase by positive cultural measures. Such measures can be taken only by the State of origin.

Mixed in distant waters, salmon runs separate to return unerringly to their home streams. In distant waters salmon runs which need special protection are mixed with runs which are abundant; only as they approach their home streams (the very streams where they were bred) can the salmon runs be cropped separately and in accordance with the catches each run can support.

Salmon reach their greatest weight as they approach their home streams. During their migrations from the open sea to the spawning grounds, salmon grow faster than they die off. The greatest yield can be obtained by fishing the runs close to their home streams.

Strict regulations are needed to let the right number of spawners through the fishery to the spawning streams. This must be done by assessments of the runs as they appear, and prompt and often drastic restriction of fishing to let the optimum spawning appear, and prompt and often drastic restriction of fishing to let the optimum spawning run through. This requires costly supervision and enforcement, as well as co-operation of the fishermen. Only the State of origin of the salmon can carry out this essential function.

Salmon must have unobstructed access to their spawning grounds, which may be as much as 1,500 miles inland from the sea. This involves heavy direct expenses in removal of natural obstructions (e.g. landslides) and construction of fish passes. There is also much indirect cost to the State of origin in foregoing hydro-electric development, irrigation projects, flood control and other benefits, all of which would involve dams obstructing the passage of salmon. For example, power dams of great potential value have been kept off the Fraser River in British Columbia in order to maintain the productivity of one of the world's great salmon rivers. The State of origin must also protect salmon waters from pollution.

Artificial means of increasing salmon production are becoming ever more effective. Large scale projects to increase salmon production include provision of artificial channels where natural spawning grounds are inadequate, hatcheries to increase the numbers and proportions of fry produced from salmon eggs, and associated facilities for rearing small salmon safe from the enemies and fluctuations in water levels which threaten them in nature. These salmon culture techniques have, in recent years, passed the experimental stage to that of demonstrated effectiveness. In North America alone, hundreds of millions of dollars will be spent in such efforts.

Both the management of the fishery and the development of artificial means of producing more salmon have required and continue to require intensive scientific research. The States of origin of salmon have already spent hundreds of millions of dollars in research on salmon.

Only the State of origin can protect and culture salmon and effectively manage the fishery. All the steps noted above can be carried out only by the State in whose rivers the salmon breed - the State of origin. No other State can see that the right number of salmon get through the fishery to spawn. No other State can keep salmon rivers and lakes unobstructed and unpolluted. No other State can take positive measures to increase salmon production by artificial means such as man-made spawning channels, hatcheries and rearing facilities. Without these effective and costly actions by the State of origin, there would be no commercial salmon runs.

A regime must be found which assures for the State of origin the fruits of its efforts and so encourages it to continue to bear the costs. This requires curtailment of the fishing of salmon on the open sea outside national jurisdictions and co-operation with the State of origin by other States through whose zones the salmon may migrate.

1982 UNITED NATIONS CONVENTION ON THE LAW OF THE SEA

Article 66
Anadromous stocks

1. States in whose rivers anadromous stocks originate shall have the primary interest in and responsibility for such stocks.

2. The State of origin of anadromous stocks shall ensure their conservation by the establishment of appropriate regulatory measures for fishing in all waters landward of the outer limits of its exclusive economic zone and for fishing provided for in paragraph 3(b). The State of origin may, after consultations with the other States referred to in paragraphs 3 and 4 fishing these stocks, establish total allowable catches for stocks originating in its rivers.

3.(a) Fisheries for anadromous stocks shall be conducted only in waters landward of the outer limits of exclusive economic zones, except in cases where this provision would result in economic dislocation for a State other than the State of origin. With respect to such fishing beyond the outer limits of the exclusive economic zone, States concerned shall maintain consultations with a view to achieving agreement on terms and conditions of such fishing giving due regard to the conservation requirements and the needs of the State of origin in respect of these stocks.

(b) The State of origin shall co-operate in minimizing economic dislocation in such other States fishing these stocks, taking into account the normal catch and the mode of operations of such States, and all the areas in which such fishing has occurred.

(c) States referred to in subparagraph (b), participating by agreement with the State of origin in measures to renew anadromous stocks, particularly by expenditures for that purpose, shall be given special consideration by the State of origin in the harvesting of stocks originating in its rivers.

(d) Enforcement or regulations regarding anadromous stocks beyond the exclusive economic zone shall be by agreement between the State of origin and the other States concerned.

4. In cases where anadromous stocks migrate into or through the waters landward of the outer limits of the exclusive economic zone of a State other than the State of origin, such State shall co-operate with the State of origin with regard to the conservation and management of such stocks.

5. The State of origin of anadromous stocks and other States fishing these stocks shall make arrangements for the implementation of the provisions of this article, where appropriate, through regional organizations.

> William L. Sullivan, Jr., "Special Problems Concerning Fishing," in *United States Law of the Sea Policy: Options for the Future, Oceans Policy Study Series*, No. 6 (November 1985), New York: Oceana Publications, Inc., pp. 260-261. Reprinted by permission.

The U.S. has long held that high seas salmon fishing should be prohibited, or where existing ones continue they should be managed by agreement. For example, a strongly worded statement issued simultaneously by the U.S. and Canada on December 24, 1971 began with the statement: "The Governments of Canada and the United States have viewed with grave concern the failure of the North Atlantic fishing nations to agree completely on a ban on the high seas fishery for Atlantic salmon . . ." [Department of State, Press Release, No. 304, December 24, 1971] That statement was issued the day after the so-called "Pelly Amendment" was signed into law [Amendment to the Fishermen's Protective Act, Public Law 92-219, December 23, 1971], and those actions led to a ban on high seas salmon fishing by the two fisheries commissions in the North Atlantic and later to the signing of the Atlantic salmon treaty in 1982 which bans all salmon fishing beyond twelve miles with two very limited exceptions. In the North Pacific, the existing high seas fishery is governed by international agreement. The salmon producing nations could be expected to react strongly to the initiation of any new high seas salmon fishery in the North Pacific. Thus, the current situation in the North Atlantic and North Pacific coupled with the Article 66 prohibition on the initiation of new high seas salmon fisheries, the requirements that existing ones be conducted by agreement, and that the state of origin establish the TAC [Total Allowable Catch] (after appropriate consultations) makes a strong case that under customary international law new high seas salmon fisheries may not be initiated. Existing high seas salmon fisheries may be conducted only by agreement, and the basic management authority of the state of origin of salmon extends to the high seas range of their stocks. Hence, Article 66 generally reflects common state practice with regard to salmon and reflects customary international law in most if not all aspects.

REFERENCES

Philip C. Jessup, "The Pacific Coast Fisheries," *American Journal of International Law*, Vol. 33 (1939), pp. 129-138; Edward W. Allen, "Developing Fishery Protection," *American Journal of International Law*, Vol. 36 (1942), pp. 115-116; J.A. Crutchfield and G. Pontecorvo, *The Pacific Salmon Fisheries: A Study of Irrational Conservation*, Baltimore: Johns Hopkins Press, 1969; "Special Considerations Regarding the Management of Anadromous Fishes and Highly Migratory

Oceanic Fishes," working paper submitted by the United States, U.N. Doc. A/AC. 138/SC.II/L. 20 (April 2, 1973), in *Report of the Committee on the Peaceful Uses of the Seabed and the Ocean Floor Beyond the Limits of National Jurisdiction*, Vol. III, pp. 11-19; P. Copes, "The Law of the Sea and Management of Anadromous Fish Stocks," *Ocean Development and International Law*, Vol. 4 (1977), pp. 233-260; *Northwest Salmon Enhancement Program -- Salmon Interception*, Hearings before Subcommittee on Fisheries and Wildlife Conservation and the Environment of the House Committee on Merchant Marine and Fisheries (96th Congress, October 15, 16, 1979 and May 28, 1980; interceptions of Alaskan Salmon, September 18, 1980); *Pacific Salmon Treaty*, Hearings before the Senate Foreign Relations Committee (99th Congress, 1st Session, February 22, 1985); F. Lorraine Bodi and Eric Erdheim, "Swimming Upstream: FERC's Failure to Protect Anadromous Fish," *Ecological Law Quarterly*, Vol. 13 (1986), pp. 7-49; Symposium on Salmon Law, *Environmental Law*, Vol. 16 (1986), pp. 343-773; Jill L. Bubier, "International Management of Atlantic Salmon: Equitable Sharing and Building Consensus," *Ocean Development and International Law*, Vol. 19 (1988), pp. 35-58; Marlyn Twitchell, "Implementing the U.S.-Canada Pacific Salmon Treaty: The Struggle to Move from 'Fish Wars' to Cooperative Fishery Management," *Ocean Development and International Law*, Vol. 20 (1989), pp. 409-427.

f. Catadromous Species

1982 UNITED NATIONS CONVENTION ON THE LAW OF THE SEA

Article 67
Catadromous species

[Species such as eels which spawn at sea but spend most of their lives in fresh waters.]

1. A coastal State is whose waters catadromous species spend the greater part of their life cycle shall have responsibility for the management of these species and shall ensure the ingress and egress of migrating fish.

2. Harvesting of catadromous species shall be conducted only in waters landward of the outer limits of exclusive economic zones. When conducted in exclusive economic zones, harvesting shall be subject to this article and the other provisions of this Convention concerning fishing in these zones.

3. In cases where catadromous fish migrate through the exclusive economic zone of another State, whether as juvenile or maturing fish, the management, including harvesting, of such fish shall be regulated by agreement between the State mentioned in paragraph 1 and the other State concerned. Such agreement shall ensure the rational management of the species and take into account the responsibilities of the State mentioned in paragraph 1 for the maintenance of these species.

g. Sedentary Species

Sedentary species are considered to be part of the natural resources of a coastal state's continental shelf (Article 77, paragraph 4) and the coastal shelf is under no obligation to take either management or conservation measures, nor to accommodate foreign fishermen, so Article 68 specifically provides that Part V (Exclusive Economic Zone) is not applicable to sedentary species.

h.   Right of Land-locked or Geographically Disadvantaged States

1982 UNITED NATIONS CONVENTION ON THE LAW OF THE SEA

Article 69
Right of land-locked States

1. Land-locked States shall have the right to participate, on an equitable basis, in the exploitation of an appropriate part of the surplus of the living resources of the exclusive economic zones of coastal States of the same sub-region or region, taking into account the relevant economic and geographical circumstances of all the States concerned and in conformity with the provisions of this article and of articles 61 and 62.

2. The terms and modalities of such participation shall be established by the States concerned through bilateral, subregional or regional agreements taking into account, *inter alia:*

(a) the need to avoid effects detrimental to fishing communities or fishing industries of the coastal State;

(b) the extent to which the land-locked State, in accordance with the provisions of this article, is participating or is entitled to participate under existing bilateral, subregional or regional agreements in the exploitation of living resources of the exclusive economic zones of other coastal States;

(c) the extent to which other land-locked States and geographically disadvantaged States are participating in the exploitation of the living resources of the exclusive economic zone of the coastal State and the consequent need to avoid a particular burden for any single coastal State or a part of it;

(d) the nutritional needs of the populations of the respective States.

3. When the harvesting capacity of a coastal State approaches a point which would enable it to harvest the entire allowable catch of the living resources in its exclusive economic zone, the coastal State and other States concerned shall co-operate in the establishment of equitable arrangements on a bilateral, sub-regional or regional basis to allow for participation of developing land-locked States of the same subregion or region in the exploitation of the living resources of the exclusive economic zones of coastal States of the subregion or region, as may be appropriate in the circumstances and on terms satisfactory to all parties. In the implementation of this provision the factors mentioned in paragraph 2 shall also be taken into account.

4. Developed land-locked States shall, under the provisions of this article, be entitled to participate in the exploitation of living resources only in the exclusive economic zones of developed coastal States of the same subregion or region having regard to the extent to which the coastal State, in giving access to other States to the living resources of its exclusive economic zone, has taken into account the need to minimize detrimental effects on fishing communities and economic dislocation in States whose nationals have habitually fished in the zone.

5. The above provisions are without prejudice to arrangements agreed upon in subregions or regions where the coastal States may grant to land-locked States of the same subregion or region equal or preferential rights for the exploitation of the living resources in the exclusive economic zones.

Article 70
Right of geographically disadvantaged States

1. Geographically disadvantaged States shall have the right to participate, on an equitable basis, in the exploitation of an appropriate part of the surplus of the living resources of the exclusive economic zones of coastal States of the same subregion or region, taking into account the relevant economic and geographical circumstances of all the States concerned and in conformity with the provisions of this article and of articles 61 and 62.

2. For the purposes of this Part, "geographically disadvantaged States" means coastal States, including States bordering enclosed or semi-enclosed seas, whose geographical situation makes them dependent upon the exploitation of the living resources of the exclusive economic zones of other States in the subregion or region for adequate supplies of fish for the nutritional purposes of their populations or parts thereof, and coastal States which can claim no exclusive economic zones of their own.

3. The terms and modalities of such participation shall be established by the States concerned through bilateral, subregional or regional agreements taking into account, *inter alia:*

(a) the need to avoid effects detrimental to fishing communities or fishing industries of the coastal State;

(b) the extent to which the geographically disadvantaged State, in accordance with the provisions of this article, is participating or is entitled to participate under existing bilateral, subregional or regional agreements in the exploitation of living resources of the exclusive economic zones of other coastal States;

(c) the extent to which other geographically disadvantaged States and land-locked States are participating in the exploitation of the living resources of the exclusive economic zone of the coastal State and the consequent need to avoid a particular burden for any single coastal State or part of it;

(d) the nutritional needs of the populations of the respective States.

4. When the harvesting capacity of a coastal State approaches a point which would enable it to harvest the entire allowable catch of the living resources in its exclusive economic zone, the coastal State and other States concerned shall co-operate in the establishment of equitable arrangements on a bilateral, sub-regional or regional basis to allow for participation of developing geographically disadvantaged States of the same subregion or region in the exploitation of the living resources of the exclusive economic zones of coastal States of the sub-regional or region, as may be appropriate in the circumstances and on terms satisfactory to all parties. In the implementation of this provision the factors mentioned in paragraph 3 shall also be taken into account.

5. Developed geographically disadvantaged States shall, under the provisions of this article, be entitled to participate in the exploitation of living resources only in the exclusive economic zones of developed coastal States of the same subregion or region having regard to the extent to which the coastal State, in giving access to other States to the living resources of its exclusive economic zone, has taken into account the need to minimize detrimental effects on fishing communities and economic dislocation in States whose nationals have habitually fished in the zone.

6. The above provisions are without prejudice to arrangements agreed upon in subregions or regions where the coastal States may grant to geographically disadvantaged States of the same subregion or region equal or preferential rights for the exploitation of the living resources in the exclusive economic zones.

Article 71
Non-applicability of articles 69 and 70

The provisions of articles 69 and 70 do not apply in the case of a coastal State whose economy is overwhelmingly dependent on the exploitation of the living resources of its exclusive economic zone.

Article 72
Restrictions on Transfer of rights

1. Rights provided under articles 69 and 70 to exploit living resources shall not be directly or indirectly transferred to third States or their nationals by lease or licence, by establishing joint ventures or in any other manner which has the effect of such transfer unless otherwise agreed by the States concerned.

2. The foregoing provision does not preclude the States concerned from obtaining technical or financial assistance from third States or international organizations in order to facilitate the exercise of the rights pursuant to articles 69 and 70, provided that it does not have the effect referred to in paragraph 1.

NOTE

For rights of landlocked or geographically disadvantaged states, see also relevant part of Chapters on High Seas, Economic Zones and Deep Seabed. The two most comprehensive coverages of this subject are A. Mpazi Sinjela, *Land-Locked States and the UNCLOS Regime*, Dobbs Ferry, N.Y.: Oceana, 1983; and S.C. Vasciannie, *Land-Locked and Geographically Disadvantaged States in the International Law of the Sea*, New York: Oxford University Press, 1990. The most comprehensive bibliography on the subject is Martin Ira Glassner, *Bibliography on Land-Locked States*, Alphen aan den Rijn: Sijthoff & Noordhoff, 1980. For fishing rights of the landlocked or geographically disadvantaged states, see Farin Mirvahabi, "The Rights of the Landlocked and Geographically Disadvantaged States in Exploitation of Marine Fisheries," *Netherlands International Law Review*, Vol. 26 (1979), pp. 130-162; Ibrahim J. Wani, "An Evaluation of the Convention on the Law of the Sea from the Perspective of the Landlocked States," *Virginia Journal of International Law*, Vol. 22 (1981-82), pp. 627-665; M. Dahmani, "Access of Landlocked and Geographically Disadvantaged-States to the Fisheries Resources of the Economic Exclusive Zone [sic] (EEZ) under the New Convention on the Law of the Sea," *Maritime Policy and Management*, Vol. 10 (1983), pp. 265-273; Surya Prasad Subedi, "The Marine Fishery Rights of Land-locked States with Particular Reference to the EEZ," *International Journal of Estuarine and Coastal Law*, Vol. 2 (1987), pp. 227-239.

i.   **Enforcement of Laws and Regulations of the Coastal State**

1982 UNITED NATIONS CONVENTION ON THE LAW OF THE SEA

Article 73
Enforcement of Laws and Regulations of the Coastal State

1. The coastal State may, in the exercise of its sovereign rights to explore, exploit, conserve and manage the living resources in the exclusive economic zone, take such measures, including boarding, inspection, arrest and judicial proceedings, as may be necessary to ensure compliance with the laws and regulations adopted by it in conformity with the Convention.

2. Arrested vessels and their crews shall be promptly released upon the posting of reasonable bond or other security.

3. Coastal State penalties for violations of fisheries laws and regulations in the exclusive economic zone may not include imprisonment, in the absence of agreements to the contrary by the States concerned, or any other form of corporal punishment.

4. In cases of arrest or detention of foreign vessels the coastal State shall promptly notify the flag State, through appropriate channels, of the action taken and of any penalties subsequently imposed.

2.   **On the High Seas**

1982 UNITED NATIONS CONVENTION ON THE LAW OF THE SEA

Article 116
Right to fish on the high seas

All States have the right for their nationals to engage in fishing on the high seas subject to:

(a) their treaty obligations;

(b) the rights and duties as well as the interests of coastal States provided for, inter alia, in article 63, paragraph 2, and articles 64 to 67; and

(c) the provisions of this section.

Article 117
Duty of States to adopt with respect to their nationals measures for the
conservation of the living resources of the high seas

All States have the duty to take, or to co-operate with other States in taking, such measures for their respective nationals as may be necessary for the conservation of the living resources of the high seas.

Article 118
Co-operation of States in the conservation and management of living resources

States shall co-operate with each other in the conservation and management of living resources in the areas of the high seas. States whose nationals exploit identical living resources, or different living resources in the same area, shall enter into negotiations with a view to taking the measures necessary for the conservation of the living resources concerned. They shall, as appropriate, co-operate to establish subregional or regional fisheries organizations to this end.

Article 119
Conservation of the living resources of the high seas

1. In determining the allowable catch and establishing other conservation measures for the living resources in the high seas, States shall:

(a) take measures which are designed, on the best scientific evidence available to the States concerned, to maintain or restore populations of harvested species at levels which can produce the maximum sustainable yield, as qualified by relevant environmental and economic factors, including the special requirements of developing States, and taking into account fishing patterns, the interdependence of stocks and any generally recommended international minimum standards, whether subregional, regional or global;

(b) take into consideration the effects on species associated with or dependent upon harvested species with a view to maintaining or restoring populations of such associated or dependent species above levels at which their reproduction may become seriously threatened.

2. Available scientific information, catch and fishing effort statistics, and other data relevant to the conservation of fish stocks shall be contributed and exchanged on a regular basis through competent international organizations, whether subregional, regional or global, where appropriate and with participation by all States concerned.

3. States concerned shall ensure that conservation measures and their implementation do not discriminate in form or in fact against the fishermen of any State.

REFERENCES

(National Practice)

Nicholars M. Poulantzas, "Recent Developments in Canada Relating to Enforcement Measures in An Expanded Fisheries Zone," *Revue Hellenique de Droit International*, Vol. 30 (1977), pp. 109-119; R.D.S. "Inshore Fishing Interests on the Atlantic Coast: Their Response to Extended Jurisdiction by Canada," *Marine Policy*, Vol. 3 (1979), No. 3, pp. 171-189; Shoichi Tanaka, "Japanese Fisheries and Fishery Resources in the Northwest Pacific," *Ocean Development and International Law*, Vol. 6 (1979), pp. 163-235; G. Moore, "National Legislation for the Management of Fisheries Under Extended Coastal State Jurisdiction," *Journal of Maritime Law and Commerce*, Vol. 11 (1980), pp. 153-182; Manjula R. Shyam, "The Emergency Fisheries Regime: Implications for India," *Ocean Development and International Law*, Vol. 8 (1980), pp. 35-55; Food and Agricultural Organization, *Legislation on Coastal State Requirements for Foreign Fishing*, Rome: FAO Legislative Study No. 21, 1981; M. K. Nawaz, "The Legal Regime of Fisheries: A Case Study of India," *Derecho Pesquero (Mexico)*, No. 1 (October 1981), pp. 227-239; R. R. Churchhill, A Review of United Kingdom Fisheries Law: Resume," *Derecho Pesquero*,

No. 2 (February 1982), pp. 7-28; John Winn, "Alaska v. F/V Baranof: State Regulation Beyond the Territorial Sea After the Magnuson Act," *British Columbia Environmental Affair Law Review*, Vol. 13 (1986), pp. 281-327.

(Regional Cooperation and Problems)

Pieter Korringa, "European Fisheries: An Object Lesson in Economic and Ecological Mismanagement," *Interdisciplinary Science Review* (London), Vol. 3 (December 1978), pp. 335-345; John P. Grant, "The Conflict between the Fishing and the Oil Industries in the North Sea: A Case Study," *Ocean Management* (Amsterdam), Vol. 4 (December 1978), pp. 137-149; J.E. Carroz and M. J. Savini, "The New International Law of Fisheries Emerging from Bilateral Agreements," *Marine Policy*, Vol. 3 (1979), No. 2, pp. 79-98; Phiphat Tangsubkul, "ASEAN States: The Law of the Sea and Fisheries Jurisdiction," in *Southeast Asian Affairs*, 1979, Singapore: Institute of Southeast Asian Studies, 1979, pp. 79-92; J.W.C. Tomlinson and P.S. Brown, "Joint Ventures with Foreigners as a Method of Exploiting Canadian Fishery Resources Under Extended Fisheries Jurisdiction, *Ocean Management*, Vol. 5 (1979), pp. 251-261; M. Fitzmaurice-Lachs, "The Legal Regime of the Baltic Sea Fisheries, "*Netherlands International Law Review*, Vol. 29 (1982), pp. 174-251; S. H. Amin," The Law of Fisheries in the Persian-Arabian Gulf," *Journal of Maritime Law and Commerce*, Vol. 14 (1983), pp. 581-594; Ronald Frank, "The Convention on the Conservation of Antarctic Marine Living Resources," *Ocean Development and International Law*, Vol. 13 (1983), pp. 291-346; Yu A. Zamansky, "International Agreements of the USSR on Fisheries," *Soviet Yearbook of Maritime Law 1984*, pp. 19-30; Donald Barry, "The Canada-European Community Long Term Fisheries Agreement: Internal Politics and Fisheries Diplomacy," *Revue de Integration European*, Vol. 9 (1985), No. 1, pp. 5-28; Marc L. Miller and Charles F. Broches, "U.S. Fishery Negotiation with Canada and Mexico," *Ocean Development and International Law*, Vol. 14 (1985), pp. 417-451; Gordon R. Munro, "Coastal States, Distant-Water Fleets and EFJ [Exclusive Fishery Jurisdiction]," *Marine Policy*, Vol. 9 (1985), No. 1, pp. 2-15; John E. Bardach, "Fish Far Away: Comments on Antarctic Fisheries," *Ocean Yearbook*, Vol. 6, Chicago: University of Chicago Press, 1986, pp. 38-54; Cameron Crone, "U.S.-Soviet Fishing Agreement, Treaty Authorizing Soviet Fishing in U.S. Waters," *Marine Policy*, Vol. 10 (1986), No. 1, pp. 51-56; Ted L. McDorman, "Thailand's Fisheries: A Victim of 200-mile Zones," *Ocean Development and International Law*, Vol. 16 (1986), pp. 183-209; W. M. Sutherland, "Coastal State Cooperation in Fisheries: Emergent Regional Custom in the South Pacific," *International Journal of Estuarine and Coastal Law*, Vol. 1 (1986), pp. 15-28; Andrea Wagner-Liebzeit, "Joint Ventures in Fisheries," *Marine Policy*, Vol. 9 (1986), No. 2, pp. 7-11.

(1982 United Nations Convention on the Law of the Sea and General Problems)

Ross D. Eckert, *The Enclosure of Ocean Resources: Economics and the Law of the Sea*, Stanford, Calif.: Hoover Institution Press, 1979; Shabtai Rosenne, "Settlement of Fisheries Disputes in the Exclusive Economic Zone," *American Journal of International Law*, Vol. 73 (1979), pp. 89-104; Farin Mirvahabi, "A Proposed Fisheries Code of Conduct," *Revue de Driot International de Sciences Diplomatiques et Politiques*, Vol. 58, No. 2 (April/June 1980), pp. 89-104; Wilfried Prewo, "Ocean Fishing: Economic Efficiency and the Law of the Sea," *Texas International Law Journal*, Vol. 15 (1980), pp. 261-285; S.P. Balasubramanian, "Fishery Provisions of the ICNT, (I)," *Marine Policy*, Vol. 5 (1981), No. 4, pp. 313-321 and ". . . (II)", **ibid.*, Vol. 6 (1982), No. 1, pp. 27-42; Parzival Cope, "The Impact of UNCLOS III on Management of the World's Fisheries," *Marine Policy*, Vol. 5 (1981), No. 3, pp. 217-228; Tony Loftas, "FAO's EEZ Programme-Assisting a New Era in Fisheries," *Marine Policy*, Vol. 5 (1981), No. 3, pp. 229-239; R. P. Arand, "The Politics of a New Legal Order for Fisheries," *Ocean Development and International Law*, Vol. 11 (1982), pp. 265-295; Rama Puri, "Legal

Regime of Marine Fisheries," *Indian Journal of International Law*, Vol. 22 (1982), pp. 240-250; Manjula R. Shyam, "The New International Economic Order and the New Regime for Fisheries Management," *Ocean Management*, Vol. 8, No. 1 (June 1982), pp. 51-64; Gunnar Saetersdal, "Problems of Managing and Sharing Living Resources under the New Ocean Regime," *Ocean Yearbook*, Vol. 4, Chicago: University of Chicago Press, 1983, pp. 45-49; E.A. Keen, "Common Property in Fisheries: Is Sole Ownership an Option?," *Marine Policy*, Vol. 7 (1983), No. 3, pp. 197-211; Shigeru Oda, "Fisheries under the United Nations Convention on the Law of the Sea," *American Journal of International Law*, Vol. 77 (1983), pp. 739-755; Richard B. Pollanac and Susan J. Littlefield," Socio-cultural Aspects of Fisheries Management," *Ocean Development and International Law*, Vol. 12 (1983), pp. 209-246; Jon L. Jacobson, "International Fisheries Law in the Year 2010," *Lousiana Law Review*, Vol. 45 (1985), pp. 1161-1199; S. Garcia, J.A. Gulland and E. Miles, "The New Law of the Sea, and the Access to Surplus Fish Resources, Bioeconomic Reality and Scientific Collaboration," *Marine Policy*, Vol. 10 (1986), No. 3, pp. 192-200; Warren H. Lieberman, "Towards Improving Fishery Management Systems," *Marine Policy*, Vol. 10 (1986), No. 1, pp. 42-50; Leslie M. MacRae, "Preemption in the Fisheries and the United Nations' Law of the Sea Treaty," *Dickinson Journal of International Law*, Vol. 4 (1986), pp. 143-166; G. Kevin Jones, "Harvesting the Ocean's Resources: Oil or Fish?" *Southern California Law Review*, Vol. 60 (1987), pp. 585-648.

3. The Driftnet Fishing Issue

Since mid-1980's, fishermen from some East Asian countries, such as Japan, the Republic of Korea and the Republic of China (Taiwan), have used driftnet for fishing on the high seas. The nets are made of lightweight filament that is largely invisible underwater. They can stretch up to 40 miles, hanging vertically to a depth of about 30 feet, catching fish by their gill covers and trapping marine mammals who are then unable to get to air. Many countries have charged that the nets seriously deplete stocks of sought-after commercial fish and indiscriminately trap and kill porpoises, seabirds and a wide variety of fish not sought by fishermen. International efforts have been launched to ban the use of driftnet in fishing.

CONVENTION FOR THE PROHIBITION OF FISHING WITH
LONG DRIFT NETS IN THE SOUTH PACIFIC
November 23, 1989
Law of the Sea Bulletin, No. 14 (December 1989), pp. 31-36.

The Parties to this Convention,

RECOGNIZING the importance of marine living resources to the people of the South Pacific region;

PROFOUNDLY CONCERNED at the damage now being done by pelagic drift-net fishing to the albacore tuna resource and to the environment and economy of the South Pacific region;

CONCERNED ALSO for the navigational threat posed by drift-net fishing;

NOTING that the increasing fishing capacity induced by large scale drift-net fishing threatens the fish stocks in the South Pacific;

MINDFUL OF the relevant rules of international law, including the provisions of the United Nations Convention on the Law of the Sea, done at Montego Bay on 10 December 1982, in

Nations Convention on the Law of the Sea, done at Montego Bay on 10 December 1982, in particular Parts V, VII and XVI;

RECALLING the Declaration of the South Pacific Forum at Tarawa, 11 July 1989, that a Convention should be adopted to ban the use of drift nets in the South Pacific region;

RECALLING ALSO the Resolution of the 29th South Pacific Conference at Guam, which called for an immediate ban on the practice of drift-net fishing in the South Pacific Commission region;

HAVE AGREED as follows:

Article 1
Definitions

For the purpose of this Convention and its Protocols:

(a) the "Convention Area",

(i)   Subject to subparagraph (ii) of this paragraph, shall be the area lying within 10 degrees North latitude and 50 degrees South latitutde and 130 degrees East longitude and 120 degrees West longitude, and shall also include all waters under the fisheries jurisdiction of any Party to this Convention;

(ii)   In the case of a State or Territory which is party to the Convention by virtue of paragraph 1(b) or 1(c) of article 10, it shall include only waters under the fisheries jurisdiction of that Party, adjacent to the Territory referred to in paragraph 1(b) or 1(c) of article 10.

(b)   "drift net" means a gillnet or other net or a combination of nets which is more than 2.5 kilometers in length the purpose of which is to enmesh, entrap or entangle fish by drifting on the surface of or in the water;

(c)   "drift net fishing activities" means:

(i)   catching, taking or harvesting fish with the use of a drift net;

(ii)   attempting to catch, take or harvest fish with the use of a drift net;

(iii)   engaging in any other activity which can reasonably be expected to result in the catching, taking or harvesting of fish with the use of a drift net, including searching for and locating fish to be taken by that method;

(iv)   any operations at sea in support of, or in preparation for, any activity described in this paragraph, including operations of placing, searching for or recovering fish aggregating devices or associated electronic equipment such as radio beacons;

(v)   aircraft use, relating to the activities described in this paragraph, except for flights in emergencies involving the health or safety of crew members or the safety of a vessel; or

(vi)   transporting, transshipping and processing any drift-net catch, and cooperation in the provision of food, fuel and other supplies for vessels equipped for or engaged in drift-net fishing.

(d)   the "FFA" means the South Pacific Forum Fisheries Agency; and

(e)   "fishing vessel" means any vessel or boat equipped for or engaged in searching for, catching, processing or transporting fish or other marine organisms.

Article 2
Measures Regarding Nationals and Vessels

Each Party undertakes to prohibit its nationals and vessels documented under its laws from engaging in drift-net fishing activities within the Convention Area.

Article 3
Measures Against Drift-net Fishing Activities

1.   Each Party undertakes:

(a) not to assist or encourage the use of drift nets within the Convention Area; and

(b) to take measures consistent with international law to restrict drift-net fishing activities within the Convention Area, including but not limited to:

    (i)   prohibiting the use of drift nets within areas under its fisheries jurisdiction; and

    (ii)   prohibitint the transshipment of drift-net catches within areas under its jurisdiction.

2.   Each Party may also take measures consistent with international law to:

(a) prohibit the landing of drift-net catches within its territory;

(b) prohibit the processing of drift-net catches in facilities under its jurisdiction;

(c) prohibit the importation of any fish or fish product, whether processed or not, which was caught using a drift net;

(d) restrict port access and port servicing facilities for drift-net fishing vessels; and

(e) prohibit the possession of drift nets on board any fishing vessel within areas under its fisheries jurisdiction.

3.   Nothing in this Convention shall prevent a Party from taking measures against drift-net fishing activities which are stricter than those required by the Convention.

Article 4
Enforcement

1.   Each Party shall take appropriate measures to ensure the application of the provisions of this Convention.

2.   The Parties undertake to collaborate to facilitate surveillance and enforcement of measures taken by Parties pursuant to this Convention.

3.   The Parties undertake to take measures leading to the withdrawal of good standing on the Regional Register of Foreign Fishing Vessels maintained by the FFA against any vessel engaging in drift-net fishing activities.

Article 5
Consultation with Non-parties

1. The Parties shall seek to consult with any State which is eligible to become a Party to this Convention on any matter relating to drift-net fishing activities which appear to affect adverseley the conservation of marine living resources within the Convention Area or the implementation of the Convention and its protocols.

2. The Parties shall seek to reach agreement with any State referred to in paragraph 1 of this article, concerning the prohibitions established pursuant to articles 2 and 3.

Article 6
Institutional Arrangements

1. The FFA shall be responsible for carrying out the following functions:

(a) the collection, preparation and dissemination of information on drift-net fishing activities within the Convention Area;

(b) the facilitation of scientific analyses on the effects of drift-net fishing activities within the Convention Area, including consultations with appropriate regional and international organizations; and

(c) the preparation and transmission to the Parties of an annual report on any drift-net fishing activities within the Convention Area and the measures taken to implement this Convention or its Protocols.

2. Each Party shall expeditiously convey to the FFA:

(a) information on the measures adopted by it pursuant to the implementation of the Convention; and

(b) information on, and scientific analyses on the effects of, drift-net fishing activities relevant to the Convention Area.

3. All Parties, including States or Territories not members of the FFA, and the FFA shall cooperate to promote the effective implementation of this article.

Article 7
Review and Consultation Among Parties

1. Without prejudice to the conduct of consultations among Parites by other means, the FFA, at the request of three Parties, shall convene meetings of the Parties to review the implementation of this Convention and its Protocols.

2. Parties to the Protocols shall be invited to any such meeting and to participate in a manner to be determined by the Parties to the Convention.

Article 8
Conservation and Management Measures

Parties to this Convention shall cooperate with each other and with appropriate distant water fishing nations and other entities or organizations in the development of conservation and management meausres for South Pacific albacore tuna within the Convention Area.

Article 9
Protocols

This Convention may be supplemented by Protocols or associated instruments to further its objectives.

[Articles 10 to 14 omitted].

DONE at Wellington this twenty-third day of November 1989 in the English and French languages, each text being equally authentic.

IN WITNESS WHEREOF the undersigned, being duly authorized by their Governments, have signed this Convention.

NOTE

Seven South Pacific countries, New Zealand, Cook Islands, Micronesia, Palau, Marshall Islands, Niue and Tokelau, signed on the Convention. *Shih-jie Jih-pao* (World Journal), New York, November 30, 1989, p. 12.

Paragraph 6 of the Preamble of the Convention refers to parts V, [Exclusive Economic Zone], VII [High Seas], and XVI [General Provisions] of the 1982 United Nations Convention on the Law of the Sea but does not specify the relevant articles. In the Tarawa Declaration of July 11, 1989 [referred to in paragraph 7 of the Preamble of the Driftnet Convention], it specifically refers to [Part V], Article 63. Stocks occurring within the exclusive economic zones of two or more coastal States or both within the exclusive economic zone and in an area beyond and adjacent to it, 64 (Highly migratory species), [Part VII] 87 (Freedom of the High Seas), 116 (Right to fish on the high seas), 117 (Duty of states to adopt with respect to their nationals measures for the conservation of the living resources of the high seas), 118 (cooperation of states in the conservation and management of living resources) and 119 (conservation of the living resources of the high seas) of the 1982 Convention. Text of the Tarawa Declaration is reprinted in *Law of the Sea Bulletin*, Nov. 14 (December 1989), p. 29.

UNITED NATIONS GENERAL ASSEMBLY RESOLUTION 44/225--
LARGE-SCALE PELAGIC DRIFTNET FISHING AND ITS IMPACT ON
THE LIVING MARINE RESOURCES OF THE WORLD'S OCEAN AND SEAS
December 22, 1989 U.N. Doc. A/RES/44/225, reprinted in
Law of the Sea Bulletin, No. 15 (May 1990), p. 15.

The General Assembly,

Noting that many countries are disturbed by the increase in the use of large-scale pelagic driftnets, which can reach or exceed 30 miles (48 kilometers) in total length, to catch living marine resources on the high seas of the world's oceans and seas,

Mindful that large-scale pelagic driftnet fishing, a method of fishing with a net or a combination of nets intended to be held in a more or less vertical position by floats and weights, the purpose of which is to enmesh fish by drifting on the surface of or in the water, can be a highly indiscriminate and wasteful fishing method that is widely considered to threaten the effective conservation of living marine resources, such as highly migratory and anadromous species of fish, birds and marine mammals,

Drawing attention to the fact that the present resolution does not address the question of small-scale driftnet fishing traditionally conducted in coastal waters, especially by developing countries, which provides an important contribution to their subsistence and economic development,

Expressing concern that, in addition to targeted species of fish, non-targeted fish, marine mammals, seabirds and other living marine resources of the world's oceans and seas can become entangled in large-scale pelagic driftnets, either in those in active use or in those that are lost or discarded, and as a result of such entanglement are often either injured or killed. . . .

1. Calls upon all members of the international community, particularly those with fishing interests, to strengthen their cooperation in the conservation and management of living marine resources;

2. Calls upon all those involved in large-scale pelagic driftnet fishing to cooperate fully with the international community, and especially with coastal States and the relevant international and regional organizations, in the enhanced collection and sharing of statistically sound scientific data in order to continue to assess the impact of such fishing methods and to secure conservation of the world's living marine resources;

3. *Recommends* that all interested members of the international community, particularly within regional organizations, continue to consider and, by 30 June 1991, review the best available scientific data on the impact of large-scale pelagic driftnet fishing and agree upon further cooperative regulation and monitoring measures, as needed;

4. *Also recommends* that all members of the international community, bearing in mind the special role of regional organizations and regional and bilateral cooperation in the conservation and management of living marine resources as reflected in the relevant articles of the United Nations Convention on the Law of the Sea, agree to the following measures:

(a) Moratoria should be imposed on all large-scale pelagic driftnet fishing by 30 June 1992, with the understanding that such a measure will not be imposed in a region or, if implemented, can be lifted, should effective conservation and management measures be taken based upon statistically sound analysis to be jointly made by concerned parties of the international community with an interest in the fishery resources of the region, to prevent unacceptable impact of such fishing practices on that region and to ensure the conservation of the living marine resources of that region;

(b) Immediate action should be taken to reduce progressively large-scale pelagic driftnet fishing activities in the South Pacific region with a view to the cessation of such activities by 1 July 1991, as an interim measure, until appropriate conservation and management arrangements for South Pacific albacore tuna resources are entered into by the parties concerned;

(c) Further expansion of large-scale pelagic driftnet fishing on the high seas of the North Pacific and all the other high seas outside the Pacific Ocean should cease immediately, with the understanding that this measure will be reviewed subject to the conditions in paragraph 4 (a) of the present resolution. . . .

NOTE

In July 1990, it was reported that Japan would suspend its driftnet fishing in the 1990-91 season and would ban the use of such net in 1992. "Tokyo Is to Ban Fish Nets Early," *New York Times*, July 18, 1990, p. A12. The Republic of China also announced in July 1990 that its driftnet fleet would be banned from the South Pacific after July 1, 1991. "'Wall of Death' Ban Announced," *Free China Journal*, Vol. 7, No. 49 (July 2, 1990), p. 2. For a discussion of this issue, see Douglas M. Johnson, "The Driftnetting Problem in the Pacific Ocean: Legal Consideration and Diplomatic Options," *Ocean Development and International Law*, Vol. 21 (1990), pp. 5-40. It was, however, reported that some Asian fishing vessels move their driftnets to the Atlantic Ocean. See William K. Stevens, "Fishermen Moving Nets to Atlantic," *New York Times*, August 14, 1990, pp. A3, C4. For U.S. and driftnet fishing issue, see Section D, Subsection 4 [pp. 617-626] of this Chapter.

F. PROTECTION OF MARINE MAMMALS

1. Definition and Status of Marine Mammals

> "UNEP: The FAO/UNEP Global Plan of Action for the Conservation, Management, and Utilization of Marine Mammals," *Ocean Yearbook*, Vol. 6, Chicago: University of Chicago Press, 1986, pp. 466-468.

What are Marine Mammals?

For the purposes of the FAO/UNEP Plan of Action, the term marine mammal includes those mammals which spend all, or a large proportion, of their time in the sea and obtain their food predominantly from it. The term also includes a few species whose ancestors were marine but which have moved back into fresh water.

There are several groups of marine mammals.

The Cetaceans (whales and dolphins)

This term covers two groups:

1. *Odontoceti* (toothed cetaceans). This includes the sperm whale and all the dolphins, including the larger species of dolphin commonly referred to as whales, killer whale, bottlenose whale, pilot whale, etc.

2. *Mysticeti* (baleen whales). This group includes five "rorquals" (blue, fin, Bryde's, sei, and minke), the humpback, right whales and grey whale.

All members of this group are totally marine. They mate, give birth to young and rear their young entirely at sea.

The Pinnipeds (seals, sea lions)

This term also covers two groups:

1. *Otariidae*. The walking or eared seals: fur seals, sea lions, walruses.

2. *Phocidae*. The crawling or earless seals, including elephant seals, monk seals, and many others.

The members of this group usually come to shore for breeding. Mating, the birth of pups, and nurturing of young for the first few months of life take place on land.

Sirenia (sea cows)

These are all tropical mammals which live in coastal habitats. All are totally herbivorous and are the only herbivorous sea mammals.

1. *The Manatees*. These live on shores that border the Atlantic. Three distinct species of the genus *Trichechus* (family *Trichechidae*) are recognized: the Amazonian manatee, the Caribbean manatee, and the West African manatee. This genus is known to travel up rivers to feed and lives in sheltered coastal sites.

2. *The Dugong*. A single species, *Dugong dugon* of the family *Dugongidae*, exists in scattered populations across the Indo-Pacific. They inhabit sheltered areas of tropical coasts.

Otters

Some otters are marine. They belong to the family *Mustelidae* and feed on invertebrate animals like sea urchins and shellfish, as well as fish.

PARTICULAR PROBLEMS FACING THE DIFFERENT GROUPS OF MARINE MAMMALS

Cetaceans

Many species of large cetaceans are now severely depleted as a result of heavy commercial exploitation. The bowhead and right whales, the blue, and humpback whales have all declined in recent years. Some populations are so low that, despite full protection, it is uncertain whether their numbers can recover. One problem is that, as populations are so low, they may be unable to find each other to mate. This problem is heightened because the noise from oceangoing vessels interferes with the whales' acoustic communication system.

Now that the larger whales are extremely reduced in numbers, commercial exploitation of smaller species is under way--fin whales and Bryde's whales are being hunted at the present time, and even the small Minke whale is being hunted, particularly in the Antarctic.

The smaller cetaceans, commonly referred to as dolphins and porpoises, are declining because they clash with fishermen and are killed both at sea and offshore, sometimes in huge numbers.

Pinnipeds

The pinnipeds, seals, sea lions, and their relatives are hunted by man at their breeding grounds or nursery areas. Huge commercial hunts are based on the harp seal nurseries of Newfoundland and Greenland. In this case, there has been a large public outcry about the methods used in the hunts.

Sirenia

Sea cows are threatened largely by indigenous hunting. Many populations of both dugong and manatee occur in developing countries where regulations are difficult or impossible to enforce; where local inhabitants may exist at subsistence levels, and where there may be problems of protein deficiencies in human populations. Sea cows, docile and nonagressive, are very easily caught by indigenous methods of hunting.

Otters

Marine otters have long been hunted for their thick lustrous pelts and are severely depleted over much of their range. They are now officially protected in some areas, but are still persecuted by fishermen who would like to exploit the sea urchins or marine molluscs on which the otters feed.

GROWING CONCERN FOR AND APPRECIATION OF MARINE MAMMALS

Public concern about the threatened status of many marine mammals, particularly the large whales, has grown since the early 1970s. Whales have almost become symbolic of the growing ecological awareness and a movement toward greater responsibility for the environment.

This new appreciation of marine mammals has developed in the last few decades. . . .

2.   **International Protection of Marine Mammals--The Case of the Whale**

Gregory M. Travalio and Rebecca J. Clement, "International Protection of Marine Mammals," *Columbia Journal of Environmental Law*, Vol. 5 (1979), pp. 207-213. Footnotes omitted. Reprinted in modified form by permission.

Only in the twentieth century has mankind demonstrated any concern for the diminishing numbers of marine mammals, and the impetus for most regulatory attempts has been economic. In 1924, whaling was added to the agenda of the League of Nations Committee on International Law. Due to its belief that whales were in small danger of extermination, however, the League initially did virtually nothing to promote their conservation. The threat of diminishing stocks was not recognized until 1931, when the League developed the International Convention for the Regulation of Whaling.

The 1931 Convention regulated commercial whaling in all oceans and in the territorial waters of the contracting countries, and implemented a system of licensing for the flag states engaged in whaling. Its main purpose was to curtail competition in the whaling industry; as a protective device it was grossly deficient. First, enforcement provisions were inadequate. Law enforcement officers who inspected the ports and handled the licensing had jurisdiction only in their territorial seas and ports. Therefore, whaling on the high seas, where the bulk of the killing occurred, remained unpoliced by international forces. Moreover, the officers were lax in patrolling their native boats. A second critical deficiency in the 1931 Convention was the refusal of many of the major whaling nations--Japan, Chile, Argentina, and the USSR--to sign. The contracting states therefore felt unfairly constrained, and consequently enforced the provisions with less vigor than was required to achieve its purposes. Most important, the failure of the 1931 Convention either to institute a quota system or specifically to define "immature whales," which qualified for special protection, thwarted any conservationalist thrust.

By 1937 the inadequacy of the 1931 Convention had become generally acknowledged, and a new covenant was signed in London. This covenant, the Agreement for the Regulation of Whaling, increased the scope of supervision to include right and gray whales, and continued the protection afforded by the previous Convention to sperm whales and the small blue, fin, and humpback species. It also set quotas and established sanctuaries in the Atlantic, Pacific, and Indian Oceans. Improved fishing techniques, coupled with refusals by Chile, Japan, and the USSR to sign, however, rendered the Agreement almost worthless.

Although the Second World War gave whales some respite, by 1946 whale catches were again rising precipitously. The threatened extinction of the blue whale prompted the United States to convene an international conference on whaling in 1946. That conference resulted in the International Convention for the Regulation of Whaling which became effective in 1948, and continues to supervise whaling activity and regulation.

The 1946 Whaling Convention expressly recognizes a common interest in achieving an optimum level of whale stocks in a manner that allows orderly development of the whaling industry. To achieve these goals, it provides for the establishment of the International Whaling Commission, (IWC). The IWC, composed of one member from each contracting government, is authorized to acquire and disseminate information on whales and whaling. It also performs the crucial function of adopting regulations that fix the annual scope of whaling activities.

Despite conservationists' accusations of IWC inefficacy and irresponsibility, its achievements and those of the Convention deserve credit. Most notably, the International Observer Scheme, whereby a foreign observer is stationed on each whaling ship and at each whaling port to ensure compliance with IWC regulations, has greatly improved the enforcement capacity of the IWC. Moreover, the IWC has developed more expertise in the study of whales, has become more independent of commercial whaling interests, and has fostered a more protectionist attitude towards whales.

Several factors, however, impede IWC efforts to promote conservation. First, while it is commendable that all major whaling nations have signed the Whaling Convention of 1946, their interests have dominated IWC policies. The Whaling Convention of 1946 purports to achieve the optimum utilization of whale resources, and expressly requires the IWC to consider the interests of consumers of whale products and the development of the whaling industry towards this end. These requirements pose an internal constitutional barrier to the IWC's attempts to conserve marine mammal resources, another stated goal of the Convention. In attempting to reconcile these goals, the IWC has consistently compromised conservation concerns in favor of policies favoring

the IWC has consistently compromised conservation concerns in favor of policies favoring consumers.

A second factor curtailing the conservationist function of the IWC is the ease with which contracting states can avoid compliance with inconvenient regulations. If any contracting state objects to a regulation within ninety days of enactment, the objection period is automatically extended an additional ninety days. Any government that objects during this extended period is not bound by the regulation. Another, more drastic method for a contracting state to escape the regulations is to opt out of the Convention altogether pursuant to Article XI of the 1946 Whaling Convention. Moreover, certain IWC nations have conducted unregulated operations under "flags of convenience" in order to circumvent IWC quotas. These operations, in addition to the whaling activities of non-IWC nations and at least one known pirate ship, threaten to exhaust various geographically distinct stocks and to further endanger those species that are nearly extinct.

A third major impediment to the effective functioning of the IWC as a conservationist organ is its adherence to the methodology of Maximum Sustainable Yield (MSY) in determining quotas. This methodology has been deemed scientifically invalid. A fourth factor hampering the IWC is that it has no power to restrict the number and nationality of factory ships or stations, and cannot allocate specific quotas to such ships or stations.

The uncertainty of the IWC's ability to protect whales is underscored by the fact that certain IWC measures originally viewed as promising have proven to be short-lived. For example, the protection of all whale stocks in 1974 and a 1977 moratorium on all bowhead whale killing presaged additional moves toward greater protection. The 1978 and 1979 quotas, however, and the reinstatement of a limited bowhead quota, represent a regression from a conservationist attitude.

> Kimberly S. Davis, "International Management of Cetaceans Under the New Law of the Sea Convention," *Boston University International Law Journal*, Vol. 3 (1985), pp. 484-488. Footnotes omitted. Reprinted by permission of the author.

During the 1960's the vast majority of IWC [International Whaling Commission] members were whaling nations. By the mid-1970's, however, many of the traditional whaling nations discontinued their whaling operations with the result that by 1977 fewer than half of all IWC members carried on commercial whaling. Also, in recent years many non-whaling states have joined the IWC, further diminishing the dominance of whaling states. This change in membership and an increased international concern with conservation of cetaceans has led the IWC to promulgate increasingly stringent regulations. These regulations have included prohibitions on the taking of the most endangered species of cetaceans, reduced catch quotas for less endangered species, and in 1982, the adoption by the IWC of an amendment to the Schedule of regulations providing for a complete moratorium on commercial whaling to become effective during the 1985/86 pelagic whaling season.

Conservationists have applauded the efforts of the IWC to increase protection for cetaceans. The IWC is, however, institutionally ill-equipped to gain compliance with truly effective regulations. Whaling nations have threatened to withdraw from the ICRW because their interests are no longer adequately represented in the IWC. Also, the right to object to amendments to the Schedule has been invoked with increasing frequency over the past several years. In particular objections have been lodged against the commercial whaling moratorium as well as the ban on sperm whaling passed at the 1981 meeting of the IWC. Concern has been voiced within the IWC that the ability of the IWC to regulate effectively is weakened by such objections.

The nullifying effect of the freedom to object to IWC regulatory action on the IWC's ability to regulate is mitigated somewhat by the influence exerted by member states on whaling nations. Notably, the United States has threatened to invoke sanctions (and on occasion has actually done so) authorized by domestic legislation against nations which have not complied with IWC regulations. Sanctions are authorized by the Packwood-Magnuson Amendment to the Magnuson Fishery Conservation and Management Act of 1976. This Amendment requires reduction by at least fifty percent of the fishing allocation within the United States 200-mile exclusive economic zone (EEZ) of any nation whose fishing operations "diminish the effectiveness" of the ICRW. Additional sanctions are provided by the Pelly Amendment to the Fishermen's Protective Act of 1967, which prescribes the prohibition of importation of fish products from any nation whose actions similarly "diminish the effectiveness" of the ICRW.

In practice, the administrative bodies responsible for invoking these sanctions, the Commerce Department and the State Department, have been reluctant to do so, preferring instead to slowly negotiate reduced quotas using the threat of sanctions as leverage. However, in *American Cetacean Society v. Baldrige*, a group of conservation organizations successfully argued in the United States District Court for the District of Columbia that application of sanctions under the Pelly and Packwood-Magnuson Amendments is mandatory and non-discretionary. This decision was upheld on appeal. Under this ruling the Secretary of State and the Secretary of Commerce must certify Japan under these statutes for failure to comply with IWC quotas. This decision may have the effect of forcing Japan, the leading hunter of whales for commercial purposes, into compliance with IWC regulations, particularly the commercial whaling moratorium which becomes effective during the coming pelagic whaling season. It should be noted, however, that this outcome is not certain and that the *American Cetacean Society* decision has the effect of scuttling an agreement between the United States and Japan to end Japanese whaling in 1988.

Even if, as a result of the imposition of sanctions, Japan complies with IWC quotas, uniform regulation of whaling activities is not assured under the auspices of the ICRW. Nations against whom invocation of such sanctions are ineffective remain free to lodge objections to regulations or withdraw from or remain outside of the IWC. To illustrate, the United States threatened to sanction the USSR under the Packwood-Magnuson Amendment for non-compliance with the IWC catch quota of 1,941 southern hemisphere minke whales for the 1984/85 harvest. However, unlike Japan, the USSR did not depend heavily on United States waters for its fish catch. Consequently, the threat of reduced fishing allocation was ineffective and the Soviet whaling fleet exceeded its quota of minke whales by about five hundred animals.

NOTE

On February 10, 1988, U.S. Commerce Secretary C. William Verity, Jr. declared Japan in violation of a moratorium on commercial whaling imposed by the International Whaling Commission in 1986 because of evidence that the commercial hunt was severely depleting the global population of the whales. See Philip Shabecoff, "U.S. Declares Japan in Violation on Whaling and May Curb Trade," *New York Times*, February 11, 1988, pp. A1, D2. In making such a finding against Japan, Verity brought into place the Packwood-Magnuson Amendment which called for an automatic reduction of at least 50% in Japan's fishing quota in U.S. waters. Under the Pelly Amendment [22 U.S.C. §1978] the U.S. could ban imports of Japanese fisheries products at the President's discretion. "U.S. Resists Japan Whaling," *Facts on File*, Vol. 48, No. 2465 (February 19, 1988), p. 101. On April 6, 1988, President Reagan denied Japan fishing privileges in U.S. waters. "U.S. Ban Japanese Fishing," *Facts on File*, Vol. 48, No. 2475, (April 29, 1988), pp. 299-300.

REFERENCES

Hughes Griffies, "The Conservation of Whales," *Cornell International Law Journal*, Vol. 5 (1972), pp. 99-112; William E. Schevill, ed., *The Whale Problem: A Status Report*, Cambridge, Mass.: Harvard University Press, 1974; Everhard J. Slijper, *Whale*, Ithaca, New York: Cornell University Press, 1979; Carl Q. Christol, John R. Schmidhauser & George O. Totten, "The Law and the Whale: Current Developments in the International Whaling Controversy," *Case Western Reserve Journal of International Law*, Vol. 8 (1976), pp. 149-167; John R. Smidhauser and George O. Totten, III, eds., *The Whaling Problem: A Status Report*, Boulder, Colorado: Westview Press, 1978, Sydney Frost, ed., *The Whaling Question*, San Francisco: Friends of the Earth, 1979; David M. Levin, "Toward Effective Cetacean Protection," *Natural Resources Lawyer*, Vol. 12 (1979), pp. 549-497; Ronald M. Lockley, *Whales, Dolphins and Porpoises*, New York: Norton Press, 1979; Note, "International Whaling Commission Regulations and the Alaskan Eskimo," *Natural Resources Journal*, Vol. 19 (1979), pp. 943-956; Everhard J. Slijper, *Whales*, Ithaca, New York: Cornell University Press, 1979; George M. Travalio and Robecca J. Clement, "International Protection of Marine Mammals," *Columbia Journal of Environmental Law*, Vol. 5 (1979), pp. 199-235; Kenneth R. Allen, *Conservation and Management of Whales*, Seattle: University of Washington Press, 1980; Don Bonker, "U.S. Policy and Strategy in the International Whaling Commission: Sinking or Swimming?" *Ocean Development and International Law*, Vol. 10 (1981), pp. 41-59; John N. Tonnessen and Arne O. Johnsen, *The History of Modern Whaling*, Berkeley, Calif.: University of California Press, 1982; Patricia Birnie, "The International Organization of Whales," *Denver Journal of International Law and Policy*, Vol. 13 (1984), pp. 309-333; Patricia Birnie, "The Role of Developing Countries in Nudging the International Whaling Commission from Regulating Whaling to Encouraging Nonconsumptive Uses of Whales," *Ecological Law Quarterly*, Vol. 12 (1985), pp. 937-975; Kimberly S. Davis, "International Management of Cetaceans under the New Law of the Sea Convention," *Boston University International Law Journal*, Vol. 3 (1985), pp. 477-518; John Warren Kindt and Charles J. Wintheiser, "The Conservation and Protection of Maritime Mammals, "*University of Hawaii Law Review*, Vol. 7 (1985), pp. 301-375; Sidney Holt, "Whale Mining, Whale Saving," *Marine Policy*, Vol. 9 (1985), No. 3, pp. 192-213; Philip Shabecoff, "U.S. Warns Japan Not to Kill Whales in Antarctic," *The New York Times*, January 22, 1988, p. A7 and "Japan and Iceland Will Defy Ban on the Killing of Whales," *The New York Times*, January 24, 1988, p. 18.

3.   1982 United Nations Convention on the Law of the Sea
and the Protection of Marine Mammals

1982 UNITED NATIONS CONVENTION ON THE LAW OF THE SEA

Article 65
Marine Mammals

Nothing in this Part [V Exclusive Economic Zone] restricts the right of a coastal State or the competence of an international organization, as appropriate, to prohibit, limit or regulate the exploitation of marine mammals more strictly than provided in this part. States shall cooperate with a view to the conservation of marine mammals and in the case of cetaceans shall in particular work through the appropriate international organizations for their conservations, management and study.

Article 120
Marine Mammals

Article 65 also applies to the conservation and management of marine mammals in the high seas.

4.   The Coastal State's Protection of Marine Mammals--The Case of Incidental Catch of Small Cetaceans

John Warren Kindt, *Marine Pollution and the Law of the Sea*, Vol. 3, Buffalo, New York: William S. Hein & Co., 1986, pp. 1334-1337. Notes omitted. Reprinted with th permission of William S. Hein & Co. and the author.

Tuna fishermen have been using purse seines since 1916, although bait-fishing was the principal method of fishing until the late 1950s, when nylon nets were introduced. This development allowed the tuna fishermen to utilize purse seines to a greater degree than had been possible before. Use of the purse seines also allowed the fishermen to take advantage of the "tuna/dolphin phenomenon." For some as yet unknown reason yellowfin tuna and dolphins are often found together. When tuna fishermen sight dolphins, a skiff is launched with a purse seine attached. The skiff circles the dolphins along with the tuna, and the net is closed around them. The net is then drawn together at the bottom trapping both the tuna and dolphins. Inevitably, many dolphins become entangled in the net, or the net itself may roll up, trapping the dolphins inside. Being mammals, the dolphins may drown. Small cetaceans are also killed incidentally by other net fishing. For example, the Japanese kill a large number of Dall's porpoises each year in their salmon fishery in the North Pacific. New England trawlermen may incidentally catch harbor porpoises, and the La Plata dolphin is caught in the shark net fishery off Uruguay. . . .

The United States has attempted to reduce dolphin mortality via the Marine Mammal Protection Act of 1972, MMPA, 16 U.S.C. §1361 et seq. (1976 & Supp. V 1981)]. The MMPA requires that each species which may be exploited under the provisions of the MMPA must be maintained at an optimum sustainable population (OSP) level. With regard to the incidental catch of the small cetaceans, the goal of the MMPA is to reduce such takings to insignificant levels approaching zero mortality. This goal has been modified by the 1981 amendments to the MMPA, which require that for the purse seining of yellowfin tuna, fishermen must use "the best marine mammal safety techniques and equipment that are economically and technologically practicable."

The National Marine Fisheries Service (NMFS) sets the annual quota for incidental takings (established at 20,500 animals per year for the period 1981 through 1985). The NMFS has issued a general permit (which allows the incidental taking of animals up to the quota limit) to the American Tunaboat Association, whose members may set their purse seines around dolphin and porpoise schools as long as they abide by other regulations. Incidental takings have decreased dramatically under the MMPA--from 368,600 in 1972 to 22,736 in 1982. However, over 2,000 of those animals killed in 1982 were under the MMPA, and in accordance with an agreement between Japan and the United States, the NMFS also issued a permit allowing the taking of 5,500 Dall's porpoises, but the NMFS required the Japanese to accept U.S. government observers on board their fishing vessels and to assist in research programs sponsored by the two governments. The U.S. Congress has voted to require Japanese vessels fishing in Alaskan coastal waters to adopt fishing gear and techniques which reduce the incidental taking of the Dall's porpoise. In 1982, an estimated 4,187 Dall's porpoises were taken by Japanese fishermen within U.S. waters, and a total of 5,903 were taken within and outside U.S. waters. These figures represent an increase from

1981, but they are down considerably from an estimated 20,000 kills annually during the late 1970s.

REFERENCES

Laurel Lee Hyde, "Dolphin Conservation in the Tuna Industry: The United States Role in An International Problem," *San Diego Law Review*, Vol. 16 (1979), pp. 565-704. F. James A. R. Nafziger, "Global Conservation and Management of Marine Mammals," *San Diego Law Review*, Vol. 17 (1980), pp. 591-615; Laura L. Lones, "The Marine Mammal Protection Act and the International Protection of Cetaceans: A Unilateral Attempt to Effectuate Transnational Conservation," *Vanderbilt Journal of Transnational Law*, Vol. 22 (1989), pp. 997-1028.

CHAPTER XII

MARINE POLLUTION

A. DEFINITION AND SOURCES OF MARINE POLLUTION

1. Definition

1982 UNITED NATIONS CONVENTION ON THE LAW OF THE SEA

Article 1, paragraph 1 (4)

(4) "pollution of the marine environment" means the introduction by man, directly or indirectly, of substances or energy into the marine environment, including estuaries, which results or is likely to result in such deleterious effects as harm to living resources and marine life, hazards to human health, hindrance to marine activities, including fishing and other legitimate uses of the sea, impairment of quality for use of sea water and reduction of amenities.

REFERENCE

P. Van Heijnsbergen, "The 'Pollution' Concept in International Law," *Environmental Policy and Law*, Vol. 5 (1979), pp. 11-13; M. Tomczak, Jr., "Defining Marine Pollution, A Comparison of Definitions Used by International Conventions," *Marine Policy*, Vol. 8 (1984), pp. 311-322.

2. Sources of Marine Pollution

R.R. Churchill and A.V. Lowe, *The Law of the Sea*, 2nd ed., Manchester: Manchester University Press, 1988, pp. 242-244. Reprinted by permission.

Shipping. There are four main sources of marine pollution: shipping, dumping, sea-bed activities and land activities. As far as shipping is concerned, some pollution results from the operation of ships. Ships which are driven by oil-burning diesel engines (the vast majority) may discharge some oil with their bilge water; and the fumes discharged through their funnels into the atmosphere will eventually return to the sea. Some ships other than oil tankers also use their fuel tanks for ballast water and subsequently may discharge this oily ballast water into the sea. The few nuclear powered ships (mainly submarines) may also cause some pollution. All ships, however propelled, will pollute the sea if they throw their garbage overboard or discharge their sewage directly into the sea. By far the greatest amount of pollution from ships, however, comes from their cargoes. Oil, the commodity which is transported most extensively by sea, is often deliberately discharged at sea, notably when seawater which has been pumped into an empty oil tanker to clean out the tanks or serve as ballast is later pumped out again. This practice is gradually declining as more tankers come to use the 'load on top' system. Some oil, as well as other noxious cargoes like chemicals, liquid gas and radioactive matter, enter the sea as a result of accidents, such as collisions, strandings and explosions, as happened in the case of the *Torrey Canyon* and *Amoco Cadiz*. The growing number of ships . . . has increased the risk of such accidents, and the trend to larger ships makes the result of any accident more serious.

Dumping. In the 1950s and 1960s dumping at sea became an increasingly popular way of disposing of waste resulting from land-based activities. This was partly because of its relative cheapness and ease, and partly as a reaction to the tightening up of pollution controls on land. The main kinds of waste dumped include radioactive matter, military materials (including obsolete weapons and explosives), dredge spoils, sewage sludge and industrial waste, which contains a variety of different pollutants, many of them highly toxic. Although waste is dumped from ships, international conventions treat dumping as a source of pollution separate from shipping. This is partly because dumping, unlike other pollution from ships, is always deliberate and usually the *raison d'être* of a particular voyage, and partly because dumping is an extension of pollution from land (although it has to be considered separately from land-based sources because the areas where dumping takes place are obviously juridically different from land).

Sea-bed activities. As far as installations for exploring and exploiting oil and gas from the sea bed are concerned, little deliberate pollution results from such structures, except for the disposal into the sea of domestic refuse, industrial debris and small amounts of oily and chemical wastes. Accidental pollution may result from blow-outs (as in the case of the Ekofisk and Ixtoc wells mentioned above); from collisions between ships and installations; or from the breaking of pipelines, either through natural wear and tear or through being fouled by a trawl. Some pollution may result from the mining of manganese nodules in the international sea-bed area, but until commercial production begins it is difficult to assess what the impact of this will be.

Land-based and atmospheric pollution. The last source--but far and away the most important, accounting for about three-quarters of all marine pollution--is the polluting matter entering the sea from land. This includes sewage and industrial wastes discharged into rivers or directly into the sea; chemicals used as fertilizers and pesticides in agriculture running off from the land into rivers; warm water from power stations (some of them nuclear) built on coasts and estuaries; and discharges into the atmosphere of vehicle exhaust, fumes from chimneys (domestic and factory) and sprayed agricultural chemicals, all of which may eventually be precipitated into the sea.

The primary approach of administrators and legislators has generally been to tackle the problems of marine pollution according to the source of such pollution, rather than dealing with the problems according to the nature of particular pollutants. The differing jurisdictional natures of land and sea make such an approach readily understandable. At the same time, however, whatever the particular source of marine pollution, attention has concentrated on tackling the more noxious and the more visible--which is not always the same--pollutants.

REFERENCES

Susan H. Anderson, "The Role of Recreation in the Marine Environment," *Ocean Yearbook*, Vol. 2, Chicago: University of Chicago Press, 1980, pp. 183-198; Sonja Boehmer-Christiansen, "The Scientific Basis of Marine Pollution Control," *Marine Policy*, Vol. 6 (1981), No. 1, pp. 2-10.

3.   Marine Pollutants

Thomas A. Clingan, "Law Affecting the Quality of the Marine Environment," *University of Miami Law Review*, Vol. 26 (1971-72), pp. 224-231. Reprinted with the permission of University of Miami Law Review which holds copyright on this article.

Pollutants are resources where they do not belong. These unwanted resources can be introduced into the oceans deliberately or inadvertently. The wastes most commonly dumped into the oceans include dredge spoils, industrial wastes, sewage sludge, construction and demolition debris, solid waste, explosive and chemical munitions, and radioactive wastes. Those inadvertently finding their way to the sea include oil (although this should also be included among deliberate introductions) and various other organic and inorganic toxic substances such as lead, cadmium, mercury, vanadium, nitrilotracetic acid, orthonitrochlorobenzene, and polychlorinated biphenyls.

Also among the forms of pollutants affecting the marine environment are excessive nutrients, heat from power and industrial plants, and sediments from land erosion, all of which exert their own peculiar influence on the totality of water quality. Complicating the pollution problem is the fact that some chemicals tend to react synergistically causing problems that would not exist had each chemical been introduced into the water by itself . . . a brief survey of some of the more threatening pollutants will be provided [below].

A. *Oil*

Oil spills attract a great deal of attention and have, to be sure, influenced the quality of the marine environment. . . . Perhaps the greater threat is the pervasive oil pollution from underwater activities and operational spills in connection with the routine transport of oil by sea. Routine spills originating from the operations of oil-carrying tankers, other ships, refineries, petrochemical plants, and submarine oil wells represent, according to one source, 90 percent of the estimated 2.1 million metric tons of oil introduced annually into the oceans. The remaining ten percent represents the spectacular spills caused by major marine accidents.

. . . In general, there are five principal ways in which oil may affect marine animals: (1) tainting of the flesh; (2) poisoning by ingestion; (3) disturbance of food chains; (4) physical fouling with coats of oil; and (5) repellent effects. . . . Limited information is available with respect to the effect of oil on filter-feeding mollusks, such as clams, oysters, scallops, and mussels, and there are indications that concentrations of 25 parts of oil per million parts of water may be toxic to these animals. At any rate, there definitely is an impact on the shellfish market in economic terms due to tainting. The effect of oil on seabirds is probably the most dramatic. The coating of feathers with oil can cause death by drowning, loss of body heat, or inability to feed. Oil pollution also damages aquatic plants and other forms of life that constitute a part of the marine food chain.

Two other special effects of oil spills should be mentioned. First, a possibly serious result could accrue from the fact that chlorinated hydrocarbons such as DDT and dieldrin are highly soluble in oil. Measurements of the effects of an oil slick on Biscayne Bay, Florida, indicated that the concentration of dieldrin in the top one millimeter of water containing the slick was more than 10,000 times higher than the rest of the water. Because many animals within the food chain feed near or on the surface, this effect can be of significant magnitude. Second, deleterious consequences for marine life have been noted to result from the use of detergents and similar compounds used for dispersing oil which are sometimes improperly attributed to the oil itself.

B. *Toxic Substances*

This category covers a wide range of organic and inorganic materials having varying effects on portions of the environment. Man produces more than a million kinds of products, many of which eventually wind up as waste in one form or another. Toxic substances among these products can be classified as metallic or organic. Among the metals, lead is perhaps the oldest known pollutant, and its presence in the oceans is steadily increasing. One of the major factors contributing lead to the environment is the automobile. According to one estimate, in 1968, 180,000 tons of lead were emitted from internal combustion engines, representing 14 percent of all the lead consumed in the U.S. during that year. Much of this lead ultimately reaches the sea.

However, the more spectacular cases of heavy metal poisoning in recent years involve mercury. It was long thought that mercury was environmentally inert and simply settled to the bottom of a river or estuary when discharged there. Mercury-caused deaths at Minimata, Japan, between 1953 and 1960 served to dispel this misconception and indicated that mercury can be changed by sea-borne bacteria into methylmercury. Methylmercury is an extremely toxic compound that enters the food chain and may reach hazardous concentrations. Newspapers have recently carried a number of stories concerning the concentrations of mercury discovered in tuna and swordfish. . . .

Among the common organic compounds, the most notorious threat to the marine environment is DDT. It has been shown that DDT in sea water affects growth, reproduction, and mortality of marine animals at concentrations currently found in some coastal aquatic environments. While all pesticides present a threat, the so-called "hard" pesticides, the chlorinated hydrocarbons such as DDT, aldrin, dieldrin, endrin, heptaclor, and toxaphene, are especially dangerous because they are extremely persistent and easily concentrated in the food chain. Plankton, at the base of the food chain, are primary concentrators, hence marine fish are almost universally contaminated to one degree or another. Shrimps, crabs, and zooplankton are killed by exposure to DDT, and the growth of oysters is inhibited by such exposure.

Other synthetic organic compounds which are being deposited in the oceans include dyes and pigments (which may also include heavy metals), plastics and associated resins, rubber products, and surface active agents such as solvents, detergents, dispersing agents, and emulsifiers). Much of these are deposited as a result of the use of household and industrial detergents. Other deposits come from the processing of leather and textiles, or the manufacture of a variety of other products.

The effects of toxic substances on man are not fully understood. While standard texts list the toxicity of more than 1,000 commercial chemical compounds at high levels of exposure, little is known of the longer range effects of exposure at lower levels. Further, the toxicity of a compound can be a function of the form it takes, as well as the metabolism and other physical characteristics of the individual exposed to it. The recent report on toxic substances of the Council on Environmental Quality refers to the effects of a few of the better known compounds. It points out that compounds of nickel and beryllium, accumulated in the lungs, may cause fatal diseases. Barium may cause respiratory disease, or heart, intestinal, or nervous disorders. Lead has been thought to produce sterility, child mortality, and permanent mental impairment. Mercury compounds destroy brain cells, cause tremors, and produce birth defects. The inescapable conclusion seems to be that the effects of toxic substances are probably sufficiently severe to call for the careful monitoring of the oceans and their products to detect the presence of these substances.

C. Heat

The increasing population in the United States creates a constant demand for more electrical power. Standard power plants generate electricity through the utilization of steam produced by the combustion of various fuels. Each plant condenses its steam for re-use through the utilization of large quantities of cooling water. The amount of water which is necessary depends on the efficiency of the plant and the designed temperature differential between intake and outfall. The temperature rise due to steam condensation is normally 10 to 20 degrees Fahrenheit, with an average increase of about 13 degrees. The demand on fresh water for cooling is so great that it is estimated that by 1980, the power industry will require about one-fifth of the total fresh water run-off of the United States for cooling. Today, approximately 68 percent of the heat produced by nuclear-fueled plants and 50 percent of the heat produced by fossil-fuel plants is removed by cooling water. It takes approximately 129 billion gallons of water a day to accomplish this task.

. . . It has been fairly well established, however, that a ten degree increase in water temperature can be expected to produce certain ecological imbalances. Some of the possible effects on fish are: (1) internal injury or inability to escape predators due to decreased mobility; (2) starvation due to inability to catch food; (3) starvation because of a decrease in food supply; (4) thermal shock due to the rapid rise in surrounding water temperature; (5) inability to digest food; (6) insufficient oxygen supply to sustain life; and, (7) disruption or cessation of the reproductive process. . . .

D. *Nutrients*

An apt example of pollutants resulting from excess resources is the presence of excess nutrients in the marine environment. Nitrates, phosphates, and potassium compounds, introduced into the water from sewage and agricultural wastes, nourish algal growth. An excess of algal growth constitutes a threat to marine life, particularly in the vital estuarine regions where almost 90 percent of the commercially important species of fish spend at least a part of their life cycle. . .
.

Injection of sewage into the environment also creates problems of oxygen depletion. Organic wastes demand oxygen to decompose. If the waste loads from sewage are heavy, the oxygen is nearly, or completely, depleted from the water and this depletion causes anaerobic bacteria to produce malodorous amounts of hydrogen sulfide and methane. An example of overnutrition can be found in the reports of the Moriches Bay, New York, experience. Moriches Bay, prior to 1950, was fed in part by a continual flow of salt water through Moriches Inlet. About 1951, the inlet became closed due to tidal action resulting in reduced salinity of the Bay. At the same time, the area was heavily fertilized with nitrates and phosphates caused by the runoff of duck wastes from the large number of poultry farms nearby. The resulting bloom of a microscopic unicellular plankton called *Nannachloris* destroyed the once prosperous oyster industry and affected the supply of clams and other fish. In 1953, the inlet was reopened, salinity increased, and the counts of algae declined to near zero. The filling of Moriches Inlet poses a continuing problem to the area, however, and an effort is being made to control the amount of nitrates and phosphates allowed to run off from the duck farms in order to reduce the threat of a repeat performance.

E. *Sediments*

Sediments, the product of erosion, constitute the greatest volume of waste materials entering surface waters. In the United States this volume has been estimated at 700 times the total sewage discharge into these waters. Normal erosion carry-away plus sediments resulting from dredge and fill operations sometimes cause severe local problems in estuaries. Light for photosynthesis is reduced, increased turbidity interferes with visibility of marine species, and most important, sediments often interfere with oyster larval attachment and egg survival in other species. A serious example of this type of effect has been observed in the New York Bight area as the result of sewage sludge and dredge spoil dumping. The "Crown of Thorns" starfish plague in the Pacific has also been attributed to sediments from blasting, dredging, and dumping which protect the larval starfish from their natural predators. The potential damage from this type of pollution is quite high, and legislation is pending to control ocean dumping through a permit system. This legislation, of course, will solve only a part of the problem.

REFERENCES

See John Warren Kindt, *Marine Pollution and the Law of the Sea*, Vol. II, Buffalo, New York: William S. Hein & Co., Inc., 1986, pp. 723-1032 and the references cited. See also, Douglas J. Cusine and John P. Grant, eds., *The Impact of Marine Pollution*, Montclair, N.J.: Allandheld,

Osmun, 1980; "The Dirty Seas, Threatened by Rising Pollution, The Oceans are Sending Out an SOS," *Time*, August 1, 1988, pp. 44-50; "Don't Go Near the Water, After Decades of Abuse, Our Coastal Waters are Dying. Is it Too late to Save Them?" *Newsweek*, August 1, 1988, pp. 42-47; P.G. Wells and R.P. Cote, "Protecting Marine Environmental Quality from Land-Based Pollutants: The Strategic Role of Ecotoxicology," *Marine Policy*, Vol. 12 (1988), pp. 9-21.

B. THE FRAMEWORK AND GENERAL PRINCIPLES OF THE INTERNATIONAL LAW RELATING TO MARINE POLLUTION

1.   Overview of Customary International Law and Treaties

R.R. Churchill and A.V. Lowe, *The Law of the Sea*, 2nd ed., Manchester: Manchester University Press, 1988, pp. 245-247. Notes omitted. Reprinted by permission.

Custom. Customary international law contains few rules relevant to the question of marine pollution. In the *Corfu Channel* case (*I.C.J. Reports*, 1949, p. 3, at p. 22) the International Court of Justice said that each State was under an obligation 'not to allow knowingly its territory to be used for acts contrary to the rights of other States'; and in the *Trail Smelter arbitration* (1938-41) [Reports of International Arbitral Awards, Vol. 3, p. 1911], a case involving damage to property in the USA caused by noxious fumes emitted by a smelter in Canada, the arbitral tribunal held that 'no State has the right to use or permit the use of its territory in such a manner as to cause injury by fumes in or to the territory of another State. Article 2 of the High Seas Convention, which is stated to be declaratory of customary international law, provides that States must exercise the freedoms of the high seas 'with reasonable regard to the interests of other States in their exercise of the freedom of the high seas.' It could be argued that, taking the principles enunciated in Article 2 and in the *Corfu Channel* case together and extending the principle in the *Trail Smelter* case by analogy, there is a general rule of customary international law that States must not permit their nationals to discharge into the sea matter that could cause harm to the nationals of other States. However, this rule appears to be too vague to be very effective, and certainly would seem incapable of being developed, given the nature of customary international law, into the detailed emission standards or liability regimes that are required.

Customary international law also defines the extent of States' legislative and enforcement jurisdiction, a question which, as we shall see, is particularly important as far as marine pollution is concerned. However, the customary rules on jurisdiction have been considered by many States to be both inadequate and incapable of sufficiently speedy or extensive development to sustain effective action against pollution. One State taking this view is Canada. In 1970 the Canadian Parliament, alarmed at the possible harm to the delicate Arctic environment which might result from the passage of oil tankers through Arctic waters, passed the Arctic Waters Pollution Prevention Act, which prohibits all pollution and regulates shipping within 100 miles of Canada's Arctic coasts. The USA protested that the Act was an infringement of the freedoms of the high seas.

Treaties. Given these deficiencies of customary international law, it is not surprising to find that the international law relating to marine pollution is contained almost wholly in treaties, of which there is now a considerable number. The first of these treaties was adopted in 1954-- although a draft treaty dealing with oil pollution from ships was drawn up in 1926 but was never opened for signature. Little attention was paid to pollution at UNCLOS I, apart from the general obligations imposed on States to prevent marine pollution by oil and radioactive waste, in articles

24 and 25 of the High Seas Convention; but since 1969, in response to growing international concern over pollution of the marine environment, a steady stream of treaties has been concluded.

Marine pollution treaties can be divided into four categories: general multilateral treaties, regional treaties, bilateral treaties and the Law of the Sea Convention. Of the general multilateral treaties, there are some half a dozen concerned with pollution from ships and one concerned with dumping. There are no general multilateral treaties dealing with marine pollution from land-based sources or sea-bed activities. The treaties concerned with pollution from ships were all adopted under the auspices of the IMO [International Maritime Organization] and the IMO exercises certain supervisory functions in the relation to them.

At the regional level there are a number of treaties dealing with all the sources of marine pollution within a single framework treaty. Such treaties have been adopted for the Baltic, Mediterranean, Arabian/Persian Gulf and Gulf of Oman, West Africa, South-East Pacific, Red Sea and Gulf of Aden, Caribbean, East Africa and South Pacific. Many of these areas are suffering particularly badly from the effects of marine pollution. With the exception of the Baltic Convention, the initiative for these agreements has largely come from, and much of the preparatory work has been done by, the United Nations Environment Programme (UNEP), as part of its Regional Seas Programme, and to a rather more limited extent the IMO. Each of the agreements is accompanied by an Action Plan. Such Plans have also been adopted for the East Asian and South Asian Seas, although there are not (as yet) any legal instruments accompanying them.   In the north-east Atlantic and North Sea there is no equivalent single framework convention, but a number of *ad hoc* agreements have been adopted, dealing with cooperation in oil pollution emergencies, dumping, land-based sources and liability for pollution resulting from seabed activities. On a smaller scale, the four Nordic States (Denmark, Finland, Norway and Sweden) have concluded two agreements dealing with marine pollution, while France, Italy and Monaco in 1976 signed an Agreement relating to the Protection of the Waters of the Mediterranean Coast.

In a number of cases States have also found it desirable to conclude bilateral agreements to deal with more specific or local questions of marine pollution. Thus, for example, Italy and Yugoslavia have signed an Agreement on Cooperation for the Protection of the Waters of the Adriatic Sea and Coastal Zones from Pollution (1974); Denmark and Sweden an Agreement concerning Protection of the Sound from Pollution (1974); Canada and the USA an Agreement relating to the Establishment of Joint Pollution Contingency Plans for Spills of Oil and other Noxious Substances (1974); and Canada and Denmark an Agreement for Cooperation relating to the Marine Environment (1983).

In view of this extensive treaty action, it was not necessary for UNCLOS III to consider detailed standards relating to marine pollution, nor perhaps would the conference have been well suited to the elaboration of such technically complex matters. Instead, having for the first time laid down a general duty to protect and preserve the marine environment (LOSC, art. 192, *et seq.*) from pollution from all sources (LOSC, arts. 207-12), the conference concentrated on defining the jurisdictional rights and obligations, both legislative and enforcement, of flag, coastal and port States. Provisions on these matters are now found in articles 207-34 and 236 of the Law of the Sea Convention. The remainder of the articles in Part XII (Protection and Preservation of the Marine Environment) deal with general principles (arts. 192-6), global and regional cooperation (arts. 197-201), technical assistance (arts. 202-3), monitoring and environmental assessment (arts. 204-6) and responsibility and liability (art. 235).

DECLARATION OF THE UNITED NATIONS
CONFERENCE ON THE HUMAN ENVIRONMENT

U.N. Doc.A/Conf. 48/14 (Stockholm 1972),
International Legal Materials, Vol. 11 (1972), p. 1418.

States shall take all possible steps to prevent pollution of the seas by substances that are liable to create hazards to human health, to harm living resources and marine life, to damage amenities or to interfere with other legitimate uses of the sea.

2.   **General Principles of Protection and Preservation of the Marine Environment**

1982 UNITED NATIONS CONVENTION ON THE LAW OF THE SEA
PART XII
PROTECTION AND PRESERVATION OF THE
MARINE ENVIRONMENT

SECTION 1. GENERAL PROVISIONS

Article 192
General Obligation

States have the obligation to protect and preserve the marine environment.

Article 193
Sovereign right of States to exploit
their natural resources

States have the sovereign right to exploit their natural resources pursuant to their environmental policies and in accordance with their duty to protect and preserve the marine environment.

Article 194
Measures to prevent, reduce and control
pollution of the marine environment

1. States shall take, individually or jointly as appropriate, all measures consistent with this Convention that are necessary to prevent, reduce and control pollution of the marine environment from any source, using for this purpose the best practicable means at their disposal and in accordance with their capabilities, and they shall endeavor to harmonize their policies in this connection.

2. States shall take all measures necessary to ensure that activities under their jurisdiction or control are so conducted as not to cause damage by pollution to other States and their environment, and that pollution arising from incidents or activities under their jurisdiction or control does not spread beyond the areas where they exercise sovereign rights in accordance with this Convention.

3. The measures taken pursuant to this Part shall deal with all sources of pollution of the marine environment. These measures shall include, *inter alia*, those designed to minimize to the fullest possible extent:

(a) the release of toxic, harmful or noxious substances, especially those which are persistent, from land-based sources, from or through the atmosphere or by dumping;

(b) pollution from vessels, in particular measures for preventing accidents and dealing with emergencies, ensuring the safety of operations at sea, preventing intentional and unintentional discharges, and regulating the design, construction, equipment, operation and manning of vessels;

(c) pollution from installations and devices used in exploration or exploitation of the natural resources of the sea-bed and subsoil, in particular measures for preventing accidents and dealing with emergencies ensuring the safety of operations at sea, and regulating the design, construction, equipment, operation and manning of such installations or devices;

(d) pollution from other installations and devices operating in the marine environment, in particular measures for preventing accidents and dealing with emergencies, ensuring the safety of operations at sea, and regulating the design, construction, equipment, operation and manning of such installations or devices.

4. In taking measures to prevent, reduce or control pollution of the marine environment, States shall refrain from unjustifiable interference with activities carried out by other States in the exercise of their rights and in pursuance of their duties in conformity with this Convention.

5. The measures taken in accordance with this Part shall include those necessary to protect and preserve rare or fragile ecosystems as well as the habitat of depleted, threatened or endangered species and other forms of marine life.

Article 195
Duty not to transfer damage or hazards or
transform one type of pollution into another

In taking measures to prevent, reduce and control pollution of the marine environment, States shall act so as not to transfer, directly or indirectly, damage or hazards from one area to another or transfer one type of pollution into another.

Article 196
Use of technologies or introduction
of alien or new species

1. States shall take all measures necessary to prevent, reduce and control pollution of the marine environment resulting from the use of technologies under their jurisdiction or control, or the intention or accidental introduction of species, alien or new, to a particular part of the marine environment, which may cause significant and harmful changes thereto.

2. This article does not affect the application of this Convention regarding the prevention, reduction and control of pollution of the marine environment.

SECTION 2. GLOBAL AND REGIONAL COOPERATION

Article 197
Cooperation on a global or regional basis

States shall cooperate on a global basis and, as appropriate, on a regional basis, directly or through competent international organizations, in formulating and elaborating international rules, standards and recommended practices and procedures consistent with this Convention, for the protection and preservation of the marine environment, taking into account characteristic regional features.

Article 198
Notification of imminent or actual damage

When a State becomes aware of cases in which the marine environment is in imminent danger of being damaged or has been damaged by pollution, it shall immediately notify other States it deems likely to be affected by such damage, as well as the competent international organizations.

Article 199
Contingency plans against pollution

In the cases referred to in article 198, States in the area affected, in accordance with their capabilities, and the competent international organizations shall cooperate, to the extent possible, in eliminating the effects of pollution and preventing or minimizing the damage. To this end, States shall jointly develop and promote contingency plans for responding to pollution incidents in the marine environment.

Article 200
Studies, research programs and exchange
of information and data

States shall cooperate, directly or through competent international organizations, for the purpose of promoting studies, undertaking programs of scientific research and encouraging the exchange of information and data acquired about pollution of the marine environment. They shall endeavor to participate actively in regional and global programs to acquire knowledge for the assessment of the nature and extent of pollution, exposure to it, and its pathways, risks and remedies.

Article 201
Scientific criteria for regulations

In the light of the information and data acquired pursuant to article 200, States shall cooperate, directly or through competent international organizations, in establishing appropriate scientific criteria for the formulation and elaboration of rules, standards and recommended practices and procedures for the prevention, reduction and control of pollution of the marine environment.

SECTION 3. TECHNICAL ASSISTANCE

Article 202
Scientific and technical assistance
to developing States

States shall, directly or through competent international organizations:

(a) promote programs of scientific, educational, technical and other assistance to developing States for the protection and preservation of the marine environment and the prevention, reduction and control of marine pollution. Such assistance shall include, *inter alia*:

(i)   training of their scientific and technical personnel;

(ii)   facilitating their participation in relevant international programs;

(iii)   supplying them with necessary equipment and facilities;

(iv)   enhancing their capacity to manufacture such equipment;

(v)   advice on and developing facilities for research, monitoring, educational and other programs;

(b) provide appropriate assistance, especially to developing States, for the minimization of the effects of major incidents which may cause serious pollution of the marine environment;

(c) provide appropriate assistance, especially to developing States, concerning the preparation of environmental assessments.

Article 203
Preferential treatment for developing States

Developing States shall, for the purposes of prevention, reduction and control of pollution of the marine environment or minimization of its effects, be granted preference by international organizations in:

(a)   the allocation of appropriate funds and technical assistance; and

(b)   the utilization of their specialized services.

SECTION 4. MONITORING AND ENVIRONMENTAL ASSESSMENT

Article 204
Monitoring of the risks or effects of pollution

1. States shall, consistent with the rights of other States, endeavor, as far as practicable, directly or through the competent international organizations, to observe, measure, evaluate and analyze, by recognized scientific methods, the risks or effects of pollution of the marine environment.

2. In particular, States shall keep under surveillance the effects of any activities which they permit or in which they engage in order to determine whether these activities are likely to pollute the marine environment.

Article 205
Publication of reports

States shall publish reports of the results obtained pursuant to article 204 or provide such reports at appropriate intervals to the competent international organizations, which should make them available to all States.

Article 206
Assessment of potential effects of activities

When States have reasonable grounds for believing that planned activities under their jurisdiction or control may cause substantial pollution of or significant and harmful changes to the marine environment, they shall, as far as practicable, assess the potential effects of such activities on the marine environment and shall communicate reports of the results of such assessments in the manner provided in article 205.

. . . .

SECTION 9. RESPONSIBILITY AND LIABILITY

Article 235
Responsibility and Liability

1. States are responsible for the fulfillment of their international obligations concerning the protection and preservation of the marine environment. They shall be liable in accordance with international law.

2. States shall ensure that recourse is available in accordance with their legal systems for prompt and adequate compensation or other relief in respect of damage caused by pollution of the marine environment by natural or juridical persons under their jurisdiction.

3. With the objective of assuring prompt and adequate compensation in respect of all damage caused by pollution of the marine environment, States shall cooperate in the implementation of existing international law and the further development of international law relating to responsibility and liability for the assessment of and compensation for damage and the settlement of related disputes, as well as, where appropriate, development of criteria and procedures for payment of adequate compensation, such as compulsory insurance or compensation funds.

. . . .

SECTION 11. OBLIGATIONS UNDER OTHER CONVENTIONS ON
THE PROTECTION AND PRESERVATION OF THE MARINE ENVIRONMENT

Article 237
Obligations under other conventions on the protection
and preservation of the marine environment

1. The provisions of this Part are without prejudice to the specific obligations assumed by States under special conventions and agreements concluded previously which relate to the protection and preservation of the marine environment and to agreements which may be concluded in furtherance of the general principles set forth in this Convention.

2. Specific obligations assumed by States under special conventions, with respect to the protection and preservation of the marine environment, should be carried out in a manner consistent with the general principles and objectives of this Convention.

Restatement on the Foreign Relations Law of the United States, Third Revision, Vol. 2, St. Paul, Minn.: American Law Institute, 1987, pp. 128, 136.

§ 603.   State Responsibility for Marine Pollution

(1)   A state is obligated

(a)   to adopt laws and regulations to prevent, reduce, and control any significant pollution of the marine environment that are no less effective than generally accepted international rules and standards; and

(b)   to ensure compliance with the laws and regulations adopted pursuant to clause (a) by ships flying its flag, and, in case of a violation, to impose adequate penalties on the owner or captain of the ship.

(2)   A state is obligated to take, individually and jointly with other states, such measures as may be necessary, to the extent practicable under the circumstances, to prevent, reduce, and control pollution causing or threatening to cause significant injury to the marine environment.

Source Note: This section is based on Articles 194, 207-12, 217, and 220 of the 1982 Convention on the Law of the Sea. . . .

§ 604. Remedies for Marine Pollution

(1)   A state responsible to another state for a violation of the principles of § 603 is subject to general interstate remedies to prevent, reduce, or terminate the activity threatening or causing pollution, and to pay reparation for injury caused.

(2)   A state is obligated to ensure that a remedy is available, in accordance with its legal system, to provide prompt and adequate compensation or other relief for an injury to private interests caused by pollution of the marine environment resulting from a violation of § 603. . . .

REFERENCES

(Pollution in General)

L.F.E. Goldie, "International Principles of Responsibility for Pollution," *Columbia Journal of Transnational Law*, Vol. 9 (1970), pp. 283-330; W.O. Douglas, "Environmental Problems of the Oceans: The Need for International Controls," *Environmental Law Review*, Vol. 1 (1971), pp. 149-166; Michael Hardy, "International Control of Marine Pollution," *Natural Resources Journal*, Vol. 11 (1971), pp. 296-348; Pacem in Maribus, *The Ocean Environment*, Vol. V, Malta: Royal University of Malta, 1971; "The Sea: Prevention and Control of Marine Pollution," Report of the Secretary-General, UN Document E/5003 (May 7, 1971); S.A. Bleicher, "An Overview of International Environmental Regulation," *Ecology Law Quarterly*, Vol. 2(1) (1972), pp. 1-190; Allan I. Mendelsohn, "Ocean Pollution and the 1972 U.N. Conference on the Environment," *Journal of Maritime Law and Commerce*, Vol. 3 (1972), pp. 385-398; Ludwik A. Teclaff, "The Impact of Environmental Concern on the Development of International Law," Natural Resources Journal, Vol. 13 (1973), pp. 357-390; Ludwik A. Teclaff, "International Law and the Protection of the Oceans from Pollution," *Fordham Law Review*, Vol. 40 (1972), pp. 529-564; Ian Brownlie, "A Survey of International Customary Rules of Environmental Protection," *Natural Resources Journal*, Vol. 13 (1973), pp. 179-189; M. Hardy, "Definition and Forms of Marine Pollution," in R. Churchill, *et al.*, eds., *New Directions in the Law of the Sea: Collected Papers*, Vol. 3, Dobbs Ferry, New York: Oceana Publications, Inc., 1973, pp. 73-77; I.C. Jain, "Legal Control of Marine Pollution," *Indian Journal of International Law*, Vol. 13 (1973), pp. 411-424; G. Matthews, "Pollution of the Oceans: An International Problem?," *Ocean Management*, Vol. 1 (1973), pp. 161-170; Ludwik A. Teclaff, "The Impact of Environmental Concern on the Development of International Law," *Natural Resources Journal*, Vol. 13 (1973), pp. 357-390; Peter S. Thacher, "Assessment and Control of Marine Pollution: The Stockholm Recommendations and Their Efficacy," *Stanford Journal of International Studies*, Vol. 8 (1973), pp. 79-98; W. Bascom, "The Disposal of Waste in the Ocean," *Scientific American*, Vol. 231 (August, 1974), pp. 17-25; A. D'Amato and J.L. Hargrove, "An Overview of the Problem," in J.L. Hargrove, ed., *Who Protects the Ocean?*, St. Paul, Minn.: West Publishing Co., 1975, pp. 1-35; E.D. Goldberg and D. Manzel, "Oceanic Pollution," in J.L. Hargrove, ed., *Who Protects the Ocean?*, St. Paul, Minn.: West Publishing Co., 1975, pp. 37-61; National Petroleum Council, "Protection of the Marine Environment," *Natural Resources Lawyer*, Vol. 8 (1975), pp. 511-543; C.S. Pearson, *International Marine Environmental Policy: The Economic Dimension*, Studies in International Affairs, No. 25, Baltimore, Maryland, Johns Hopkins University Press, 1975; R.E. Stein, *Excerpts from Critical Environmental Issues on the Law of the Sea*, Washington, D.C.: International Institute for Environment and Development, 1975; R.B. Bilder, "The Settlement of International Environmental Disputes," *University of Wisconsin Sea Grant Technical Report*, WISCU-U-75-001, (Feb. 1976), p. 321; Ved P. Nada and William K. Rio, Jr., "The Public Trust Doctrine: A Viable Approach to International Environmental Protection," *Ecology Law Quarterly*, vol. 5 (1976), pp. 291-319; I.A. Ostrovskii, "International Legal Protection of the Seas from Pollution," *Ocean Development and International Law*, Vol. 3 (1976), pp. 287-302; Gr. J. Timagenis, *Marine Pollution and the Third United Nations Conference on the Law of the Sea: The Emerging Regime of Marine Pollution*, London: Lloyd's of London Press, 1977; Jan Schneider, "Something Old, Something New: Some Thoughts on Grotius and the Marine Environment," *Virginia Journal of International Law*, Vol. 18 (1977), pp. 147-164; Edward Goldsmith, "Can We Control Pollution?" *The Ecologist*, Vol. 10 No. 10 (December 1979), pp. 316-328; R.P. Anand, "Development and Environment: The Case of the Developing Countries," *Indian Journal of International Law*, Vol. 20 (1980), pp. 1-19; Thomas A. Clingan, Jr., "Environmental Problems and the New Order of the Oceans," *Columbia Journal of World Business*, Vol. 15, No. 4 (Winter 1980), pp. 45-51; John Warren Kindt, "The Effect of Claims by

Developing Countries on LOS Intermarine Pollution Negotiations," *Virginia Journal of International Law*, Vol. 20 (1980), pp. 313-345; John Warren Kindt, "Prolegomenon to Marine Pollution and the Law of the Sea, An Overview of the Pollution Problem," *Environmental Law*, Vol. 11 (1980), pp. 67-96; L. Speranskaya, "International Legal Safeguards for the Marine Environment," *International Affairs* (Moscow), 1980, No. 10, pp. 86-93; Vincenzo, "Protection and Preservation of the Marine Environment in the United Nations Convention on the Law of the Sea: An Appraisal," *Italian Yearbook of International Law*, Vol. 5 (1980/81), pp. 52-64; Sonja Boehmer-Christiansen, "Marine Pollution Control, UNCLOS as the Partial Codification of International Practice," *Environmental Policy and Law*, Vol. 7 (1981), No. 2, pp. 71-74; Dean E. Cycon, "Calming Troubled Waters: The Developing International Regime to Control Operational Pollution," *Journal of Maritime Law and Commerce*, Vol. 13, No. 1 (October 1981), pp. 35-51; Edward D. Goldberg, "The Oceans as Waste Space: The Argument," *Oceanus* (Woods Hole, Mass.), 1981, pp. 2-9; Kenneth S. Hamlet, "The Oceans as Waste Space: The Rebuttal," *Oceanus, ibid.*, pp. 10-17; Jan Schneider, "Codification and Progressive Development of International Environmental Law at the Third United Nations Conference on the Law of the Sea: The Environmental Aspects of the Treaty Review," *Columbia Journal of Transnational Law*, Vol. 20 (1981), pp. 243-275; "The Fight Against Marine Pollution," *IMO News*, 1982, No. 3, pp. 8-15; Clifton E. Curtis, "The United States and the Law of the Sea--Marine Environmental Concerns," *Oregon Law Review*, Vol. 63 (1984), pp. 139-150; John Warren Kindt, "The Law of the Sea: The Environmental Goals Governing Marine Pollution," *Suffork Transnational Law Journal*, Vol. 8 (1984), pp. 1-44; John Warren Kindt, "Ocean Resources and Marine Pollution: Putting the Development of Ocean Resources in Proper Perspective," *Houston Journal of International Law*, Vol. 6 (1984), pp. 111-158; Alan E. Boyle, "Marine Pollution under the Law of the Sea Convention," *American Journal of International Law*, Vol. 79 (1985), pp. 347-372; Christopher C. Joyner, "The Southern Ocean and Marine Pollution: Problems and Prospects," *Case Western Reserve Journal of International Law*, Vol. 17 (1985), pp. 165-194; K. Ramakrishna, "Environmental Concerns and the New Law of the Sea," *Journal of Maritime Law and Commerce*, Vol. 16 (1985), pp. 1-19; John Warren Kindt, "Particular Pollution and the Law of the Sea," *British Columbia Environmental Affairs Law Review*, Vol. 12 (1985), pp. 273-311; Ramanlal Soni, *Control of Marine Pollution in International Law*, Cape Town, South Africa: Juta & Co., 1985; John Warren Kindt, *Marine Pollution and the Law of the Sea*, Buffalo, New York: William S. Hein, 1986-88; Brian D. Smith, *State Responsibility and the Marine Environment: The Rules of Decision*, Oxford, United Kingdom: Clarendon Press, 1988; *Law of the Sea: Protection and Preservation of the Marine Environment*, New York: The United Nations, 1990.

(International Cooperation And Regional Pollution Arrangement)

C.O. Okidi, *Regional Control of Ocean Pollution: Legal and Institutional Problems and Prospects*, Alphen aan den Rijn, Netherlands: Sijthoff and Noordhoff, 1978; Saeed Sulaiman Sagat, "The Kuwait Convention for Cooperation on the Protection from Pollution of the Marine Environment of the Arabian Gulf Area, April 1978," *Revue Egyptienne De Droit International*, Vol. 34 (1978), pp. 149-158; Jose Antonio de Yturriaga Barberan, "Regional Conventions on the Protection of the Marine Environment," in *Recueil Des Cours* (Hague Academy of International Law), Leyden, Vol. 162(I), 1979, pp. 319-449; Marise Cremona, "The Role of the EEC in the Control of Oil Pollution," *Common Market Law Review*, Vol. 17 (1980), No. 2, pp. 171-189; Jean-Pierre Dobbert, "Protocol to Control Pollution in the Mediterranean," *Environmental Policy and Law*, Vol. 6 (1980), No. 3, pp. 110-114; Alexandre Charles Kiss, "International Cooperation for the Control of Accidental Marine Pollution," *German Yearbook of International Law*, Vol. 23 (1980), pp. 231-254; James P. Lester, "Domestic Structure and International Technological Collaboration: Ocean Pollution Regulation," *Ocean Development and International Law*, Vol. 8

(1980), pp. 299-335; Helena Rytovuori, "Structure of Détente and Ecological Interdependence: Cooperation in the Baltic Sea Area for the Protection of Marine Environment and Living Resources," *Cooperation and Conflict* (Oslo), Vol. 15, No. 2 (June 1980), pp. 85-102; Peter S. Thacher and Nikki Meith, "Approaches to Regional Marine Problems: A Progress Report on UNEP's Regional Seas Program" *Ocean Yearbook*, Vol. 2, Chicago: University of Chicago Press, 1980, pp. 153-182; Dominique Alheritiere, "Marine Pollution Control Regulations, Regional Approaches," *Marine Policy*, Vol. 6 (1982), No. 3, pp. 162-174; S.H. Amin, "Marine Pollution Regulation in the Persian Gulf," *Marine Policy Report*, Vol. 5 (1982), No. 1, pp. 1-4; Baruch Boxer, "Mediterranean Pollution: Problem and Response," *Ocean Development and International Law*, Vol. 10 (1982), pp. 315-356; Louise J. Saliba, "Mediterranean Pollution, Health Related Aspects," *Marine Policy*, Vol. 7 (1983), No. 2, pp. 109-117; Boleslaw Adam Boczek, "Global and Regional Approaches to the Protection and Preservation of the Marine Environment," *Case Western Reserve Journal of International Law*, Vol. 16 (1984), pp. 39-70; Sonia Boehmer-Christiansen, "Marine Pollution Control in Europe, Regional Approaches, 1972-80," *Marine Policy*, Vol. 8 (1984), No. 1, pp. 44-55; Peter Hayward, "Environmental Protection, Regional Approaches," *Marine Policy*, Vol. 8 (1984), No. 2, pp. 106-119; H. Lindpere, "On the International Legal Regime of the Baltic Sea and Some Problems of Regional Cooperation in the Protection of the Marine Environment," *Soviet Yearbook of Maritime Law*, 1984, pp. 116-119; Thomas A. Mensah, "Environmental Protection, International Approaches," *Marine Policy*, Vol. 8 (1984), No. 2, pp. 95-105; Mark J. Valencia and A.B. Joafu, "Environmental Management of the Malacca/Singapore Straits: Legal and Institutional Issues," *Natural Resources Journal*, Vol. 25 (1985), pp. 195-232; Mark J. Valencia, "The Yellow Sea: Transnational Marine Resource Management Issue," *Marine Policy*, Vol. 12 (1988), pp. 373-381.

(National Practice)

R.A. Malviya, "Marine Pollution in India: Its Prospects and Control," *Indian Journal of International Law*, Vol. 19 (1979), pp. 344-371; L. Diane Schenke, "The Marine Protection, Research, and Sanctuaries Act: The Conflict Between Marine Protection and Oil and Gas Development," *Houston Law Review*, Vol. 18 (1981), pp. 987-1035; Catherine A. Cooper, "The Management of International Environmental Disputes in the Context of Canada--United States Relations: A Survey and Evaluation of Techniques and Mechanism," *Canadian Yearbook of International Law*, Vol. 24 (1986), pp. 247-312; *I* M.A. Rabie and J.A. Lusher, "South Africa Marine Pollution Control Legislation," *Acta Juridica* (Cape Town), 1986, pp. 161-192; Erik Franckx, "The New USSR Legislation on Pollution Prevention in the Exclusive Economic Zone," *International Journal of Estuarine and Coastal Law*, Vol. 1 (1986), pp. 155-183.

C. VESSEL SOURCE POLLUTION

1.   Ways of Introducing Pollutants by Vessels into the Marine Environment

COMPETENCE TO ESTABLISH STANDARDS FOR THE CONTROL OF VESSEL SOURCE POLLUTION: WORKING PAPER PRESENTED BY THE UNITED STATES OF AMERICA U.N. Doc. A/AC.138/SC.III/L.36 (April 2, 1973) General Assembly, *Official Records*, 28th Session, Supplement No. 21 (A/19021).

Vessels introduce pollutants into the marine environment in three principal ways - through oil and other cargoes entering the water due to collisions or other maritime casualties, through loading, unloading and bunkering operations, and through the intentional operational discharge of oil. There are, of course, other pollutants released from vessels such as sewage and garbage but these do not present problems of the same magnitude (there are international efforts underway to develop technical means of control for such pollutants).

A.   *Collisions and Other Maritime Casualties*

Most casualties occur in congested areas in internal waters, at port entrances or in heavily traveled shipping lanes close to the coast. Thus, individual States can and should act effectively to reduce pollution from such incidents by the provision of adequate navigational aids, warnings of dangers to navigation and other assistance to the mariner to ensure that collisions, groundings and other casualties are minimized. Also, such international actions as provision of compulsory traffic separation schemes in congested areas, and requiring double-bottom construction for large tankers . . . can assist in solving these problems. In addition, authority to take remedial action is given to coastal States in the Convention Relating to Intervention on the High Seas in Cases of Oil Pollution Casualties . . . . Oil spills resulting from casualties contribute about 10 percent of vessel source oil pollution and methods for preventing such spills must continue to be developed.

B.   *Loading and Bunkering Operations*

It is estimated that approximately 5 to 10 percent of vessel source oil pollution is caused by spills occurring during bunkering and loading operations. This source of pollution is being reduced through provision of automatic loading controls on large tankers and improved personnel training. Also, significant advances are being made in the development of new techniques to clean up spills. Many ports are now providing the equipment and personnel to deal rapidly and effectively with such spills but continuing efforts are needed by maritime and port States.

C.   *Operational Discharges*

The major source of vessel pollution is the intentional operational discharge of oily wastes from commercial vessels. Operational discharge is due to the pumping of oily bilge wastes, tanker ballasting operations, and the cleaning of tanker cargo tanks prior to a change in the type of cargo or prior to overhaul. Such discharges are estimated to account for approximately three-fourths of all oil pollution from vessels, with tank washings and ballasting providing about twice as much oil pollution as bilge pumping.

After discharging a cargo of oil, a tanker must take aboard seawater in her cargo tanks for use as ballast to facilitate handling in port and to provide proper seakeeping characteristics. For example, safe navigation requires ballast of approximately 40 percent of dead weight tonnage under normal conditions and as much as 80 percent in extreme weather conditions. Since some oil remains in the tanks by adhering to the tank surface, the ballast water will mix with that residue and become "oily." As the tanks must be empty before a new cargo of oil can be taken aboard, the oily ballast water is disposed of in one of two ways - direct discharge at sea or separation of the oil and its retention on board under the "load-on-top" system. In tankers structurally equipped for "load-on-top", the tanks are washed with sea water which is then collected in a slop tank (the other tanks are then clean and can take on water for ballast). During the ballast voyage the oily water in the slop tank slowly separates into a layer of oil and a layer of water, after which the water can be discharged. A new cargo can then be loaded on top of the retained oil or the retained oil can be discharged into a shore reception facility. This procedure is not fully effective since settling is affected by turbulent sea conditions and other factors and since some voyages are simply not lengthy enough for the process to be completed, but it is estimated that the system is 80 percent effective. Although "load-on-top" tankers carry three-fourths of the oil transported by sea, they produce only about one-fourth of the operational oil discharge due to ballasting and tank cleaning.

REFERENCES

David Michael Collins, "The Tanker's Right of Harmless Discharge and Protection of the Marine Environment," *Journal of Maritime Law and Commerce*, Vol. 18 (1987), p. 275-291.

2.   **Necessity for Establishing International Standards to Control Vessel Source Pollution**

COMPETENCE TO ESTABLISH STANDARDS FOR THE CONTROL OF
VESSEL SOURCE POLLUTION: WORKING PAPER PRESENTED BY THE
UNITED STATES OF AMERICA U.N. Doc. A/AC.138/SC.III/L.36
(April 2, 1973), General Assembly, *Official Records*,
28th Session, Supplement No. 21 (A/9021).

A principal issue in the consideration of standards to control vessel source pollution is the authority to establish standards which will eliminate or minimize environmental damage caused by vessels. Only a system of exclusively international standards will provide an effective means to control vessel source pollution while protecting the community interest in both of these fundamental objectives. There are at least five principal reasons which support exclusively international standards.

First, the international community has basic interests which should be represented in the formulation of such standards. One basic concern, of particular interest to coastal States, is to protect the marine environment from pollution. A second basic concern, of particular interest to exporting States, importing States, and maritime States, is the avoidance of unnecessary increases in transportation costs. Participation by these concerned States in the establishment of standards will ensure that a proper balance is maintained.

On the other hand, if coastal States were to be given the authority to establish standards by themselves, such standards might not adequately reflect either the interests of existing maritime States or the developing States as they become maritime nations or the interests of the international community in effective protection of the marine environment.

Second, because of the difficulty or impossibility of a vessel complying with several sets of different, and possibly inconsistent standards, there should be a single set of uniform standards observed by all States. Although vessels utilizing major ocean routes pass close to shore for only a fraction of a normal voyage, they could be subject to many separate sets of standards if coastal States were authorized to establish standards in an area adjacent to the territorial sea. For example, on a voyage from the Persian Gulf to Europe, a heavily traveled oil transport route, a vessel might be subject to as many as 15 different sets of standards. Since compliance with differing standards would be difficult and costly, vessels may try to avoid these areas, if possible, thus increasing voyage length and time. Avoidance of these areas might even force a vessel into a different load line area, thus requiring a lighter cargo load. The result would be higher shipping costs, which in the end would be passed on to producers and consumers. A legal regime which accords coastal States the authority to supplement international standards does not avoid these problems. Moreover, it should be kept in mind that the higher costs associated with divergent standards will not necessarily result in improved protection for the marine environment.

Third, exclusively international standards are required for effective protection of the full marine environment. Since ocean currents carry some amounts of pollution from one ocean area to another and from far offshore to inshore areas, individual coastal State standards could not as effectively reduce such pollution. All of the principal oceans have major currents flowing generally from one continent to another and across broad expanses of open ocean. To demonstrate the magnitude of these currents, the major North American current system washes the shores of 23 coastal states of Africa, South America, North America and Europe. In crossing any major oceans, ships will encounter one or more of these major currents and may discharge oil into them many miles from shore. Inshore currents may carry quantities of oil onto beaches and inshore areas hundreds of miles away from the point of discharge. Because of the size of the areas and the distances involved, individual coastal State pollution control standards cannot possibly cope with the entire problem. Moreover, individual coastal State standards may simply transfer the effects of pollution from one State to another. Such a transfer could add to friction between nations and would not meaningfully contribute to the protection of the marine environment. Certain areas, of course, may require special measures for effective protection. Such measures, however, could and should be internationally established.

Fourth, an exclusively international approach is better able to respond to changes in the technology for the control of pollution and to new knowledge about threats to the marine environment. Our concern, of course, must be protection of the entire marine environment. In meeting that concern, it is far more efficient to continually update one set of international standards than to alter over 100 national standards. Moreover, an international approach provides a focus for utilizing the expertise of all nations in establishing international standards.

Fifth, concerns regarding economic advantage and disadvantage among States are increasingly evident in attempts to deal effectively with environmental problems. Individual States may fear the economic effects on themselves of imposing environmental controls that others may not impose. A system of exclusively international standards would largely eliminate these competitive economic concerns and would encourage a willingness to impose higher standards on an agreed basis.

REFERENCES

Ludwik A. Teclaff, "International Law and the Protection of the Oceans from Pollution," *Fordham Law Review*, Vol. 40 (1972), pp. 529-564; Ved P. Nanda, "The Establishment of International Standards for Transnational Environmental Injury," *Iowa Law Review*, Vol. 60 (1975), pp. 1089-1127; A. Kirton, "Developing Country View of Environmental Issues," in E. Miles and J.K. Gamble, eds., *Law of the Sea: Conference Outcomes and Problems of Implementation*, Cambridge, Mass.: Ballinger, 1977, pp. 279-283; R. McManus, "Environmental Provisions in the Revised Single Negotiating Text," in E. Miles and J.K. Gamble, eds., *Law of the Sea: Conference Outcomes and Problems of Implementation*, Cambridge, Mass., Ballinger, 1977, pp. 269-277.

3.   **International Regulations on Controlling Vessel Source Pollution**

INTERNATIONAL CONVENTION FOR THE PREVENTION OF
POLLUTION OF THE SEA BY OIL, May 12, 1954.
12 UST 2989; TIAS 4900; 327 UNTS 3, As Amended
1962 (17 UST 1523; TIAS 6109; 600 UNTS 332), 1969
(28 UST 1205, TIAS 8505) and 1971 (*International
Legal Materials*, Vol. 11 (1972), pp. 267-275.)

. . . .

Article III

Subject to the provisions of Articles IV and V:

(a) the discharge from a ship to which the present Convention applies, other than a tanker, of oil or oily mixture shall be prohibited except when the following conditions are all satisfied:

(i) the ship is proceeding en route;

(ii) the instantaneous rate of discharge of oil content does not exceed 60 liters per mile;

(iii) the oil content of the discharge is less than 100 parts per 1,000,000 parts of the mixture;

(iv) the discharge is made as far as practicable from land;

(b) the discharge from a tanker to which the present Convention applies of oil or oily mixture shall be prohibited except when the following conditions are all satisfied:

(i) the tanker is proceeding en route;

(ii) the instantaneous rate of discharge of oil content does not exceed 60 liters per mile;

(iii) the total quantity of oil discharged on a ballast voyage does not exceed 1/15,000 of the total cargo-carrying capacity;

(iv) the tanker is more than 50 miles from the nearest land;

(c) the provisions of sub-paragraph (b) of this Article shall not apply to:

(i) the discharge of ballast from a cargo tank which, since the cargo was last carried therein, has been so cleaned that any effluent therefrom, if it were discharged from a stationary tanker into clean calm water on a clear day, would produce no visible traces of oil on the surface of the water; or

(ii) the discharge of oil or oily mixture from machinery space bilges, which shall be governed by the provisions of sub-paragraph (a) of this Article.

Article IV

Article III shall not apply to:

(a) the discharge of oil or of oily mixture from a ship for the purpose of securing the safety of a ship, preventing damage to a ship or cargo, or saving life at sea;

(b) the escape of oil or of oily mixture resulting from damage to a ship or unavoidable leakage, if all reasonable precautions have been taken after the occurrence of the damage or discovery of the leakage for the purpose of preventing or minimizing the escape.

Article V

Article III shall not apply to the discharge of oily mixture from the bilges of a ship during the period of twelve months following the date on which the present Convention comes into force for the relevant territory in accordance with paragraph (1) of Article II.

Article VI

(1) Any contravention of Articles III and IX shall be an offense punishable under the law of the relevant territory in respect of the ship [registered] . . . .

(2) The penalties which may be imposed under the law of any of the territories of a Contracting Government in respect of the unlawful discharge from a ship of oil or oily mixture outside the territorial sea of that territory shall be adequate in severity to discourage any such unlawful discharge and shall not be less than the penalties which may be imposed under the law of that territory in respect of the same infringements within the territorial sea.

(3) Each Contracting Government shall report to the [International Maritime] Organization the penalties actually imposed for each infringement.

Article VI [Amendment adopted in 1971]

(1) Every tanker to which the present Convention applies and for which the building contract is placed on or after the date of coming into force of this Article shall be constructed in accordance with the provisions of Annex C [on Requirements Relating to Tank Arrangements and to the Limitation of Tank Size]. . . .

(2) A tanker required under paragraph (1) of this Article to be constructed in accordance with Annex C and so constructed shall carry on board a certificate issued or authorized by the responsible Contracting Government attesting such compliance. . . .

(3) Certificates issued under the authority of a Contracting Government shall be accepted by the other Contracting Governments for all purposes covered by the present Convention. They shall be regarded by the other Contracting Governments as having the same force as certificates issued by them.

(4) If a Contracting Government has clear grounds for believing that a tanker required under paragraph (1) of this Article to be constructed in accordance with Annex C entering ports in its territory or using off-shore terminals under its control does not in fact comply with Annex C, such

Contracting Government may request consultation with the Government with which the tanker is registered. If, after such consultation or otherwise, the Contracting Government is satisfied that the tanker does not comply with Annex C, such Contracting Government may for this reason deny such a tanker access to ports in its territorial waters or to off-shore terminals under its control until such time as the Contracting Government is satisfied that the tanker does comply.

Article VII

(1) As from a date twelve months after the present Convention comes into force for the relevant territory in respect of a ship [registered there] . . . such a ship shall be required to be so fitted as to prevent, as far as reasonable and practicable, the escape of oil into bilges, unless effective means are provided to ensure that the oil in the bilges is not discharged in contravention of this Convention.

(2) Carrying water ballast in oil fuel tanks shall be avoided if possible.

. . . .

Article IX

(1) Of the ships to which the present Convention applies, every ship which uses oil fuel and every tanker shall be provided with an oil record book, whether as part of the ship's official log book or otherwise. . . .

(2) The oil record book shall be completed on each occasion, on a tank-to-tank basis, whenever any of the following operations take place in the ship:

(a) *for tankers*:

(i)	loading of oil cargo;
(ii)	transfer of oil cargo during voyage;
(iii)	discharge of oil cargo;
(iv)	ballasting of cargo tanks;
(v)	cleaning of cargo tanks;
(vi)	discharge of dirty ballast;
(vii)	discharge of water from slop-tanks;
(viii)	disposal of residues;
(ix)	discharge overboard of bilge water containing oil which has accumulated in machinery spaces whilst in port, and the routine discharge at sea of bilge water containing oil unless the latter has been entered in the appropriate log book.

In the event of such discharge or escape of oil or oily mixture as is referred to in Article IV, a statement shall be made in the oil record book of the circumstances of, and the reason for, the discharge or escape.

(3) Each operation described in paragraph (2) of this Article shall be fully recorded without delay in the oil record book so that all the entries in the book appropriate to that operation are completed. Each page of the book shall be signed by the officer or officers in charge of the operations concerned and, when the ship is manned, by the master of the ship. The written entries in the oil record book shall be in an official language of the relevant territory in respect of the ship

in the oil record book shall be in an official language of the relevant territory in respect of the ship [registered] . . . or in English or French.

(4) Oil record books shall be kept in such a place as to be readily available for inspection at all reasonable times, and, except in the case of unmanned ships under tow, shall be kept on board the ship. They shall be preserved for a period of two years after the last entry has been made.

(5) The competent authorities of any of the territories of a Contracting Government may inspect on board any ship to which the present Convention applies, while within a port in that territory, the oil record book required to be carried in the ship in compliance with the provisions of this Article, and may make a true copy of any entry in that book and may require the master of the ship to certify that the copy is a true copy of such entry. Any copy so made which purports to have been certified by the master of the ship as a true copy of an entry in the ship's oil record book shall be made admissible in any judicial proceedings as evidence of the facts stated in the entry. Any action by the competent authorities under this paragraph shall be taken as expeditiously as possible and the ship shall not be delayed.

Article X

(1) Any Contracting Government may furnish to the Government of the relevant territory in respect of the ship [registered . . .] particulars in writing of evidence that any provision of the present Convention has been contravened in respect of that ship, wheresoever the alleged contravention may have taken place. If it is practicable to do so, the competent authorities of the former Government shall notify the master of the ship of the alleged contravention.

(2) Upon receiving such particulars, the Government so informed shall investigate the matter, and may request the other Government to furnish further or better particulars of the alleged contravention. If the Government so informed is satisfied that sufficient evidence is available in the form required by its law to enable proceedings against the owner or master of the ship to be taken in respect of the alleged contravention, it shall cause such proceedings to be taken as soon as possible. That Government shall promptly inform the Government whose official has reported the alleged contravention, as well as the Organization, of the action taken as a consequence of the information communicated.

Article XI

Nothing in the present Convention shall be construed as derogating from the powers of any Contracting Government to take measures within its jurisdiction in respect of any matter to which the Convention relates or as extending the jurisdiction of any Contracting Government.

Article XII

Each Contracting Government shall send to the Bureau and to the appropriate organ of the United Nations: --

(a) the text of laws, decrees, orders and regulations in force in its territories which give effect to the present Convention;

(b) all official reports or summaries of official reports in so far as they show the results of the application of the provisions of the Convention, provided always that such reports or summaries are not, in the opinion of that Government, of a confidential nature.

Article XIII

Any dispute between Contracting Governments relating to the interpretation or application of the present Convention which cannot be settled by negotiation shall be referred at the request of either party to the International Court of Justice for decision unless the parties in dispute agree to submit it to arbitration.

. . . .

REFERENCES

Joseph C. Sweeney, "Oil Pollution of the Oceans," *Fordham Law Review*, Vol. 37 (1968), pp. 155-208; "Comments: Oil Pollution of the Sea," *Harvard International Law Journal*, Vol. 10 (1969), pp. 316-359; N.D. Shutler, "Pollution of the Sea by Oil," *Houston Law Review*, Vol. 7 (1970), pp. 415-441; W.W. Maywhort, "International Law--Oil Spills and Their Legal Ramifications," *North Carolina Law Review*, Vol. 49 (1970), pp. 996-1003; Peter Rawlinson, "International Problems Concerning Pollution and the Environment," *Natural Resources Lawyer*, Vol. 4 (1971),p. 804-808; Peter N. Swan, "International and National Approaches to Oil Pollution Responsibility: An Emerging Regime for a Global Problem," *Oregon Law Review*, Vol. 50 (1971), pp. 506-586; W.J. Tearle, "Oil Pollution from Shipping: The International Response," *University of Queensland Law Journal*, Vol. 7 (1971), pp. 303-310; L.C. Caflisch, "Some Aspects of Oil Pollution from Merchant Ships," *Annals of International Studies*, Vol. 4 (1973), pp. 213-236; R. Sandbrook and A. Yurchyshyn, "Marine Pollution from Vessels," in P.W. Birnie and R.E. Stein, eds., *Critical Environmental Issues on the Law of the Sea*, Washington, D.C.: International Institute for Environment and Development, 1975, pp. 19-29; R.M. M'Gonigle and M.W. Zacher, *Pollution, Politics, and International Law*, Berkely: University of California Press, 1979; Ian J. Booth, "International Ship Pollution Law: Recent Developments at UNCLOS," *Marine Policy*, Vol. 4 (1980), No. 3, pp. 215-28; Richard J. Payne, "Flags of Convenience and Oil Pollution: A Threat to National Security?" *Houston Journal of International Law*, Vol. 3 (1980), pp. 67-99; Alfred H.E. Popp, "Recent Developments in Tanker Control in International Law," *Canadian Yearbook of International Law*, Vol. 18 (1980), pp. 3-30; John Warren Kindt, "Vessel-Source Pollution and the Law of the Sea," *Vanderbilt Journal of Transnational Law*, Vol. 17 (1984),*1* pp. 287-328; Richard J. Payne, "Flags of Convenience and Oil Pollution: A Threat to National Security?" *Houston Journal of International Law*, Vol. 3 (1980), pp. 67-99; Alfred H.E. Popp, "Recent Developments in Tanker Control in International Law," *Canadian Yearbook of International Law*, Vol. 18 (1980), pp. 3-30; Ian J. Booth, "International Ship Pollution Law, Recent Developments at UNCLOS," *Marine Policy*, Vol. 4 (1980), No. 3, pp. 215-228; John Warren Kindt," Vessel-Source Pollution and the Law of the Sea," *Vanderbilt Journal of Transnational Law*, Vol. 17 (1984), pp. 287-328.

INTERNATIONAL CONVENTION FOR THE PREVENTION OF POLLUTION
FROM SHIP (MARPOL), WITH ANNEXES AND PROTOCOLS
Done on November 2, 1973, IMCO Doc. MP/Conf/ WP.35, reprinted in
International Legal Materials, Vol. 12 (1973), pp. 1319-1444.

The MARPOL Convention was adopted in 1973 and is intended to deal with all forms of intentional pollution of the sea from ships, other than dumping. Detailed pollution standards are set out in five annexes. These are concerned with oil (Annex I), noxious liquid substances in bulk (Annex II), harmful substances carried by sea in packaged forms (Annex III), sewage (Annex IV), and garbage (Annex V). The acceptance of Annexes I and II is obligatory for all contracting parties, but acceptance of the remaining annexes is optional. By 1978 the Convention was still a long way from receiving the necessary number of ratifications to enter into force, mainly because of the considerable economic cost and technical difficulties of complying with its provisions. In an effort to speed up ratification, a Protocol to the Convention was adopted at the IMO's Conference on Tanker Safety and Pollution Prevention, held in February 1978. The effect of the Protocol was to provide that a State could become a party to the MARPOL Convention initially by accepting only Annex I. Annex II would not become binding until three years after the entry into force of the Protocol or such longer period as might be decided by the parties to the Protocol. In this modified form the Convention and Annex I came into force in October 1983 and Annex II in April 1987. As between the parties to it, the MARPOL Convention supersedes the 1954 Convention.

The detailed regulations dealing with oil pollution contained in Annex I (as amended by the 1978 Protocol and further amendments adopted in 1984) are similar to those described above in the 1954 Convention as amended, but with some significant additions. The most important of these are: the reintroduction of special areas (the Mediterranean, Baltic, Black and Red Seas, and the Arabian Gulf. The areas are not the same as those which had been done away with by the 1969 amendments to the 1954 Convention) where no discharges at all are permitted, even by tankers operating the load-on-top system; the requirement for ships other than tankers to be fitted with oily water separating or filtering equipment and adequate sludge tanks; the requirement for most tankers to be fitted with segregated ballast tanks and for crude oil washing, and for new non-tankers over 4,000 GRT to be fitted with segregated ballast tanks; and, finally, making the obligation on parties to provide reception facilities more effective.

The provisions of the remaining annexes to the MARPOL Convention (of which only Annex II is yet in force) . . . [is] briefly summarized here. Under Annex II (which was substantially amended in 1985) the discharge of residues containing noxious liquid substances must be made to a reception facility, unless they are adequately diluted, in which case they may be discharged into the sea in accordance with detailed regulations. The annex also contains provisions for minimizing pollution in the event of an accident. This last is the chief concern of Annex III, which seeks to prevent or minimize pollution from harmful substances carried in packaged forms by laying down regulations concerning packaging, marking, labelling, documentation, stowage and quantity limitations. Annex IV prohibits the discharge of sewage within four miles of land unless a ship has in operation an approved treatment plant. Between four and twelve miles from land, sewage must be comminuted and disinfected before discharge. Finally, Annex V sets specified minimum distances from land for the disposal of all the principle kinds of garbage, and prohibits the disposal of all plastics. For the substances covered by Annexes II, IV and V contracting States are obliged

of all plastics. For the substances covered by Annexes II, IV and V contracting States are obliged to provide adequate reception facilities in their ports.

[The Protocol referred to in the above summary was done at London on February 17, 1978 and entered into force on October 2, 1983 IMCO Doc. TSPP/CONF/11 (February 16, 1978), reprinted in *International Legal Materials*, Vol. 27 (1978), pp. 546-578. As of October 2, 1983 the regime to be applied by the states parties to the 1978 protocol will be the regime contained in the 1973 Convention as modified by the 1978 Protocol. This Protocol supersedes the International Convention for the Prevention of Pollution of the Sea by Oil of May 12, 1954 as between the contracting parties to the 1978 Protocol. *Treaties in Force*, 1989, Washington, D.C.: U.S. Government Printing Office; 1987, p. 335, n.1].

Article 3

. . . .

(3) The present Convention shall not apply to any warship, naval auxiliary or other ship owned or operated by a State and used, for the time being, only on government non-commercial service. However, each Party shall ensure by the adoption of appropriate measures not impairing the operations or operational capabilities of such ships owned or operated by it, that such ships act in a manner consistent, so far as is reasonable and practicable, with the present Convention.

Article 4

(1) Any violation of the requirements of the present Convention shall be prohibited and sanctions shall be established therefor under the law of the Administration of the ship concerned wherever the violation occurs. If the Administration is informed of such a violation and is satisfied that sufficient evidence is available to enable proceedings to be brought in respect of the alleged violation, it shall cause such proceedings to be taken as soon as possible, in accordance with its law.

(2) Any violation of the requirements of the present Convention within the jurisdiction of any Party to the Convention shall be prohibited and sanctions shall be established therefor under the law of that Party. Whenever such a violation occurs, that Party shall either:

(a) cause proceedings to be taken in accordance with its law; or

(b) furnish to the Administration of the ship such information and evidence as may be in its possession that a violation has occurred.

(3) Where information or evidence with respect to any violation of the present Convention by a ship is furnished to the Administration of that ship, the Administration shall promptly inform the Party which has furnished the information or evidence, and the Organization, of the action taken.

(4) The penalties specified under the law of a Party pursuant to the present Article shall be adequate in severity to discourage violations of the present Convention and shall be equally severe irrespective of where the violations occur.

. . . .

Article 6

(1) Parties to the Convention shall cooperate in the detection of violations and the enforcement of the provisions of the present Convention, using all appropriate and practicable measures of detection and environmental monitoring, adequate procedures for reporting and accumulation of evidence.

(2) A ship to which the present Convention applies may, in any port or off-shore terminal of a Party, be subject to inspection by officers appointed or authorized by that Party for the purpose of verifying whether the ship has discharged any harmful substances in violation of the provisions of the Regulations. If an inspection indicates a violation of the Convention, a report shall be forwarded to the Administration for any appropriate action.

(3) Any Party shall furnish to the Administration evidence, if any, that the ship has discharged harmful substances or effluents containing such substances in violation of the provisions of the Regulations. If it is practicable to do so, the competent authority of the former Party shall notify the master of the ship of the alleged violation.

(4) Upon receiving such evidence, the Administration so informed shall investigate the matter, and may request the other Party to furnish further or better evidence of the alleged contravention. If the Administration is satisfied that sufficient evidence is available to enable proceedings to be brought in respect of the alleged violation, it shall cause such proceedings to be taken in accordance with its law as soon as possible. The Administration shall promptly inform the Party which has reported the alleged violation, as well as the Organization, of the action taken.

(5) A Party may also inspect a ship to which the present Convention applies when it enters the ports or off-shore terminals under its jurisdiction, if a request for an investigation is received from any Party together with sufficient evidence that the ship has discharged harmful substances or effluents containing such substances in any place. The report of such investigation shall be sent to the Party requesting it and to the Administration so that the appropriate action may be taken under the present Convention.

Article 7

(1) All possible efforts shall be made to avoid a ship being unduly detained or delayed under Articles 4, 5, and 6 of the present Convention.

(2) When a ship is unduly detained or delayed under Articles 4, 5, and 6 of the present Convention, it shall be entitled to compensation for any loss or damage suffered.

NOTE

The International Convention for the Safety of Life at Sea, done at London on November 1, 1974, *International Legal Materials*, Vol. 14 (1975), pp. 963-978, (SOLAS Convention), in Chapter VII of its Annex, contains provisions relating to the packing, marking, labelling, documentation and stowage of dangerous goods, which have the objective *inter alia* of reducing the risk of pollution resulting from the carriage of such goods by ships. Chapter VIII of Annex of this Convention also lays down regulations governing non-military nuclear-powered ships. These regulations, and the Code of Safety for Nuclear Merchant Ships, adopted by IMO in November 1981, IMO Assembly Resolution A. 491 XII, attempt to reduce the risk of accidental or deliberate pollution arising out of the operation of such ships. This question has also been dealt with by several bilateral agreements, such as the Anglo-American Agreement Relating to Visits by the N.S. Savannah to Ports in the United Kingdom Territory, June 19, 1964, 15 UST 1511; TIAS 5633; 530 UNTS 99.

Some regional conventions deal with pollution from ships by simply referring their parties to the applicable multilateral conventions. For instance, Article 6 of the Convention for the Protection of the Mediterranean Sea Against Pollution, February 16, 1976, *International Legal Materials*], Vol. 15 (1976), pp. 290-312, provides: "The Contracting Parties shall take all measures in conformity with international law to prevent, abate and combat pollution of the Mediterranean Sea Area caused by discharges from ships and to ensure the effective implementation in that Area of the rules which are generally recognized at the international level relating to the control of this type of pollution." Article 5 of the Convention for Cooperation in the Protection and Development of the Marine Coastal Environment of the West and Central African Region, March 23, 1981, *International Legal Materials*, Vol. 20 (1981), pp. 746-756, contains similar provisions. However, the Convention on the Protection of the Marine Environment of the Baltic Sea Area (with Annexes II-VI), March 22, 1974, *International Legal Materials*, Vol. 13 (1974), pp. 544-585, contains more detailed regulations on oil pollution.

4.   Liability and Compensation

Robert H. Stansfield, "The Torrey Canyon," in R. Bernardt, ed., *Encyclopedia of International Law*, Vol. 11, *Law of the Sea, Air and Space*, Amsterdam: Elsevier Science Publishers, 1989, pp. 333-334. Reprinted with the permission of the publisher and Dr. R. Bernardt.

The *Torrey Canyon* was an American-owned and chartered merchant ship, a super-tanker, registered under the Liberian flag, a flag of convenience. While sailing from Mina Al Ahamadi in the Persian Gulf to Milford Haven, Great Britain, the ship ran aground on March 18, 1967 on the Seven Stones Reef between the Isles of Scilly and Lands End off the southwest coast of Britain in international waters.

At the time of the incident, the ship was carrying 119,328 tons of crude oil. Immediately, it was recognized that the *Torrey Canyon* presented a major pollution threat to the British and French coasts and the ocean environment. The British and French governments took prompt action to prevent and mitigate the pollution caused by leaking oil.

Because of rough seas salvage operations were hindered. A plan to pump the oil off the distressed vessel had to be abandoned because of the danger of explosion. Attempts to refloat the tanker were unsuccessful and ceased when the worsening weather and high seas broke the ship into three pieces. After exhausting all other possibilities, on March 27, 1967 the British Government decided to burn the oil slicks and destroy the remaining cargo by bombing the vessel. The government stated that its intention was not to destroy the ship, but only to open the cargo tanks and burn the oil therein.

After informing the owners, British war planes bombed the wreck, setting her afire. Neither the owners nor Liberia made a protest against the British Government's action. By March 30, 1967 all oil in the vicinity of the ship had been destroyed. However, 80,000 tons of oil escaped into the ocean polluting the British and French coasts. A Liberian board of inquiry determined that the sole cause of the accident was the master's negligence. The board recommended that his sailing papers be revoked.

Traditionally, flag States have almost absolute jurisdiction over their vessels on the high seas, whereas coastal States have only limited authority over ships in adjacent international waters. The British Government made it quite clear that its primary concern had been the prevention of oil pollution and that neither domestic legal, international legal nor financial constraints were considered. Members of the opposition in Parliament strongly attacked the government's failure to consider the legal ramifications, both domestic and international.

Subsequent supporters of the British Government's action asserted that it was permissible under the doctrines either of self-defense or necessity. However, the applicability of these doctrines is questionable as no unlawful act was performed to invoke self-defense, and the peace and security of Britain was not threatened to the degree needed to support a plea of necessity. Nevertheless, in 1980 the U.N. International Law Commission (ILC) concluded that Britain's actions against the Torrey Canyon were an expression of the doctrine of "necessity". The ILC's characterization of the *Torrey Canyon* incident reflects its elevation of environmental concerns and a liberalization of the grounds supporting the defense of necessity [*Yearbook of the International Law Commission*, 1980, Vol. II, Part Two, p. 39]. Other advocates claimed that as the wreck occurred in Britain's contiguous zone, Britain was permitted to intervene under Art. 24 of the 1958 Geneva Convention on the Territorial Sea and the Contiguous Zone. Art. 24 of the Convention allows coastal States to exercise the control necessary to prevent the infringement of sanitary regulations. However, at the time of the incident, Britain had not declared a contiguous zone. Other existing oil pollution conventions were not applicable as they were not concerned with oil pollution arising from such maritime incidents.

A host of other admiralty law problems arose when France and Britain brought actions against the owners and charterers for damages. Of particular concern was the limited liability of the owners and charterers. This question and others were left unresolved as the owners and charterers settled with the two governments. Each defendant paid each government 1.5 million pounds sterling.

The two issues of coastal State intervention and civil liability were presented by Britain to the Inter-Governmental Maritime Consultative Organization (now the International Maritime Organization) at an extraordinary meeting on May 4, 1967. The efforts of this organization culminated in the adoption of two conventions which addressed these issues. The Convention relating to Intervention on the High Seas in Cases of Oil Pollution Casualties of November 29, 1969 (UNTS, Vol. 970, p. 212) authorizes States parties to take "such measures on the high seas as may be necessary to prevent, mitigate or eliminate grave and imminent danger to their coastline" from pollution by oil (Art. 1). The treaty requires consultation with all interested parties and provides for mandatory conciliation an arbitration for disputes arising out of such incidents.

The Convention on Civil Liability for Oil Pollution Damage of November 29, 1969 (UNTS, Vol. 973, p. 3) establishes a régime of limited liability for owners of ships registered in contracting States, whereby the owner of a vessel which causes oil pollution damage may limit his liability by establishing a fund for compensation. All judgments against the ship owner for oil pollution damage rendered by courts of contracting States are to be satisfied from this fund.

REFERENCES

Secretary of State, *The Torrey Canyon*, British Command Papers, Cmnd. 3246 (1967); "Liberian Board of Investigation Report in the Matter of the Standing of the SS Torrey Canyon on March 18, 1967," *International Legal Materials*, Vol. 6 (1967), pp. 480-487. V.P. Nanda, "The

Torrey Canyon Disaster: Some Legal Aspects," *Denver Law Journal*, Vol. 44 (1967), pp. 400-425; A. Utton, "Protective Measures and the Torrey Canyon," *Boston College Industrial and Commercial Law Review*, Vol. 9 (1967/1968), pp. 613-632; E. Brown, "The Lessons of the Torrey Canyon: International Law Aspects," *Current Legal Problems*, Vol. 21 (1968), pp. 113-136; G.W. Keeton, "The Lessons of the Torrey Canyon: English Law Aspects," *Current Legal Problems*, Vol. 21 (1968), pp. 94-112; J.C. Sweeney, "Oil Pollution of the Oceans," *Fordham Law Review*, Vol. 37 (1968/1969), pp. 155-208; N. Healy, "The CMI & IMCO Draft Conventions on Civil Liability for Oil Pollution," *Journal of Maritime Law and Commerce*, Vol. 1 (1969/1970), pp. 93-106; L.F.E. Goldie, "International Principles of Responsibility for Pollution," *Columbia Journal of Transnational Law*, Vol. 9 (1970), pp. 283-330; N. Healy, "The International Convention on Civil Liability for Oil Pollution Damage, Journal of Maritime Law and Commerce, Vol. 1 (1970), pp. 317-332; Brian P. Smith, *State Responsibility and the Marine Environment: The Rules of Decision*, London & New York: Oxford University Press, 1988.

INTERNATIONAL CONVENTION ON CIVIL LIABILITY
FOR OIL POLLUTION DAMAGE
Done at Brussels, November 29, 1969 *International
Legal Materials*, Vol. 9 (1970), pp. 45-64; as amended
by a protocol done at London on November 19, 1976,
ibid., Vol. 16 (1977), pp. 617-621 and a Protocol
done at London on May 25, 1984, (MD Doc. LEG/CONF.6/66,
Environmental Policy and Law, Vol. 13 (1984), pp. 66-68.

ARTICLE II

This Convention shall apply exclusively to pollution damage caused on the territory including the territorial sea of a Contracting State and to preventive measures taken to prevent or minimize such damage.

The 1984 Protocol extends the application of the Convention to Exclusive Economic Zone extending not more than 200 nautical miles from the baselines from which the breadth of its territorial sea is measured.

. . . .

ARTICLE V

1. The owner of a ship shall be entitled to limit his liability under this Convention in respect of any one incident to an aggregate amount of 2,000 francs for each ton of the ship's tonnage. However, this aggregate amount shall not in any event exceed 210 million francs.

[The 1976 Protocol modified the limit of the owner's liability to 133 units of account for each ton, with maximum limit of liability to 14 million units of account. The 1984 Protocol made further revision on the limits of the ship's owner's liability as follows:

(a)   3 million units of account for a ship not exceeding 5,000 units of tonnage;

(b)   for a ship with a tonnage in excess thereof, for each additional unit of tonnage, 420 units of account in addition to the amount mentioned in subparagraph (a);

provided, however, that this aggregate amount shall not in any event exceed 59.7 million units of account.]

2. If the incident occurred as a result of the actual fault or privity of the owner, he shall not be entitled to avail himself of the limitation provided in paragraph 1 of this Article.

The 1984 Protocol modified the above provision as follows:

[The owner shall not be entitled to limit his liability under this Convention if it is proved that the pollution damage resulted from his personal act or omission, committed with the intent to cause such damage, or recklessly and with knowledge that such damage would probably result.]

3. For the purpose of availing himself of the benefit of limitation provided for in paragraph 1 of this Article the owner shall constitute a fund for the total sum representing the limit of his liability with the Court or other competent authority of any one of the Contracting States in which action is brought under Article IX. The fund can be constituted either by depositing the sum or by producing a bank guarantee or other guarantee, acceptable under the legislation of the Contracting State where the fund is constituted, and considered to be adequate by the Court or another competent authority.

4. The fund shall be distributed among the claimants in proportion to the amounts of their established claims.

5. If before the fund is distributed the owner or any of his servants or agents or any person providing him insurance or other financial security has as a result of the incident in question, paid compensation for pollution damage, such person shall, up to the amount he has paid, acquire by subrogation the rights which the person so compensated would have enjoyed under this Convention.

. . . .

9. The franc mentioned in this Article shall be a unit consisting of sixty-five and a half milligrams of gold of millesimal fineness nine hundred. The amount mentioned in paragraph 1 of this Article shall be converted into the national currency of the State in which the fund is being constituted on the basis of the value of that currency by reference to the unit defined above on the date of the constitution of the fund.

[In the 1976 Protocol the franc is replaced by the "unit of account" which is the Special Drawing Right (SDR) as defined by the International Monetary Fund. SDR is an international reserve asset created by the International Monetary Fund (IMF) and allocated to its members as a supplement to existing reserve assets. The valuation of the SDR is determined on the basis of a basket of five currencies -- the U.S. dollars, the Deutsche mark, the French franc, the Japanese yen, and the pound sterling. See John H. Jackson and William J. Davey, *Legal Problems of International Economic Relations*, 2nd ed., St. Paul, Minn.: West Publishing Co., 1986, p. 856. The conversion rate can vary from day to day and from country to country. In August 1987 one SDR was worth about £0.80 or U.S. $ 1.26. See R.R. Churchill and A.V. Lowe, *The Law of the Sea*, 2nd ed., Manchester: Manchester University Press, 1988, p. 265.]

ARTICLE VI

1. Where the owner, after an incident, has constituted a fund in accordance with Article V, and is entitled to limit his liability,

(a)   no person having a claim for pollution damage arising out of that incident shall be entitled to exercise any right against any other assets of the owner in respect of such claim;

(b)   the Court or other competent authority of any Contracting State shall order the release of any ship or other property belonging to the owner which has been arrested in respect of a claim for pollution damage arising out of that incident, and shall similarly release any bail or other security furnished to avoid such arrest.

2.   The foregoing shall, however, only apply if the claimant has access to the Court administering the fund and the fund is actually available in respect of his claim.

ARTICLE VII

1. The owner of a ship registered in a Contracting State and carrying more than 2,000 tons of oil in bulk as cargo shall be required to maintain insurance or other financial security, such as the guarantee of a bank or a certificate delivered by an international compensation fund, in the sums fixed by applying the limits of liability prescribed in Article V, paragraph 1 to cover his liability for pollution damage under this Convention.

. . . .

ARTICLE VIII

Rights of compensation under this Convention shall be extinguished unless an action is brought thereunder within three years from the date when the damage occurred. However, in no case shall an action be brought after six years from the date of the incident which caused the damage. Where this incident consists of a series of occurrences, the six-years period shall run from the date of the first such occurrence.

ARTICLE IX

1. Where an incident has caused pollution damage in the territory including the territorial sea of one or more Contracting States, or preventive measures have been taken to prevent or minimize pollution damage in such territory including the territorial sea, actions for compensation may only be brought in the Courts of any such Contracting State or States. Reasonable notice of any such action shall be given to the defendant.

[The 1984 Protocol extends the application of this provision to exclusive economic zone.]

2. Each Contracting State shall ensure that its Courts possess the necessary jurisdiction to entertain such actions for compensation.

3. After the fund has been constituted in accordance with Article V, the Courts of the State in which the fund is constituted shall be exclusively competent to determine all matters relating to

which the fund is constituted shall be exclusively competent to determine all matters relating to the apportionment and distribution of the fund.

ARTICLE X

1. Any judgment given by a Court with jurisdiction in accordance with Article IX which is enforceable in the State of origin where it is no longer subject to ordinary forms of review, shall be recognized in any Contract State, except:

(a)   where the judgment was obtained by fraud; or

(b)   where the defendant was not given reasonable notice and a fair opportunity to present his case.

2. A judgment recognized under paragraph 1 of this Article shall be enforceable in each Contracting State as soon as the formalities required in that State have been complied with. The formalities shall not permit the merits of the case to be re-opened.

ARTICLE XI

1. The provisions of this Convention shall not apply to warships or other ships owned or operated by a State and used, for the time being, only on Government non-commercial service.

2. With respect to ships owned by a Contracting State and used for commercial purposes, each State shall be subject to suit in the jurisdictions set forth in Article IX and shall waive all defenses based on its status as a sovereign State.

INTERNATIONAL CONVENTION ON THE ESTABLISHING OF AN INTERNATIONAL FUND FOR COMPENSATION FOR OIL POLLUTION DAMAGE
Done at Brussels, December 18, 1971
International Legal Materials, Vol. 11 (1972), pp. 284-302.

. . . .

Article 2

1. An International Fund for compensation for pollution damage, to be named "The International Oil Pollution Compensation Fund" and hereinafter referred to as "The Fund", is hereby established with the following aims:

(a)   to provide compensation for pollution damage to the extent that the protection afforded by the Liability Convention is inadequate;

(b)   to give relief to shipowners in respect of the additional financial burden imposed on them by the [1969] Liability Convention, such relief being subject to conditions designed to insure compliance with safety at sea and other conventions;

(c)   to give effect to the related purposes set out in this Convention.

2. The Fund shall in each Contracting State be recognized as a legal person capable under the laws of that State of assuming rights and obligations and of being a party in legal proceedings before the courts of that State. Each Contracting State shall recognize the Director of the Fund (hereinafter referred to as "The Director") as the legal representative of the Fund.

Article 3

This Convention shall apply:

1. with regard to compensation according to Article 4, exclusively to pollution damage caused on the territory including the territorial sea of a Contracting State, and to preventive measures taken to prevent or minimize such damage.

2. with regard to indemnification of shipowners and their guarantors according to Article 5, exclusively in respect of pollution damage caused on the territory including the territorial sea of a State party to the [International Convention on Civil] Liability Convention, by a ship registered in or flying the flag of a Contracting State and in respect of preventive measures taken to prevent or minimize such damage.

Compensation and Indemnification

Article 4

1. For the purpose of fulfilling its function under Article 2, paragraph 1(a), the Fund shall pay compensation to any person suffering pollution damage if such person has been unable to obtain full and adequate compensation for the damage under the terms of the Liability Convention,

(a)   because no liability for the damage arises under the Liability Convention;

(b)   because the owner liable for the damage under the Liability Convention is financially incapable of meeting his obligations if full and any financial security that may be provided under Article VII of that Convention does not cover or is insufficient to satisfy the claims for compensation for the damage; an owner being treated as financially incapable of meeting his obligations and a financial security being treated as insufficient if the person suffering the damage has been unable to obtain full satisfaction of the amount of compensation due under the Liability Convention after having taken all reasonable steps to pursue the legal remedies available to him;

(c)   because the damage exceeds the owner's liability under the Liability Convention as limited pursuant to Article V, paragraph 1, of that Convention or under the terms of any other international Convention in force or open for signature, ratification or accession at the date of this Convention.

Expenses reasonably incurred or sacrifices reasonably made by the owner voluntarily to prevent or minimize pollution damage shall be treated as pollution damage for the purposes of this Article.

2. The Fund shall incur no obligation under the preceding paragraph if:

(a)   it proves that the pollution damage resulted from an act of war, hostilities, civil war or insurrection or was caused by oil which has escaped or been discharged from a warship or other ship owned or operated by a State and used, at the time of the incident, only on Government noncommercial service; or

(b)   the claimant cannot prove that the damage resulted from an incident involving one or more ships.

3. If the Fund proves that the pollution damage resulted wholly or partially either from an act or omission done with intent to cause damage by the person who suffered the damage or from the negligence of that person, the Fund may be exonerated wholly or partially from its obligation to pay compensation to such person provided, however, that there shall be no such exoneration with regard to such preventive measures which are compensated under paragraph 1. . . .

4.   (a)   Except as otherwise provided in sub-paragraph (b) of this paragraph, the aggregate amount of compensation payable by the Fund under this Article shall in respect of any one incident be limited, so that the total sum of that amount and the amount of compensation actually paid under the Liability Convention for pollution damage caused in the territory of the Contract States, including any sums in respect of which the Fund is under an obligation to indemnify the owner pursuant to Article 5, paragraph 1, of this Convention, shall not exceed 450 million francs.

(b)   The aggregate amount of compensation payable by the Fund under this Article for pollution damage resulting from a natural phenomenon of an exceptional, inevitable and irresistible character, shall not exceed 450 million francs.

5. Where the amount of established claims against the Fund exceeds the aggregate amount of compensation payable under paragraph 4, the amount available shall be distributed in such a manner that the proportion between any established claim and the amount of compensation actually recovered by the claimant under the Liability Convention and this Convention shall be the same for all claimants.

6. The Assembly of the Fund (hereinafter referred to as "the Assembly") may, having regard to the experience of incidents which have occurred and in particular the amount of damage resulting therefrom and to changes in the monetary values, decide that the amount of 450 million francs referred to in paragraph 4, sub-paragraph (a) and (b), shall be changed, provided however, that this amount shall in no case exceed 900 million francs or be lower than 450 million francs. The changed amount shall apply to incidents which occur after the date of the decision effecting the change. . . .

Article 5

1. For the purpose of fulfilling its function under Article 2, paragraph 1(b), the Fund shall indemnify the owner and his guarantor, for that portion of the aggregate amount of liability under the Liability Convention which:

(a)   is in excess of an amount equivalent to 1,500 francs for each ton of the ship's tonnage or of an amount of 125 million francs, whichever is the less,

(b)   is not in excess of an amount equivalent to 2,000 francs for each ton of the said tonnage or an amount of 210 million francs whichever is the less,

provided however, that the Fund shall incur no obligation under this paragraph where the pollution damage resulted from the willful misconduct of the owner himself.

2. The Assembly may decide that the Fund shall, on conditions to be laid down in the Internal Regulations, assume the obligations of a guarantor in respect of ships referred to in Article 3, paragraph 2, with regard to the portion of liability referred to in paragraph 1 of this Article. However, the Fund shall assume such obligations only if the owner so requests and if he maintains adequate insurance or other financial security covering the owner's liability under the Liability Convention up to an amount of 125 million francs, whichever is the less. If the Fund assumes such obligations, the owner shall in each Contracting State be considered to have complied with Article VII of the Liability Convention in respect of the portion of his liability mentioned above.

3. The Fund may be exonerated wholly or partially from its obligations under paragraph 1 towards the owner and his guarantor, if the Fund proves that as a result of the actual fault or privity of the owner:

(a)   the ship from which the oil causing the pollution damage escaped, did not comply with the requirements laid down in;

(i)   the International Convention for the Prevention of Pollution of the Sea by Oil, 1954, as amended in 1962; or

(ii)   the International Convention for the Safety of Life at Sea, 1960; or

(iii)   the International Convention on Load Lines, 1966; or

(iv)   the International Regulations for Preventing Collisions at Sea, 1960; or

(v)   any amendments to the above-mentioned Conventions which have been determined as being of an important nature in accordance with Article XVI(5) of the Convention mentioned under (i), Article IX(e), of the Convention mentioned under (ii) or Article 29(3)(d) or (4)(d) of the Convention mentioned under (iii), provided, however, that such amendments had been in force for at least twelve months at the time of the incident;

and

(b)   the incident or damage was caused wholly or partially by such non-compliance.

The provisions of this paragraph shall apply irrespective of whether the Contracting State in which the ship was registered or whose flag it was flying, is a Party to the relevant Instrument. . . .

NOTE

Under a Protocol to the Fund Convention adopted on November 19, 1976, *International Legal Materials*, Vol. 16 (1977), pp. 621-625), the limit for compensation is converted to 30 million SDRs and the shipowner's liability which is in excess of 1500 francs per ton to 100 SDRs or 125 million francs to 8.333 million SDRs. At an IMO conference held on May 25, 1984, another Protocol to amend the Fund Convention, *Environmental Policy and Law*, Vol. 13 (1984), pp. 61-65, was adopted.

TANKER OWNERS VOLUNTARY AGREEMENT
CONCERNING LIABILITY FOR OIL POLLUTION*
Signed January 7, 1969
International Legal Materials, Vol. 8 (1969), pp. 497-501.
Explanation of the Tanker Owners Voluntary Agreement
Concerning Liability for Oil Pollution (TOVALOP)

This memorandum is designed to serve as a brief summary of the principal points of the Tanker Owners Voluntary Agreement Concerning Liability for Oil Pollution, which, for the sake of convenience, is called "TOVALOP"....

TOVALOP originated from the determination of certain tanker owners to take constructive action with respect to oil pollution. These owners recognized that marine casualties may, on occasion, lead to pollution of coast lines, at least when crude oil, fuel oil, heavy diesel oil or lubricating oil is discharged. (For convenience these materials will be referred to simply as "oil"). These owners were aware of the fact that traditional maritime laws and practice do not always provide an adequate means for reimbursing national governments who incur expenditures to avoid or mitigate damage from such pollution, as well as tanker owners who, on their own initiative incur this kind of expenditure. They recognized also that traditional maritime law and practice do not encourage voluntary action by tanker owners, or joint measures by governments and tanker owners, against such pollution.

In an effort to establish responsibility to national governments with respect to these matters, to assure that there will be financial capability to fulfill this responsibility and otherwise to alleviate this situation, these tanker owners have developed an Agreement called "TOVALOP" which is available to all tanker owners throughout the world.

TOVALOP provides that a Participating Tanker Owner will reimburse national governments for expenses reasonably incurred by them to prevent or clean up pollution of coast lines as the result of the negligent discharge of oil from one of his tankers. The tanker causing the discharge is presumed to be negligent unless the owner can establish that discharge occurred without the tanker's fault. The Participating Owner would not, under TOVALOP, reimburse prevention or clean-up costs incurred by private parties. However, if a national government spends monies to remove oil from privately owned coast lines, it could, in the case of negligence of the discharging tanker, recover these expenses from the tanker owner.

---

*Reproduced from *TOVALOP*, a booklet published by The International Tanker Owners Pollution Federation Limited in London. The original signatories to the agreement are B.P. Tanker Company Limited, Esso Transport Company, Inc., Gulf Oil Corporation, Mobil Oil Corporation, Shell International Petroleum Company Limited, Standard Oil Company of California, and Texaco, Inc.

In the event of a negligent discharge of oil, where the oil pollutes or causes grave and imminent danger of pollution to coast lines within the jurisdiction of a national government, the tanker owner involved is obligated to reimburse the national government concerned for oil removal costs reasonably incurred by it up to a maximum of $100.00 (U.S.) per gross registered ton of the tanker discharging the oil, or $10,000,000 (U.S.), whichever is lesser. If the owner himself also helps remove the oil, his costs in effect result in prorating the government's claim where the combined costs exceed these limits.

TOVALOP also contains provisions for reimbursing a tanker owner for any expenses reasonably incurred by him to prevent or clean up pollution from a discharge of oil. These provisions are designed to encourage a tanker owner to take prompt action to remove or mitigate pollution damage.

TOVALOP applies only to physical contamination to land adjoining waters navigated by tankers including structures built on this land. It doesn't cover fire or explosion damage, consequential damage, or ecological damage.

TOVALOP will be administered by a limited company registered in England, and headquartered in London, which will be called The International Tanker Owners Pollution Federation Limited and each tanker owner who becomes a party to TOVALOP would be a member of this Federation. TOVALOP requires each tanker owner who becomes a party to establish and maintain financial capability to fulfill his contractual obligations described above. The parties to TOVALOP have made provision to establish their financial capability for forming another limited company registered in Bermuda called International Tanker Indemnity Association Limited. This Association will provide insurance coverage for all tankers owned by the Parties to TOVALOP, and thus assure that they would be capable of fulfilling their financial commitments. Alternative coverage may be provided should the Association consider this necessary.

TOVALOP is structured so that all tanker owners of the world can at any time become participants. Tanker owners owning at least 50 percent of the tankers of the world (excluding tankers owned by a government or government agency and tankers of under 5,000 d.w.t.) as measured by deadweight tonnage must become parties before the principal obligations of an owner under TOVALOP come into existence and TOVALOP itself becomes fully effective, and TOVALOP will lapse if 80 percent (with the same exclusions just mentioned) do not become parties at the end of two years after its effective date.

In the case of any disputes, a national government can enforce the liability of a tanker owner who is a party to TOVALOP through arbitration under the Rules of the International Chamber of Commerce. This latter feature should avoid the problems of establishing jurisdiction and effecting collection which exist at present in maritime law and practice.

When a tanker owner becomes a party to TOVALOP he continues in the Agreement for an initial period of five years from its effective date and for successive two-year periods, unless he elects to withdraw at the end of one of these periods. All tanker tonnage (including barges capable of seagoing service) owned or bareboat chartered by a party to the Agreement will be covered, excluding LNG and LPG carriers.

In summary, TOVALOP does the following:

(1) Encourages immediate remedial action by Participating Tanker Owners in the event of a discharge of oil,

(2) Assures financial capability of Participating Tanker Owners to fulfill their obligations under TOVALOP through insurance coverage,

(3) Avoids jurisdictional problems under existing maritime law and practice,

(4) Places on tanker owner the burden of disproving negligence,

(5) Provides a national government with machinery for making valid claims notwithstanding the fact that such government might not, under international or local law, have a legal obligation to remove oil discharged from a tanker or a legal right to recover removal expenses.

[Text of the Agreement omitted.]

NOTE

In 1986, the maximum amount of compensation was increased to US $40,000,000. See R.R. Churchill and A.V. Lowe, *The Law of the Sea*, 2nd ed., Manchester: Manchester University Press, 1988, p. 267.

CONTRACT REGARDING AN INTERIM SUPPLEMENT TO TANKER LIABILITY FOR OIL POLLUTION (CRISTAL)
January 14, 1971
International Legal Materials, Vol. 10 (1971), pp. 137-142.

PREAMBLE

The Parties to this Contract are various Oil Companies and the Oil Companies Institute For Marine Pollution Compensation Limited, an entity organized and existing under the Laws of Bermuda (hereinafter referred to as the "Institute").

The Parties recognize that marine casualties involving tankers carrying bulk oil cargoes can, on occasion, cause extensive pollution damage on the escape or discharge of oil into the sea. They believe that by increasing the responsibility of tanker owners with respect to pollution damage, the occurrence of such incidents can be reduced, and therefore they strongly favor ratification by the nations of the world of the International Convention on Civil Liability for Oil Pollution Damage adopted at Brussels on November 29, 1969 (hereinafter referred to as "CLC").

The Parties further recognize that in some instances persons sustaining pollution damage may be unable, even after ratification of CLC, (as under current legal regimes), to recover adequate compensation for pollution damage.

The Parties accordingly advocate, in addition to ratification of CLC, the adoption and ratification by the nations of the world of a Convention creating an International Compensation Fund or its equivalent whereby persons who sustain pollution damage for which a tanker owner is liable under CLC would have available supplemental compensation beyond the limits established in CLC. Moreover, the Parties have decided, pending the enactment of such a Convention, to establish by contract a means for providing supplemental compensation for pollution damage beyond the limits of liability presently available under existing legal regimes, including Tanker

Owners Voluntary Agreement Concerning Liability for Oil Pollution (TOVALOP), and beyond the limits of liability that will be applicable under CLC, once it enters into force.

In view of the above considerations, the Parties who, as of this 14th day of January, 1971, have executed this Contract and those Oil Companies who later become Parties, have agreed, and do hereby agree, that the Institute will pay such supplemental compensation and that the Oil Company Parties will assure the availability of funds to permit payment thereof, upon the following terms and conditions:

. . . .

IV. *Functions of the Institute.*

(A)--After the Effective Date, the Institute shall compensate persons for pollution damage sustained by them as the result of an incident when at the time of the incident the oil was owned by an Oil Company Party as follows:

(1) Prior to the time CLC enters into force, whenever (i) the Owner or Bareboat Charterer of the ship from which the oil escaped or was discharged was a Party to TOVALOP at the time of the incident and (ii) the Owner of said ship would have been liable to said persons sustaining pollution damage under the provisions of CLC for the damage if CLC had been in force at the time of the incident and had been applicable to the incident.

(2) After the time CLC comes into force whenever the provisions of CLC apply to the incident, and by reason thereof the Owner of the ship from which the oil escaped or was discharged was, in fact, liable to said persons sustaining pollution damage for said damage.

(B)--The compensation to be paid by the Institute under Clause IV (A) to all persons sustaining pollution damage as a result of said incident (regardless of the number of ships from which oil has escaped or been discharged) shall in no event exceed Thirty Million U.S. Dollars (U.S. $30,000,000.00) less the sum of the following:

(1) The Owner's or Bareboat Charterer's maximum liability for said pollution damage under TOVALOP, *plus*

(2) The amount of expenditures that the Owner or Bareboat Charterer was entitled to make for "Removal of Oil" (as defined in TOVALOP) and to receive reimbursement for as provided in TOVALOP, *plus*

(3) The maximum liability of Owner or Bareboat Charterer with respect to such damage under applicable law, statutes, regulations or conventions, *plus*

(4) The maximum amount to which such persons sustaining pollution damage were entitled from any other person or from the ship or from any other vessel under applicable law, statutes, regulations or conventions providing for compensation for all or part of said damage.

(C)--If the total pollution damage resulting from an incident exceeds the net amount referred to in Clause IV (B), then said net amount shall be prorated by the Institute among the persons sustaining said damage.

(D)--Notwithstanding the foregoing, if a person sustaining pollution damage fails to exercise due diligence to recover compensation for such damage from (i) the Owner or Bareboat Charterer of the ship from which the escape or discharge of oil occurred, or (ii) any other person, or (iii) the ship or any other vessel, then to the extent that said Owner, Bareboat Charterer, person, ship or other vessel are liable for part of all of said damage, the Institute shall not compensate said person sustaining pollution damage under this Clause IV.

(E)--The net amount provided for in Clause IV(B) shall be reduced by any amounts paid, or agreed to be paid, by the Institute in settlement of claims made under this Contract.

V. *The Fund.*

The Institute, in order to assure its financial capability to pay compensation under Clause IV hereof, shall maintain and administer a Fund created as follows:

(1) The Fund shall initially be constituted in the amount of Five Million U.S. Dollars (U.S. $5,000,000.00) (hereinafter referred to as the "Initial Call").

(2) As soon as practicable after the Effective Date the Institute shall assess each Oil Company Party to this Contract as of the Effective Date and each such Party shall pay to the Institute that portion of the Initial Call calculated by dividing its total Crude/Fuel Oil Receipts for the calendar year immediately preceding the Effective Date by the total Crude/Fuel Oil Receipts during such preceding calendar year of all Oil Companies who were Parties to this Contract at the Effective Date and by multiplying this percentage by said Initial Call.

(3) Any Oil Company becoming a Party to this Contract subsequent to the Effective Date shall be assessed by the Institute and shall pay to the Institute that portion of the Initial Call calculated in the same manner as under Clause V(2). At such time appropriate adjustment shall be made in the portion of the Initial Call of all Oil Companies then Parties to this Contract and, at the discretion of the Institute, such Oil Companies shall receive an appropriate refund or a credit against future assessments.

(4) The Institute shall, from time to time during each Contract Year estimate the amount reasonably required by it to pay compensation in accordance with Clause IV and shall determine what portion of any such amount ("such amount" being hereinafter referred to as a "Periodic Call"), shall be in cash and what portion shall be in other forms.

(5) The Institute shall, at such times as are appropriate during each Contract Year, assess each Oil Company Party and each such Party shall pay to the Institute that portion of any Periodic Call made during said Contract Year calculated by dividing its total Crude/Fuel Oil Receipts for the calendar year first preceding the commencement of said Contract Year by the total of the Crude/Fuel Oil Receipts during such preceding calendar year of all Oil Companies who were Parties to this Contract at the date of such assessment and by multiplying this percentage by the amount of said Periodic Call, provided however, that notwithstanding the foregoing, (i) each such Oil Company Party (whether or not it had any Crude/Fuel Oil Receipts in such preceding calendar year) shall pay a minimum charge determined by the Institute for each Contract Year, which minimum charge may be offset against any portions of an assessment otherwise payable hereunder, and (ii) no Oil Company Party shall be liable for that portion of an assessment which relates to payment of compensation by the Institute in excess of Five Hundred Thousand U.S. Dollars (U.S. $500,000.00) with respect to any one incident which occurred prior to the date upon which it becomes a Party to this Contract.

NOTE

TOVALOP is of great benefit to the victim of oil pollution damage in approximately 80 coastal states which are not parties to the 1969 Civil Liability Convention. It now covers over 90 percent of the world's oil tankers. The CRISTAL can operate in conjunction with the 1969 Civil Liability Convention in the case where the 1971 Fund Convention is not applicable, thus providing additional compensation and relieving the ship owner of part of his liability. As of 1988, only about two-thirds of the contracting parties to the 1969 Civil Liability Convention are parties to the 1971 Fund Convention. By the end of 1986 CRISTAL had paid out some $ 60 million in compensation. Its maximum amount of compensation was increased fourfold. R.R. Churchill and A.V. Lowe, *The Law of the Sea*, 2nd ed., Manchester: Manchester University Press, 1988, p. 267.

POLLUTION LIABILITY AGREEMENT AMONG TANKER OWNERS (PLATO)
June 5, 1985
Kenneth R. Simmonds, ed., *New Directions in the Law of the Sea*,
New York: Oceana Publications, Inc., New Series, Release 86-2,
Issued September 1986, J. 24, pp. 3-14. Reprinted by permission.

Preamble

The Parties to this Agreement, as Participating Owners, recognize that (i) while the Liability Convention has established, in many jurisdictions, a legal system providing for the compensation of Persons (including Governments) who sustain Pollution Damage resulting from the Discharge of Oil from Tankers it does not provide for the compensation of costs incurred to remove a Threat of an escape or discharge of Oil from a Tanker and it, as well as its voluntary counterpart Tovalop, does not provide for adequate compensation in respect of legitimate claims for Pollution Damage and, (ii) it is unlikely that revisions to the Liability Convention, adopted in 1984, will come into force for some time.

Accordingly, the Parties of this Agreement, and such others as may hereinafter become Parties, in consideration of their mutual promises have agreed with one another and do hereby agree as follows:

. . . .

IV. Responsibility of a Participating Owner

(A) If an incident occurs in a jurisdiction where the provisions of the Fund Convention are not in force, but irrespective as to whether the provisions of the Liability Convention are in force, the Participating Owner shall, with respect to his Participating Tanker involved in that Incident, but subject to the applicable provisions of Paragraph (C) of this Clause IV, exercise his best efforts to take such Preventive Measures and Threat Removal Measures as are practical and appropriate under the circumstances and compensation any Person who (i) sustains Pollution Damage or (ii) incurs Costs in taking Preventive Measures and Threat Removal Measures.

(B) If an Incident occurs in a jurisdiction where the provisions of both the Liability Convention and the Fund Convention are in force, the Participating Owner shall, with respect to his Participating Tanker involved in that Incident, but subject to the applicable provisions of Paragraph (C) of this Clause IV, exercise his best efforts to take such Preventive Measures and

Paragraph (C) of this Clause IV, exercise his best efforts to take such Preventive Measures and Threat Removal Measures as are practical and appropriate under the circumstances and compensate:

(1) the Fund in an amount equal to the amount that the fund has paid or intends to pay as compensation as a result of the Incident, (irrespective as to whether said Participating Owner bears or would bear any liability under the Liability Convention with respect to the Incident); and,

(2) to the extent any Person remains uncompensated, any Person who (i) sustains Pollution Damage or (ii) incurs Cost in taking Preventive Measures and Threat Removal Measures.

(C) The responsibilities which a Participating Owner has assumed, pursuant to Paragraphs (A) and (B) of this Clause IV, shall be subject to the terms and conditions set forth herein.

(1) A Participating Owner shall not be obligated to take Preventive Measures or Threat Removal Measures or pay Costs or make any compensation to a Person if the Incident (i) resulted from an act of war, hostilities, civil war, insurrection or a natural phenomenon of an exceptional, inevitable and irresistible character, or (ii) was wholly caused by an act or omission done with intent to cause damage by the Person or any other third person, or (iii) was wholly caused by the negligence or other wrongful act of any Government or other authority responsible for the maintenance of lights or other navigational aids in the exercise of that function; however, nothing set forth herein shall affect the Participating Owners' responsibility to compensate the Fund pursuant to Paragraph B(1) of this Clause IV.

(2) If Pollution Damage or the circumstances which gave rise to Threat Removal Measures resulted partially from the negligence of the Person who sustained the Pollution Damage or who took the Threat Removal Measures, the Participating Owner shall be partially exonerated from any responsibility he would otherwise have to such Person; however, nothing set forth herein, shall be applicable if the Incident was caused wholly or partially by the negligence of the Participating Owner nor affect the Participating Owner's responsibility to compensate the Fund pursuant to Paragraph B(1) of this Clause IV.

(3) The maximum amount of Costs to be incurred in respect of Preventive Measures and Threat Removal Measures and compensation to be paid by a Participating Owner under Paragraph (A) or (B) of this Clause IV, in respect of any one incident, shall not exceed:

(i) with respect to an Incident occurring after the Effective Date but prior to January 1, 1990, an amount equal, in the case of a Tanker of Five Thousand (5,000) Tons or less to Ten Million United States Dollars (U.S. $ 10,000,000.00) and for a Tanker in excess of Five Thousand (5,000) Tons Ten Million United States Dollars (U.S. $ 10,000,000.00) plus Five Hundred United States Dollars (U.S. $ 500.00) for each Ton in excess of said Five Thousand (5,000) Tons, subject to a maximum of Sixty Million United States Dollars (U.S. $ 60,000,000.00); and

(ii) with respect to an Incident occurring on or after January 1, 1990 an amount equal, in the case of a Tanker of Five Thousand (5,000) Tons or less to Fifteen Million United States Dollars (U.S.$ 15,000,000.00) and for a Tanker in excess of Five Thousand (5,000) Tons Fifteen Million United States Dollars (U.S. $ 15,000,000.00) plus Six Hundred United States Dollars (U.S. $ 600.00) for each Ton in excess of said Five Thousand (5,000) Tons, subject to a maximum of Seventy Five Million United States Dollars (U.S. $ 75,000,000.00);

including Costs incurred and compensation paid as a result of the application of the Liability Convention and/or by the terms of TOVALOP.

(4) When Oil has escaped or been discharged from two or more Participating Tankers and/or there is a Threat of an escape or discharge of Oil from two or more Participating Tankers, the Participating Owners concerned, subject to the remaining provisions of Paragraph (C) of this Clause IV, shall be jointly and severally responsible for all said Costs and compensation under Paragraphs (A) and (B) of this Clause IV, which are not reasonably separable.

(5) If the maximum amount that can be paid by the Participating Owner(s), pursuant to sub-paragraph (3) of this Paragraph (C) of this Clause IV, is insufficient to meet the financial responsibilities assumed under Paragraphs (A) and (B), of this Clause IV, then the Participating Owner(s) shall first compensate in full the Fund and second prorate the remaining amount then available among all other Persons.

[Signed by Amoco Transport Co., B.P. Shipping Ltd., Chevron Shipping Co., Esso International Shipping (Bahamas) Co., Fina Marine S.A., Mobil Shipping and Transportation Co., Shell International Marine Ltd., and Texaco Inc.]

REFERENCES

Thomas R. Post, "A Solution to the Problem of Private Compensation in Oil Discharge Situations," *University of Miami Law Review*, Vol. 28 (1973-1974), pp. 524-550; L.F.E. Goldie, "Liability for Oil Pollution Disaster, International Law and the Delimitation of Competence in a Federal Policy," *Journal of Maritime Law and Commerce*, Vol. 6 (1975), pp. 303-329; John L. Pedrick, "Liability, Compensation and Prevention of Oil Spills: A North American Perspective," *Earth Law Journal*, Vol. 1 (1975), pp. 301-322; A.N. Roushdy, "Marine Pollution and the Absolute Civil Liability of the Shipowner Under the Laws of the United States and Egypt," *Journal of International Law and Economics*, Vol. 10 (1) (1975), pp. 117-182; P.W. Bernie and R.E. Stein, eds., *Critical Environmental Issues on the Law of the Sea*, Washington, D.C.: International Institute for Environment and Development, 1975; A.L. Makovsky, "Liability for Marine Environment Pollution Damage in Contemporary International Sea Law," *Georgia Journal of International and Comparative Law*, Vol. 6 (1976), pp. 59-71; R.E. Stein, "Responsibility and Liability for Harm to the Marine Environment," *Georgia Journal of International and Comparative Law*, Vol. 6 (1976), pp. 41-57; V.E. Fitzmaurice, "Liability for North Sea Oil Pollution," *Marine Policy*, Vol. 2(2) (1978), pp. 105-112; S.J. Byers, "Civil Liability for Oil Pollution at Sea," *Journal of Planning and Environment Law*, January 1979, p. 5-12; Boyd N. Boland, "Vessel Traffic Services and Liability for Oil Spills and Other Maritime Accidents," *Columbia Journal of Transnational Law*, Vol. 18 (1980), pp. 482-524; Ann Blackwood Crain, "Troublesome Aspects of the Sedco 135 Disaster: Has the Plight of the Transnational Pollution Victim Really Improved in the Wake of Torry Canyon?" *Houston Journal of International Law*, Vol. 2 (1980), pp. 387-423; Paul Stephen Dempsey and Lisa L. Helling, "Oil Pollution by Ocean Vessels--An Environmental Tragedy: The Legal Regime of Flags of Convenience, Multilateral Conventions, and Coastal States," *Denver Journal of International Law & Policy*, Vol. 10 (1980), pp. 37-87; Brainimir Luksic, "Limitation of Liability for the Raising and Removal of Ships and Wrecks: A Comparative Survey," *Journal of Maritime Law and Commerce*, Vol. 12 (1980), pp. 47-64; Henri G. Nagelmackers, "Aftermath of the Amoco Cadiz: Why Must the European Community Act?" *Marine Policy*, Vol. 4 (1980), No. 1, pp. 3-18; Alfred Rest, "Draft Convention on Liability and Compensation Concerning the Carriage of Noxious and Hazardous Substances by Sea, The Legal Concept and Perspectives," *Environmental Policy and*

Law, Vol. 6 (1980), pp. 82-85; Faith Halter, "Recovery of Damages by States for Fish and Wildlife Losses Caused by Pollution," *Ecology Law Quarterly*, Vol. 10 (1982), pp. 5-35; Gordon L. Becker, "Acronyms and Compensation for Oil Pollution Damage from Tankers," *Texas International Law Journal*, Vol. 18 (1983), pp. 475-481; *International Oil Pollution: Current and Alternative Liability and Compensation Arrangements Affecting the United States*, Washington, D.C.: U.S. General Accounting Office, GAO/ID-83-19, February 3, 1983; Joseph W. Dellapenna and Ar-Young Wang,"Protecting the Republic of China from Oil Pollution in the Sea: Accounting for Damages from Oil Spills," *Texas International Law Journal*, Vol. 19 (1984), pp. 115-138; Volkmar J. Hartje, "Oil Pollution Caused by Tanker Accidents: Liability Versus Regulation," *Natural Resources Journal*, Vol. 24 (1984), pp. 41-60.

THE AMOCO CADIZ INCIDENT OF 1978

Douglas A. Jacobsen and James D. Yellen, "Oil Pollution: The 1984 London Protocols and the AMOCO CADIZ," *Journal of Maritime Law and Commerce*, Vol. 15 (1984), pp. 467, 483-485. Footnotes omitted. Reprinted with the permission of Anderson Publishing Co. and the authors.

On March 16, 1978, the Liberian flag supertanker AMOCO CADIZ lost control of her rudder and subsequently grounded off the Brittany Coast. . . . Both the vessel and her $24 million cargo of Middle East crude oil were totally lost. In the days to follow, over 65 million gallons of crude created a slick approximately 18 miles wide and 80 miles long, polluting 130 miles of French coastline. . . .

The super tanker AMOCO CADIZ was transporting 68 mi!'ion gallons of crude oil from Kharg Island in the Persian Gulf to Rotterdam when her hydraulic steering gear system malfunctioned and she lost control of her steering. Despite efforts by the vessel's crew to repair the steering gear and salvage attempts by the West German Tug PACIFIC, the vessel went aground and her entire cargo of crude oil was released into the sea. For days, the oil washed ashore along the Breton coastline.

The cargo on board the AMOCO CADIZ was owned by local affiliates of the Shell International Petroleum Co. The registered owner of the vessel was Amoco Transport Company, a Liberian corporation indirectly owned by Standard Oil Company of Indiana. The vessel had been designed and constructed in Cadiz, Spain, by the Spanish firm of Astilleros Espanoles. The Tug PACIFIC was owned and operated by Bugsier Reederei und Bergungs, A.G.

Actions for pollution damages and clean-up costs were filed by the French Government, by the French administrative departments of Finistere and Conseil Cotes du Nord, and by numerous municipalities, French individuals, businesses and associations. Suits were commenced against several Amoco companies, and all the United States actions were eventually consolidated by the Multidistrict Litigation Panel for hearing in the District Court for the Northern District of Illinois. Limitation of liability proceedings were filed by all the Amoco parties, and also by Bugsier. In April 1979, however, the district court granted the claimants' motion to dismiss the limitation complaint as to Standard Oil and Amoco International Oil Co., since they were technically not the owners of the tanker. [In re Amoco Transport Co., 1979, AMC 1017 (N.D. Ill., 1979].

The Amoco parties and the French claimants also filed suit against Astilleros Espanoles. Astilleros refused to make a general appearance in the action, and a default judgment against it was rendered by the trial court [In re Oil Spill by the AMOCO CADIZ, 491 F. Supp. 170, 1983 AMC 925 (N.D. Ill. 1979)] and affirmed by the Seventh Circuit [In re Oil Spill by the AMOCO CADIZ, 699 F.2d 909, 1983 AMC 1633 (7th Cir. 1983), cert. denied, 104 S.Ct. 196 (1983)].

IN RE: OIL SPILL BY THE "AMOCO CADIZ"
OFF THE COAST OF FRANCE ON MARCH 16, 1978
MDL Docket No. 376, U.S. District Court for the
Northern District of Illinois, Eastern Division,
Slip Opinion, April 18, 1984

II. CONCLUSIONS OF LAW

A. Jurisdiction And Applicable Law

. . . .

2. Any damage sustained by the claimant in this case were sustained in French territorial waters or on the coast of France; the substance law applicable to such claims would therefore have been French law if it had been proved different from that of the United States. However, it was not proved different. Claimants Cotes du Nord, in open court, stipulated that United States law applied, and claimants Bretagne-Angleterre-Irlande, et al., ("Bretagne") made no objection. The claims will be decided in accordance with United States law. . . .

B. The Claims Against Bugsier

3. Bugsier had no contractual or other relationship with claimants Cotes du Nord or claimants Bretagne and owed no warranties of any kind to the said claimants. . . . Therefore, the only grounds on which the claimants could base a claim against Bugsier would be actionable negligence.

4. The said claimants had the burden of proving that any oil pollution damage consequent upon the grounding of the Amoco Cadiz was caused or contributed to by actionable negligence on the part of Bugsier, its agents or servants. . . .

5. A salvor whose efforts are unsuccessful is not liable for losses sustained either by the owners of the property he has endeavored to salve or by third parties, in the absence of proof of causative gross negligence or willful misconduct. . . .

6. Since Bugsier is being exonerated from liability to the claimants whose claims are before the court, any question that might otherwise have arisen concerning its right to limitation of liability in accordance with the Limitation of Liability Act, 46 U.S.C. §§ 183-189, has become moot.

7. The claims of the Cotes du Nord and Bretagne against Bugsier are denied.

8. The stay of proceedings brought against Bugsier by Transport [Amoco Transport Company], and AIOC [Amoco International Oil Company], is continued, pending completion of arbitration now pending.

9. The claims against Bugsier filed by claimants Cotes du Nord and Bretagne are accordingly dismissed.

C.   The International Convention on Civil Liability for Oil Pollution Damage

10. The Amoco parties argue that the International Convention on Civil Liability for Oil Pollution Damage, Brussels 1969 ("the CLC"), to which France and Liberia were parties, but not the United States, operates to limit their liability.

11. Whether AIOC and Standard may be sued is determined by United States law.

12. The CLC is the law of France and not the law of the United States; it thus does not apply to a determination of whether AIOC and Standard may be sued in this country.

13. Even if French law, including the CLC, were applicable to this issue, none of the provisions of the CLC would bar suits against Standard or AIOC.

14. The CLC is not the exclusive remedy available to victims of oil pollution damage and does not prohibit such victims from bringing an action in tort outside the CLC against anyone other than the registered owner of the vessel or its mandataires or preposes ("agents" and "servants" in the English text of the CLC). All other parties may be sued and held liable, without limitation, independent of the CLC.

15. None of the plaintiffs is precluded by French law, including the CLC, from suing Standard or AIOC because neither Standard nor AIOC, both parent corporations of Transport was the registered owner of the Amoco Cadiz or a mandatory or prepose, or an agent, or servant, of the registered owner.

16. The CLC must be interpreted in light of its legislative history and French law.

17. Article III, section 4 of the CLC was not intended by the drafters to immunize from suit major companies operating vessels, such as AIOC. The terms mandataires and preposes were intended to refer to and immunize the master and crew of a vessel, individuals who would be unable to bear the financial expense of liability and whom it would therefore be futile and unfair to sue.

18. Pursuant to French law, the consulting agreement was not a contract de mandat and, in any case, AIOC was not the mandataire of Transport with respect to the tortious acts and omissions which led to the grounding of the Amoco Cadiz because those were material acts, which cannot be performed in the capacity of mandataire.

19. AIOC also was not and could not possibly have been the mandatory of Transport in connection with AIOC's negligent acts with respect to design and construction, which occurred prior to the existence of the consulting agreement on June 1, 1974.

20. AIOC was also not the "agent" of the registered owner, Transport. Although United States law cannot be used to interpret the CLC, which is not a United States law, the consulting agreement by its terms does not purport to create the relation of principal-agent, but that of owner-independent contractor. Furthermore, Transport did not and could not exercise any direction or control over the operations of AIOC, which therefore was not Transport's "agent."

21. AIOC therefore, is not entitled to claim immunity from suit under French law, including the CLC, for its negligence which resulted in oil pollution damage.

D.   The Liability of AIOC

22. As the party which exercised complete control over the operation, maintenance and repair of the Amoco Cadiz and the selection and training of its crew, AIOC had a duty to ensure that the vessel was seaworthy and adequately maintained and repaired, and that the crew was properly trained.

23. AIOC negligently performed its duty to ensure that the Amoco Cadiz in general and its steering gear in particular were seaworthy, adequately maintained and in proper repair.

24. AIOC was privy to and had knowledge of the scored rams, slipping belts, maintenance practices and steering gear problems on the Amoco Cadiz which made the vessel unseaworthy. . . .

25. The failure of Amoco Cadiz's steering gear is directly attributable to an improperly designed, constructed and maintained steering gear system and AIOC knew or should have known of the unseaworthy condition. . . .

26. AIOC failed to carry its burden relative to the steering gear failure on Amoco Cadiz that it was without privity or knowledge. . . .

27. The negligence of AIOC in failing reasonably to perform its obligations of maintenance and repair of the steering gear system was approximate cause of the breakdown of the system on March 16, 1978, the grounding of the vessel and the resulting pollution damage.

28. AIOC negligently performed its duty to ensure that the crew of the Amoco Cadiz was properly trained.

29. The crew's improper training with respect to the maintenance, operation, inspection and repair of the steering gear system was a proximate cause of the grounding of the Amoco Cadiz and the resulting pollution damage.

30. AIOC, as the party which supervised and approved the design and construction of the Amoco Cadiz, had a duty to ensure that the design and construction were properly carried out so as to result in a seaworthy vessel. It failed in that duty.

31. AIOC was negligent in operating the Amoco Cadiz without a redundant steering system or any other means of controlling the rudder in the event of complete failure of the hydraulic steering system.

32. The lack of a redundant steering system was a proximate contributing cause of the grounding of the Amoco Cadiz and resulting pollution damage.

33. For each and all of the reasons expressed above, AIOC is liable for the damages suffered by the plaintiff parties as a result of the grounding of the Amoco Cadiz.

34. AIOC failed to make Amoco Cadiz seaworthy prior to the last voyage and, for that reason among others, cannot limit its liability. . . .

E.   The Liability of Transport [Amoco Transport Company of Monrovia which is registered in Liberia]

35. Transport, the nominal owner of the Amoco Cadiz, failed to meet its burden of proving that it was free from privity and knowledge with respect to the negligence which proximately caused the grounding of the vessel.

36. Transport, as nominal owner of the Amoco Cadiz, had a non-delegable duty to ensure that the vessel was seaworthy, properly maintained and repaired, and that the crew was adequately trained at the time of her final voyage, and on March 16, 1978. Transport therefore is liable, without limitation, for AIOC's negligent operations, maintenance and crew training with respect to the Amoco Cadiz.

37. Transport negligently failed to ensure that the Amoco Cadiz was seaworthy on her final voyage.

38. Transport, as nominal owner of the Amoco Cadiz, had a duty to control and supervise the maintenance, repair and crew training on the vessel. Transport negligently failed to exercise any control or supervision whatsoever over AIOC with respect to those activities. Transport therefore is liable, without limitation, for the damage suffered by claimants as a result of the grounding of the Amoco Cadiz.

39. Transport knew and should have known of the unseaworthy condition of the Amoco Cadiz and of the negligence of AIOC which caused and contributed to the grounding.

40. Transport, as registered owner of the Amoco Cadiz, failed to use due diligence to provide a seaworthy vessel and failed to exercise control over its vessel and the activities of AIOC in order to prevent unseaworthy conditions and negligence.

41. Transport had actual knowledge of the unseaworthy condition of the Amoco Cadiz, as evidenced by the following:

(a) Reports of the ship's inspectors were sent to Transport's offices in Bermuda.

(b) Transport's ship inspectors knew of or negligently failed to ascertain the unseaworthy condition of the Amoco Cadiz.

42. Transport presented no evidence which would tend to establish its freedom from privity or knowledge of AIOC's negligence and the conditions which resulted in the grounding of the vessel.

F.   The Liability of Standard [Standard Oil Company of Indiana]

43. As an integrated multinational corporation which is engaged through a system of subsidiaries in the exploration, production, refining, transportation and sale of petroleum products throughout the world, Standard is responsible for the tortious acts of its wholly owned subsidiaries and instrumentalities AIOC and Transport.

44. Standard exercised such control over its subsidiaries AIOC and Transport, that those entities would be considered to be mere instrumentalities of Standard. Furthermore, Standard itself was initially involved in and controlled the design, construction, operation and management of the Amoco Cadiz and treated that vessel as if it were its own.

45. Standard therefore is liable for its own negligence and the negligence of AIOC and Transport with respect to the design, operation, maintenance, repair and crew training of the Amoco Cadiz.

46. Standard therefore is liable to the French claimants for damages resulting from the grounding of the Amoco Cadiz.

G.   Limitation of Liability

47. In an earlier opinion of the court, the right to limit damages was denied to Standard and AIOC for the reason that they were not owners. Transport, as the owner of the Amoco Cadiz, was not affected by that ruling.

48. However, for the additional reasons stated in this opinion, Standard, AIOC and Transport are liable without limitation.

H.   The Amoco Counterclaims and Third-Party Claims

49. The Amoco parties have asserted counter- and third-party claims against France, the Departments of Finistere and Cotes du Nord, and the communes for their negligence in failing to prevent or contain the oil spill. A pretrial motion to dismiss the claims was denied. In re Oil Spill by the Amoco Cadiz off the Coast of France on March 16, 1978, 491 F. Supp. 161 (N.D. Ill. 1979).

50. At the conclusion of the trial, these claims are ripe for resolution. It becomes apparent that these claims are unfounded in law and in fact.

51. No duty which France may have had to its citizens could run to the benefit of Amoco. No action or lack of action on France's part could result in a right accruing to Amoco to sue for lack of planning or ineffectual cleanup efforts. Amoco's counterclaims and third-party claims against the French claimants are denied. . . .

52. It remains true, however, that in the assessment of damages Amoco cannot be liable for damage resulting from any inept cleanup effort which in fact exacerbated the harm.

. . . .

J.   Sanctions Against France

54. On March 15, 1982, this court in the circumstances of France's refusal to produce certain testimony and documents pursuant to order of court ordered France to pay the reasonable fees and expenses, including attorneys' fees, incurred by the Amoco parties as a result of that refusal. The Amoco parties may, within 60 days of the date of this opinion, petition the court for such sums are as appropriate under that order.

III. SUMMARY

Both the French claimants and the Amoco parties have asserted the liability of Astilleros, and the court has found that design and construction faults contributed to the grounding of the Amoco Cadiz thus rendering Astilleros liable, in part, for the consequent damage.

The French claimants and PIL [Petroleum Insurance Limited] are entitled to the full extent of their incurred damages against Standard, AIOC and Transport which latter defendants are jointly and severally liable therefor.

Amoco is entitled to damages against Astilleros to the extent that its own liability was contributed to by the negligence and fault of the shipbuilder.

All claims against Bugsier are denied.

The court asserts continuing jurisdiction over the matters in controversy and the taking of further evidence for the purpose of resolving the damage issues. . . .

IN RE OIL SPILL BY THE "AMOCO CADIZ" OFF
THE COAST OF FRANCE MARCH 16, 1978
U.S. District Court for the Northern District of Illinois, Eastern Division, MDL Docket No. 376,
Memorandum Opinion, April 18, 1988, pp. 1-6, 10-16, 19-21, 23, 25-26, 459.

I.   INTRODUCTION

This opinion addresses and resolves the issues in one of a handful of the most complex and lengthy cases to be addressed by the United States courts. . . .

. . . .[This] was not a case appropriate for trial by jury, although that decision had a basis in law, had an additional and compelling basis in fact. Putting aside the enormous problems of obtaining and maintaining a jury for a trial which occupied virtually an entire year, the decision-making process of this court, assisted by a roomful of exhibits, summaries and memoranda, took several months and could not have been replicated by a jury.

Another extraordinary aspect of the trial arose from the special problems concerning the admissibility of evidence. The plaintiffs had an enormous information-gathering task to enable them to present to the court some appropriate measure of damages. If each individual claiming injury were to be presented to the court to hear direct evidence on the claim, lifetimes would have been insufficient for trial. The result was that individuals represented groups of complainants, and information gatherers and compilers presented testimony concerning events which they had not personally witnessed. A great deal of the testimony in the trial was hearsay. While the admission of hearsay is not fatal to a fair trial in the absence of a jury, the court's major concern in this case was the fact that the defendant Amoco was limited in its cross examination opportunities because of the lack of personal knowledge of the witness presenting the evidence. It was necessary to balance this deprivation against the pragmatic realization that plaintiffs had no other feasible way to present a case for damages which, liability having been established, plaintiffs were entitled to present. This dilemma is adverted to many times hereafter in this opinion, and it was never out of the mind of the court as the many difficult damage decisions were made. . . .

At the conclusion of this opinion, it will become obvious that the plaintiffs, while receiving a very substantial judgment by way of recompense for damages suffered, received considerably less than they sought. This is true in part because several theories of damage were rejected by the court, thus eliminating in toto very substantial claims. It is true also because, in the preparation of detailed damage claims in 1984 after this court's finding of Amoco's liability, exaggeration of claims became the norm, particularly on the part of the communes. The extent of this exaggeration was dramatically highlighted by a comparison of the final claims for damages with much earlier estimates of damages prepared by the communes or arrived at by governmental agencies. This circumstance explains the significant disparity between the total amount claimed by the individuals, communes, departments, and the French State and the amount actually granted, which amount reflects what the court views as non-speculative damages, damages actually suffered and reasonably ascertainable.

Finally, in contemplating the damage awards to communes and many other claimants, it should be noted that their total damages were reduced by the court by substantial amounts which were paid by the French State through various indemnity programs. The cost of these programs is, of course, part of the French State claim.

II. CONCLUSIONS OF LAW

. . . .

In applying, as this court must, the law of France on the subject of damages, the court observes initially that the law of damages in France is substantially identical to the law of the United States. The exigencies of civilized life and the reason and logic common to all men dictate that the laws of all nations, including France and the United States, result in an almost total commonality of principles of law, with such differences as do occur being most often procedural rather than substantive.

The French Civil Code, Code Civil (C. civ.) art. 1382, creates liability based on fault; C. civ. art. 1383 creates liability based upon intentional and negligent acts. The plaintiff has the burden of proving that the conduct of the defendant caused damage to the plaintiff which it has or will certainly suffer, and which can be measured and compensated for by sums of money. Causation must be proved; there is no presumption favoring the victim, who is entitled to indemnification only upon meeting his or her burden of proof of proximate causation.

A plaintiff may not profit from his or her injury beyond full indemnification for damages suffered, and amounts which a plaintiff has received as indemnification from other sources must be deducted from the damages sought from the defendant based upon the presumption that the indemnification paid resulted in the transfer of the right to claim damages to the indemnor.

The principal object of this section of the opinion is to address specific issues concerning various categories of damages claimed in this case and to examine their basis in French law. In pursuit of this goal, the court turns first to the principle asserted by defendants under the rubric of the free public services rule. It is Amoco's contention that the response of any sovereign to an emergency threatening the health or well-being of its citizens or their property is a duty assumed by that sovereign and that, therefore, any expenses incurred in the course of the plaintiffs furnishing public services, which they were obligated to furnish in ordinary course, is not chargeable to Amoco. Examples of the type of activity involved in the claimed application of this rule would be the utilization of fire fighters and military personnel to respond to the oil spill emergency, and to work toward the protection of health and property by cleanup activities. The plaintiffs respond that there is no application of a free public service rule in the instance where the defendants are tort-feasors. . . .

It is the conclusion of the court that the principle of free public services, which, in the ordinary case, bars a municipality or other sovereign from charging the beneficiary of services which the sovereign has an obligation to generally provide, is not applicable to discharge Amoco from liability for the public services furnished in furtherance of the cleanup efforts of the various

from liability for the public services furnished in furtherance of the cleanup efforts of the various plaintiffs after the March, 1978 oil spill.

The court turns to the next question which involves certain specific damage claims. The parties have advanced, with some disagreement, the content of the French law on damages, with the plaintiffs relying on the concept that all damages are recoverable as long as they are direct, personal and certain. This statement is true, but only by adding to it the concept that such damages are recoverable from a defendant only if fault and causation can be demonstrated. The issue arises, *inter alia*, in the context of the validity of the claim by the plaintiffs for the costs of the services of public employees utilized in cleanup activities, or of public officials who expended time in supervision of cleanup activities, or other responses to the cleanup emergency. It is the conclusion of the court that French law allows public bodies, whose employees devoted time to the cleanup or repair or prevention of damage resulting from a defendant's negligence, to claim the value of the expenditure of that time, but only to the extent that the cleanup activities of those employees diverted them from other duties which their sovereign employers would normally expect of them. . . .

A. Public Employee Time and Expenses

To the extent that public employees took time from their regular duties to devote their efforts to the cleanup activity, the communes have a valid claim for the value of that time. To the extent that public employees expended overtime hours on cleanup activities, the communes have a claim for the reasonable value of those overtime hours measured by such amounts as the communes paid for those overtime hours. The voluntary contribution to the cleanup by employees of the communes, other than expenditure of the employee's regular time or compensated overtime, is not a valid claim of the employer. These principles apply not only to the communal employees, but to all public employees including the military.

B. Elected Officials (Communes)

The above principles are the same with regard to elected officials. . . .

C. Travel Costs (Communes)

The travel costs incurred by employees and elected officials of the commune, if the travel was indeed devoted to the necessary activity in connection with the oil spill cleanup, constitute a valid basis for a damage claim.

D. Volunteers (Communes)

. . . .

Money spent in accommodating the volunteers, feeding them, housing them, and providing them with transportation costs are, if appropriately demonstrated by the evidence, compensable items. The value of the volunteers' time, however, computed, is not compensable. . . .

E. Gifts (Communes)

. . .[G]ifts made by governmental bodies to volunteers or expenditures for celebrations in their honor are not appropriate subjects for damage claim. Expenditures arising out of the presence of the volunteers and the military and the necessity of maintaining them, such as food and housing, are compensable items. . . .

F. Costs of Material and Equipment

Claimants are clearly entitled to recover the costs of material and equipment which they were forced to purchase in order to further their cleanup efforts. They are entitled to recover the purchase price of such material and equipment, less the residual value. This assumes that the purchase was reasonable, that the equipment was, in fact, used during the cleanup of the oil spill, and that a residual value in the hands of the commune is demonstrable by the evidence. With respect to the equipment already owned by the claimants, the claimants are entitled to recover a sum measured either by the value of the equipment before the commencement of the use and the value thereafter, or by an imputed reasonable rental value for the equipment during the term of its use, whichever theory is appropriately supported by the evidence.

G.   Costs of Using Public Buildings

. . .[T]he ability of the commune to claim damage to the buildings, if any, resulting from the oil spill cleanup use and to claim as they have extra expenses arising out of that use, such as increased consumption of water, power and telephones, represent adequate compensation for the availability of public buildings for use in service of a public activity. This view does not preclude, however, the claim for rental value damages for the use of buildings if the cleanup use precluded their use for some other profitable purpose.

H.   Coastline and Harbor Restoration (Communes)

Coastline and harbor restoration claims are . . . for work that the communes have already done to repair damage to harbor works, docks, access ways, and the beach as the result of the oil spill, work yet to be done to repair and restore as required by the damages consequent to the cleanup activities, and the work of repair and restoration represented by the Setame program, which reflects what remains to be done to repair the claimed coastline damage. . . .

I.   Lost Enjoyment

. . .[T]he loss of enjoyment claim by the communes is not a claim maintainable under French law. . . .

J.   Effect of Delayed Investment

The delayed investment claim represents the value of the lost use and enjoyment of facilities damaged during the oil spill and the cleanup which, due to insufficient available resources, could not be repaired, restored or replaced immediately subsequent to the oil spill. . . . The court is cognizant of the difficulty of addressing this type of damage in any event, since the roads and other facilities in question were, for the most part, continuously used by the communal public after the oil spill, and some not repaired for several years and some not at all, thus suggesting that the claim for loss of enjoyment of these facilities was not based upon any extensive actual loss of enjoyment, or at least upon a considerably lesser inconvenience to the public than the amount of the claims would suggest.

It is the view of the court that the delay on the part of the commune, whatever its cause, to effectuate appropriate repairs to the facilities damaged by the oil spill cleanup, is an intervening factor which relieves the Amoco parties of the responsibility for the consequences of that delay. Amoco is indeed liable for the damage done to the roads and other facilities, as measured by the cost of repair thus necessitated and the anticipated cost of repair for those damaged facilities which had not yet been repaired due to lack of funds. Such intervening loss of use, however, as delay in repair may have occasioned, is not the responsibility of the Amoco parties nor are they liable therefor.

K.   Lost Image

This element of damage covers the claimed loss by the communes of their reputation and public image resulting from the oil spill. . . . The loss of image harm to the commune is based upon the supposition that persons who would normally have visited the commune for vacation and other recreational purposes were deterred by the loss of image of the commune to the commune's detriment. Yet, within the commune, individual claims by hotels, restaurants, and others address the same issue in a more specific context. Plaintiffs claim that loss of image is compensable in measurable damage, to the extent that it can be demonstrated that this loss of image resulted in specific consequential harm to the commune by virtue of tourists and visitors who might otherwise have come staying away. Yet this is precisely the subject matter of the individual claims for damages by hotels, restaurants, campgrounds, and other businesses within the communes. To award the communes additional damages for this reason would be duplicative. The loss of image claim of the communes will not be recognized.

[L.   Departmental Union of Family Associations Claim [on behalf of its members for loss of enjoyment of life for the families in Finistere] omitted.]

M.   Ecological Damage

    . . . .

The court has recognized the claims of fishermen and fishing associations based upon the reduction in their catches and their resultant profits, as the result of the damage done to the ecosystem by the oil spill, and these claims represent the total entitlement of the plaintiffs. . . .

The claim is in the amount of 164.7 million francs for the estimated cost of a program to implant nine different marine species along the north Brittany coast. This claim is for a program that has not yet been undertaken. Amoco argues, and the court agrees, that the program was not designed to restore the ecosystem to pre-spill conditions but was rather a restoration program motivated in significant part by the marine scientists' desire to bring about improvements in an ecosystem which was deteriorating as the result of causes unconnected to the oil spill.

Because the implantation program has not been undertaken in any significant measure and a large portion of the cost claimed is for planned and not executed programs, the court must take cognizance of the natural restoration of the ecosystem due to intervening time which, in significant measure, has precluded the necessity for much of the implantation programs. Finally, the restoration of the ecosystem for which this claim is made contemplates the restoration of species for which catch statistics reveal no basis for the conclusion that a species decline justifies implantation.

It was reasonable of the French authorities and the interested scientific organizations to cooperate in the contemplation of and experiments with species implantation programs to restore the ecosystem. The cost of such studies was a valid cost incurred under the circumstances and justified by the exigencies of the moment. The anticipated cost of implantation programs not undertaken and no longer justified, by virtue of the natural recovery of or ultimate disclosure of minimal damage to the species involved, is not a recoverable cost.

The claim of 164.7 million francs is unreasonable and is disallowed. The court will recognize . . . certain early efforts in the direction of contemplating and planning implantation programs and some experiments conducted in that regard, and will award the reasonable costs of these programs. . . .

[INTEREST AND CURRENCY QUESTION]

The court has determined that both pre-judgment and post-judgment interest are allowable and should be awarded in this case. The currency of the judgment is determined to be French francs with a date of exchange and exchange rate defined if the parties elect and agree to pay and receive the judgment in dollars. Costs are allowable and will be awarded upon the presentation of appropriate proof. The petition for attorneys fees has been disallowed.

SUMMARY TOTAL [OF AWARDS]

REPUBLIC OF FRANCE	201,993,707.39
COMMUNES	46,191,289.00
CALVEZ CLAIMANTS	2,273,468.00
SPEISER & KRAUSE CLAIMANTS	841,576.73
STERNS, WALKER & GRELL CLAIMANTS	259,000.00
OYSTER GROWERS	813,327.00
FISHERMEN'S ASSOCIATION	-0-
LOCAL FISHING COMMITTEE OF BREST	165,000.00
M. LE BITOUX	-0-
S.A. LA LANGOUSTE	-0-
ENVIRONMENTAL ASSOCIATIONS	300,457.00
TOTAL	252,837,825.12

NOTE

The total award, including prejudgment interest, is 433.6 million francs, approximately U.S. $85.2 million. The total claim of the plaintiffs was in the amount of U.S. $2 billion. See Dirk Johnson, "$85.2 million Fine Levied on Amoco for 1978 Oil Spill," *New York Times*, January 12, 1988, pp. A1, A16. Judge McGarr later added $32.5 million to the damage award because two communes, Cotes-du-Nord and Finistere, were overlooked in the initial litigation. Therefore, the total award now stands at U.S. $117.50 million.

REFERENCES

N.J.J. Gaskell, "The Amoco Cadiz: (II) Limitation and Legal Implications," *Journal of Energy and Natural Resource Law*, Vol. 3 (1985), No. 4, pp. 225-242; R. Kbaier and V. Sebek, "New Trends in Compensation for Oil Pollution Damage, Amoco Cadiz Legal Proceedings and the 1984 Diplomatic Conference on Liability and Compensation," *Marine Policy*, Vol. 9 (1985), pp. 269-279; L. Rosenthal and C. Raper, "Amoco Cadiz and Limitation of Liability for Oil Spill Pollution: Domestic and International Solutions," *Virginia Journal of Natural Resources Law*, Vol. 5 (1985), pp. 259-295; Lothar Gündling, "Amoco Cadiz Incident," R. Bernhardt, ed.,

Encyclopedia of International Law, Vol. 11, *Law of the Sea, Air and Space*, Amsterdam: Elsevier
Science Publishers, 1989, pp. 31-33.

5.   **Emergency Measures**

INTERNATIONAL CONVENTION RELATING TO INTERVENTION ON THE
HIGH SEAS IN CASES OF OIL POLLUTION CASUALTIES, WITH ANNEX.
Done at Brussels, November 29, 1969
26 UST 765; TIAS 8068.

. . . .

Article I

1. Parties to the present Convention may take such measures on the high seas as may be
necessary to prevent, mitigate or eliminate grave and imminent danger to their coastline or related
interests from pollution or threat of pollution of the sea by oil, following upon a maritime
casualty or acts related to such a casualty, which may reasonably be expected to result in major
harmful consequences.

2. However, no measure shall be taken under the present Convention against any warship or
other ship owned or operated by a State and used, for the time being, only on government non-
commercial service.

Article II

For the purposes of the present Convention:

1. "maritime casualty" means a collision of ships, stranding or other incident of navigation,
or other occurrence on board a ship or external to it resulting in material damage or imminent
threat of material damage to a ship or cargo;

. . . .

4. "related interests" means the interests of a coastal State directly affected or threatened by the
maritime casualty, such as:

(a) maritime coastal, port or estuarine activities, including fisheries activities, constituting an
essential means of livelihood of the persons concerned;

(b) tourist attractions of the area concerned;

(c) the health of the coastal population and the well-being of the area concerned, including
conservation of living marine resources and of wildlife;

. . . .

Article III

When a coastal State is exercising the right to take measures in accordance with Article I, the following provisions shall apply:

(a) before taking any measures, a coastal State shall proceed to consultations with other States affected by the maritime casualty, particularly with the flag State or States;

(b) the coastal State shall notify without delay the proposed measures to any persons physical or corporate known to the coastal State, or made known to it during the consultations, to have interests which can reasonably be expected to be affected by those measures. The coastal State shall take into account any views they may submit;

(c) before any measure is taken, the coastal State may proceed to a consultation with independent experts, whose names shall be chosen from a list maintained by the Organization;

(d) in cases of extreme urgency requiring measures to be taken immediately, the coastal State may take measures rendered necessary by the urgency of the situation, without prior notification or consultation or without continuing consultations already begun;

(e) a coastal State shall, before taking such measures and during their course, use its best endeavors to avoid any risk to human life, and to afford persons in distress any assistance of which they may stand in need, and in appropriate cases to facilitate the repatriation of ships' crews, and to raise no obstacle thereto;

(f) measures which have been taken in application of Article I shall be notified without delay to the States and to the known physical or corporate persons concerned, as well as to the Secretary-General of the Organization.

. . . .

Article V

1. Measures taken by the coastal State in accordance with Article I shall be proportionate to the damage actual or threatened to it.

2. Such measures shall not go beyond what is reasonably necessary to achieve the end mentioned in Article I and shall cease as soon as that end has been achieved; they shall not unnecessarily interfere with the rights and interests of the flag State, third States and of any persons, physical or corporate, concerned.

3. In considering whether the measures are proportionate to the damage, account shall be taken of:

(a) the extent and probability of imminent damage if those measures are not taken; and

(b) the likelihood of those measures being effective; and

(c) the extent of the damage which may be caused by such measures.

Article VI

Any Party which has taken measures in contravention of the provisions of the present Convention causing damage to others, shall be obliged to pay compensation to the extent of the damage caused by measures which exceed those reasonably necessary to achieve the end mentioned in Article I . . . .

NOTE

For intervention on the high sea in cases of non-oil pollution casualties, see Protocol Relating to Intervention on the High Seas in Cases of Pollution by Substances Other Than Oil, Done at London on November 2, 1973, TIAS 10561; *International Legal Materials*, Vol. 13 (1974), pp. 615-620.

1982 UNITED NATIONS CONVENTION ON THE LAW OF THE SEA

Article 221
Measures to avoid pollution arising from maritime casualties

1. Nothing in this Part [XII Protection and Preservation of the Marine Environment (Articles 192-237)] shall prejudice the right of States, pursuant to international law, both customary and conventional, to take and enforce measures beyond the territorial sea proportionate to the actual or threatened damage to protect their coastline or related interests, including fishing, from pollution or threat of pollution following upon a maritime casualty or acts relating to such a casualty, which may reasonably be expected to result in major harmful consequences.

2. For the purposes of this article, "maritime casualty" means a collision of vessels, stranding or other incident of navigation, or other occurrence on board a vessel or external to it resulting in material damage or imminent threat of material damage to a vessel or cargo.

REFERENCES

Dennis M. O'Connell, "Reflections on Brussels: IMCO and the 1969 Pollution Conventions," *Cornell International Law Journal*, Vol. 3 (1970), pp. 161-188; R.P. Cundick, "Oil Pollution: Negotiation--An Alternative to Intervention," *International Lawyer*, Vol. 6 (1972), pp. 34-41; Y. Dinstein, "Oil Pollution by Ships and Freedom of the High Seas," *Journal of Maritime Law and Commerce*, Vol. 3 (1972), pp. 363-374; R.P. Cundick, "High Seas Intervention; Parameters of Unilateral Action," *San Diego Law Review*, Vol. 10 (1973), pp. 514-558; *Intervention on the High Seas Act*, Senate Report 93-482; 93rd Cong., 1st Sess., November 2, 1973); W.K. Bissell, "Intervention on the High Seas: An American Approach Employing Community Standards," *Journal of Maritime Law and Commerce*, Vol. 7 (1976), pp. 718-735; D.W. Abecassis, *The Law and Practice Relating to Oil Pollution from Ships*, London: Butterworths, 1978; Trevor O'Neill, "Oil Spill Contingency Plans and Policies in Norway and the United Kingdom," *Coastal Zone Management Journal*, Vol. 8 (1980), pp. 289-317.

6.   **Jurisdiction and Enforcement**

1982 UNITED NATIONS CONVENTION ON THE LAW OF THE SEA

Article 211
Pollution from vessels

1. States, acting through the competent international organization or general diplomatic conference, shall establish international rules and standards to prevent, reduce and control pollution of the marine environment from vessels and promote the adoption, in the same manner, wherever appropriate, of routing systems designed to minimize the threat of accidents which might cause pollution of the marine environment, including the coastline, and pollution damage to the related interests of coastal States. Such rules and standards shall, in the same manner, be re-examined from time to time as necessary.

2. States shall adopt laws and regulations for the prevention, reduction and control of pollution of the marine environment from vessels flying their flag or of their registry. Such laws and regulations shall at least have the same effect as that of generally accepted international rules and standards established through the competent international organization or general diplomatic conference.

3. States which establish particular requirements for the prevention, reduction and control of pollution of the marine environment as a condition for the entry of foreign vessels into their ports or internal waters or for a call at their off-shore terminals shall give due publicity to such requirements and shall communicate them to the competent international organization. Whenever such requirements are established in identical form by two or more coastal States in an endeavor to harmonize policy, the communication shall indicate which States are participating in such cooperative arrangements. Every State shall require the master of a vessel flying its flag or of its registry, when navigating within the territorial sea of a State participating in such cooperative arrangements, to furnish, upon the request of that State, information as to whether it is proceeding to a State of the same region participating in such cooperative arrangements and, if so, to indicate whether it complies with the port entry requirements of that State. This article is without prejudice to the continued exercise by a vessel of its right of innocent passage or to the application of article 25, paragraph 2.

4. Coastal States may, in the exercise of their sovereignty within their territorial sea, adopt laws and regulations for the prevention, reduction and control of marine pollution from foreign vessels, including vessels exercising the right of innocent passage. Such laws and regulations shall, in accordance with Part II, section 3, not hamper innocent passage of foreign vessels.

5. Coastal States, for the purpose of enforcement as provided for in section 6 [articles 213-222], may in respect of their exclusive economic zones adopt laws and regulations for the prevention, reduction and control of pollution from vessels conforming to and giving effect to generally accepted international rules and standards established through the competent international organization or general diplomatic conference.

6. (a) Where the international rules and standards referred to in paragraph 1 are inadequate to meet special circumstances and coastal States have reasonable grounds for believing that a particular, clearly defined area of their respective exclusive economic zones is an area where the adoption of special mandatory measures for the prevention of pollution from vessels is required for recognized technical reasons in relation to its oceanographical and ecological conditions, as well as

its utilization or the protection of its resources and the particular character of its traffic, the coastal States, after appropriate consultations through the competent international organization with any other States concerned, may, for that area, direct a communication to that organization, submitting scientific and technical evidence in support and information on necessary reception facilities. Within 12 months after receiving such a communication, the organization shall determine whether the conditions in that area correspond to the requirements set out above. If the organization so determines, the coastal States may, for that area, adopt laws and regulations for the prevention, reduction and control of pollution from vessels implementing such international rules and standards or navigational practices as are made applicable, through the organization, for special areas. These laws and regulations shall not become applicable to foreign vessels until 15 months after the submission of the communication to the organization.

(b) The coastal States shall publish the limits of any such particular, clearly defined area.

(c) If the coastal States intend to adopt additional laws and regulations for the same area for the prevention, reduction and control of pollution from vessels, they shall, when submitting the aforesaid communication, at the same time notify the organization thereof. Such additional laws and regulations may relate to discharges or navigational practices but shall not require foreign vessels to observe design, construction, manning or equipment standards other than generally accepted international rules and standards; they shall become applicable to foreign vessels 15 months after the submission of the communication to the organization, provided that the organization agrees within 12 months after the submission of the communication.

7. The international rules and standards referred to in this article should include *inter alia* those relating to prompt notification to coastal States, whose coastline or related interests may be affected by incidents, including maritime casualties, which involve discharges or probability of discharges.

Article 217
Enforcement by flag States

1. States shall ensure compliance by vessels flying their flags or of their registry with applicable international rules and standards, established through the competent international organization or general diplomatic conference, and with their laws and regulations adopted in accordance with this Convention for the prevention, reduction and control of pollution of the marine environment from vessels and shall accordingly adopt laws and regulations and take other measures necessary for their implementation. Flag States shall provide for the effective enforcement of such rules, standards, laws and regulations, irrespective of where a violation occurs.

2. States shall, in particular, take appropriate measures in order to ensure that vessels flying their flag or of their registry are prohibited from sailing, until they can proceed to sea in compliance with the requirements of the international rules and standards referred to in paragraph 1, including requirements in respect of design, construction, equipment and manning of vessels.

3. States shall ensure that vessels flying their flag or of their registry carry on board certificates required by and issued pursuant to international rules and standards referred to in paragraph 1. States shall ensure that vessels flying their flag are periodically inspected in order to verify that such certificates are in conformity with the actual condition of the vessels. These certificates shall be accepted by other States as evidence of the condition of the vessels and shall be

regarded as having the same force as certificates issued by them, unless there are clear grounds for believing that the condition of the vessel does not correspond substantially with the particulars of the certificates.

4. If a vessel commits a violation of rules and standards established through the competent international organization or general diplomatic conference, the flag State, without prejudice to articles 218, 220, and 228, shall provide for immediate investigation and where appropriate institute proceedings in respect of the alleged violation irrespective of where the violation occurred or where the pollution caused by such violation has occurred or has been spotted.

5. Flag States conducting an investigation of the violation may request the assistance of any other State whose cooperation could be useful in clarifying the circumstances of the case. States shall endeavor to meet appropriate requests of flag States.

6. States shall, at the written request of any State, investigate any violation alleged to have been committed by vessels flying their flag. If satisfied that sufficient evidence is available to enable proceedings to be brought in respect of the alleged violation, flag States shall without delay institute such proceedings in accordance with their laws.

7. Flag States shall promptly inform the requesting State and the competent international organization of the action taken and its outcome. Such information shall be available to all States.

8. Penalties provided for by the laws and regulations of States for vessels flying their flag shall be adequate in severity to discourage violations wherever they occur.

Article 218
Enforcement by Port States

1. When a vessel is voluntarily within a port or at an off-shore terminal of a State, that State may undertake investigations and, where the evidence so warrants, institute proceedings in respect of any discharge from that vessel outside the internal waters, territorial sea or exclusive economic zone of that State in violation of applicable international rules and standards established through the competent international organization or general diplomatic conference.

2. No proceedings pursuant to paragraph 1 shall be instituted in respect of a discharge violation in the internal waters, territorial sea or exclusive economic zone of another State unless requested by that State, the flag State, or a State damaged or threatened by the discharge violation, or unless the violation has caused or is likely to cause pollution in the internal waters, territorial sea or exclusive economic zone of the State instituting the proceedings.

3. When a vessel is voluntarily within a port or at an off-shore terminal of State, that State shall, as far as practicable, comply with requests from any State for investigation of a discharge violation referred to in paragraph 1, believed to have occurred in, caused, or threatened damage to the internal waters, territorial sea or exclusive economic zone of the requesting State. It shall likewise, as far as practicable, comply with requests from the flag State for investigation of such a violation, irrespective of where the violation occurred.

4. The records of the investigation carried out by a port State pursuant to this article shall be transmitted upon request to the flag State or to the coastal State. Any proceedings instituted by the port State on the basis of such an investigation may, subject to section 7 [articles 223-233], be

suspended at the request of the coastal State when the violation has occurred within its internal waters, territorial sea or exclusive economic zone. The evidence and records of the case, together with any bond or other financial security posted with the authorities of the port State, shall in that event be transmitted to the coastal State. Such transmittal shall preclude the continuation of proceedings in the port State.

Article 219
Measures relating to seaworthiness of vessels to avoid pollution

Subject to section 7 [articles 223-233], States which, upon request or on their own initiative, have ascertained that a vessel within one of their ports or at one of their offshore terminals is in violation of applicable international rules and standards relating to seaworthiness of vessels and thereby threatens damage to the marine environment shall, as far as practicable, take administrative measures to prevent the vessel from sailing. Such States may permit the vessel to proceed only to the nearest appropriate repair yard and, upon removal of the causes of the violation, shall permit the vessel to continue immediately.

Article 220
Enforcement by coastal States

1. When a vessel is voluntarily within a port or at an off-shore terminal of a State, that State may, subject to section 7 [articles 223-233], institute proceedings in respect of any violation of its laws and regulations adopted in accordance with this Convention or applicable international rules and standards for the prevention, reduction and control of pollution from vessels when the violation has occurred within the territorial sea or the exclusive economic zone of that State.

2. Where there are clear grounds for believing that a vessel navigating in the territorial sea of a State has, during its passage therein, violated laws and regulations of that State adopted in accordance with this Convention or applicable international rules and standards for the prevention, reduction and control of pollution from vessels, that State, without prejudice to the application of the relevant provisions of Part II, section 3, [Innocent Passage in the Territorial Sea, articles 17-32] may undertake physical inspection of the vessel relating to the violation and may, where the evidence so warrants, institute proceedings, including detention of the vessel, in accordance with its laws, subject to the provisions of section 7.

3. Where there are clear grounds for believing that a vessel navigating in the exclusive economic zone or the territorial sea of a State has, in the exclusive economic zone, committed a violation of applicable international rules and standards for the prevention, reduction and control of pollution from vessels or laws and regulations of that State conforming and giving effect to such rules and standards, that State may require the vessel to give information regarding its identity and port of registry, its last and its next port of call and other relevant information required to establish whether a violation has occurred.

4. States shall adopt laws and regulations and take other measures so that vessels flying their flag comply with requests for information pursuant to paragraph 3.

5. Where there are clear grounds for believing that a vessel navigating in the exclusive economic zone or the territorial sea of a State has, in the exclusive economic zone, committed a violation referred to in paragraph 3 resulting in a substantial discharge causing or threatening significant pollution of the marine environment, that State may undertake physical inspection of the vessel for matters relating to the violation if the vessel has refused to give information or if the

information supplied by the vessel is manifestly at variance with the evident factual situation and if the circumstances of the case justify such inspection.

6. Where there is clear objective evidence that a vessel navigating in the exclusive economic zone or the territorial sea of a State has, in the exclusive economic zone, committed a violation referred to in paragraph 3 resulting in a discharge causing major damage or threat of major damage to the coastline or related interests of the coastal State, or to any resources of its territorial sea or exclusive economic zone, that State may, subject to section 7, provided that the evidence so warrants, institute proceedings, including detention of the vessel, in accordance with its laws.

7. Notwithstanding the provisions of paragraph 6, whenever appropriate procedures have been established, either through the competent international organization or as otherwise agreed, whereby compliance with requirements for bonding or other appropriate financial security has been assured, the coastal State if bounded by such procedures shall allow the vessel to proceed.

8. The provisions of paragraphs 3, 4, 5, 6, and 7 also apply in respect of national laws and regulations adopted pursuant to article 211, paragraph 6.

Article 223
Measures to facilitate proceedings

In proceedings instituted pursuant to this Part, States shall take measures to facilitate the hearing of witnesses and the admission of evidence submitted by authorities of another State, or by the competent international organization, and shall facilitate the attendance at such proceedings of official representatives of the competent international organization, the flag State and any State affected by pollution arising out of any violation. The official representatives attending such proceedings shall have such rights and duties as may be provided under national laws and regulations or international law.

Article 224
Exercise of powers of enforcement

The powers of enforcement against foreign vessels under this Part may only be exercised by officials or by warships, military aircraft, or other ships or aircraft clearly marked and identifiable as being on government service and authorized to that effect.

Article 225
Duty to avoid adverse consequences in the exercise of the powers of enforcement

In the exercise under this Convention of their powers of enforcement against foreign vessels, States shall not endanger the safety of navigation or otherwise create any hazard to a vessel, or bring it to an unsafe port or anchorage, or expose the marine environment to an unreasonable risk.

Article 226
Investigation of foreign vessels

1. (a) States shall not delay a foreign vessel longer than is essential for purposes of the investigations provided for in articles 216, 218 and 220. Any physical inspection of a foreign vessel shall be limited to an examination of such certificates, records or other documents as the vessel is required to carry by generally accepted international rules and standards or of any similar documents which it is carrying; further physical inspection of the vessel may be undertaken only

documents which it is carrying; further physical inspection of the vessel may be undertaken only after such an examination and only when:

(i) there are clear grounds for believing that the condition of the vessel or its equipment does not correspond substantially with the particulars of those documents;

(ii) the contents of such documents are not sufficient to confirm or verify a suspected violation; or

(iii) the vessel is not carrying valid certificates and records.

(b) If the investigation indicates a violation of applicable laws and regulations or international rules and standards for the protection and preservation of the marine environment, release shall be made promptly subject to reasonable procedures such as bonding or other appropriate financial security.

(c) Without prejudice to applicable international rules and standards relating to the seaworthiness of vessels, the release of a vessel may, whenever it would present an unreasonable threat of damage to the marine environment, be refused or made conditional upon proceeding to the nearest appropriate repair yard. Where release has been refused or made conditional, the flag State of the vessel must be promptly notified, and may seek release of the vessel in accordance with Part XV [Settlement of Disputes, articles 279-299].

2. States shall cooperate to develop procedures for the avoidance of unnecessary physical inspection of vessels at sea.

Article 227
Non-discrimination with respect to foreign vessels

In exercising their rights and performing their duties under this Part, States shall not discriminate in form or in fact against vessels of any other State.

Article 228
Suspension and restrictions on institution of proceedings

1. Proceedings to impose penalties in respect of any violation of applicable laws and regulations or international rules and standards relating to the prevention, reduction and control of pollution from vessels committed by a foreign vessel beyond the territorial sea of the State instituting proceedings shall be suspended upon the taking of proceedings to impose penalties in respect of corresponding charges by the flag State within six months of the date on which proceedings were first instituted, unless those proceedings relate to a case of major damage to the coastal State or the flag State in question has repeatedly disregarded its obligation to enforce effectively the applicable international rules and standards in respect of violations committed by its vessels. The flag State shall in due course make available to the State previously instituting proceedings a full dossier of the case and the records of the proceedings, whenever the flag State has requested the suspension of proceedings in accordance with this article. When proceedings instituted by the flag State have been brought to a conclusion, the suspended proceedings shall be terminated. Upon payment of costs incurred in respect of such proceedings, any bond posted or other financial security provided in connection with the suspended proceedings shall be released by the coastal State.

2. Proceedings to impose penalties on foreign vessels shall not be instituted after the expiry of three years from the date on which the violation was committed, and shall not be taken by any State in the event of proceedings having been instituted by another State subject to the provisions set out in paragraph 1.

3. The provisions of this article are without prejudice to the right of the flag State to take any measures, including proceedings to impose penalties, according to its laws irrespective of prior proceedings by another State.

Article 229
Institution of civil proceedings

Nothing in this Convention affects the institution of civil proceedings in respect of any claim for loss or damage resulting from pollution of the marine environment.

Article 230
Monetary penalties and the observance of recognized rights of the accused

1. Monetary penalties only may be imposed with respect to violations of national laws and regulations or applicable international rules and standards for the prevention, reduction and control of pollution of the marine environment, committed by foreign vessels beyond the territorial sea.

2. Monetary penalties only may be imposed with respect to violations of national laws and regulations or applicable international rules and standards for the prevention, reduction and control of pollution of the marine environment, committed by foreign vessels in the territorial sea, except in the case of a willful and serious act of pollution in the territorial sea.

3. In the conduct of proceedings in respect of such violations committed by a foreign vessel which may result in the imposition of penalties, recognized rights of the accused shall be observed.

Article 231
Notification to the flag State and other States concerned

States shall promptly notify the flag State and any other State concerned of any measures taken pursuant to section 6 [articles 213-222] against foreign vessels, and shall submit to the flag State all official reports concerning such measures. However, with respect to violations committed in the territorial sea, the foregoing obligations of the coastal State apply only to such measures as are taken in proceedings. The diplomatic agents or consular officers and where possible the maritime authority of the flag State, shall be immediately informed of any such measures taken pursuant to section 6 against foreign vessels.

Article 232
Liability of States arising from enforcement measures

States shall be liable for damage or loss attributable to them arising from measures taken pursuant to section 6 [articles 213-222] when such measures are unlawful or exceed those reasonably required in the light of available information. States shall provide for recourse in their courts for actions in respect of such damage or loss.

Article 233
Safeguards with respect to straits used for international navigation

Nothing in sections 5 [articles 207-212], 6 [articles 213-222], and 7 [articles 223-233] affects the legal regime of straits used for international navigation. However, if a foreign ship other than those referred to in section 10 [article 236] has committed a violation of the laws and regulations referred to in article 42, paragraph 1(a) and (b), causing or threatening major damage to the marine environment of the straits, the States bordering the straits may take appropriate enforcement measures if so shall respect *mutatis mutandis* the provisions of this section.

Article 236
Sovereign immunity

The provisions of this Convention regarding the protection and preservation of the marine environment do not apply to any warship, naval auxiliary, other vessels or aircraft owned or operated by a State and used, for the time being, only on government non-commercial service. However, each State shall ensure, by the adoption of appropriate measures not impairing operations or operational capabilities of such vessels or aircraft owned or operated by it, that such vessels or aircraft act in a manner consistent, so far as is reasonable and practicable, with this Convention.

REFERENCES

J. Peter A. Bernhardt, "A Schematic Analysis of Vessel-Source Pollution: Prescriptive and Enforcement Regimes in the Law of the Sea Conference," *Virginia Journal of International Law*, Vol. 20 (1980), pp. 265-311; W.J. Fenwick, "Legal Limits on the Use of Force by Canadian Warships Engaged in Law Enforcement," *Canadian Yearbook of International Law*, Vol. 18 (1980), pp. 113-145; Sally A. Messe, "When Jurisdiction Interests Collide: International, Domestic, and State Efforts to Prevent Vessel Source Oil Pollution," *Ocean Development and International Law*, Vol. 12 (1982), pp. 71-139; Paul Stephen Dempsey, "Compliance and Enforcement in International Law--Oil Pollution of the Marine Environment by Ocean Vessels," *Northwest Journal of International Law & Business*, Vol. 6 (1984), pp. 459-561; I.A. Shearer, "Problems of Jurisdiction and Law Enforcement Against Delinquent Vessels," *International and Comparative Law Quarterly*, Vol. 35 (1986), pp. 320-343; Michael A. Titz, "Port State Control Versus Marine Environmental Pollution," *Maritime Policy and Management*, Vol. 16, No. 3 (July-September 1989), pp. 189-211.

D. OCEAN DUMPING.

CONVENTION ON THE PREVENTION OF MARINE POLLUTION BY DUMPING OF WASTES AND OTHER MATTERS
Done at London on December 29, 1972
26 UST 2403; TIAS 8165.

Article I

Contracting Parties shall individually and collectively promote the effective control of all sources of pollution of the marine environment, and pledge themselves especially to take all practicable steps to prevent the pollution of the sea by the dumping of waste and other matter that is liable to create hazards to human health, to harm living resources and marine life, to damage

is liable to create hazards to human health, to harm living resources and marine life, to damage amenities or to interfere with other legitimate uses of the sea.

Article II

Contracting Parties shall, as provided for in the following Articles, take effective measures individually, according to their scientific, technical and economic capabilities, and collectively, to prevent marine pollution caused by dumping and shall harmonize their policies in this regard.

Article III

For the purposes of this Convention:

1. a. "Dumping" means:

> (i) any deliberate disposal at sea of wastes or other matter from vessels, aircraft, platforms or other man-made structures at sea;

> (ii) any deliberate disposal at sea of vessels, aircraft, platforms or other man-made structures at sea;

b. "Dumping" does not include:

> (i) the disposal at sea of wastes or other matter incidental to, or derived from the normal operations of vessels, aircraft, platforms or other man-made structures at sea and their equipment, other than wastes or other matter transported by or to vessels, aircraft, platforms or other man-made structures at sea, operating for the purpose of disposal of such matter or derived from the treatment of such wastes or other matter on such vessels, aircraft, platforms or structures;

> (ii) placement of matter for a purpose other than the mere disposal thereof, provided that such placement is not contrary to the aims of this Convention;

c. The disposal of wastes or other matter directly arising from, or related to the exploration, exploitation and associated off-shore processing of seabed mineral resources will not be covered by the provisions of this Convention.

. . . .

Article IV

1. In accordance with the provisions of this Convention, Contracting Parties shall prohibit the dumping of any wastes or other matter in whatever form or condition except as otherwise specified below:--

a. The dumping of wastes or other matter listed in Annex I is prohibited;

b. The dumping of wastes or other matter listed in Annex II requires a prior special permit;

c. The dumping of all other wastes or matter requires a prior general permit.

2. Any permit shall be issued only after careful consideration of all the factors set forth in Annex III, including prior studies of the characteristics of the dumping site, as set forth in Sections B and C of that Annex.

3. No provision of this Convention is to be interpreted as preventing a Contracting Party from prohibiting, insofar as that Party is concerned, the dumping of wastes or other matter not mentioned in Annex I. That Party shall notify such measures to the Organization.

Article V

1. The provisions of Article IV shall not apply when it is necessary to secure the safety of human life or of vessels, aircraft, platforms or other man-made structures at sea in cases of force majeure caused by stress of weather, or in any case which constitutes a danger to human life or a real threat to vessels, aircraft, platforms or other man-made structures at sea, if dumping appears to be the only way of averting the threat and if there is every probability that the damage consequent upon such dumping will be less than would otherwise occur. Such dumping shall be so conducted as to minimize the likelihood of damage to human or marine life and shall be reported forthwith to the Organization.

2. A Contracting Party may issue a special permit as an exception to Article IV (1)(a), in emergencies, posing unacceptable risk relating to human health and admitting no other feasible solution. Before doing so the Party shall consult any other country or countries that are likely to be affected and the Organization which, after consulting other Parties, and international organizations as appropriate, shall, in accordance with Article XIV promptly recommend to the Party the most appropriate procedures to adopt. The Party shall follow these recommendations to the maximum extent feasible consistent with the time within which action must be taken and with the general obligation to avoid damage to the marine environment and shall inform the Organization of the action it takes. The Parties pledge themselves to assist one another in such situations.

3. Any Contracting Party may waive its rights under Paragraph 2 at the time of, or subsequent to ratification of, or accession to this Convention.

Article VI

1. Each Contracting Party shall designate an appropriate authority or authorities to:

a. issue special permits which shall be required prior to, and for, the dumping of matter listed in Annex II and in the circumstances provided for in Article V (2);

b. issue general permits which shall be required prior to and for the dumping of all other matters;

c. keep records of the nature and quantities of all matter permitted to be dumped and the location, time and method of dumping;

d. monitor individually, or in collaboration with other Parties and competent international organizations, the condition of the seas for the purposes of this Convention.

2. The appropriate authority or authorities of a Contracting Party shall issue prior special or general permits in accordance with paragraph 1 in respect of matter intended for dumping:

a. loaded in its territory;

b. loaded by a vessel or aircraft registered in its territory or flying its flag, when the loading occurs in the territory of a State not party to this Convention.

3.   In issuing permits under sub-paragraphs 1a and b above, the appropriate authority or authorities shall comply with Annex III, together with such additional criteria, measures and requirements as they may consider relevant.

4.   Each Contracting Party, directly or through a Secretariat established under a regional agreement, shall report to the Organization, and where appropriate to other Parties, the information specified in sub-paragraphs c and d of paragraph 1 above, and the criteria, measures and requirements it adopts in accordance with paragraph 3 above.   The procedure to be followed and the nature of such reports shall be agreed by the Parties in consultation.

Article VII

1.   Each Contracting Party shall apply the measures required to implement the present Convention to all:

a. vessels and aircraft registered in its territory or flying its flag;

b. vessels and aircraft loading in its territory or territorial seas matter which is to be dumped;

c.   vessels and aircraft and fixed or floating platforms under its jurisdiction believed to be engaged in dumping.

2.   Each Party shall take in its territory appropriate measures to prevent and punish conduct in contravention of the provisions of this Convention.

3.   The Parties agree to cooperate in the development of procedures for the effective application of this Convention particularly on the high seas, including procedures for the reporting of vessels and aircraft observed dumping in contravention of the Convention.

4.   This Convention shall not apply to those vessels and aircraft entitled to sovereign immunity under international law.   However, each party shall ensure by the adoption of appropriate measures that such vessels and aircraft owned or operated by it act in a manner consistent with the object and purpose of this Convention. . . .

5.   Nothing in this Convention shall affect the right of each Party to adopt other measures, in accordance with the principles of international law, to prevent dumping at sea.

. . . .

ANNEX I

1.   Organohalogen compounds.

2.   Mercury and mercury compounds.

3. Cadmium and cadmium compounds.

4. Persistent plastics and other persistent synthetic materials, for example, netting and ropes, which may float or may remain in suspension in the sea in such a manner as to interfere materially with fishing, navigation or other legitimate uses of the sea.

5. Crude oil, fuel oil, heavy diesel oil, and lubricating oils, hydraulic fluids, and any mixtures containing any of these, taken on board for the purpose of dumping.

6. High-level radioactive wastes or other high-level radioactive matter, defined on public health, biological or other grounds, by the competent international body in this field, at present the International Atomic Energy Agency, as unsuitable for dumping at sea.

7. Materials in whatever form (e.g., solids, liquids, semi-liquids, gases or in a living state) produced for biological and chemical warfare.

8. The preceding paragraphs of this Annex do not apply to substances which are rapidly rendered harmless by physical, chemical or biological processes in the sea provided they do not:

(i) make edible marine organisms unpalatable, or

(ii) endanger human health or that of domestic animals. . . .

9. This Annex does not apply to wastes or other materials (e.g., sewage sludges and dredged spoils) containing the matters referred to in paragraphs 1-5 above as trace contaminants. Such wastes shall be subject to the provisions of Annexes II and III as appropriate.

ANNEX II

The following substances and materials requiring special care are listed for the purposes of Article VI 1a.

A. Wastes containing significant amounts of the matters listed below:

arsenic
lead
copper and their compounds
zinc
organosilicon compounds
cyanides
fluorides
pesticides and their by-products not covered in Annex I.

B. In the issue of permits for the dumping of large quantities of acids and alkalis, consideration shall be given to the possible presence in such wastes of the substances listed in paragraph A and to the following additional substances:

beryllium
chromium
nickel and their compounds

vanadium

C. Container, scrap metal and other bulky wastes liable to sink to the sea bottom which may present a serious obstacle to fishing or navigation.

D. Radioactive wastes or other radioactive matter not included in Annex I. In the issue of permits for the dumping of this matter, the Contracting Parties should take full account of the recommendations of the competent international body in this field, at present the International Atomic Energy Agency.

ANNEX III

Provisions to be considered in establishing criteria governing the issue of permits for the dumping of matter at sea, taking into account Article IV 2 include:

A. Characteristics and Composition of the Matter.

1. Total amount and average composition of matter dumped (e.g., per year).

2. Form (e.g., solid, sludge, liquid, or gaseous).

3. Properties: physical (e.g., solubility and density), chemical and biochemical (e.g., oxygen demand, nutrients) and biological (e.g., presence of viruses, bacteria, yeasts, parasites).

4. Toxicity.

5. Persistence: physical, chemical and biological.

6. Accumulation and biotransformation in biological materials or sediments.

7. Susceptibility to physical, chemical and biochemical changes and interaction in the aquatic environment with other dissolved organic and inorganic materials.

8. Probability of production of taints or other changes reducing marketability of resources (fish, shellfish, etc.).

B.   Characteristics of Dumping Site and Method of Deposit

1. Location (e.g., coordinates of the dumping area, depth and distance from the coast), location in relation to other areas (e.g., amenity areas, spawning, nursery and fishing areas and exploitable resources).

2. Rate of disposal per specific period (e.g., quantity per day, per week, per month).

3. Methods of packaging and containment, if any.

4. Initial dilution achieved by proposed method of release.

5. Dispersal characteristics (e.g., effects of currents, tides and wind on horizontal transport and vertical mixing).

6. Water characteristics (e.g., temperature, pH, salinity, stratification, oxygen indices of pollution--dissolved oxygen (DO), chemical oxygen demand (COD), biochemical oxygen demand (BOD)--nitrogen present in organic and mineral form including ammonia, suspended matter, other nutrients and productivity).

7. Bottom characteristics (e.g., topography, geo-chemical and geological characteristics and biological productivity).

8. Existence and effects of other dumpings which have been made in the dumping area (e.g., heavy metal background reading and organic carbon content).

9. In issuing a permit for dumping, Contracting Parties should consider whether an adequate scientific basis exists for assessing the consequences of such dumping, as outlined in this Annex, taking into account seasonal variations.

C.   General Considerations and Conditions

1. Possible effects on amenities (e.g., presence of floating or stranded material, turbidity, objectionable odor, discoloration and foaming).

2. Possible effects on marine life, fish and shellfish culture, fish stocks and fisheries, seaweed harvesting and culture.

3. Possible effects on other uses of the sea (e.g., impairment of water quality for industrial use, underwater corrosion of structures, interference with ship operations from floating materials, interference with fishing or navigation through deposit of waste or solid objects on the sea floor and protection of areas of special importance for scientific or conservation purposes).

4. The practical availability of alternative land-based methods of treatment, disposal or elimination, or of treatment to render the matter less harmful for dumping at sea.

NOTE

On October 12, 1978, the Third Consultative Meeting of the Contracting Parties to the 1972 London Convention adopted a resolution on incineration at sea which made the following amendments to Annex I and Annex II of the Convention:

The following paragraph shall be added to Annex I:

10. Paragraphs 1 and 5 of this Annex do not apply to the disposal of wastes or other matter referred to in these paragraphs by means of incineration at sea. Incineration of such wastes or other matter at sea requires a prior special permit. In the issue of special permits for incineration the Contracting Parties shall apply the Regulations for the Control of Incineration of Wastes and Other Matter at Sea set forth in the Addendum to this Annex (which shall constitute an integral part of this Annex) and take full account of the Technical Guidelines on the Control of Incineration of Wastes and Other Matter at Sea adopted by the Contracting parties in consultation.

The following paragraph shall be added to Annex II:

E. In the issue of special permits for the incineration of substances and materials listed in this Annex, the Contracting Parties shall apply the Regulations for the Control of Incineration of Wastes and Other Matter at Sea set forth in the Addendum to Annex I and take full account of the Technical Guidelines on the Control of Incineration of Wastes and Other Matter at Sea adopted by the Contracting Parties in consultation, to the extent specified in these Regulations and Guidelines [Addendum omitted.]

International Legal Materials, Vol. 18 (1979), pp. 510-516 [Addendum in pp. 511-516].

The sub-seabed disposal of high-level radioactive wastes completely isolated from the biosphere is not covered by the 1972 London Convention, see Hubertus Welsh, "The London Dumping Convention and Sub-Seabed Disposal of Radioactive Wastes," *German Yearbook of International Law*, Vol. 28 (1985), pp. 322-354. For a discussion of the question of dumping nuclear or radioactive wastes at sea, see also David A. Deese, *Nuclear Power and Radioactive Waste: A Sub-Seabed Disposal Option?* Lexington, Mass.: Lexington Books, 1978; Robert A. Frosch, Charles D. Hollister and David A. Deese, "Radioactive Waste Disposal in the Ocean," *Ocean Yearbook*, Vol. 1, Chicago: University of Chicago Press, 1977, pp. 340-349; Anthony M. Michaelis, "Nuclear Waste: The Battle for Gorleben," *Interdisciplinary Science Reviews* (London), Vol. 5, No. 4 (December 1980), pp. 255-259; Daniel P. Finn, "Ocean Disposal of Radioactive Wastes: The Obligation of International Cooperation to Protect the Marine Environment," *Virginia Journal of International Law*, Vol. 21 (1981), pp. 621-690; George D. Haimbaugh, Jr., "Protecting the Seas from Nuclear Pollution," *South Carolina Law Review*, Vol. 33 (1981), pp. 197-225; Gunther Handl, "Managing Nuclear Wastes: The International Connection," *Natural Resources Journal*, Vol. 21 (1981), pp. 267-314; G.T. Needler, "Radioactive Waste: The Need to Calculate an Oceanic Capacity," in G.T. Needler and W.L. Templeton, *Oceanus*, Woods Hole, Mass.: 1981, pp. 60-67; Sonja Boehmer-Christiansen, "Nuclear Waste in the Marine Environment," *Marine Policy Report*, Vol. 6, No. 2 (1983), pp. 1-5; S.A. Boehmer-Christiansen, "Nuclear Waste in the Sea, International Control and the Role of Science and Law," *Marine Policy*, Vol. 7 (1983), No. 1, pp. 25-36; Daniel P. Finn, "Nuclear Waste Management Activities in the Pacific Basin and Regional Cooperation on the Nuclear Fuel Cycle," *Ocean Development and International Law*, Vol. 13 (1983), pp. 213-246; David G. Spak, "The Need for a Ban on All Radioactive Waste Disposal in the Ocean," *Northwest Journal of International Law & Business*, Vol. 7 (1986), pp. 803-832.

1982 UNITED NATIONS CONVENTION ON THE LAW OF THE SEA

Article 1, Paragraph 1 (5)

(5)(a) "dumping" means:
      (i) any deliberate disposal of wastes or other matter from vessels, aircraft, platforms or other man-made structures at sea;
      (ii) any deliberate disposal of vessels, aircraft, platforms or other man-made structures at sea;

(b) "dumping" does not include:
      (i) the disposal of wastes or other matter incidental to, or derived from the normal operations of vessels, aircraft, platforms or other man-made structures at sea and their equipment, other than wastes or other matter transported by or to vessels, aircraft, platforms or other man-made structures at sea, operating for the purpose of disposal

of such matter or derived from the treatment of such wastes or other matter on such vessels, aircraft, platforms or structures;

(ii) placement of matter for a purpose other than the mere disposal thereof, provided that such placement is not contrary to the aims of this Convention.

. . . .

Article 210
Pollution by dumping

1. States shall adopt laws and regulations to prevent, reduce and control pollution of the marine environment by dumping.

2. States shall take other measures as may be necessary to prevent, reduce and control such pollution.

3. Such laws, regulations and measures shall ensure that dumping is not carried out without the permission of the competent authorities of States.

4. States, acting especially through competent international organizations or diplomatic conference, shall endeavor to establish global and regional rules, standards and recommended practices and procedures to prevent, reduce and control such pollution. Such rules, standards and recommended practices and procedures shall be re-examined from time to time as necessary.

5. Dumping within the territorial sea and the exclusive economic zone or onto the continental shelf shall not be carried out without the express prior approval of the coastal State, which has the right to permit, regulate and control such dumping after due consideration of the matter with other States which by reason of their geographical situation may be adversely affected thereby.

6. National laws, regulations and measures shall be no less effective in preventing, reducing and controlling such pollution than the global rules and standards.

. . . .

Article 216
Enforcement with respect to pollution
by dumping

1. Laws and regulations adopted in accordance with this Convention and applicable international rules and standards established through competent international organizations or diplomatic conference for the prevention, reduction and control of pollution of the marine environment by dumping shall be enforced:

(a) by the coastal State with regard to dumping within its territorial sea or its exclusive economic zone or onto its continental shelf;

(b) by the flag State with regard to vessels flying its flag or vessels or aircraft of its registry;

(c) by any State with regard to acts of loading of wastes or other matter occurring within its territory or at its off-shore terminals.

2. No State shall be obliged by virtue of this article to institute proceedings when another State has already instituted proceedings in accordance with this article.

REFERENCES

E. Bohme, "The Use of the Seabed as a Dumping Site: Viewed from the Outcome of the FAO Technical Conference on Marine Pollution, Rome, 1970," in E. Bohme and M.I. Kehden, eds., *From the Law of the Sea Towards an Ocean Space Regime: Practical and Legal Implications of the Marine Revolution*, Hamburg, 1972, pp. 93-121; C.S. Pearson, "Control of Ocean Dumping," *S.A.I.S. Review*, Vol. 17 (1972) No. 1, p. 31; "The Question of an Ocean Dumping Convention: Conclusions of the Working Group on an Ocean Dumping Convention and Background Paper by L.A.W. Hunter," *American Society of International Law Occasional Paper*, No. 2, 1972; David S. Silverstein, "The Trouble with Mercury: Can Domestic Laws Contain an International Threat?," *Cornell International Law Journal*, Vol. 5 (1975), pp. 219-241; T.L. Leitzell, "The Ocean Dumping Convention--A Hopeful Beginning," *San Diego Law Review*, Vol. 10 (1973), pp. 502-513; R.J. McManus, "The New Law on Ocean Dumping: Statute and Treaty," *Oceans Magazine*, Vol. 6 (Sept. 1973), p. 25; H.C. Miller, "Ocean Dumping--Prelude and Fugue," *Journal of Maritime Law and Commerce*, Vol. 5 (1973), pp. 51-75; C.S. Pearson, "Extracting Rent from Ocean Resources: Discussion of a Neglected Source," *Ocean Development and International Law*, Vol. 1 (1973), pp. 221-237; J.W. Seller, "Solid Waste Disposal and Ocean Dumping," *Marine Affairs Journal*, Vol. 1 (1973), pp. 52-77; W. Bascom, "The Disposal of Waste in the Ocean," *Scientific American*, Vol. 231 (August 1974), pp. 17-25; R.N. Duncan, "The 1972 Convention on the Prevention of Marine Pollution by Dumping of Wastes at Sea," *Journal of Maritime Law and Commerce*, Vol. 5 (1974), pp. 299-315; M.S. Schenker, "Saving a Dying Sea? The London Convention on Ocean Dumping," *Cornell International Law Journal*, Vol. 7 (1974), pp. 32-48; G.E.B. Kullenberg, "Ocean Dumping Sites," *Ocean Management*, Vol. 2 (1975), pp. 189-209; Stuart Weinstein-Bacal, "The Ocean Dumping Dilemma, *Lawyer of the Americas*, Vol. 10 (1978), pp. 868-920; William L. Lahey, "Ocean Dumping of Sewage Sludge: The Tide Turns from Protection to Management," *Harvard Environmental Law Review*, Vol. 6 (1982), pp. 395-431; Robert L. O'Halloran, "Ocean Dumping: Progress Toward A Rational Policy of Dredged Waste Disposal," *Environmental Law*, Vol. 12 (1982), pp. 745-772; C.L. Osterberg, "Why Not in the Ocean?" *IAEA Bulletin*, Vol. 24 (1982), No. 2, pp. 30-34; William L. Lahey, "Economic Charges for Environmental Protection: Ocean Dumping Fees," *Ecological Law Quarterly*, Vol. 11 (1984), pp. 305-342; Julian H. Spirer, "The Ocean Dumping Deadline: Easing the Mandate Millstone," *Fordham Urban Law Journal*, Vol. 11 (1983/84), pp. 1-49; Allan Bakalian, "Regulation and Control of United Ocean Dumping: A Decade of Progress, An Appraisal for the Future," *Harvard Environmental Law Review*, Vol. 8 (1984), pp. 193-256; John Warren Kindt, "Ocean Dumping," *Denver Journal of International Law & Policy*, Vol. 13 (1984), pp. 335-376; Mary-Lynne Hoffmeyer, "Ocean Dumping Provisions of the Convention on the Law of the Sea," *Brooklyn Journal of International Law*, Vol. 11 (1985), pp. 355-377; Marc A. Zeppetello, "National and International Regulation of Ocean Dumping: The Mandate to Terminate Marine Disposal of Contaminated Sewage Sludge," *Ecological Law Quarterly*, Vol. 12 (1985), pp. 619-664; Charles Osterberg, "Old Submarines and Ocean Dumping Policy," *Marine Policy Report*, Vol. 8 (1986), No. 5, pp. 1-6; Maxwell Bruce, "The London Dumping Convention, 1972: First Decade and Future," *Ocean Yearbook*, Vol. 6, Chicago: University of Chicago Press, 1986, pp. 298-318.

NOTE

There are several regional treaties on ocean dumping concluded since the early 1970's. The Convention for the Prevention of Marine Pollution by Dumping from Ships and Aircraft, done at

Oslo on February 15, 1972, 932 UNTS 5, which applies to the northeast Atlantic and North Sea, and the Protocol to the Convention for the Prevention of Pollution of the Mediterranean Sea by Dumping from Ships and Aircraft, done at Barcelona on February 16, 1976, *International Legal Materials*, Vol. 15 (1976), pp. 300-306, adopt similar approach of the London Convention in dealing with dumping. The Convention on the Protection of the Marine Environment of the Baltic Sea Area, done at Helsinki on March 22, 1974, *International Legal Materials*, Vol. 13 (1974), pp. 544-585, takes a much stricter approach to dumping. Article 9 prohibits all dumping, except of dredged spoils, and even this is prohibited if the wastes contain significant quantities of certain listed noxious substances. Where such dumping is permitted, a special prior permit must be obtained. All three conventions, however, permit dumping if it appears to be the only way of averting a threat to the safety of life or of a vessel.

The Council of the Organization for Economic Cooperation and Development (OECD) adopted on July 22, 1977 a Decision establishing a Multilateral Consultation and Surveillance Mechanism for Sea Dumping of Radioactive Waste, *International Legal Materials*, Vol. 17 (1978), pp. 445-452. This Mechanism involves the establishment of guidelines and recommendations to be applied to the dumping of radioactive waste by OECD member states; procedures for notification and consultation concerning proposed dumping; international surveillance of dumping and recording and reporting on actual dumping.

E. SEABED ACTIVITIES

1. Within National Jurisdiction

1982 UNITED NATIONS CONVENTION ON THE LAW OF THE SEA

Article 194
Measures to prevent, reduce and control pollution of the marine environment

. . . .

3. The measures taken pursuant to this Part XII [Protection and Preservation of the Marine Environment] shall deal with all sources of pollution of the marine environment. These measures shall include, *inter alia*, those designed to minimize to the fullest possible extent: . . .

(c) pollution from installations and devices used in exploration or exploitation of the natural resources of the sea-bed and subsoil, in particular measures for preventing accidents and dealing with emergencies, ensuring the safety of operations at sea, and regulating the design, construction, equipment, operation and manning of such installations or devices; . . . .

Article 208
Pollution from sea-bed activities subject to national jurisdiction

1. Coastal States shall adopt laws and regulations to prevent, reduce and control pollution of the marine environment arising from or in connection with seabed activities subject to their jurisdiction and from artificial islands, installations and structures under their jurisdiction, pursuant to articles 60 and 80.

2. States shall take other measures as may be necessary to prevent, reduce and control such pollution.

3. Such laws, regulations and measures shall be no less effective than international rules, standards and recommended practices and procedures.

4. States shall endeavor to harmonize their policies in this connection at the appropriate regional level.

5. States, acting especially through competent international organizations or diplomatic conference, shall establish global and regional rules, standards and recommended practices and procedures to prevent, reduce and control pollution of the marine environment referred to in paragraph 1. Such rules, standards and recommended practices and procedures shall be re-examined from time to time as necessary.

. . . .

Article 214
Enforcement with respect to pollution from sea-bed activities

States shall enforce their laws and regulations adopted in accordance with article 208 and shall adopt laws and regulations and take other measures necessary to implement applicable international rules and standards established through competent international organizations or diplomatic conference to prevent, reduce and control pollution of the marine environment arising from or in connection with sea-bed activities subject to their jurisdiction and from artificial islands, installations and structures under their jurisdiction, pursuant to articles 60 and 80.

REFERENCES

Dennis M. O'Connell, "Continental Shelf Oil Disasters: Challenge to International Pollution Control," *Cornell Law Review*, Vol. 55 (1969), pp. 113-128; R.B. Krueger, "International and National Regulation of Pollution from Offshore Oil Production," *San Diego Law Review*, Vol. 7 (1970), pp. 541-573; V.P. Nanda and K.R. Stiles, "Offshore Oil Spills: An Evaluation of Recent United States Responses," *San Diego Law Review*, Vol. 7 (1970), pp. 519-540; Joseph F. Singleton, "Pollution of the Marine Environment from Outer Continental Shelf Oil Operations," *South Carolina Law Review*, Vol. 22 (1970), pp. 228-240; Albert E. Utton, "A Survey of National Laws on the Control of Pollution from Oil and Gas Operations on the Continental Shelf," *Columbia Journal of Transnational Law*, Vol. 9 (1970), pp. 331-361; A.F. Walch, "Pollution of the High Seas Resulting from Drilling and Producing Operations: Federal Jurisdiction and Operator Liability," *South Texas Law Review*, Vol. 12 (1970), pp. 73-91; R.B. Krueger, "International and National Regulation of Pollution from Offshore Oil Production," in D.W. Hood, ed., *Impingement of Man on the Oceans*, Wiley, 1971, p. 603; Frederic L. Kirgis, Jr., "Technological Challenge to the Shared Environment: United States Practice," *American Journal of International Law*, Vol. 66 (1972), pp. 301-307; D.J. Walmsley, "Oil Pollution Problems Arising Out of Exploitation of the Continental Shelf: The Santa Barbara Disaster," *San Diego Law Review*, Vol. 9 (1972), pp. 514-568; M. Hardy, "Offshore Development and Marine Pollution," *Ocean Development and International Law Journal*, Vol. 1 (1973), pp. 239-273; Moritaka Hayashi, "Comparative National Legislation on Offshore Pollution," *Syracuse Journal of International Law and Commerce*, Vol. 1 (1973), pp. 250-256; S.H. Lay, "Pollution from Offshore Oil Wells," in R. Churchill, *et al.*, eds., *New Directions in the Law of the Sea: Collected Papers*, Vol. III, Dobbs Ferry, New York: Oceana Publications, Inc., 1973, pp. 103-105; V.E. McKelvey, "Environmental Protection in Offshore Petroleum Operations," *Ocean Management*, Vol. 1 (1973), pp. 119-128; B.A. Dubois, "Compensation for Oil Pollution Damage Resulting from Exploration and Exploitation of Hydrocarbons in the Seabed," *Journal of Maritime Law and Commerce*, Vol. 6 (1975), pp. 549-573; R.M. Hallman, "Environmental

Regulation of Marine-Based Activities (Non-Vessel) in Areas of National Jurisdiction," in P.W. Birnie and R.E. Stein, eds., *Critical Environmental Issues on the Law of the Sea*, Washington, D.C." International Institute for Environment and Development, 1975, pp. 9-13; Richard Lewandowski, "Civil Liability for Oil-Pollution Damage on the Norwegian Continental Shelf," *Ocean Development and International Law*, Vol. 5 (1978), pp. 397-420; A.L.C. DeMestral, "The Prevention of Pollution of the Marine Environment Arising from Offshore Mining and Drilling," *Harvard International Law Journal*, Vol. 20 (1979), pp. 469-518; John Warren Kindt, "Offshore Siting of Nuclear Power Plants," *Ocean Development and International Law*, Vol. 8 (1980), pp. 57-103; Kenneth G. Robert, "Offshore Petroleum Exploitation and Environmental Protection: The International and Norwegian Response," *San Diego Law Review*, Vol. 17 (1980), pp. 629-660; Barbara Kwiatkowska, "Marine-based Pollution in the Exclusive Economic Zone: Reconciling Rights, Freedoms and Responsibilities," *Hague Yearbook of Interantional Law*, Vol. 1 (1988), pp. 111-140.

2. Beyond National Jurisdiction

1982 UNITED NATIONS CONVENTION ON THE LAW OF THE SEA

Article 142
Rights and legitimate interests of coastal States

1. Activities in the Area [sea-bed and ocean floor and subsoil thereof beyond the limits of national jurisdiction], with respect to resource deposits in the Area which lie across limits of national jurisdiction, shall be conducted with due regard to the rights and legitimate interests of any coastal State across whose jurisdiction such deposits lie.

2. Consultations, including a system of prior notification, shall be maintained with the State concerned, with a view to avoiding infringement of such rights and interests. In cases where activities in the Area may result in the exploitation of resources lying within national jurisdiction, the prior consent of the coastal State concerned shall be required.

3. Neither this Part [XI, The Area, articles 133-191] nor any rights granted or exercised pursuant thereto shall affect the rights of coastal States to take such measures consistent with the relevant provisions of Part XII [Protection and Preservation of the Marine Environment, articles 192-237] as may be necessary to prevent, mitigate or eliminate grave and imminent danger to their coastline, or related interests from pollution or threat thereof or from other hazardous occurrences resulting from or caused by any activities in the Area.

Article 145
Protection of the marine environment

Necessary measures shall be taken in accordance with this Convention with respect to activities in the Area to ensure effective protection for the marine environment from harmful effects which may arise from such activities. To this end the Authority shall adopt appropriate rules, regulations and procedures for *inter alia*:

(a) the prevention, reduction and control of pollution and other hazards to the marine environment, including the coastline, and of interference with the ecological balance of the marine environment, particular attention being paid to the need for protection from harmful effects of such activities as drilling, dredging, excavation, disposal of waste, construction and operation or maintenance of installations, pipelines and other devices related to such activities.

(b) the protection and conservation of the natural resources of the Area and the prevention of damage to the flora and fauna of the marine environment.

. . . .

Article 209
Pollution from activities in the Area

1. International rules, regulations and procedures shall be established in accordance with Part XI to prevent, reduce and control pollution of the marine environment from activities in the Area. Such rules, regulations and procedures shall be re-examined from time to time as necessary.

2. Subject to the relevant provisions of this section, States shall adopt laws and regulations to prevent, reduce and control pollution of the marine environment from activities in the Area undertaken by vessels, installations, structures and other devices flying their flag or of their registry or operating under their authority, as the case may be. The requirements of such laws and regulations shall be no less effective than the international rules, regulations and procedures referred to in paragraph 1.

. . . .

Article 215
Enforcement with respect to pollution from activities in the area

Enforcement of international rules, regulations and procedures established in accordance with Part XI to prevent, reduce and control pollution of the marine environment from activities in the Area shall be governed by that Part.

NOTE

The United States does not accept the deep seabed mining regime provided in the Convention, but the 1980 Deep Seabed Hard Mineral Resources Act [Chapter X, section E *supra*], incorporates extensive rules relating to the protection of the marine environment against pollution which might result from deep seabed activities carried on by persons subject to United States jurisdiction.

REFERENCES

B. Johnson, "Environmental Controls in the Deep Seabed Under International Jurisdiction, in P.W. Birnie and R.E. Stein, eds., *Critical Environmental Issues on the Law of the Sea*, Washington, D.C.: International Institute for Environment and Development, 1975, pp. 31-39; A.F. Amos and O.A. Roels, "Environmental Aspects of Nodule Mining," *Marine Policy*, Vol. 1 (1977), pp. 156-163; R.A. Frank, *Deep Sea Mining and the Environment*, A Report of the Working Group on Environmental Regulation of Deep Sea Mining--Sponsored by the American Society of International Law, St. Paul: West Publishing Co., 1977; R.A. Frank, "Environmental Consequences of Deep-Sea Mining," in E. Miles and J.K. Gamble, eds., *The Law of the Sea: Conference Outcomes and Problems of Implementation*, Cambridge, Mass., Ballinger, 1977, pp. 319-325; K.M. Keith, "Manganese Nodule Processing in Hawaii: An Environmental Prospectus," *Hawaii Bar Journal*, Vol. 14 (1978), pp. 103-121; Virginia A. Pruitt, "Unilateral Deep Seabed Mining and Environmental Standards: A Risky Venture," *Brooklyn Journal of International Law*, Vol. 8 (1982), pp. 345-363; Frank, "Deep Sea Mining and the Environment," *Studies in Transnational Legal Policy*, (No. 10), John Warren Kindt, "The Environmental Aspects of Deep

Transnational Legal Policy, (No. 10), John Warren Kindt, "The Environmental Aspects of Deep Seabed Mining," *UCLA Journal of Environmental Law & Policy*, Vol. 8 (1989), pp. 125-144.

F. POLLUTION FROM LAND-BASED SOURCES

1982 UNITED NATIONS CONVENTION ON THE LAW OF THE SEA

Article 194
Measures to prevent, reduce and control pollution of the marine environment

. . . .

3. The measures taken pursuant to this Part [XII Protection and Preservation of the Marine Environment] shall deal with all sources of pollution of the marine environment. These measures shall include, *inter alia*, those designed to minimize to the fullest possible extent:

(a) The release of toxic, harmful or noxious substances, especially those which are persistent, from land-based sources, from or through the atmosphere or by dumping; . . . .

. . . .

Article 207
Pollution from land-based sources

1. States shall adopt laws and regulations to prevent, reduce and control pollution of the marine environment from land-based sources, including rivers, estuaries, pipelines and outfall structures, taking into account internationally agreed rules, standards and recommended practices and procedures.

2. States shall take other measures as may be necessary to prevent, reduce and control such pollution.

3. States shall endeavor to harmonize their policies in this connection at the appropriate regional level.

4. States, acting especially through competent international organizations or diplomatic conference, shall endeavor to establish global and regional rules, standards and recommended practices and procedures to prevent, reduce and control pollution of the marine environment from land-based sources, taking into account characteristic regional features, the economic capacity of developing States and their need for economic development. Such rules, standards and recommended practices and procedures shall be re-examined from time to time as necessary.

5. Laws, regulations, measures, rules, standards and recommended practices and procedures referred to in paragraphs 1, 2 and 4 shall include those designed to minimize, to the fullest extent possible, the release of toxic, harmful or noxious substances, especially those which are persistent, into the marine environment.

. . . .

Article 213
Enforcement with respect to pollution from land-based sources

States shall enforce their laws and regulations adopted in accordance with article 207 and shall adopt laws and regulations and take other measures necessary to implement applicable international rules and standards established through competent international organizations or diplomatic conference to prevent, reduce and control pollution of the marine environment from land-based sources.

NOTE

There are several regional treaties dealing with pollution from land-based sources, such as: Convention for the Prevention of Marine Pollution from Land-Based Sources [Relating to the North Atlantic Ocean and Arctic Sea], done at Paris on June 4, 1974, International Legal Materials, Vol. 13 (1974), pp. 352-372; Article 6 of the Convention on the Protection of the Marine Environment of the Baltic Sea Area, done at Helsinki on March 22, 1974, International Legal Materials, Vol. 13 (1974), pp. 544-585, and Protocol of the Mediterranean Sea Against Pollution from Land-Based Sources, done at Athens on May 17, 1980, International Legal Materials, Vol. 19 (1980), pp. 869-878. In these treaties, generally the introduction of hazardous substances into the sea is to be eliminated, while the introduction of noxious substances into the sea is to be strictly controlled and generally may be done in significant quantities only after the issuance of a permit by designated national authorities. Each treaty establishes a regional commission to administer the treaty.

The U.S. law governing pollutants from land-based sources into navigable waters of the United States is strictly regulated under the 1972 Clean Water Act, as amended, 33 U.S.C. §§ 1251 et seq.

REFERENCES

James E. Hickey, Jr., "Customs and Land-Based Pollution of the High Sea," *San Diego Law Review*, Vol. 15 (1978), pp. 409-476; Gr. J. Timagenis, "Protocol for the Protection of the Mediterranean Sea Against Pollution from Land-Based Sources, Athens," *Hellenic Review of International Relations*, Vol. 1 (1980), pp. 123-136; Patricia A. Bliss-Guest, "The Protocol Against Pollution from Land-Based Sources: A Turning Point in the Rising Tide of Pollution," *Stanford Journal of International Law*, Vol. 17 (1981), pp. 261-279; Tadeusz Jasudowicz, "International Legal Problems of the Protection of Maritime Environment Against Land-Based Pollution," *Polish Yearbook of International Law*, Vol. 11 (1981/82), pp. 155-176; John Warren Kindt, "Marine Pollution and Hydrocarbons: The Goal of Minimizing Damage to the Marine Environment," *California Western International Law Journal*, Vol. 14 (1984), pp. 233-288; Barbara Kwiatkowska, "Marine Pollution from Land-Based Sources: Current Problems and Prospects," *Ocean Development and International Law*, Vol. 14 (1984), pp. 315-335; John W. Warner and John Warren Kindt, "Land-Based Pollution and the Chesapeake Bay," *Washington and Lee Law Review*, Vol. 42 (1985), pp. 1099-1138; Meng Qing-nan, *Land-based Marine Pollution*, Dordrecht, Boston, London: Martinus Nijhoff Publishers, 1987.

G. POLLUTION FROM OR THROUGH THE ATMOSPHERE

1982 UNITED NATIONS CONVENTION ON THE LAW OF THE SEA

Article 212
Pollution from or through the atmosphere

1. States shall adopt laws and regulations to prevent, reduce and control pollution of the marine environment from or through the atmosphere, applicable to the air space under their sovereignty and to vessels flying their flag or vessels or aircraft of their registry, taking into account internationally agreed rules, standards and recommended practices and procedures and the safety of air navigation.

. . . .

Article 222
Enforcement with respect to pollution
from or through the atmosphere

States shall enforce, within the air space under their sovereignty or with regard to vessels flying their flag or vessels or aircraft of their registry, their laws and regulations adopted in accordance with article 212, paragraph 1, and with other provisions of this Convention and shall adopt laws and regulations and take other measures necessary to implement applicable international rules and standards established through competent international organizations or diplomatic conference to prevent, reduce and control pollution of the marine environment from or through the atmosphere, in conformity with all relevant international rules and standards concerning the safety of air navigation.

TREATY BANNING NUCLEAR WEAPON TESTS IN THE ATMOSPHERE, IN OUTER SPACE AND UNDER WATER
Done at Moscow on August 5, 1963
14 UST 1313, TIAS 5433, 480 UNTS 43

ARTICLE 1

(1) Each of the Parties to this Treaty undertakes to prohibit, to prevent, and not to carry out any nuclear weapon test explosion, or any other nuclear explosion, at any place under its jurisdiction or control:

(a) in the atmosphere; beyond its limits, including outer space; or underwater, including territorial waters or high seas; or

(b) in any other environment if such explosion causes radioactive debris to be present outside the territorial limits of the State under whose jurisdiction or control such explosion is conducted. It is understood in this connection that the provisions of this subparagraph are without prejudice to the conclusion of a treaty resulting in the permanent banning of all nuclear test explosions, including all such explosions underground, the conclusion of which, as the Parties have stated in the Preamble to this Treaty, they seek to achieve. . . .

H. PROTECTION OF FRAGILE ECOSYSTEMS

1982 UNITED NATIONS CONVENTION ON THE LAW OF THE SEA

Article 194
Measures to prevent, reduce and control pollution of marine environment

5. The measures taken in accordance with this Part [XII Protection and Preservation of the Marine Environment] shall include those necessary to protect and preserve rare or fragile ecosystems as well as the habitat of depleted, threatened or endangered species and other forms of marine life.

. . . .

Article 234
Ice-covered areas

Coastal States have the right to adopt and enforce non-discriminatory laws and regulations for the prevention, reduction and control of marine pollution from vessels in ice-covered areas within the limits of the exclusive economic zone, where particularly severe climatic conditions and the presence of ice covering such areas for most of the year create obstructions or exceptional hazards to navigation, and pollution of those marine environment could cause major harm to or irreversible disturbance of the ecological balance. Such laws and regulations shall have due regard to navigation and the protection and preservation of the marine environment based on the best available scientific evidence.

NOTE

In 1970, Canada enacted the Arctic Water Pollution Prevention Act [18-19 Elizabeth II, c. 47 (1969-70), Canada Revised Statute, Chapter C-2; *International Legal Materials*, Vol. 9 (1970), pp. 543-554] for the purpose of "preservation of the peculiar ecological balance that now exists in the water, ice and land area of the Canadian arctic." It seeks to establish pollution zones in Arctic Waters up to 100 miles from every point of Canadian coastal territory above the 60th parallel. United States protested this Act as violation of the principle of the freedom of the high seas [See *International Legal Materials*, Vol. 9 (1970), pp. 605-606], but the protest was rejected by Canada [see *ibid.*, pp. 607-615]. The issue is now moot as Canada is entitled to enact such legislation under the 1982 United Nations Convention on the Law of the Sea.

For further references on protecting Arctic and Antarctica environment, see Donat Pharand, "The Northwest Passage in International Law," *Canadian Yearbook of International Law*, Vol. 17 (1979), pp. 99-133; Philip Newbury, "The International Environmental Law of the Sea: The Canadian Arctic Waters Pollution Prevention Act and Its Effects, 1970-1980," *Suffork Transnational Law Journal*, Vol. 4 (1980), pp. 139-161; Elizabeth Young, "The Arctic--In Need of an International Regime," *Marine Policy*, Vol. 5 (1981), No. 2, pp. 154-156; Christopher C. Joyner, "Antarctica and the Law of the Sea: An Introductory Overview," *Ocean Development and International Law*, Vol. 13 (1983), pp. 277-289; M.J. Peterson, "Antarctic Implications of the New Law of the Sea," *Ocean Development and International Law*, Vol. 16 (1986), pp. 137-181; Francesco Francioni and Tullio Scovazzi, eds., *International Law* for Antarctica, Milan, Italy: Giuffre Editore, 1987; Cynthia Lamson, "Arctic Shipping, Marine Safety and Environmental Protection," *Marine Policy*, Vol. 11 (1987), No. 1, pp. 3-15; W.M. Bush, *Antarctica and International Law: A Collection of Inter-State And National Documents*, London, Rome, New

York: Oceana Publications, 1988, 3 vols.; Nicholas C. Howson, "Breaking the Ice: The Canadian-American Dispute Over the Arctic's Northwest Passage," *Columbia Journal of Transnational Law*, Vol. 26 (1988), pp. 337-375; Christopher C. Joyner, and Sudhir K. Chopra (eds.), *The Antarctic Legal Regime*, Dordrecht, Boston, London: Martinus Nijhoff Publishers, 1988; John Warren Kindt, "Ice-covered Areas and the Law of the Sea: Issues Involving Resources Exploitation and the Antarctic Environment, *Brooklyn Journal of International Law* Vol. 14 (1988), pp. 27-71; Francisco Orrego Vicuna, Antarctic Mineral Exploitation: The Emerging Legal Framework, Cambridge, United Kingdom, and New York: Cambridge University Press, 1988; M.J. Peterson, *Managing the Frozen South: The Creation and Evolution of the Antarctic Treaty System*, Berkely, Los Angeles, London: University of California Press, 1988; Henry C. Burmester, "Liability for Damage from Antarctic Mineral Resource Activities," *Virginia Journal of International Law*, Vol. 29 (1989), pp. 621-660; Christopher P. Davis, "Hiding Our Heads In the Snow: The Dilemma of Non-Living Resources in Antarctica," *Syracuse Journal of International Law and Commerce*, Vol. 15 (1989), pp. 431-450.

Although the 1982 United Nations Convention on the Law of the Sea does not mention marine parks, reserves and sanctuaries, their creation is spreading around the world as part of the broader environmental movement, and already there have been conflicts over them between environmentalists on one side and shipping and fishing interests on the other. See Daniel P. Finn, *Managing the Ocean Resources of the U.S.: The Role of the Federal Marine Sanctuaries Program*, Berlin: Springer-Verlag, 1982; Jon Lien and Rebert Graham, eds., *Marine Parks and Conservations: Challenge and Promise*, Ottawa: The National and Provincial Parks Association of Canada, 1985, "U.S. Marine Sanctuaries," *Oceanus*, Vol. 31, No. 1 (Spring 1988), pp. 5-10.

REFERENCES

Lauriston R. King, "The Coastal Upwelling Ecosystems, Analysis Program as An Experience in International Cooperation," *Ocean Development and International Law*, Vol. 9 (1981), pp. 269-288; Louis B. Sohn and Kristen Gustafson, *The Law of the Sea in A Nutshell*, St. Paul, Minn.: West Publishing Co., 1984, pp. 205-206, Christopher C. Joyner, "The Exclusive Economic Zone and Antarctica: The Dilemmas of Non-Sovereign Jurisdiction," *Ocean Development and International Law*, Vol. 19 (1988), pp. 489-492; Martin H. Belsky, "The Ecosystem Model Mandate for A Comprehensive United States Ocean Policy and the Law of the Sea," *San Diego Law Review*, Vol. 26 (1989), pp. 417-495.

CHAPTER XIII

MARINE SCIENTIFIC RESEARCH AND TRANSFER OF MARINE TECHNOLOGY

A. THE IMPORTANCE OF MARINE SCIENTIFIC RESEARCH AND ITS IMPACT ON OTHER MARINE ACTIVITIES AND THE MARINE ENVIRONMENT

> Charles Maechling, Jr., "Freedom of Scientific Research: Stepchild of the Ocean," *Virginia Journal of International Law*, Vol. 15 (1975), pp. 552-554. Reprinted by permission.

The importance of scientific research to a better understanding of the marine environment is axiomatic. What requires repeated and painstaking elaboration is the fact that this knowledge rebounds to the benefit of all mankind--not merely to the profit of the advanced industrial state . . .

In the area of long-range weather forecasting, the constant accumulation and verification of data derived from the ocean-atmosphere is essential for the accurate prediction of seasonal climatic variations. Although atmospheric winds determine primary ocean currents, the heat that actually drives the atmosphere comes mainly from the surface of the ocean, either in the form of long-wave radiation or evaporation. Thus, close and continuing observation of ocean temperature changes from year to year is a key to climate prediction. When one considers the effect of climate change on patterns of drought and rainfall, and consequently on crops and world food stocks, the importance of oceanographic research to better understanding of such apparently unrelated social and economic phenomena as fluctuation of commodity prices and their effect on the international balance of payments becomes less fanciful than it might seem.

Better knowledge of ocean temperature and currents is also necessary to broadening our knowledge of the world's fish supply. . . . [W]e are so ignorant of the environment in which fish stocks multiply and migrate that the data base to devise a rational scheme of allocation is entirely lacking.

One example of this deficiency is our inadequate knowledge of El Nino, a warm "counter-current" that periodically deflects the northward-flowing Humboldt current and cuts off the West Coast of South America from the rich supplies of phytoplankton on which the largest single-species fishery in the world, the anchoveta of Peru, depends for sustenance. Another area of comparative ignorance is the migratory pattern of deep-sea food fish, which congregate in distinct temperature layers that shift with the ocean's currents. Maximization of the sustainable fish yield of the ocean to provide growing populations with cheap protein is supposed to be an economic goal that every state endorses, but to attain this on a scientific basis will require much greater knowledge of fishery dynamics than can be obtained from the meager data currently available.

Another subject area where basic data is lacking is marine pollution. It is well-known, for example, that levels of mercury and lead pollution in the oceans are constantly rising, and that pollution emanating from offshore garbage and waste disposal has largely destroyed the marine life of inland seas like the Mediterranean and the Baltic. But man's ability to predict the consequences of this pollution on a global scale is virtually nonexistent, and his understanding of ecological relationships in the ocean is frankly primitive. If mankind is to have adequate warning of the long-term effects of pollution on the environment, more knowledge and hence more research of ocean-atmosphere interactions is essential.

Finally, the proper allocation and exploitation of deepsea mineral resources is dependent on knowledge of the geology of the seabed and the dynamics of mineral resource production. Exploratory drilling and subsurface mapping provide crude information about the location of petroleum and mineral reserves, but they do not provide adequate information either about their extent or accessibility. Nor do the most sophisticated exploratory techniques provide data on mineral resource formation, ecological inter-relationships, and safety of exploitation. In fact, most of the information the world needs for rational exploitation and allocation of undersea mineral resources is still rudimentary, and can only be amplified and evaluated as part of an integrated research program, containing many elements superficially unrelated to the immediate objective.

It has become trite to point out how dependent the global community is on science and technology. If the less-developed countries are ever to escape from the iron cycle of over-population, poverty, and starvation, they will need every bit of know-how that can be brought to bear on the development of new energy sources, improvement of crop yields, prevention of disease, and control of population. The rich promise that the seabed and oceans offer for the attainment of these goals will be effectively stultified if restrictions, red-tape and artificial constraints are imposed on the acquisition and verification of the data necessary to guide the technology for developing these resources. It is absurd for less-developed coastal states to suppose that science can help them to develop their resources if they deny science access to the information necessary to the exploitation process. It is equally absurd for the advanced industrial countries, especially the United States, to believe that the scientific enterprise can be treated as an expendable bargaining chip.

REFERENCES

Eric Linklater, *The Voyage of the Challenger*, London: Murray; New York: Doubleday, 1972; Lord Ritchie Calder, "Perspectives on the Sciences of the Sea," Elisabeth Mann Borgese and Norton Ginsburg, eds., *Ocean Yearbook*, Vol. 1, Chicago and London: University of Chicago Press, 1978, pp. 271-292; Francisco J. Palacio, "The Development of Marine Science in Latin America," *Oceanus* (Woods Hole, Mass.), Vol. 23, No. 2 (Summer 1980), pp. 39-49; Intergovernmental Oceanographic Commission [of UNESCO], "Ocean Sciences for the Year 2000," Elisabeth Mann Borgese and Norton Ginsburg, eds., *Ocean Yearbook*, Vol. 4, Chicago and London: University of Chicago Press, 1983, pp. 176-259.

Alfred H.A. Soons, *Marine Scientific Research and the Law of the Sea*, Deventer, The Netherlands: Kluwer Law and Taxation Publishers, 1982, pp. 28-29. Notes omitted. Reprinted with the permission of the Kluwer Academic Publishers Group.

4.3 Potential conflicts with other marine activities

An important consequence of the greatly expanded scale of marine scientific research is the increased possibility of conflicts with other uses of ocean space. In the early days of oceanography, when vessels were the only platforms used for scientific observations, and other activities in the marine environment were limited to navigation and fishing, there was little chance of mutual interference. Still, at present, the operations of a single research vessel will not normally cause any serious difficulties. The introduction of new platforms, however, combined with the intensification of other ocean uses, has changed the former situation. Particularly buoys, both moored and drifting, and fixed installations can be hazards to navigation and fishing. The dangers involved in a collision between such devices and vessels should not be underestimated. Drifting buoys could cause serious damage to mining installations on the continental shelf, and to fixed fishing gear. The operation of research submersibles also requires special precautions.

The deployment of instruments involving physical contact with the sea bottom, such as coring and dredging, can cause damage to submarine cables and pipelines, fixed fishing gear, military devices and so on. Certain research activities, such as deep drilling, require the exclusive use of a specific area for longer periods. Large-scale investigations, involving a large number and variety of platforms may require that vast areas are temporarily closed to other uses. Finally, it may become desirable to establish marine reserves for protection and study of natural marine communities, within which human activities would be restricted to observation and research.

4.4 Potential harmful effects on the marine environment

The use of modern technology has greatly enhanced the capability to conduct marine scientific research. At the same time, however, it has increased the possibility of research activities causing damage to the marine environment.

For example, seismic explosions for geophysical research can do damage to living organisms. Dredging may disturb life on the sea bottom. The excessive taking of specimens might affect the nature equilibrium in a particular area. Deep drilling provides another example. Although the drilling itself disturbs only a very small area of sea floor, there is a risk of oil seepage, blow-out, or fire. If a hole is abandoned, it must be plugged or sealed to avoid the danger of snagging fishing gear, and the risk of oil seepage and pollution.

Some kinds of research may involve the introduction of potentially harmful substances into the marine environment, for example, the use of dyes to trace currents or the spraying of detergents when testing oil pollution abatement methods.

Finally, the use of radioactive materials for generating power or in the equipment, especially in buoys and fixed platforms, involves a risk of contaminating the marine environment, for example, as a result of a collision.

B. THE REQUIREMENTS OF SCIENTIFIC RESEARCH

Alfred H.A. Soons, *Marine Scientific Research and the Law of the Sea*, Deventer, The Netherlands: Kluwer Law and Taxation Publishers, 1982, pp. 16-20. Notes omitted. Reprinted with the permission of the Kluwer Academic Publishers Group.

3.1 Access to data

Marine scientific research, like all scientific research, can be divided into two phases: (1) the collection of basic data; and (2) the interpretation of such data. Since marine science essentially is an environmental science, which means that it looks at man's natural environment as it actually exists, the data with which it is concerned consist primarily of measurements made in the marine environment. In some cases marine scientific research can be conducted on the basis of data which already exist, either because they had been collected for earlier research projects or because they are being collected on a routine basis for multiple purposes. Very often, however, the necessary data (all, or additional) will have to be collected in the ocean. . . .

An important source of already existing data is the scientific literature. A basic characteristic of open scientific research indeed is the fact that the results are made generally available by publishing them. Almost all scientific work is somehow based on the application of the results of earlier investigations. The exchange of data therefore is an important condition for scientific progress. Publications, however, generally only include interpreted data, whereas scientists often need access to the raw data. This requires the cooperation of the persons and institutions which have collected the data. In the early days of marine scientific research personal contacts on an *ad hoc* basis between the scientists or institutions concerned were sufficient for this purpose. However, the recent expansion of marine scientific research and the use of newly developed techniques have resulted in an enormous increase in the volume of oceanographic data. This has led to the establishment of international systems for data management.

The International Council for the Exploration of the Sea (ICES) has been operating successfully for many years a system for exchanging oceanographic data on a regional basis. The area covered by this system includes the North Sea and the North Atlantic Ocean. When the programme of the International Geophysical Year (1957-1958) made necessary the creation of a world-wide system, World Data Centers A and B (Oceanography) were established, located in Washington, D.C., and Moscow respectively. Later it became clear that the original idea of World Data Centers, maintained by large nations as an international service for holding all data, would be impracticable. A more recent trend has resulted in the establishment of a network of national centers, with the World Data Centers acting as inventory-referral centers, and linked with a series of specialized disciplinary centers. Under the present global oceanographic data exchange system, as recommended by the Intergovernmental Oceanographic Commission (IOC) of UNESCO, individual nations may designate the whole or part of their oceanographic activities as Declared National Programmes, which entails an obligation to forward all data to the appropriate international depositories where they are available to all qualified requesters in the scientific community. This system largely fulfills the scientist's need for access to already existing data.

3.2 Access to ocean areas, flexibility of movement and
access to ports

For most marine scientific research, the collection of new data is an absolute condition. This requires access to the ocean areas where the measurements or other observations must be made. Consequently, the accessibility of the ocean for the conduct of scientific investigations is a fundamental element of the international legal regime of marine scientific research.

Because of the physical and ecological unity of the marine environment, marine scientists require access to all parts of the ocean. Many of the living inhabitants of the sea migrate over long distances, and the waters of the sea together with the materials dissolved or suspended therein are transported freely by ocean currents over vast reaches. In a great many cases the marine scientists cannot adequately study the object of his research unless he can work with the same freedom and disregard for man-made frontiers as are enjoyed by the natural phenomena he seeks to understand. The part of the ocean that is especially important for marine scientific research is the coastal zone. This is a result of its special natural characteristics and its particular significance for man. The coastal zone includes the continental shelf and overlying waters; it extends generally several tens of nautical miles offshore.

Most of man's marine activities take place in the coastal zone. The productivity of marine life is highest in coastal regions, because the upwelling of nutrient rich waters occurs mostly there. About 90 percent of the present world's fish catch comes from this area. The mineral resources of the sea now being exploited come exclusively from the continental shelf and the waters above it. A large amount of maritime transport is coastal, and all transoceanic transport begins and ends at ports. Partly as a consequence of these factors the shores of the ocean are often densely populated. Human and industrial wastes are introduced into coastal waters, where they mix with other pollutants resulting from man's marine activities. Coastal waters differ chemically from those of the open sea, even in areas where man's impact is minimal. Generally, coastal water can be identified at least to the edge of the continental shelf, but the influence of major rivers may extend beyond this boundary.

It is not easy to evaluate quantitatively the extent to which marine scientific research depends on access to coastal waters. Wooster and Bradley have made an attempt to do this by analyzing the recommended projects listed in the UN Long-term and Expanded Programme of Oceanic Exploration and Research (LEPOR). Of the 53 projects, 10 (19%) were found to be dependent on access to coastal areas, 34 (64%) were partially dependent on access, and 9 (17%) were independent of access. . . . the results of a survey conducted in 1973 by the United States Department of Defense . . . indicated that approximately 50% of the research undertaken by U.S. marine scientists in the last few years before 1973 took place over the continental shelf. Another 30% was conducted in areas beyond the continental shelf, but within a distance of 200 miles from the coast. Thus, 80% of the U.S. research activities was carried out inside the 200-mile limit. If a similar survey would be undertaken on a world-wide basis, these figures would certainly even be higher. This is a result of the fact that the United States and a few other industrially advanced nations conduct almost all of the open ocean research, whereas the research activities of most other countries are confined to near-shore waters, which has the effect of increasing the absolute share of coastal marine scientific research in the total world marine research effort.

Of particular significance for the international legal regime of marine scientific research is the extent to which research is carried out by institutions or nationals from one State in the coastal waters of another State. These are the activities with which the international legal regime of marine scientific research is primarily concerned, since research conducted in coastal waters by institutions or nationals from the coastal State itself in principle has few international aspects and is governed primarily by the national laws of that coastal State. Most marine scientific research in coastal areas is conducted by institutions or nationals from the coastal State because the coastal State has the greatest need for information concerning its offshore areas, and because this region is easiest accessible for scientists from the coastal State. Frequently, however, scientists from one State need access to the coastal waters of a neighboring State in order to be able to adequately study certain phenomena or processes, for example pollution studies in estuaries of boundary rivers. Moreover, often research projects are undertaken which require field work off more distant foreign shores. . . .

Apart from access to ocean areas, marine scientists also require a certain flexibility of movement at sea. Although research cruises are generally planned far in advance, often even two or three years, it may still sometimes be necessary to change schedules at the last minute. This can be the result of changes in the research project itself (e.g., as a consequence of new scientific developments), or can be due to ship repairs or equipment failure. Even while at sea, schedules might have to be changed for such reasons. It could also be desirable to change the preconceived route of the research vessel because of the observations made earlier during the cruise. Such flexibility of movement could be seriously hampered when a research project is carried out in an area under the jurisdiction of a coastal State which had permitted access under conditions requiring

area under the jurisdiction of a coastal State which had permitted access under conditions requiring precise specification of time, place and activity.

Finally, it should be noted that research vessels often need access to foreign ports for logistical purposes. Both while underway to areas distant from their home ports, and during prolonged research operations in such distant areas, port calls will be necessary to take in fuel and other supplies. Frequently scientists, ship personnel and equipment are to be exchanged in foreign ports, and samples and specimens unloaded for shipment back to the laboratory. Availability of ports for these purposes is very important; their unavailability can seriously affect the scientific effectiveness of a cruise.

C. THE TECHNOLOGY FOR MARINE SCIENTIFIC RESEARCH

> Alfred H.A. Soons, *Marine Scientific Research and the Law of the Sea*, Deventer, The Netherlands: Kluwer Law and Taxation Publishers, 1982, pp. 23-26, 28. Notes omitted. Reprinted with the permission of the Kluwer Academic Publishers Group.

4.1 Platforms

The actual collection of oceanic data depends on the availability of platforms capable of carrying and deploying the instruments required for the various investigations. The platforms from which marine scientific research is being conducted include vessels, submersibles, moored and drifting buoys, fixed installations, aircraft and satellites. These will be briefly discussed in the following paragraphs.

(A) Vessels

The traditional, and still the most important, platforms are vessels. These can be divided into two categories: (1) vessels which are at sea exclusively for the conduct of scientific investigations; and (2) vessels conducting scientific research only as an incidental activity during regular voyages. The latter are called "ships of opportunity." The vessels of the first category can be either regular research vessels, employed full-time for scientific research, or they can be temporary research vessels, such as merchant or navy ships, or fishing vessels, chartered for one or more cruises. Most ships of opportunity are merchant vessels, although naval and fishing vessels are also being used. The scientific observations are made by a few scientists or by regular crew members; in some cases automatic recording instruments are employed. Drilling ships have also been used for marine scientific research, principally because of their ability to obtain deeper samples of the earth's crust. Disadvantages of the use of vessels for marine scientific research are the relatively low speed (time-consuming to cover large areas), the inability to work in all-weather conditions or in ice-covered seas, and the sometimes tremendous costs involved in their operation, particularly for longer periods. . . .

(B) Submersibles

The idea of using submarine platforms for making scientific observations is not new; for example, submarines have already been used for gravity measurements during the 1930's. In recent years, however, increasing use is being made of smaller submersibles, specifically designed for scientific work. A main advantage of subsurface platforms is their stability. This is a result of the fact that they are not affected by the motion produced by the varying sea surface, and they are therefore better suited for delicate measurements. In addition, they provide a means for subsurface visual observations. Perhaps the greatest limitation on their use is the high cost of operation. This explains why unmanned submarine vehicles, which can be remotely controlled or towed and are less expensive, have become more popular. It should be noted that research submersibles, as well as unmanned submarine vehicles, always require support by a surface vessel.

(C) Buoys

Continuous monitoring of the ocean has become very important for marine scientific research. Since this cannot be accomplished by research vessels alone, a system of placing instruments in the ocean which can record the change in such features as water movement, temperature, salinity, density, etc., on a continuous basis has been developed. These instruments are supported by buoys at or near the sea surface which are moored or anchored to the bottom. The sensing elements, which can be located at any depth extending to the bottom, record their signals either internally or transmit them to the surface float for recording or for further telemetering to shore or shipboard receiving stations. The buoys vary in size from six to over forty feet in diameter. Drifting, or free-floating, buoys are also being widely used. They can be divided in surface and subsurface types. In general, the subsurface types are neutrally buoyant and designed to float at an intermediate depth. They contain sonic devices permitting the buoys to be tracked, thus identifying ocean current trajectories. Free-floating surface buoys range in size from small drift bottles to large manned ocean laboratories. It is expected that the use of the various types of buoys will be greatly expanded in the near future. The various categories of buoys described in this paragraph, and the installations to be discussed next, together are referred to as "ODAS" (Ocean Data Acquisition Systems, Aids and Devices).

(D) Installations

The number of fixed, bottom-bearing installations specifically employed for making oceanographic observations is still very small. Most surface penetrating installations are large and heavily constructed, and usually manned. Subsurface systems are generally limited to bottom or near-bottom devices which are self-recording or connected to shore by electrical cables. Often the self-recording systems must be recalled to the surface for retrieval by means of acoustically-activated releases. Experiments have already been carried out with manned stations on the sea floor to test their usefulness for scientific work.

(E) Aircraft

The collection of oceanic data is not restricted to platforms operating on or in the water column. Some of these data can also be obtained by means of remote sensing from aircraft and satellites. Aircraft can be used for measuring such parameters as the earth's magnetic field, sea surface temperature, surface and subsurface currents, as well as for biological observations, such as tracking and observing schools of fish. The main advantage of aircraft over ships is that large areas can be covered much more rapidly and at substantially lower costs. In addition, fixed-wing aircraft as well as helicopters can be used for the deployment of expendable instruments, such as bathythermographs, and of instruments which are subsequently retrieved by the same aircraft.

(F) Satellites

Satellites are already used extensively for remote sensing. Among the advantages offered by satellite platforms are the ability to provide more continuous and complete coverage of the ocean's surface, the potential to obtain uniform data over very large areas in a very short time, and the accessibility of remote areas. Manned space vehicles offer some additional advantages, such as the possibility of adjusting instruments in the course of observations and of concentrating on sudden-appearing phenomena. Disadvantages of the use of space platforms are the high costs involved and the complex ground facilities required for data processing. But although a satellite is a tremendously expensive platform, it gets so many data in such a short period of time that each piece of information costs less than it would if acquired in any other way.

4.2 Instruments and techniques

(A) Geological measurements

Water depth is generally measured by an echo sounder. This device measures the time for a sound pulse transmitted from a vessel to travel to the seabed and return to a listening device. Since the speed of sound in seawater is known, the travel time can be converted to a distance indicating the water depth. Continuous bottom profiles are provided by vessels making continuous soundings while sailing. The sidescanning sonar scans the sea floor beneath and to the sides of the research vessel.

Observation of the sea floor is carried out with cameras which can be lowered from a research vessel to any depth. Such cameras can take several hundred photographs, either automatically or upon command. Direct observation by divers is feasible in water no deeper than 45 meters. Research submersibles can take scientists to the deepest parts of the ocean.

Sediment samples can be taken with a variety of instruments. Dredges are box-like devices dragged along the bottom of the sea. A mesh is placed inside the dredge to keep sedimentary material from being lost. . . .

(D) Biological measurements

For collecting benthic organisms (i.e., those organisms that live on or below the ocean bottom), dredges and grab samplers are used. The ocean bottom and the benthic organisms living there can be observed by underwater cameras. Plankton is sampled by dragging fine-mesh nets behind a moving ship, or by pumping seawater through a hose lowered from the ship. Nekton (i.e., those animals that are able to swim freely, independent of current movement) are gathered with various trawls or nets. Marine scientists use trawls and nets similar to those used by fishermen.

(E) Remote sensing techniques

Remote sensing methods used with aircraft or satellites depend at present upon the reception, or emission and reflection, of electromagnetic radiation. Every substance having a temperature above absolute zero (-273°C) selectively absorbs, transmits, reflects, emits, or can be made to emit, electromagnetic radiation at characteristic wavelengths peculiar to its composition. These wavelengths can be in the visible range, but many are in the non-visible ultraviolet, infra-red or microwave parts of the spectrum. When the spectral characteristics are collected, compared, and analyzed, it is possible to distinguish objects from each other, and furnish information relating to their size, shape, density and other properties. There is, however, one severe limitation on the use of electromagnetic energy for remote sensing of the marine environment. Since electro-magnetic radiation does not penetrate water to any great depth, 100 meters being the most that can be expected in the foreseeable future, only the upper layer of the oceanic environment can be sampled.

The methods of remote sensing can be divided into two major groups: active and passive ones. Active methods of remote sensing use sensors capable of generating radiation which, after interaction with an object, return a signal which is measured by on-board receivers. Examples of such methods are radar and laser systems. Passive methods of remote sensing use sensors which do not rely on self-generated radiation. Most of the methods presently employed are passive ones. They include visual observations, photographs and images on film and TV-cameras, radiometric measurements and images from scanning radiometers.

D. GENERAL PRINCIPLES OF MARINE SCIENTIFIC RESEARCH

1982 UNITED NATIONS CONVENTION ON THE LAW OF THE SEA

PART XIII
MARINE SCIENTIFIC RESEARCH
SECTION 1. GENERAL PROVISIONS

Article 238
Right to conduct marine scientific research

All States, irrespective of their geographical location, and competent international organizations have the right to conduct marine scientific research subject to the rights and duties of other States as provided for in this Convention.

Article 239
Promotion of marine scientific research

States and competent international organizations shall promote and facilitate the development and conduct of marine scientific research in accordance with this Convention.

Article 240
General principles for the conduct of marine scientific research

In the conduct of marine research the following principles shall apply:

(a) marine scientific research shall be conducted exclusively for peaceful purposes;

(b) marine scientific research shall be conducted with appropriate scientific methods and means compatible with this Convention;

(c) marine scientific research shall not unjustifiably interfere with other legitimate uses of the sea compatible with this Convention and shall be duly respected in the course of such uses;

(d) marine scientific research shall be conducted in compliance with all relevant regulations adopted in conformity with this Convention including those for the protection and preservation of the marine environment.

Article 241
Non-recognition of marine scientific research
activities as the legal basis for claims

Marine scientific research activities shall not constitute the legal basis for any claim to any part of the marine environment or its resources.

REFERENCES

Herman Pollack, "National Interest, Foreign Affairs, and the Marine Sciences," *Department of State Bulletin*, Vol. 58, No. 1494 (February 12, 1968), pp. 211-215; Milners B. Schaefer, "Freedom of Scientific Research and Exploration in the Sea," *Stanford Journal of International Studies*, Vol. 4 (1969), pp. 46-70; E.D. Brown, "Freedom of Scientific Research and the Legal Regime of Hydrospace," *Indian Journal of International Law*, Vol. 9 (1969), pp. 327-380; Femke Groustra, "Legal Problems of Scientific Research in the Oceans," *Journal of Maritime Law and Commerce*, Vol. 1 (1970), pp. 603-620; William T. Burke, *Marine Science Research and International Law*, Kingston [now Honolulu]: Occasional Paper No. 8, Law of the Sea Institute, University of Rhode Island [now University of Hawaii], 1970; R. Munier, "The Politics of Marine Science: Crisis and Compromise," Lewis M. Alexander, ed., *The Law of the Sea: Needs and Interests of Developing Countries*, Kingston, R.I.: The University of Rhode Island, 1973, pp. 219-223; Warren S. Wooster, ed., *Freedom of Ocean Research*, New York: Crane, Russak and Co., Inc., 1973; Herman Franssen, "Understanding the Ocean Science Debate," *Ocean Development and International Law*, vol. 2 (1974), pp. 187-202; John A. Knauss, "Marine Science and the 1974 Law of the Sea Conference," *Science*, Vol. 184, No. 4144 (June 28, 1974) pp. 1335-1341; Charles Maechling, Jr., "Freedom of Scientific Research: Stepchild of the Oceans," *Virginia Journal of Inter-national Law*, Vol. 15 (1975), pp. 539-559; Richard R. Baxter, "The International Law of Scientific Research in the Ocean," *Georgia Journal of International and Comparative Law*, Vol. 6 (1976), pp. 27-39; A.F. Vysotsky, "Freedom of Scientific Research in the World Ocean," *ibid.*, pp. 7-25; National Academy of Sciences, Ocean Policy Committee, Commission on International Relations, *Marine Scientific Research and the Third Law of the Sea Conference: 2nd Substantive Session* (report prepared by the Freedom of Ocean Research Group), Washington, D.C.: National Academy of Sciences, 1976; John A. Knauss, P. Frye and Warren S. Wooster, "The Marine Scientific Research Issue in the Law of the Sea Negotiations," *Science*, Vol. 197, No. 4300 (July 15, 1977) pp. 230-233; A.H.A. Soons, "The International Legal Regime of Marine Scientific Research," *Netherlands International Law Review*, Vol. 24 (1977), pp. 393-444; Warren S. Wooster, "Some Implications of Ocean Research," *Ocean Development and International Law*, Vol. 4 (1977), pp. 39-50; Russ Winner, "Science, Sovereignty, and the Third Law of the Sea Conference," *ibid.*, pp. 297-342; Manik Talwani, "Marine Research and the Law of the Sea," *Columbia Journal of World Business*, Vol. 15 (1980), pp. 84-91; A.H.A. Soons, *Marine Scientific Research and the Law of the Sea*, Hingham, Mass.: Kluwer Academic Publishers [for Kluwer Law and Taxation Press], 1983; Christopher K. Vanderpool, "Marine Science and the Law of the Sea," *Social Studies of Science*, Vol. 13 (1983), pp. 107-129; Alexander Yankov, "A General Review of the New Convention on the Law of the Sea: Marine Science and Its Application," Elizabeth Mann Borgese and Norton Ginsburg, eds., *Ocean Yearbook*, Vol. 4, Chicago and London: University of Chicago Press, 1983, pp. 150-175.

E. INTERNATIONAL COOPERATION

Alfred H.A. Soons, *Marine Scientific Research and the Law of the Sea*,
Deventer, The Netherlands: Kluwer Law and Taxation Publishers,
1982, pp. 20-23. Notes Omitted. Reprinted with the permission of the
Kluwer Academic Publishers Group.

There can be several reasons for international cooperation in scientific research in general.
First, the very nature of the research topic can be such that the field work required cannot be
restricted to the territory of one nation. Secondly, international cooperation may also be necessary
to make possible the cross-fertilization of ideas, particularly in newer and highly specialized fields
where only close collaboration by scientists from a number of countries is likely to provide the
necessary critical mass of activity. And thirdly, the provision of the very expensive equipment and
operations required by large-scale scientific research may only be possible by cost sharing between
countries.

These general reasons are all applicable to marine scientific research. In particular,
international cooperation is required in the compilation and exchange of information, the
standardization and inter-calibration of instruments and methods, and in the organization of field
investigations. The importance of international data exchange has already been dealt with above.
Standardization and inter-calibration of instruments and methods is essential in order to improve
the comparability of data. Since many investigations require the pooling of data from a number of
sources, synthesis can be particularly difficult when different methods and standards have been used.
The need for international cooperation in the organization of field investigations is a result of the
fact that some oceanic research projects can only be carried out by means of simultaneous
observations on short time scales, requiring many ships or other platforms. Few nations are
capable of providing these on their own. Other research projects may require only a few platforms,
but for long periods. Such projects can often only be carried out if the costs are shared by several
nations. An additional advantage of joining forces in international operations is that the cost-
effectiveness of the research for each participating nation will be substantially increased.

Cooperative research programs can be either "problem oriented", i.e., concerned with specific
scientific problems, or "area oriented", i.e., concerned with a particular geographical region. . . .

The basis, however, for all international cooperation in marine science is provided by a
number of international organizations. A distinction must be made between governmental
international organizations and non-governmental international organizations. The latter will be
dealt with first.

The functions performed by non-governmental international organizations in the marine
science field are threefold. In the first place they facilitate communications, in order to help
scientists exchange their ideas and experience. Secondly, they bring together scientists from
different countries to work out agreements on methodology or on other technical problems where
an exchange of views and accepted opinion is required. Their third function is monitoring,
evaluation and comment on intergovernmental programs.

The most important non-governmental international organization in the area of marine science
is the Scientific Committee on Oceanic Research (SCOR), established in 1957 by the International
Council of Scientific Unions (ICSU), an organization having consultative status with UNESCO
("A" status). Other scientific organizations in this field, operating within the framework of ICSU,
include:

- the Commission on Marine Geology (CMG), of the International Union of Geodesy and Geophysics (IUGG),

- the International Association of Biological Oceanography (IABO), of the International Union of Biological Science (IUBS);

- the International Association for the Physical Sciences of the Ocean (IAPSO), of the International Union of Geological Sciences (IUGS); and

- the Scientific Committee for Antarctic Research (SCAR).

Intergovernmental organizations concerned with marine scientific research can be either regional or global. Apart from a number of regional fisheries commissions having competence in the field of scientific research, two regional intergovernmental organizations established specifically to promote and coordinate marine research exist. In 1906 the International Council for the Exploration of the Sea (ICES) was founded. ICES, which now has 17 members, is primarily concerned with the North Atlantic Ocean and deals particularly with research related to the living resources. A similar organization was established in 1919 for the Mediterranean Sea area: the International Commission for the Scientific Exploration of the Mediterranean Sea (ICSEM), also now having 17 members.

The only global intergovernmental organization exclusively concerned with marine scientific research is the Intergovernmental Oceanographic Commission (IOC). The IOC was established as an autonomous body within UNESCO in 1960. Its purpose is "to promote scientific investigation with a view to learning more about the nature and resources of the ocean through the concerted action of its members." It further functions as the coordinating body within the UN system for marine science and related activities. Cooperative scientific investigations of the ocean as well as world-wide ocean services, combined with a program of training, education and mutual assistance, form the chief components of IOC's work. Membership is open to any member State of any one of the organizations of the UN system; on 1 March 1979 103 States were members of the IOC. The Secretariat of the IOC is located in UNESCO Headquarters in Paris.

A number of other global intergovernmental organizations is concerned with marine research. Of these, the most important ones are:

- the Food and Agriculture Organization of the United Nations (FAO), active in the fields of fisheries research, marine biological research and marine pollution research;

- the World Health Organization (WHO), mainly interested in marine pollution research;

- the World Meteorological Organization (WMO), which is involved in meteorological and physical oceanographic research;

- the Intergovernmental Maritime Consultative Organization (IMCO), interested in marine pollution research;

- the International Atomic Energy Agency (IAEA), active in the field of marine pollution research; and
- the United Nations Environment Program (UNEP), also interested in marine pollution research.

Coordination between these organizations in the area of marine scientific research programs is ensured through the Inter-secretariat Committee on Scientific Programs Relating to Oceanography (ICSPRO).

1982 UNITED NATIONS CONVENTION ON THE LAW OF THE SEA

PART XIII. MARINE SCIENTIFIC RESEARCH
SECTION 2. INTERNATIONAL CO-OPERATION

[Article 242 refers to promotion of international cooperation; Article 243 refers to creation of favorable conditions and Article 244 refers to publication and dissemination of information and knowledge.]

REFERENCES

Guilio Pontecorvo, "Ocean Science and Mutual Assistance: An Uneasy Alliance," *Ocean Development and International Law*, Vol. 1 (1973), pp. 51-64; Warren S. Wooster, "Interactions Between Intergovernmental and Scientific Organizations in Marine Affairs," *International Organization*, Vol. 27 (1973), pp. 103-113; "Oceanology International '80," *Ocean Management*, Vol. 7 (1981), 352 pp. [This special issue presents a selection of the proceedings of the Oceanology International '80 Conference held in Brighton, United Kingdom, from March 2-7, 1980]; Warren S. Wooster, "International Cooperation in Marine Science," Elisabeth Mann Borgese and Norton Ginsburg, eds., *Ocean Yearbook*, Vol. 2, Chicago and London: University of Chicago Press, 1980, pp. 123-136; Lewis M. Alexander, "Organizational Response to New Ocean Science and Technology Developments," *Ocean Development and International Law*, Vol. 9 (1981), pp. 241-268; Lee Kimball, "Regional Marine Resources Development: Growth by Necessity," Elisabeth Mann Borgese and Norton Ginsburg, ed., *Ocean Yearbook*, Vol. 3, Chicago and London: University of Chicago Press, 1982, pp. 157-197; Norton Ginsburg, "On the Nature of a Model Global Maritime Research Organization," *ibid.*, Vol. 5, 1985, pp. 109-116; Velimir Pravdic, "International Cooperation in Marine Sciences: The Nongovernmental Framework and the Individual Scientist," *ibid.*, pp. 117-129; Roger Revelle, "The Need for International Cooperation in Marine Science and Technology," *ibid.*, pp. 130-149.

F. CONDUCT OF MARINE SCIENTIFIC RESEARCH IN THE TERRITORIAL SEA AND BEYOND

1.   The Interest of the Coastal State in Regulating Scientific Research in its Maritime Zone

Alfred H.A. Soons, *Marine Scientific Research and the Law of the Sea*,
Deventer, The Netherlands: Kluwer Law and Taxation Publishers,
1982, pp. 30-33. Notes omitted. Reprinted with the permission of the
Kluwer Academic Publishers Group.

5.2 Economic interests

The economic interests of coastal States have probably had a greater influence on the international legal regime of marine scientific research than any other single factor. The protection of these interests certainly was the original reason why coastal States began to exercise control over the conduct of scientific investigations in maritime areas under their jurisdiction beyond the territorial sea. As a direct consequence of the coastal State's rights with respect to the exploration and exploitation of its offshore natural resources, it was felt that certain scientific research activities could no longer be left unregulated, for several reasons.

In the first place, a certain degree of control over marine scientific research is considered necessary in order to prevent that commercial exploration (an activity which falls under complete coastal State jurisdiction) is carried out under the guise of marine scientific research. The activities of commercial exploration vessels are sometimes not distinguishable from those of scientific research vessels. Such unauthorized exploration can be prevented by, for example, requiring prior notification to the coastal State, or by requiring coastal State consent and/or by requiring the presence of observers from the coastal State on board the research vessel.

A second reason for coastal States to claim control over the conduct of marine scientific research in maritime areas under their jurisdiction is related to the fact that certain *bona fide* scientific research activities can provide valuable information concerning the natural resources. It is, for instance, possible that the results of certain scientific investigations (such as seismic surveys during a marine geophysical research program) indicate that existence of geological structures likely to contain petroleum or gas or indicate the occurrence of other exploitable minerals. A coastal State, particularly a smaller developing State, may consider it to be not in its best interests to have such information generally available because it might fear that it could result in pressure by foreign governments or companies for further exploration of the areas in question. If the exploration is successful, there could be further pressure for exploitation of the resources, while the coastal State would prefer to develop them later, when it can make better use of the resources itself. Another possibility is that the results of scientific research indicate that certain areas are highly unlikely to contain any mineral resources. As a result, commercial enterprises will not apply for exploration licenses for such areas, which means a loss of income for the coastal State. Such interference with coastal State interests can be prevented by not permitting the research to be conducted (which presupposes a coastal State right to require its prior consent), or by restricting the scientist's right to publish all or certain results of the research.

Thirdly, coastal States require some kind of control over marine scientific research in order to ensure that they will receive all results. It will be obvious that a coastal State has an interest in any information concerning its offshore areas, because it may be valuable, for e.g., its economic development plans, its environmental policy or the management of its resources. The coastal State must also have this information in order to prevent that others know more about its offshore areas than it does itself. It is a well-known fact that geologists from oil companies regularly visit academic oceanographic institutions to examine the results of recent research cruises. Often it takes several years before the results of the research are published, and become available to the coastal State. As a result, the coastal State could be at a disadvantage during negotiations for exploration or exploitation licenses, when the oil company has a better idea of the potentials of the area in question. Such situations can be prevented from happening if researchers are under an obligation to provide access to all data obtained, and to all results of the research, to the coastal State involved.

5.3 Military interests

The international legal regime of marine scientific research is also influenced by the military interests of coastal States.

In the first place, the security of a coastal State could be affected by the conduct of military intelligence or subversive activities under the guise of, or along with, marine scientific research. A research vessel operating near the coast of a foreign country could provide a cover for such activities. This, in fact, was the case with the United States naval vessel *Pueblo*, which was conducting intelligence activities off the coast of North Korea when it was seized by North Korean warships in 1969. The *Pueblo* was officially classified as an environmental research ship. Such intelligence vessels, disguised as research vessels, might even be used to seek easier and/or more frequent access to certain foreign ports.

Another possibility is the discovery, accidentally or not, and maybe even damaging, of military installations on the seabed near the coast by a research vessel from a foreign State. Research vessels may also be used to implant sonar arrays or other sensing devices to monitor movements of submarines or other activities occurring on or above the continental shelf.

Finally, there is a possibility that during *bona fide* research activities by foreign vessels scientific information about a coastal State's offshore areas is collected which is also valuable for foreign navies, and which the coastal State therefore wishes not to be made generally available. For example, surveys of the seasonal distribution of characteristics such as temperature, salinity, and sound velocity, as well as geological characteristics of the sea floor, are necessary to evaluate the local performance of sonar.

Like the case of economic interests, such military interests of coastal States can be protected by, for example, requiring prior notification to the coastal State, or by requiring prior coastal State consent and/or by requiring the presence of observers from the coastal State on board the research vessel.

5.4 Other interests

Apart from the protection of economic and military interests there may be other reasons for coastal States to claim some kind of control over marine scientific research to be conducted in offshore areas under their jurisdiction. One such reason could be the prevention of interference by research with other marine activities. Another reason for claiming control could be the prevention of harmful effects of research on the marine environment, for example, the prevention of pollution that might result from scientific drilling.

2. In the Territorial Sea, Straits and Archipelagic Sea Lanes

1982 UNITED NATIONS CONVENTION ON THE LAW OF THE SEA

Article 245
Marine scientific research in the territorial sea

Coastal States, in the exercise of their sovereignty, have the exclusive right to regulate, authorize and conduct marine scientific research in their territorial sea. Marine scientific research therein shall be conducted only with the express consent of and under the conditions set forth by the coastal State.

NOTE

Article 19(2)(j) of the Convention provides that "the carrying out of research or surveying activities" in the territorial sea as not within the meaning of "innocent passage." Article 40 provides: "During transit passage, foreign ships, including marine scientific research and hydrographic survey ships, may not carry out any research or survey activities without the prior authorization of the States bordering straits." Article 54 provides that Article 40 applies *mutatis mutandis* to archipelagic sea lanes passage.

3.   Beyond the Territorial Sea

1982 UNITED NATIONS CONVENTION ON THE LAW OF THE SEA

Article 246
Marine scientific research in the exclusive
economic zone and on the continental shelf

1.   Coastal States, in the exercise of their jurisdiction, have the right to regulate, authorize and conduct marine scientific research in their exclusive economic zone and on their continental shelf in accordance with the relevant provisions of this Convention.

2.   Marine scientific research in the exclusive economic zone and on the continental shelf shall be conducted with the consent of the coastal State.

3.   Coastal States shall, in normal circumstances, grant their consent for marine scientific research projects by other States or competent international organizations in their exclusive economic zone or on their continental shelf to be carried out in accordance with this Convention exclusively for peaceful purposes and in order to increase scientific knowledge of the marine environment for the benefit of all mankind. To this end, coastal States shall establish rules and procedures ensuring that such consent will not be delayed or denied unreasonably.

4.   For the purpose of applying paragraph 3, normal circumstances may exist in spite of the absence of diplomatic relations between the coastal State and the researching State.

5.   Coastal States may, however, in their discretion withhold their consent to the conduct of a marine scientific research project of another State or competent international organization in the exclusive economic zone or on the continental shelf of the coastal State if that project:

(a) is of direct significance for the exploration and exploitation of natural resources, whether living or non-living;

(b) involves drilling into the continental shelf, the use of explosives or the introduction of harmful substances into the marine environment;

(c) involves the construction, operation or use of artificial islands, installations and structures referred to in articles 60 and 80;

(d) contains information communicated pursuant to article 248 regarding the nature and objectives of the project which is inaccurate or if the researching State or competent international organization has outstanding obligations to the coastal State from a prior

objectives of the project which is inaccurate or if the researching State or competent international organization has outstanding obligations to the coastal State from a prior research project.

6.   Notwithstanding the provisions of paragraph 5, coastal States may not exercise their discretion to withhold consent under subparagraph (a) of that paragraph in respect of marine scientific research projects to be undertaken in accordance with the provisions of this Part on the continental shelf, beyond 200 nautical miles from the baselines from which the breadth of the territorial sea is measured, outside those specific areas which coastal States may at any time publicly designate as areas in which exploitation or detailed exploratory operations focused on those areas are occurring or will occur within a reasonable period of time. Coastal States shall give reasonable notice of the designation of such areas, as well as any modifications thereto, but shall not be obliged to give details of the operations therein.

7.   The provisions of paragraph 6 are without prejudice to the rights of Coastal States over the continental shelf as established in article 77.

8.   Marine scientific research activities referred to in this article shall not unjustifiably interfere with activities undertaken by coastal States in the exercise of their sovereign rights and jurisdiction provided for in this Convention.

Article 247
*Marine scientific research projects undertaken by
or under the auspices of international organizations*

A coastal State which is a member of or has a bilateral agreement with an international organization, and in whose exclusive economic zone or on whose continental shelf that organization wants to carry out a marine scientific research project, directly or under its auspices, shall be deemed to have authorized the project to be carried out in conformity with the agreed specifications if that State approved the detailed project when the decision was made by the organization for the undertaking of the project, or is willing to participate in it, and has not expressed any objection within four months of notification of the project by the organization to the coastal State.

Article 248
Duty to provide information to the coastal State

States and competent international organizations which intend to undertake marine scientific research in the exclusive economic zone or on the continental shelf of a coastal State shall, not less than six months in advance of the expected starting date of the marine scientific research project, provide that State with a full description of:

(a) the nature and objectives of the project;

(b) the method and means to be used, including name, tonnage, type and class of vessels and a description of scientific equipment;

(c) the precise geographical areas in which the project is to be conducted;

(d) the expected date of first appearance and final departure of the research vessels, or deployment of the equipment and its removal, as appropriate;

(e) the name of the sponsoring institution, its director, and the person in charge of the project; and

(f) the extent to which it is considered that the coastal State should be able to participate or to be represented in the project.

Article 249
Duty to comply with certain conditions

1.   States and competent international organizations when undertaking marine scientific research in the exclusive economic zone or on the continental shelf of a coastal State shall comply with the following conditions:

(a) ensure the right of the coastal State, if it so desires, to participate or be represented in the marine scientific research project, especially on board research vessels and other craft or scientific research installations, when practicable, without payment of any remuneration to the scientists of the coastal State and without obligation to contribute towards the costs of the project;

(b) provide the coastal State, at its request, with preliminary reports, as soon as practicable, and with the final results and conclusions after the completion of the research;

(c) undertake to provide access for the coastal State, at its request, to all data and samples derived from the marine scientific research project and likewise to furnish it with data which may be copied and samples which may be divided without detriment to their scientific value;

(d) if requested, provide the coastal State with an assessment of such data, samples and research results or provide assistance in their assessment or interpretation;

(e) ensure, subject to paragraph 2, that the research results are made internationally available through appropriate national or international channels, as soon as practicable;

(f) inform the coastal State immediately of any major change in the research program;

(g) unless otherwise agreed, remove the scientific research installations or equipment once the research is completed.

2.   This article is without prejudice to the conditions established by the laws and regulations of the coastal State for the exercise of its discretion to grant or withhold consent pursuant to article 246, paragraph 5, including requiring prior agreement for making internationally available the research results of a project of direct significance for the exploration and exploitation of natural resources.

Article 250
Communications concerning marine scientific research projects

Communications concerning the marine scientific research projects shall be made through appropriate official channels, unless otherwise agreed.

Article 251
General criteria and guidelines

States shall seek to promote through competent international organizations the establishment of general criteria and guidelines to assist States in ascertaining the nature and implications of marine scientific research.

Article 252
Implied consent

States or competent international organizations may proceed with a marine scientific research project six months after the date upon which the information required pursuant to article 248 was provided to the coastal State unless within four months of the receipt of the communication containing such information the coastal State has informed the State or organization conducting the research that:

(a) it has withheld its consent under the provisions of article 246; or

(b) the information given by that State or competent international organization regarding the nature or objectives of the project does not conform to the manifestly evident facts; or

(c) it requires supplementary information relevant to conditions and the information provided for under articles 248 and 249; or

(d) outstanding obligations exist with respect to a previous marine scientific research project carried out by that State or organization, with regard to conditions established in article 249.

Article 253
Suspension or cessation of marine scientific research

1.   A coastal State shall have the right to require the suspension of any marine scientific research activities in progress within its exclusive economic zone or on its continental shelf if:

(a) the research activities are not being conducted in accordance with the information communicated as provided under article 248 upon which the consent of the coastal State was based; or

(b) the State or competent international organization conducting the research activities fails to comply with the provisions of article 249 concerning the rights of the coastal State with respect to the marine scientific research project.

2.   A coastal State shall have the right to require the cessation of any marine scientific research activities in case of any non-compliance with the provisions of article 248 which amounts to a major change in the research project or the research activities.

3.   A coastal State may also require cessation of marine scientific research activities if any of the situations contemplated in paragraph 1 are not rectified within a reasonable period of time.

4.   Following notification by the coastal State of its decision to order suspension or cessation, States or competent international organizations authorized to conduct marine scientific research activities shall terminate the research activities that are the subject of such a notification.

5.   An order of suspension under paragraph 1 will be lifted by the coastal State and the marine scientific research activities allowed to continue once the researching State or competent international organization has complied with the conditions required under articles 248 and 249.

Article 254
Rights of neighboring land-locked and geographically disadvantaged States

1.   States and competent international organizations which have submitted to a coastal State a project to undertake marine scientific research referred to in article 246, paragraph 3, shall give notice to the neighboring land-locked and geographically disadvantaged States of the proposed research project, and shall notify the coastal State thereof.

2.   After the consent has been given for the proposed marine scientific research project by the coastal State concerned, in accordance with article 246 and other relevant provisions of this Convention, States and competent international organizations undertaking such a project shall provide to the neighboring land-locked and geographically disadvantaged States, at their request and when appropriate, relevant information as specified in article 248 and article 249, paragraph 1(f).

3.   The neighboring land-locked and geographically disadvantaged States referred to above shall, at their request, be given the opportunity to participate, whenever feasible, in the proposed marine scientific research project through qualified experts appointed by them and not objected to by the coastal State, in accordance with the conditions agreed for the project, in conformity with the provisions of this Convention, between the coastal State concerned and the State or competent international organizations conducting the marine scientific research.

4.   States and competent international organizations referred to in paragraph 1 shall provide to the above-mentioned land-locked and geographically disadvantaged States, at their request, the information and assistance specified in article 249, paragraph 1(d), subject to the provisions of article 249, paragraph 2.

Article 255
Measures to facilitate marine scientific research and assist research vessels

States shall endeavor to adopt rules, regulations and procedures to promote and facilitate marine scientific research conducted in accordance with this Convention beyond their territorial sea and, as appropriate, to facilitate, subject to the provisions of their laws and regulations, access to their harbors and promote assistance for marine scientific research vessels which comply with the relevant provisions of this Part.

Article 256
Marine scientific research in the area

All States, irrespective of their geographical location, and competent international organizations have the right, in conformity with the provisions of Part XI, to conduct marine scientific research in the Area.

Article 257
Marine scientific research in the water column beyond the exclusive economic zone

All States, irrespective of their geographical location, and competent international organizations have the right, in conformity with this Convention, to conduct marine scientific research in the water column beyond the limits of the exclusive economic zone.

> Jorge Vargas, "Marine Scientific Research and the Transfer of Technology," in Jon M. Van Dyke, ed., *Consensus and Confrontation: The United States and the Law of the Sea Convention*, Honolulu: The Law of the Sea Institute, University of Hawaii, 1985, pp. 453-455, 458-460. Reprinted by permission of The Law of the Sea Institute, University of Hawaii.

Part XIII of the Convention on marine scientific research contains 28 articles. Prior to this Convention, the topic of marine scientific research was not discussed in a systematic way. It is mentioned in the 1958 Convention on the Continental Shelf. Article 5(8) creates a consent regime--no state can conduct scientific research on the continental shelf unless they have the consent of the coastal states, which should be normally granted.

The debate over Part XIII of the 1982 Convention focused on the controversy between developed nations and developing nations over the freedom of marine scientific research. For a number of years, developed nations, using Article 2 of the 1958 High Seas Convention, argued that the paragraph at the end of the article indicating that other freedoms might exist implicitly included freedom of scientific research. This view was questioned by developing nations arguing that there was no such freedom. [See R.K. Dixit, "Freedom of Scientific Research in and on the High Seas," *Indian Journal of International Law*, Vol. 11 (1971), pp. 1-8, in which the author argues that freedom of scientific research is *not* envisioned in the 1958 Convention on the High Seas. For a contrary view, see A.F. Vysotsky, "Freedom of Research on the High Seas: A Generally Recognized Rule of International Sea Law," in *The Legal Regime of the World Ocean*, Moscow: U.S.S.R. Academy of Sciences, Institute of State and Law, 1973, pp. 85-90.]

One of the first proposals presented to Committee Three in UNCLOS III by the developed nations was a proposal recognizing a notification regime. Because there was this freedom of marine scientific research, the developed nations argued, it was only necessary to notify the coastal states in order to conduct marine scientific research activities off the shores of those states.

As the discussion progressed, the strategy of the developed nations changed, and we were presented with a second proposal stating that for the conduct of marine scientific research activities relating to the resources of the marine environment, coastal states could require consent prior to research activities, but if the marine scientific research related to basic research or pure research, namely, research activities not relating to the resources, it would be enough only to notify the coastal state.

The 1982 Convention, as it finally developed, has a provision that establishes the freedom of marine scientific research on the high seas. This is one of the new freedoms added to the four traditional freedoms of Article 2 of the High Seas Convention. This new freedom is explicitly listed in Article 87(1)(f) of the Convention along with the freedom to construct artificial islands in Article 87(1)(d).

Article 143 also stipulates that all states have the right to conduct marine scientific research activities for peaceful purposes and for the benefit of humankind as a whole in the Area. . . .

Within any area under the jurisdiction or the sovereignty of the coastal state, no marine scientific research activities can take place unless the coastal state gives its consent or authorization to the researching state. . . . The principle of consent depart from the traditional notion of the so-called freedom of marine scientific research. Articles 245 and 246 have a very clear set of provisions applicable to the territorial sea, the continental shelf, and exclusive economic zone to control and regulate access of researching states.

In my opinion, the principle of consent applicable to scientific research in coastal-state zones is one of the clearest emerging principles of customary international law. I hope coastal nations will not use this requirement to limit the activities of scientists. Some observers may not classify this as an emerging principle of customary international law, but rather as an example of the instant generation of a principle of customary international law.

This important principle of consent is probably going to require the scientific community to coordinate its research and increase the cost of the conduct of marine scientific research. It will pose some coordination problems. No system is a perfect system, and Part XIII of the Convention is the best we have. The advantage of these new provisions is that they establish very clear principles. This is a tremendous advantage. We are eliminating one of the irritants between developed countries and developing countries. I think these principles are going to promote direct communication and international cooperation between developed countries and developing countries.

DISCUSSION

Scientific Research

Anatoly Kolodkin: . . . . If we turn to the marine scientific research in the EEZ and on the continental shelf, I agree that the most important provision is that coastal states now enjoy the right to give consent before scientific research can take place. Under Article 246(3) "Coastal States shall, in normal circumstances, grant their consent for marine scientific research projects by other states or competent international organizations. . . ." The "coastal States shall establish rules and procedures ensuring that such consent will not be delayed or denied unreasonably." We can now conclude that the requirement that coastal states consent to such research is a rule of customary international law. Article 246(5), however, limits coastal states' discretion to withhold their consent to four circumstances. Moreover, Article 246(6) says coastal states may not withhold consent for scientific research on the continental shelf beyond 200 nautical miles unless they are specifically engaged in resource exploitation.

What Does "Consent" Mean?

Anthony D'Amato: May I comment on Professor Vargas's notion that the consent regime in Article 246 is now a principle of customary law and on Professor Kolodkin's reply? I think if we look at Article 246 closely, it gives us a strained use of the word *consent* when it says consent *must* be given in certain circumstances. There were diplomatic reasons for using this language, but from a logical and linguistic standpoint, it really means that the researching state's activities are not *dependent* on the consent of the coastal states at all. Unless the listed circumstances exist, the researching nation can proceed after it gives notice, because the coastal state cannot then withhold consent. The requirement of consent is not therefore really a principle of customary law. Notification is required, and consent can be withheld in certain circumstances.

The Consent Regime

William Burke: . . . . I do not think we need to debate whether the consent regime is the greatest invention since fire. Entirely apart from the Convention, I think today we have a consent regime. The United States put its stamp of approval on that in its Oceans Policy Statement in March 1983. There might be some questions about the details, but a consent regime now exists as a part of customary international law because so many states have made it evident that that is what they expect.

I do not believe, however, that the implied consent concept in Article 252 has become customary international law. In fact, I do not believe we will be able to confirm any time soon whether or not implied consent is a part of customary international law. Very few oceanographic institutions will risk losing an oceanographic research vessel on implied consent. The problem now is how to operate under a consent regime, and my expectation is that there will be a number of parts of the world where no consent will be given.

I doubt if you will see American research vessels operating off the coast of India, for example, unless there are private agreements changing Indian law. The requirements of Indian law for prior consent to publication will turn off all American research because no American scientist will submit to those provisions. Science assumes publication. Recently surveys of U.S. scientists indicate that approximately 99% of them would not engage in research under those conditions. Trinidad and Tobago in the Caribbean present similar problems. Research will occur where it is most feasible and convenient. Where coastal states implement a regime that requires delay and costly expenditures for assessments, the research will simply go elsewhere. This is unfortunate, but it follows from the nature of the regime.

I hope none of these predictions is true, that states are reasonable in the requests they make and do act promptly in response to requests for consent. I do not, however, believe that many states would feel obliged to respond to requests from research institutions in the United States.

I disagree completely with Jorge Vargas about the freedom of scientific research on the high seas. I think most observers viewed it as a real freedom of the sea both prior to and subsequent to 1958. Its place in the Convention (Article 87(1)(f)) is highly desirable, but I do not believe it is innovative in the sense of creating a freedom that did not exist prior to that time.

Basis for U.S. Policy on Marine Scientific Research

Brian Hoyle: The United States will not assert jurisdiction over marine science in our coastal areas, but we will recognize the right of other states to exercise jurisdiction over marine science in compliance with international law. We did not assert jurisdiction because our marine scientists came to us and said they do not trust the United States government to act reasonably. If we were to regulate foreign marine scientists, we might begin to regulate domestic scientists. We really do not have any immediate need to regulate marine science, so we have left it alone.

NOTE

The 1982 Convention does not address issues arising from the use of aircraft or satellite technology in marine scientific research, such as remote sensing from space. See D. James Baker,

"Satellite Measurements of the Oceans: A New Global View," *Impact of Science on Society*, 1983, Nos. 3/4, pp. 271-277; Joint Oceanographic Institutions, Inc., *Oceanography from Space: A Research Strategy for the Decade 1985-1995*, 1984, pp. 3-6; G.M. Danilenko, "Space Technology and the Legal Regime of Marine Scientific Research," *Marine Policy*, Vol. 13 (1988), pp. 247-255.

REFERENCES

Bill Woodhead, "A Drag Anchor on Knowledge: The Law of the Sea and Marine Science Research," *Utah Law Review*, 1971, pp. 524-544; Robert L. Friedhaim and Joseph B. Kadane, "Ocean Science in the United Nations Political Arena," *Journal of Maritime Law and Commerce*, Vol. 3 (1972), pp. 473-512; U. Jenisch, "A Comparative Study of Current Draft Convention and Proposals for a New Ocean Regime from the Point of View of Scientific Research," in E. Bohme, and M.J. Kehden, eds., *From the Law of the Sea Towards an Ocean Space Regime: Practical and Legal Implications of the Marine Revolution*, Hamburg, 1972, pp. 141-154; John A. Knauss, "Developing the Freedom of Scientific Research Issue of the Law of the Sea Conference," *Ocean Development and International Law*, Vol. 1 (1973), pp. 93-120; Conrad H. Cheek, "Law of the Sea: Effects of Varying Coastal State Controls on Marine Research," *ibid.*, pp. 209-219; Gisele Ringeard, "Scientific Research: From Freedom to Deontology," *ibid.*, pp. 121-136; George S. Robinson, "Evolution of the Law of the Seas: Destruction of the Pristine Nature of Basic Oceanographic Research," *Natural Resources Journal*, Vol. 13 (1973), pp. 504-510; John Norton Moore, "The Future of Scientific Research in Contiguous Resources Zones: Legal Aspects," *International Lawyer*, Vol. 8 (1974), pp. 242-261; John King Campbell, et al., "Implementation of the Scientific Provisions of the Revised Single Negotiating Text," Edward Miles and John King Gamble, Jr., eds., *Law of the Sea: Conference Outcomes and Problems of Implementation*, Cambridge, Mass.: Ballinger Publishing Co., 1977, pp. 295-306; Thomas John Scotto, "Marine Scientific Research Amid Troubled Political Waters," *Hastings International and Comparative Law Review*, Vol. 1 (1977), pp. 139-165; John Norton Moore, "Some Specific Suggestions for Resolving Two Lingering Law of the Sea Problems: Packages of Amendments on 'The Status of Economic Zone' and Marine Scientific Research," *Virginia Journal of International Law*, Vol. 19 (1979), pp. 401-409; Abdulqawi A. Yusuf, "Toward a New Legal Framework for Marine Research: Coastal State Consent and International Coordination," *ibid.*, pp. 411-429; J.C. Phillips, "The Economic Resources Zone: Progress for the Developing Coastal States," *Journal of Maritime Law and Commerce*, Vol. 11 (1980), pp. 349-365; Wesley S. Scholz, "Oceanic Research: International Law and National Legislation," *Marine Policy*, Vol. 4 (1980), pp. 91-127; Warren S. Wooster, "Research in Trouble Waters: U.S. Research Vessel Clearance Experience, 1972-1978," *Ocean Development and International Law*, Vol. 9 (1981), pp. 219-239; Louwine Van Meurs, "Regulations Relating to Marine Scientific Research Conducted for the Purpose of Preservation of the Environment or Aimed at Locating Natural Resources," *South African Yearbook of International Law*, Vol. 10 (1984), pp. 96-120; V.I. Andrianov, "The Regime of Marine Scientific Research on the Continental Shelf and in the Exclusive Zone," *Soviet Yearbook of Maritime Law*, 1984, pp. 89-95; John Warren Kindt, "The Claim for Limiting Marine Research: Compliance with International Environmental Standards," *Ocean Development and International Law*, Vol. 15 91985), pp. 13-35; Erik Franckx, Marine Scientific Research and the New USSR Legislation on the Economic Zone," *International Journal of Estuarine and Coastal Law*," Vol. 1 (1986), pp. 367-390.

4.   Marine Archaeology and Historical Objects

Not all research carried out in the ocean is an investigation of the ocean environment or seabed. Investigation may include archaeological finds and recovery of historical objects.

1982 UNITED NATIONS CONVENTION ON THE LAW OF THE SEA

Article 303
Archaeological and historical objects found at sea

1. States have the duty to protect objects of an archaeological and historical nature found at sea and shall co-operate for this purpose.

2. In order to control traffic in such objects, the coastal State may, in applying article 33, presume that their removal from the sea-bed in the zone referred to in that article without its approval would result in an infringement within its territory or territorial sea of the laws and regulations referred to in that article.

3. Nothing in this article affects the rights of identifiable owners, the law of salvage or other rules of admiralty, or laws and practices with respect to cultural exchanges.

4. This article is without prejudice to other international agreements and rules of international law regarding the protection of objects of an archaeological and historical nature.

REFERENCES

James Kevin Meenan, "Cultural Resources Preservation and Underwater Archaeology: Some Notes on the Current Legal Framework and A Model Underwater Antiquities Statute," *San Diego Law Review*, Vol. 15 (1978), pp. 623-662; Patrick J. O'Keefe, and Lyndel V. Prott, Australian Protection of Historic Shipwrecks," *Australian Year Book of International Law*, Vol. 6 (1978), pp. 119-138. Lyndel V. Prott and Patrick J. O'Keefe, "International Legal Protection of the Underwater Cultural Heritage," *Revue Belge de Droit International*, Vol. 14 (1978-79), pp. 85-103; David A. Balinsky, "Treasure Salvors, Inc. v. Unidentified Wrecked and Abandoned Sailing Vessel, etc., Atocha." 5 *Brooklyn Journal of International Law*, Vol. 5 (1979), pp. 178-190; George F. Bass, "Marine Archaeology: A Misunderstood Science," 2 *Ocean Yearbook*, Vol. 2 (1980), pp. 137-152; Beth Read, "Open Season on Ancient Shipwrecks: Implications of the 'Treasure Salvors' Decisions in the Fields of Archaeology, History and Property Law," *Nova Law Journal*, Vol. 4 (1980), pp. 213-236; Anthony Clark Arend, "Archaeological and Historical Objects: The International and Legal Implications of UNCLOS III," *Virginia Journal of International Law*, Vol. 22 (1981-82), pp. 777-803; Lucius C. Caflisch, "Submarmine Antiquities and the International Law of the Sea," *Netherlands Yearbook of International Law*, Vol. 13 (1982), pp. 3-32; Charles A. Cerise, Jr., "Treasure Salvage: The Admiralty Court 'Finds' Old Law," *Loyola Law Review*, Vol. 28 (1982), pp. 1126-1145; Robert A. Koenig, "Property Rights in Recovered Sea Treasure: The Salvor's Perspective," *Journal of International and Comparative Law*, Vol. 3 (1982), pp. 271-305; Piers Davies, "Wrecks on the New Zealand Coast," *New Zealand Law Journal*, 1983, pp. 202-205; Douglas B. Shallcross and Anne G. Giesecke, "Recent Developments in Litigation Concerning the Recovery of Historic Shipwrecks," *Syracuse Journal of International Law and Commerce*, Vol. 10 (1983), pp. 371-404; David R. Watters, "The Law of the Sea Treaty and Underwater Cultural Resources," *American Antiquity*, Vol. 48 (1983), pp. 808-816; United States Congress, Senate

Committee on Energy and Natural Resources, Subcommittee on Public Lands and Reserved Water, *Protection of Historic Shipwrecks and the National Maritime Museum; Hearings*, 98th Congress, 1st Session, on S. 1504, October 21, 1983, Washington: U.S. Government Printing Office, 1984; Charles A. Szypszak, "The Protection, Salvage, and Preservation of Underwater Cultural Resources in the Chesapeake Bay," 4 *Virginia Journal of Natural Resources Law*, Vol. 4 (1984-85),pp. 373-395; Dean E. Cycon, "Legaland Regulatory Issues in Marine Archaeology," *Oceanus* (Boston, Mass.), Vol. 28(1) (Spring 1985) pp. 78-84; Charles Mazel, "Technology for Marine Archaeology," *Oceanus*, Vol. 28(1) (Spring 1985), pp. 85-89; Luigi Migliorino, The Recovery of Sunken Warships In InternationalLaw," in *Essays on the New Law of the Sea*, Zagreb [Yugoslavia]: Sveucilisna naklada Liber, 1985, pp. 244-258; David R. Owen, "Some Legal Troubles with Treasure: Jurisdiction and Salvage," *Journal of Maritime Law and Commerce*, Vol. 16 (1985),pp. 139-179; Cynthia Newton Furrer, "Finders Keepers?: The Titanic and the 1982 Law of the Sea Convention," *Hasting International and Comparative Law Review*, Vol. 1 10 (1986), pp. 159-197; L. Van Meus, "Legal Aspects of Marine Archaeological Research," *Acta Juridica* (Cape Town), 1986, pp. 102-123; Anne G. Giesecke, "Shipwrecks: The Past in the Present," *Coastal Management: An International Journal of Marine Environment, Resources, Law and Society*, Vol. 15(3) (1987), pp. 179-195; John P. Fry, "The Treasure Below: Jurisdiction Over Salvaging Operations in International Waters," *Columbia Law Review*, Vol. 88 (1988),pp. 863-881; David R. Owen, "The Abandoned Shipwreck Act of 1987: Good-bye to Salvage in the Territorial Sea," *Journal of Maritime Law and Commerce*, Vol. 19 (1988), pp. 499-516.

G. SCIENTIFIC RESEARCH INSTALLATIONS, RESPONSIBILITY AND LIABILITY AND SETTLEMENT OF DISPUTES

1982 UNITED NATIONS CONVENTION ON THE LAW OF THE SEA

Part XIII

MARINE SCIENTIFIC RESEARCH

SECTION 4. SCIENTIFIC RESEARCH INSTALLATIONS OR EQUIPMENT IN THE MARINE ENVIRONMENT

Article 258
Deployment and use

The deployment and use of any type of scientific research installations or equipment in any area of the marine environment shall be subject to the same conditions as are prescribed in this Convention for the conduct of marine scientific research in any such area.

Article 259
Legal Status

The installations or equipment referred to in this section do not possess the status of islands. They have no territorial sea of their own, and their presence does not affect the delimitation of the territorial sea, the exclusive economic zone or the continental shelf.

Article 260
Safety zones

Safety zones of a reasonable breadth not exceeding a distance of 500 meters may be created around scientific research installations in accordance with the relevant provisions of this Convention. All States shall ensure that such safety zones are respected by their vessels.

Article 261
Non-interference with shipping routes

The deployment and use of any type of scientific research installations or equipment shall not constitute an obstacle to established international shipping routes.

Article 262
Identification markings and warning signals

Installations or equipment referred to in this section shall bear identification markings indicating the State of registry or the international organization to which they belong and shall have adequate internationally agreed warning signals to ensure safety at sea and the safety of air navigation, taking into account rules and standards established by competent international organizations.

SECTION 5. RESPONSIBILITY AND LIABILITY

Article 263

Responsibility and liability

1. States and competent international organizations shall be responsible for ensuring that marine scientific research, whether undertaken by them or on their behalf, is conducted in accordance with this Convention.

2. States and competent international organizations shall be responsible and liable for the measures they take in contravention of this Convention in respect of marine scientific research conducted by other States, their natural or juridical persons or by competent international organizations, and shall provide compensation for damage resulting from such measures.

3. States and competent international organizations shall be responsible and liable pursuant to article 235 for damage caused by pollution of the marine environment arising out of marine scientific research undertaken by them or on their behalf.

SECTION 6. SETTLEMENT OF DISPUTES AND
INTERIM MEASURES

Article 264
Settlement of disputes

Disputes concerning the interpretation or application of the provisions of this Convention with regard to marine scientific research shall be settled in accordance with Part XV [Settlement of Disputes], sections 2 and 3.

Article 265
Interim measures

Pending settlement of a dispute in accordance with Part XV, sections 2 and 3, the State or competent international organization authorized to conduct a marine scientific research project shall not allow research activities to commence or continue without the express consent of the coastal State concerned.

REFERENCES

Nikos Papadokis, "Some Legal Problems Associated with the Ocean Data Acquisition Systems, Aids, and Devices (ODAS)," *International Relations*, Vol. 5 (1975), pp. 825-837; R. Jaganmohan Rao, "The International Legal Regime of ODAS [Ocean Data Acquisition System] and Other Offshore Research Installations," *Indian Journal of International Law*, Vol. 22 (1982), pp. 375-395.

H. EFFECT OF THE 1982 UNITED NATIONS CONVENTION ON THE LAW OF THE SEA ON FUTURE MARINE SCIENTIFIC RESEARCH

John A. Knauss, "The Effects of the Law of the Sea on Future Marine Scientific Research and of Marine Scientific Research on the Future Law of the Sea," *Louisiana Law Review*, Vol. 45 (1985), pp. 1208-1211. Footnotes omitted. Copyright 1985, The Louisiana Law Review. All rights reserved. Reprinted by permission.

Based on recent trends it seems evident that the 1982 Law of the Sea Convention will strongly affect where marine scientific research is done and how it is done. It will even influence the techniques and instrumentation. The adjustments are already evident. It is assumed that whether or not the Convention is ever widely adopted, the EEZ provisions of the Convention, including the right of the coastal state to control marine scientific research within its EEZ, will become part of customary international law.

International Agreements: Increasingly, marine scientists from researching States such as the United States attempt to develop joint efforts with their colleagues from those States in whose waters they wish to work. One consequence is that such research programs are longer in the planning and are often more elaborate in their execution than was the case previously. Joint plans often have at least a semi-official sponsorship from organizations within the two States.

Some feel that we will soon see an increase in large, internationally sanctioned research programs by U.N. sponsored groups such as the Intergovernmental Oceanographic Commission (IOC), or the World Meteorological Organization (WMO), or by such nongovernmental international science organizations as the Special Committee on Oceanographic Research (SCOR) of the International Council of Scientific Unions. Two such programs for the future are the World Ocean Circulation Experiment (WOCE) and a major new program called Global Change which encompasses the land and the atmosphere as well as the oceans.

Large programs of the scope of WOCE require several years of planning, but once States have agreed through the IOC or similar organizations to participate in WOCE, it becomes much easier for scientists from those States to develop joint programs. Perhaps as important, a program such as WOCE provides an umbrella under which a number of "spin-off" scientific programs can often find a home. Small additional programs often can be accommodated at the last minute as long as these last-minute programs are in the spirit of the original plan. When significant changes must be made (including major changes in ship schedules or ship programs) it may be possible to reach agreement within the international scientific steering committee without having to resubmit formal requests to the coastal State involved. In other words, large international science programs take time to establish, but once all participating States have agreed, the detailed planning and execution of the program can be facilitated. For these reasons, I believe we will see an increase in internationally sponsored marine scientific research.

Areas in which marine scientific research is undertaken: A dozen years ago, before there were significant constraints on scientific research in most parts of the world, an estimate was made of approximately how much time U.S. academic research vessels spent in waters which would come under coastal State jurisdiction. Both the Woods Hole Oceanographic Institution and the University of Rhode Island reviewed several years of their research ship programs and each came up with about the same answer. Some forty percent of the time was being spent in waters which would soon be some States' exclusive economic zone, and which henceforth would require permission if we were to work there. We are now in a transition stage between the old and the new, and it may be a bit early to make a careful survey of what effect the new 200-mile exclusive economic zones have had on where marine science is done. A quick survey of programs run from the University of Rhode Island's research vessel Endeavor during the four year period 1980-1984 shows that less than ten percent of the ship time was spent doing work in another State's EEZ. Part of that dramatic change could simply be a change in interests; for example, concentration on the Gulf Stream, deep ocean spreading centers, and equatorial currents--all of which can be studied without entering a foreign EEZ. However, as noted earlier, all things being equal, scientists will concentrate their efforts on problems that require minimum bureaucratic entanglements. The procedures which must be followed in many States to work in their EEZs add both problems and uncertainty of success to what is already a difficult work program. Thus, the trend we have observed in the work program of our own research vessel may not be an exception.

Research techniques: One of the important new tools of oceanography is the satellite. Sensors aboard satellites allow us to measure the surface temperature of the ocean and to determine the "color" of the ocean and thus gain an indirect measure of its biological productivity. Satellite sensors can also determine the detailed shape of the ocean surface as well as the surface roughness, from which we can infer information about currents and waves. Most importantly, satellite sensors allow one to measure large areas of the ocean almost simultaneously. In a way never before possible, one can see the detailed structure of the entire length of the Gulf Stream at a single pass, or see the spatial patterns of biological productivity. Satellite information has one very important limitation. All the information comes from the surface skin of the ocean. Inferences can often be drawn about what is occurring beneath the surface, but the data are surface data. Considerable research is now underway to attempt to develop relationships between what can be seen on the surface with the often more important processes that occur beneath the surface. For example, scientists are now attempting to correlate the highly visible superficial scar that marks the edge of the Gulf Stream as seen by satellite with the "real" Gulf Stream that one observes from the more detailed measurements one can make from a ship.

The 1982 Law of the Sea Convention is silent on marine scientific research from satellites. In fact, the subject was never formally raised during the negotiations. It is also noteworthy that nowhere in the Convention is marine scientific research defined. Research vessels wishing to do marine scientific research in a foreign EEZ must request permission, but satellites passing overhead do not need to request permission to collect information about the surface of the ocean.

The improvements in satellite technology in the past decade would have insured increasing interest of marine scientists in these kinds of data under any circumstances; the fact that these data are not subject to the constraints of the Law of the Sea Convention enhances the interest.

Marine scientists sometimes inadvertently gather information from a coastal State's EEZ without processing formal request forms. These are the data from drifting buoys, both surface buoys and subsurface buoys. A typical one might work as follows: a cylindrical tube, perhaps a few inches in diameter and several feet long, is designed to float with the currents at a depth of 1000 feet or so. It carries sensors to measure the temperature and salinity of the water, and perhaps such information as dissolved oxygen, or bioluminescence. By recording the time of arrival of sound pulses from a number of acoustic beacons scattered in the area, it is able to determine its position several times a day and this information is recorded on magnetic tape. After recording position information and data about the ocean for a period of several weeks a weight is dropped by a preprogrammed clock, and the buoy floats to the surface and radios the information it has stored to a communications satellite which in turn transmits the information to the scientist in the laboratory.

The use of these floating instrument packages is growing, both those that float on the surface and those that float at mid-depth. As far as the 1982 Law of the Sea Convention is concerned, the problem is that there is no way to guarantee which way they will float. There is little problem for buoys with a life span of a few weeks, but one set of buoys was tracked in the central North Atlantic for more than two years. Most stayed in the vicinity, but a few wandered off into the Caribbean. Although they were often out of range of the acoustic network, they occasionally sent back information about subsurface currents from one or another foreign EEZ. If these systems grow in popularity in the future, it seems likely that some misunderstandings between researchers and coastal States will occur. What effect this will have on the continued use of the technique is uncertain.

REFERENCES

G.F. Humphrey, "UNCLOS and the Marine Scientist," *Marine Policy*, Vol. 5 (1981), pp. 270-271; Jon L. Jacobson, "Marine Scientific Research Under Emerging Ocean Law," *Ocean Development and International Law*, Vol. 9 (1981), pp. 187-199; Gerard J. Mangone, "The Effect of Extended Coastal States Jurisdiction Over the Seas and Seabed upon Marine Science Research," *ibid.*, pp. 201-218; Allen Manzur, "Large-scale Ocean Research Projects: What Makes Them Succeed or Fail?" *Social Studies of Science*, Vol. 11 (1981), pp. 425-449; Maria Eduarda Goncalves, "Science, Technology and the New Convention on the Law of the Sea," *Impact of Science on Society*, 1983 Nos. 3/4, pp. 347-355; Jacques Richardson, ed., "Research, International Law and the Sea in Man's Future," *Impact of Science on Society*, 1983, Nos. 3/4, pp. 243-503; Joint Oceanographic Institutes, Inc., Satellite Planning Committee of Joint Oceanographic Institutions, *Oceanography from Space: A Research Strategy for the Decade 1985-1995*, 2 volumes, Washington, D.C.: Joint Oceanographic Institutions, 1984-1985; Ocean Studies Board (National Academy of Sciences/National Research Council), *Marine Scientific Research--Law of the Sea Constraint and Emerging State Practice*, 1986.

I. TRANSFER OF MARINE TECHNOLOGY

Boleslaw A. Boczek, *The Transfer of Marine Technology to Developing Nations in International Law*, Honolulu: The Law of the Sea Institute, University of Hawaii, 1982, pp. 23-24, 26, 28-30, 33-34. Notes omitted. Reprinted by permission of The Law of the Sea Institute, University of Hawaii.

[The provisions of the Draft Convention referred to in this article are the same as later adopted in the 1982 Convention, though editorial changes were made in Articles 274(c) and 276(1).]

Compared with other "Parts" of the Draft Convention, Part XIV, entitled "Development and Transfer of Marine Technology," is of medium size, consisting of 13 articles in four sections. Section 1 (General Provisions) spells out in Article 266 the principle of states' duty to cooperate within their capabilities to promote actively the development and transfer of marine science and technology; in Article 267 the protection of all legitimate interests; in Article 268 the operational goals of the cooperation; and in Article 269 measures to achieve these objectives. Section 2 (International Cooperation) deals with ways and means of such cooperation in Article 270; guidelines, criteria and standards in Article 271; coordination of international programs in Article 272; cooperation with international organizations, including the Seabed Authority, in Article 273; and objectives of the Authority in Article 274, the last two articles, which interject the Authority into Part XIV, being the most controversial in an otherwise relatively easy part of the Draft Convention. The non-controversial Section 3 regulates national and regional marine scientific and technological centers in Articles 275 and 276 respectively. The final Section 4 is Article 278 on cooperation among international organizations. . . .

C.   *The Legal Nature of Part XIV*

It will be recalled that one of the hard core issues at UNCTAD [United Nations Conference on Trade and Development] negotiations for a Code of Conduct on the Transfer of Technology has been the legal nature of that document: should it be legally binding or only voluntary guidelines. In principle, such a problem should not have arisen at UNCLOS III negotiations whose objective was to draft an international treaty, that is, legal rules. Still there was enough latitude in the possibility of using more or less stringent verbal phrases, from clearly mandatory verbs to watered down obligations or, at most, hortatory language in the articles of the Draft Convention concerning technology transfer. In general, that is what happened to Part XIV. Whereas, for example, the embryonic draft of the Group of 77 used such strong formulations as "shall actively promote," the ISNT, like the present Draft Convention, has a slightly weaker language "shall cooperate to . . . actively promote." Generally speaking, throughout the debates the developing countries favored more direct formulations whereas the developed nations would try to modify it by introducing indirect and milder formulas, like "endeavor to," for example . . . .

E.   *Protection of Private Commercial Interests*

Although Part XIV does not expressly guarantee industrial property rights, such guarantee can be implied from Article 267, Protection of Legitimate Interests, dating back to the ISNT and derived from a proposal of Denmark on behalf of the European Community. Under this provision, in promoting cooperation concerning the development and transfer of marine science and marine technology, states shall have "due regard for all legitimate interests including, *inter alia*, the rights and duties of holders, suppliers and recipients of marine technology." It is remarkable that except for the adjective "due" instead of "proper" this clause, suggested by the EXEC, is a copy of a phrase in the Charter of the Economic Rights and Duties. Despite this most respectable origin, a number of developing countries (Nigeria, Algeria, Egypt, for example), unsuccessfully tried to delete the relevant article or, like Peru, at least replace it by a less comprehensive formula. An additional guarantee for commercial technology suppliers appears in the initial article of Part XIV on the cooperation in promoting the development and transfer of marine technology which--as proposed by Denmark--should take place "on fair and reasonable terms and conditions," a compromise formula which met the minimum concerns of both the developed and developing countries. This formula is virtually the same as the one found in the principles and the guarantees of the Draft Code of Conduct on the Transfer of Technology.

F.   *The Role of the International Seabed Authority*

The most controversial question, and the last to be resolved, in the debates on the transfer of technology was the very mention and role of the International Seabed Authority in a part designed to deal with technology transfer in general. It was this issue that most prominently exposed the North-South conflict on this matter. The tactical goal of the developed countries was to concede to the Authority as little power as possible or, preferably, eliminate any mention of this body. They believed that the Authority was a threat to their interests and preferred to tackle it exclusively in the context of the deep seabed mining issue in the First Committee. The origin of the brief article where the name of the Authority is first mentioned dates back to Article 4 of the Nigerian proposal at Caracas taken over without any essential changes by the Drafts of 28 and the Group of 77. It appeared in the ISNT and Rev. SNT. Following their tactic, the developed countries moved that the mention of the Authority be replaced by "competent international organizations," playing down this motion as a small amendment of a drafting nature. As usual, a compromise was reached and both "competent international organizations" and "the Authority" are now in the text. The deep seabed mining orientation of the article was stressed by naming the Enterprise as another recipient of technology with regard to the "activities in the Area."

The origin of Article 274 shows equal if not sharper controversy. The Draft of 28 endowed the Authority with functions going beyond its activities in the Area, for example, marine scientific research and setting up a special fund to finance all marine activities of the developing countries. The former was strongly opposed by the industrialized countries as well as by the Soviet bloc. Moreover, the Western nations found it unacceptable and a dangerous precedent in view of the UNCTAD negotiations that the Authority should have the power to ensure that all blueprints and patents be made available to developing nations. This united opposition of the industrialized world was taken into account in the ISNT where "blueprints and patents" were replaced by "technical documentation" to "be made available to all States, in particular developing States which may need and request technical assistance in this field," and the scope of the Authority's competence was limited to the Seabed Area. The Revised SNT deleted any mention of a "special fund" but introduced "financial arrangements provided for in [the] Convention." Finally, from the Western point of view the key change produced in the draft of the future Article 274 (Article 86 of the Revised SNT) was adding the guarantee clause of Article 267, that is, a reference to "all legitimate interests including, *inter alia*, the rights and duties of holders, suppliers and recipients of marine technology." This means that in pursuing its objectives under Article 274, that is, ensuring training, technical assistance, technical documentation, and financial arrangements for developing states, the Authority as well as states must respect all legitimate interests. Attempts by developing states to delete this clause at the 5th Session (1976) failed against counter-arguments adduced by developed nations that retaining a reference to the rights and duties of holders and suppliers of technology lay also in the interest of recipients. "If the reference was deleted," argued the Australian representative, "the International Authority might not fully recognize those rights, and that would inevitably impede the transfer of technology. The acquired rights of holders and suppliers of technology must therefore be recognized and protected if the transfer of technology was really to be encouraged". . . .

J.   *Final Remarks*

In summing up the discussion of the provisions on the transfer of marine technology in the Law of the Sea Draft Convention, the point must be stressed that these provisions do not lay down clear legal obligations but only establish certain standards of conduct which to a large extent reflect the already existing practice. The developing nations concentrated their attention in the First Committee where they perceived a much more vital aspect of technology transfer. It is significant that the most controversial problem debated in the Third Committee's work on technology transfer was related to the International Seabed Authority. The inclusion in Part XIV of provisions on the Authority is structurally alien to this part of the Draft Convention, but to a certain extent it represents a success for the Group of 77 . . . It is also important that Part XIV recognized the legitimate rights of the parties to technology transfer transactions: holders, suppliers, and recipients alike. In conclusion, the provisions on technology transfer of the Draft Convention are not likely to have any immediate discernible legal effect upon the transfer of marine technology.

REFERENCES

C. Weiss, Jr., "Technology Transfer and the Oceans," in John King Gamble and Giulio Pontecorvo, eds., *Law of the Sea: The Emerging Regime of the Oceans*, Cambridge, Mass.: Ballinger Publishing Co., 1974, pp. 81-98; I.J. Silva, "The Transfer of Technology and the Role of the Indian Ocean Fishery Survey and Development Programme," *ibid.*, pp. 113-124; David A. Ross and Leak J. Smith, "Training and Technical Assistance in Marine Science--A Viable Transfer Product," *Ocean Development and International Law*, Vol. 2 (1974), pp. 219-253; Giulio Pontecorvo and Maurice Wilkinson, "An Economic Analysis of the International Transfer of Marine Technology," *ibid.*, pp. 255-283; John Liston and Lynwood Smith, "Fishing and the Fishing Industry: An Account with Comments on Overseas Technology Transfer," *ibid.*, pp. 285-312; David Kay, "International Transfer of Marine Technology: The Transfer Process and International Organizations," *ibid.*, pp. 351-377; Vinod Dar and Marcia Levis, "Effective Communication in Technology Sharing," *ibid.*, pp. 379-401; Victor T. Neal, "Transfer of Marine Science and Technology: A Case History," *Interciencia* (Caracas), Vol. 6 (1981), pp. 324-328; "Offshore Oil Drilling," *Environmental Science and Technology*, Vol. 15 (1981), pp. 1259-1263; W. M. Reisman, "Key International Legal Issues with Regard to Ocean Thermal Energy Conversion Systems," *California Western International Law Journal*, Vol. 11 (1981), pp. 425-444; Harvey B. Silverstain," Ocean Surveillance Technologies and International Payoffs," *Ocean Development and International Law*, Vol. 10 (1981), pp. 187-198; Jonathan I. Charney, "Technology and International Negotiations," *American Journal of International Law*, Vol. 76 (1982), pp. 78-118; Jon M. Van Dyke and David L. Teichmann, "Transfer of Seabed Mining Technology: A Stumbling Block to U.S. Ratification of the Law of the Sea Convention?," *Ocean Development and International Law*, Vol. 13 (1984), pp. 427-456; Douglas Yarn, "The Transfer of Technology and UNCLOS III," *Georgia Journal of International and Comparative Law*, Vol. 14 (1984), pp. 121-153; Rahmatulah Khan, "Transfer of Marine Technology," *Indian Journal of International Law*, Vol. 25 (1985), pp. 262-269; M.C.W. Pinto, "Transfer of Technology under the UN Convention on the Law of the Sea," Elisabeth Mann Borgese and Norton Ginsburg, ed., *Ocean Yearbook*, Vol. 6, Chicago and London: University of Chicago Press, 1986, pp. 241-270 [only pp. 264-267 deal with Part XIV of the Convention, the remaining part of the article discusses the seabed mining technology transfer problem].

NOTE

For various problems relating to marine technology, see *Marine Technology Society Journal.*

CHAPTER XIV

SETTLEMENT OF DISPUTES RELATING
TO THE LAW OF THE SEA

A. INTERNATIONAL DISPUTE SETTLEMENT IN GENERAL

> Thomas Buergenthal and Harold G. Maier, *Public International Law*,
> 2nd ed., St. Paul, Minn.: West Publishing Co., 1990, pp. 65-79, 82-
> 86. Some references omitted. Reprinted with the permission of the
> West Publishing Co.

I. INTRODUCTION

. . . Article 33(1) of the UN Charter provides a useful list of the methods used to deal with international disputes. The article reads as follows:

> The parties to any dispute, the continuance of which is likely to endanger the maintenance of international peace and security, shall, first of all, seek a resolution by negotiation, enquiry, mediation, conciliation, arbitration, judicial settlement, resort to regional agencies or arrangements, or other peaceful means of their own choice. . . . .

II. NON-JUDICIAL METHODS

§ **4-1. Introduction.** The traditional non-judicial methods for the resolution of international disputes are negotiations, inquiry, mediation and conciliation. Depending upon the dispute, its context and the attitude of the parties to it, one or more and sometimes all of these methods may come into play. In short, they are not necessarily distinct or exclusive techniques for the resolution of a conflict. Each of these methods has domestic institutional counterparts which function much the same way.

§ **4-2. Negotiation.** Bilateral and multilateral negotiations to resolve differences between one or more states or between groups of states may be carried out by diplomatic correspondence, face-to-face encounters by permanent diplomatic envoys or by specially designated negotiators. Negotiation is the traditional and most commonly employed method. It tends to be the first stage in a process that may require resort to other, more formal, dispute-resolution methods. Prior negotiation is often also required as a condition precedent to the exercise of jurisdiction by an international court.

§ **4-3. Inquiry.** The reference of a dispute to a process of inquiry involves the designation of a group of individuals or an institution to act as an impartial fact-finding or investigatory body. This method can be extremely effective under certain circumstances. An inquiry undertaken with the consent of the parties that results in an unambiguous finding of fact is more likely than not to lead to the resolution of the dispute when the disagreement between the parties involves only issues of fact.

§ **4-4. Mediation or good offices.** This technique consists of third-party efforts to assist the parties to a dispute to resolve their disagreements through negotiation. The role of mediator is to bring the parties together, to serve as intermediary between them, to propose solutions and to explore opportunities for settlement. Today these techniques take on many different forms. Mediators may serve as a bridge between contending states whose representatives do not even talk to each other--the Middle East shuttle diplomacy provides a good example. Mediators may sit in on negotiations, chair meetings, suggest solutions, cajole, etc.

§ 4-5. Conciliation. This is a more formal process than the other dispute resolution techniques described above. It requires an agreement by the parties to the dispute to refer the controversy to a group of individuals or to an institution to make appropriate findings of fact and recommendations. As a rule, the parties do not obligate themselves to accept the recommendations, but the existence of a report containing the findings tends to make it more difficult for the parties to disregard it or to reject the recommendations, particularly if they wish to avoid the appearance of acting in an arbitrary or lawless manner.

§ 4-6. Negotiation, mediation, conciliation combined. There exist today numerous international institutions and mechanisms in which the above mentioned techniques are structured into one formal dispute-resolution process that consists of a combination of negotiation, fact-finding, mediation and conciliation. Institutions that have been established to resolve disputes concerning claims of human rights violations are but one example of this phenomenon. They normally consist of a committee or commission created by a treaty, which as a rule also contains a catalog of the protected rights. Disputes concerning violations of these rights may be referred by the state parties to a committee. That body then initiates a formal process which moves from negotiations and fact-finding to efforts to bring about a friendly settlement, followed by a report containing conclusions and, if a friendly settlement is not reached, recommendations. See, e.g., UN Racial Convention, arts. 11-13; International Covenant on Civil and Political Rights, arts. 41-42. In some of these treaties, provisions are even made for adjudication, which is resorted to as a final step in the dispute-settlement process. This possibility exists, for example, under the European and American Conventions of Human Rights. . . . The UN Charter itself envisages a dispute resolution process in which the Security Council and the General Assembly play different roles in activating resort to the various methods listed in Article 33 of the Charter. UN Charter, chs. VI & VII.

III. QUASI-JUDICIAL METHODS

§ 4-7. Arbitration and adjudication distinguished. International arbitration and international adjudication differ from the dispute-resolution techniques discussed in the preceding sections in one very important respect: both the arbitral and judicial decisions are binding on the parties. In international law, arbitration is a form of adjudication, the difference being that an arbitral tribunal or panel is as a rule not a permanent judicial body. Its composition as well as its jurisdiction and the rules of procedure it applies, must be agreed upon by the parties. (The agreement in which all of these matters are settled is known as a *compromis*.) International adjudication, by contrast, takes place in the context of a permanent court, which has a fixed composition and operates under preexisting jurisdictional standards and rules of procedure. . . .

§ 4-9. Consent to arbitrate. It is a basic rule of international law that states cannot be required to arbitrate a dispute unless they have given their consent thereto, either before or after the controversy has arisen. . . . [Some] arbitral agreements . . . contain provisions permitting either party to the dispute to require the other party to arbitrate. But where this is not true, the subsequent consent of both parties will be needed for arbitration to take place. In the third type, the consent to arbitrate is contained in the *compromis*.

§ 4-10. The *compromis*. This agreement contains provisions for the designation of the arbitral panel, if that subject has not been previously agreed upon. It will identify the issues that are to be decided, specify the rules of procedure to be followed, and state the undertaking of the parties to abide by and implement the award. Since the *compromis* is a binding international agreement, a party's failure to abide by the award would constitute a separate breach of international law. The vast majority of international arbitral awards are complied with.

§ 4-11.   **Composition of arbitral tribunals.**   Usually, arbitral tribunals are composed of three members. Each party to the dispute may name one member, with the third member to be designated by agreement of the parties or, failing such agreement, by the President of the International Court of Justice or some other person of international stature. If the parties are unable to agree on the third member and the arbitral agreement does not contain an alternative method for his selection, there may be no way to implement the agreement to arbitrate because international courts have no general power under international law to impose an arbitrator. While arbitral tribunals vary in size--the U.S.-Iranian Claims Tribunal, for example, consists of nine members--the tripartite structure described above is usually maintained. Arbitral tribunals are established either to deal with a specific dispute or to decide a variety of claims. In some instances, so-called *ad hoc* international arbitral tribunals have continued to function for decades.

§ 4-12.   **The arbitral award.**   Unless the agreement provides otherwise, arbitral awards are binding on the parties to the dispute and not subject to appeal. Some arbitral clauses permit judicial review of the decree by the International Court of Justice. See, e.g., Appeal Relating to the Jurisdiction of the ICAO Council (India v. Pakistan), 1972 ICJ Rep. 46. The validity of arbitral awards may be challenged, moreover, in certain special circumstances. The four most commonly accepted bases for such a challenge, codified in the UN's Model Rules of Arbitral Procedure, are that the tribunal has exceeded its powers; that there was corruption on the part of a member of the tribunal; that there has been failure to state the reasons for the award or a serious departure from a fundamental rule of procedure; that the undertaking to arbitrate or the *compromis* is a nullity. UN Model Rules on Arbitral Procedure, art. 35. These rules were approved by the UN General Assembly in 1958. . . .

§ 4-13.   **Applicable law and sources of law.**   Arbitral tribunals apply international law unless the parties specify that some other law should be applied. In the 19th and early 20th century and before, international law case law consisted principally of decisions of arbitral tribunals and judgments of domestic courts applying international law. . . .

Although the authority of the older arbitral decisions has diminished with time and some have been characterized by new states as relics of colonialism and imperialism, they remain a valuable secondary source of law. The legal authority of contemporary arbitral decisions is much greater, of course. In the absence of a decision by the International Court of Justice or one of the other permanent courts, these decisions are the best judicial evidence of international law.

§ 4-14.   **International arbitration and the individual.**   Although international arbitration is a method for the adjudication on the international plane of disputes between states, the facts giving rise to such disputes often involve claims by nationals of one state against another state. Here the states are said to be "espousing" the claims of their nationals. Over the years, international arbitral tribunals have developed a whole body of international law, both procedural and substantive, bearing on the various legal issues that arise in the litigation of such claims. . . . Much of that law, particularly its procedural and jurisdictional components, has found its way into the constitutions and rules of procedures of existing international courts.

IV. INTERNATIONAL COURTS

§ 4-15.   **Introduction.** . . . Today there exist a number of permanent international courts, including the International Court of Justice (ICJ) and various specialized regional tribunals. . . .

One very important rule applicable to international adjudication needs to be emphasized at this point: under international law, states cannot be required to submit disputes to international adjudication unless they have consented to it.   Thus, the threshold question for an international tribunal hearing a case always is the issue whether its jurisdiction has been accepted by the states parties to the dispute.   States are free, as a rule, to accept jurisdiction either before a dispute has arisen or thereafter, to limit their acceptance of certain disputes, and to attach various conditions to the acceptance.   Jurisdictional issues consequently always loom large in the work of international tribunals.

A. The International Court of Justice

§ 4-16.   **Historical development.**   The ICJ is the successor to the Permanent Court of International Justice (PCIJ), which was established in 1920 under the auspices of the League of Nations.   The PCIJ stopped functioning during the Second World War in 1939, although it was not formally dissolved until 1946.   That tribunal rendered some 30 judgments, 27 advisory opinions, and various interlocutory orders.   These decisions continue to be cited as authority by international lawyers and judges.

The ICJ, which is the principal judicial organ of the UN, came into being in 1945.   Its Statute or constitution, modelled on that of the PCIJ, is annexed to and forms an integral part of the UN Charter.   All member states of the UN are *ipso facto* parties to the Statute of the Court. States that are not UN members may adhere to the Statute under conditions that the UN has prescribed.   UN Charter, arts. 92-94.

§ 4-17.   **Composition and institutional structure.**   The ICJ consists of 15 judges, no two of whom may be nationals of the same state.   The judges are elected by the UN General Assembly and the Security Council; they have to receive an absolute majority of the votes in both bodies.   The regular term of the judges is nine years; they may be reelected.   There is no formal rule allocating a seat on the Court to each of the permanent members of the Security Council, although this is done in practice.

The Court has two distinct types of jurisdiction: contentious jurisdiction and advisory jurisdiction.   Different rules and procedures apply to each.

1. *Contentious Jurisdiction*

§ 4-18.   **Bases of contentious jurisdiction.**   The contentious jurisdiction of the ICJ applies only to disputes between states which have accepted that jurisdiction.   The Court lacks contentious jurisdiction to deal with disputes involving individuals or entities that are not states. ICJ Statute, art. 34(1).

In discussing the Court's jurisdiction, it is important not to confuse adherence to the Court's Statute with jurisdiction.   The doors of the Court are open to a state which is a party to its Statute-

-that is what adherence to the Statute signifies. But whether the Court may hear a case filed by a state party to the Statute against another state party depends upon whether both have accepted the tribunal's jurisdiction.

Article 36 of the Statute deals with the Court's contentious jurisdiction. There are basically three ways in which states can submit to the jurisdiction of the ICJ. First, they can accept the Court's jurisdiction on an *ad hoc* basis for the adjudication of an existing dispute. ICJ Statute, art. 36(1). Second, they can adhere to a treaty, be it bilateral or multilateral, in which the Court's jurisdiction is accepted, expressly or by implication, for cases relating to the interpretation or application of the treaty or for any other disputes that might arise. Ibid. Provisions of this type may be limited to specific disputes or be general in character. Third, under article 36(2), which is known as the "optional clause," the states parties to the Statute may by means of a unilateral declaration undertake that "they recognize as compulsory *ipso facto* and without special agreement, in relation to any other state accepting the same obligation, the jurisdiction of the Court in all legal disputes . . ." involving issues of law or fact governed by rules of international law. The Court lacks jurisdiction to hear cases that are governed by domestic law rather than international law. ICJ Statute, art. 38(1).

§ 4-19. **Reciprocity.** A state's unilateral declaration accepting the Court's jurisdiction under article 36(2) is applicable "in relation to any other state accepting the same obligation." By filing this declaration, a state accepts the Court's jurisdiction on the basis of reciprocity and, consequently, is required to respond only if sued by a state that has made a similar declaration.

Moreover, whatever jurisdictional defenses the appellant state might have been able to assert against the respondent under its declaration if the roles were reversed, are open to the respondent because of reciprocity. . . .

The question whether a state, which accepts the Court's jurisdiction "unconditionally," will be deemed to have waived reciprocity under article 36(2), has been answered in the negative by a majority of commentators. . . .

§ 4-22. **National security considerations.** Issues of national security are usually perceived to be the most sensitive and, thus, least likely to be submitted to international adjudication. For example, in recent decades several nations have modified their acceptance of the compulsory jurisdiction of the ICJ to exclude matters related to national security or self-defense. The U.S., which had not made such a modification, cited these considerations, *inter alia*, as reasons for its withdrawal from the *Nicaragua* case after the Court ruled against it on the jurisdictional issue. See U.S. Statement of January 8, 1985, 24 Int'l Leg. Mat. 246 (1985). Similar considerations explain the French position in the *Nuclear Test Cases* (*Austria v. France*; *New Zealand v. France*), 1973 ICJ 99 and 135; 1974 ICJ 253 and 257. In the *Nicaragua* case, the ICJ rejected the view that disputes involving issues of national security or self-defense were *ipso facto* not suitable for adjudication by the Court or inadmissible. Nicaragua v. U.S., supra, at 433-37. . .

§ 4-23. **Effect and enforcement of judgments.** Judgments rendered by the ICJ in contentious cases are binding on the parties thereto. ICJ Statute, art. 59. They are also deemed to be "final and without appeal." ICJ Statute, art. 60. The Statute of the Court does not specify how its judgments are to be enforced. That subject is governed by article 94 of the UN Charter. In article 94(1), each UN member state "undertakes to comply with the decision of the International Court of Justice in any case to which it is a party." A state which fails to abide by the Court's judgment would thus violate the UN Charter. This point is reinforced by article 94(2), which permits a party to a suit to appeal non-compliance to the UN Security Council, "which may, if it deems necessary, make recommendations or decide upon measures to be taken to give effect to the judgment." It should be emphasized that the Security Council "may" but need not take any action. Moreover, if it acts, it may do so by means of a recommendation or decision; only the latter is binding. The failure of a member state to comply with a Security Council decision may in certain circumstances give rise to enforcement measures. See UN Charter, arts. 39, 41, 42. Since the veto power of the permanent members applies to enforcement measures, that action will only be taken in cases in which these states are prepared to cooperate in forcing compliance with a judgment of the Court. . . .

2. Advisory Jurisdiction

§ 4-24. Scope of advisory jurisdiction. The advisory jurisdiction of the ICJ may be invoked only by UN organs and by the specialized agencies of the UN. ICJ Statute, art. 65(1). States and individuals have no standing to request advisory opinions. Article 96(1) of the UN Charter expressly authorizes the UN General Assembly and the Security Council to seek advisory opinions. Other UN organs and the specialized agencies of the UN may do so with the approval of the General Assembly. UN Charter, art. 96(2). The Assembly has given this authorization not only to the principal organs listed in article 7 of the UN Charter, but also to various subsidiary organs. As for the authority of the specialized agencies to request advisory opinions, the requisite approval is, as a rule, contained in their cooperative agreements with the UN. . .

§4 25. Legal character. Advisory opinions are by definition non-binding. Whether the requesting institution will be guided by or accept as obligatory the Court's ruling is a matter that is governed by the institution's internal law. In the UN it is customary for the requesting organ to vote on whether to accept the opinion. Some international agreements provide that the advisory opinion requested by an organization is binding on the organization and the states parties. . . . The non-binding character of advisory opinions should not be confused with their juridical authority, the legitimating effect they may have on the conduct of states and organizations, or with their value as precedent in a legal system in which there is a scarcity of judicial pronouncements. In practice, advisory opinions are relied upon and cited as legal authority as frequently as are judgments rendered in contentious cases. Since the doctrine of *stare decisis* (binding precedent) is not a doctrine of international law and since it does not apply to contentious decisions of the ICJ, the Court's advisory opinions have in theory no less precedential value than judgments rendered in contentious cases. The fact that the latter are binding on the parties to the case and that the former are not does not affect their value as legal precedent in future controversies involving other parties.

B. SETTLEMENT OF DISPUTES UNDER THE 1958 GENEVA CONVENTIONS ON THE LAW OF THE SEA AND OTHER CONVENTIONS

OPTIONAL PROTOCOL OF SIGNATURE CONCERNING
THE COMPULSORY SETTLEMENT OF DISPUTES
Done at Geneva on April 29, 1958
United Nations Treaty Series, Vol. 450, pp. 170, 172.

The States Parties to this Protocol and to any one or more of the Conventions on the Law of the Sea adopted by the United Nations Conference on the Law of the Sea held at Geneva from 24 February to 27 April 1958,

Expressing their wish to resort, in all matters concerning them in respect of any dispute arising out of the interpretation or application of any article of any Convention on the Law of the Sea of 29 April 1958, to the compulsory jurisdiction of the International Court of Justice, unless some other form of settlement is provided in the Convention or has been agreed upon by the Parties within a reasonable period,

Have agreed as follows:

Article I

Disputes arising out of the interpretation or application of any Convention on the Law of the Sea shall lie within the compulsory jurisdiction of the International Court of Justice, and may accordingly be brought before the Court by an application made by any party to the dispute being a Party to this Protocol.

Article II

This undertaking relates to all the provisions of any Convention on the Law of the Sea except, in the Convention on Fishing and Conservation of the Living Resources of the High Seas, articles 4, 5, 6, 7 and 8, to which articles 9, 10, 11 and 12 of that Convention remain applicable.

Article III

The Parties may agree, within a period of two months after one party has notified its opinion to the other that a dispute exists, to resort not to the International Court of Justice but to an arbitral tribunal. After the expiry of the said period, either Party to this Protocol may bring the dispute before the Court by an application.

Article IV

1. Within the same period of two months, the Parties to this Protocol may agree to adopt a conciliation procedure before resorting to the International Court of Justice.

2. The conciliation commission shall make its recommendations within five months after its appointment. If its recommendations are not accepted by the parties to the dispute within two months after they have been delivered, either party may bring the dispute before the Court by an application.

Article V

This Protocol shall remain open for signature by all States who become Parties to any Convention on the Law of the Sea adopted by the United Nations Conference on the Law of the Sea and is subject to ratification, where necessary, according to the constitutional requirements of the signatory States.

CONTRACTING PARTIES TO THE OPTIONAL PROTOCOL
Multilateral Treaties Deposited with the Secretary-
General, Status as at 31 December 1988,
New York: United Nations, 1989, p. 750.

Participant	Signature[1]	Definitive signature(s)[1] ratification, succession (d)[2]
Australia		14 May 1963s
Austria	27 Oct 1958	
Belgium		6 Jan 1972s
Bolivia		17 Oct 1958s
Canada	29 Apr 1958	
China[3]		
Colombia		29 Apr 1958s
Costa Rica		29 Apr 1958s
Cuba		29 Apr 1958s
Democratic Kampuchea	22 Jan 1970	
Denmark	29 Apr 1958	26 Sep 1968
Dominican Republic		29 Apr 1958s
Finland		27 Oct 1958s 16 Feb 1965
France		30 Oct 1958s
Germany, Federal Republic of		30 Oct 1958s 26 Jul 1973
Ghana		29 Apr 1958s
Haiti		29 Apr 1958s 29 Mar 1960
Holy See		30 Apr 1958s
Indonesia	8 May 1958	
Israel	29 Apr 1958	

---

[1]It will be noted that certain signatures, although they were affixed without reservation as to ratification, were followed by the deposit of an instrument of ratification: in such cases, the two corresponding dates will be found in the third column.

The States listed herein are bound by this Protocol to the extent that they have signed it definitively, ratified it or succeeded to it, and that they are bound by one at least of the four Law of the Sea Conventions to which it related.

[2]"d" means succession.

[3]Signature affixed without reservation as to ratification on behalf of the Republic of China on 29 April 1958. [The Republic of China ratified the Convention on the Continental Shelf, 499 UNTS 311, on October 12, 1970. However, on October 26, 1971, the General Assembly of the United Nations decided that the People's Republic of China should represent China in all United Nations organs and its affiliated agencies. The People's Republic of China has not ratified any of the four Geneva Conventions.]

Liberia		27 May 1958s
Madagascar		10 Aug 1962s
Malawi		17 Dec 1965s
Malaysia		1 May 1961s
Malta		19 May 1966d
Mauritius		5 Oct 1970d
Nepal		29 Apr 1958s
Netherlands	31 Oct 1958	18 Feb 1966
New Zealand		29 Oct 1958s
Pakistan		6 Nov 1958s
Panama		2 May 1958s
Portugal	28 Oct 1958	8 Jan 1963
Sierra Leone		14 Feb 1963s
Solomon Islands		3 Sep 1981d
Sri Lanka		30 Oct 1958s
Sweden	1 Jun 1966	28 Jun 1966
Switzerland	24 May 1958	18 May 1966
Uganda		15 Sep 1964s
United Kingdom		9 Sep 1958s
United States of America	15 Sep 1958	
Uruguay		29 Apr 1958s
Yugoslavia	29 Apr 1958	28 Jan 1966

NOTE

With respect to the conservation of fishery and other living resources provided in Articles 4 to 8 of the 1958 Geneva Convention on Fishery and Conservation of the Living Resources of the High Sea, done on April 29, 1958, 559 UNTS 285, Article 9 of this Convention provides for the organization of a special commission of five members to be agreed between states in dispute. Failing agreement on the composition of the commission, "they shall, upon the request of any State party, be named by the Secretary-General of the United Nations, within a further three-month period, in consultation with the States in dispute and with the President of the International Court of Justice and the Director-General of the Food and Agriculture Organization of the United Nations, from amongst well-qualified persons being nationals of States not involved in the dispute and specializing in legal, administrative or scientific questions relating to fisheries, depending upon the nature of the dispute to be settled." Article 10 provides for the criteria to be applied by the commission, Article 11 provides for the binding character of the commission's decision and Article 12 deals with the situation of subsequent factual change after the rendering of the commission's decision.

Several conventions concluded under the auspices of the Intergovernmental Maritime Consultative Organization (now International Maritime Organization) contain provisions authorizing the submission of disputes to the International Court of Justice or to an arbitral tribunal. E.g., see Article 13 of the International Convention for the Prevention of Pollution of the Sea by Oil, done at London, May 12, 1954, 327 UNTS 3 and Article 8 and Annex and Articles 13 to 19 of the International Convention on the High Seas in Cases of Oil Pollution Casualties (usually referred to as Intervention on the High Seas Convention), done at Brussels, November 29, 1969, 26 U.S.T. 765, T.I.A.S. No. 8068.

C. SETTLEMENT OF DISPUTES UNDER THE 1982 UNITED NATIONS CONVENTION ON THE LAW OF THE SEA

J.G. Merrills, *International Dispute Settlement*, London: Sweet & Maxwell, 1984, pp. 118-136. Some notes omitted or renumbered. Reprinted with the permission of the publisher and the author.

The Convention proceeds from the basic principle that the states which are parties shall settle any dispute between them concerning its interpretation or application by peaceful means in accordance with Article 2(3) of the United Nations Charter (Article 279), and goes on to provide that nothing in this part of the Convention impairs their right to settle such a dispute by any peaceful means of their own choice (Article 280). This emphasis on the parties' autonomy is of course consistent with general practice and was not controversial. However, the principle of free choice of means is elaborated in later articles which underline its implications.

When a dispute arises the parties are under an obligation to "proceed expeditiously to an exchange of views" as to the means of settlement to be adopted (Article 283(1)). This important provision is clearly designed to provide the obligation to use peaceful means with a procedural buttress. However a similar duty arises when a procedure has been tried unsuccessfully (Article 283(2) [:The parties shall also proceed expeditiously to an exchange of views where a procedure for the settlement of such a dispute has been terminated without a settlement or where a settlement has been reached and the circumstances require consultation regarding the manner of implementing the settlement]) and this . . . tends to de-emphasize the Convention's own arrangements.

No less significant is the provision laying down that when the parties have selected a particular means of peaceful settlement the procedures laid down later in the Convention apply only if such means prove unsuccessful *and* the agreement between the parties does not exclude any further procedure (Article 281). Moreover, any agreement of a general, regional, bilateral, or other nature providing for the submission of a dispute to a procedure involving a binding decision supplants the procedures laid down later in the Convention, unless the parties otherwise agree (Article 282). The effect of these articles is to enable the parties by agreement in advance to avoid the settlement machinery provided in the Convention.

Thus the Convention's first principle is peaceful settlement with free choice of means. But what happens if the parties cannot agree upon a means of settlement, or choose a means which proves unsuccessful? At this stage, after the exchange of views required by Article 283, section 2 of Part XV, entitled "Compulsory Procedures Entailing Binding Decisions," comes into play.

Whether the Convention should incorporate articles providing for the compulsory settlement of disputes provoked considerable disagreement. The corresponding provisions of the 1958 Conventions on the Law of the Sea are merely an optional protocol to the Conventions and one view was that the same approach should be adopted in the new Convention. However many found this unacceptable on the ground that the interpretation and application of an instrument containing so many innovations was bound to generate disputes which could only be resolved by the use of obligatory third-party procedures. . . .the knowledge that recourse to such procedures is ultimately possible also discourages unreasonableness and so acts as a means of dispute avoidance and this too was no doubt a salient consideration. It was therefore eventually decided that compulsory procedures of some kind should be incorporated.

The first problem in establishing a procedure for securing binding decisions in an instrument such as the Convention is to find a method which all the parties to the treaty can accept. The International Court . . . is not universally supported, yet may be preferred by some states to alternatives such as permanent tribunals with specialised jurisdiction, or ad hoc arbitration. The Convention accepts that this problem exists and resolves it by again invoking the principle of freedom of choice, this time in the form of a choice of methods of binding settlement.

The Convention provides for states to make a written declaration accepting that disputes may be referred to one or more of the following tribunals: a new "International Tribunal for the Law of the Sea;" the International Court of Justice; an arbitral tribunal; or a special arbitral tribunal, with both forms of arbitral tribunal to be constituted in accordance with the Convention. Where both parties to a dispute have accepted the same procedure that procedure is to be used, unless the parties otherwise agree. Where, however, they have accepted different procedures (or one party has not accepted any procedure), then the dispute may be referred to arbitration. These arrangements, which are set out in Article 287 of the Convention, represent a neat solution to the problem of choice of forum and, subject to a point considered below, can be said to establish a useful and flexible system of compulsory jurisdiction.

The articles which comprise the remainder of section 2 of the Convention deal with a number of matters relevant to the functioning of the system of obligatory settlement. The crucial question of jurisdiction is dealt with in Article 288, which provides for the reference of disputes concerning the interpretation or application of the Convention and any international agreement "related to the purposes" of the Convention. Article 289 provides for the appointment of scientific or technical experts, with a role similar to that of assessors in the International Court. Another provision reminiscent of the Court's Statute, Article 290, authorises the prescribing of provisional measures of protection (though only at the request of a party to the dispute), while Article 292 deals with the particular problem of securing the prompt release of vessels and crews detained by national authorities.

The question of choice of law is dealt with by a directive to courts and tribunals having jurisdiction to apply "this Convention and other rules of international law not incompatible with this Convention" (Article 293). The parties may agree to request a decision *ex aequo et bono*, but unless they do so, the clear intention is that the Convention will prevail over other sources of obligation. In . . . arbitration and judicial settlement it was seen that the basis of an international tribunal's decisions is a matter to which states, for obvious reasons, attach very great importance. Bearing in mind the widely held view that the reluctance of "new" states to use the International Court stems from a distrust of traditional international law, it is not difficult to see why the "new" law of the sea, reflecting as it does the influence of those states in many of its elements, should have been given such priority in the Convention.

The third and final section of Part XV is headed "Limitations and Exceptions to the Applicability of Section 2" and concerns disputes which are not, or need not, be subject to the procedures just described, and in certain cases may be referred to another compulsory procedure instead. Thus if the principle of section 2 is that disputes which the parties have failed to settle by means of their own choice are, as a general rule, to be submitted to some form of legal tribunal, section 3 proceeds on the assumption that certain disputes ought not to be subject to obligatory settlement at all, while others call for a procedure unassociated with adjudication.

The details of section 3 are complex and closely bound up with the substantive provisions of the Convention. Their significance, however, can be grasped without an exhaustive analysis of each provision. Article 297 reflects the view of coastal states that certain decisions relating to the exercise of sovereign rights or jurisdiction, especially those concerning the exercise of discretion, should not be subject to challenge in any form of adjudication. Thus after providing that the procedures of section 2 apply to disputes involving an abuse or infringement of traditional maritime freedoms, the Convention lays down that disputes involving coastal states' rights with respect to marine research and fisheries shall be submitted conciliation. The important point here is that while the use of conciliation in the cases specified is obligatory, the Convention is careful to state that the coastal state's exercise of its discretion cannot be questioned, and the commission's report is in any event not binding on the parties. . . .

Article 298 . . . deals with three types of disputes which states may exclude from any or all of the procedures of section 2 by written declaration. These are disputes involving sea-boundary delimitations or historic bays or titles, disputes concerning military activities or law enforcement connected with Article 297, and disputes in respect of which the United Nations Security Council is exercising its functions under the Charter.

In the case of sea-boundary delimitations and other disputes in the first category, the Convention provides that a dispute may be subject to compulsory conciliation and ultimately to the procedures provided for in section 2. However, this elaborate procedure has no application to such a dispute if it also involves sovereignty or other rights over land territory, and there is no corresponding provision concerning disputes in the second and third categories.

The intricate provisions of section 3 are an attempt to balance the desire to be a judge in one's own cause against the principle of binding third party settlement. The exclusion of certain types of disputes from the procedures of section 2 in Article 297 and the opportunity to exclude others provided by Article 298 reflect both traditional sensitivities--territorial sovereignty and military activities, for example--and the special concerns of developing states, whose voting power at the Conference as the so-called "Group of 77," secured the exclusions relating to fishing and research. It is arguable, of course, that for certain disputes--over the exercise of discretion, for example-- conciliation is a more appropriate means of settling disputes than adjudication. Be that as it may, it is clear that without the limitations and exceptions provided for in section 3, the adoption of machinery for the binding settlement of disputes as an integral part of the Convention would not have been generally accepted.

Conciliation

Conciliation is the only method of third party settlement specifically mentioned in section 1 of Part XV, dealing with the settlement of disputes by any means chosen by the parties. Moreover, . . . it is obligatory for certain types of disputes excluded from adjudication in section 3. Conciliation can therefore be said to occupy a prominent place in the Convention, a conclusion which is confirmed in Annex V, where the procedure to be followed in voluntary or mandatory conciliation is set out. In general the articles which make up Annex V follow those of other recent multilateral treaties, though they are more elaborate in certain respects and also differ in certain details.

. . . The Convention provides for the submission of disputes to ad hoc commissions rather than to permanent bodies. A commission is established by each party appointing two members, who then appoint an additional member as chairman. Thus a commission will normally contain five members. In the event of a failure to agree the chairman may be appointed by the Secretary-General of the United Nations, who can also act should a party fail to appoint its own members. To facilitate the appointment of commissions, each party to the Convention is entitled to nominate four conciliators to a list to be compiled by the Secretary-General. In setting up a commission, preference is to be given to candidates on the list, though only the Secretary-General is bound by it, and a state cannot select more than one of its own nationals. The qualification for nomination to the list is "the highest reputation for fairness, competence and integrity" (Article 2). A conspicuous, but not unprecedented, omission is the absence of any reference to legal qualification.

In accordance with the usual practice, a commission determines its own procedure and takes decisions relating to its report, its recommendations and other matters by majority vote. With the consent of the parties to the dispute it may invite any party to the Convention to submit its views orally or in writing and in the course of its proceedings may also draw attention to any measures which might facilitate an amicable settlement.

The functions of a commission are to "hear the parties, examine their claims and objections and make proposals to the parties with a view to reaching an amicable settlement" (Article 6). This formula . . . was originally put forward to emphasize the point that although conciliation is not arbitration, legal, as well as factual, issues may be examined. The directive that the commission's report shall record "its conclusions on all questions of fact or law relevant to the matter in dispute" is also reminiscent of the Vienna Convention and was similarly intended to underline the judicial element in the commission's work by obliging it to present its conclusions. The earlier Convention, however, envisaged conciliation by "qualified jurists." Whether the conciliators appointed under the new Convention will in practice be competent to draw conclusions on questions of law remains to be seen.

The provisions just discussed incline towards what was termed . . . "quasi-arbitration." However there is no lack of emphasis on conciliation as a distinctive process. In addition to the fact, already noted, that in certain cases a state's discretion cannot be challenged, the commission's conclusions are only to be presented when the parties, despite the commission's assistance, have failed to reach agreement. Moreover, any conclusions must be accompanied by "such recommendations as the commission may deem appropriate for an amicable settlement" (Article 7). And the commission's report, including its conclusions and recommendations, is, of course, not binding on the parties.

The fact that in certain circumstances the Convention envisages conciliation as a compulsory procedure is reflected in both the arrangements for filling vacancies on a commission and articles providing that a state is obliged to submit to such proceedings and cannot prevent them by non-cooperation. As might be expected, any disagreement as to whether a commission has competence is to be decided by the commission. If the prospect of obligatory conciliation discourages unreasonableness it will have done its job. . . .

Arbitration

According to the Convention, law of the sea disputes may be referred to arbitration in three different ways. Under section 1 of Part XV the parties may by agreement select any peaceful means and so can decide to set up an arbitration tribunal along traditional lines. Under section 2 both parties may make declarations nominating arbitration as a preferred means of settlement in which case arbitration will be governed by the provisions of the Convention. Alternatively, if there is no common declaration under section 2, arbitration under the Convention will be deemed to have been accepted as the relevant obligatory procedure. It is arbitration under the Convention, the arrangements for which are set out in Annex VII, with which we are here concerned.

The arrangements for constituting a tribunal resemble the earlier provisions concerning conciliation. A list of arbitrators is to be drawn up by the Secretary-General and each party to the Convention may make four nominations. The persons nominated are to be "experienced in maritime affairs and enjoying the highest reputation for fairness, competence and integrity" (Article 2(1)). While these qualifications are clearly most desirable, the omission of any reference to the legal competence of prospective arbitrators is again disquieting. Unless a dispute involves more than two parties, a tribunal is to consist of five members, one nominated by each party and three, including the president, appointed by agreement. The "neutral" element, it will be noticed, is larger here than in conciliation commissions and will normally consist of non-nationals. In constituting a tribunal preference is to be given to arbitrators on the Secretary-General's list.

[The question] that the failure of a state to appoint its members of an arbitration tribunal, or disagreement between the parties as to the neutral element, are matters that must be expressly provided for to guard against difficulties in getting an arbitration under way. The Convention deals with the problem by providing that unfilled places on the tribunal, and disagreement over the president, shall be resolved either by a person or third state chosen by the parties, or by the President of the International Tribunal for the Law of the Sea. All such appointments are to be made from the Secretary-General's list and in consultation with the parties. In an obvious attempt to provide assurance on the crucial issue of neutrality, the Convention lays down that members of the tribunal appointed in this way must also be of different nationalities and may not be "in the service of, ordinarily resident in the territory of, or nationals of, any of the parties to the dispute" (Article 3(e)).

The provisions dealing with procedure and related matters contain a number of points of interest. The tribunal is to decide its own procedure and take decisions by majority vote. Frustration of the proceedings by members of the tribunal is discouraged by an unusual provision that "the absence or abstention of less than half the members shall not constitute a bar to the tribunal reaching a decision" (Article 8). In accordance with the usual practice the tribunal's expenses will normally be borne by the parties. The parties to the dispute are also obliged to facilitate the work of the tribunal by providing it with documents, facilities, access to witnesses, etc. However the Convention's directive here is qualified by a provision that such assistance shall be "in accordance with their law and using all means at their disposal" (Article 6), a formula which permits a state to plead lack of resources and, more seriously, to set up its own law to restrict its obligations.

Failure to appear or to defend a case is dealt with in terms similar to those of Article 53 of the I.C.J. Statute. While such default cannot prevent a decision, before making an award the tribunal must satisfy itself that it has jurisdiction and that the claim is well founded in fact and in law. The award, which is binding on the parties, must be reasoned and limited to the subject-matter of the dispute and may include separate and dissenting opinions. As is generally the case with arbitration, the award is final and without appeal unless the parties otherwise agree, though, surprisingly, disagreements relating to interpretation or implementation may apparently be submitted by either party to the original tribunal at any time, or to another court or tribunal by agreement. Like several other parts of the Convention, the provisions of Annex VII apply *mutatis mutandis* to disputes involving international organizations.

Special Arbitration

The maritime activities of states, like many aspects of the contemporary international scene, are so complex that disputes often involve technical issues which arbitrators with no qualification as specialists may find difficult to handle. A partial attempt to meet this problem was made

[Geneva Convention on Fishing and Conservation of the Living Resources of the High Seas 1958, Articles 9-12, see Note in p. 14-12] which provides for the appointment of experts to decide disputes relating to fishing and conservation. This functional approach to dispute settlement is taken considerably further in Annex VIII of the new Convention concerning special arbitration.

Special arbitration is one of the binding methods of settlement which a party to the Convention can accept in advance by a declaration under section 2 of Part XV. It may therefore be initiated unilaterally whenever a dispute of the appropriate type arises and both parties have deposited a declaration in appropriate terms. The disputes for which special arbitration may be employed are those concerning the interpretation or application of the articles of the Convention relating to: fisheries; protection and preservation of the marine environment; marine scientific research; and navigation, including pollution from vessels and by dumping. Since a state is free to accept special arbitration for all or any of these categories, it is essential for jurisdictional purposes that both parties' declarations cover the type of dispute in question.

To assist states in setting up a tribunal, lists of experts in each of the four fields are to be maintained by, respectively, the Food and Agriculture Organization, the U.N. Environment Programme, the Inter-Governmental Oceanographic Commission and the International Maritime Organization. Each state party may nominate to each list two experts "whose competence in the legal, scientific or technical aspects" of the field is established and "who enjoy the highest reputation for fairness and integrity" (Article 3). The inclusion here of a reference to legal competence and the corresponding omission in the provisions on conciliation and arbitration perhaps suggest that law is regarded more as another type of useful expertise, than, as might be thought, a primary qualification for interpreting and applying a major international convention.

The arrangements for constituting a tribunal essentially follow the pattern of conciliation, rather than arbitration, *i.e.* each party selects two members, preferably from the appropriate list, and the president is chosen by agreement. Similarly, vacant places must be filled from the appropriate list by the Secretary-General, not the President of the I.T.L.S. However, as might be expected, the provisions concerning the disqualification of certain candidates follow those on arbitration, and in exercising his powers of appointment the Secretary-General must consult with both the parties and the relevant international organisation.

The job of a special arbitral tribunal, as the name implies, will normally be adjudication. However the last provision of Annex VIII (Article 5) provides that in certain circumstances its functions can be broadened to include fact-finding and conciliation. By agreement the parties may set up a special arbitral tribunal to carry out an inquiry into the facts of any dispute of a type amenable to special arbitration. An interesting point here is that unless otherwise agreed, such a tribunal's findings of fact are conclusive as between the parties . . . if the parties so request, such a tribunal may formulate non-binding recommendations to provide the basis for a review by the parties of the questions giving rise to the dispute. Thus in a suitable case and with the parties' agreement, the machinery of special arbitration can be employed as an additional form of conciliation. The term "special arbitration" seems hardly appropriate to describe either inquiry or inquiry with conciliation. . . .

The International Tribunal for the Law of the Sea

Among the several new institutions created by the Convention is a new court, the International Tribunal for the Law of the Sea (I.T.L.S.). The idea that disputes of a particular type are best handled by tribunals set up for the purpose is nothing new--the machinery of the European Convention on Human Rights is a well-established example--and the Convention's arrangements for special arbitration clearly reflect the same impulse. However, since the law of the sea can scarcely be said to be so specialised as to be beyond the competence of existing tribunals, the creation of the I.T.L.S. may be thought to indicate a certain lack of confidence in the International Court. In the light of this it is interesting to compare the new Tribunal's Statute, which forms Annex VI of the Convention, with that of the I.C.J.

The I.T.L.S., whose seat is in Hamburg, has 21 members, elected for a nine year term. They are to be "persons enjoying the highest reputation for fairness and integrity and of recognised competence in the field of the law of the sea" (Article 2(1)). The vital matter of distribution of seats is dealt with by requiring that "the representation of the principal legal systems of the world and equitable geographical distribution shall be assured" (Article 2(2)). To clarify this point it is provided that "there shall be no fewer than three members from each geographical group as established by the General Assembly of the United Nations" (Article 3(2)). Election is by a two-thirds majority of the parties to the Convention. This is of course a quite different arrangement from that governing elections to the I.C.J., and one which makes it unlikely that permanent members of the Security Council (assuming they are parties to the Convention) will be assured of a seat on the new Tribunal.

The provisions dealing with disqualification of a member in a particular case contain the usual reference to previous participation as agent, counsel, etc., and are modelled on Article 17 of the Statute of the I.C.J. The treatment of incompatible activities of members of the Tribunal, however, expands the earlier Statute's prohibition on political and administrative functions to include active association or financial interest "in any of the operations of any enterprise concerned with the exploration for or exploitation of the resources of the sea or other commercial use of the sea or the sea-bed" (Article 7). As with the I.C.J., a member of the Tribunal is not disqualified by being a national of one of the parties to a dispute and an ad hoc member may be appointed by a party or parties currently unrepresented.

In the light of the I.C.J.'s recent efforts to encourage the use of Chambers it is interesting to note that the new Tribunal's Statute provides for these in terms very similar to those of the earlier instrument. Chambers of three or more members may be formed for dealing with particular categories of cases. A five member chamber of summary procedure is to be formed for the "speedy despatch of business" (Article 15(3)). And a chamber may be formed to deal with a particular dispute if the parties so request. In the last case the Statute makes it clear that the composition of the chamber is to be determined by the Tribunal "with the approval of the parties" (Article 15(2)). . . .

The competence of the I.T.L.S. raises a number of points of interest. As already noted, a dispute may be referred to the Tribunal when both parties have made a declaration accepting its jurisdiction. It will also have jurisdiction when any agreement so provides, or when all the parties to any treaty concerning the law of the sea already in force agree that disputes may be so referred. Unlike the I.C.J., the Tribunal is open to international organisations in certain circumstances (Article 20(2)) and under the same provision may be used by states which are not parties to the Convention. Its choice of law, as we have seen, is governed largely by the Convention.

Procedural arrangements are straightforward and in general resemble those of the I.C.J. Statute. Each party to a case normally bears its own costs, while the running expenses of the Tribunal are borne by the parties to the Convention and the International Sea-Bed Authority on terms to be agreed. Article 31, allowing a state which considers that it has an interest of a legal nature in the outcome of a case to request permission to intervene and Article 32, giving parties to the Convention, or to other treaties before the tribunal, the right to intervene in proceedings, are both modelled on the I.C.J. Statute. The provision governing default (Article 28) is likewise very similar to the Statute and the Convention's own articles on arbitration. Decisions, for which a quorum is nine, are by majority vote and may include separate opinions. Like I.C.J. decisions, they are final, but may be interpreted by the Tribunal at the request of any party. Similarly, they are binding only as between the parties and in respect of the particular dispute.   The Sea-Bed Disputes Chamber concerning the complex arrangements envisaged in the Convention for the exploration and exploitation of the deep sea-bed are dealt with in a series of provisions separate from those relating to other types of disputes. Indeed it was originally suggested that because sea-bed disputes raise a variety of special problems they should be handled by a distinct tribunal with no connection with the I.T.L.S. However, it was eventually decided that though such disputes required a functional approach, the best arrangement would be to create a Sea-Bed Disputes Chamber of the I.T.L.S. with its own constitution and jurisdiction. As a result of this change of policy, the provisions governing the S.B.D.C. are to be found in two places in the Convention, Part XI, section 5, dealing with the administration of the International Sea-Bed Area, and Annex VI, setting up the I.T.L.S.

The S.B.D.C. is to consist of 11 members chosen for a three year term by the 21 elected members of the I.T.L.S. from among their number. In electing the Chamber they are required to ensure that the principal legal systems of the world are represented and that equitable geographical distribution is achieved. At one time it was proposed that elections should be in the hands of a political body, the Assembly of the International Sea-Bed Authority, and traces of this proposal can be discerned in a provision permitting recommendations of a general nature relating to representation and the distribution of seats to be made by the Assembly.

A quorum in the S.B.D.C. is seven, but for certain purposes a smaller ad hoc chamber of three may be formed. The composition of this "chamber of a chamber" is to be determined by the S.B.D.C. with the approval of the parties. If they cannot agree it is to be set up in the same way as an arbitral tribunal, with each party appointing one member and the third appointed by agreement, or, if necessary, by the President of the S.B.D.C.

The competence of the S.B.D.C. is bound up with the complex arrangements for the administration of the International Sea-Bed Area. . . .the Chamber's jurisdiction, which is set out in Article 187,[1] covers disputes between states; between a state and the Authority; between the Authority and a prospective contractor; and between the parties to a contract, including state enterprises and natural or juridical persons. Thus although the privileges traditionally accorded to states are by no means ignored,[2] the Convention seeks to ensure that machinery for the settlement of disputes is available to all prospective participants in the International Sea-Bed Area.

The law to be applied by the S.B.D.C. corresponds to the nature of its jurisdiction. In addition to the provisions of Article 293 which, as we have seen, all tribunals are to apply, the S.B.D.C. is to apply "the rules, regulations and procedures of the Authority" adopted in accordance with the Convention, together with "the terms of contracts concerning activities in the Area in matters relating to those contracts" (Annex VI, Article 38). While it can perhaps be argued that the scope of Article 293 is wide enough to make such particularisation unnecessary, the aim here was presumably "to specify with a view to greater clarity by means of emphasis, those parts of the

---

[1]In addition to the jurisdiction conferred by Art. 187, the S.B.D.C. is competent to prescribe provisional measures under Art. 290.

[2]In proceedings involving natural or juridical persons Art. 190 gives a right of appearance and participation to sponsoring states.

law of the Convention itself which would be likely always to be relevant in proceedings before the Sea-Bed Disputes Chamber, but which would be less likely to be of significance in proceedings before the full Tribunal."

The S.B.D.C., unlike the I.T.L.S., has a jurisdiction which is automatically accepted by all parties to the Convention.   In respect of certain disputes there are nevertheless alternative procedures available. Thus the principle of freedom of choice, already encountered in the general provisions of the Convention, emerges again in the treatment of sea-bed disputes.   As an alternative to the S.B.D.C., a dispute between states concerning the sea-bed articles of the Convention may be referred to an ordinary chamber of the I.T.L.S. by agreement.   As a further alternative, it may, at the request of any party to the dispute, be referred to the type of ad hoc chamber of the S.B.D.C. already described.   Similarly, unless the parties otherwise agree, disputes concerning the application or interpretation of a contract can be referred at the request of either party to binding commercial arbitration in accordance with the UNCITRAL Arbitration Rules. The Arbitral Tribunal, however, has no authority to interpret the Convention and any such issue must be referred to the S.B.D.C. for a ruling.   This unusual arrangement, which may give rise to difficulties in practice, is clearly an attempt to combine the established advantages of commercial arbitration with the need for a uniform interpretation of the Convention.

The exclusion of certain issues on grounds of non-justiciability provides another parallel between the general provisions of the Convention and those relating to the S.B.D.C.   Article 189 prohibits the latter from questioning the exercise by the Authority of its discretionary powers under the Convention.   Moreover, unless the S.B.D.C. is asked for an advisory opinion on the point,[3] it may not "pronounce itself on the question of whether any rules, regulations and procedures of the Authority are in conformity with this Convention, nor declare invalid any such rules, regulations and procedures."   Essentially, therefore, its jurisdiction is confined to questions concerning the application of the Convention and its associated legislation. Like the provisions on the discretion of coastal states considered earlier, these prohibitions are an uncompromising assertion of the controversial proposition that certain disputes concerning the exercise of legal powers are unsuitable for adjudication.   Within its allotted sphere decisions of the S.B.D.C. are binding and the Convention provides that in the territories of the states parties such decisions shall be enforceable "in the same manner as judgments or orders of the highest court of the State Party in whose territory the enforcement is sought" (Annex VI, Article 39). Usually, of course, there is no question of enforcing the decisions of international tribunals through municipal law. In the case of the S.B.D.C., however, the commercial orientation of its work and the fact that effective decisions are essential to the whole sea-bed enterprise, explain this unusual provision.

REFERENCES

Comment, "Toward Peaceful Settlement of Ocean Space Disputes: A Working Paper," San Diego Law Review , Vol. 11 (1974), pp. 733-756; Louis B. Sohn, "Settlement of Disputes Arising out of the Law of the Sea Convention," San Diego Law Review , Vol. 12 (1975), pp. 495-517; A. O. Adede, "Settlement of Disputes Arising Under the Law of the Sea Convention," *American Journal of International Law*, Vol. 69 (1975), pp. 798-818; Louis B. Sohn, "U.S. Policy Toward the Settlement of the Law of the Sea Disputes," *Virginia Journal of International Law*, Vol. 17 (1976), pp. 9-21; John Lawrence Hargrove, "Settlement of Disputes Under the Law

---

[3]The duty to give advisory opinions at the request of the Assembly or the Council "on legal questions arising within the scope of their activities" is laid down by Art. 191.

of Ocean Use, with Particular Reference to Environmental Protection," *Georgia Journal of International and Comparative Law*, Vol.6 (1976), pp. 181-196; John King Gamble, Jr., "The Law of the Sea Conference: Dispute Settlement in Perspective," *Vanderbilt Journal of Transnational Law*, Vol. 9 (1976), pp. 323-341; Maxwell Cohen, "Canada and the United States: Dispute Settlement and International Joint Commission -- Can This Experience be Applied to Law of the Sea Issues?" *Case Western Reserve Journal of International Law*, Vol. 8 (1976), pp. 69-83; A. O. Adede, "Law of the Sea: The Scope of the Third Party, Compulsory Procedures for Settlement of Disputes," *American Journal of International Law*, Vol. 71 (1977), pp. 305-311; Mark W. Janis, "Dispute Settlement in the Law of the Sea Convention: The Military Activities Exception," *Ocean Development and International Law*, Vol. 4 (1977), pp. 51-65; Louis B. Sohn, "Problems of Dispute Settlement," in Edward Miles and John King Gamble, Jr., eds., *Law of the Sea: Conference Outcomes and Problems of Implementation*, Cambridge, Mass.: Ballinger Publishing Co., 1977, pp. 223-244; Roger H. Hull, "Much Ado About Something -- Dispute Settlement and the Law of the Sea Convention," *International Lawyer*, Vol. 11 (1977), pp. 365-375; A. O. Adede, "Law of the Sea--The Integration of the System of Settlement of Disputes under the Draft Convention as a Whole," *American Journal of International Law*, Vol. 72 (1978), pp. 84-95; Louis B. Sohn, "Settlement of Disputes Relating to the Interpretation and Application of Treaties," in *Recuiel des Cours*, Vol. 150-II (1976), pp. 195, 280-290 ("The Compromissory Clause in the Law of the Sea Negotiations"); A. O. Adede, "Prolegomena to the Dispute Settlement Part of the Law of the Sea Convention," *New York University Journal of International Law and Politics*, Vol. 10 (1977), pp. 253-393; Shabtai Rosenne, "Settlement of Fisheries Disputes in the Exclusive Economic Zone," *American Journal of International Law*, Vol. 73 (1979), pp. 88-104; J. Peter A. Bernhardt, "Compulsory Dispute Settlement in the Law of the Sea Negotiations: A Reassessment," *Virginia Journal of International Law*, Vol. 19 (1978), pp. 69-105; A. R. Carnegie, "The Law of the Sea Tribunal," *International and Comparative Law Quarterly*, Vol. 28 (1979), pp. 669-684; Andreas J. Jacovides, "Three Aspects of the Law of the Sea: Islands, Delimitation, and Dispute Settlement," *Marine Policy*, Vol. 3 (1979), pp. 278-288; Paul C. Irwin, "Settlement of Maritime Boundary Disputes: An Analysis of the Law of the Sea Negotiations," *Ocean Development and International Law*, Vol. 8 (1980), pp. 105-148; S. Rama Rao, "Towards a Dispute Settlement Mechanism for the International Seabed Area: An Enquiry," in Ram Prakash, ed., *Law of the Sea: Caracas and Beyond*, The Hague: Martinus Nijhoff, 1980, pp. 343-372; J. N. Saxena, "Limits of Compulsory Jurisdiction in Respect of the Law of the Sea Disputes," in *ibid.*, pp. 320-342; A. O. Adede, "Environmental Disputes under the Law of the Sea Convention," *Environmental Policy and Law* (Lausanne), Vol. 7, No. 2 (May 6, 1981), pp. 63-66; George A. Pierce, "Dispute Settlement Mechanisms in the Draft Convention on the Law of the Sea," *Denver Journal of International Law and Policy*, Vol. 10 (1981), pp. 331-354; A. O. Adede, "The Basic Structure of the Disputes Settlement Part of the Law of the Sea Convention," *Ocean Development and International Law*, Vol. 11 (1982), pp. 125-148; Stanley Anderson, "Peaceful Dispute Resolution and A Common Heritage," *Center Magazine* (Santa Barbara, California), March/April 1982, pp. 57-59; Marianne P. Gaertner, "The Dispute Settlement Provisions of the Convention on the Law of the Sea: Critique and Alternatives to the International Tribunal for the Law of the Sea," *San Diego Law Review*, Vol. 19 (1982), pp. 577-597; Gunther Jaenicke, "Dispute Settlement under the Convention on the Law of the Sea," *Zeitschrift fÅr AuslÑdisches Offentliches Recht und Vîlkerrecht*, Vol. 43 (1983), pp. 813-827; Louis B. Sohn, "The Role of Arbitration in Recent International Multilateral Treaties, Complex Clauses: Law of the Sea," *Virginia Journal of International Law*, Vol. 23 (1983), pp. 171-189; Louis B. Sohn, "Peaceful Settlement of Disputes in Ocean Conflicts: Does UNCLOS III Point the Way?," *Law and Contemporary Problems*, Vol. 46 (1983) pp. 195-200; Hungdah Chiu, "The 1982 United Nations Convention on the Law of the Sea and the Settlement of China's Maritime Boundary Dispute," in T. Buergenthal, ed., *Contemporary Issues in International Law, Essays in Honor of Louis B. Sohn*, Kehl, Strasbourg and Arlington: N.P. Engel, 1984, pp. 189-208; A. L. C. De

Mestral, "Compulsory Dispute Settlement in the Third United Nations Convention on the Law of the Sea: A Canadian Perspective," *ibid.*, pp. 169-188; Andreas J. Jacovides, "Peaceful Settlement of Disputes in Ocean Conflicts: Does UNCLOS III point the Way?" *ibid.*, pp. 165-168; Elliot L. Richardson, "Dispute Settlement under the Convention on the Law of the Sea: A Flexible and Comprehensive Extension of the Rule of the Law to Ocean Space," *ibid.*, pp. 149-163; Eero J. Manner, "Settlement of Sea-Boundary Delimitation Disputes According to the Provisions of the 1982 Law of the Sea Convention," in Jerzy Makarczyk, ed., *Essays in International Law in Honour of Judge Manfred Lachs*, The Hague, Boston and Lancaster: Martinus Nijhoff, 1984, pp. 625-643; Shigeru Oda, "Some Reflections on the Dispute Settlement Clauses in the United Nations Convention on the Law of the Sea," *ibid.*, pp. 645-655; Jorge R. Coquia, "Settlement of Disputes in the UN Convention on the Law of the Sea, New Directions in the Settlement of International Disputes," *Indian Journal of International Law*, Vol. 25 (1985), pp. 171-190; Yogesh K. Tyagi, "The System of Settlement of Disputes under the Law of the Sea Convention: An Overview," *Indian Journal of International Law*, Vol. 25 (1985), pp. 191-209; Gerhard Erasmus, "Dispute Settlement in the Law of the Sea," *Acta Juridica* (Cape Town), 1986, pp. 15-27; Bernard H. Oxman, "Dispute Settlement with and Among Non-parties to the Law of the Sea Convention: Navigation and Pollution," Thomas A. Clingan, ed., *The Law of the Sea: What Lies Ahead?* Honolulu: Law of the Sea Institute, 1988, pp. 479-493. A. O. Adede, *The System for Settlement of Disputes under the United Nations Convention on the Law of the Sea: A Drafting History and a Commentary*, Dordrecht, Boston and Lancaster: Martinus Nijhoff Publishers, 1987; Leonard Lukaszuk, "Settlement of International Disputes Concerning Marine Scientific Research," *Polish Yearbook of International Law*, Vol. 16 (1987), pp. 39-56; John E. Noyes, "Compulsory Third-Party Adjudication and the 1982 United Nations Convention on the Law of the Sea," *Connecticut Journal of International Law*, Vol. 4 (1989), pp. 675-696.

CHAPTER XV

THE LAW OF THE WAR AND
NEUTRALITY IN WARFARE AT SEA

A. THE CHARTER OF THE UNITED NATIONS AND THE LAW OF WAR AND NEUTRALITY IN NAVAL WARFARE

Patrick M. Norton, "Between the Ideology and the Reality: The Shadow of the Law of Neutrality," *Harvard International Law Journal,* Vol. 17 (1976), pp. 249-252, 276-77, 307, 309-311. Reprinted by permission.

Since the signing of the United Nations Charter, the customary law of neutrality has been caught between an international legal order which purports to outlaw war and hence make neutrality obsolete, and an international political environment characterized by frequent armed conflicts in which there is a need to regulate the relations of belligerent and non-belligerent states. The results have been confused, if not chaotic. With the juridical status of armed conflicts uncertain, third states have most often refrained from taking a formal stance of neutrality. But where the need for *some* legal rule has been acute and where the particular rule of the customary law has suited their interests, states have invoked that customary law and defended its continued vitality. Neutrality has for some three decades, therefore, led a sort of "juridical half-life," suspended between an ideology which denies its premises and a reality which finds it useful, if not necessary. . . .

Under the international legal order established by the Charter, resort to armed force by a state was . . . to be regarded as aggression. The objects of such aggression would be entitled to defend themselves, but self-defense was to be primarily an interim measure until the collective security mechanism of the United Nations could be organized to meet the armed aggression. There were envisioned, then, three essential categories of the use of armed force: aggression; self-defense; and collective self-defense. Future international armed conflicts would be between an aggressor and either an individual state exercising its right of self-defense or the United Nations acting collectively. In either event, an attitude of impartiality toward the belligerents, the very essence of traditional neutrality, would be impermissible.

Most commentators recognized from the outset that this system was not seamless, and accordingly that there still might be a place in the interstices for the traditional law of neutrality. The principal problem was the authoritative designation of the aggressor. In every instance of armed conflict each party might be expected to characterize its opponent as the aggressor. The Security Council was empowered to make authoritative determinations on this issue and then to authorize collective security actions or make other recommendations binding on member states. But in the absence of a Security Council decision, individual states might not wish to be able to ascertain for themselves which of the belligerents was the aggressor. In such a situation, it was recognized that assuming the status of a traditional neutral was probably permissible. This was, however, expected to be an unusual situation.

The unusual situation soon became the rule. Because of the Cold War split among the permanent members of the Security Council, that body never assumed the collective security role initially envisioned for it. For the same reason, and because in most instances of armed conflict designation of an aggressor was impossible or likely to have adverse political consequences, the Security Council never designated aggressors. The originally anticipated interstitial situation in which assumption of a neutral status might be permissible under the Charter has arisen, therefore, in every international armed conflict of the last three decades.

But, despite this development, it has not proven possible simply to revert to the earlier system in which non-belligerent states were always entitled, if not obligated, to become neutrals. War is still outlawed. This ideological premise creates difficult issues for non-belligerent states in several respects. First, every instance of international armed conflict is still subject to United Nations debate and theoretically to authoritative resolution by the Security Council. To declare neutrality may to some extent legitimize the legal status of the conflict and impede its potential resolution by the appropriate international bodies. Secondly, belligerents no longer uniformly characterize armed hostilities as "war." It is, therefore, no longer certain under exactly what circumstances a non-belligerent is entitled to declare itself a neutral for legal purposes. In the absence of a formal acknowledgement of a state of war by the belligerents, it is unclear whether a non-belligerent, by the very fact of its non-belligerence, is automatically entitled to any of the rights or subject to any of the duties of the traditional law of neutrality. But if a non-belligerent does issue a declaration of neutrality under these circumstances, it creates the possible anomaly of applying the law of neutrality between belligerents and neutrals despite the fact that the belligerents do not themselves recognize a legal state of war. Finally, the outlawry of aggressive war raises the classical issues of the *bellum justum* for third states: may they unilaterally designate the aggressor and discriminate in favor of its victim; or, alternatively, are they *obligated* under certain circumstances to so designate and discriminate? . . .

Practical considerations have also dissuaded non-belligerents from becoming neutrals in the legal sense:

> It is advantageous for third States not to be forced to apply rules of neutrality, which only serve to restrict commercial relations between these States and their citizens on the one hand and conflicting States and other neutral States on the other, without, however, conferring any real additional benefits. In peacetime conditions, they are able to protect themselves and their citizens quite as well and even better.

*   *   *

It would, however, seem indisputable that under some circumstances--notably the absence of binding Security Council decisions--the customary law of neutrality retains its legal validity and should be applicable. Moreover, practice suggests that states will sometimes find it mutually advantageous to apply the customary law, and that on other occasions non-belligerents should at least have the option of relying upon that law to protect their interests.

> D.P. O'Connell, *The International Law of the Sea*, edited by I.A. Shearer, Vol. 2, New York: Oxford University Press, 1984, pp. 1194-1196. Footnotes omitted. Reprinted with the permission of Oxford University Press.

The outlawry of the resort to force in the United Nations Charter has profoundly affected the law of war at sea. Since the condition of war, in the traditional sense, is no longer lawful, questions arise as to the legal viability of the traditional rules of maritime warfare. Two things need to be said about this. First, if general war should occur, contrary to the Charter, these rules would undoubtedly be resuscitated, since the alternative would be a totally unregulated conflict and belligerents would be deprived of the advantages of useful devices of economic warfare: for this reason, defence planners need to take into account the whole range of traditional rules of maritime warfare. Secondly, the concept of limited war, upon which contemporary naval operations are based, utilizes certain of the traditional institutions, and, because of the limited character of the hostilities, these have enhanced rather than diminished significance in current international law, although they need to be discriminately employed. Far from being moribund, therefore, the law of war at sea remains a matter of preoccupation, and the real question is the extent to which it is modified by contemporary circumstances. . . .

There have been roughly one hundred situations since 1945 in which naval power has been exerted in a coercive role, involving about fifty different navies. Each of these could be described as "limited", although they have varied enormously in the scale of intensity or the level of violence. The factor common to them all is the limited operational goal, not the way the parties have conducted themselves. Strategic options in the contemporary world are more restricted than formerly because the political circumstances have changed. War is no longer an option, and hence the political goal of subjugation is no longer available to those who seek to influence others. That limitation upon strategy requires limitations upon tactics too, so that there are curbs upon the deployment and use of the vehicles of warfare that were unfamiliar to previous ages.

If war is no longer a political option, how are the conflicts which have occurred, and continue almost daily to occur, to be rationalized? The answer is that they are justified on the theory of "self-defence" by both sides, and it is this that enables us to assimilate the one hundred-odd naval incidents since 1945, so diverse in character and degree of violence, for the purpose of analysis. "Self-defence" is a concept of international law, and one endowed with certain qualifications and conditions by the law which politicians have to take into account. . . .

This fundamental shift in international relations is reflected in two paragraphs of the United Nations Charter that stand in uneasy conjunction. Article 2(4) outlaws the use of force, and does so in plain, absolute, and peremptory terms. If it stood alone there would be no plausible justification within the framework of United Nations membership for resort to force. But it stands in relation to Article 51, which reserves the inherent right of individual or collective self-defence if an armed attack "occurs".

. . . If the right of self-defence is, as the Article says, "inherent", does it import the classical doctrine of pre-1945 international law that self-defence, to be justified, must be limited to what is "necessary and proportional" in order to defend oneself? These concepts, necessity and proportion, embody limitations upon conduct, and these can be classified for the purpose of analysis into limitations as to:

      (a) the theatre of operations;
      (b) the scale of operations and the level of weaponry;
      (c) the graduation of force and the scale of response.

All of the one hundred-odd naval operations since 1945 have been characterized by the factor of such limitation. To begin with the theatre of operations: until 1945 all wars at sea were fought without inherent geographical limitation. Indeed, the contrary was the case: sea power was best deployed to destroy an enemy's sea-borne commerce and deny him access to the sea as an avenue of communications and strategic advantage. Although the opportunities for the flexible use of sea power in waters distant from the focus of conflict have been available, they have not, since 1945, in fact been taken advantage of. None of the limited wars at sea since 1945 has spilled over into the oceans at large.

The formal reason for this is that such an extension of the conflict could not plausibly be presented as necessary and proportional to resist an armed attack, but behind that reason lies the incubus of world opinion, which, rightly or wrongly, has been supposed by naval planners and their political masters to be tolerant towards localized conflict but apt to be dangerously alarmed by eruptions of violence in the sea-lanes of international commerce. The advantages of sea power in this respect are thought to be outweighed by the disadvantages of political complications and embarrassment.

REFERENCES

R. Artar, "Development of Laws of Maritime Warfare Since World War II," *Civil and Military Law Journal*, Vol. 16 (1980), pp. 173-178; Yoram Dinstein, "The Law of War at Sea," *Israel Yearbook on Human Rights*, Vol. 10 (1980), pp. 38-69; Bruce A. Harlow, "The Law of Neutrality at Sea for the 80's and Beyond," *UCLA Pacific Basin Law Journal*, Vol. 3 (1984), Nos. 1/2, pp. 42-54; Francis V. Russo, Jr., "Neutrality at Sea in Transition: State Practice in the Gulf War as Emerging International Customary Law," *Ocean Development and International Law*, Vol. 19 (1988), pp. 381-400; "The Persian/ Arabian Gulf Tanker War: International Law or International Chaos," *Ocean Development and International Law*, Vol. 19 (1988), pp. 299-322; Boleslaw Adam Boczek, "Law of Warfare at Sea and Neutrality: Lessons from the Gulf War," *Ocean Development and International Law*, Vol. 20 (1989), pp. 239-271.

B. WAR ZONE OR EXCLUSIVE ZONE

D. P. O'Connell, *The International Law of the Sea*, edited by I.A. Shearer, Vol. 2, New York: Oxford University Press, 1984, pp. 1109-1112. Some footnotes omitted or renumbered. Reprinted with the permission of Oxford University Press.

5. WAR ZONES AND EXCLUSION ZONES

The rule that neutral shipping may not be denied the right of navigation on the high seas is one of the fundamentals of the law of war at sea, and it is especially rigid in times of limited war or states of belligerency short of formal war. Yet it is precisely in these circumstances that the problem of positive identification in the exercise of self-defence is most acute. For modern naval planning, therefore, the condition of tension between these two requirements of the law leads to inevitable perplexity. If all shipping could be excluded from an operational area, or around a convoy or task force, the designation of a contact as potentially hostile would be easier, and that would tend to solve the problem of identification. But if shipping may not be so excluded, the risk of successful attack against such convoy or task force is magnified by the latter's need to take care in identifying a contact.

Defence sea area zones have been established during several of the modern wars. The first was that created by Japan during the Russo-Japanese War, up to ten miles from the coast, when foreign shipping was required to follow routes that kept it away from the main operational areas. In 1914 this was regarded as a precedent by the United States Naval War College on the basis of reasonableness, and when the United States entered the War in 1917 similar defence sea areas, up to ten miles from the coast, were designated around focal American points. The United States *Law of Naval Warfare* states that within the immediate vicinity of naval operations, a belligerent may establish special restrictions and prohibit shipping altogether from the area. Neutral vessels and aircraft which fail to comply with such an exclusion are said to be liable to be fired upon and to be

aircraft which fail to comply with such an exclusion are said to be liable to be fired upon and to be captured.

The line between areas proclaimed as sea defence zones or operational zones and war zones such as were proclaimed in both World Wars is thin. On 3 November 1914 Great Britain proclaimed the North Sea to be a military area within which exceptional measures would be taken in response to indiscriminate minelaying by Germany. On 4 February 1915 Germany declared a war zone around the British Isles in which every ship, regardless of nationality, would be liable to attack. Great Britain retaliated by laying minefields to establish a North Sea barrage, albeit with channels for passage, and by Order in Council on 16 February 1917 ships which failed to comply were liable to be seized. The "reasonableness" of this was defended by the United States Naval War College in a study in 1937, although at the time it occurred the British action was justified as rendered necessary by alleged German illegalities.

The pattern of the First World War was repeated in the Second. Germany initiated indiscriminate mining with magnetic mines, and at the end of 1939, as a counter-measure, a British mine barrage between twenty and fifty miles wide was laid along the east coast of Britain, with a channel for coastal navigation, and after the conquest of Norway this was extended. The Skaggerak and Kattegat were also mined, with a twenty-mile wide open channel. The United Kingdom claimed the right to remove ships from the barred zone, to sequestrate wireless used contrary to the zoning order, and to capture neutral ships for unneutral service in conveying information from the zone.

The legal evaluation of the British-proclaimed war zones is complicated by the fact that the exclusion was effected by means of minefields which were laid and notified in accordance with The Hague Convention No. XIII, so that it could not, of itself, be illegal. The dubious feature of the exclusion is that it went beyond notifying risk and embodied prohibitions and penalties for breach.

The War Zones proclaimed by Germany fall into a different category. These were zones within which all shipping would be attacked at sight, and the exclusion was compounded by the means employed to enforce it, namely unrestricted submarine warfare. The justification proffered in defence was that such zones were created as a reprisal to Great Britain's failure to abide by the unratified Declaration of London of 1908 respecting the legal conditions for blockade; and also that if mining is legal, and a war zone can be so established, the same must be true of the use of the torpedo for that end. At the Nuremberg trial of major German war criminals Admiral Doenitz was found guilty of war crimes for authorizing the establishment of the war zone around the British Isles. That decision seems to settle the question of legality, but it has not ended speculation on the naval utility of exclusion zones either fixed around particular operations, or itinerant around a moving focus (PIM) such as a convoy or task force.

In either case legal evaluation would need to proceed, not from the concepts of reprisals or belligerency but from that of self-defence. Provided that publicity is given to the creation of an exclusion zone, and neutral shipping is not put unduly at risk, self-defence can conceivably justify a proclamation that contacts within a zone will be treated as hostile. Such an argument is more plausible in the case of submerged contacts than in the case of surface contacts because the problem of positive identification is acute in the former instance but hardly arises in the latter because of the available technologies of surveillance.

The proclamation of an exclusion zone by the United Kingdom in 1982 around the Falkland Islands after Argentina had forcibly invaded and occupied the islands illustrates how use can be made of such zones in political as well as military terms. The 200-mile "Maritime Exclusion

Zone", proclaimed on 12 April 1982, declared that "any Argentine warships and Argentine naval auxiliaries found within this zone will be treated as hostile and are liable to be attacked".[1] The absence of any reference to Argentine aircraft, or to ships and aircraft of third countries acting in support of the Argentine occupation, indicated the limited nature of the zone, and leads to the supposition that the British intention was as much to demonstrate political resolution to insist on an Argentine withdrawal as to seek justification for the immediate use of force against Argentine units. With the failure of Argentina to accept Security Council Resolution 502, calling on it to withdraw from the Falkland Islands, the British Government proclaimed a "Total Exclusion Zone" on 28 April 1982, within the same geographical boundaries as the earlier zone, applying to "all ships and aircraft, whether military or civil, operating in support of the illegal occupation of the Falkland Islands".[2] This proclamation presaged a more active use of the zone to treat mere presence within it as prima facie constituting a hostile act justifying immediate measures in self-defence. In the event, the first attack against a surface unit took place outside the Total Exclusion Zone when, on 2 May, the Argentine cruiser *Belgrano* was torpedoed by a British submarine. The justification given was the belief that the *Belgrano*, although outside the zone, was about to attack the British aircraft carriers within it, and that it was a self-defensive measure falling within the proviso to the original proclamation of 11 April that the establishment of the zone was "without prejudice to the right of the United Kingdom to take whatever additional measures may be needed in exercise of its right of self-defence under Article 51 of the United Nations Charter". Whether British warships would have been spared attack within the zone, had the *Belgrano* not been sunk, remains highly problematical; until then, at least, it seemed that the zone had been achieving what is generally thought to be a major purpose of such zones: that, proclaimed by one party in a self-defensive posture, it places the political onus of escalation on the other party to the conflict. Since the end of active hostilities, the Total Exclusion Zone has been lifted, and replaced by a "Protection Zone" of 150 miles similar in nature to the original Maritime Exclusion Zone.

NOTE

On February 15, 1990, the United Kingdom and Argentina reached an agreement to resume full diplomatic relations, which had been broken since the Falkland War in 1982. The agreement stipulates that both nations must give prior notice of air and maritime military maneuvers in the vicinity of South Atlantic islands (Falkland Islands, which the Argentines call the Malrinas) and the lifting of the 150-mile exclusion zone. Both the lifting of the exclusion zone and the new security system are to go into effect on March 31, 1990. "Falkland Enemies Resume Relations," *New York Times*, February 16, 1990, p. A3. For analysis of legal issues relating to the Falkland Islands War, see W.J. Fenwick, "Legal Aspects of the Falklands Naval Conflict," *Revue de Droit Militaire et de Droit de la Guerre* (Brussels), Vol. 24 (1985), Nos. 3/4, pp. 241-268.

---

[1]The British Defence Secretary announced to Parliament on 7 April 1982: "Through appropriate channels the following notice is being promulgated to all shipping forthwith: 'From 0400 Greenwich Mean Time on Monday April 12, 1982, a maritime exclusion zone will be established around the Falkland Islands. The outer limits of this zone is a circle of 200 nautical miles radius from latitude 51 degrees 40 minutes south, 59 degrees 30 minutes west, which is approximately the centre of the Falkland Islands. From the time indicated, any Argentine warships and Argentine naval auxiliaries found within this zone will be treated as hostile and are liable to be attacked by British forces. This measure is without prejudice to the right of the United Kingdom to take whatever additional measures may be needed in exercise of its right of self defence under Article 51 of the United Nations Charter'." Hansard, 7 April 1982, col. 1045.

[2]This zone was described by the British Prime Minister also as a 'blockade' . . . .

The Iran-Iraq War arose over a major border dispute between the two countries: in a 1975 agreement, the Shatt al Arab waterway had been designated as the southern border, which is Iraq's only route to the Persian Gulf--between Iraq and Iran. On September 17, 1980, Iraq abrogated the 1975 agreement and wanted to return to the 1913 Constantinople Accords, which Iraq considered as recognizing the entire waterway as Iraqi territory. Iraqi forces then occupied the waterway and also invaded Iranian territory and thus started the war. Iraq in February, 1984, announced an "exclusion war zone" embracing a 50-mile radius area around Iran's Kharg Island oil terminal. Iraq stated that vessels entering that zone would risk attacks by Iraqi aircraft or naval units. On June 6, 1984, Iran in turn announced a war zone within which commercial shipping would be searched and Iraq-bound vessels seized. Both countries, however, attacked on neutral oil tankers and merchant vessels on the high seas outside the limits of the Iranian war zone. The situation is described by a scholar as follows:

> Following the first escalation of the tanker war in 1984, sporadic attacks on merchant shipping continued throughout 1985 . . . .

> A marked deterioration in the Gulf War at sea followed in 1986 when 111 and in 1987 when as many as 174 ships were targets of attack. Whereas the Iraqis continued using missiles launched from aircraft until the end of the hostilities, most Iranian attacks in 1986 were carried out by missiles from helicopters. In 1987, however, out of 62 Iranian attacks, 32 originated from the Revolutionary Guards' speedboats and other vessels and 14 from missiles launched from ships. Eight were due to mines; one to helicopters, and the origin of five could not be ascertained.

> The year 1987 brought a dangerous escalation of the Gulf War at sea. The Iranian navy received orders to fire missiles at any neutral ship on its way to Kuwait. Occasionally, Iranian warships did so even after having stopped a ship in search of contraband according to the traditional rules. Iran also laid mines in several international shipping lanes of the Gulf, ostensibly to "defend its coastlines." Although some ships were damaged by mines, the increasing hit-and-run raids by patrol boats and speedboats, manned by Revolutionary Guards and armed with heavy machine guns and rocket-propelled grenades, were more dangerous.

> In response to the Iranian attacks on neutral shipping, a number of countries, namely France, Italy, Belgium, the United Kingdom, the United States, and the Soviet Union, sent warships to the region to escort their respective shipping to neutral ports in the Gulf. Especially the U.S. Navy increased its profile following an apparently accidental attack by Iraqi missiles upon the U.S. destroyer *Stark*. Kuwait, transferred 11 oil tankers to the U.S. flag, thus obtaining the U.S. Navy's protection against attacks. Despite that, one reflagged tanker, the *Bridgeton*, struck a mine while passing through a waterway near the Iranian island of Farsi under the first U.S. convoy to Kuwait.

> In the tense atmosphere of the Gulf, the U.S. Navy could not escape going beyond its mission of an armed escort of a neutral convoy and soon got involved in armed exchanges with the Iranian armed forces. In these clashes Iranian boats and mine-layers were sunk or captured and unidentified boats suspected of hostile intent were fired at. In one case, in response to an Iranian attack in Kuwait territorial waters on a reflagged tanker, the *Sea Isle City* in October 1987, with 18 crew wounded and the captain blinded, the U.S. warships, after a warning, destroyed an Iranian military ocean platform in the Gulf, but outside of Iran's territorial sea. Whereas this action could be qualified as a

reprisal, it was justified by the United States as self-defense under Article 51 of the UN Charter. In early 1988 during the resumed "war of the cities," neutral shipping enjoyed a brief lull of some 3 weeks in attacks by either side in the war. However, the respite soon ended and the tanker war was resumed with 96 ships becoming targets of attack before the ceasefire entered into effect on August 20 (see Figure 15-1). There also occurred an armed confrontation between the U.S. Navy and Iranians, in which some Iranian oil platforms were destroyed and six Iranian warships sunk or severely damaged.

Boleslaw Adam Boczek, "Law of Warfare at Sea and Neutrality: Lessons from the Gulf War," *Ocean Development and International Law*, Vol. 20 (1989), pp. 247-248. Reprinted with the permission of the Hemisphere Publishing Corporation.

REFERENCES

Maxwell Jenkins, "Air Attacks on Neutral Shipping in the Persian Gulf: The Legality of the Iraqi Exclusion Zone and Iranian Reprisals," *Boston College International and Comparative Law Review*, Vol. 8 (1985), pp. 517-549.

C. MAJOR TREATIES ON NAVAL WARFARE AND NEUTRALITY

D. P. O'Connell, *The International Law of the Sea*, edited by I. A. Shearer, Vol. 2, New York: Oxford University Press, 1984, pp. 1101-1105. Footnotes omitted. Reprinted with the permission of Oxford University Press.

Two general principles have infused the law of war at sea: the first is the right of neutrals to pursue, as far as is consistent with the circumstances of war, their commerce and national interest; and the second is the humane treatment of belligerents, so far as the exigencies of war permit. Both principles necessarily yield elastic judgments when applied to actual situations. . . .

Neutrality is . . . not an absolute right, for if it were it would negate belligerency. An accommodation is to be arrived at between the two conditions simply because of the coexistence of neutral and belligerent nations in community, and the accommodation will inevitably reflect the technological and commercial factors of the moment, and is not a static condition.

[Major treaties on naval warfare and neutrality are as follows:]

(a)   *The Declaration of Paris, 1856*

[The Declaration was adopted at the Paris Peace Conference among France, Great Britain, Turkey and Russia in 1856. It contains four rules:]

1.   Privateering is and remains abolished.

2.   The neutral flag covers enemy's goods, with the exception of contraband of war.

3.   Neutral goods, with the exception of contraband of war, are not liable to capture under the enemy's flag.

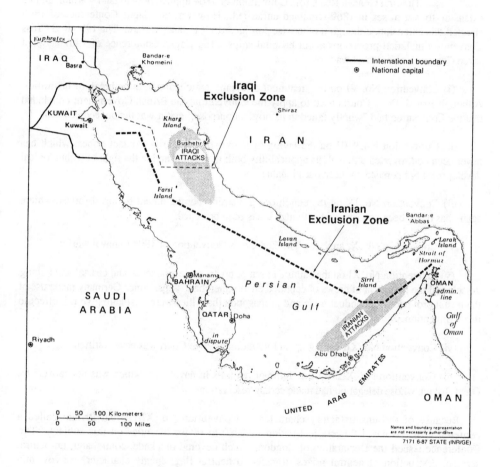

EXCLUSION ZONES OF THE IRAQ-IRAN WAR, 1984 - 1989
Figure 15-1

Source: Revised from "U.S. Policy in the Persian Gulf," *Department of State Bulletin*, Vol. 87, No. 2127 (October 1987), p. 40.

4.   A blockade, in order to be binding, must be effective; that is to say, maintained by a force sufficient really to prevent access to the coast of the enemy.

The United States did not subscribe to the Declaration because it did not go far enough in guaranteeing private property from seizure at sea.

(b)   *The Hague Conferences, 1899 and 1907*

The first Geneva Red Cross Convention of 1864 applied only to land warfare, and its extension to war at sea in 1869 remained unratified. However, the Hague Conference of 1899 effected this extension, although it otherwise confined itself to land warfare. The 1906 Red Cross Convention included provisions about hospital ships. The Hague Conference of 1907 adopted seven Conventions on naval warfare:

(i) Convention No. VI on the treatment of enemy merchantmen at outbreak of hostilities. Although British Prize Courts tried to apply the Convention, the British Government concluded that the Convention had "wholly failed in its original purpose," and it was denounced in 1926.

(ii) Convention No. VIII on the laying of automatic submarine contact mines, which has never been controverted although its applicability both in practice and in the light of technological development has persistently been questionable.

(iii) Convention No. IX on the conditions governing bombardment by naval forces, which, again, has never been controverted, although it has been breached.

(iv) Convention No. X, applying The Red Cross Convention of 1906 to naval warfare.

(v) Convention No. XI on the capture at sea of postal correspondence and coastal and fishing vessels and the treatment of crews of captured enemy merchant ships. Since Germany made use of the postal provisions to conduct trade and propaganda the Allies were unable to give full effect to this Convention.

(vi) Convention No. XII setting up an International Prize Court was never ratified.

(vii) Convention No. XIII on the rights of neutrals in naval war, which was not ratified by Great Britain, whose delegation had made certain reservations.

Because of the unsatisfactory character of Convention No. XIII Great Britain called a conference of the naval Powers in London in 1980 to revise the rules on this subject. The Conference issued the Declaration of London, which covered blockade, contraband, un-neutral service, destruction of neutral prizes, transfer to neutral flag, enemy character, convoy, and resistance to search. Although Great Britain participated in the making of the Declaration, strong resistance to the curbs it would impose upon her capacity to maintain a blockade and to decide what would constitute contraband led to a negative vote in Parliament, and so to a failure of the British Government to proceed to ratification.

On the outbreak of war in 1914 France and Russia undertook to comply with the Declaration, Germany and Austria adopted particular provisions of it, and Great Britain adopted it with additions and modifications, which were then imitated by France, Russia, and Italy. The status of the Declaration became a propaganda issue for the Central Powers in seeking neutral sympathy. After further modifications in 1914 and 1915, the whole Declaration was withdrawn in 1916 by Great

Britain and France and new rules were made concerning contraband and continuous voyage. The explanation given was that "the rules laid down in the Declaration could not stand the strain imposed by the test of rapidly changing conditions and tendencies which could not have been foreseen". It was explained that Great Britain was abandoning the innovations of the Declaration and returning to "the historic and admitted rules of the Law of Nations".

(c)   *The Washington Treaty, 1922*

This was intended to reaffirm the principles which Germany's policy of unrestricted submarine warfare was alleged to have infringed. It emphasized the rule of international law forbidding the sinking of enemy or neutral merchant ships at sight and requiring that their crews and passengers be placed in safety if a vessel is destroyed, and that submarines are obliged to conduct warfare according to the same rules as surface ships, which was intended to minimize their availability as commerce raiders. The Treaty was not ratified.

(d)   *The London Protocol, 1936*

The rules in the Washington Treaty were adopted in substance at the London Naval Conference of 1930, and embodied in the London Protocol of 1936, to which forty-five countries were parties at the outbreak of war in 1939.

(e)   *The Geneva Conventions (Red Cross), 1949*

One of the 1949 Red Cross conventions concerns the Amelioration of the Condition of the Wounded, Sick, or Shipwrecked Members of the Armed Forces at Sea. This is made effective by the general requirement that the High Contracting Parties prohibit and penalize "grave breaches," which are defined as "wilful killing, torture, or inhuman treatment, including biological experiments, wilfully causing great suffering or serious injury to body or health, and extensive destruction and appropriation of property, not justified by military necessity and carried out unlawfully and wantonly." This is so general as to be available as a generic principle of the conduct of naval warfare. In that sense, the Red Cross Conventions have developed from being arrangements for the protection of captured enemy forces to being Laws of War supplementing and completing the Hague Conventions. Protocol No. 1 adopted in 1977 makes this evident.

HAGUE CONVENTION XIII ON THE RIGHT AND
DUTIES OF NEUTRAL POWERS IN NAVAL WAR
October 18, 1907
36 Stat. 2415; Treaty Series 545; partial text reprinted from Charles I. Bevans, compiler,
Treaties and Other International Agreements of the United States of America 1776-1949, Vol. 1,
Multilateral, Washington, D.C.: U.S. Government Printing Office, 1968, pp. 731-735.

Article 1

Belligerents are bound to respect the sovereign rights of neutral Powers and to abstain, in neutral territory or neutral waters, from any act which would, if knowingly permitted by any Power, constitute a violation of neutrality.

Article 2

Any act of hostility, including capture and the exercise of the right of search, committed by belligerent war-ships in the territorial waters of a neutral Power, constitutes a violation of neutrality and is strictly forbidden.

Article 3

When a ship has been captured in the territorial waters of a neutral Power, this Power must employ, if the prize is still within its jurisdiction, the means at its disposal to release the prize with its officers and crew, and to intern the prize crew.

If the prize is not in the jurisdiction of the neutral Power, the captor Government, on the demand of that Power, must liberate the prize with its officers and crew.

Article 4

A Prize Court cannot be set up by a belligerent on neutral territory or on a vessel in neutral waters.

Article 5

Belligerents are forbidden to use neutral ports and waters as a base of naval operations against their adversaries, and in particular to erect wireless telegraphy stations or any apparatus for the purpose of communicating with the belligerent forces on land or sea.

Article 6

The supply, in any manner, directly or indirectly, by a neutral Power to a belligerent Power, of war-ships, ammunition, or war material of any kind whatever, is forbidden.

Article 7

A neutral Power is not bound to prevent the export or transit, for the use of either belligerent, of arms, ammunition, or, in general, of anything which could be of use to an army or fleet.

Article 8

A neutral Government is bound to employ the means at its disposal to prevent the fitting out or arming of any vessel within its jurisdiction which it has reason to believe is intended to cruise, or engage in hostile operations, against a Power with which that Government is at peace. It is also bound to display the same vigilance to prevent the departure from its jurisdiction of any vessel intended to cruise, or engage in hostile operations, which had been adapted entirely or partly within the said jurisdiction for use in war.

Article 9

A neutral Power must apply impartially to the two belligerents the conditions, restrictions, or prohibitions made by it in regard to the admission into its ports, roadsteads, or territorial waters, of belligerent war-ships or of their prizes.

Nevertheless, a neutral Power may forbid a belligerent vessel which has failed to conform to the orders and regulations made by it, or which has violated neutrality, to enter its ports or roadsteads.

Article 10

The neutrality of a Power is not affected by the mere passage through its territorial waters of war-ships or prizes belonging to belligerents.

Article 11

A neutral Power may allow belligerent war-ships to employ its licensed pilots.

Article 12

In the absence of special provisions to the contrary in the legislation of a neutral Power, belligerent war-ships are not permitted to remain in the ports, roadsteads, or territorial waters of the said Power for more than twenty-four hours, except in the cases covered by the present Convention.

Article 13

If a Power which has been informed of the outbreak of hostilities learns that a belligerent war-ship is in one of its ports or roadsteads, or in its territorial waters, it must notify the said ship to depart within twenty-four hours or within the time prescribed by local regulations.

Article 14

A belligerent war-ship may not prolong its stay in a neutral port beyond the permissible time except on account of damage or stress of weather. It must depart as soon as the cause of the delay is at an end.

The regulations as to the question of the length of time which these vessels may remain in neutral ports, roadsteads, or waters, do not apply to war-ships devoted exclusively to religious, scientific, or philanthropic purposes.

Article 15

In the absence of special provisions to the contrary in the legislation of a neutral Power, the maximum number of war-ships belonging to a belligerent which may be in one of the ports or roadsteads of that Power simultaneously shall be three.

Article 16

When war-ships belonging to both belligerents are present simultaneously in a neutral port or roadstead, a period of not less than twenty-four hours must elapse between the departure of the ship belonging to one belligerent and the departure of the ship belonging to the other.

The order of departure is determined by the order of arrival, unless the ship which arrived first is so circumstanced that an extension of its stay is permissible.

A belligerent war-ship may not leave a neutral port or roadstead until twenty-four hours after the departure of a merchant-ship flying the flag of its adversary.

Article 17

In neutral ports and roadsteads belligerent war-ships may only carry out such repairs as are absolutely necessary to render them seaworthy, and may not add in any manner whatsoever to their fighting force. The local authorities of the neutral Power shall decide what repairs are necessary, and these must be carried out with the least possible delay.

Article 18

Belligerent war-ships may not make use of neutral ports, roadsteads, or territorial waters for replenishing or increasing their supplies of war material or their armament, or for completing their crews.

Article 19

Belligerent war-ships may only revictual in neutral ports or roadsteads to bring up their supplies to the peace standard.

Similarly these vessels may only ship sufficient fuel to enable them to reach the nearest port in their own country. They may, on the other hand, fill up their bunkers built to carry fuel, when in neutral countries which have adopted this method of determining the amount of fuel to be supplied.

If, in accordance with the law of the neutral Power, the ships are not supplied with coal within twenty-four hours of their arrival, the permissible duration of their stay is extended by twenty-four hours.

Article 20

Belligerent war-ships which have shipped fuel in a port belonging to a neutral Power may not within the succeeding three months replenish their supply in a port of the same Power.

Article 21

A prize may only be brought into a neutral port on account of unseaworthiness, stress of weather, or want of fuel or provisions.

It must leave as soon as the circumstances which justified its entry are at an end. If it does not, the neutral Power must order it to leave at once; should it fail to obey, the neutral Power must employ the means at its disposal to release it with its officers and crew and to intern the prize crew.

Article 22

A neutral Power must, similarly, release a prize brought into one of its ports under circumstances other than those referred to in Article 21.

Article 23

A neutral Power may allow prizes to enter its ports and roadsteads, whether under convoy or not, when they are brought there to be sequestrated pending the decision of a Prize Court. It may have the prize taken to another of its ports.

If the prize is convoyed by a war-ship, the prize crew may go on board the convoying ship.

If the prize is not under convoy, the prize crew are left at liberty.

Article 24

If, notwithstanding the notification of the neutral Power, a belligerent ship of war does not leave a port where it is not entitled to remain, the neutral Power is entitled to take such measures as it considers necessary to render the ship incapable of taking the sea during the war, and the commanding officer of the ship must facilitate the execution of such measures.

When a belligerent ship is detained by a neutral Power, the officers and crew are likewise detained.

The officers and crew thus detained may be left in the ship or kept either on another vessel or on land, and may be subjected to the measures of restriction which it may appear necessary to impose upon them. A sufficient number of men for looking after the vessel must, however, be always left on board.

The officers may be left at liberty on giving their word not to quit the neutral territory without permission.

Article 25

A neutral Power is bound to exercise such surveillance as the means at its disposal allow to prevent any violation of the provisions of the above Article occurring in its ports or roadsteads or in its waters.

Article 26

The exercise by a neutral Power of the rights laid down in the present Convention can under no circumstances be considered as an unfriendly act by one or other belligerent who has accepted the Article relating thereto.

Article 27

The Contracting Powers shall communicate to each other in due course all Laws, Proclamations, and other enactments regulating in their respective countries the status of belligerent war-ships in their ports and waters, by means of a communication addressed to the Government of the Netherlands, and forwarded immediately by that Government to the other Contracting Powers.

Article 28

The provisions of the present Convention do not apply except to the Contracting Powers, and then only if all the belligerents are parties to the Convention.

AMERADA HESS SHIPPING CORPORATION V. ARGENTINE REPUBLIC
U.S. Court of Appeals for the Second Circuit
September 11, 1987, 830 F.2d 421, at 423-424.

[A Liberian registered vessel sailing on the high seas was attacked by Argentina during the 1982 Falklands War, and after the owner unsuccessfully attempted to get a hearing on its claims in Argentina, brought suit in the United States. They held that it has jurisdiction under the Alien Tort Statute [28 U.S.C. § 1350], and that the Foreign Sovereign Immunities Act [28 U.S.C.A. § 1602-11] would not bar the suit. The U.S. District Court for the Southern District of New York dismissed complaint for lack of jurisdiction, 638 F. Supp. 73 (May 5, 1986). The Court of Appeal for the Second Circuit revised and remanded, 830 F.2d 421 (September 11, 1987). The Supreme Court reversed the case on the ground that the exception for noncommercial tort provided in the Foreign Sovereign Immunity Act is not applicable here as the damage to or loss of property did not occur in the U.S., 109 S.Ct. 683 (January 23, 1989). The Court of Appeals for the Second Circuit's discussion on the rights of neutrals' vessels on the high seas during armed conflict is reproduced below:]

II. Violation of International Law

The facts alleged by appellants, if proven, would constitute a clear violation of international law. "The law of nations "may be ascertained by consulting the works of jurists, writing professedly on public law; or by the general usage and practice of nations; or by judicial decisions recognizing and enforcing that law.'" Filartiga v. Pena-Irala, 630 F.2d 876, 880 (2d Cir. 1980) (quoting United States v. Smith, 18 U.S. (5 Wheat.) 153, 160-61 (1820)). Of course, the mere fact that many or even all nations consider an act a violation of their domestic law does not suffice to create a principle of international law. IIT v. Vencap, Ltd., 519 F.2d 1001, 1015 (2d Cir. 1975). "It is only where the nations of the world have demonstrated that the wrong is of mutual, and not merely several, concern, by means of express international accords, that a wrong generally recognized becomes an international law violation." Filartiga, 630 F.2d at 888. In this case, treaties, case law and treatises establish that Argentina's conduct, as alleged by appellants, violates settled principles of international law.

International treaties and conventions dating at least as far back as the last century recognize the right of a neutral ship to free passage on the high seas. Broad international recognition of the rights of neutrals can be found in paragraph 3 of The Declaration of Paris of 1856: "Neutral goods, with the exception of contraband of war, are not liable to capture under enemy's flag."

A more contemporary statement of the international concern and accord on this issue may be found in The Geneva Convention on the High Seas of 1958 (Convention on the High Seas), to which both Argentina and the United States were signatories. The Convention on the High Seas maps the general usage and practice of nations with regard to the rights of neutral ships in time of war. Article 22 of that treaty states that a warship encountering a foreign merchant vessel on the high seas may not board her without grounds for suspecting her of engaging in piracy, or the slave trade, or traveling under false colors. Even when there are grounds for such suspicion, the proper course is to investigate by sending an officer to inspect the ship's documents or even to board her, not to commence an attack. If such inspection fails to support the suspicions, the merchant vessel shall "be compensated for any loss or damage that may have been sustained." Article 23 of the Convention on the High Seas makes similar provisions for aircraft that have grounds to suspect a neutral vessel. Clearly, Argentina's alleged conduct in this case, bombing HERCULES and refusing compensation, violates the Convention on the High Seas. More recently, the Law of the Sea Convention of 1982 explicitly incorporated these provisions into its text. Argentina is a signatory to the Law of the Sea Convention and the United States has endorsed the relevant sections of it.

Other international accords adopted by the United States supporting a similar view of the rights of neutral ships include The London Naval Conference of 1909, the International Convention Concerning the Rights and Duties of Neutral Powers in Naval War (Hague Convention, 1907) and the Pan-American Convention Relating to Maritime Neutrality of 1928, to which Argentina was a signatory. No agreement has been called to our attention that would cast doubt on this line of authority.

As to "judicial decisions recognizing and enforcing" the rights of neutral ships on the high seas, federal courts have long recognized in a variety of contexts that attacking a merchant ship without warning or seizing a neutral's goods on the high seas requires restitution. See, e.g., Talbot v. Jansen, 3 U.S. (3 Dall.) 133, 161 (1795); The Lusitania, 251 F. 715, 732-36 (S.D.N.Y. 1918) (dictum); cf. The I'm Alone (Canada v. United States), 3 U.N. Rep. Int. Arb. Awards 1609 (1933). Similarly, the academic literature on the rights of neutrals is of one voice with regard to a neutral's right of passage. See, e.g., Rappaport, "Freedom of the Seas," 2 Encyclopedia of Amer. For. Policy 387 (1978); Restatement of Foreign Relations Law of the United States (Revised) § 521 reporters' note 1, § 522 (Tent. Draft No. 6 1985).

In short, it is beyond controversy that attacking a neutral ship in international waters, without proper cause for suspicion or investigation, violates international law. Indeed, the relative paucity of cases litigating this customary rule of international law underscores the longstanding nature of this aspect of freedom of the high seas. Where the attacker has refused to compensate the neutral, such action is analogous to piracy, one of the earliest recognized violations of international law. See 4 W. Blackstone, Commentaries 68, 72. Argentina has cited no contrary authority. Accordingly, we turn to the jurisdictional ramifications of our holding that appellants have stated a claim of a violation of international law.

REFERENCES

L. Oppenheim, *International Law*, edited by H. Lauterpacht, Vol. 2, 7th ed., London: Longmans, Green and Co. 1952; C. John Colombos, *The International Law of the Sea*, 6th ed., London: Longman Group Ltd., 1967, Part II (The International Law of the Sea in Time of War), pp. 477-853; N. Ronzitti, *The Law of Naval Warfare: A Collection of Agreements and Documents with Commentaries*, Dordrecht, Boston, Lonon: Martinus Nijhoff Publishers, 1988; Adam Boleslaw Boczek, "Law of Warfare at Sea and Neutrality: Lessons from the Gulf War," *Ocean Development and International Law*, Vol. 20 (1989), pp. 239-271.

D . MINE WARFARE

1907 HAGUE CONVENTION (VIII) RELATIVE TO THE
LAYING OF AUTOMATIC SUBMARINE CONTACT MINES
36 Stat. 2332; T.S. 541; 1 Bevans 669

Article 1

It is forbidden:

1. To lay unanchored automatic contact mines, except when they are so constructed as to become harmless one hour at most after the person who laid them ceases to control them;

2. To lay anchored automatic contact mines which do not become harmless as soon as they have broken loose from their moorings;

3. To use torpedoes which do not become harmless when they have missed their mark.

Article 2

It is forbidden to lay automatic contact mines off the coast and ports of the enemy, with the sole object of intercepting commercial shipping.

Article 3

When anchored automatic contact mines are employed, every possible precaution must be taken for the security of peaceful shipping.

The belligerents undertake to do their utmost to render these mines harmless within a limited time, and, should they cease to be under surveillance, to notify the danger zones as soon as military exigencies permit, by a notice addressed to ship owners, which must also be communicated to the governments through the diplomatic channel.

Article 4

Neutral Powers which lay automatic contact mines off their coasts must observe the same rules and take the same precautions as are imposed on belligerents.

The Neutral Power must inform ship-owners, by a notice issued in advance, where automatic contact mines have been laid. This notice must be communicated at once to the Governments through the diplomatic channel.

Article 5

At the close of the war, the Contracting Powers undertake to do their utmost to remove the mines which they have laid, each Power removing its own mines.

As regards anchored automatic contact mines laid by one of the belligerents off the coast of the other, their position must be notified to the other party by the Power which laid them, and each Power must proceed with the least possible delay to remove the mines in its own waters.

THE CORFU CHANNEL CASE (UNITED KINGDOM V. ALBANIA)
Judgement on the Merits, April 19, 1949.
I.C.J. Reports 1949, p. 4, at pp. 18-20.

[The Facts as summarized in H. Lauterpacht, ed., *Annual Digest and Reports of Public International Law Cases*, Vol. 16 (1949), p. 155, are as follows (Reproduced with permission from the *International Law Reports*.):

On October 22, 1946, a squadron of British warships, the cruisers *Mauritius* and *Leander* and the destroyers *Saumarez* and *Volage*, left the port of Corfu and proceeded northward through a channel previously swept for mines in the North Corfu Strait. The cruiser *Mauritius* was leading, followed by the destroyer *Saumarez*; at a certain distance thereafter came the cruiser *Leander* followed by the destroyer *Volage*. Outside the Bay of Saranda, *Saumarez* struck a mine and was heavily damaged. *Volage* was ordered to give her assistance and to take her in tow. Whilst towing the damaged ship, *Volage* struck a mine and was much damaged. Nevertheless, she succeeded in towing the other ship back to Corfu.

Three weeks later, on November 13, the North Corfu Channel was swept by British minesweepers and twenty-two moored mines were cut. Two mines were taken to Malta for expert examination. It was subsequently established that they were of the German GY type.

The Court considered first the question whether the two explosions that occurred on October 22, 1946, were caused by mines belonging to the minefield discovered on November 13. The documents produced by the Government of the United Kingdom and the statements made by the Court's experts and based on those documents showed that the minefield had been recently laid. The Court considered that fact as established.

The Government of the United Kingdom contended that the mines which struck the two ships on October 22 were part of this minefield. This was contested by the Albanian Government, which argued that these mines might have been floating mines, coming from old minefields in the vicinity, or magnetic ground mines.

The Court found the following facts to have been established: The two ships were mined in Albanian territorial waters in a previously swept and check-swept channel just at the place where a newly laid minefield consisting of moored contact German mines was discovered three weeks later. The Court arrived at the conclusion that the explosions were due to mines belonging to that minefield.

While in the light of the information available to it the authors of the minelaying remained unknown, the Court considered that the task before it, as defined by the Special Agreement, was to decide whether Albania was responsible, under international law, for the explosions which occurred on October 22, 1946, and to give judgment as to the compensation to be paid, if any.]

It is clear that knowledge of the minelaying cannot be imputed to the Albanian Government by reason merely of the fact that a minefield discovered in Albanian territorial waters caused the explosions of which the British warships were the victims. It is true, as international practice shows, that a State on whose territory or in whose waters an act contrary to international law has occurred, may be called upon to give an explanation. It is also true that that State cannot evade such a request by limiting itself to a reply that it is ignorant of the circumstances of the act and of its authors. The State may, up to a certain point, be bound to supply particulars of the use made by it of the means of information and inquiry at its disposal. But it cannot be concluded from the mere fact of the control exercised by a State over its territory and waters that that State necessarily knew, or ought to have known, of any unlawful act perpetrated therein, nor yet that it necessarily knew, or should have known, the authors. This fact, by itself and apart from other circumstances, neither involves prima facie responsibility nor shifts the burden of proof.

On the other hand, the fact of this exclusive territorial control exercised by a State within its frontiers has a bearing upon the methods of proof available to establish the knowledge of that State as to such events. By reason of this exclusive control, the other State, the victim of a breach of international law, is often unable to furnish direct proof of facts giving rise to responsibility. Such a State should be allowed a more liberal recourse to inferences of fact and circumstantial evidence. This indirect evidence is admitted in all systems of law, and its use is recognized by international decisions. It must be regarded as of special weight when it is based on a series of facts linked together and leading logically to a single conclusion.

The Court must examine, therefore, whether it has been established by means of indirect evidence that Albania has knowledge of minelaying in her territorial waters independently of any connivance on her part in this operation. The proof may be drawn from inferences of fact, provided that they leave *no room* for reasonable doubt. The elements of fact on which these inferences can be based may differ from those which are relevant to the question of connivance.

In the present case, two series of facts, which corroborate one another, have to be considered: the first relates to Albania's attitude before and after the disaster of October 22nd, 1946; the other concerns the feasibility of observing minelaying from the Albanian coast. . . .

As the Parties agree that the minefield had been recently laid, it must be concluded that the operation was carried out during the period of close watch by the Albanian authorities in this sector. This conclusion renders the Albanian Government's assertion of ignorance a *priori* somewhat improbable. . . .

Another indication of the Albanian Government's knowledge consists in the fact that that Government did not notify the presence of mines in its waters at the moment when it must have known this, at the latest after the sweep on November 13th, and further, whereas the Greek Government immediately appointed a Commission to enquire into the events of October 22nd, the Albanian Government took no decision of such a nature, nor did it proceed to the judicial investigation incumbent, in such a case, on the territorial sovereign.

This attitude does not seem reconcilable with the alleged ignorance of the Albanian authorities that the minefield had been laid in Albanian territorial waters. It could be explained if the Albanian Government, while knowing of the minelaying, desired the circumstances of the operation to remain secret. . . .

From all the facts and observations mentioned above, the Court draws the conclusion that the laying of the minefield which caused the explosions on October 22nd, 1946, could not have been accomplished without the knowledge of the Albanian Government.

The obligations resulting for Albania from this knowledge are not disputed between the Parties. Counsel for the Albanian Government expressly recognized that [translation] "if Albania had been informed of the operation before the incidents of October 22nd, and in time to warn the British vessels and shipping in general of the existence of mines in the Corfu Channel, her responsibility would be involved. . . ."

The obligations incumbent upon the Albanian authorities consisted in notifying, for the benefit of shipping in general, the existence of a minefield in Albanian territorial waters and in warning the approaching British warships of the imminent danger to which the minefield exposed them. Such obligations are based, not on the Hague Convention of 1907, No. VIII, which is applicable in time of war, but on certain general and well-recognized principles, namely: elementary considerations of humanity, even more exacting in peace than in war; the principle of the freedom of maritime communication; and every State's obligation not to allow knowingly its territory to be used for acts contrary to the rights of other States.

In fact, Albania neither notified the existence of the minefield, nor warned the British warships of the danger they were approaching. . . .

"U.N. Notified of New Measures Against North Viet-Nam," *U.S. Department of State Bulletin*, Vol. 66, No. 1718 (May 29, 1972), pp. 750-751.

Following is the text of a letter dated May 8 from George Bush, U.S. Representative to the United Nations, to the President of the Security Council.

MAY 8, 1972.

DEAR MR. PRESIDENT: The President of the United States of America today announced that he had directed United States forces in Southeast Asia to take additional measures, in conjunction with the forces of the Republic of Vietnam, in response to the new armed attacks launched by North Vietnam. The President directed that the entrances to the ports of North Vietnam be mined and that the delivery of seaborne supplies to North Vietnam be prevented. These measures of collective self-defense are hereby being reported to the United Nations Security Council as required by Article 51 of the United Nations Charter.

The massive invasion across the demilitarized zone and international boundaries by the forces of North Vietnam and the continuing aggression of those forces against the people and territory of the Republic of Vietnam, have created unprecedented dangers to the forces of the Republic of Vietnam, to the Republic of Vietnam itself, and to those United States forces which remain in that country. This invasion has been carried out in blatant violation of the understandings negotiated in 1968 in connection with the cessation of bombing of territory of North Vietnam. The extent of this renewed aggression and the manner in which it has been directed and supported demonstrate with great clarity that North Vietnam has embarked on an all-out attempt to take over South Vietnam by military force and to disrupt the orderly withdrawal of United States forces.

At the same time that North Vietnam has launched this massive invasion, it has refused, both in public and in private, to negotiate to bring about a peaceful settlement of the conflict in Southeast Asia.

A major portion of the supplies through which the invasion of South Vietnam is being supported enters North Vietnam from the sea. It is essential that this delivery of supplies from the sea be prevented so that North Vietnam cannot continue to resupply both its forces in the field and its logistics base.

Accordingly, as the minimum actions necessary to meet this threat, the Republic of Vietnam and the United States of America have jointly decided to take the following measures of collective self-defense: The entrances to the ports of North Vietnam are being mined, commencing 0900

Saigon time May 9, and the mines are set to activate automatically beginning 1800 hours Saigon time May 11. This will permit vessels of other countries presently in North Vietnamese ports three daylight periods to depart safely. The mines will be so positioned within the internal waters and claimed territorial waters of North Vietnam as to prevent access to North Vietnamese ports and North Vietnamese naval operations from these ports. In addition, the Republic of Vietnam and the United States are advising their respective naval and air forces to take appropriate measures within the internal and claimed territorial waters of North Vietnam to prevent the delivery of seaborne supplies to North Vietnam.

In addition to this and other general notices of these measures, the naval forces of the Republic of Vietnam and of the United States will notify any vessels approaching the internal and claimed territorial waters of North Vietnam of these measures.

As can be seen from the foregoing, the measures being taken by United States and South Vietnamese forces are restricted in extent and purpose. The President also announced that as soon as there is an internationally supervised cease-fire throughout Indochina and prisoners of war have been released, we will terminate all acts of force throughout Indochina, and United States forces will be withdrawn from South Vietnam within four months.

I request that this letter and the text of President Nixon's announcement, which is enclosed, be circulated as a Security Council document.

Sincerely,
GEORGE BUSH.

MILITARY AND PARAMILITARY ACTIVITIES IN AND AGAINST NICARAGUAY (NICARAGUAY v. UNITED STATES OF AMERICA).
Judgement on the Merits, June 27, 1986.
I.C. J. Reports 1986, p. 14, at p. 112.

215. The Court has noted above (paragraph 77 *in fine*) that the United States did not issue any warning or notification of the presence of the mines which had been laid in or near the ports of Nicaragua. Yet even in time of war, the Convention relative to the laying of automatic submarine contact mines of 18 October 1907 (the Hague Convention No. VIII) provides that "every possible precaution must be taken for the security of peaceful shipping" and belligerents are bound

> "to notify the danger zones as soon as military exigencies permit, by a notice addressed to ship owners, which must also be communicated to the Governments through the diplomatic channel" (Art. 3).

Neutral Powers which lay mines off their own coasts must issue a similar notification, in advance (Art. 4). It has already been made clear above that in peacetime for one State to lay mines in the internal or territorial waters of another is an unlawful act; but in addition, if a State lays mines in any waters whatever in which the vessels of another State have rights of access or passage, and fails to give any warning or notification whatsoever, in disregard of the security of peaceful shipping, it commits a breach of the principles of humanitarian law underlying the specific provisions of Convention No. VIII of 1907. Those principles were expressed by the Court in the *Corfu Channel* case as follows:

"certain general and well recognized principles, namely: elementary considerations of humanity, even more exacting in peace than in war" (I.C.J. Reports 1949, p. 22).

REFERENCES

C. John Colombos, *The International Law of the Sea*, 6th ed., London: Longman Group Ltd., 1967, 531-534; Marjorie M. Whiteman, *Digest of International Law*, Vol. 10, Washington, D.C.: U.S. Government Printing Office, 1968, pp. 676-681; Howard S. Levie, "Mine Warfare and International Law," *Naval War College Review*, Vol. 24 (April 1972), pp. 27-35; Katrina J. Church, "The Briar Patch of Reality: A Legal Analysis of the Mining of Nicaragua's Harbors," *New York University Journal of International Law and Politics*, Vol. 18 (1985), pp. 169-227; A. G. Y. Thorpe, "Mine Warfare at Sea--Some Legal Aspects of the Future," *Ocean Development and International Law*, Vol. 18 (1987), pp. 255-278.

"U.S. Attacks, Seizes Iranian Mine Ship," *Facts on File*, Vol. 47, No. 2444 (September 25, 1987), p. 685. Reprinted by permission.

Helicopter Strafed Vessel In Night Raid. A U.S. helicopter on Sept. 21 attacked and disabled an Iranian naval vessel that was allegedly laying mines in the Persian Gulf, after which American forces seized the ship and its crew. Three Iranian sailors were killed, two others were missing and presumed dead and four were wounded. . . .

The Reagan administration described the attack as a legitimate defensive act sanctioned by international law. Iran denied that the ship was a mine-layer and threatened revenge against the U.S. . . .

The U.S.-Iranian clash occurred at night in international waters 50 miles (80 km) northeast of Bahrain. The *Iran Ajr*--variously described as an amphibious landing craft and a roll-on, roll-off cargo vessel--had been under surveillance by a helicopter based on the frigate U.S.S. *Jarrett*. The aircraft was actually an Army special operations helicopter assigned to the gulf fleet because of its sophisticated night-vision capabilities.

The Iranian ship was observed dropping mines into the water, an act that merited an armed response according to the Navy's revised rules of engagement for the gulf. Washington had warned that it would respond forcefully if it could prove Iranian involvement in mine-laying. (The U.S. said it had not been able to do so when the supertanker *Bridgeton* struck a mine during the first escort operation.)

After receiving authority from Rear Adm. Harold Bernsen, commander of the U.S. gulf fleet, the helicopter's pilots opened fire on the Iranian vessel with rockets and machine guns. Contrary to some initial reports, no effort was made to communicate with the *Iran Ajr* and no warning shots were fired.

Bernsen told reporters in a Pentagon media pool Sept. 22 that the Iranian crew resumed dropping mines after the first attack, so the ship was strafed again 34 minutes later. The second attack left the ship dead in the water with its stern in flames, and the crew abandoned ship.

26 Iranians Rescued, Detained--U.S. forces, fearful of hitting one of the mines dropped by the ship, waited until daybreak on Sept. 22 before moving in to begin rescue operations. A team of Navy SEAL commandos boarded and seized the ship. They found three dead crewmen and 10 remaining contact mines. Reporters were later brought aboard and allowed to film the devices, which were shown to be large spiked spheres mounted on wheeled canisters. (The ensemble was designed to be rolled into the water together, after which the canister acted as a mooring anchor for the mine, which would float just beneath the surface.)

Later, as U.S. warships gathered near the disabled vessel, the *Jarrett* fired warning shots at an Iranian navy hovercraft when it refused warnings to cease its high-speed approach. The hovercraft then turned away.

Ten Iranians were found in a lifeboat and 16 others were rescued from the sea. The most seriously wounded crewmen were transferred to hospital facilities aboard the U.S.S. *Guadalcanal*. Some of the other captives were filmed by the American media pool aboard the command ship U.S.S. *LaSalle* as they lay bound on stretchers under guard by armed sailors.

Asked if the detainees were being treated humanely, a U.S. official told the Washington Post, "Well, they weren't beaten."

The precise status of the *Iran Ajr* and its crew was unclear. While said to be a naval vessel, it was officially registered as a commercial ship. U.S. Defense Secretary Caspar Weinberger, on the eve of a trip to the gulf, Sept. 23 said the crew was from the regular Iranian navy. Previously, Iranian mine-laying had been attributed to the more fanatical Revolutionary Guards, which operated separately from the professional navy . . . .

The U.S. Navy Sept. 24 concluded an agreement to repatriate the captives to Iran by way of Oman. (Oman, a pro-Western sultanate, had maintained strong trade links with Iran at the same time that it quietly provided limited landing rights to U.S. military aircraft.) However, the Reagan administration said it had no intention of returning the *Iran Ajr* to Iran.

U.S. officials, meanwhile, had bragged of catching the Iranians "red-handed" with videotape footage of the mine-laying that preceded the attack. The tape was to have been offered to the United Nations as definitive evidence against Iran. But embarrassed Pentagon officials admitted Sept. 24 that the tape made by the U.S. helicopter's supposedly night-capable cameras had come up blank. . . .

NOTE

For a description of Iranian mining activities in the Persian Gulf before this incident, see "The Gulf, Here a Mine, There a Mine," *Time*, Vol. 130, No. 8 (August 24, 1987), pp. 24-27 and "The Mines of August," *Newsweek*, Vol. CX, No. 8 (August 24, 1987), pp. 22-24.

E. BLOCKADE

> J. G. Starke, *Introduction to International Law*, 9th ed., London: Butterworths, 1984, pp. 566-568. Footnotes omitted. Reproduced with the permission of Butterworth & Co. (Publishers) Ltd.

A blockade occurs when a belligerent bars access to the enemy coast or part of it for the purpose of preventing ingress or egress of vessels or aircraft of all nations. The blockade is an act of war, and if duly carried out in accordance with the rules of warfare, is effective to deny freedom of passage to the shipping or aircraft of other states. Under the Declaration of Paris 1856, which is declaratory of prior customary international law, a blockade is binding only if effective, and the effectiveness of a blockade is conditioned by the maintenance of such a force by the belligerent as is "sufficient really to prevent access to the enemy coast".

Ships which break a blockade by entering or leaving the blockaded area are liable to seizure by the belligerent operating the blockade in the same way as contraband cargoes, and after capture must be sent to a port for adjudication on their character as lawful prize. Generally, the cargoes carried by such ships will also suffer condemnation by a Prize Court unless those who shipped the goods prove to the court's satisfaction that the shipment was made before they knew or could have known of the blockade.

The practice of states varies greatly as to what is deemed to constitute a breach of blockade. For instance, practice is not uniform on the point whether a neutral vessel must have actual formal notice of the blockade. According to Anglo-American juristic opinion and practice, it is sufficient to establish presumptively that those in charge of the neutral vessel knew that a blockade had been established. The commander of a neutral vessel who sails for an enemy port knowing that it is blockaded at the beginning of the voyage ought to expect that it will be in the same state when he arrives in the vicinity of the port; and anything which can be proved to affect him with knowledge at the date of departure, for example, publication of a declaration of blockade, will render the vessel and its cargo liable to the penalties for breach of blockade. According to the French theory, the neutral vessel is not affected by presumptions as to continuance or cesser of blockade, but the commander of the vessel on approaching the blockaded area is entitled to individual warning from one of the blockading squadrons, the fact of the notification being entered in the vessel's log-book with specific mention of the hour, date, and place of notification. It is only for subsequent attempts to enter the blockaded area that the neutral vessel is liable to seizure.

Apart from the matter of actual or constructive notice to neutral vessels, it is an established rule of international law that a blockade must be properly declared and notified to neutral states with a specific statement as to the date when the blockade begins and the geographical limits of the coastline to which access is barred. Secondly, in accordance with the rule of effectiveness, the blockade must be maintained by a sufficient and properly disposed force, rendering ingress or egress by other vessels a matter of material danger. . . .

The size of the blockading force and the distance at which it operates from the blockaded coast are alike immaterial, provided this test of danger to neutral vessels be satisfied. Thus in the Crimean War in 1854, a single British cruiser commanding the one navigable approach to the Russian port of Riga at a distance of 120 miles was deemed sufficient to constitute a blockade of the port. United States judicial decisions and practice are to the same effect as the British authorities.

In the First World War, the British Navy enforced a "long-distance" blockade of Germany through ships and squadrons operating often more than one thousand miles from German ports. The objections raised to this type of blockade were that it extended across the approaches to the ports and coastline of neighbouring neutral countries and that it was in many respects ineffective. It was first instituted in 1915 as a reprisal for the German decision to attack British and Allied merchantmen in the waters surrounding the British Isles without regard for the personal safety of the passengers or crew. Under British Orders-in-Council, neutral vessels carrying goods of presumed enemy destination, origin, or ownership could be required to proceed to a British port to discharge their cargoes, and might be forbidden to move to a German port. If neutral vessels under colour of permission to proceed to a neutral port, sailed for a German port, they were liable to seizure and condemnation if subsequently caught. Such a blockade was probably not justified according to the rules followed in the nineteenth century, either as a retaliatory measure or as a blockade in the strict sense of that term. The British Government, however, justified the "long-distance" blockade of Germany by reference to the changed conditions of war, stating that a modern blockade could only be effective by covering commerce with the enemy passing through neutral ports. The "long-distance" blockade was reinstituted in 1939 in the Second World War, and its rational justification was likewise the necessity for waging "total" economic warfare against the enemy. In both wars, France took action similar to that of Great Britain. Without Great Britain's predominant naval power in relation to the enemy, the blockade could not have been enforced.

> D.P. O'Connell, *The International Law of the Sea*, edited by I. A. Shearer, Vol. 2, New York: Oxford University Press, 1984, pp. 1154-1156. Some footnotes omitted. Reprinted with the permission of Oxford University Press.

(3) THE PRESENT STATUS OF THE LAW OF BLOCKADE

The practice during the two World Wars has left the law of blockade devoid of most of its traditional characteristics, so that its present applicability and content are questionable. Close blockade, in the sense of visible investment, was made obsolete by long-range coast defences, torpedo-boats, and minefields even before the London Conference of 1909, but its obsolescence has been compounded by the development of means of trade other than by sea and by commercial transactions which put economic weapons and defences in the hands of belligerents so making discharge of cargoes less important in the conduct of economic warfare than was hitherto the case. The notion of the long-distance blockade accommodated not only the need to control traffic to and from enemy out of range of his defences, but also the need to control strategic commodities, their price mechanisms and the credit to gain access to them. In fact, the policy of long-range blockade was only the compulsory side of a strategy of global control of shipping that involved other forms of encouragement, duress, palliative, and persuasion. . . .

There has been practically no experience of blockade since 1945 to test the matter. India proclaimed a blockade of Pakistan during the Indo-Pakistan War of 1971, but that was so short-lived, and so aberrant in its purposes and enforcement, as to offer scant lessons; there was no investment of Pakistan ports, nor even visitation on the high seas, but neutral ships were attacked *en route* to Pakistan. In 1982 the United Kingdom proclaimed a 'Total Exclusion Zone' around the Falkland Islands, prohibiting the entry of all ships and aircraft "operating in support of the illegal occupation of the Falkland Islands" by Argentina. This zone did not constitute a blockade of Argentina itself, and was an extension of the earlier proclaimed "Maritime Exclusion Zone", the purpose of which was defensive rather than economic.[1] No blockade was instituted during the

---

[1]The Total Exclusion Zone was announced on 28 April 1982. The British Prime Minister informed Parliament: "The latest of our military measures is the imposition of the total exclusion zone around the Falkland Islands, of which we gave forty-eight hours notice yesterday. The new zone has the same geographical boundaries as the maritime exclusion zone which took effect on 12 April. It will apply from noon London time tomorrow [30 April 1982] to all ships and aircraft, whether military or civil, operating in support of the illegal occupation of the Falkland Islands. A complete blockade will be placed on all traffic supporting the occupation forces of Argentina. Maritime and aviation authorities have been informed of the imposition of the zone, in accordance with our international obligations." Hansard, 29 April 1982, cols. 980-1. [For subsequent

Vietnam War, although no great significance attaches to that. In the case of international traffic to Haiphong this is explicable on political grounds, and in the case of the minor ports of North Vietnam the tactics of surveillance, harassment, and interdiction were an effective substitute for blockade. The mining of Haiphong in 1972, however, demonstrates the difficulty of keeping blockade and methods of waging warfare conceptually discrete.

In fact, the hypothesis of limited war upon which all naval operations since 1945 have been founded, tends rather to rigidify these rules than to relax them. This is because the theory of self-defence which underlies the concept tends to insulate the high seas and neutral shipping therein from the state of hostilities, if not absolutely, then certainly to a much greater extent than conditions of general war. It is unlikely that the international community would tolerate interference with neutral shipping not actually seeking ingress and egress to and from a belligerent port, and such interferences would be argued to be a use of armed force contrary to the United Nations Charter. These considerations tend to emphasize the requirement of close blockade.

Since close blockade is likely in the missile age to be a tactically unavailable option, and long-distance blockade is likely to be a politically unavailable one, blockade may no longer be feasible except where, because of remoteness or want of defensive weapons to keep a blockading fleet away from its station, it can be instituted without disproportionate risk. A close blockade in these circumstances is likely to be combined with a mine-warfare policy. In 1972 it became tactically feasible to blockade Haiphong by relatively close methods, because the range of coastal defence was limited and the blockading force maintained complete air cover.

The extension of the territorial sea to twelve miles has had the consequence of extending a close blockade to a distance from the coast out of range of anything less than air or missile defence. For, as in the Vietnam War, the territorial sea can be regarded as territory of the enemy for the purpose of waging war, and ingress and egress thereto and therefrom can be indicted form the high seas. In practice, therefore, the law may have facilitated naval operations in finding a compromise between close and long-distance blockade.

REFERENCES

L. Oppenheim, *International Law*, Vol. II, 7th ed. by H. Lauterpacht, London: Longman Group Ltd., 1952, pp. 767-797; C. John Colombos, *International Law of the Sea*, 6th ed., London: Longman Group Ltd., 1967, pp. 714-752; Sally V. Mallison and W. Thomas Mallison, Jr., "A Survey of the International Law of Naval Blockade," *U.S. Naval Institute Proceedings*, Vol. 102 (February 1976), pp. 44-53; David Thomas Jones, "The International Law of Maritime Blockade--A Measure of Naval Economic Interdiction," *Howard Law Journal*, Vol. 26 (1983), pp. 759-779.

development, see NOTE in section B.]

F. BLOCKADE OR CLOSURE OF PORTS IN CIVIL WAR

PRIZE CASES
67 U.S. (2 Black) 635, 17 L. Ed. 459 (1863).
Reprinted from Francis Deak and Frank S. Ruddy, editors, *American International Law Cases,*
1783-1968, Vol. 17, Dobbs Ferry, New York: Oceana Publications, Inc., 1977, pp. 381-387.
Reprinted with the permission of Oceana Publications, Inc.

[Facts: The Confederated-owned brig Amy Warwick had been seized and condemned as enemy property. The Confederate schooner Crenshaw, the British barque Hiawatha, and the Mexican Schooner Brilliante had all been seized and condemned for violating the blockade of the Confederate States. In rejecting appeals from these condemnations, the Supreme Court confirms that a state can institute a blockade against the coasts held by rebels in a civil war.]

Mr. Justice GRIER. There are certain propositions of law which must necessarily affect the ultimate decision of these cases, and many others, which it will be proper to discuss and decide before we notice the special facts peculiar to each.

They are, 1st. Had the President a right to institute a blockade of ports in possession of persons in armed rebellion against the Government, on the principles of international law, as known and acknowledged among civilized States? . . . .

I. Neutrals have a right to challenge the existence of a blockade *de facto*, and also the authority of the party exercising the right to institute it. They have a right to enter the ports of a friendly nation for the purposes of trade and commerce, but are bound to recognize the rights of a belligerent engaged in actual war, to use this mode of coercion, for the purpose of subduing the enemy.

That a blockade *de facto* actually existed, and was formally declared and notified by the President on the 27th and 30th of April, 1861, is an admitted fact in these cases.

That the President, as the Executive Chief of the Government and Commander-in-chief of the Army and Navy, was the proper person to make such notification, has not been, and cannot be disputed.

The right of prize and capture has its origin in the "*jus belli*," and is governed and adjudged under the law of nations. To legitimate the capture of a neutral vessel or property on the high seas, a war must exist *de facto*, and the neutral must have a knowledge or notice of the intention of one of the parties belligerent to use this mode of coercion against a port, city, or territory, in possession of the other.

Let us enquire whether, at the time this blockade was instituted, a state of war existed which would justify a resort to these means of subduing the hostile force.

War has been well defined to be, "That state in which a nation prosecutes its right by force."

The parties belligerent in a public war are independent nations. But it is not necessary to constitute war, that both parties should be acknowledged as independent nations or sovereign States. A war may exist where one of the belligerents, claims sovereign rights as against the other.

Insurrection against a government may or may not culminate in an organized rebellion, but a civil war always begins by insurrection against the lawful authority of the Government. A civil war is never solemnly declared; it becomes such by its accidents--the number, power, and organization of the persons who originate and carry it on. When the party in rebellion occupy and hold in a hostile manner a certain portion of territory; have declared their independence; have cast off their allegiance; have organized armies; have commenced hostilities against their former sovereign, the world acknowledges them as belligerents, and the contest a *war*. *They* claim to be in arms to establish their liberty and independence, in order to become a sovereign State, while the sovereign party treats them as insurgents and rebels who owe allegiance, and who should be punished with death for their treason.

The laws of war, as established among nations, have their foundation in reason, and all tend to mitigate the cruelties and misery produced by the scourge of war. Hence the parties to a civil war usually concede to each other belligerent rights. They exchange prisoners, and adopt the other courtesies and rules common to public or national wars.

"A civil war," says Vattel, "breaks the bands of society and government, or at least suspends their force and effect; it produces in the nation two independent parties, who consider each other as enemies, and acknowledge no common judge. Those two parties, therefore, must necessarily be considered as constituting, at least for a time, two separate bodies, two distinct societies. Having no common superior to judge between them, they stand in precisely the same predicament as two nations who engage in a contest and have recourse to arms.

"This being the case, it is very evident that the common laws of war--those maxims of humanity, moderation, and honor--ought to be observed by both parties in every civil war. Should the sovereign conceive he has a right to hang up his prisoners as rebels, the opposite party will make reprisals, &c., &c.; the war will become cruel, horrible, and every day more destructive to the nation."

As a civil war is never publicly proclaimed, *eo nomine* against insurgents, its actual existence is a fact in our domestic history which the Court is bound to notice and to know.

The true test of its existence, as found in the writing of the sages of the common law, may be thus summarily stated: "When the regular course of justice is interrupted by revolt, rebellion, or insurrection, so that the Courts of Justice cannot be kept open, *civil war exists* and hostilities may be prosecuted on the same footing as if those opposing the Government were foreign enemies invading the land.". . .

It is not the less a civil war, with belligerent parties in hostile array, because it may be called an "insurrection" by one side, and the insurgents be considered as rebels or traitors. It is not necessary that the independence of the revolted province or State be acknowledged in order to constitute it a party belligerent in a war according to the law of nations. Foreign nations acknowledge it as war by a declaration of neutrality. The condition of neutrality cannot exist unless there be two belligerent parties. In the case of the *Santissima Trinidad*, (7 Wheaton, 337,) this Court say: "The Government of the United States has recognized the existence of a civil war between Spain and her colonies, and has avowed her determination to remain neutral between the parties. Each party is therefore deemed by us a belligerent nation, having, so far as concerns us, the sovereign rights of war." (See also 3 Binn., 252.)

As soon as the news of the attack on Fort Sumter, and the organization of a government by the seceding States, assuming to act as belligerents, could become known in Europe, to wit, on the 13th of May, 1861, the Queen of England issued her proclamation of neutrality, "recognizing hostilities as existing between the Government of the United States of America and *certain States* styling themselves the Confederate States of America." This was immediately followed by similar declarations or silent acquiescence by other nations.

After such an official recognition by the sovereign, a citizen of a foreign State is estopped to deny the existence of a war with all its consequences as regards neutrals. They cannot ask a Court to affect a technical ignorance of the existence of a war, which all the world acknowledges to be the greatest civil war known in the history of the human race, and thus cripple the arm of the Government and paralyze its power by subtle definitions and ingenious sophisms.

The law of nations is also called the law of nature; it is founded on the common consent as well as the common sense of the world. It contains no such anomalous doctrine as that which this Court are now for the first time desired to pronounce, to wit: That insurgents who have risen in rebellion against their sovereign, expelled her Courts, established a revolutionary government, organized armies, and commenced hostilities, are not *enemies* because they are *traitors*; and a war levied on the Government by traitors, in order to dismember and destroy it, is not a *war* because it is an "insurrection."

Whether the President in fulfilling his duties, as Commander-in-chief, in suppressing an insurrection, has met with such armed hostile resistance, and a civil war of such alarming proportions as will compel him to accord to them the character of belligerents, is a question to be decided *by him*, and this Court must be governed by the decisions and acts of the political department of the Government to which this power was entrusted. "He must determine what degree of force the crisis demands." The proclamation of blockade is itself official and conclusive evidence to the Court that a state of war existed which demanded and authorized a recourse to such a measure, under the circumstances peculiar to the case. . . .

On this first question therefore we are of the opinion that the President had a right, *jure belli*, to institute a blockade of ports in possession of the States in rebellion, which neutrals are bound to regard.

NOTE

The consequence of instituting a blockade against the coasts held by rebels in a civil war is the granting to the rebels belligerent status in international law, as explained by Professor Briggs:

> If a State invokes belligerent rights by instituting a blockade *jure belli* against any of its ports in the hands of rebels or insurgents, this constitutes a recognition of the belligerency of the insurgents and justifies the application of the laws of war by both contestants and of the laws of neutrality by third States. . . .

> During the American Civil War, Secretary of State Seward protested bitterly against Queen Victoria's Proclamation of Neutrality of May 13, 1861, as an unwarranted concession of belligerent rights to the Confederacy. The British Government quite correctly maintained that, by proclaiming, on April 19, 1861, a blockade of the coasts and ports of the Southern states "in pursuance of the laws of the United States, *and of the law of nations in such case provided*," the United States had itself recognized the belligerency of the insurgents prior to British recognition. A later claim by the United States for indemnity, based, in part, upon the alleged prematurity of British recognition of the belligerency of the Confederacy, was rejected by the British Government. See 51 B.&

F.S.P., 165 ff., 185 ff.; 57 *id.* 1119 ff. The legal situation has been summarized succinctly by Philip Jessup: "A blockade can be enforced against ships flying foreign flags only through the exercise of belligerent rights. Belligerency is never a unilateral position; there must be at least two belligerents. By asserting belligerent rights on the high seas, the North thereby recognized the belligerency of the Confederates, as the British Government was quick to point out." Jessup, "The Spanish Rebellion and International Law," 15 *Foreign Affairs* (1937), 260, 273. Herbert W. Briggs, ed., *The Law of Nations, Cases, Documents, and Notes*, 2nd ed., New York: Appleton-Century-Crofts, Inc., 1952, p. 991. Reprinted with the permission of Prentice Hall.

In order to avoid granting belligerent status in international law through declaration of blockade in a civil war, a legal government sometimes simply declares the closure of the rebel-held ports. The United States in several cases considered that such a measure was in fact a blockade and therefore must be effective. The following cases illustrate this position of the United States.

CLAIMS COMMISSION--UNITED STATES AND MEXICO. THE
ORIENTAL NAVIGATION COMPANY v. THE UNITED MEXICAN STATES
(Docket No. 411) Opinion rendered October 3, 1928
American Journal of International Law, Vol. 23 (1929), pp. 434-437.
Reprinted with the permission of the American Society of International Law.

On April 15, 1924, the steamship *Gaston*, owned by the Southgate Marine Corporation, and, according to a time charter dated February 28, 1924, operated by the Orient Navigation Company, an American corporation, cleared the port of New Orleans with a cargo of general merchandise consigned to Frontera, Tabasco, Mexico. When this cargo was unloaded, the vessel was to load a cargo of bananas, consisting of fifteen or sixteen thousand bunches, which had been purchased by agents of the Oriental Navigation Company and was to be transported from Frontera to New Orleans for the purpose of sale at the latter place for the company's account.

At that time the port of Frontera and some other Mexican ports were in the hands of insurgents. The Government of the United Mexican States had decreed that those ports should be closed to international trade, and had officially informed the Government of the United States of America about the closure. In reply the Government of the United States of America had declared that it felt obliged to respect the requirements of international law according to which a port in the hands of insurgents can be closed by an effective blockade only, and, further, that it felt obliged to advise American citizens engaged in commerce with Mexico that they might deal with persons in authority in such ports with respect to all matters affecting commerce therewith.

The *Gaston* arrived at Frontera on April 20, and anchored in the roadstead. The following day the unloading of her cargo was begun. In the afternoon the Mexican gunboat *Agua Prieta* was noticed cruising in the offing and ordering the *Gaston* to put to sea. On April 22 this order, accompanied by some random shots, was repeated, and subsequently the *Gaston*, having communicated with the *U.S.S. Cleveland* and the *U.S.S. Tulsa*, put to sea, having unloaded only part of her cargo, and without having loaded any part of the cargo of bananas. The vessel went back to New Orleans, where the rest of her cargo was unloaded. The cargo of bananas became a total loss.

On behalf of the Oriental Navigation Company the United States of America are now claiming that the United Mexican States should indemnify the company for the loss suffered by it from the action of the gunboat *Agua Prieta*. The loss is alleged to amount to $15,400.91, which

claiming that the United Mexican States should indemnify the company for the loss suffered by it from the action of the gunboat *Agua Prieta*. The loss is alleged to amount to $15,400.91, which sum is claimed with the allowance of interest thereon.

The respondent government refers to the fact that the belligerency of the insurgents in question had been recognized by no foreign power. It follows therefrom, the respondent government contends, that the Federal Government of Mexico, notwithstanding the revolution, was vested with full and undivided sovereignty over all her territory, so that it was a question solely dependent upon domestic Mexican law whether or not the Federal Government was entitled to close a Mexican port. But according to the General Customs Regulations of Mexico, whenever a port is occupied by rebels, it will be deemed closed to legal traffic, no Federal consul or other official will authorize shipment of merchandise to it, and persons violating this law will be liable to the punishment prescribed for smugglers.

In the opinion of the Commission it cannot be said to depend solely on domestic Mexican law whether or not the government of the United Mexican States was entitled to close the port of Frontera. In time of peace, it no doubt would be a question of domestic law only. But in time of civil war, when the control of a port has passed into the hands of insurgents, it is held, nearly unanimously, by a long series of authorities, that international law will apply, and that neutral trade is protected by rules similar to those obtaining in case of war. It is clear also, that if this principle be not adopted, the conditions of neutral commerce will be worse in case of civil war than in case of war.

Now, it has been submitted by the respondent government that the law protecting neutral commerce is not the same after the World War 1914-19 as it was before. The old rules of blockade were not followed during the war, and they cannot, it is submitted, be considered as still obtaining. Indeed, this seems to be the view of most post-war authors. They point to the fact that the use of submarines makes it almost impossible to have blockading forces stationed or cruising within a restricted area that is well known to the enemy. On the other hand, they argue, it cannot be assumed that there will be no economic warfare in future wars. Is it not a fact that Article 16 of the Covenant of the League of Nations even makes it a duty for the members of the League, under certain circumstances, to carry on economic war against an enemy of the League? But the economic warfare of the future, it must be assumed, will apply means that are entirely different from the classical blockade, and the old rule of the Paris declaration of 1856 will have to yield to the needs of a belligerent state subjected to modern conditions of naval war.

If the view above set forth were accepted, there would seem to be little doubt that the rather moderate action of the *Agua Prieta*, consisting in simply forcing off the port a neutral vessel without doing any harm to the vessel or her crew, must be considered to be lawful. The Commission, however, deems it unnecessary to pass an opinion as to the correctness of that view, which, at any rate, for obvious reasons could not be adopted without hesitation. The Commission is of the opinion that the action of the *Agua Prieta* can hardly be considered as a violation of the law obtaining before the World War. It is true that, according to that law, the trading of the *Gaston* to the port of Frontera was perfectly lawful. The Federal Mexican authorities would not be justified in capturing or confiscating the vessel, or in inflicting any other penalty upon it. Neither would a Mexican warship have a right to interfere, if, for example on the high seas, it met with a neutral vessel bound for a port in the hands of insurgents. But, on the other hand, the authorities do not show, and the Commission is of the opinion that it cannot be assumed that the Federal Mexican authorities should be obliged to permit the unloading and the subsequent loading of a neutral vessel trading to an insurgent port without such clearance documents as are prescribed by Mexican law, even in case control of the port should have been obtained again by those authorities before the arrival of the vessel to the port or be reobtained during her stay there. Now, in the present case, it cannot fairly be said that the port of Frontera was in the hands of insurgents at the time when the events in question took place. It was in fact partly commanded by the *Agua Prieta*. That being the case, and none of the authorities invoked by the claimants bearing upon a situation of this nature, the Commission holds that the lawfulness of the action taken by the *Aqua Prieta* in forcing off the *Gaston*, which had not applied to the Mexican consul at New Orleans for clearance, can hardly be challenged.

Decision

The claim of the United States of America on behalf of the Oriental Navigation Company is disallowed.

Done in Mexico, D. F., this 3rd day of October, 1928.

KRISTIAN SINDBALLE,
Presiding Commissioner.

C. FERNANDEZ MACGREGOR,
Commissioner.

[*Dissenting opinion* by NIELSEN, *Commissioner:* Established principles of international law with regard to blockade were not observed, and a ship engaged in trading in a perfectly lawful manner was the victim of an interference which was an invasion or confiscation of property rights. The pronouncements of governments, the opinions of international tribunals, and the writings of authorities all support the view that effective blockade is necessary to close an insurgent port. The brief visit of the *Agua Prieta* to the waters outside of Frontera was not an effective blockade of ingress and egress. The communication sent to the Government of the United States with respect to the closing of the port of Frontera, which made no mention of blockade, was neither notice nor proclamation of blockade. The firing of some shots in the direction of the *Gaston* lying in the harbor, and the signal sent to it ordering it to depart, were not a proper substitute for capture or prize court proceedings or warning. There is no distinction in international law and practice, or in logic, between a port held by insurgents whose belligerency has been recognized, and a port occupied by insurgents to whom that status has not been accorded.]

"Closure of Insurgent Ports in Spain: Policy of the United States,"
U.S. Department of State, *Press Release*, No. 361 (August 29, 1936),
p. 192; reprinted from Herbert W. Briggs, ed., *The Law of Nations,
Cases, Documents, and Notes*, 2nd ed., New York: Appleton-Century-
Crofts, Inc., 1952, pp. 995-996.

On August 21 Mr. Eric C. Wendelin, in charge of the American Embassy in Madrid, received a *note verbale*, dated August 20, 1936, from the Spanish Foreign Office at Madrid which stated:

Spanish ports in the power of the rebels as well as those of Ceuta and Melilla and the ports of our proscription zone in Morocco, Balearic and Canary Islands, have all been declared a war zone and therefore it is not possible for the ships of our fleet to permit the entry into them of merchant ships in order in this way to prevent furnishing of provinces of Almeria, Murcia, Alicante, and Badajoz and supplies to the rebels.

The Spanish Foreign Office requested that this information be transmitted to the American Government in order that American merchant ships may be warned and that thus "possible incidents may be avoided.

Mr. Wendelin reported that he believed that the same communication had been sent to all other governments.

The Secretary of State, on August 25, instructed Mr. Wendelin to address the following note to the Minister of State in reply to the Minister's *note verbale* of August 20:

Sir:
I have the honor to acknowledge the receipt of your note of August 20, 1936, requesting me to inform my Government, in order that American merchant ships might be warned and possible incidents thus avoided, that your Government has declared Spanish ports in control of the insurgents, both on the Spanish mainland and in Morocco and the Balearic and Canary Islands, a war zone into which merchant vessels will not be permitted to enter.

My Government directs me to inform you in reply that, with the friendliest feelings toward the Spanish Government, it cannot admit the legality of any action on the part of the Spanish Government in declaring such ports closed unless that Government declares and maintains an effective blockade of such ports. In taking this position my Government is guided by a long line of precedents in international law with which the Spanish Government is doubtless familiar.

"Regions in China Closed to Foreign Vessels, "*Department of State Bulletin*, Vol. XXI, No. 523 (July 11, 1949), pp. 34-36.

Note From Chinese Ministry of Foreign Affairs to American Embassy in Canton, dated June 20, 1949 [Released to the Press June 23]

[Translation]

The Ministry of Foreign Affairs presents its compliments to the American Embassy and has the honor to state that the Government of China has now decided that the following regions from the north bank of the mouth of the Min River, longitude 119 degrees, 40 minutes east and latitude 26 degrees, 15 minutes north to the mouth of the Liao River, longitude 122 degrees, 20 minutes east and latitude 40 degrees, 30 minutes north, which lie along the coast and within the territorial water of China shall be temporarily closed, and entry therein of foreign vessels shall be strictly forbidden. Instructions have already been issued by the Government of China that, beginning from midnight of June 25 of this year, prompt actions shall be taken to prevent violations of this decision by foreign vessels. All foreign vessels shall themselves be responsible for any danger resulting from their violation of this decision.

The Ministry of Foreign Affairs also wishes to call the Embassy's attention to the fact that, during the period of rebellion suppression, the Government of China decided on June 18 of this year to close all ports originally declared open but no longer under the actual control of the Government of China. Included in this category are Yungchia [Wenchow], Ningpo, Shanghai, Tientsin and Chinghuangtao [Chinwangtao], where no commercial shipping by sea shall be

Tientsin and Chinghuangtao [Chinwangtao], where no commercial shipping by sea shall be permitted.

The Ministry of Foreign Affairs requests the Embassy to give due consideration to this matter and to transmit the contents of this note to the American Government, and promptly notify the American shipping companies concerned to act accordingly.

Note From U.S. Embassy at Canton to the Chinese Ministry of Foreign Affairs, dated June 28, 1949

[Released to the Press June 29]

The Embassy of the United States of America presents its compliments to the Ministry of Foreign Affairs of the Republic of China and has the honor to refer to the latter's note No. 5938 of June 20 stating that the Government of China has now decided that the regions from the north bank of the mouth of the Min River, longitude 119 degrees 40 minutes east and latitude 26 degrees 15 minutes north, to the mouth of the Liao River, longitude 122 degrees 20 minutes east and latitude 40 degrees 30 minutes north, which lie along the coast and within the territorial waters of China shall be temporarily closed, and entry therein of foreign vessels shall be strictly forbidden. The note under reference adds that instructions have been issued by the Government of China for the enforcement of this decision beginning from midnight June 25, 1949, and calls attention to a decision by the Government of China on June 18, 1949, to close all ports originally declared open but no longer under the actual control of the Government of China.

As requested therein, the Ministry's note was transmitted to Washington. The Embassy is now instructed to state in reply that, despite the friendliest feelings toward the Chinese Government, the United States Government cannot admit the legality of any action on the part of the Chinese Government in declaring such ports and the territorial waters adjacent thereto closed to foreign vessels unless the Chinese Government declares and maintains an effective blockade of them. In taking this position, the United States Government has been guided by numerous precedents in international law with which the Chinese Government is doubtless familiar and has noted that the ports referred to are not under the actual control of the Chinese Government.[1]

---

[1]On Nov. 21, 1908, the Government of Haiti declared the port of Aux Cayes blockaded. Upon receipt of the telegram Secretary of State Root directed the American Minister to Haiti (Furniss) "to convey to the Haitian Government the usual notice that blockade must be proclaimed and maintained by an adequate force in order to be respected." (1908 *For. Rel.* p. 439.)

The Department of State was informed in 1912 that the port of Veracruz, Mexico, which was in the hands of insurgents, had been ordered closed by the Federal Government. It thereupon instructed the American Chargé d' Affaires to inform the Mexican Foreign Office as follows:

"As a general principle a decree by a sovereign power closing to neutral commerce ports held by its enemies, whether foreign or domestic, can have no international validity and no extraterritorial effect in the direction of imposing any obligation upon the governments of neutral powers to recognize it or to contribute toward its enforcement by any domestic action on their part. If the sovereign decreeing such a closure have a naval force sufficient to maintain such a blockade, then he may seize, subject to the adjudication of a prize court, vessels which may attempt to run the blockade. But his decree or acts closing ports which are held adversely to him are by themselves entitled to no international respect. The Government of the United States must

Note From Chinese Ministry of Foreign Affairs to American Embassy at Canton, dated June 30, 1949

[Translation]

The Ministry of Foreign Affairs of the Republic of China presents its compliments to the Embassy of the United States of America, and has the honor to refer to the latter's note, No. 265, of June 28, 1949, setting forth the position of the United States Government with regard to the closure by the Chinese Government of certain parts of its territorial waters and the ports therein.

In reply, the Ministry has the honor to state that the Chinese Government deems it within the sovereign right of a state to declare open or closed any part of its territories, whenever conditions necessitate. In fact, the Chinese Government has exercised in the past on more than one occasion the right to close some of its ports, and no question of legality has been raised by any government,

---

therefore regard as utterly nugatory such decrees or acts closing ports which the United States of Mexico do not possess, unless such proclamations are enforced by an effective blockade." (VII Hackworth, *Digest of International Law*, 1943, p. 166.)

When the Mexican Government decreed that in addition to the ports of Veracruz and Manzanillo, in the hands of insurgents, the ports of Frontera and Puerto Mexico were closed and notified the United States of its action, Secretary of States Hughes replied, February 1, 1924, that --

". . . this Government, with the friendliest disposition toward the Mexican Government, feels obliged, following a long line of precedents, to respect what are believed to be the requirements of international law, to the effect that a port of a foreign country declared by the government thereof to be outside of its control, cannot be closed by such government save by an effective blockade maintained by it." (VII Hackworth, *Digest of International Law*, 1943, p. 167.)

During the revolution in Sao Paulo in 1932, the Brazilian Government closed all ports of that State to foreign and domestic shipping. On July 16, 1932, Secretary of State Stimson instructed the Embassy in Rio de Janeiro:

"If Santos is in the control of insurgents the Brazilian Government would have no right to close this port by decree as reported . . . unless this decree is enforced by an effective blockade." (VII Hackworth, *Digest of International Law*, 1943, p. 168.)

In reply to a *note verbale* of August 20, 1936, from the Spanish Foreign Office to the American Embassy advising the Embassy that certain ports in the possession of the Government had "been declared a war zone" and that consequently entry into them by merchant ships would not be permitted, the Department of State instructed the Embassy on August 25 to reply as follows:

"My Government directs me to inform you in reply that, with the friendliest feelings toward the Spanish Government, it cannot admit the legality of any action on the part of the Spanish Government in declaring such ports closed unless that Government declares and maintains an effective blockade of such port. In taking this position my Government is guided by a long line of precedents in international law with which the Spanish Government is doubtless familiar." Department of State, XV *Press Releases*, weekly issue 361, pp. 192-193 (Aug. 27, 1936).

including that of the United States. Port Dairen, for instance, was declared closed at a time when it was not under the actual control of the Chinese Government. The closure order under reference is, in effect, of a similar nature and is, therefore, enforceable independently of a declaration of blockade, which has never been, and is not, under the contemplation of the Chinese Government.

In stating its position, the Chinese Government also wishes to assure the United States Government that in the execution of the closure order it will undertake to do its best to avoid any unnecessary hardship or loss to the nationals of the United States. The Chinese Government hopes, therefore that in view of the friendly feelings happily existing between the two peoples, the United States Government will see its way to cooperate with it so as to prevent any untoward incident.

The Chinese Government has the honor to request the Embassy of the United States of America to be good enough to transmit at its earliest convenience the above reply to the Government of the United States.

NOTE

On June 25, 1950, north Korean forces crossed the 38th parallel of the Korean peninsula and invaded the territory controlled by the Government of the Republic of Korea. The United States decide to intervene to prevent the Communists' taking over of the entire Korean peninsula. On June 27, 1950, American President Harry S. Truman declared that he had "ordered the Seventh Fleet to prevent any attack on Formosa"; and in the meantime he requested the Chinese Government on Taiwan to cease military operations against the mainland. *American Foreign Policy, 1950-1955, Basic Documents*, Vol. 2, Washington, D.C.: U.S. Government Printing Office, 1957, p. 2468. On June 28, 1950, the Chinese Government accepted the proposal of the United States. *China Handbook 1951*, Taipei: China Publishing Co., 1951, p. 115. The Chinese Government decrees on closing the Chinese Communists' held ports were since then in fact terminated.

REFERENCES

Edwin D. Dickson, "Closure of Ports in Control of Insurgents," *American Journal of International Law*, Vol. 24 (1930), pp. 69-78; C. John Colombos, *International Law of the Sea*, 6th ed., London: Longman Group Ltd., 1967, pp. 336-338.

G. PACIFIC BLOCKADE, "QUARANTINE" AND SIMILAR MEASURES

> J.G. Starke, *Introduction to International Law*, 9th ed., London: Butterworths, 1984, pp. 497-498. Footnotes omitted. Reproduced with the permission of Butterworth & Co. (Publishers) Ltd.

The pacific blockade . . . is a measure employed in time of peace. Sometimes classed as a reprisal, it is generally designed to coerce the state whose ports are blockaded into complying with a request for satisfaction by the blockading states. Some authorities have doubted its legality. If not now obsolete, its admissibility as a unilateral measure is questionable, in the light of the United Nations Charter.

The pacific blockade appears to have been first employed in 1827, since that date there have been about 20 instances of its employment. It was generally used by very powerful states, with naval forces, against weak states. Although for that reason liable to abuse, in the majority of cases it was employed by the Great Powers acting in concert for objects which were perhaps in the best interests of all concerned, for example, to end some disturbance, or to ensure the proper execution of treaties, or to prevent the outbreak of war, as in the case of the blockade of Greece in 1886 to secure the disarming of the Greek troops assembled near the frontiers and thus avoid a conflict with Turkey. From this standpoint the pacific blockade may be regarded as a recognised collective procedure for facilitating the settlement of differences between states. Indeed, the blockade is expressly mentioned in article 42 of the United Nations Charter as one of the operations which the Security Council may initiate in order to "maintain or restore international peace and security."

There are certain obvious advantages in the employment of the pacific blockade. It is far less violent means of action than war, and is more elastic. On the other hand, it is more than an ordinary reprisal, and against any but the weak states who are usually subjected to it, might be deemed an act of war. It is perhaps a just comment on the institution of pacific blockade that the strong maritime powers who resort to it do so in order to avoid the burdens and inconveniences of war.

Most writers agree, and on the whole the British practice supports the view, that a blockading state has no right to seize ships of third states which endeavour to break a pacific blockade. It follows also that third states are not duty bound to respect such a blockade. The principle is that a blockading state can only operate against ships of other states if it has declared a belligerent blockade, that is, where actual war exists between the blockading and blockaded states and accordingly it becomes entitled to search neutral shipping. But by instituting merely a pacific blockade, the blockading state tacitly admits that the interests at stake were not sufficient to warrant the burdens and risks of war. On principle, therefore, in the absence of an actual war, the blockading state should not impose on third states the obligations and inconveniences of neutrality. In other words, a blockading state cannot simultaneously claim the benefits of peace and war.

NOTE

The legality of the pacific blockade under the United Nations Charter, which in Article 2, paragraph 4, prohibits "the threat or use of force against the territorial integrity or political independence of any State," is now highly questionable. Cf. D. P. O'Connell, *International Law of the Sea*, edited by I. A. Shearer, Vol. 2, New York: Oxford University Press, 1984, p. 1158. However, a form of pacific blockade can be instituted by the Security Council acting under Chapter VII of the Charter, as indicated by the following case relating to Rhodesia:

> In the course of the sanctions imposed by the British Government against the carriage of oil to Rhodesia, following her Unilateral Declaration of Independence in 1965, a Greek-owned tanker *Joanna V* ran the blockade by entering the port of Beira with the avowed intention of discharging her cargo of crude oil at that port for conveyance to Rhodesia. The timely action of the Royal Navy frustrated this attempt and *The Joanna V* eventually sailed for Durban with her cargo on her way to the Canary Islands, escorted by the frigate *Zulu*.

> A second, also Greek-owned tanker *Manuela*, with a similar intention, was intercepted in April 1966, by the frigate *Berwick*, when about 150 miles south-east of Beira, and a "back-up party" placed on her, thus preventing the leakage of her cargo of oil until she left for Santa Cruz, Tenerife, in July 1966. In both instances, the Royal Navy acted in full accord with the Resolution passed, for the "maintenance of international

peace and security" under chapter VII of its Charter, by the Security Council of the United Nations on April 7, 1966, and which reads as follows: "The British Government is authorized to prevent by the use of force if necessary the arrival at Beira of vessels reasonably believed to be carrying oil destined for Rhodesia.

C. John Colombos, *The International Law of the Sea*, 6th ed., London: Longmans Group Limited, 1967, p. 470.

> William W. Bishop, Jr., *International Law, Cases and Materials*, 3rd ed., Boston and Toronto: Little, Brown and Co., 1971, pp. 926-928. footnotes omitted. Reprinted with the permission of Little, Brown and Co.

In a radio and television address to the nation on the evening of October 22, 1962, President Kennedy said in part: "This Government . . . has maintained the closest surveillance of the Soviet military buildup on the island of Cuba. Within the past week unmistakable evidence has established the fact that a series of offensive missile sites is now in preparation on that imprisoned island. The purpose of these bases can be none other than to provide a nuclear strike capability against the Western Hemisphere. . . . [Pointing out that these missile sites were in part for missiles capable of carrying a nuclear warhead 1000 miles, and in part for those capable of traveling twice that far, and that "jet bombers, capable of carrying nuclear weapons, are now being uncrated and assembled in Cuba, while the necessary air bases are being prepared," he stated that this action] contradicts the repeated assurances of Soviet spokesmen, both publicly and privately delivered, that the arms buildup in Cuba would retain its original defensive character and that the Soviet Union had no need or desire to station strategic missiles on the territory of any other nation. . . .

"Neither the United States of America nor the world community of nations can tolerate deliberate deception and offensive threats on the part of any nation, large or small. We no longer live in a world where only the actual firing of weapons represents a sufficient challenge to a nation's security to constitute maximum peril. Nuclear weapons are so destructive and ballistic missiles are so swift that any substantially increased possibility of their use or any sudden change in their deployment may well be regarded as a definite threat to peace.

"For many years both the Soviet Union and the United States, recognizing this fact, have deployed strategic nuclear weapons with great care, never upsetting the precarious status quo which insured that these weapons would not be used in the absence of some vital challenge. . . .

"Acting, therefore, in the defense of our own security and of the entire Western Hemisphere . . . I have directed that the following initial steps be taken immediately:

"First: To halt this offensive buildup, a strict quarantine of all offensive military equipment under shipment to Cuba is being initiated. All ships of any kind bound for Cuba from whatever nation or port will, if found to contain cargoes of offensive weapons, be turned back. This quarantine will be extended, if needed, to other types of cargo and carriers. . . .

"Second: I have directed the continued and increased close surveillance of Cuba and its military buildup. . . .

"Third: It shall be the policy of this nation to regard any nuclear missile launched from Cuba against any nation in the Western Hemisphere as an attack by the Soviet Union on the United

against any nation in the Western Hemisphere as an attack by the Soviet Union on the United States, requiring a full retaliatory response upon the Soviet Union."

Later portions of the address announced reinforcement of the Guantanamo base, the calling of a meeting of the Organ of Consultation of the Organization of American States, and the calling of an emergency meeting of the U.N. Security Council.

On October 23 the Council of the OAS, acting as the Organ of Consultation under the Rio Treaty, unanimously resolved: "1. To call for the immediate dismantling and withdrawal from Cuba of all missiles and other weapons with any offensive capability; 2. To recommend that the member states, in accordance with Articles 6 and 8 of the Inter-American Treaty of Reciprocal Assistance, take all measures, individually and collectively, including the use of armed force, which they may deem necessary to ensure that the Government of Cuba cannot continue to receive from the Sino-Soviet powers military material and related supplies which may threaten the peace and security of the Continent and to prevent the missiles in Cuba with offensive capability from ever becoming an active threat to the peace and security of the Continent; 3. To inform the Security Council of the United Nations of this resolution in accordance with Article 54 of the Charter. . . ."

At 7:06 p.m. on October 23, President Kennedy signed a proclamation ordering forces to "interdict, subject to the instructions herein contained, the delivery of offensive weapons and associated material to Cuba." Meanwhile on October 23 the matter had been laid before the Security Council, and the Secretary-General cooperated with the United States and Soviet Governments in working out a solution. After the interchange of messages between Chairman Khrushchev and President Kennedy on October 26, 27, and 28, the former announced that instructions had been issued "to take appropriate measures to discontinue construction of the aforementioned facilities, to dismantle them, and to return them to the Soviet Union," and that they were prepared to work out arrangements for United Nations verification of the dismantling. Although Cuba refused such verification, United States overflights were the method of observation used. By a proclamation of November 21, 1962, the earlier order interdicting deliveries of offensive weapons to Cuba was terminated.

> Abram Chayes, "The Legal Case for U.S. Action on Cuba,"
> *Department of State Bulletin*, Vol. XLVII, No. 1221 (November 19,
> 1962), pp. 763-765.

. . . The question was not, as most of my friends in and out of the press seemed to think, "Is it a legal blockade?" The effort to name and classify things has its place in the law as in other disciplines, but this audience needs no reminder that legal problems are something more than a search for pigeon-holes within which to encase living phenomena.

In wartime the establishment of a blockade, of course, with all its classical elements, is justified according to the books. It represents minimal interference with neutral commerce consistent with the necessities of war. But even in the most hallowed of the texts, war is not the sole situation in which such interference is permissible.

It is instructive to examine the rules of blockade. They were developed in the 19th century. They reflect very accurately the problems of the international order--as well as the weapons technology--that then prevailed. The typical subjects of international law were European nation-states. Their relations with each other were episodic and largely bilateral.

The age of total war was only beginning; so the application of force as an instrument of national policy was recognized as legitimate, if not positively beneficial. When force was applied it was, at least in theory, a bilateral affair or, at most, something between small and temporary groupings of nations on each side. The operating legal rules--always nicer and more coherent in retrospect than at the time--had two principal objects: first, to help assure that these affrays were carried out with the smallest disturbance of the normal activities of all concerned; and second, to permit a state to make an unambiguous choice whether to join with one of the belligerents--and so have a chance to share in any political gains--or to remain uninvolved and make its profits commercially, which were in any event likely to be both larger and safer.

International law addresses different problems today and in a different context. Its overriding object is not to regulate the conduct of war but to keep and defend the peace. If nonalinement continues to be a goal for some countries, noninvolvement has become a luxury beyond price. We remember that war in this century has twice engulfed us all, willy-nilly. Paper commitments to right conduct did not stop it. Above all we are burdened with the knowledge and the power to destroy the world. The international landscape today, too, looks quite different than it did a century ago. It is peopled with permanent organizations of states--some more comprehensive, some less, some purely for defense, and some with broader purposes. It is through these organizations that we hope to give reality to our pledges to maintain the peace.

The Soviet Union's threat in Cuba was made in the context of this international system, and it was answered in the same context.

The United States saw its security threatened, but we were not alone. Our quarantine was imposed in accordance with the recommendation of the Organization of American States acting under the Rio Treaty of 1947. This treaty, together with related agreements, constitutes the inter-American system. Twenty-one countries, including Cuba, are parties to that treaty. None has ever disaffirmed it.

The Rio Treaty provides for collective action not only in the case of armed attack but also "if the inviolability or the integrity of the territory or the sovereignty or political independence of any American State should be affected . . . by any . . . fact or situation that might endanger the peace of America. . . ." In such cases, a special body, the Organ of Consultation, is to "meet immediately in order to agree on the measures . . . which should be taken for the common defense and for the maintenance of the peace and security of the Continent." The Organ of Consultation acts only by a two-thirds vote.

The treaty is explicit as to the measures which may be taken "for the maintenance of the peace and security of the Continent." The "use of armed force" is specifically authorized, though "no State shall be required to use armed force without its consent."

On October 23d, the Organ of Consultation met, in accordance with the treaty procedures, and considered the evidence of the secret introduction of Soviet strategic nuclear missiles into Cuba. It concluded that a situation existed which endangered the peace of America. It recommended that member states "take all measures, individually and collectively, including the use of armed force, which they may deem necessary to ensure that the Government of Cuba cannot continue to receive from the Sino-Soviet powers military material and related supplies . . . ." The quarantine was imposed to carry out this recommendation.

Action by regional organizations to keep the peace is not inconsistent with the United Nations Charter. On the contrary, the charter assigns an important role to regional organizations in carrying out the purposes of the United Nations. Article 52(1) prescribes the use of "regional arrangements or agencies for dealing with such matters relating to the maintenance of international peace and security as are appropriate for regional action. . . ." And it is certainly not irrelevant in the present context that provisions dealing with regional organizations were written into the charter at San Francisco at the insistence of the Latin American countries and with the inter-American system specifically in mind.

The activities of regional organizations, of course, must be "consistent with the Purposes and Principles of the United Nations." It may seem self-evident that action to deal with a threat to the peace meets this requirement. But the principles of the United Nations are stated in article 2 of the charter and include the undertaking of all members to

> . . . refrain in their international relations from the threat or use of force
> against the territorial integrity or political independence of any state, or
> in any other manner inconsistent with the Purposes of the United
> Nations.

The quarantine action involves a use of force and must be squared with this principle.

The promise not to use force is not absolute. One qualification comes readily to mind. Article 51 affirms that nothing in the charter, including article 2(4), impairs "the inherent right of individual or collective self-defense if an armed attack occurs." The quarantine action was designed to deal with an imminent threat to our security. But the President in his speech did not invoke article 51 or the right of self-defense. And the OAS acted not under article 3, covering cases of armed attack, but under article 6, covering threats to the peace other than armed attack.

Self-defense, however, is not the only justifiable use of force under the charter. Obviously, the United Nations itself could sanction the use of force to deal with a threat to the peace. So it did in Korea and in the Congo. We accept use of force in these instances as legitimate for two reasons. First, all the members have constituted the United Nations for these purposes. In signing the charter they have assented to its powers and procedures. Second, the political processes by which the U.N. makes a decision to use force give some assurance that the decision will not be rashly taken.

I submit that the same two factors legitimize use of force in accordance with the OAS resolution dealing with a threat to the peace in the hemisphere. The significance of assent is attested by the fact that, though Cuba is now and has been for some time the object of sanctions and hostility from the OAS and has been suspended from participation in its agencies, she has remained a party to the treaties and a member of the inter-American system, as, in a like case, did the Dominican Republic. The significance of the political processes in the Organization is attested by the fact that, despite the disproportion of power between the United States and its neighbors to the south, it was not until the danger was clear and present that the necessary majority could be mustered to sanction use of armed force. But when that time came, the vote was unanimous.

Some have asked whether we should not first have gone to the Security Council before taking other action to meet the Soviet threat in Cuba. And I suppose that in the original conception of the United Nations, it was thought that the Security Council would be the agency for dealing with situations of this kind. However, the drafters of the charter demonstrated their wisdom by making Security Council responsibility for dealing with threats to the peace "primary" and not "exclusive." For events since 1945 have demonstrated that the Security Council, like our own electoral college, was not a viable institution. The veto has made it substantially useless in keeping the peace.

The withering away of the Security Council has led to a search for alternative peacekeeping institutions. In the United Nations itself the General Assembly and the Secretary-General have filled the void. Regional organizations are another obvious candidate.

Regional organizations, even when they employ agreed processes and procedures, remain subject to check. They are subordinate to the U.N. by the terms of the charter, and in the case of the OAS, by the terms of the relevant inter-American treaties themselves. Like an individual state, it can be called to account for its action in the appropriate agency of the parent organization. In recognition of this relation, the President ordered that the case be put immediately before the Security Council. The U.N., through the Council and the Secretary-General, is, as a result, actively engaged in the effort to develop a permanent solution to the threat to the peace represented by the Soviet nuclear capability in Cuba. . . .

NOTE

There has been much discussion as to the legality of the Cuban "quarantine" instituted by the United States. See Leonard C. Meeker, "Defensive Quarantine and the Law," *American Journal of International Law*, Vol. 57 (1963), pp. 515-524; Carl Q. Christol and Charles R. Davis, "Maritime Quarantine: The Naval Interdiction of Offensive Weapons and Associated Materiel to Cuba," *ibid.*, pp. 525-545; Quincy Wright, "The Cuban Quarantine," *ibid.*, pp. 546-565 and "Panel: Cuban Quarantine: Implications for the Future," *Proceedings of the American Society of International Law, 57th Annual Meeting, 1963*, pp. 1-18.

The Cuban "quarantine" instituted by the United States cannot be fitted within the traditional pattern of pacific blockade described before, as explained by Professor J. G. Starke:

> First, it was more than a blockade of the coast of a country as such. Its express purpose was to "interdict" the supply of certain weapons and equipment to Cuba, in order to prevent the establishment or reinforcement of missile bases in Cuban territory, but not to preclude all entry or exit of goods to or from Cuba. Second, vessels of countries other than Cuba, en route to Cuba, were subject to search and, if necessary, control by force, and could be directed to follow prescribed routes or avoid prohibited zones; but it was not in terms sought to render weapon-carrying vessels or their cargoes subject to capture for breach of the "interdiction". Third, among other grounds, the President of the United States purported to proclaim the quarantine pursuant to a recommendation of an international organisation, namely the Organisation of American States. Fourth, the quarantine was conducted in a manner unlike that characteristic of traditional pacific blockades; e.g. under a "Clearcut" scheme, shippers could obtain beforehand a clearance certificate to send cargoes through the zone subject of the quarantine.
>
> Assuming that such a blockade is, in all the circumstances, permitted by the United Nations Charter, nevertheless because of the very special geographical and other conditions, no general conclusions can be drawn from it as a precedent. If not permissible under the Charter, the effect of the "quarantine" in interfering with the freedom of the high seas raised serious issues as to its justification under customary international law.

J.G. Starke, *Introduction to International Law*, 9th ed., London: Butterworths, 1984, pp. 498-499.

See also Marcella M. Agerholm, "Domestic and International Law Implications of a Presidential Declared Blockade of Cuba," *New York University Law School Journal of International and Comparative Law*, Vol. 3 (1982), pp. 547-580.

NOTE ON NAVAL FORCE TO ENFORCE UNITED NATIONS EMBARGO AGAINST IRAQ

On August 1, 1990, Iraq invaded Kuwait and the next day, the Security Council of the United Nations adopted Resolution 660 demanding the immediate, unconditional withdrawal of all Iraqi forces from Kuwait. Paul Lewis, "U.N. Condemns the Invasion With Threat to Punish Iraq," *New York Times*, August 3, 1990, p. A10. On August 6, the Security Council, in accordance with Chapter 7 of the United Nations Charter, adopted Resolution 661 to impose economic sanctions on Iraq, which states:

THE SECURITY COUNCIL,

REAFFIRMING ITS RESOLUTION 660 (1990),

DEEPLY CONCERNED that this resolution has not been implemented and that the invasion by Iraq against Kuwait continues with further loss of human life and material destruction,

DETERMINED to bring the invasion and occupation of Kuwait by Iraq to an end and to restore the sovereignty, independence and territorial integrity of Kuwait. . . .

AFFIRMING the inherent right of individual or collective self-defense, in response to the armed attack by Iraq against Kuwait, in accordance with Article 51 of the Charter.

ACTING under Chapter 7 of the Charter of the United Nations,

1.   DETERMINES that Iraq has failed to comply with operative paragraph 2 of Resolution 660 (1990) and has usurped the authority of the legitimate Government of Kuwait;

2.   DECIDES, as a consequence to take the following measures to secure compliance of Iraq with operative paragraph 2 and to restore the authority of the legitimate Government of Kuwait;

3.   DECIDES that all states shall prevent:

a.   The import into their territories of all commodities and products originating in Iraq or Kuwait exported therefrom after the date of this resolution;

b.   Any activities by their nationals or in their territories which would promote or are calculated to promote the export or transshipment of any commodities or products from Iraq or Kuwait; and any dealings by their nationals or their flag vessels or in their territories in any commodities or products originating in Iraq or Kuwait and exported therefrom after the date of this resolution. . . .

c. The sale or supply by their nationals or from their territories or using their flag vessels of any commodities or products. . . but not including supplies intended strictly for medical purposes, and, in humanitarian circumstances, foodstuffs, to any person or body in Iraq or Kuwait. . . .

5. CALLS UPON all states, including states nonmembers of the United Nations, to act strictly in accordance with the provisions of this resolution notwithstanding any contract entered into or license granted before the date of this resolution. . . .

"Text of the Resolution For Sanctions on Iraq," *New York Times*, August 7, 1990, p. A9.

The United States maintained that it had the authority under the Charter of the United Nations to enforce the economic sanction imposed by the above Resolution on Iraq and occupied Kuwait. But other Security Council members considered that any military action in the name of the United Nations would require another vote by the Council. On August 12, 1990, U.S. Administration officials said that President Bush had ordered the large Navy fleet assembling in the Mideast to be prepared to use force to prevent any ships from breaking the economic embargo of Iraq and occupied Kuwait imposed by the Council. This policy was referred as "interdiction." This interdiction began on August 16, 1990 and the main zones for intercepting ships would be inside the gulf near Kuwait, in the Gulf of Oman and in the northern Red Sea, including the Jordanian part of Aqaba. See *Facts On File*, Vol. 50, No. 2595 (August 17, 1990), pp. 597, 599.

On August 25, 1990, the Security Council adopted Resolution 665 authorizing the use of force to enforce its embargo, which states:

THE SECURITY COUNCIL

. . . .

1. CALLS UPON those member states cooperating with the Government of Kuwait which are deploying maritime forces to the area to use such measures commensurate to the specific circumstances as may be necessary under the authority of the Security Council to halt all inward and outward maritime shipping in order to inspect and verify their cargoes and destinations and to insure strict implementation of the provisions related to such shipping laid down in Resolution 661 (1990). . . .

"Text of Resolution by U.N. Security Council," *New York Times*, August 26, 1990, p. 15.

To enforce the Security Council imposed embargo, the United States warships were authorized by the United States government to use "minimal force," such as shooting out a suspect vessel's

by the United States government to use "minimal force," such as shooting out a suspect vessel's rudder, to disable it. *Facts on File*, Vol. 50, No. 2597 (August 31, 1990), p. 633.

H. CONTRABAND

> J. G. Starke, *Introduction to International Law*, 9th ed., London: Butterworths, 1984, pp. 561-566, 568-569. Footnotes omitted.

Contraband is the designation for such goods as the belligerents consider objectionable because they may assist the enemy in the conduct of war.

The importance of the conception of contraband is due to certain rules enunciated by the Declaration of Paris 1856, which are now recognised to be part of international law. The effect of these may be stated as follows: Belligerents may seize enemy contraband goods which are being carried to an enemy destination on neutral ships, or neutral contraband goods which are being carried to an enemy destination on enemy ships. These rights of seizure are conceded by international law in view of the obvious necessity for belligerents, in the interests of self-preservation, to prevent the importation of articles which may strengthen the enemy.

A distinction is drawn between *absolute* and *relative* contraband. Articles clearly of a warlike or military character are considered to be absolute contraband; for example, arms of all kinds, military clothing, camp equipment, machinery for the manufacture of munitions, and gun mountings. Articles useful for purposes of peace as well as of war are considered to be relative contraband, for example, food, fuel, field-glasses, railway rolling stock, and if intercepted on their way to the enemy government or to the enemy forces are treated as absolute contraband and are liable to seizure by a hostile belligerent. It is doubtful if the distinction is now of any practical value.

Besides absolute and relative contraband, there is a third class of goods, known as "free articles", which must never be declared contraband, inasmuch as they are not susceptible to use in war; for example, chinaware and glass, soap, paint and colours, and fancy goods.

So far states have not reached general agreement on what articles fall within each of the three categories mentioned, except that by universal admission instruments of war or warlike materials are absolute contraband. Even jurists and Prize Court judges have seldom been in accord on the matter, and the practice of the states shows little uniformity and many anomalies.

For the sake of self-preservation, belligerents had necessarily to adapt themselves to these exigencies, and the old rules and usages as to contraband were disregarded by them when official lists of contraband covering every conceivable kind of article or material were drawn up. . . . The very extensive lists of contraband drawn up by Great Britain in both wars were eloquent testimony to the desuetude of former rules and usages. By the time of the Second World War, both by practice and according to British judicial decisions, the Declaration of London was regarded as devoid of any authority. The impact of "total war", at first in 1914, and then with much greater effect in 1939, completely revolutionised the conditions of warfare. In view of the enormous range of equipment required for modern war, of the much more advanced use of scientific weapons and instruments, and of the possible production of ersatz or substitute war materials, it could scarcely be predicted of any article or substance that it did not have a warlike use. For the sake of self-preservation, belligerents had necessarily to adapt themselves to these exigencies, and the old rules and usages as to contraband were disregarded by them when official lists of contraband covering every conceivable kind of article or material were drawn up.

Destination of contraband; Doctrine of continuous voyage or continuous transportation

Usually the simplest case of seizure of contraband is one in which the goods are clearly of hostile destination. A number of cases invariably arise in which the purpose of supplying the enemy is sought to be achieved more indirectly, as where citizens in a neutral state adjacent to enemy territory purchase contraband for resale to the enemy in order to avoid interception at sea.

In circumstances such as these the doctrine of continuous voyage or continuous transportation becomes applicable. This consists in treating an adventure which involves the carriage of goods in the first instance to a neutral port, and then to some ulterior and hostile destination as being for certain purposes one transportation only to an enemy destination, with all the consequences that would attach were the neutral port not interposed. Accordingly, if these goods are contraband, they are liable to seizure. The doctrine was expounded in classical terms by Lord Stowell in *The Maria*.

In the American Civil War, the United States Supreme Court applied the doctrine systematically to nearly all cases of breach of blockade or of contraband. Furthermore, United States courts took it upon themselves to draw presumptions as to hostile destination from all kinds of unexplained facts, for example, if the bill of lading were made out to order, or the manifest of cargo did not disclose the whole cargo, or a consignee were not named, or if the ship or cargo were consigned to a firm known to have acted as an enemy agent, or if there were a notorious trade in contraband between a neutral port and enemy territory.

Till 1909, it was nevertheless doubtful whether the doctrine was subject to general approval; at all events, it was not supported by a uniform practice. However, the Declaration of London 1909, which as mentioned above did not come into force, laid it down that the doctrine applied to absolute contraband, but did not apply to conditional contraband except in a war against an enemy possessing no seaboard.

In the First World War, the doctrine received its fullest executive and judicial application by Great Britain. British Orders-in-Council enunciated the doctrine in the widest terms, going far beyond the terms of the Declaration of London 1909. British courts also applied the doctrine systematically to a large number of cases, and in *The Kim* it was declared that:

> . . . the doctrine of continuous voyage or transportation, both in
> relation to carriage by sea and to carriage over land, had become part of
> the law of nations at the commencement of the present war, in
> accordance with the principles of recognised legal decisions, and with
> the views of a great body of modern jurists, and also with the practice
> of nations in recent maritime warfare.

As illustrating the wide scope of the doctrine the following principles were accepted by British courts: (1) that contraband goods might be seized, on their way to a neutral country if there existed an intention to forward them to any enemy destination after their undergoing a process of manufacture; (2) that, notwithstanding that the shippers of contraband goods might be innocent of any intention of an ultimate hostile destination, yet if on the "consignees" side the goods were in fact purchased for delivery to the enemy they were liable to confiscation.

The courts of other belligerents also accepted and applied the doctrine of continuous transportation.

In practice, the system of cargo and ship "navicerts", i.e. certificates given by a diplomatic or consular or other representative in a neutral country to a neutral shipper, testifying, as the case might be, that the cargo on board a neutral vessel was not liable to seizure as contraband, or that the voyage of a particular ship was innocent, left little room for the application of the doctrine of continuous transportation. "Navicerts" were first introduced by the Government of Queen Elizabeth in 1590, but were not used on a large scale in modern conditions of maritime warfare until 1916 when they were instituted by the Allies. "Navicerts" were again introduced on the outbreak of the Second World War in 1939. Vessels using "navicerts" were normally exempted from search, although there was no complete guarantee against interception or seizure, which might take place because of the discovery of fresh facts or because the destination of the cargo had become enemy occupied territory. A "navicert" might, of course, be refused on grounds which would not be sufficient to justify belligerent seizure of a ship or its cargo, and subsequent condemnation by a Prize Court. For example, at certain stages of the war, "navicerts" were, temporarily, not granted for the consignment to neutral territory of commodities needed by the Allies, such as rubber and tin.

Originally the mere absence of a "navicert" was not in itself a ground for seizure or condemnation. However, after the occupation of France and the Low Countries by Germany in June 1940 changed the whole circumstances of the Allied maritime blockade, Britain issued the Reprisals Order-in-Council (dated 31 July 1940), the effect of which was:

a.   that goods might become liable to seizure in the absence of a "navicert" to cover them; and

b.   that there was a presumption that "unnavicerted" goods had an enemy destination.

The Order did not make "navicerts" compulsory in every sense for neutral shippers, but it heightened the risk of interception and seizure of cargoes by putting the onus on the shipper of establishing the innocence of the shipment. The legality of the Order was of course questioned, but it was justified as a legitimate act of reprisal to simplify the blockade, and to put increased pressure on the enemy, and also possibly as a method of regulating neutral trade through a system of passes.

Neutral vessels were also required to equip themselves with ship warrants, which were granted upon covenants, inter alia, not to engage in contraband trading, to search the ship for smuggled contrabands, etc. In the absence of a ship warrant, "navicerts" might be refused, and bunkering and other facilities at Allied ports withheld.

By the system of "navicerts" and ship warrants, British authorities were able inter alia to police the smuggling of small contraband objects or articles, the employment of undesirable seamen, and the transport of technicians who might assist the enemy war effort. . . .

Consequences of Carriage of contraband; Condemnation by Prize Courts

Contraband is, in the circumstances mentioned above, liable to seizure, and under certain conditions even the vessel carrying the contraband cargo is liable to seizure. Seizure by a belligerent is admissible only in the open sea or in the belligerent's own territorial waters; seizure

conditions even the vessel carrying the contraband cargo is liable to seizure. Seizure by a belligerent is admissible only in the open sea or in the belligerent's own territorial waters; seizure in neutral territorial waters would be a violation of neutrality.

According to British and continental practice, the right of a belligerent state to seize contraband cargoes or vessels carrying them is not an absolute one but requires confirmation by the adjudication of a Prize Court established by that state. The origin of Prize Courts and of Prize Law goes back to the Middle Ages when there were frequent captures of piratical vessels. In England, for example, the Court of Admiralty would inquire into the authority of the captor and into the nationality of the captured vessel and of the owners of her goods. This practice was extended to captures made in time of war and it gradually became a recognized customary rule of international law that in time of war the maritime belligerents should be obliged to set up courts to decide whether captures were lawful or not. These courts were called Prize Courts. They are not international courts but municipal courts, although they apply international law largely. Every state is bound by international law to enact only such regulations, or statutes, to govern the operation of Prize Courts, as are in conformity with international law.

The structure of Prize Courts varies in different countries. In certain states, Prize Courts are mixed bodies consisting of judges and administrative officials, but in the United Kingdom and the United States they are exclusively judicial tribunals.

If the Prize Court upholds the legitimacy of the seizure, the cargo or vessel is declared to be "good prize" and to be confiscated to the captor's state. Jurisdiction is exercised in accordance with international law, unless otherwise directed by statute. The decree of condemnation is accompanied by an order for sale under which the purchaser acquires a title internationally valid. Thenceforward, what becomes of the prize is no concern of international law, but is solely a matter for municipal law to determine.

Seized ships or goods in the custody of the Prize Court pending a decision as to their condemnation or release, may be requisitioned subject to certain limitations, one of which is that there is a real issue to be tried as to the question of condemnation. . . .

Belligerent right of visit and search

Co-extensive with the right of seizing contraband or of capturing ships in breach of blockade, belligerents have by long established custom the right to visit and search neutral vessels on the high seas in order to determine the nature of the cargo and to check the destination and neutral character of the vessel. This right must be exercised so as to cause neutral vessels the least possible inconvenience. If suspicious circumstances are disclosed in the case of a particular neutral vessel, that vessel may be taken into port for more extensive inquiry and if necessary for adjudication before a Prize Court.

Formerly the right of visit and search was qualified by severe restrictions, designed to protect neutrals from unnecessary or burdensome interference with their commerce. In both the First and Second World Wars, the exigencies of "total war" caused belligerents to disregard these limitations. Contrary to the rules that search should precede capture and that it should generally not go further than an examination of the ship's papers and crew and cursory inspection of the cargo, neutral vessels could be required to call at contraband-control bases, or if intercepted on the high seas might be sent to port for thorough searching even in the absence of suspicious circumstances, considerable delays occurring while the vessels were so detained. On the British side, this practice of searching in port instead of on the high seas was justified on three main grounds:

a.   the growth in size of modern cargo vessels, rendering concealment easier and a thorough search more lengthy and difficult;

b.   the danger from submarines while the search was being conducted;

c.   the need for considering the circumstances of the shipment in conjunction with civilian authorities, for example, of the Ministry of Economic Warfare.

Several international law purists criticised the British defence of the practice, but the overpowering circumstances which rendered the practice necessary could not be gainsaid.

This inconvenience to neutral vessels could, for all practical purposes, be avoided by obtaining a "navicert".

REFERENCES

L. Oppenheim, *International Law*, Vol. II, 7th ed. by H. Lauterpacht, London: Longman Group Ltd., 1952, pp. 798-830; C. John Colombos, *International Law of the Sea*, 6th ed., London: Longman Group Ltd., 1967, pp. 675-699; T. Baty, "The History of Continuous Voyage," *University of Pennsylvania Law Review*, Vol. 90 (1941), pp. 127-136; J. H. Zeeman, "The Netherlands, the Law of Neutrality and Prize Law," in *International Law in the Netherlands*, Vol. III, Alphen ad Rijn/Dobbs Ferry, New York: Oceanna, 1981, pp. 337-371.

States	Convention Ratification	Territorial Sea	Contiguous Zone	Exclusive Economic Zone	Fishery Zone	Continental Shelf
Albania		12				200m/EXP
Algeria		12				
Angola		20			200	200/CM
*Antigua and Barbuda	2/2/89	12	24	200		200m/EXP
Argentina[2]		12		200		
Australia		3			200	200m/EXP
*Bahamas	29/7/83	3			200	200m/EXP
*Bahrain	30/5/85	3				
Bangladesh		12	18	200		CM
Barbados		12		200		
Belgium		12			Up to the median line with neigh-boring States	Up to the median line with oppposite and adjacent states
*Belize	12/8/83	3				
Benin		200				
*Brazil[3]	22/12/88	200				
Brunei Darussalam		12			200	

* States indicated with an asterisk have ratified the United Nations Convention on the Law of the Sea.

[1] The table is based on the maritime legislation of 144 coastal States, compiled as of 31 December 1989. Four of these States fall under article 305 (1) (c), (d) and (e) of the Convention.

[2] A press release dated 6 November 1989 issued by the Governor of Argentina explicitly mentions a 12-nm territorial sea and 200-nm exclusive economic zone, although Argentinian legislation has not yet been changed.

[3] It should be noted that Brazil adopted on 5 October 1988 a new constitution establishing a territorial sea and an exclusive economic zone. Brazil has also ratified the United Nations Convention on the Law of the Sea. On that basis it could be assumed that Brazil intends to establish the limits of its territorial sea and exclusive economic zone of 12 nm and 200 nm respectively.

851

States	Convention Ratification	Territorial Sea	Contiguous Zone	Exclusive Economic Zone	Fishery Zone	Continental Shelf
Bulgaria		12	24	200		
Burma (see Myanmar)						
Cambodia4		12	24	200		200nm
*Cameroon	19/11/85	50				
Canada		12			200	200/CM
*Cape Verde	10/8/87	12		200		200/CM
Chile5		12	24	200		200/350
China		12				
[China, Republic of (Taiwan)]		[12]	[24]	[200]		200m/EXP
Columbia		12		200		
Comoros		12		200		
Congo		200				
Costa Rica		12		200		200m/EXP
*Cote d'Ivoire	26/3/84	12		200		200nm
*Cuba	15/8/84	12		200		
*Cyprus	12/12/88	12				
Dem. People's Rep. of Korea6		12		200		
*Democratic Yemen	21/7/87	12	24	200		200/CM
Denmark		3			200	
Djibouti		12	24	200		
Dominica		12	24	200		
Dominican Republic		6	24	200		200/CM

4 Cambodia was previously known as Democratic Kampuchea.

5 A 350-nm continental shelf limit applies to Sala y Gomez and the Easter Island.

6 An army command announcement has established a 50-nm "nautical boundary line" within which foreign vessels cannot enter without authorization.

States	Convention Ratification	Territorial Sea	Contiguous Zone	Exclusive Economic Zone	Fishery Zone	Continental Shelf
Ecuador		200				200/iso
*Egypt	26/8/83	12	24	200		200m/EXP
El Salvador		200				
Equatorial Guinea		12		200		
Ethiopia		12				
*Fiji	10/12/82	12		200		200m/EXP
Finland		4	6		12	200m/EXP
France		12	24	200		
Gabon		12	24	200		
*Gambia	22/5/84	12	18		200	
German Democratic Repulic		12			Up to equidistance line with neighboring States	200m/EXP
Germany, Federal Rep. of[7]		3			200	
*Ghana	7/6/83	12	24	200		200m/EXP
Greece[8]		6				200nm
Grenada		12		200		200m/EXP
Guatemala		12		200		200m/EXP
*Guinea	6/9/85	12		200		
*Guinea-Bissau	25/8/86	12		200		
Guyana		12			200	200/CM
Haiti		12	24	200		EXP

7 A Decree for Preventing Tanker Casualties in the German Bight was promulgated on 12 November 1984 extending the territorial sea of the Federal Republic of Germany in the North Sea to 16 nm.

8 Decree 6/18 of September 1931 extended the territorial sea to 10 nm for the purposes of aviation and the control thereof.

States	Convention Ratification	Territorial Sea	Contiguous Zone	Exclusive Economic Zone	Fishery Zone	Continental Shelf
Honduras		12		200		200m/EXP
*Iceland	21/6/85	12		200		200/CM
India		12	24	200		200/CM
*Indonesia	3/2/86	12		200		EXP
Iran		12			50	
Iraq	30/7/85	12				
Ireland		12			200	EXP
Israel		6				
Italy		12				200m/EXP
*Jamaica	21/3/83	12				200m/EXP
Japan[9]		12			200	
Jordan		3				
*Kenya	2/3/89	12		200		200m/EXP
Kiribati		12		200		
*Kuwait	2/5/86	12				
Lebanon		12				
Liberia		200				
Libyan Arab Jamahiriya		12				
Madagascar		12	24	200		200/iso
Malaysia		12		200		200m/EXP
Maldives[10]		12				
Malta		12	24		25	200m/EXP
Mauritania		12	24	200		200/CM
Mauritius		12		200		200/CM
*Mexico	18/3/83	12	24	200		200/CM

9 There is a 3-nm territorial sea in certain designated areas (Soya strait, Tsugaru strait, eastern channel of Tsushima strait and western channel of Tsushima and Osumi straits).

10 Maldives has proclaimed an exclusive economic zone which is defined by coordinates (see Status of the United Nations Convention on the Law of the Sea (United Nations publication, Sales no. E.85.V.10, p. 1730)).

States	Convention Ratification	Territorial Sea	Contiguous Zone	Exclusive Economic Zone	Fishery Zone	Continental Shelf
Monaco		12				
Morocco		12	24	200		
Mozambique		12		200		
Myanmar[11]		12	24	200		200/CM
Nauru		12			200	
Netherlands		12		200	200	200m/EXP
New Zealand		12				200/CM
Nicaragua		200				
*Nigeria	14/8/86	30				200m/EXP
Norway		4		200		200nm
*Oman	17/8/89	12	24	200		200/CM
Pakistan		12	24	200		
Panama		200				
Papua New Guinea		12			200	200m/EXP
Peru		200				200nm
*Philippines	8/5/84	12		200		EXP
Poland					Up to a line to be determined by international agreement	
Portugal		12		200		200m/EXP
Qatar		3			Up to median line with neighboring states or international agreement	
Republic of Korea		12				

11 Myanmar was previously kown as Burma.

855

States	Convention Ratification	Territorial Sea	Contiguous Zone	Exclusive Economic Zone	Fishery Zone	Continental Shelf
Romania		12		200		200m/EXP
Saint Kitts and Nevis		12	24	200		200/CM
*Saint Lucia	27/3/85	12	24	200		200/CM
Saint Vincent and the Grenadines		12	24	200		200nm
Samoa		12		200		
*Sao Tome and Principe	3/11/87	12		200		
Saudi Arabia		12	18			
*Senegal	25/10/84	12	24	200		200/CM
Seychelles		12		200		200/CM
Sierra Leone		200				200m/EXP
Singapore		3				
Solomon Islands		12		200		200nm
*Somalia	24/7/89	200		200	200	
South Africa		12				200m/EXP
Spain		12		200		200m/EXP
Sri Lanka		12	24	200		200/CM
*Sudan	23/1/85	12	18			200m/EXP
Suriname		12		200		
Sweden		12			Up to equi-distance line wih neighboring States	200m/EXP
Syrian Arab Republic		35	41			200m/EXP
Thailand	16/4/85	12		200		200m/EXP
*Togo		30		200		
Tonga		12		200		200m/EXP
*Trinidad and Tobago	25/4/86	12	24	200		
*Tunisia	24/4/85	12				

States	Convention Ratification	Territorial Sea	Contiguous Zone	Exclusive Economic Zone	Fishery Zone	Continental Shelf
Turkey[12]		6			12	
Tuvalu		12	24			
Ukrainian SSR		12		200		200m/EXP
USSR		12		200		200m/EXP
United Arab Emirates[13]		3		Up to the boundary with neighboring States. If no boundary, up to median line.		
United Kingdom		12			200	200m/EXP
*United Republic of Tanzania	30/9/85					
United States of America		12	12	200		200m/EXP
Uruguay		200		200		200m/EXP
Vanuatu		12	24	200		200/CM
Venezuela		12	15	200		200m/EXP
Viet Nam		12	24	200		200/CM
Yemen		12				200m/EXP
*Yugoslavia	5/5/86	12				
*Zaire	17/2/89	12		200		
Others under article 305 (1) (c), (d) and (e)						
Cook Islands		12		200		200/CM
Niue		12		200		
Marshall Islands		12	24	200		
*Micronesia, Federated States of		12		200		

12 A limit of 12 nm applies in the Mediterranean Sea and the Black Sea.

13 A limit of 12 nm applies to Sharga.

857

Summary of claims to maritime zones (cont.)

EXCLUSIVE ECONOMIC ZONE

Breadth (nautical miles)	Number of States
200	79***
Proclamation with coordinates	1
Up to median line with neighboring States	1

*** 80, if includes the Republic of China (Taiwan).

FISHERY ZONE

Breadth (nautical miles)	Number of States
12	2
25	1
50	1
200	16
Up to median line with neighboring States	5

CONTINENTAL SHELF

Criteria	Number of States
Depth (200 m) plus exploitability (200m/EXP)	42
Breadth (200 nm) plus continental margin (200/CM)	21
Continental margin (CM)	1
Exploitability (EXP)	4
Breadth (200 nm or 100 nm from the 2,500-nm isobath) (200/iso)	2
Breadth (200/350 nm) (200/350)	1
Breadth (200 nm) (200nm)	6

Source: Law of the Sea Bulletin, No. 15 (May 1990), pp. 29-40.

SUMMARY OF CLAIMS TO MARITIME ZONES

TERRITORIAL SEA

Breadth (nautical miles)	Number of States
3	10
4	2
6	4
12	110*
20	1
30	2
35	1
50	1
200	12

* 111, if includes the Republic of China (Taiwan).

CONTIGUOUS ZONE

Breadth (nautical miles)	Number of States
6	1
12	1
18	4
24	32**

** 33, if includes the Republic of China (Taiwan).

SELECTED BIBLIOGRAPHY

This Bibliography provides only basic reference materials, it does not include books on special subject matter or articles, which are listed in the appropriate places of this book.

General Work

Andreyev, E.P., general editor, *The International Law of the Sea*, Moscow: Progress Publishers, 1988.

Bernhardt, R. ed., *Encyclopedia of Public International Law*, Vol. 11, *Law of the Sea, Air and Space*, Amsterdam: North-Holland, 1989; Vol. 12, *Geographical Issues*, 1990.

Churchill, R.R., and A.V. Lowe, *The Law of the Sea*, 2nd ed., Manchester: Manchester University Press, 1988.

Colombos, C. John, *The International Law of the Sea*, 6th ed., London: Longman Group Ltd., 1967.

Glassner, Martin Ira, *Neptune's Domain, A Political Georgraphy of the Sea*, Boston: Unwin Hyman, 1990.

Kindt, John Warren, *Marine Pollution and the Law of the Sea*, Buffalo: William S. Hein & Co., 1986-1988. 4 vols. and 2 vols. of Appendices.

Mangone, Gerard J., Mangone's Concise Marine Almanac, New York: Taylor & Francis, 1991.

McDougal, Myres S. and William T. Burke, *The Public Order of the Oceans, A Contemporary International Law of the Sea*, New Haven and London: Yale University Press, 1962.

O'Connell, D.P., *The International Law of the Sea*, edited by I.A.Shearer, New York and London: Oxford University Press, 1982, 1984. 2 vols.

Sohn, Louis B. and Kristen Gustafson, *The Law of the Sea in A Nutshell*, St. Paul, Minn.: West Publishing Co., 1984.

United Nations Conferences and Related Work

Report of the Committee on the Peaceful Uses of the Sea-Bed and the Ocean Floor Beyond the Limits of National Jurisdiction (United Nations General Assembly: *Official Records*, 28th Session, Supplement No. 21 (A/9021)), 6 vols., New York: The United Nations, 1973.

[First] United Nations Conference on the Law of the Sea: Official Records, 7 vols., New York: The United Nations, 1958.

Second United Nations Conference on the Law of the Sea: Official Records, New York: The United Nations, 1960.

Third United Nations Conference on the Law of the Sea: Official Records, 17 vols., New York: The United Nations, 1975-1984.

The Law of the Sea: United Nations Convention on the Law of the Sea with Index and Final Act of the Third United Nations Conference on the Law of the Sea, New York: The United Nations, 1983.

The Law of the Sea, Status of the United Nations Convention on the Law of the Sea, New York: The United Nations, 1985.

Law of the Sea: Master File Containing References to Official Documents of the Third United Nations Conference on the Law of the Sea, New York: United Nations, 1985.

The Law of the Sea: Multilateral Treaties Relevant to the United Nations Convention on the Law of the Sea, New York: The United Nations, 1985.

Crowded Agendas, Crowded Rooms, Institutional Arrangements at UNCLOS III: Some Lessons in Global Negotiations, New York: The United Nations, 1981.

Nordquist, Myron H., ed., *United Nations Convention on the Law of the Sea 1982, A Commentary*, Dordrecht/Boston/Lancaster: Martinus Nijhoff Publishers, 1985-89, 5 vols.

Nordquist, Myron H. and Choon-ho Park, eds., *Reports of the United States Delegation to the Third United Nations Conference on the Law of the Sea*, Honolulu: Law of the Sea Institute, University of Hawaii, 1983.

Collection of National Legislation, Treaties/Agreements and Documents

Laws and Regulations on the Regime of the High Seas (United Nations Legislative Series, ST/LEG/SER.B/1 and 2), 2 vols., New York: The United Nations, 1951-1952.

Laws and Regulations on the Regime of the Territorial Sea (United Nations Legislative Series, ST/LEG/SER.B/6), New York: The United Nations, 1957.

Laws Concerning the Nationality of Ships (United Nations Legislative Series, ST/LEG/SER.B/5 and Add. 1), New York: The United Nations, 1956.

National Legislation and Treaties Relating to the Territorial Sea, the Contiguous Zone, the Continental Shelf, the High Seas and to Fishing and Conservation of the Living Resources of the Sea (United Nations Legislative Series, DT/LEG/SER.B/15), New York: The United Nations, 1970.

National Legislation and Treaties Relating to the Law of the Sea (United Nations Legislative Series, ST/LEG/SER.B/16), New York: The United Nations, 1974.

_____, (ST/LEG/SER.B/18), 1976.

_____, (ST/LEG/SER.B/19), 1980.

Supplement to Laws and Regulations on the Regime of the High Seas (Volumes I and II) and Laws Concerning the Nationality of Ships (United Nations Legislative Series, ST/LEG/SER.B/8), New York: The United Nations, 1959.

The Law of the Sea: Current Developments in State Practice, No. 1 (1987) and No. 2 (1989), New York: The United Nations.

The Law of the Sea: Maritime Baselines, New York: The United Nations, 1988.

The Law of the Sea: Maritime Boundary Agreements (1970-1984), New York: The United Nations, 1987.

The Law of the Sea: National Legislation on the Continental Shelf, New York: The United Nations, 1989.

The Law of the Sea: National Legislation on the Exclusive Economic Zone, the Economic Zone and the Exclusive Fishery Zone, New York: The United Nations, 1986.

The Law of the Sea: National Legislation, Regulation and Supplementary Documents on Marine, Scientific Research in Areas Under National Jurisdiction, New York: The United Nations, 1989.

The Law of the Sea: Navigation on the High Seas, New York: The United Nations, 1989.

The Law of the Sea: Pollution by Dumping, New York: The United Nations, 1985.

The Law of the Sea: Regime of Islands, New York: The United Nations, 1987.

The Law of the Sea: Rights of Access of Land-locked States to and from the Sea and Freedom of Transit, New York: The United Nations, 1987.

Private Compilations

Butler, William E., ed., *The USSR, Eastern Europe and the Development of the Law of the Sea*, Dobbs Ferry, New York: Oceana, 1983-, 2 vols.

Durante, Francesco and Walter Rodino, eds., *Western Europe and the Development of the Law of the Sea*, Dobbs Ferry, New York: Oceana, 1979-, 4 vols.

Moore, John Norton, ed., *International and United States Documents on Ocean Law and Policy*, 5 vols., Buffalo, New York: William S. Hein & Co., Inc., 1986.

Nordquist, Myron H. and Choon Ho Park, eds., *North America and Asia-Pacific and the Development of the Law of the Sea*, Dobbs Ferry, New York: Oceana, 1981-.

Nordquist, Myron (vols. 1-8), S. Houston Lay (vols. 1-8) and Kenneth R. Simons, eds., *New Directions in the Law of the Sea*, Dobbs Ferry, New York: Oceana, 1973-1981, 11 vols.

Sebek, Victor, ed., *The Eastern European States and the Development of the Law of the Sea*, Dobbs Ferry, New York: Oceana, 1979-, 2 vols.

Simmonds, Kenneth R., *Cases on the Law of the Sea*, 4 vols., Dobbs Ferry, New York: Oceana, 1976-1980.

Simmonds, Kenneth R., ed., *New Directions in the Law of the Sea* [looseleaf], New York: Oceana, 1983-, 5 vols.

Szekely, Alberto, ed., *Latin America and the Development of the Law of the Sea*, Dobbs Ferry, New York: Oceana, 1986-, 2 vols.

Periodicals/Yearbooks

Annual Review of Ocean Affairs: Law and Policy, Main Documents, Vol. 1 (1985)-. (This is compiled and edited by the United Nations Office for Ocean Affairs and the Law of the Sea, Sarasota, Florida: UNIFO Publihers, Inc./London: Lloyd's of London Press, Ltd.)

International Journal of Estuarine and Coastal Law, quarterly, 1986-.

International Organizations and the Law of the Sea, Documentary Yearbook, Vol. 1 (1985)- . (This is compiled and edited by the Netherlands Institute for the Law of the Sea, Dordrecht, The Netherlands: Martinus Nijhoff, 1987 ____.)

Journal of Maritime Law and Commerce, quarterly, 1969-.

Law of the Sea Bulletin, 1983-. (This is published by the Special Representative of the Secretary-General for the Law of the Sea irregularly).

Lloyd's Maritime and Commercial Law Quarterly, 1974-.

Lloyd's Maritime Law Yearbook, Vol. 1 (1987)-.

Marine Policy, quarterly, 1977-.

Ocean Development and International Law, quarterly, 1973-.

Ocean Yearbook, annually, Chicago: University of Chicago Press, 1978-.

San Diego Law Review. (Since 1971, each volume contains a special issue on the law of the sea.)

Bibliography

Books

Wiktor, Christian L. and Leslie A. Foster, *Marine Affairs Bibliography 1980-1985*, Dordrecht/Boston/Lancaster: Martinus Nijhoff Publishers, 1987.

Papadakis, Nikos, *International Law of the Sea: A Bibliography*, Alphen aan den Rijn, The Netherlands; Germantown, Maryland: Sijthoff & Noordhoff, 1980.

Papadakis, Nikos and Martin Ira Glassner, eds., *International Law of the Sea and Marine Affairs: A Bibliography, Supplement to the 1980 Edition*. The Hague: Martinus Nijhoff, 1984.

United Nations Bibliography

The Sea: Legal and Political Aspects, A Selected Bibliography, New York: The United Nations, 1974.

The Sea: A Selected Bibliography on the Legal, Political, Economic and Technological Aspects, 1974-1975. New York: The United Nations, 1975.

_____, 1975-1976 (1976).

_____, 1976-1978 (1978).

_____, 1978-1979 (1980).

Law of the Sea, A Selected Bibliography, New York: The United Nations, 1985.

_____, [1987] (1987).

_____, 1988 (1989).

_____ , 1989 (1990).

Periodicals

Marine Affairs Bibliography, vols. 1-8 (1980-1987), annually, Dalhousie University Law School. Vol. 9 (1988-), quarterly, University of Virginia Law Library.

Public International Law, A Current Bibliography of Articles, semi-annually 1975-. (Each issue contains a section on the law of the sea.)

CASE INDEX

The following special abbreviations are used to indicate the source of certain cases/incidents:

ICJ: International Court of Justice;
ILM: International Legal Materials;
ILR: International Law Reports (Vols. 1-16's title is Annual Digest of Public International Law Cases);
Moore: J.B. Moore, History and Digest of the International Arbitration to Which the United States has been a Party;
PCIJ: Permanent Court of International Justice;
RIAA: Reports of International Arbitral Awards; and
RGDIP: Revue Generale de Droit International Public.

Amerada Hess Shipping Corporation v. Argentine Republic, 830 F.2d 421 (2d Cir. 1987): 816

American Cetacean Society v. Baldridge, 604 F.Supp. 1398 (D.D.C. 1985), aff'd; 768 F.2d 426 (D.C. Cir. 1985): 657

Anglo-Norwegian Fisheries Case [1951] ICJ Rep. 116: 20, 39, 41, 42, 83, 92, 248

Anna, The, 5 C. Rob 373 (1805), 165 Eng. Rep. 809: 67-68

Arbitration between the US and UK concerning the Ship Washington (1853), 4 Moore 4342: 70

Attorney General v. Chambers, 4 De G. M. & G. 206: 61

Award by the Arbitral Tribunal on the Maritime Delimitation (Guinea/ Guinea-Bissau), (1986), 25 ILM 252; 77 ILR 635: 202-208

Behring Sea Fur Seals Arbitration (1895), 1 Moore 75: 15

Borax Consolidated v. City of Los Angeles, 296 US 10 (1935): 60-62

California v. Watt, 668 F.2d 1290, 1325 (D.C. Cir. 1981): 450

California v. Watt, 712 F.2d 584 (D.C. Cir. 1983): 450

Cape Horn Pigeon Arbitration (US-Russia), U.S. Foreign Realtions, 1902, Appendix 1, p. 451 et seq.: 15

Case concerning Military and Paramilitary Activities and Against Nicaraguay (Nicaraguay v. United States), [1986] ICJ Rep. 14: 785, 822-823

Case concerning the Continental Shelf (Tunisia v. Libyan Arab Jamahiriya), [1982] ICJ Rep. 18: 180-186, 207, 211, 214

Case of Maksymilllian K. (Poland, Supreme Court, February 20, 1964), 47 ILR 118: 231

Case of St. Pierre et Miquelon (1973) (Canada v. France), Arbitral Award of July 17, 1986, 90 RGDIP 713: 214

Church v. Hubbart, 6 US (2 Cranch) 187 (1804): 237, 304

Constitution of the Maritime Safety Committee of the Inter-Governmental Maritime Consultative Organization, Advisory Opnion of June 8, 1960, [1960] ICJ Rep. 150: 349-351

Continental Shelf Case (Libyan Arab Jamahiriya v. Malta, 1985), [1985] ICJ Rep. 13: 189-193, 212

Cook v. US, 288 US 102; 53 S.Ct. 305; 77 L.Ed. 641 (1932): 434

Corfu Channel Case (Merit) (UK v. Albania), [1949] ICJ Rep. 4: 285-287, 666, 819-821, 822

Costa Rica Packet Arbitration (1897), 5 Moore 4948: 15

Croft v. Dunphy (1932), 6 ILR 157: 305

Cunard S.S. Co. v. Mellon, 262 US 101 (1923): 236-237

Delimitation of Continental Shelf Arbitration (UK-France) (1977) [Channel Continental Shelf Case], 18 ILM 395; 54 ILR 6: 21, 174-178, 214

Delimitation of the Maritime Boundary of the Gulf of Maine (Canada/US) [1984] ICJ Rep. 246: 47, 196-200

Employers Mutual Casualty Co. v. Samuels, 407 S.W.2d 839 (Tex. Civ. App. 1966): 245-247

Empresa Hondureana de Vapores, S.A. v. Mcleod, 300 F.2d 222 (2d Cir. 1962): 348

Filartiga v. Pena-Irala, 630 F.2d 876 (2d Cir. 1980): 816

Fisheries Case (UK v. Norway) (1951), [1951] ICJ Rep. 116: 53, 56, 72-79, 81, 82, 107, 119

Fisheries Jurisdiction Case (United Kingdom v. Iceland), [1973] ICJ Rep. 3; [1974] ICJ Rep. 3 (Federal Republic of Germany v. Iceland): 39, 40, 43, 585-586, 594-597

Franconia, The, (1876) 2 Ex.D. 63: 15

Gillam v. US, 27 F.2d 296 (4th Cir. 1928): 389-390

Guess v. Read, 290 F.2d 622 (1961), cert. denied, 386 US 957; 82 S.Ct. 394; 7 L.Ed. 2d 388 (1962): 433

I'm Alone, (Canada v. US, 1941), 3 RIAA 1609: 387-389, 817

IIT v. Venecap, Ltd., 519 F.2d 1001 (2d Cir. 1975): 816

In Re: Oil Spill by the "Amoco Cadiz" off the Coast of France on March 16, 1978, MDL Docket No. 376, US District Court for the Northern District of Illinois, Eastern Division, slip opinion, April 18, 1984: 706-716

India v. Pakistan, [1972] ICJ Rep. 46: 783

James Hamilton Lewis and C. H. White (US-Russia), U.S. Foreign Relations, 1902, Appendix 1, p.451 et seq.: 15

Johnson v. Mexico (The Daylight), (US-Mexican Claims Commission, April 15, 1927), 21 AJIL 794: 242-243

Jones v. US, 137 US 202; 11 S.Ct. 80; 34 L.Ed. 691 (1890): 437

Kate and Anna Arbitration (US-Russia), U. S. Foreign Relations, 1902, Appendix 1, p.451 et seq.: 15

Khedivial Line, S.A.E. v. Seafarers' International Union, 278 F.2d 49 (2d Cir. 1960): 279

Latham v. US, 2 F.2d 208 (4th Cir., 1924): 276

Le Louis (France v. Great Britain) 2 Dodson 210; 615 Eng. Rpt. 1464 (1817): 16-17

Lotus Case, PCIJ Ser. A No. 10 (1927): 42, 370

Louisiana v. Mississippi, 202 US 1; 26 S.Ct. 408; 50 L.Ed 913 (1906): 113-114, 237

Lusitania, The, 251 F. 715, (S.D.N.Y. 1918): 817

Maine v. Kreps, 563 F.2d 1043 (1st Cir. 1977): 610

Manchester v. Massachusetts, 139 US 240 (1891): 237

Marianna Flora, The, (US. v. Portugal) 11 Wheat. (24 U.S.) 1 (1826): 17

McCulloch v. Sociedad Nacional de Marineros de Honduras, 372 US 10; 83 S.Ct. 671; 9 L.Ed. 2d 547 (1962): 348

Merkur Island Shipping co. v. Laughton, [1983] 2 All E.R. 189 (H.L.): 348

Molvan v. Attorney General for Palestine, (1948) A.C. 351: 341

N.W.L. Ltd. v. Woods [1979] 3 All E.R. 614 (H.L.): 348

Natural Resources Defense Council Inc. v. Morton, 458 F.2d 827 (D.C. Cir. 1972): 450

North Atlantic Coast Fisheries Arbitration (US-Great Britain) (1910), 11 RIAA 167: 15, 102

North Sea Continental Shelf Cases (Federal Republic of Germany v. Denmark & Federal Republic of Germany v. Netherlands), [1969] ICJ Rep. 4: 35, 40, 167-170, 175-176, 180, 181, 198, 207, 414, 420-421, 424, 586

Nuclear Test Case (Australia v. France), [1973] ICJ 99: 785

Nuclear Test Case (New Zealand v. France), [1974] ICJ 253: 785

Oriental Navigation Co. v. the United Mexican States, US-Mexico Claims Commission, (Docket No. 411, 1928), 23 AJIL 434: 831-833

Paterson v. Bark Eudora, 190 US 169; 23 S.Ct. 821; 47 L.Ed. 1002 (1903): 279

People of the State of New York v. Paul Nissen and Alan Van Horn, 412 N.Y.S.2d 999 (1979): 274-276

Plaisance v. US, 433 F.Supp 936 (E.D. La. 1977): 435-438

Prize Cases, 67 US (2 Black) 635, 17 L.Ed. 459 (1863): 828-830

R. v. Kent Justices [1967] 1. All E. R. 560 (Q.B.): 141-143

Re Martinez and Others, (Italy, Court of Cassation, Nov. 25, 1959), 28 ILR 170: 310-312

Republic of El Salvador v. Republic of Nicaragua, Central American Court of Justice, March 9, 1917, 11 AJIL 674: 133

Saudi Arabia v. Arabian American Oil company (ARAMCO), Award of Aug. 23, 1958, 27 ILR 117: 278

Secretary of the Interior v. California, 104 S.Ct. 656 (1984): 450

Snyder v. Motorists Mutual Ins. Co., 2 Ohio App. 2d 19; 206 N.E.2d 227 (1965): 243-245, 246

Souza v. Commissioner of Internal Revenue, 33 T.C. 817 (1960): 591

Talbot v. Jansen, 3 US (3 Dall.) 133 (1795): 817

Texas Overseas Petroleum Co. v. Libyan Arab Republic (1977), 17 ILM 1: 38

Trail Smelter arbitration (1938-41), 2 RIAA 1911: 666

Treasure Slavors v. Unidentified Wrecked, Etc., 569 F.2d 330 (5th Cir. 1978): 432-435

US v. Alaska, 422 US 184 (1975): 126-131

US v. Black, 291 F.Supp. 262 (S.D.N.Y. 1968): 375

US v. California, 332 US 19; 67 S.Ct. 1658; 91 L.Ed 1889 (1947): 433, 448

US v. California, 381 US 139 (1964): 86-87, 137-138

US v. Conroy, 589 F.2d 1258 (5th Cir. 1979); 594 F.2d 241 (1979); 100 S.Ct. 60 (1979): 270-273

US v. F/V Taiyo Maru No. 28, 395 F.Supp. 413 (1975): 391-394

US v. Florida, 363 US 1 (1959): 449

US v. Holmes, 18 US 412 (1820): 342

US v. Kaiyo Maru No. 53, 503 F.Supp. 1075 (D. Alaska 1980): 610

US v. Klintok, 18 US 144 (1820): 342

US v. Louisiana, 339 US 699; 70 S.Ct. 914; 94 L.Ed. 1216 (1950): 441, 448

US v. Louisiana, 394 US 11 (1969): 87, 108-114, 128, 138-139, 143-145

US v. Maine, 420 US 515; 95 S.Ct. 1155; 43 L.Ed. 2d 363 (1975): 433

US v. Monroy, 614 F.2d 61 (5th Cir., 1980): 340

US v. Ray, 423 F.2d 16 (5th Cir. 1970): 434, 438-442

US v. Republic of Steel Corp., 362 US 482; 80 S.Ct. 884; 4 L.Ed. 2d 903 (1960): 441

US v. San Jacinto Tin Co., 125 US 273; 8 S.Ct. 850; 31 L.Ed. 747: 441

US v. Smith, 18 US (5 Wheat.) 153 (1820): 816

US v. States of Louisiana, Texas, Mississippi, Alabama and Florida, 363 US 1 (1959): 449

US v. Texas, 339 US 707; 70 S.Ct. 918; 94 L.Ed. 1221 (1950): 441, 448

Wildenhus's Case, 120 US 1 (1886): 229-230

CHRONOLOGICAL TABLE OF TREATIES

The various treaties, convention or agreements referred to in this book are listed in chronological order. In each case, information is given as to the place and date of signature or adoption; and references to the source of the convention, treaty or agreement. The following abbreviations are used for the reference to the source:

AJIL: American Journal of International Law;
Bevans: Charles I. Bevans, ed., Treaties and Other International Agreements of the United States of America 1776-1949;
BFSP: British and Foreign State Papers;
Cmnd.: [British] Command Papers;
CTS: Consolidated Treaty Series;
CYILA: Chinese Yearbook of International Law and Affairs;
ILM: International Legal Materials;
IMO: International Maritime Organization;
LNTS: League of Nations Treaty Series;
LOSMBA: The Law of the Sea, Maritime Boundary Agreements (1970-1984);
Misc: [UK] Miscellaneous;
ND: New Directions in the Law of the Sea;
RGDIP: Revue Generale de Droit International Public;
Stat.: United States Statutes at Large;
TIAS: [US] Treaties and Other International Acts Series;
TS: [US] Treaty Series;
UKTS: United Kingdom Treaty Series;
UN: United Nations;
UNTS: United Nations Treaty Series; and
UST: United States Treaties and Other International Agreements

---

1494 Spain-Portugal Treaty of Tordesillas, [G.F. de Martens, Supplement (1802-1808), I, 373]: 12

1818 Convention Respecting Fisheries, Boundaries and Restoration of Slaves, [Anglo-American Fishery Convention], London, Oct. 20, 1818 [8 Stat. 248; TS 112; 12 Bevans 57]: 15, 102

1825 Great Britain-Russia Convention concerning the Limits of Their Respective Possessions on the North-West Coast of America and the Navigation of the Pacific Ocean, St. Petersburg, February 16, 1825 [75 CTS 95]: 70

1839 Great Britain-France Convention for Defining the Limits of Exclusive Fishing Rights [Fishery Convention], Paris, August 2, 1839 [89 CTS 221]: 15

1856 The Declaration of Paris, April 16, 1856 [115 CTS 1]: 808, 810, 816, 825, 832, 846

1864	Convention for the Amelioration of the Condition of the Wounded in Armies in the Field [Red Cross Convention], Geneva, August 22, 1864 [22 Stat. 940; TS 377; 1 Bevans 7]: 810
1867	US-Russia Convention Ceding Alaska [Treaty of Cession], Washington, March 30, 1867 [15 Stat. 539; TS 301; 11 Bevans 1216]: 127
1882	Convention for Regulating the Police of the North Sea Fisheries [North Sea Fisheries Convention], The Hague, May 6, 1882 [160 CTS 219]: 15, 70, 104
1886	France-Portugal Convention for the Delimitation of the African Possessions of the Parties, Paris, May 12, 1886 [167 CTS 485]: 204, 208
1901	Denmark-Great Britain Convention for Regulating the Fisheries Outside Territorial Waters in the Ocean Surrounding the Faroe Islands and Iceland [Anglo-Danish Convention], London, June 24, 1901, [189 CTS 429]: 594
1906	Amelioration of the Condition of the Wounded and Sick on the Field of Battle [Red Cross Convention], Geneva, July 6, 1906 [35 Stat. 1885; TS 464; 1 Bevans 516]: 810
1907	Convention VIII relative to the Laying of Automatic Submarine Contact Mines, The Hague, October 18, 1907, [36 Stat. 2332; TS 541; 1 Bevans 669]: 18, 818, 821-822
	Convention XIII concerning the Right and Duties of Neutral Powers in Naval War, The Hague, October 18, 1907 [36 Stat. 2415; TS 545; 1 Bevans 723]: 811-817
1910	Convention for the Unification of Certain Rules of Law with respect to Collisions between Vessels, Brussels, September 23, 1910 [103 BFSP 434]: 363
	Convention for the Unification of Certain Rules of Law respecting Assistance and Salvage at Sea, Brussels, September 23, 1910 [37 Stat. 1658; TS 576; 1 Bevans 780]: 363
1912	US-Great Britain Agreement Adopting, with Certain Modifications, the Rules and Method of Procedure Recommended in the Award of September 7, 1910, of the North Atlantic Coastal Fisheries Arbitration, Washington, July 20, 1912 [37 Stat. 1634; TS 572; 12 Bevans 357]: 103
1919	Covenant of the League of Nations, Versailles, June 28, 1919 [225 CTS 195]: 832

Convention on the Regulation of Aerial Navigation [Air Navigation Convention], Paris, October 13, 1919 [11 LNTS 173]: 241

1922   Treaty for the Limitation of Naval Armament [Washington Treaty], Washington, February 6, 1922 [43 Stat. 1655; TS 671; 25 LNTS 202]: 811

1924   US-Great Britain Convention for Prevention of Smuggling of Intoxicating Liquors, Washington, January 23, 1924 [43 Stat. 1761; TS 685; 12 Bevans 414]: 238

1926   International Convention for the Unification of Certain Rules relating to Immunity of State-owned Vessels, Brussels, April 10, 1926 [176 LNTS 199]: 365

1928   Convention on Maritime Neutrality [Pan-American Convention relating to Maritime Neutrality], Havana, February 20, 1928 [47 Stat. 1989; TS 845; 135 LNTS 187]: 817

Colombia-Nicaragua Treaty concerning Territorial Questions at Issue between the Two States, Managua, March 24, 1928 [105 LNTS 337]: 146

1931   Convention for the Regulation of Whaling, Geneva, September 24, 1931 [49 Stat. 3079; TS 880; 3 Bevans 26; 155 LNTS 349]: 604, 654-655

1936   Protocol of Signature of the Treaty for the Limitation of Naval Armament [London Protocol], London, March 25, 1936 [50 Stat. 1363 (Protocol at p.1395); TS 919 (Protocol at p.37); 3 Bevans 257 (Protocol at p.272)]: 811

Convention regarding the Regime of the Straits, [Dardanelles-Bosphorus Convention concerning the Regimes of Straits], Montreux, July 20, 1936 [173 LNTS 213]: 291

1937   International Agreement for the Regulation of Whaling, London, June 8, 1937 [52 Stat. 1460; TS 933; 190 LNTS 79]: 655, 656

1944   Convention on International Civil Aviation, Chicago, December 7, 1944 [61 Stat. 1180; TIAS 1591; 3 Bevans 944; 15 UNTS 295]: 241, 257

1947   Inter-American Treaty of Reciprocal Assistance [Rio Treaty], Rio de Janerio, September 2, 1947 [62 Stat. 1681; TIAS 1838; 4 Bevans 559; 21 UNTS 77]: 307, 840-841

1948   International Convention on the Safety of Life at Sea, London, June 10, 1948 [3 UST 3450; TIAS 2495]: 363

1949	Geneva Conventions (Red Cross): Convention for the Amelioration of the Condition of the Wounded and Sick in Armed Forces in the Field, Geneva, August 12, 1949 [6 UST 3114; TIAS 3362; 75 UNTS 31]; Convention for the Amelioration of the Condition of the Wounded, Sick and Ship-Wrecked Members of Armed Forces at Sea, Geneva, August 12, 1949 [6 UST 3217; TIAS 3363; 75 UNTS 85]; Convention relative to the Treatment of Prisoners of War, Geneva, August 12, 1949 [6 UST 3316; TIAS 3364; 75 UNTS 135]; Convention relative to the Protection of Civilian Persons in Time of War, Geneva, August 12, 1949 [6 UST 3516; TIAS 3365; 75 UNTS 287]: 811
1950	European Convention for the Protection of Human Rights and Fundamental Freedoms, Rome, November 4, 1950 [213 UNTS 221]: 782
1952	International Convention for the Unification of Certain Rules relating to the Penal Jurisdiction in Matters of Collisions and Other Incidents of Navigation, Brussels, May 10, 1952 [439 UNTS 233]: 370
1954	International Convention for the Prevention of Pollution of the Sea by Oil, London, May 12, 1954 [12 UST 2989; TIAS 4900; 327 UNTS 3]: 789
1956	US-Germany Treaty of Friendship, Commerce and Navigation, Washington, October 29, 1954 [7 UST 1839; TIAS 3593; 273 UNTS 3]: 228-229
1958	Geneva Conventions on the Law of the Sea, April 29, 1958: generally 5, 20-22, 24, 36, 40, 44, 47-48, 50, 185; history 19-21, 392

Convention on Fishing and Conservation of the Living Resources of the High Seas, Geneva, April 29, 1958 [559 UNTS 285]: 20-21, 579, 587

Convention on the Continental Shelf, Geneva, April 29, 1958 [15 UST 471; TIAS 5578; 449 UNTS 311]:
generally 20, 47-48, 211, 216, 246, 412, 433, 434, 436, 439; Norway 424; natural sources 438; art.(1) 166, 212, 414, 415-418, 420, 436, 439, 586; art.(2) 208, 246, 414, 418, 431, 434, 440, 583, 586; art.(3) 246, 414, 436, 443, 494, 495, 586; art.(4) 396, 443; art.(5) 65-67, 436, 443-444, 495, 767; art.(6) 166-168, 174-177, 417; art.(7) 415

Convention on the High Seas, Geneva, April 29, 1958 [13 UST 2312; TIAS 5200; 450 UNTS 82]:
generally 20-21, 340, 361; reflagging 361; dispute settlement 122; art.(1) 43, 319, 325; art.(2) 330, 395, 576, 584, 587, 595, 597, 666, 767; art.(3) 330-331; art.(4) 330, 331, 342, 787, 789; art.(5) 342, 344, 345, 348, 787, 789; art.(6) 339, 342-343, 346, 787, 789; art.(7) 343, 787, 789; art.(8) 364, 789; art.(9) 364, 368, 789, 795; art.(10) 369,

789, 795; art.(11) 369, 795; art.(12) 363, 789, 795; art.(13) 370; art.(14) 371; art.(15) 371; art.(16) 371; art.(17) 372; art.(18) 372; art.(19) 372; art.(20) 372; art.(21) 372; art.(22) 371, 372, 374, 816; art.(23) 384, 386, 391-393, 395, 817; art.(24) 667; art.(25) 667; art.(26) 395-396; art.(27) 396; art.(28) 396; art.(29) 396

Convention on the Territorial Sea and Contiguous Zone, Geneva, April 29, 1958 [15 UST 1606; TIAS 5639; 516 UNTS 205]:
generally 20-21, 85, 86, 96, 113, 114, 142, 272, 290, 393; boundaries 143; art.(1) 241; art.(2) 241; art.(3) 56; Art.(4) 80, 84-85, 87, 92, 93, 114, 147; art.(5) 80-81, 133, 141, 227-228; art.(6) 151, 249; art.(7) 106-109, 111-112, 114-115, 147-148; art.(8) 137-139; art.(9) 140; art.(10) 63, 64, 66, 212; art.(11) 141, 143-146; art.(12) 156, 121; art.(13) 147-149; art(14) 256-257, 272, 277, 330, 331; art.(15) 257; Art.(16) 258, 261, 272, 289; art.(17) 258; art.(18) 258; art.(19) 267; art.(20) 267

Optional Protocol of Signature concerning the Compulsory Settlement of Dispute, Geneva, April 29, 1958 [450 UNTS 169]: 786-789

1960   International Convention for the Safety of Life at Sea, London, June 17, 1960, [16 UST 185; TIAS 5780; 536 UNTS 27]: 696

International Regulation for Preventing Collisions at Sea, approved by the International Conference on Safety of Life at Sea, London, May 17-June 17, 1960 [16 UST 794; TIAS 5813]: 696

1961   US-Belgium Treaty of Friendship, Establishment and Navigation, Brussels, February 21, 1961 [14 UST 1284; TIAS 5432; 480 UNTS 149]: 279

1962   Convention on the Liability of Operators of Nuclear Ships, Brussels, May 25, 1962 [57 AJIL 268]: 265, 279

1963   Treaty Banning Nuclear Weapon Tests in the Atmosphere, in Outer Space and Under Water, Moscow, August 5, 1963 [14 UST 1313; TIAS 5433; 480 UNTS 43]: 321, 743

1964   Fisheries Convention, London, March 9, 1964 [581 UNTS 57]: 585

US-UK Agreement relating to Visits by the N.S. Savannah to Ports in the United Kingdom Territory, London, June 19, 1964 [15 UST 1511; TIAS 5633; 530 UNTS 99]: 688

1965   Convention on Transit Trade of Landlocked States, New York, July 8, 1965 [19 UST 7383; TIAS 6952; 597 UNTS 42]: 331-332

International Convention on the Elimination of All Forms of Racial Discrimination [UN Racial Convention], New York, December 21, 1965 [660 UNTS 195]: 782

1966   International Convention on Load Lines, London, April 5, 1966 [18 UST 1857; TIAS 6331; 640 UNTS 133]: 696

International Convention for the Conservation of Atlantic Tunas, Rio de Janeiro, May 14, 1966 [20 UST 2887; TIAS 6767; 673 UNTS 63]: 608

International Covenant on Civil and Political Rights, New York, December 16, 1966 [999 UNTS 171]: 782

1967   Convention on Conduct of Fishing Operation in the North Atlantic, London, June 1, 1967 [1977 UKTS 40]: 587

1968   Convention concerning Minimum Standards in Merchant Ships, Geneva, October 29, 1976 [15 ILM 1288]: 351-352

1969   Convention on the Law of Treaties, Vienna, May 23, 1969 [1980 UKTS 58]: 35, 50

American Convention of Human Rights, San Jose, Costa Rica, November 22, 1969 [65 AJIL 679]: 782

Convention on Civil Liability for Oil Pollution Damage, Brussels, November 29, 1969 [9 ILM 45]: 689, 690-695, 699-700, 702

International Convention relating to Intervention on the High Seas in Cases of Oil Pollution Casualties, Brussels, November 29, 1969 [26 UST 765; TIAS 8068]: 677, 789

1970   US-Mexico Treaty to Resolve Pending Boundary Differences and Maintain the Rio Grande and Colorado River as the International Boundary between the United States and Mexico, Mexico City, November 23, 1970 [23 UST 371; TIAS 7313]: 161

1971   Italy-Tunisia Agreement concerning the Delimitation of the Continental Shelf between the Two countries, Tunis, August 20, 1971 [LOSMBA 174]: 215, 217, 219

International Convention on the Establishing of an International Fund for Compensation for Oil Pollution Damage, Brussels, December 18, 1971 [1978 UKTS 95]: 693-696

1972   Convention for the Prevention of Marine Pollution by Dumping from Ships and Aircraft, Oslo, February 15, 1972 [932 UNTS 5]: 736-737

US-Colombia Treaty concerning the Status of Quita Sueno, Rencador and Serrana, Bugota, September 8, 1972 [33 UST 1405; TIAS 10120]: 145-146

878

Convention on the Regulation of Marine Pollution by Dumping of Waters and Other Matters, London, December 29, 1972 [26 UST 2403; TIAS 8165]: 727-733

1973   USSR-USA Agreement relating to the Consideration of Claims resulting from Damage to Fishing Vessels or Gear and Measures to Prevent Fishing Conflict, Moscow, February 21, 1973 [24 UST 669; TIAS 7575]: 588

International Convention for the Prevention Oil Pollution from Ships, London, November 2, 1973 [12 ILM 1319]: 685-687

Protocol relating to Intervention on the High Seas in case of Pollution by Substances other than Oil, London, November 2, 1973 [1983 UKTS 27]: 719

1974   Italy-Yugoslavia Agreement on Cooperation for the Protection of the Waters of the Adriatic Sea and Coastal Zones from Pollution, Belgrade, February 14, 1974 [6 ND 456]: 667

Convention on the Protection of the Marine Environment of the Baltic Area, Helsinki, March 22, 1974 [13 ILM 546]: 688, 737, 742

Denmark-Sweden Agreement concerning Protection of the Sound from Pollution, Copenhagen, April 5, 1974 [6 ND 459]: 667

Convention for the Prevention of Marine Pollution from Land-Based Sources, Paris, June 4, 1974 [1978 UKTS 64]: 742

US-Canada Agreement relating to the Establishment of Joint Pollution Contingency Plans for Spills of Oil and Other Noxious Substances, Ottawa, June 19, 1974 [25 UST 1280; TIAS 7861]: 667

International Convention for the Safety of Life at Sea, London, November 1, 1974 [32 UST 47; TIAS 9700]: 687

1975   Iceland-Belgium Fisheries Agreement relating to the Extension of the Icelandic Fishery Limits to 200 Nautical Miles, Reykjavik, November 28, 1975 [15 ILM 1]: 598

Iceland-Germany Fisheries Agreement relating to the Extension of the Icelandic Fishery Limits to 200 Nautical Miles, Reykjavik, November 28, 1975 [15 ILM 43]: 598

1976   Convention for the Protection of the Mediterranean Sea against Pollution, Barcelona, February 16, 1976 [15 ILM 290]: 688

Protocol to the Convention for the Prevention of Pollution of the Mediterranean Sea by Dumping from Ships and Aircraft, Barcelona, February 16, 1976 [15 ILM 300]: 737

India-Sri Lanka Agreement on the Maritime Boundary between the Two Countries in the Gulf of Manaar and the Bay of Bengal, New Delhi, March 23, 1976 [5 ND 333]: 215

France-Italy-Monaco Agreement relating to the Protection of Waters of Mediterranean Coast, Monaco, May 10, 1976 [85 RGDIP 647]: 667

Iceland-Great Britain Agreement concerning British Fishing in Icelandic Waters, June 1, 1976 [15 ILM 878]: 598

1978   US-Venezuela Maritime Boundary Agreement, Caracas, March 28, 1978 [TIAS 9890; 32 UST 3100]: 213

International Convention on Standards of Training, Certification and Watchkeeping for Seafarers, London, July 7, 1978 [Misc 6 (1979); Cmnd. 7543]: 352

Convention on Future Multilateral Co-operation in the North-West Atlantic Fisheries, [International Convention for the Northwest Atlantic Fisheries], Ottawa, October 24, 1978 [Misc 9 (1979); Cmnd. 7569]: 576

1979   US-Great Britain Agreement relating to Jurisdiction over Vessels Utilizing the Louisiana Offshore Oil Port, Washington, May 25, 1979 [30 UST 5926; TIAS 9525]: 471-472

1980   US-New Zealand Maritime Treaty on the Delimitation of the Maritime Boundary between Tokelan and the U.S.A., Atutu, December 2, 1980 [TIAS 10775]: 219-220

1981   Convention for Cooperation in the Protection and Development of the Marine Coastal Environment of the West and Central African Region, Abidjan, March 23, 1981 [20 ILM 746]: 688

Agreement to Facilitate the Interdiction by the US of Vessels of the UK Suspected of Trafficking in Drugs, London, November 13, 1981 [33 UST 4224; TIAS 10296]: 374

1982   Convention for the Conservation of Salmon in the North Atlantic Ocean [Atlantic Salmon Treaty], Reykjavik, March 2, 1982 [Cmnd. 8830]: 638

France-Germany-Great Britain-US Agreement concerning Interim Arrangements relating to Polymetallic Nodules of the Deep Sea Bed, Washington, September 2, 1982 [TIAS 10562]: 561-568

1983   Canada-Denmark Agreement for Cooperation relating to the Marine Environment, Copenhagen, August 26, 1983 [23 ILM 269]: 667

1984 Belgium-France-Germany-Italy-Japan-Netherlands-Great Britain-US Provisional Understanding regarding Deep Seabed Mining, Geneva, August 3, 1984 [23 ILM 1354]: 566-568

US-Bulgaria Agreement on Fisheries off the US Coast, Washington, September 22, 1983 [TIAS 10816]: 614-615

1986 UN Convention on Condition for Registration of Ships, Geneva, February 7, 1986 [7 LOSB 87]: 356-361

1988 Convention for the Suppression of Unlawful Acts against the Safety of the Maritime Navigation, Rome, March 10, 1988 [11 LOSB 14]: 380-383

Protocol for the Suppression of Unlawful Acts against the Safety of Fixed Platforms Located on the Continental Shelf, Rome, March 10, 1988 [11 LOSB 24]: 447

US-USSR Agreement on Mutual Fisheries Relations, Moscow, May 31, 1988 [TIAS number not yet available]: 615-617

UN Convention against Illicit Traffic in Narcotic Drugs and Psychotropic Substances, Vienna, December 19, 1988 [UN Doc. E/CONF. 82/15]: 379-380

1989 International Convention on Salvage, London, April 28, 1989 [IMO Doc. LEG/CONF. 7/26]: 364

AIT-CCNAA Sea Driftnet Fishing Agreement, Arlington, Virginia, July 13, 1989 [8 CYILA 512]: 620-625

Convention for the Prohibition of Fishing with Long Drift Nets in the South Pacific, Wellington, November 23, 1989 [14 LOSB 31]: 646-650

INDEX TO THE 1982 UNITED NATIONS CONVENTION ON THE LAW OF THE SEA

generally 5, 23-24, 50, 97, 206, 269, 296, 774, 776; history 24-28; text 28-31; U.S. with, 47; 200 mile EZ 248, 461, 464, 581, 583; territorial water 254; sea-bed production policy 525-526; International Sea-Bed Authority 54; marine pollution 667

Text of the Convention

886

894

SUBJECT INDEX

Access to ports; see also ports
278-279

Aegean Sea
216

Aqaba, Gulf of
134, 136

Air defense areas
325

Air Defense Identification Zone (ADIZ)
3, 325

Alaska
126-131

Albania
ten-mile territorial sea 239; Corfu Channel dispute with the UK 285-288

Alexander, Lewis
147

Allowable catch
in EEZ 627, 629, 631, 640; in high seas 644; total 638

Alluvium and increment, principle of
68

American Samoa
219-221

American Tunaboat Association
659

Amoco Cadiz incident
705-706; damage amount 711-716

Anadromous species/stocks
conservation of 483, 582, 601, 605-606, 611-612, 616; in high seas 582-583; outer limit of EEZ 637-638

Anderson, Andrew W.
339-342

Arbitral Tribunal
174-177, 202-208, 666, 783

Archipelagic baseline
69, 98; maximum length 97

Archipelagic sea-lane passage; see also transit passage
28, 49, 99, 303; definition 100; marine scientific research 762

Archipelagic states
23, 25, 69, 97, 247, 322; straight baseline exception 98; sovereignty of 98-99; delimitation of internal waters 99; right of innocent passage 99

Archipelagic waters
25, 28, 99-100, 247, 319, 322; legal status of 98

Archipelagos; see also group of islands
69, 77, 97-98, 113; types 95; oceanic 97; delimitation of territorial sea 95

Arcs of circle method; see also delimitation
151

Argentina
816-817; Declaration with USA 148-149; temporary/transitory zones of mineral reserves 412, 454; 200 miles conservation zone 589

Artificial island; see also installation
64-65, 139, 213, 408-409, 438; on continental shelf 446; in EEZ 467, 488; marine scientific research 483; jurisdiction 541, 738

Attard, David
212-215, 453-462, 492-496

Australia
maritime boundary with Papua New Guinea 222; sedentary fishery dispute 583

897

Automatic contact mines
818; warning 822-823

Bab el Mandeb, Straits of
281

Bahrain
313

Baltic Sea
12, 326, 747

Bangladesh
territorial waters 93

Baseline; see also location of baseline,
straight baseline, archipelagic baseline,
coastline; generally 28; normal 84, 85;
methods determining 28, 67, 70, 203;
territorial sea 56, 69, 78, 141, 227, 690;
large-scale charts 56-57, 167; intermediate
scales 57; small scales 57; length of 77,
83; permissible deviation 70; delimiting
fishery zone 73; delimitation of 92;
drawing of 82, 92, 144; history 70;
restriction of 83; rocks 213

Basepoint
65-66, 92-93

Bays; see also inland waters, internal waters
generally 105, 131, 147; definition 77,
102-103, 106, 113-114; well defined 77,
81; three miles 103, 143; six mile wide
102-103; ten miles 77, 106-107;
exceeding fifteen miles 108; twenty-four
miles 106, 109; characteristics of 103,
107; straight baseline 104, 107; historic
107-108; closing line 107, 109, 112;
relations with islands 111; multiple
mouths to 112, 113 ; natural entrance
point to 112; enclosed by two or more
states 131; semi-circle test 106, 108-111,
114

Belgium
fishery agreement with Iceland 598;
friendship treaty with the US 279; deep
sea mining treaty 566-568; jurisdiction
issue with the US 229-230

Bernardt, R.
688-689

Billfish
608-509

Bishop, Jr., William W.
839-840

Black Sea
326

Blockade; see also reprisal, quarantine
824, 831-833; breach of 825, 828-830,
838, 847; publication of 825, 830, 837;
long distance 826, 827; close 827;
effective 835; pacific 837-838, 843; Indo-
Pakistan War 826; of Greece 838; Cuba
crisis 839-840

Boczek, Boleslaw A.
777-779, 807-808

Bolivia
333-334

Bosphorus, Strait of
291

Bouchez, L.J.
117-118, 131

Bowett, D.W.
314-316, 346

Brazil
seizure of a vessel 304; 200 miles
territorial sea 457; fishing zone 457, 588;
lobster dispute with France 577, 583; 200
miles conservation zone 589, 591; fishery
accord with the US 591

Briggs, Herbert W.
830-831

Buergenthal, Thomas
781-786

Bulgaria
fishery agreement with the US 614-615

Burke, William T.
5-54, 629-631, 769

Bush, George
821-822

Bynkershoek, Comelins
232-234

Bynkershoek's principle; see also cannon shot rule
14, 233

California
137

Canada
maritime boundary with US 196, 202; Customs Act of 305; fishery agreement with Japan and USA 611-613; marine pollution treaty with USA 667; legislation of marine pollution 666, 744; salmon 636-637

Cannon-shot rule; see also Bynkershoek's principle
14, 18, 127, 304; history 234-235

Case of Edisto and Eastwind
289-290

Catadromous species
633; outer limit of EEZ 639

CCNAA
fishery agreement with AIT 620-625

Central American Court of Justice
133

Chayes, Abram
840-843

Channel
69, 138-139

Chile
transit 333-334; 200-n.m. maritime zone 454, 588, 589; fishery dispute with the US 577

China, Republic of
island dispute with Japan 215-216; continental shelf dispute with Japan 424; control of foreign warships passage 269; closures of ports at wartime 834-837

Chiu, Hungdah
95-97, 179-180

Chosen Strait
297

Churchill, R.R.
65-66, 68-69, 564, 585-588, 661-662, 666-667

Clement, Rebecca J.
654, 656

Clingan, Thomas
540-541, 662-665

Closed sea
13, 325

Coastal states
duties of 20, 260; notice of straight baseline 80; notice of danger 257, 260; charts of 105, 140; rights of 260, 269; fishery regulation 643; fishing jurisdiction 19, 247, 406, 477, 596, 629, 632, 640; criminal jurisdiction 266; civil jurisdiction 266-267; general jurisdiction/ sovereignty 67, 133, 241, 247, 541; EEZ jurisdiction 458, 465-466, 483, 541, 626-627; preferential rights 40, 44, 586, 596, 642; historic bays 115; bay generally 131; rights/duties over continental shelf 208, 399, 414, 418, 420-421, 431, 442-443, 477, 495, 586, 762; pollution control 723, 735, 759-760; security 760-761

Coastal waters
14; of Greece 10; of Italy 10; of Norway 73; resource management 25; jurisdiction 129

Coastline; see also baseline
53-54, 74, 168, 191; normal baseline of 84; indented 92; concave 204, 213; ratio of 199; of island 219

Cod war
594-597

Code of Safety for Nuclear Merchant Ships (1981)
687

Codification of customary norms
23, 35

Codification of the law of the sea
18-23

Collisions; see also marine casualty
18, 370, 717

Common heritage of mankind
28, 337, 461, 508-510, 515, 521, 543

Colombos, C. John
838-839

Commission on the Limits of the Continental Shelf
427-429; delimitation of boundaries 429

Committee on the Peaceful Uses of the Sea-Bed and the Ocean Floor beyond the Limits of National Jurisdiction
513

Compromis
782-783

Conflict of interest
346

Conflict of laws
18

Constantinople Accords (1913)
Iran-Iraq 807

Contiguous zone; see also vigilance zone
generally 14, 227, 305-306, 310-312; jurisdiction 3, 307, 308, 310-312, 315; extent of 314, 588; outer limit 55; beyond twelve miles 252; hot pursuit 384-386, 392-394; exploration 509

Continental margin
400, 402, 404, 425, 430

Continental rise
49, 400

Continental shelf; see also platform, submarine areas, natural prolongation
generally 14, 44, 206, 244-245, 399-401, 403, 411, 412, 415-416, 488, 494, 509, 544; categories 422; development of 406-408; doctrine 20, 211, 399; 200 meters 415-416, 418, 421; 200 nautical miles 49, 190, 425-426, 428, 492; inner limit 55; outer limit 182, 425, 426, 449; exploration of 63, 66-67, 184, 395, 396, 426, 434, 437, 443, 446, 449, 488; activities in 489; island 166, 213; delimitation of 167-168, 170, 174-179, 182, 189-193, 195, 196-200, 213, 217, 219, 399, 417, 426; relations with EEZ 189, 492; hot pursuit 386; trough problem 424-425

Continental slope
49, 400, 418, 508

Contraband; see also doctrine of continuous voyage/ transportation
generally 816, 846-847; categories 846-847; seizure of 847, 848; seizure in neutral territorial waters 849

Contract regarding an Interim Supplement to Tanker Liability for Oil Pollution, see CRISTAL

Conventional line; see also delimitation
152

Cook Inlet
132

900

Delimitation; see also maritime boundary
generally 39, 77, 81-82, 200, 205, 248;
adjustment 192; internal waters from
territorial waters 53-54, 77, 00; territorial
sea 138, 156, 166, 203, 227, 249; tidal
boundaries 59-60; artificial island 66-67;
methods 76, 81, 191, 199, 204-205, 215;
equitable principle 181-183, 190, 205-
206; proportionality test 186; multi-
purpose 196; fishery zone 78-79, 212;
archipelagos 95; continental shelf 166-
167, 169-170, 174-179, 180-186, 189-
193, 195, 203, 212, 217, 219, 417

Delta
84

Demersal species
583

Denmark
delimitation of contintental shelf with
Germany 167-171, 173, 414, 420-421, 423;
fishing zone with Norway 208; marine
pollution treaty 667; marine scientific
research 777

Disparate jurisdiction; see also jurisdiction
French revolution 14

Dispute settlement; see also maritime
disputes, International Court of Justice;
International Sea Bed Authority,
International Tribunal for the Laws of Sea
generally 28; non-judicial methods 781-
782; quasi-judicial methods 782-783; int'l
conventions 786-798; compulsory
settlement 786-787, 790, 792-793;
conciliation 782, 792, 795; arbitration
782, 783, 793; special arbitration 794-
795; freedom of choice 791, 798

Distant early warning identification zone
(DEWIZ)
325

Distant water fishing
581, 586, 589, 632, 650

Diurnal inequality
59

Doctrine of Abstention; see also new
entrants of fishery
582

Doctrine of continuous voyage/ transportation; see also contraband
847-848

Doctrine of effectiveness
41

Doctrine of necessity; see also self defense
689

Doctrine of shared use/utilization
319

Doctrine of the jurists
10

Dover Strait
283

Driftnet fishing; see also fishing technique
617-626, 646-652

Drilling
exclusive right of coastal state 442

Drug, illicit traffic in
379-380

Dubach, Harold W.
57-58

Due notice of hazard
28

Dumping; see pollution

Economic Planning Commission
525, 530

Economic zone
generally 47; development 21, 329, 453-
462, 477; living resources in 476

902

Ecuador
territorial sea 88; fishery dispute with the US 577, 588-590; 200 miles fishing zone 588, 589; maritime zone declaration 588; US assistance to 592-594

Edisto and Eastwind, the Case of
289-290

EEZ; see exclusive economic zone

El Salvador
jurisdiction over 200-n.m. 455; 200 miles conservation zone 589

Emergency measures
717-719

Enclosed sea; see also semi-enclosed sea, marginal sea
326-327, 327-329, 641

Enemy merchantmen
treatment of 810

Enlarged Seabed Committee
509

Enterprise; see also International Sea Bed Authority
523-525, 527-528, 530-532, 537, 539; Statute of 520

Entry in distress
228, 273-274, 274-276, 277

Envelope line/ trace parallele
152, 153-154

Envelope of all arcs/circle; see also estuary
105, 219

Epicontinental sea
454, 461

Equality of states
191, 214-215

Equidistance line
182, 184, 204, 214; distortion of 176

Equidistance method; see also principle of equidistance
169, 174, 178, 184, 190-192, 205, 213

Equidistance principles; see also equidistance method
162, 167, 169-170, 174-176, 178, 179-180, 423-424; combined with special circumstance rule 175

Equitable principle; see also delimitation
181-183, 190-191, 196, 200, 203, 411; exploration of continental shelf 426, 495; fishery resources 578, 580

Estuary; see also bays
105, 147

European Economic Community
559; fishery policy 585

Evensen, Jen
95

Exclusion zone; see also Maritime Exclusion Zone
804, 806; UK 805-806; 150 miles 806; Iran-Iraq war 807

Exclusive economic jurisdiction zone
459

Exclusive Economic Zone (EEZ)
generally 39, 41, 298-299, 313, 319, 322, 465, 493, 509, 615; history 453-462; two hundred miles 28, 47, 51, 125, 227, 248, 460-462, 466, 477, 480, 488, 582, 621, 632; twelve miles 39, 581; distance principle of 212; fishing in 627-628, 631, 633; jurisdiction 125, 482, 485, 488; delimitation of 179, 203, 208, 212-214, 217; relations with continental shelf 189, 206, 211, 492; relations with high sea 465; rights/ duties of coastal states 322, 466, 627; hot pursuit 386; activities in 466, 489; countries proclaimed 479; pollution control 720

Exclusive fisheries zone/ jurisdiction
392, 393, 581, 585, 586, 596, 601; 200
miles 585, 588, 591; twelve miles 585,
596

Exclusive Fishery Management Authority
601

Exploitability tests
494

Exploitation beyond national jurisdiction,
principle of
514-516

Exploration
544, 556, 561; license/permit 546-547,
552, 556-557; transfer of license 548,
559; duration of license/permit 548, 558;
termination of license/ permit 558

Falkland Islands
805-806

FCN treaties
228-229, 231

Finland
marine pollution treaty 667

Fishery conflict
578, 587-588

Fishery conservation zone; see also fishery
zone
453, 455, 601, 605-606, 608

Fishery management; see also fishery
operation
allowable catch 571, 573, 578, 597, 629;
total authorized catch 483; maximum
sustainable yield 571, 573, 576-577, 579,
581, 600, 644, 656, 747; optimum
sustainable yield 576, 579, 600, 630;
optimum utilization 483, 630-631, 634,
655; optimum sustainable population
659; permissible yield 629, 631; quotas
581; problems 575-584; int'l fishery
agreement 601-602, 607-608; foreign
fishing 603-607; fishery violation 615-
616, 624, 643

Fishery operation; see also fishery
management
fleet limit 613; time limit 613; location
limit 613, 621; species limit 622

Fishery resources; see also fishing rights
in territorial sea 581; in EEZ 581; in
continental shelf 601, 605-606; allocation
of 578, 580-583, 597, 603

Fishery zone; see also fishery conservation
zone
generally 492; extent of 76, 102;
delimitation of 78-79, 196-200, 208, 212;
three miles 102; six miles 238; twelve
miles 248, 392, 393, 459; 100 miles
457; 200 miles 612; US/ Canada joint
proposal 252; regional 476

Fishing rights
250, 407; archipelagic state 99; offshore
area of other states 249; traditional 581

Fishing technique
driftnet 617-618, 620, 622, 646-650, 651-
652; others 659

Fishing vessel
229, 648

Flag of convenience; see also nationality of
ships
generally 315, 345, 347-348, 688; causes
344, 346, 351

Flag state
generally 267; jurisdiction of 587;
exclusive jurisdiction on high seas 342,
346, 353, 370, 379-380, 689; duties of
353-354, 358-359; consent of seizure
374; fishery regulation 586-587;
pollution control 721-722, 726

Floating territory
231

Fonesca, Gulf of
133-134, 135

Food and Agriculture Organization (FAO)
582, 789, 795

Force majeure
276, 277, 299

Four-mile limit
244; adopted by Belgium, Holland, Greece
and France 14-15

Four-mile league
Scandinavian states 238

Fragile ecosystems
744-745

France
delimitation of continental shelf with the
United Kingdom 174-178; convention
with Portugal 208; views on adjacent area
to continental shelf 417; treaty of
polymetallic nodules 561-566; lobster
dispute with Brazil 577, 583; marine
pollution treaty 667; Civil Code 712;
neutrality treaty 808; view on enclosed or
semi-enclosed sea 328; use iceberg as a
spy base 324

Franklin, C.M.
400-403

Freedom of commerce
26

Freedom of communication
26, 133, 458, 460

Freedom of fishing
595, 633; in high sea 244, 506, 573, 586-
588, 595, 643

Freedom of laying submarine
cables/pipeline; see also submarine
cables/pipelines
320, 322, 395-397, 443-444, 459; EEZ
464, 466, 480, 483, 489; continental
shelf 444, 489; int'l seabed 541

Freedom of marine scientific research
767-768; high seas 769

Freedom of navigation
13, 26, 125, 134, 240, 244, 248, 280,
291, 299, 313, 322, 330, 342, 379, 446,
595; through continental shelf 411, 442,
445, 489; through fishery conservation
zone 453; interruption on high sea 16;
semi-enclosed seas 328; through EEZ
454, 455, 457-460, 464, 466, 480, 483,
489; int'l seabed 541

Freedom of overflight; see also overflight
125, 257, 296, 299, 322; semi-enclosed
seas 328; EEZ 457-460, 464, 466, 480,
483, 489; through continental shelf 489;
int'l seabed 541

Freedom of the high [open] sea
generally 43, 49, 66, 129, 248, 313, 319,
330, 337, 341-342, 395, 546, 666; limit
28; activities 319-320, 323, 395, 542;
jurisdiction of a foreign state 344; exploit
subsoil 417; pollution control 744;
quarantine 843

Freedom of the seas; See also freedom of
navigation
generally 9-11, 19-21, 39, 79, 240, 250-
251, 306; history 12-13, 507; beyond
three miles 244; exploration of natural
resources 432, 444-445, 506; continental
shelf 444-445; EEZ 465

Freedom of transit; see also transit passage,
strait
331, 337, 338; exception 332; blockade
824-825

French Doctrine
234

Fulton, Thomas Wemyss
11-12

Gambling ships
US jurisdiction over 375

Garcia-Amador, F.V.
305-307

General Agreement of Tariff and Trade (GATT)
fishery conservation 599

General direction of the coastline
77, 81, 84, 157, 204-205; change of 181

Geneva Conventions
21-22, 24, 44, 48; Optional Protocol 43

Gentleman's Agreement
25

Genuine link; see also nationality of ships, flag of convenience
343, 345-348, 353

Geographically disadvantaged states; see also land-locked states
generally 23, 478, 479; access to resources 475, 640-641; exploitation exception 642; transit right 476; EEZ 477; seabed activities 523; marine scientific research 766

German Democratic Republic, see Germany

Germany
friendship treaty with the US 228-229; treaty of polymetallic nodules 561-566; cod war with Iceland 594; fishery agreement with Iceland 598; long distance blockade 826; East Germany's view on contiguous zones 312-313

Ghana
475-476

Gibraltar, Strait
282

Gidel, G.
straight baseline method 72

Government non-commercial ships
categories 368; immunity of jurisdiction 364

Government ships
268, 289-290

Governmental commercial ships
immunity on high seas 365

Great Britain, see United Kingdom

Great Lakes (US-Canada)
326

Greece
continental shelf dispute with Turkey 216; blockade of 838

Griffin, W.L.
56-57

Group of 77
777, 792

Groups of islands; see also archipelagos
77, 95-96

Guinea
202-208, 209-210

Guinea-Bissau
202-208, 209-210

Gulf War (1986); see also Iraq-Iran War
807-808

Gustafson, Kristen
448-450

Hackworth, Green H.
79, 387-389, 408-409

Hague Codification Conference (1930)
19, 56, 96, 107, 140, 147, 241-242, 268, 306, 308-309, 385, 386

Haiti
270-273

Harbour works
137-139

Harvard Draft on the Law of the Territorial Sea (1929)
96

Headland; see alos baseline
113

Headland-to-headland doctrine; see also baseline
103

Heinzen, Bernard G.
238-240, 250-251

High seas; see also open sea
generally 53, 126, 137, 237, 298-299; definition 43; inner limit 55; scope of 319, 494, 509; access to 134; jurisdiction 320-321, 402, 437; nuclear weapon test 320-322; hot pursuit 388; relations with EEZ 465; exploration of natural resources 509

High tide
generally 82; causation of 57-58; elevation 91

High-water mark/line
55-56; ordinary 60-61, 439; island 63

Highly migratory fisheries/ species
460, 480, 601, 605, 607, 631, 633, 634-635

Historic fishing rights
449

Historic waters/bays
generally 115, 118, 126, 133, 184; Norwegian 92; Cook Inlet 127; Seychelles 487, 489; requirements of 117-118, 125-126; title to 118-121; jurisdiction 118-120, 489; legal status of 121; US position 122-123

Hodgson, R.D.
63-65, 83-84, 147

Honduras
sovereignty over shelf 455

Hormuz, Strait of
284

Hot pursuit
384-386, 388-390, 392, 394-395; compensation 395

Hsu Mo
79

Hudson Bay
326

Hydrogen bomb test
44-46

Iceland
fishing right dispute with UK 577; extension of fishing limit 586, 594, 598; cod war with UK and Germany 594; legislation of fishery conservation 594-595; fishery agreements with Germany, UK and Belgium 598

Immunity of jurisdiction; see also government commercial ships, jurisdiction
364-366; state owned commercial vessels 367; waiver 693, 727

India
EEZ boundary with Sri Lanka 215

Indo-Pakistan War (1971)
826

Indonesia
294

Informal Composite Negotiating Text (ICNT)
26

Informal Single Negotiating Text (ISNT)
97

Inland sea/water; see also interior waters, internal waters
generally 10, 104, 114, 126, 128; jurisdiction 53, 87, 103, 128; straight baseline method 87, 96, 114; ten miles 103; maximum area of 112; historic title to 128

Innocent passage
generally 20, 28, 256, 272, 277, 330; high seas 81, 228, 302; territorial waters 81, 128, 134, 228, 240, 248, 254-255, 257, 263-264, 302, 457, 487, 541, 585; internal waters 82, 85, 228, 585; archipelagic waters 99; historic bays 118, 125; straits 290, 294, 296, 298, 302; EEZ 302; roadsteads 140; air space 257, 458; maritime zone 456; suspension of 258, 260-262, 289, 302, 487-488; restriction of 258-259, 272; exception 264; warships 268, 285-287; pollution control 720; marine scientific research 762

Installations; see also island
continental shelf 443-446; EEZ 467, 488; jurisdiction 445, 67, 541; legal status 468, 522, 772; marine scientific research 483, 772; pollution from 737-738

Inter-Governmental Maritime Consultive Organization (IMCO)
349, 689, 789

Intergovernmental Oceanographic Commission of UNESCO
428, 795

Interior waters; see also internal waters, inland waters
88, 105

Internal waters; see also interior waters
generally 53, 55, 80-81, 84, 128, 227, 322; relationship with territorial waters 28, 80, 105, 137, 228, 241; Norwegian 76; bays 107; roadsteads 140; within a strait 298; hot pursuit 385

International Atomic Energy Agency (IAEA)
353, 732

International Civil Aviation Organization (ICAO)
35, 300

International Court of Justice (ICJ)
generally 203, 207, 784-786; history 784; jurisdiction 784-787; judgment enforcement 785-786

International Court of Justice Statute
art. (17) 796; art. (26) 196; art. (31) 196; art. (36) 785; art. (53) 794; art. (57) 79; Art. (59) 785; Art. (38) 33, 37, 183, 195, 217

International Hydrographic Organization
428

International Law
evidence 34, 37; sources 34-37

International Law Commission commentary
island in the bay 111-112; draft art. (1) 141, 241-242; article (6) 151; art. (7) 107-108; art. (8) 137; art. (9) 140; art. (10) 63-65; art. (11) 144-145; art. (12) 156-157; art. (13) 147; art. (14) 157-158; art. (29) 343; art. (33) 364-365; art. (35) 370; art. (36) 363; art. (66) 308-309; art. (67) 415-416, 421; art. (69) 444; art. (70) 396-397, 444; art. (71) 67, 445-446; art. (68) 431-432; art. (72) 167

International law of the sea; see also law of sea
evidence 34; sources 33-36; secondary sources 36-37

International Maritime Organization (IMO)
667, 689, 789, 795

International minimum standard
fishing 627, 644

International Monetary Fund
35; Special Drawing Right 691

International North Pacific Fisheries Commission
611

International Observer Scheme
655

International Oil Pollution Compensation Fund
693-696; exemption of payment 695

International Regulations for Preventing Collisions at Sea
300

International Sea-Bed Area
generally 66, 521, 523, 797; land-locked state 477; pollution control 739-740; marine scientific research 766

International Sea-Bed Authority; see also dispute settlement
520, 522, 537, 777-779, 796; Preparatory Commission 525, 527-528, 535-536; organs 529-530, 797

International Tribunal for the Law of the Sea
30, 527-528, 535, 791, 795-798

International Whaling Commission
655-657

Interpretation of contract
243

Iran
view on enclosed sea 327-328, view on landlocked states 477; mine ships seized by US 823-824

Iraq
844-846

Iraq-Iran War
807, 809

Island states
23, 213, 215; EEZ 215

Island; see also rocks, archipelagos, artificial island, installation
definition 213; uninhabited 213; high water mark 63; sizes 63-64; oceanic 64; territory of 68; fringe of 80, 83-84, 91, 114; string of 109; relations with bays 111-112; drying rocks 141; coastal 204; scattered 204; offshore 213; continental shelf 166, 197, 213; EEZ 212, 215

Isobath line
93

Italy
continental shelf with Libya 193; shelf with Tunisia 215, 217- 219; territorial sea 310-312; Customs Law 312; legislation of exploration of hard mineral resource of seabed 556-561; treaty of deep seabed mining 566-568; marine pollution treaty 667

Japan
island dispute with China 215-216; continental shelf dispute with China 424; Law of the Territorial Sea 296; treaty of deep seabed mining 566-568; sedentary fisheries dispute with USSR 577, 583; fishery agreement with Canada and USA 611-613; driftnet agreement with US 626, 659; seizure of a fishing vessel by the US 391-394; violation of whaling 657

Jessup, P.C.
231, 234, 268, 272, 831

Jurisdiction; see also sovereignty of states
adjacent to coast 11; over foreign ship 14; among ships 18; high seas 15, 20, 342, 346, 353, 372; EEZ 485; seabed 222; continental shelf 246; over resources 85, 244-245; fisheries 222; beyond three miles 244; limits 28; immunity of 273-274, 274-276, 301, 364-366; subject matter 340

Jus gestionis
367

Jus imperii
367

Just and equitable share
176

Kenya
200 miles EEZ 459

Kindt, John Warren
659-660

909

Magnuson Act; see also US law
600, 604, 608

Maier, Harold G.
781-786

Mainland
144, 166

Malacca, Strait of
294-295

Malaysia
294

Malone, James L.
536-539, 539-540

Malta
continental shelf with Libya 189-194

Maramara, Sea of
292

Mare liberum
13

Marginal sea; see also territorial sea
128, 151, 327; measurement of 95, 151-152; three miles 151

Marine archaeology
771

Marine casualty; see also collision
717, 719

Marine data management; see also marine scientific research
organizations 750; system 753

Marine geology
498-500

Marine league rule
305

Marine mammals; see also whaling
categories 652-653; problems 653-654; int'l protection of 654-657, 658-659

Marine resources; see also natural resources, non-living resources, living resources
generally 487, 618; protection of 9, 24; exploitation of 20, 54

Marine scientific research; see also marine data management
generally 46, 300, 495, 516, 545, 747, 749-751, 756; principles 755; in EEZ 483-484, 762-766, 768, 774; in territorial sea 761; in continental shelf 762-766, 768; peaceful purpose 484, 515, 521, 755, 768; conflict 748-749, 773; technology 749, 752-755, 769, 775-776; int'l cooperation organizations 757-759, 763, 765, 774-775; coastal states' regulations 759-760, 766, 774, 792; consent of coastal states 762-763, 765, 767-769; responsibility and liability 773

Maritime belt
233-234, 273

Maritime boundary; see also delimitation
three miles 14; low-water mark 14; Guinea/ Guinea-Bissau 202-208; Papua New Guinea/ Australia 222; territorial waters 234

Maritime commerce
16

Maritime disputes; see also dispute settlement
generally 12; Belgium/ Great Britain 15; Norway/Sweden 157; Denmark/Netherlands 168; Libya/ Malta 189-193; coastal zone 74; submerged lands 108-114; island 215-216; continental shelf 216; EEZ disputes 467; marine scientific research 773-774

Maritime Exclusion Zone; see also exclusive zone
805-806, 826

MARPOL
685-687

911

Netherlands, The
167-171, 173, 414; treaty of deep seabed mining 566-568

Neutral goods
816

Neutral port
825

Neutral shipping
804

Neutral ships
rights of 817, 825, 828, 848; search on high seas 849

Neutral trade
832

Neutral waters
war time 234

Neutrality
20, 235, 801-804, 808; US independence war 14; UK 830; war time 234; treaties 808-816; rights and duties of neutral powers 811-816

New entrants of fishery; see also Doctrine of Abstention
581

New Zealand
baseline 213, maritime boundary with US 219-220

Newton, Frank R.
408-409

Nicaragua
jurisdiction over continental shelf 454; 200 miles fishing zone 456, 589; mining by the US in Nicaragua harbor 822-823

Nigeria
261-262

Nine-mile
Mexico 239

Non-encroachment principle
190

Non-living resources; see also living resources, natural resources
generally 28, 487; exploration 426, 448-449; exploration beyond 200 miles of shelf 494; difference with living resources 476; in EEZ 493

Non-pollution zone
212 miles 459

North Atlantic Coast Fisheries Tribunal
102, 103

North Sea
172, 435

Northern Mariana Island
481

Norton, Patrick M.
801-802

Norway
coast of 75, fishing zone with Denmark 208; view on continental shelf 424; marine pollution treaty 667; maritime boundary 73; delimitation of maritime boundary dispute 72-79

Nuclear-power ship
264

Nuclear-weapon test
321-322, 743

Nuclear/ dangerous substances
innocent passage 264; treaty banning nuclear weapon test 743

O'Connell, D.P.
9, 12-13, 13-16, 18-22, 38-44, 506-507, 507-510, 802-804, 804-806, 808-811, 826-827

913

Ocean Data Acquisition Systems, Aids and Devices (ODAS)
753

Ocean dumping; see also pollution
definition 728, 734; exception 728, 734; incineration 733; radioactive waste 734; treaties 736-737

Ocean floor
peaceful use of 416-419, 515; activities 508

Oceans and seas
generally 1; nature 2-3; space 3-4, 53; values 3-4; jurisdiction zone in 5-7

Oda, Shigeru
248-249

Offenses
generally 380-381, 447, 490-491; committed in ports or territorial waters 230-231; jurisdiction 382

Oil pollution
limited liability 689, 690-693, 703; limited liability exception 691; owners' joint liability 704; treaties/agreements 690-699, 699-701, 702-704; statute of limitation 692; compensation fund 693-696; maximum compensation 703; violation of treaties 696

Okhotsk, Sea of
326

One league limit; see also three-mile rule
238-239, 250; states claiming one league territorial sea 239, 240

Open seas; see also high seas
10, 104, 111; jurisdiction 142

Operational zone; see also war zone, sea defense zone
805

Opinion juris
39-41

Ordre public
243

Organ of Consultation of the Organization of American States
840-841

Organization for Economic Cooperation and Development (OECD)
34; marine pollution 737

Overflight; see also freedom of overflight
100, 257, 296, 840

Pacific blockade; see also blockade
843, 837-839

Panama
security zone 307, 454; fishing jurisdiction 454; 200 miles territorial sea 457; 200 miles conservation zone 589

Papua New Guinea
maritime boundary with Australia 222

Paracel Islands
216

Paria, Gulf of
409, 410

Passage; see also transit passage
definition 255-256; prejudicial 256; submerged 296, 303; neutral ships 817

Patrimonial sea
generally 461-462; 200 miles 458

Peaceful uses/purpose; see also sea-bed
generally 24; of seabed/ocean floor 416-419, 514-515, 521; marine scientific research 484, 755, 762, 768

Pearcy, G.E.
55

Pelly Amendment; see also US law
599, 638

915

Quasi-land-locked states
access to resources 460

Quita Sueno
145-146

Reagan, Ronald
254-255, 479-480

Reasonable use
44

Reciprocity
access to EEZ 483; exploration of hard
mineral 551-552, 556-557, 560-561;
foreign fishing 604; Int'l Court of
Justice's jurisdiction 785

Reefs
439; US rights to 441

Regional Sea Programme
667

Regulations for the Control of Incineration
of Wastes and Other Matter at Sea
733

Replica line; see also delimitation
152, 153

Reprisal; see also blockade
837

Res communis
13

Research; see marine scientific research

Resolution Governing Preparatory
Investment in Pioneer Activities Relating to
Polymetallic Nodules
561

Resolution of the Inter-American Juridical
Committee (1973)
458

Resolutions of the Institute of International
Law
278

Rift zone
189-190

Right of navigation; see also freedom of
navigation
100, 352

Right of passage; see also transit passage
internal waters 82

Right of search; see also right of visitation
16-18; wartime 849

Right of visitation; see also right of search
17-18, 372-373; consent 374; grounds
377-378, 816; compensation 378;
wartime 849

Rio de la Plata
148-150

Roadsteads
140; outer limit of territorial sea 140

Rockall
216

Rocks/shoals
68, 82; drying 141, 144-145; sedimentary
425; uninhabited 198, 212; baseline 213

Romania
legislation of EEZ 482-486

Roncador
145-146

Safe harbour theory
276

Safety zone
137, 443, 445-446, 468-469, 522; 500
meters 468, 483, 773; prohibited
activities 469; deepwater ports 470;
scientific research installation 773

Salmon
613; fishing management 636-637; high seas fishing 638

Samoa, see American Samoa

Santiago Declaration on the Maritime Zone (Peru-Chile-Ecuador) (1952)
588-589

Savannah, N.S.
264-265

Scientific Council for Africa
459

Sea defense zone; see also war zone, operational zone
805

Sea-Bed Committee
24, 511-512; EEZ 460-461; exploration beyond national jurisdiction 508, 514

Sea-bed Dispute Chamber
30, 535, 797-798

Sea-bed mining; see also mining technology
generally 38, 47, 49, 498-502, 508-509, 525, 748; reserved area 527; Commercial/non-commercial 527; US position 536-540; mineral resources 542, 553, 556, 566; protection of interim investment 554; pollution from 737-738, 740

Seabed
generally 26, 65, 98, 189, 439; abyssal 506; use/value of 4, 417; within territorial sea 144; beyond three miles 433; peaceful use of 416-419, 514-515, 521

Seabed exploration beyond national jurisdiction; see also pioneer investor
506-507, 514, 523, 527; regulation of 540; license 542

Sealane; see also traffic separation scheme
259, 300-301, 490; recognized 468

Seaworthy
708; pollution control 723

Security zone; see also Panama
307, 454

Sedentary fisheries
407, 431, 586; in EEZ 493; in continental shelf 586, 639; dispute 577, 583

Self-defense
16-17, 308, 390, 689, 803-804, 808, 821, 827, 842; collective 801, 844

Self-determination
219-220

Semi-circle test; see also bays
106, 108-111, 114

Semi-enclave approach; see also maritime boundary
215

Semi-enclosed sea; see also enclosed sea, marginal sea
326-327, 327-329, 641; fishery zone 328

Senkaku Gunto, see T'iao-yu Tai Islets

Serrana
145-146

Seychelles
legislation of maritime zones 487-491, 495

Shalowitz, A.L.
57, 58-60, 61, 75, 102-104, 151-154, 158-161

Shearer, I.A.
38-44, 506-507, 507-510, 802-804, 804-806, 808-811, 826-827

Shelik Strait incident
129-130

Ships/vessels
  master's responsibility 363, 383; search
  of 16, 271-272, 275, 306; condemnation
  of 16; seizure of 17, 67, 129, 272-273,
  275, 304, 389, 391; seizure of US ships
  607; arrest 20, 369; forfeiture of foreign
  vessels 610; discipline of 229-330,
  registration of 356-360; US ship
  registration requirements 362; slave trade
  370; pollution control violation 723-726;
  transfer of ownership 342, 346, 353

Sidra, Gulf of, see Sirte, Gulf of

Simmonds, Kenneth R.
  702-704

Singapore
  294

Sirte, Gulf of
  123-126

Six mile limit
  Spain 14, 238; general jurisdiction 239;
  countries claiming six-mile territorial sea
  239; registered tonnage 350-351

Skjaergaard
  74, 77; in Norway 81, 95

Slavery
  370-371

Sohn, Louis B.
  448-450

Soons, Alfred H.A.
  748-755, 757-761

Sorensen, Max
  344-346

South China Sea
  216

South Pacific Forum Fisheries Agency
(FFA)
  648, Regional register of Foreign Fishing
  Vessels 649

Sovereign and permanent appropriations,
principle of
  18

Sovereignty of States; see also jurisdiction
  generally 13, 24, 207, 215, 237; inland
  waters 228; coastal sea 232; air space
  247; fishing 632; immunity waiver 693,
  727; marine scientific research 763

Soviet Union, see USSR

Soya Strait
  296

Spain
  territorial sea 238; six-mile fishing zone
  238; Act concerning Nuclear Energy 264;
  closure of insurgent ports 833-834

Special circumstances rule; see also
equidistance principle
  174-176; combined with equidistance 175

Spratly Islands
  216

Spring tides
  59

Sri Lanka
  EEZ boundary with India 215

Stansfield, Robert H.
  688-689

Stare decisis
  786

Starke, J.G.
  824-826, 847-838, 843-844

Stateless ships; see also nationality of ships
  339-340, 353; universal jurisdiction 341-
  342

Statute of the International Court of Justice;
see International Court of Justice Statute

Statute on the International Regime of
Maritime Ports of 1923
278

Straddling stock; see also transboundary
stock
632-633

Straight baseline; see also delimitation
generally 56, 70, 73, 77, 79-80, 83-86,
91-93, 102, 141, 151, 156, 192;
maximum length 81-82; drawing of 82,
84; land/water ratio 84, 94; restriction of
84; internal waters 85, 114, 228; bays
104; river 147; territorial waters 423, 425

Straits
generally 77, 279; overflight of 3;
passage 280, 290, 291, 294; pollution
control 727

Submarine areas; see also continental shelf,
submerged land
401, 409, 415, 416; 200 meters 416,
421; submarine canyons 422, 423;
submarine elevations 425; submarine
valleys 422

Submarine cables/pipelines
99, 320, 322, 395, 397; responsibility
exception 396, 397; on continental shelf
446

Submerged lands; see also submarine areas
138, 411, 412; legal status of 494

Subsoil
generally 98, 439; use/value of 4, 198,
416-417, 443, 515

Sudan
Territorial Waters and Continental Shelf
Act 269

Sui generis
EEZ 464

Sullivan, Jr., William L.
632-633, 638

Sweden
667

Switzerland
476-477

T'iso-yu Tai Islets
215-216

Taber, Robert W.
57-58

Tanker Owners Voluntary Agreement
concerning Liability for Oil Pollution; see
TOVALOP

Tarawa Declaration of the South Pacific
Forum (1989)
647, 650

Technical Guidelines on the Control of
Incineration of Wastes and Other Matter at
Sea
733

Technology transfer
521, 523, 526, 528, 777-779; mandatory
538-540; fishery 628; Code of Conduct
on the Transfer of Technology 777

Teclaff, L.A.
70, 72

Ten-mile
Albania 239

Territorial sea; see also territorial waters,
internal waters
13-14, 128, 144, 227, 241, 322;
measurement of 55, 69-70, 76, 80, 84,
92, 96, 105, 125, 142, 156, 167;
extent/breadth of 15, 20, 39, 54, 56, 69,
107, 143, 227, 247, 425, 596, 690;
countries claiming specific breadths of
territorial sea 253-254; three miles 28,
104-105, 239, 245, 250, 263, 453, 588;
twelve miles 28, 43, 125, 250, 253, 312,
458, 461-462, 827; two hundred miles
459; outer limit of 140, 151, 249, 253;
seizure outside 15, 272, 304-305;
jurisdiction/sovereignty 20, 239, 247,

589; hot pursuit 385; island 66, 80, 105, 111; beyond median line 166

Territorial waters; see also territorial sea, marginal seas
generally 10, 53, 241; difference with internal waters 28; belt of 76-77, 81, 105

Three marine leagues (nine miles)
449

Three-mile rule; see also cannon shot rule, one league limit
14-15, 18, 127, 128, 143, 234-235, 250, 412, 437, 591; Denmark, Belgium, Holland 15; UK 239; fishery 19; measurement 15, 102, 143; U.S. 67, 436, 453, 588; history 238-239; criminal jurisdiction 239

Tokelau
219-221

Torrey Canyon incident
668-669

Total Exclusion Zone
Falkland Islands War 806, 826

Total war
846, 849

TOVALOP
697-699, 702; maximum liability 700

Traffic separation scheme; see also sea lanes
100, 259-260, 300-301, 490

Transboundary stock; see also straddling stock
632, 633

Transit passage; see also passage
28, 299, 301, 303, 331, 337-338; straits 49, 100, 156, 227, 280, 296, 298, 328, 461; high seas 100; EEZ 100; territorial sea 254, 258; charges/ payments 258, 260; warship 280; duties of ships 299-300; aircraft 300; law/ regulations 301; marine scientific research 762

Transit state
331, 337

Travalio, Gregory M.
654-656

Trawl fishing
406

Tributary waters; see also bays
109

Truman. Harry S.
433, 453

Tsugaru Strait
296

Tsushima Strait
296

Tuna
international organizations 635

Tuna war; see also US-CEP dispute
577, 583, 588, 591; Quadriparties Fisheries Conference 590

Tuna/ dolphin phenomenon
659

Tunisia
continental shelf with Libya 180-188; shelf with Italy 215, 217, 219

Turkey
continental shelf dispute with Greece 216; neutrality treaty 818, 810

Turkish Straits
291-293

Twelve miles limit
162; countries claiming twelve-mile territorial sea 239, 251

Two hundred miles
200, 239

UN Charter
  generally 508, 515; use of force 35-36,
  299, 577, 806, 841; blockade 837, 843;
  art.(2) 838; art.(7) 786; art.(33) 516;
  art.(39) (41-42) 786, 838; art.(51) 806,
  808, 821, 842, 844; art.(52) 842; art.(94)
  785; art.(96) 786; art.(103) 35

UN resolutions
  (502) 806; (660) 844; (661) 844; (665)
  845; (1105) 392; (2467) 512-514; (2340)
  513, 514; (2574-D) 513; (2749) 514-516;
  (44/225) 651-652

Unauthorized broadcasting; see also pirate
broadcasting
  377, 379-380

UNCITRAL Arbitration Rules
  798

UNCLOS
  generally 23-24, 47, 52, 97; history 24-
  28, 179; discussion of 32nd meeting 475-
  477; deep seabed exploration 561

UNCLOS I (First United Nations Conference on the Law of Sea)
  24, 40, 69, 96, 249, 251, 303, 365, 436,
  EFZ 585, fishery conservation 587

UNCLOS II (Second United Nations Conference on the Law of Sea)
  96, 249, 251

UNCLOS III (Third United Nations Conference on the Law of Sea, 1982)
  21, 25-26, 39-40, 50-51, 97, 212-215,
  269, 461-462, 492-493; sea-bed question
  497, 509

UNESCO (United Nations Educational,
Scientific and Cultural Organization)
  421-423

United Kingdom (UK)
  three-mile rule 239; territorial sea 255;
  1878 Territorial Water Jurisdiction Act
  15, 142-143, 239; continental shelf
  legislation 436-437; delimitation of
  continental shelf with France 174-178;

treaty of polymatallic nodules 561-566;
treaty of deep seabed mining 566-568;
fishery dispute with Norway 72-79;
fishing right dispute with Iceland 577,
594; 200 miles fishing limit agreement
with Iceland 598; pollution control
agreement with USA 688; neutrality
treaty 818, 810

United Nations Conference on Trade and
Development (UNCTAD)
  777-778

United Nations Environment Programme
(UNEP)
  667

United Nations Security Council
  792, 796, 806

Upper Volta (now Bukina Faso)
  475

Uruguay
  generally 148; 200 miles territorial sea
  457; 200 miles conservation zone 589

US law
  Alien Fishing Act 128; Alien Tort
  Statute 816; Anti-smuggling Act of 1935
  306; Antiquities Act 432, 434; Bartlett
  Act 591; Coastal Zone Management Act
  450; Code of Federal Regulations 230-
  231; Constitution 373; Contiguous
  Fisheries Zone Act(1966) 393; Deep
  Seabed Hard Mineral Resources Act 542-
  555; Deepwater Port Act of 1974 468-
  471; Driftnet Impact Monitoring,
  Assessment and Control Act of 1987 and
  Related Int'l Agreement 617-620;
  Fishermen's Protective Act 589-592, 599,
  619, 638, 657; Fishery Conservation and
  Management Act 591, 600, 608, 617,
  657; Foreign Assistance Act 592, 593-
  594; Foreign Assistance and Related
  Program Appropriation Act 593-594;
  Foreign Military Sales Act 590, 592;
  Foreign Relations Law 436, 542; Foreign
  Sovereign Immunities Act 368, 816;
  Gambling Act of 1948 375; Internal
  Revenue Code 435, 438; Marine Mammal

Protection Act 659; Limitation of Liability Act 706; National Prohibition Act 236; Outer Continental Shelf Lands Act 244-246, 432-433, 438-440, 447-448; Regulation of Exploration and Commercial Recovery by United States Citizens 545-546; Rivers and Harbors Act of 1899 448; Submerged Lands Act 108, 137, 143, 145, 227, 244-246, 432-433, 440, 449; Wireless Telegraphy Act (1949) 142

US-CEP [Chile-Ecuador-Peru] Dispute; see also tuna war
577, 583, 588

US-Mexico Claims Commission
831-833

USA
territorial sea 70, 235-236, 242, 251, 254-255, 309, 390, 436, 588; internal waters 229; continental shelf 244, 245, 409, 410, 433-434, 438-442, 448, 588; contiguous zone 309-310, 391, 588; EEZ 461, 479, 493, 617-618, 657; extent of jurisdiction 245, 408, 410, 433, 440, 447, 471, 480; jurisdiction on the high seas 339; position on historic bays 122-123; position on rivers flowing into bays 148; position on deep seabed mining 536-541; policy on marine scientific research 769; fishery dispute with Chile, Ecuador and Peru 577, 583, 588, 590; seizure of Iranian mine ships 823-824; seizure of s Japanese fishing vessel 391-394; friendship treaty with Germany 228-229; Immunity of governmental commercial ships 367

USA fishery agreements
Declaration with Argentina 148-149; Brazil 591; Bulgaria 614-615; Canada 611-613, 638, 667; driftnet fishing agreement with CCNAA/ Taiwan 620-625; Japan 611-613, 659; pollution agreement with UK 688; USSR 588, 615-617; treaty of polymetallic nodules 561-568; treaty of deep seabed mining 566-568

USA maritime boundary with
Mexico 161-163; Canada 196-200; Venezuela 213; Cook Islands 215; New Zealand 219-220

Use of force; see also UN Charter
299, 577, 801, 838, 841; authorized by UN 845

USSR
sedentary fisheries dispute with Japan 577; fishery agreement with US 588, 615-617; neutrality treaty 818, 810; Cuba crisis 839-842; shot down a Korean airplane 257; refusing US ships passage through Vilkitsky 289-290; view on enclosed or semi-enclosed sea 328-329; use of an iceberg as a spy base 324; immunity of governmental ships 365-366, 368

Varagas, Jorge
767-768

Vessel source pollution; see also pollution, oil pollution
categories 676-678; int'l standards 678-679, 685, 720; int'l regulations 680-687, 722; in ice-covered areas 744

Vietnam
north 821; south 262; war 827

Vigilance zone; see also contiguous zone
310, 312

Wachenfeld, Margaret
361-362

Walker, Wyndham
234-235

Wang, Frank F.H.
498-500

War zone; see also operational zone, sea defense zone
804; UK 805; Germany 805